Philippe Barbour,
Dana Facaros and Michael Pauls

FRANCE

that spirit of *élan*, that shot of Gallic
pepper sauce, that daring to go an extra
mile, often right over the top,
that sets the French apart in Europe...

CADOGANguides

Contents

About the authors

Dana Facaros and Michael Pauls (*History, Culture, Topics, Paris and the Ile de France, the Southwest, Gascony, the Basque Lands and the Pyrenees, Provence and the Côte d'Azur, Languedoc-Roussillon*) lived for eight years in a leaky old farmhouse in southwest France, and now they're back...at least for a while. They have written over 30 guides for Cadogan.

Philippe Barbour (*Normandy, Brittany, Loire Valley, Atlantic Coast, the North, the Northeast, Burgundy, the Rhône Valley and the Auvergne, the Alps and the Jura*) may have been born half-English and half-French, but his loyalties aren't divided. While England gives him a solid base, he is madly in love with France. He studied French and German literature at Oxford University and has since worked in publishing. He has written several other books for Cadogan, including their guide to Brittany and their guide to the Loire.

Cadogan Guides
Network House, 1 Ariel Way, London W12 7SL
cadoganguides@morrispub.co.uk
www.cadoganguides.com

The Globe Pequot Press
246 Goose Lane, PO Box 480, Guilford,
Connecticut 06437–0480

Updated by Rosemary Bailey, Jacqueline Chnéour,
   Paul Grieve, Vanessa Letts, Linda McQueen,
   Linda Rano, Mathieu Touchard

Cover and photo essay design by Kicca Tommasi
Book design by Andrew Barker
Cover photographs by John Ferro Sims
Maps © Cadogan Guides, drawn by Map Creation
   Ltd; map on p.86 courtesy of SNCF; Paris metro
   map © TCS
Editorial Director: Vicki Ingle
Series Editor: Linda McQueen
Editor: Catherine Charles
Proofreading: Lorna Horsfield
Indexing: Judith Wardman
Production: Book Production Services

Printed in Italy by Legoprint
A catalogue record for this book is available
   from the British Library
ISBN 1-86011-978-6

The author and publishers have made every effort to ensure the accuracy of the information in this book at the time of going to press. However, they cannot accept any responsibility for any loss, injury or inconvenience resulting from the use of information contained in this guide.

Please help us to keep this guide up to date. We have done our best to ensure that the information in this guide is correct at the time of going to press. But places and facilities are constantly changing, and standards and prices in hotels and restaurants fluctuate. We would be delighted to receive any comments concerning existing entries or omissions. Authors of the best letters will receive a copy of the Cadogan Guide of their choice.

France
a photo essay

by John Ferro Sims

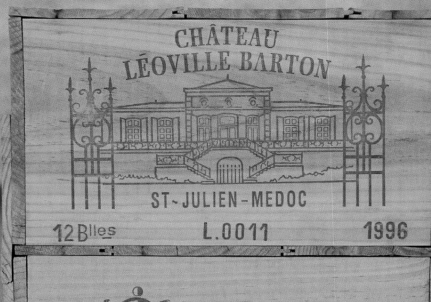

CHÂTEAU
LÉOVILLE BARTON

ST-JULIEN-MEDOC

12 B^{lles}   L.0011   1996

CHATEAU-FIGEAC

SAINT-ÉMILION

FRANCE   1996

CHATEAU
GRAND MAYNE

GRAND CRU CLASSE
SAINT-EMILION

12 B^{lles}   1996

CHATEAU SOUTA

Moselle, near Dieuze
Reims Cathedral

Place des Vosges, Paris
Centre Pompidou, Paris

Josselin, Morbihan

Cayeux-sur-Mer, Somme
Nice

Laon Cathedral
Cathedral of St-Front,
Périgueux

Château de Biron,
Dordogne

village perché,
Provence

wine crates, St-Emilion
vineyards near Dijon

St-Rémy-de-Provence

Mont St-Michel,
Normandy

rket, Sarlat-la-Canéda
café, Nice
vineyard, St-Emilion
marzipan, Périgueux

Pra-Loup, Hautes-Alpes

About the photographer

John Ferro Sims was born of Anglo-Italian parents in Udine, Italy. He worked successfully for five years as an investment analyst before quitting the world of money for a career as a professional photographer which has taken him around the world. He has published 9 books.

Introduction

'As happy as God in France,' is an old German saying, and the rest of us merrily concur by making France the most visited country in the world, number one in the tourist sweepstakes. Its charms are legion, ranging from mighty Mont Blanc to a sliver of truffle in a foie gras, and all are marked with a style and *savoir faire* that make other countries seem like amateurs.

France, after all, was born with every grace geography could bestow. Three distinct climates (Mediterranean, Atlantic and Continental), abundant rivers and springs, rich plains and sunlit hills, make it the most fertile country in Europe, producing the wherewithall for its legendary cuisine as well as the world's most famous wines. On these lovely landscapes, wealth and talent have left an artistic legacy second only to Italy's, with a prehistoric headstart in the painted caves of the Dordogne and the Neolithic stone alignments of Brittany. Celtic metalwork and the Gallo-Roman monuments of Provence are a prelude to Romanesque works of pure imagination, followed by perhaps France's great invention, soaring Gothic cathedrals with walls of glass. Enchanting châteaux in Renaissance variations along the Loire give way to the classic and rococo styles of the big Louies. In the 19th century Paris was remade as Europe's first modern city, where Impressionism and its aftershocks brought the old art world to the ground. The five-sixths of the French population who don't live in or around Paris have countless beautiful cities, towns and villages to call home: Avignon and Aix, Tours and Nantes, Bordeaux and Toulouse, Dijon and Strasbourg, to name just a few.

As heirs of the highly individualistic tribes of Gaul, picked off one by one by Caesar, the French like to do as they please. De Gaulle got it right when he said that 'The French will only be united under the threat of danger. Nobody can simply bring together a country that has 265 kinds of cheese' – only, as has often been noted, he grossly underestimated the number of cheeses. The complusion to melt the French down into some kind of centrally controlled fondue is a constant throughout the monarchy, the Revolution, the Napoleons, and the old-style *classe politique*: France, after all, wrote the book on centralization. There is, however, a growing restlessness with the schoolbook image of a culturally and politically homogenous France. You only need to look into the corners of the Hexagon, as France is often nicknamed, to see how unFrench France can be. In Alsace, German is still widely spoken. In the northwest, the Bretons cling on to their Celtic roots. In the far southwest, the Basque country retains its language, culture and fierce nationalists, even if the Catalans, another group scooped up by the Pyrenees, tend to be more pragmatic. In the south-east, Savoy and Nice only voted to become a part of France (rather than Italy) in 1860. Not forgetting Corsica, the biggest political thorn in the national side, recently, momentously, given a measure of autonomy.

Change is in the air, and as power fitfully devolves from Paris – a process encouraged under Mitterrand – France may well become even more colourful, even more fun to visit and even more enjoyable to live in. Already it is more determined than most countries to dig in its heels to save its soul. If anyone can resist the bland siren song of globalization, it'll be the French. After all, ensconced in their earthly paradise, they have the most to lose.

Guide to the Guide

Paris and the Ile de France The City of Light glitters brighter than ever at the dawn of the 21st century, spruced up and bursting with a lion's share of France's art and culture, restaurants, shops and myths, plus Versailles and Disneyland Paris.

Normandy Explore the coastal glamour of Honfleur and Deauville, the moving D-Day landing beaches, the Bayeux tapestry and otherworldly Mont St-Michel.

Brittany Even Neolithic men couldn't resist the region's tough granite charms, as Carnac most memorably recalls. Virtually every inch of the Breton shore can still seduce you; inland, up the river estuaries, hide delightful historic towns and chapels.

Loire Valley With its pure French accent and its plethora of fantasy châteaux, the Loire sums up refined French living. It also boasts numerous wine villages, and a whole hidden underground world from which the region's white stone was quarried.

Atlantic Coast A dark horse, hiding gorgeous islands; the splendid old ports of La Rochelle and Rochefort; the pilgrimage churches of inland Poitou; the Marais Poitevin, which can knock spots off the Camargue; and the shock of Futuroscope cinema park.

The Southwest A gentle land of rivers, from the quiet wooded Limousin through the honeyed villages, châteaux and prehistoric caves of the Dordogne and Lot to Bordeaux, wine capital of the world, and its upriver dynamic rival, Toulouse.

Gascony and the Pyrenees Under the snowy citadels of the Pyrenees, the land of the Gascons and Basques offers *la France profonde* at its most genial, with the Cathedral of Auch and the lively cities of Biarritz, St-Jean-de-Luz, Bayonne and Pau.

The North Head for pretty St-Omer, Montreuil and Bergues, or, further inland, the high drama of Lille and Arras, the cathedral cities of Amiens and Senlis, or the many grand castles. More moving than all these are the war cemeteries of the Somme.

The Northeast Champagne and its wine route fills many a visitor with joy. Troyes, old capital of the region, conceals startling artistic riches. In the fortified territories of French Ardenne, Charleville's Place Ducale proves more than a match for Paris' Place des Vosges. In Lorraine, Nancy screeches style, both Ancien Régime and Art Nouveau. The beautiful red-stoned, forested Vosges mountains separate Lorraine from Alsace, which looks sweetly across the Rhine to Germany, while offering splendid cities such as Strasbourg, Colmar and Mulhouse.

Burgundy Renowned above all for its wine and its religious legacy, here you'll find ducal Dijon and Beaune in the winey east; ancient sites such as Bibracte, Alésia and Autun; misunderstood Vichy and Moulins; and religious Brionnais and Charlieu.

Rhône Valley and the Auvergne These are sensational, little-explored areas, hiding the weird and wonderful volcanic landscapes of the Auvergne; the secretive upper Loire and upper Allier valleys; staggering Le Puy-en-Velay and its stairways to heaven; the hillside paradise of the Ardèche and the Drôme; and France's second city, Lyon.

Alps and the Jura Mont Blanc is the crowning glory of the Savoy Alps. The most famous French ski resorts lie way up above the Isère valley, circling the great Vanoise range. The southern Alps of the Dauphiné, centred on the Ecrins mountains, come as an exceptionally sunny surprise. North of genteel Lake Geneva, the Jura mountains are a better-kept secret, along with Besançon and the Jura wine route.

Chapter Divisions

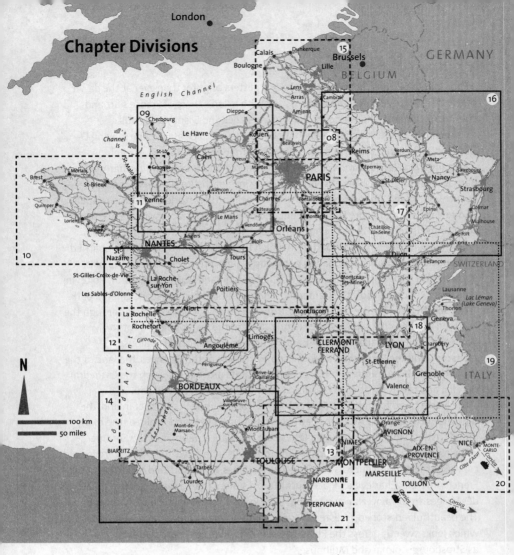

Provence and Côte d'Azur This region attracts tourists like bees to a honeypot with its glittering resorts, modern art, Roman monuments, landscapes painted by Cézanne and Matisse, and its *villages perchés*. Off the coast lies **Corsica**, the Ile de Beauté.

Languedoc-Roussillon France's other, less-visited Mediterranean region, with bigger and better beaches, plus the fascinating cities of Narbonne, Montpellier, Nîmes, Carcassonne and Perpignan, and the vertiginous castles of the Cathars.

History

–AD 260

A precocious prehistory, inherited by Celts and then Romans

Cro-Magnon is the name of a hamlet in the Dordogne, only one of many terms to describe early man that come from finds in France. Someone was tramping around these green valleys around a million years ago, and the upper Palaeolithic cultures called the **Perigordian** (from Périgord), the **Aurignacian** (from Aurignac, near Toulouse) and the **Magdalenian** (from a cave in the Tarn; 15–9,000 BC) left the famous cave paintings that are the world's oldest art. France continued its precocious start in Europe's first real civilization, the **Neolithic** (4500–2000 BC), a period that saw the beginnings of agriculture, astronomy and architecture. Situated at the heart of the Neolithic world, the country has more than its share of dolmens, tumuli and menhirs, as well as the spectacular alignments at Carnac in Brittany.

After a rather sleepy millennium, things pick up again c. 1000 BC with the beginnings of the 'Iron Age'; this, probably not coincidentally, is also the earliest date proposed for the arrival of the **Celts** from central Europe. Long neglected by historians and archaeologists, the Celts were not quite as backward as is commonly believed. 'Gaul', as the Romans would call it, was a distinctly prosperous land, supporting some ten million people. Though the Celts never cared much for urban life and organization, throughout Gaul many of their *oppida* (trading centres) grew into proper little towns as trade increased. In metallurgy, and especially the making of weapons, the Celts were at least as advanced as the Mediterranean civilizations. They also had better chariots and wagons, and they built a network of good roads for them.

Gaul was never exclusively Gaulish; the Celts had to share the land with earlier inhabitants in the south: the Iberians and Basques in the southwest, and the Ligurians in the southeast. The **Greeks** arrived in c. 600, with the founding of Marseille, which became the mother to a string of towns along the coast: Nice, Antibes and Agde among them. The Greeks introduced the olive and vine, and probably roses from Persia to give Provence's perfume industry a start.

Rome became interested in Gaul from its need to control a land route to Spain, newly acquired in the Punic Wars. With the support of its long-time ally Marseille, Rome occupied southeastern Gaul in 121 BC, and the region became Rome's first 'province' outside Italy, hence **Provence**. It assimilated so rapidly that the Romans also liked to call it Gallia Togata ('Gaul with the toga on'), as opposed to Gallia Comata ('Hairy Gaul') further north.

By the 1st century BC, the first Germanic tribes were already infiltrating across the Rhine, and worries about these fierce warriors were one factor that finally spurred Rome to complete the conquest. Another was the ambition of **Julius Caesar**, in an age when the only sure way to power was to gain control of an army, grab someone else's land, and use the booty to purchase influence back in Rome. Starting in 58, he did the job with impressive brutality, tackling one Celtic tribe at a time. When the Gauls finally united under **Vercingétorix**, their last revolt was crushed at the siege of Alésia (Alise-Ste-Reine in the Côte d'Or) in 52. Gaul offered Caesar little else in the way of booty, but it had people, and Caesar sold a tenth of them into slavery and pocketed the profits.

For all that, Hairy Gaul proved remarkably receptive to Roman language, religion and ways of life. Old Celtic centres, such as Lutetia (Paris), grew into modest provincial capitals, while the greatest city of all was Lugdunum (Lyon), a key crossroads both for trade and defence. Rome's enormous investment in maintaining the Rhine frontier against the Germans was always a key factor in eastern Gaul's prosperity.

AD 260–687

Gaul becomes a Teutonic playground, and the Franks found a kingdom in it

The Roman 'crisis of the 3rd century' was felt in Gaul as much as any part of the Empire. Troubles started when two German tribes, the Franks and Alemanni, broke through the Rhine frontier in 260. It took sixteen years to chase them out, and after that a series of civil wars and imperial pretenders raised by the legions kept the land in turmoil. Many rural districts became depopulated and, for the first time since the Roman conquest, the already hard-pressed cities had to add to their burdens the building of defensive walls.

By the 4th century, Gaul had become a very different place. The old Gallo-Roman aristocracy, largely wiped out in the previous century, had been replaced by a class of new men, mostly Romans with ties to the emperor. They owned nearly everything, including the people, as free farmers and tradesmen came under increasing pressure to sell themselves into serfdom to escape worse fates at the hands of the Roman taxman. While the rest of Gaul deteriorated into an economic vacuum, the small elite, defended by private armies, lived in luxury in their palatial rural villas, and supported a last flowering of Latin culture, centred on the famous school of Bordigala (Bordeaux); many among the elite also converted to Christianity, which took hold more strongly in Gaul than anywhere in the west.

But history does not like vacuums, and the Germans were desperate to fill this one. The Rhine frontier finally collapsed in 406, and the next decades saw Gaul overrun by **Franks**, **Burgundians** and **Visigoths**. These 'barbarians' had not come to pull down the temples and rape the women. Pushed from behind by other Germans, who were themselves being pushed by the rampaging Huns, they chiefly wanted enough to eat, and a safe and cosy place to settle; all of them made their arrangements with Rome, and with the landowners, who kept considerable control by means of their wealth and their monopoly of positions in the now-established Church. A committee of them effectively ran much of Provence, which they shared with the Visigoths; this tribe, along with the Burgundians in what is now Burgundy, were the most advanced Germans, and accepted Roman culture and Christianity easily. Up north, the Franks and Alemanni stayed pagan and continued to coat their bodies in bear grease.

No doubt that is what gave the Franks the extra virtue they needed to gain ascendency over all of Gaul. One Frankish tribe, at Tournai, was ruled by a formidable chieftain named Merovech, and he and his sons first unified the Franks and then went after their German cousins. **Clovis** (ruled 482–511) devoured the Alemanni, snuffed out the Roman 'King' Syagrius, conquered Aquitania (the southwest) and drove the Visigoths into Spain. He also converted to Christianity, with the aid of a nagging pious wife and St Remigius, bishop of Reims. When Remigius told him the story of Christ's crucifixion, Clovis sighed and said 'Ah, if only my Franks had been there!'

One more fateful decision of Clovis's – he made a little town on the Seine called **Paris** his capital. The advantages of the strategically located, fertile and defensible Ile-de-France were becoming apparent, and as the centre of Frankish power, the region came to be called Francia, and its dialect Francien, the embryo of modern French. So much about these **Merovingian kings** (the descendants of Merovech) is wonderfully strange: their sacred status, and the long hair that symbolized it, or the scores of tiny golden bees that turn up in their burials. For a time, they prevailed over their enemies, though their own customs made the job difficult. Clovis divided up his lands among four sons, mixed up in patches around the map. **Clotaire I** (d. 561) reunited them all, and then left it all to his four sons. Such behaviour leaves the 6th and 7th centuries wildly cluttered with names and dates and battles, in which most of the protagonists were Merovingian brothers and cousins. Two new peoples, both beyond Frankish control, appear in this period to add further complications: British refugees, fleeing from Angles and Saxons in great numbers to make **Brittany** a Celtic redoubt, and the **Gascons**, or Vascones – slightly Romanized Basques in fact, who had long ago owned the lands between the Pyrenees and the Garonne, and now in unsettled times came back to reclaim them.

687–840
A short-lived Carolingian Empire, followed by feudal anarchy

The Merovingians were slipping. Not the least of their mysteries is how such a virile dynasty could decline so rapidly into the line of 'do-nothing kings', the *rois faineants*. By the mid-7th century, real power in the Frankish courts was held by the 'mayors of the palace', the kings' chief ministers. Strongest of these was Pepin II of Herstal, who was boss of nearly all the Frankish lands by 687; from then on his descendants ruled, and the anointed kings were their puppets. Pepin's grandson **Charles Martel** – the 'Hammer' – took power at a time when the Franks were facing their greatest threats. Charles was equal to the challenge. He reasserted control over Aquitaine, pushed the invading Saxons back into Saxony and, most importantly, defeated the hitherto invincible Arabs, rolling northwards after their conquest of Spain, at Poitiers in 732.

It was left to Charles' son **Pepin III the Short** to take the logical final step: disposing of the last feeble Merovingian and having himself proclaimed king. This was accomplished with the aid of the pope, and in return Pepin had to cross the Alps and sort out the Lombards in Italy. Pepin the Short's son and successor in the new Carolingian dynasty, apparently legitimate, was a seven-foot cracker who has gone down in history as **Charlemagne**, though he might have answered as readily to Karl der Grosse – half of Charles/Karl's lands were in Germany and his preferred capital was at Aachen. Above all, Charlemagne was a warrior. He made his authority felt in every part of old Gaul, intervened in Spain, destroyed the Lombards and seized all northern Italy, and pushed his frontiers far out into the German lands, treating any tribes who refused conversion to Christianity with a policy that would charitably be described as genocide. At home, he was a loving paterfamilias and a great patron of learning, though all the efforts of his learned English culture minister Alcuin were not quite enough to teach him how to write his own name. He ruled his vast kingdom like a paterfamilias too, sending agents called the *missi domenici* to every corner to see if officials were doing their jobs and justice was secure.

Something very significant in the history of the west was happening, though Charlemagne may not have realized it until Christmas Eve in Rome in the year 800. While he was kneeling at Mass, a scheming Pope Leo III sneaked up behind him and placed an imperial crown on his head. Whether or not he expected it to happen, or even desired it, the Empire of the West had been reborn, and the papacy had created the pretension that the crown was theirs to give.

Unfortunately, all this new Carolingian empire was good for was falling apart. Poor communications, a lack of resources and a lack of ingrained unity ensured that the vast areas tied together by Charlemagne's conquests could never be held together for long. Even while Charlemagne was alive, the **Vikings** had begun their raids, and there was little he could do about it. A speedy dissolution was made certain by the old Germanic habit of dividing everything between one's sons. Thus, after the death of Charlemagne's only son Louis the Pious in 840, the empire was split into three king-doms for each of Louis' sons. The arrangement was confirmed at the **Treaty of Verdun** in 843. Lothair, the strongest, got the territories in the middle, including Flanders, Burgundy and northern Italy, as well as the now nearly worthless imperial title; this far-flung collection of lands could never survive, though its name Lotharingia did, in Lorraine. Louis II got Francia Orientalis, which would one day be Germany, and Charles the Bald got the west, Francia Occidentalis, the lands that would one day be France.

In a sense, the brothers were carving up a corpse. The collapse of the Carolingian order was swift and complete, and Francia Occidentalis in particular was in a bad way. The 9th century, which had started with such promise, turned out to be the very darkest stretch of the Dark Ages. Other bugbears, notably the Magyars, came roaring through the land, but it was the Vikings who provided the greatest menace, repeat-edly ravaging the country as far inland as rivers were navigable. One of their favourite raiding grounds was the valley of the lower Seine. In 885 they besieged Paris, and **Count Eudes**, depending entirely on the city's own resources, held them off – the first time anyone had ever managed to do so. Eudes' heirs, the counts of Paris (later dukes), would for the next century be the most powerful lords of France.

After thoroughly wrecking the lower Seine, about 896 the Vikings began to settle it. The 'northmen' were becoming **Normans**, and in 911 under their chief Rollo they turned Christian in exchange for recognition of their right to what is now Normandy.

Elsewhere, great lords were finding opportunity in disorder, carving out effectively independent states: besides Paris, **Aquitaine**, **Provence**, **Burgundy**, and **Toulouse** were the strongest. In one sense it was the triumph of Germanic law and customs over Roman, personal relations over state control – in short, feudalism. Nor was the atomization of society limited to the few grandees. The castellans, originally royal or ducal agents, began everywhere to think of themselves as lords in their own right. Power accrued to men with castles, or indeed anyone with a horse and armour.

Still, feudalism gave the country a paradoxical stability in the midst of the chaos of battling barons, and the 10th century was a time of slow, gradual recovery. One of the Counts of Paris, **Hugues Capet**, became king in 987. His royal domain was limited to a thin strip between Paris and Orléans, and passing from one town to the other he had to worry about ambushes from any castle along the way. No one at the time could have noticed that something important had begun, but Hugues Capet's descendants would hold that throne for the next 805 years.

1000–1328

Paris becomes the capital of the Middle Ages, and France becomes a nation

The year 1000 found the first French pope, the learned Sylvester II, ruling at Rome, the Ottonian dynasty (inheritors of Charlemagne's imperial title) bringing stability and prosperity to Germany, and the new Europe's first commercial cities in Flanders and Italy providing an impetus to trade. The lands that were coming to be known as 'France' shared fully in the ascent. Cities were growing here too, and by 1050 some, such as Laon and Le Mans, were asserting their independence. New wealth brought new life to the Church; 'the world was clothing itself in a white mantle of churches', as one chronicler put it, while the great Abbey of Cluny, founded in 910, contributed much to the growth of education. The revival of learning gathered momentum at Laon, at the cathedral school of Chartres, and in Paris, with its school that developed into the most renowned of Europe's new universities.

While the feudal order permitted such progress, it continued to have its drawbacks – most of all, a simple overabundance of knights, all striving to impress. Constant feudal warfare was the curse of the age. The Church responded with such initiatives as the late 10th-century Truce of God and the 1120 Peace of God, but the problem was finally resolved by the Crusades. Pope Urban II proclaimed the **First Crusade** in 1095 not in Rome, but in Clermont-Ferrand, and he was correct in his assumption that French knights would be the most numerous and enthusiastic Crusaders. France, this chaotic new country without a central government to speak of, had quite suddenly become a powerhouse in European affairs. In 1066 thirty years before the Crusaders had sailed off to found 'Frankish' states in the Middle East, **Duke William of Normandy** had conquered England at a blow, and Norman knights who missed out on that escapade would later carve out a kingdom for themselves in southern Italy and Sicily.

If the new powerhouse did not have a head, at least it was developing a worthy capital. By organizing the towns of northern France into a powerful economic unit, **Paris** in the 12th century surpassed Venice to become the biggest city in Europe. Besides its university, the intellectual centre of Christendom, and its revolutionary Gothic architecture, Paris also created the schools of painting, sculpture and music that created so much of the style of the Middle Ages.

For all its energy and strength, this 'France' was still more a geographical expression than a political reality, and the 'King' in Paris was only one player on an extremely complicated chessboard. Louis VI, in 1137, thought he had achieved a master stroke by marrying off his son, the future Louis VII, to **Eleanor of Aquitaine**, heiress to the biggest state in the land. But Eleanor was a lively girl, and she found life with the pious, slow-witted Louis intolerable. From this family soap opera came a conflict that would spring the plot of French history for the next 300 years. In 1152 they divorced; Eleanor had found someone she liked better – **Henry II**, Duke of Normandy and soon to be King of England. It was the ultimate nightmare for the king in Paris, now nearly surrounded by the possessions of a vassal far more powerful than himself.

Louis VII wasn't up to the challenge, but he did leave an heir who would be. **Philippe Auguste**, also a descendant of Charlemagne on his mother's side, battled the Plantagenets for three decades, first against Henry and then his sons Richard the Lionheart and John. He manoeuvered the hapless John into appearing a disloyal vassal (as Duke of Normandy, Philippe was his lord) and used that as an excuse to confiscate the fief. Success in battle made it stick. The Plantagenets gathered a formidable European coalition of allies, but Philippe whipped them all at the **Battle of Bouvines** (1214); Paris celebrated with a week-long party in the streets.

No one did more to build France. By the end of his reign Philippe had gained for the crown not only Normandy, but Touraine, Poitou and Brittany besides; for the first time, there was enough land, and enough men, under direct royal control to make Paris' ruler a king not only in name, but in fact. Philippe reformed and reorganized his state along Norman lines; with a strong and capable bureaucracy, he chartered cities and fostered commerce and learning. Fittingly, in his own time he was the first to be called not 'King of the Franks', but King of France.

This new France was still largely limited to the north. No one in the south thought of themselves as French at all. They didn't even speak the same language, but the various related tongues (Languedocien, Provençal, Gascon) that are now called **Occitan** – the language of the troubadours, and of an accomplished civilization that looked more to the Mediterranean than to Paris. One of Occitania's peculiarities was its tolerance for religious heresy, especially the dualistic faith of the **Cathars**, imported from the Balkans. The growth of this sect, with its own bishops and church organization in the southwest, was the excuse for the **Albigensian Crusade** of 1209, in which the Pope and the French combined to conquer much of the south, notably the powerful County of Toulouse. Mass slaughters of Cathars and the introduction of the Inquisition accompanied a vast and blatant land grab by the northern knights.

Philippe Auguste's son Louis IX (1226–70) mopped up the remaining heretics, and became **St Louis** for his trouble. But while he may look something of a thug from the southern point of view, the French regard him with some justification as their all-time model monarch. Louis's obsession with crusading abroad detracted somewhat from the good he did at home, but he did possess a sincere concern for the welfare of his people – old French school histories would always have a picture of the wise, thoughtful king dispensing justice from under an oak in his palace garden on the Ile de la Cité (near the spot where Paris' law courts are located today).

St Louis also continued his father's policy of building a strong, centralized state, and this trend would reach its culmination in the reign of his grandson, **Philippe IV le Bel** (Philip the Fair, 1285–1314). A decidedly modern character, this Philippe in 1302 convoked the first **Estates-General**, a national parliament divided into the three 'estates' of nobles, clergy and bourgeois. What he wanted from them was, of course, money. Philippe always needed more, especially for his epic battle with the papacy, which had been meddling in French affairs for centuries. He was fortunate to be up against the most arrogant and grasping of all popes, Boniface VIII, at a time when all Europe was fed up with the impostures of Rome, and he won. Philippe gained considerable control over the French Church and its revenues, and he had the papacy in his pocket; a French pope, Clement V, fled Roman anarchy in 1309 for Provence – not part of France until 1481, but still close enough for Philippe to keep an eye on him. The **'Babylonian Captivity'**, as Italians called it, would keep the popes in Avignon until 1377.

1328–1453
A century of war, and the ruin of medieval France

Medieval France was the richest and most populous country in Europe, the land of chivalry, scholarly authority and artistic innovation – and quite suddenly, it all started to come apart. France had beaten the English under Philippe Auguste, and now the old National Enemy was coming back for its revenge. King Charles le Bel, last of the direct line of Hugues Capet, died in 1328. A cousin, Philippe de Valois, had a reasonable claim to the throne, but so did Edward III of England, and the result would be the **Hundred Years' War**. At first, the war proceeded fitfully in the southwest, in Aquitaine, held by England since the days of the Plantagenets. In 1346, however, Edward invaded France proper, and he brought his Welsh and English archers with him. Though the French took a very long time to realize it, a revolution in warfare was occurring, and Edward's bowmen chopped down French knights like grass at the **Battle of Crécy**. Ten years later, they repeated the performance at Poitiers, and took King Jean II prisoner.

France was down, and leaderless. The war played hell with commerce and culture in the cities, while an epochal change in Europe's main trade route helped finish off France's medieval prosperity; where once merchants linked Italy and Flanders by way of Lyon and the great fairs of Champagne, now the fighting made them take a new route, over the Alps and down the Rhine. In the country things were even worse. Every region of France was devastated at least once in the war, and the mercenary companies that sprung up spread terror when no king was paying them, often setting themselves up as freebooters in captured castles. Add to that the waves of peasant rebellions, the *jacqueries* in Picardy and elsewhere, and the **Black Plague** of 1347–8, which carried off a third of the population, and France's misery was complete.

France nearly had a real revolution in these dark times, one that might have set the nation on the same course of constitutional evolution as England. In 1356 the provost of the Paris merchants, **Etienne Marcel**, proposed to the Estates-General that they meet on a regular basis, and assume more power over the king's government and his purse. Royal resistance led to a revolt, and Marcel ruled Paris, with some help from the English, until his assassination in 1358.

The dauphin who put down Paris' revolt (while his father was imprisoned in London) became **Charles V** (1364–80), and despite this unpromising start he ruled with caution and skill, even winning some territories back from the English with his talented commander Bertrand du Guesclin. For the French, it would be only the eye of the hurricane in the endless war.

In the next round, most of France's injuries would be self-inflicted. It did not help that the next king, Charles VI, went mad, but while the English waited in the wings the French, quite irresponsibly, collapsed into a bitter and pointless civil war. The two sides were called 'Armagnacs' and 'Bourguignons' after their noble leaders, and as they tore up the country the English came back. They played one faction off against the other, and in 1415 crushed the French army once again at the **Battle of Agincourt**. When Charles VI died in 1422, most of France recognized Henry V of England as king. His brother, the Duke of Bedford, ran the occupation government from a half-abandoned Paris, while the rightful king, young, indecisive Charles VII, held on to Berry and the Auvergne; contemporaries mocked him as the 'King of Bourges'.

At France's darkest hour, history seems to dissolve into myth with the appearance of **Joan of Arc**, the shepherd girl from Lorraine who came to tell the king of her visions, gained a horse and some men from a sympathetic commander, and chased the English out of Orléans in 1429. Captured by the Bourguignons at Compiègne in 1430, she was sold to the English, who burned her as a witch the following year (while King Charles did nothing to help her). But the revival of the French spirit she began soon swept all before it. In 1436 Paris fell, and by 1453 the English had lost all of their possessions in France, save only the town of Calais.

1453–1562
Recovery, and a touch of royal Renaissance opulence

Much of France, including Paris, was a desolation, but economic recovery came with surprising pace, speeded along by Charles' son, **Louis XI** (1461–83). Eccentric and miserly, often living in near solitude, his huge nose and dusty felt hat made him a butt of jokes in Europe's courts, but Louis attended to business with wily tenacity. England, preoccupied with the Wars of the Roses, was no longer a threat, but a powerful new foe appeared in **Burgundy**, which had taken advantage of French setbacks in the Hundred Years' War to become a kingdom in all but name. Duke Charles the Bold (le Téméraire) even managed once to capture Louis in battle, but when he died without a male heir in 1477, Burgundy and Picardy reverted to the king. Three years later, Louis acquired Provence, Maine and Anjou in the same way.

By the late 15th century France was back on its feet and making trouble for its neighbours. Charles VIII (1483–98), Louis XII (1498–1515) and **François I** (1515–47) all spent most of their time meddling south of the Alps. But instead of conquering Italy, the Renaissance Italians conquered France – with their art, music, poetry, clothes and cuisine. In the palaces of the Marais in Paris and suburban digs such as Fontainebleau, François I and his son Henri II held the showiest courts France had yet seen – also the most expensive; besides the innumerable scrimmaging nobles (who for the first time were addressing their king as 'votre Majesté' instead of simply 'vous') François supported 12,000 hunting dogs and 12,000 horses.

The long **Wars of Italy** proved a waste of effort, and at the Battle of Pavia in 1527 François himself became the third French king in two centuries to be captured in battle. This time, the tormentor was Charles V, Holy Roman Emperor and King of Spain, who had amassed the largest European empire since Charlemagne. The French were lucky to hold their own against him and his ally Henry VIII of England, and although they gave up their designs in Italy (1559), they managed to snatch Calais from the English, and also pick up some imperial territories in the east (Metz and Verdun) by paying German barons to oppose the emperor.

Also in 1559, Henry II took a shot through the visor at a mock tournament, and France came under the rule of a queen-regent, the unstable but always interesting **Catherine de' Medici**. This was a woman who took her political advice from sorcerers and seers (Nostradamus among them); and whose actions were largely expressed in plots, poison and intrigues. After bringing up three boys who would each be untalented, unfortunate and short-lived kings (François II, Charles IX and Henri III), Catherine often continued to pull all the strings.

1562–1610
In the Wars of Religion, France nearly destroys itself again

It was not a propitious time for France to be without a strong king. The **Reformation** was turning once-calm souls into partisan zealots, especially after French-born **Jean Calvin** made Geneva the main centre for exiled Protestants in 1541. François I, that perfect Renaissance prince, had done much to turn religious difference into a mortal struggle; he incinerated whatever Protestants he could catch, and sent an army into Provence to destroy the communities of Waldensian dissenters who had been living peacefully there for centuries – 24 villages burned and 10,000 slaughtered. Meanwhile, mobs of peasants and labourers would occasionally sack a church and smash the images of the Virgin and saints, and powerful princes, even some close to the royal family, were lining up on the Protestant side. France divided into two parties, the Catholics under the Duc de Guise (who had been the liberator of Calais), supported by Spain; and the Protestants (or **Huguenots**, from the German word *eidgenossen*, or 'comrades') under Antoine de Bourbon, king of the small Pyrenean state of Navarre, supported by England.

In 1562, three years after the death of Henri II, the long-threatened civil war broke out. Factional armies, some little more than thugs, roamed the countryside, while both sides strove to outdo the other in atrocities, paticularly in the Midi; throughout the troubles, Paris stayed under the control of the crown, though this rapidly turned into a dictatorship of fear run by the Duc de Guise and, after his assassination, by his successors. A truce was agreed in 1576, and many of the principal Protestant leaders, including Admiral de Coligny, returned to the capital. Two nervous years later, Queen Catherine, who had once sincerely worked for peace and accommodation, arranged the **St Bartholomew's Day Massacre**, which took care of the moderate leaders and some 10,000 followers across France, and guaranteed another 26 years of war.

For most of this time Paris continued to be dominated by the Guises, who hoped to be kings themselves, and kept the wars going when nearly everyone else wanted them to stop. The decadent court of Henri III, a flouncing gay queen, shocked both sides; Henri at first played little part in events, but he showed some steel when the designs of the Duc de Guise became apparent. Exiled to Tours, he finally ordered Guise's assassination, and was assassinated by one of their followers in turn. As luck would have it, the rightful heir to the throne was now Henri of Navarre, son of Antoine, and the leader of the Protestant cause.

And as luck would have it, **Henri IV** turned out to be just the man France needed. A courageous commander, tried in over a decade of campaigns, his kindness, natural charm and good sense made him popular even among Catholics (and he had a special way with women; historians have counted at least 56 of them). While the Catholic League, propped up by the money and troops of Philip II of Spain, still held Paris and plotted to give the crown to one of their own, Henri marched north with a small force, beat the Catholics in Normandy, and besieged Paris. His conversion to Catholicism in 1593 – in fact, his third conversion to the old faith in the course of a busy life – removed the last obstacles to peace. After the four years it took him to chase the Spaniards out of France, he issued the Edict of Nantes, decreeing religious tolerance, and allowing Protestants the control of the 150 towns and forts they already held.

Rebuilding a devastated country proved more difficult, but again Henri was fortunate to have the model for that stock character of French history, the wise and prudent minister. His friend Maximilien de Béthune, whom he made **Duc de Sully**, squeezed corrupt officials, reformed the administration, rebuilt bridges and roads, worried the nobles and defended the peasants, and went far to realize Henri's wish for every Frenchman to 'have a chicken in the pot' every Sunday. Sully started the gracious French habit of planting avenues of trees by roadsides, and he built the nation a silk industry, beginning the tradition of state initiative and state control that has dominated the French approach to economic policy, for better or worse, ever since.

1610–1715
France's Grand Siècle, in which all was not as grand as it seemed

Henri ended his reign tragically, knifed by a Catholic fanatic named Ravaillac in 1610 while his carriage was caught in a Paris traffic jam. His son, **Louis XIII**, took the throne at the age of 11. Louis' mother, fat and silly Marie de' Medici (immortalized by an incredible cycle of paintings by Rubens in the Louvre) controlled the government at first. Lacking any idea of how to govern, Marie called the Estates-General in 1614. The third estate, the bourgeoisie, demanded lower taxes and reforms so loudly that the Estates were sent home and not called again for another 175 years. Finally, in 1624, after a bizarre attempted maternal coup d'état that has gone down in history as the 'Day of the Dupes', the weak-willed king was finally able to ease Mum out of power, with the help of his immensely capable and devoted minister, **Cardinal Richelieu**.

Sully's heir concentrated less on economics than on control, making sure that the nobles would never again challenge the king's power. He knocked down their castles wherever he could manage it, and set middle-class *intendants* to watch over every corner of the kingdom, all of whom were directly responsible to him. Richelieu also put an end to the strongholds Henri IV had left the Protestants, which were beginning to look like a state within the state. The climactic event was a dramatic and successful siege of La Rochelle (1628). Both king and minister died in 1642; they left France the strongest and most intelligently run state in Europe.

Louis XIV (1643–1715) became king at the age of five; the regent was his mother, Anne of Austria, and the minister was Richelieu's protégé, **Cardinal Mazarin**, whose father had been a Roman butler. Though corrupt to the core, Mazarin did well by France in extremely perilous times, beating back a Spanish invasion, organizing the peace of Europe, and surviving the civil wars of the Fronde (1648). 'Fronde' means a slingshot, a children's toy; this name, which the Parisians conferred on the affair, captures perfectly its lack of seriousness. In succession, the useless Parlement de Paris, a cabal of scheming court ladies called the 'Amazons', the greedy nobility, and the long-oppressed bourgeoisie of Paris tried to take advantage of the child-king's weakness. Though briefly forced to flee Paris, Mazarin and the royal cause prevailed by 1661.

Young Louis, enjoying total, personal power over France when he reached his majority, chose as his new minister **Jean-Baptiste Colbert**. A relentless overachiever, Colbert assumed control of the economy and tried to reform everything. None of the money Colbert made for Louis rested in the king's pocket for long. As Louis grew older, his conceit and ambitions ballooned to incredible proportions, disturbing Europe with wars of aggression for almost 50 years.

At home, meanwhile, Louis had put an end to the independence of the nobles once and for all. Following the example of Henri IV, he simply lavished money upon them, bribing them to spend all their time at court, where he could hold the chits for their gambling debts. Turning the entire ruling class into complaisant, mincing lapdogs ensured unity and civil peace. But surrounded by sycophants – some 10,000 of them – Louis rapidly lost all touch with reality. Perhaps he never really believed himself to be the Sun incarnate, illuminating this poor planet all by himself, but he did act the part, every hour of every day, and seemed to enjoy it. The bottom line for all the expenses of his court, and the insane new playpen that Louis built for it at Versailles, plus the costs of the wars, is simple – France nearly went bust again.

The realm of the Roi-Soleil had never exactly been paradise for the poor. Besides the grinding taxes and forced labour, Colbert locked up the indigent in workhouses to provide slave labour for his new industries, and even religious pilgrims without expensive permits from the police were likely to get pressed into the navy. By the end of Louis' long reign, misery was widespread and terrible famines gripped town and country alike. As if this wasn't enough, Louis also destroyed Henri IV's religious compromise. The Edict of Nantes was revoked in 1685, and torture and prison or exile became the lot of Protestants once more.

1715–89
The Enlightenment, and the twilight of the Ancien Régime

Another century, another Louis. After 72 years of the Roi-Soleil, his great-grandson **Louis XV** ascended the throne in 1715, at the age of five; this time the regent was the Duke of Orléans, who allowed France a refreshing interlude of Edwardian decadence after the Victorian coma of the 'Great Reign'. The regent fell for John Law's speculative schemes, and the bursting of his 'Mississippi Bubble' in 1720 nearly bankrupted the entire nation. When Louis XV began to reign in his own right, his people called him *le bien-aimé*, 'the well-beloved'. Unfortunately, no. Louis XV turned out to be an indolent, pleasure-loving fool, who allowed France to be governed by flouncing favourites and court ladies, most notably the famous Madame de Pompadour.

France was stirring. This was the age of the salons and the philosophes: Voltaire, Diderot and Montesquieu, importing English political thought and common sense to the continent. The ills of France were discussed endlessly. Most flagrant of these were the incredible privileges of the all-devouring nobility and Church. The middle classes were exasperated by the economic oppression of every productive effort, and the total lack of justice, fairness and political rights.

Despite high taxes and forced labour, France hovered near bankruptcy for most of Louis' reign. Military defeats, notably the loss of the American empire in the **Seven Years' War** (1756-63), added to the disturbing sense that the France which had loomed so large under Louis XIV no longer counted for much. The solutions were obvious, but reform depended on the king, and he wasn't having any of it. Louis really did say, 'Après moi, le déluge'. When he finally died in 1774, curses and rotten vegetables followed his coffin to St-Denis. Voltaire died four years later, regretting the coming Revolution he would not live to enjoy.

Under **Louis XVI** (1774–92) the last years of the Ancien Régime saw well-intentioned ministers Anne Robert Turgot and Jacques Necker try to push through reforms, only to be let down by the weak-willed, slow-witted king. Louis did allow his ministers to give the crucial support that led to the success of the American Revolution. Beating the Brits lifted national morale, but it also gave the French a dangerous whiff of liberty from across the Atlantic. And it left the nation in the poorhouse. By 1789 the financial situation was desperate; Louis, having failed miserably on his own, made the fatal step of doing what every Frenchman demanded – he called the Estates General. They met at Versailles on 5 May 1789, for the first time in 179 years.

1789–1815
History's noisiest Revolution, followed by the original Man on Horseback

As was traditional, the Estates voted by orders, not by individuals, and the noble and church delegates at first stymied the reforms proposed by the Third Estate, the bourgeoisie. On 20 June the king ordered the Third Estate locked out of the sessions, whereupon they assembled at the real tennis court and swore the 'Tennis Court Oath', declaring themselves the **National Assembly** and promising not to break up until they gave France a constitution. After some typical indecision, the king surrounded Versailles with foreign troops, mostly Swiss and German. But things were already getting out of hand. Radical agitators in Paris had inflamed the population, and on 12 July the mob sacked the customs barriers on the hated Farmers-General wall around the city. Two days later, they took the **Bastille**, the prime symbol of arbitrary authority, even though it was nearly empty and scheduled for demolition. After that, the Parisians formed a militia, commanded by the Marquis de Lafayette, and invented the tricolour, taking Paris' red and blue, and adding the white of the royal flag (Lafayette's idea).

More and more liberal-minded nobles and clergy were joining the Assembly and accepting its principles. On the dramatic night of 4 August they spontaneously renounced all their old feudal exemptions and privileges. The Declaration of the Rights of Man was voted in, along with a liberal constitution. Meanwhile, the émigrés, reactionary nobles who had fled France, were conspiring with foreign governments to overthrow the Revolution. The king was now obviously on their side. Louis and his family attempted to flee Paris in June 1791 – the 'flight to Varennes', and after that they were kept as prisoners.

The émigrés' invasion from across the Rhine in June 1792 brought war with their protectors, Austria and Prussia. At first things went badly for the hastily formed citizen army, but they checked the Prussian advance at the Battle of Valmy; the next day the newly elected National Convention declared France a republic. The Convention, led at first by the moderate faction of the Girondins, was captured in 1793 by the radical Jacobins, backed by the Paris mob and the new Paris government, the Commune. Its vote to execute Louis was the prelude to the **Reign of Terror**, overseen by the 'incorruptible' Maximilien Robespierre from September 1793, until he himself became its last victim in July 1794.

The government passed to a five-man executive, the **Directoire**, as provided by the new constitution. By 1797 the mood of the nation had changed. Reaction was in the air, and a royalist party began to manoeuvre semi-openly. In Paris few cared for poli-tics after such a glut of it; the workers who had supported the Commune were silent, battered by rampant inflation, and still without the right to vote. The new govern-ment had difficulty gaining any authority or respect.

The victorious army had both authority and respect, and its most able general, **Napoleon Bonaparte**, had already saved the Republic from a royalist revolt in Paris. Having beaten the English at Toulon, and conquered northern Italy from the Austrians in a campaign against overwhelming odds, he was the man of the hour. With his brother Jérôme as speaker of the national legislature, and his ally, the intriguer Siéyès, in control of the Directoire, the road was prepared for a coup that many clever politicians found desirable; like the German conservatives in 1933, they were sure they could 'handle' their man. In November 1799 Napoleon took power, and his control was solid enough for him to declare himself Emperor in 1804.

As long as Napoleon was winning, and loot and art flowed into Paris, there was little need for a heavy hand. His government consolidated the work of the Revolution at home, adopting the metric system and the law code that came to be known as the Code Napoléon, and creating such enduring institutions as the first of the Grandes Ecoles, the Ecole Polytechnique and the Ecole Normale. The real oppression came after 1810, when the economy was in disarray and the cemeteries were starting to fill up. Eight new state prisons, meant for political dissenters, had just opened when the game was up in 1814.

1815–71
France tries out every imaginable government, and finds them all wanting

The Revolution had shaken France so thoroughly, and created so many opinions and grudges, that no regime of whatever stripe could govern impartially and effectively. The rest of the nineteenth century would be an impossible search for consensus and legitimacy; from 1790 to 1875, the Gallic banana republic/empire/monarchy lurched through 13 regimes and 17 constitutions.

The king imposed by the allies at the Congress of Vienna was Louis XVI's gouty brother, **Louis XVIII** (1814–24): 'partly an old woman, partly a capon, partly a son of France and partly a pedant'. But France as a whole was content, and Louis had mellowed enough in his long exile not to exact too much revenge, even permitting a charter (not quite a constitution) and a parliament. His successor was the youngest brother, **Charles X** (1824–30). As Count of Artois he had been the head of the émigrés, and the most reactionary of the lot, the proverbial Bourbon who 'learned nothing and forgot nothing'. When he tried to gut the charter, in July 1830, Paris revolted. A move-ment of journalists, secret political societies and Napoleonic veterans seized the Hôtel de Ville, won over the troops, and tossed out the Bourbons once and for all.

The new king was **Louis-Philippe** of the Orléans branch of the family, who had fought briefly in the Revolutionary army and later ended up teaching French in

Boston. The 'bourgeois king', in his drab coat that became the prototype for the businessman's uniform of today, entrusted government to Gradgrinds like the liberal Guizot, with his message to the poor: 'Enrichissez-vous'! ('Get rich!'), and after him Adolphe Thiers. The rich alone had the right to vote, while the workers were rewarded with laws more oppressive than anything the Bourbons ever dreamed of, such as the 1838 decree forbidding them even to discuss politics.

Increasing prosperity had buoyed the regime since its birth, but the depression of the late 1840s brought discontent into the open. A provocative Washington's Birthday Dinner in Paris started the 'Revolution of Contempt' on 21 February 1848. The next day students and workers occupied the Place de la Concorde; Louis-Philippe soon abdicated, and the **Second Republic** was proclaimed. The winner of the first presidential elections turned out to be Napoleon's nephew Louis-Napoleon (as one old veteran put it: 'How could I fail to vote for this gentleman, I whose nose froze at Moscow?'). Louis made a coup three years later and declared himself **Emperor Napoleon III**, sending some 26,000 political opponents off to the prison hulks in 1851 alone.

Under the influence of his Spanish wife, the ambitious and reactionary Eugénie, the new emperor who had previously written a book called *The Extinction of Pauperism* now found himself pampering a court of nouveaux riches, and presiding over a vulgar orgy of conspicuous consumption unmatched since Louis XIV's court at Versailles. Paris, naturally, was the Second Empire's showcase, with the first of the great Expositions (1867), grandiose new monuments such as the Opéra, and the total replanning of the city by Napoleon III's prefect of the Seine, Baron Georges Haussmann. The reign of Napoleon III also saw a new overseas empire based on the occupation of Algeria (begun 1830, but not finished until 1870), Indochina, and the intervention in Italy's war of independence that gained France Nice and its hinterlands.

But by the end of Napoleon III's reign, the glitter was fading fast. The 1870 **Franco-Prussian War,** cleverly instigated by Bismarck, proved no contest; the French army was immediately surrounded at Sedan, and within three weeks most of it had surrendered, including the emperor himself. Two weeks later began the **Siege of Paris**, where a citizens' militia held the city behind its strong fortifications, while Parisians ate the animals in the zoo and the rats from the sewers, and Léon Gambetta made his dramatic escape by balloon to raise a new army in the south. A self-proclaimed government at Bordeaux – led by old Adolphe Thiers – signed an armistice and made a humiliating peace with Bismarck and the Kaiser. When Thiers tried to disarm the Parisians, the result was the rebellion of the **Paris Commune**, a name that recalled the brave days of Etienne Marcel as well as the Revolution of 1789. 'Bloody Week', the taking of Paris, began in May 1871; the revolutionaries responded to the bombardments and massacres by murdering the archbishop among others and burning down the Tuileries Palace. When it was over, some 50,000 Parisians had been killed or sent to prison camps in French Guiana. Thomas Cook was organizing special 'Ruins of Paris' tours.

1871–1940
A solid Republic prevails in one Great War, and folds up in the next

Despite its bloody start, the **Third Republic** worked with a will to make itself a stable and popular regime. Given France's turbulent history since the revolution, this was no mean accomplishment. The new regime had to contend with a strong sentiment for monarchy—the romantic young pretender who could have been Henri V only lost his chance when he refused to accept the tricolour as the national flag.

In this period, like the other powers, France rushed to grab whatever loose territories were still available around the globe, and greatly increased its colonial empire in Africa and southeast Asia. While stealing other peoples' land, the Third Republic never let Frenchmen forget the 'great crime' of 1870 – the loss of Alsace and Lorraine to Germany. Military security and hopes for revenge filled the Republic's debates, and in 1888 came the bizarre episode of another 'Man on Horseback', General Boulanger, a dummy for rightist factions that at one point seemed ready to make a coup d'état. The Republic survived that too, and its governments dominated by the Left under such leaders as Gambetta, Jules Ferry and Georges Clemenceau pushed through the first social welfare acts and vastly improved education all over the country.

More tribulations were in store for a regime that still had not entirely won the nation's confidence. The Panama Company, engineer Ferdinand de Lesseps' attempt to duplicate his triumph at Suez by digging a canal through the Isthmus of Panama, collapsed in 1889, leaving investors ruined and angry, and government ministers compromised by corruption. Worse, the **Dreyfus Affair** divided the nation on bitter partisan lines after 1894. A false accusation of spying against a Jewish army officer turned into a consuming issue when the army not only tried to cover up its mistakes, but convicted Dreyfus in a new trial against all evidence. Rightists felt compelled to line up on the side of injustice, from the old royalists to the new Action Française of Charles Maurras, Europe's prototype for the Fascist movements of the future.

The Left, aided by Emile Zola's famous *J'Accuse*, finally won the fight with Dreyfus' exoneration, recompense and promotion ten years later, but the old leftist parties found themselves increasingly pushed from their left by a burgeoning Socialist movement. France's confederation of trade unions, the CGT, appeared in 1895, and the Socialist party was founded by Jean Jaurès in 1905. Frequent strikes and anarchist terrorism, including the assassination of President Sadi Carnot in 1894, did not seriously disturb the dreams of most Frenchmen in a period of increasing prosperity and contentment.

No one doubted that the showdown with Germany would eventually come. French politicians made a cult out of 'martyred' Alsace and Lorraine, while school histories reminded children that someday they would have to be good soldiers to redeem them. When war did come, in 1914, the Germans were stopped outside Paris at the 'Miracle of the Marne', the battle that saw the famous ride of the Paris taxis carrying the reserves up to the front. Then followed the heartbreaking war of the trenches, with the familiar names of failed offensives on both sides: Ypres, the Somme, Verdun, and in 1917 Chemin des Dames, a French attack so bloody and pointless it caused mutinies all across the line; order was restored, just barely, by Marshal Philippe Pétain. **Georges Clemenceau**, the 76-year-old 'Tiger', came back to power in 1917 and rallied the nation – asked about his policies, he said, 'Moi, je fais la guerre'. In 1918 German exhaustion and the arrival of fresh American divisions won the war. France had contributed more than any nation to the victory; Allied troops had been under French command (Marshal Joffre), and French forces not only held most of the line, but delivered another decisive blow by opening up a second front in the Balkans.

The nation had restored its honour, and its two lost provinces, but at a cost proportionally greater than that of any country except Serbia, some 1,400,000 dead. What's more, the war left France a stricken economy and a tremendous debt. Paris may have had one of its most colourful decades in the '20's, jumping with avant-garde painters, Dadaist pranksters and expatriate Americans, but under the façade was an exhausted nation, increasingly bitter about a victory that brought no one anything good. The **Depression** made everything worse, and the '30's were a grim time indeed, with strikes and agitation coming from the increasingly powerful Communists (who had broken away from the Socialist party and unions in 1920), and at the other extreme from an increasingly venomous Right, which found its inspiration in Italy and Germany. In 1934, during a corruption scandal known as the 'Stavisky affair', a neo-Fascist mob besieged the Assembly in the Palais Bourbon – a clumsy attempt at a coup, with some shadowy figures behind it, that still puzzles historians.

To defend the Republic, the leftist parties combined in a **Popular Front** to win the elections of 1936 under Léon Blum. Lacking a majority in the Senate, and tormented by his Communist partners, Blum was unable to push through promised reforms (or aid Loyalist Spain in the Civil War) and his government fell before the year was out. Divided, disgruntled and confused, France drifted towards its appointment with Hitler as if in a dream.

1940–the present
A difficult convalescence

Many nations suffered more death and destruction in the Second World War, but France's experience contained a unique dose of humiliation. Europe's biggest army was annihilated by concentrated tank and air attacks in four weeks, as refugees clogged every road of northeastern France, making counterattacks nearly impossible, and a dithering, witless government decamped first for Tours, then Bordeaux. **Charles de Gaulle**, a hitherto little-known officer, made his famous speech of defiance over the BBC on 18 June 1940, four days before France's formal surrender.

In the armistice, the Nazis made all of northern France and a strip along the Atlantic coast into their occupied zone, leaving the rest to be governed from **Vichy** by Marshal Pétain, who had been granted dictatorial powers by what was left of the Assembly. Pétain and the rest of the old anti-Dreyfus Right now created a model Fascist 'French State', and efficiently aided the Nazis in the deportation of Jews and political opponents. After the North African landings in 1942 the Nazis put an end to Vichy and occupied all of France, while the **Resistance**, its strongest units dominated by the Communists, became an effective force in many areas. Liberation came with the Normandy invasions in 1944, the biggest amphibious landing in history; Eisenhower's army graciously stepped aside to let the French under General Leclerc be the first to enter Paris, on 24 August, following a frenetic week in which local Resistance forces had largely liberated the city themselves. At the same time, a highly efficient landing in Provence opened a second front that allowed the rapid liberation of most of the Midi.

The postwar **Fourth Republic**, with its Italian-style revolving-door governments, cut a poor figure on the international stage. While recovery at home made great progress, France's attempts to maintain its colonial empire led to embarrassing disasters. First in **Vietnam**, with total military defeat at Dien Bien Phu in 1954, and next in **Algeria**. The illusion of treating Algeria as a part of metropolitan France, and the presence of over a million French settlers, made this possession harder to let go, resulting in a divisive, exhausting and quite dirty war – the army's long-buried history of torture and civilian massacres is still slowly leaking out today. When the government seemed ready to negotiate with the Algerians in 1958 the army nearly staged a coup, and all sides turned to de Gaulle as the only hope.

So was born the **Fifth Republic**, with the strong executive that de Gaulle had always believed necessary. Instead of indulging the army, however, the old general worked to end the war, and his reward was the the formation by army officers of the sinister OAS, the 'Secret Army' in Algeria which staged a revolt in 1961 and made attempts on de Gaulle's life. He survived this crisis with the help of a referendum that turned out a huge 'yes' vote for allowing Algerian independence. De Gaulle saved French democracy, but his years in the presidency were a grim and nervous time for France, with a government run by colourless technocrats, a state-run radio and television worthy of a dictatorship, and an erratic, independent foreign policy that amused France's allies when it did not irritate them.

Many Frenchmen, especially the leftists and old Resistance members, had hoped for a freer, more modern society in the postwar era. Gaullism let them down, and the lid finally blew off in **May 1968** with the students' revolt in Paris, eventually joined by some nine million striking workers. With his control over the media, de Gaulle was able to mobilize the 'silent majority' and survive, though he torpedoed his own presidency soon after by staking it on a rather trivial referendum that failed. The urge to reform died on the vine under the tedious reigns of Gaullist Georges Pompidou and UDF (centrist) Valéry Giscard d'Estaing, but hopes revived with the election of Socialist **François Mitterrand** in 1981, bringing the left to power for the first time since the late '40's.

Mitterrand's years produced some welcome initiatives, notably the creation of **regional governments**, reversing, if only a little, the centuries-old habit of Parisian centralism. His pharaonic building projects in Paris, the *Grands Projets*, put a veneer of modernist gloss on what turned out to be a boisterous 14-year orgy of corruption and sleaze; an honest Socialist prime minister, Pierre Bérégovoy, shot himself in 1993 when the details started leaking out. Mitterrand, the old cynic who had served Vichy and protected war criminals while in office, admitted just before his death that he had been a man of the Right all along. His place in the Socialist leadership has been taken by the owlish and decidedly non-sleazy Prime Minister Lionel Jospin, while since 1995 the presidency has belonged to former Paris mayor **Jacques Chirac** of the old Gaullist party, now called the RPR. The Right has sleaze problems of its own, and Chirac himself has been caught up in them, along with many of his cronies, joining several Socialist nabobs facing appointments with a judiciary that has shown increasing independence and integrity.

France has definitely become a more open society since 1968. The ruling *classe politique*, a club to whose members party labels mean little, may be the last to learn it. It has been said that they instinctively feel the breath of the guillotine on the back of their necks, and their weakness in dealing with the increasing mass protests of farmers, fishermen and truckers – at the head of a long list – suggests that this is true. Much of the action today is outside the old power centres in Paris, in the regions and in progressive, go-ahead cities such as Toulouse, Lille and Strasbourg, seat of the European Parliament. Amidst great prosperity, the nation is faced with the difficult task of finding its role in a changed world, and plotting a path between Anglo-Saxon economic determinism and its own sense of tradition and social solidarity. After the grand disasters and confusions of this century, and after some grumpy and out-of-sorts postwar decades, at least it is a country that is learning to smile again.

Culture

Palaeolithic and Neolithic

The world's art, as far as has yet been discovered, begins in France, with Palaeolithic cave paintings, some 35,000 years old. These startling, sophisticated works have been aptly described as 'the infancy of art, not an art of infancy' (Lascaux, Font-de-Gaume, Pech Merle around the Dordogne, Niaux in the Ariège). The more-than-voluptuous 'fertility goddesses' common throughout the era also turn up in many of France's museums. Culture seems to take a nap – at least from the archaeological evidence – until the advent of Neolithic civilization *c.* 4000 BC. Neolithic peoples, with a cultural continuity that stretched for over 2,000 years along Europe's western coasts, were the first serious builders; in France their major monument is the enigmatic stone avenues of Carnac in Brittany, though their dolmens and menhirs, as well as some passage-grave tombs, can be seen at innumerable sites, mostly in the west and south.

Roman Gaul to Romanesque

In Roman times, the south was the richest and most cultured part of Gaul, and that is where most of the major surviving monuments are to be found: the Pont du Gard, one of the greatest surviving works of Roman engineering; the theatre of Orange, with the only intact stage building in the West; the Maison Carrée and amphitheatre at Nîmes; the amphitheatre and cryptoporticus in Arles; the elegant 'Antiques' of St-Rémy; the Pont Flavien at St-Chamas; the trophy at La Turbie; the excavated towns at Vaison-la-Romaine and Glanum (St-Rémy).

Most of the early Christian buildings that remain are baptistries, as at Fréjus, Aix-en-Provence and Marseille, all from the 5th century. Such art as was possible in the centuries after the Germanic invasions mixed classical Roman styles with a Germano-Celtic fancy for abstraction and geometric and floral patterns. Like most barbarians of the time, France's were most interested in jewellery; a few illustrated manuscripts and *objets d'art* have survived, and precious little of architecture or sculpture, though Merovingian carved capitals and reliefs can often be found recycled into later churches.

Charlemagne's dream of recreating the empire was accompanied by a style of art and architecture that closely copied surviving Roman examples. Carolingian artists did well at ivories, metalwork and manuscript illumination (there was an important workshop at Reims). They also tried their hand at painting and mosaic; little survives, apart from a rare, lovely apse mosaic (*c.* 800) at Germigny-des-Prés, near Orléans.

'Romanesque' is a catch-all term that covers a wide variety of styles, all born with the great upsurge of culture and wealth that created medieval Europe after the year 1000. Its sources are more complex than simple copying of the monuments left by ancient Rome. Influences range from the court architecture of Charlemagne to early churches in the east, in Syria and Armenia, and buildings of the Byzantine and the Islamic world.

Wealthy, cultured Burgundy was one of the places where the new architecture and sculpture made their greatest advances, including the stone barrel vault. Cluny created a church style (Cluny II) that proved equally influential; it provided the model for other Burgundian churches, notably at Autun, Paray-le-Monial, Tournus and Vézelay, all begun in the early 12th century. Cluny was soon rebuilt, as the biggest church ever attempted in medieval Europe (Cluny III, 1088, demolished in 1810). Other important early Romanesque churches survive at Toulouse (St-Sernin), Reims (St-Rémi) and Conques in the Aveyron (Ste-Foy). The Loire valley has several, including those at La Charité-sur-Loire, Nevers and St-Benoît-sur-Loire.

As the Romanesque developed, distinctive regional styles rapidly appeared all over France: ornate, domed churches in Périgord (St-Front at Périgueux, also Angoulême cathedral); in the Auvergne, octagonal crossing towers and delicately patterned exterior decoration in coloured stone (St-Nectaire, Clermont-Ferrand, Orcival, Issoire). In and around Poitou, the fashion was 'hall churches' with narrow, steep naves (St-Savin-sur-Gartempe, Talmont, Cunault); other southern buildings show a great liberty, even eccentricity of styles, as at the round church of Rieux-Minervois in Languedoc, or the fortress-like Stes-Maries-de-la-Mer in the Camargue. In Roussillon, then part of Catalunya, churches and monasteries naturally followed the heavy, yet graceful Catalan Romanesque (St-Michel-de-Cuxa, St-Martin-du-Canigou).

While most of the new architecture appeared in the service of the Church, secular building also participated in the great revival. Early medieval architects created engineering works to compete with the ancient Romans, such as the bridge across the Rhône at Avignon. It was also a great age for castle building, witnessing the development of the residential keep. Château-Gaillard in Normandy, the Key of France, was contested by Capetians and Plantagenets; other large concentrations are in the Loire valley (Chinon) and in western Languedoc.

From the beginning, architecture and sculpture were inseparable. French Romanesque sculpture, a mixture of transcendent spirituality and fairy-tale strangeness, had its beginnings in Burgundy and the Pyrenees, and it sprouted somewhat magically as a fully mature art in the early 1100s. Burgundy, under the influence of Cluny, developed the most distinctive style, with a high degree of stylization and abstraction in both figures and draperies. The greatest works were the unearthly Christs in Majesty and ferocious Last Judgements, as on the spectacular portals at Autun and Vézelay. A similar, brilliant style was evolved by the 'School of Toulouse'; its finest works can be seen there and at Moissac and Souillac in the Lot.

There is more to Romanesque sculpture than the tremendous scenes on the great portals. The period witnessed the rebirth of tomb sculpture, as at Fontrevault, the Plantagenet pantheon where Henry II, Eleanor of Aquitaine and Richard the Lionheart are buried. Even in some of the less ambitious village churches, you will see good sculptural work on capitals, on the modillons around the cornice of an apse, and hidden in unexpected places where you have to look twice to find them.

Here you will meet all the monsters of the medieval bestiary, allegorical figures that often defy explanation, or occasionally a little medieval joke; the freshness and freedom of subject matter in sculptural decoration gives Romanesque buildings much of their charm.

Gothic

The word 'Gothic' itself is a disparagement invented by 16th-century Italian critics, an attempt to make the most technically sophisticated architecture the world had ever seen seem somehow barbarous. 'Gothic' might better be called the 'Parisian' style, since Paris and the Ile-de-France is where it was developed.

The transition from early medieval civilization to the great world of the High Middle Ages was accompanied by a rapid evolution of architecture. The landmarks along the way included technical advances such as the ribbed vault, the pointed arch and the flying buttress. Never before could so much space, so much height, be enclosed with so little stonework; the walls, no longer required to carry the load, offered great opportunities to the new medium of stained glass.

The first complete 'Gothic' church was St-Denis, the traditional resting place of the Capetian kings outside Paris, begun in 1140. The new system of building spread rapidly; among the early Gothic cathedrals, Sens' was begun the same year as St-Denis, followed by Noyon (1145), Notre-Dame-de-Paris (1163), and Laon (1165). High Gothic – more elaborate vaulting, carved stone traceries and crockets, flying buttresses to make possible even greater height, and greater areas of glass – begins with Chartres, rebuilt beginning in 1194, and continued through Reims (1211), Amiens (1220) and Troyes (1262). Aspirations culminated at Beauvais, with the tallest nave ever attempted, 155ft – its collapse while still under construction dampened enthusiasm somewhat.

Replacing the diversity of Romanesque, this first national style imposed itself every-where just as the French monarchy was imposing its rule over the lands that now make up France. Only very slight regional variations ever appeared, in Poitou and Anjou, and in the south at the unusual cathedral of Albi (1282).

In the 13th century Gothic evolved more in decoration than structure. The period roughly from 1230 to 1350 is called the Rayonnant ('Decorated Style' in Britain), applying increasingly complex decoration in pinnacles and window traceries, including the great rose windows. This was the style of one of the greatest Gothic achievements, Sainte-Chapelle in Paris (1241). The Flamboyant (roughly 1350–1500, the equivalent of the English Perpendicular) brought even more elaborate traceries, carved stonework on as many surfaces as possible, a love of sinuous curves in stonecarving, and ornate, web-like rib vaulting – Gothic taken to its extremes, at its best in Rouen (the Tour de Beurre of the Cathedral, St-Ouen, St-Maclou).

In Gothic the marriage of architecture and sculpture begun in the Romanesque was perfected. The two arts evolved hand in hand, and Gothic sculpture presents an increasing confidence and skill, and a new delight in nature, as in the motifs of buttercup and lettuce leaves that adorn windows and columns. A complex, detailed iconography grew up, dictated by the Church, in which all the universe was the sculptor's province; scenes of everyday life (the Labours of the Months), and a love of fantasy continued from the Romanesque, as in the monsters atop Notre-Dame. Some of the finest sculpture can be seen in the cathedrals of Reims and Amiens.

Gothic architecture ironically retarded the art of painting in France; even had painters wanted to compete with the stained glass, in the important churches there simply wasn't much wall surface to be painted. In Avignon, however, the 14th-century papal court attracted some of Italy's finest artists, especially Simone Martini of Siena and Matteo Giovanetti of Viterbo, whose frescoes inspired the graceful, colourful style known as International Gothic. A distinct school of painting developed from International Gothic and the influence of Flemish painters favoured by the last popes: the early 15th-century School of Avignon. The school's greatest masters were from the north: the exquisite Enguerrand Quarton (c. 1415–66) from Laon, and Nicolas Froment. The little that has come down from the 15th century continues to show a strong Flemish influence, as in court painter Jean Fouquet (c. 1420–75), and in the so-called 'Maître de Moulins'; it was Flemish miniaturist monks who illuminated one of the masterpieces of the century, the little book called the *Très Riches Heures du Duc de Berry* (1416).

Medieval Literature

Written French (really Francien, the dialect of the Franks around Paris) traditionally begins in 842 with the Oath of Strasbourg, signed by Charles the Bald and Louis the German, both grandsons of Charlemagne, though Latin remained the unchallenged language of scholars at the Sorbonne and elsewhere all through the Middle Ages. Already, the *jongleurs*, itinerant minstrels, were developing an oral tradition of narrative poetry, consisting mostly of stirring tales of feudal valour and the lives of saints. Some of these were written down c. 1100: the *Chansons de Geste*, many dealing with the deeds of Charlemagne and his knights. The most famous of them, the *Chanson de Roland*, is still read for pleasure today.

By the early Middle Ages, the old Latin vernacular of Gaul had divided into two distinct languages, the northern *langue d'oïl* and southern *langue d'oc* (from their two ways of saying 'yes'). The southerners, who would have laughed in derision to hear themselves called 'French', were closer to the Muslim world, which provided much of the inspiration for the first European poetry, and they produced the *troveres*, or troubadours. One of the first was a powerful duke, William IX of Aquitaine (1071–1127); other notables included Bertran de Born, Jaufré Rudel, Peire Vidal and Bernard de Ventadour.

The 'Courts of Love' in which this ideal of chivalry was perfected were brought to the north by Eleanor of Aquitaine, granddaughter of William IX. The subject of chivalry found its most mature expression in the high medieval masterpiece, the *Romaunt de la Rose*, begun by Guilaume de Lorris c. 1230 and finished by the more cynical Jean de Meun. Much later, the proto-feminist writer Christine de Pisan (1364–1430) would speak up for women (*Le Livre de la Cité des Dames*), in a time when the chivalric ideal had become an occasion for literary argument more than inspiration – a good deal of misogyny was in the air.

The 12th century also witnessed an increasing interest in the legends of the Celts; these too had always been present in the oral tradition. Chrétien de Troyes gave form to the Arthurian cycle in the 1160s and '70s, with *Lancelot*, *Erec et Enide*, and *Perceval*, in which the legend of the Holy Grail first appears. Medieval France always enjoyed a laugh, and the *fabliaux*, verse satires on everyday life, on haughty nobles and grasping friars, became increasingly popular. The love of animal fables created one master-piece, the stories of Reynard the Fox, the *Roman de Renart*, begun c. 1175 by Pierre de St-Cloud and carried on by other hands over the next 200 years until it became a veri-table epic cycle.

In the late Middle Ages, literature became less fantastical and more down-to-earth, especially as France suffered the continuing disaster of the Hundred Years' War. That period also saw the beginnings of French historical writing; François Villon (b. 1431), the Baudelaire of his day, left an intensely personal, topical, mocking portrait of life in medieval Paris. This was also a great age for the theatre, not only the mystery plays and miracle plays (dramatized lives of the saints) acted out inside churches, but secular theatre – farces, tragedies and morality plays put on by *confréries* or the guilds of lawyers and clerks, or (in Paris) the goldsmiths.

The Renaissance

The onset of the Wars of Religion retarded the progress of the new art in France, and in any case the country was slow in absorbing the lessons of the Italians. It did produce a few exceptional architects: Pierre Lescot, who designed the Cour Carrée of the Louvre (1546); Philibert Delorme (1514–70), whose few surviving works include the Château d'Anet, made for Diane de Poitiers; Jean Bullant (Petit Château at Chantilly, Château d'Ecouen); and Jacques du Cerceau and his son Baptiste. To most people, the term 'French Renaissance' conjures up visions of the great châteaux of the Loire. These were architectural hybrids, combining traditional French ideas, with an emphasis on turrets and gables, and some elements of the new Italian architecture (Blois, Chambord, Azay-le-Rideau, as well as some *hôtels particuliers* in the Marais, Paris).

Paralleling the arts, the classical revival begins in the 16th century with the poets called the *grands rhétoriquers*, and especially with the most famous of them, Clément Marot (1496–1544). A humanist and a Protestant, Marot wrote classical allegories and lyrics, and was constantly in trouble with the Church authorities and the Sorbonne.

Love poetry, though increasingly precious, was never out of fashion (Marot once wrote a sonnet in honour of his lady's nipple); something beyond came from the group of poets that came to be known as La Pléiade, refined, scholarly Humanists with a classical bent, including Pierre de Ronsard (*Odes* 1550), and Joachim du Bellay, a friend and protector of Rabelais remembered for his poems mourning the lost glories of ancient Rome (*Regrets*, 1558).

In prose, a bitter century produced two refreshingly sane writers: François Rabelais (1494–1553), a mocker and a scholarly sceptic in an age when both were dangerous, concealed his talent behind a career as a Franciscan friar. Later in life, he dropped out and became a physician, while writing his *Pantagruel* and *Gargantua* under the pen name Alcofribas Nasier. French literature before or since has produced nothing like this rare spirit, capable of mixing spectacular scatological humour and the praise of drink (on one level, the thirst is for wisdom), with a vision of the Abbey of Thélème, the ideal of a civilized, tolerant community. Another voice for good sense and tolerance was Michel de Montaigne (1533–92), who invented the term 'essay' and developed its literary form. From his book-lined tower on the family estate, Montaigne restated classical stoicism in a wholly original form.

17th-century Literature

The early 17th century was a turning point in French cultural life, a time that first expressed a national craving for order, authority and common sense after the tumults of the Wars of Religion. The tone for a restrained, reasonable (though oft over-decorated) literature was set by François de Malherbe, a mediocre and pedantic poet, and later by Jean Chapelain, critic and habitué of the salons, who came to control the pensions handed out by Louis XIV to favoured writers. So began the classical ideal of harmony and order that was to dominate the nation's cultural life for 200 years.

This was the age of alexandrines and well-polished clichés, and of the 'three unities' (time, place and action). While the theatres of England and Spain were enjoying real golden ages, France made do with the more formal, measured drama of Pierre Corneille (*Le Cid*, 1637, and a string of well-received plays in the 1640s), capturing the 'heroic ideal' of the time as an alternative to true tragedy.

This heroic ideal didn't last long. Popular opinion was more in tune with works like the worldly, cynical *Maximes* of François de la Rochefoucauld (1665). The influence of women, both in the salons and as writers, such as Madame de Sévigné and the novelist Madame de Lafayette, brought delicacy and urbanity, as well as a bit of new freedom. A great variety of miscellaneous literature appeared, from the sonorous volumes of sermons of the conservative Bishop Bossuet to Jean de la Fontaine's delightful verse fables. Charles Perrault, a protagonist in the great literary battle of the day, the 'Quarrel of the Ancients and Moderns', also gave the world the first collection of *Contes de ma mère l'oie – Mother Goose*, including fairy tales such as *Little Red Riding Hood*, *Sleeping Beauty* and *Puss-in-Boots*. One of the most popular figures of the day was poet and critic Nicolas Boileau, whose 'Le Lutrin' was the model for Pope's 'Rape of the Lock'.

Jean Racine (1639–99) restored tragedy from the formalism of Corneille. Racine took his themes from Greek mythology (*Iphigénie in Aulis*, and *Phédre*, his greatest work), from classical history (*Britannicus*, *Mithridate*), the Bible (*Esther*), and even from the contemporary Turks (*Bajazet*); all his dramas are noted for their strongly drawn characters with tragic flaws. The greatest Grand Siècle name of all is Molière

(Jean-Baptiste Poquelin, 1622–73), the master of farces and comedies of manners, and a breath of fresh air in an overdecorous age. Molière spent most of his life with his theatre troupes, like Shakespeare, whom he rivals in the rich humanity and wit of his comedies (*Tartuffe*, *Le Misanthrope*, *Le Médecin malgré lui*).

For all its fussiness, the age of Louis XIV maintained a strong interest in science – *Provinciales* and *Pensées* by Blaise Pascal (1623–62), scientist and philosopher, found a wide audience despite their tacit condemnation of the worldliness and watered-down piety of the court and aristocracy. Then there was Pascal's contemporary, René Descartes (1596–1650). Besides his contributions to mathematics, his analytic philosophy and logic have influenced everything written and thought in France since the publication of his *Discours de la méthode* in 1637.

French Baroque and Art in the Grand Siècle

The massive rebuilding of Paris in the 17th century created a tremendous demand for art of all kinds. The first of the remarkable *places royales* (squares built as unified architectural ensembles) emerged in the 1610s: Place des Vosges and Place Dauphine, while Henri IV had made it easy to find talented painters by converting the Long Gallery of the Louvre into lodgings and studios for artists. Patrons, however, continued to regard them as their servants, and imposed on them not only the subject matter but their own taste. The greatest French painters of the day, Claude Lorrain (1600–82) and Nicolas Poussin (1594–1665), fled Paris like the plague and spent most of their lives in Italy.

So Louis XIII was stuck with the insipid Simon Vouet (1590–1649) for his *premier peintre du roi*. All the court artists who followed – Le Sueur, Mignard and Lebrun – painted in his workshop. The greatest artist to work in Paris under Louis XIII had been Rubens, in town to do the queen-sized scenes of Marie de' Medici's life for the Palais de Luxembourg (now in the Louvre). Some of his Flemish and Dutch assistants stayed behind; they influenced a notable set of non-court painters to tackle similar everyday subjects, especially the Le Nain brothers – Antoine, Louis and Mathieu. An even greater realistic artist was Georges de La Tour (1593–1652), whose solemn figures captured in candlelight and shadow are the most distinctive of the period. But Louis XIV's opinion of the Flemish and realist painters was well known: '*Enlevez-moi ces magots*' ('Get these apes away from me').

Meanwhile the Counter-Reformation Church was promoting a new wave of religious building; with St-Paul-St-Louis in the Marais (1627) began the fashion for tepid reworkings of Roman Baroque, and Italianate domes began springing up all over Paris. In secular buildings, imported Baroque translated into a more restrained, more French manner; its leading exponents were François Mansart (1598–1666, Château de Blois) and Louis le Vau (Vaux-le-Vicomte, 1657–61, the beginnings of Versailles, 1669, and the Institut de France on the left bank of the Seine, 1661).

Together with the painter Lebrun, Le Vau and Le Nôtre created the style of the Grand Siècle. For the long postponed completion of the Louvre, though, Louis and Colbert had called upon the King of Baroque himself, Gianlorenzo Bernini, in 1664. Bernini's foreign ideas and arrogance caused endless disputes; finally his plans were abandoned and the project was entrusted to Claude Perrault. The result was a classicist revelation, a remarkably original colonnade that has had a tremendous influence over everything built in France since.

In 1648 the king founded the Académie Royale de Peinture et de Sculpture to govern his artists. The Académie lay dormant until 1661, when the indefatigable Colbert took over its direction. Colbert believed that art had but one purpose: to enhance the glory of his master, Louis XIV, and France. To make the propaganda credible, Colbert demanded that the Académie dictate the highest standards to painters and sculptors, and to the weavers and furniture-makers at the the newly established Gobelins. Astute flattery in the right places by Charles Lebrun (1619–90) earned him the position as the Académie's first director-dictator, and in 1675 he issued the magnificently flatulent *Tables de Préceptes*, the Académie's rules for art.

At the same time Colbert and Lebrun were snapping up paintings and sculptures for the royal collection (in the Louvre since 1681, where the academicians could study them). Lebrun, *premier peintre du roi*, spent his last 12 years directing the decoration of Versailles – painting the tedious Hall of Mirrors' ceiling with the glory of the Sun King.

The Enlightenment

Even in the last comatose decades of the 'Great Reign', there were stirrings of thought and change. The protestant Pierre Bayle spoke up for religious freedom and toleration (*Dictionnaire historique et critique*, 1697), while his contemporary the Sieur de Fontanelle spread new scientific ideas to the general public with his *Entretiens sur la pluralité des mondes* (1697). Only six years after the Sun King's death, the Baron de Montesquieu (1689–1755) wrote a book that would not have much pleased him: the *Lettres persanes* (1721), a satirical critique of French society. In 1748 came *De l'esprit des lois*, expounding a liberal political philosophy that would help inspire the Revolution.

Voltaire (François-Marie Arouet, 1694–1778) embodied the whole of Enlightenment beliefs and aspirations. His admiration for the freer climate and more progressive outlook of England, where he spent two years in the 1720s, resulted in his *Lettres philosophiques* (1734). The eternal enemy of the Church, its dogmas and its privileges, for over sixty years he was the voice of France's intellect and conscience against the rotting, medieval complex of crown, church and aristocracy. Besides his role as social critic and philosopher, he also found time to write volumes of poetry and letters, magisterial histories, and novels (*Candide*, 1759).

In the wake of Voltaire came the other *philosophes*, the men of new ideas, of whom the most prominent was Denis Diderot (1713–84), encyclopedist, dramatist, art critic, novelist and philosopher. He oversaw the creation of the famous 28 volume *Encyclopédie* (1772), to which most of the leading figures of the Enlightenment contributed; it was a summation of the scientific knowledge and philosophical speculation of the day, as well as a complete course in the new radical ideas. The other great influence of the age came from Jean-Jacques Rousseau (1712–78), a watch-maker's son from Geneva. Rousseau was the eternal opposite to urban, urbane Voltaire, the first since the pastoral poets of the Renaissance to celebrate nature, and along with it everything in humanity that could be called 'natural' – simplicity, spon-taneity and sincerity, as remedies for a culture that had been too studied and too artificial for too long. Foreshadowing the Romantic era, he was the champion of the creative spirit over artistic rules. His novels of sensibility (*Julie: ou la nouvelle Héloïse* and *Emile*) caused a sensation, while his *Du Contrat social* applied the same ideas to politics, with an analysis of the artificial bases of inequality and a revolutionary vision of liberty.

As the crisis of society built up steam through the century, many works took on more of an edge; most notoriously, there was the Marquis de Sade (*Justine, ou les malheurs de vertu*, 1791) who came along just in time to suggest that Rousseau's vision of natural virtue might somehow be flawed.

Neoclassicism and the Art of the Salons

As the Revolution approached, Paris was full to bursting with hack painters, and in 1791 the National Assembly opened the salon to all, bringing in a flood of art. The leading painter and art dictator of the Revolution, Jacques-Louis David (1748–1825), closed down the Académie's salon the next year and opened up a carbon copy called the Académie des Beaux-Arts. It held competitions for Neoclassical patriotic pictures like his own, evocations of austere civic virtue, modelled on a ludicrous fantasy of ancient Rome. He led the government's nationalizing of art from royal palaces, churches (at least the bits that somehow escaped the anti-clerical fury of the *sans-culottes*) and the châteaux of the *émigrés*.

In 1804 Napoleon made himself Emperor, instigating grandiose Neoclassical proj-ects in Paris, such as the building of the Arc de Triomphe (1806). He mandated the new Empire style to decorate his residences, and to create political propaganda pieces more repugnant even than Louis XIV's. Besides imitating Louis XIV's use of art to sanc-tify tyranny, Napoleon shared his mania for the prestige of sheer accumulation. Advised by David, he cleaned out a number of Italian collections and even stripped Venice's San Marco of its famous horses as a prize for Paris; he booted the artists out of the Louvre and made it the Musée Napoléon. But thanks to the little hoodlum, all the artists and art-lovers in Paris could freely go to study the Grand Masters – a crucial first step for the artistic revolutions that were to follow.

The 1819 salon was shocked by its first Romantic painting, a barn-burner called the *Radeau de la Méduse* (now in the Louvre) by Théodore Géricault (1791–1824). In 1822 Eugène Delacroix (1798–1863), putative son of Talleyrand, made his salon debut and quickly became the leader of the Romantics. Like Géricault he painted topical subjects that moved him; his *La Liberté guidant le peuple* (in the Louvre), the well-known image of the people of Paris at their barricades, was painted after the Revolution of 1830. Considered as an incitement to riot, it was hidden away until the Exposition of 1855.

The Romantic emphasis on the emotions and the individuality of the artist created the image of the artist as a bohemian, an eccentric outside respectable society. One group of painters – led by Théodore Rousseau (1812–67), went off to paint landscapes in Barbizon, a hamlet in the Forest of Fontainebleau. But the greatest landscape painter of the day was Camille Corot (1796–1875). As lyrical as his landscapes are, Corot was also the first painter inspired by photography; by mid-century, when the Académie and salon public had tacitly accepted the fact that the best an artist could do was mimic the camera, Corot was extremely popular, and artists were instructed to paint in his style, in various tones of grey.

'Paint what your eyes see' became the slogan of the realist painters who followed, although the first exponent, Gustave Courbet (1819–77) carefully composed his pictures to improve on it. Courbet's declarations that his own judgement and appreciation of his art was all that mattered infuriated the salon and its public. After Courbet, the salon next declared war on Edouard Manet (1832–83), who, like Corot, had sufficient means to withstand the thundering hostility his works provoked. When the salon jury of 1863 turned out so blatantly conservative that Napoleon III permitted a Salon des Refusés, Manet made Paris howl with outrage at the unclassical naked women in his *Déjeuner sur l'herbe* and *Olympia* (1866). Manet's bold new technique, and his novel but masterful handling of paint may have offended the smoothies in the salon, but it would make him the idol of the Impressionists.

19th-century Literature: Romanticism and Realism

If Rousseau was Romanticism's godfather, the movement in France hung considerably behind Britain and Germany. Exhausted, overstimulated, and confused – suffering its Revolutionary and Napoleonic double hangover – France had little to contribute, except perhaps André Chenier, the poet executed under the Terror whose works were not published until 1819. In most writing the prevailing tone was emptiness, loss and regret, the *mal du siécle*: The Vicomte de Chateaubriand (1768–1848), who reawakened intellectual interest in Christianity with his *Génie du Christianisme*, also redeemed the Middle Ages, leading to a great age of historical novels: Stendhal's *Chartreuse de Parme* (1839), and Alexandre Dumas' *Les Trois Mousquetaires* (1844). The growth of the middle class led naturally to a more popular literature, melodramas that could be serialized in newspapers such as Eugène Sue's *Mystères de Paris* (1842). The *mal du siècle* did bring forth some incisive historical writing, such as Jules Michelet's seminal *Histoire de France* (1844), though its greatest achievement was dedicated to another land – Alexis de Tocqueville's *De la démocratie en Amérique* (1844), still uncannily up to date after more than a century and a half.

Romanticism, still gathering momentum, eventually spawned native poets following in the wake of Byron and Shelley and Schiller. Victor Hugo (1802–85) had his first great success with a novel, *Notre-Dame de Paris* (*The Hunchback of Notre-Dame*) in 1831. His *Le roi s'amuse* became the libretto for Verdi's *Rigoletto*. Although politically radical, Hugo nevertheless exerted himself mightily to be elected to the Académie, finally succeeding on the third attempt in 1841. He wrote little else until *Les Misérables* in 1862. Much of his finest poetry also appeared in this late period, when Hugo was in voluntary exile from Napoleon III; by his death he had become a national institution.

Along with Romantic poets came Romantic novelists: Prosper Mérimée (1803–70), with his *Carmen* and *Colomba*, specialized in violent passions in exotic settings; George Sand (*Aurore Dupin*, 1804–76) began with socialist and feminist themes, and ended writing rustic romances. Honoré de Balzac (1799–1850), like Hugo, was capable of exhausting even the most devoted readers by the sheer volume of his work (*Père Goriot*, 1835, *Illusions Perdues, Splendeurs et misères des courtsanes*). An obsessive observer of every detail of contemporary society, Balzac arranged some 90 stories and novels into an all-encompassing overview of French society called *La comédie humaine*.

Under the gilded dictatorship of Napoleon III, many of France's intellectuals turned to the sturdier truths of science, or at least pseudo-science, as in the woolly Positivism of philosophers Auguste Comte and Hippolyte Taine, who sought to rationalize human life into narrow and poorly digested biological concepts. Another alternative was art for art's sake, as in the aestheticism of poet-novelists such as Théophile Gautier. Yet another was disgust and withdrawal; Charles Baudelaire (1821–67) a rebellious youth, led a life of drug-fuelled excess, at turns ribald and melancholy. A translator of Poe, a child alone in the modern city, Baudelaire set the pattern for the solitaire wrestling with the problem of modern evil. Parts of his *Les Fleurs du Mal* (1857) remained suppressed for obscenity until 1949. Disenchantment on a more down-to-earth level found expression in the novels of Gustave Flaubert (1821–80). Haunted by the difference between ideals and reality, between the vast complex facade of modern life and the elemental, Flaubert explored the none-too-flattering motives that govern our behaviour in *Madame Bovary* (1857) and *L'éducation sentimentale* (1870). Guy de Maupassant (1850–93), protégé of Flaubert, added to the roll of classic 19th-century novels of passion and greed with *Bel-Ami*, though he is better known for his collections of short stories.

The scientific bent of late 19th-century thought reached fiction in a tendency variously called 'realist' or 'naturalist'. Emile Zola churned out a cycle of 20 novels called *Les Rougon-Macquart* (1871–93). The subtitle, *Histoire naturelle et sociale d'une famille sous la second Empire*, gives away Zola's intention to put social relations under a 'scientific' scrutiny. One of the first to interest himself in the tribulations of the new working class, as in *Germinal* and *L'Assommoir*, Zola became the conscience of France when he intervened in the Dreyfus affair with his famous manifesto *J'accuse* (1898).

In Paris, at least, the bohemian idyll was contagious. The *décadents*, heirs of Baudelaire, took in absinthe and turned it into free verse. Mostly self-obsessed types who met bad ends, they shook up the dusty old metres and style of French verse while distilling poetic atmosphere and radiating subjectivity. The best were Paul Verlaine (1844–96) and his lover Arthur Rimbaud (1854–91) (the affair ended famously with pistol shots). Rimbaud, who preferred to be thought of as a 'Symbolist', was a precocious genius seeking the 'alchemy of word and sense' in poems ('Le Bateau Ivre') and prose poems ('Illuminations'). Rimbaud stopped writing at 20 and became a drunken bum; Verlaine kept writing and became a Catholic.

Impressionism and Beyond

In 1874 the Société Anonyme des Artistes held its first exhibition – yet another protest against exclusion from the salon. What set it apart from other protest shows were the artists exhibiting: Edgar Degas (1834–1917), Auguste Renoir (1841–1919), Camille Pissarro (1830–1903) and Claude Monet (1840–1926). Monet's painting of a sunrise entitled *Impression: Soleil Levant* inspired the papers to call the whole group *Impressionistes* – a name the painters adopted for their next seven exhibitions. The Impressionists were not as interested in the realism of photography as in the science behind it, the discovery that colour completely owes its existence to light, and they made it their goal to record objectively what their eye saw in an instant. Their works achieved considerable critical acceptance by the 1880s – although soreheads at the salon made sure that the state never spent any money to purchase their works; nearly all the magnificent paintings in Paris' Musée d'Orsay are later gifts.

The crucial role the south was to play in modern art dates from the 1880s, thanks to the two artists most closely associated with Provence today, Vincent Van Gogh (1853–90) and Paul Cézanne (1839–1906). Van Gogh was influenced at first by the Impressionists and Japanese prints he saw in Paris; after his move to Arles in 1888 he responded to the heightened colour and light of Provence on such an intense, personal level that colour came less and less to represent form (as it did for the Impressionists), but instead took on a symbolic value; colour became the only medium Van Gogh found powerful enough to express his extraordinary moods and visions. Cézanne's innovations were as important as Van Gogh's, although his response to Provence was analytical rather than emotional, perhaps because he was born in the south. Loosely associated with the Impressionists in the 1860s and '70s, by the 1880s he had undertaken his stated task of 'making Impressionism solid and enduring, like the art of the museums', exploring underlying volumes, planes and structure not through perspective, but through amazingly subtle variations of colour. A third important figure, Paul Gauguin (1848–1903) echoed Van Gogh in finding spirituality in colour. After leaving Paris for Pont-Aven in Brittany, his search for the primitive sources of creativity led him off to the South Pacific in 1891.

In these 'Post-impressionist' decades, plenty of artists remained in Paris, including Georges Seurat (1859–91), the most scientific of painters, who invented pointillism to bring a new classical structure to art. In 1884 he took part in the founding of the Salon des Indépendants, open to all; those exhibiting included Henri de Toulouse-Lautrec (1864–1901), whose portraits of Montmartre and Paris' underworld have so powerfully affected the way the world looks at Paris, and Henri Rousseau (1844–1910), the first and greatest of naïve painters. At the same time, the expressive Romantic Auguste Rodin (1840–1917) was shaking sculpture awake from its stale neoclassical doldrums, causing furious controversies with his powerful, often radically distorted works.

In the 1890s artists searched for ever more rare, exotic and exquisite stimulation – most interesting of all are the works of Odilon Redon (1840–1916), who painted from his pre-Freudian dreams, and was much admired by Mallarmé and the Symbolists. An unfortunate side effect of the 'decadents' with their languid maidens and ambiguous sexuality is that they retarded a genuine renaissance in European design, the Art Nouveau. Best known for its long flowing line inspired by plants and the geometry of natural growth, Art Nouveau's complete devotion to craftsmanship put prices out of reach of the masses, and it never caught the popular fancy. The little success Art Nouveau had in France outside of architecture was in vases by Gallé, curvilinear furniture by Prouve, Vallin and Majorelle, and the virtuoso creations of Lalique, whose intricate, fairy-like jewellery, often in the form of dragonflies or beetles, delighted Sarah Bernhardt.

Beaux-Arts, and a Revolution in Iron

As in art, the result of the Revolutionary/Napoleonic experience for architecture was to replace one kind of academicism with another. The opening of the Ecole Polytechnique in 1794 created the new model, entirely separating the engineering side of architecture from the artistic. To be an architect, you had to attend the Ecole des Beaux-Arts, the proud bastion of academicism. The real action was elsewhere. Paris, far ahead of any other European city, was on the verge of beginning a new architectural age, using durable, versatile iron and glass to make buildings fit for the Industrial Revolution and the new century dawning. Glass roofs were being put up over narrow shopping streets as early as 1776; the first of Paris' *passages*, or arcades, were probably built in the 1790s, and the first iron bridges appeared shortly after 1800. Other uses for iron and glass included churches, greenhouses, market buildings and the railway stations, prime symbols of the Industrial Revolution that tried to marry the new technology to traditional French monumental architecture. The most surprising application was supplied by the visionary architect Henri Labrouste (1801–75) in the main reading room of the Bibliothèque Nationale, an enormous, soaring ceiling of lovely intersecting domes, perching on the slenderest of iron columns.

In the reign of Napoleon III, Paris was transformed under the direction of the brilliant and forceful Prefect of the Seine department, Georges Haussmann. To facilitate traffic, to enrich the unsavoury swarm of speculators that buzzed about the imperial throne, and to get the poor out of sight and out of mind, central Paris was nearly obliterated by a gargantuan programme of slum clearance and boulevard-building. It might have been a perfect opportunity for a new architecture to take hold, but despite the new ideas and new advances, the Second Empire was the heyday of the Beaux-Arts, with eclectic regime showpieces like the completion of the Louvre wings and Charles Garnier's mammoth Opéra, begun in 1861. Recovery from the disasters of

1870–1 was slow, but by the 1880s the Third Republic was fostering inspired architecture once more. The 1889 Exposition was the apotheosis of iron, producing not only engineer Gustave Eiffel's tower but also the incredible Galerie des Machines (over 1,300ft long), demolished in 1910. The Eiffel Tower was a magical apparition: a symbol for Paris, for its century, for all of modern industrial civilization – a building with no purpose, an ornament, yet one that delights everyone and makes intellectuals discuss and contemplate endlessly.

20th-century Literature

With the turn of the century, ideas of the avant-garde began spreading from the artists and poets to the novelists; a wave of experimentation in style and language was pioneered by Marcel Proust (1871–1922), another old Dreyfusard, with his huge rumination on memory and eternity (*A la recherche du temps perdu*, 1913–27), and André Gide (1869–1951), whose works sought a 'new humanism' in themes of freedom and commitment.

Among the poets of the new century, the most popular was Paul Valéry (1871–1945), whose most famous poem 'Le Cimitiére marin' was a memory of his home town, Sète. Other poets were breaking moulds: Guillaume Apollinaire (1880–1918), friend of Picasso, Derain and other young artists, tried to translate their Cubist inspiration into poetry, and became a fantastical forebear of the Surrealists ('L'Enchanteur pourrissant', 1909; 'Alcools', 1913).

Surrealism, a term Apollinaire invented to describe his play *Les mamelles de Tirésias* (1917), attempted to subvert a perverse society from within, by attacking its perception and processes of thought. The assault was led by Andre Breton (*Nadja*, 1928), Louis Aragon and Paul Eluard. Another early Surrealist was Jacques Prévert (1900–77) who later became widely popular for his humorous, politically radical poems and song lyrics (*Paroles*, 1950). Eluard and Aragon too came to write more direct poetry, circulated clandestinely during the Occupation. This rare phenomenon – serious poets finding common ground with a mass audience – would lead to the postwar success of the *chanson française*, most memorably in the songs of Georges Brassens and Jacques Brel.

Paris' busy, creative 1920s also saw a revival of theatre. Most of the impetus came from Jean Cocteau (1889–1963) who not only wrote plays (*Orphée*, 1926) but collaborated on ballets with Satie and Milhaud. Jean Giraudoux (1882–1944) added a touch of the absurd, along with some high seriousness and poetic stylization, though in the age-old French tradition his plays dealt with classical themes and subjects as well as modern ones (*La Guerre de Troie n'aura pas lieu*, 1935; *Ondine*, 1939, *La Folle de Chaillot*, 1946).

Politically and philosophically, French letters remained divided along the lines of the Dreyfus case for decades. Put the extremes of left and right together, add a good dose of misanthropy, and you get Louis-Ferdinand Céline (1894–1961) who caused a sensation in the '30s with his *Voyage au bout de la nuit* (*Journey to the End of Night*) and

Mort à crédit (*Death on the Instalment Plan*), violent, nihilistic rejections of everything in a rotten modern world.

Interesting theatre picked up directly after the war. The more traditional works of writers such as Jean Anouilh (1910–87) maintained favour, though the spotlight soon turned to the more experimental works of Jean Genet (*Les Bonnes*, 1947) and especially to the 'theatre of the absurd' pioneered by Romanian-born Eugene Ionesco with *La Cantatrice Chauve* (1949, *The Bald Soprano*) and Irishman Samuel Beckett (*En attendant Godot*, *Waiting for Godot*, 1952).

No one mistook Jean-Paul Sartre (1905–80) for an absurdist; he first gained attention with plays (*Huis-clos*, 1944) and novels (*La Nausée*, 1938) as misanthropic as anything by Céline. Not content with describing an empty universe, he also developed existentialist philosophy to tell us what to do about it, beginning with *L'Etre et le néant* (1943). Albert Camus (1913–60), who grew up in Algeria, echoed Sartre's conclusions, but caught the dark postwar mood of alienation better with a series of remarkable novels (*L'Etranger*, 1942, *La Peste*, 1947) and plays (*Caligula*, 1945). Sartre's companion and collaborator Simone de Beauvoir (1908–86) became an important novelist in her own right, though she is best known for her groundbreaking feminist work *La Deuxième Sexe* (1949).

Much of the Baroque, relentlessly didactic flavour of French discourse in the postwar decades can be traced to the 'Structuralist' anthropology of Claude Lévi-Strauss (*Mythologiques*, 1964–71). His ideas were carried into the realm of contemporary culture by Roland Barthes (1915–80) and Jacques Derrida (1930–) with his idea of 'deconstruction': concentrating on the 'text' as an object in itself, something to be 'decoded'. The French approach has proved useful in the examination of the hidden codes by which our society operates, especially in the work of Michel Foucault (1926–84): studying the history of prisons and madhouses to discover society's 'principles of exclusion', compiling the history of sexuality, and 'archaeologies' of knowledge and science.

Few Frenchmen in the postwar years were moved to serious poetry, or by it, and by the '70s critics were speaking of the 'crisis of verse'. Such works as did appear were often little more than intellectual word games, as in Georges Perec, who wrote a long poem ('La Disparition') without using the letter 'e'. Even in fiction writing there had to be 'movements', complete with manifestos, and a little of all the ideas of the postwar ferment became grafted on to novel writing. As a counterpart to *nouvelle vague* cinema, there was the *nouveau roman*. Novelists such as Alain Robbe-Grillet, Nathalie Sarrante, Marguerite Duras and Claude Simon exploded the traditional framework of fiction, and played games with narrative and time, in settings of intentional vagueness and indeterminate reality. Not all readers were happy with a diet of constant polemics, and the traditional French novel lived on in the works of Françoise Sagan, Jean-Marie Le Clézio, Marcel Pagnol, the historical novels of Marguerite Yourcenar, the first woman elected to the Académie, and the endless list of detective novels by Georges Simenon (1903–89).

Movements in 20th-century Art

Among the poor bohemians living in Paris at the turn of the century were three painters inspired by the intense, pure colours of Van Gogh and the decorative Nabis group that followed Gauguin. Henri Matisse (1869–1954), André Derain (1880–1954) and Maurice de Vlaminck (1876–1958) first became known to the Paris public at an exhibition in 1905, when a critic labelled them 'wild beasts', or Fauves, for their uninhibited use of colour. Although Fauvism only lasted another three years, it was the first great avant-garde movement of the century and, as Matisse said, the one that made all the others possible.

The next movement followed quickly on its heels and lasted longer. In 1907 two hungry artists in Montmartre, admirers of the recently deceased Cézanne, Pablo Picasso (1881–1973) and Georges Braque (1882–1963), formulated Cubism, which liberated form in the same way that the Fauves had liberated colour. They aimed to depict the permanent structure of objects, and not the transitory appearance of the moment, by showing them from a number of angles at the same time.

In 1910 Robert Delaunay (1885–1941) began his vibrant Cubist paintings of the Eiffel Tower, and two years later went a step further from the austere Cubism of Picasso, Braque and Gris to a lyrical style of brightly coloured, non-representational abstraction which the poet Apollinaire called Orphism. Orphism had a strong influence on German Expressionism and Italian Futurism, if little in Paris. More new influences came with refugees from Eastern Europe: sculptors Constantin Brancusi (1876– 1957) and Osip Zadkine (1890–1967), who borrowed the multi-faceted aspect of Cubism to create powerful, expressive works; Marc Chagall (1887–1985), who, with his dreamy Russian-Jewish paintings, brought figurative painting into the avant-garde; and the Lithuanian-born Expressionist Chaim Soutine (1893–1943).

Meanwhile, Parisian Marcel Duchamp (1887– 1968) made the tradition of shocking the bourgeoisie a goal in itself (most famously at the 1913 New York Armoury Show, America's introduction to modern art). In 1915 he outraged the public even further with his 'ready-mades' – everyday items such as toilet seats displayed as art to challenge the typical attitudes towards taste. His anti-art ideas had followers on both sides of the Atlantic: Dada, founded in Zurich in 1916, arrived in Paris after the war with Francis Picabia and Tristan Tzara.

In 1924 a new manifesto announced that Dadaism was dead and a new movement with deeper aims, known as Surrealism, would take its place. As its theoretician, André Breton, explained it, Surrealism was 'to resolve the previously contradictory conditions of dream and reality into an absolute reality, a super-reality'. The police had to be called to stop the riots at the first Surrealist show in 1925: exhibitors included the American photographer Man Ray, Picasso, the Catalan Joan Miró (1893–1983) and Max Ernst (1891–1976); in 1929 the group was joined by another Catalan, Salvador Dalí (1904–89), whose knack for self-publicity made him the most famous and controversial member of the group.

After the war and occupation, the Paris art scene reflected the grey, postwar malaise. In the 1940s the explosion of Abstract Expressionism in New York stripped

Paris of its position in the avant-garde, leaving Paris with pale imitators – but also with refreshing 'anti-artists', such as Jean Dubuffet (1901–85), who engaged in open warfare with France's culture czars; in his art he rejected professional technique in favour of spontaneity and authenticity, which he called *art brut* (raw art), inspired by the works of children, prisoners and the insane. In the early 1960s a playful group of artists known as the Nouveaux Réalistes emerged, inspired by the everyday items presented as art in Duchamp's 'ready-mades', and by a disgust for contemporary culture: Niki de Saint-Phalle (b. 1930), Jean Tinguely (1925–92), Bulgarian-American Christo (b. 1935), César (b. 1921), Ben and Arman (b. 1928) gave Paris in the 1980s some of its most important (and amusing) monuments.

French Cinema

Photography is a field where France has made important contributions since the time of pioneers Niepce (1816) and Jacques Daguerre, who perfected daguerrotypy in 1839. It was only natural that the French should also have been at the forefront of the cinema. The Lumière brothers of Besançon perfected the first practical film projector, their *cinématographe* (from which the word cinema derives), in 1895.

Their early films inspired Georges Méliès, a magician by trade who pioneered in putting actual stories on the screen, beginning in 1896. He made one of cinema's first artistic triumphs with the magical *Le Voyage dans la lune* (1902), which included animated sequences. The Pathé Company , founded in 1896, had the best technology of its time, the first big studio, at Vincennes, and the first specially built luxury theatre, in Paris (1906). Its rival Gaumont, founded a year earlier, employed the first woman director, Alice Guy. These studios produced some of the first full-length features, including such international successes as Louis Mercanton's *Les Amours de la Reine Elisabeth*.

Before the First World War, the French film industry was the world's largest along with Italy's. It produced the popular comedian Max Linder, whose persona was the inspiration for Charlie Chaplin's, along with the elegant productions of directors such as Louis Feuillade (*Fantomas*, 1914), as well as 'art films', such as Comédie Française productions brought to the screen. The industry nearly closed down during the war because of a film shortage; it never recovered its leading role, though the '20s saw such memorable productions as Abel Gance's epic eight-hour *Napoléon*. Some recovery did take place in the '30s, and at the end of the decade France's industry was second only to America's. Many of the best films of the period were in a manner described as 'poetic realism', as in the works of Jean Renoir (1894–1979), son of the painter (*Boudu sauvé des eaux*, 1932, the anti-war *La Grande Illusion*, 1937, *La Règle du jeu*, 1939), as well as those of René Clair, who made one of the first important sound movies, *Sous les toits de Paris* (1930), Julien Duvivier (*Pépé le Moko*, 1937), Marcel Carné (*Le Jour se lève*, 1937, *Hôtel du Nord*, 1938), and Jean Vigo (*Zéro de Conduite*, 1933).

Ironically, French filmmaking did better under occupation in the Second World War than it had in the First. Marcel Carné was able to make *Les Enfants du Paradis*, a big-budget spectacular with screenplay by Jacques Prévert, in the middle of the war. Poet Jean Cocteau, who made the Surrealist film, *Sang d'un Poète* in 1930, returned to film-making after the war with a French classic, *La Belle et la bête* (1946). Robert Bresson continued a 50-year career of stylish films full of psychological insight (*Le Journal d'un curé de campagne*, 1950). Some of the most popular postwar films were made by Jacques Tati (1907–82), a former professional rugby player who provided some rare fun in a time when the French were not easily amused (*Les Vacances de Monsieur Hulot*, 1953, *Mon oncle*, 1958, *Playtime*, 1967). Max Ophüls, a German who directed sophisticated films in four different countries, gave France *La Ronde* (1950) and *Lola Montès* (1955).

The French began to take cinema more seriously in these years, seeing a necessity for an alternative to the more commercial American approach, and they went about it in a way that was typically French: the establishment of film schools and *cinema-thèques* (film museums), and the influential review, Andre Bazin's *Cahiers du Cinéma*, founded in 1951. A conscious 'movement' in cinema could not be far behind. The *nouvelle vague* (new wave) of films that were cheaply made (of necessity), shot on location and with less narrative continuity, made its breakthrough in 1959, with the works of François Truffaut (*Les Quatre cents coups*, 1959, *Jules et Jim*, 1961), Alain Resnais (*Hiroshima mon amour*, 1959), and Jean-Luc Godard (*Alphaville*, 1965, and plenty of Marxist-oriented works in the '60s and '70s). Along with these pioneers came a whole generation of directors: Claude Chabrol, Eric Rohmer, Agnès Varda and Louis Malle, names that dominated the French cinema for the next three decades, treating audiences to the blank face of Jean-Luc Belmondo and countless hours of Parisians smoking cigarettes and discussing their relationships. In many ways it was the counterpart of the *nouveau roman*, and there was a strong connection between the two; Alain Robbe-Grillet wrote screenplays for Alain Resnais (*L'Année dernière à Marienbad*, 1961), and directed films of his own.

The 1970s heralded the rise of a French star system, that aped the Hollywood model with Belmondo and Alain Delon at the outset, giving way to Gérard Depardieu and Isabelle Adjani by its close. With *L'Amour en fuite*, in 1978, François Truffaut completed a remarkable series of four films made over 20 years charting the life of Antoine Doinel – the character played by his alter ego, actor Jean-Pierre Léaud. But with the shock of Truffaut's death in 1984, his spirit of romantic humanism gave way to the more gritty, psychological nature of films by Maurice Pialat and Jacques Doillon. By contrast, the glossy *cinéma du look*, begun by Luc Besson (*Diva*, 1981), took hold in the mid-80s – epitomized by films like Jean-Jacques Beineix's *Betty Blue*, in 1985, and Besson's own first English language hit *The Big Blue* in 1988. It was perceived that the French industry needed to up its budgets to compete with Hollywood, and this led to a series of super-production, heritage films such as Claude Berri's Pagnol adaptations, *Jean de Florette*, and *Manon des Sources*, in 1985–6. French producers were still not averse to taking risks, however, giving one of the new generation of filmmakers, Léos Carax, the then biggest French film budget to date to make the modern fable *Les Amants du Pont Neuf*, with Juliette Binoche, in 1990. France scored its biggest domestic success to date with the medieval comedy *Les Visiteurs*, in 1993. More recently, a new breed of young filmmakers have begun to make their mark with widely diverging styles – from Matthieu Kassovitz's angry debut *La Haine* (1995) through Gilles Mimouni's stylishly complex *L'Appartement* (1996) to the poetic naturalism of Erick Zonca's *La Vie Rêvée des Anges* (1998).

Architecture: from Classicism to the *Grands Projets*

On the whole, it was a miserable century for French architecture, and the best works around are mostly by foreigners. With the turn of the 20th century, instead of carrying bravely on with modern styles, architecture inexplicably decayed into another heavy, tedious classicism – Louis XIV without the frills, as exemplified in the work of Auguste Perret (1874–1954; the first Frenchman to fall in love with bare concrete) and in the 1937 Exposition (Palais de Chaillot). France may have invented the term Art Deco, but no French architect ever caught its spirit.

France is largely exempt from blame for the beginnings of architectural Modernism, if only because early pioneer Tony Garnier was rarely allowed to build anything, and because Le Corbusier (Charles Jeanneret, 1887–1965) was really Swiss. The great theorist of the movement (*Vers une architecture*, 1923) built several houses in and around Paris in the '20s and '30s, and the Unité d'habitation in Marseille (1947) before turning to an abstract, curvilinear style (church at Ronchamp, 1950). More influential than his individual buildings were his plans for Paris; his Voisin Project proposed demolishing much of central Paris and replacing it with tidy rows of tower blocks. Paris' élite saved the city for itself, but after the Second World War it imposed Le Corbusier's totalitarian vision on hundreds of thousands of Frenchmen, 'rehoused' in grim suburban concrete wastelands. Today, scenes of the dynamiting of tower blocks are still a regular feature at the end of the French television news, but the damage inflicted on the fabric of France by the Modernist architects and planners will take at least a century to repair.

Until 1968 architects were still being trained almost exclusively in the Beaux-Arts, guaranteeing a maximum of conformity and an allergy to creativity. This shows best in Paris' huge office project of La Défense, begun in 1958. In the 1970s, though, the steadfast modernist President Pompidou stood Paris on its ear by commissioning Richard Rogers' and Renzo Piano's Centre Pompidou, a controversial, high-tech structure that has won fans even among traditionalists.

With the 1980s and President François Mitterrand, both Paris and its tutelary state were desperate to make up for so much lost time. Thus the Pharaonic era of the Grands Projets: the Grande Arche at La Défense, the Bastille Opéra, the Grand Louvre renovation that includes I. M. Pei's Pyramid, the Science Park at La Villette, the museum conversion of the Gare d'Orsay, almost all by foreign architects. For a glimmer of optimism on the state of French architecture, the building that won the widest acclaim in the last two decades has been Jean Nouvel's elegant Institut du Monde Arabe (1987) on the Left Bank.

Topics

The Names on the Pedestal

Every village has one. Some, for reasons that nobody remembers, have two. To any American, they will seem familiar, since they closely resemble the monuments that every town in the eastern states erected for the dead of the Civil War. Only instead of a slouch-capped Union or Confederate soldier, the statue on top will be a *poilu* in an iron helmet from the First World War. Some villages could only afford a simple stone plaque, and some chose to commemorate the war with allegories featuring naked ladies, as Frenchmen will do (and at least one village has a stone obelisk with a rooster on top). Still, in the 1920s the studios and foundries of Paris were cranking out bronze or iron *poilus* by the hundred. On the pedestal, usually, will be inscribed the names of the local boys who died in the Marne or the Somme or Verdun or Chemin-des-Dames. Just what all this means to the French may dawn on you, in a little village that scarcely counts two hundred people, when you look at the names and realize that there are over thirty of them.

'Eleven-eleven', Armistice Day, is still observed here. At noon, in almost every village, people will congregate by reflex at the monument to the *poilus*. Only a few years ago, one might still see a stooped old veteran or two, with ribbons on his coat. Today, any one still around would have to be a centenarian at least. The mayor, with or without his sash, will make a short speech, and maybe read a letter from a government minister or the head of a veterans' organization. Then, in our village and many others, comes the part that seems somewhat strange to us outsiders. The mayor reads the list of the soldiers who died, and after each name the assemblage gives the response like a congregation: '*Mort pour la France*'.

As in many nations, Armistice Day has become a day of remembrance for the dead of all the wars. The names listed may include a few from the Second World War, the Resistance, Vietnam or Algeria, but the overwhelming majority will always be from the War to End All Wars. In the beginning, they went off to war in sky-blue uniforms with bright red trousers – a Gallic gesture perhaps designed to impress the enemy in some strange way, but one that instead merely made the *poilus* better targets. The shooting gallery would be open for the next four years, a war that didn't seem to be about anything in particular, conducted by generals on both sides who didn't mind casualties in the tens of thousands, in the cause of trying out some new tactical ideas. When it was over, 1,400,000 Frenchmen were dead – roughly a fifth of the nation's young men.

In the years before the war, France had never seemed more prosperous and content. A stable government, the first since the Revolution, presided over an age of social progress and techological marvels, of ice cream and the first holidays on the beach and the bright colours of the avant-garde painters, an age epitomized by the Paris of the great World Fairs, the Moulin Rouge and the Eiffel Tower. When it was over, France had been bled white. Besides the sheer loss of life, the wreck of an entire generation, the war left much of the northeast of the country in ruins (in Picardy the farmers are still finding unexploded shells). France's economy was in ruins too; after 1918 business, along with the government's tax revenue, contracted by a sixth; recovery would really only start in the 1950s.

In the '20s France watched Germany rebuild, and complained that the Americans were giving it better terms on the war debts than her allies. The inter-war decades were filled with strikes and dissension even before the Depression came along to leave the country even lower. When the next war came, France was still dealing with the shocks of the first one. Though not entirely exhausted in a physical sense, emotionally and physically something seemed to have died. When the challenge came, France simply collapsed.

It was definitely a rough century, here as much as any part of Europe. The noted historian André Maurois, however, repeats over and over the fact of his country's 'wonderful powers of recuperation'. There have been other disasters, and worse ones: the Hundred Years' War, and the Wars of Religion. Maurois, writing in the '60s, was no doubt fondly wishing that the charm would work again. Perhaps it has, though these things take time, and the disasters of the early 20th century are the central fact of the nation's life, more so than the long ago age of cathedrals, or the Grand Siècle of Louis XIV, or even the Revolution. So it is entirely fitting that a tiny village, each year, should come out and dedicate a few minutes to the memory of Louis, Laurent, Cyprien, Armand, Auguste, Daniel, Abel, Alphonse, Paul, Omer, Isidore, Jean, Joseph, Germain, Ernest and Charles.

North and South

'Well, what about us?' regionalist partisans of the Bretons, Corsicans, Catalans and Basques might ask. They have a case, but for the moment, let us consider this surprisingly diverse France as essentially two nations. According to most histories, it all started in the Dark Ages, when Gaulish Latin vernacular was evolving, or maybe decomposing, into two languages. Latin didn't have a word for yes, surprisingly (the Romans were never the most agreeable of peoples). To indicate affirmation, they would say *hic*, literally 'thus', and through the prisms of the two opposite ends of Gaul this came out *oc*, in the south, and *oïl* in the north, where people even at this early date showed a deplorable sloppiness about their consonant sounds. Eventually the northern version would be spelled *oui*, but people as early as the Middle Ages came to call the two nations after their languages, the *langue d'oc* and the *langue d'oïl*.

It would, however, be a mistake to say that the north-south division is as old as history. It's older. Recent research (through aerial photography, place names and archaeology) has discovered faint traces of a line of fortifications that once cut a nearly straight line clean across what is now France. It may have been built by the prehistoric Ligurians, an unsuccessful try at keeping out the Celts. The Romans refortified it, as a second line of defence against any Germans who broke through the Rhine frontier, and later it would mark the southern boundary of the Franks. South of the line was always the more civilized part, the Gallia Togata of the great Romanized cities: Lyon, Marseille, Arles, Nîmes, Narbonne. To the north lay forests and bears, little Gaulish villages probably quite like Asterix's, and scubby backwater outposts such as Lutetia ('Mudville') on the Seine, one day to be Paris.

By one of history's tricks, this wilderness was to give birth to a creative and powerful civilization in the Middle Ages. For the first time, the south was falling behind. Occitania (a word invented only in the 18th century to describe the Provençal-Languedocien-Gascon-Aquitanien-Auvergnat cultural world) was thriving too – this after all was the home of the troubadours. But the north suddenly had bigger ideas, greater resources, and, most important of all, a huge surplus of well-armed knights. These came south to stay in the Albigensian Crusade, in which the pretence of extinguishing Languedoc's Cathar 'heretics' made possible a land-grab of monumental proportions. The Crusaders' leader was northerner Simon de Montfort – grim-visaged, incredibly lucky and always victorious. After his death at the siege of Toulouse other captains took up the fight, and often kept the land they won. For many southerners, the castle of Montségur is the Alamo, the last hurrah of not only the Cathars (1244) but all the tolerant, sophisticated world of medieval Occitania. Other parts fell to Paris later on; Provence did not become part of France until 1481.

The cultural effacement of Occitania came later. Landmarks along the way include the Edict of Villars-Cotterets in 1539 that made French the legal language of all the kingdom, and the dividing of France into homogenous *départements* in the Revolution, erasing all the old regional boundaries and names. Despite these, north and south carried on as essentially separate countries. Until the Revolution, there were actually customs barriers, and tolls to pay, between north and south. In our time, Paris was still treating the south like a conquered province. The new schools of the Third Republic taught in French only, and until very recently students were punished if they were caught speaking their own language in the schoolyard; the Parisians created the myth that the Occitan languages were not languages at all, but mere *patois*. The south's politics were carefully managed by northerners; in radical, Catalan Roussillon, for example, they long manipulated the vote to keep one of their own sitting for the *département* in the National Assembly; no natives need apply.

The south is the Midi, the Noonday, in the same way Italians call their south the Mezzogiorno, and like the good burghers of Milan and Turin, many northern Frenchmen have always found it unaccountable that they should be sharing a country with such outlandish and foreign-seeming people, that there should be a France where palm trees and lemons grow. The stereotypical view was voiced by Ernst Renan: 'Our foolishness comes from the south, and if France had never drawn Languedoc and Provence into her sphere of activity, we should be a serious, active, Protestant and parliamentary people'.

Today the Occitan/Provençal languages of the troubadours are seeing a modest revival, and even some state schools are teaching them – for the first time ever. Some towns put up street signs in Occitan, and when you see a car with a white oval sticker on the back that says OC instead of F, you've found a partisan for the cause. Contacts between nationalistic Occitans and Catalans have already begun to create a kind of cross-border cultural union – an eastern counterpart to the relationship between French and Spanish Basques.

Especially since the introduction of regional governments in the '80s, southerners have shown new confidence, and a new willingness to re-examine their identity, their interests and their future. Their olive oil and duck fat-fuelled cuisine is triumphant everywhere, and even the economy is reviving in many places. Some think that France might have a long-sustained 'sunbelt' boom like America's. Some of the big southern cities, moribund for centuries, are on their way up, notably Toulouse, Montpellier and Nice, while some rural areas that became severely depopulated a century ago are filling up again with people from all over France and Europe, who find them simply delightful places to live or retire. The south, perhaps, shall rise again.

Microtourism

To keep it smaller than a breadbox, this book by necessity concentrates on France's more obvious charms – its Eiffel Towers, the awe-inspiring cathedrals, its most stunning châteaux. While visiting them, however, you may feel swept up in a tide of tourists, of hordes shooting the big-game monuments of France with Nikons or camcorders to add them like trophies to their collections. Behind this dazzling surface, however, is another, less chic and arty place, an eminently rural, slow France, that is far from boring. Getting the most out of it requires learning to look at the country the way the French themselves do – on a small scale. Connoisseurs of every particularity of *village* and *pays*, the French are passionately interested in the detail of traditional life and local history. Painstaking cartographers have compiled maps showing traditional roof styles in France: where they are high-pitched or shallow, and where the boundary is between slate and canal tiles (which roughly corresponds to the boundary between the *langue d'oil* and *langue d'oc* – it's all connected). Other maps display the types of construction used for *pigeonniers*, or dovecotes.

Get the locals talking about these subjects and they'll go on for hours, explaining how in some areas only nobles were allowed to keep pigeons, which went out every day and ate all the peasants' grain and so caused the Revolution, which allowed everyone to keep pigeons, and farmers let the poo pile up for their daughters' dowries, but later they planted groves of poplars when a girl was born, because the trees would mature just in time for her marriage, by which time chemical fertilizers had made pigeon droppings less valuable than firewood... you get the idea. And by the way, you've probably noticed how the poplars are always planted in orderly quincunxes, but scholars are divided on whether this fashion, invented by King Cyrus of Persia, came into France in the Middle Ages or in the time of Louis XIV...

If you want to play too, the first thing to do is pick up the Cartes IGN: Série Bleue map for the area that interests you. Drawn on a scale of 1:25,000, these are the equivalent of the Ordnance Survey or US Geodetic Survey maps. You'll find them in any good newsagent or bookshop; walkers and mushroom-hunters probably account for much of the demand. From the first glance, you'll get a feeling for the traditional life and the slowly evolving fabric of your area: the villages and hamlets, each with its patch of cleared farmland, like islands in the vast green of the forests, along with the works that kept life going: sawmills, remains of old water mills, *pigeonniers*, sandpits and quarries, sources and fountains.

The map will show you some surprises, even if you think you already know the area well. Naturally it will help you find the nearest swimming hole, and some nice places for a walk in the woods, but there will be other surprises too: maybe a dolmen or menhir, a collection of *gariottes* or a fortified tower, or a medieval chapel in an unlikely place that may turn out to have seven devils frescoed on the walls inside. Ruins, by the score, are generally marked on the map – without further detail, so take pot luck; ruins can mean anything from bits of a Roman aqueduct to a routiers' stronghold destroyed at the end of the Hundred Years' War, or a barn abandoned by some poor farmer who gave up when the phylloxera hit.

Once you get to know the country and its history better, you'll be able to read these maps like a detective. That village surrounded by a circuit of roadside crosses – it must have been a *sauveté* of the Church in the 1100s; the crosses marked the limits within which knights were forbidden to bash each other or molest the peasants. Crosses of all kinds grow thick along the roadsides. People from Brittany to the Alps have various folk stories to explain them, but in fact many are simply the latest incarnation of markers that go back to Neolithic times.

Not least among the virtues of rural France is modesty. This doesn't mean a lack of pride; on the contrary nearly everyone here is convinced that their particular coin is Paradise on Earth. But rather, modesty as an outlook, as a way of life. As historian Emmanuel LeRoy Ladurie has noted, France is the country where bars are called *Au Petit Bonheur* or *Au Petit Profit*. Ladurie and others have developed an equally modest and original way of looking at the past. 'Microhistory', studying a single place and time in the minutest detail, not only flushes out unwarranted generalities and clichés, but adds real depth to our understanding. And a little understanding is all that the rural French, the 'provincials' so disdained by the Parisians, ask of the visitor. Deeply in love with their country, they are concerned that we learn to appreciate it as they do. With understanding, the *petits bonheurs* and sweet surprises begin to add up, secret doors into a country where the roots of life are rich and deep.

Big Mac Attack

Jose Bove and his nine co-defendants absolutely denied that they 'wrecked' that McDonald's in Millau, in the Aveyron, back in August 1999. Rather, they called it 'a festive dismantling with collateral damage'. Whatever that means, they did a pretty thorough job of it, over $100,000 damage and entirely without the use of any such potential pollutants as dynamite or nitroglycerin. The leader of *Confédération Paysanne* and his followers were out to make a point, and no one doubts they succeeded. Now everybody in France knows who they are, and 20,000 people came out to show their support when Mr Bove went on trial. That didn't stop the court from sending him down for three months but at last report Bove is still out leading demonstrations and adding spice to the talk show circuit while appeals continue.

Though festively dismantling a McDonald's might seem like good clean family fun, opinions in the Anglophone world found the whole exercise a bit immature. The French, it was often claimed, just couldn't understand 'globalization', and it was all a matter of some grumpy peasants venting some steam at a common symbol of American hegemony. Thanks to the congenital laziness of most of the media, though (especially television), most Americans in particular never got to hear the real story. It's about cows, all right, but not about the indisputably Gallic ones that get turned into McDo's burgers here. The cows in question are American, nice fat ones pumped full of growth hormones. France, and Europe, won't let them into their markets. They believe in the precautionary principle – that more should be known about the health effects of artificially juiced-up food before they are put on sale. America says rather, you've got to eat our beef whether you like it or not, and it's none of your business what we put in it. That's what free markets are all about.

The US has invented a nice new shiny World Trade Organization, where it can sue countries that let health, environmental or social concerns get in its way. But in the meantime, while the issue of hormone-laced cows is being fought out there, Washington has used its favourite tactic of 'revolving sanctions' against France, cleverly designed to annoy as many Frenchmen as possible. For a year it might be 100 per cent tariffs on champagne, and then on perfume, or perhaps Roquefort cheese. That, in fact is what it was. Mr Bove's sheep happen to be signed up with the Société Roquefort, and he has been getting screwed by Uncle Sam over a quarrel that has nothing to do with him.

French politicians do not like to argue with Mr Bove, or with any farmer. This is after all the country where every new president traditionally forgives all outstanding traffic fines on his first day in office, a country where the art of governance has become almost all carrot and no stick. Like the truckers who can now shut down France any time they feel like when fuel prices go up, and the trade unions that stop the railroads every now and then just to remind the government that they can do it, France's farmers are politically unassailable. They can close borders, tie up roads, or trash warehouses full of imported wine while the *gendarmes* stand and watch. Local officials are always in their corner; farmers do vote, and besides, no mayor really needs ten tons of manure dumped on the steps of his *mairie*.

For decades now, France's farmers have had the temerity to demand that they be allowed to make a good living in the old-fashioned way, in the face of all the trends, and defying all the economists' prattle about markets and the inevitability of more efficient means of production. While fighting for their livelihoods, they have also been fighting to keep their communities alive – as when the government tries to close village schools or cut transport services. In trying to preserve a way of life, they have suffered a good deal of condecension from the economic planners, but things are changing fast. In a time when issues of food seem to crystallize the big issues, the farmers of *Confédération Paysanne* suddenly look very much like the cutting edge. They have made the connection between healthy food, a healthy environment, and healthy communities. Europe's 'mad cow' crisis, very much in the public eye, is their Exhibit A. France's record of protecting consumers, like that of most European countries, is hardly more virtuous that America's; fate just led the two systems to foul up in different ways. The framers point out that whenever agriculture is corporatized and indusrialized, this is what happens: chemical, potentially fatal food, a poisoned environment, and dying villages. Now they have a philosophy, and they know who the enemy is. France and the rest of the world will be hearing from them again.

That World Record Breaking Spirit

As far as we know, Jean Gimpel in his Medieval Machine was the first to use this expression to describe a key trait of the French, that spirit of *élan*, that shot of Gallic pepper sauce, that daring to go an extra mile, often right over the top, that sets them apart in Europe. No one else does it with such panache. Rugby and football fans know it well. Les Bleus are playing a sloppy game, the other side looks sure to win, when suddenly the French rustle up their old *esprit de corps* with the flair of d'Artagnan, with something of the fire that kindled Jeanne d'Arc or rallied Napoleon's diehards against the odds, and proceed to steamroll the bewildered opposition.

The first true sign of the World Record Breaking Spirit is in Brittany. Alignments of a few dozen menhirs sufficed for other Neolithic folk, but in Carnac there are thousands. Charlemagne was a big one-off spark in the Dark Ages, but in the 11th century the juices really began to flow. Adventure was there. The Normans grabbed it in Britain and southern Italy; in the Crusades, France responded with more enthusiasm than anyone to the papal jihad and set up one of their own, Geoffroy de Bouillon, as king of Jerusalem. The biggest Romanesque churches in the world were built at Cluny (destroyed), followed by Toulouse's St-Sernin (still there); French monasteries sponsored the great pilgrimage routes to Compostela. A century later in the Ile-de-France, Abbot Suger built the first Gothic church at St-Denis. Gothic really ignited the WRBS, in the first romances, in the intellectual challenges of Abelard's dialects, in sheer walls of stained glass, and as the cathedrals grew like the tower of Babel ever closer to God – at least until Beauvais', the tallest ever, which collapsed.

The Hundred Years' War, itself something of a record-breaking war, put the kibosh on all that (indeed the mind boggles to think what France might have done if it hadn't been Europe's favourite battleground). Later the concentration of power in one man – the king – also concentrated the WRBS. The court's Loire châteaux, and François I's personal collection of the same, still dazzle today, although it was Louis XIV who created the yardstick for modern megalomania in Europe. So much of the nation's resources were sucked into Versailles that the gilt, the marble vases, the dainty tables might as well be made of blood. A far more useful project of his reign, the linking of the Mediterranean and the Atlantic with the Canal du Midi, was achieved by Paul Riquet, an engineer who spent his own money on his idea when Louis refused to help, and inevitably went broke.

As the sap began to rise again in the 18th century, France was on its way to starting the Industrial Revolution. In 1778 Jouffroy invented the first steam boat, and the French got a steam car on the road in 1792; it immediately crashed into a wall. Instead, France chose to have another kind of Revolution – a World Record Breaking Revolution – before the bottled-up talent and ambition of the nation was hijacked by Napoleon, whose extra private helping of WRBS cost, by his own account, the lives of a million Frenchmen. When the dust settled, the Parisians invented the department store and much of what we call modern society; Eiffel erected his daredevil tower, the tallest structure in the world, and built a skeleton for the Statue of Liberty. The French invented, although they didn't always get to the patent office first: photography, the hot air balloon, automobiles, motion pictures, the phonograph, and the aeroplane. As the 19th century marched on, the restless, feverish impetus to go beyond the limits led to the first great -isms of modern art and literature as French daring and freedom sucked in avant garde talent from around the world. Even the cancan and the Moulin Rouge were world record breaking in their way.

After a prolonged postwar hangover, France didn't really get back into its groove until the 1970s, when speed became an obsession: high-speed trains, rockets and jets made in Toulouse, followed by two co-productions with Britain, the Concorde super-sonic jets and the Channel Tunnel. France Telecom came up with the Minitel before there was an Internet. Pharaonic WRBS *Grands Projets* changed the face of Paris.

The French (wisely, if the Millennium Dome and World Fair in Hanover are any indi-cation) avoided seeing in 2000 with any more *Grands Projets*, but not without WRBS: turning the Eiffel Tower into the world's biggest Roman candle on New Year's Eve was perhaps the most brilliant single image of the world celebrations, and it was followed, on Bastille Day, with the fondest: *L'Incroyable Pique-Nique*, a 1,000km-long picnic straight down the heart of France along the Paris Meridian (which, in 1884, lost its honour of anchoring all the world's lines of longitude to Greenwich). Renamed the Green Meridian for the Millennium, it was planted with trees by children and deco-rated with plinths by artists. The Badoit company supplied miles of plastic checked tablecloth in the name of '*Amour, Fraternité, Mayonnaise*'. A 24-hour relay race along its length was part of the *fête*, while each of the 337 *communes* along the Green Meridian organized their own individual celebrations (the Picnic of the Nap, the e-Picnic, a Picnic of the Kiss, a picnic on in-line skates). The weather didn't cooperate as it might have, but nothing could dampen a feeling that was mostly a stranger to war-wounded, existential, cynical, deconstructed France in the 20th century: optimism.

The Most Improved Nation

Nearly everybody of a certain age has fond memories of their first trip to France. Trying to buy bread, for example, and mistaking the gender of the word. '*C'est une baguette! Une baguette!*' shrieks the shopkeeper, wagging her finger while the other customers viciously smile. Back in the '70s, it seemed the streets were full of pinch-faced sods who quite literally, we all found, wouldn't give you the time of day. We learned to appreciate, if only as a kind of surreal comic relief, the jaded bureaucrats who pretended not to understand anything you said, while they tried to think of another piece of paper to send you out hunting for, or the impossible middle-aged women with hairdos from hell and the inevitable poodles whose expressions matched theirs exactly. Many of these belonged to France's unique class of shop-keepers, those desiccated souls who thought of customers only as nuisances who open the door and let in a draught, and who used to hang up *Entrée libre* signs by the door, knowing we would feel honoured by the privilege.

The spirit of the age was captured in the *minuterie*, the arch-French device that, when you turned on the light in the hotel lobby, would give you just enough of it to let you reach your floor in total darkness. Non-smokers, not having lighters, would then knock on doors and try their key whenever nobody answered.

Back in the '50s, Paris was looking pretty shabby. Culture Minister André Malraux made Paris' building owners clean off all the grimy façades, though it didn't seem to cheer anyone up. It was a difficult time. The music was rotten, nothing got built except concrete monstrosities, and cultural life was dominated by the Stalinist-existentialist spleen of Monsieur Sartre; foreigners were not forgiven for thinking it all looked like boredom and angst masquerading as art and philosophy. Modern art had moved on to New York, and in Paris' galleries nothing much was happening. Even after France finally got fed up with Charles de Gaulle, in 1968, the tone was still set by the National Nose and his governments of nervous grey technocrats with sticks up their heinies, the fellows who built the public housing *cités* and knocked down Les Halles, Paris' beloved market.

When the technocrats built a horrific new home for the state-controlled radio and television on the banks of the Seine, its own employees named the place 'Alphaville', after the cold, clinical and thoroughly sinister fantasy city in the 1965 film of the same name by Jean-Luc Godard. That film made quite an impression on the French; like all the best science fiction, it showed them exactly where they were headed.

It was a common Anglo-American misconception at the time that France's ill-humour came from smoking Gauloises; another is that they were mad at us for liberating them. The fact is, France had reason to be grumpy. The traumas of the early 20th century were murder on a country that has always been rather highly strung. We like to imagine that France in the late 1400s, after the Hundred Years' War, was much the same, and the art of the time does hint of neurosis, just like Alphaville on the Seine and the other creations of the postwar decades. The good news is that the fit does seem to be passing. All of us foreigners who have been around a while have noticed it, so it must be true. Now, even Parisians occasionally smile.

What has happened to France's ill-humour? It hasn't all disappeared, and there are still plenty of poodle ladies and reptilian bureaucrats to remind you where you are. And the country still has its share of bizarre habits, like the brown (yes, brown) chrysanthemums people give their dear departed on All Souls' Day, or the beige bathroom tiles with pictures of tropical fish on them, which in *la France profonde* are the only kind you can get. Even *bal musette* music (cue the accordions) is making a comeback, though considering the musical alternatives in this country that might not be such a bad thing.

The signs are everywhere. A French director has made a successful comedy. The *cités*, the poverty traps that became the sites of so much violence and *anomie* in the last thirty years, are dynamited almost daily. Following the political sleaze is delicious; everyone seems to enjoy it, and this is one area where the French know they can successfully compete with the Americans. The French are more open to new ideas than they have been for a long time, and they definitely seem happier and more relaxed. Shame about the bathroom tiles.

Travel

06

Getting There

By Air

From the UK and Ireland

The main international airports are at Paris (Roissy-Charles de Gaulle and Orly), Bordeaux, Brest, Grenoble, Lille, Lyon, Marseille, Montpellier, Nantes, Nice, Rennes, Strasbourg and Toulouse. It takes around 50mins to fly from London to Paris, or a mere 90mins to Nice, deep in the south of France. Prices depend on how and when you wish to travel. To be sure of a seat and to save money (especially in the summer and during the Easter holidays), it's well worth shopping around and trying to book as far ahead as possible.

For the latest bargains, check with your preferred travel agency or in your major Sunday newspaper, *Time Out* or the *Evening Standard*. To get an idea of the lowest fares available you could also take a look on the Internet at the useful sites found at *www.cheapflights.com*, *www.travelocity.co.uk* or *www.lastminute.com*.

There are a number of low-cost charters from London to France's regional airports, but from the rest of the UK and Ireland it can work out cheaper to fly to Paris and from there catch a cheap flight or train onwards (*see* 'Getting Around', below).

Airline Carriers

UK and Ireland

Major Carriers

Air France, t 0845 0845 111, **f** (020) 8782 8115, *www.airfrance.co.uk*. Regular flights from Heathrow, Birmingham, Edinburgh, Glasgow, Humberside, Manchester, Newcastle, Southampton and Teesside to Paris Charles de Gaulle. Also flies from Heathrow to Lyon and Toulouse; from Gatwick to Brest, Caen, Nantes and Strasbourg; and from London City to Paris Charles de Gaulle, Le Havre and Rennes.

AOM French Airlines, t (01293) 596663, **f** (01293) 596658. Flies from Paris Orly to Marseille, Nice, Perpignan and Toulon, with connecting flights to and from London if required.

British Airways, t 0345 222 111, **f** (0161) 247 5707, *www.britishairways.com*. Daily flights from Gatwick or Heathrow to Paris, Bordeaux, Lyon, Marseille, Montpellier, Nantes, Nice, Perpignan and Toulouse. Also flies directly to Paris Charles de Gaulle from Aberdeen, Belfast, Birmingham, Bristol, Cardiff, Edinburgh, Glasgow, Inverness, Jersey, Manchester, Newcastle, Newquay and Plymouth.

British Midland, t 0870 6070 555, *www.british midland.com*. Flights from Aberdeen, Belfast, Edinburgh, Glasgow, Heathrow, Leeds, Manchester and Teesside to Nice and Paris Charles de Gaulle.

Love Air, t (01279) 681434, **f** (01279) 680356, *loveair@lineone.net*. Flights from Birmingham to Caen, Le Havre, Nantes and Rennes.

Scotairways, t 0870 606 0707, **f** (01223) 292160, *www.scotairways.co.uk*. Flights from Norwich to Paris Charles de Gaulle.

Low-cost Carriers

The cheap no-frills low-cost carriers such as Go, Buzz, Ryanair and EasyJet can get you to Paris or Nice from London for upwards of £39 single if you book well in advance. You can book directly over the Internet. Prices go up the closer you get to your leaving date; fares booked last minute are, in fact, not much cheaper than those of the major carriers. All services may be less frequent in the winter.

Buzz, t 0870 240 7070, *www.buzzaway.com*. Flights from Stansted to Paris Charles de Gaulle, Bordeaux, Lyon, Marseille, Montpellier and Toulouse.

EasyJet, t 0870 600 0000, **f** (01582) 443355, *www.easyjet.com*. Daily flights from Luton and Liverpool to Nice.

Go, t 0845 605 4321, *www.go-fly.com*. Flights from Stansted to Lyon.

Ryanair, t 08701 569 569, *www.ryanair.com*. Regular flights from Stansted to Biarritz, Carcassonne, Dinard (coach to Rennes) and St-Etienne (coach to Lyons); also from Glasgow to Paris Beauvais.

From the USA and Canada

There are frequent flights to Paris, the gateway to France, on most of the major airlines. During off-peak periods (the winter months and fall) you should be able to get a scheduled economy flight from New York to Paris from as little as around $370–$460, and for an extra $100 or so a transfer to one of the regional airports (for instance, Bordeaux, Grenoble, Lyon, Marseille, Strasbourg or Toulouse). Delta flies regularly from New York to Nice, and in the summer you may also be able to get non-stop charters to some of the regional destinations (especially Marseille or Lyon – call Nouvelles Frontières for details).

Check the Sunday-paper travel sections for the latest deals, and if possible research your fare initially on some of the US cheap-flight websites: *www.priceline.com* (bid for tickets), *www.expedia.com, www.hotwire.com, www.bestfares.com, www.travelocity.com, www.eurovacations.com, www.cheaptrips .com, www.courier.com* (courier flights), *www.fool.com* (advice on booking over the net) or *www.ricksteves.com*.

It may work out cheaper to fly to London and then continue your journey to Paris from there. In which case, you could fly onwards using some of the British low-cost carriers such as Go and Buzz; *see* the box below for website details.

Charter Flights

Though the likes of Go and EasyJet are slightly cheaper, charter flights can be good value, and offer the added advantage of departing from a wider range of regional airports. Companies such as Thomson, Airtours and Unijet can offer return flights from as little £80. Check out your local travel agency, the Sunday papers and TV Teletext. In London, look in the *Evening Standard* and *Time Out*. Remember, there are no refunds for missed flights – most travel agencies sell insurance so that you don't lose all your money if you become ill.

Nouvelles Frontières, Heritage House, 35 Watling St, Canterbury CT1 2UD, **t** (01227) 785451. Charter flights from nearly all the UK airports.

USA and Canada

Major Carriers

Air France, 125 West 55th St, New York, NY 10019, **t** 800 237 2747, Canada **t** 800 667 2747, *www.airfrance.com*. Non-stop flights from New York to Lyon, daily flights to Paris from Philadelphia, twice a day from Cincinnati, and three times a day from Atlanta. Regular services also from Boston, Chicago, Houston, Miami, San Francisco and Washington.
American Airlines, **t** 800 433 7300, *www.im.aa.com*. Flights from Boston, Chicago, Dallas, JFK, Los Angeles and Miami.

British Airways, **t** 800 AIRWAYS, *www.britishairways.com*.
Continental, **t** 800 231 0856, **t** 800 343 9195 (hearing impaired), Canada **t** 800 525 0280, *www.continental.com*. Flights from Houston and Newark.
Delta, **t** 800 241 4141, *www.delta.com*. Flights from Cincinnati and Atlanta to Paris, and regularly from New York to Nice.
Northwest Airlines, **t** 800 225 2525, *www.nwa.com*. Flights from Detroit to Paris.
Nouvelles Frontières, 6 East 46th St, New York, NY 10017, with branches on the West Coast and Canada, **t** 800 677 0720, **t** (212) 986 3343, *www.newfrontiers.com*. Discounted scheduled and charter flights on Corsair from LA, Oakland and New York to Paris (from around $400), and non-stop to some French provincial cities.
TWA, **t** 800 892 4141, *www.twa.com*.
United Airlines, **t** 800 241 6522, *www.ual.com*.

Students, Discounts and Special Deals

UK and Ireland

Besides saving 25% on regular flights, young people under 26 have the choice of flying on special discount charters. Students with the relevant ID cards are eligible for considerable reductions, not only on flights but also on trains and admission fees to museums, concerts and more. Agencies specializing in

By Sea

The ferry is a good option if you're travelling by car or with young children (children of four–14 get reduced rates; under-fours go free), or if you want to nip across the Channel to do some shopping (it takes 35mins from Dover to Calais by seacat). Fares can be expensive and do vary according to season and demand (these days, annoyingly, the brochures will only print a rough 'price guide'). The most expensive booking period runs from the first week of July to mid-August; other pricey times include Easter and the school holidays. Book as far ahead as possible and keep your eyes peeled for special offers. Some good-value five-day mini breaks for a car and up to nine people (Caen and Cherbourg from £65) and 10-day saver-breaks (Caen and Cherbourg from £88) are available. On many sailings, bicycles go free. You will have to pay extra to bring a motorcycle or a trailer.

Brittany Ferries, The Brittany Centre, Wharf Road, Portsmouth PO2 8RU, t 08705 360 360, *www.brittany-ferries.com*. Sailings from Portsmouth to Caen (6hrs) and St-Malo, from Poole to Cherbourg (4.25hrs), and from Plymouth to Roscoff (6hrs).

Condor Ferries, The Quay, Weymouth, Dorset DT4 8DX, t (01305) 761551, *www.condor ferries.co.uk*. Sailings from Weymouth and Poole to St-Malo.

student and youth travel can supply ISIC cards. Try:

STA, 6 Wright's Lane, London W8 6TA, *www.statravel.com*, t (020) 7361 6161; Bristol, t (0117) 929 4399; Leeds, t (0113) 244 9212; Manchester, t (0161) 834 0668; Oxford, t (01865) 792 800; Cambridge, t (01223) 366 966; and many other branches in the UK.

Trailfinders, 194 Kensington High St, London W8 6BD, t (020) 7937 1234, *www.trailfinder.com*.

Usit Campus Travel, 52 Grosvenor Gardens, London SW1 0AG, t (020) 7730 3402, *www.usitcampus.co.uk*; branches at most UK universities, including Bristol, t (0117) 929 2494; Manchester, t (0161) 833 2046; Edinburgh, t (0131) 668 3303; Birmingham, t (0121) 414 1848; Oxford, t (01865) 242 067; Cambridge, t (01223) 324 283.

Europe Student Travel, 6 Campden St, London W8, t (020) 7727 7647. Kindly travel agency, catering to non-students as well.

USA and Canada

If you're resilient, flexible and/or youthful and prepared to shop around for budget deals on stand-bys or even courier flights (you can usually only take hand luggage on the latter), you should be able to get yourself some rock-bottom prices. Check out Airhitch (stand-by tickets), Council Travel (student discounts) or the *Yellow Pages* for courier companies (Now Voyager is one of the largest in the USA). For discounted flights, try the small ads in newspaper travel pages (e.g., *New York Times, Chicago Tribune, Toronto Globe and Mail*). Numerous travel clubs and agencies also specialize in discount fares, but may require an annual membership fee. Also see the websites at *www.xfares.com* (carry-on luggage only) and *www.smarterliving.com*.

Airhitch, 2472 Broadway, Suite 200, New York, NY 10025, t (212) 864 2000, *www.airhitch.org*. Last-minute tickets to Europe from around $170.

Council Travel, 205 East 42nd St, New York, NY 10017, t 800 743 1823, t (212) 822 2700, *www.counciltravel.com*. Major specialists in student and charter flights; branches all over the USA. Can also provide Eurail and Britrail passes.

Last Minute Travel Club, 132 Brookline Av, Boston, MA 02215, t 800 527 8646.

Now Voyager, 74 Varick St, Suite 307, New York, NY 10013, t (212) 431 1616.

STA, t 800 781 4040, *www.statravel.com*, with branches at most universities and also at 10 Downing St, New York, NY 10014, t (212) 627 3111, and ASUC Building, 2nd Floor, University of California, Berkeley, CA 94720, t (510) 642 3000.

TFI, 34 West 32nd St, New York, NY 10001, t 800 745 8000, t (212) 736 1140.

Travel Cuts, 187 College St, Toronto, Ontario M5T 1P7, t (416) 979 2406. Canada's largest student travel specialists; branches in most provinces.

Rail Passes

If you're planning on taking some long train journeys, it may be worth investing in a rail pass.

Available in the UK and Ireland

The excellent-value **Euro Domino** pass entitles EU citizens to unlimited rail travel through France for three–eight days in a month for £99–£198, or £79–£159 for 12–25-year-olds.

These days, EU citizens of any age and non-EU citizens who've been resident in Europe for more than six months are all eligible for the **InterRail** pass (currently £269 if you're over 26, or £129 if you're under 26). Passes entitle holders to 22 days' unlimited second-class travel through France, Belgium, Luxembourg and Holland (one zone), plus 30–50% discounts on trains to cross-Channel ferry terminals, and returns on Eurostar from £59. InterRail cards are not valid on trains in the UK.

Contact: Rail Europe, 179 Piccadilly, London W1V 0BA, **t** 08705 848 848, *www.raileurope. co.uk* or *www.inter-rail.co.uk*.

Available in the USA and Canada

The North American **Eurail** pass allows unlimited first-class travel through 17 European countries for 15-, 21-, 30-, 60- or 90-day periods; it saves the hassle of buying numerous tickets, but will only pay for itself if you use it a lot. It is not valid in the UK, Morocco or countries outside the European Union. Two weeks' travel is $388 for those under 26; those over 26 can get a 15-day pass for $554, a 21-day pass for $718, 30 days for $890 or three months for $1,558.

Other passes for North Americans include the **France Railpass**, which gives three days of unlimited travel throughout the country in a one-month period for $180 (reducing to $146 per person for two people travelling together). The equivalent **France Youthpass** gives under-26s four days' unlimited travel through France over a two-month period, including reduced rates on Eurostar, for $164. The **Europass** gives unlimited first-class travel through France, Germany, Italy, Spain and Switzerland for 5, 6, 8, 10 and 15 days in a two-month period for $348–728, or $233–513 if you're under 26. You may also wish to invest in a Paris Museum Pass ($20 for one day), a Bus and Metro Paris Pass ($40 for two days) or a five-day **Rail 'n' Drive** pass giving three days' unlimited rail travel through France and two days' car rental for $175.

Contact: Rail Europe USA, **t** 1 800 438 7245, *www.raileurope.com*.

Hoverspeed Ferries, International Hoverport, Dover CT17 9TG, **t** 08705 240 241, **f** (01304) 240 088, *www.hoverspeed.co.uk*. Seacats Dover–Calais (35mins), Folkestone–Boulogne (55mins), Newhaven–Dieppe (2hrs).

Norfolkline, **t** (01304) 218 410, **f** (01304) 218 420, *www.norfolkline.com*. An alternative option to consider between Dover and Dunkerque, but for cars only, not foot passengers.

P&O Portsmouth, Peninsular House, Wharf Rd, Portsmouth PO2 8TA, **t** 0870 242 4999, **f** (01705) 864 211, *www.poportsmouth.com*. Day and night sailings from Portsmouth to Le Havre (5.5hrs) and Cherbourg.

P&O Stena Line, Channel House, Channel View Rd, Dover CT17 9TJ, **t** 0870 600 0600, **f** (01304) 863 464, *www.posl.com*. Ferry and superferry from Dover to Calais (45mins).

SeaFrance, Eastern Docks, Dover, Kent CT16 1JA, **t** 08705 711 711, **f** (01304) 240033, *www.seafrance.com*. Sailings from Dover to Calais (1.5hrs).

Southern Ferries/SNCM, 179 Piccadilly, London W1V 9DB, **t** (020) 7491 4968, **f** (020) 7491 3502. Sailings from Marseille/Nice/Toulon to Corsica/Sardinia/Livorno/Genoa.

Useful Numbers

Parking information in Dover: **t** 0839 401 570.
Shopping information in Calais: **t** 0839 401 577.
Weather forecast for Dover: **t** 0839 444 069.
Weather forecast for France: **t** 0891 575 577.

By Train

Air prices and the sheer brain-mushing awfulness of airports make travelling by high-speed train an attractive alternative. Eurostar (**t** 0990 186 186) trains leave from London Waterloo or Ashford International, in Kent, and

French Railway Routes

© SNCF

there are direct connections to Paris (Gare du Nord; 3hrs; £70), Brussels (2hrs 40mins; £70) and Lille (2hrs; £60). Eurostar also goes directly to Disneyland Paris (3hrs) and the French Alps. Fares are cheaper if booked at least seven days in advance and you include a Saturday night away. Check in 20mins before departure, or you will not be allowed on to the train.

When they're not breaking world records, France's legendary TGVs (*trains à grande vitesse*) zip along at an average speed of 180mph: from Paris there are swift connections to Avignon, Nice and Montpellier in the south; Limoges, Bordeaux, Biarritz and Lourdes in the southwest; and Reims, Nancy and Strasbourg in the east. The journey from Paris's Gare de Lyon to Marseille takes only 4hrs 25mins; to Dijon and Poitiers 3hrs; to Avignon 3hrs 35mins; to Montpellier 4hrs 25mins; to Nice 6hrs 30mins. Ticket prices from London range from £95 to Dijon and Reims, to £125 to Nice, Toulouse and Marseille.

Another pleasant if slower way of getting deep into France is by overnight sleeper after dinner in Paris (and SNCF have recently been cracking down on robberies in the compartments at night by introducing security patrols and eliminating many of the train stops between midnight and 5am). People under 26 are eligible for a 30 per cent discount on fares (*see* the travel agencies in the box on pp.83–4) and there are discounts if you're 60 or over, available from major travel agencies. Details, advance reservations and car hire information are available at:

Rail Europe, 179 Piccadilly, London W1V 0BA, t 08705 848 848, *www.raileurope.co.uk*.
Rail Europe, 226 Westchester Av, White Plains, NY 10064, t 1 800 438 7245, *www.raileurope.com*. Take your passport.

By Coach

Eurolines has regular coach services from London to over 65 destinations, including Paris, Bordeaux, Chamonix, Grenoble, Perpignan, Roscoff, St-Malo and Strasbourg. If you book a week in advance, return tickets to Paris are as low as £33. The journey to Paris takes 8hrs, to Avignon and Marseille 19hrs, and to Toulouse 22hrs. Peak-season fares between 22 July and 4 September are slightly higher. There are discounts for anyone under 26, senior citizens, and children under 12. In the summer, the coach can be the best bargain for anyone over 26; off-season you may be able to find an equivalently priced flight.

Contact: Eurolines, 52 Grosvenor Gardens, London SW1Q 0AU, t 0990 143 219.

By Car

Putting your car on a Eurotunnel train is the most convenient way of crossing the Channel. It takes only 35mins to get through the tunnel from Folkestone to Calais, and there are up to four departures an hour 365 days of the year. In low season, tickets for a car and passengers should cost around £170 return, rising to £200 return at peak times. If you travel at night (*10pm–6am*), it will be slightly cheaper. Special-offer day returns (look for them on the website)

range from £15 to £50. The price for all tickets is per car less than 6.5m in length, plus the driver and all passengers.

Contact: Eurotunnel, t 0990 353 535, *www.eurotunnel.com*.

A fairly comfortable but costly option is to put your car on a Motorail train. Accommodation is compulsory, in a four-berth (1st class) or six-berth (2nd class) carriage. Linen is provided, along with washing facilities. Compartments are not segregated by sex. The Motorail services operate from May to September running from Calais to Avignon, Brive, Narbonne, Nice and Toulouse.

Contact: Rail Europe (*see* 'By Train', above).
French Motorail, t 08702 415 415.

If you prefer a dose of bracing sea air, you've plenty of choice, although changes and mergers may be on the horizon. Short ferry crossings currently include Dover–Calais with P&O Stena, t 0870 600 0600, SeaFrance, t 08705 711 711, or Hoverspeed, t 08705 240 241, which offers the fastest crossing, at 35mins. See 'By Sea', above, for information on other routes. Prices vary considerably according to season and demand, and, as always, it pays to shop around for the best deal.

For information on rules and regulations when driving in France, *see* 'Getting Around', pp.89–90.

Entry Formalities

Passports and Visas

Holders of full, valid EU, USA, Canadian, Australian and New Zealand passports do not need a visa to enter France for stays of up to three months. If you intend to stay longer, the law says you need a *carte de séjour*, a requirement EU citizens can easily get around as passports are rarely stamped. Non-EU citizens had best apply for an extended visa before leaving home, a complicated procedure requiring proof of income, etc. You can't get a *carte de séjour* without the visa, and obtaining that is a trial run in the *ennuis* you'll undergo in applying for a *carte de séjour* at your local *mairie*. For further information contact your nearest French consulate (*see* p.102).

Customs

Those arriving from another EU country do not have to declare goods imported into France for personal use if they have paid duty on them in the country of origin. You are allowed to bring in, duty paid, up to 800 cigarettes or 400 cigarillos, 200 cigars or 1kg of tobacco; plus 10 litres of spirits, 90 litres of wine and 110 litres of beer.

Travellers from the US are allowed to bring home duty-free goods to the value of $400, including 200 cigarettes or 100 cigarillos, 50 cigars or 250g of tobacco; plus 1 litre of spirits (or 2 litres of fortified wine or other spirits under 22% alcohol); plus 2 litres of wine.

For more information, telephone the US Customs Service at t (202) 354 1000, or see the pamphlet *Know Before You Go* available from *www.customs.gov*. You're not allowed to bring back absinthe or Cuban cigars.

Getting Around

By Air

Air France (in the UK, t 0845 0845 111) has a very extensive nationwide network with daily connections to 27 cities from Paris Orly, and another 17 cities from Paris Charles de Gaulle. Show-up-and-fly 'Navette' shuttles leave Orly at frequent intervals: every 30mins for Marseille and Toulouse, every hour for Nice, several times a day for Bordeaux.

Scheduled domestic flights on Corsair, France's second national carrier, can be booked in England via their agents Nouvelles Frontières (t (01227) 785451). To get the best prices be sure to book at least 14 days in advance and include a Saturday night. Ask about reduced prices for under-26s and over-60s, and discount family fares for anyone who has a husband, wife or children tugging at their coat-tails.

By Train

The SNCF's France-wide information number is t 08 36 35 35 35 (3.35F/min), or check out *www.sncf.com* (you can book advance tickets from the USA or UK prior to departure

on this website, and pay by credit card at an SNCF machine in France).

The SNCF runs a decent and efficient network of trains through all the major cities. Prices have recently gone up but are still reasonable. If you plan on making only a few long hauls the Euro Domino or France Railpass (*see* 'Rail Passes', p.85) will save you money. Other possible discounts hinge on the exact time of your departure.

For ordinary trains (excluding TGVs and *couchettes*), SNCF has divided the year into blue (off-peak) and white (peak) periods, based on demand: white periods run from Friday noon to midnight, and from Sunday 3pm to Monday 10am, and during holidays (all stations give out little calendars).

If you depart in a Période Bleue with a return ticket, travel over 200km and stay at least a Saturday night, you'll get a 25% discount (**Découverte Séjour**). Couples are eligible for a **Découverte à Deux** tariff, which gives a discount of 25% on all trains when travelling together in a blue period.

Anyone over 60 can purchase a **Carte Sénior** (290F) valid for a year and giving 25–50% off individual journeys according to availability, and 25% off train journeys from France to 25 countries in Europe. There is also a **12–25 Carte** which offers 50% reductions in blue periods and a 25% reduction in white periods.

Anyone can save money by buying a second-class ticket at least a week to a month in advance (**Découverte J8 or J30**), the only condition being that you must use it at the designated time on the designated train, with no chance for reimbursement if you miss it.

Tickets must be stamped in the little orange machines by the entrance to the lines that say *Compostez votre billet* (this puts the date on the ticket, to keep you from using the same one over and over again). Any time you interrupt a journey until another day, you have to re-compost your ticket. Long-distance trains (Trains Corail) have snack trolleys and bar-cafeteria cars; some have play areas for small children.

Nearly every station has large computerized lockers (*consignes automatiques*) which take about half an hour to puzzle out the first time you use them, so plan accordingly;

also note that any recent terrorist activity in France tends to close them down across the board.

By Coach

There is no national bus network. Though local services can work out, do not count on seeing any part of rural France by public transport. The bus network is just about adequate between major cities and towns (places often already well served by rail), but can be rotten in rural areas – where the one bus a day fits the school schedule, leaving at the crack of dawn and returning in the afternoon. More remote villages are linked to civilization only once a week or not at all.

Buses are run either by the SNCF (replacing discontinued rail routes) or private firms. Rail passes are valid on SNCF lines, and buses generally coincide with trains. Private bus firms, especially when they have a monopoly, tend to be more expensive than trains. Some towns have a *gare routière* (coach station), usually near the train station, though many lines start from any place that catches their fancy.

For details on local bus services, enquire at your local tourist office in France.

By Car

Unless you plan to stick to the major cities or the coast, a car is the only way to see some of the remoter parts of France. This has its drawbacks: expensive petrol and car hire rates, and an accident rate double that of the UK (and much higher than in the USA). The vaunted French logic and clarity breaks down completely on the asphalt. Never expect any French driver to be aware of the possibility of a collision.

Roads are generally excellently maintained, but anything of less status than a departmental route (D road) may be uncomfortably narrow. Mountain roads are reasonable except in the vertical *département* of Alpes-Maritimes, where they inevitably follow old mule tracks. Shrines to St-Eloi, patron of muleteers, are common here, and a quick prayer is a wise precaution. Conditions vary widely: in rural Languedoc you may catch up on your sleep while you drive; traffic in the Côte d'Azur, the 'California of Europe', can be diabolically Californian, and parking a nightmare; in Paris, parking is forbidden in many streets in the centre. Many towns now have pricey guarded car parks underneath their very heart, spectacularly so in Nice. Everywhere else, the blue 'P' signs infallibly direct you to a village or town's already full car park.

Rules and Regulations

You will need your vehicle registration document, full driving licence and an up-to-date insurance certificate. Green cards are no longer compulsory, but are worth getting as they give fully comprehensive cover – your home insurance may only provide minimum cover. If you're coming from the UK or Ireland, you'll need headlight converters to adjust the dip of the headlights to the right. Carrying a warning triangle is mandatory if you don't have hazard lights, and advisable even if you do. In the mountains you may need to buy (or hire from a garage) snow chains. Drivers with a valid licence from an EU country, Canada, the USA or Australia do not need to have an international driving licence.

France has over 8,000km of motorways and most of these are privately run toll roads or *autoroutes à péage* which can be paid for by cash or credit card. Speed limits are 130km/80mph (110km/h in wet weather) on the *autoroutes* (toll motorways); 110km/69mph on dual carriageways (divided highways and motorways without tolls); 90km/55mph on other roads; 50km/30mph in an 'urbanized area' – as soon as you pass a white sign with a town's name on it and until you pass another sign with the town's name barred. Fines for speeding, payable on the spot, begin at 1,300F and can reach an astronomical 10,000F if you fail the breathalyser (the limit is 0.05% alcohol).

If you wind up in an accident, the procedure is to fill out and sign a *constat amiable*. If your French isn't sufficient to deal with this, hold off until you find someone to translate for you so you don't accidentally incriminate yourself. If you have a breakdown and are a member of

Car Hire

Car hire in France can be an expensive proposition. To save money, look into air and holiday package deals as well as combination 'Train and Auto' rates (*see* 'Rail Passes', p.85). Prices vary widely from firm to firm: beware the small print about service charges and taxes. The minimum age for hiring a car in France is around 21 to 25, and the maximum around 70. Your local tourist office will have a list of car hire agencies.

UK and Ireland

Avis, t 0990 900500, f 0870 6060 100.
Budget, t 0541 565 656, f (01442) 280092.
Europcar, t 0870 607 5000, f (01132) 429495, *www.europcar.com*.
Hertz, t 0990 996699, f (020) 8679 0181.
Thrifty, t 0990 168 238, f (01494) 751 601, *thrifty@thrifty.co.uk*.

USA and Canada

Auto Europe, 39 Commercial St, Portland, ME 04101, t 888 223 5555, t (207) 842 2000, *www.autoeurope.com*.
Auto France, 211 Shadyside Rd, Ramsey, NJ 07446, t 800 572 9655, t (201) 934 6994, f (201) 934 7501, *www.autofrance.com*.
Avis Rent a Car, 900 Old Country Rd, Garden City, NY 11530, t 800 331 1084, t (516) 222 3000, *www.avis.com*.
Europe by Car, 1 Rockefeller Plaza, New York, 10020 NY, t 800 223 1516, t (212) 581 3040, f (212) 246 1458, California t 800 252 9401, t (213) 272 0424, f (310) 273 9247, *www.europebycar.com*.
Europcar, 5330 E. 31st St, P.O. Box 33167, Tulsa, OK 74153 1167, t 800 800 6000, t (918) 669 2823, f (918) 669 2821, *www.europcar.com*.
Hertz, 225 Brae Bd, Park Ridge, NJ 07656, t 800 654 3001, *www.hertz.com*.

France used to have a rule of giving priority to the right at every intersection. This has largely disappeared, although there may still be intersections, usually in towns, where it applies – these will be marked.

Watch out for the *Cedez le passage* (Give way) signs and be careful. Generally, as you'd expect, give priority to the main road, and to the left on roundabouts. If you are new to France, think of every intersection as a new and perilous experience. Watch out for Byzantine street-parking rules (which would take pages to explain, so do as the natives do, and be especially careful about village centres on market days). When you (inevitably) get lost in a town or city, the *Toutes directions* or *Autres directions* signs are like Get Out of Jail Free cards. Watch out for the tiny signs indicating which streets are meant for pedestrians only (with complicated schedules in even tinier print).

Petrol (*essence*) at the time of writing is 7.4F a litre for unleaded, 7.8F a litre leaded, 5.3F for diesel (gasoil), but varies considerably, with motorways always more expensive. Petrol stations keep shop hours (most close Sunday and/or Monday) and are rare in rural areas, so consider your fuel supply while planning any forays into the mountains – especially if you use unleaded. If you come across a garage with petrol-pump attendants, they will expect a tip for oil, windscreen-cleaning or air.

Contact: Europ Assistance, Sussex House, Perrymount Rd, Haywards Heath, West Sussex RH16 1DN, t (01444) 442211. They offer help with motorcar insurance for travelling abroad.

Useful Websites

Route planner: *www.iti.fr*.
Autoroute information: *www.autoroutes.fr*.
Roads and traffic information: *www.equipment.gouv.fr*.

a motoring club affiliated with the Touring Club de France, ring the latter; if not, ring the police.

The French have one delightfully civilized custom of the road: if oncoming drivers unaccountably flash their headlights at you, it means that the gendarmes are lurking just up the way.

By Bicycle

Cycling signals more pain than pleasure in most French minds. That said, one of the hazards of driving in the Alps and Pyrenees is suddenly coming upon bands of cyclists pumping up the kinds of inclines that most people require escalators for. If you mean to cycle in the south during the summer, start early and stop early to avoid heatstroke. French drivers, not always courteous to fellow motorists, usually give cyclists a wide berth; and yet, on any given summer day, half the patients in a French hospital are from accidents on two-wheeled transport. Consider a helmet. Also be aware that bike thefts are fairly common, so make sure your insurance covers your bike or the one you hire.

Getting your own bike to France from the UK and Ireland is fairly easy: Air France, British Airways and some of the ferry operators will carry them free. From the USA or Australia most airlines will carry them as long as they're boxed and are included in your total baggage weight. In all cases, telephone ahead. Certain French trains (called Autotrains, with a bicycle symbol in the timetable) carry bikes for free; otherwise you have to send it as registered luggage, and pay a 40F fee, with delivery guaranteed within five days.

You can hire bikes of varying quality (most of them 10-speed) at most SNCF stations and in major towns. The advantage of hiring from a station means that you can drop it off at another, as long as you specify where when you hire it. Rates run at around 50F a day, with a deposit of 300–400F or a credit card number. Private firms hire mountainn bikes (VTTs or *vélos tout terrain*) and racing bikes. There are cycling paths and shelters in most French towns, and cycle hire points in some car parks.

Those aged between 14 and 16 need to pass a road safety test before they can ride a moped up to 50cc.

For more information on cycle touring abroad contact:

Cyclists' Touring Club, Cotterell House, 69 Meadrow, Godalming, Surrey GU7 3HS, t (01483) 417217, f (01483) 426994, *cycling@ctc.org.uk*.

On Foot

A massive 40,000km network of long-distance paths, or Sentiers de Grandes Randonnées, **GRs** for short (marked by distinctive red and white signs), takes in some of France's most spectacular scenery.

Each GR is described in a Topoguide, with maps and details about campsites, refuges and so on, available in area bookshops or from the Comité National des Sentiers de Grande Randonnée, 8 Av Marceau, ✉ 75008 Paris, t 01 47 23 62 32, or the Fédération Française de la Randonnée Pédestre, 64 Rue Gergovie, ✉ 75014 Paris, t 01 45 45 31 02.

The complete set, plus English translations covering GRs in Alsace and Provence, is available from Stanfords, Long Acre, London WC2, t (020) 7836 1321.

Otherwise, the best maps for local excursions, based on ordnance surveys, are put out by the Institut Géographique National (1:50,000 or 1:100,000), available in most French bookshops.

Of special interest are: GR5 from Holland to Nice; GR3 following the entire length of the Loire; GR65, the Chemin de St-Jacques, from Le Puy-en-Velay to Santiago de Compostela (in Spain); GR52 from Menton up to Sospel, the Vallée des Merveilles to St-Dalmas-Valdeblore (in the Provençal Alps); GR52a and GR5 through Mercantour National Park (*both of which are only open end of June–beginning Oct*); GR51, nicknamed 'the balcony of the Côte d'Azur', from Castellar (near Menton), taking in the Esterel and Maures before ending at Bormes-les-Mimosas; GR9, beginning in St-Tropez and crossing over the region's most famous mountains – Ste-Baume, Ste-Victoire, the Luberon and Ventoux; GR4, which crosses the Dentelles de Montmirail and Mont Ventoux en route to Grasse; and GR42, which descends the west bank of the Rhône from near Bagnols-sur-Cèze to Beaucaire.

For a description in French of the *Sentier Cathare* (which is well marked and well endowed with places to eat and stay en route) via the famous Cathar citadels of Padern, Peyrepertuse and Puilaurens to Montségur, *see* Louis Salavy's excellent *Le Sentier Cathare*.

For other walks in the Pyrenees you could also consult the excellent *Randonnées Pyrénéennes* by J. L. Sarret.

Tour Operators and Special-interest Holidays

For a complete list of tour operators, see the Maison de France website at *www.franceguide.com* or the US website at *www.francetourism.com*, or get in touch with a French government tourist office (*see* pp.108–9). Other sources of information are The French Centre, 164–6 Westminster Bridge Rd, London SE1 7RW, **t** (020) 7960 2600, or the Cultural Services of the French Embassy, 23 Cromwell Rd, London SW7 2EL, **t** (020) 7838 2088/9, or at 972 Fifth Av, New York, NY 10021, **t** (212) 439 1400. Alternatively, check out the information at *www.fr-holidaystore.co.uk*.

French universities are easy to enter if you're already enrolled in a similar institution at home; tuition fees are nominal but room and board are up to you. The Cultural Services can send a prospectus and tell you what paperwork is required.

France

Archaeology

Institut de Paléontologie Humaine, 1 Rue René Panhard, 75013 Paris, **t** 01 43 31 62 91, **f** 01 43 31 22 79. Palaeontology students or fans can spend a minimum of 15 or 30 days excavating caves in southeast France (address your letter to M. Henry de Lumley).

Art

Atelier du Safranier, 2 bis Rue du Cannet, 06600 Vieil Antibes, **t** 04 93 34 53 72. Year-round courses in painting, engraving, lithography, etc.

Ballooning

Air Adventures, Rue du Chat Fou, 21320 Pouilly en Auxois, **t** 03 80 90 74 23, **f** 03 80 90 72 86. Balloon rides over Burgundy and elsewhere.

Champagne Air Show, 9 Rue Thiers, 51100 Reims, **t** 03 26 87 89 12, **f** 03 26 87 89 14. Deluxe ballooning trips in Champagne, Alsace, Paris, Ile de France and the Loire; also vintage car and helicopter tours.

Cooking and Wine

Ecole Ritz Escoffier, 15 Place Vendôme, 75041 Paris Cedex, **t** 01 43 16 30 50, **f** 01 43 16 31 50, *ecole@ritzparis.com*. Cookery courses at the Ritz.

L'Ecole du Moulin, Restaurant L'Amandier, Mougins 06250, **t** 04 93 90 11 90. Year-round week-long Cuisine du Soleil cookery courses.

Vedel, 30 Rue Pierre Euzeby, 13200 Arles, **t/f** 04 90 49 69 20, *act.vedel@provnet.fr*. Courses in Provençal cuisine from a meal to a week, including trips to the Camargue, a winery and the hills to pick herbs.

Language

Accord, 52 Rue Montmartre, 75002 Paris, **t** 01 42 21 17 44, **t** 01 42 36 24 95, **f** 01 42 21 17 91, *www.accordlangues.com*. Year-round intensive language courses.

Alliance Française, 2 Rue Paris, 06000 Nice, **t** 04 93 62 67 66, **f** 04 93 85 28 06. French classes at all levels. Courses last a month but they will tailor to your needs.

C.A.V.I.L.A.M, 14 Rue du Maréchal Foch, 03206 Vichy, **t** 04 70 58 82 58, *www.cavilam.com*. Intensive language courses in Vichy.

Centre Etudes Linguistiques d'Avignon, 16 Rue Ste-Catherine, **t** 04 74 78 01 31, **f** 04 90 85 92 01. French courses at all levels.

Centre International d'Etude des Langues, Rue du Gue Fleuri, B.P. 35, 29480 Le Relecq Kerhuon, **t** 02 98 30 57 57, *www.ciel.com*.

By Boat

France has around 8,000km of navigable waterways: travelling along the network of rivers and canals at an average speed of 6km/h can be the best of all ways of getting to the heart of some ravishing French country-side (especially in the south, where travelling by road can be hot purgatory). The main barging areas are in Brittany, Anjou (the beautiful Canal de Nantes à Brest), Burgundy, Nivernais and Franche-Comté in central France (you can riverbathe and fish, and cross the Loire via Eiffel's aqueduct at Briare); Alsace

Language courses in Brittany, accommodation provided.

Eurocentres Foundation, 13 Passage Dauphine, 75006 Paris, t 01 40 46 72 00, in the US t (703) 684 1494 or t 800 648 4809, *www.eurocentres.com*. Non-profit organization: intensive general and business French in professionally equipped centres in Paris, Amboise and La Rochelle. DELF and Paris Chamber of Commerce diplomas; accommodation with families or in hotels.

Limousine

Aristo's Limousine, 12 Rue Martissot, 92110 Clichy, t 01 47 37 53 70, f 01 47 37 91 99, *aristos@infonie.fr*. Sightseeing tours of Paris, Normandy, the Loire and Champagne, all by luxury limousine.

UK and Ireland

General Interest

Abercrombie & Kent, Sloane Square House, Holbein Place, London SW1W 8NS, t (020) 7559 8500, f (020) 7730 9376. Quality city breaks.

American Express Europe, Destination Services, 19–20 Berners St, London W1P 4AE, t (020) 7637 8600, f (020) 7631 4803. City breaks and fly-drives.

Kirker Travel, 3 New Concordia Wharf, Mill St, London SE1 2BB, t (020) 7231 3333, f (020) 7231 4771. Tailor-made itineraries and packages, such as Paris/Ile de France and the Riviera.

Page & Moy, 135–40 London Rd, Leicester LE2 1EN, t (0116) 250 7000, f (0116) 250 7123. City breaks, gastronomy and cultural tours throughout France.

Trailfinders, 194 Kensington High St, London W8 6BD, t (020) 7937 1234, *www.trailfinder.com*. City breaks, flights, car hire, etc.

Canal Tours and River Cruises

Abercrombie & Kent, Sloane Square House, Holbein Place, London SW1W 8NS, t (020) 7559 8500, f (020) 7730 9376. Barges and houseboats.

French Country Cruises, t (01572) 821330, f (01572) 821072. Canal and river cruises.

Hoseasons Holidays, Sunway House, Lowestoft NR32 2LW, t (01502) 500555, f (01502) 500532, *www.hoseasons.co.uk*. Canal tours and river cruises.

Cooking and Wine

Allez France, 27 West St, Storrington, West Sussex RH20 4DZ, t (01903) 748100, f (01903) 745044, *www.allezfrance.com*. Wine and gastronomic holidays, plus city breaks in Nice, and short breaks in Antibes, Juan-les-Pins and Gorges du Verdon.

Arblaster & Clarke, Clarke House, Farnham Rd, West Liss GU33 6JQ, t (01730) 895 353, f (01730) 892 888. Escorted wine tours of major wine regions: Alsace, Burgundy, the Loire, Champagne-Ardennes, Languedoc-Roussillon, Provence, Rhône-Alps and Corsica.

Language

Euro Academy, 77a George St, Croydon CR0 1LD, t (020) 8686 2363. French courses with activities or sports options.

Languages Abroad (C.E.S.A.), Western House, Malpas, Truro, Cornwall TR1 1SQ, t (01872) 225300, f (01872) 225400. Language courses in group classes, with accommodation in college residences or with host families.

Music, Art and History

Andante, Grange Cottage, Winterbourne Dauntsey, Salisbury, Wiltshire SP4 6ER,

and the Ardennes in the east; Charentes and Périgord in the southwest; and the Lot et Garonne, Camargue and Midi in the south (where the Canal du Midi takes you past the 549m aqueduct at Agen and the towers of Carcassonne). It's possible, though complicated, to get by water from the Channel to the Mediterranean, via Le Havre, Paris, Burgundy and the Camargue.

Yacht, motorboat and sailing-boat charters are big business (France has the longest coastline – nearly 2,000 miles – of any European country). Companies hire boats out by the hour or day, or, in the case of yachts, by the

t (01980) 610555, f (01980) 610002, *andante* *.travel@virgin.net*. Archaeological, walking and historical study tours in Brittany, Limousin, the Pyrenees and Provence.

J.M.B. Travel, 'Rushwick', Worcester WR2 5SN, t (01905) 425628, f (01905) 420219. Opera and music festivals in Provence, Western Loire, Paris and Ile de France.

LSG Theme Holidays, 201 Main St, Thornton LE67 1AH, t (01509) 231713, t (01509) 239857 (24hrs). Painting, photography, language, cookery and horse-riding courses.

Martin Randall, 10 Barley Mow Passage, London W4 4PH, t (020) 8742 3355, f (020) 8742 7766. Varying programme of lecturer-accompanied cultural tours.

Prospect Music and Art Tours, 36 Manchester St, London W1M 5PE, t (020) 7486 5704, f (020) 7486 5863. Cultural breaks and cruises throughout France.

Specialtours, 81a Elizabeth St, London SW1W 9PG, t (020) 7730 2297. Fully escorted cultural tours through Champagne-Ardennes and Burgundy.

Singles

Solo's Holidays, 54–8 High St, Edgware, Middx HA8 7ED, t (020) 8951 2800, f (020) 8951 2848. Singles holidays throughout France.

Walking and Cycling

Alternative Travel Group, 69–71 Banbury Rd, Oxford OX2 6PE, t (01865) 515678, f (01865) 315697. Walking and cycling holidays.

Headwater Holidays, 146 London Rd, Northwich CW9 5HH, t (01606) 813333, f (01606) 813334. Accompanied and in-dependent cycling, walking, canoeing and rafting holidays throughout France.

InnTravel, Hovingham, York YO6 4JZ, t (01653) 628811, f (01653) 628 741. Walking and cycling holidays throughout France.

Sherpa Expeditions, 131a Heston Rd, Hounslow, Middlesex TW5 0RD, t (020) 8577 2717, f (020) 8572 9788. Treks.

Susi Madron's Cycling for Softies, 2–4 Birch Polygon, Rusholme, Manchester M14 5HX, t (0161) 248 8282, f (0161) 248 5140. Easy cycling.

USA and Canada

General Interest

Abercrombie & Kent, 1520 Kensington Rd, Oakbrook, IL 60521, t 800 323 7308, t (630) 954 2944, f (630) 954 3324, *www* *.abercrombiekent.com*. Quality city and country breaks throughout France.

Europe Train Tours, 198 E. Boston Post Rd, Mamaroneck, NY 10543, t 800 551 2085, t (914) 698 9426, f (914) 698 9516, *www.abn1.net/etttours*. Escorted tours by train and car in Provence and the Riviera.

Maupintour, 1421 Research Park Drive, Suite 300, Lawrence, KS 66049, t 800 255 4266, t (785) 331 1000, f (785) 331 1057, *www.maupintour.com*. Barge cruises and escorted tours.

Archaeology

Past Times Archaeological Tours, 800 Larch Lane, Sacramento, CA 95864, t (916) 485 8140, f (916) 488 4804, *www.pasttimes* *tours.com*. Escorted historical tours focusing on Lascaux, Cathar castles, etc.

Ballooning

The Bombard Society, 333 Pershing Way, West Palm Beach, FL 33401, t 800 862 8537, t (561) 837 6610, f (561) 837 6623, *bombard@* *compuserve.com*. Five-day luxury ballooning 'adventures' in Burgundy and the Loire.

week or fortnight. The average cost per week for a 16m yacht that sleeps six, including food, drink and all expenses, is about what six people would pay for a week in a luxury hotel. If things are slow you may dicker the price down. For a 20m crewed yacht, you would be looking at paying a cool $25,000 for a week.

Contact individual tourist offices for boat-hire companies in their area. For a full list of companies contact the Syndicat National des Loueurs de Bateaux de Plaisance, Port de la Bourdonnais, 75007 Paris, t 01 45 55 10 49. For crewed yachts try Camper & Nicholsons, 25 Bruton St, London W1X 7DB, t (020) 7491 2950,

Canal Tours and River Cruises

Abercrombie & Kent, 1520 Kensington Rd, Oakbrook, IL 60521, t 800 323 7308, t (630) 954 2944, f (630) 954 3324, *www.abercrombie kent.com*. Barges and river cruises.

Alden Yacht Charters, 1909 Alden Landing, Portsmouth, RI 02871, t 800 253 3654, t (401) 683 4200, f (401) 683 3668, *www.alden yachts.com*. Deluxe private yachts on the Côte d'Azur.

Elegant Cruises and Tours, 31 Central Drive, Port Washington, NY 11050, t 800 683 6767, t (516) 767 9302, f (516) 767 9303. River cruises on the Rhône and Seine, plus barges.

Etoile de Champagne, 88 Broad St, Boston, MA 02110, t 800 280 1492, f (617) 426 4689, *www.etoiledechampagne.com*. Privately owned luxury barge.

French Country Waterways, P.O. Box 2195, Duxbury, MA 02331, t 800 222 1236, t (781) 934 2454, f (781) 934 9048. Hotel barges in Alsace, Burgundy, Champagne and the Loire.

Cooking and Wine

Avalon, P.O. Box 8911, Newport Beach, CA 92658, t 888 499 9463, t (949) 673 7376, f (949) 673 6533, *www.avalontours.com*. Wine and gastronomy tours in Bordeaux, Burgundy, Rhône-Alps and the Loire Valley.

La Varenne, P.O. Box 25574, Washington, DC 20007, t 800 537 6486, t (202) 337 0073, f (703) 823 5438, *www.lavarenne.com*. Cookery school in a château in Burgundy.

Savour of France, 2450 Iroquois Av, Detroit, MI 48214, t 800 827 4635, t (313) 331 4568, f (313) 331 1915. Gourmet food and wine holidays.

Gay and Lesbian

Alyson Adventures, P.O. Box 180179, Boston, MA 02118, t 800 825 9766, t (617) 542 1177, *www.alysonadventures.com*. Bike tours through Provence, the Loire and Burgundy.

L'Arc en Ciel Voyages, P.O. Box 234, 997 Old Eagle School Rd, Suite 207, Wayne, PA 19087 0234, t 800 965 LARC, t (610) 964 7888, f (610) 964 8220, *www.larcenciel.com*. Tailor-made and escorted tours.

Horticulture

Expo Garden Tours, 70 Great Oak, Redding, CT 06896, t 800 448 2685, t (203) 938 0410, f (203) 938 0427. Fully escorted tours for gardening enthusiasts.

Language

Accent, 870 Market St, Suite 1026, San Francisco, CA 94102, t 800 869 9291, t (415) 835 3744, f (415) 835 3749, *sfaccent@aol.com*. Semester/year-long programmes at the Sorbonne for all abilities.

International Studies Abroad, 817 W. 24th St, Austin, TX 78705, t 800 580 8826, t (512) 480 8522, f (512) 480 8866, *www.studiesabroad .com*. Courses in Angers and Tours.

National Registration Centre for Study Abroad, 823 N. 2nd St, Milwaukee, WI 53203, t (414) 278 0631, *www.nrcsa.com*. Language and culture courses.

Vacances Jeunesse, 60 E. 42nd St, Suite 1166, New York, NY 10165, t (212) 370 7981. At the Sorbonne.

Music, Art and History

Art Horizons, 330 W. 58th St, Suite 608, New York, NY 10019, t (212) 969 9410, f (212) 969 9416. Tailor-made art and history tours.

Dailey Thorp Travel, 330 W. 58th St, Suite 610, New York, NY 10019, t (212) 307 1555, f (212) 974 1420. Luxury escorted tours to opera and music festivals in Paris, Aix-en-Provence, Orange, Nice, Lyon and Strasbourg.

Elderhostel, 75 Federal St, Boston, MA 02110, t (617) 426 7788, f (617) 426 8351, *www.elderhostel.org*. Courses in art, history, music, wine, etc. for older adults.

www.cnconnect.com. For canal boats and barges, contact Locaboat Plaisance, Port au Bois, B.P. 150, 89303 Joigny Cedex, t 03 86 91 72 72, *www.locaboat.com*, and *see* 'Tour Operators and Special-interest Holidays' above.

The French tourist authority produces a pamphlet called *Boating on the Waterways*.

Books on sailing include *Reeds' Mediterranean Navigator* (Thomas Reed Publications) and *South France Pilot* by Robin Brandon (Imray Laurie). These and other nautical books and maps in English may be found at Le Silmar, 10 Rue Jean Braco, 06310 Beaulieu-sur-Mer, t 04 93 01 36 71.

Skiing

Central Holidays, 120 Sylvan Av, Englewood Cliffs, NJ 07632, t 800 935 5000, t (201) 228 5200, f (201) 228 5267. Meribel, Courchevel, Chamonix, Val Thorens, Val d'Isère, Tignes.

Lindenmeyr Travel, 19 E. 37th St, Suite 4R, New York, NY 10016, t 800 248 2807, t (212) 725 2807, f (212) 779 2239, *www.lindenmeyr travel.com*. Ski vacations staying in family-run hotels and inns.

Ski Europe, 1535 W. Loop St, Suite 319, Houston, TX 77027, t 800 333 5533, t (713) 960 0900, f (713) 960 8966, *www.skieurope.com*. Group tours to the French Alps.

Snow Tours, 1281 Paterson Plank Rd, Secaucus, NJ 07094, t 800 222 1170, t (201) 348 2244, f (201) 348 0545. Organized by ski profes-sionals, and staying in quality hotels.

Sports and Activities

Adventure Sport Holidays, 815 North Rd, Westfield, MA 01085, t 800 628 9655, t (413) 568 2855, f (413) 562 3621, *www.advonskis .com*. Skiing, biking, hiking, mountaineering and mountain biking throughout France.

Cross Country International, P.O. Box 1170, Millbrook, NY 12545, t 800 828 8768, t (914) 677 6000, f (914) 677 6077, *www.equestrian vacations.com*. Horse-riding in Provence and the Camargue.

Custom Spa Vacations, 1318 Beacon St, Suite 20, Brookline, MA 02446, t 800 443 7727, t (617) 566 5144, f (617) 731 0599, *www.spa tours.com*. Health spas in Antibes, Biarritz, Cannes, Deauville, Eugenie-les-Bains, etc.

Elite Golf Tours, P.O. Box 1091, Commack, NY 11725 1091, t 800 711 8089, t (516) 462 1946, f (516) 462 1339. Luxury golf tours.

Sportstours, P.O. Box 457, New York, NY 10185 0457, t 800 879 8647, t (305) 535 0007, f (305) 535 0008, *www.sportstours.com*. Racing, tennis, Formula One, Tour de France, etc.

Veterans

Galaxy Tours, P.O. Box 234, 997 Old Eagle School Rd, Suite 207, Wayne, PA 19087 0234, t 800 523 7287, t (610) 964 8010, f (610) 964 8220, *www.galaxytours.com*. First and Second World War veterans' tours.

Walking and Cycling

Backroads, 801 Cedar St, Berkeley, CA 94701 1800, t 800 462 2848, t 800 GO ACTIVE, f (510) 527 1444, *www.backroads.com*. Bicycling, hiking and multisport holidays in Burgundy, the Loire Valley, Dordogne, Brittany, Normandy, Provence, etc.

Breakaway Adventures, 3148 Dumbarton St N.W., Washington, DC 20007, t 800 567 6286, t (202) 944 5006, f (202) 944 5009, *brkaway@clarkinet*. Self-guided walking and cycling trips staying in small country inns, with full vehicle support; destinations include Provence, the Dordogne, the Loire and Burgundy.

Brooks Country Cycling Tours, 140 W. 83rd St, New York, NY 10024, t (212) 874 5151, f (212) 874 5286, *brookscct@aol.com*. Guided cycling tours in Brittany, Normandy, the Dordogne and the Loire Valley.

CBT Tours, 415 W. Fullerton, Suite 1003, Chicago, IL 60614, t 800 736 2453, t (773) 404 1710, f (773) 404 1833, *www.cbttours.com*. Hiking, biking, mountain biking and skiing tours for all abilities.

Country Walkers, P.O. Box 180, Waterbury, VT 05676, t 800 464 9255, t (802) 244 1387, f (802) 244 5661, *www.countrywalkers.com*. Walking holidays during the summer, in Burgundy, Dordogne and Provence, led by expert local guides.

DuVine Adventures, 635 Boston Av Somerville, MA 02144, t 888 396 5383, t (781) 395 7440, f (781) 395 8472, *info@duvine.com*. Bicycling tours through French vineyards.

Practical A–Z

07

Calendar of Major Events

January
Late Jan–early Feb Festival of short films, Clermont-Ferrand

February
Week prior to Lent Nice has the most famous Mardi Gras in France; Feria du Carnival, Nîmes

March
Throughout month Strasbourg film festival

April
Good Friday Traditional processions in Corsica, especially Bonifacio, Sartène and Bastia
Easter Bullfights in Arles
Mid-month Paris marathon; ham fair, Bayonne
Last Sunday Fête des Gardians, traditional rodeo in Arles

May
Early Festival of French song, Montauban
2nd week Cannes International Film Festival
16–17 Bravade de St-Torpes, St-Tropez
24–25 Gypsy pilgrimage, Stes-Maries-de-la-Mer
Ascension Day week Monte Carlo Grand Prix
Whitsun Féria de Pentecôte, Nîmes
Last week–early June Roland Garros tennis tournament, Paris

June
Throughout month Festival de la Danse et de l'Image, Toulon; Festival Mondiale du Théâtre, Nancy
June and July Contemporary arts festival, La Rochelle
Mid-month Le Mans 24-hour rally
Last fortnight Jazz and chamber music, Aix; Nuits Musicales, Uzès
20 Courses landaises, Aire-sur-Adour
21 Summer equinox gatherings, Montségur
23–24 St Jean: bonfires, dancing and fireworks in Perpignan and Céret
Late June–early July Festival International de Danse, Montpellier; Quinzaine Celtique, Nantes; Festival de Pau; international film festival, La Rochelle; festival of the giants, Douai

July
Early July Flamenco festival, Mont-de-Marsan; festival of European theatre, Grenoble
1st 10 days Tombées de la Nuit theatre and music festival, Rennes
1st fortnight Jazz à Vienne
Last Sunday Fête de la Tarasque, Tarascon
July–August International fireworks festival, Monaco; modern music festival, St-Paul-de-Vence
Throughout month International music festival, Vence; music festival, Carcassonne
Mid-month Aix international dance festival; world music and gypsy festival, Arles; blues festival, Cahors

Children

France is a very child-friendly country, and there are few places – mostly very hoity-toity bars and restaurants – where children aren't welcome. Under-fours travel for free on the trains and most buses, and four- to eleven-year-olds go for half-price; long-distance trains often have a special play area.

Hotels will put a cot (child's bed) in a room for a small fee, and family-orientated ones often provide an array of special activities, watersports and baby-sitting services. Most restaurants offer a low-cost menu enfant with kid-pleasing dishes (invariably including frites), although high chairs are still rare outside family resort areas.

Although all baby supplies are available in supermarkets and pharmacies, you may want to bring powdered formulas and prepared foods along if exact matches are important to you (or the pipsqueak).

Climate and When to Go

France has a full deck of climates. Continental cold winters and hot summers prevail in the east and centre; the north is as changeable as Britain, while the west is tempered and wettened by the Atlantic.

Mid-July–mid-Aug International theatre festival, Avignon; Festival Pablo Casals, Prades; dance festival, Vaison-la-Romaine

14 Fireworks in many places for Bastille Day: Paris, Avignon, Arcachon and Carcassonne put on excellent shows

Third week End of the Tour de France, in Paris; Basque festival and surfing, Biarritz; Festival de Cornouaille, Quimper; Vannes Festival de Jazz; national festival of street artists, Chalon-sur-Saône; jazz festival, Souillac

Last three weeks Music festival, Aix; Festival de Radio France, classical music and jazz in Montpellier

Last two weeks International jazz festival, Juan-les-Pins

Late July–early Aug Theatre festival, Sarlat

August

Early Aug St-Malo Festival de Jazz

Throughout month Tournois de Joutes, nautical jousts at Sète; chamber music festival, Menton

First two weeks Festival Interceltique, Lorient; jousts and medieval costumes, Carcassonne; international mime festival, Périgueux

Second week Medieval festival, Foix; Grande Fête des Menhirs, Carnac

Second and third week Jazz in Mauriac

End of August Bullfights at Béziers; Fête de St Louis, with historical re-enactment, at Aigues-Mortes; street theatre festival, Aurillac

September

Throughout month Sigma theatre, dance and music festival, Bordeaux

First week Dijon wine and folk festival

6–8 Santa di U Niolu, with traditional songs and fair, Casamaccioli (Corsica)

Mid-month Festival du Roi de l'Oiseau, Puy-en-Velay; Napoleon Days, Ajaccio

Third week Feria des Vendanges, bullfights at Nîmes

Last week–first week Oct Nioulargue, yacht race in St-Tropez

Sun nearest the 29th Festival de St Michel, Mont-St-Michel

October

Throughout month Jazz festival, Paris

Early Oct Montmartre grape harvest, Paris

Mid-month International theatre festival, Bayonne

Last week Festiventu, Calvi (Corsica), a popular event dedicated to the wind

November

Throughout month International mime and clown festival, Strasbourg

Mid-month International contemporary music festival, Metz

December

Throughout month Music festival, Marseille; Les Transmusicales rock festival, Rennes

24 Fêtedes Bergers and midnight mass, Les Baux

Provence, Languedoc and Corsica have a Mediterranean climate, cooled by the mistral and other winds. The Pyrenees get more rain than most places on the planet – nearly 7ft a year – while the Camargue barely gets 500mm a year, the least in France. In an average year, it rains as much in Nice as in Brest, and more in Marseille than Paris, but in Provence it tends to come down all at once, especially in the autumn.

France is the world's top tourist destination, and avoiding the crowds can be a prime consideration when deciding when you go. The Easter school break in April and the months of July and August are the busiest, when temperatures and prices soar, tempers flare, and weekend traffic is abominable, but it's also the season of the great festivals.

From December to March most of the tourists are in the mountains; in February the mimosa and almonds bloom on the Côte d'Azur. By April and May you can sit outside at restaurants in most places and start to swim in the Med. June is usually warm and a relatively quiet month, and the beginning of the walking season in the mountains. In August, the cities empty out except for tourists; shops and restaurants close, while getting any kind of room on the coast can be impossible if you haven't booked well ahead.

Once French school holidays end in early September, prices and crowds decrease with

Average Daily High Temperatures in °C (°F)

	Jan	Feb	Mar	April	May	June	July	Aug	Sept	Oct	Nov	Dec
Ajaccio (Corsica)	13 (55)	14 (56)	15 (59)	17 (63)	20 (70)	24 (75)	27 (81)	27 (81)	25 (77)	21 (70)	17 (63)	14 (56)
Biarritz	13 (55)	14 (56)	16 (61)	18 (64)	21 (70)	25 (77)	28 (82)	27 (81)	26 (79)	24 (75)	19 (66)	13 (55)
Grenoble	3 (37)	3 (37)	8 (45)	14 (56)	16 (61)	22 (71)	27 (81)	26 (79)	22 (71)	16 (61)	11 (51)	6 (42)
La Rochelle	10 (50)	9 (48)	12 (54)	18 (64)	16 (61)	22 (71)	25 (77)	25 (77)	22 (71)	18 (64)	14 (56)	10 (50)
Lyon	7 (44)	6 (42)	11 (51)	16 (61)	17 (63)	25 (77)	27 (81)	27 (81)	24 (75)	17 (63)	10 (50)	8 (45)
Nice	12 (54)	12 (54)	14 (56)	18 (64)	21 (70)	26 (79)	27 (81)	28 (82)	25 (77)	22 (71)	16 (61)	14 (56)
Paris	7 (44)	7 (44)	10 (50)	16 (61)	17 (63)	24 (75)	25 (77)	26 (79)	21 (70)	17 (63)	12 (54)	8 (45)
Périgueux	10 (50)	12 (54)	14 (56)	17 (63)	19 (66)	23 (73)	25 (77)	26 (79)	22 (71)	18 (64)	15 (59)	12 (54)
Rennes	9 (48)	9 (48)	11 (51)	17 (63)	16 (61)	23 (73)	25 (77)	24 (75)	21 (70)	16 (61)	12 (54)	9 (48)
Strasbourg	5 (41)	5 (41)	9 (48)	13 (55)	16 (61)	23 (73)	24 (75)	26 (79)	21 (70)	15 (59)	8 (45)	4 (39)

the temperature. In October the weather is often mild on the coast, although torrential downpours and floods are not unknown; the first snows fall in the Pyrenees and Alps. November is generally a bad month to visit: it rains, and many museums, hotels and restaurants close down.

For day-to-day information, see the comprehensive Meteo France website at *www.meteo.fr.*

Crime and the Police

France is a safe and very policed country, but it's important to be aware that thieves target visitors, especially their holiday homes and cars – they see foreign number plates or a rental car as easy pickings. Leave anything you'd really miss at home, carry travellers' cheques, insure your property, and be especially careful in large cities or on the Côte d'Azur. Report thefts to the nearest *gendarmerie* or *police national* – it's not a pleasant task but the reward is the bit of paper you need for an insurance claim. If your passport is stolen, contact the police and your nearest consulate for emergency travel documents. Carry photocopies of your passport, driver's licence, etc. – it makes it easier when reporting a loss.

By law, the police in France can stop anyone anywhere and demand to see ID; in practice, they tend to do it only to harass minorities, the homeless and the scruffy (the Paris police are notorious for this). The drug situation is the same in France as anywhere in Western Europe: soft and hard drugs are widely available, and the police only make an issue of victimless crime when it suits them – being a foreigner may be reason enough, and there is little that your consulate can or will do about it.

Disabled Travellers

When it comes to providing access for all, France is not exactly in the vanguard of nations, but things are beginning to change. The SNCF, for instance, now publishes a pamphlet, *Guide Pratique du Voyageur à Mobilité Réduite*, covering travel by train for the disabled (all TGVs are equipped) – contact the French Railways office in your country for details. The Channel Tunnel is a good way to travel by car since disabled passengers are allowed to stay in their vehicle. By train, Eurostar gives wheelchair passengers first-class travel for second-class fares. Most ferry companies will offer facilities if contacted beforehand. Vehicles fitted to accommodate transport for disabled people pay reduced tolls on *autoroutes*. An *autoroute* guide for disabled travellers (*Guides des Autoroutes à l'Usage des Personnes à Mobilité Réduite*) is available free from **Ministère des Transports**, Direction des Routes, Service du Contrôle des Autoroutes, La Défense, 92055 Cedex, Paris, t 01 40 81 21 22. The *Gîtes Accessibles aux Personnes Handicapées*, published by Gîtes de France, lists self-catering possibilities (*see* below, p.110, for their address). Other useful contacts:

Access Ability, *www.access-ability.co.uk*. Information on travel agencies catering specifically to disabled people.

Access Tourism, *www.accesstourism.com*. Pan-European website with information on hotels, guesthouses, travel agencies and specialist tour operators, etc.

Access Travel, 6 The Hillock, Astley, Lancashire M29 7GW, t (01942) 888844, *info@access-travel.co.uk*, *www.access-travel.co.uk*. Travel agent for disabled people: special airfares, car hire and wheelchair-accessible *gîtes* in Calais, Normandy and the Loire.

Alternative Leisure Co, 165 Middlesex Turnpike, Suite 206, Bedford, MA 01730, t (718) 275 0023, *www.alctrips.com*. Organizes vacations abroad for disabled people.

Association des Paralysés de France, t 01 40 78 69 00. A national organization with an office in each *département*, with in-depth local information; headquarters are in Paris.

Australian Council for Rehabilitation of the Disabled (ACRODS), PO Box 60, Curtin, ACT 2605, Australia, t/TTY (02) 6682 4333,

www.acrod.org.au. Information and contact numbers for specialist travel agencies.

Comité National Français de Liaison pour la Réadaptation des Handicapés, 236B Rue Tolbiac, 75013 Paris, t 01 53 80 66 66. Provides information on access, and produces useful guides to various regions in France.

Disabled Persons Assembly, PO Box 27-254, Wellington 6035, New Zealand, t (04) 472 2626, *www.dpa.org.nz*. All-round source for travel information.

Emerging Horizons, *www.emerging horizons.com*. International on-line travel newsletter for people with disabilities.

Global Access, *www.geocities.com*. On-line network for disabled travellers, with links, archives and information on travel guides for the disabled, etc.

Holiday Care Service, Imperial Building, Victoria Rd, Horley, Surrey, RH6 7PZ, t (01293) 774535, f (01293) 784647, Minicom t (01293) 776943, *holiday.care@virgin.net*, *www.holidaycare.org.uk*. Publishes an information sheet on holidays in France (£1).

Mobility International USA, PO Box 10767, Eugene, OR 97440, USA, t/TTY (541) 343 1284, f (541) 343 6812, *www.miusa.org*. Information on international educational exchange programmes and volunteer service overseas for the disabled.

RADAR (Royal Association for Disability and Rehabilitation), 12 City Forum, 250 City Rd, London EC1V 8AF, t (020) 7250 3222, f (020) 7250 0212, Minicom t (020) 7250 4119, *www.radar.org.uk*. Information and books on all aspects of travel.

SATH (Society for the Advancement of Travel for the Handicapped), 347 5th Av, Suite 610, New York, NY 10016, t (212) 557 0027, f (212) 725 8253, *www.tenonline.com/sath*. Travel and access information.

The Able Informer, *www.sasquatch.com/ableinfo*. International on-line magazine with tips for travelling abroad.

Electricity

France is all 220v. British and Irish appliances will need an adapter with two round prongs; North American appliances usually need a transformer as well.

Embassies and Consulates

In France

Australia: 4 Rue Jean Rey, 75015 Paris, t 01 40 59 33 00.

Canada: 35 Av Montaigne, 75008 Paris, t 01 44 43 29 00; Lyon t 04 72 77 64 07; Nice t 04 93 92 93 22.

Ireland: 4 Rue Rude, 75016 Paris, t 01 44 17 67 00; Monaco t 07 93 15 70 00.

New Zealand: 7 Rue Léonard de Vinci, 75116 Paris, t 01 45 01 43 43.

UK: 18 bis Rue d'Anjou, 75008 Paris, t 01 44 51 31 00, f 01 44 51 31 27; the rest of France is divided into five main regions: Marseille and Nice t 04 91 15 72 10; Bordeaux t 05 57 22 21 10; Lille t 03 20 12 82 72; and Lyon t 04 72 77 81 70.

USA: 2 Rue St-Florentin, 75001 Paris, t 01 43 12 22 22; 12 Bd Paul Peytrel, Marseille 13286, t 04 91 54 92 00; 15 Av d'Alsace, 67082 Strasbourg, Cedex, t 03 88 35 31 04.

Abroad

Canada: 25 Rue St Louis, Québec, QC G1R 3Y8, t (418) 688 0430.

Ireland: 36 Ailesbury Rd, Ballsbridge, Dublin 4, t (01) 260 1666.

UK: 21 Cromwell Rd, London SW7 2DQ, t (020) 7838 2000, *www.ambafrance.org.uk.* 11 Randolph Crescent, Edinburgh EH3 7TT, t (131) 225 7954.

USA: 737 North Michigan Av, Suite 2020, Chicago, IL 60611, t (312) 787 5359/60/61. 10990 Wilshire Bd, Suite 300, Los Angeles, CA 90024, t (310) 235 3200. 934 Fifth Av, New York, NY 10021, t (212) 606 3688, *www.amb-usa.fr, citizeninfo@ state.gov.*

Festivals

Festivities in France range from the village fête, celebrating the patron saint, with feasting, dancing, music, various amounts of *animation* (jumping motorbikes, dogs pulling sleds on wheels, etc.) and fireworks, to the glittering Cannes film festival. Traditional events, however, are rare outside Brittany, Corsica and a few places in the south. Local tourist offices will be happy to fill you in on what's happening in the area, as well as give you precise dates.

Besides Bastille Day, another nationally celebrated affair is the **Fête de la Musique** on 21 June, an initiative of former culture minister Jack Lang that fills the streets of France with music. The first three weeks of July are taken up with the **Tour de France**. Then there's the **Fête de la Patrimoine**, on the third weekend of September, which throws open the doors of usually inaccessible monuments (especially in Paris) and offers free admission to state museums.

Food and Drink

Food

French restaurants generally serve between noon and 2pm and in the evening from 7 to 10pm, with later summer hours; brasseries in the cities often stay open continuously. Most post menus outside the door so you know what to expect, and offer a choice of set-price (*prix fixe*) menus; if prices aren't listed, it's usually not because they're a bargain. If you summon up the appetite to eat the biggest meal of the day at noon, you'll spend a lot less money, as many restaurants offer special lunch menus – an economical way to experience some of the finer gourmet temples. Some of these offer a set-price gourmet *menu dégustation* – a selection of chef's specialities, which can be a great treat. At the humbler end of the scale, bars and brasseries often serve a simple *plat du jour* (daily special) and the no-choice *formule*, which is more often than not steak and *frites*. Eating *à la carte* anywhere will always be more expensive, in many cases twice as much.

Menus sometimes include the house wine (*vin compris*). If you choose a better wine anywhere, expect a big mark-up; the French wouldn't dream of a meal without wine, and the arrangement is a simple device to make food prices seem lower. If service is included it will say *service compris* or s.c.; if not, *service non compris* or s.n.c.

Restaurants, especially the cheaper ones in rural areas, presume everyone has the appetite of Gargantua. A full meal consists of:

an *apéritif*, *hors d'oeuvres* and/or a starter (typically, soup, pâté or *charcuterie*), an *entrée* (usually fish or an omelette), a main course (usually meat, poultry, game or offal, *garni* with vegetables, rice or potatoes), often followed by a green salad-(to 'lighten' the stomach), then cheese, dessert, coffee, chocolates and *mignardises* (or *petit fours*) and perhaps a *digestif* to round things off. Most people only devour the whole whack on Sunday afternoons, and at other times condense this feast to a starter, main course, and cheese or dessert. Vegetarians will have a hard time in France, especially if they don't eat fish or eggs, but most establishments will try to accommodate them somehow. Pizzas, salads and bushels of *frites* are the old stand-bys.

When looking for a restaurant, homing in on the one place crowded with locals is as sound a policy in France as anywhere. Don't overlook hotel restaurants, some of which are absolutely top notch even if a certain red book refuses on some obscure principle to give them more than two stars. To avoid disappointment, call ahead in the morning to reserve, especially at the smarter restaurants, and particularly in the summer. Cities and resorts have a plethora of ethnic restaurants, mostly North African (a favourite for couscous), Asian (usually Vietnamese, sometimes Chinese, Cambodian or Thai) and Italian.

Each region of France is proud of its local cuisine, or *cuisine de terroir*. Some of these are so popular that you'll find them throughout France: Breton *crêperies* or *galetteries* (with buckwheat pancakes); restaurants from Alsace serving *choucroute* (sauerkraut and sausage); Périgordin restaurants featuring duck, foie gras and truffles; and Lyonnaise *haute cuisine*. For general help in ordering, *see* **Language**, pp.1021–8.

Restaurant Prices

In this book, recommended restaurants have prices listed for their set menus, to give a rough idea of cost. Alternatively, restaurants are split into four price categories (prices are for a three-course meal without wine per person):

luxury	over 400F
expensive	200–400F
moderate	100–200F
cheap	under 100F

Markets, Picnic Food and Snacks

The food markets of France are justly celebrated for the colour and perfumes of their produce and flowers. They are fun to visit, and become even more interesting if you're cooking or gathering the ingredients for a picnic. In the larger cities, markets take place every day, while smaller towns and villages have markets once a week which double as a social occasion for the locals. Most finish around noon.

Other good sources for picnic food are the *charcuteries* or *traiteurs*, both of which sell prepared dishes sold by weight in cartons or tubs, a service also provided by the larger supermarkets. Cities are snack-food wonderlands, with outdoor counters selling pastries, *crêpes*, pizza slices, *frites*, *croque-monsieurs* (toasted ham and cheese sandwiches) and a wide variety of sandwiches made from *baguettes* (long thin loaves of bread).

Drink

You can order any kind of drink at any bar or café – except cocktails, unless the bar has a certain cosmopolitan flair. Cafés are also a home from home, places to read the papers, play cards, meet friends, and just unwind, sit back and watch the world go by. Prices are listed on the *Tarif des Consommations*: note they are progressively more expensive depending on whether you're served at the bar (*comptoir*), at a table (*la salle*) or outside (*la terrasse*). French coffee is strong and black, but lacklustre next to the aromatic brews of Italy or Spain (you'll notice an improvement in the coffee near their respective frontiers). If you order *un café* you'll get a small black espresso; if you want milk, order *un crème*. If you want more than a few drops of caffeine, ask them to make it *grand*. For decaffeinated, the word is *déca*. Some bars offer cappuccinos, but again they're only really good near the Italian border. In the summer, try a *frappé* (iced coffee). The French only order *café au lait* (a small coffee topped off with lots of hot milk) when they stop in for breakfast, and, if what your hotel offers is expensive or boring, consider joining them. There are baskets of croissants and pastries, and some bars will make you a baguette with butter, jam or honey. If you want to go native, try the

Frenchman's Breakfast of Champions: a pastis or two, and five non-filter Gauloises. *Chocolat chaud* (hot chocolate) is usually good. If you order *thé* (tea), you'll get an ordinary bag. An *infusion* is a herbal tea – camomile, *menthe* (mint), *tilleul* (lime or linden blossom) or *verveine* (verbena). These are kind to the all-precious *foie*, or liver, after you've over-indulged.

Mineral water (*eau minérale*) can be addictive, and comes either sparkling (*gazeuse* or *pétillante*) or still (*non-gazeuse* or *plate*). If you feel run down, Badoit has lots of peppy magnesium in it. The usual international corporate soft drinks are available, and all kinds of bottled fruit juices (*jus de fruits*). Some bars also do fresh lemon and orange juices (*citron pressé* or *orange pressée*). The French are also fond of fruit syrups – red grenadine and ghastly green *diabolo menthe*.

Beer (*bière*) in most bars and cafés is run-of-the-mill big brands from Alsace, Germany and Belgium. Draft (*à la pression*) is cheaper than bottled beer. Nearly all resorts have bars or pubs offering wider selections of drafts, lagers and bottles.

The strong spirit of the Midi comes in a liquid form called *pastis*, first made popular in Marseille as a plague remedy, now drunk as an *apéritif* before lunch and in rounds after work. Most people drink their '*pastaga*' with lots of water and ice (*glaçons*), which makes it almost palatable. Spirits include the familiar cognac and armagnac brandies, liqueurs and *digestifs* made from walnuts, cherries, pears and herbs (these are a speciality of the Alps), and fiery marc, the grape spirit that is the same as Italian grappa (but usually better).

Wine

One of the pleasures of travelling in France is drinking great wines for a fraction of what you pay at home, and discovering new ones you've never seen in your local shop. Wines labelled AOC (Appellation d'Origine Contrôlée) come from a certain defined area and are made from certain varieties of grapes, guaranteeing a standard of quality. *Cru* on the label means vintage; a *grand cru* is a great, noble vintage. Descending in the vinous hierarchy are those labelled VDQS (Vin de Qualité Supérieure), followed by Vin de Pays (guaran-

teed to originate in a certain region; some are excellent), with Vin Ordinaire (or Vin de Table) at the bottom, which may not send you to seventh heaven but is usually drinkable and cheap. In a restaurant if you order a *rouge* (red), *blanc* (white) or rosé (pink), this is what you'll get, either by the glass (*un verre*), by the quarter-litre (*un pichet*) or bottle (*une bouteille*). *Brut* is very dry, *sec* dry, *demi-sec* and *moelleux* sweetish, *doux* sweet, and *méthode champenoise* is sparkling.

If you're buying direct from the producer (or a wine co-operative, or *syndicat*, a group of producers), you'll be offered glasses to taste, each wine older than the previous one until you are feeling quite jolly and ready to buy the oldest (and most expensive) vintage. On the other hand, some sell loose wine *à la petrol pump*, *en vrac*; many *caves* even sell the little plastic barrels to put it in.

Health and Emergencies

Ambulance (SAMU) t 15
Police and ambulance t 17
Fire t 18

France has one of the best healthcare systems in the world. Local hospitals are the place to go in an emergency (*urgence*). Doctors take turns going on duty at night and on holidays: ring one to listen to the recorded message to find out what to do.

To be on the safe side, always carry a phone card. If it's not an emergency, pharmacists are trained to administer first aid, and dispense advice for minor problems. In rural areas there is always someone on duty if you ring the bell of a pharmacy; in cities, pharmacies are open on a rota and addresses are posted in their windows and in the local newspaper.

In France, however you're insured, you pay up front for everything, unless it's an emergency, when you will be billed later. Doctors will give you a brown and white *feuille de soins* with your prescription; take both to the pharmacy and keep the *feuille*, the various medicine stickers (*vignettes*) and prescriptions for insurance purposes at home. *See* 'Insurance', below, for more information.

Insurance

Citizens of the EU should bring an E111 form (available from post offices before you travel), entitling you to the same emergency health services and treatments as French citizens. This means paying up front for medical care and prescriptions, of which 75 to 80 per cent of the costs are reimbursed a week to 10 days later. In the UK, see the Department of Health website at *www.doh.gov.uk/ traveladvice*.

Many of the larger credit card companies will also offer free travel insurance for health and theft, etc. when you use them to book a package holiday or aeroplane/train tickets. Read the small print very carefully, especially if you're travelling with expensive equipment (laptops, cameras, etc.).

If you're not covered on your credit card, you may want to consider taking out extra insurance, covering theft and losses and offering 100 per cent medical refund and emergency repatriation if necessary; check to see if it covers extra expenses should you get bogged down in airport or train strikes.

Beware that accidents resulting from sports are rarely covered by ordinary insurance.

Canadians may or may not be covered in France by their provincial health coverage; Americans and others should check their individual policies.

Maps

If you plan to cover a lot of territory in France by car, you can't do better than the Michelin *Atlas Routier* (1:200 000), which binds together Michelin's yellow regional maps. They also do one of the best sheet maps for the entire country, No.989. These are all readily available in French service stations or newsagents. The yellow regional maps are also widely available abroad.

Walkers, cyclists and micro-tourists who are serious about exploring a certain patch of France should have a look at the IGN ordnance survey maps; the most common blue series (1:25 000), almost always carried by local newsagents or stationers, marks every path, building and roadside cross.

Money and Banks

1 Jan 1999 saw the start of the transition to the euro. It became the official currency in France (and 10 other nations of the European Union) and the official exchange rate was set at 1euro=6.55957F. Shops and businesses are increasingly indicating prices in both currencies. You can open euro accounts, and some places will accept payment in euros by cheque or credit card, although euro coins and notes will not be circulated until 2002. Beware high bank charges for cashing cheques for euros from other countries. Travellers' cheques are also available in euros. Until 2002, you'll still be using the franc (abbreviated with an F), which consists of 100 centimes. Banknotes come in denominations of 500, 200, 100, 50 and 20F; coins in 20, 10, 5, 2 and 1F, and 50, 20, 10, and 5 centimes.

Travellers' cheques are the safest way of carrying money, but the wide acceptance of credit or debit cards and the presence of ATMs (*distributeurs de billets*) even in small villages make them a convenient alternative. Major international credit cards are widely used in France; Visa (in French, Carte Bleue) is the most readily accepted, although, for the French, Carte Bleue is a direct-debit bank card. American Express is often not accepted, however. Smaller hotels and restaurants and bed and breakfasts may not accept cards at all. For debit/cash cards, ask at your bank before you leave. In any case, bring some travellers' cheques in case you lose your card or go over its daily or weekly limits. Some shops and supermarkets experience difficulties reading UK-style magnetic strips (French credit cards now contain a chip or *puce* containing ID information), so arm yourself with cash in case. However, your card is valid, and the French Government Tourist Office suggests you use the following phrase to explain the problem:

'*Les cartes internationales ne sont pas des cartes à puce, mais à bande magnetique. Ma carte est valable et je vous serais reconnaissant d'en demander la confirmation auprès de votre banque ou de votre centre de traitement.*'

Under the Cirrus system, withdrawals in francs can be made from bank and post office automatic cash machines, using your UK PIN.

The specific cards accepted are marked on each machine, and most give instructions in English. Credit card companies charge a fee for cash advances, but rates are often better than those at banks.

In the event of **lost or stolen credit cards**, call the following emergency numbers:

Mastercard t 0800 901387
American Express t Paris, **t** 01 47 77 72 00
Visa (Carte Bleue) **t** Paris, **t** 01 42 77 11 90
Barclaycard t (00 44) 1604 230 230
(UK number)

Banks are generally open 8.30am–12.30pm and 1.30–4pm; they close on Sunday, and most close either on Saturday or Monday as well. Exchange rates vary, and nearly all take a commission of varying proportions. *Bureaux de change* that do nothing but exchange money (and hotels and train stations) usually have the worst rates or take the heftiest commissions.

Opening Hours, Museums and National Holidays

While many **shops and supermarkets** are now open continuously Tuesday–Saturday from 9 or 10am to 7 or 7.30pm, businesses in smaller towns still close down for lunch from 12 or 12.30pm to 2 or 3pm, or in the summer 4pm. There are local exceptions, but nearly everything shuts down on Mondays, except for grocers and *supermarchés* that open in the afternoon. In many towns, Sunday morning is a big shopping period. Markets (daily in the cities, weekly in villages) are usually open mornings only, although clothes, flea and antique markets run into the afternoon.

Most **museums** close for lunch, and often all day on Mondays or Tuesdays, and sometimes for all of November or the entire winter. Hours change with the season: longer summer hours begin in May or June and last until the end of September – usually. Most museums close on national holidays. We've done our best to include opening hours in the text, but don't sue us if they're not exactly right. Most museums give discounts if you have a student ID card, or are an EU citizen under 18 or over 65 years old; most charge admissions ranging from 10 to 30F. National museums are free if

National Holidays
January 1 New Year's Day
Easter Sunday March or April
Easter Monday March or April
May 1 Fête du Travail (Labour Day)
May 8 VE Day, Armistice 1945
Ascension Day usually end of May
Pentecost (Whitsun) and the following
  Monday beginning of June
July 14 Bastille Day
August 15 Assumption of the Virgin Mary
November 1 All Saints'
November 11 Remembrance Day (First World War Armistice)
25 December Christmas Day

you're under 18. **Churches** are usually open all day, or closed all day and only open for Mass. Sometimes notes on the door direct you to the *mairie* or priest's house (*presbytère*) where you can pick up the key. There are often admission fees for cloisters, crypts and special chapels.

On French national holidays, banks, shops, businesses and some museums close; but most restaurants stay open. The French have a healthy approach to holidays: if there is a holiday on a Tuesday or Thursday, they 'make a bridge' (*faire un pont*) to the weekend and make Monday or Friday a holiday too.

Post Offices, Telephones and the Internet

Known as the PTT or Bureaux de Poste, easily discernible by a blue bird on a yellow background, post offices are open in the cities Monday–Friday 8am–7pm, and Saturdays 8am until noon. In villages, offices may not open until 9am, then break for lunch, and close at 4.30 or 5pm. You can receive letters *poste restante* at any of them; the postal codes in this book should help your mail get there in a timely fashion. To collect it, bring ID; you may have to pay a small fee. You can purchase stamps in tobacconists as well as post offices.

Nearly all public telephones have switched over from coins to *télécartes*, which you can purchase at any post office or newsstand for 40F for 50 *unités* or 96F for 120 *unités*. The French have eliminated area codes, giving everyone a 10-digit telephone number (the following regional numbers have gained a prefix: Paris and Ile de France region 01, Northwest 02, Northeast 03, Southeast and Corsica 04, and Southwest 05). If **ringing France from abroad**, the international dialling code is 33, and drop the first 'o' of the number. For **international calls** from France, dial 00, wait for the change in the dial tone, then dial the country code (UK 44; US and Canada 1; Ireland 353; Australia 61; New Zealand 64), and then the local code (minus the 0 for UK numbers) and number. The easiest way to reverse charges is to spend a few francs ringing the number and giving your number in France, which is always posted by public phones; alternatively, ring your national operator and tell him or her that you want to call reverse charges (for the UK dial 00 33 44; for the USA 00 33 11). For directory enquiries, dial **t** 12, or try your luck and patience on the free, slow, inefficient Minitel electronic directory in every post office.

The old saying that it doesn't pay to be first certainly applies to France with its national computer system, the Minitel, which was distributed to every phone subscriber in the 1980s. Next to the Internet, it seems a Neanderthal, but its presence considerably slowed French interest in the Internet. This is changing fast: most cities and towns now have cybercafés, and the French have some of the most remarkable websites on the information highway – one, for instance, pinpoints every address in Paris, with a photo of the building.

Racism

Unfortunately, in France the forces of bigotry and reaction are strong enough to make racism a serious concern. It's especially bad in the south, where Jean-Marie Le Pen's Front National is a powerful political force: in places such as Orange, Marseille, Nice, Toulon and Perpignan, campsites, hotels and restaurants may suddenly have no places if the colour of your skin doesn't suit the proprietor; the bouncers at clubs may say it's really the cut of your hair or trousers they find offensive; police may stop you for no reason and demand to check your papers. If any place recommended in this book is guilty of such behaviour, please

let us know: we will remove it in the next edition and forward your letter to the regional tourist office and relevant authorities in Paris.

Sport and Leisure Activities

Basque Sports

Summer in the Pays Basque is a great time to watch its special sports: tug of war, stone lifting, or running with 100lb weights. But there's more to the Basques than brute strength: every town has an outdoor *fronton*, or court for *pelote*, the fastest ball game in the world; the indoors version, *cesta punta* or *jaï alaï*, is even more fast and furious. If you want to get in a little action yourself, you might try to talk your way into it at any village *fronton* when they're practising (they'd be charmed), or else contact the **Fédération de Pelote Basque** at the Trinquet Moderne in Bayonne, 60 Av Dubrocq, **t** 05 59 59 05 22; they set up training courses in summer for beginners. Matches take place at least once a week in towns throughout the Pays Basque, but times and days change, so ring the local tourist office to ask for the most up-to-date schedule.

Boules/Pétanque

Even the smallest village has a rough, hard court for *boules* or *pétanque*. Nearly all players are male and of a certain age, although women are welcome to join in. The object is to get your metal ball closest to the wooden marker (*bouchon* or *cochonnet*). Tournaments are frequent and well attended.

Bullfights

The Roman amphitheatres at Nîmes and Arles had hardly been restored when they once again became venues for *tauromachie*. However, most bullfights in Provence, Languedoc and Gascony are not bloody: the object is to remove a round cockade from between the horns of the bull (or cow) by cutting its ribbons with a blunt razor comb – a sport far more dangerous to the human players than the animals. You will see other types of bullfight advertised: the *corrida*, or traditional Spanish bullfight, in which the bull is put to death, and the *corrida portuguaise*, in which the bullfighter is on horseback but doesn't kill the bull.

Cycling

No country on earth respects cycling more, or follows the flying Lycra with such passion as in the Tour de France. If you find yourself along the route in July, it's fun to see what the fuss is all about. If you do it yourself, you'll get plenty of respect (see 'Getting Around', pp.90–91).

Football/Soccer

The dazzling success of the French national team in the World Cup in 1998 and Euro 2000 has given the country a boost of self-confidence and pride, and the fact that its stars came in all shades brought home the fact that a multicultural France is a tremendous asset. At other times, almost all of its stars play outside of the country, where TV deals shower clubs with megatons of money. Nevertheless, the French follow *le foot* with the same passion as everyone else in Europe: Paris St-Germain, Auxerre, Monaco and Olympique Marseille are the most exciting teams in the First Division.

Rugby

Rugby is the national sport of Southwest France, which is the cradle of most of the players on the national team, famous for its virtuosity. Although the best teams lately have been Toulouse, Brive, Dax, Agen and Bayonne, you can still see fiery matches in Béziers, long-time champions, and Carcassonne. In some places they play 'Cathar rugby' – 13 to a side instead of 15.

Skiing

The French Alps are famous for their skiing, and the most economical way of joining in is to book a package ski holiday from a local travel agency. Snowfall is less reliable in the Pyrenees, although the atmosphere is generally more relaxed and *sympa*. Here cross-country skiing (*ski de fond*) is as popular as downhill skiing, as it is in the Massif Central. For more information, contact the **Fédération Française de Ski**, 50 Rue des Marquisats, 74000 Annecy, t 04 50 51 40 34, f 04 50 51 75 90.

Water Sports and Beaches

France has beaches for all tastes: sheltered nooks in Brittany, endless miles of sand and big waves along the Bay of Biscay, long beaches in Languedoc, short ones with paying concessions on the Côte d'Azur. Legally, and often in spite of appearances, all are public up to 15ft of the high-tide mark. Green flags mean that swimming is permitted and that a lifeguard is on duty (*baignade autorisée et surveillée*). Orange flags mean that swimming is not advised, but that there is a lifeguard on duty (*baignade surveillée mais déconseillée*). Red flags mean that swimming is forbidden and that there is no lifeguard on duty (*baignade interdite*). Topless bathing is accepted everywhere; areas are set aside for *les naturistes*, or nudists.

Every town on the coast hires out equipment for water sports, often for hefty prices. Some of the best diving is in the clear waters off Ile Port-Cros National Park and around Corsica; for a list of diving clubs, contact the **Fédération Française d'Etudes et de Sports Sous-Marins**, 24 Quai de Rive Neuve, 13007 Marseille, t 04 91 33 99 31, f 04 91 54 77 43.

Time

France is usually an hour ahead of the UK and Ireland, and six hours ahead of US Eastern Standard Time.

Tourist Information

Every city and town, and most villages, have a tourist information office, usually called a Syndicat d'Initiative or an Office de Tourisme. In smaller villages this service is provided by the town hall (*mairie*). They distribute free maps and town plans, and hotel, camping and self-catering accommodation lists for their area, and can inform you about sporting events, leisure activities, wine estates open for visits, and festivals. Addresses and telephone numbers are listed in the text, and if you write to them they'll post you their booklets to help you plan your holiday.

French government tourist offices abroad:

Australia: 25 Bligh St, Level 22, NSW 2000
Sydney, t (02) 9231 5244, f (02) 9221 8682.
Canada: 1981 Av McGill College, No.490,
Montreal, PQ H3A 2W9, t (514) 288 4264,
f (514) 845 4868, *mfrance@attcanada.net*.
Ireland: 10 Suffolk St, Dublin 1, t (01) 679 0813,
f (01) 679 0814, *frenchtouristoffice@tinet.ie*.
UK: 178 Piccadilly, London W1V OAL,
t 0891 244 123 (calls charged at 60p/min),
info@mdlf.co.uk, *www.franceguide.com*.
Normandy Tourist Board, The Old Bakery,
44 Bath Hill, Keynsham, Bristol BS31 1HG,
t (0117) 986 0386,
stevenrodgers@compuserve.com.
Picardy Tourist Board, c/o THF, PO Box 21352,
London WC2H 9SR, t (020) 7836 2232,
picardie@thehatfactory.com.
Tarn Tourist Board, 39 Neal St, London WC2H
9PJ, t (020) 7379 6891.
USA: 444 Madison Av, New York, NY 10022,
t (410) 286 8310, f (212) 838 7855, *info@france
tourism.com*, *www.francetourism.com*.
676 N. Michigan Av, Chicago, IL 60611, t (312)
751 7800, f (312) 337 63 39, *fgto@mcs.net*.
9454 Wilshire Bd, Suite 715, Beverly Hills, CA
90212, t (310) 271 6665, f (310) 276 2835,
fgto@gte.net

Where to Stay

Hotels

In France you can find some of the most
splendid hotels in Europe and some genuine
fleabags, with the vast majority of establishments falling somewhere between. As in most
countries, the tourist authorities grade them
by their facilities (not by charm or location)
with stars. Hotels with no stars are not
necessarily dives: their owners probably
never bothered filling out a form for the
tourist authorities.
Most hotels have a wide range of rooms and
prices – a very useful and logical way of doing

Hotel Price Ranges

*Note: all prices listed here and elsewhere in
this book are for a double room.*
luxury 1,500F and over
expensive 600–1,500F
moderate 400–600F
inexpensive 200–400F
cheap under 200F

things, once you're used to it. In some the
difference in quality and price can be enormous: a large room with antique furniture, a
television, a balcony over the sea and a bathroom will cost much more than a poky back
room in the same hotel, with a window overlooking a car park, no antiques, and the WC
down the hall. Some proprietors will drag out
a sort of menu for you to choose the level of
price and facilities you would like.
Standards vary so widely that it's impossible
to be more precise, but we can add a few more
generalizations. Single rooms are relatively
rare, and usually two-thirds the price of a
double, and rarely will a hotelier give you a
discount if only doubles are available (again,
because each room has its own price); on the
other hand, if there are three or four of you,
triples or quads or adding extra beds to a
double room is usually cheaper than staying
in two rooms. Flowered wallpaper, usually
beige, comes in all rooms with no extra charge
– it's an essential part of the French experience. Breakfast (usually coffee, a croissant,
bread and jam) is nearly always optional.
Rates rise considerable in the busy season
(Easter holidays and summer, and in the
winter around ski resorts), when many hotels
with restaurants will require that you take
half-board (*demi-pension* – breakfast and a set
lunch or dinner). Many hotel restaurants are
superb and described in the text, and non-
residents are welcome. At worst the food will
be boring, and it can be monotonous eating in
the same place every night. In the off-season,
board requirements vanish into thin air.
Your holiday will be much sweeter if you
book ahead, especially in popular areas from
May to October when the few reasonably
priced rooms are snapped up very early across
the board. Phoning a day or two ahead is
always a good policy, although hotels will only
confirm a room with the receipt of a cheque or
a credit card number covering the first night.
Tourist offices have complete lists of accommodation in their given areas or even
département which come in handy during the
peak season; many will even call around and
book a room for you on the spot for free or a
nominal fee.
Chain hotels (Sofitel, Formula One, etc.) are
in most cities, but always dreary and geared to

the business traveller, so you won't find them in this book. Don't confuse chains with the various **umbrella organizations**, such as Logis et Auberges de France, Relais de Silence or the prestigious Relais et Châteaux, which promote and guarantee the quality of independently owned hotels. Many are recommended in the text. Larger tourist offices usually stock their booklets, or you can pick them up before you leave from the French National Tourist Office.

Chambres d'hôtes, or bed and breakfasts, are in private homes, châteaux or farms, or may be connected to restaurants or wine estates. Local tourist offices can provide listings. Prices tend to be moderate to inexpensive. Also try **B & B France**, PO Box 66, Bell St, Henley-on-Thames, Oxon RG9 1XS, **t** (01491) 578803, **f** (01491) 410806, *bookings@bedbreck. demon.co.uk* (catalogue £13.99); or in France, 6 Rue d'Europe, 95470 Fosses, **t** 01 34 68 83 15 (catalogue 50F).

Youth Hostels, *Gîtes d'Etape* and *Refuges*

Most cities and resort areas have youth hostels (*auberges de jeunesse*) which offer simple dormitory accommodation and breakfast to people of any age for 40–70F a night. Most offer kitchen facilities as well, or inexpensive meals. They are the best deal if you're travelling on your own; for people travelling together, a one-star hotel can be just as cheap. Another downside is that many are in the most ungodly locations – in the suburbs where the last bus goes by at 7pm, or miles from any transport at all in the country. In the summer the only way to be sure of a room is to arrive early in the day. Most require a Hostelling International card, which you can often purchase on the spot, although regulations say you should buy them in your home country (UK: from YHA, 14 Southampton St, London WC2, **t** 0870 870 8808; USA: from AYH, P.O. Box 37613, Washington DC 20013, **t** (202) 737 2333; Canada: from 75 Nicholas St, Ottawa, Ont K1N 7B9, **t** (613) 235 2595; Australia: from AYHA, 11 Royston Place, opposite Central Station, Sydney, New South Wales, **t** (2) 928 19 111).

A *gîte d'étape* is a simple shelter with bunk beds and a rudimentary kitchen set up by a village along GR walking paths or a scenic bike route. Again, lists are available for each *département*. In the mountains, similar rough shelters along the GR paths are called *refuges*, most of them open summer only. Both charge around 40 or 50F a night.

Camping

Camping is a very popular among the French themselves, and there's at least one campsite in every town, often an inexpensive, no-frills place run by the town itself (*camping municipal*). Other campsites are graded with stars from four to one: at the top of the line you can expect lots of trees and grass, hot showers, a pool or beach, sports facilities, a grocer's, a bar and/or restaurant, and, on the coast, prices rather similar to one-star hotels (although these, of course, never have all the extras). But be aware that July and August are terrible months to camp near the most popular beaches, when sites become so overcrowded that the authorities have begun to worry about health problems.

Tourist offices have complete lists of campsites in their regions, or if you plan to move around a lot pick up a *Guide Officiel Camping/Caravanning*, available in French bookshops. A number of UK holiday firms book camping holidays and offer discounts on Channel ferries: Canvas Holidays, **t** (01383) 644000; Eurocamp Travel, **t** (01606) 787878; Keycamp Holidays, **t** 0870 700 0123.

Gîtes de France and Other Self-catering Accommodation

France offers a vast range of self-catering accommodation: inexpensive farm cottages, history-laden châteaux with gourmet frills, sprawling villas, flats in modern beach resorts or even on board canal boats. The Fédération Nationale des Gîtes de France is a French government service offering inexpensive accommodation by the week in rural areas. Lists with photos arranged by *département* are available from the Maison des Gîtes de France, 59 Rue St-Lazaire, 75009 Paris, **t** 01 48 70 75 75, or in the UK from their official agents, Brittany Ferries, **t** 08705 360360 . If you want to stay in châteaux, request the *Chambres d'Hôtes et Gîtes de Prestige*. Other options are advertised in the Sunday papers, or contact one of the firms listed below. The accommodation they offer will nearly always be more costly than a *gîte*, but the discounts holiday firms can offer on ferries, plane tickets or car hire can make up for the difference.

In France

Château de la Guillonnière, La Guillonnière, Dienne 86410, t 05 49 42 05 46, f 05 49 42 48 34, *www.rent-a-castle.com*. Cottages, B&B and castles in the Loire Valley.

Eurovillage-Groupe VVF, 172 Bd de la Villette, 75918 Paris, Cedex 19, t 01 44 52 48 68/66, f 01 44 52 68 64. Gîtes, B&B, holiday clubs and youth centres. English spoken.

Locaflat, 63 Av de la Motte Picquet, 75015 Paris, t 01 43 06 78 79, f 01 40 56 99 69, *www.locaflat.com*. Apartments in central Paris.

Maeva, 92 Route de la Reine, 92100 Boulogne-Billancourt, t 01 46 99 53 53, f 01 41 22 10 46. Self-catering apartments and other accommodation combined with sports activities such as skiing.

In the UK

Allez France, 27 West St, Storrington, West Sussex RH20 4DZ, t (01903) 742345, *www.allezfrance.com*. Wide variety of accommodation all over France, from cottages to châteaux.

Angel Travel, 34 High St, Borough Green, Sevenoaks TN15 8BJ, t (01732) 884109. Villas, gîtes and flats.

Belvedere Holiday Apartments, 5 Bartholomews, Brighton BN1 1HG, t (01273) 323404. Studio flats and apartments in the south of France.

Bowhills, Mayhill Farm, Swanmore, Southampton SO32 2QW, t (01489) 877627, *www.bowhills.co.uk*. Luxury villas and farmhouses, mostly with pools.

Chez Nous, Spring Mill, Earby, Barnoldswick, Lancashire BB94 0AA, t 08700 781 400, f (01282) 445158, *www.cheznous.com*. Over 3,000 privately owned holiday cottages and B&Bs.

Crystal Holidays, King's Place, Wood St, Kingston-upon-Thames, Surrey KT1 1JY, t (020) 8241 4000. Villas all over France.

Dominique's Villas, 13 Park House, 140 Battersea Park Rd, London SW11 4NB, t (020) 7738 8772, f (020) 7498 6014. Large villas and châteaux with pools.

French Affair, 517 Humbolt Rd, London W6 8QH, t (020) 7381 8519, *www.french affair.com*. Traditional cottages, villas, manors and châteaux in the Dordogne, Lot, Languedoc-Roussillon and Provence.

French Villa Centre, 175 Selsdon Park Rd, South Croydon CR2 8JJ, t (020) 8651 1231. *Gîtes, villages de vacances* and coastal villas.

InnTravel, Hovingham, York YO6 4JZ, t (01653) 628811, *www.inntravel.co.uk*. Apartments and villas with pools in Aquitaine and Queyras.

International Chapters, 47–51 St John's Wood High St, London NW8 7NJ, t (020) 7722 9560, *www.villa-rentals.com*. Farmhouses, châteaux and villas.

LSG Theme Holidays, 201 Main St, Thornton, Coalville LE67 1AH, t (01509) 231713. Seaside gîtes.

Meon Villas, Meon House, College St, Petersfield GU32 3JN, t (01730) 268411, f (01730) 230399, *www.meontravel.co.uk*. Villas with pools.

Palmer and Parker Villa Holidays, Bank Rd, Penn, Bucks 8P10 8LA, t (01494) 815411. Upmarket villas with pools on the Riviera from Nice to St-Tropez.

The Apartment Service, 5–6 Francis Grove, London SW19 4DT, t (020) 8944 1444, f (020) 8944 6744, *www.apartmentservice.com*. Selected apartment accommodation in cities for long or short stays.

Vacances en Campagne, Bignor, Pulborough, West Sussex RH20 1QD, t (01798) 869433, *www.indiv-travellers.com*. Farmhouses, villas and gîtes all over France and Corsica.

VFB Holidays, Normandy House, High St, Cheltenham GL50 3FB, t (01242) 240339, *www.vfbholidays.co.uk*. From rustic gîtes to luxurious farmhouses.

In the USA

Absolutely B&Bs, Box 703, South Miami, FL 33143, t 800 380 7420, t (305) 666 0710, f (305) 666 0173. B&Bs, from châteaux to carefully selected private homes.

At Home Abroad, 405 E. 56th St, Suite 6C, New York, NY 10022 2466, t (212) 421 9165, f (212) 752 1591, *www.athomeabroad.com*. Private villas and apartments in Côte d'Azur, Provence and the Dordogne.

At Home in France, P.O. Box 643, Ashland, OR 97520, t (541) 488 9467, f (541) 488 9468, *www.athomeinfrance.com*. Apartments, cottages, farmhouses, manor houses and villas; moderate to deluxe.

Doorways Lt., P.O. Box 151, Bryn Mawr, PA 19010 3105, t 800 261 4460, t (610) 520 0806, f (610) 520 0807, *www.villavacations.com*. Villas and farm apartments in Provence, Languedoc and Paris.

Families Abroad, 194 Riverside Drive, New York, NY 10025, t (212) 787 2434, t (718) 768 6185, f (212) 799 8734. Sabbatical and vacation rentals, in apartments, villas and châteaux in Paris, Normandy, Loire, Provence, Dordogne, Alpes Maritimes and the Riviera.

France by Heart, P. O. Box 614, Mill Valle, CA 94942, t (415) 331 3075, f (415) 331 3076, *www.francebyheart.com*. Over 200 properties throughout the country.

Global Home Network, 1110 D Elden St, Suite 205, Herndon, VA 20170 5527, t 800 528 3549, t (703) 318 7081, f (703) 318 7086, *www.globalhomenetwork.com*. Apartments in Paris, from luxury to budget.

Heaven on Earth, 39 Radcliffe Rd, Rochester, NY 14617, t 800 466 5605, t (716) 342 5550, f (716) 266 1425. Properties in Paris, the Riviera, Provence and the Dordogne; moderate to luxury.

Hideaways International, 767 Islington St, Portsmouth, NH 03802, t 800 843 4433, t (603) 430 4433, f (603) 430 4444, *www.hideaways.com*. Apartments in Paris, plus villas, farmhouses and châteaux throughout France.

Loire Tours, 158 Crosby St, Suite 3B, New York, NY 10012, t 800 755 9313, f (212) 254 0654. Studios, apartments and villas.

New York Habitat, 307 7th Av, Suite 306, New York, NY 10001, t (212) 255 8018, f (212) 627 1416, *www.nyhabitat.com*. Five hundred apartments throughout Paris.

Overseas Connection, Long Wharf Promenade, P.O. Box 2600, Sag Harbor, NY 11963, t (516) 725 9308/1805, f (516) 725 5825, *www .overseasvillas.com*. Villas and apartments in Paris, Provence, the French Alps, Côte d'Azur, Loire Valley, Dordogne and Brittany.

Prestige Villas, P.O. Box 1046, Southport, CT 06490, t 800 336 0080, t (203) 254 1302, f (203) 254 7261. Luxury villas in Provence, Dordogne, the Côte d'Azur and Normandy.

Vacances Provencales, 1425 Bayview Av, Suite 204, Toronto, Ontario M4G 3A9, t 800 263 7152, f (416) 322 0706. Moderate to luxury villas, country homes, châlets and apartments in Provence, Dordogne and Paris.

Villas of Distinction, P.O. Box 55, Armonk, NY 10504, t (914) 273 3331, t 800 289 0900, f (914) 273 3184, *www.villasofdistinction.com*. Private villas, cottages and châteaux mainly in Provence and the Côte d'Azur.

Paris and the Ile de France

Getting Around

Tickets and Passes

Buying single tickets is crazy – always get a *carnet* of 10 from any métro window or machine for 58F, a 40% discount from the individual rate – good for buses too. A weekly pass (*carte hebdo*) is 85F; a monthly (*carte orange*) is 285F (good for two zones only; for more zones the fee is higher; you need a passport photo and be sure to write the number of your carrying pouch on your ticket or you'll end up with a fine). All these passes expire at the end of the week or month, so purchase them at the beginning of the period. There is a special travel card, *Paris Visite*, starting at 55F per day. This is a rotten deal – you'll need to ride seven or eight times a day just to break even, and none of the major attractions is included.

Always keep your ticket until the end, not only for spot checks, but because some of the bigger stations have automatic exit gates that require it to let you out.

By Métro

The métro is a godsend to disorientated visitors; not only quick and convenient for travelling, but its stations serve as easy reference points for finding addresses. Contrasts with the London Underground are unavoidable. A ride in Paris costs less than half as much, and for that you get cleaner stations and faster service, although the *direction* system is harder to read: to find the right train you'll need to look at the map and remember the name of the station at the *end of the line*, in the direction you wish to travel. You can change métro lines as often as you want on the same journey for the same ticket.

There is a new automatic line, the *Météor*, Line 14, from Bibliothèque F. Mitterrand to the Gare St-Lazare, super efficient and hi-tech, but very noisy.

RER: The Réseau Express Régional is Paris' suburban commuter train system, and you can use métro tickets on it within the Paris boundaries. It can come in handy for getting across town fast or for visiting places like the Musée d'Orsay or the Jardin du Luxembourg, where it has the closest station. From almost all the other stations, you can easily change on to the métro. The RER can also take you to Versailles or the airports.

The *Régie Autonome des Transports Parisiens* is the authority controlling the buses and the métro. For information in French call t 08 36 68 77 14, in English t 08 36 68 41 14 (both 2.21F a minute), *www.ratp.fr*.

Lost property, t 01 40 30 52 00.

By Bus

Bus routes are more of a challenge than the métro, but much more fun. An unused métro ticket is equally valid for the bus, but you'll need a fresh ticket with each bus you catch. Enter from the front of the bus and leave from the middle or the rear; press the *arrêt demandé* button just before your stop; you'll need to stamp your ticket (*oblitérer*) in the machine next to the driver as you enter.

The *Noctambus*, Paris' **night bus** network, can be useful; there are 16 lines, many converging at Place du Châtelet from points around the edge of the city.

Route 29, through the Marais (from Gare St-Lazare to Gare de Lyon), features a modern version of the old Paris buses with open back platforms.

Sightseeing: *L'Open Tour*, a system of tourist buses with an open upper deck, follows a circular route of the principal sites with further loops out to Montmartre and to Bercy, 160F for two days, get on and off anywhere; *Balabus* (operated by RATP) runs from the Grande Arche along the river to the Gare de Lyon and back (*15 April–15 Sept Sun and hols 1pm–8pm*), requiring three tickets for the full one-way journey; *Montmartrobus* (route 64), another circular route, runs up, down and around Montmartre, get on or off anywhere, one ticket per journey; ride the *Funiculaire de Montmartre* instead of climbing the steps of the Sacré Cœur, one ticket each way.

By Taxi

There are 14,900 taxis in Paris, and on the whole the service is competent and they're a pleasure to ride. Most taxi drivers will get you to the station on time if it kills you both, while forcing you to defend your government's policies or telling you about their daughter's trip to Oklahoma City.

Radio taxis can be especially helpful in rush hours, when cabs are hard to find (credit cards accepted, charged from time of call).

Taxis Bleus, t 01 49 36 10 10.

G7, t 01 47 39 47 39.

By Car

This is, of course, absurd. Parking is almost impossible in Paris, and battalions of the world's most elegant meter maids cheerfully await your every indiscretion. None of the smaller hotels and few even of the luxury variety have a garage. Underground car parks are fairly common, though (shown on the Michelin map with a blue P).

By Boat

The famous *bateaux-mouches* got their name (literally, fly boats) because the first ones were built in Lyon, on the Quai des Mouches. Most charge 40–50F for a 1hr tour, and most also offer lunch and dinner cruises.

Canauxrama, t 01 42 39 15 00. Reserve for 3hr tours of Canal St-Martin.

Bateaux Parisiens. From the Port de La Bourdonnais, 7e, ⓜ Bir-Hakeim/Iéna.

Vedettes de Pont Neuf, t 01 46 33 98 38. From Sq du Vert-Galant, Ile de la Cité, 1er, ⓜ Pont-Neuf.

Vedettes de Paris. From the Port de Suffren, 7e, ⓜ Bir-Hakeim.

Bateaux-Mouches de Paris, t 01 42 25 96 10. From Pont de l'Alma, RER Pont de l'Alma (north side, 8e); night tours in summer and a fancy dinner cruise for 500F; lunch Sat 300F, public hols 350F.

Paris Canal, t 01 42 40 96 97. From the Musée d'Orsay up the Canal St-Martin to La Villette, passing through old locks and under tunnels.

The Batobus, t 01 40 58 27 90. River bus service operating up and down the Seine in the heart of Paris (*April–Oct*), with six stops along the quais.

Tourist Information

127 Av des Champs-Elysées, 8e, **t** 08 36 68 31 12 (2.23F a minute), near the Arc de Triomphe (*open daily 9am–8pm; low season same, but Sun 11–6*). Bilingual and helpful, the staff can help you find a hotel room, sell you a museum pass, fill you in on events, and tell you about places to see in the Ile de France. A second office is at the Gare du Nord.

Maps: For detailed information, the Michelin *Paris-Plan 14* (the little blue book) is indispensable. For day trips into the outskirts of the city, Michelin's green *Environs de Paris 106* is the best. Otherwise, most stationery stores sell the useful *Plan de Paris*, a little book that details every tiny street, métro station, and attraction you could ever hope to visit.

Shopping

People who think shopping is an art have long regarded Paris as Europe's masterpiece when it comes to consumption; throughout its history, the city has enjoyed an enviable reputation for craftsmanship, especially in luxury goods and high fashion. If you find designer *prêt-à-porter* too dear, there are a number of shops that sell last season's clothes and accessories, or you can tackle Paris' huge department stores. Paris has endless little speciality shops tucked into nearly every *arrondissement*; for the bargain hunter there are mega-flea markets and some interesting second-hand shops. The big sales take place in January and July. Remember, most shops close on Sundays and Mondays.

If in one place you fork out over 2,000F (non-EU resident) or 4,200F (EU resident), you are entitled to a rebate on the VAT you've paid. The shop gives you the form (the magic word is *détaxe*), which you present to French customs as you depart. A few weeks later they post you the rebate.

Opéra and Bd Haussmann

The area around the Opéra is one of Paris' liveliest shopping districts, where the managers still send hucksters out on to the street to demonstrate vegetable choppers and dab cologne on the ladies.

Galeries Lafayette, 40 Bd Haussmann, 9e. A bit of Art Nouveau splendour with a wonderful glass dome. Better than anyone, they know what the Parisiennes like. The store puts on its own free fashion show, with selections from its various designer boutiques (*Tues 11am; 1 April–Oct 31 also Fri 2.30pm; reserve, t 01 42 82 34 56*). ⓦ Chaussée d'Antin.

Printemps, 64 Bd Haussmann, 9e. A wee bit posher, stuffier and nearer the cutting edge of fashion for women's designer clothes and accessories than Galeries Lafayette. Good household and linen departments, lovely cupolas and a good view from the café on the top floor. ⓦ Havre-Caumartin.

Brentano's, 37 Av de l'Opéra, 2e, t 01 42 61 52 50. New books and magazines in English; American interests; novels, guides, children's and art sections too. ⓦ Opéra.

Madeleine, Faubourg-St-Honoré

The area around Place de la Madeleine is one of Paris' gourmet paradises, with famous restaurants such as Lucas Carton, and many of the city's finest food shops. The window displays are entirely over the top.

There is also a small but cheerful flower market (*daily exc Mon*).

Chanel, Rue Cambon, 1er. Probably the most famous house in Paris, now under the design wand of Karl Lagerfeld. ⓦ Madeleine.

Fauchon, 26 Pl de la Madeleine, 8e. The most famous and snobbish grocery in Paris, with the best of everything you can imagine. ⓦ Madeleine.

Ladurée, 16 Rue Royale, 8e, ⓦ Madeleine; 75 Av des Champs-Elysées, ⓦ Franklin Roosevelt. Heavenly chocolates.

Institut Géographique National, 107 Rue La Boétie, 8e. Superb collection of maps, ordnance surveys, guidebooks, etc. ⓦ Miromesnil.

Artcurial, 9 Av Matignon, 8e. Largest collection of glossy art and coffee-table books, in French and English. ⓦ Franklin D. Roosevelt.

Anna Lowe, 35 Av Matignon, 8e. One of the oldest high fashion discount houses in Paris, selling Chanel, Escada, Lacroix, YSL, etc. at 50% off. ⓦ Miromesnil.

Au Nain Bleu, 408–10 Rue St-Honoré, 1er. Paris' oldest and most magical toy store. ⓦ Concorde.

St-Laurent Rive Gauche, Rue du Fbg-St-Honoré. The new flagship of the king of Paris fashion. ⓦ Concorde.

Hermès, 24 Rue du Fbg-St-Honoré, 8e. Pay a month's rent for a scarf. ⓦ Madeleine.

Versace, 62 Rue du Fbg-St-Honoré, 8e. One of the first and most opulent 'mega-boutiques' in Paris: fashion-as-theatre in a glass-domed Roman temple. ⓦ Madeleine.

Dalloyau, 99–101 Rue du Fbg-St-Honoré, 8e. Napoleon's *pâtissier*. ⓦ St-Philippe-du-Roule.

Champs-Elysées

Still the street to stroll down, to see and be seen, looking glitzier and shinier than ever. The perfect avenue to indulge in a little *lèche-vitrine* (window shopping) and take home the ultimate Parisian souvenir.

Mugler, 49 Av Montaigne, 8e. Off-the-peg fashion. ⓦ Franklin D. Roosevelt.

Caron, 34 Av Montaigne, 8e. Posh perfumes. ⓦ Franklin D. Roosevelt.

Guerlain, 68 Av des Champs-Elysées, 8e. A beautiful shop, displaying Guerlain's famous range of perfumed seduction. ⓦ Franklin D. Roosevelt.

La Maison du Chocolat, 56 Rue Pierre-Charron, 8e. Chocolates to buy, and rich hot chocolate to drink. ⓦ Franklin D. Roosevelt.

Rue de Rivoli

A long, busy street, lined with imposing, if not beautiful, buildings, and arcades.

W. H. Smith, 248 Rue de Rivoli, 1er, t 01 44 77 88 99. Especially good for their English-language magazines; fiction, children's and travel sections. ⓦ Concorde.

Galignani, 224 Rue de Rivoli, 1er, t 01 42 60 76 07. Cosy place founded in 1802 – the oldest English bookshop on the Continent; new titles, children's and glossy art books. ⓦ Tuileries.

Louvre des Antiquaires, next to the Louvre, 1er. The poshest, biggest antiques centre and a great place for browsing. ⓦ Palais Royal.

Bazar de l'Hôtel de Ville (BHV), 52 Rue de Rivoli, 4e. BHV has been around since 1854 and lacks the pretensions of other department stores. A good bet for practical items, and other services, like tool rental, which you'll probably manage to do without. ⓦ Hôtel de Ville.

La Samaritaine, 19 Rue de la Monnaie, 1er. The most beautiful department store in Paris, with its Art Nouveau façade, skylight and balconies (in the old building). The café on its 10th-floor terrace (*open April–Sept*) has one of the most gratifying of views over Paris, across the Pont Neuf. Ⓜ Louvre-Rivoli.

Gosselin, 123 Rue St-Honoré, 1er. Voted best baguette in Paris in 1996. Ⓜ Louvre-Rivoli.

Philippe Model, 33 Pl du Marché-St-Honoré, 1er. Paris' top glove, hat and shoe designer. Ⓜ Pyramides.

Les Halles

Once Les Halles was a vast colourful wholesale distribution market (moved to Rungis near Orly airport) surrounded by slums. Today the Forum is a subterranean labyrinthine 'new town' of shops and fast food outlets. The streets around and to the north are also full of shops.

FNAC, Forum des Halles, Rue Pierre-Lescot. A Paris institution – the city's biggest and fullest book chain (including some titles in English); also CDs, etc. Other outlets across the city. Ⓜ Châtelet-Les Halles.

Agnès B, 10 Rue du Jour, 2e. Fashion, cosmetics and accessories. Ⓜ Les Halles.

Marie Mercié, 56 Rue Tiquetonne, 2e. For the kind of hat you see in films and have always dreamed of on your own head. Ⓜ Etienne Marcel.

St-Germain and Latin Quarter

Although you'll have to save up your pocket money just to be able to afford a *café au lait* in St-Germain, the bustling narrow streets, legendary cafés and trendy bookshops invite you to explore and tempt you to spend. The Latin Quarter is where Abelard taught, Villon fought, Erasmus thought and Mimi coughed. This is also the *quartier* of publishers and bookshops, and where Paris' students hang out and smoke Gauloises: the streets are lively by day and night.

Librairie de l'Ecole Supérieure des Beaux-Arts, 17 Quai Malaquais, 6e. Architecture books from around the world. Ⓜ St-Germain-des-Prés.

The Village Voice, 6 Rue Princesse, t 01 46 33 36 47. Where Odile Hellier carries the banner of American literature in Paris, hosting scores of readings by contemporary writers; has anglophone Paris' most discriminating collections of books. Ⓜ Mabillon.

Stéphane Kélian, 13 bis Rue de Grenelle, 7e. Perhaps the most extraordinary and

certainly the most expensive women's shoes in Paris. Ⓜ Sèvres Babylone.

Barthélemy, 51 Rue de Grenelle, 7e. The *ne plus ultra* of *fromageries*: only the most refined classic French cheeses. Ⓜ Rue du Bac.

Brûlerie de l'Odéon, 6 Rue Crébillon, 6e. One of Paris' oldest coffee-roasters, still providing fresh roasted coffees and teas for picky java junkies. Ⓜ Odéon.

Debauve et Gallais, 30 Rue des Sts-Pères, 7e. Oldest and most beautiful *chocolatier* in Paris; the unusual displays are worth a trip in themselves. Ⓜ St-Germain-des-Prés.

Poilâne, 8 Rue du Cherche-Midi, 7e. Tasty sourdough country bread, the most famous in Paris; used in the best sandwiches across the city. Ⓜ Sèvres-Babylone.

Au Bon Marché, 38 Rue de Sèvres, 7e. The only department store on the Left Bank, but the grand-daddy of them all, still puts on a pretty good show of desirable stuff – its extraordinary food halls are an unrivalled gourmet cornucopia, and its prices for clothes and other goods tend to be a bit lower than its big-name rivals. Ⓜ Sèvres-Babylone.

L'Artisan Parfumeur, 24 Bd Raspail, 6e. A range of perfumes based around single flower or fruit notes, plus blends. Ⓜ Rue du Bac.

Shakespeare & Co, 37 Rue de la Bûcherie, 5e, t 01 43 26 96 50. Just what a bookshop should be – a convivial treasure hunt, crammed full of inexpensive second-hand and new books in English (*see* p.169). Ⓜ St-Michel.

Marais

The most ambitious restoration effort in Paris has spruced up the elegant streets and old palaces of the Marais, ready for your inspection (*see* pp.144–8). The shops are small, exclusive and individual: antiques, jewellery and unusual *objets*.

L'Apache, 45 Rue Vieille-du-Temple, 4e. Great, reasonable second-hand clothes and hats from the 1930s and '40s (*open every pm*). Ⓜ St-Paul.

Art Depot, 3 Rue du Pont-Louis-Philippe, 4e. Lots of fun (and packable) Art Deco pieces. Ⓜ St-Paul.

A la Bonne Renommée, 26 Rue Vieille-du-Temple, 4e. Beautiful, richly coloured satins, silks and velvets with a folkloric touch. ⓂSt-Paul.

Tehen, 5 bis Rue des Rosiers, 4e. Stylish jersey and knitwear co-ordinates. Ⓜ St-Paul.

Goldenberg's, 7 Rue des Rosiers, 4e. Paris' best Jewish deli and a godsend to any New Yorker in Paris. Ⓜ St-Paul.

Mariage Frères, 30 Rue du Bourg-Tibourg, 4e. 400 different types of tea and tea-flavoured goodies. Ⓜ St-Paul.

Arcades and Passages

Most of Paris' covered, glass-ceilinged arcades were built in the early 19th century.

Galerie Véro-Dodat, 19 Rue J.-J. Rousseau. One of the prettiest (see p.157). Ⓜ Palais-Royal.

The Galerie Vivienne, 4 Rue des Petits-Champs, and the adjacent Galerie Colbert, 6 Rue Vivienne. Glass-ceilinged elegance passage complex (see p.157). Well restored, although the Colbert has had most of the life squeezed out of it by the Bibliothèque Nationale. Ⓜ Bourse.

Passage des Panoramas, 11 Bd Montmartre. Paris' largest arcade complex. Five distinct arcades intersect (Galeries Feydeau, St-Marc, des Variétés, Montmartre and the Passage des Panoramas), to make a little self-contained city of a hundred shops. Mostly utilitarian, with a few stamp and coin shops, printers and even a Turkish bath. Graveur Stern, a print shop in business here since 1840, loves to put its best work in its window. Ⓜ Rue-Montmartre.

Passage Jouffroy, 10 Bd Montmartre. If you still haven't come to love the peculiar little world of the passages, this one might do the trick. A pretty play of dappled shadows lights up the faded grandeur of this busy 1846 arcade, which boasts its own hotel, and a wax museum, as well as antique toys, oriental rugs, cinema memorabilia, and an outlandish selection of antique walking sticks and canes. Ⓜ Rue Montmartre.

Markets

Flea, Books, Flowers and Birds

Les Puces de Saint-Ouen. The mother of all flea markets (open Sat, Sun and Mon). Ⓜ Porte de Clignancourt.

Puces de Montreuil. Great junky flea market (open Sat, Sun and Mon). Ⓜ Porte de Montreuil.

Puces de Vanves. The most humble, and potentially most exciting market for the eagle-eyed (open Sat and Sun). Ⓜ Porte de Vanves.

Marché aux Fleurs: Place de la Madeleine, 8e (open daily exc Mon); Place des Ternes, 8e (open daily exc Mon); and Place Lépine, 4e (open Mon–Sat).

Marché du Livre Ancien et d'Occasion, Rue Brancion, Parc Georges-Brassens, 15e. Second-hand book market (open Sat and Sun). Ⓜ Porte de Vanves.

Marché aux Timbres. Stamp market (the one that co-starred in Charade with Audrey Hepburn and Cary Grant), north of Théâtre Marigny, 8e. Ⓜ Champs-Elysées.

Marché aux Vieux Papiers de St-Mandé, Av de Paris, 12e. Old books, postcards and prints (open Wed). Ⓜ Porte de St-Mandé Tourelle.

Food

Paris' permanent street markets are intoxi-cating to visit (open daily exc Sun pm and all day Mon), and usually lined with shops that spill out into the street (some shops close for lunch out of season). The tourist office has a complete list of all the covered markets and the 60 travelling street markets (open one or two days a week).

Place d'Aligre, 12e. Colourful, with a strong North African presence. Ⓜ Ledru Rollin.

Buci, 6e. One of the liveliest, with a good selec-tion; best Sun am. Ⓜ Mabillon.

Rue Cler, 7e. The market of the aristocratic Faubourg, noted for its high quality. Ⓜ Ecole Militaire.

Montorgueil, Rue Montorgueil, 1er. North of Rue Etienne-Marcel, convivial and fun, a whiff of the old atmosphere of nearby Les Halles. Ⓜ Etienne Marcel.

Mouffetard, 5e. Lower end of Rue Mouffetard, with lots of character and characters. Ⓜ Censier Daubenton.

Where to Stay

There are basically three kinds of hotels in the centre of Paris: big luxury and grand hotels, mainly on the Right Bank; business hotels, scattered everywhere; and small privately owned hotels, some very fashionable and some dogged dives, mostly on the near Left Bank.

Advance bookings are essential in June, and in September and October when Paris is awash in salons and conventions. July and August are low season, and some expensive hotels offer discounts. If you arrive without a reservation, booking services in the tourist offices will find you a room.

The categories relate to prices for an average double room. In most places each room has its own price, depending on its view, plumbing, heated towel racks, etc. This is the French way of doing things, and it's also perfectly normal to visit rooms or press the proprietor for details and negotiate. The one hitch is that there are few single rooms.

Optional continental breakfast costs from 25F at the cheapie places to 180F a head at the Ritz. Many proprietors pretend not to know it's optional, but the same cup of coffee and croissant in the bar across the street will be more fun and save you lots of francs.

The annual hotel list for Paris available from the Tourist Office indicates all hotels with facilities for the disabled, as well as the most current prices. Parisian postcodes include the arrondissement, so an address with the postcode 75004 is in the 4th arrondissement.

Ile de la Cité and Ile St-Louis
****Jeu de Paume, 54 Rue St-Louis-en-l'Ile, 75004, t 01 43 26 14 18, f 01 40 46 02 76, www.hoteldujeudepaume.com (luxury–expensive). Paris' last real-tennis venue is now the most enchanting little inn on the Seine, complete with a sunny garden. ⓜ Pont Marie.
***Des Deux Iles, 59 Rue St-Louis-en-l'Ile, 75004, t 01 43 26 13 35, f 01 43 29 60 25, hotel.2.iles@free.fr (expensive). Smallish rooms in an 18th-century house, decorated with period pieces and Provençal fabrics. Late-night bar in the cellar. ⓜ Pont Marie.
***Lutèce, 65 Rue St-Louis-en-l'Ile, 75004, t 01 43 26 23 52, f 01 43 29 60 25 (expensive). Charming, tasteful and small, many rooms with beams. ⓜ Pont Marie.

***St-Louis, 75 Rue St-Louis-en-l'Ile, 75004, t 01 46 34 04 80, f 01 46 34 02 13, www.hotelsaintlouis.com (expensive). Fashionable, antique furniture, but smallish rooms (no Amex). ⓜ Pont Marie.
*Henri IV, 25 Pl Dauphine, 75001, t 01 43 54 44 53 (inexpensive–cheap). Four hundred years old, frumpy flowered wallpaper, and toilets and showers down the hall, but visitors book months in advance to stay in all simplicity in this most serendipitous square (no credit cards). ⓜ Pont Neuf/Cité.

Marais/Bastille
**St-Louis Marais, 1 Rue Charles-V, 75004, t 01 48 87 87 04, f 01 48 87 33 26, slmarais@cybercable.fr (expensive). An 18th-century Celestine convent offering romantic if monk-sized rooms. Five floors, but no lift. ⓜ Sully Morland/Bastille/St Paul.
**Place des Vosges, 12 Rue de Birague, 75004, t 01 42 72 60 46, f 01 42 72 02 64, hotel.place.des.vosges@gofornet.com (expensive). Well restored, and just a few steps from the Place. ⓜ Bastille.
**Grand Hôtel Jeanne d'Arc, 3 Rue de Jarente, 75004, t 01 48 87 62 11, f 01 48 87 37 31, www.parishotels.com (moderate). Not so Grand any more – but ancient, cute and well run, close to the Place des Vosges; book far ahead. ⓜ St-Paul.
**Sévigné, 2 Rue Malher, 75004, t 01 42 72 76 17, f 01 42 78 68 26 (inexpensive). Nice place right around the corner from the nosher's paradise of Rue des Rosiers. ⓜ St-Paul.

Les Halles/Beaubourg
****Grand Hôtel de Besançon, 56 Rue Montorgueil, 75002, t 01 42 36 41 08, f 01 45 08 08 79 (expensive). Views over the Montorgueil market. ⓜ Châtelet/Les Halles.
***Hôtel de la Bretonnerie, 22 Rue Ste-Croix-de-la-Bretonnerie, 75004, t 01 48 87 77 63, f 01 42 77 26 78, hotel@bretonnerie.com (expensive). A very popular small hotel with Louis XIII furnishings. ⓜ Hôtel de Ville.
***St-Merri, 78 Rue de la Verrerie, 75004, t 01 42 78 14 15, f 01 40 29 06 82 (expensive–moderate). A stone's throw from the Centre Pompidou, this was once St Merri's presbytery and later a bordello. Its latest

metamorphosis as a hotel stands out for the beautiful Gothic rooms. ⓦ Hôtel de Ville.

★★Andrea, 3 Rue St-Bon, 75004, t 01 42 78 43 93, f 01 44 61 28 36 (*moderate*). Decent quiet choice near the Rue de Rivoli. ⓦ Hôtel de Ville.

★La Vallée, 84–6 Rue St-Denis, 75001, t 01 42 36 46 99, f 01 42 36 16 66, *hvallee@cybercable.fr, www.perso.cybercable.fr/hvallee* (*inexpensive*). Excellent bargain choice, between Les Halles and Beaubourg. ⓦ Châtelet/Les Halles.

Palais Royal

★De Rouen, 42 Rue Croix-des-Petits-Champs, 75001, t/f 01 42 61 38 21 (*inexpensive*). A good choice: old and comfortable. ⓦ Palais Royal.

Hôtel de Lille, 8 Rue du Pélican, 75001, t 01 42 33 33 42 (*inexpensive*). A rare bargain hotel between the Louvre and Palais Royal. Old and plain. ⓦ Palais Royal.

Opéra/Faubourg St-Honoré

★★★★Intercontinental, 3 Rue de Castiglione, 75001, t 01 44 77 11 11, f 01 44 77 14 60, *paris@interconti.com, www.interconti.com* (*luxury; 3,250–3,850F*). Built by Garnier nearly as lavishly as his Paris Opéra. Three of the seven grand imperial ballrooms are listed as national monuments. The hotel takes up a whole city block; 390 rooms and 62 suites. ⓦ Tuileries/Concorde.

★★★★The Ritz, 15 Pl Vendôme, 75001, t 01 43 16 30 30, f 01 43 16 31 78, *resa@ritzparis.com, www.ritz.com* (*luxury; 4,000–4,500F*). One of the most famous hotels in the world. Sound-proof and bullet-proof glass on the ground floor, tiled pool and health centre, free cookery classes in the tradition of the legendary chef Escoffier, and exclusive nightclub. ⓦ Opéra.

★★★Tuileries, 10 Rue St-Hyacinthe, 75001, t 01 42 61 04 17, f 01 49 27 91 56, *htuileri@aol.com, www.members@ aol.com/htuileri* (*expensive*). A quiet 18th-century *hôtel particulier* with antiques. ⓦ Tuileries/Pyramides.

★★★Brébant, 30–32 Bd Poissonnière, 75009, t 01 47 70 25 55, f 01 42 46 65 70, *hotel.brebant@wanadoo.fr* (*expensive*). Smart, stylish, crisply run hotel midway between the striped suits in the Bourse and the Folies-Bergère girlie shows. ⓦ Grands Boulevards.

★★Cité Rougemont, 4 Cité Rougemont, 75009, t 01 47 70 25 95, f 01 48 24 14 32 (*moderate–inexpensive*). The best economy bet in the area, located in a traffic-free street off Rue Bergères. ⓦ Grands Boulevards.

Grand Axe

★★★★★Crillon, 10 Pl de la Concorde, 75008, t 01 44 71 15 00, f 01 44 71 15 02, *reservations@crillon.com, www.crillon.com* (*luxury; 3,500–3,900F*). Behind the classic 18th-century façade stands the last luxury hotel in Paris to remain completely in French hands. Inside are some of the most exquisite and prestigious suites in town, and rooms, if not always grand, done up choicely with marble baths to match. ⓦ Concorde.

★★★★George V, 31 Av George-V, 75008, t 01 49 52 70 00, f 01 49 52 70 20, *par.reservations@fourseasons.com, www .fourseasons.com* (*luxury; 3,608–4,756F*). Recently restored Art Deco hotel minutes from the glittering shops of the Champs-Elysées, with 18th-century tapestries, a restaurant, bar and coffee lounge, health club, pool and spa, and some private terraces with fantastic views over Paris. ⓦ Georges V.

★★★★Plaza Athénée, 25 Av Montaigne, 75008, t 01 53 67 66 65, f 01 53 67 66 66, *fpoli@plaza-athenee-paris.com* (*luxury; 3,700–4,800F*). Celebrated for its voluptuous luxury and superb service – there are twice as many staff as rooms, and more money spent on fresh flowers than lights. Mata Hari was arrested in its bar, but the spies have since given way to celebrities and corporate bosses. ⓦ Franklin D. Roosevelt/Alma Marceau.

★★★★Raphaël, 17 Av Kléber, 75016, t 01 44 28 00 28, f 01 53 64 32 01, *reservation@raphael-hotel.com, www.raphael-hotel.com* (*luxury; 2,400–5,050F*). Built in the 1920s, élite, intimate, splendid and artsy, plus an English bar and garden terrace with view over Paris. ⓦ Kléber.

★★★★De Vigny, 9–11 Rue Balzac, 75008, t 01 42 99 80 80, f 01 42 99 80 40 (*luxury; doubles 2,500F, suites from 4,500F*), *de-vigny@wanadoo.fr, www.relaischateaux.fr/vigny*. One of Paris' most sumptuous small hotels, its bar evoking the Paris of the 1930s *salons*. Soundproof, marble bathrooms, library, cable TV. ⓜ George V.

Montmartre

Note that, due to the steps, disabled access is very limited.

****Terrasse**, 12 Rue Joseph-de-Maistre, 75018, t 01 46 06 72 85, f 01 42 52 29 11, *terrasse@francenet.fr*, (*luxury–expensive*). Montmartre's most luxurious hotel, overlooking the cemetery and the rest of Paris. Also has two restaurants, one of them with a terrace for summer dining. ⓜ Place Clichy.

****Timhotel Montmartre**, 11 Rue Ravignan, 75018, t 01 42 55 74 79, f 01 42 55 71 01 (*expensive*). Henry Miller knew it when it was called Paradis. It's still one of the most romantic hotels in Paris, overlooking delightful Place Emile-Goudeau. ⓜ Abbesses.

"Hôtel de Charme" Ermitage, 24 Rue Lamarck, 75018, t 01 42 64 79 22, f 01 42 64 10 33 (*moderate*). A charming little white hotel under the gardens around Sacré-Coeur (no credit cards). ⓜ Lamarck-Caulaincourt.

****Prima Lepic**, 29 Rue Lepic, 75018, t 01 46 06 44 64, f 01 46 06 66 11 (*moderate*). Pleasant and pretty rooms on the slope of the Butte. ⓜ Abbesses/Blanche.

****Régyn's Montmartre**, 18 Place des Abbesses, 75018, t 01 42 54 45 21, f 01 42 23 76 69, *hotel@regynsmontmartre.com* (*moderate*). A simple but good address in the heart of Montmartre, with good views over Paris. ⓜ Abbesses.

Latin Quarter

*****Grands Hommes**, 17 Pl du Panthéon, 75005, t 01 46 34 19 60, f 01 43 26 67 32 (*expensive*). André Breton defined Surrealism here in the 1920s. Furnishings, however, are more in the spirit of Voltaire and Rousseau. Small garden, cable TV and baby-sitting. ⓜ Cardinal Lemoine, RER: Luxembourg.

*****Le Colbert**, 7 Rue de l'Hôtel-Colbert, 75005, t 01 43 25 85 65, f 01 43 25 80 19 (*expensive*). Elegant, peaceful hotel with tea room south of Place Maubert. ⓜ Maubert-Mutualité, St-Michel.

*****Grand Hotel St-Michel**, 19 Rue Cujas, 75005, t 01 46 33 33 02, f 01 40 46 96 33, *grand.hotel.st.michel@wanadoo.fr* (*expensive*). Fully renovated, fairly quiet choice with a garden, near the Panthéon. RER: Luxembourg.

Les Degrés de Notre-Dame, 10 Rue des Grands-Degrés, 75005, t/f 01 55 42 88 88 (*expensive*). Ten charming rooms on a quiet street, many with prize views over Notre-Dame. Restaurant. ⓜ Maubert-Mutualité.

****Les Argonautes**, 12 Rue de la Huchette, 75005, t 01 43 54 09 82, f 01 44 07 18 84 (*moderate*). Perfect for Latin-Quarter night-owls, on the corner of Paris' narrowest street; not all rooms ensuite. ⓜ St-Michel.

****Familia**, 11 Rue des Ecoles, 75005, t 01 43 54 55 27, f 01 43 29 61 77 (*moderate*). Comfortable, with frescoes in some rooms and great views of Notre-Dame from the top floors. ⓜ Cardinal Lemoine.

***Esmeralda**, 4 Rue St-Julien-le-Pauvre, 75005, t 01 43 54 19 20, f 01 40 51 00 68 (*moderate*). Endearing, romantic hotel in a 16th-century building with a *classé* stairway and 19th-century furnishings. ⓜ St-Michel.

***Delhy's**, 22 Rue de l'Hirondelle, 75006, t 01 43 26 58 25, f 01 43 26 51 06 (*inexpensive*). Modest choice on a quiet lane tucked near busy Place St-Michel. ⓜ St-Michel.

Mouffetard/Jussieu

****Jardin des Plantes**, 5 Rue Linné, 75005, t 01 47 07 06 20, f 01 47 07 62 74, *jardin-des-plantes@tinhotel.fr* (*expensive*). The best choice in the area, with its sauna, cheerful décor, and 5th-floor terrace overlooking the botanical gardens. ⓜ Jussieu.

*****Grandes Ecoles**, 75 Rue du Cardinal-Lemoine, 75005, t 01 43 26 79 23, f 01 43 25 28 15, *hotel.grandes.ecoles@wanadoo.fr*, *www.hotel-grandes-ecoles.com* (*expensive–moderate*). One of the most amazing settings in Paris, a peaceful cream-coloured villa in a beautiful garden courtyard. Reserve weeks ahead. ⓜ Cardinal Lemoine/Place Monge.

***Alliés**, 20 Rue Berthollet, 75005, t 01 43 31 47 52, f 01 45 35 13 92 (*inexpensive*). Simple place in a quiet street by the Val de Grâce. ⓜ Censier Daubenton.

★Le Central, 6 Rue Descartes, 75005, **t** 01 46 33 57 93 (*inexpensive*). Family-run haven. **Ⓜ** Maubert-Mutualité/Cardinal Lemoine.

St-Germain

★★★★L'Hôtel, 13 Rue des Beaux-Arts, 75006, **t** 01 44 41 99 00, **f** 01 43 25 64 81 (*luxury; 1,800–4,300F suite*). Besides seeing the last of Oscar Wilde, this is one of the most romantic hotels in Paris; the honeymoon suite is outrageously furnished. **Ⓜ** St-Germain-des-Prés.

★★★★Relais Christine, 3 Rue Christine, 75006, **t** 01 40 51 60 80, **f** 01 40 51 60 81, *relaisch@club-internet.fr, www.relaischristine.com* (*luxury; double 2,000–2,500F, suite 2,800–4,400F*). Luxurious, colourful rooms in a 16th-century Augustinian cloister, a quiet oasis. **Ⓜ** Odéon.

★★★★Lutétia, 45 Bd Raspail, 75006, **t** 01 49 54 46 46, **f** 01 49 54 46 00, *lutetia-paris@lutetia-paris.com, www.lutetia-paris.com* (*luxury; double 1,900–2,900F, suite 15,000F*). Renovated early Art Deco palace, a favourite for honeymoons since Pablo and Olga Picasso, and Charles and Yvonne de Gaulle canoodled here. When it was requisitioned by the Nazis, the staff walled up the prize wine cellars, and never gave away the secret. **Ⓜ** Sèvres-Babylone.

★★★De l'Abbaye, 10 Rue Cassette, 75006, **t** 01 45 44 38 11, **f** 01 45 48 07 86, *hotel.abbaye@wanadoo.fr, www.hotel-abbaye.com* (*luxury–expensive*). One of the swankiest small Left-Bank hotels – originally a monastery – and despite the traffic serenely quiet, especially if you get one of the bedrooms over the lovely garden courtyard. **Ⓜ** St-Sulpice.

★★★Duc de St-Simon, 14 Rue de St-Simon, 75007, **t** 01 44 39 20 20, **f** 01 45 48 68 25 (*luxury–expensive*). In a 17th-century house in a quiet side street off Bd St-Germain, one of the most fashionable little hotels on the Left Bank, all antiques, old beams, stone walls and snob appeal, its cellars converted into a string of bars and salons. **Ⓜ** Rue du Bac.

★★★★La Villa, 29 Rue Jacob, 75006, **t** 01 43 26 60 00, **f** 01 46 34 63 63, *hotel@villa-stgermain.com* (*luxury–expensive*). *Le dernier cri* in St-Germain, with precocious

bathrooms of chrome, glass and marble and chi-chi piano bar. **Ⓜ** St-Germain-des-Prés.

★★★Angleterre, 44 Rue Jacob, 75006, **t** 01 42 60 34 72, **f** 01 42 60 16 93, *anglotel@wanadoo.fr* (*luxury–expensive*). A former British embassy, now a hotel with character. Some rooms have vertiginously high ceilings; huge double beds. **Ⓜ** St-Germain-des-Prés.

★★★Marronniers, 21 Rue Jacob, 75006, **t** 01 43 25 30 60, **f** 01 40 46 83 56 (*expensive*). An enchanting hotel at the bottom of a courtyard, with a garden at the back, but book well in advance (Visa and MasterCard only). **Ⓜ** St-Germain-des-Prés.

★★★Université, 22 Rue de l'Université, 75007, **t** 01 42 61 09 39, **f** 01 42 60 40 84, *hoteluniversite@gofornet.com* (*expensive*). In a refurbished 17th-century town house, a few minutes from St-Germain-des-Prés – 27 stylish, quiet rooms. **Ⓜ** Rue du Bac/St-Germain-des-Prés.

★★Quai Voltaire, 19 Quai Voltaire, 75007, **t** 01 42 61 50 91, **f** 01 42 61 62 26, *info@hotelduquaivoltaire.com* (*expensive*). A hotel since the 19th century, overlooking the Seine and the Louvre, a favourite of Baudelaire, Sibelius and Richard Wagner. RER: Musée d'Orsay.

★★★Lenox Montparnasse, 15 Rue Delambre, 75014, **t** 01 43 35 34 50, **f** 01 43 20 46 64, *www.parishotel.com* (*expensive*). A large, elegant hotel, just off Bd Raspail. **Ⓜ** Vavin/Edgar Quinet.

★★★Villa des Artistes, 9 Rue de la Grande-Chaumière, 75006, **t** 01 43 26 60 86, **f** 01 43 54 73 70, *hotel@villa-artistes.com* (*expensive*). Where Samuel Beckett stayed; recent Art Deco facelift – some of Montparnasse's artists had studios across the street. **Ⓜ** Vavin.

★★Welcome, 66 Rue de Seine, 75006, **t** 01 46 34 24 80, **f** 01 40 46 81 59 (*moderate*). Renovated, simple, soundproofed, and a warm welcome. **Ⓜ** Mabillon/Odéon.

★Nesle, 7 Rue de Nesle, 75006, **t** 01 43 54 62 41 (*moderate*). Slightly dilapidated but welcoming hotel that hasn't accepted reservations since it was an international be-in in the 1960s. Each room is in a different style: no.9 is Egyptian. Some rooms with shower or bath. **Ⓜ** Odéon/Pont Neuf.

Stanislas, 5 Rue du Montparnasse, 75006, t 01 45 48 37 05, f 01 45 44 54 43 (*inexpensive*). A well-kept, agreeable hotel in crêpe alley – TV, WC, shower, hairdryer and phones in each room. **Ⓜ** Notre-Dame des Champs.

*Des Académies**, 15 Rue de la Grande-Chaumière, 75006, t 01 43 26 66 44, f 01 43 26 03 72 (*inexpensive*). Simple, unpretentious, family hotel near the Luxembourg gardens. **Ⓜ** Vavin.

Exhibition Paris

***Bourdonnais**, 111 Av de la Bourdonnais, 75007, t 01 47 05 45 42, f 01 45 55 75 54, *htlbourd@club-internet.fr, www.hotella bourdonnais.fr* (*expensive*). Airy, elegant and comfortable, and breakfast is served in a sunlit indoor garden. **Ⓜ** Ecole Militaire.

***Jardins d'Eiffel**, 8 Rue Amélie, 75007, t 01 47 05 46 21, f 01 45 55 28 08, *eiffel@acom.fr* (*expensive*). Built at the same time as the 1889 Exposition. Rooms are cosy in an old-fashioned way, and there's a sauna; book a room on the top floor for a view of Mr Eiffel's flagpole. **Ⓜ** La Tour Maubourg.

***Varenne**, 44 Rue de Bourgogne, 75007, t 01 45 51 45 55, f 01 45 51 86 63 (*expensive*). An attractive converted town house with an interior courtyard in a peaceful corner of Paris; comfortable rooms. **Ⓜ** Varenne.

Kensington, 79 Av de la Bourdonnais, 75007, t 01 47 05 74 00, f 01 47 05 25 81, *hk@hotel-kensington.com, www.hotel-kensington.com* (*moderate*). Pleasant and friendly, small and tidy. **Ⓜ** Ecole Militaire.

Grand Hôtel Lévèque, 29 Rue Cler, 75007, t 01 47 05 49 15, f 01 45 50 49 36, *info@hotelleveque.com* (*moderate*). Friendly and pleasant and in the middle of Rue Cler market. **Ⓜ** Ecole Militaire.

Centre-La Serre, 24bis Rue Cler, 75007, t 01 47 05 52 33, f 01 40 62 95 66, *laserre@easynet.fr* (*moderate–inexpensive*). Recently refurbished old-fashioned hotel on Faubourg-St-Germain's liveliest market street, and one of the cheapest in the quarter. **Ⓜ** Ecole Militaire.

Eating Out

Cooking styles, like everything else in Paris, go in and out of fashion. What some enthusiastic food writers call *haute cuisine* is really what the French call *cuisine bourgeoise* – elaborate dishes concocted as much to impress as to please in the pretentious *boulevard* restaurants a century ago. Lots of places still cook this way, for tourists or for nostalgic Parisians.

Nouvelle cuisine (expensive ingredients, strange combinations, minute portions artily presented on huge plates at indigestible prices) began as a reaction to bourgeois cooking; you won't see much of it now, but the fad did much to turn the French back to a more natural way of cooking. Although vegetarians still have a hard time in restaurants, at home Parisians eat more seafood and vegetables than ever before.

Nearly all the restaurants listed below offer set-price menus; little adventures *à la carte* are liable to double prices. As anywhere in France, inexpensive/moderate restaurants expect that most of their clients will order one of the menus, especially at lunch, and they do their best to offer a good deal. The easiest way to tell a useless restaurant or a tourist-exploiter is to look at the menus – any place that offers *crudités* and a *steak frites* for over 100F, for example. Some expensive restaurants put on an inferior, inexpensive lunch menu just to get people in the door. On the other hand, some of the most famous places offer excellent bargain lunch menus that even budget-balancers can treat themselves to perhaps once or twice.

For dinner, bookings are essential – weeks in advance (lunch too) for real gourmet citadels on popular dates (or be flexible). For the moderate/inexpensive-range restaurant, you will probably get a table weekday nights without booking, but don't try it on weekends. Brasseries tend to have lots of tables, and spare ones aren't difficult to find except at the most famous.

What restaurants choose to call themselves means little, whether it's an *auberge*, a *relais* or, most fashionable these days, a *bistrot*. The original *bistrots* evolved from the old *bougnats bois-et-charbons* run by rough-edged

Auvergnats, who sold wine and snacks along with wood and coal; real ones have a friendly, neighbourhood feel, where you wait for a table over a glass of wine at the bar, and dine on hearty country classics like sausages and *andouillettes, bœuf bourguignon* and salt cod. A few examples of the big, working-class restaurants called *bouillons* still survive. *Brasseries* were founded by refugees from Alsace-Lorraine after the war with Prussia in 1871, and specialized in beer and *choucroute* (sauerkraut), along with such Paris classics as *steak/frites, moules/frites, plâteau de fruits de mer* and *steak tartare.*

Brasseries usually serve meals around the clock until midnight, rather like American diners, and many offer breakfast. Other restaurants open more or less from 12 with last orders at 2pm and from 7 until 10.30 or 11; in Paris though, the trend is towards staying open later and later. Remember that many restaurants are closed in August.

Restaurants

Ile de la Cité and Ile St-Louis

Expensive
L'Orangerie, 28 Rue St-Louis-en-l'Ile, 4e, t 01 46 33 93 98. One of the most elegant and romantic dining rooms in Paris, founded by actor Jean-Claude Brialy as an after-theatre rendezvous for his colleagues; refined *cuisine bourgeoise (menu 380F, wine included). Dinner only; book.* **Ⓜ** Pont Marie.
Au Monde des Chimères, 69 Rue St-Louis-en-l'Ile, 4e, t 01 43 54 45 27. A pretty *bistrot* with a *brandade de morue* just the way *maman* prepared it on a good day *(lunch menu 90–160F with wine; dinner around 350F). Closed Sun and Mon.* **Ⓜ** Pont Marie.

Moderate–cheap
Brasserie de l'Ile St-Louis, 55 Quai de Bourbon, 4e, t 01 43 54 02 59. For lovers of old-fashioned *choucroute.* **Ⓜ** Pont Marie.
Au Rendez-vous des Camionneurs, 72 Quai des Orfèvres, 1er, t 01 43 54 88 74. Good French-truckers' style cooking at very reasonable prices. **Ⓜ** Cité.

Marais/Bastille

Luxury
L'Ambroisie, 9 Pl des Vosges, 4e, t 01 42 78 51 45. Under the supreme fine touch and imagina-tion of master chef Bernard Pacaud, one of the top gastronomic addresses in the country, in the elegant Hôtel de Luynes; a short *carte* but every dish a winner from the succulent *feuillantine de langoustines* with sesame to the bitter cocoa tart (*more than 700F per head). Closed Sun and Mon.* **Ⓜ** Bastille.
Le Train Bleu, Gare de Lyon, first floor, 12e, t 01 43 43 97 96. Built for the 1900 World Fair, and after Maxim's perhaps the most spec-tacular decoration in a Paris restaurant; frescoes and gilt everywhere. Cuisine not memorable but good enough (*lunch menu 250F).* **Ⓜ** Gare de Lyon.

Expensive
Chez Julien, 1 Rue Pont Louis Phillipe, 4e, t 01 42 78 81 64. Well-cared-for Belle Epoque restau-rant. Excellent, traditional fare *(menus from 165F). Closed Sun.* **Ⓜ** Hôtel de Ville.
Chez Janou, 2 Rue Roger-Verlomme, 3e, t 01 42 72 28 41 (north of Pl des Vosges). Friendly tiled *bistrot* from 1900 with inventive dishes from Provence *(menu 100F; no credit cards).* **Ⓜ** Chemin Vert, Bastille.
La Biche au Bois, 45 Av Ledru-Rollin, 12e, t 01 43 43 34 38. Some of the best moderately priced traditional cuisine *(menus from 120F). Closed Sat and Sun.* **Ⓜ** Gare de Lyon/Ledru-Rollin.
Bofinger, 5 Rue de la Bastille, 4e, t 01 42 72 87 82. One of the prettiest brasseries; wonderful seafood specialities. A great place *(menu 169F).* **Ⓜ** Bastille.

Moderate
Chez Paul, 13 Rue de Charonne, 11e, t 01 47 00 34 57. Solid family cooking (rillettes, duckling with prunes) in an old Paris setting straight out of a Doisneau photo, complete with a pretty terrace. **Ⓜ** Bastille.
Chez Nénesse, 17 Rue de Saintonge, 3e, t 01 42 78 46 49. A popular neighbourhood *bistrot* run by husband and wife, with better-than-average cooking *(lunch menu 80F; dinner more expensive). Closed Sat and Sun.* **Ⓜ** Filles-du-Calvaire.

Piccolo Teatro, 6 Rue des Ecouffes, 4e, t 01 42 72 17 79. Not an Italian restaurant, but the best vegetarian place in the area. Imaginative dishes with pretentious titles (*45F and 55F lunch menus*). Ⓜ St-Paul.

Le P'tit Gavroche, 15 Rue Ste-Croix-de-la-Bretonnerie, 4e, t 01 48 87 74 26. An old *bistrot* that has remained popular by never changing; *confits* and *coq au vin*. Ⓜ Hôtel-de-Ville.

Cheap

Aquarius, 54 Rue St-Croix-de-la-Bretonnerie, 4e, t 01 48 87 48 71. Vegetarian, non-smoking but non-ideological; good salads and desserts. Produce counter. *Closed Sun.* Ⓜ Hôtel-de-Ville.

Dame Tartine, 59 Rue de Lyon, 12e, t 01 44 68 96 95. A snack restaurant better than any chain and handy for the opera (*hot or cold, 15–40F*). *Closed Sun.* Ⓜ Bastille.

Le Grand Appétit, 9 Rue de la Cerisaie, 4e, t 01 40 27 04 95. A rare macrobiotic restaurant in Paris. Friendly, good (especially the desserts) and no doubt good for you; also a macrobiotic food store. Ⓜ Bastille.

Le Temps des Cerises, 31 Rue de la Cerisaie, 4e, t 01 42 72 08 63. Small friendly *bistrot à l'ancienne*. Ⓜ Bastille.

Le Trumilou, 84 Quai de l'Hôtel-de-Ville, 4e, t 01 42 77 03 98. Popular old Auvergnat *bistrot*, on the quai although a view of the Seine is blocked by a store wall; lamb chops or duck with prunes (*menus under 100F*). Ⓜ Hôtel-de-Ville.

Les Halles/Beaubourg

Luxury–Expensive

Benoît, 20 Rue St-Martin, 4e, t 01 42 72 25 76. Considered by many the most genuine Parisian *bistrot*, opened by current owner Michel Petit's grandfather, devoted to the most perfectly prepared dishes of *la grande cuisine bourgeoise française* with a wondrous *boeuf mode* (*more than 700F per head*). Ⓜ Châtelet.

Ambassade d'Auvergne, 22 Rue du Grenier-St-Lazare, 3e, t 01 42 72 31 22. Mouthwatering *cuisine de terroir* from the Auvergne (*soupe aux choux et au roquefort, Charlotte aux marrons*), near Beaubourg. Ⓜ Rambuteau.

La Tour de Montlhéry (Chez Denise), 5 Rue des Prouvaires, 1er, t 01 42 36 21 82. An old-fashioned *bistrot* with character and excellent cooking, full of locals not tourists; try the mutton with white beans. *Open 24hrs, but closed Sat–Mon.* Ⓜ Les Halles, Louvre-Rivoli.

Moderate

Caveau François Villon, 64 Rue de l'Arbre-Sec, 1er, t 01 42 36 10 92. A *bistrot* in a 15th-century cellar, delicious fresh salmon with orange butter. *Closed Sun and Mon.* Ⓜ Louvre-Rivoli.

Pharamond, 24 Rue de la Grande-Truanderie, 1er, t 01 42 33 06 72. Established 1832; its Belle Epoque interior is a national monument. Roast pheasant and rich *tripes à la mode de Caen* (*lunch menu 180F*). *Closed Sun, Mon lunch, first half Aug.* Ⓜ Etienne Marcel, Les Halles.

L'Alsace aux Halles, 16 Rue Coquillère, 1er, t 01 42 36 93 89. A brasserie that never closes, with shellfish, *choucroute* and Alsatian whites (*menus from 167F*). Ⓜ Les Halles.

Georges, top floor, Centre Pompidou, 4e. Shiny new restaurant-with-a-view; dress up (in clothes or confidence) to run the gauntlet of black-clad waiters. Range of food from simple 55F lunch salads to full evening push-the-boat-out; short well-chosen wine list.

Cheap

Les Forges, 3/5 Rue des Forges, 2e, t 01 42 36 40 83. The true Sentier restaurant: owners, models and drivers all eating together. Fresh fish a speciality. *Closed Sun.* Ⓜ Sentier.

Chez Léon de Bruxelles, 120 Rue Rambuteau, 3e. Chain with acceptable Belgian cuisine – mussels, *pommes frites* and good beer. Ⓜ Les Halles.

La Tavola Calda, 39 Rue des Bourdonnais, 1er, t 01 45 08 94 66. The place for decent pizza – a rare thing in Paris. Ⓜ Chatelet.

Palais Royal

Luxury

Le Grand Véfour, 17 Rue de Beaujolais, 1er, t 01 42 96 56 27. The grandest of grand old restaurants with one of the loveliest dining rooms in Paris (*lunch menu 360F, dinner 670–830F*). *Closed Sat and Sun.* Ⓜ Palais Royal, Bourse.

Pile ou Face, 52 Rue Notre-Dame-des-Victoires, 2e, t 01 42 33 64 33. A great restaurant, where many of the ingredients come from the proprietors' farm in Normandy. Innovative cooking, along with simple roast fowls and lots of wild mushrooms; good wine list (*up to 650F per head*). *Closed Sat and Sun.* Ⓜ Bourse.

Chez Georges, 1 Rue Mail, 2e, t 01 42 60 07 11. This fine establishment is at the very pinnacle of the *bistrot* range. Not cheap, with main dishes over 100F, but the equal of many with much heftier prices. *Closed Sun.* Ⓜ Sentier/Etienne Marcelle.

Expensive

Le Poquelin, 17 Rue Molière, 1er, t 01 42 96 22 19. Opposite Molière's birthplace and popular with actors from the Comédie Française who enjoy Michel Guillaumin's light, innovative cooking – salmon with cream of chives sauce and warm *tarte aux pommes* (*menu 189F, carte 270–370F*). *Closed Sat lunch and Sun.* Ⓜ Pyramides.

La Gaudriole, Jardin du Palais-Royal, 1er, t 01 42 97 55 49. Delicious terrace dining in fair weather (*generous 160F menu with wine*). Ⓜ Louvre, Palais Royal.

Moderate

Le Gavroche, 19 Rue St-Marc, 2e, t 01 42 96 89 70. The archtypical family-run *bistrot à vins* of old; authentic without even trying. Hearty country cooking from *cassoulet* to *pot-au-feu*, and a very good wine list. Ⓜ Bourse.

Entre Ciel et Terre, 5 Rue Hérold, 2e, t 01 45 08 49 84. When the moment arrives and you can't even face another slice of *foie gras*, this is your place. Vegetarian, light, homemade and totally non-smoking. *Closed Sat and Sun.* Ⓜ Bourse.

L'Incroyable, 26 Rue de Richelieu, 2e, t 01 42 96 24 64. Cheap *bistrot* in an alley just off the street. *Only open until 9pm; closed Sun, Sat lunch and Mon eve.* Ⓜ Richelieu Drouot.

Chez Danie, 5 Rue de Louvois, 2e, t 01 42 96 64 05. Another great bargain with goulash a speciality and homemade deserts. Always packed. *Lunch only; closed Sat and Sun.* Ⓜ Richelieu Drouot.

Opéra/Faubourg St-Honoré

Luxury–Expensive

Lucas Carton, 9 Pl de la Madeleine, 8e, t 01 42 65 22 90. The perfect marriage of tradition, beautiful surroundings and one of the top-rated modern chefs, Alain Senderens (*dinner more than 700F per head; or splurge on the lunch 395F menu*). *Closed Sat lunch, Sun.* Ⓜ Madeleine.

Drouant, 18 Place Gaillon, 2e, t 01 42 65 15 16. Since 1914 the seat of the Académie Goncourt, where it bestows France's most sought-after literary prize. Sumptuous Art Deco interior; famous for its elegant sauces, wine cellar and its *grand dessert Drouant* (*650F and up; 290F lunch menu*). *Open daily inc Aug.* **Café Drouant** (*menu 200F*). *Open daily inc Sun.* Ⓜ Opéra, Quatre Septembre.

Goumard, 9 Rue Duphot, 1er, t 01 42 60 36 07, near the Madeleine. A top-rated seafood restaurant since the 1890s, recently completely renovated, though the original bathrooms are a listed monument (*more than 700F per head*). *Closed Sun, Mon and 10–23 Aug.* Ⓜ Madeleine.

Pierre à la Fontaine Gaillon, Pl Gaillon, 2e, t 01 47 42 63 22. Seasonal menus based on seafood in the mansion of the Duc de Lorgues; tables out on the terrace by the Fontaine d'Antin. *Closed Sat lunch, Sun and Aug.* Ⓜ Opéra.

À la Grille St-Honoré, 15 Pl Marché St-Honoré, 1er, t 01 42 61 00 93. Guaranteed quality lunch in the middle of businessman's bistroland. *Closed Sun, Mon and 1–25 Aug.* Ⓜ Opéra, Quatre Septembre.

Moderate

Le Roi du Pot au Feu, 34 Rue Vignon, 9e, t 01 47 42 37 10. Entirely devoted to the most humble and traditional of all French dishes, but here raised to an art form. *Open 12 noon–10pm; closed Sun, end July to mid-Aug.* Ⓜ Madeleine.

La Ferme St-Hubert, 21 Rue Vignon, 8e, t 01 47 42 79 20. The restaurant annexe to the famous *fromager*, serving a variety of delicious cheese dishes based on country recipes (*menus 160–200F*). *Closed Sun; open Aug.* Ⓜ Madeleine.

Grand Axe

Luxury

Taillevent, 15 Rue Lamennais, 8e, t 01 44 95 15 01. M. Vrinat is still at the top, despite all the young hot-shots, with his brilliantly prepared classic dishes and his care of the customer. In handsome *hôtel* of the Duc de Morny; booking essential (*menus 650–900F*). Ⓜ George V.

Maxim's, 3 Rue Royale, 8e, t 01 42 65 27 94. Still the most beautiful restaurant in the galaxy, with perfectly preserved Belle Epoque rooms, and the food isn't bad either – but it is the fate of any place so famous to become more of a tourist attraction than a mere restaurant. Overpriced (*more than 700F per head*). *Closed Sun.* Ⓜ Concorde.

Les Ambassadeurs, Hôtel de Crillon, 10 Place de la Concorde, 8e, t 01 44 71 16 16. Highly rated cuisine in a sumptuous setting (*bargain 380F menu*). *Book well ahead.* Ⓜ Concorde.

Expensive

Androuët, 6, Rue Arsène Houssaye, 8e, t 01 42 89 95 00. If, like gastronome Brillat-Savarin, you believe 'a meal without cheese is like a beauty with one eye', come to this mouse heaven, with its cheese platters, cheese dishes and cheese *dégustation* from over 200 varieties. *Closed Sat lunch and Sun.* Ⓜ Etoile.

La Fermette Marbeuf 1900, 5 Rue Marbeuf, 8e, t 01 53 23 08 00. Over-the-top Art Nouveau décor – redeemed by an honest 178F menu. Ⓜ George V.

Montmartre

Luxury–Expensive

A. Beauvilliers, 52 Rue Lamarck, 18e, t 01 42 54 54 42. Montmartre's gourmet restaurant and one of the oldest restaurants in France – 1787 (*more than 700F per head; good value lunch menus 185F and 285F*). *Closed Sun, and Mon lunch.* Ⓜ Lamarck Caulaincourt.

Charlot Roi des Coquillages, 12 Place Clichy, 9e, t 01 53 20 48 00. A 1930s brasserie; a fishy kitsch-palace. You would have to go to Marseille for better seafood. *Open daily until 1am.* Ⓜ Place Clichy.

La Pomponnette, 42 Rue Lepic, 18e, t 01 46 06 08 36. Classic *bistrot*, lively atmosphere; homemade desserts. *Closed Mon.* Ⓜ Blanche.

Le Restaurant, 32 Rue Véron (south of Rue des Abbesses), 18e, t 01 42 23 06 22. A *typique* of high-quality Montmartre with dishes such as *canette rotie au miel* (*2 course menu 120F*). *Closed Sat lunch, Sun lunch and Mon.* Ⓜ Abbesses.

Moderate–Cheap

Chez Ginette, 101 Rue Caulaincourt, near the *métro*, 18e, t 01 46 06 01 49. Very reasonable, with plenty of fun; a complete night out (*lunch menu 65F; dinner around 100F*). *Closed Sun and Aug.* Ⓜ Lamarck Caulaincourt.

Le Montagnard, 102 Rue Lepic, 18e, t 01 42 58 06 22. Good-quality traditional country cooking in an old Montmartre grill. Impressive attention to detail and excellent value (*menu Club Affaire 98F*). Ⓜ Abbesses.

Au Rendez-vous des Chauffeurs, 11 Rue des Portes-Blanches (northern end of Bd Barbès), 18e, t 01 42 64 04 17. Out of the way, perhaps, but good home cooking at reasonable prices (*menu 63F*). *Closed Wed.* Ⓜ Marcadet-Poissoniers.

Latin Quarter

Luxury–Expensive

La Tour d'Argent, 15 Quai de la Tournelle, 5e, t 01 43 54 23 31. Established here in 1582 and recently brought back to splendour by a new chef, who has added his own innovations to the classic *canard au sang* (pressed duck). Add unforgettable, romantic views of Notre-Dame, unique atmosphere and a superlative wine cellar (*menus 750–980F; lunch menu 350F*). *Closed Mon.* Ⓜ Maubert-Mutualité.

Balzar, 49 Rue des Ecoles, 5e, t 01 43 54 13 07. An institution from the 1930s. Where stars and Sorbonne *intellectuels* rub shoulders – you might find yourself sitting next to Gwyneth Paltrow! Limited menu, but superb. Ⓜ Cluny-Sorbonne.

Atelier de Maître Albert, 1 Rue Maître-Albert, 5e, t 01 46 33 13 78. Stone walls, exposed beams and an open fire create one of Paris' most medieval environments (*menus around 250F*). *Closed Mon lunch, Sun.* Ⓜ Maubert-Mutualité.

La Rotisserie Galande, 57 Rue Galande, 5e, t 01 46 34 70 96. Succulent roasts of all kinds. Good for a winter meal. Ⓜ St-Michel/Maubert-Mutualité

Chez Maître Paul, 12 Rue Monsieur-le-Prince, 6e, t 01 43 54 74 59. Ordinary looking but highly recommended, with dishes from the Franche-Comté – *poulette à la crème gratinée* and delicious apple or walnut desserts, washed down with wines from the Jura (*lunch menu with wine 155F, 190F*). *Closed Sat lunch and Sun.* Ⓜ Odéon.

Au Pactole, 44 Bd St-Germain, 5e, t 01 43 26 92 28. Fashionable and excellent restaurant, ghastly decor, but terrace and a delectable *côte de boeuf* (*good-value menus lunch 150F, dinner 280F*). *Closed Sat lunch and Sun.* Ⓜ Maubert-Mutualité.

Moderate–Cheap

Perraudin, 157 Rue St-Jacques, 5e, t 01 46 33 15 75. Comfortable and old-fashioned, fresh tarts – sweet and savoury – a speciality (*lunch menu 63F*). RER: Luxembourg.

Chez Hamadi, 12 Rue Boutebrie, 5e, t 01 43 54 03 30. Not much to look at but good North African cuisine (*menu 85F with wine*). Ⓜ St-Michel.

La Petite Hostellerie, 35 Rue de la Harpe, 15e, t 01 43 54 47 12. Excellent inexpensive restaurant (*lunch menus 59F and 89F*). Ⓜ Cluny-Sorbonne.

Mouffetard/Jussieu

Expensive

Le Petit Marguery, 9 Bd de Port-Royal, 13e, t 01 43 31 58 59. Innovative brasserie run by the Cousin brothers, using seasonal ingredients; black truffles in the spring, game dishes and wild mushrooms in the autumn, and a heavenly *crème cassonade* (*lunch menu 165F; dinner from 210F*). *Closed Aug, Sun and Mon.* Ⓜ Gobelins.

Cheap

Crêperie Belliloise, 11 Rue des Boulangers, 5e, t 01 43 25 57 24. Popular with students from the nearby Paris VI-VII complex; an unpretentious place with a wide selection of *crêpes* and *galettes* from Brittany. Excellent value (*daily specials from 49F*). Ⓜ Jussieu.

St-Germain

Luxury–Expensive

Jacques Cagna, 14 Rue des Grands-Augustins, 6e, t 01 43 26 49 39. One of Paris' most gracious institutions for an unforgettable culinary experience (*lunch menu 270F; dinner 550F*). Ⓜ Odéon.

Lapérouse, 51 Quai des Grands-Augustins, 6e, t 01 43 26 68 04. Luscious Second Empire décor and alcoves for romantic rendezvous; some highly innovative dishes from the new Basque chef. *Closed Sat lunch, Sun.* Ⓜ St-Michel.

Le Récamier, 4 Rue Récamier, 7e, t 01 45 48 86 58. In a quiet cul-de-sac, an Empire dining room where writers and publishers dawdle over a perfect Chateaubriand or *boeuf bourguignon*, or linger over a lobster salad on the delightful terrace in summer (*dinner 300–450F, wine included*). *Closed Sun.* Ⓜ Sèvres Babylone.

Moderate–Cheap

Aux Charpentiers, 10 Rue Mabillon, 6e, t 01 46 33 07 98. Located in the former carpenters' guild hall (with a little museum about it), serving excellent *pot-au-feu*, *boudin* and other everyday French basics; economical *plats du jour*. Ⓜ Mabillon.

Le Petit Vatel, 5 Rue Lobineau, 6e, t 01 43 54 28 49. When they say *petit* they mean minuscule but good *grand-mère*-style meat and vegetable dishes that rarely hit 90F. Ⓜ Mabillon.

Chez Germaine, 30 Rue Pierre-Leroux, 7e, t 01 42 73 28 34. Delicious: not to be missed by gourmets on a budget (*lunch 65F*). *Closed Sun.* Ⓜ Vaneau.

Exhibition Paris

Luxury–Expensive

Alain Ducasse, 59 Av Raymond-Poincaré, 16e, t 01 47 27 12 27. The only *chef de cuisine* in France to have three Michelin stars in two places at once, here and at the Louis XV in the Hôtel de Paris in Monaco. Book months in advance and take out a loan for the experience of a lifetime (*dinner menus 880F and 1,100F*). *Closed Sat, Sun, half of July, and Aug.* Ⓜ Victor Hugo.

Jules Verne, Eiffel Tower (private lift to 2nd floor),15e, t 01 45 55 61 44. Highly rated *haute cuisine* high above Paris (*more than 700F per head*). Ⓜ Bir-Hakeim.

Morot-Gaudry, 6 Rue de la Cavalerie, 15e, t 01 45 67 06 85. An epicurean delight with a hanging terrace far from the tourist crowds; perfect food with a Mediterranean touch (*excellent weekday lunch menu 500F*). *Closed Aug, Sat and Sun.* Ⓜ La Motte Picquet.

Don Juan, Pont de Grenelle, 15e, t 01 44 54 14 70. A wood-panelled 1930s yacht, now refitted as a floating restaurant with a two-Michelin-star chef working his magic (*dinner cruises down the Seine 950F per head*). *Closed lunch.* Ⓜ Av Président Kennedy, Maison de Radio France.

La Bourdonnais, 113 Av de la Bourdonnais, 7e, t 01 47 05 47 96. Beautifully prepared dishes from the Midi: *croustillant de homard risotto safrané, turbot à la crème de citron confit* and delicious raspberry desserts (*great-value lunch menu 240F, wine included, dinner from 320F*). Ⓜ Ecole Militaire.

Tan Dinh, 60 Rue de Verneuil, 7e, t 01 45 44 04 84. Excellent Vietnamese cooking – steamed crab pâté, lobster triangles with ginkgo nuts. *Closed Sun.* Ⓜ Solférino.

Moderate

Au Pied de Fouet, 45 Rue de Babylone, 7e, t 01 47 05 12 27. Le Corbusier's favourite restaurant, shared table and long queues for its tasty and very affordable meals (*under 100F*). *Closed Sat night, Sun and Aug.* Ⓜ St François-Xavier.

Le Scheffer, 22 Rue Scheffer, 16e, t 01 47 27 81 11. Neighbourhood restaurant serving good *entrecôte bordelaise* and dark *mousse au chocolat. Closed Sun.* Ⓜ Trocadéro.

Montparnasse

Expensive

La Coupole, 102 Bd du Montparnasse, 14e, t 01 43 20 14 20. The police had to control the crowds when it opened its doors in the 1920s, and it's still a sight to behold in full flight. Wide variety of dishes on the menu, and old-fashioned dancing on Sat and Sun afternoons (*lunch menu 155F; also after 10pm*). *Open until 2am.* Ⓜ Vavin.

Dominique, 19 Rue Bréa, 6e, t 01 43 27 08 80. Restaurant, bar and deli; a favourite of Paris' Russians since the '20s, with *chachlick caucasien* and *vatrouchka* – Russian cheesecake (*200F dinner menu*). *Closed Sun and Mon.* Ⓜ Vavin.

Le Restaurant Bleu, 46 Rue Didot, 14e, t 01 45 43 70 56. A piece of old working-class Paris now taken on by a smart young chef. Fresh produce and dishes from the Aveyron (*lunch menu 120F, dinner 160F*). *Closed Sat lunch, Sun, Mon lunch.* Ⓜ Plaisance.

Moderate–Cheap

L'Amuse Bouche, 186 Rue du Château, 14e, t 01 43 35 31 61. A minute restaurant run by the former chef of Jacques Cagna, serving lovely ravioli filled with langoustines in a white leek sauce and much more to warm the cockles of your heart (*lunch menu only 120F, dinner 160F*). *Closed Sun but open Sat lunch.* Ⓜ Mouton-Duvernet.

Le Vin des Rues, 21 Rue Boulard, 14e, t 01 43 22 19 78. Idiosyncratic traditional *bistrot* with delicious food *à la Lyonnaise. Open dinner Wed, Fri and Sat, lunch Tues–Sat. Reservation recommended.* Ⓜ Mouton-Duvernet.

Aux Artistes, 63 Rue Falguière, 15e, t 01 43 22 05 29. Named after Montparnasse's bohemians, and prices are still on the bohemian level; popular neighbourhood atmosphere (*good 80F menu, inc wine*). *Closed Sat and Sun lunch.* Ⓜ Pasteur.

Bois de Boulogne

Luxury

La Grande Cascade, Allée de Longchamps, Bois de Boulogne, t 01 45 27 33 51. Napoleon III's pavilion in the park, gloriously redecorated; excruciatingly snotty cuisine and service, with one of the biggest wine cellars in town. Overpriced (*menus 285–600F*). *Closed mid-Dec to mid-Jan.*

Le Pré Catelan, Rte de Suresnes, Bois de Boulogne, t 01 44 14 41 14. Lovely Belle Epoque restaurant far from the hubbub. Food fit for an emperor – pressed pigeon, succulent langoustines, heavenly chocolate desserts (*menu 295F, carte 550–750F*). *Closed Sun night, Mon and Feb.* Ⓜ Porte Dauphine.

Wine Bars

Sometimes called *bistrots à vin* or like the English, *bars à vin*, this once-common city institution is enjoying a revival as Parisians have begun to expand their wine-consciousness. There are even some chains, like L'Ecluse, that aim to recreate the old *bistrot à vin* environment.

It isn't always clear where to draw the line between a wine bar and a restaurant; any old traditional *bistrot à vin* will serve something to go along with the wine: plates of sausages or paté, onion soup, cheese, sandwiches or even three-course meals.

Right Bank

A La Cloche des Halles, 28 Rue Coquillière, 1er. Wine bar of renown; excellent choices to go with solid country snacks of cheese and *charcuterie*. *Closed Sat night and Sun.* Ⓜ Châtelet.

L'Entracte, 47 Rue Montpensier, 1er. A favourite of Diderot when it was called La Pissotte, now specializing in wines from the Loire and plates of tasty *charcuterie*; reasonable prices. *Open daily until 2am or so.* Ⓜ Palais Royal.

Willi's Wine Bar, 13 Rue des Petits-Champs, 1er. A well-regarded British wine bar in Paris, and one of the few to serve wines from around the world (*good lunch menu 140F*). *Open until 11pm; closed Sun.* Ⓜ Pyramides.

La Gavroche, 19 Rue St-Marc, 2e. Near the Bourse and with a sign on the wall exclaiming that wine banishes sadness, excellent food (*côte de boeuf*, etc.) accompanies good Beaujolais. Ⓜ Richelieu-Drouot.

La Tartine, 24 Rue de Rivoli, 4e. Unchanged more or less for over 90 years, though newly fashionable. *Closed Tues.* Ⓜ St-Paul.

Café Mélac, 42 Rue Léon Front, 11e. Jovial proprietor ages his Château Mélac plonk (from his drainpipe vine) in the fridge, and has even organized a cooperative of urban wine-growers, the Vignerons de Paris; also has a range of very drinkable wines not made in Paris, and Auvergnat snacks. *Closed Sat and Sun, and Mon night.* Ⓜ Charonne.

A la Courtille, 1 Rue Envierges, 20e. Near Parc Belleville, with a top selection of *crus* for wine-lovers and superb views over Paris from the summer terrace (*good lunch menu 100F*). Ⓜ Pyrénées.

Le Baratin, 3 Rue Jouye-Rouve, 20e. Popular new *bistrot à vin*, with delicious, hearty snacks. *Open until midnight.* Ⓜ Pyrénées.

Islands and Left Bank

Henri IV, 13 Pl du Pont Neuf, 1er. Long established and good snacks with a southwest flavour; Beaujolais and Loire wines. *Closed Sat night and Sun.* Ⓜ Pont Neuf.

Millésimes, 7 Rue Lobineau, 6e. Little *bistrot à vin* with an international list of wines to choose from, and cold snacks to keep them company; reasonable prices. *Open until 1am.* Ⓜ Odéon.

Le Sancerre, 22 Av Rapp, 7e. Red, white, rosé: pick your Sancerre and chow down at the oyster bar. Cosy, classy atmosphere with warmth. Ⓜ Ecole Militaire.

Le Rallye Peret, 6 Rue Daguerre, 14e. Owned by the same family for over 80 years, with the biggest variety of bottles to choose from on the Left Bank (especially Beaujolais). *Closed Sun afternoon and Mon.* Ⓜ Denfert Rochereau.

Bars, Beer Cellars, Pubs, Tapas

Cafés are Parisian, bars are not, except for the old working-class watering holes that have completely disappeared from the city landscape. Therefore almost all the bars you will find in this city have one sort of angle or another: immigrant bars, gay bars, beer bars, music bars or whatever (for those offering entertainment, *see* pp.136–7).

Beer is definitely trendy in this city, and more places devoted to it are opening up all the time. In recent years the institution of the happy hour has hit Paris in a big way – keep an eye out for signs in the windows; discounts on drinks can be spectacular. The biggest current fad is the 'Irish Pub', with Guinness, Irish music, and often a genuine Irishman in attendance. One gets the impression that what Parisians really want are English pubs, except for the fact that they are English.

Right Bank

Conway's, 73 Rue St-Denis, 1er. One of the best American bars in Paris, run by the daughter of a New York boxer. *Happy hour 6pm–9pm; open until 3am.* Ⓜ Les Halles.

Gambrinus, 62 Rue des Lombards, 1er. The 'God of Beer', offering 30 draught beers in a medieval crypt built by the Templars; T-bone steaks, country and rhythm and blues nightly. Ⓜ Châtelet-Les Halles.

Le Sous Bock, 49 Rue St-Honoré, 1er. Complicated cocktails and the best imported beers; snacks of mussels and *frites* at all hours. Includes a booze boutique that is a tippler's dream– 180 varieties of whisky. Ⓜ Châtelet.

Arco, 12 Rue Daunou, 2e. Some of Paris' tastiest and most authentic *tapas*, washed down with Spanish wines; expensive. *Open until 1 or 2am; closed Sun.* Ⓜ Opéra.

Le Baragouin, 17 Rue Tiquetonne, 2e. Lively, affordable Breton bar. *Open until 2am; closed afternoons.* Ⓜ Les Halles.

La Champmeslé, 4 Rue Chabanais, 2e. Intimate, feminine and romantic. *Open 6pm–10pm; closed Sun.* Ⓜ Pyramides, Bourse.

Harry's Bar, 5 Rue Daunou, 2e. Since 1911 the most famous American bar in Paris, home of the Bloody Mary and Side Car, where a big international business clientele gathers to discuss making more do-re-mi over one of 180 different brands of whisky or *Pétrifiant* – a slightly less lethal version of the Mickey Finn. *Open daily until 4am.* Ⓜ Opéra.

Kitty O'Shea's, 10 Rue des Capucines, 2e. Popular Irish bar – a scrum when Ireland plays France in the Five Nations; Guinness, good Irish coffees and beers. *Open until 2am.* Ⓜ Opéra.

La Micro-Brasserie, 106 Rue de Richelieu, 2e. Serving 50 kinds of beer – including the house's own Morgane, brewed here since 1987. *Open until 2am.* Ⓜ Richelieu-Drouot.

Le Fouquet's, 99 Av des Champs-Elysées, 8e. A Paris institution for the rich and famous. Ⓜ George V.

Café Moustache, 138 Rue du Faubourg-St-Martin, 10e. Relaxed gay bar, popular with the international set. *Open until 1.30am.* Ⓜ Gare de l'Est.

China Club, 50 Rue de Charenton, 12e. In an old ice house, one of the trendiest bars in a trendy area; elegant atmosphere, Chinese snacks. *Open until 2am.* Ⓜ Bastille.

Left Bank

Académie de la Bière, 88 bis Bd de Port-Royale, 5e. German beer specialists, with over 50 different varieties, mussels and *frites*. *Open until 3am.* RER: Port-Royal.

Le Crocodile, 5 Rue Royer-Collard, 5e. Cosy, intimate night haunt for serious cocktail aficionados, with over 120 varieties – also Irish coffees. *Open until 2am; closed Sun.* RER: Luxembourg.

La Gueuze, 19 Rue Soufflot, 5e. Extremely popular café with Paris' most impressive *carte des bières* – over 400 kinds of brew from around the world. RER: Luxembourg.

Polly Magoo, 11 Rue St-Jacques, 5e. Sleazy down-at-heel fun in the modern equivalent to the old haunts of Villon, practically unchanged since it opened in 1970. *Open until 4 or 5am.* Ⓜ St-Michel.

Birdland Club, 8 Rue Guisarde, 6e. Castel's, the most exclusive nightclub in Paris, has moved St-Germain's sophisto-trendy nightlife scene to Rues Princesse and Guisarde; stylish cocktails and good jazz records. *Open till dawn.* Ⓜ Mabillon.

La Closerie des Lilas, 171 Bd de Montparnasse, 6e. Unchanged since Verlaine and Hemingway boozed here; great cocktails but at a price. *Open until 2am.* RER: Port-Royal.

Le Mazet, 61 Rue St-Andre-des Arts, 6e. A serious beer cellar (15 kinds on tap) where you can also get a bowl of onion soup in the wee small hours. Ⓜ Odéon.

Pub St-Germain (or Parrot's tavern), 17 Rue de l'Ancienne-Comédie, 6e. A popular non-stop Left Bank haven for beer connoisseurs, with over 100 varieties in bottles and some 20 on tap. *Open 24hrs; ring the bell if it looks closed.* Ⓜ Odéon.

Café Thomieux, 4 Rue de la Comète, 7e. Plush tapas bar associated with high-quality restaurant around the corner. *Open 12pm–2am.* Ⓜ Invalides.

Cafés, *Salons de Thé, Glaciers*

Nearly every crossroads in Paris has its café, an institution dating back to the 17th century, where people could shed their social and class distinctions and speak their minds about politics and start revolutions. Since Haussmann's creation of the Grands Boulevards, cafés became what many remain to this day: passive grandstands, a place to meet friends and be at once private and yet public. A *salon de thé*, on the other hand, tends to be more inward-looking, concentrating on light (and often overpriced) luncheons, but good for a quality coffee or tea and pastries.

Right Bank and Islands

Angelina, 226 Rue de Rivoli, 1er. A Viennese confection, vintage 1903 (when it was called Rumpelmayer), with a special rich African chocolate and the world's best *montblanc* (chestnut cream, meringue and chantilly). Ⓜ Tuileries.

Café Marly, in the Louvre, facing the Pyramid, 1er. New, beautifully designed chic hangout in the old ministries vacated for the Grand Louvre project (*also lunch and dinner for 200F and up*). Especially pretty at night. Ⓜ Palais Royal-Musée du Louvre.

A Priori Thé, 36 Galerie Vivienne, 2e. Take a trip back in time over a cup of English tea and cheesecake under the glass-roofed passage. Ⓜ Bourse.

Ma Bourgogne, 19 Pl des Vosges, 4e. Vortex of café life in the Place des Vosges (*passable lunch menu 185F*). Ⓜ St-Paul.

Mariage Frères, 30 Rue du Bourg-Tibourg, 4e. Paris' best-known purveyors of tea; hundreds of blends to sample with a pastry. Ⓜ St-Paul.

Ladurée, 16 Rue Royale, 8e. Exquisite and precious *salon de thé*, famous for its macaroons. Bring your laciest great-aunt along for tea. Ⓜ Madeleine. Also at 75 Av des Champs-Elysées. Ⓜ Franklin-Roosevelt.

Mollard, 113 Rue St-Lazare, 8e. Beautiful Art Nouveau café-brasserie. Ⓜ St-Lazare.

Baggi, 33 Rue Chaptal, 9e. The best homemade ice cream on the Right Bank, founded in 1850 and still going strong, using 100 per cent natural ingredients. Ⓜ Pigalle.

Café de la Paix, 12 Bd des Capucines, 9e. An historic landmark; if you can't afford a ticket to the Opéra, you might just be able to manage the price of a coffee here; architect Garnier's second-best effort in the outlandish style he invented – Napoleon III. Ⓜ Opéra.

Au Rêve, 89 Rue Caulaincourt, 18e. Old-fashioned Montmartre café, inexpensive and friendly. Lunch served. *Open until 2am; closed Sun.* Ⓜ Lamarck Caulaincourt.

Left Bank and Islands

Berthillon, 31 Rue St-Louis-en-l'Ile, Ile St-Louis, 4e. Paris' best ice creams and sorbets with a list of flavours a mile long; you can also enjoy them sitting down in most of the island's cafés. Ⓜ Pont Marie.

Le Flore en l'Ile, 42 Quai d'Orléans, Ile St-Louis, 4e. Great view over Notre-Dame, great tea, great Berthillon ice cream (straight and in exotic cocktails). Ⓜ Pont Marie.

La Fourmi Ailée, 8 Rue du Fouarre, 5e. A cosy atmosphere in a former glassworks, fire in the fireplace, good salads, scones and excellent desserts. Ⓜ St-Michel or Maubert-Mutualité.

Les Deux Magots, 6 Pl St-Germain-des-Prés, 6e. A hoot for all its pretensions, and usually full of tourists, but the chocolate and ice cream are compensations. Note, however, if it's crowded, you may be pressured into making a second order or leaving – *zut alors*! Ⓜ St-Germain-des-Prés.

Le Flore, 172 Bd St-Germain, 6e. Fabled literary café, everything just so Parisian, but full of tired vampires trying to suck out your soul with their cool, discerning eyes. So popular with tourists that they've opened their own boutique. Ⓜ St-Germain-des-Prés.

Le Pol'Noir, 39 Rue Monsieur-le-Prince, 6e. Next to Polidor, a superb *glacier* serving fresh, homemade ice cream. *Open until 3am, 4am on Sat.* Ⓜ Odéon.

Calabrese Glacier, 15 Rue d'Odessa, 14e. The Leonardo da Vinci of ice cream inventions, home of the famous vanilla and cinnamon *soupe anglaise*. Ⓜ Montparnasse.

Entertainment and Nightlife

When the last museums and shops close, the City of Light turns on the switch for a night of fun. There are several main circuits: from the Latin Quarter and across the Seine to Les Halles, Bastille to République, the Butte de Montmartre and Pigalle, St-Germain, Rue Mouffetard, Montparnasse and the Plaisance-Pernety area in the 14e. In a city as full of fashion slaves as Paris, the most *branché* ('plugged-in', literally) clubs change fairly rapidly.

Besides the plethora of posters that cover the métro stations, cafés and Morriss columns, weekly entertainment guides come out on Wednesdays: *Pariscope* (3F; including exhibitions and museum hours, etc. and in summer an English-language section written by *Time Out*, a nightlife hotline t 08 36 68 88 55, and a website *www.Pariscope.fr*), the similar *L'Officiel des Spectacles* (only 2F), and *7 à Paris* (listings, articles and reviews). The Wednesday *Figaro* has weekly listings; *Libération* has good pieces on art and music; the Wednesday *Le Monde* has ADEN, a listing of cinemas and exhibitions; the monthly *Paris Free Voice* has reviews in English.

Ticket Agents

FNAC has ticket offices all over the city and a general number, t 01 49 87 50 50; Virgin Megastore, 52 Av des Champs-Elysées, t 01 42 56 52 60, Ⓜ Georges V, is similar and open until midnight.

Concerts, shows, plays, sporting events, etc. may also be booked through the tourist office's Billetel ticket counter, 127 Av des Champs-Elysées, Ⓜ Charles de Gaulle-Etoile, t 01 49 52 53 53 (*open daily 9am–8pm*).

Kiosque Théâtre, near 15 Place de la Madeleine, 8e, Ⓜ Madeleine; also on the Parvis de la Gare Montparnasse. Same-day, half-price theatre tickets, plus a 16F commission; expect a queue (*open Tues–Sat 12.30–8 and Sun 12.30–4; July and Aug closed Sun*).

Film

The Parisians may well be the biggest film junkies in the world, and chances are that in one of their 320 screens, one will show that obscure flick you've been dying to see for years.

Films in French are labelled v.f. (*version française*); in English, *version anglaise*; if in the original language, with French subtitles, v.o. (*version originale*).

Average admission prices are between 25 and 50F; students and senior citizens are often eligible for discounts at weekday matinées. In some larger cinemas, the usherette should be tipped between 5 and 10F.

Vidéothèque de Paris, Porte St-Eustache, Forum des Halles, t 01 40 26 34 30. Shows films and documentaries (*30F adm for the day*). Open 2.30–9pm; closed Mon. Ⓜ Châtelet-Les Halles.

The Salle Garance, Centre Pompidou, t 01 42 78 37 29. Shows international films with French subtitles (*adm 27F and 20F*). Closed Tues.

Dôme IMAX, 1 Pl du Dôme, La Défense, t 08 36 67 06 06. 'Largest Wraparound Movie Theatre in the World'. Ⓜ/RER: Grande Arche de La Défense.

Le Grand Rex, 1 Bd Poissonnière, 2e, t 08 36 68 70 23. Films are all dubbed into French, but the Rex is a must for lovers of old Hollywood Busby Berkeley 1930s extravaganzas with one of the biggest screens in Europe, 2750 seats and a great ceiling. Ⓜ Bonne Nouvelle.

Gaumont Kinopanorama, 60 Av de La Motte-Picquet, 15e. Very popular, 180° cinema, 70mm film, equipped for high definition Showscan (60 images per second) and extraordinary sound (*53F*). Ⓜ La Motte Picquet.

Studio 28, 10 Rue Tholozé, 18e, t 01 46 06 36 07. Founded in 1928, charming, family-run and still going strong. Decorations by Cocteau. Films always in v.o. Ⓜ Abbesses.

La Géode, 26 Av Corentin-Cariou, 19e, t 01 40 05 12 12. Extraordinary OMNIMAX cinema of the Cité des Sciences (see p.187) puts on shows with fish-eye-lens cameras that make you feel as if you were in the centre of the action (*hourly showings daily exc Mon 10–7; 57F; book in advance for the 7pm, 8pm and 9pm showings, same day only, t 01 42 05 50 50*). Ⓜ Porte de la Villette.

Music

Opera, Classical and Contemporary

Paris has traditionally been ambivalent towards classical music. It is the only great European capital without a proper symphony auditorium – or a great orchestra to play in it. However, there is more interest in music than before: lunchtime concerts in the churches (listed in Pariscope), medieval music at Sainte-Chapelle, and chamber music at the Orangerie at La Bagatelle, plus festivals year-round.

Théâtre du Châtelet, Pl du Châtelet, 1er, t 01 40 28 28 40. 130-year-old theatre with better opera than the Bastille, and a vast range of other innovative offerings. Ⓜ Châtelet.

Opéra Comique, 5 Rue Favart, 2e, t 01 42 44 45 46. Opéra Comique repertoire from Lully to Carmen, and the occasional operetta. Ⓜ Richelieu Drouot.

Théâtre de la Ville, 2 Pl du Châtelet, 4e, t 01 42 74 22 77. Every kind of music, from piano recitals to jazz to African songs. Ⓜ Châtelet.

Opéra de Paris Bastille, Pl de la Bastille, 12e, t 01 44 73 13 00. Mixed reviews, but the acoustics are great (see pp.147–8); 60–600F. Ⓜ Bastille.

Théâtre des Champs-Elysées, 15 Av Montaigne, 16e, t 01 49 52 50 50. Where Josephine Baker first danced in Paris; a favourite of big-name classical performers; also some opera. Ⓜ Alma Marceau.

Cité de la Musique, 221 Av Jean Jaurès, 19e, t 01 44 84 44 84. Two high-tech venues, one home to Pierre Boulez's Ensemble Inter-Contemporain. Ⓜ Porte de Pantin.

Jazz, Blues, Rock and World

Still considered the jazz capital of Europe, Paris is also in the forefront of world music – African, North African, Latin, Brazilian and Caribbean. Major hot spots are around Odéon, the Marais, Rue du Trésor, the Butte aux Cailles (behind Place d'Italie), Rue Oberkampf and Rue St-Maur (behind Bastille and République), and of course Place Pigalle. Clubs tend to charge admission or an exorbitant price for a first drink (around 100F).

Au Duc des Lombards, 42 Rue des Lombards, 1er, t 01 42 33 22 88. One of the best; popular, friendly, dimly lit lounge, with jazz piano, trios and crooners ranging from excellent to competent. Open 10pm–3am. Ⓜ Châtelet.

Slow Club, 130 Rue de Rivoli, 1er, t 01 42 33 84 30. The late Miles Davis' favourite jazz club in Paris, and a must for lovers of swing, New Orleans and traditional jazz. Ⓜ Châtelet-Les Halles.

Le Bilboquet, 13 Rue St-Benoît, 6e, t 01 45 48 81 84. St-Germain club, vintage 1947; popular with tourists remembering the golden days. Pricey, for average French jazz. Doors open 8pm. Ⓜ St-Germain-des-Prés.

Buddha Bar, 8 Rue Boissy d'Anglas, 8e. Chic bar with a huge dance floor and a 20ft Buddha. Drinks are pretty expensive. Ⓜ Concorde.

Cithea, 114 Rue Oberkampf, 11e, t 01 40 21 70 95. Live soul, blues, jazz, funk, etc. A favourite of local musicians: overcrowded but fun (usually free). Open Thurs–Sat nights. Ⓜ Ménilmontant.

Le Petit Journal Montparnasse, 13 Rue du Commandant-René-Mouchotte, 14e, t 01 43 21 56 70. One of the best, with enough space for big bands from France and abroad. Ⓜ Gaîté.

La Flèche d'Or, 102 Rue de Bagnolet, 20e, t 01 43 72 04 23. Roots, rock, reggae and funk in a charming setting in a former train station. Also live performers and jam sessions. During the day, you can read the papers, play chess or cards; there are sometimes exhibitions of local artists. Ⓜ Alexandre-Dumas/Gambetta.

Nightclubs and Discothèques

Unfortunately, most discos in Paris take themselves seriously, your appearance tends to be all-important and the bouncers at the door picky if you're not their type. In summer many Parisians like to waltz to the schmaltzy accordion tunes of their grandparents (bal musette) especially at the festivals.

Entrance fees and first drinks are usually 100F, 120F weekends.

Les Bains, 17 Rue du Bourg-L'Abbé, 3e, t 01 48 87 01 80. The ultimate place for beautiful people (entrance 80–100F). Open 11pm–6am; restaurant open until 1am. Ⓜ Etienne Marcel.

La Java, 105 Rue du Faubourg-du-Temple, 10e, t 01 42 02 20 52. A grand old music hall opened in the 1920s, where Piaf got her first break; Thurs and Fri live salsa, Sat bal musette, Sun night is Brazilian night. Ⓜ République.

Le Neil's, 27 Av des Ternes, 17e, **t** 01 47 66 45 00. Sophisto-sister disco of the one in New York, with bookcases, plush sofas, and the occasional celebrity; good restaurant (*250–350F*) and disco after 12.30am. **M** Ternes.

Elysée Montmartre, 72 Bd de Rochechouart, 18e, **t** 01 42 52 25 15. Alternative and world music bands in a hall designed by Eiffel, where La Goulue first cancanned, with one of the best dance floors in Paris. Golden oldies, twist, disco, reggae every other Sat. **M** Anvers.

Chansonniers and Cabarets

The *chansonnier* is Paris' own art form, first popularized by Aristide Bruant, revived in the 1950s and '60s by Jacques Brel, Georges Brassens and Juliette Greco, and now for both Parisians and tourists. Paris rivals Las Vegas for over the top kitsch-and-glitter-oozing, tit-and-feather spectaculars, invariably advertised as 'sophisticated'.

Le Paradis Latin, 28 Rue du Cardinal-Lemoine, 5e, **t** 01 43 25 28 28. In an old theatre built by Eiffel, this is the one music hall-cabaret with Parisian customers (*at least 700F for dinner and show*). **M** Cardinal-Lemoine.

Lido, 116 Av des Champs-Elysées, 8e, **t** 01 40 76 56 10. The best special effects perk up the act of the 60 Bluebell Girls (*dinner and show 805F; show only 540F with champagne, or 365F at the bar at 10 and midnight*). **M** George V.

Moulin-Rouge, 82 Bd de Clichy, 11e, **t** 01 53 09 82 82. The most famous and the most Las-Vegasey of the lot, with its guest stars and cancanning Doriss Girls (*dinner and show 750F; 10pm show and champagne only 510F, midnight 450F*). **M** Blanche.

Au Lapin Agile, 22 Rue des Saules, 18e, **t** 01 46 06 85 87. A valiant attempt at bringing old French traditional song back to life to busloads of Japanese tourists (*show and first drink 110F; 90F for students*). *Open 9pm–2am; closed Mon.* **M** Lamarck Caulaincourt.

Michou, 80 Rue des Martyrs, 18e, **t** 01 46 06 16 04, **f** 01 42 57 20 37. Funny satirical drag show that draws even the celebrities to see themselves being parodied (*dinner and show 550F*). *Show starts 8.30pm. Reserve.* **M** Pigalles.

Dance

Many of the already listed theatres and concert halls also schedule dance performances, often by visiting companies.

Opéra de Paris-Garnier, Place de l'Opéra, 9e, **t** 01 44 73 13 00. Home of the Ballet de l'Opéra de Paris. The exterior has just been renovated and looks fantastic. Guided tour during the week; call for info. **M** Opéra.

Studio Regard du Cygne, 210 Rue de Belleville, 20e, **t** 01 43 58 55 93. Devoted to innovative international companies. **M** Place des Fêtes.

Café de la Danse, 5 Passage Louis-Philippe, 11e, **t** 01 47 00 01 79. The place to see small innovative contemporary companies. **M** Bastille.

Theatre and Performance Arts

There's plenty of Racine and Molière from the excellent Comédie-Française and frequent revivals of Ionesco, Anouilh, Genet and co.

Les Bouffes du Nord, 37 bis Bd de la Chapelle, 10e, **t** 01 46 07 34 50. Peter Brook's acclaimed experimental productions. **M** La Chapelle.

Théâtre National de Chaillot, Pl du Trocadéro, 16e, **t** 01 47 27 81 15. Lavish productions of Brecht et al. **M** Trocadéro.

Comédie Française, 2 Rue de Richelieu, 1er, **t** 01 40 15 00 15. Founded in 1680, in the beautiful Salle Richelieu in the Palais Royal; excellent productions of classics by Molière, Beaumarchais, Marivaux and Racine, also foreign classics in translation; seats sold two weeks in advance. **M** Palais-Royal.

Comédie Italienne, 17 Rue de la Gaîté, 14e, **t** 01 43 21 22 22. Goldoni, Commedia dell'Arte and Pirandello in French in a poky theatre amongst 'live sex' shops. **M** Edgar Quinet.

Palais-Royal, 38 Rue de Montpensier, 1er, **t** 01 42 97 59 81. Boulevard comedy (*dinner-spectacle 350F*). **M** Palais Royal/Bourse.

Théâtre de la Huchette, 23 Rue de la Huchette, 5e, **t** 01 43 26 38 99. Ionesco's *La Cantatrice Chauve* and *La Leçon* for over 40 years (*under-26s half-price*). **M** St-Michel.

Théâtre de Nesle, 8 Rue de Nesle, 6e, **t** 01 46 34 61 04. English language performances. **M** Odéon.

Théâtre de la Porte St-Martin, 16 Bd St-Martin, 10e, **t** 01 42 08 00 32. Often sparkling, very Parisian productions and one-man shows. **M** Strasbourg St-Denis.

Prince, aux dames Parisiennes
De beau parler donne le pris;
Quoy qu'on die d'Italiennes,
Il n'est bon bec que de Paris.
                         François Villon

Paris has been a wonder for nearly a thousand years, from the time when masons came to learn the magic numbers of Gothic architecture to the present day when we come to ponder the fearful symmetry of its latest geometric tricks – a pyramid of glass, a hollow cube, a sphere of a thousand mirrors. Squeezed into one place are the brains, mouth, piggy bank and bossy-stick of a wealthy and talented nation that fondly regards itself as the most rational and sensible land on Earth; the Ville Lumière is France's collective dream, the vortex of all its vanity, its parasite and its showcase. The results are there for all to enjoy, for Emerson's statement that 'England built London for its own use, but France built Paris for the world' is true in both senses: as a monumental show-off, but a generous and cosmopolitan one.

Like a cactus flower, Paris blooms only now and then, but when it does it captures the heart and mind as no other city can. In the last twenty years the government has lavished billions on it to coax it into bud, and in many ways Paris has rarely been more delightful: *nouvelle cuisine* is out of fashion, the new museums are spectacular, the plonk in the cafés is better, the street markets are more seductive than ever; even rear-platform buses are back. Best of all, the Parisians themselves have shed their grumpy postwar xenophobia and chauvinism to embrace the rest of the world.

Precocious and exasperating, a shining light and dire warning, Paris 'changes faster', as Baudelaire sighed 150 years ago, 'than a mortal heart'. Never destroyed by enemies or act of God, it has been perpetually devouring and re-creating itself, a restless metamorphosis. After inventing so much of modern society and modern art in the 19th century, Paris is preening itself to become the 'culture pole of the 21st' (vanity has always been its worst sin). Yet at the same time its ruling technocrats are doing their best to turn the city, once so beloved for its earthy spirited life, into an arty shopping mall, a safety-tested playground for trendies and tourists. It's a battle for Paris' soul, but things are always changing. 'Paris is bored', they'd murmur in the 1800s – right before a revolution in art or in politics, or both.

Ile de la Cité and Ile St-Louis

Paris made its début on the Ile de la Cité and, in their congenital chauvinism, the Parisians regard their river islet to this day not only as the centre of the city, but the centre of all France. Baron von Haussmann's mid-19th-century rebuilding of Paris banished 25,000 people who lived on a hundred colourful tiny streets and, like the City of London and Wall Street, the area is deserted at night. But two of the most luminous Gothic churches ever built are reason alone for visiting, and there are other delights – shady squares and *quais*, panoramic bridges and the perfect symmetry of neighbouring Ile St-Louis, an island-village of the *haute bourgeoisie*, concocted by

17th-century speculators and architecturally little changed since. On a Sunday morning you can hear an echo of the old din in Place Louis-Lépine's bird market.

Ile de la Cité

Notre-Dame

Open 8–6.45; part or all of the cathedral will occasionally be closed for services.

This site has been holy ever since Paris was Lutetia, when a temple to Jupiter stood here. In the 6th century a small church was erected; sacked by the Normans in 857, it was reconstructed but on the same scale, hardly large enough for the growing population. A proper cathedral had to wait for Maurice de Sully, who became bishop of Paris in 1160.

Cities all over France were beginning great cathedrals. Notre-Dame came along on the crest of the wave; its architecture was destined to become the consummate work of the early Gothic, the measuring stick by which all other cathedrals are judged. Because it was in Paris, the cosmopolitan centre of learning, Notre-Dame had a considerable influence in diffusing Gothic architecture throughout Europe; for over two centuries its construction site was a busy, permanent workshop, through which passed the continent's most skilled masons, sculptors, carpenters and glassmakers. Plans changed continually, as new problems came up. Henry VI of England was crowned here in 1430; seven years later Charles VII was present at a solemn Te Deum to celebrate the retaking of Paris from the English. French coronations commonly took place at Reims; the next one here would not come until 1804, the pompous apotheosis of Emperor Napoleon, brilliantly captured in the famous propaganda painting by David.

During the Revolution, the Parisians had first trashed Notre-Dame, wrecking most of its sculptures; then they decided to demolish it. A few subtle voices stood up for its 'cultural and historical value' and the cathedral was saved to become the 'Temple of Reason', where Reason's goddess, a former dancer, held forth. Little upkeep took place for centuries. The building was literally falling to bits when Victor Hugo, with his novel *Notre-Dame de Paris*, contributed immeasurably to a revival of interest in the city's medieval roots. Serious restoration work only began in the 1840s. Viollet-le-Duc, a man who spent his life trying to redeem centuries of his countrymen's ignorance and fecklessness, worked the better part of two decades on the site. His approach to restoration was not scientifically perfect, but still far ahead of its time. Viollet-le-Duc's workshops produced original sculpture, attempting to capture the spirit of what had been destroyed or damaged instead of merely copying it.

To see the **façade** as it was intended, remember that, as with the temples of ancient Greece, originally all the statues and reliefs of a Gothic church were painted in bright colours. The statuary begins at the level of the rose window: *Adam and Eve*, on either side of the rose, and the *Virgin Flanked by Angels*. Below these, running the length of the façade, is a row of 28 *Kings of Judah and Israel*, the ancestors of Jesus.

Below the kings are the three portals, interspersed with four framed sculptural groups: *St Stephen* on the left; the *Church and Synagogue* on the two centre piers, representing the 'true and false revelations'; and on the right pier, *St Denis*. The **left portal** is dedicated to the Virgin Mary, a lovely composition *c*. 1210. The **right portal** is dedicated to St Anne, and is the earliest of the portals (mostly *c*. 1170); and the **central portal**, the largest and most impressive of the three, finished *c*. 1220, is of the *Last Judgement*. Such fine portals deserve **doors** to match. The hardware and hinges for those on the left and right are still in good nick today.

We can only guess what the **interior furnishings** looked like in the days before the Revolution. In the Middle Ages, when cathedrals were the great public living rooms of the cities and always open, there would have been no chairs, of course, just rushes strewn on the floor to soak up the mud from the hordes of people who passed through daily, gabbing, gambling, making business deals, eating their lunch, waiting for the rain to stop or listening to the choir practice – throughout the Middle Ages Notre-Dame was the musical centre of Europe, where much of the new polyphonic method was invented. The decorations of the altar and chapels were more colourful and artistic than anything there now. Besides the gifts of kings and nobles, for centuries the city guilds competed ardently to embellish the cathedral.

Today, we must be content with the architecture and the remnants of the stained glass, but it's more than enough. And it's big enough: 430ft long, with room for some 9,000 people. The plan set the pattern for the other cathedrals of the Ile de France: a wide nave with four side aisles, which curve and meet around the back of the altar. The side chapels were not original, but added in the 13th century to hold all the gifts pouring in from the confraternities and guilds. Today, sadly, there is not a single noteworthy painting or statue in any of them.

Most of the chapels were remodelled to suit the tastes of the 17th and 18th centuries, or wrecked in the Revolution. But this is nothing compared to the vandalism committed in the age of the Big Louies. In the 18th century nearly all of the stained glass was simply removed, to let in more light. To thank the Virgin for his birth, the Sun King ordered the florid, carved-wood choir stalls, and a complete rebuilding of the choir, including a new altar, flanked by statues of His Majesty himself and his father. Thank God at least he spared the original choir enclosure, lined with a series of 23 beautiful **reliefs of the life of Christ** (c. 1350) by Jean Ravy and his nephew Jean le Bouteiller.

We can be even more thankful they didn't take out the three great **rose windows**. The one in the west front, heavily restored by Viollet-le-Duc, expresses the message of this cathedral's art even better than the portals: the Virgin sits in majesty at the centre, surrounded by the virtues and vices, the signs of the zodiac and the works of the months – all the things of this world. In the left transept rose, Mary is again at the centre, in the company of Old Testament prophets, judges and kings. In the right transept rose, a truly remarkable composition, she dominates the New Testament, amid the Apostles (in the square frames) and saints.

Leaving the cathedral, turn right and right again, following the north side of the cathedral along Rue du Cloître-Notre-Dame. Originally all of the island east of Rue d'Arcole was occupied by Notre-Dame's **cloister**. At the beginning of Rue du Cloître signs beckon you to ascend the **Tours de Notre-Dame** for the Quasimodo's-eye view over Paris and a chance to eyeball the gargoyles at close quarters (*open daily 9.30–6.30; adm*). No one has ever come up with a satisfactory explanation for the hordes of fanciful beasts that inhabit medieval churches, though if you can pick these out from ground level, they are disconcerting enough. Rue du Cloître continues to the little **Musée de Notre-Dame** at no.10 (*open Wed, Sat and Sun 2.30–6; adm*), run by a society of friends of Notre-Dame, charming people who like to explain things to visitors and tell stories. The exhibits, mostly old prints, views, photos and plans, are fascinating, offering a wealth of detail on the history of the building and the quarter.

The **Place du Parvis-Notre-Dame** extends in front of the cathedral. In the Middle Ages the miracle plays and mystery plays put on by the confraternities were one of the major public entertainments. Often they were held here, where the magnificent porch of the cathedral could serve as 'Paradise', a word that over the centuries got mangled into Parvis.

Traced in the Parvis is the former route of Rue Neuve de Notre-Dame, laid out by Louis VII in the 12th century. When new, this was the widest street in Paris – all of 21ft across. If you want to see what was underneath it, go down to the **Crypte Archéologique du Parvis-Notre-Dame** (*open daily 10–6; Oct–Mar daily 10–5.30; closed Mon and hols; adm; discount ticket with the towers of Notre-Dame available; free Sun 10–1*). What was begun as an underground car park in 1965 had to become a museum when the excavations revealed the 3rd-century wall of Lutetia, traces of Roman and medieval houses, 17th-century cellars, the Merovingian cathedral that preceded Notre-Dame, and foundations of the 1750 Enfants Trouvés, or foundlings hospital, where unwanted children were left on a revolving tray.

Around Ile de la Cité

The **Conciergerie** (*Quai de l'Horloge; open April–Sept daily 9.30–6.30; Oct–Mar daily 10–5; adm; joint ticket with Ste-Chapelle available*) was known as the 'Antechamber of Death'. To set the mood, the first of three round towers you pass along the Quai de l'Horloge is the Tour Bonbec (1250), or 'babbler', where prisoners presumed guilty were 'put to the question'. A trap door under the prisoners' feet waited to pitch them into an *oubliette* lined with razor-sharp steel spikes; the Seine washed their mangled bodies away.

The Conciergerie wasn't always so grim. In its first, 4th-century incarnation it was the palace of Lutetia's Roman governors. Clovis requisitioned the palace *c.* AD 500, and established the Frankish monarchy within its walls; in 987 Hugues Capet moved in, and it stayed in the family for the next 800 years. As the kings grew wealthy, their palace grew ever more splendid, so that by the time Richard the Lionheart came to call on Philippe-Auguste, it resembled a fairy-tale miniature from the Duc de Berry's *Très Riches Heures*. In 1358 Etienne Marcel's partisans stormed the palace and assassinated the king's ministers as the Dauphin Charles V stood helplessly by. It was a lesson in the vulnerability of the royal person in Paris, and the result was the construction of the better fortified Louvre. Abandoned by the kings, the palace evolved into Paris' seat of justice and its prison.

Architecturally, the highlight of the Conciergerie is Philippe le Bel's **Salle des Gens d'Armes** (1314), or guardroom, one of the largest Gothic halls ever built. A large percentage of the guillotine's fodder passed through the dreary **Galerie des Prisonniers**: Marie Antoinette, Danton, Desmoulins, Charlotte Corday and St-Just. All would have their collars torn and hair cut in Paris' grimmest **Salle de la Toilette** before boarding the tumbrils.

At the **Sainte-Chapelle** (*Cour du Mai, Palais de Justice, 4 Bd du Palais; same opening hours as Conciergerie*), as at Notre-Dame, you will lose any notion you might have had about the Middle Ages being quaint and backward. Every inch declares a perfect mastery of mathematics and statistics, materials and stresses. The Sainte-Chapelle, finished in 1248, has an unusual plan, somewhat like a beaver lodge: the important part, the spectacular **upper chapel**, can only be entered from below. Emerging from the narrow stair into the upper chapel is a startling, unforgettable experience. The other cliché in the books is that the Sainte-Chapelle is a 'jewel box' for St Louis' treasured relics; this too is entirely apt: awash in colour and light from the tall windows, the chapel glitters like the cave of the Forty Thieves. The glass is the oldest in Paris (13th-century), though much was restored a century ago. The atmosphere of the chapel is heightened by the lavish use of gold paint and the deep-blue ceiling painted with golden stars.

Paris' oldest hospital, the **Hôtel-Dieu** was founded in AD 660 by Bishop St-Landry. Despite the very best of intentions, it was for centuries a ripe subject for horror and black humour even beyond the borders of France. Patients could count on food and spiritual comfort, but until the 18th century medical ignorance ensured that few who checked in ever checked out again.

A **flower market** in Place Louis-Lépine offers a haven of dewy green fragrances in the desert of offices. The orchid stalls (in the first barn, off Rue de la Cité) are definitely worth a detour. On Sunday mornings a **bird market** takes over, a tradition dating back to the birds sold in the Middle Ages on the Pont au Change.

The **Pont Neuf** is the longest and oldest bridge in Paris. By the late Middle Ages the ancient umbilical bridges tying the mother island to the banks of the Seine had become eternally jammed with traffic, and on 31 May 1578 the cornerstone for a new bridge was laid by Henri III. It was completed in 1605 and, although often restored, retains its original form. Reliefs and grotesques decorate the Pont Neuf (visible from the river), portraying the pickpockets, charlatans and tooth extractors who harangued, amused and preyed on the passing crowds.

Behind the equestrian statue of Henri IV, steps lead down to the **Square du Vert-Galant**, the leafy prow of the Ile de la Cité. The Vert-Galant, or 'gay old spark', was a fond nickname for Henri IV, whose incessant skirt-chasing endeared him to his subjects. The weeping willow at the tip, trailing into the river, is traditionally the first tree in Paris to burst into leaf. The Square affords good views back to the Pont Neuf and its carvings, and ahead to the Pont des Arts (1803), one of the first, and most elegant, iron bridges in France. You can embark for a tour of the Seine's other bridges on a *vedette du Pont Neuf*, moored at the end of the square. In the Middle Ages the Square was the tip of a muddy islet called Ile de Juif, a favourite place for burning Jews and witches, and used on 12 March 1314 for the execution of Jacques de Molay, the Grand Master of the Templars. Before going up in smoke, de Molay cursed his accusers, Pope Clement V and Philippe le Bel, and predicted (accurately) they would follow him to the grave within a year. After the Templar barbecue, the Ile de Juif was joined to Ile de la Cité and made into a royal garden; in 1607 Henri IV allowed Achille de Harlay, president of the Paris *Parlement*, to convert it into a square, **Place Dauphine**, named after the dauphin, the future Louis XIII, on condition that he make it a set architectural piece like Place des Vosges. The design, a triangle of identical houses of brick and stone, has been sorely tried over the centuries: only nos.14 and 16 preserve something of their original appearance. Now it is quiet, a leafy triangle in the cold stone officialdom that has usurped the Cité.

Ile St-Louis

Nearly all the houses on Ile St-Louis went up between 1627 and 1667, bestowing on the island an architectural homogeneity rare in Paris. Although it charmed the Parisians of the Grand Siècle, it fell out of fashion in the 18th century, and in the 19th enjoyed a Romantic revival among bohemians such as Cézanne, Daumier, Gautier and Baudelaire, who were drawn by its poetic solitude. Since the last war property prices have rocketed to the stars. The fine *hôtels* have nearly all been restored or divided into flats; bijou restaurants sprout at every corner, and during Paris' big tourist invasions its famous village atmosphere decays into the gaudy air of an ice-cream-spattered 17th-century funfair.

The **Rue St-Louis-en-L'Ile** has always been the island's main commercial street, with enough little village shops to keep an islander from ever really having to cross over to the mainland. But there is one striking building as well, at no.51, the **Hôtel de Chenizot** (1730). A bearded faun's head and pot-bellied chimeras enliven its doorway, one of Paris' rare rococo works. The first chapel on the island, dedicated to the Virgin, was deemed too dinky and common by the new islanders, and in 1664 Le Vau designed a new **parish church** (*19 bis; open Tues–Sun 9–12 and 3–7*), which remained unfinished until 1725; its boxy exterior conceals a perfect Baroque society church. At no.2, on the corner of Quai d'Anjou, is the **Hôtel Lambert**. Designed in 1641 by Le Vau for Jean-Baptiste Lambert, secretary to Louis XIII, it was given lavish interiors painted by the top decorators of the day; most of these decorations are still in place. Today the Hôtel Lambert belongs to the Rothschilds, and sometimes on weekdays they leave the gate open so you can sneak a peek at the *cour d'honneur*.

The **Hôtel de Lauzun** (*17 Quai d'Anjou; open mid-April to mid-Sept Sun 10–5.40; adm*), once home to the Duc de Lauzun, a favourite of Louis XIV, is the only private 17th-century mansion in Paris open to the public. In 1842 the *hôtel* was purchased by Jérôme Pichon, a bibliophile, who rented the extra rooms out to Baudelaire and

Théophile Gautier, and to the Club des Haschischins, or 'hashish eaters'. The interior surprises with the exuberance of its original painted ceilings and woodwork; you can't help imagining what the hash-heads must have dreamt, with ceilings such as *Time Discovering Truth* or the *Triumph of Venus*.

The Marais and Bastille

One of the less frantic corners of old Paris, the Marais is the aristocratic quarter *par excellence*. The main attractions are the grand *hôtels particuliers* of the 16th to 18th centuries and the museums they contain. In the area that has perhaps changed the least over the last 300 years, take time to look at details, like the 17th-century street signs carved into many old buildings or the subtle sculptural decoration on the scores of old *hôtels*.

When the Seine changed its present course, the old bed remained as low, marshy ground, especially in its eastern edge, the Marais of today. Left mostly outside the original walls of Paris, the Marais was home to several monasteries while other parts were little more than a dump for garbage and dead animals. The religious orders owned most of the land, and they undertook the slow work of reclamation. Charles V enclosed the Marais within his new wall in the 1370s, and set the tone by moving in himself, taking residence for a period at the Hôtel St-Pol near the Seine (now vanished). Nobles and important clerics followed and the old swamplands began to sprout imposing *hôtels particuliers*.

What really made the Marais' fortune was Henri IV's construction of the Place des Vosges in 1605. During the Revolution most of the great *hôtels* were confiscated and divided up, starting them on a career as homes for clothing makers and warehouses. They were still serving the same purpose in the 1950s and '60s, falling into ever more decay, when Parisians finally rediscovered what had become a lost world. The 'Malraux Law' of 1962 allowed the city to create preservation districts and today almost all the *hôtels* of the Marais have been restored and put to good use. The old working population is long gone and the Marais has settled into a mixture of gay bars, hip boutiques and Hasidic Jews around Rue des Rosiers (with recent additions from new immigrants from North Africa and the Middle East).

The **Place des Vosges'** association with royalty began long before the Place ever appeared. The Hôtel des Tournelles, a turreted mansion built here in the 1330s, had belonged to a chancellor of France, a bishop of Paris and a pair of dukes before Charles VI purchased it in 1407. Catherine de' Medici had the palace demolished when her husband Henri II was killed there in a joust, and she seems to have had the original inspiration to replace it with Paris' first proper square. The idea was probably a memory of the fashionable, arcaded Piazza S. Annunziata back home in Florence. In 1605 Henri IV finally began the building of what would be known as the 'Place Royale', a centrepiece that the sprawling Marais badly needed. The architect credited with building it is Louis Métezeau; the square is Italian in concept, the adaptation became something a 17th-century Frenchman could love – elegant, hierarchical and rigorously

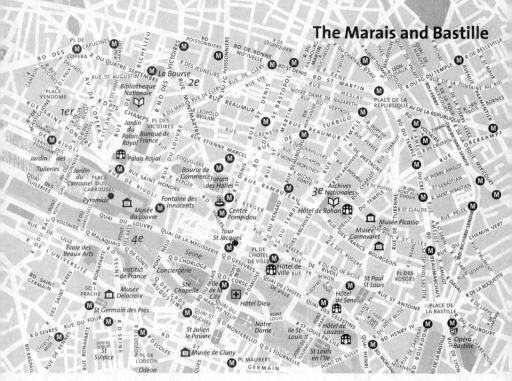

symmetrical. After the Revolution, when all the names of Ancien Régime streets were changed, Napoleon gave it its present name in honour of the first *département* of France to pay its share of the new war taxes. Today the Place is a favourite with tourists, Parisians, schoolchildren and everyone else. It's utterly pleasant under the clipped linden trees, and the statue of Louis XIII looks fondly foolish with his pencil moustache and Roman toga. The architecture, totally French and refreshingly free of any Renaissance imitation, invites contemplation. If you do so, you'll notice a lot of the 'brick' is really painted plaster; even aristocrats can cut corners.

It is only fitting that the **Musée Carnavalet** (*23 Rue de Sévigné; open Tues–Sun 10–5.40; closed Mon and hols; adm*), the city museum of Paris, should be housed in the grandest of all the *hôtels* of the Marais. Begun in 1548, the Hôtel Carnavalet was rebuilt in the Grand-Siècle style by François Mansart in 1660. *Carnavalet*, besides being the name of a former owner, also means a carnival mask; you'll notice one of these carved over the entrance. It is a reminder of how the streets of old Paris, or any other city, were an empire of symbols and pictorial allusions in the days before everyone could read. The first room of the museum is entirely devoted to the charming **shop signs** of this Paris. The rooms that follow, devoted to ancient and medieval Paris, are rather scanty. After these there's an abrupt jump to modern times, such as the faithfully reproduced **bedchamber of Marcel Proust**, where he would accept his morning *madeleine* and muse on fate and memory.

If you're nodding off after too much bourgeois plushness, the **ballroom of the Hôtel Wendel** will startle you back awake. This hotel, formerly on Avenue de New-York, gave

Spanish artist José-María Sert *carte blanche* in 1924 to create a venue that would draw the avant-garde. After that comes an earlier monument of abstruse modernism, the entire **Fouquet jewellery shop** from Rue Royale, *c.* 1901. Fouquet's baubles would have been displayed to advantage in the next tableau, a private room from the **Café de Paris** (formerly 41 Avenue de l'Opéra), showing Art Nouveau at its sweetest. The next section is devoted to paintings. Those of Jean Béraud (1849–1936) stand out, faithful recordings of Parisian life of photographic quality.

The **Hôtel de Rohan** (*Association pour l'Action Sociale, t 01 44 78 09 09; 87 Rue Vieille-du-Temple; open to the public during special exhibitions Mon–Fri 12.30–5.30*) is one of the last and most ambitious of all the Marais mansions. In the courtyard, over the door to the Rohans' stables, is a masterpiece of rococo sculpture, Robert le Lorrain's theatrical **Horses of Apollo** (through the arch to the right of the door). The interior is one of the best preserved in Paris, and it's worth keeping an eye out for when the Hôtel is open.

The huge neoclassical bulk on the Rue des Archives is the **Archives Nationales** (*open Mon and Wed–Fri 10–5.45, Sat and Sun 1.45–5.45; closed Tues; adm*). The oldest part of the complex is a turreted gateway built in the 1370s. The truly grand horseshoe-shaped courtyard facing the Rue des Francs-Bourgeois belongs to the main part of the Archives, the **Hôtel de Soubise**. The part you can visit is called the Musée de l'Histoire de France, which isn't for everyone, but with a little knowledge of French this collection of documents can be utterly fascinating. The best thing in the museum is a painting on the far wall: a funny 16th-century allegory of the *Ship of Faith*, piloted by the Jesuits, and rowed by priests and nuns, smiling beatifically down at the drowning sinners.

The **Musée Picasso** (*5 Rue de Thorigny; open daily 9.30–5.15, Thurs till 8pm;closed Tues; adm*) is in the Hôtel Salé, the 'Salted Palace', which takes its name from its original occupant, Jean Bouiller, a collector of the hated *gabelle* (salt tax) for Louis XIV. Picasso's heirs donated most of the works here to the state in the 1970s in lieu of inheritance taxes. There are few really famous pictures, but representational works can be seen from all Picasso's diverse styles: a 'blue-period' *Self-portrait* of 1901 through the *Cubist Man with a Guitar* (1912) and beyond. Works from the early 1920s, such as the *Pan's Flute*, show a classicizing tendency, while those from the later '20s and '30s are the most abstract of all. This is Picasso at the top of his art, exquisite draughtsman-ship and the most skilful use of colour, especially in the series of corridas and minotauromachies, employing mythological elements later seen in *Guernica*. One room of the museum contains paintings from Picasso's personal collection, including works by Corot, Matisse and Cézanne. There is also a covered sculpture garden of Picasso's work from many periods, and an audiovisual room with slide shows and films.

Centre of a small Jewish community since the 1700s, a wave of immigration from Eastern Europe in the 1880s and '90s made the **Rue des Rosiers** what it is today – one of the liveliest, most picturesque little streets in Paris. Recently, a number of Sephardic Jews from North Africa have moved in, adding to a scene that includes bearded

Hasidim, old-fashioned *casher* (kosher) grocery shops, and famous delicatessen restaurants. There are several synagogues, including one around the corner at 10 Rue Pavée, designed with a stunning curvilinear façade by Hector Guimard.

Strangely enough, Paris did not become an archiepiscopal see until 1623; for over a thousand years, its bishops were subject to the archbishops of the little town of Sens (*see* pp.726–7). In the Middle Ages these influential clerics spent most of their time in the capital. One of them, *c.* 1475, built the **Hôtel de Sens** (*Square de l'Ave Maria; exhibitions Tues–Sat 1–8; you can view the palace gardens round the back off Rue du Figuier*), a medieval confection overlooking the Seine (today the river is two streets away). One archbishop, Rénaud de Béarn, rented it to Henri IV. Henri used it to park Queen Margot (Marguerite de Valois) who was becoming too much of an embarrassment at court. Almost completely reconstructed, it is one of the loveliest buildings in Paris, an impertinently asymmetrical fantasy of gables, turrets and pinnacles. The palace is now the Bibliothèque Forney, a remarkable institution dedicated to the old crafts and industries of France.

In the late 16th century there developed in Italy the architectural fashion that art historians used to call the 'Jesuit Style'. Combining the confident classicism of the decaying Renaissance with a sweeping bravura that would soon be perfected in the dawning Baroque, this architecture was a key part of the Jesuits' plan to forge a swank, modern image for the Counter-Reformation Church. From its opening, the church of **St-Paul-St-Louis** was the showcase of the new Catholicism in Paris: the most sumptuous interior decoration, the Jesuits' best orators delivering vague but sonorous sermons, music supplied by Lully and Charpentier (both organists here), and all the lights of Parisian society present among the congregation.

Place de la Bastille

There's nothing to see of the famous fortress, of course – unless you arrive on the no.5 métro, coming from the Gare d'Austerlitz, where some of the foundations survive around the platform. The square has been redesigned, with the outline of the fortress set into the pavement. It is the only square in town created not by kings nor planners but by the people of Paris. Since they cleared the space back in 1789, the Place has been the symbolic centre of leftist politics, the setting for monster celebrations like the one that followed Mitterrand's election in 1981.

As part of Mitterrand's notions of 'bringing culture to the people', he conjured up the startling façade of the **Opéra Bastille** (*for excellent guided tours (in French only), call t 01 40 01 19 70, for times; buy a ticket from the office. Box office for performance tickets open daily 11–6.30 (exc Sun); tickets available on sale two weeks in advance, t 01 43 43 96 96*). There used to be a small railway station here, and the buildings included a métro pavilion that was one of the finest works of Hector Guimard. The government planners levelled it without a second thought when they began clearing the site for the Opéra in 1985. Uruguayan-Canadian architect Carlos Ott was chosen personally by President Mitterrand in 1983 as the winner of the design competition. The architectural criticism has been harsh; Ott was up against popular ideas about

The Storming of the Bastille

On the morning of the 14th July 1789, after a rousing speech by Camille Desmoulins in the Palais Royal (*see* p.157), some 600 people, including women and children, advanced across Paris to the grim fortress that had become a symbol of royal despotism. They battled all afternoon against a small garrison of Swiss Guards and retired veterans until, at about 5pm, the arrival of a detachment of revolutionary militia decided the issue. The gates were forced, the governor and many of the defenders massacred, and the last seven inmates of the Bastille were acclaimed as heroes among the crowd: the prisoners comprised four swindlers who were about to be transferred to another prison, an English idiot named Whyte, a gentleman whose family had petitioned the king to lock him up for incest, and one genuine political prisoner – who had been in the Bastille since some obscure conspiracy in 1759 and didn't want to leave. The demolition commenced the following day.

Today, the centrepiece of the Place de la Bastille is the 153ft **Colonne de Juillet**. The 'July column', restored for the bicentennial of the Revolution, was erected over the elephant's pedestal in honour of those who died in the 1830 revolt. On top is a figure of the 'Genius of Liberty' – familiar from the obverse of the 10-franc piece.

what an opera house should look like. On the inside, Ott did everything you could ask of an architect – the sight lines and acoustics are excellent – but the auditorium is hardly intimate: this is a stage meant for spectacle rather than the singer-to-audience and heart-to-heart communication of classic Italian (or French) opera.

Le Viaduc and the Promenade Plantée

A short walk from Place de la Bastille down Rue de Lyon, or bus no.20, takes you to Avenue Daumesnil and one of Paris' latest not-so-grand projects. The old railway viaduct high above the north side of the avenue has been planted up into a charming garden walk, which will eventually lead all the way from Bastille to the Bois de Vincennes; as you follow the long-gone tracks, the garden narrows and opens out in a series of flowery vistas, cuts right through the middle of apartment blocks, and affords views into the second-floor windows of houses that used to rattle to the passing of trains. Below, along the length of Avenue Daumesnil, every single railway arch now houses an *atelier* of high-class specialized craft: furniture, glass, art paper, wood, aromatherapy oils, lampshades, and even Le Viaduc restaurant and bar at no.43, modishly making the most of its reclaimed setting.

Les Halles and Beaubourg

This is the site of the old Paris of merchants and markets, the only *quartier* on the Right Bank without either a royal palace or a royal square. It was – at least until recently – the Paris of the Parisians, the place you would go to buy your turnips, pick up a strumpet or start a revolution. The streets are medieval, or older, and their names betray the gritty workaday spirit of the place: Street of the Knifesmiths, of the Goldsmiths, Goose Street.

Only 30 years ago, these streets were crowded with handcarts and barrels night and day. No part of Paris has seen greater changes in those 30 years and certainly not for the better. Once Les Halles was a vast colourful wholesale distribution market for all Paris, and surrounded by slums. Today its replacement, the Forum des Halles, is a subterranean labyrinthine 'new town' of failing shops, the park is as full of life as a cinder cemetery, and the streets are bleak un-spaces of plannerized compromise dominated by skateboarders and fast food outlets. Only the streets untouched by re-development are fun for ambling and observing.

Les Halles, the 'Belly of Paris' as Emile Zola called it, was an 800-year-old institution before it was sacrificed in 1969. Les Halles began in the reign of Louis VI, a simple open place. About 1183, Philippe Auguste laid out a proper market; the people, organized in their various corporations, felt themselves representative of Paris as a whole, and they often played a hand in political affairs. Napoleon reacted to this just as you'd expect he would. After a brief tour in 1810, he said, 'I don't like this mess...there is no discipline here.' His architects made the first plans for a covered market but it was not until the reign of Napoleon III that anything was done. Architect Victor Baltard designed the famous, graceful green pavilions in 1851.

This Halles was in its way as much fun as its medieval predecessor. It lived by night, when the loads of meat and produce came rolling in from across France. Bars and *bistrots* thrived on its fringes; they stayed up all night too, giving the poets and prostitutes and insomniacs a place to refresh themselves while they relaxed in the company of the market people. In the 1920s and through to the 1950s, Parisian toffs and English and American swells liked to end up here after a night of carousing. But, convivial and informal as they are, markets make politicians nervous. A perverse conspiracy grew up between the government, developers and property interests. Here was an opportunity to redevelop a huge space in the very heart of Paris. Although the vast majority of Parisians were shocked by the proposed scheme, little organized opposition appeared until it was too late. By 1977 the last of Baltard's pavilions had disappeared – the same year London closed down Covent Garden.

The planners did go to great lengths to make this something more than just another shopping mall. Besides the ice-cream and chain stores, there is plenty of modern art to study, as well as questionable cultural amenities like the 'Pavillon des Arts' and the 'Maison de la Poésie'; you can shoot a game of inscrutable French billiards (no pockets) or watch the young at the indoor swimming pool next to a tropical garden. At the **Vidéothèque de Paris**, you can while away an afternoon watching old French television shows, movies or newsreels (*open daily 12.30–9*).

About three-quarters of the new Forum is underground, and most of the old marketplace is now the **Jardin des Halles**. It isn't a very inviting park; habitués come with a bottle of beer, and sit quietly with looks of dismal resignation on their faces. One curious fragment of Catherine de' Medici's palace remains: the tall column called the **Colonne des Médicis**, now standing at the southeastern corner of the building on Rue de Viarmes. Inside, a spiral staircase leads to a platform where Catherine and her astrologers (including, briefly, Nostradamus) would contemplate the destinies of the dynasty and of France.

The entrance to the market's own parish church, **St-Eustache**, is on Place du Jour. The façade, a pathetic neoclassical pudding, was added in the 1750s. St-Eustache, begun in 1532, soon became one of the most important churches in the city, second only to Notre-Dame. Richelieu, Molière and Madame de Pompadour were baptized here, and Louis XIV had his first communion. The interior shows the plan typical of great Parisian churches since Notre-Dame. The art inside, meticulously detailed at the entrance, is disappointing. Don't miss the forlorn chapel in the left aisle, entirely filled with Raymond Mason's 1969 work, *The Departure of the Fruits and Vegetables from the Heart of Paris*, a funny, moving diorama of solemn, dignified market people, carrying their leeks and tomatoes and turnips in a sort of funeral procession, away from the Baltard pavilions and into suburban exile.

The crowds of young people who have made the **Square des Innocents** their main city-centre rendezvous can be seen literally dancing on the graves of their ancestors. At one time, the entire neighbourhood was perfumed by a ripe stench of decaying corpses from Les Halles' neighbour, the Cimetière des Innocents. In 1786 the cemetery was demolished, and the cleared site was converted into a market. Later it was remodelled into the present square, and the **Fontaine des Innocents** installed at its centre. The only surviving Renaissance fountain in Paris (1549) is a work of Pierre Lescot, though the decorative reliefs are by Jean Goujon.

Centre Pompidou

Place Georges-Pompidou and Rue St-Martin, www.centrepompidou.fr.
Open Mon and Wed–Sun 11am–10pm, for guided visits call t 01 44 78 46 25.
Museum open 11am–9pm, last adm 8pm; adm. English audioguides extra.
Atelier Brancusi open 1pm–9pm. Closed Tues.

The 'Beau Bourg' was a village, swallowed up by Paris in the Middle Ages, that ever since has lent its name to the neighbourhood. By the 1920s it had become a grey, unloved place; the government cleared a large section, meaning to relocate the flower market from Les Halles. Nothing happened, leaving the void as a challenge to Paris planners until the end of the 1960s, when grey, unloved President Georges Pompidou came up with the idea of a 'department store for culture', accessible to the widest possible public.

After the Centre opened in 1977, Parisians and tourists voiced their opinion by making it overnight the most visited sight in the city, surpassing even the Eiffel Tower. The 'Plateau' in front, redesigned by Piano into an austere, sloping rectangle, became an instant happening that even Georges Pompidou might have enjoyed (from a safe distance), where Paris' old coterie of repulsive oral tricksters – sword swallowers, cigarette munchers and bicycle eaters – performed amid buskers, tramps, backpackers and portrait sketchers.

Inside, you won't need a ticket for the **escalator** to the top, by far the most popular attraction, which runs along the outside, providing a spectacular view over Paris that changes dramatically as you ascend; for a special treat, come back and do it at twilight, when the monuments of the city are illuminated.

The major permanent feature of the Centre is the newly reopened millennium-edition **Musée National d'Art Moderne**. This superlative collection of 20th-century art (*excellent audioguide available*) has been re-presented over two floors of open white space, punctuated at every turn with plate glass windows, alternating stunning views over Paris with flat, still lakes of water setting off stone and iron sculptures.

The **top floor**, 'Art 1905–1960', takes up where the Musée d'Orsay leaves off: at the turning point of modernity, when the Fauves (Derain, Vlaminck, Matisse, Marquet) liberated colour from its age-old function of representing nature. Van Gogh had blazed a trail by using colour to express emotions. The Fauves went a step beyond, applying colour and line on a two-dimensional surface as an intellectual expression, the way a poet uses words on a piece of paper. Fauvism flickered out after only four years, but set off an immense burst of creative energy. Picasso formulated the creed of modern art when he wrote, 'I don't work after nature, but before nature – and with her.' New developments happened at a dizzying pace. As Van Gogh was a prophet for the Fauves, Cézanne's experiments in rendering volume with nuances of colour inspired Cubism. The Cubist works of Picasso, Braque, Juan Gris and Duchamp analyse form by depicting it simultaneously from a hundred points of view on a flat surface, destabilizing our perception in order to broaden it. A prism of aftershocks fills the next rooms, especially the first abstract works, born of Wassily Kandinsky, imaginative Expressionism and the geometric fundamentals of Mondrian and his de Stijl followers. And there are important works from most of the artists who continued modernism's enquiry into art, expression and meaning: stylized figurative painters Chagall, Soutine and Rouault, the Dadaists Picabia and Man Ray, the Surrealists Dalí, Magritte, Tanguy, Masson and Ernst. At every point the display and organization of the museum's works explores the cross-pollination between pure and applied art, combining a Mondrian canvas of flat squares and defined boundaries with sculptures composed of squares and flat planes, alongside 1920s architectural models by Paul

The Museum that was Built Inside Out

The design finally chosen was the most radical of all those submitted. The architects, Richard Rogers and Renzo Piano, turned traditional ideas of building upside down – or rather, inside out. To allow larger, more open spaces on the inside, and to expose what a modern structure really is, they came up with a big rectangle of girders, from which the insides are hung, a kind of invertebrate architecture, with an insect's shell instead of a skeleton. Much more provocative was the idea of putting the technological guts of the building on the outside – celebrating the essentials instead of hiding them, and painting them in bright colours keyed to help the observer understand how it all works: electrics in yellow, air conditioning in blue, white for ventilation ducts, etc. These are best seen on the back of the building, along Rue Beaubourg.

Nelson and Le Corbusier, where the same principles have been used to transform the spaces we live in. Further on are more naturalistic paintings such as Bonnard's *L'Atelier au mimosa*, whose vibrating colours are only barely contained by the vertical and diagonal lines of the window-frames and balustrade, and Fernand Léger, whose chunky human forms mark a return to figure painting but stylized into ovals and squares edged in thick black lines. The effect of war and the collapse of political idealism is painfully clear, and from the '50s on you can see the rapid hurtling towards the modern art of today, with monochrome canvases of pure texture, white on rippling white by Piero Manzoni like Lazarus' bandages or Tracey Emin's rumpled bedsheet, or Yves Klein's wall-sized rectangle of deep blue to drown in.

> *La vérité changera l'art.*
>
> Ben, 1935, *Le magasin de Ben*

The audioguide is especially helpful on the lower floor, 'Post 1960', where the familiar images of Pop Art and new realism and displays of space-age plastic furniture give way to the explorations of artists' cautionary responses to new technology in the 1960s: Robert Rauschenberg's *Oracle* and Sigmar Polke's *Pasadena*, questioning the truth of the sudden flood of media images, information and advertising pouring over an unprepared public. The art on this floor is participatory, kinetic, interactive – Yaacov Agam's *L'Antichambre à l'Elysée* and Dorothea Tanning's *La Chambre 202, Hôtel du Pavot* shift their colours with each changing viewpoint – and there are installations such as Joseph Beuys' 1985 *Plight*, two rooms of rolled felt enclosing a silenced and sick piano, that embrace a particularly modern and self-absorbed kind of uncertainty. Also on this floor are a Graphic Art Gallery and a New Media Centre.

On other floors of the Centre are a major public reading library (the BPI) and musical research institute (IRCAM), a gift shop with goods inspired by the modern art collections, a bookshop, a café, a swanky new restaurant, Georges (*see* p.127), halls for temporary exhibitions, two cinemas, two concert spaces, and, outside on the Plateau, the **Atelier Brancusi**, a reconstruction of the Paris studio where the Romanian sculptor lived from 1925 to 1957.

Around the Centre Pompidou

St Merri, or Medericus, was an abbot of Autun buried here in the early 8th century. A chapel was built over his relics, then on the outskirts of the city; in the Middle Ages, with all the bankers and cloth merchants in this area, it became one of the richest parish churches of Paris. The present **St-Merri** was begun *c.* 1500, in the same late-Flamboyant Gothic style as St-Eustache, and not completed until 1612. The last part to be finished was the bell tower, which contains a 14th-century bell called the Merri, the oldest in the city. What you see on it today are largely replacements from the 1840s, including the statues of saints and the little, winged, supposedly hermaphroditic demon that leers over the main portal. There are frequent concerts on Sunday afternoons; after these, you can have a free guided tour (*first and third Sun of each month, and Sat eves before*).

Behind the Centre Pompidou, the broad sheet of water of the **Stravinsky Fountain** serves as a play pool for a collection of monsters created by that delightful sculptress from Mars, Niki de Saint-Phalle. Her colourful gadgets are each dedicated to one of Stravinsky's works; at any moment, they are likely to start spinning around and spraying you with water. The black metal mobiles between them are by Jean Tinguely.

The Louvre

Open daily 9–6, Mon and Wed eve until 9.45 (Wed eve everything is open; Mon eve Richelieu wing only); closed Tues; adm lower on Sun and after 3pm; under-18s free; free for everyone on first Sun of every month.
At weekends or on any day in summer, come early to avoid the long queues. For details on which rooms are closed, call t 01 40 20 51 51.

Here it is, the delicious, often indigestible 99-course feast that sooner or later all visitors to Paris must swallow. 'Biggest Museum in the World' they call it, certain they have surpassed the Vatican, the Smithsonian, the British Museum and the other monsters. It isn't even as big as it used to be, for all post-1848 art has been moved to the Musée d'Orsay.

'Louvre' was the name of the area long before any palaces were dreamt of. The original castle was built some time after 1190 by Philippe Auguste. Charles V rebuilt and extended it in the 1360s. During the worst of the Hundred Years' War (1400–1430) the kings abandoned the Louvre and Paris; the first to return was François I, in 1527; he demolished the old castle and began what is known today as the *Vieux Louvre*, the easternmost part of the complex, in 1546. Henri IV, Louis XIII and Louis XIV all contributed in turn to the palace. The next royal resident was a reluctant Louis XVI, brought here by force from Versailles in October 1789 and installed in the Tuileries, where the National Assembly could keep a close eye on him.

Republican governments kept their offices in the Tuileries after 1795; they consolidated the art collections and made them into a public museum in 1793. Napoleon moved in in 1800, and started work on the northern wing. During the next 15 years his men looted the captive nations of Europe for their finest paintings and statues, most of which ended up here.

The Louvre was 350 years in the building, and the best parts are the oldest. Start on the eastern end, on Rue de l'Amiral de Coligny. The majestic **colonnade** (begun 1668) marks the beginning of the French classical style; its architect was Claude Perrault, brother of Charles, the famous writer of fairy tales. The outer façades of the **north wing**, facing Rue de Rivoli, are contributions of Napoleon (right half, viewed from the street) and Napoleon III (left half); both lend much to the imperial dreariness of that street. As for the **south wing**, facing the Seine, the left half is the beginning of Catherine de' Medici's long extension; its completion (right half) was done under Henri IV. The Napoleons, with their symmetrical brains, naturally had to make the Louvre symmetrical too; between them they more than doubled the size of the palace, expanding the south wing and building the northern one to mirror it.

Before a *carrousel* became a merry-go-round, the word meant a knightly tournament, involving races, jousts and even singing. The **Arc du Carrousel**, like the other monument Napoleon built to himself, the Vendôme column, is a mere copy, in this case of the Arch of Septimius Severus in the Roman Forum. A sculptural ensemble in bronze in the **Jardin du Carrousel** appears to represent a crack ladies' rugby team at practise. In fact these are a collection of separate works by **Aristide Maillol**, a wonderful turn-of-the-20th-century, Catalan-French sculptor who started his career aged 40 and believed that any conceivable subject could be most effectively represented by female nudes of heroic proportions.

In 1981, his first year in office, President Mitterrand decided to shake it up a bit with the *Projet du Grand Louvre*, a total refurbishing of the palace, museum and the adjacent Tuileries gardens. The entire north wing, which had housed the Ministry of Finance, was cleared to expand the museum space, and a giant underground car park and plush shopping mall was burrowed under the Jardin du Carrousel.

And then there's the **Pyramid** – for a simple geometric bagatelle, architect I. M. Pei's 1988 entrance to the Louvre has certainly generated a lot of ink. *Le Figaro* called the Pyramid controversy a revival of the 17th-century literary battle, the 'Quarrel of the Ancients and Moderns'. The structure is the crowning achievement or the ultimate atrocity from a decade of *grands projets* that transformed Paris. To some it was a cause célèbre of classical pure form, to others the Pyramid was a chilly, inhuman blast of rude geometry in the sacred precincts of art. The Pyramid and the Hall Napoléon beneath it are open until 9.45pm, and that is the best time to come and see for yourself. Illuminated from inside the structure is undeniably beautiful, inspiring almost. Behind the glass, the metal struts and cables make an intricate and delicate pattern, a marvel of intelligence and grace.

Once through the door and down the long curving stairway, you are in the **Hall Napoléon**, where you can buy your ticket. From here you have a choice of three entrances into the labyrinth, up escalators marked **Denon**, **Sully** and **Richelieu**, the three sections into which the Louvre has been divided: Sully is the old Louvre, Denon the south wing, Richelieu the north wing. A free, colour-coded **orientation guide** is available at the front desk.

Highlights of the Collections

Egyptian Art: The finest and most complete collection outside Egypt itself. (Thanks to Napoleon, of course, the French got a head start. His 1798 expedition to the land of the pharaohs took along a fair-sized platoon of scientists and scholars interested in Egyptian antiquities. The army carted tons of art and mummies back to Paris, where Champollion, the director of the Louvre's new Egyptian department, first deciphered the hieroglyphics.)

Sarcophagi there are a plenty, but keep an eye out for the surprises that make the subtle Egyptians come to life – like the dog with a bell around his neck, a sort of Alsatian, with a quizzical look. The **Mastaba of Akhetep** is a complete small funeral chapel (*c.* 2300 BC) from Saqqara. Exceptional exhibits of **Coptic Art** up to the Middle Ages are here, too.

Middle Eastern Art: The various civilizations of **Mesopotamia** (*Richelieu 3, 4, ground floor*) are well represented. You may never have heard of **Mani**, a great civilization centred on the Euphrates, now in Syria, that reached its height *c.* 1800 BC, but its people were some of the Middle East's most talented artists, represented here by statues and a rare surviving fresco. From **Babylon**, which destroyed Mani, there is a black monument carved with the **Code of Hammurabi**, the oldest known body of laws. **Medieval Islamic** ceramics and metalwork (*Richelieu entresol*) include the *Font of St Louis*, used to baptize future kings of France.

Classical Antiquity: The **Venus de Milo** (*Sully 12*), for whom neither date nor provenance is known, only that the islanders of Milos sold her to the French in 1820 to keep the Turks from getting her. There are **Roman-era copies** of Greek works, **Etruscan art**, and from **Rome**, penetrating, naturalistic portrait busts including *Caligula, Nero, Hadrian* and *Marcus Aurelius*. The large **Cour du Sphinx** assembles some of the best antique works from all periods, including the *mosaic of the Four Seasons* and a huge anthropomorphized *River Tiber*, from the Isis temple in Rome. The 5th–7th-century **early Christian art** is mostly from Syria.

Sculpture: From the Middle Ages onwards (*entresol and ground floor of Denon and Richelieu*). See especially the **French Renaissance sculpture**, not only for the quality of the work but also because there's hardly any in the rest of Paris. Guillaume Costou's *Marly Horses* (*c.* 1740, the originals of the ones in the Place de la Concorde) are naturalistic, virtuoso productions as intellectually challenging as a chocolate éclair.

French Painting: Highlights are the earliest known French easel painting, a 1350 portrait of *King Jean le Bon*; works by Georges de la Tour, greatest of the French followers of Caravaggio, with his startling contrasts of light and shadow; Watteau's *Gilles*; delightful landscapes by Corot and the Barbizon school, forerunners of Impressionism. David's unfinished *portrait of Madame Récamier*, the famous Paris beauty, offers a glimpse of everything that was best about the era. Delacroix's iconic *Liberty Leading the People* was painted after the revolt of 1830, where the bourgeoisie and workers fight side by side; Géricault's dramatic *Raft of the Medusa* was painted after a shipwreck that was in the news at the time.

Flemish, Dutch and German Painting: A feast of fine 15th-century altarpieces by van Eyck, van der Weyden and Memling, Hieronymous Bosch's delightful *Ship of Fools*, Joachim Patinir's gloomy *St Jerome in the Desert*, and beautiful, meticulous works of Quentin Metsys. From the height of the Renaissance, from Duke Federico's Palace at Urbino, come 14 remarkable *Portraits of Philosophers*. There are two masterpieces of light and depth by Jan Vermeer, joyous scenes of peasant life by David Teniers and others, odd allegories from Jan Brueghel, and 15 Rembrandts. Then there's the *Life of Marie de' Medici*, over 1,000 sq metres of unchained Peter Paul Rubens. Rubensian buttocks fly every which way, in colours that Cecil B. De Mille would have died for.

Italian Painting: The Grande Galerie (*Denon 8, first floor*) has the third (and least well preserved) part of the three-piece *Battle of San Romano* by Paolo Uccello, greatest and strangest of the Early Renaissance's slaves of perspective, some fine late altarpieces by Botticelli, an eerie *Crucifixion* by Mantegna, and good works by da Messina, Baldovinetti, Piero della Francesca, Carpaccio, Perugino, Raphael's dreamlike

St Michael and the Dragon and his portrait of the perfect Renaissance courtier, *Baldassare Castiglione*, and Leonardo da Vinci's haunting *Virgin of the Rocks* and *Virgin and Child with St Anne*. A major attraction is the room itself, running the length of the Louvre's south wing, flooded with light.

The Salle des Etats: The Louvre's undisputed superstar, *Mona Lisa*, 'the most famous artwork in the world', as a local guide trumpets her, smiles from behind the glass (installed after she was slashed a few years back), as the tourists with their flash machines close in like paparazzi. In the same room are Titian's smiling portrait of *François I* and works by Correggio, Pontormo, del Sarto and others, and Paolo Veronese's room-sized *Wedding at Cana*, which besides Jesus and Mary includes nearly all the political and artistic celebrities of the day: Emperor Charles V, François I and Suleiman the Magnificent sit at the table, while Titian, Tintoretto and other artists play in the band – Veronese himself is on viola.

Late Italian and Spanish Painting: Francesco Guardi's colourful series of 12 works on *Venetian Festivals* (1763) is a sweet document of the Serenissima near the end of its career. On the grand staircase, next to the *Winged Victory of Samothrace*, don't miss a detached Botticelli fresco called **Venus and the Graces**: five perfect Botticelli maidens maintaining their poise and calm amid the crowds. El Greco checks in with a *Crucifixion*, and from the golden age of Spanish painting, there's at least one work by each of the masters: Velázquez (*Infanta Margarita*), Ribera, and two Zurbaráns from the cycle of *St Bonaventure* (from Seville – among Napoleon's thefts that never were returned), and several Goyas.

Objets d'Art: Blinding jewels and heavy gold gimcracks, tapestries, Renaissance bronzes, Merovingian treasure, sardonyx vases... In the extravagantly decorated **Salle d'Apollon** (*Denon 8, first floor*) are Louis XIV's crown jewels, Henri II's rock crystal chess set, Napoleon's crown and Josephine's earrings, Charlemagne's dagger, St Louis' ring, Louis XV's crown, and a 107.88 carat ruby in the shape of a dragon called *La Côte de Bretagne*. The rest of the collection is separate, on the first floor. Don't miss it.

Musée des Arts Décoratifs: Rue de Rivoli, Ⓜ Palais-Royal. Part of the Louvre, the museum (*open Wed–Sat 12.30–6 and Sun 12–6; adm*) was founded in 1877, its purpose to show the public beautiful things so that people would be more demanding about what they bought for themselves.

Palais Royal

Welcome to the most unabashedly retro area of Paris. Dusty, dignified, and thoroughly obsolete in a number of unimportant ways, it hasn't been popular with Parisians or anybody else since the 1830s. But you may find it one of the most unexpected delights Paris has to offer. This *quartier* is about old books, pretty things and good architecture; in other words, the elements of civilization. Though not a well-defined quarter like the Marais, it has assumed and thrown off various identities over the centuries: it was an area of court servants, artists and hangers-on when kings lived at the Louvre or Tuileries, and briefly Paris' tenderloin when the Palais Royal was full of bordellos. Though containing the Bourse and the Banque de France, it has miraculously been spared the fate of becoming a soulless business centre.

Originally Cardinal Richelieu built the Palais Royal for himself, beginning in 1629. Naturally he willed it to the king, whose money he was playing with, long before his death in 1642. Anne of Austria and four-year-old Louis XIV moved in soon after, but left for the more defensible Louvre when the uprising of the Fronde got hot, and gave it to his brother Philippe, Duc d'Orléans. Much rebuilt, the Palais Royal currently houses the *Conseil d'Etat*, which advises on proposed laws and serves as an appeal court. Next door is the **Théâtre Français**, attached to the Palais-Royal complex in 1786. Ever since, it has been the home of the Comédie Française, the company founded by Louis XIV out of Molière's old troupe. In the lobby, Houdon's famous statue of Voltaire is displayed along with the chair on which Molière died.

But the real attraction is not these mournful buildings, but the sweet surprise behind them. Pass under the arch between the theatre and the palace into the **Jardin du Palais Royal**. The last descendant of the Duke of Orléans had in 1781 hit on the idea of cutting down his enormous debts by selling off part of the gardens for building lots. His architects chopped the greenery down by a third, and enclosed it with an arcaded quadrangle of terraced houses, à la Place des Vosges. Under the arcades, several cafés soon opened; gambling houses and bordellos thrived. The latter were quite refined, fronting as hat, or even furniture, shops. The police couldn't do a thing about it. They could not, in fact, even enter the Palais grounds without the duke's permission – such were the privileges of princely families before 1789.

Ironically enough, this privilege helped make the Palais Royal gardens, and the cafés that proliferated around its arcades, one of the birthplaces of the Revolution. Like the Tuileries, this was one of the bastions of the *nouvellistes*, or news-mongers. You came here if you wanted to argue politics. Typically, the attack on the Bastille was spontaneously conceived here, when Camille Desmoulins jumped on to a café table and started talking, on the morning of 14 July.

Fashion and vice both moved to the Grands Boulevards after 1838, when Louis-Philippe closed the gambling houses. Later, because the Dukes of Orléans were pretenders to his throne, Louis-Napoleon confiscated both the gardens and the palace. Ever since, the garden has kept well out of the mainstream of popularity. The arcades that were once packed day and night now hold only a few quietly fascinating shops, selling antiques, military models or recycled designer clothing from the 1950s. The gardens themselves are well clipped and neat.

One of the oldest and prettiest of Paris' *passages*, built in 1826, the **Galerie Véro-Dodat**, east of the Jardin, wowed the Paris crowds with its mahogany, marble and bronze decoration, as well as its use of a new technological marvel – gas lighting. Véro and Dodat were two butchers who made it big and went out of their way to impress. There are some interesting shops both new and old. The **Galeries Vivienne and Colbert**, just north of Place des Victoires, were built in the 1820s, and along with the Véro-Dodat they are the most luxurious and well-restored survivors of the genre in Paris. Light and airy, with neoclassical reliefs and mosaic floors, these arcades make a dreamy setting for their little shops and cafés.

The second of Paris''royal' squares (after Place des Vosges), **Place des Victoires** was laid out by Hardouin-Mansart in 1685 to accommodate an equestrian statue of Louis XIV. Like its predecessor, the piazza was planned as an intimate, enclosed public space. Over the last century, the Parisians have done their best to spoil the effect. Façades were altered, and in 1883 Rue Etienne-Marcel was cut through, entirely wrecking the dignified atmosphere. By the 1950s it reached a nadir of tackiness, but lately there has been a clean-up; the place now attracts fashion shops.

The **Bibliothèque Nationale** (*Rue de Richelieu; entrance on Rue Vivienne; open Tues–Sat 1–5, Sun 12–6; adm*) was born in 1537 when a decree inaugurated the *dépôt légal*, the requirement that anyone publishing a book must send a copy to the king – who was concerned with seeing anything that might be seditious. Louis XIV's minister, Colbert, put the library on a sound footing when he consolidated all the king's holdings in two adjacent *hôtels particuliers*. You can't use the facilities without a reader's card, but have a look inside at the old building. The main reading room has been transferred to the new site at Quai François-Mauriac; here you can see a museum of coins and medals. The exit on the opposite side of the Bibliothèque takes you to Rue de Richelieu, facing the **Square Louvois**, with a pretty fountain (1844) allegorizing the 'Four Rivers of France': the Seine, Loire, Garonne and Saône.

Opéra and Faubourg-St-Honoré

This area was to the Paris of the early 1800s what the Champs-Elysées would be later in the century: the city's showcase and playground of the élite. It's still the home of all luxury, the main source of what the French call *articles de Paris*; here you'll find the gilded fashion houses and the jewellers whose names are known around the galaxy and beyond. Close to the Louvre and the *Grand Axe*, this corner of town attracted monumental projects from three of France's most unpleasant despots: Louis XIV's Place Vendôme, Napoleon's self-memorial that became the Madeleine, and Little Napoleon's incomparable Opéra, a popular subject for wallpaper patterns on both sides of the Atlantic. These men, and the style of the buildings they left behind, set the tone for the area, which is a little stuffy, a little faded, more than a little over the top, and eternally, unashamedly Parisian.

Construction of **La Madeleine** was begun in 1764, but this church was fated to see many changes before its completion. The death of the architect in 1777 occasioned a complete rethink; the new man opted for a neoclassical Greek cross plan, imitating Soufflot's Panthéon. Only a quarter finished by 1792, the revolutionary government pondered over a new use for the project – perhaps the seat of the National Assembly, the Banque de France or the National Library. But Napoleon knew what was best: a Temple of Glory, dedicated to himself and his Grand Army. The previous plans were scrapped, the foundations razed, and in 1806 architect Barthélemy Vignon came up with an imitation Greek temple. Napoleonic efficiency got the colonnades up in nine years, but once more, political change intervened; after 1815 the restored Bourbons decided to make it a church after all.

After the chilly perfection of the Madeleine's exterior, the inside comes as a surprise: windowless and overdecorated, creamy and gloomy, more like a late-Baroque Italian church – or ballroom. The rustic cane chairs contrast strangely with the gilded Corinthian columns and walls covered with a dozen varieties of expensive marble. The combined efforts of these 19th-century artists will never convince you that this building, the scene of Paris' high-society marriages and funerals, could possibly have anything to do with the Christian religion.

Place Vendôme, the second of Louis XIV's 'royal squares', after Place des Victoires, was laid out in 1699 by the same architect, Jules Hardouin-Mansart. The most satisfactory of all 17th-century French attempts at urban design, the square seems the utter antithesis of a building like the Opéra – but both were built to impress. Here, however, Hardouin-Mansart does it with absolute decorum. Only two streets lead into the square, which was conceived as a sort of enclosed urban parlour for the nobility. Balls were sometimes held in it, but cafés or anything else that would encourage street life or spontaneity were strictly forbidden.

Originally, the square was to house embassies and academies, but the final plan proposed the present octagon of eight mansions, with uniform façades, and an equestrian statue of – guess who – in the centre. Today the square still has a not-too-discreet aroma of money about it, home to the Ritz Hotel, Cartier, Van Cleef & Arpels and a fleet of other jewellers who never put prices in the window displays.

The **Opéra** (*tours of the interior daily 10–4.30; guided tour at 1pm; museum open daily 10–4.30; separate adm for both. Tours include the main hall on days when there is no performance; check beforehand, t 01 40 01 22 63, if you want to see Chagall's ceiling*) is the supreme monument of the Second Empire, conceived in 1858, after Napoleon III was leaving a slightly more intimate theatre and one of the rabble got close enough to try and assassinate him. A competition was organized for a new Opéra, and the plan chosen was the largest, submitted by a fashionable young architect named Charles Garnier. After winning the competition, Garnier still had to convince a sceptical Napoleon and Eugénie. Asked what style his work was supposed to be, the architect replied: 'It is no style. Not Greek or Roman; it is the style of Napoleon III.' That won the Emperor over immediately.

Finally open in 1875, three years after Napoleon's death, the biggest and most sumptuous theatre in the world soon passed into legend, much of it due to Gaston Leroux's novel *Fantôme de l'Opéra*. There were controversies, such as the one over Carpeaux's flagrant statuary outside. The artist's rivals pretended to be shocked (naked women, in Paris!) and threw bottles of ink at them. Anarchists plotted to blow the place up, and everyone whispered about the famous Opéra masked balls ('great festivals of pederasty'). Envied and copied throughout the world, this building contributed much to the transformation of opera into the grand spectacle and social ritual it became in the Belle Epoque. It may have seemed that way to François Mitterrand when, in the 1980s, he decided on the overtly political gesture of sentencing opera to the proletarian Bastille. Today the behemoth sits a bit forlorn, home only to its dance company, run until a few years ago by the late Rudolf Nureyev.

The inside is impressive, awash with gold leaf, frescoes, mosaics and scores of different varieties of precious stone, from Swedish marble to Algerian onyx. The highlight of the tour may be the hall itself, with its **ceiling** (1964) painted by Marc Chagall; the nine scenes, lovely if perhaps incongruous in this setting, are inspired by some of the artist's favourite operas and ballets. The **Musée de l'Opéra** is in the Imperial Pavilion (enter from main entrance); it has a collection of memorabilia and art, including a portrait of Wagner by Renoir.

Outside, the **Place de l'Opéra** was one of the status addresses of late 19th-century Paris; it included the original Grand Hôtel, opened for the World Fair of 1867. To your left and right stretch the western **Grands Boulevards**: Boulevard des Italiens, Boulevard des Capucines and Boulevard de la Madeleine. A century ago these were the brightest promenades of Paris, home of all the famous cafés and restaurants. Today the glamour is gone but the streets are popular and crowded just the same; they're a good place to take in a movie – and have been since the world's first public film show was put on by the Lumière brothers at no.14 Boulevard des Capucines, on 28 December 1895.

The **Musée Jacquemart-André** (*158 Bd Haussmann; closed for renovation; open by appointment only*), assembled by Edouard André and his wife Nélie Jacquemart in the early 1900s, is the place to go if you feel like looking at beautiful pictures, but don't care to tackle the terrible Louvre. Nélie was a painter herself, and had a sharp eye. The works from the Italian Renaissance rival the Louvre's own collection. Don't miss Tiepolo's fresco on the stairway, the *Reception of King Henri III in Venice*. French painters of the 17th and 18th centuries are also well represented, as are the Dutch, including two works of Rembrandt. Their country home is also a museum (*see* p.665).

The Grand Axe

This is a part of Paris that every first-time visitor feels obliged to see. From the Louvre to La Défense, the monuments line up like pearls on a string – some natural, some cultured and some fake. Paris' main drag recalls destiny and de Gaulle; its breadth and majesty still proclaim to the world that this is the place to be. It has been an irresistible magnet for parades ever since it was built: Napoleon's Grande Armée did it, and Bismarck made a Champs-Elysées promenade part of the armistice terms in 1870 – even though the Prussians couldn't capture Paris. And on both sides of the Atlantic, there are still plenty of stout fellows who will never forget the day they did this walk in uniform, on 26 August 1944.

Jardin des Tuileries

The first gardens on this site were built at the same time as the Tuileries palace, in the 1560s. It was Catherine de' Medici's idea, following the latest fashions in land-scaping from Renaissance Italy; she purchased a large tract of land behind the palace, part of which had been a rubbish dump and part a tile works – hence the name. Her new pleasure park, designed by Philibert de l'Orme and others, was soon the wonder of Paris; symmetrical and neat, it became the model for Le Nôtre's work and all the classical French landscaping that followed. Contemporary accounts suggest it must have been much more beautiful, and more fun, than the present incarnation, with such features as a hedge maze, elaborate sundials, a 'grotto' lined with Sèvres porcelain and statuary, and a semicircle of trees cleverly planted to create an echo effect.

Louis XIV opened the park to the public and the new Tuileries became Paris' most fashionable promenade; it continued as such through the 18th century, featuring such novelties as Paris' first public toilets and first newspaper kiosk. The first gas airship took off from a spot near the octagonal pond in 1783, the same year as the Montgolfiers' pioneer hot-air balloon.

The centre of the park is shaded by avenues of chestnut trees, the *Quinconces des Marroniers*. Further up the Grande Allée (heading for the Place de la Concorde) is the **octagonal basin**, surrounded by some statues that have survived from the days when the Tuileries was a royal park: allegories of the seasons, and of French rivers, also the Nile and the Tiber. The **Chevaux Ailés**, two winged horses at the gates facing Place de la Concorde, are by Louis XIV's chief sculptural propagandist, Coysevox: *Mercury* and *Fame* (both copies).

Le Nôtre's plan included narrow raised terraces at the northern and southern ends, the *Terrasse des Feuillants* and the *Terrasse du Bord de l'Eau*, both favourite tracks for Parisian joggers. At the Concorde end, the terraces expand into broader plateaux supporting buildings from the time of Napoleon III. To the north is the **Galerie Nationale du Jeu de Paume** (*open Wed–Fri 12–7, Sat and Sun 10–7, Tues 12–9.30; adm*), built for real tennis, the crazy medieval game where the ball bounces off walls, roofs and turrets. The building was once the Impressionists' museum in Paris; the collection has since been consolidated at the Musée d'Orsay. It now sits a bit forlorn, hosting contemporary art exhibitions. But its counterpart in the southwest corner, the **Musée National de l'Orangerie** (*open daily exc Tues 9.45–5; adm*), offers a fine permanent collection, complementary to the Musée d'Orsay, with a large lower level devoted to Monet. Many of the big-name artists of the 20th century are represented, but be warned that the works are seldom among their best: dissolving landscapes of Chaim Soutine, Cézanne still lifes and portraits, rosy Renoir *fillettes*, Paris scenes by Utrillo, and a trio of Modigliani weird sisters. The highlights are the luminous canvases of Monet, including one of the *Nymphéas* (Water Lilies), and two wonderful pictures by the Douanier Rousseau: a nasty-looking *Little Girl with a Doll* (1907), and the pinched-faced provincial family on *Père Junier's Cart* (1910).

Place de la Concorde

Without the cars the Place de la Concorde would be a treat, the most spacious square and the finest architectural ensemble in Paris. Jacques-Ange Gabriel won the competition for its design by coming up with something utterly, unaccountably original. Breaking completely with the enclosed, aristocratic ethos of the other royal

The Obelisk

The obelisk in the Place de la Concorde comes from Luxor on the Nile, *c*. 1250 BC in the time of Ramses II. It was a gift from France's ally Muhammad Ali, semi-independent Ottoman viceroy of Egypt in the 1830s, and this spot was chosen for it because any political monument would have been a sure source of controversy in the future. Accepting an obelisk is one thing; floating the 221-tonne block to Paris and getting it upright again a different matter. Look at the inscriptions on the base: scenes of the erection carved in intricate detail, with thanks in big gold letters to M. LEBAS, INGENIEUR, for managing the trick, 'to the applause of an immense crowd'.

squares, Gabriel laid out an enormous rectangle, built up on one side only (the north), with the Seine facing opposite and the two ends entirely open, towards the parklands of the Tuileries and the Champs-Elysées.

Later generations perfected the Place. The Pont de la Concorde over the Seine opened in 1790; under Napoleon, the Madeleine and Palais Bourbon were added to close the views and complete the brilliant architectural ensemble. A new exclamation mark along the Grand Axe, the Egyptian obelisk, appeared in 1836. But in the meantime the Place had changed its name six times, and seen more trouble than any square deserves. In 1782 the spot where the obelisk stands today held a guillotine, the venue for all the most important executions under the Terror; Louis and Marie were the most famous victims; Danton, Desmoulins, Charlotte Corday and finally Robespierre himself held centre stage here while Madame Defarge knitted.

This is a square made for strollers and carriages. The fumes and menace of six lanes of traffic, zooming around the obelisk as fast as they can, have made its enjoyment nearly impossible – come at dawn on Sunday morning, or right after a rare big snow-fall if you want some idea of the original effect. The centre island is an octagon, as Gabriel designed it, with allegorical statues of eight French cities at the corners. Baron Haussmann's architect, Jacques Hittorff, added the ornate lamp-posts and two incredible bronze **fountains**, with rows of perplexed marine deities sitting on benches and cradling fishes.

On the western edge of the Place stands a pair of winged horses to complement those on the Tuileries side. These familiar landmarks are copies of the **Marly horses**, sculpted by Coysevox's nephew, Guillaume Coustou, in the 1740s. Like their counter-parts across the Place they originally came from Louis XIV's château at Marly, destroyed in the Revolution.

Champs-Elysées

Just off the beginning of the Champs-Elysées, the **Grand Palais** (*t 01 44 13 17 17; open daily 10–8, Wed 10–10; reservation obligatory if visiting 10–1; closed Tues; adm*), built for the 1900 exhibition, is one of the biggest surprises in Paris, and beyond any doubt the capital's most neglected and unloved monument. The main entrance on Avenue

Winston-Churchill has been barricaded for years and whatever renovations were underway have been stalled. But you can peek through the glass doors at the grandest interior space in Paris, if not all Europe: a single glass arcade 1,100ft long with a glass dome at the centre, flanked by several levels of balconies and a magnificent grand stair. Even now, standing forlorn, it astounds like an Egyptian pyramid. Its architects and the fair promoters built their folly in a pompous, eclectic style already obsolete, and adorned it with an allegorical jungle of florid sculpture and sententious figurines.

The building itself was an allegory: 'A Monument Consecrated by the Republic to the Glory of French Art'. In 1900, for a novelty, 22 works of the major Impressionists – already a bit dated – were included in a separate room, something that would have been unthinkable in 1878 or 1889. When President Emile Loubet came to see the show, he thought he might take a look at the work of such notorious, anti-social radicals as Pissarro, Renoir and Degas. A fashionable academician named Gérôme was showing him around; when they came to the Impressionists' room, Gérôme flung himself in front of the doorway, crying: 'Go no further, Monsieur le Président; here France is dishonoured!' It was too late.

The 1900 show in fact proved a turning point, where modern art made its first big breakthrough to a wider public. As much as the Eiffel Tower, the Grand Palais is a symbol of an age, of both France and Europe at the height of their power, empire and confidence. It reflects, more than any building except the lost Crystal Palace in London, the exuberance of an architecture that had just realized its technological capabilities. Special world-touring art exhibitions are held in the northern end of the Grand Palais.

The rear of the Grand Palais has been declared a palace in itself, the **Palais de la Découverte** (*open daily 9.30–6, Sun and hols 10–7; closed Mon; adm; separate charge for planetarium shows Tues-Fri 11.00, 2.00, 3.15 and 4.30, Sat and Sun 11.30, 2.00, 3.15, 4.30 and 5.30*), a science museum. Before you go in, take a minute to look at one of the glories of the Grand Palais' original decoration, a colourful frieze of Sèvres terracotta designed by Joseph Blanc. It represents *The Triumph of Art*, beginning in earliest times and passing through Greece, Rome, Charlemagne's Empire, Renaissance Florence, Rome and Venice, and ultimately, of course, Paris.

Neither you nor the children will be bored, even if you can't read much French; there are lasers to play with, ant colonies, and computers. Whatever your age, the best part may be the **Eureka** rooms: hands-on games and tricks to learn about colours, optics and elementary physics. The scary stuff is kept at the back of the ground floor and mezzanine: big Van de Graaff generators that crank out a million and a half volts and make your hair stand on end, and a nuclear exhibit where the kids can make various objects radioactive.

The **Musée du Petit Palais** (*open daily 10–5.40; closed Mon and hols; adm*) has a 'permanent collection' inside, but not quite a 'museum' – restorations and rearrangements have been going on for years. It consists of a large collection of 18th-century art and furniture (busts of Voltaire and Franklin by Houdon), a selection of medieval art and a smattering of works from the Renaissance, including Italian majolica and Venetian glass. The main attraction is 19th-century French painting and sculpture, including some from a vast collection of prints and engravings.

The **Avenue des Champs-Elysées** was the second step in the creation of the Grand Axe, the long radian that stretches, perfectly straight, from central Paris west to La Défense. Catherine de' Medici had fixed its eastern point with her Louvre extensions and the Tuileries gardens in the 1560s. In 1616 everything west of the Louvre was royal meadows and hunting preserves; in that year Marie de' Medici ordered the first improvement, a tree-lined drive along the Seine called the *Cours la Reine*. In 1667 Louis XIV had Le Nôtre lay out a long straight promenade through the area, continuing the perspective of the Tuileries' Grande Allée.

For the next few decades, the Champs-Elysées was a less aristocratic promenade; all Paris came on Sundays for a bit of fresh air, and in 1709 the pleasure promenade took its present name, the 'Elysian Fields'. The upper part of the avenue, already partly built-up, saw a speculative boom in the reign of Napoleon III. The lower part, below the Rond-Point, was saved only because it served as a pleasure ground for all the late 19th-century exhibitions, a delightful bower of groves and avenues, Chinese lanterns, brightly painted pavilions, ice cream and lemonade. There was a glassed-in Winter Garden with banana trees; dances were held there at night. Outside there were *café-concerts* under the trees. Parisians and visitors agreed that it was the pleasantest place in the world.

The upper Champs-Elysées, after decades of decline, has been the subject of a major renovation which included everything from pavement surfaces to a second row of *platanes* (plane trees) on each side. Even the car dealers, hamburger stands, banks and obscure airline offices that took over the once-fashionable street in the 1970s have cleaned themselves up. The scheme is working well; the great avenue is always packed, and it's a considerably more lively and interesting place than ten years ago. The north side is the more popular, usually in the sun and where most of the shops are to be found. A *café crème* sitting outside is a famous treat, while the world turns about you on its axe.

Arc de Triomphe

Place Charles-de-Gaulle. Open Oct–Mar daily 10–5.30;
April–Sept daily 9.30–6.30, Fri 9.30am-10pm; adm.
Pedestrian tunnel on righthand side of Champs-Elysées.

The Arc de Triomphe is not a tribute to Napoleon, although it certainly would have been if the Emperor had been around to finish it. The arch commemorates the armies of the Revolution: the heroic, improvised citizen levy that not only protected their new freedoms against the Anciens Régimes of the rest of Europe, but actually liberated other peoples.

In the 18th century the Etoile was a rustic *rond-point* on the boundaries of the city. Napoleon did have the idea for the arch, after his smashing victories of 1805–6; originally he wanted it in Place de la Bastille, but his sycophants convinced him that this

Calendar of Events

Dates for nearly all the events listed below change every year. The tourist office provides precise dates.

Mar Festival des Instruments Anciens – medieval, Renaissance and Baroque music, mostly in the city's churches.

Late April Waiters' race – 8km circuit holding their trays, beginning and ending at the Hôtel de Ville; Foire du Trône – ancient traditional fun fair, Porte Dorée, Bois de Vincennes.

Late April–May Foire de Paris at the Porte de Versailles – the closest equivalent of the old St-Germain fair, with all kinds of new-fangled gadgets, food, wine and more.

1 May Trade unions march and people buy sprigs of *muguet* (lily of the valley) for good luck while the National Front rallies around the statue of Joan of Arc in Place des Pyramides.

Some time in May Salon de Montrouge – one of Paris' more intriguing annual art shows; Marathon International de Paris – 42km race from Place de la Concorde, which ends at the Hippodrome de Vincennes.

Late May–June French Open Tennis Championships at Roland Garros.

Pentecost Dual pilgrimages by modern Catholics and traditionalist Lefèbvrites from Chartres to Sacré-Coeur.

Mid-June International fireworks contest, in Chantilly.

Mid-June–July Festival de St-Denis – classical music concerts.

Late June St John's Eve – fireworks at Sacré-Coeur; Fête du Marais – jazz and classical music and drama.

21 June Fête de la Musique – free concerts across town.

Early July La Villette Jazz Festival – 2wk-long, big-name jazz fest at Parc de la Villette.

14 July Military parade on the Champs-Elysées; fireworks at Trocadéro; Bastille Ball, rollicking all-night gay party.

A few days later End of the Tour de France on the Champs-Elysées.

Sept Fête de l'Humanité – lively national Communist festival, in suburban La Courneuve.

Sept–Dec Festival de l'Automne – music dance and drama.

Oct FIAC – Foire Internationale de l'Art Contemporain – choice selections from galleries around the world.

First Sat Oct Wine harvest in Montmartre – lots of good clean fun.

Mid-Oct 20km de Paris race, open to all and sundry – entries in past years have numbered over 20,000.

Nov Salon d'Automne – major art salon in the Grand Palais.

25 Nov Les Catherinettes – women in the fashion trade who are 26 and single don outrageous hats made by co-workers – '*coiffer la Ste-Catherine*'.

Christmas Eve Midnight *Réveillon* feast – Parisians eat out and gorge like geese. Billions of oysters meet their maker.

New Year's Eve St-Sylvestre – occasion for another ultra-rich midnight feast – in a week, Paris downs 2,000 tons of foie gras.

prominent spot in the fashionable west end would be much more fitting. A life-size model was erected in 1810, during the celebrations for Napoleon's marriage to Marie-Louise of Austria.

Not surprisingly, work stopped cold in 1815. Eight years later, Louis XVIII had the really contemptible idea of finishing it as a monument to his own 'triumph' – sending an army to put down a democratic revolt in Spain. But by the reign of Louis-Philippe, the 'myth of Napoleon' had already begun its strange progress. Times were dull; Frenchmen had forgotten the huge numbers of their countrymen Napoleon had sent to die for his glory. A massive effort to complete the arch was mounted in 1832, and they had it finished four years later. And four years after that Napoleon's remains rolled under the arch, on a grey November day where the silence of the crowds was broken only by a few old veterans croaking 'Vive l'Empereur!' Napoleon III had Baron Haussmann make the Etoile into the showcase of Paris.

It isn't just the location and the historical connotations that make this such an important landmark. It's also a rather splendid arch. Any Frenchman would recognize the group on the right side, facing the Champs-Elysées: the dramatic *Departure of the Volunteers* in 1792, also known as the *Marseillaise*. Inside is a small **museum** of the arch; from there you can climb up to the roof for a remarkable view of the *Grand Axe* and the pie-slice blocks around the Etoile (especially recommended after dark).

Montmartre

From the Eiffel Tower or the top of the Centre Pompidou , gleaming white Montmartre resembles an Italian hill town from Mars. A closer inspection reveals honky-tonk tourist Paris at its ripest, churning francs from the fantasy-nostalgia mill for the good old days of Toulouse-Lautrec, can-can girls, Renoir and Picasso. On the other hand, the area has some of Paris' last secret alleys and picturesque streets, just as pretty as they were when Utrillo painted them.

The Romans called this 423ft 'mountain' *Mons Mercurii*, after its hilltop shrine to the god of commerce, but he lost his billing in the 9th century when the abbot of St-Denis renamed it the Hill of Martyrs, Montmartre, the *Butte Sacrée*. Montmartre became a commune (pop. 638) during the Revolution, renamed Mont Marat. The population of the hill soared as workers took refuge from Baron Haussmann's demolitions, but Paris came after them and gobbled up Montmartre itself in 1860.

The first artists, poets and composers had already moved into Montmartre with the workers, drawn by cheap rents and the quality of its air and light. The police knew the village rather as the resort of *apaches*, gangs of Parisian toughs distinguished by their wide berets and corduroy trousers; when Erik Satie began his career playing piano in a Montmartre cabaret, he came to work armed with a hammer. After the First World War the bohemians moved off to the lower rents of Montparnasse, leaving their reputation to the sideshow artists.

Sacré-Cœur

Open daily 6.45–11; free. Dome and crypt open daily 9–6; adm.

The story goes that between 1673 and 1689 Jesus Christ appeared to a nun from the Royal Abbey of Montmartre, demanding a church to the glory of his Divine Heart 'to serve France and repair the bitterness and outrages that have wasted her'. The project was put to every regime that followed, but nothing happened until the Commune and the fall of Rome (Napoleon III had been protecting the pope from the Italians, who captured Rome in 1870).

Many Parisians regard the result with some embarrassment, and not only for its preposterous Romano-Byzantine architecture. The national vow promising its

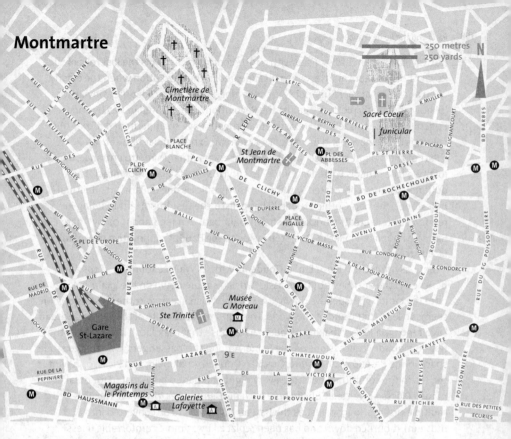

construction was imposed on the city by a vote in the National Assembly in 1873, despite opposition by radicals and many Montmartrois, who claimed it would ruin the character of the Butte (as indeed it has, drawing 6 million visitors a year). In the design competition the most pompous entry, by Paul Abadie, was chosen. It drove Adolphe Willette (the designer of the Moulin-Rouge) crazy: 'It isn't possible that God, if he exists, would consent to live there,' he declared. On the day the first bit, the crypt chapel, opened, he ran in and shouted: '*Vive le diable!*' The Montmartrois have honoured him with a square at the foot of Sacré-Cœur's stairs.

For a real descent into the abyss, visit the clammy **crypt**, with its neglected chapels, broken chairs, dingy cases of relics salvaged from the Royal Abbey of Montmartre, overgrown statues of praying cardinals, and a slide show on the building of Sacré-Cœur. The view from the dome isn't that much more spectacular than the view from the parvis, but you can look vertiginously down into the interior of the basilica.

The Streets of Montmartre

The **Place du Tertre** was once the main square of Montmartre village. It's hard to imagine a more blatant parody of the Butte's hallowed artistic traditions: unless you come bright and early, you can scarcely see this pretty square for the easels of a couple of hundred artists. At the east end of the Place is **St-Pierre de Montmartre**, the

Butte's oldest church, disguised with a 19th-century façade. It is the last relic of the Royal Abbey of Montmartre, which disappeared in the Revolution when the elderly, blind and deaf Mother Superior was condemned to death by Fouquier-Tinville for 'blindly and deafly plotting against the Revolution'. Consecrated in 1147 by Pope Eugenius III, the tunnels and quarries underneath have so undermined it that the columns of the nave bend inwards like a German Expressionist film set.

Part of the delight of little **Place des Abbesses** is Guimard's métro entrance, one of just two (the other is Porte-Dauphine) to survive with its glass roof intact. The outlandish church decorated with turquoise mosaics is one of Paris' architectural milestones, the neo-Gothic **St-Jean l'Evangéliste**, the first important building in reinforced concrete (the bricks are sham), built between 1894 and 1904 by Anatole de Baudot, a pupil of Viollet-le-Duc; step inside to see Baudot's innovative play of interlaced arches.

Leafy, asymmetrical **Place Emile-Goudeau**, with its Wallace fountain, steps and benches, is the antithesis of the classic Parisian square down on the 'plain' below; note the curious perspective down Rue Berthe, which like many other streets up here, seems to lead to the end of the world. This square was the site of the famous **Bateau Lavoir** (no.13), a leaky, creaking wooden warehouse that Max Jacob named after the floating laundry concessions on the Seine. Among the 'passengers' who rented studio space in the Bateau were Braque, Gris, Van Dongen, Apollinaire and Picasso; in winter the tea in the communal pot froze every night and had to be reheated for breakfast. In 1907 Picasso invented Cubism here with his *Demoiselles d'Avignon*, the girls with multiple profiles. In 1970, just as the Bateau Lavoir was to be converted into a museum, it burned down and has been replaced by 25 more comfortable if less picturesque studios; there's a small display on its predecessor in the window.

The last two of Montmartre's 30 windmills, **Moulin du Radet** (now an Italian restaurant) and to the left, **Moulin de la Galette**, are on Rue Lepic, built in 1640 and currently being restored. In the 1814 occupation (according to local legend) the miller of the Galette, his three brothers and eldest son defended their property against the Cossacks. Only the son survived, and converted the windmill into a *guinguette*, painted by Renoir (*The Ball at the Moulin de la Galette* (1876), Musée d'Orsay). **Avenue Junot**, the 'Champs-Elysées of Montmartre', was laid out in 1910, now a rare street of peaceful Art Deco houses with gardens.

The **Musée de Montmartre** (*12 Rue Cortot; open Tues–Sun 11–6; closed Mon; adm*) is a genuine neighbourhood museum, set up and run by the people of Montmartre. Behind a pretty courtyard full of giant fuchsias, you'll see prints, pictures and souvenirs that tell the real Montmartre story. There are plenty of old photos and maps of the area, some of Toulouse-Lautrec's posters and even the original sign from the *Lapin Agile*.

Le Lapin Agile on Rue des Saules opened in 1860 as the Cabaret des Assassins, but in 1880 a painter named Gil painted the mural of a nimble rabbit avoiding the pot, a play on his name: the *lapin à Gil*. In the early days, when it was a favourite of Verlaine, Renoir and Clemenceau, customers would set the table themselves and join in singsongs, originating an informal style the French call *à la bonne franquette*. In 1903

Aristide Bruant purchased the place to save it from demolition and, thanks to the good humour of his friend Frédé, it enjoyed a second period of success. Artists could pay for their meals with paintings – as Picasso did with one of his *Harlequins*, now worth millions. Now, every evening, *animateurs* attempt to recapture that first peerless rapture. Opposite, **Montmartre's Vineyard** was planted by the Montmartrois in 1886 in memory of the vines that once covered the Butte. If nothing else the harvest is an excuse for a colourful neighbourhood wine crush, which results in some 400 bottles of weedy gamay called Clos de Montmartre, the perfect accompaniment, perhaps, for a roast Paris pigeon fed on cigarette butts.

The Latin Quarter

The Latin Quarter is one of Paris' great clichés. Its name was bestowed by a student named Rabelais, for Latin (with an excruciating nasal twang) was the only language permitted in the university precincts until Napoleon said *non*. Napoleon's 19th-century successors tended to regard the Latin Quarter itself as an anachronism, and rubbed most of its medieval abbeys, colleges and slums off the map. But once you too have dispersed any lingering romantic or operatic notions that the Latin Quarter evokes, it can be good fun, especially at night when it becomes the headquarters for an informal United Nations of goodwill.

This is one of the rare corners of Paris to preserve the pre-Haussmann higgledy-piggledy. To see it all, wander the streets bordered by the Seine to the north and Boulevard St-Germain to the south, with Boulevard St-Michel to the west and the tip of the Ile de la Cité to the east. **Rue du Fouarre**, a mere stump of a street, in the 12th century was the very embryo of the university. **Rue Galande** was once the start of the bustling Roman road to Lyon; its houses are medieval, but have been much restored. On **Rue de la Bûcherie** is what must be the most famous English-language second-hand bookshop on the continent, **Shakespeare and Company** (*open daily noon to midnight*). This is the namesake of Sylvia Beach's English bookshop that stood in Rue de l'Odéon between the wars. Beach's kindness and free lending library made her a den mother for many expat writers, but none owed her as much as James Joyce. After the *Ulysses* obscenity trial in 1921 precluded the publication of the book in Britain or the US, Beach volunteered to publish it herself.

At the end of Rue de la Bûcherie, **Square René-Viviani** has Gothic odds and ends, melted by wind and rain, found near Notre-Dame; the tree on concrete crutches is the oldest in Paris. It's a false acacia, called a *robinier*, after Robin the botanist who planted it in 1602. Next to it is one of the oldest churches in Paris, the diminutive transitional Gothic **St-Julien le Pauvre** (*open daily 9–1 and 2.30–6.30; sung Mass Sun at 11am*), first built in 587. Enlarged in 1208, it became the university's assembly hall, an association that went sour when a student riot in 1524 left the church half-ruined. All members of the university were henceforth banned, and so they migrated up the hill to St-Etienne du Mont (*see* below, p.173), while poor St Julien was practically abandoned. In 1651 it was on the verge of collapse when the roof was lowered and the nave lopped off and it became a chapel for the Hôtel-Dieu.

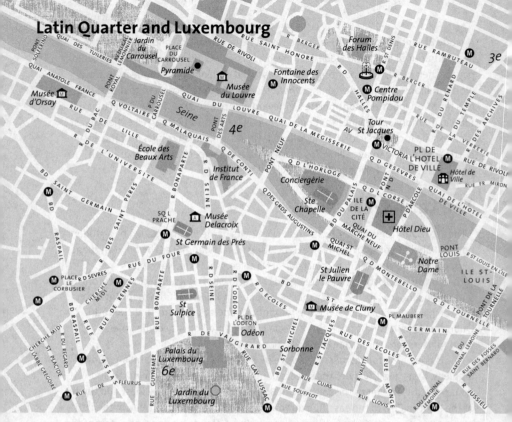

On the other side of Rue St-Jacques, **St-Séverin** (*open Mon–Sat 11–7.30*), with the menacing gargoyles, is named after a 6th-century hermit. The original Merovingian church here was rebuilt in 1031, though its replacement took 450 years to complete and gradually evolved into Flamboyant Gothic. St-Séverin's most remarkable feature is a palm-ribbed double ambulatory that seems to unwind organically from the twisted spirals of the centre column. The peaceful garden, enclosed by arcades, is actually the last charnel house in Paris. When the graveyard became too crowded, bones were dug up and embedded in the arches.

The 13th-century **Rue de la Huchette**, 'street of the little trough', is a suitable name for a vocation the lane holds to this very day: on weekend evenings the aroma of greasy spoons draws half of the students in the world. If Rue de la Huchette seems a squeeze, take a look down the first right, **Rue du Chat-qui-Pêche** (named after a long-ago inn sign of a fishing cat). At 6ft it's the narrowest street in Paris, and the last really medieval one. Rue de la Huchette peters out in Place St-Michel, a traffic vortex laid out under Napoleon III and decorated with a striking fountain by Davioud of St Michael slaying the Dragon. It marks the beginning of the Latin Quarter's main artery, **Boulevard St-Michel**, or simply Boul' Mich, laid out in 1859. What you can't see any longer are its paving stones, which proved too convenient for slinging at the police in May 1968 and now lie under a thick coat of asphalt.

Musée National du Moyen Age (Musée de Cluny)

6 Place Paul-Painlevé. Open daily 9.15–5.45; closed Tues; adm, half-price Sun.

Above the corner of Boulevards St-Michel and St-Germain rise the baths, or Thermes, the oldest surviving Roman monument in Paris, standing next to the Hôtel de Cluny, the Paris residence of the powerful abbots, itself one of only two Gothic mansions still standing in Paris. Fittingly, the two contain one of the world's great collections of medieval art, a continuous trove of the rare and the beautiful in exquisite detail to linger over all afternoon.

Among the highlights: in **Salle III**, a gorgeous English leopard embroidery believed to have been the saddlecloth of Edward III; in **Salle IV**, a delightful series of six tapestries called *La Vie Seigneuriale* on the good life 500 years ago, contemporary with the Hôtel de Cluny itself; in **Salle V**, 15th-century alabasters from Nottingham. Beyond, in the Roman section of the museum, **Salle VIII** contains the museum's newest exhibit: 21 sad, solemn, erosion-scarred heads of the kings of Judea from the façade of Notre-Dame. Revolutionaries, mistaking them for French kings, had beheaded the statues in 1793; a Catholic Royalist buried them face down in a courtyard in Rue de la Chaussée-d'Antin, where they lay until their rediscovery in 1977.

Lofty, vast **Salle XII** is the *frigidarium* of the Roman baths. Wide-arched openings admit light; there are niches in the walls for statues, and remains of drains in the floor. It is the only Roman bath in France to keep its roof – three barrel vaults linked by a groin vault in the centre, ending at the corners with capitals carved with ships' prows. In the centre are five large blocks from an altar to Jupiter, erected under Tiberius and discovered under the choir of Notre-Dame.

Salle XIV, a long gallery of retables, painting and sculpture, contains two masterpieces: the *Pietà de Tarascon* (1450s), influenced by Italian and Flemish artists who painted in the papal entourage of Avignon, and a moving figure of *Marie Madeleine*, sculpted in Brussels *c.* 1500. Other rooms contain ivories, crowns, a rare golden rose, reliquaries, 4th-century lion heads in rock crystal, and exquisite works in gold and enamel. In **Salle XVIII**, where you can leaf through a 15th-century Book of Hours, the walls are hung with the first of 23 tapestries on the *Life of St Stephen* (1490). The chapel (**Salle XX**) is a flamboyant gem.

The Lady and the Unicorn

Upstairs, Salle XIII is a rotunda containing Cluny's greatest treasure: the six Aubusson tapestries of **La Dame à la Licorne**, dating from the late 15th century. Woven for Le Viste, a Lyonnese noble family, the tapestries were only rediscovered in the 19th century, rolled up and mouldering away in an obscure château in the Limousin. The lady, unicorn and lion appear in each scene, on a blue foreground and red background called *millefleurs*, strewn with a thousand flowers, birds and animals in the early Renaissance's fresh delight in nature. The first scenes appear to be allegories of the five senses, but the meaning of the sixth, where the legend on the tent reads *A mon seul désir*, will always remain a charming mystery.

The Sorbonne

The high standards of inquiry and scholarship at the University of Paris were set by Peter Abelard, one of the great thinkers of the Middle Ages, and it made the Left Bank a 'paradise of pleasure' for intellectuals and students from across Europe. In 1180 Philippe-Auguste enclosed the whole area in his *enceinte*. Paris' first college, supplying room and board to poor students, was founded at the same time, and among the scores of others that followed was the Sorbonne, founded in 1257 by Robert de Sorbon, chaplain to St Louis.

The heady freedom of thought that made Paris University great in the 13th century drew the greatest minds of the day. But when Philippe le Bel convinced the theological judges at the Sorbonne that they should condemn the Knights Templars in 1312, he cursed the university with a political role that compromises its independence to this day. At the trial of Joan of Arc the Sorbonne supplied the prosecutor, Pierre Cauchon, who sent the Maid to the stake.

In 1470 three Germans were invited to the Sorbonne to start the first printing press in France, beginning a renaissance of intellectual life on the Left Bank, although the Sorbonne itself proved too reactionary to satisfy the new thirst for knowledge. Richelieu, appointed chancellor in 1622, tried to revive its flagging status with extensive rebuilding of the college. Nothing he could do, however, halted the Latin Quarter's decline into a volatile slum. The Revolution had no qualms about closing the whole university down as the rubber stamp of King and Church. Napoleon resuscitated the university, but there was no going back to the old ways – if the Sorbonne was political, so were its students, who played roles in the upheavals of the 19th century, who battled the Nazis in Place St-Michel, protested against the war in Algeria, and in May 1968 shocked the government with their famous uprising. But the government has accomplished its agenda anyway: the rebellious Sorbonne has been blasted into a centreless prism of thirteen campuses scattered throughout Paris.

Enter the *cour d'honneur* at 17 Rue de la Sorbonne to see what survives from Richelieu's day: the domed **Chapelle de Ste-Ursule de la Sorbonne** (*1630; open only (and rarely) for temporary exhibitions*). The interior decoration was destroyed when the *sans-culottes* converted it into a Temple of Reason, except for paintings in the spandrels by Philippe de Champaigne and the white marble tomb of Richelieu. If you come between lectures (or can manage to sit through one – they're free), take a look in the **Grand Amphithéâtre** to see the celebrated fresco in lollipop colours of *Le Bois Sacré* by Puvis de Chavannes.

Panthéon

Place du Panthéon. Open daily Oct–Mar 10–6.15; last ticket 5.30; April–Sept 9.30–6.30, last ticket 5.45; adm; under-18s free.

Old Ste-Geneviève, housing the relics of the patron saint of Paris (*see* below), was demolished because Louis XV, after a close call with the grim reaper in 1744, had vowed to construct her a new basilica. Some French critics trumpet the result, by Jacques-Germain Soufflot, as 'the first example of perfect architecture', when in fact the Panthéon is a textbook case of how *not* to build, an impoverished bastard of a design that has always had difficulties fulfilling even the most basic tenet of architecture: standing up.

It had just been completed in 1790 when the Revolution kicked off its muddled history by co-opting it as a Panthéon to honour its Great Men. Even this didn't start on the right foot, when two of the first pantheonized corpses, those of Mirabeau and Marat, were given the bum's rush in the changing political climate. Napoleon reconverted the Panthéon to a church, and the remains of two other inmates, Rousseau and Voltaire, were shunted off into a closet. Louis-Philippe thought the church was better as a Panthéon; in 1851 Napoleon III made it back into a church. In 1871 the cross was turned into a pole for the red flag when the Panthéon became the Left-Bank headquarters of the Commune. It was a church again until 1885, when Victor Hugo died. Hugo was so inflated that no ordinary tomb would hold him, and his funeral inaugurated the building's current status.

The Panthéon stands on the summit of the Gallo-Roman Mont Leucotitius (Mont Lutèce), which has been known since the Middle Ages as **Montagne Ste-Geneviève**. In 451, fresh from pillaging and deflowering 11,000 virgins in Cologne, Attila and the Huns marched towards Lutèce looking for more fun. Paris' Romans fled in terror to Orléans, but the native Celts, the Parisii, stuck around when Geneviève, a holy virgin, assured them that God would spare the city. She was right; at the last minute, the Huns veered off and sacked Orléans.

When Clovis converted to Christianity, he built on Montagne Ste-Geneviève a basilica dedicated to SS Peter and Paul. In 512 he was buried there, next to his wife Clotilde, and Geneviève, but such a cult grew around the miracle-working tomb of Geneviève that the church was expanded and renamed. In 1220 Philippe Auguste's wall around the Latin Quarter was finished – at no.3 Rue Clovis you can see a stretch of it, minus its original crenellations – and by the next year, so many students had moved into the quarter that a new chapel, St-Etienne, was built next to Ste-Geneviève to accommodate them. In 1802 old Ste-Geneviève was demolished to make way for Rue Clovis. Fortunately, **St-Etienne du Mont** (*open daily 7.45–12 and 2–7.30*) remains charming, asymmetrical and intact. This St-Etienne was begun in 1492, to squeeze in the great press of students. It retains a very fetching *jubé*, or rood screen, the only one left in Paris. In the ambulatory are the graves and epitaphs of Blaise Pascal (d. 1662) and Racine (d. 1699) and, just beyond them, surrounded by *ex-voto* plaques and paintings, is the **Chapel of Ste-Geneviève**, still one of the busiest pilgrimage sites in Paris.

Mouffetard and Jussieu

This *quartier*, east of the medieval walls that cradled the Latin Quarter for most of its history, offers an unusual cocktail of sights and smells that hardly seems to belong to the same city as the Eiffel Tower and Champs-Elysées – gossipy village streets, a tropical garden, a Maghrebi mosque and old geezers playing *boules* in a Roman arena.

Picturesque and piquant, the **Place de la Contrescarpe** (a bit behind St-Etienne) dates only from 1852, when the 14th-century Porte Bourdelle was demolished. For the next hundred years Paris' tramps flocked here, and now, even though most of the houses have been restored, it still has a bohemian atmosphere, especially at week-ends. Rabelais, Ronsard, du Bellay and the other Renaissance poets of the Pléiade would come to make merry at the Cabaret de la Pomme de Pin, at the corner of Rue Blainville (plaque at no.1). Just off the Contrescarpe, at no.50 Rue Descartes, a plaque shows the position of Porte Bourdel with its drawbridge; further along, there's a 'Hemingway-was-here' plaque, and one at no.39 (now a restaurant) commemorates Paul Verlaine, who died in 1896 in a squalid hotel. In his last years, after his fiery love affair with Rimbaud ended with pistol shots and a prison term, the poet had become Paris' most famous anti-hero, a wasted, pathetic figure, haunting Left Bank cafés to extinguish his brain cells in absinthe.

Leading off Place de la Contrescarpe is **Rue Rollin**, a treeless street of blonde houses more Mediterranean than Parisian. A plaque at no.14 marks Descartes' address in Paris. A good Catholic, he nevertheless preferred the Protestant Netherlands, and sniffed that while in France 'what most disgusted me was that no one seemed to want to know anything about me except what I looked like, so I began to believe that they wanted me in France the way they might want an elephant or a panther, because it is rare, and not because it is useful.' The **Arènes de Lutèce**, on the other side of Rue Monge, are the slight remains of Lutetia's Roman amphitheatre (now a garden, football pitch and *boules* court) dating from the 2nd century. Originally it could seat 10,000 – half the entire population of Lutetia, which if nothing else proves that Parisians have always been inveterate theatre-goers. The amphitheatre was too convenient a quarry to survive the Dark Ages, when its stone went into fortifying the Ile de la Cité. What remained was forgotten until rediscovered in 1869, restored in 1917 and, incredibly, almost demolished in 1980 for a housing project. Don't miss the knotty beech in the gardens: famous as the crookedest tree growing in Paris.

Rue Mouffetard

Place de la Contrescarpe also stands at the top of Rue Mouffetard, named after the *mofette* or stench that rose from the tanners and dyers along the Bièvre, a once bucolic tributary of the Seine which became an open sewer and was covered over. The street itself is one of the most ancient in Paris, following the path of the Roman road to Lyon. Ever since then it has been lined with inns and taverns for the wayfarer; while strolling down the 'Mouff' and poking in its capillary lanes and courtyards you can pick out a number of old signs, such as the carved oak at no.69 for the Vieux Chêne, which began as a Revolutionary club. Rue du Pot-de-Fer owes its name to the Fontaine du Pot-de-Fer, one of fourteen fountains donated by Marie de' Medici. In 1928, 25-year-old George Orwell moved into a seedy hotel at no.6 Rue du Pot-de-Fer to live off his meagre savings while he learned the craft of writing; when he was robbed he was reduced to washing dishes in a big hotel in the Rue de Rivoli – the source for his first published book *Down and Out in Paris and London*. Further south, beyond Rue de l'Epée-de-Bois, begins Rue Mouffetard's **market** (*closed Mon*), where shops spill out to join pavement stalls, cascading with fruit and vegetables, cheeses, seafood, pâtés, sausages, bread and more, with an occasional exotic touch such as the African market in Rue de l'Arbalète.

The **Grande Mosquée de Paris** (*Rue Georges-Desplas; open for visits daily 9–12 and 2–6; closed Fri; adm*) was built between 1922 and 1926 in remembrance of the Muslim dead in the First World War and as a symbol of Franco-Moroccan friendship, and is nominally the central mosque for France's 4 million-plus faithful. A series of interior courtyards gives on to the sumptuous prayer room, where the domes were decorated by rival teams of Moroccan artisans competing in geometric ingenuity. During Ramadan the mosque is well attended and a fair of religious items is held in the main courtyard, but at other times the place is almost deserted. Short tours of the building are available in French, on request. Behind the mosque, at nos. 39 and 41 Rue Geoffroy-St-Hilaire, there's a Turkish **hammam** (*men Fri and Sun, women on other days 11–8; closed Tues*), a quiet courtyard café serving mint tea and Middle Eastern pastries, a couscous restaurant and an arts and crafts shop.

Jardin des Plantes

In 1626 doctors Jean Hérouard and Guy de La Brosse convinced their best-known patient, Louis XIII, to establish a botanical garden of medicinal plants in the capital, and the country's greatest botanists were sent around the world to collect 2,500 species of plants and exotic trees. In 1793 the Convention created the School and Museum of Natural History, and galleries and research laboratories went up along the flanks of the gardens.

The most endearing feature of the Jardin des Plantes is a 17th-century dump that one of the botanists, the Comte de Buffon, converted into a garden **labyrinth** (up on the little hill), topped by a bronze temple with a sundial called the **Gloriette de Buffon** (1786). Near the maze towers a cedar of Lebanon, a seedling from Kew Gardens brought to Paris in 1734 by Bernard de Jussieu. And south of the Grand Amphitheatre (a small neoclassical building near the entrance), look for one of the oddest trees, the ironbark from Iran. The tropical forest in the **Serre Tropicale** just to the south (*open daily 10–5; closed Tues; adm*) is sheltered in one of the world's first iron and glass pavilions, complete with mini-waterfall, stream and turtles; a second hothouse at the back bristles with cacti. In front, a fence encloses the 2,600 labelled plants of the **Botanical School gardens** (*open summer daily 7.30am–7.45pm; winter daily 10–12 and 2–5; closed Tues, Sun and hols*).

At the far west end of the formal parterres looms the impressive Zoology Building, the centrepiece of the Jardin des Plantes' ensemble of natural history museums. After being closed for thirty years, the former zoology section is back with a vengeance as the **Grande Galerie de l'Evolution** (*entrance Rue Censier; open daily 10–5; closed Tues; adm*), full of every sort of 'interactive exhibit' and audio-visual trick, all on the theme of evolution and the diversity of life (pull-out English translations are slotted in the benches). The long building beyond it houses the **Galerie de Minéralogie** (*open daily 10–5; closed Tues; adm*), displaying giant quartz crystals from Brazil, as well as meteorites, and the museum treasure – two rooms of precious gems, on their own and in schmaltzy objets d'art that belonged to Louis XIV.

Opposite the formal parterres, and east beyond the rose gardens, Allée de Jussieu leads to the **Ménagerie** (*open summer Mon–Sat 9–6, Sun 9–6.30; winter 10–5; closed hols; adm*). In 1793 the Commune ordered all the wild beasts in circuses and travelling zoos to be sent to the Jardin des Plantes to form a public ménagerie. Nowadays larger zoo creatures are kept at Vincennes, while the Ménagerie has smaller animals, to be viewed up close – reptiles, birds of prey, foetus-like albino axolotls, insects (in the micro-zoo) deer, monkeys and a pair of bears.

Last and most surreal is the massive, eclectic **Galerie de Paléontologie**, overlooking Place Valhubert and the Gare d'Austerlitz (*open daily 10–5; closed Tues; adm*). The bas-reliefs of bugs, scorpions and violent battles (man v. bear, man v. crocs) that decorate the exterior reach a climax just inside the door, with a huge statue of an orang-utan strangling a man. The displays – skeletons of mammoths, mammals and giant birds, burdened with names like Mégaptère Boops – march in frozen ranks down the centre of the galleries. Along the walls, glass cases contain a nightmarish collection of disembodied, greyish organs in bottles – a tiger's liver; a giraffe's uterus; camel, elephant and rhino willies; and a two-headed baby named Marie et Christine.

Institut du Monde Arabe

1 Rue des Fossés St-Bernard. Open Tues–Sun 10–6; closed Mon.

The coolly elegant riverside Institut du Monde Arabe, completed in 1987, is nearly everyone's favourite contemporary building in Paris. The competition for the design was won in 1981 by Jean Nouvel (a Frenchman, for once), who came up with a pair of long, thin buildings, one gracefully curved to follow the line of the quay. Their walls are covered with window panels inspired by ancient Islamic geometric patterns, but equipped with photo-electric cells that activate their dilation or contraction according to the amount of sunlight – with a gentle high-tech whoosh. The Institut is financed by the French government and 22 Arab countries, with the goal of introducing Islamic civilization to the public and facilitating cultural exchanges. Besides an extensive library (on the third floor, around a great spiral ramp), there are rotating exhibitions, a shop of books and crafts, and recordings and films to see in the *Espace Son et Image*. The **museum** (*adm*), spread out on several floors, displays examples of the art and exquisite craftsmanship of the Arab world.

St-Germain

France is one country where brainy philosophers get respect, and St-Germain is their citadel; in the postwar decades there were enough eggheads here to make omelettes, sizzling and puffing away with the latest fashionable philosophy. Since the 1960s it has cooled considerably; and, in the inevitable urban cycles, the haunts of the avant-garde have now been gentrified. But despite the absurd rents and surplus posers, St-Germain's essential conviviality remains intact. Its narrow streets, scarcely

A Literary Rendez-vous

Whether **Les Deux Magots** is '*le rendez-vous de l'élite intellectuelle*', according to its own menu, or the 'Two Maggots' of American teenagers, the café does offer grandstand views of St-Germain. Inside, the two statues of Chinese mandarins or *magots* date from the shop's original vocation – selling silks. The name was retained when it became a café in 1875; Mallarmé, Verlaine and Rimbaud gave it its literary seal of approval in the 1880s, and the café has distributed its own literary prize since 1933. A few doors down Boulevard St-Germain, its rival **Le Flore** opened in 1890. It too attracted a brainy clientele: Picasso and Apollinaire would edit art magazines in the back, Sartre and Camus were regulars, but stalwartly ignored each other's presence. On the south side of the boulevard, 'Le Drugstore', a groovy hangout in the 1960s, has recently succumbed to changing tastes, although its neighbour, **Brasserie Lipp**, still packs in Paris' Who's Who with a *choucroute* unchanged since 1920.

violated by the planners of the last two centuries, its art galleries, cafés and bookshops, and the Luxembourg Gardens cluttered with chairs, all invite you to gas the day away in the scholarly spirit of those first eggheads, Voltaire and Diderot, if not Camus, Sartre, Simone de Beauvoir and Foucault.

If urbanity is St-Germain's middle name, it owes much to its parent, the Benedictine abbey of St-Germain-des-Prés. The monks, specialists in ancient manuscripts, set the intellectual tone of the quarter; art, food and fashion from the rest of Europe and the East were introduced into Paris through the abbey's month-long fair. Theatres prospered; the first coffee houses opened here; and actors, Protestants and foreign artists could live in peace in the then independent town of St-Germain. Ideas circulated more freely as well; if Rousseau and Voltaire got short shrift at the Sorbonne, they were published and discussed in St-Germain. In its cafés Paris' intellectuals kept the spark alive in a circle around Jean-Paul Sartre and Simone de Beauvoir, the notebook-scribbling high priest and priestess of St-Germain. Everyone was tremendously cool, which meant being tremendously bored; jaded youth stewed in existential *ennui*. Today jaded youth can hardly afford a coffee on Boulevard St-Germain, and switched-on couples go deep into debt to buy a former maid's rooms tucked under a steep mansard roof. Meanwhile, the contemporary Parisian art world has flown over the river to the Marais, Beaubourg and Bastille, while the arteries of St-Germain's galleries harden around well-established artists and plain old antiques.

When Childebert I, son of Clovis, returned from the siege of Saragossa in 543, his booty included a piece of the True Cross and the tunic of St Vincent. Germanus, bishop of Paris, convinced Childebert that he should found an abbey to house the relics. When Germanus himself was canonized, the church became **St-Germain-des-Prés**. It was one of the most important Benedictine monasteries in France, and until Dagobert (d. 639) it was the burial place of the Merovingian kings. Of this early church little has survived: capitals, now in the Musée de Cluny, and the base of the massive tower on the west front. The rest was rebuilt in 1193; architect Peter de Montreuil added a Lady Chapel, as beautiful as his Sainte-Chapelle. In 1789 St-Germain's precious tombs and reliquaries were destroyed, and the famous library confiscated, while the church was converted into a saltpetre factory. In 1840 Victor Hugo led a campaign for St-Germain's restoration, and for the next 20 years much of what the Revolutionaries missed fell victim to the hacks hired to save it. The marble shafts in the columns above the arcade are the only Merovingian work *in situ* in Paris.

Serene Place Furstemberg with its delicate paulownia trees is a dainty gem of urban design that traces the ancient cloister of the abbots' palace. In the old abbey stable is the **Musée Delacroix** (*open daily 9.30–5; closed Tues; adm*), the last home of Eugène Delacroix, who moved here in 1857. Sketches, etchings and a dozen minor paintings hang in his lodgings and atelier, and there's a quiet garden that suited the old bachelor to a T. For, despite the romantic, exotic pre-Impressionistic fervour of his paintings, Delacroix liked his peace and quiet.

Down Rue Bonaparte, the **Ecole des Beaux-Arts** (*courtyards open 8am–8pm; other adm only during exhibitions*) holds exhibitions in the oldest buildings on this site: Queen Marguerite de Valois' Chapelle des Louanges (1606; the first dome in Paris) and a chapel (1619; with elegant doors by Goujon) built for an Augustine monastery after Marguerite's death. In 1816 this convent became the school of fine arts. The main courtyard contains a collage of architectural fragments, most notably the central façade of Henri II's Château d'Anet (1548), with another fine door by Goujon. The **Rue des Beaux-Arts** is one of the main axes of the slowly churning St-Germain art world. The original galleries opened in the 1920s and shocked the public by being the first to show modern and abstract works. In 1900 Oscar Wilde, aged 46 but broken by his prison term, came to die 'beyond his means' in the former Hôtel d'Allemagne (no.13). At least he kept his good taste to the very end. 'Either this wallpaper goes, or I do,' he grumbled and, never failing a cue, went.

Off Rue St-André-des-Arts is the **Carrefour de Buci**, in the 18th century one of the most fashionable crossroads of the Left Bank, and now the city's most fashionable market, particularly at weekends. When you can pull yourself away from the meticulous displays of smoked salmon and *pâtés en croûte*, backtrack a few giant steps along Rue St-André-des-Arts for a look at the cobblestoned **Cour du Commerce St-André**, opened in 1776. This is Paris' oldest *passage*, built before new iron and glass engineering techniques were to make them the marvel of the Right Bank. Midway, to your left, extend three courtyards known as the **Cour de Rohan**. In the first courtyard, the gentle Dr Joseph-Ignace Guillotin and a carpenter named Schmidt used sheep to test their decapitation machine. There's a pretty Renaissance house covered with vines in the second courtyard, part of the *hôtel* of Diane de Poitiers; the iron tripod in the corner was a once common urban sight, a *pas de mule* (horse mount).

The quartier's other big church, **St-Sulpice**, dates from 1646; by the time the builders reached the façade in 1732, the original Baroque plan seemed old-fashioned, resulting in a competition, won by an even more antique design by a Florentine named Servandoni. Inside the grey, cavernous nave, railway clocks tick down the minutes to the next TGV to heaven. The organ is one of the most seriously overwrought in Paris; the holy water stoups are two enormous clam shells, gifts from Venice to François I. In such a setting, the lush, romantic murals by Delacroix in the first chapel on the right radiate warmth. The last chapel before the right transept contains the Hallowe'en *tomb of Curé Languet de Gergy* (1750) by Michelangelo Slodtz. The copper strip across the transept traces the Paris meridian, and if you come at the winter solstice you'll see a sunray strike the centre of the obelisk.

Built by Louis XV in 1782, the neoclassical **Théâtre de l'Odéon** was the first public theatre in Paris designed exclusively for drama. Its austere Doric temple façade is attractively set in the semicircular Place de l'Odéon, while porticoes on either flank integrate the building into the square. After fires in 1807 and 1818, the theatre was faithfully reconstructed to the original design. For decades, however, the Odéon was a commercial flop. During the Revolution its troupe split, the pro-Republican actors going off to the Comédie Française and the Royalists sticking it out here until they were carted off to the slammer. In the next century the theatre had a few successes (Bizet's *L'Arlésienne*, in 1872), but it only became popular after the Second World War when Jean-Louis Barrault and Madeleine Renaud quickened its pulse with contemporary drama. In May 1968 Barrault and Renaud even took their enthusiasm to the streets, distributing Roman helmets from the wardrobe to protect student skulls from billy clubs. They were immediately sacked.

Jardin du Luxembourg

The Jardin du Luxembourg is a welcome Left Bank oasis of greenery. Metal chairs are scattered under the trees and around a shady café and bandstand, although the scarce lawns are out of bounds. But the kids have all the fun, on an opulent carousel designed by Charles Garnier, riding pony carts and mini-cars, sailing boats in the Grand Bassin, or watching performances of *guignol* in the **Théâtre des Marionettes du Luxembourg** (*shows daily exc Tues from 11am; call* **t** *01 43 26 46 47; adm*).

Near the gate, the park remembers its foundress, Marie de' Medici, with the long pool of the **Fontaine de Médicis** (just east of the Palais du Luxembourg), a romantic rendezvous under the plane trees, dating from 1624 and adorned with 19th-century statuary of the lovers Acis and Galatea about to be ambushed by the jealous cyclops Polyphemus. They are only the first of the Luxembourg's numerous marble men and women. Marie de' Medici herself figures among the Great Women of France posing around the central basin; in the trees towards Rue Guynemer, there's a midget *Statue of Liberty* by Bertholdi, who modelled her on his monolithic mom and gradually made her bigger (on the Ile des Cygnes) and bigger (in New York).

Palais du Luxembourg

Jardin du Luxembourg, entrance Rue de Vaugirard. Interior open one or two Sun per month for guided tours; contact Monuments Historiques, **t** *01 44 61 20 84.*

'Twas a dark and stormy night when the newly widowed Marie de' Medici, Regent of France, ordered coachman to drive her to the Bastille, where she brazenly pinched all the money her husband, Henri IV, had set aside in case of war. Marie used it to buy land south of Rue de Vaugirard. And in 1612, on the death of the Duke of Luxembourg,

Marie added his *hôtel* (now the Petit Luxembourg) to her estate. But the regent's ambitions were hardly *petit*; in fact, she dreamed of a replica of her girlhood home, Florence's enormous Pitti Palace. Architect Salomon de Brosse managed to dissuade her in favour of a more traditional French mansion, but decorated it with Florentine touches – especially the rusticated bands of stone that give it a corrugated look, and its 'ringed' Tuscan columns. At the west end of the big Palace, at Rue de Vaugirard, the delightful **Petit Luxembourg** was Paris' first public art gallery, and the **Musée de Luxembourg** (*open daily 11–7; Thurs till 10pm; adm*) still puts on temporary exhibitions.

Montparnasse

Paris' Mount Parnassus began its career as a weedy heap of tailings dug up from the many Roman quarries in the area, a mound where students came to frolic with bottles of wine and buxom muses – hence its tongue-in-cheek name taken from the holy mountain of Apollo, the god of art and poetry. In the Middle Ages Montparnasse ground the flour for the Left Bank's baguettes; in 1780 there were still 18 working windmills. The first houses date from the 17th century, when Louis XIV built the Observatoire to create an *axe* or prospect with the Palais du Luxembourg, and laid out the Grand Cours du Midi (now Boulevard du Montparnasse). Land was still cheap enough in the early 1800s for Montparnasse to experience a first flash of fashion with its dance halls, *guingettes* and cabarets. After the construction of the Gare Montparnasse (the terminus from Brittany), a piquant workers' quarter grew up south of the Boulevard du Montparnasse; the area still boasts a strong Breton flavour.

In the 1870s Verlaine, Anatole France and Sully-Prudhomme called themselves 'The Parnassians', giving Montparnasse its first real association with the arts. Other Parnassians arrived in the early 1900s: Modigliani and Apollinaire in the lead, fleeing rising prices in Montmartre. Art connoisseurs Gertrude and Leo Stein moved in just behind them; Lenin, Trotsky and so many other revolutionaries lived in the area that the Tsarist police had a special Montparnasse unit to keep an eye on them.

After the First World War these pioneer *Monparnos* were followed by artistic and literary pilgrims and refugees from all over the world. The Hemingways, Fitzgeralds and so on, came as refugees from Prohibition; made instantly rich thanks to the dollar exchange rate, they helped to create the frenzy of *les années folles* – as the French call the 1920s – partying the night away in Montparnasse's cafés.

After the Second World War the scene changed again; the culture vultures retreated back to St-Germain and the north side of Boulevard du Montparnasse, while the neighbourhood where Americans drank themselves silly was singled out for Paris' first experiment in American-style property development, in a toadstool project called Maine-Montparnasse. Planned back in 1934, but begun only in 1961, this incorporated Paris' first skyscraper, a new railway station, a shopping mall and a concrete wasteland of urban anomie. This and similar displacements since 1975 have resulted in the 14e losing a fifth of its population, nearly all of them workers forced out into deathly suburbs.

Until the advent of London's Canary Wharf, the **Tour Montparnasse** (*viewing platforms open summer daily 9.30am–11.30pm; winter daily 9.30am–10pm; last ascent 30min before closing; adm*) was the tallest skyscraper in Europe, 656ft high and perched at the top of Rue de Rennes; visible for miles around, it sticks up like a sore tombstone, way out of proportion to the rest of the skyline. The closed-in 56th floor offers not only views but a bar, *Ciel de Paris*, and a film of aerial views over Paris; the 59th floor is an open terrace. On a clear day you can see for 25 miles; for many people this has the added plus of *not* seeing the Tour Montparnasse. The ungainly, submerged shopping mall in front overlooks Place du 18 Juin 1940, the date of de Gaulle's famous BBC speech encouraging the French to fight on.

The nearby **Mémorial de Maréchal Leclerc de Hauteclocque et de la Libération de Paris et Musée Jean Moulin** (*Bâtiment Nord-Parc; open Tues–Sun 10–5.40; adm*) has exhibits and audio visuals on the wartime careers of the general and the Resistance leader. The surrender in 1945 was signed in the **Gare Montparnasse**, first built in 1852. It had already entered Parisian mythology in 1898, when the brakes of a train speeding at 37 miles an hour failed just as it approached the station. The guard applied the Westinghouse brake and saved the passengers, but the engine went hurtling through the glass wall and came to a halt halfway across the square, crashing into a kiosk where it killed an old woman. A postcard showing the accident was so popular it had to be reprinted seven times.

Exhibition Paris

This isn't the cosy Paris of quaint *bistrots* and narrow streets; this is Paris, the national capital and showcase of France. Here at the self-designated centre of civilization both the buildings and the spaces between them are on an heroic scale, a magnitude first set by the Roi Soleil with the Invalides and Esplanade, monuments baked through the centuries then iced and glazed by a succession of world fairs.

Musée d'Orsay

1 Rue de la Légion d'Honneur, www.musee-orsay.fr.
Open Tues, Wed, Fri, Sat 10–6, Sun and 20 June–20 Sept 9–6,
Thurs 10–9.45pm; closed Mon; adm, half-price Sun.

The Gare d'Orsay is a monument born on the cusp of the 19th century: a daring work of iron weighing more than the Eiffel Tower, with a nave taller than Notre-Dame, thrown up in two years for the 1900 World Fair. The architect, Victor Laloux, professor at the Ecole des Beaux-Arts, was hired to make the façade a dignified foil for the Louvre across the river. The net result is pure Napoleon III rococola; unfortunately its platforms were too short for modern trains, and the station was abandoned in 1960. It opened as a museum in 1986. The core exhibits came from the former Jeu-de-Paume Museum and the 19th-century rooms of the Louvre. Here under one huge roof are gathered all the combative schools of painting and sculpture from 1848 to 1910, rounded out with a magnificent array of furniture, decorative arts, architectural exhibits and photography. You could easily spend a day here, and neither thirst nor starve, thanks to the museum's restaurant and rooftop café.

Highlights of the Collections

Sculptures command the entrance: Rude's piece of Romantic hyperbole, *Génie de la Patrie*, from the Arc de Triomphe, is followed inside the main door by a *Lion assis* by Barye (d. 1875), animal sculptor extraordinaire, and Rude's *Napoleon Awaking to Immortality*.

The **Salle de l'Opéra**, dedicated to Garnier's extraordinary folly, has Carpeaux's original *La Danse* pixies from the façade. A model of the Opéra (from the 1900 World Fair) is cross-sectioned so you can see all the machinery behind the scenes. The several floors of a tower called the *Pavillon Amont* offer a compendium of Second Empire and Third Republic Paris façades and architecture from Viollet-le-Duc to Frank Lloyd Wright. Best of all is a massive 1855 *View of Paris* painted by Victor Navlet from a balloon floating over the Observatoire.

There are plenty of paintings that shocked in their day: the works of **Gustave Courbet**, the formulator of Realism and the first artist to buck completely the salon system. **Manet**'s *Olympia* (1865) made people spit venom when it was shown in the Salon des Refusés: not because of the nude but because Manet merely sketched in the flowers – a photograph-inspired blur that damned it in the eyes of critics.

The **Impressionists** on the upper floor (with the best natural light) are one of the museum's glories: **Manet**'s *Le Déjeuner sur l'Herbe* (1863), an updated version of Giorgione's *Concert Champêtre* in the Louvre, was a key inspiration for the Impressionists with its masterly, experimental handling of paint. The same room has a portrait by an arty American dandy and friend of Manet and Baudelaire, who called it *Arrangement in Grey and Black no.1*, although everyone knows it as *Whistler's Mother*.

Next come **Monet**'s *Régates à Argenteuil* and steam-filled *Gare St-Lazare*, **Pissarro**'s *Les Toits Rouges* and *L'Inondation à Port-Marly*, the masterpiece of **Albert Sisley**, who was born in Paris of English parents and concentrated on the nuances of the changing colours and sensations of water, sky and mists. The *Bal du Moulin de la Galette* (1876) is **Renoir**'s irresistible evocation of the city's *bal-dansants*. Manet's *Sur la Plage*, as well as his slices of everyday life in Paris (*La Serveuse de Bocks*) influenced many, especially **Berthe Morisot**, the grande dame of Impressionism, whose subjects from her life and that of her friends form a woman's diary in paint (*Le Berceau*).

Unlike the other Impressionists **Degas** never painted out of doors or from life, but from memory; his unusual compositions *A la Bourse, L'Absinthe, Les Repasseuses* were inspired in part by the spontaneity of photography and Japanese prints. The ballet and race track became special interests of Degas after 1874, affording opportunities for even more 'spontaneous' compositions and for the study of movement.

Late Impressionists (after 1880) star Monet's series that portray the same subject at different times of day: *Les Meules* (Haystacks), five of *Les Cathédrales de Rouen* and two versions of the *Nymphéas* (waterlilies) painted at Giverny, where representation of form is so minimal as to verge on abstract constructions of pure colour. Of the many Renoirs, *Les Grandes Baigneuses* is perhaps the most extraordinary, done by an old man paralysed by rheumatism, with his brushes strapped to his wrists.

Van Gogh is well represented with *La Guinguette, L'Arlésienne, La Chambre de Van Gogh à Arles*, the merciless *Portrait de L'Artiste*, painted during his first fit of madness in Arles, and the darkly foreboding *L'Eglise d'Auvers-sur-Oise* (1890). There are early works by **Cézanne**, *La Maison du Pendu* and *Une Moderne Olympia*, inspired by Manet. The other Impressionists were not very impressed by him or vice versa, and after 1877 Cézanne spent most of his time in Aix, becoming a legend towards the end of his life. The Musée d'Orsay has masterpieces of his three favourite subjects: a landscape (*L'Estaque*), figures (*La Femme à la Cafetière, Les Joueurs de Cartes* and *Baigneurs*) and still lifes.

The **Postimpressionists** include **Georges Seurat**'s weirdly compelling *Cirque*. The most scientific of painters, Seurat set out to rescue Impressionism from the charges of frivolity by developing his distinctive pointillist style, based on the theories of the optic mixing of tones and the action of colour; when viewed from a distance, each dot of colour takes on the proper relationship with the dots around it, although remaining visible as an optic vibration.

The Salle Redon is devoted to the works of the elusive **Odilon Redon**, master colourist and pre-Freudian painter of dreams, who belonged to no school but greatly inspired the Symbolists, Surrealists and Metaphysical painters who followed (*Portrait de Gauguin*). Another room is devoted to **Toulouse-Lautrec**, who broke both legs as a child, which seriously impeded his growth. His physical afflictions may have contributed to his empathy in the penetrating portraits of 'occupationally distorted souls', especially of the prostitutes he lived with. Paintings by the intuitive 'naif' painter **Douanier Rousseau** follow (the *Charmeuse des Serpents*), along with **Gauguin**'s lush paintings from the South Seas, where he fled to escape 'diseased' civilization to rejuvenate art by becoming 'one with nature'. Chronologically the last -ism in the museum, **Fauvism** is represented by **André Derain**'s *Le Pont de Charing Cross* (1902) in the Kaganovitch collection in the last room on this floor.

The middle level hops back in time. Here among the **Symbolists** you'll find *The Wheel of Fortune* by **Burne-Jones**, who made the Pre-Raphaelites popular in France, *Summer Night* by **Winslow Homer**, the famous *Portrait of Proust* by **Jacques-Emile Blanches**, *Le Rêve* by **Puvis de Chavannes**, *Nuit d'Eté* by **Munch**, and the extraordinary, pastel-coloured *Ecole de Platon* by **Jean Delville**, where naked youths with Gibson girl hairdos languidly listen to philosophy under the wisteria.

The **Art Nouveau** section has dragonfly jewellery by **Lalique**, furniture by **Guimard** (*Banquette avec Vitrine*), a desk by **Henry Van de Velde**, and glass by **Tiffany** and **Gallé**, while the Tour Guimard contains furniture designed by architects – beautiful chairs by Guimard, **Gaudí**, **Bugatti**, **Mackintosh** and **Frank Lloyd Wright**.

Musée Rodin

77 Rue de Varenne (in the Hôtel Biron). Open Tues–Sun 9.30–5.45;
Oct–Mar Tues–Sun 9.30–4.45; closed Mon; adm, reduced price Sun;
small fee to visit the gardens only.

The Hôtel Biron (1731) is one of the most charming and best-preserved mansions in Paris from the period, fitted with distinguished façades overlooking the front courtyard and back gardens. When Auguste Rodin moved here in 1908, he was 68; his reputation as France's greatest sculptor was in the bag, and it was agreed that he would leave the state his works after he died (in 1917, ten days after marrying his mistress of over 50 years).

Rodin was the last of the great Romantics. He sculpted the literary subjects of the day, but with a personal vision that liberated sculpture from its stagnant rut as portraiture, public decoration or propaganda. He studied Michelangelo in Italy and caused his first sensation in 1876 with *The Age of Bronze* (*L'Age d'Airain*) – so realistic that he was accused of casting a live man in bronze.

In 1880 Rodin was commissioned to make a bronze door for a museum of decorative arts, resulting in the *Gates of Hell* (in the garden). Studies are scattered throughout the museum: the *Three Shadows*, Paolo Malatesta and Francesca da Rimini in *The Kiss* and *The Thinker* (outside), in a pose reminiscent of the Lost Soul in Michelangelo's *Last Judgement*. The famous *La Main de Dieu* (1898) inaugurated Rodin's departure from academic tradition in a composition purely from his imagination.

One room is dedicated to sculptor Camille Claudel, sister of poet Paul, and Rodin's mistress and model for *La France* and *L'Aurore*; here too are examples of her work before she went mad. Upstairs are paintings that Rodin owned and left to the state. Outside, amid the roses of the *Cour d'Honneur*, are *The Thinker* and other master-pieces, a delightful **garden** and a serene duck pond containing the most harrowing sculpture of all, *Ugolin and his Sons*.

Hôtel des Invalides

In 1670 Louis XIV's under-minister of war, Louvois, persuaded his warmongering king to provide a hospital for old soldiers, which could just incidentally double as a monument to the military glory and triumphs of Louis himself. Set at the head of an enormous Esplanade stretching to the Seine, the Invalides has Siamese-twin churches, back to back, originally sharing the same altar and chancel: St-Louis for the old soldiers and staff, and the Eglise-du-Dôme for royals.

St-Louis des Invalides (*open daily 10–6*) closes the south end of the majestic Cour d'Honneur, guarded by the statue of Napoleon as 'the Little Corporal', in his old grey coat and hat. As you leave the church, the arcade to your left enshrines one of the 700 Paris taxicabs requisitioned during the night of 6 September 1914 to transport 7,000 soldiers 35km to the front and save Paris at the Battle of the Marne.

It's a preview for the vast collections of the **Musée de l'Armée** (*open daily 10–6; Oct–Mar daily 10–5; adm; tickets are good for two consecutive days*). A large section is devoted to Napoleon, his stuffed dog and white horse, paintings of his retreat from

Moscow, and *Napoleon at Fontainebleau*, where the abdicating Emperor resembles a little boy slouching in his chair. The top floor, under the massive joists of the roof of the Invalides, houses the **Musée des Plans-Reliefs** (*open daily 10–5; adm*). Louis XIV began to collect these huge scale relief models of France's fortified cities and towns upon Louvois' advice in 1686. Some fill entire rooms; until 1927 they were considered a military secret.

Save your ticket for the **Eglise-du-Dôme**. Designed by Hardouin-Mansart and completed in 1706, the pointy dome is so impressive that the church itself is named after it, and so prominent on the Paris skyline that it was freshly gilded with 27½ lb of gold for the bicentennial of the Revolution. The greatest main-chancer in history, responsible on his own estimate for the death of 1,700,000 Frenchmen, Napoleon died on 21 May 1821. His wish, inscribed over the bronze doors to the crypt – 'I wish to be buried on the banks of the Seine, in the midst of the people of France, whom I have loved so dearly' – was imprudently granted by Louis-Philippe in 1840 as a bid to gain popularity. The big porphyry sarcophagus of **Napoleon's tomb** contains no fewer than six coffins fitted tightly together; one can't be too careful.

Eiffel Tower and Trocadéro

Open winter daily 9.30am–11pm; summer daily 9am–midnight; adm exp.
If you arrive later in the day, count on a good hour's wait for the lift.

The incomparable souvenir of the 1889 Fair, the Eiffel Tower was built to celebrate the Revolution's centenary and the resurrection of France after her defeat by Prussia in 1870. Derided over the last hundred years as 'a suppository', 'a giraffe', 'a criminal, sinister pencil-sharpener', it is 1,000ft (300m) of graceful iron filigree; belly-up between its four spidery paws, its 9,700 tons may look menacing, but they sit with extraordinary lightness on the soft clay of Paris, exerting as much pressure as that of a man sitting in a chair.

It was erected in two years, for less than the estimated 8 million francs, welded together with 2,500,000 rivets and built without a single fatal work accident. Until 1930, when it was surpassed by the Chrysler Building in New York, it was the tallest structure in the world. Originally the tower was painted several tints, lightening to yellow-gold at the top, so its appearance dissolved and changed according to the time of day and weather; now every five or six years, forty painters cover it with 7,700lb of a sombre maroon colour called *ferrubrou*.

The competition for the design of a 1,000ft tower resulted in 700 proposals. Gustave Eiffel was already famous for his daring bridges and viaducts; in 1886 he had designed the structural frame of the Statue of Liberty, defying all the nay-sayers who said her arm would surely blow off. In its day, the Tower's engineering daredevilry bent quite a few Parisians out of shape. Residents around the Champ de Mars feared it would fall on their heads. The artistic élite, led by Charles Gounod, Charles Garnier and Alexandre Dumas, signed a vitriolic petition against the profanation and dishonour of the capital; Guy de Maupassant left Paris for good so as never to look upon its 'metallic carcass' again. For the 1925 Exposition des Arts Décoratifs, André Citroën paid to make the Eiffel Tower the world's largest advertising sign. In 1986 sodium lamps were installed; it's usually lit up until midnight.

The Eiffel Tower has proved a litmus test of modernity. Georges Seurat painted it soon after it was built, anarchists tried to blow it up, Hitler saw it and sniffed 'Is that all?' René Clair may have had the last word in his 1924 film *Paris qui Dort*, in which an evil spell puts the whole world to sleep – except for a handful of people visiting the top of the Eiffel Tower.

To reach the **Jardins du Trocadéro**, cross the Pont d'Iéna, commissioned after Napoleon I's victory at Jena in Prussia, and decked out with imperial eagles. The gardens stretching down to the Seine were laid out for the 1878 fair and restored in 1937; today they are home to a 1900s *carrousel* and on Bastille Day they are filled with *son et lumière* followed by a blaze of fireworks.

Palais de Chaillot

Facing Place du Trocadéro are the entrances to the Palais de Chaillot's four museums. The oldest, in the east wing, is the **Musée National des Monuments Français** (*currently closed for restoration*), a collection of exact, lifesize copies of France's finest architectural features, sculptures and mural paintings from the early Romanesque period to the 19th century.

The **Musée de l'Homme** (*open daily 9.45–5.15; closed Tues; adm*) is an excellent anthropology museum, offering dusty display cases and long explanations in French of things you never dreamed existed. The best part is the gallery of African cultural anthropology, with fascinating exhibits on the life and architecture of the mysterious Dogon of the Sahel (who told anthropologist Marcel Griaule lots of things he didn't know about astronomy), a facsimile of the 1858 Royal Palace façade of King Gleté of Dahomey, and brilliant art from all over the continent. Other galleries contain excellent artefacts from Australian aborigines, Maoris and Inuits; ivories; jewellery from Yemen; kites from Malaysia; and literally tons more.

Haughty Brits may turn a blind eye, like Nelson, but France has its own proud tradition on the sea, and you'll get an extra helping of it here. As you might expect, gloriously detailed ship models make up the bulk of the exhibits in the **Musée de la Marine** (*open daily 10–5.45; closed Tues and May 1; adm*): Cousteau's *Calypso*, the carrier *Clemenceau*, pride of the modern French fleet, a room-sized 120-gun *L'Océan* from Napoleon's time, and on and on. Don't miss the collection of navigational instruments, and compasses, all pointing in different directions.

Peripheral Attractions

Many of the sights of Paris are within walking distance of one another. However, this section includes attractions located just beyond the city centre, starting at La Villette in the northeast corner, just inside the Boulevard Périphérique, and continuing clockwise around the city.

Parc de la Villette

🅜 Porte de la Villette; 19e. Cité des Sciences et de l'Industrie open Tues–Sat 10–6, Sun 10–7; adm 50F, under 7s free – the Cité des Enfants, Techno City, exhibitions, Music City, the Argonaute, Cinaxe and the Géode require separate adm. Musée de la Musique (🅜 Porte de Pantin) open Tues–Sat 12–6, Sun 10–6; adm. You can sail to La Villette in a catamaran from the Musée d'Orsay.

When the slaughterhouse was metamorphosed into the **Cité des Sciences et de l'Industrie**, a rectangle of glass and exposed girders reminiscent of the Centre Pompidou, Mitterrand's critics had their fun. As a science museum it duplicates the Palais de la Découverte (*see* p.163), only it's a little flashier and more up to date. It has its own internal television station, a staff of smartly costumed *animateurs* speaking 15 different languages, computerized magneto-sensitized tickets, 'infra-red headphones', and lasers, buzzing gimcracks and whirling gizmos. Bring children to help you get through alive. There are **Planétarium** shows (with English translations) and 3-D films in the **Louis Lumière cinema**.

On the ground floor, the **Cité des Enfants** is a brilliant place for children to experiment with plants, animals and computers, with expert attendants to help. There are two sections: one for ages 3–5, one for 5–12; **Techno Cité** is designed for children from age 11 up (*but open only on Wed and Sat during the school year*).

Across the Canal de l'Ourcq, the southern half of the Parc de La Villette is occupied by the two new white asymmetrical buildings of the **Cité de la Musique**, designed by Christian de Portzamparc: they contain concert halls (one with hyper-acoustics designed by Pierre Boulez), the Conservatoire of dance and music, and a **Musée de la Musique** with 4,500 instruments, including Stradivarius and Guarnieri violins, and Beethoven's clavichord, all cosily gathered together in one place.

Parc des Buttes-Chaumont

🅜 Buttes-Chaumont; 19e.

A rocky haunt of outlaws in the Middle Ages, well known to François Villon, the park, now Paris' loveliest, was begun in 1867. In an age when the 'picturesque' was fully in vogue, the natural charms of the Buttes weren't quite good enough. Haussmann's designers brought in thousands of tons of rock and created the artificial cliffs that are its fame today. The centrepiece is a familiar landmark, a steep island in a lake, crowned by a small classical temple, modelled after the Temple of the Sybil in Tivoli. The climb rewards you with a seldom-seen view over Montmartre and the northern parts of Paris; before the Eiffel Tower was built this was the favourite spot for suicides. Edith Piaf was literally born on the streets below, under a street-lamp, shielded behind the cloak of a kindly gendarme (there's a plaque at 72 Rue de Belleville).

Canal St-Martin

Once home to Paris' less than affluent, the long banks of the old canal between Rue du Faubourg-du-Temple and Rue Louis-Blanc (**ⓜ** *République/Goncourt/Louis Blanc; 10ᵉ*) are fast coming to life as hip Paris' new 'in' zone. The Quai de Valmy and Quai de Jemmapes are being developed into modern apartment blocks clearly competing for the oddest balcony prize; fathers and sons on in-line skates race between the raised gardens, and fishermen dangle their feet along the cobbled banks beneath the green iron bridges. At 95 Quai de Valmy, the pink, green and yellow façades of the assorted Antoine et Lili shops and wholefood café make a colourful splash between the green trees. At 102 Quai de Jemmapes is the site of the **Hôtel du Nord**, famous for being the location of Marcel Carné's 1938 film with Arletty and Louis Jouvet; it now serves traditional French cuisine in its setting full of *atmosphère*; 167 Quai de Valmy hops after 10pm to the strains of live jazz. Despite its ambitions it's not quite Amsterdam, and there are still long stretches of building sites punctuating the clusters of trendy bars, but it's a relaxing place for a summer evening stroll.

Père-Lachaise Cemetery

ⓜ *Père-Lachaise; 20ᵉ. Open Mon–Fri 7.30–6, Sat 8.30–6, Sun 9–6; 6 Nov–15 Mar daily 8–5.30.*

Père Lachaise had the best job in France. As Louis XIV's confessor, he held the keys to heaven for a king who was both superstitious and rotten to the core. It isn't surprising that Lachaise got lots of presents, which he converted to real estate here. In 1804, under Napoleon's orders, Prefect of Paris Nicholas Frochot bought the land for cemetery space. To popularize the new development, the prefect invited in a couple of celebrity corpses – Molière's and La Fontaine's.

The 'most famous cemetery in the world', and the largest in Paris, Père-Lachaise has always been a favourite place for a stroll; Balzac said he liked to come here to 'cheer himself up'. In design, it is a cross between the traditional, urban sort of French cemetery, with ponderous family mausolea in straight rows, and the modern, suburban-style model. Brongniart, the architect of the Bourse, laid it out like an English garden.

At the main entrance you can buy a good map to all the famous stiffs for 10F. There are few signs to help you find the graves you're looking for, except rock poet Jim Morrison's: his fans have thoughtfully decorated everybody else's tombs with directions in felt pen.

Père-Lachaise's senior residents are **Héloïse and Abelard**. In the 17th century prudish abbesses would pry their remains apart and put them in separate tombs, only for romantic abbesses to reunite them. In 1792 they were moved and placed in a double coffin. Other residents of note include **Chopin** (sec 11), **Balzac** (sec 48), **Bizet** (sec 68) and **Delacroix** (sec 48). To the right of the chapel is the oldest and loveliest part of Père-Lachaise, where you'll find **Corot** (sec 24), **Hugo** (sec 27), and **Molière** and **La**

Fontaine (sec 25). The wide Avenue Transversale No.1 neatly bisects the cemetery. Just beyond it, near the centre, you can visit **Simone Signoret** (sec 44), keeping company with fellow actress **Sarah Bernhardt** (sec 91). Nearby are **Proust** (sec 85) and **Apollinaire** (sec 86). The large structure in section 87 is the **Columbarium**, in which are kept the ashes of **Isadora Duncan**. One of the grandest tombs of all is Sir Jacob Epstein's tribute to **Oscar Wilde**, a sort of looming Egyptian Art Deco deity.

Bois de Vincennes

Ⓜ *Porte Dorée for the zoo;* Ⓜ *Château de Vincennes for the castle.*

Like the Bois de Boulogne, its matching bookend at the other end of Paris, Vincennes owes its existence to the French kings' love of hunting. They set it aside for that purpose in the 1100s, and even built a wall around it to keep out poachers. In the 14th century the Valois kings built its castle – a real fortified castle, not just a château, for this was the time of the Hundred Years' War. As long as the nearby Marais was fashionable, so was Vincennes, but when Louis XIV left Paris in the opposite direction, for Versailles, the neglected hunting ground was turned into a public park. During the Revolution most of it became a space for military training grounds and artillery practice, and it had to be almost completely reforested in the 1860s.

Besides the open spaces, the main attraction is the **zoo**, one of the largest in Europe (*open summer daily 9–6 or 6.30; winter daily 9–5 or 5.30; adm*), which offers giant pandas and a 220ft artificial mountain (which has started to collapse). Adjacent is one of the prettier parts of the park: the **Lac Daumesnil** with its islands, one blessed with a fake romantic ruin like the one in Buttes-Chaumont. Further east (Ⓜ *Château de Vincennes, then bus no.112*) is the **Parc Floral** (*open summer daily 9.30–8; winter till 5.30, adm*): water lilies, orchids and dahlias, and a good place to bring the kids at weekends, with rides and special entertainments.

The Castle

Open Oct–Mar daily 10–12 and 1.15–5; April–Sept daily 10–12 and 1.15–6.30; long and short guided tours; adm, free to under-18s.

The finest example of medieval secular architecture in Paris, this 'Versailles of the Middle Ages' shows what the French could build even in the sorrows of the 1300s. Begun under Philippe IV in 1337, it was completed in 1380. Under Cardinal Mazarin the complex was modernized, just in time for Louis XIV to go off to Versailles and forget about it. Louis was always short of prison cells – no king in French history locked up so many political prisoners – and Vincennes made a convenient calaboose. Napoleon, another ruler who liked to keep his cells full, made it a prison again while rebuilding the fortifications just in case. Unwittingly he provided Vincennes with a chance for a short but brilliant military career – the only bit of Paris that never surrendered in the Napoleonic Wars. The hero of the story is General Daumesnil, who had lost his leg fighting the Austrians and was given the easy job of commandant here. When the

Allies took Paris in 1814, peg-legged Daumesnil refused to submit; he sent them a message:'The Austrians got my leg at Wagram; tell them to give it back or else come in and get the other one.' During the First World War the trenches around the castle were used for shooting spies – Mata Hari was one of them.

The highlight of the tour is the **donjon,** the 14th-century keep, strong and taciturn outside, but a beautiful residence within, containing stained glass and excellent sculptural work. The **Salle des Gens d'Armes** is a lovely Gothic vaulted space. In the bedroom on the second floor Henry V of England died in 1422; they parboiled him in the kitchen to keep him nice for the trip home to London. Besides these, the tour inside takes you through the **Résidence Royale**, built by Le Vau for Louis XIV, and the **Sainte-Chapelle**, a copy of the famous one.

The Catacombes

Ⓜ *Denfert-Rochereau; 14e. Open Tues–Fri 2–4; Sat and Sun 9–11 and 2–4; closed Mon and hols; adm.*

Down, down the 90 steps of a spiral stair, and a tramp through damp and dreary tunnels to a vicious blue puddle called the *source de Léthé*, inhabited by little pale-eyed creatures who dine on bone moss. Then the doorway inscribed:'Halt! This is the empire of the dead', beyond which is the main attraction: the last earthly remains of Mirabeau, Rabelais, Madame de Pompadour and five to six million other Parisians removed here beginning in 1786 from the putrid, overflowing cemetery of the Innocents and nearly every other churchyard in Paris. Tibias are stacked as neatly as tinned goods in a supermarket. Skulls, with a nice patina of age, are arranged decoratively in cross or heart shapes. The ossuary, with its remarkable acoustics, was dubbed the catacombs in Paris' eternal effort to ape Rome, and has been a tourist attraction since the day it opened.

Bois de Boulogne

After the Eiffel Tower, the Bois de Boulogne was not so long ago the most visited place in Paris – 'the world capital of prostitution' no less, where every day over a million francs changed hands. It was a venerable tradition. François I built the Château de Boulogne here, where he installed his mistress, La Ferronnière; it is said he died of loving her too fervently. Other kings installed their own loves – Diane de Poitiers and Gabrielle d'Estrées lived here. Even after the Revolution, when the château was razed, the Bois kept its reputation. Now all the access roads are blocked off at night, and things are considerably more staid.

The Bois de Boulogne owes its current appearance to Napoleon III, who spent his early years in London and gave it to the city as its own Hyde Park. Roads, riding and walking paths crisscross it, but for anyone with children in tow the biggest attraction is on the Neuilly side, to the north (Ⓜ *Les Sablons*) where the **Jardin d'Acclimatation** (*open daily 10–6, till 7 in summer; special activities at weekends and during school hols; adm*) has nearly every possible activity for kids – camel and canal-boat rides, playgrounds, a small zoo, a doll's house with antique toys, a *guignol* (puppet show), children's theatre, bumper cars, crafts and games. Catch a small train from ⓜ Porte Maillot in summer for extra fun.

The most scenic spots in the Bois include the **Lac Inférieur**, with its islets and emperor's kiosk (*near RER Av Henri-Martin or* ⓜ *Ranelagh*); the **Shakespeare garden** by the open-air theatre in the **Pré Catelan**; the **Grande Cascade**, an artificial Swiss Alps waterfall, just east of Longchamp; and for garden and rose lovers, the sumptuous **Parc de Bagatelle** (*a 15min walk or bus 43 from* ⓜ *Pont de Neuilly or take bus 244 from* ⓜ *Porte Maillot or RER Rueil-Malmaison; open Wed and Thurs 8.30–8, Fri–Tues 8.30–7; closed Mon; adm*).

The **Musée Marmottan** (*2 Rue Louis-Boilly,* ⓜ *La Muette; open Tues–Sun 10–5.30; closed Mon; adm*) is on the edge of the Bois. The Marmottan family collected medieval miniatures, tapestries and Napoleonic art and furniture, but the Monets are the highlight: some of the *Nymphéas* ('Water Lilies'), one of the *Cathédrales de Rouen* and a view of the British Houses of Parliament.

La Défense

ⓜ/*RER La Défense. Open summer daily 9am–8pm; winter daily 9am–7pm; ticket office closes one hour earlier.*

Forty years ago this was a dismal suburban industrial area, its only feature a *rond-point*, laid out by Madame de Pompadour's brother back in 1765 when it was a hunting reserve. After the siege of 1870 a statue commemorating the defence of Paris was set up here, and *La Défense* gradually gave its name to the whole area. In 1955 the national government decided to make a modern, American-style business district out of the vacant land, and a state development corporation called EPAD was set up. By 1960 glass towers were sprouting like toadstools. French directors were not slow to seize on La Défense's cinematic potential: Jacques Tati's poor bewildered Monsieur Hulot was baffled by its glass doors. In *The Little Theatre of Jean Renoir* there is a vignette of a modern woman who falls hopelessly in love with her electric floor polisher; the tidy corporate people of La Défense provide a sort of Greek chorus. Today, about 150,000 people work here and there are about 55,000 residents.

The **Parvis**, also called the Podium or the Dalle, is the long pedestrian mall aligned with the *Grand Axe*. Sorry monoliths dubbed with corporate acronyms are interspersed with a wealth of abstract sculptures and mosaics. At the eastern end, with a broad view over Paris, is the **Takis Fountain**, illuminated in the evenings with coloured lights. In the centre, near the Agam Fountain, is the original sculpture. Since its opening in 1989, though, the star of the show has unquestionably been François Mitterrand's personal monument, the **Grande Arche**. A competition was proclaimed for its design; the winner was an obscure architect named Otto von Spreckelsen. In the late 1980s work went on at a furious pace in an attempt to get the monster ready for the Revolutionary Bicentennial; on one memorable day the girders went up for eight entire storeys. The Arche opened in grand style on 14 July 1989, with the president hosting a meeting of the (then) G-7 heads of state at the top. Visiting it is a surreal experience, while speakers hidden in the trees regale you with Serge Gainsbourg tunes. There's a lift, running up a glass tube; take the ride through the air to the top for a panoramic view of the city.

Parc de Monceau

Ⓜ *Monceau; 8e.*

As with the Palais Royal, Paris owes this rare oasis to Philippe d'Orléans (Philippe-Egalité) who had it landscaped in the 1770s – and redone a decade later, shocking Parisians by hiring a Scotsman named Blakie to turn the grounds into the city's first large English garden. History was made here in 1797 when a man named Garnerin made the world's first parachute jump: 1,000ft from one of the Montgolfiers' balloons, and he lived to tell the tale. The park is lovely and immaculately kept; it includes a large pond called the *Naumachie* near a colonnade believed to have originally stood at St-Denis, from a failed project of Catherine de' Medici to build a mausoleum for the Bourbons.

Ile de France

This is the cradle of the Capet kings, of France and of *francilien*, the medieval dialect that evolved into modern French. But how did the Ile-de-France get its name? In the Middle Ages any place between rivers could be an island, while Francia was the name given to the Paris basin under the Merovingians, long before it encompassed the entire country. In later years it maintained a quintessential quality: its gentle hills produce Brie, the Frenchiest of French cheeses, while its architects produced Gothic, the ultimate French style, leaving great cathedrals at Beauvais (*see* p.666), Amiens (*see* p.651), Soissons (*see* p.659–62), Laon (*see* p.656) and Chartres (*see* p.399–401), all day trips out of Paris. In the last 150 years it has become quintessential in another way. While the Impressionists found bucolic subjects to paint here in the 1870s, the Ile de France has since been covered with urban sprawl; over one out of every five people in France now live in the region, too many in the dire state housing estates of the *banlieue*, others, mostly to the west, in chichi retreats. In between are the following easy daytrips from Paris.

Versailles

Un chef-d'œuvre de mauvais goût et de magnificence.
(A masterpiece of bad taste and magnificence.)

Voltaire

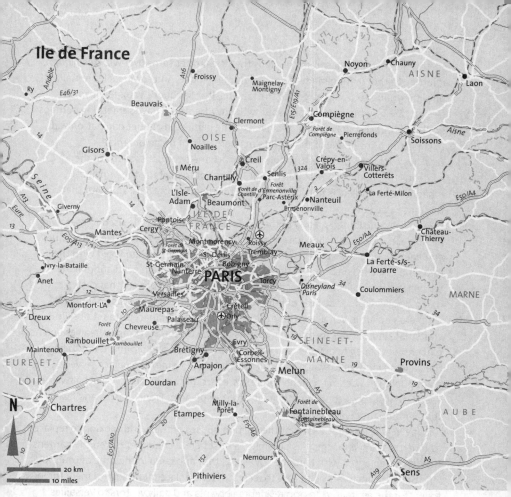

Getting there is easy by RER C or train from the Gare Montparnasse or from Gare St-Lazare to Versailles-Rive Droite, followed by a 15min walk. The château is open April–Oct Tues–Sun 9–6.30; Nov–Mar Tues–Sun 9–5.30; closed hols; guided tours in English from 10am. **Grands Appartements** (entrance A) adm 45F, some reduced tarifs. Another 25F at entrance C will get you into the **Apartments of Louis XIV** and the **Apartments of the Dauphin and Dauphine**, with an audioguide in English; you can also visit the **Opéra Royal**, a gem designed by Gabriel for Louis XV in 1768, which is all wood, painted as marble, but designed 'to resonate like a violin' (adm extra). From April–mid-Oct the garden's **musical fountains** are turned on (all still using their original plumbing); 25F adm, free 5pm–dusk. A **Passport** gives access to the Château, Grand Trianon, Petit Trianon, Coach Museum and the Groves (exc during the fountain show) for 90F (70F low season); 3 July–18 Sept four Sats in summer occasion the extravagant **Grandes Fêtes de Nuit**: fireworks, illuminated fountains and an 'historical fresco'; book with FNAC or Spectacles Châteaux, t 01 30 83 78 88, f 01 30 83 78 96; Versailles Tourist Office t 01 39 24 88 88.

Versailles' name comes from the clods that the farmer turns over with his plough, referring to the clearing made for a royal hunting lodge. And so Versailles remained until the young Louis XIV attended the fatal bash at Fouquet's Vaux-le-Vicomte (*see* pp.198–9), which turned him sour with envy. He would have something perhaps not better but certainly bigger, and hired all the geniuses Fouquet had patronized to create for himself one of the world's masterpieces of megalomania – 123 acres of rooms. They are strikingly void of art; the enormous façade of the château is as monotonous as it is tasteful, so as not to upstage the principal inhabitant. The object is not to think of the building, but of Louis, and with that thought be awed.

Versailles contributed greatly to the bankruptcy of France: Louis, used to overawing his subjects, began to hallucinate that he could bully nature as well. He ordered his engineers to divert the Loire itself to feed his fountains, and when faced with the impossible, settled on bringing the waters of the Eure through pestilent marshes to Versailles by way of the aqueduct of Maintenon, a ten-year project that cost 9,000,000 livres and the lives of hundreds of workmen before it was abandoned.

If there's no art in Versailles, there is certainly an extraordinary amount of skilful craftsmanship. Besides its main purpose as a stage for the Sun King (Versailles and its gardens were open to anyone who was decently dressed and promised not to beg in the halls; anyone could watch the king attend Mass, or dine), the palace served as a giant public showroom for French products, especially luxury ones. As such it was a spectacular success, contributing greatly to the spread of French tastes and fashions throughout Europe.

Today, Versailles' curators haunt the auction houses of the world, looking to replace as much of the original gear as possible – a bust here, a chair there. Even the gardens have been replanted with Baroque bowers, as they appeared in the time of Louis XIV. One thing the restorers don't care to recreate is the palace plumbing – a mere three toilets for the estimated 20,000 residents, servants and daily visitors to Versailles. After Louis XVI and Marie-Antoinette were evicted by the Paris mob on 6 October 1789, Versailles was left empty, and there was talk of knocking it down when Louis-Philippe decided to restore it as a museum.

The Grands Appartements are the public rooms open to all in Louis XIV's day. There's the elliptical, two-storey **Chapelle Royale**, architecturally the highlight of Versailles; a historical gallery of rooms lined with portraits of royal relatives and views of Versailles; the **Grands Appartements**, a series of tiresome gilded drawing rooms, each dedicated to a Roman deity; the **Salon d'Hercule**, designed around Veronese's *Repas du Christ chez Simon le Pharisien*, the one good painting in the palace. The **Salon de Diane** has the gutsy bust of Louis by Bernini.

Beyond are the **Salle de Guerre** and **Salle de Paix**, linked by the famous 241ft **Hall of Mirrors**, still crowned with Lebrun's paintings of the first 17 years of Louis XIV's reign, but minus the original solid-silver furniture, which Louis had to melt down to pay his war debts. The famous 17 mirrors with 578 panes are post-1975 copies, put in place after a disgruntled Breton blew up the originals; facing the windows, they reflect the sunlight into the gardens, a fantastical conceit intended to remind visitors that the Sun himself dwelt within.

Beyond the Salle de Paix are the formal apartments of the queen; their current appearance required a colossal reconstruction – shreds of fabric were found and rewoven in the original designs, and Savonnerie carpets copied from old designs. The **Chambre de la Reine** was used for the public birthing of Enfants de France. In the Antechamber, note the portrait of *Marie-Antoinette and Her Children* by Madame Vigée-Lebrun. The **Salle du Sacre** was created by Louis-Philippe to receive a copy of David's painting of Napoleon's coronation in the Louvre – a copy David preferred to his original.

Then there are the **gardens**, last replanted by Napoleon III, with their 13 miles of box hedges to clip, and the 1,100 potted palms and oranges of the Orangerie, all planted around the 'limitless perspective' from the terrace fading into the blue horizon of the Grand Canal. Not by accident, the sun sets straight into it on St Louis' day, 25 August, in a perfect alignment with the Hall of Mirrors. On either side Le Nôtre's original garden design – more theatrical and full of surprises than any of his other creations – is slowly being restored while hundreds of trees have been sacrificed in the name of new vistas of the château, inspired by Louis XIV's own guidebook to his gardens, the *Manière de Montrer les Jardins de Versailles*. In it he devised a one-way route for his visitors to take, for even at their best Le Nôtre's gardens are essentially two-dimensional; to appreciate them they must be seen from just the right angle.

Louis kept a flotilla of gondolas on his Grand Canal, to take his courtiers for rides; today the gondoliers of Venice come to visit every September for the *Fêtes Vénitiennes*. The rest of the year you can hire a boat to paddle yourself about or a bike to pedal through the gardens, or even catch a little zoo train to a building far more interesting than the main palace, the **Grand Trianon** (*adm 25F*). An elegant, airy Italianate palace of pink marble and porphyry with two wings linked by a peristyle, it was designed in 1687 for Louis XIV ('I built Versailles for the court, Marly for my friends, and Trianon for myself,' he said). After his divorce, Napoleon brought his new Empress Marie-Louise here, who did it up quite attractively in the Empire style.

The gardens in this area were laid out by Louis XV's architect, Jacques-Ange Gabriel, who also built the Rococo **Pavillon du Jardin des Français** and the refined **Petit Trianon** nearby (*adm 15F*), intended for Louis XV's meetings with Mme de Pompadour. Louis XVI gave the Petit Trianon to Marie-Antoinette, who spent much of her time here. Beyond the Petit Trianon is the **Hameau de la Reine,** the delightful operetta farm-house built for Marie-Antoinette, where she could play shepherdess.

Nothing escaped Louis XIV's attention, and even his carrots and cabbages were planted in geometric rigidity in his immaculate vegetable garden, **Le Potager du Roi** (*entrance at 6 Rue Hardy, on the left side of Place des Armes, the square in front of the château; guided tours with fruit and jam tastings April–Oct Sat and Sun 10–6; group tours all year by reservation; adm; book on t 01 39 24 62 62*). The visit includes the adjacent **Parc Balbi**, a romantic park planted by the Comte de Provence (future Louis XVIII) for his mistress. As an antidote to Versailles, you can try to visit the nearby **Salle du Jeu de Paume**, 1 Rue du Jeu-de-Paume (*open May–Sept usually two afternoons a week; ring to check, t 01 39 67 07 73*), where the Third Estate made its famous Tennis Court Oath to give France a constitution on 29 July 1789.

St-Germain-en-Laye

West of La Défense, the old town of St-Germain-en-Laye (RER A) grew up around a priory founded by Robert the Pious in 1050. The priory became a château lavishly rebuilt in brick by François I, and it saw the dawn of the Sun King, who spent most of his first 40 pre-Versailles years here and hired Le Nôtre to lay out the long gardens. There are regular tours of the château, and the excellent **Musée des Antiquités Nationales** (*open daily 9–5.15; closed Tues; adm*), an archaeological collection of treasures ranging from Lower Paleolithic to Merovingian France. The Marquise de Montespan's old digs house the **Musée Départemental Maurice Denis-La Prieuré** (*2 bis Rue Maurice Denis; open Wed–Fri 10–12.30 and 2–5.30, Sat and Sun 10–12.30 and 2–6.30; closed Mon and Tues; adm*), containing Symbolist and Nabis paintings by Denis, Bonnard, Vuillard, and company.

St-Denis: the Original Gothic Church

St-Denis, with its great abbey that was the necropolis of the kings of France, is today one of the classic *banlieues défavorisées*. Communist-run, gritty and poor, it saw its transformation from rural idyll to industrial inferno in the 19th century, when some 60 factories making everything from cars to pianos moved in. Today the old village is only the centre of a suburban agglomeration of over 100,000 people. It's well run, and still has a noticeable sense of civic pride.

The Abbey Basilica

St Denis, who after being decapitated at Montmartre shambled up here with his head tucked under his arm to begin his career as patron of France, is a truly shadowy character. Like so many other French saints – St Pol (Apollo) or St Saturnin (Saturn) – he may be a half-conscious fabrication, papering over survivals of paganism that early missionaries had assimilated. And what would be more natural than retaining Denis – really Dionysus – as guardian deity of the wine-quaffing Gauls?

In any case, there was a cemetery here from Roman times, and an abbey from perhaps the 5th century, favoured by Dagobert and other Merovingian kings, who began the tradition of making it the site for royal burials. St-Denis' present glory is entirely due to its rebuilding under the remarkable Abbot Suger (1081–1151). Diplomat, counsellor to Louis VI and Louis VII, and ruler of France while the latter was away on the Crusades, Suger also found time, according to his own accounts, to invent Gothic architecture single-handedly. Perhaps his architects had something to do with it too, but the good abbot, constantly cajoling, suggesting, kibitzing over the sculptor's shoulder and even helping hoist the stones, must get a fair share of the credit; his ideas may well have been decisive in the use of pointed-arch vaulting and rose windows in the new architecture.

To promote his beloved abbey, Suger wrote influential works on history and government, practically creating by himself the mythology of the sacred kings of France, while emphasizing the importance of the abbey and the role of St Denis as protector of all the kings since Clovis. After his death, St Denis seems to have become a regular forgery factory, as monks cranked out false chronicles, charters and bequests dating from as early as Charlemagne's time to prove certain rights of the abbey and its royal patrons. Wealth, influence and royal cadavers accumulated, and not surprisingly St-Denis became one of the chief targets of the revolutionaries of 1793. Twelve hundred years' worth of anointed bones were tossed into a pit; the revolutionaries trashed the tombs and carted off France's richest church treasure (much of which finally found its way into the Bibliothèque Nationale). Under the restoration, Louis XVIII started fixing the place up, and Viollet-le-Duc came to finish the job in 1859.

The basilica's **façade** is one of the triumphs of Suger and his architects, a marvel of clarity and order that pointed the way to all the Gothic cathedrals that followed; the sculptural trim on the upper levels and the three carved portals became a Gothic commonplace; thanks to the revolutionaries almost all the reliefs and statues are copies. Inside, notice that the nave and transepts are in a different style, a confident mature Gothic – they weren't completed until the mid-13th century. The unassuming **choir** is the real Gothic revolution, with its ribbed vaulting. From the west portals you can see how the walls now tilt backwards a bit. The lovely **rose window**, with seasons and signs of the zodiac, is one of the few remaining bits of medieval glass, as are the *Tree of Jesse* and *Life of the Virgin* in the apse behind the main altar.

From the right aisle, you begin the tour of the **royal tombs** (*open daily 10–5, Sun 12–5; adm*). These too were heavily restored after the desecrations of 1793 and few are of interest, even though they go as far back as Dagobert, who died in 639 (for all the early kings, *gisants* – horizontal effigies atop the sarcophagi – were remade during the Middle Ages). In the right ambulatory hangs the **oriflamme**, flame-covered battle standard of the French kings, a 15th-century copy of the medieval original, lost in the Hundred Years' War.

Musée de l'Art et de l'Histoire de la Ville de St-Denis

St-Denis has a delightful museum, housed in an old Carmelite convent (*Rue Gabriel-Péri; open daily 10–5.30, Sun 2–6.30; closed Tues; adm*). From nun memorabilia and an exhibit on medieval daily life, the scene changes to modern industrial St-Denis: paintings by local artists of the canals and gas works, old shop fronts and the *roulottes* (caravans) many workers lived in. The biggest exhibit is devoted to the 1871 Commune: a floor of paintings, posters, cartoons and newspapers relates the story more thoroughly than you'll ever see it in Paris.

Disneyland Paris

32km east of Paris at Marne-la-Vallée; RER A4: Marne-la-Vallée/Chessy.
Open daily, although hours change according to season and school
holidays; t 08705 03 03 03 (UK residents), t (1) 407 934 7639 (US residents),
for all information, events schedules, and hotel/bungalow reservations;
high season adm 220F; 170F for children 3–11; 'multipass' available, good
for two or three days.

'A cultural Chernobyl at the heart of Europe,' snarled theatre director Ariane
Mnouchkine although, as the French themselves admitted, culture in Europe must be
pretty thin gruel if it can be threatened by a cartoon mouse. The French government
helped bring the fox into the chicken coop – an RER line and TGV line linked up to
Marseille, Lyon, Lille, Charles de Gaulle airport and eventually London, and land made
available on very favourable terms. Disneyland Paris opened on 12 April 1992 and the
first three years were characterized by a brutal baptism in red ink and farcical Franco-
American misunderstandings. However, it appears to have settled down under the
French management which has none of the hip-shooting swagger of the American
years, and no one frets any more about cultural pollution leaking out.

The park is a fifth the size of the city of Paris – 1,943 hectares (4,800 acres),
protected from the outside world by 30ft sloped dikes. Six large theme hotels are run
with that guaranteed 'Have a nice day' friendliness and chocolates on the pillow
approach. Besides the rides, the corporate-processed fun includes infinite 'shopping
opportunities', special shows, food (American, Mexican, Italian and other European),
discos and weird American nightlife at the Festival Disney complex. If you go in
summer, bring a good book: Tinkerbell herself must have designed the enchanted
queue routes for the rides that curl in and out, up and down, all the better to keep you
believing you're almost there when there's still half the population of Europe waiting
in front of you. For more chills and thrills and less mouse, try **Parc Astérix** (*see* p.665).

Vaux-le-Vicomte

Get there by train from the Gare de Lyon to Melun (61km), then take a
taxi 6km to the château. Open 1 April–1 Nov daily 10–6; for other times
by appointment, t 01 64 14 41 90. Fountains play the 2nd and last Sat of
each month 3–6; romantic candlelight tours June–Sept Sat 8.30pm–11pm;
adm. Pets not allowed.

Vaux was the prototype for Versailles but is much prettier: designed by Louis Le Vau
and decorated by Charles Lebrun, set in the original *jardin à la française* by André Le
Nôtre – who for the first time had a scale vast enough to play with vanishing points
and perspectives to his heart's content. The whole shebang was masterminded by
Nicolas Fouquet, Louis XIV's minister of finances, who adopted Hercules as his patron,
just as Louis saw himself as Apollo.

Even if Fouquet aped a decorative mythology on the level of Disney's *Fantasia*, the concept of Vaux was undeniably Herculean. Not only did Fouquet unite the greatest talents of his time (Mme de Sévigné and La Fontaine were among his other 'discoveries'), but he created this country palace and gardens in only five years, employing 20,000 masons, decorators and gardeners, all with one aim in mind: to form a suitable stage for a grand fête to impress one single person, the king, on 17 August 1661. It was, by all accounts, the most splendid party in the history of France. The choicest dishes were prepared on gold and silver plates by Vatel, the famous maître d'hôtel; the great Lully composed music for the occasion; the *comédie-ballet* was by Fouquet's friend Molière; 1,200 jets of water danced from the fountains; elephants decked in jewels lingered among the orange trees; while Italian fireworks wizards astounded all with their artistry. The 23-year-old Louis was certainly impressed – and so miffed that he refused to sleep in the *chambre du roi* built just for him.

Vaux was used as lavish proof of Fouquet's graft, and cited in his embezzlement trial three years later, but it wasn't the expense that got Louis' goat that famous night – after all, limitless graft by treasurers was built into the still feudal system, and Cardinal Mazarin had filched much more. What niggled Apollo was that Hercules, a mere mortal, had upstaged him not only in extravagance but as an arbiter of taste (Vaux suggests that *style Louis XIV* should really be called *style Fouquet*). And like Apollo, who was often cruel, Louis punished Fouquet's hubris, personally intervening in his trial to insist on a sentence of solitary confinement for life. The king confiscated all Fouquet's property. Then he confiscated Fouquet's ideas to create Versailles, hiring Le Vau, Lebrun and Le Nôtre to repeat their work at Vaux, but on an appalling scale; Fouquet's tapestry weavers and furniture makers were employed to form the nucleus of the Gobelins factories; Louis hired Fouquet's fireworks makers to light his own fêtes; he even carted off Fouquet's 1,200 orange trees for his Orangerie at Versailles.

In the 19th century Le Nôtre's gardens, with their clipped hedges, statues and elaborate waterworks, were restored. Period furnishings and tapestries from the Gobelins and Savonnerie complement the surviving decorations, which include Lebrun's portraits of Fouquet in the **Salon d'Hercule** and his poignantly unfinished ceiling in the **Grand Salon**. Vaux's stables contain the **Musée des Equipages** full of beautiful antique carriages. Lastly, look for the carved squirrels – Fouquet's family symbol (because they hoard all their goodies).

Fontainebleau

*The train to Melun continues to **Fontainebleau**, 65km from Paris; get off at Fontainbleau-Avon, where bus A or B from the station will whisk you to the centre. The **Tourist Office**, 4 Rue Royale, **t** 01 60 74 99 99, hires out bikes, an ideal way to explore ancient forest paths (they also sell a map). The **Château de Fontainebleau** is open June, Sept and Oct daily 9.30–5; July and Aug daily 9.30–6; Nov–May daily 9.30–12.30 and 2–5; closed Tues; adm; **t** 01 60 71 50 70.*

At weekends half of Paris seems to be here; the **forest**, with its wonderful variety of flora – including 2,700 species of mushrooms and fungi – oak and pine woods, rocky escarpments and dramatic gorges, is the wildest place near the metropolis. It was always exceptionally rich in game and by 1150 had already been set aside as the royal hunting reserve of Louis the Fat. The medieval kings managed with a fortified castle-hunting lodge, but along came François I, who chose Fontainebleau to be his artistic showcase; down went most of the old castle and up went an elegant **château**, fit to be decorated by the artists the king had imported from Italy, especially the great Rosso Fiorentino, a student of Michelangelo. Work on the château continued under Henri II and the exquisite architect Philibert de l'Orme. Henri IV added two courts decorated by Flemish artists. Every subsequent ruler to Napoleon added their bit; the Revolution destroyed most of its furnishings, while Louis-Philippe hired ham-handed restorers, who left much of the art a shadow of itself.

With contributions from so many monarchs, the Château de Fontainebleau makes an interesting style book. Enter through the **Cour des Adieux**, where Napoleon bid farewell to his Imperial Guard after his abdication on 20 April 1814, and Louis XIII built the magnificent horseshoe staircase. The tour of the **Grands Appartements** includes the famous **Galerie François I** (1533–7), with Rosso's repainted frescoes framed in the original stuccoes; the Michelangelo-influenced **Chapelle de la Trinité** and the extraordinary, sumptuous **Salle de Bal**, both built under Henri II; the **Chambre de l'Impératrice**, with Marie-Antoinette's elaborate bed; and the **Salle du Trône**, designed for Napoleon. Other rooms were used by Pius VII during his stay in Paris. The **Petits Appartements** are less grand, but just as interesting (*tours only, June–Aug, 10, 11, 2.15 and 3*); the **Musée Napoléon I** concentrates on the daily life of a self-made emperor.

Fontainebleau's gardens, notably the Parterre, were first laid out by François; Henri IV added the water, dubbed the Tibre, and Le Nôtre rearranged the whole into geometric gardens. In 1812 Napoleon ordered English gardens to be planted around the Fontaine Belle-Eau.

Normandy

09

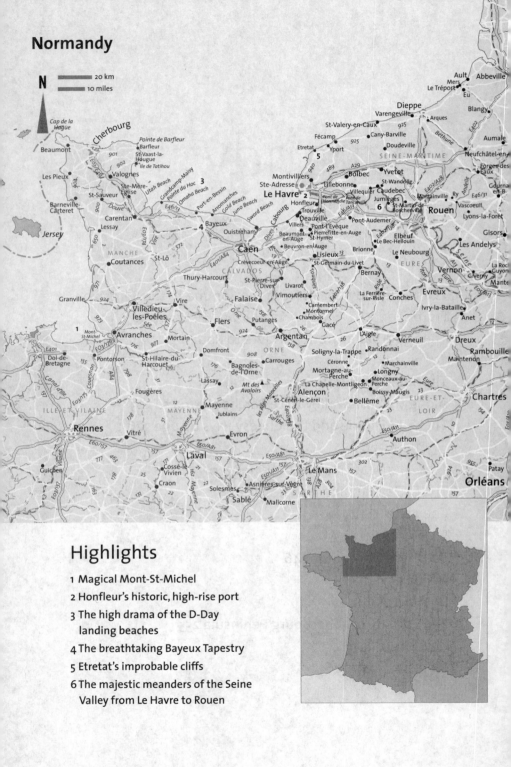

Normandy

N

20 km
10 miles

Cap de la Hague
Cherbourg
Pointe de Barfleur
Barfleur
St-Vaast-la-Hougue
Île de Tatihou
Beaumont
901
902
Les Pieux
904
Valognes
Ste-Mère-Église
Utah Beach
Grandcamp-Maisy
Pointe du Hoc
Omaha Beach
St-Sauveur
E46/13
Port-en-Bessin
Barneville-Carteret
909
Douve
Carentan
Lessay
650
Jersey
MANCHE
E03/74
Vire
St-Lô
Coutances
572
Granville
924
971
Villedieu-les-Poêles
973
Sée
1
Mont-St-Michel
Avranches
176
977
Mortain
E401
E03/176
Dol-de-Bretagne
155
A84
Pontorson
798
St-Hilaire-du-Harcouet
176
Canal d'Ille
157
E03/N175
Couesnon
Fougères
E03/N12
ILLE-ET-VILAINE
A84
178
Rennes
Vitré
E60/157
Vilaine
777
463
Guichen
78
25
E03/N137
Ault
Mers
Le Tréport
Abbeville
Eu
Dieppe
Varengeville
925
Arques
Blangy
E402
St-Valery-en-Caux
925
Cany-Barville
Aumale
Fécamp
925
Doudeville
Béthune
Etretat
Yport
SEINE-MARITIME
Neufchâtel-en-
5
489
A29
Yvetot
Forges-les-Eaux
Montivilliers
Bolbec
Ste-Adresse
Lillebonne
St-Wandrille
E402/A28
Gournay-en-B
Le Havre
2
Villequier
Caudebec
Martainville
Ry
E46/31
Honfleur
Pont de Normandie
Pont de Brotonne Tancarville
Jumièges
St-Martin-de-Boscherville
Vascoeuil
Trouville
Deauville
E46/A13
6
Rouen
Lyons-la-Forêt
Villers
Pont-l'Évêque
Pont-Audemer
Elbeuf
Gisors
Bayeux
Beaumont-en-Auge
Pierrefitte-en-Auge
St-Hymer
Le Bec-Hellouin
Les Andelys
Ouistreham
Dives
Cabourg
Beuvron-en-Auge
Le Neubourg
La Roch
Guyon
Caen
Lisieux
13
Brionne
EURE
Vernon
Crèvecoeur-en-Auge
St-Germain-du-Livet
13
Giverny
Mante
CALVADOS
Bernay
Évreux
Thury-Harcourt
St-Pierre-sur-Dives
Livarot
Role
13
Falaise
Vimoutiers
La Ferrière-sur-Risle
Conches
Ivry-la-Bataille
Vire
158
Camembert
Montormel
Anet
12
Flers
Putanges
Chambois
Gacé
924
Argentan
26
L'Aigle
Verneuil
Dreux
Domfront
908
ORNE
158
Soligny-la-Trappe
Randonnai
Rambouille
Carrouges
Céronne
Marchainville
Maintenon
Bagnoles-de-l'Orne
176
Mortagne-au-Perche
Longny
Lassay
Mt des
Avaloirs
La Chapelle-Montligeon
Monceaux-au-Perche
Boissy-Maugis
23
Chartres
Alençon
Bellême
EURE-ET-LOIR
Mayenne
St-Céneri-le-Gérei
23
MAYENNE
Jublains
LOIR
12
Sarthe
Authon
Evron
E50/A11
Laval
157
E50/A81
302
Patay
Cossé-le-Vivien
163
Le Mans
157
955
Craon
22
Asnières-sur-Vègre
SARTHE
924
Orléans
Solesmes
22
157
Sablé
Malicorne

Highlights

1 Magical Mont-St-Michel
2 Honfleur's historic, high-rise port
3 The high drama of the D-Day landing beaches
4 The breathtaking Bayeux Tapestry
5 Etretat's improbable cliffs
6 The majestic meanders of the Seine Valley from Le Havre to Rouen

Normandy is a land of heroes and conquerors, but the Norsemen who came from Scandinavia, and gave Normandy its name, were the terrors of the Dark Ages. In 911 one Viking, Wrolf, was granted lands around the lower Seine by the Carolingian king of France; he converted to Christianity and the precocious duchy was born. In 1066, with one rather famous conquest, the dukes of Normandy became kings of England. In 1204, Philippe Auguste won back Normandy from King John, leaving the English only the islands known to the French as the Iles Anglo-Normandes, to the British as the Channel Islands. In modern times, North American and British soldiers proved their heroism on Normandy's beaches.

Normandy has its art heroes, with Monet leading the charge, and more than its share of literary heroes. Corneille, heroic playwright par excellence, came from Rouen. André Gide mounted a brilliant challenge to provincial Catholic morality and hypocrisy in a series of novels for which he won the Nobel Prize. Maupassant wrote the sharpest, bitterest short stories in the French language, many as redolent of Normandy as the finest Calvados. Then of course there's Flaubert, whose Madame Bovary wastes away so despondently in Normandy, desperate for passion. On the whole Normandy's native *literati* have hardly given the province a good name, but the region's most stinking heroes are, of course, its cheeses.

Normandy, lush with orchards and horsey meadows, has more than its fair share of superlative sights. In Haute Normandie, Monet's garden at Giverny, the stunning modern bridges over the Seine estuary, and Honfleur, the smartest of all French historic ports stand out. However, the most famous sights are found in Basse Normandie: the Bayeux tapestry, the D-Day beaches and Mont-St-Michel.

Food and Drink

Anathema to the cholesterol-conscious, Normandy cuisine is often heightened by a rich dollop of cream and a dash of cider or calvados (apple brandy). But it is best known for its **cheeses**, although Camembert in particular has suffered from cheap imitations. Normandy cheeses are soft and creamy; they start off smelly and get more pungent and tastier with age. Most come from the Pays d'Auge and the Pays de Bray; the latter has produced Neufchâtel since the time of William the Conqueror. Normandy also makes fine butter; Isigny butter has even been awarded its own *appellation d'origine contrôlée*.

Normandy produces a considerable quantity of **cider**, and apples feature large in Normandy cooking. **Calvados** (nicknamed *calva*) can be added to just about anything, and is renowned as one of France's most densely flavoured brandies. The *Trou Normand* – a pause in a meal – is when diners drink a drop of *calva* to help the digestion. You'll still find it on some of the more elaborate menus in the region's restaurant, normally in the form of a light sorbet.

Normandy has excellent **seafood**: try mussels (with cream), oysters and scallops, and sole – *à la Normande*, cooked with cider, butter and mussels, or *dieppoise*, with wine and cream. Local meat dishes might turn your stomach, but locals love *tripes à la mode de Caen*, black puddings from Mortagne-au-Perche, or *canetons* (ducklings) from Rouen, stuffed with liver and served up in a blood and cream sauce.

Getting Around

By Ferry or Other Boat

Normandy has four major cross-Channel ports, Dieppe, Le Havre, Caen-Ouistreham and Cherbourg, going east to west. See **Travel** for details.

By Plane

Normandy has small airports at Rouen, Le Havre, Deauville, Caen and Cherbourg.

If you're coming from the UK, Air France runs twice-daily flights in each direction between London City Airport and Le Havre (reservations, **t** 0845 0845 111, *www.airfrance.co.uk*).

Otherwise, the two major Paris airports lie quite close to eastern Normandy, Roissy linked to the region by the new A14 motorway.

Ryanair (**t** 0870 156 9569) offer direct flights between Beauvais airport, north of Paris, and Glasgow-Prestwick.

By Train

From the UK, it's generally easiest to travel via Paris. Most trains leave from Gare St-Lazare for Le Havre via Rouen; some of the more southerly services leave from Gare de Montparnasse for Cherbourg via Lisieux, Caen and Bayeux, or for Granville.

Le Mans is well served by high-speed trains. The Normandy coast has only very limited train transport.

By Road

The main motorway through the region is the arc formed by the A13 and A83, from Paris via Rouen and Caen down to Avranches. Coming from Calais or Boulogne, there's now motorway all the way to Normandy – take the A16 motorway, branch off on to the A28 just before Abbeville, then choose between the A28 to Rouen and the A29 down almost as far as Mont-St-Michel via Le Havre.

The Normandy Coast from the Somme to the Seine

The white cliffs of Haute Normandie stretch unbroken from the bay of the Somme to the estuary of the Seine. This coast has been dubbed the Côte d'Albâtre: the churning waters often have a milky alabaster quality, with subtle tinges of beiges and turquoises, like the chalk cliffs above. Settled in the breaks in the cliffs, the resorts resemble one another. They sprawl slightly messily behind pebbly beaches provided with a few beach huts. A small 'casino' often takes pride of place along the beach front. There may be a hotel or two, a stretch of modern blocks even, but the slopes will be mainly occupied by neo-Gothic Norman mansions.

The ports of Dieppe and Le Havre have strong connections with England. Dieppe has the advantage of its pretty, protected harbour set among the cliffs, and a greater historical legacy. Le Havre, although badly war-torn, stretches along a splendid site overlooking the Seine estuary. Its industrial chimneys and petroleum depots may come as a bit of a shock, but the place has some attractions as a big city on the seashore. The real star of this piece of French coast, though, is Etretat with its fabulous cliffs.

Dieppe

Dieppe's name comes from the old Norse for 'deep'; its deep-water harbour at the mouth of the Arques reaches right into the heart of town. This natural advantage made Dieppe an important port, especially after the Norman conquest. It continued to grow through the Middle Ages, in part because pilgrims to Santiago de Compostela disembarked here, but it suffered repeatedly in the English and French wars. The Dieppois sailors gained a formidable reputation : in 1338 a band led a terrible raid on Southampton, and in 1372 they helped in the French victory at La Rochelle. When the English occupied the town after Agincourt, the Dieppois were made to pay for supporting the French, until the town liberated itself from the English in 1435.

Dieppe's greatest times came in the period of exploration and exploitation of the New World. A Dieppe sailor, Jean Cousin, is claimed as one of the discoverers of Brazil. The Florentine explorer Verrazano worked for the most famous of all Dieppe's merchants, Jean Ango, who had other irons in the fire: François I authorised him to raise a fleet of privateers to challenge the supremacy of the Portuguese and Spanish in Africa and the New World. Ango made a killing: one of his captains grabbed Cortés' treasure-filled fleet in 1522. Ango has been portrayed as a local hero ever since.

A powerful English naval fleet bombarded the gritty port in 1694 and reduced it to rubble, but as warring between Britain and France diminished, Dieppe assumed its role as a popular cross-Channel port. In the 1820s it became the first coastal town in France to follow Brighton and become a seaside resort. The artists were not long behind. In the 1820s Richard Bonington encouraged his friends Turner and Delacroix to visit Dieppe and paint its seas and skies. Monet, Pissarro, Renoir, Gauguin, Whistler, Degas, and especially the latter's friend Walter Sickert, also came. Sickert invited Oscar Wilde to visit in 1878; when Wilde returned in 1897, he was a broken man following his imprisonment. He stayed several months in Dieppe while writing the moving *Ballad of Reading Gaol*.

On 19 August 1942 the Allies sent a predominantly Canadian force of 6,000 men into Dieppe to test a possible invasion strategy. Tragically, three-quarters of the troops were killed, wounded or captured in the so-called Dieppe Raid.

Old Dieppe, its Beaches and Château

The ferries from Newhaven used to sail right into Dieppe's **Avant-Port** to dock, allowing passengers to step straight out into a historic port at **Quai Henri IV**. With the sea terminal's move to the eastern end of Dieppe, part of the Avant-Port has now become a marina, but even so the business of the wider port is still an integral feature of the centre of town. The pedestrianized **Grande Rue**, running into town from the Quai Henri IV, offers a tempting choice of luxury food shops. The pinnacles and buttresses of Dieppe's largest church, **St-Jacques**, loom up at the end of many of the streets and alleys in this area. The Sacré Cœur chapel inside is held up by very fine late-Gothic vaulting while another chapel contains the tomb of Jean Ango. The **Place**

Tourist Information

Dieppe: Pont Jehan Ango, Quai du Carénage,
t 02 32 14 40 60, f 02 32 14 40 61.

Where to Stay and Eat

Dieppe ✉ 76200
A practical place to stay if you cross the
Channel for a short break.
***Présidence, Bd Verdun, **t** 02 35 84 31 31, **f** 02
35 84 86 70 (*moderate*). Of the handful of
hotels looking out to sea, this is the nicest, in
a smartish quite recent block by the castle.
***L'Aguado, 30 Bd de Verdun, **t** 02 35 84 27
00, **f** 02 35 06 17 61 (*moderate*). Close to the
harbour, but with some rooms facing the
Channel. Has tried to brighten up the other-
wise uninspiring modern architecture. .
**Les Arcades, 1–3 Arcades de la Bourse,
t 02 35 84 14 12, **f** 02 35 40 22 29 (*inexpensive*).
Some rooms overlook the pretty harbour.
Countless restaurants stick out glass-fronted
extensions on to the pavement of the Quai
Henri IV.

du Puits-Salé, the hub of Dieppe town life, is presided over by the **Café des Tribunaux**.
First built as a cabaret hall in the 18th century, it looks much more official, and in fact
served as Dieppe's town hall at one time.

Dieppe's **seafront** is disappointing. The hotels lie a considerable distance from the
water. The no-man's-land in between has been taken over by an outdoor swimming
pool, tennis courts, and so on. Children seem to like the **Cité de la Mer** (*open May–Aug
daily 10–7; rest of year daily 10–12 and 2–6; adm*), but it isn't as sophisticated as
Nausicàa in Boulogne. Dieppe's beach may be of shingle, but as one of the closest
to Paris it prompted the Duchesse de Berry to introduce the English fad for sea-
bathing into France here in 1824. Dieppe remained fashionable for the next century.
The seafront grandeur may have disappeared, but there's still fun in the sun here
every summer.

West along the shore, the roads climb a steep hill crowned by Dieppe's daunting
castle. At its foot, the **Square du Canada** commemorates two lots of Canadians: Jesuit
missionaries killed by Indians in Quebec in the 17th century and servicemen killed in
the 1942 Dieppe Raid. The **Château-Musée** (*open June–Sept daily 10–12 and 2–6; rest of
year daily exc Tues 10–12 and 2–5; adm*) glowers down on the coast. Built mainly in the
14th and 15th centuries, it consists of a rambling complex and has great views. Apart
from nautical exhibits and an entertaining display on the history of sea bathing in
Dieppe, it contains paintings by artists associated with Dieppe and an extraordinary
array of carved ivories. When Dieppe was at its height its sailors wandered the coast
of Africa trading for tusks, brought back to be decorated by skilled local craftsmen.
They produced combs, fans, crucifixes, thimbles, pens and decorative scenes, all in
intricate detail.

Around Dieppe

The once mighty medieval **Château d'Arques** (*free*) stands a short way southeast of
Dieppe and still looks daunting on the crest of its hill, surrounded by a rectangular dry
moat of staggering proportions. An uncle of William the Conqueror, one Count
William d'Arques, had the trench dug. He was foolish enough to take on his nephew,
and needless to say his upstart of a relative won, sending him into exile. A royal

descendant of William's, King Henry I of England (also duke of Normandy), ordered the stone ramparts and the flint keep within. The castle was then ready to play its part in medieval clashes, and was the last Norman place to fall to Philippe Auguste's troops in 1204. During the 16th-century Wars of Religion, the leader of the Protestant side, Henri de Navarre (the future Henri IV of France), took on one of the toughest Catholic commanders, the Duc de Mayenne, here in 1589 and defeated him. A stone frieze over one gateway, just about the last detail of decoration left in the château ruins, shows a flying equestrian figure of Henri de Navarre racing to victory.

The **Château de Miromesnil** (*open May–mid-Oct daily exc Tues 2–6; adm*), set in the lush gardens just west of Arques, is best known as the birthplace in 1850 of Guy de Maupassant who came into the world in this elegant Henri IV-style brick and stone château . His father was given to living above his means and the family had to move on from Miromesnil four years later. The other famous resident, the enlightened Marquis de Miromesnil, served as a minister under Louis XVI, trying ineffectually to bring in reforms. The marquis' study and bedroom are the best part of the quirky visit. The main cider-producing area of the Seine Maritime lies to the south of here, home to major firms such as Duché de Longueville at Anneville-sur-Scie which offers tours and tastings. The tourist authorities have marked out a clear **Route de la Pomme et du Cidre** to follow.

Back by the coast, **Varengeville** presents swish village houses in a variety of Norman styles strung along winding lanes. Swisher still, and turning its back on the village, the Renaissance **Manoir d'Ango** (*open April–Sept daily 10–12.30 and 2–6.30; rest of year Sat pm, Sun and hols only; adm*) stands aloof, looking determinedly inland. By the time Jean d'Ango commissioned this summer residence (1530–45) he had amassed enough money to pay for the finest craftsmen. Although parts were badly damaged at the Revolution, splendid elements remain, most notably a Florentine loggia with busts of French royals and of Ango and his wife. Inside, some of the original features are still in place, plus sumptuous later furnishings. The **Parc du Bois des Moutiers** (*open 15 Mar–15 Nov 10–12 and 2–6; adm*) offers the charms of an English country garden and house designed by Lutyens, one of the most famous English architects of the late 19th and early 20th centuries. But the best thing in Varengeville is the **church**, at the end of a lane leading to the cliffs. From the churchyard you get splendid views down towards Dieppe and the Channel, and at the right time, you can see boats heading into or out of port. Then enter the church by the side door and you're greeted by a man who appears to be throwing up! The vomiting voyager is carved on one of the most extraordinary columns inside. Striking stained glass adds colour to the interior. It turns out to be the work of Georges Braque, who is buried in the cemetery.

From Dieppe to Fécamp, Etretat and Le Havre

Eu

East up the coast from Dieppe and straddling the river Bresle on the border with Picardy, **Eu** is a traditional gateway into Normandy. Today this town with its odd

Getting Around

Dieppe and Le Havre are Channel ferry ports (*see Travel*). From Dieppe, there's only one direct train to Paris a day; otherwise, trains go via Rouen. The port of Le Havre is connected to Paris-St-Lazare by regular services (1hr 50mins).

There aren't any trains to take you along the coast from the Somme to the Seine. Instead, branch lines off the main track between Rouen and Le Havre will take you up to Le Tréport, St-Valéry-en-Caux, Fécamp and Etretat. You'll need to rely on local bus services to get you elsewhere along the coast if you don't have a car.

Tourist Information

Eu: B.P.82, 41 Rue P. Bignon, t 02 35 86 04 68, f 02 35 50 16 03.
Le Tréport: Quai Sadi Carnot, t 02 35 86 05 69, f 02 35 86 73 96.
Fécamp: B.P.112, 113 Rue Alexandre Le Grand, t 02 35 28 51 01, f 02 35 27 07 77.
Etretat: B.P.3, Place Maurice Guillard, t 02 35 27 05 21, f 02 35 29 39 79.
Le Havre: B.P.649, 186 Bd Clemenceau, t 02 32 74 04 04, f 02 35 42 38 39.

Where to Stay and Eat

Eu/Le Tréport ✉ 76260

★★★**Le Domaine de Joinville**, Route du Tréport, t 02 35 50 52 52, f 02 35 50 27 37 (*expensive–moderate*). Set in its own little valley off the road from Eu to Le Tréport, with bags of style, originally constructed as outbuildings for King Louis-Philippe's château in Eu. Restaurant (*menus 215–450F*)
★★**La Vieille Ferme**, ✉ 76910 Creil-sur-Mer, t 02 35 86 72 18, f 02 35 86 12 67 (*inexpensive*). West down the coast at Mesnil-Val Plage. Somewhat cheaper, but an upmarket two-star in timberframe Norman style. The restaurant is in a converted 18th-century farmhouse; in summer you can eat in the garden (*menus 110–240F*).
Le Tréport's quayside is lined with some tempting seafood restaurants.

Varengeville ✉ 76119

★★**Hôtel de la Terrasse**, Route de Vastérival, t 02 35 85 12 54, f 02 35 85 11 70 (*inexpensive*). A well-placed, peaceful hotel by the sea.

Offranville ✉ 76550

Le Colombier, Parc du Colombier, t 02 35 85 48 50. Serves surprisingly exciting modern French cuisine in an archetypal Norman

grunting name has a noticeably out-of-the-way provincial charm. Eu crops up in the history of France and the British Isles in a curious variety of circumstances. It took off in the 10th century, when the dukes of Normandy built a castle here as the north-eastern bastion of their new territories. In 1050 William brought Matilda, daughter of the count of Flanders, to the castle of Eu to marry her. She wasn't keen, and only submitted to William after he had dragged her around by the hair.

Central Place Guillaume le Conquérant is dominated by a **church** dedicated to an Irishman: Laurence O'Toole was archbishop of Dublin at the time of the first Anglo-Norman invasion of Ireland in 1169. In 1180 he was sent to England by the Irish lords to intercede with Henry II. The king refused to see him and went off to Normandy. Laurence, old and sick, followed, but only got as far as the abbey at Eu where he died. His canonization was set rapidly in motion, in part because of the papacy's arguments with Henry II. Laurence's shrine immediately became an important pilgrimage centre; his church, known as the **Collégiale**, was begun in 1186, but the choir and apse provide an extravagant display of Flamboyant Gothic, added after a fire in 1426. The Collégiale contains fine statuary, including an altarpiece depicting St Laurence

timbered house in this attractive village with its twisted spire (*menus 100–170F*).

Sassetot-Le-Mauconduit ✉ 76540

**Château de Sassetot, t 02 35 28 00 11, f 02 35 28 50 00 (*moderate*). Its long 18th-century façade makes a grand sight. It pleased the 19th-century Austrian Empress 'Sissi' who took it on as her Normandy holiday home. Now its rooms are very comfortable. Restaurant (*menus 110–350F*).

Fécamp ✉ 76400

***La Ferme de la Chapelle, t 02 35 10 12 12, f 02 35 10 12 13 (*moderate*). Best hotel in Fécamp, up on the cliffs, developed from a 16th-century farm. Restaurant (*menus 95–210F*).

**Auberge de la Rouge, Route du Havre, t 02 35 28 07 59, f 02 35 28 70 55, at St-Léonard, 2km south of town (*inexpensive*). Leafy garden, elegant restaurant serving complex dishes, and pleasant rooms.

Etretat ✉ 76790

One of the stars of the Normandy coast. *****Le Donjon**, Chemin de St-Clair, t 02 35 27 08 23, f 02 35 29 92 24 (*expensive*). Set back a bit from the sea, and exclusive; a very comfortable little neo-Gothic castle. *****Dormy House**, Route du Havre, t 02 35 27 07 88, f 02 35 29 86 19 (*moderate*). Large

modern hotel with views, attached to Etretat's golf course.

La Résidence, 4 Bd du Président Coty, t 02 35 27 02 87, f 02 35 27 04 31 (*moderate*). Prices are surprisingly reasonable at this fabulously beam-fronted hotel.

**Le Corsaire, Rue du Général Leclerc, t 02 35 10 38 90, f 02 35 28 89 74 (*moderate*). Some rooms have splendid views of the cliffs – though they cost a lot more than the others.

**L'Escale, Place Foch, t 02 35 27 03 69, f 02 35 28 05 86 (*inexpensive*). Above a brashly lit pizza parlour (attached to the hotel), but the rooms are sweet, cosy little cabins with varnished wood everywhere.

Le Havre ✉ 76600
Ste-Adresse ✉ 76310

***Bordeaux, 147 Rue Brindeau, t 02 35 22 69 44, f 02 35 42 09 27 (*moderate*). Offers more comfort than the rest.

***Marly, 121 Rue de Paris, t 02 35 41 72 48, f 02 35 21 50 45 (*moderate*). Well located in the shopping heart of town.

***Hôtel des Bains, 3 Place Clemenceau, Ste-Adresse, t 02 35 54 68 9, f 02 35 54 68 91 (*expensive*). Best located hotel in the area, with sea views, terrace and restaurant (*menus 110–150F*).

Le Nice Havrais, 6 Place Frédéric Sauvage, Ste-Adresse, t 02 35 46 14 59. Good food and spectacular views over the Seine estuary.

coming to Eu and Our Lady of Eu, but its greatest treasure is an exquisite 16th-century Entombment in polychrome stone.

In 1430 Eu was one of the places where Joan of Arc was held on the way to her trial in Rouen. Little of the medieval town survived the fires started on the orders of King Louis XI to prevent it falling into the hands of the English. If, however, you walk from the south side of Place Guillaume up Rue Paul Bignon, you'll enter an area of winding streets built during a revival in the town's fortunes in the 16th and 17th centuries, with many fine Louis XIII-style merchants' houses in brick. The **Chapelle du Collège des Jésuites** recalls the fact that Eu became a Catholic stronghold with the French Wars of Religion. Henri de Guise founded a Jesuit college here in 1582, and his notoriously unfaithful wife Catherine de Clèves commissioned the Jesuit chapel, built between 1613 and 1624. The fine sculpture on the façade was the work of the local Anguier brothers. Inside, the most prominent features by far are two bombastic, but very finely sculpted Baroque memorial tombs in marble, made for Catherine.

The de Guises were also responsible for the Renaissance **Château d'Eu** (*open 15 Mar–8 Nov daily exc Tues 10–12 and 2–6; adm*), begun on the site of an earlier castle in

1578. In 1660 the château passed to Mademoiselle de Montpensier, cousin of Louis XIV, known as the Grande Mademoiselle, who ordered the French-style garden. However, the Château d'Eu is most associated with Louis-Philippe, who inherited it, together with the title of count of Eu, in 1821. Louis-Philippe loved the place: not only did he restore the château, he also built the Bresle Canal, restoring the town's access to the sea for the first time in centuries, in part for his yacht. The July Revolution of 1830 catapulted Louis-Philippe into the role of France's 'Citizen King'. Eu for a time became the virtual summer capital of France, and a new barracks-like Pavillon des Ministres was built next to the Collégiale to accommodate members of the government who were obliged to decamp here for several weeks each year. In September 1843 Queen Victoria and Prince Albert arrived at the château for a week of entertainments. This was apparently the first time a British monarch had set foot in France since Henry VIII met François I at the Field of the Cloth of Gold in 1520, so Eu claims to be the birthplace of the *entente cordiale*. After Louis-Philippe was deposed by another revolution in 1848, Eu fell back into its usual obscurity, but in the 1870s the Republic returned the château to the king's grandson, the Comte de Paris, pretender to the throne. Part of it now serves as town hall, part of it as an engagingly tumbledown museum. Some rooms still have the 17th-century decor of the Grande Mademoiselle.

North of Eu, the fishing port of **Le Tréport** has grand seaside houses and hotels from its late-19th-century heyday, as well as the inevitable casino and a long shingle beach. **Mers-les-Bains**, on the opposite side of the Bresle estuary – so just in Picardy – has a nicer, sandy beach than Le Tréport and a more elegant seafront, the tall houses given colourful balconies. But a hideous factory lurks in the valley just behind.

Along the Coast

The drab and scruffy resorts between Varengeville and St-Valéry-en-Caux are much of a muchness. A snake of yachts in the meandering river estuary at **St-Valéry-en-Caux** gives this small port its charm. On the quays, you can hardly fail to notice the **Maison Henri IV**, its beams richly carved with decorative motifs (*open July–Aug daily 11–1 and 3–7; June and Sept daily exc Mon and Tues same times; rest of the year exc Jan and Feb weekends and school hols same times; adm*), now serving as tourist office and local museum. Much of the rest of town was destroyed at the start of the Second World War. In a pitiful attempt to halt the German advance, a French cavalry division tried to fight it out here with Rommel's tanks, while a section of the 51st Highlanders was caught by the Nazis.

The coast road up along the top of the cliffs leads to **Fécamp**, home to that heady liqueur Benedictine, and also to one of Normandy's greatest religious foundations. Way before the invention of the liqueur, Fécamp gained its reputation thanks to a phial of Christ's blood. Legend has it that Joseph of Arimathea left it with his nephew Isaac, who hid it in the trunk of a fig tree and then launched it into the sea to entrust it to God. The log landed in lucky old Fécamp. Already in the 7th century, a convent went up and the little bottle was well protected.

Under an early duke, William Longsword, a new monastery was founded, and alongside it a hall which became one of the dukes' favourite residences. Duke Richard II made Fécamp's monastery one of the largest Benedictine abbeys in France, and here declared his intention to go on pilgrimage to the Holy Land, pronouncing his illegitimate son William as his heir. In 1067 the blessed bastard William celebrated at Fécamp his successful conquest of England. The recipe for Benedictine liqueur was invented here as a tonic by a Venetian monk in 1510. In the mid-19th century an entrepreneur revived the recipe and turned it into an international bestseller.

Fécamp's surviving monastic buildings, rebuilt in the 17th and 18th centuries, now make up the town hall. Alongside them stands the abbey church, **La Trinité**. Larger than many cathedrals, it too was altered in the 18th century, but inside it remains early Gothic. The Precious Blood is still venerated and kept on a 16th-century marble altar by the Italian sculptor Viscardo. In the south transept look out for a vivid 15th-century Entombment of the Virgin. The church contains exquisite stone screens, and in the Lady Chapel, Gothic stained glass. Last but not least, look out for a giant, ornate clock from the 17th century.

Nothing stands out at Fécamp like the **Palais Bénédictine** (*open 13 May–5 Sept daily 9.30–6; mid-Mar–mid-May and early Sept–Oct daily 10–12 and 2–5.30; 2 Jan–12 Mar 10.30am visit and 2–5; adm*), the most palatial distillery in France. With its pinnacles, baronial staircases and stained glass, it was built for Alexandre Le Grand to exploit the history of the liqueur while adding to its mystique. The grandest parts were conceived as a museum to house the family's medieval and Renaissance statuary, paintings, carved wooden chests, Nottingham alabaster altarpieces, Limoges enamels and magnificent 15th-century illuminated manuscripts.

Etretat looks as though it has sold its soul to tourism, and as soon as you see the spectacular beach you understand why. The natural rock formations, often painted by the Impressionists, take the shape of arches to the east and needles to the west, and are sensationally illuminated after dark. Etretat's lively centre has a distinctive covered market that served as a British and American military hospital in the last war. To the French, Etretat is also the setting for a much-loved children's detective story featuring Arsène Lupin, the creation of author Maurice Leblanc. Fans can try solving some of the crimes of this gentleman burglar at the **Clos Lupin** (*open June–Sept daily 9–7; rest of year weekends and hols 10–6; adm*) in Leblanc's former house.

Le Havre

France's second harbour after Marseille, Le Havre was bombed to bits in the Second World War, but don't dismiss it entirely. Its functional grid holds an excellent fine arts museum, and Brazilian architect Oscar Niemeyer's astonishing 'Volcano centre'.

Le Havre was planned for François I as a replacement for silting Honfleur and Harfleur further up the Seine estuary. The new harbour was first christened Franciscopolis before the more neutral Le Havre (The Haven) was adopted. Even back then it was designed on a grid plan. It grew from strength to strength, trading with the Americas in particular: nearly 350 slaving vessels set out in the 18th century. Before World War II, Le Havre greeted the beau monde off the ocean liners, but also featured in anti-establishment classics such as André Gide's *La Porte Etroite* and Jean-

Paul Sartre's *La Nausée*. The city was such an important industrial base and port by the Second World War that it became one of the most bombed targets in France.

In the centre, the Bassin de Commerce is crossed by an elegant footbridge, but it's the colossal **Espace Niemeyer** that steals the show. One of Oscar Niemeyer's constructions from the 1970s takes the form of a ship's funnel, the other a volcano. Unfortunately, the sunken square has suffered badly from Le Havre's depression in the 1990s and most of the shops have been abandoned. Between the Espace Niemeyer and the Bassin, a hefty monument records the names of Le Havre's civilian war dead. Find out more about Le Havre's fiery and tragic history in the **Musée de l'Ancien Havre** (*open Wed–Sun; adm*), set in an 18th-century mansion in a small pocket of prewar houses just south of the Bassin. You might also visit the **Baroque cathedral**, its well-turned yellow stone standing out curiously in the midst of concrete arcades.

On the west side of town, behind the wide strip of pebble beaches and car parks, the soaring tower of Le Havre's postwar **church of St-Joseph** marks the skyline. Designed by Perret in his beloved (and cheap) concrete, the square-plan edifice looks grim on the outside, but walk inside on a bright day and you'll feel you've been caught in a kaleidoscope. South along the shore, by the Capitainerie, a plaque commemorates the 800 passengers and crew of the *Niobe* who died when the ship was sunk by the Germans on 11 June 1940. Opposite, the smart glass block of the **Musée Malraux** (*open Mon–Fri 11–6, Sat and Sun 11–7; closed Tues*) forms a vibrant setting for its paintings, superbly rehung in 1999. Locals Eugène Boudin and Raoul Dufy expressed their love of the Normandy coast in their works, and are well represented here. A trio of wonderful Monets stand out, but there are other discoveries to be made, such as Camoin's amazing portrait of a black woman.

The Seine Valley from Le Havre to Rouen

The Seine journeys from Paris to the sea majestically, in large shapely meanders. This river has always been one of the major trading routes through France, and to this day ships chug up to the inland port of Rouen. Coming in to the Seine estuary, they first have to pass by the vast smelly industrial areas of Le Havre and Lillebonne. But after Lillebonne the banks of the Seine are rustic until Rouen. Along the way lie the evocative remnants of the medieval abbeys of St-Wandrille, Jumièges and St-Georges.

Mighty Modern Bridges to Caudebec

A splendid trio of modern toll bridges spans the Seine between Le Havre and Caudebec. The **Pont de Normandie** (1995), held in place by two towering sets of tweezers, is one of the longest bridges in the world, and takes you from the sulphurous marshes of the Seine estuary to Honfleur. The slightly more modest **Pont de Tancarville**, itself a feat of technology, lies upstream. The **Pont de Brotonne**, held up by cables in the form of sails, links Caudebec to the Brotonne forest.

Caudebec was almost wholly destroyed in the last war, but ringed by desperately drab postwar architecture stands one of the great Flamboyant Gothic churches in

France, built between 1426 and 1515. Don't be put off by the blackened appearance of the exterior. The intricacy of the Gothic canopies on the west front is as close as stone gets to lace. Little figures in period costume, the size of porcelain pieces, grace the lower canopies. Although anti-Catholic fanatics decapitated some of the statues, the musician angels and elders in the archivolts have kept their heads. An ornate balustrade running around the roof spells out in stone tracery words from hymns to the Virgin, the Magnificat and Salve Regina. Inside, the stained glass windows have miraculously survived, some attributed to the great Flemish master Arnoult de Nimègue and his successor in Normandy, Engrand le Prince: one memorable scene shows Moses leading the Israelites across the Red Sea, the Egyptian soldiers drowning in the brightest red waters, while others depict Norman saints, including St Wandrille, St Philbert, St Victrice,and St Romain. One chapel contains monumental statues saved from Jumièges abbey, and a remarkable Entombment scene.

The **Musée Victor Hugo** (*open daily exc Tues 10–12.30 and 2–6; adm*) occupies a delightful riverside spot at **Villequier** west of Caudebec. Hugo never lived in this fine bourgeois brick house overlooking the Seine: it was his daughter Léopoldine who married a local. Tragically, one afternoon she and her husband were drowned while boating on the river. There are sketches, photos and letters by Hugo, mementoes from Léopoldine's wedding, and extracts from *Les Contemplations*, the series of poems Victor Hugo wrote to remember his drowned daughter.

Three Great Seine Abbeys

Following the north bank of the Seine from Caudebec to Rouen is one of the great experiences of Normandy. Apple farms are tucked below the low white cliffs; here and there little ferries still take local traffic across the wide river. The Seine looks magnificent, tracing its confident curves through the land, and you'll see barges gliding along, and huge tankers like multi-storey apartment blocks on the move through the countryside. On special occasions, tall ships pass through to gather at Rouen.

The remnants of three massive abbeys stand between Caudebec and Rouen. **St-Wandrille** (*guided tours daily 3 and 4, Sun 11.30 and 3.30; adm*) was founded in the mid-7th century by Wandrille, who studied in Italy before serving at the Merovingian court of King Dagobert. Supported by Bishop Ouen of Rouen, his abbey became a great centre of learning, and controlled priories as far afield as Provence; 17 abbots were canonized, and today the abbey is the only one of the three still serving its original purpose behind its Baroque gate. You can wander freely around the ruins of the vast 13th-century abbey church or go to the big barn of a modern church where the monks sing plain chant. On the guided tour monks show you parts of the 18th-century Maurist monstery. For an evocation of postwar life at St-Wandrille read Patrick Leigh Fermor's *A Time to Keep Silence*.

Following the Seine, the road leads past the ruins of the enormous **abbey of Jumièges** (*open mid-April–mid-Sept daily 9.30–7; rest of year daily 9.30–1 and 2.30–5.30; adm*). Much more survives here from the Gothic period than at St-Wandrille. It too was founded in the 7th century, by Philibert, again at the

Getting Around

A good train service links the two main Norman towns along the Seine, Le Havre and Rouen, but to explore the actual banks of the Seine you'll need your own transport.

Tourist Information

Caudebec-en-Caux: Quai Guilbaud, t 02 32 70 46 32, f 02 35 95 90 26.
Parc Naturel Régional de Brotonne: Maison du Parc, 76940 Notre-Dame-de-Bliquetuit, t 02 35 37 23 16.

Where to Stay and Eat

Jumièges ✉ 76480
Auberge des Ruines, 17 Place de la Mairie, t 02 35 37 24 05. Timberframe inn on a kind of triangular square by the abbey ruins; a pretty location for a quite expensive

restaurant (*menus 88– 250 F*), while the very few rooms are basic and cheap. *Closed 2nd half Aug; Christmas; 1 Nov–15 Mar eves; Sun, Tues eves, and Wed.*
Bar du Bac, t 02 35 37 24 23, outside the village down by the local ferry crossing over the Seine. Tranquil and popular little restaurant with a terrace.

Duclair ✉ 76480
★★**Hôtel de la Poste,** 286 Quai de la Libération, t 02 35 37 50 04, f 02 35 37 39 19 (*inexpensive*). May look like an unexciting block on the outside and the rooms may be a bit dingy, but get a Seine river view and you can spend hours watching the little ferry dashing back and forth and barges and container ships slipping silently past your window. It's as atmospheric as a French movie. The traditional French restaurant also has river views (*menus 70–250F*). *Closed 2nd half July; 2nd half Feb; Mon, Sun eves.*

instigation of Ouen. As at St-Wandrille, in the mid-9th century the Vikings laid waste to the abbey but when they settled and converted to Christianity a great new Jumièges rose from the ashes. It was one of the first great Romanesque buildings in northern France, begun in 1040 under Abbot Robert Champart, who would go on to become a shortlived archbishop of Canterbury under Edward the Confessor. Champart is a reminder of the very close ties that existed between the English crown and Normandy before William's conquest – Edward the Confessor's mother was the daughter of Duke Richard of Normandy. William the Conqueror attended the consecration ceremony of Jumièges' new abbey church in 1067, just after his victory in England. The soaring ruins of the church stand like a huge disused medieval factory for God. Adjoining them are the ruins of the church of St-Pierre, part of which is an exceptional piece of late 10th-century architecture.

Nowadays, the most absorbing of the three abbeys between Le Havre and Rouen is the least known, the **abbey of St-Georges,** located at St-Martin-de-Boscherville (*open June–Sept daily 9–7; April–May daily 9.30–12 and 2–7; Oct–Mar daily 2–5; adm*). St-Georges remains fascinating both in outline and detail, with much of the giant medieval abbey church left standing. Building commenced in 1114, and the massive church is just about the only great Romanesque building in Normandy to have survived the Revolution fairly unscathed. The interior combines harmony with complexity. The detail begins to emerge as you look more closely: the stone rope that encircles the walls, the bestiary on the capitals, the crinkly geometrical patterns on the arches. Raoul de Tancarville had participated in the Norman taking of Sicily and some of the decorative ideas may have come back with him.

Beside the church, the chapterhouse has preserved sculpted capitals so fine that they look as though they've been executed in ivory rather than stone. There are magnificent scenes showing horn-blowing, knights in chainmail and monks fighting and being whipped. Among the statue-columns of the chapterhouse the most arresting shows a woman slitting her own throat. The museum in the garden tells you about the life of the Benedictine monks and the history of St-Georges.

Rouen

You may want to copy the most famous tour of Rouen: by Emma Bovary committing adultery with her lover Léon as the horse-drawn cab bumps them round the cobbled streets in Flaubert's famous novel. You certainly won't want to follow in the footsteps of Joan of Arc, whose visit to Rouen ended on the pyre. Close to the spot where the Pucelle was burnt stands a delicatessen called the Charcuterie Jeanne d'Arc which certainly deserves a prize for bad taste. Otherwise the city fairly ignores her. It also turns its back on the Seine to which it owes its existence and its success.

When the Viking leader Wrolf was accepted as duke of Normandy in 911, Rouen became his capital. Under him, the Seine quays were developed for trade. William the Conqueror died in the great city, and two of his successors as kings of England, Richard and John, were crowned dukes of Normandy in Rouen cathedral; Richard's lion's heart was buried there. But with John the English lost Normandy to Philippe Auguste at the start of the 13th century. The French king had a massive new castle built in Rouen. The English king Henry V took Rouen in 1418 after a long siege, and during the ensuing decades of English occupation Joan of Arc would be tried here and burnt at the stake. When peace came at last, commerce changed the face of the city. The archbishop Georges d'Amboise, a powerful figure in the late 15th century, was close to the French kings and Rouen benefited from the links. Textiles and pottery flourished, and in the course of the 19th century Rouen grew into a large industrial city – and as such it would suffer terribly in World War II. Although the riverside remains a mess, historic Rouen has been so well restored it's hard to imagine the true scale of the damage it suffered. It has remained by far the largest city in Normandy and one of the largest ports in France.

Place du Vieux Marché and Around

Joan of Arc was brought as a prisoner to Rouen in time for Christmas 1430. Her trial for witchcraft and heresy was conducted by Pierre Cauchon, Bishop of Beauvais. Found guilty, she recanted her claims at the scaffold, but then her obstinacy returned and she refused to recant a second time. She was burned at the stake on 30 May 1431 in the **Place du Vieux Marché**. Her ashes were chucked in the river; her heart, they say, would not burn. The fish-tailed, scaley-slated **church of Ste-Jeanne-d'Arc** twists round the spot, ready to do battle like a hooded stingray. The design by the Basque architect Arretche was executed in 1979 to include space for the 16th-century stained glass saved from the church of St-Vincent.

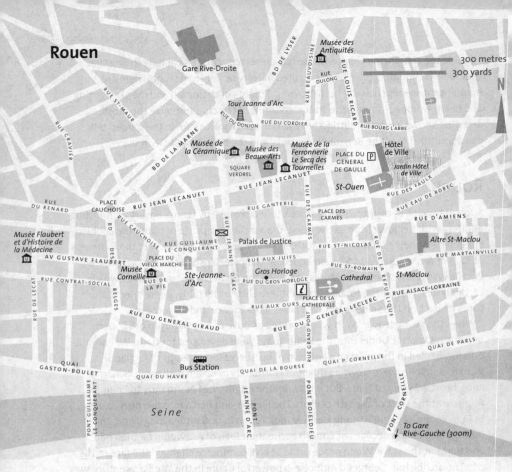

Rouen

Gare Rive-Droite

300 metres
300 yards

N

BD DE LYSER
RUE ST-MAUR
RUE CRAVIER
BD DE LA MARNE
RUE BEAUVOISINE
Musée des Antiquités
RUE DULONG
RUE LOUIS RICARD
RUE BOURG L'ABBE

Tour Jeanne d'Arc
RUE DU DONJON
RUE DU CORDIER

Musée de la Céramique
Musée des Beaux-Arts
SQUARE VERDREL
Musée de la Ferronnerie Le Secq des Tournelles
PLACE DU GENERAL DE GAULLE
Hôtel de Ville
Jardin Hôtel de Ville

RUE JEAN LECANUET
St-Ouen
RUE DES FAULX

RUE DU RENARD
PLACE CAUCHOISE
RUE JEAN LECANUET
RUE GANTERIE
RUE DES CARMES
PLACE DES CARMES
RUE EAU DE ROBEC
RUE D'AMIENS

BD DES BELGES
RUE CAUCHOISE
RUE JEANNE D'ARC

Musée Flaubert et d'Histoire de la Médecine
AV GUSTAVE FLAUBERT
RUE GUILLAUME LE CONQUERANT
Palais de Justice
RUE ST-NICOLAS
Aître St-Maclou
RUE MARTAINVILLE

RUE CONTRAT-SOCIAL
Musée Corneille
PLACE DU VIEUX MARCHE
RUE AUX JUIFS
RUE ST-ROMAIN

RUE DE LECAT
RUE DE LA PIE
Ste-Jeanne-d'Arc
Gros Horloge
RUE DU GROS HORLOGE
Cathedral
St-Maclou
RUE ALSACE-LORRAINE

RUE DU GENERAL GIRAUD
RUE AUX OURS
PLACE DE LA CATHEDRALE
RUE DE LA REPUBLIQUE

QUAI GASTON-BOULET
Bus Station
QUAI DU HAVRE
QUAI DE LA BOURSE
RUE DU GENERAL LECLERC
RUE GRAND PONT
QUAI P. CORNEILLE
QUAI DE PARIS

PONT GUILLAUME LE CONQUERANT
Seine
PONT JEANNE D'ARC
PONT BOIELDIEU
PONT CORNEILLE
To Gare Rive-Gauche (300m)

The **Musée Jeanne d'Arc** (*open May–10 Sept daily 9.30–7; rest of year daily 10–12 and 2–6.30; adm*), on the south side of the square, proves a measly, dismal thing hidden in the ugly basement of a touristy shop. Sadder still is the nearby **Musée Corneille** (*open daily exc Tues and Wed am 10–12 and 2–6; adm*) in Corneille's house west along the Rue de la Pie. It's easy to miss the entrance, and you shouldn't be too put out if you do. Flaubert too gets scant attention from his home town. The **Musée Flaubert et d'Histoire de la Médecine** (*open daily exc Sun and Mon 10–12 and 2–6; adm*) lies a long walk further west, attached to a hospital just outside the centre – Gustave's father and brother held important positions there. More a medical museum than a literary one, this is a bizarre place; you may want to read *Flaubert's Parrot*, Julian Barnes' hilarious and moving homage to the writer, before hazarding a detour yourself.

Rue du Gros Horloge, a major shopping street, links Place du Vieux Marché with the cathedral to the east, divided at one point by a gate and its elaborate **Gros Horloge**, a clock which dates back to the late 14th century. You can admire its mechanisms by climbing into the tower. North of the Rue du Gros Horloge, the **Palais de Justice** stands like an island of intricate Flamboyant Gothic stone. The building was begun in 1499 as a merchants' hall and exchequer, but when François I created a Parlement de

Normandie in 1514, the palace became its home. The exuberant architecture, despite the grime, is one of the greatest late Gothic inventions in France. Ask about possibilities for visits at the tourist office.

Rouen Cathedral, St Maclou and St Ouen

Rouen Cathedral's fame stems in good part from Monet's gorgeous series of studies of the façade in changing lights. The famous west front lords it over a square which was largely wrecked by bombing during the war and turns out to be something of a mess without Monet's beautifying brush. The sober north tower, the **Tour St-Romain**, is along with the crypt a rare survivor of the Romanesque cathedral. The vast bulk is 13th-century Gothic, from the great period of northern French cathedral building. The north portal depicts scenes from the life of John the Baptist, a Tree of Jesse decorates the central doorway, while the south portal is dedicated to St Stephen. The late 16th-century southern tower, the **Tour de Beurre**, was apparently paid for by wealthy townspeople to avoid having to give up such little luxuries as butter during Lent. The statues on this tower, their heads bent in different directions, are beautiful.

Comparing a cathedral interior to a boudoir figures among Flaubert's more outrageous descriptions in *Madame Bovary*, but you may find a certain sensuous pleasure in the shapely Gothic arches. There's some wonderful bejewelled 13th-century stained glass in the choir. Two windows are devoted to the life of Old Testament Joseph, and another to the Good Samaritan. Art historians remain intrigued by the fact that the life of Joseph was actually signed, by a certain Clément de Chartres. But the most famous windows tells the Greek-like tragedy of St Julian the Hospitaller, who tried to avoid the prediction that he would murder his parents, a powerful story retold by Flaubert in one of his *Trois Contes*. Surprisingly little attention appears to be paid to Joan of Arc in the cathedral. One modern piece of stained glass portrays her: 'From the English in homage,' it reads. The d'Amboise family made sure they were better remembered: Georges II d'Amboise, relative of the great archbishop Georges d'Amboise, ordered the exquisite Renaissance tomb for the two of them in the Lady Chapel, designed by Roulland Le Roux. The other, heavier Renaissance tomb was made for Louis de Brézé, seneschal of Normandy and husband of Diane de Poitiers, who is supposed to have ordered this piece from Jean Goujon.

Do wander round the outside of the cathedral: the rows of triangular Gothic gables down the side create a fine effect. The north transept is a superb piece of Flamboyant Gothic, but the south transept portal is even finer, with small Gothic panels telling the stories of Jacob and Joseph and local saints Ouen and Romain. The crossing is topped by a late-19th-century cast-iron tower that rockets into the sky like Rouen's answer to the Eiffel Tower. Antique shops and art galleries fill the cathedral quarter.

Two other churches, St-Maclou and St-Ouen, challenge the cathedral in the beauty stakes. **St-Maclou's** porch is a masterpiece of Flamboyant Gothic seduction, built between 1500 and 1514. The doors, affixed shortly before Georges II d'Amboise consecrated the church in 1521, represent Christ's circumcision and baptism and Old Testament figures. The beautiful relief work is attributed to Jean Goujon.

Getting Around

There are internal flights to Rouen airport. Rouen is just 1hr 10mins from Paris St-Lazare by train.

Tourist Information

Rouen: 25 Place de la Cathédrale, t 02 32 08 32 40, f 02 32 08 32 44.

Where to Stay and Eat

Rouen ☒ **76000**

Surprisingly few good choices of hotels exist in old Rouen. Exceptions are:

***Le Dandy, 93 bis Rue Cauchoise, t 02 35 07 32 00, f 02 35 15 48 82 (*moderate*). Hotel with style and warm modern rooms. No restaurant.

**La Cathédrale, 12 Rue St-Romain, t 02 35 71 57 95, f 02 35 70 15 54 (*inexpensive*). One of the best options in the very centre of town, set around a very pretty timberframe courtyard. Some of the rooms are a bit worn, but they are good value.

***Tulip'Inn, 15 Rue de la Pie, t 02 35 71 00 88 (*moderate*). Probably the best chain hotel if you can cope with a few gnomes: modern, smart, quiet and great central location.

**Les Carmes, 33 Place des Carmes, t 02 35 71 92 31, f 02 35 71 76 96 (*inexpensive*). Well-located, well-maintained little hotel with bright rooms.

Many top Rouen restaurants have taken over splendid historic houses. There are plenty around the Place du Vieux Marché.

Les Nymphéas, 7–9 Rue de la Pie, t 02 35 89 26 69. Particularly beautiful restaurant, tucked away in a timberframe courtyard, serving superlative cuisine (*menus 130–260F*).

La Couronne, 31 Place du Vieux Marché, t 02 35 71 40 90. Claims to be the oldest auberge still going in France, dating back to 1345. Warm and luxurious interior serving relatively light Norman cuisine (*menus 130–245F*).

Dufour, 67 Rue St-Nicolas, t 02 35 71 90 62. Set in a magnificent timberframe house. Coloured glass panes stop the hoi-polloi from peering in too indiscreetly. The food is as Norman as the décor (*menus 120–230F*). *Closed Sun eve and Mon.*

You'll find plenty of cheap and ethnic options between St-Maclou and St-Ouen.

St-Maclou's square is full of charm, with timberframe houses and a little fountain of peeing figures. Close by, off Rue Martainville, the delightful courtyard or **Aître St-Maclou** in the Ecole des Beaux-Arts served as a charnel house. Look at the carved beams from the 1520s and you'll get the message: each upright sports a skull and cross-bones, the crossbeams decorated with the tools of the gravedigger. Handsome streets fill the space between here and the great Benedictine abbey church **St-Ouen**, set by a pretty garden, timberframe houses, and the majestic town hall. The west front has been heavily restored, but the interior combines Gothic power with simple Gothic elegance from the 14th and 15th centuries. Enter through the south door, the Porte des Marmousets, named after the stone figures monkeying around on the portal. Inside, the nave is sober, dignified and airy, its multi-columned piers punctuated with elegant Gothic statue niches. The most impressive stained glass fills the strips of the choir chapels.

To the Museums of Fine Arts, Iron, Ceramics, and History

Monet and Sisley star in the rich **Musée des Beaux-Arts** (*open daily exc Tues 10–6; adm*), but there's plenty more in these handsome rooms, complete with descriptions in English. Several of the Flemish works are outstanding: Gérard David's *Virgin among* the *Virgins* is an extraordinarily serious piece, where the thoughtful faces of the women express the concerns of motherhood. Among the Italians, Caravaggio's *Flagellation of Christ* stands out. The Spanish school has fewer works but holds its own with some ravishing still lives and a chirpy Velázquez fool.

The substantial French collections feature superb portraits by Largillère, de Troy, and Vigée-le-Brun, busts and statues by Drouais, and a rare 16th-century Clouet of the goddess Diana. Of exceptional interest are a Poussin self-portrait, another attributed to Delacroix and a portrait by David. Views of historic Rouen feature, especially one by Paul Huet showing the pre-industrial city lying in shadow, dwarfed by the Seine valley and the cloudy sky. Several artists born along the Seine in Normandy are recalled in the museum, most famously Théodore Géricault, born in Rouen in 1791. The short-lived prodigy gets a whole room, mainly of preparatory pieces for major works, including some amazing studies of horses. Normandy-born Boudin and Normandy-influenced Jongkind also contribute fine paintings.

Housed in a Gothic church behind the museum, the **Musée de la Ferronnerie Le Secq des Tournelles** (*open daily exc Tues 10–1 and 2–6; adm*) displays an eccentric and amusing collection of wrought-iron objects from ornate gateways and inn signs to keys going back to the Dark Ages and even Gallo-Roman times.

The **Musée de la Céramique** (*open daily exc Tues 10–1 and 2–6; adm*) tells the story of ceramics-making in Western Europe, in France and in Rouen in splendid fashion. Masseot Abaquesne, in the mid-16th century, brought southern European techniques to Rouen, and production began on a major scale. All sorts of ceramic follies feature in the many rooms, including pottery, busts, shoes, clocks, lions and even a violin.

The building holding Rouen's **Musée des Antiquités** (*open daily exc Tues 10–12.30 and 1.30–5.30, Sun 2–6; adm*) has been in danger of becoming a ruin like some of its exhibits. The beautiful pointed helmet of Bernières d'Ailly (*c. 900 BC*) stands out among the pre-Roman exhibits, and the Gallo-Roman collections include two large and impressive mosaics showing Orpheus serenading wild animals and a nymph pursued by Poseidon. Further medieval tapestries may have been made to celebrate French victory in the Hundred Years' War. Some of the medieval treasures are very elaborate, such as a little book covered in enamels, a reliquary arm from the abbey of Saint-Saens, or the array of Flemish retables. You can learn a bit more about Rouen's history at the **Tour Jeanne d'Arc**, but little about Joan, who was a short-term inmate here. The tower is a solid but solitary remnant of the enormous castle Philippe Auguste built on Rouen's hillside.

The Seine from Rouen to Paris

Richard the Lionheart's Château-Gaillard and Monet's Giverny hog the limelight along this stretch of the Seine, but there are also some delightful detours east from the river, into Emma Bovary country, to Lyons-la-Forêt, or to a château built for a famed 16th-century Diana, at Anet. A visit to La Roche-Guyon takes you into the surprisingly rural Vexin Français, just outside Normandy in the Ile de France.

A Detour into Emma Bovary Country East of Rouen

The very handsome brick **Château de Martainville** stands out in flat countryside by Martainville due east of Rouen along the N31. Built in the late 15th century for Jacques Le Pelletier, intriguing emblems in darker brick add detail to the exterior. The fashionable Renaissance additions to the castle were commissioned by Le Pelletier's nephew. The rooms now serve as lovely settings for the **Musée Départemental des Traditions et Arts Normands** (*open April–Sept daily 10–12.30 and 2–6; rest of year daily 10–12.30 and 2–5; adm*). Virtually none of the items comes from the original château, but there are splendid examples of Normandy furniture.

Just east of Martainville, pretty little **Ry** is reckoned to have been the model for Yonville-l'Abbaye, the provincial Yawnville which drives Emma Bovary crazy for passion. Her story is given 3D substance at the **Galerie Bovary Musée d'Automates** (*open July–Aug daily 3–8, weekends and Mon 11–12 and 2–7; rest of period Easter–Oct just weekend and Mon times; adm*), with scenes from the novel reenacted by automata made by a local clockmaker. Flaubert would have enjoyed the absurdity. The tourist office has laid out an Emma Bovary trail you can follow through the area.

Very pretty **Vascœuil** lies a hop and a skip east of Ry. The strikingly patterned **Château de Vascœuil** (*open confusing hours; arrive May–Oct 3–6 and you should be OK; adm*) was home to that monumental figure among 19th-century historians, Jules Michelet, whose vast *Histoire de France* is one of the most famous books in the French language. The **Musée Michelet** is modest given the man's phenomenal output and importance, but there's modern art, too, including sculptures and mosaics in the garden by the likes of Calder, Vasarely and Dali.

Packed with timberframe houses, **Lyons-la-Forêt** (a little east again) is the perfect picture of a Norman village, stretching along a richly wooded valley. The covered market dates from the 17th century, as do many of the grandest dwellings. Plaques around the village record famous figures associated with Lyons-la-Forêt: Henry I of England even died here in 1135. At the edge of the village, the church dates in part from the 12th century, with its slate-helmeted tower and its stone and flint chequerboard patterning on the façade. The magnificent beech woods of the **Forêt de Lyons** were planted by the monks of the abbey of Mortemer whose ruins you can visit.

Along the Seine to Château-Gaillard, Giverny and the Vexin Français

After the industrial loops in the Seine south of Rouen, a dramatic cliff road shadows the river from Pitres on the east bank as far as **Les Andelys**.

Les Andelys are plural because there are two of them. Le Grand-Andely was founded by the Romans and is set back from the Seine. Le Petit-Andely was built next to the river to provide supplies for the medieval **Château-Gaillard** (*guided tours of keep at set times; open mid-Mar–mid-Nov daily exc Tues and Wed am 9–12 and 2–6; adm*). When Richard the Lionheart returned from imprisonment in Austria after the Third Crusade, he found that his former childhood friend, fellow crusader, and, it has often been rumoured, gay lover, King Philippe Auguste of France, was planning to take Normandy from him. To stop him, Richard resolved to build the most advanced fortifications yet

Getting Around

For Giverny, take the train to Vernon and then take a taxi or the summer bus service.

Tourist Information

Ry: Les Trois Vallées Maison de l'Abreuvoir, t 02 35 37 23 16.

Lyons-la-Forêt: Association Touristique du Pays de Lyons-Andelle, 20 Rue de l'Hôtel de Ville, t 02 32 49 31 65, f 02 32 48 10 60.

Les Andelys: Rue Philippe Auguste, B.P.242 Cedex, t 02 32 54 41 93, f 02 32 54 04 16.

Evreux: 3 Place Général de Gaulle, t 02 32 24 04 43, f 02 32 31 28 45.

Dreux: 4 Rue Porte–Chartraine, t 02 37 46 01 73, f 02 37 46 02 19.

Where to Stay and Eat

Lyons-la-Forêt ✉ 27480

A charming village to sleep in.

***La Licorne, 27 Place Bensserade, B.P. 4, t 02 32 49 62 02, f 02 32 49 80 09 (expensive–moderate). A timberframe delight. The rooms are lovely, the cooking classic Norman. Closed 20 Dec–25 Jan; Oct–Mar Sun eve and Mon.

**Hostellerie du Domaine de St-Paul, Route de Forges-les-Eaux (the D321), t 02 32 49 60 57, f 02 32 49 56 05 (moderate). Exceptionally pretty, extremely popular hotel just outside

Lyons towards Gournay – a classy two-star behind a white-fenced entrance.

Connelles ✉ 27430

****Le Moulin de Connelles, 40 Route d'Amfreville, t 02 32 59 53 33, f 02 32 59 21 83, www.cofrase.com/hotel/moulinde connelles (expensive). An extravagant 19th-century pastiche of Normandy timberframe architecture – a glorious château of a 'mill' by the Seine where everything is luxury. Restaurant (menus 140–315F). Closed 2 Jan–30 Mar and Nov.

Les Andelys ✉ 27700

***La Chaîne d'Or, 27 Rue Grande, Le Petit Andely, t 02 32 54 00 31, f 02 32 54 05 68 (moderate). 18th-century inn set apart in a lovely courtyard behind the church. The back looks on to the Seine. Closed 24 Dec– 1 Feb; Tues lunch, Sun eves and Mon.

**Moderne, 8–10 Rue Georges Clemenceau, t 02 32 54 10 41, f 02 32 54 63 63 (inexpensive). Well-established Seine-side hotel with a lovely terrace on which to appreciate classic Normandy cuisine and Seine scenery.

Giverny ✉ 27620

**La Musardière, t 02 32 21 03 18, f 02 32 21 60 00 (inexpensive). Large property with its own big garden.

Les Jardins de Giverny, t 02 32 21 60 80, f 02 32 51 93 77. Pleasing classic Normandy restaurant. Closed first half Nov; Feb and Mon.

seen in Europe, incorporating lessons taken from the Arab and crusader castles. In a prodigious effort, Château-Gaillard was built in just one year, from 1196 to 1197. Philippe Auguste was duly deterred, but after the Lionheart's death his hapless brother John seemed an easier adversary, and in 1203 a French army besieged Château-Gaillard. The castle fell in March 1204, and Normandy was soon in the hands of the French monarch. Château-Gaillard continued to be an important stronghold, so much so that Henri IV and later Richelieu ordered that it be demolished. This work and centuries of pilfering by local builders have taken their toll on the castle, but the sections still standing are awe-inspiring.

Le Petit-Andely below has narrow streets with some half-timbered old buildings and an open-air swimming pool. Le Grand-Andely has an ample market square. Not far away, the collegiate church of Notre-Dame stands on the site of a monastery founded in the 6th century by Clotilda, wife of Clovis. Inside, note the 16th-century stained glass and two fine altar paintings by Quentin Varin. Varin was the first teacher of Les Andelys' most famous son, Nicolas Poussin, born in 1594. Although he scarcely ever returned after leaving to study in Paris in his twenties, his birthplace pays its respects with a small **Musée Nicolas Poussin** (*open daily exc Tues 2–6; adm*) which boasts one of his major paintings, *Coriolanus Answering His Mother's Tears*.

Giverny, further upstream, is all too well known thanks to **Monet's House and Gardens** (*open April–Oct daily exc Mon 10–6; adm*) which the artist in fact discovered by accident, from the window of a train. Monet moved here in 1883 with Alice Hoschedé and their several children by their respective first marriages. They later married. When he first arrived, Monet only rented the house and its garden, called the Clos Normand. As he became more successful, he was able to buy them and remodel the garden to his liking; in 1895 he bought a plot on the other side of the tracks to create his famous Japanese water garden and lily pond from scratch. When Monet's son left the property to the Académie des Beaux-Arts in 1966, it was in a sorry state. The current immaculate condition of the house and gardens is due to American benefactors, including Walter Annenberg.

Monet's choice of flowers makes for one of the most intoxicating colour-saturated gardens you'll ever see. The water lily garden with its famous bridge is surrounded by white wisteria. The cosy house is beautifully light and colourful, and covered wall to wall with one of the world's finest collections of Japanese prints, hung by Monet himself. The warehouse-like studio in which Monet worked on his giant *Nymphéas*, in the years before his death in 1926, contains reproductions and a powerfully equipped souvenir shop.

The Vexin Français

Around another meander in the Seine, the **Vexin Français** is a surprisingly delightful corner of the Ile de France, declared a Parc Naturel Régional in an effort to preserve it from the encroachment of suburbia and golf courses from Paris. The great St Denis came to the Vexin in the 3rd century, and converted the noble lady at La Roche Guyon, who built a grotto oratory in the cliffside, under the sensationally located **Château de la Roche-Guyon**. One of the most vertiginous stairways in France, cut into the blindingly white Seine chalk in early Capetian times, mounts to the towering tubular keep. In the early 12th century a Norman murdered the lord Guy de la Roche while he was at Mass and took over the keep, until the king wrought his revenge and sent the Norman's body on a raft down the Seine as a warning to his countrymen not to step beyond their boundaries. A later medieval castle was built at the foot of the keep and remnants of it flank the main 16th-century block.

The château opened to the public in the mid-1990s, but as yet there's not much to see. The owners, the great family de la Rochefoucauld, are recalled in the curiously tacky displays in the dilapidated apartments. Down in the cellar Rommel is the focus of attention. When Hitler appointed him to review the Nazi coastal defences from Denmark to the Spanish frontier in 1944, La Roche-Guyon became his headquarters. Luckily it didn't suffer much when the Americans liberated it on 23 August 1944.

The Eure Valley and Evreux

The Eure joins the Seine below Rouen; its valley offers a quiet route through eastern Normandy to Chartres. **Evreux**, actually on the Iton just west of the Eure, is encased in postwar architecture, but it has a trio of attractions: an excellent museum with exceptional Gallo-Roman finds; the cathedral, with splendid Flamboyant Gothic features and stained glass that the war bombs missed; and the Abbaye de St-Taurin, concealing a memorably excessive reliquary shaped like a miniature Gothic building.

Further down the Eure, **Ivry-la-Bataille** is enlivened by the antiques dealers close to the river. **Anet** is devoted to the great 16th-century court figure, Diane de Poitiers. A star of her time, she was first married to the powerful Louis de Brézé, around 30 years her senior, who served as seneschal of Normandy. After his death Diane became the mistress of an even more powerful man, this time many years her junior, Henri II, who was married to Catherine de' Medici. The men in Diane's life lavished extraordinary gifts and riches upon her, including some of the finest châteaux ever built in France.

The king gave her Chenonceau, but had the **Château d'Anet** (*open April–Oct daily exc Tues 2–6.30; Feb, Mar and Nov Sat and Sun only 2–5*) specially created for her. The sumptuous scraps may look incoherent, but for France this château was a ground-breaking piece of Italianate architecture, designed by Philibert de l'Orme (1547–51). The gate pays extravagant homage to Diane with its references to Diana, the goddess of the hunt, represented by a recumbent nude watched over rather closely by a large-antlered stag. Anet's surviving masterpiece is the extraordinarily bold chapel. Of the château proper, only one wing out of three survived the Revolution, but the half dozen rooms on the tour are splendidly furnished. One cabinet contains some of Diane's personal possessions. Her tomb stands in a plain funerary chapel nearby.

Continue down the Eure valley to Dreux and Maintenon, with their strong French royal connections. **Dreux**'s extravagant royal chapel contains the remains of Louis-Philippe, brought back here from Weybridge, his Surrey exile, after he was deposed. The splendid, mainly 16th-century **Château de Maintenon** (*open April–Oct daily exc Tues 2–6; Feb, Mar and Nov Sat and Sun only 2–5*) was famously given by Louis XIV to his pious mistress Françoise d'Aubigné in 1674, who then became better known as the Marquise de Maintenon. She and Louis secretly married in 1683.

Along the Risle Valley to Le Perche Normand

The Risle flows up from southern Normandy to join the Seine east of the great Pont de Normandie and historic Honfleur. Further south Normandy's typical architecture goes out of the window in Le Perche where manors and farms with ochre walls and earth-brown tiles embellish the countryside. **Pont-Audemer** is a busy crossroads with a core of picturesque timberframe houses within the postwar surrounds. By contrast, **Le Bec-Hellouin**, southeast along the Risle valley, is a relaxed place dominated by a 15th-century Gothic tower soaring high above mighty beech trees. It's the only surviving relic of the briefly powerful Norman abbey and an impressive one. The statues perched high up have been helpfully named in large Gothic script.

The monastery was founded by a local lord, Herluin, around 1032, and the great Italian theologian Lanfranc moved here from the Mont-St-Michel in 1042. The monastic school he established became one of the most influential in France. In the 1040s, when William the Conqueror was besieging nearby Brionne, he met Lanfranc and was deeply impressed. Lanfranc became his ally in the religious sphere, and after William took the English crown, he became archbishop of Canterbury. Lanfranc called another famed Italian scholar of his day, Anselm, to Le Bec-Hellouin, who in his turn would become archbishop of Canterbury. The school at Le Bec-Hellouin turned out important clerics until the mid-12th century, many of whom went to England.

A vast Gothic church was built at Le Bec-Hellouin in the 14th century, but all that remains today is its outline – its stone was sold off after the Revolution. However, the 17th- and 18th-century wings of the Maurist abbey have survived, and you can visit the ex-refectory, now the abbey church, an enormous barrel-vaulted room with superb acoustics. The guided tour (*daily exc Tues, 3 or 4 tours a day*) also includes the massive cloister.

Bernay (west of the Risle along the Charentonne river) was one of the few lucky towns in Normandy to escape the bombs of the Second World War. It arose around a monastery founded by Judith of Brittany, wife of Duke Richard II of Normandy, in the early 11th century. The Romanesque **abbey church of Notre-Dame** has survived, held up on staggeringly tall arches. Bernay's best art, saved from Le Bec-Hellouin abbey at the Revolution, is in the **church of Ste-Croix** opposite the market: remarkable Gothic statues and tombstones of abbots, and a melodramatic Baroque crucifixion scene set in a semicircular colonnade in the choir.

Shapely slate roofs and patterned strips of pink brick give the **Château de Beaumesnil** (*open July–Aug daily exc Tues 10–12 and 2–6; rest of period Easter–Sept Fri–Mon 2–6; adm*) its elegant 17th-century style. Surrounded by moats and charming gardens, it feels a bit lost in a flat little village southeast of Bernay. Inside, the central tower is taken up by a grand staircase. The château contains 18th-century furniture and a museum on bookbinding, with fine covers from Renaissance times on.

In its wooded valley, **La Ferrière-sur-Risle** stretches out from its long, attractive square with a covered market. The dark nave of **St-Georges** contains an array of statues, including a charming St George on a mule. A wildly decorated retable holds an Entombment painting that some have attributed to a follower of Leonardo; but it's dark, difficult to see, and speckled with bird droppings.

The medieval castle of **Conches-en-Ouches**, east of La Ferrière-sur-Risle, looks like an enlarged sand castle, but the ruins are too dangerous to explore, with tree roots bulging out like veins on one side. It overlooks the little valley of the Rouloir, with a train line running through it and seemingly under **Ste-Foy**, a jewel box of a late Gothic church containing stunning 16th-century Renaissance glass. In the north aisle you can follow episodes in the life of the Virgin, in the south aisle, the Eucharistic story. The Mystic Wine Press shows Christ stamping on the grapes which produce a juice the colour of fresh blood. In the choir, the cycle telling the Passion of Christ, attributed to the Normandy artist Romain Buron, was inspired by Dürer's engravings. Below the Passion, scenes relate the life of the child saint Ste Foy.

Getting Around

Bernay and L'Aigle have train stations, but to reach the Perche Normand using public transport you'll have to rely on buses from either L'Aigle to the north, Alençon to the west, or Nogent-le-Rotrou to the south.

Tourist Offices

Pont-Audemer: Place Maubert, t 02 32 41 08 21, f 02 32 57 11 12.
Bernay: 29 Rue Thiers, t 02 32 43 32 08, f 02 32 45 82 68.
Mortagne-au-Perche: Place du Général de Gaulle, t 02 33 85 11 18, f 02 33 83 76 76, *office-mortagne@wanadoo.fr.*

Where to Stay and Eat

Le Bec-Hellouin ✉ 27800
The finest place to stay along the Risle valley, with several tempting restaurants.

★★★Auberge de l'Abbaye, t 02 32 44 86 02, **f** 02 32 46 32 23 (*moderate*). Only a few

rooms at this delightful timberframed inn. The restaurant serves many Norman apple specialities (*menus 140–300F*). *Closed most of Jan; Nov–Easter Mon eves and Tues; Easter–Oct Mon.*

La Ferrière-sur-Risle ✉ 27760
Roselion, 7 Route de Pont-Audemer, **t** 02 32 30 10 55, **f** 02 32 30 66 14 (*inexpensive*). B&B in just about the smartest house in town on the splendid main square.

Mortagne-au-Perche ✉ 61400
★★Hôtel du Tribunal, 4 Place du Palais, **t** 02 33 25 04 77, **f** 02 33 83 60 83 (*inexpensive*). Wonderful old hotel on the corner of a charming square, reflecting the town's historic character. Restaurant (*menus 90–190F*).

Bellême ✉ 61130
★★★Hôtel du Golf, Route du Mans, **t** 02 33 85 13 13, **f** 02 33 73 00 17 (*moderate*). Smart hotel, like the golf course by which it stands, which occupies a spot outside the town with very pretty views of the surrounding countryside (*menus 102–258F*).

Le Perche Normand

Little **Mortagne** makes a good base for Le Perche Normand. Wandering from one delightful square to another, you'll find a tiny museum paying homage to the philosopher-journalist Alain who was born here, and whose humanist attacks on the French establishment at the time of the First World War were a rare voice of sanity. Another native, Pierre Boucher, led a large number of people to Canada; Boucherville near Montréal is named after him. Numbered panels around Mortagne explain the history of each historic house, starting in the public garden with a weird statue of a baby riding a full-sized horse, which turns out to represent a tale from Ovid: Neptune emerges from the sea in the guise of a horse, and aided by Cupid, he heads off to conquer Ceres. This was one of the sculptures executed in the 19th century by Frémiet, best known for his militant St Michael atop Mont-St-Michel.

To discover the rural delights of the Perche, head north out of Mortagne on a big loop of country roads via the pretty D205 passing through Céronne and Soligny-la-Trappe to reach the 17th-century **abbey of La Trappe**, the first Trappist monastery in France. The statuary on the gate is surprisingly showy given the ascetic reputation of the Trappist order (or to be more precise, the Cistercians of the Strict Observance).

The monks do speak, but not to any old visitors. You can hear them on the explanatory video at the Accueil. The rest of the abbey is out of bounds to the public.

Continuing the country loop, head east from La Trappe for Randonnai and then southeast for Marchainville. The road down from Marchainville to Monceaux-au-Perche via Longny-au-Perche is dotted with gorgeous Percheron manor houses. Just west of Monceaux-au-Perche, the spires of the **basilica of La Chapelle-Montligeon** stand out against a wooded hillside. It was built as a place of pilgrimage at the end of the 19th century by Abbot Buguet and dedicated to souls in purgatory. The neo-Gothic excesses climax with the garish stained glass in the transepts.

The Côte Fleurie and the Cheesy Pays d'Auge

The Côte Fleurie (the Flowery Coast), west from the mouth of the Seine, became the seaside of Paris in the 19th century. Deauville took on the role of self-styled 21st *arrondissement* of the capital when it supplanted its rival Trouville and, with its famous horse-racing track, still comes in several furlongs ahead of the other seaside resorts. The resorts now mix tackiness with old glamour.

The main attraction in these parts, the historic port of Honfleur, has fine museums and quays lined with ancient high-rise houses. Inland, the Pays d'Auge lays on thick the classic clichés of the Normandy countryside: half-timbered farms and rose-covered manors among apple orchards in green valleys where horses and dappled cows graze.

Honfleur

Why would explorers ever have wished to leave for adventures from as beautiful a port as Honfleur? But they did, most famously Samuel de Champlain at the beginning of the 17th century, whose voyages led to the founding of Quebec. Less trumpeted by the port is its trading and slaving links with Africa; by the 18th century the shipping magnates of little Honfleur had mounted well over 100 expeditions. The fantastic quayside houses of Honfleur's **Vieux Bassin** date from this time. The Vieux Bassin itself was only dug in the second half of the 17th century to provide a safer inner harbour for the port.

The **Quai Ste-Catherine** has the most spectacular display of houses. They must have seemed the skyscrapers of their day. All sorts of touristy shops and restaurants do a roaring trade at ground level. At the end of the Quai Ste-Catherine the Lieutenance served as the well-positioned home of the governors of Honfleur. On one side stands a bust of Champlain, a plaque below recalling the various voyages he organized to Canada.

Behind the Quai Ste-Catherine lies a delightful timberframe neighbourhood. A funny belfry stands guard over **Ste-Catherine**, probably the finest timberframe church in France. It was built in the second half of the 15th century when, after the troubles of the Hundred Years' War, stone was reserved for the rebuilding of the port's fortifications. Inside, the hull of a roof was constructed by local shipbuilders. At the end of the 15th century, the church had to be considerably enlarged, hence the double nave. Light pours in through the diamond-shaped window panes. Some of the carving mixes a touch of sailors' earthiness with refinement; the musicians along the organ gallery display an excess of shapely legs and bottoms.

The **Musée Boudin** (*open 15 Mar–Sept daily exc Tues 10–12 and 2–6; rest of year daily exc Tues 2.30–5, weekends also 10–12; adm*) is the fine arts museum, named after Eugène Boudin, son of a sailor, who was born in Honfleur in 1824. Baudelaire came on holiday to Honfleur with his mother in 1859 and was deeply moved by meeting Boudin and seeing some of his works with 'these firmaments of black or violet satin, crumpled, rolled up or torn, these horizons in mourning or streaming with molten metal, all these depths, all these splendours...' They went to his brain 'like the eloquence of opium'. Here, along with those black horizons are studies of sunsets with touches of Turner, the wonderful *Route de Trouville* and some interesting still lives. Another of the museum's highlights is Jongkind's silvery *Entrée du port d'Honfleur*. The paintings by Dubourg, disparaged by many critics, give a good notion of the 19th-century Normandy seaside, ladies wandering along the beach hemmed in by elaborate dresses and protected by parasols, vessels with great sails colouring the background. The museum also has views by 20th-century artists. Dufy is as irrepressible as ever, and Henri de St-Delis's naïve style is quite fun. Herbo stands apart in tackling the grittier industrial side of the Seine estuary.

Honfleur was also the birthplace in 1886 of the maverick musician Erik Satie, and a new experimental museum has recently been opened in his honour, the **Maisons Satie** (*open high season daily 10–7; rest of year daily 10.30–6; adm*). Your senses are bombarded in this eccentric museum, quite in keeping with the enchanting quirkiness of Satie's music. You can finish the tour riding on a basketball on the musical merry-go-round, made for adults and children alike.

Back at the Vieux Bassin, cross to the **Quai St-Etienne** to wander around the oldest part of the port, known as the Enclos. The adorable **church of St-Etienne turned Musée Maritime** (*open July and Aug daily 10–1 and 2–6.30; April–June and Sept daily exc Mon 10–12 and 2–6; 8 Feb–Mar plus end Sept–mid-Nov daily exc Mon 2–5.30, weekends also 10–12; adm*) is hugged tightly by old houses. Inside the church, what with the clutter of large-scale models of boats, wood carvings and pictures, it's hard to focus on anything. But fragments of Honfleur's history emerge. The plaques in the choir give a chronology of French expeditions to Canada.

Tucked away off a street to one side of the church, the **Musée d'Ethnographique** (*open same times as the Musée Maritime*) presents a fragrant picture of Normandy interiors, a very pretty, cleaned-up picture, except for the prison room. In the same quarter, the 17th-century salt lofts or **Greniers à Sel** were built to supply the Atlantic shipping fleets with salt to preserve cod, but now house seasonal exhibitions. The tradition of painting, good and bad, flourishes in Honfleur to this day.

Getting Around

Deauville airport has direct flights from London in August – contact Brit Air (part of Air France).

Lisieux railway station inland has good connections with Paris (journey time a little over 1hr 30mins). There are a few trains daily from Paris to Lisieux that continue to Trouville-Deauville (allow about 20–30 mins more), but you usually have to change trains at Lisieux.

Unfortunately, Honfleur and the resorts along the coast between Deauville and Cabourg are only accessible on public transport by bus.

Tourist Information

Honfleur: Place A. Boudin, t 02 31 89 04 40, f 02 31 89 31 82.

Deauville: Place de la Mairie, t 02 31 14 40 00, f 02 31 88 78 88, *promo-lpean@deauville.org*.

Trouville: 32 Quai F. Moureaux, t 02 31 14 60 70, f 02 31 14 60 71, *o.t.trouville@wanadoo.fr*.

Cabourg: Jardins du Casino, t 02 31 91 20 00, f 02 31 24 14 49, *cabourg.tourisme@wanadoo.fr*.

Pont-l'Evêque: Rue St-Michel, t 02 31 64 12 77.

Lisieux: Rue d'Alençon, t 02 31 48 18 10, f 02 31 48 18 11, *officelx@club-internet.fr*.

Livarot: Place Georges Bisson, t 02 31 63 47 39, f 02 31 63 15 89.

Where to Stay and Eat

Honfleur ✉ 14600

Peach of a port with a stupendous array of fine hotel choices for all budgets. The three most splendid hotels lie on the Seine estuary slopes west of Honfleur.

****La Ferme St-Siméon**, Rue Adolphe Marais, below the Côte de Grâce church, t 02 31 81 78 00, f 02 31 89 48 48, *simeon@relaischateaux.fr* (*luxury*). A hotel that has it all: views of the Seine; 29 extremely luxurious rooms set in the large central manor or various thatched buildings

around it; the most refined cuisine; the most fabulous and decadent swimming pool complex; and the memories of Monet, Boudin, Sisley, Courbet and Jongkind, who used to meet here.

****La Chaumière**, Route du Littoral (the D513), t 02 31 81 63 20, f 02 31 89 59 23, *chaumiere@relaischateaux.fr* (*luxury–expensive*). Owned by the same family as La Ferme St-Siméon and just a little further west. Long low converted timberframe building offering the height of luxury, in just 9 rooms. Delicious food; a lovely garden; views; and a private path to the beach below. *Closed Wed lunch and Tues*.

****Le Manoir du Butin**, Phare du Butin, t 02 31 81 63 00, f 02 31 89 59 23 (*luxury–expensive*). 9 rooms. Neighbour of the Ferme St-Siméon, a timberframed, gabled pile set in a shaded garden. Restaurant (*menus 185–285F*). *Closed Tues lunch and Mon*.

***L'Ecrin**, 19 Rue Eugène Boudin, B.P.6, t 02 31 14 43 45, f 02 31 89 24 41 (*expensive–moderate*). A good hotel in the very centre of Honfleur, and packed full of character.

***L'Absinthe**, 10 Quai de la Quarantaine, t 02 31 89 23 23, f 02 31 89 53 60 (*expensive–moderate*). Slate-covered and flint-patterned 16th-century hotel close to the Greniers à Sel, with appealing rooms and appealing restaurant (*menus 175–380F*). *Closed 15 Nov–15 Dec*.

Le Belvédère, 36 Rue Emile Renouf, t 02 31 89 08 13, f 02 31 89 51 40 (*moderate*). Exceptionally luxurious two-star hotel.

Les Loges, 18 Rue Brûlée, t 02 31 89 38 26 (*moderate*). Lovingly decorated, slate-sided and luxurious two-star hotel.

Le Dauphin, 10 Place Pierre Berthelot, t 02 31 89 15 53, f 02 31 89 92 06, *hotel.dudauphin@wanadoo.fr* (*moderate*). Timberframe hotel by the timberframe church of Ste-Catherine, with a mix of rooms – some swankier some rather cheaper.

*Les Cascades**, 17 Place Thiers, t 02 31 89 05 83, f 02 31 89 32 13 (*inexpensive*). Reasonable value, basic and well placed.

Honfleur has plenty of splendid restaurants too to choose from:

L'Assiette Gourmande, 2 Quai des Passagers, t 02 31 89 24 88, f 02 31 89 52 80 (*expensive*). If you want to splash out a little, this is Honfleur's most exclusive restaurant.

La Terrasse de l'Assiette, 8 Place Ste-Catherine, t 02 31 89 31 33, f 02 31 89 90 17 (*moderate*). The above's fantastic little sister (*menu 139F*). Closed Nov; 1st half Jan; Wed exc July and Aug, and Tues.

Le Champlain, 6 Place Hamelin, t 02 31 89 14 91. Another excellent restaurant (*menus 128–198F*). Closed Jan and 1st half Feb; Wed and Thurs eves.

La Lieutenance, 12 Place Ste-Catherine, t 02 31 89 07 52, f 02 31 89 07 52. Good, reliable restaurant.

Au P'tit Mareyeur, 4 Rue Haute, t 02 31 98 84 23. A favourite of Normandy foodies (*menu 140F*). Closed Jan eves and Tues.

Trouville ✉ 14360

★★Les Sablettes, 15 Rue Paul Besson, t 02 31 88 10 66, f 02 31 88 59 06 (*inexpensive*). Charming and relatively cheap for this coast, but no restaurant. Closed Dec and Jan.

★★Carmen 24 Rue Carnot, t 02 31 88 35 43, f 02 31 88 08 03 (*inexpensive*). Good value rooms and cuisine (*menus 95–180F*). Closed Jan and Wed, exc school hols.

The quay by the Touques boasts some of the best brasseries in Normandy.

Les Vapeurs, 160 Quai Fernand Moureaux, t 02 31 88 15 24. Top dog, renowned for both style and cuisine.

Les Roches Noires, 16 Bd Louis Bréguet, t 02 31 88 12 19. Beautifully simple fresh fish dishes to accompany delightful sea views.

Deauville ✉ 14800

★★★★Normandy, 38 Rue Jean Mermoz, t 02 31 98 66 22, f 02 31 98 66 23, *normandy@lucienbarriere.com* (*luxury–expensive*). Palatial Deauville institution with 265 rooms by the casino, which contains the very luxurious **La Potinière** restaurant (*menus 285–325F*).

★★★★Royal, Bd Cornuché, t 02 31 98 66 33, f 02 31 98 66 34, *royal@lucienbarriere.com*

(*luxury–expensive*). Outrageously luxurious hotel with 223 rooms close to the beach, with its own flamboyant restaurant, **L'Etrier** (*menus 295–385F*).

★★Le Trophée, 81 Rue du Général Leclerc, t 02 31 88 45 86, f 02 31 88 07 94 (*moderate*). Stylish, bright bedrooms behind a Norman façade. Good food (*menus 150–295F*).

★★Le Patio, 180 Av de la République, t 02 31 88 25 07, f 02 31 88 00 81 (*inexpensive*). Stylish two-star.

Cabourg ✉ 14390

★★★★Grand Hôtel, Promenade Marcel Proust, t 02 31 91 01 79, f 02 31 24 03 20 (*expensive*). Enormous camp wedding cake-like hotel with 70 rooms on the Cabourg seafront, where Proust stayed so faithfully. Proust aficionados will probably want to dine at **Le Balbec**, its posh restaurant (*menus 230–290F*). Closed Jan Mon; Dec–Mar Tues.

★★Le Cottage, 24 Av du Général Leclerc, t 02 31 91 65 61, f 02 31 28 78 82 (*inexpensive*). Typical simple seaside Norman hotel with 14 rooms but no restaurant.

★★Hôtel de Paris, 39 Av de la Mer, t 02 31 91 31 34, f 02 31 24 54 61 (*inexpensive*). Another simpler choice.

★★Beaurivage, Allée du Château/Route du Home, t 02 31 24 08 08, f 02 31 91 19 46 (*inexpensive*). More modest seafront option.

Beaumont-en-Auge ✉ 14950

Auberge de l'Abbaye, 2 Rue de la Libération, t 02 31 64 82 31. Posh picture of a Normandy village restaurant (*menus 160–290F*). Closed 1st half Oct, 1st half Feb and Tues, Wed exc July and Aug.

Pierrefitte-en-Auge ✉ 14130

Auberge des Deux Tonneaux, t 02 31 64 09 31. Characterful inn in delightful old timberframe village tumbling down the hillside, with bulging walls, thatched roof, many plants and a fine view on to the Touques. Run as a local restaurant serving straightforward Normandy cooking. Closed 15 Nov–15 Feb and Sun eves exc school hols.

Trouville, Deauville and Cabourg

The greatest events of my life have been a few thoughts, reading,
certain sunsets at Trouville...
                                         Flaubert

Trouville may have been beaten by Dieppe as France's first seaside resort, but thanks to a better beach and good connections with Paris, it quickly became more popular. Its beach has been its fortune, a sweep of soft sand running away to the cliffs in the far distance. The first beach huts appeared in the 1840s, and when Napoleon III began to bring his court here in the 1850s its popularity was assured. The view along Trouville's boardwalk, or *planches*, with flags fluttering in the wind, must be one of the most familiar images of 19th-century French painting. After the elite had transferred their allegiance to Deauville, Trouville continued to draw crowds. It now has a relaxing, old-style seafront, with bars, ice-cream stands and some grand old villas.

Away from the beach, Trouville is an idiosyncratic town, with narrow streets winding up suddenly steep hillsides. Bizarre Norman holiday-home architecture features: half-timbering and pebbledash. On Rue Général Leclerc, the main street, the small **Musée Montebello** (*check opening hours with tourist office*) shelters some charming works by Boudin and other Trouville painters. The long quay where fishing boats moor is another focus of activity.

Fleeting glimpses of French actresses, sharply preserved matrons promenading with little dogs, Belle Epoque *roués* staggering ruined from the casino, men and women with flawless skin lolling in unbelievably comfortable chairs on café terraces, a precise sense of chic and luxury – these are the images conjured up by **Deauville**, another product of the decadent Second Empire. In 1860 Napoleon III's half-brother, the Duc de Morny, strayed across the Touques from Trouville and decided to develop the empty dunes and marshes as a much more exclusive resort. Another contributor to Deauville was a speculator called Eugène Cornuché, who rebuilt the seafront and the casino. By the early 1900s anyone who was anyone could be found each summer along Deauville's neatly clipped seafront. Since it was a totally artificial town its promoters imposed particular styles, the most common one known locally as Anglo-Norman, using lashings of mock half-timbering to build up giant mansions that look like traditional Norman manor houses on steroids. Yet Deauville's architecture has a rather sterile feel, and is separated from the beach by a no-man's-land of gardens.

The Touques estuary has two large marinas full of luxury yachts. Deauville also has two tracks where you can lose your shirt, La Touques for flat racing and the more casual Clairefontaine (*free guided tours every day in season 10.30am*) mainly used for steeplechases and trotting. Both are lavishly equipped and beautifully maintained. In August the polo tournament at La Touques and the Grand Prix de Deauville, the traditional end to the racing season, are major social events. Deauville's Festival du Cinéma Américain follows in early September, and gets in a US film star to preside. Deauville of course boasts one of the most luxurious thalassotherapy centres in France, while the golf course claims to be one of the finest in the country.

Deauville may have played around with its seafront blocks, but at **Cabourg** the feel of the Belle Epoque lives on. It served as a model for Balbec in Proust's masterpiece, and much of the attention in Cabourg centres around the Grand Hôtel where Proust stayed with his chauffeur. The hotel trades shamelessly on its associations by offering wildly expensive teas, but no refund is promised should the madeleines fail to unlock the floodgates of memory. However, Cabourg also has the free attraction of one of the finest beach fronts in Normandy, where grand old villas play their role more elegantly than the attention-seeking crowds in Deauville.

Into the Pays d'Auge: From the Coast to Lisieux

The northern Pays d'Auge, roughly above the N13 Lisieux to Caen road on the map, is perhaps the prettiest part of this prettiest area of Normandy, where the valleys are at their most verdant, half-timbered houses predominate and horse-breeding, cider and cheese making are major concerns.

With its many smart stud farms marked off by white fencing, the D118 from Villers-sur-Mer to Pont-l'Evêque takes you through the juiciest village in the area, **Beaumont-en-Auge**, full of character, with a pensive statue of the great astronomer Laplace, born here in 1749. A short distance east is **Pont-l'Evêque** of very fine and smelly cheese fame, although it lost much of its soul in Second World War bombing.

Take the D48 from Pont-l'Evêque towards Lisieux. The higgledy-piggledy collection of old houses at **Pierrefitte-en-Auge** has plenty of traditional character. Head a little way west of Pierrefitte-en-Auge and you'll discover **St-Hymer** hidden in its little valley, with a washing fountain next to the babbling stream.

Above the N13, the **Cambremer Route du Cidre** offers a well-signposted circuit round the heart of the Auge cider *appellation* area where you can visit traditional cider-making farms. The prettiness of **Beuvron-en-Auge**, with its variety of timberframe patterns and brick façades, is no secret, so it's often crawling with tourists. South of Beuvron-en-Auge, the **Château de Crèvecœur** lies close to the busy N13, but could serve as a book illustration of a Norman motte-and-bailey castle. Its oldest ramparts went up before its lord joined William in his conquest of England, while the delightful half-timbered buildings around the grassed-over courtyard date from later centuries. The dovecote is spectacular. Bizarrely, as Crèvecoeur has been lovingly restored by a foundation created by the Alsatian Schlumberger engineering family, it now houses a museum on oil exploration as well as temporary exhibitions.

Lisieux attracts intense crowds of pilgrims, thanks to Ste Thérèse de Lisieux. An outrageously large dome sticks out of the Lisieux hillside, crowning a neo-Byzantine **basilica** built to dazzle the masses. Inside the basilica, elaborate marble patterning leads up to a series of enormous mosaics. Photos of Thérèse and her parents are much in evidence. The other main place of pilgrimage in Lisieux is the bourgeois house where Thérèse Martin was reared (*open Palm Sun–Sept daily 9–12 and 2–6; Oct, Feb and Mar daily 10–12 and 2–5; Nov and Dec daily 10–12 and 2–4*) after the family had moved from Alençon where she was born. On the short guided tour you're told something of Thérèse's disturbed life, and it isn't a pretty story. Her fanaticism was provoked by several factors: the death of her mother when Thérèse was just four; a terrible childhood illness which she thought she had survived miraculously; and a crisis over Christmas presents. In 1888, aged 15, Thérèse was allowed, given her ardour, to follow two of her sisters and join the Carmelite order. In under ten years she was dead from tuberculosis, having followed the rule with exceptional rigour. She left a number of writings, including *L'Histoire d'une âme*, recording her brief but intense life and spiritual journey.

In the centre of the town you can see all too well how the heart was ripped out of Lisieux in the war. However, the mainly 13th-century **cathedral** has survived, skulking in a corner of a postwar square. Its rough interior exudes a rather purer spirituality than the kitsch Catholic places devoted to Ste Thérèse.

A short way south of Lisieux, rural **St-Germain-du-Livet** boasts one of the most playfully picturesque little châteaux in Normandy, one of its moated wings patterned with glazed green tiles. Fragments of original wall paintings survive inside, including a tournament scene and, among 16th-century biblical representations, St John the Baptist's head on a plate.

The Augean Cheese Stables South of Lisieux

Livarot, Vimoutiers, St-Pierre-sur-Dives and charming little Camembert fight it out for cheese-lovers' attention in this corner of the Auge. **Livarot**, which produces perhaps the most characterful of all the potent Normandy cheeses, has converted the basement of a little château into a museum of *fromage* and *fromage*-making (*open Mar–Oct daily 10–12 and 2–6*).

Camembert cheese, so far ahead in the cheese marketing stakes, has two museums devoted to it, one at Vimoutiers, another in the village of Camembert itself. Poor **Vimoutiers** was torn to bits in the Battle of Normandy, and to add to the devastation came the painful decapitation of the town's statue of the 'inventor' of the cheese, Marie Harnel. In the museum (*open April–Oct daily exc Mon am 9–12 and 2–6; Oct–Mar daily exc Sun and Mon am 10–12 and 2–5.30*) you discover how the goddess of gooey *fromage* was taught her techniques by a priest on the run (excuse the pun) from Brie. At both Camembert museums you learn about the important procedure whereby the curds are added in five separate ladlefuls to make true Camembert. Fake Camembert is big business, too, as labels from Iceland, Japan and New Zealand show.

However, the meltingly gorgeous village of **Camembert**, in its lush valley, remains unique, and the new Maison du Camembert (*open April–11 Nov daily 10–7*) is built in the familiar shape of an opened Camembert poplar box. After the displays and video, you can sample both AOC Camembert and the more exclusive Camembert Fermier, still produced on a few local farms.

West of Livarot, delightful **St-Pierre-sur-Dives** was another major stop on the cheese trail until it recently shut down its museum. However, its exceptional market hall remains very firmly in place, a great dark barn protected by stone walls and steep slopes of tiles, some parts of which date as far back as the 11th century. The Monday morning market here is as traditional as they come. The mutilated **abbey**, in particular its church, has various bits and pieces from different centuries. William the Conqueror was present at its original consecration.

Just south of St-Pierre-sur-Dives you can seek out a bonbon of a stately Louis XVI-style home, the **Château de Vendeuvre** (*open May–Sept daily 10–6; Mar–April and Oct–Nov weekends and hols only; adm*). Gutted in 1944, it has been lavishly restored with all of its original sugary pastel decor. It also contains a remarkable collection of furniture, bric-à-brac and life-size automata in each room. In the orangery the countess shows off the world's largest collection of miniature furniture. Much of the present count's attention is devoted to his fanciful water garden with its elaborate concealed fountains – all very twee and entertaining.

The D-Day Beaches Along the Côte de Nacre

This is surely the most famous stretch of coastline in the Western World. The successful campaign by allied American, British, Canadian and other troops to defeat Nazi Germany began with the massive military landings here in early June 1944.

The Caen Mémorial de la Paix

The state-of-the-art **Caen Mémorial de la Paix** (*open June–Aug daily 9–9; rest of year exc first fortnight Jan daily 9–7; adm*), devoted to peace as well as war, opened in 1988. A sculptural slab of a building with a gash for an entrance recalling the violence of war, it stands in a beautifully landscaped park on the north side of the Caen ring road, so you don't need to go into the town to visit it (the rest of Caen is covered from p.240). The Mémorial seeks to present a broad picture of the Second World War, including its causes going back to 1918, its political and social background, and views of life at the time. The museum portrays the D-Day landings and Operation Overlord in highly dramatic manner. Strongly visual mixed-media displays figure largely, along

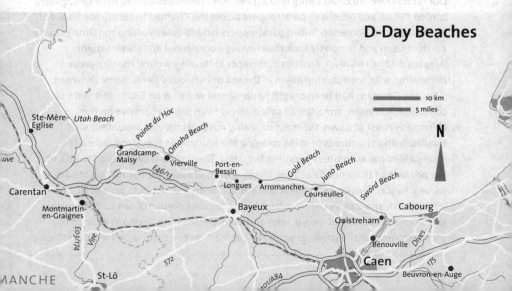

D-Day Beaches

D-Day Heroics

The daring and scale of the Allies' D-Day landings and the greater Operation Overlord still seem breathtaking today. Planning had begun in January 1943 for an Allied invasion, with General Sir Frederick Morgan in charge. He opted for Normandy as the favourable place for a landing, as the Pas de Calais coast was too obvious. The Allied commanders Montgomery and Eisenhower agreed to the plan, only insisting on increasing the scale and width of the invasion Morgan had envisaged. The Nazi leaders realized as 1943 advanced that an Allied attack was becoming more and more likely. However, through clever misinformation and superior airpower, the Allies kept the Germans guessing as to where this might be staged. Such was Allied control in the air that in the six months leading up to D-Day the Luftwaffe proved virtually incapable of achieving any surveillance flights over England. Meanwhile, the Allies were busy assembling a vast number of landing craft, although a contretemps with the uncooperative US Admiral King caused the planners to delay Overlord till June.

That gave the Germans a few extra weeks to strengthen their coastal defences. At the end of 1943 Rommel had been called in by Hitler to help organize the defence of Nazi-occupied France with Rundstedt, the latter settled somewhat too comfortably in Paris. Rommel realized that the defence of the French coasts hadn't been organized efficiently. He had large sections mined much more intensively, and obstacles placed in strategic positions. He also insisted on the importance of the Panzer tank divisions in countering any attack, having learnt in the North African campaign the ability of the Allied aeroplanes to knock out lines of reinforcement. Rundstedt hadn't experienced the pace of modern warfare and hampered Rommel's intelligent plans.

Sure enough, in the weeks leading up to the landings Allied planes carried out extensive bombings on the rail network across northern France. But not all went according to plan. D-Day had deliberately been chosen to fall on 4 June, when it had been calculated that the tides would be manageable. However, the weather let the Allies down for two days, and it was only on the evening of 5 June that it was decided Operation Overlord could swing into action. From the hours around midnight, gliders carried British and American paratroopers across the Channel to secure the flanks of the bridgehead. Some 180 British paratroopers landed quietly along the Orne estuary north of Caen and famously took the crossing now named after their insignia, Pegasus Bridge. However, American attempts at landing around the Vire proved harrowing, with men coming down in the sea or in flooded fields. Some drowned.

But the Germans had been caught napping and woke up on 6 June in a state of confusion. A massive armada had sailed across from Britain to arrive on the Normandy coast at dawn, the most daunting naval attack ever mounted, with hundreds upon hundreds of ships covering the horizon. As they approached the shore, Allied naval bombers pounded the coast. The Germans only began to pick up the advance of this armada at 2am. Blumentritt had asked for permission at 4am to move a Panzer division to the beaches, but had been instructed to wait until dawn.

The British and Canadian forces landed on the coast north of Caen and Bayeux, on the beaches codenamed Sword, Juno and Gold. Because the Germans were so ill-prepared, most of the landings were easy, at least on the eastern and western sides of the bridgehead. The British and Canadian troops arriving at Sword and Juno met with very little resistance as they came ashore. The crack American troops that landed on Utah suffered the least casualties of all. However, towards the centre, the landings met with fiercer resistance and Gold proved difficult to take. The naval bombardments hadn't managed to destroy a German-fortified village overseeing the beach, and many soldiers were mown down as they came ashore. But by nightfall the 50th Division that had landed on Gold had made the most progress of all.

The Americans landing at Omaha beach northwest of Bayeux would encounter the worst from the start. Not only did they come face to face with the only formidable German formation then stationed along this stretch of the coast, but on top of that their amphibious Shermans were launched too far from the sands and failed to provide cover for the soldiers. The vast majority of the 4,649 American casualties in the D-Day landings fell at Omaha. The Rangers who were given the impossible task of trying to take the high headland of the Pointe du Hoc to the west of Omaha were almost completely wiped out. Despite these two tragedies, by the close of 6 June the Allies had established their footholds along some 60 miles of Normandy coast.

The hinterland would prove much more difficult to take. That said, such was the vast superiority of the Allied airforce that the Germans found it painfully hard to get reinforcements through the French countryside. Meanwhile troops and supplies were coming across the Channel unimpeded. Most remarkably, two whole ports, known as Mulberries, were floated across the Channel to be put in place on the beaches. Unfortunately Channel storms from 19 to 21 June badly damaged these portable ports, although the one established at Arromanches would go on to play its part. As early as 26 June 25 Allied divisions had landed in Normandy, with a further 15 to come. The German Western Army had 14 at their disposal. Rundstedt suggested to Hitler that he sue for peace, and was immediately replaced by Kluge.

Some two million Allied soldiers in all landed on the D-Day beaches, along with around 500,000 vehicles and 3 million tonnes of supplies. Such statistics give an idea of the scale of the landing enterprise and what an extraordinary exercise it was.

After the Allies' initial success in the east along the Orne, Caen would prove devilishly difficult to take. On the western side of operations the hedgerows of the Cotentin peninsula would make the American advance northwards to take Cherbourg painstakingly difficult. But American success in the north of the Cotentin and Cherbourg was followed by a vital breakthrough in the south of the Cotentin. On 25 and 26 July 'Lightning Joe' Collins led a crucial attack on just about the finest tank division the Germans had, the Panzer Lehr division. After one awful accident when US bombs were dropped on US troops, the American soldiers moved forward to trounce the Lehr division. The Americans were ready to break through into Brittany, but Hitler, in a state of anger at the assassination attempt against him on 20 July, ordered a great defence of Normandy. This would lead to the most terrible tank battle the Western Front ever witnessed, the Battle of the Falaise Gap.

The two war museums either end of the D-Day beaches, at Caen and at Quinéville, describe the whole context of the Second World War. Other museums placed at regular intervals between them concentrate on specific D-Day actions or themes.

with more traditional exhibits. The visit culminates with an hour-long three-screen film centred on the Normandy battles.

From Ouistreham to Arromanches

Head up through the industrial sprawl between Caen and its ferry port of Ouistreham via the **Orne river**. It's along here that the liberation of France began in June 1944 with the securing of crossings over the Orne, most famously that known as Pegasus Bridge. At **Bénouville**, the **Café Gondrée** is almost as much a museum as a bar, a well-known, proudly maintained symbol. According to the plaque, it was the first house to be liberated in France, on the night of 5 to 6 June. The daring operations in this area were carried out by the Oxfordshire and Buckinghamshire light infantry. In summer 2000 the new **Musée des Troupes Aéroportées** (*open July–Aug daily 9–7; June daily 9.30–12.30 and 2–7; mid-Mar–May and Sept–mid-Oct daily 9.30–12.30 and 2–6; adm*) was opened by Prince Charles. The major exhibit is the original Pegasus Bridge which was replaced by a modern replica spanning the Orne in 1993. The museum gives visitors details on the events involved in the crucial taking of the bridge. Across the river stand memorials to Major Howard, the man who led the operation, and the 180 men who landed here. Nowadays, between April and October the bridge serves as the backdrop to a wartime *son-et-lumière* which recalls the daring start to D-Day.

An almost unbroken line of resorts have linked up from Ouistreham west to Courseulles to make the most of the sands from Sword Beach to Juno Beach. This isn't the easiest stretch along which to recall the actions of 1944, despite the occasional monument or recovered tank. Instead, old-fashioned seaside pleasures dominate.

Courseulles is an estuary port tucked away behind Juno Beach where the Canadian soldiers landed on D-Day. A memorial also recalls that it was here that General de Gaulle finally made it back to France, on 14 June 1944, after leading the French Resistance from London. A big silver cross of Lorraine rises out of the dunes. Courseulles has a sweet maritime museum, the **Musée de la Mer** (*open July–Aug daily 9–7; May–June daily 9–1 and 2–7; Sept–April daily exc Mon 10–12 and 2–6; adm*).

At Courseulles the string of resorts comes to an end. The coast to Arromanches looks wilder, the strand below known as Gold Beach from the war, another British landing beach. Many stop on the heights east of **Arromanches** to look down on the remains of its Mulberry Harbour. A modern cinema up here, **Arromanches 360 degrees** (*showings start at 10 and 40 past the hour; open June–Aug daily 9.10–6.40; May and Sept daily 10.10–5.40; Feb–April and Oct–Dec daily 10.10–4.40; adm*), presents a dramatic film about the D-Day landings on a 360 degree screen. The crude hype of the place promising '18 minutes of total emotion' could surely have been avoided, however. More soberly, the plain memorial by the white Virgin pays homage to the Sappers of the Royal Engineers who played a key role in preparations for the D-Day landings. Some came across in midget submarines, canoeing to the beaches on their reconnaissance missions. Their specialist skills were crucial, and well over 6,000 died in daring actions between D-Day and VE Day.

Getting Around

The ferry port of Caen-Ouistreham lies on the eastern side of the D-Day landing beaches. To reach the beaches via public transport, you need to catch a bus from Caen or Bayeux. The buses from Caen will take you to Sword Beach, Juno Beach and the eastern side of Gold Beach, and to the villages of Ouistreham, Riva-Bella, Colleville, Lion-sur-Mer, Luc-sur-Mer, Langrune, St-Aubin-sur-Mer, Bernières-sur-Mer, Courseulles-sur-Mer, and Ver-sur-Mer.

The buses from Bayeux serve the villages behind Omaha Beach, including Port-en-Bessin, Vierville-sur-Mer and Grandcamp.

Tourist Information

Ouistreham-Riva Bella: Jardins du Casino, t 02 31 97 18 63, f 02 31 96 87 33.
Courseulles: Rue de la Mer, t 02 31 37 46 80, f 02 31 37 29 25.
Arromanches: 4 Rue du Maréchal Joffre, t 02 31 22 36 45.
Port-en-Bessin: 2 Rue du Croiseur-Montcalm, t 02 31 21 92 33, f 02 31 22 08 40.
Vierville-sur-Mer + Omaha Beach: t 02 31 22 43 08.
Grandcamp-Maisy: 118 Rue Aristide Briand, t 02 31 22 62 44, f 02 31 22 99 95.
St-Lô: Place Général de Gaulle, t 02 33 77 60 35, f 02 33 77 60 36.

Where to Stay and Eat

Crépon ✉ 14480
**Ferme de la Rançonnière, Rte d'Arromanches, t 02 31 22 21 73, f 02 31 22 98 39 (*moderate–inexpensive*). Medieval atmosphere, but the rooms are quite luxurious. In the barn-like restaurant you can taste superlative local poultry (*menus lunch 60F, eves 98–280F*).

Arromanches ✉ 14117
**Hôtel de la Marine, Quai du Canada, t 02 31 22 34 19, f 02 31 22 98 80 (*inexpensive*). Evocative views on to the Mulberry Harbour. The rooms are dull but comfortable; the restaurant more exciting.

Tracy-sur-Mer ✉ 14117
**Hôtel Victoria, 24 Chemin de l'Eglise, t 02 31 22 35 37, f 02 31 22 93 38 (*inexpensive*). Smart little 19th-century manor in its own courtyard near Arromanches. *Closed Oct–Mar.*

Port-en-Bessin/Escures-Commes ✉ 14520
****La Chenevière, t 02 31 51 25 25, f 02 31 51 25 20, *la.chenevière@wanadoo.fr* (*luxury–expensive*). A grand-looking hotel just south of the port, with a highly regarded restaurant (*menus 150–420F*). *Closed Jan.*

Arromanches, destination for one of the Mulberry Harbours, didn't see any landing craft on D-Day – it was important that the sea here shouldn't have any wrecks in the way to hamper the construction of the harbour. Allied tanks landed on Gold Beach and made it to Arromanches by mid-afternoon on D-Day; the elements of the harbour arrived on D-Day +1. The main parts were five-storey-high concrete blocks, towed from England, then sunk on the rocks in front of Arromanches. By D-Day +9 the harbour was in operation. It survived the terrible storms of mid-June 1944, and by the end of that year, 220,000 men and around 39,000 vehicles had landed. The harbour stopped operating in mid-November. The **Musée du Débarquement** (*open summer daily 9–6.30; winter exc Jan daily 9.30–5; adm*) tells the story.

From Omaha Beach to Utah Beach

West of Arromanches at **Longues** a row of concrete batteries, several with rusting guns still in place, give an evocative picture of the Nazi defences along the coast. These guns weren't hit by the naval shelling early on 6 June and caused some difficulty for the Allies during that day.

Port-en-Bessin, unlike most of the coastal villages and towns along the Côte de Nacre, has remained a working fishing harbour. It is also home to one of the oddest of the Normandy war museums, the **Musée des Epaves Sous-marines** (*open June–Sept and May weekends 10–12 and 2–6; adm*). Since 1968, owner Jacques Lemonchois has had the sole concession from the French government to salvage the D-Day wrecks off the coast. The finds he and his team have dredged up are presented here, including whole tanks, ships' turbines, guns, plates and small items such as coat hooks, razors and old pennies, all rusted to a uniform brown.

'This embattled shore, portal of freedom, is forever hallowed by the ideals, the valor and sacrifices of our fellow countrymen.' So reads one of the memorial sentences up at the **American cemetery** overlooking Omaha Beach. With its temple of a memorial, its long, long rows of pure white crosses on immaculately kept lawns and its evocative setting by the sea, this is a war cemetery that powerfully recalls the price paid for freedom in Western Europe. The large-scale maps at the memorial show the staggering size of the Reich in 1943 and speak more eloquently of the fight which the Americans crucially joined than the camp-looking loin-clothed winged Victory. Nearly 10,000 soldiers are buried in the cemetery. In the weeks leading up to D-Day, the German 352nd Panzer tank division was moved to guard Omaha Beach and inflicted terrible casualties on the American 1st Division as it landed. But only a minority of the 10,000 buried here died on the beaches; most were brought here from other areas where the Americans fought in France and in Belgium.

The **Musée Omaha** (*open July–Aug daily 9.30–7; Mar–June and Sept–Oct daily 9.30–12.30 and 2.30–6.30; adm*) is privately run and a little tatty, but displays the everyday objects given to the US soldiers, such as toothbrushes and army-issue condoms. Down on the beach, it still seems a bit odd for people to be sandyachting on such symbolic terrain. The steep slope at the back of the beach at **Vierville** on the western end of Omaha beach recalls the scenery used in Spielberg's *Saving Private Ryan*, although the beach scenes in the film were in fact shot in Ireland.

The mix of natural beauty and war horror makes the **Pointe du Hoc** just about the most moving Second World War location along the D-Day coast. Big chunks of Nazi cement bunkers lie on their sides on the clifftop, the ground around them puckered with the big holes of heavy shelling. To either side you can see the beautiful pincers of cliffs. The squarish fishing port of **Grandcamp-Maisy** still has some fishing vessels. A small **Musée des Rangers** (*open June–Aug daily exc Mon am 10–7; April, May, Sept and Oct daily exc Mon 10–1 and 3–6; adm*) recalls the Pointe du Hoc tragedy, when the 2nd Ranger Battalion unsuccessfully tried to put the German defences out of action.

To get to Utah Beach, cross a corner of the Cotentin marshes. This is where, in the early hours of the morning of D-Day, the American parachute drop started so disastrously. **Graignes**, a quiet village with a devastated church, was the scene of another tragedy in June 1944. On the 6th, some 170 US parachutists were dropped over the marshes. A few drowned, but the others gathered, aided by metal clickers nicknamed crickets, at Graignes, where they were taken in by the villagers. Unfortunately the Germans spotted them and the village was surrounded. On Sunday 11 June, while the villagers were at Mass, the Germans began their attack. By nightfall they controlled the village. Many of the Americans were killed; any taken prisoner were executed; a few escaped. The priest was murdered, the houses pillaged.

St-Lô, some distance inland, became the most terrible victim of the Battle of Normandy in 1944, and it came to be known as the Capital of Ruins. The hill town lay at an important road junction in western Normandy, and the fighting between Americans and Germans officially left 95 per cent of the town destroyed. And yet the place retains vestiges of its past, including parts of its medieval ramparts and an eccentric Gothic church. The remnants of the prison gate have been turned into a war memorial. The town has been given a splendid curving modern building housing a fine arts museum which also pays homage to St-Lô's past. The **Musée des Beaux-Arts** (*open daily exc Tues 10–12 and 2–6; adm*) contains a special round room devoted to a delightfully saucy series of Bruges tapestries, made between 1590 and 1650, recounting the love story of shepherds Gombault and Macée with much kissing, skirt-lifting and hanky-panky. Among the other curiosities are Old Master drawings and portraits of the local Matignon-Grimaldi family, related to the present royal family of Monaco. The collection of 19th-century landscapes is particularly strong and modern art is represented by the likes of Picasso, Léger and Miro. There are also photographs and models of pre-war St-Lô and paintings of the devastation.

Only the front of St-Lô's Gothic **Notre-Dame** was savagely amputated in the war. Inside it looks as broad as a Flemish church; its most peculiar feature, the south choir, fans out from the side aisle. Some pieces of Gothic stained glass have survived, while a postwar creation retells the story of Thomas à Becket. Horse enthusiasts may enjoy a visit to the large national stud, the **Haras National** (*tours June–15 Sept daily 2.30–4.30, plus July–Aug 11am tour; adm*). On Thursday afternoons in August special horse and carriage displays are laid on.

Moving back north, before reaching Utah Beach, visit **Ste-Mère-Eglise** for its war museum, one of the most interesting in Normandy. In one of the most famous images of the D-Day landings, American parachutist John Steele came down over the town and ended up stranded in midair as his parachute got stuck on the church tower; Red Buttons memorably played his part in the film *The Longest Day*. As Steele dangled, Ste-Mère-Eglise became the first village liberated in France. The **Musée des Troupes Aéroportées** (*open Feb–mid-Nov daily; mid-Nov–mid-Dec weekends; adm*) remembers the thousands of soldiers less fortunate than John Steele (who survived his ordeal) as well as explaining the D-Day airborne operations in detail. The two large rooms centre around spectacular exhibits, in one a US WACO glider, in the other a C47 Douglas, both vital to the Allied airborne operations. The two films in English, *Getting Ready* and *Mission Accomplished*, help to give you a fuller picture of the objectives and dangers of the parachute missions in which thousands died. There's also the moving testimony of a Resistance fighter, and all sorts of related matter to pore over: rations, weapons, newspaper articles, photos, paintings... The historic **church** interior, appropriately enough, has Gothic vaults in the Angevin style which look rather like parachutes in stone. A stained glass window pays homage to the paratroopers. The streets of Ste-Mère-Eglise bear the names of US soldiers.

Cows chew the grass contentedly beside the Nazi bunkers behind long, long **Utah Beach**, the only landing beach on the Cotentin peninsula. In the southern section, behind the innocuous little dunes, the country roads also carry the names of American soldiers killed on 6 June 1944. The **Utah Beach Musée du Débarquement** (*open April–Nov daily; rest of year weekends only; adm*) lies at the southern end of the beach, housed in an ultra-modern building with a light blue landing vessel and other pieces from D-Day standing outside. The architecture is designed to give wide views across to the Pointe du Hoc. Models, documents and films give a good picture of the enormous landing operation.

Right by the beach at **Quinéville**, the rambling **Musée de la Liberté** (*open June–Sept daily 9.30–7.30; Mar–May and Oct–Nov daily 10–6; adm*) goes back to the time before France was occupied by the Nazis. There's a mass of information, on the build-up to the Second World War, on the invasion of France and the shortlived flight of civilians, on daily life under the Nazis (including a reconstituted shopping street), on Operation Otter (the Nazi plan of 1940 to invade Britain), on German policies and propaganda in France, on collaboration and the Resistance. There are separate sections on Operation Overlord, the Holocaust and the Nuremberg trials. You need to read French to be able to appreciate this museum to the full, but the basic outlines are translated into English. You can watch an hour-long film on the Second World War made for the 50th anniversary of D-Day. This reveals to what degree the *département* of La Manche suffered during the Battle of Normandy – apparently some 15,000 civilians died in the bombings, and out of a population of 440,000, 280,000 were made homeless.

Caen

Caen shot to greatness under William the Conqueror and his wife Matilda of Flanders. From a meagre village by the Orne, it grew into one of the main centres of the extraordinarily powerful Norman dukedom. As well as getting ramparts and a castle thanks to William, it received as a gift from him and his wife two enormous Romanesque abbeys. The couple were forced into their acts of benevolence. William had married Matilda, a cousin, in the early 1050s, but she proved not to be a distant enough relation to avoid the wrath of the papacy, and they were excommunicated. William's powerful friend in the Church, Lanfranc, managed to have the punishment lifted in exchange for an expiatory abbey from each of the spouses.

The abbeys have survived, but much of Caen was devastated in the bombardments and fighting after the D-Day landings. Montgomery pursued a deliberate policy around Caen of encouraging the Germans to concentrate their armoured units in the area, all the more easily, he hoped, to wipe them out and open the way to Paris. The Allies targeted the city relentlessly for a month as the Germans held on doggedly. The Allied troops in this bitter combat suffered heavy losses, particularly with Montgomery's so-called Epsom Offensive that failed to take the town. Canadian forces eventually managed to gain Caen west of the Orne on 10 July, but the Germans remained ensconced on the opposite bank. They in turn shelled Caen ceaselessly for a

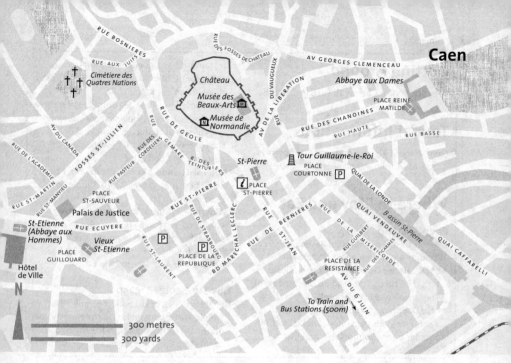

RUE BOSNIERES

RUE AUX JUIFS

RUE DES FOSSES DE CHATEAU

AV GEORGES CLEMENCEAU

†† Cimètiere des
† † Quatres Nations

Château

Musée des
Beaux-Arts

Abbaye aux Dames

PLACE REINE
MATILDE

RUE DE GEOLE

AV DE LA LIBERATION

AV DU VAUGUEUX

RUE DES CHANOINES

RUE HAUTE

RUE BASSE

RUE DE L'ACADEMIE

AV DU CANADA

FOSSES ST-JULIEN

RUE PASTEUR

RUE DES CORDELIERS

R. DES
TEINTURIERS

GEMARE

Musée de
Normandie

St-Pierre

Tour Guillaume-le-Roi

PLACE
COURTONNE P

QUAI DE LA LONDE

Bassin St-Pierre

i PLACE
ST-PIERRE

RUE ST-MARTIN

RUE ST-MANVIEU

PLACE
ST-SAUVEUR

Palais de Justice

RUE ST-PIERRE

RUE DE STRASBOURG

RUE MARÉCHAL LECLERC

RUE DE BERNIERES

RUE
DE LA

RUE
DE
ST-JEAN

QUAI VENDEUVRE

RUE GUILBERT

RUE DES CARMES

RUE DE MISERICORDE

QUAI CAFFARELLI

St-Etienne
(Abbaye aux
Hommes)

RUE ECUYERE

Vieux
St-Etienne

P

PLACE
GUILLOUARD

RUE ST-LAURENT

P

PLACE DE LA
REPUBLIQUE

BD MARECHAL LECLERC

PLACE DE LA
RESISTANCE

AV DU 6 JUIN

Hôtel
de Ville

N

To Train and
Bus Stations (500m)

300 metres
300 yards

further month. The fighting continued around the city until 20 August, at the end of the Battle of Normandy.

From afar, the town looks at first like a mass of postwar blocks dominated by a towering modern hospital. But in fact a great many historic buildings have survived or been rebuilt in the centre of Caen. The city's most popular site is the Mémorial de la Paix on the northern edge of town (see pp.233–6). In the centre, the mighty castle walls that remain standing today actually date from the time of Henry I, William's successor as duke of Normandy and king of England. The bailey walls hide a couple of good museums. The **Musée de Normandie** (open daily exc Tues 9.30–12.30 and 2–6; adm) has particularly beautiful Gallo-Roman and Merovingian artefacts, but sadly little seems to have survived from the Viking period. Traditional crafts are well represented, and the separate Salle des Echiquiers, the great hall built for Henry I, provides a grand setting for temporary exhibitions.

The **Musée des Beaux-Arts** (open daily exc Tues 10–6; adm), in a modern sunken bunker within the bailey, contains a colourful collection, surprisingly rich in Italian art. The two Veroneses are vibrant and dramatic; Perugino's famous Marriage of the Virgin directly inspired Raphael's even more famous one. Among the Flemish paintings highlights are a serene Van der Weyden Virgin and Child, a Breughel the Younger tax-collecting scene full of detail and Rubens's bold ruddy-faced Abraham and Melchior. Still lifes include an amazing goose hanging like a reflection of a crucified Christ by Frans Snyders. The 17th-century French school features a disappointingly dark Venus crying over the death of Adonis by Poussin, and Philippe de Champaigne's depiction of Louis XIII thanking Christ and the Virgin for finally receiving a son. Robert Tournières, born in Caen in 1668, painted piercing portraits, most notably that of the glistening-eyed engraver Andran. The museum also has an extensive collection of old

Getting Around

Fast trains link Caen with Paris in just 2hrs.

Tourist Information

Caen: Place St-Pierre, t 02 31 27 14 10, f 02 31 27 14 13, tourisminfor@ville-caen.fr.

Where to Stay and Eat

Caen ✉ 14300

Better to stay in or around Bayeux if you can, although staying in Caen is better value.

****Relais des Gourmets**, 15 Rue de Geole, t 02 31 86 06 01, f 02 31 39 06 00 (*expensive*). The town's one luxury hotel.

***Le Dauphin**, 29 Rue Gemare, t 02 31 86 22 26, f 02 31 86 35 14 (*moderate*). 22 roms in a fomer priory. Comfortable hotel; its restaurant has a good reputation (*menus 120–380F*). *Closed Sun, Sat lunch. Hotel closed 16 Jul–8 Aug.*

**Les Cordeliers, 4 Rue des Cordeliers, t 02 31 86 37 15, f 02 31 39 56 51 (*inexpensive*). Hotel with plenty of character, occupying one of the old town houses that escaped war destruction. Good value.

*Hôtel St-Etienne, 2 Rue de l'Académie, t 02 31 86 35, f 02 31 85 57 69 (*cheap*). Simple hotel in an old town house.

La Bourride, 15 Rue du Vaugueux, t 02 31 93 50 76, f 02 31 93 29 63 (*luxury*). Small, expensive restaurant of the highest order, in an historic building (*menus 250–600F*). *Closed Jan; some of Aug; Sun and Mon.*

Tilly-sur-Seule ✉ 14250

The Ameys' B&B of La Londe, t 02 31 80 81 12. Simple, rustic bargain lost in the countryside off the D9 some way below the main road connecting Caen and Bayeux.

master drawings, plus a Courbet view of the sea and a Monet *Nymphéas* and other later works.

St-Pierre and its elaborate Gothic spire at the foot of the castle ramparts were rebuilt after the war. The stonework becomes lace-like in the choir with its kink. A short walk east beyond the lively café-surrounded **Place Courtonne**, overseen by the old Tour Guillaume-le-Roi, you come to the **Bassin St-Pierre**, the broad marina in the centre of Caen.

Coyly distant from its twin, the **Abbaye aux Dames** was built for William's wife Matilda, east of the castle in what is now a quiet administrative quarter. More subdued than the church of the Abbaye aux Hommes, it is also more harmonious, most of what you see dates from the start of the 12th century. The façade is sober. Inside, the decoration is limited to little heads and animals on the capitals and to the crinkly patterning around the arches. The false ambulatory in the apse gives the scrubbed interior added depth. A black marble slab in the choir marks Matilda's tomb.

The most famous and forceful church in Caen is **St-Etienne** attached to the **Abbaye aux Hommes** in the western administrative quarter of town. Two towers rocket up above the stern Romanesque nave and the enormous wing added to the abbey in the 18th century. Lanfranc was the first abbot of St-Etienne, and the church was chosen to be William's burial place. His funeral in 1087 turned into a fiasco, with various factions causing mayhem during the ceremony, until his putrefying body broke up as it was being lowered into the tomb and the stench caused the mourners to flee. Architecturally, St-Etienne was a ground-breaking building. The sheer vertical wall of masonry of the façade is formidably daunting; inside, try not to let the greyness of the stone distract you from the power of the architecture. Although the choir was redone in Gothic style in the 13th century, the rest is the Romanesque original. The three different levels with the tribune and clerestory above the nave arches prefigure northern Gothic. An extraordinary lantern tower lets in light above the crossing. William the Conqueror's tomb was desecrated in the Wars of Religion.

The 18th-century abbey wing has been turned into the town hall, and some of the rooms are open to the public at certain hours. Traffic races madly around the **Place Guillouard** in front of it. The other major buildings overlooking the Place Guillouard include the skeleton of the Gothic church of Vieux St-Etienne and the pompous Ancien Régime Palais de Justice. Not far away to the north, the triangular **Place St-Sauveur** has retained its grandeur too, with elegant houses looking on to a statue of Louis XIV in one of his favourite fancy-dress guises, as a Roman emperor.

Bayeux

Capital of a small rich territory known as the Bessin, Bayeux was one of the very few cities in Normandy to be spared large-scale destruction in the war. So close to the D-Day landing beaches, it was the first town in France to be liberated, on D-Day +1. Thanks to this good fortune, many fine streets and houses survive, although restorers have sometimes been heavy-handed with the plaster.

The Bayeux Tapestry

Open May–Aug daily 9–7; 15 Mar–April and Sept–17 Oct daily 9–6.30; rest of year daily 9.30–12.30 and 2–6.

The most famous tapestry in the world is not in fact a tapestry but an embroidery, and although the exact facts of its origin are unknown, the most convincing story as to its creation runs something like this. Odo de Conteville, William the Conqueror's half-brother, bishop of Bayeux and a powerful Normandy landowner, seemingly commissioned the work, no doubt before 1082, when he was imprisoned by William. Odo, a battling bishop, took part in the conquest of England and he features a couple of times in the embroidery. After the conquest he acquired estates in southern England; similarities in style between the embroidery and certain Anglo-Saxon manuscripts suggest that it may have been made across the Channel. Some experts reckon that women in a nunnery connected either with Canterbury or with Winchester executed the work. In France, however, it was long believed that William's wife Matilda had commissioned the work, and it is commonly referred to in French as the *Tapisserie de la Reine Matilde*.

Many places in Normandy and neighbouring Brittany feature, depicted in stylized but still recognizable form, indicating that someone with a reasonable knowledge of northwest France played an important part in the conception. The crucial event, Harold's oath (presumably promising the English throne to William, as the then king of England – Edward the Confessor – had stipulated) is reckoned to be shown taking place in Bayeux.

Visiting the embroidery begins with an in-depth introduction, although it hasn't kept up with recent scholarship. The copy of the embroidery and explanatory commentaries are, however, very helpful. Best of all are the accounts quoted from the contemporary chroniclers Guillaume de Poitiers and Guillaume de Jumièges. The film, though, peddles outdated, inaccurate stories.

The embroidery has 55 'panels' in all, over half of which are devoted to the period before William's invasion, explaining the reasons for his actions. Edward the Confessor of England gives a mission to Harold, his most trusted earl, who sets sail for Normandy. But blown off course, he is captured by Guy de Ponthieu (alias Wido) when he lands in France. The powerful William organizes Harold's release and invites him to his Norman court. They then go on an expedition together to put down the obstreperous Conan of Brittany to the west. The two friendly warriors William and Harold return to Bayeux where Harold swears on holy reliquaries the crucial oath regarding the succession of the English crown. Harold then returns to England where King Edward is soon to die. Harold accepts the crown of England although he has promised that he will allow William to succeed.

Following the appearance of Halley's comet, considered a bad omen for Harold, William swings into action to assert his right. Ships are prepared for the invasion and land at Pevensey in Sussex; the Norman troops set up camp and frighten the local population. The chaotic Battle of Hastings is where the embroidery ends, in the midst of fierce fighting. At one point it is rumoured that William has been killed but he lifts his vizor to show that he is still alive. Harold is mortally wounded by an arrow in the eye. The very final scene shows the English army fleeing.

Artistically, the blue, green, beige and red horses steal the show, while the Viking-prowed ships in stripy beach colours come a delightful second. The men, with their vague features and bonnets for hats, look rather comical; the spies in the first part of the story could not look more inept. Unlike the stallions, the soldiers seem sexless, emaciated creatures in chainmail mesh rendered in fashionable pretty colours. The violent combat looks acrobatic rather than distressing, although the curious frieze of the dead below the battle scenes is a reminder that this was no circus.

The Cathedral Quarter

Bayeux's second trump card is its **cathedral**. Construction began under Odo's prede-cessor, but Odo's wealth no doubt helped the project to advance rapidly and it was consecrated in 1077, with all the major figures of the Norman court in attendance, including William the Conqueror and his Archbishop of Canterbury, Lanfranc. It is often said that the embroidery was originally made to hang in the cathedral, although this is now hotly disputed. A fire in 1105 destroyed important Romanesque sections, which explains the daunting Gothic of the exterior, although the soaring spires are Romanesque originals. Inside, the Gothic nave is superb, but the upper levels are supported on Romanesque arches, most decorated with crinkly patterns, one covered in devils' heads, their tongues sticking out over the edge. The carved panels between the arches have ornamental details influenced by Middle Eastern art.

Getting Around

Fast trains link Bayeux with Paris via Caen (2hrs 20mins).

Tourist Information

Bayeux: Pont St-Jean, **t** 02 31 51 28 28, **f** 02 31 51 28 29, *bayeux-tourisme@mail.cpod.fr*.

Where to Stay and Eat

Bayeux ✉ 14400

Bayeux has some fine hotels, but it's a fairly expensive place to stay.

★★★Château de Bellefontaine, 49 Rue de Bellefontaine, **t** 02 31 22 00 10, **f** 02 31 22 19 09 (*expensive–moderate*). Just on the outskirts of town in a pretty garden with waterways. Spacious rooms

★★★Le Churchill, 14 Rue St-Jean, **t** 02 31 21 31 80, **f** 02 31 21 41 66 (*moderate*). Stylish hotel in the centre.

★★★Le Lion d'Or, 71 Rue St-Jean, **t** 02 31 92 06 90, **f** 02 31 22 15 64 (*moderate*). Former posting inn which serves up good rooms and food for modern-day travellers.

★★Hôtel d'Argouges, 21 Rue St-Patrice, **t** 02 31 92 88 86, **f** 02 31 92 69 16, *argouges@mail.cpod.fr* (*inexpensive*). Elegant but slightly cheaper 18th-century retreat right in the centre of Bayeux.

★Hôtel Notre-Dame, 44 Rue des Cuisiniers, **t** 02 31 92 87 24, **f** 02 31 92 67 11. A cheerful stop for those on a smaller budget.

Around Bayeux

There's a clutch of fine country hotels set in charming little 18th-century châteaux and manors within 10 miles of Bayeux.

★★★★Château d'Audrieu, ✉ 14250 Audrieu, **t** 02 31 80 21 52, **f** 02 31 80 24 73, *audrieu@relaischateaux.fr* (*luxury*). Luxurious 18th-century style and elegance in the countryside southwest of Bayeux, with fine restaurant (*menus from 280F*) and gardens.

★★★Château de Sully, Route de Port-en-Bessin, ✉ 14400 Sully, **t** 02 31 22 29 48, **f** 02 31 22 64 77, *chsully@club-internet.fr* (*moderate*). Just northwest of Bayeux, this is very smart too, with tasteful rooms in the château and annexe. Restaurant (*menus 150–350F*).

★★★Château de Goville, ✉ 14330 Le Breuil-en-Bessin, **t** 02 31 22 19 28, **f** 02 31 22 68 74 (*moderate*). More a romantic little manor than a château, with sweet rooms and a fine collection of dolls' houses. Restaurant (*menus 145–195F*).

★★Château du Baffy, ✉ 14480 Colombiers-sur-Seulles, **t** 02 31 08 04 57, **f** 02 31 08 08 29, *baffy@ pacwan.mm.soft.fr* (*moderate*). Substantial country house turned pleasing simple country hotel with plenty of space and facilities. Restaurant (*menus 135–175F*).

The **Musée Baron Gérard** (*open June–15 Sept daily 9–7; 16 Sept–May daily 10–12.30 and 2–6; adm*) in the former bishops' palace displays the collection of the 19th-century baron: ceramics, archaeological artefacts and paintings, with local artists well represented. Lace is displayed here and in **L'Hôtel du Doyen** (*open July–Aug daily 10–12.30 and 2–7; rest of year daily 10–12.30 and 2–6; adm*), which includes both a lace conservatory and a more specialist museum of religious art.

Bayeux has the largest British war cemetery in Normandy; opposite stands the big **Musée-Mémorial 1944, Bataille de Normandie** (*open May–mid-Sept daily 9.30–6.30; rest of year daily 10–12.30 and 2–6; adm*), where the overwhelming mass of military memorabilia is in danger of making the war itself fade into a blur. In amongst the plethora of objects, certain personal items cut to the quick, such as the papers informing the family of Canadian airman James Lanfranchi that he wouldn't be coming home. Newspaper cuttings seem to follow the campaign day by day.

Southern Normandy

The Suisse Normande and Falaise

The pallid stone of the Calvados coast gives way to darker and darker rock as you head south from Caen down the Orne valley. The **Suisse Normande** is the name given to a small, charming stretch of the Orne valley from around Thury-Harcourt to Putanges. The crests of the hills don't reach very high, but the banks of the Orne become dramatically rocky as you climb up from the Caen plain. Around the hairpin meander of the Boucle du Hom is **Thury-Harcourt** from where the roads west take you up to some of the highest 'peaks', the Mont Pinçon winning the prize at 1197ft.

Continue south down the Orne to the prettiest and liveliest stop in the Suisse Normande, **Clécy**, beyond the striking **Pain de Sucre**, or Sugarloaf rock. Narrow roads clamber up to the old village on the hill, but the riverbank sees most of the action with its tightly packed shoal of restaurants and its boats and pedalo-hire. Further riverside meanders bring you out at **Pont-d'Ouilly**. Follow the west bank up past St-Philbert-sur-Orne to best appreciate the craggy scenery around the Roche d'Oëtre and the Gorges de St-Aubert. You soon come into riverside **Putanges**, southern gateway of the Suisse Normande; here too it's easy to hire boats.

Falaise

A path above an equestrian statue of William leads to the very top of this town named 'Cliff', occupied by the remnants of a massive **medieval castle** (*open April–Sept daily 9.30–4.30; Oct–Mar daily exc Wed 9.30–4.30; daily guided tour in English at 1.30; adm*) which miraculously survived 1944. It remains one of the best examples of medieval military architecture in northern France. The impressive keeps were built for William's successors, Henry I and Henry II, and the big barrel of the Tour Talbot was added for the French king who seized Normandy, Philippe Auguste. It's a shame that the town saw fit to add an Eastern European-style block of flats on one side of the fort. You can visit the interiors, but all you will find inside are recently restored rooms.

Back on William's square, the one edifice that stands out is the **church of La Trinité** with its triangular entrance porch. Inside, don't miss the scenes of martyrdoms and medieval life on the nave capitals, the Flamboyant Gothic window with its wild petal tracery, and the raised ambulatory on tubular columns. At the opposite end of town, the grand **church of St-Gervais** by a busy road junction had to be much restored after the war, but preserves some Gothic angels and howling gargoyles on the outside and some mischievous medieval carving inside. The **Musée Août 44 La Bataille de la Poche de Falaise** (*open June–Aug daily; rest of period April–11 Nov daily exc Tues; adm*) is a short way out of town.

To Montormel and the Battle of the Falaise Gap or Falaise Pocket

Montormel, southeast of Falaise, with its splendid views over the Normandy *bocage*, is the best place to learn about the Allied actions after D-Day that led to

Getting Around

Public transport is limited in these parts. There are no trains, but there is a fairly regular bus service from Caen to Falaise, Thury-Harcourt and Clécy. You'll probably do best to travel by car if at all possible.

Tourist Information

Thury-Harcourt: Place St-Sauveur, t 02 31 79 70 45, f 02 31 79 15 42.
Putanges: Place de la Mairie, t 02 33 35 86 57, f 02 33 67 17 52.
Falaise: Forum, t 02 31 90 17 26, f 02 31 90 98 70, *falaise-tourisme@mail.cpod.fr*.
Chambois: Place Boulais, t 02 33 67 64 17.

Where to Stay and Eat

Clécy ✉ 14570
***Le Moulin du Vey**, t 02 31 69 71 08, f 02 31 69 14 14 (*moderate*). The most appealing place to stay or eat, in a converted mill, with terraces by the Orne river (*menus 140–390F*).

Pont-d'Ouilly ✉ 14690
Auberge St-Christophe, t 02 31 69 81 23, f 02 31 69 26 58 (*inexpensive*). An appealing, unpretentious address.

Falaise/St-Martin-de-Mieux ✉ 14700
***Le Château du Tertre**, t 02 31 90 01 04, f 02 31 90 33 16 (*expensive*). Exclusive hotel in a delightfully self-important little brick château with stylish rooms and cuisine.

Hitler's fall. This vital campaign has gone down in history as the Battle of the Falaise Gap or Falaise Pocket.

The **Mémorial de Montormel** (*open May–Sept daily 9–6; Oct–mid-Dec and mid-Jan–April Wed and weekends 10–5; adm*), located in a bunker of a modern building, looks down on to the now tranquil countryside of the Cauldron. This museum gives some idea of how violent the conflict was. The soldiers who witnessed the horror compared it with a vision of hell or the Apocalypse. Extracts from soldiers' writings speak of rivers obstructed by the corpses of men and horses, of the most appalling stench of death, of the Normandy lanes turned into yawning graves.

Down on the flat, the village of **Chambois** still feels drained by war. A memorial recalls the final hours of the Battle of Normandy here, for it was at Chambois that the Allied forces came together after 77 days of fighting. An empty medieval keep towers over the rather vacant main square.

As an antidote to the battle sites, take a guided tour round the Ancien Régime **Haras National du Pin** (*open April–8 Oct daily 9.30–6; rest of year daily 2.30–5*), set in delightful countryside. The main château is surrounded by brick stables laid out in a horseshoe shape. In spring and summer you won't see many stallions as they are packed off elsewhere, but on Thursday afternoons in summer there are horse parades.

Other stud farms lie scattered around the area. Lovers of French architecture should head south to the **Château d'O** (*open July–Aug daily 10.30–12 and 2.30–6; April–July and Sept daily exc Tues 2.30–6; rest of year daily exc Tues 2.30–5*), built between the late 15th and late 16th centuries, whose long, slender roofs and turrets look irresistibly sexy. It's said that François d'O, royal servant to Henri III and Henri IV, fleeced his masters to pay for the embellishments. The interiors have later decoration, including an amazing *trompe-l'œil* series of Apollo and the Nine Muses.

The Battle of the Falaise Gap

After the success of the D-Day landings, the time came, early in August 1944, for the Allies to try to break out southwards and liberate the rest of France. Hitler, however, decided on a massively concentrated counteroffensive, codenamed Operation Lüttich, to confine the Allies to Normandy. He reckoned the best opportunity was to catch the US divisions in the gap between Mortain and the sea. Mortain was the place where the Battle of the Falaise Gap would commence on 7 August 1944. The opening proved a disaster for the Germans. Although already weakened by the Allied offensive and air bombardments, four of the best Nazi tank divisions were sent to surprise the Americans in the Sée valley on 7 August. Unfortunately for them, the Allied decryption service had already informed Allied command of this plan on 5 August, and the Americans were ready and waiting. The Nazi divisions met with a shattering defeat.

On the same day, Montgomery just happened to have launched Operation Totalise from the eastern end of the Allied bridgehead. The idea was for Canadian troops, backed by an émigré Polish division, to storm south from the Caen area to Falaise. Although not entirely successful, the Allied forces in Operation Totalise advanced far enough to present a major threat to the rear of the German divisions. The Allied commanders suddenly found themselves in a position of power, with the Germans trapped. They changed their plan from advancing down to the Loire to encircling the Germans in southern Normandy in the beautiful bowl of land west of Montormel. It became known to the Germans as the dreaded Cauldron.

Hitler tried to insist that Kluge, the main German commander, try another attack, refusing to accept the increasingly desperate situation for over half a million German soldiers who risked being trapped. On 15 August, the day Hitler described as the worst in his life, Kluge was replaced by Model, but it was too late for any commander to reverse the situation. The bulk of the German armies in Normandy were now surrounded between Mortain, Falaise and Argentan. By mid-August just a small corridor between Falaise and Argentan to the south would remain open by which 300,000 soldiers and 25,000 vehicles were able to retreat under cover of night. The remaining Germans were caught in the Allied encirclement: around 50,000 Germans died, while 200,000 were taken prisoner. More than 1,300 German tanks were lost.

Meanwhile on 19 August a US section under Patton had raced as far east as Mantes on the Seine just beyond the Normandy frontier, closing in on Paris. The liberation of the capital, and the rest of France, now looked possible.

Between Alençon and Mortain

This seductive slice of Normandy lies within the protective boundaries of the Parc Régional Normandie-Maine. In the east, around the upper Sarthe valley, lace-making is a speciality particularly associated with Alençon.

Alençon and the Upper Sarthe Valley

The grubby little local stones give a grey tinge to some of the buildings of historic **Alençon**, the first French town to be liberated by French forces at the end of the war. Alençon has long been known in France for its lace, a tradition which was started by Colbert in the late 17th century. Until then Venice had a virtual monopoly, but the *point d'Alençon* began to satisfy the huge French demand.

The sister of François I, Marguerite d'Angoulême, married Duke René of Alençon in the late 15th century, and patronized the splendid Flamboyant finishings of **Notre-Dame**. Inside small Gothic dogs and dragons scamper along the ribs of the elaborate vaults, done in a style introduced from England in the Hundred Years' War. The Renaissance puts in an appearance in some extremely refined stained glass from the early 16th century, illustrations of Old Testament stories on one side, on the other the life of the Virgin Mary. The glaziers may have come from Alençon and Le Mans, but they were clearly familiar with the German and Italian Renaissance – Alençon was a cosmopolitan place back then.

By the river Sarthe, the small **Maison de la Dentelle** (*open daily exc Sun and public hols 10–12 and 2–6; adm*) tells the story of Alençon point lace. Part of Colbert's plan to revive the economy by making France self-sufficient in luxuries, lace-making was supported from 1665. You can buy pieces at phenomenal prices – once you hear the number of hours required to make them you'll understand why. At one time 8,000 people in the area made lace for the aristocracy and clergy; in fact, before the Revolution no one else was supposed to wear it. There is a lace-making school in town now, with only some 10 pupils. Above the Maison de la Dentelle, a second museum recalls Alençon in the war, from its initial bombing by the Germans on 14 June 1940 to its liberation on 12 August 1944.

Alençon's **Musée des Beaux-Arts et de la Dentelle** (*open daily exc Mon outside July and Aug 10–12 and 2–6; adm*) has taken over a former Jesuit college to display its attractive collections of second-rate paintings and first-class lace. The techniques of lace-making are clearly explained, while the showcases include representative pieces from across Europe. Next door is the shapely curve of the former Jesuit seminary, now the public library, with a splendid reading room. The Halle au Blé, a striking 19th-century domed corn exchange close to the museum, holds temporary exhibitions.

A short way west of Alençon you enter a hilly area known as the Alpes Mancelles. The story goes that a couple of brothers from Italy, Cénéri and Cénéré, arrived in the course of the 6th or 7th century and settled in the area as it supposedly reminded them of the Alps. They set about converting the locals. Utterly picturesque **St-Cénéri-le-Gérei**, perched above a hairpin bend in the Sarthe river, lost its castle to English soldiers in the Hundred Years' War, but its 11th–12th-century chapel survived, albeit only after undergoing a lot of surgery in the past two centuries. Some of the cutest devils in any French church are among the medieval wall paintings heavy-handedly restored in the 19th century. Other images include a Virgin protecting her praying flock under her cape. She looks a bit cross-eyed with anxiety. By contrast the Christ in majesty exudes serenity. Go down from the church to the meander in the

Getting Around

Trains to Alençon from Le Mans (linked by TGV from Paris) take under an hour. A handful of buses a day link Alençon with Bagnoles-de-l'Orne, and there are buses to Domfront from Flers (on the Paris–Granville line).

Tourist Information

Alençon: Place Lamagdelaine, t 02 33 80 66 33, f 02 33 32 10 53.
Carrouges: 24 Place du Général Leveneur, t 02 33 27 40 62.
Bagnoles-de-l'Orne: Place du Marché, t 02 33 37 85 66, f 02 33 30 06 75.
Domfront: 12 Place de la Roierie, t 02 33 38 53 97, f 02 33 37 40 27.

Where to Stay and Eat

Bagnoles-de-l'Orne ✉ 61140
Some surprisingly fun hotels here. Stay in the centre to sample the bizarre atmosphere of this spa town.

*****Manoir du Lys,** Route de Juvigny-sous-Andaine, t 02 33 37 80 69, f 02 33 30 05 80 (*expensive–moderate*). Very appealing, brightly converted manor house with 25 rooms, next to a golf course, actually in the forest of Andaine. High standard, including the cuisine (*menus 150–360F*). *Closed Jan and some of Feb; Nov–Easter Sun eves and Mon.*
Le Celtos, Rue des Casinos, t 02 33 38 44 44, f 02 33 38 46 23 (*moderate–inexpensive*). Modern, 75-room hotel in the centre with its main windows cascading down its façade.. Restaurant (*menus 95–200F*).
****La Potinière du Lac,** 2 Rue des Casinos, t 02 33 30 65 00, f 02 33 38 49 04 (*inexpensive*). Central hotel with chequered pepperpot tower and modern timberframe building overlooking the lake. Restaurant (*menus 85–175F*). *Closed mid-Nov–mid-Mar.*

Mortain ✉ 50140
****Hôtel de la Poste,** 1 Place des Arcades, t 02 33 59 00 05, f 02 33 69 53 89 (*inexpensive*). Thirty rooms within large granite walls.

river and in the lower meadow you're greeted by the charming sight of the 15th-century **Chapelle du Petit-Saint-Célerin**, set against a steep theatre of woods.

West from Carrouges to Mortain

Northwest of Alençon the mammoth, moated **Château de Carrouges** (*open mid-June–Aug daily 9.30–12 and 2–6.30; April–mid-June and Sept daily 10–12 and 2–6; Oct–Mar daily 10–12 and 2–4.30; adm*) is a delightful rough-brick château. The tour starts in the courtyard decorated with playful waves and lozenges of black brick. It then takes you through rooms with big fireplaces, fine tapestries and painted beams, while stories are told about the families who lived here, notably the Le Veneurs. Cardinal Le Veneur was a confidant of François I and a friend of Rabelais, who presented the Breton explorer and discoverer of Canada, Jacques Cartier, to the king. The Le Veneurs survived the Revolution and lived in the château until recent times.

Centred around a small lake set amongst picturesque woods, the little spa town of **Bagnoles-de-l'Orne** is appealing in a chichi kind of way. Swans glide around the lake, weeping willows weep beside it, streams cascade away among shaded rocks...and people with circulatory problems come to take the radioactive waters. Local legends spur them on, like the tale of the medieval lord whose flagging old steed Rapide found a new lease of life after lapping up the water here, or that of a Franciscan who managed, after taking the waters, to jump across the highest rocks above the town, known now as the Saut du Capucin. The town has a low white casino with a dome, an Art Deco church with its colonnaded spire, and a couple of particularly showy hotels.

Domfront stands aloof on its rocky spine west of Bagnoles-de-l'Orne through the beech woods of the Forêt des Andaines. The ruins of the haughty medieval castle date as far back as Henry I of England; while Henry II and Eleanor of Aquitaine were frequent visitors as they travelled up and down their little empire. Domfront is associated with a couple of reconciliation attempts betwen Henry II and his friend turned over-zealous Archbishop of Canterbury, Thomas à Becket. A dozen or more towers still stand guard over the streets of town. Far down below, lorries trundle noisily past the Romanesque **Notre-Dame-sur-l'Eau**, which has lost a large part of its nave, although the choir end contains some remarkable Romanesque frescoed faces, possibly apostles, and a splendid medieval effigy of a knight with pinched waist and natty garb.

West of Domfront you enter pear-growing territory, with attractive orchards of tall, unkempt trees. Heavy Normandy cows laze in the shade. You can follow an official **Route de la Poire**, and visit several little fruit museums.

From **Mortain** there are gorgeous views down on to the patchwork of fields and hedges leading west to Mont-St-Michel. The town's Romanesque-Gothic church of St-Evroult has held on to several impressive reliquaries, most prized of which is the Chrismale, a 7th-century Celtic Christian casket probably made at the Scottish monastery of Iona (*only on display July and Aug Tues and Thurs at 3pm*). Others are permanently displayed around the altar.

Maine

Le Mans, the Plantagenet city with its world-famous car race, is the highlight of Eastern Maine – the *département* of the Sarthe – but a tour down the Sarthe river south of Le Mans offers a taste of some of the area's smaller attractions.

Le Mans

Le Mans has a superbly restored historic centre occupying a thin spur of rock. One side of the old town overlooks the Sarthe river, while a colossal many-buttressed cathedral lords it over the other side. The car museum stands by the race track south of town.

History

The vestiges of the walls of Le Mans' Gallo-Roman predecessor are incorporated into houses overlooking the Sarthe, and are said to be among the best-preserved in Europe. As William the Conqueror expanded his duchy, his troops took hold of Le Mans. It went on to become an important centre of the Angevin kings who succeeded the Normans on the throne of England. Geoffrey Plantagenet, the founder of the dynasty, came from here, and Henry II Plantagenet of England was born here in 1135; he kept an affection for his birthplace throughout his life. The French king, Jean le Bon, was born in Le Mans in 1319. The brilliant array of 16th-century houses in the upper town proves that Le Mans prospered after the Hundred Years' War. From the 17th to the 19th centuries it was, among other things, a major producer of pewter-ware. At the end of the 19th century the local Bollée family started making motor vehicles. The first major car race at Le Mans took place in 1906, but the internationally famed 24-hour competition only took off in 1923.

Touring Le Mans

The exterior of the **cathedral** looks an incoherent mess, although the flying buttresses around the choir give it a spectacular spidery quality. The inside, however, is extraordinary, divided into two parts. The narrow, dark nave is Romanesque, held up on pillars with beefy primitive-leaved capitals. The arches were replaced by Gothic ones after a terrible fire in 1134. The Ascension stained glass window, from around 1140, has been heavily restored and Christ has gone missing altogether, but it still represents one of the earliest surviving examples of stained glass in France. From the crossing and transepts, the style suddenly changes, with a viciously sharp opening arch and the light of Gothic flooding in. The transepts are in fact mainly 14th and 15th century, but the choir is older, completed in 1254. The side chapels of the double-colonnaded apse seem to be made of walls of light.

The **Musée de Tessé** (*open daily 9–12 and 2–6; closed Mon; adm exc Sun*), the city's fine arts museum, lies just outside the historic centre. The pride of the collection is the so-called **Plantagenet Enamel**, the largest piece of luxury medieval enamel work in Western Europe. Made in the mid-12th century for the tomb of Geoffrey Plantagenet in the cathedral, its style clearly reflects the influence of Byzantine art. The cautious-looking duke is shown wearing a bonnet, and has a rather feminine curve to the hip. More gorgeous Limoges enamel work features in the museum, which contains a surprising number of Italian paintings. The most cherished local pieces are the triptych panels by the so-called Master of Vivoin; the Virgin's radically combed-back hair recalls Loire courtly fashions in the mid-15th century, while the wizened baby Christ has an inquisitive look.

Up in the handsome old town (used as a setting in the film *Cyrano de Bergerac* star-ring Gérard Depardieu), some houses are covered with beams carved with Gothic figures. One mansion contains the **Musée de la Reine Bérengère** (*open daily 9–12 and 2–6; closed Mon; adm exc Sun*) recalling Le Mans' history through painting, pottery and pewterware. The Gothic **church of La Couture** in the lower town has domed vaulting, unusual statues in the apse, and a Virgin thought to be by the great 16th-century sculptor Germain Pilon.

The son of Henry II, Richard the Lionheart, married one Berengaria of Navarre, much ignored by her adventuring bisexual husband and by history, but well remembered in Le Mans for founding the **Abbaye de la Piété Dieu de l'Epau** after Richard's death The abbey stands in a walled park east of town. Although destroyed in the Hundred Years' War, the abbey was rebuilt in the 14th century and provides a fine example of a sober and beautiful Cistercian monastery. The pleasing golden-brown architecture enclosing magnificent examples of Gothic window tracery survived the Revolution

Getting Around

Le Mans is well served by rail. It's on a high-speed TGV line from Paris-Montparnasse (under an hour) and on a direct train line from Lille (2hrs 30mins). Local bus services radiate out from Le Mans. The fastest way to reach Le Mans and the Sarthe from Paris by car is via the A10 and A11 motorways.

Tourist Information

Le Mans: Hôtel des Ursulines, Rue de l'Etoile, **t** 02 43 28 17 22, **f** 02 43 23 37 19.
Malicorne: 3 Place Duguesclin, **t** 02 43 94 74 45.
Asnières-sur-Vègre: 3 Rue du Temple, **t/f** 02 43 92 40 47.
Sablé-sur-Sarthe: Place Raphael Elizé, **t** 02 43 95 00 60, **f** 02 43 92 60 77.

Where to Stay and Eat

Le Mans ✉ 72000
★★★Concorde, 16 Av du Général Leclerc, **t** 02 43 24 12 30, **f** 02 43 24 85 74 (*moderate*). Large, modern and stylish (*menus 95–195F*).
Chez Jean, 9 Rue Dorée, **t** 02 43 28 22 96. Refined regional cuisine (*menus 152–210F*)

Asnières-sur-Vègre ✉ 72430
Manoir des Claies, **t** 02 43 92 40 50, **f** 02 43 92 65 72. Delightful B&B in gorgeous 15th-century house, lovingly done up by its owner.

Solesmes ✉ 72300
★★★Grand Hôtel de Solesmes, 16 Place Dom Guéranger, **t** 02 43 95 45 10, **f** 02 43 95 22 26 (*inexpensive*). Large, comfortable hotel opposite the abbey, with a terrace for sunny days, and delicate cuisine (*menus 120–175F*).

almost intact. Now an exhibition and conference centre, the abbey offers an interesting presentation of Cistercian life and thinking peppered with good quotes. 'Build as you believe. Rigour in prayer makes for rigour in construction,' says one. Berengaria's restored tomb effigy is in the chapter house, big-nosed, reading a book.

To find the excellent **Musée de l'Automobile** (*open June–Sept daily 10–7; Mar–May and Oct daily 10–6; rest of year check with tourist office*) and race track follow signs south of town for the 'Circuit des 24 Heures'. The local heroes, the Bollées, are well represented by early models of their cars and some hilarious archive film. There's also a gleaming collection of cars from the late 19th-century to the present day. The 24-hour race takes place in mid-June.

Down the Sarthe from Le Mans

Malicorne-sur-Sarthe is the first obvious stop along the Sarthe river southwest of Le Mans. With the friendly remnants of a château on its outskirts, the main attraction within this scrappy town are its pottery shops. It is best known for copying the styles of the major schools of French ceramics, as the local museum shows very clearly. Medieval **Asnières-sur-Vègre**, west of Malicorne, has been delightfully preserved with yellow-stone houses and a 12th-century bridge. Its church contains remarkable 13th-century frescoes only rediscovered after the war. The back wall scene of hell shows demons stirring a soup of human heads.

The **abbey of Solesmes** looms large and menacing over the Sarthe river nearby. Celebrated for its development of plainchant, it was a priory for nearly a thousand years, then acquired much greater significance when it was transformed into a Benedictine abbey in 1837, by order of Pope Gregory XVI, although in the early part of the 20th century, as Church and state clashed, the monks of Solesmes went into exile on the Isle of Wight for over 20 years. You can hear the monks sing plainchant Mass in the abbey church. Made up of a wide mix of styles, some dating back to the 11th century, this church contains some truly extravagant sculpture. The two great set pieces represent Christ's and the Virgin's Entombments. The first (end 15th century) demonstrates the finesse of late-Gothic sculpting, although the figures show a stony, static grief. The group round the Virgin (mid-16th century) teems with movement and texts – it's been described as an early example of Counter-Reformation propaganda art. It's even said that the Jewish doctors whom the boy Jesus is shown lecturing represent leading Protestants, including Luther and Calvin.

Western Maine

Western Maine – or the *département* of the Mayenne – is divided by the Mayenne river like a piece of paper roughly torn down the middle. A handful of historic villages and unspoilt countryside are the main attractions. Unlike eastern Maine, taken over by large, monotonous fields, western Maine has preserved its *bocage* – the old fields divided up by oaks and hedges.

The enormous rounded towers of the 15th-century castle of **Lassay-les-Châteaux** (*open Pentecost–Sept daily 2.30–6.30; also Easter weekend and May weekends 2.30–6.30*) are an impressive introduction to northern Mayenne. The short tour affords a good lesson in late medieval fortification. The historic village is built in gritty granite with ruddy tinges like the castle. **Mayenne**, the town, may have lost much of its appeal as a river port, but you can hire river boats here. A short way southeast, the sophisticated Gallo-Roman settlement of Noviodunum has been unearthed at the quiet village of **Jublains**. The most unusual structure to have survived is the so-called fortress, thought to have been built to protect the provisions and precious metals passing through the region. Portions of the baths have been well preserved thanks to a church built over them. You can also take a look at the outlines of the theatre and of the walls of a fanum or temple. An archaeological museum (*open May–Sept daily 9–12.30 and 1.30–6; rest of year daily exc Feb and Mon 9.30–12.30 and 1.30–5.30*) tells the story.

Tourist Information

Laval: Rue du Vieux St–Louis, t 02 43 49 46 46, f 02 43 49 46 21.

Lassay-les-Châteaux: 8 Rue du Château, t 02 43 04 74 33.

Mayenne: Quai Waiblingen, t 02 43 04 19 37.

Jublains: Impasse de l'Eglise, t 02 43 04 41 42, f 02 43 00 01 99, tourism-pays-mayenne@wanadoo.fr.

Evron: Place de la Basilique, t 02 43 01 63 75.

Ste-Suzanne: Place Ambroise de Loré, t 02 43 01 43 60, f 02 43 01 42 12, ste-suzanne.53@wanadoo.fr.

Where to Stay and Eat

Laval ☒ **53000**

Le Bas du Gast, 6 Rue de la Halle aux Toiles, t 02 43 49 22 79, f 02 43 56 44 71. Luxurious B&B with 3 rooms – a wonderful place to stay with many period features. Delightful garden and views over old Laval. Monsieur speaks excellent English. *Closed 1 Dec–31 Jan.*

**Grand Hôtel de Paris, 22 Rue de la Paix, t 02 43 53 76 20, f 02 43 56 91 83. Central, with some spacious and quite stylish rooms.

Bistro de Paris, 22 Quai Jehan Fouquet, t 02 43 56 98 29, f 02 43 56 52 85. Swanky décor.

The centre of **Evron** southeast of Jublains is dominated by a great abbey church in golden stone, built to house a holy thorn. In the 14th-century stained glass of the choir you can follow its story. Delightful hilltop **Ste-Suzanne** has a ruined Romanesque keep and little streets that exude charm. The Dolmen des Erves, nearby, is the biggest in the area.

Back by the Mayenne river, **Laval** is capital of the *département*. Remnants of a medieval castle survey the valley, and its interior has been turned into a museum with a large collection of Art Naïf works, inspired by the great Henri 'Le Douanier' Rousseau, a native of Laval, although only one of his paintings is here. For more artistic exuberance, head southwest for Cossé-le-Vivien, and the nearby **Musée Robert Tatin** (*open April–15 Oct daily exc Tues am 10–7; rest of year exc Jan, Sat am, Sun am and Tues 10–12 and 2–6*), devoted to one man's extraordinary vision of the world. Set in an unremarkable patch of countryside, Tatin's creations include large outdoor sculptures, the design of the building and the decoration of the interiors. The alley of giants at the entrance include homages to Alfred Jarry, the nutty dramatist who was also born in Laval, and Rousseau, as well as to other figures who influenced the artist, such as Joan of Arc. These wacky painted cement figures, a bit like Polynesian totems, are typical of Tatin's work with their sculptures within sculptures and heads popping out all over the place in a chaotic *joie de vivre*.

The Cotentin or Cherbourg Peninsula

The coast of this peninsula, sticking its head into the Channel, is not unlike neighbouring Brittany with its tough but lovable granite edge and character, dotted with pretty ports and the up-and-coming resort of Granville. Cherbourg, long able to claim the largest man-made harbour in the world, has a fine war museum and will soon boast a new Cité de la Mer (*to be completed by 2002*). The nuclear power station of the Cap de la Hague is the one enormous blip in the northwest of the Cotentin, an aberration sited along one of the most romantic stretches of French coastline.

St-Vaast-la-Hougue, the Ile Tatihou and Barfleur

St-Vaast-la-Hougue and Barfleur compete for the prize of prettiest port in western Normandy. **St-Vaast-la-Hougue** has more eccentric character than Barfleur, with a confusion of low spits stretching into the sea around it. Forts to the south and on the island of Tatihou add a military twist to the horizon. They went up in 1694, after the Battle of La Hougue when much of the French fleet was set alight by the Anglo-Dutch enemy. Today St-Vaast's pretty port has been developed into a massively popular marina.

The Fort de La Hougue on the spit south of St-Vaast remains in military hands but you can visit the **island of Tatihou** in an amphibious craft (*book tickets in advance from Accueil Tatihou, Quai Vauban at St-Vaast, t 02 33 23 19 92*). The funny name derives from that of a Viking leader, Tati. It makes a delightful excursion, with a sea fort to visit as well as the former *lazare*, the quarantine hospital for crews struck by

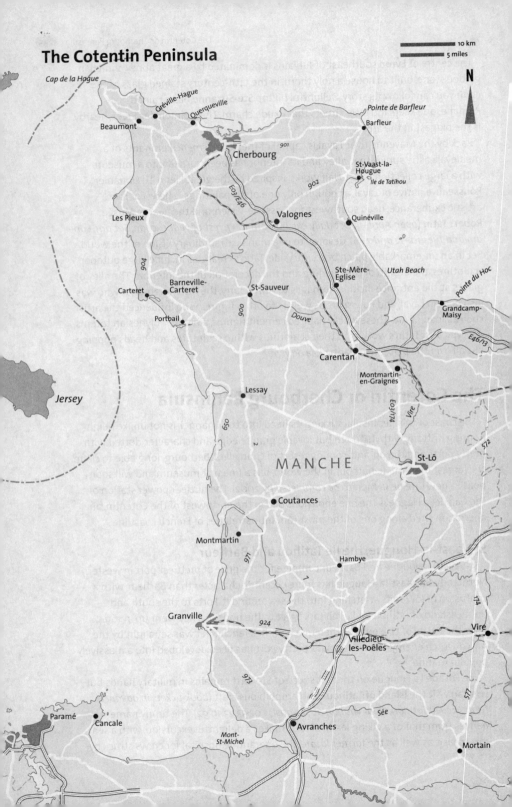

The Cotentin Peninsula

10 km
5 miles

N

Cap de la Hague

Gréville-Hague
Querqueville
Beaumont

Pointe de Barfleur
Barfleur

Cherbourg
901

St-Vaast-la-
Hougue
Ile de Tatihou

902

Les Pieux

Valognes

Quinéville

904

Ste-Mère-
Eglise
Utah Beach

Pointe du Hoc

Barneville-
Carteret
Carteret

St-Sauveur

Grandcamp-
Maisy

E46/13

Portbail

900

Douve

Carentan

Montmartin-
en-Graignes

Jersey

Lessay

650

2

E03/174

Vire

572

MANCHE

St-Lô

Coutances

Montmartin

971

Hambye

7

774

Granville

924

Villedieu-
les-Poêles

Viré

973

577

Paramé

Cancale

Mont-
St-Michel

Sée

Avranches

Mortain

the plague or suspected of bringing home infectious diseases and, after the Revolution, when an extra ring of walls was added, for crews affected by cholera. Men and merchandise could be forced to stay on the island for between 8 and 40 days. Today, within its walls, there is an active ship repair yard, a maritime museum (*open Easter–Oct daily 10–5.30; rest of year weekends only 2–5.30*) and a walled maritime garden – Tatihou has a distinguished history of research into marine biology. It also hosts a summer festival of coastal music from around the world.

Cherbourg

The ferry port of Cherbourg may not look immediately appealing, but it has a dramatic natural setting and, beyond the chaotic jumble of its ports and the apartment blocks on the steep hill, it has some gripping stories to tell.

High up, reached by hairpin bends worthy of the Alps, is the excellent **Musée de la Libération** (*open April–Sept daily 10–6; rest of year daily exc Mon 9.30–12 and 2–5.30; adm*) occupies the mid-19th-century Fort du Roule which still bears the scars of shells from the vicious but remarkably short battle in June 1944 which liberated the town of Cherbourg. It very rapidly became a key port for the Allies; a vital oil pipe line from the Isle of Wight was already down and running by mid-August. Inside the fort you'll find just about the best Second World War museum in Normandy. The build-up to the D-Day landings and the taking of Cherbourg are presented with a rare clarity. In the section devoted to commemorating the war, the urn containing ashes and earth from concentration camps is deeply moving, an appalling Nazi poster tellingly displayed behind it.

The views from the fort over the harbour are spectacular, giving a good picture of the town's strategic importance. It was Louis XIV's genius of a military engineer, Vauban, who developed it into a key French naval base. Down by the water, the new **Cité de la Mer** is taking shape. Cherbourg's enormous and once glamorous transatlantic liner station is being converted for the purpose, with a large aquarium and the submarine *Redoutable* to feature among the many highlights. On the seafront behind the marina, the much-restored Gothic church of La Trinité stands by a square with an equestrian statue of Napoleon bearing one of the emperor's more dubious quotes : 'I resolved to renew the marvels of Egypt in Cherbourg'.

The old shopping quarters, packed with shops and restaurants, surround the elaborate theatre and the glass- and steel-covered market. Behind the theatre, the **Musée Thomas Henry** (*open daily exc Mon and public hols 9 (10 on Sun)–12 and 2–6; adm*) has a rather confusing display of fine Old Masters: Filippino Lippi (*The Entombment*), Fra Angelico (*The Conversion of St Augustine*) and the Master of the Legend of St Ursula (*The Enthroned Madonna*). A 16th-century portrait of a beautiful coiffed woman attributed to Clouet stands out. The French portraits display much more decorum. Some (not the best) are by the most famous Cotentin artist of them all, Millet. More interesting are a few landscapes, including the almost cubist *Falaise de la Hague*.

To the Cap de la Hague and the Western Cotentin

Heading west along the coast from Cherbourg you enter a world of increasingly high cliffs and narrow lanes sometimes virtually enclosed by towering hedgerows. Stone village houses huddle together for comfort. La Hague was a major area of Viking settlement in Normandy, and most of the place-names ending in -*ville* indicate villages founded by Norsemen. **Querqueville**, with a great view back over Cherbourg, has preserved the rare, tiny Chapelle de St-Germain, that dates in part to before the Viking invasions. It is dedicated to a British saint who helped convert the Bessin in the 5th century but was martyred by Saxons. Some of the walls may go back to the 6th century, but the patterned east end dates from after the year 1000.

The copper-green statue of Jean-François Millet at **Gréville-Hague** makes clear this was his place of birth. Millet painted the squat Norman church several times before moving on to his more familiar themes of peasant life in the Seine valley. The **Maison Natale du Peintre Jean-François Millet** (*open July–Aug daily 11–7; Easter–June and Sept same but closed Tues; Oct Sun only 2–7; adm*) has been converted into a museum recalling his work through reproductions and 19th-century rural artifacts.

Omonville-la-Petite was the last home of the popular poet Jacques Prévert, author of *Paroles*, deceptively simple pieces whose wit emphasizes the writer's criticisms of the uncaring side of society. Prévert also wrote the scripts for several cinema classics, including *Les Enfants du paradis*. He died in his house here in 1977 and after his widow's death in 1993 it was opened as the **Maison Jacques Prévert** (*open April–15 Nov daily 10–12 and 2–6.30; adm*). Much of the house has been turned into an space suitable to host an annual exhibition on a theme of his work.

The sensational west side of the Cap de la Hague looks out to the distant Channel Islands. Watch the sun set at **Goury** on the very tip of the peninsula, the Gros du Raz lighthouse in the foreground, the Channel Island of Alderney looming out to sea. Long a refuge for endangered mariners, Goury has a lifeboat station, a few boats, a shingle beach, six or seven houses and, sometimes, a van selling sandwiches. At the southern end of the magnificent arc of sand and surf of the **Baie d'Ecalgrain** some of the tallest cliffs in Europe rise out of the sea at the **Nez de Jobourg**.

As you turn the corner, the views remain breathtaking, but the **nuclear reprocessing plant of La Hague** is a disastrous blight on the countryside, an unforgivable piece of crass planning by an insensitive central government. Environmentalists are concerned about the abnormally high levels of radioactivity in the waters on the north side of the bay, and on the southern end at Flamanville where there's a nuclear power station. Unsurprisingly the beaches are unspoilt, backed by precipitous dunes. The popular resorts of **Carteret** and **Barneville-Plage** face each other across a wide inlet. Barneville has a good beach, and the port from which boats leave for Jersey.

Below Barneville-Carteret, the coast flattens out, and right down to the bay of the Mont-St-Michel the sea recedes an awfully long way at low tide, leaving vast expanses of sandy flats. **Portbail**, an historic little port, is well protected from the sea; the waterside church of Notre-Dame has a defensive tower which comes with crenellations. The remains of a 6th-century baptistry were unearthed here after the war.

Long stretches of sand and dunes reach south to the inlet above **Lessay**, best-known for its Romanesque abbey which suffered much in the Second World War, but which has been lovingly restored. Amusing Romanesque figures run along the outside, but the interior is held up on sober pillars and capitals.

Inland the little, hilltop city of **Coutances** suffered badly in the liberation of Normandy but has held on to its dramatic Gothic cathedral. The massive octagonal crossing tower stands out, a triumph of Norman Gothic architecture. The interior is more showy, although it was rather heavily restored. The transepts and very light ambulatory chapels contain fine stained-glass windows. South of Coutances, the quirky little 17th-century **Manor of Saussey** (*open Easter–Sept daily 2–6.30; Oct, Nov and Mar weekends only 2.30–6*) is topped by pottery finials and surrounded by neat little themed gardens. It contains a curious pack of collections: amazingly sophisticated glass; some more rustic pottery; and some very naff cribs.

Heading further inland towards Villedieu-les-Poêles, the ruined Benedictine **church of Hambye** (*open Feb–15 Dec daily 10–12 and 2–6; adm*), although battered and roofless, remains one of the finest examples of Norman Gothic architecture. A massive tower rises 100ft above the giant but unusually narrow arches on which it remains improbably perched. At the Revolution Hambye abbey was plundered by locals for stone. Some of the monastic buildings have fared better than the church. You can only see them on guided tours (*May–15 Oct only; adm*). The monks' parlour has a 13th-century decorated ceiling, painted with flowers, while the kitchen has a magnificent fireplace. The chapter house has survived virtually undamaged, its vaulting similar to that at Norwich, with which Hambye had close links.

Charming medieval **Villedieu-les-Poêles**, the 'City-of-God-the-Cooking-Pots', got its funny name from specializing in the metal industries. Several museums and workshops showcase its trades, notably the **Fonderie des Cloches** (*open 15 Feb–15 Nov Tues–Sat 8–12 and 1.30–5.30; mid-June–mid-Sept also Sun and Mon; adm*), one of the last completely traditional bell foundries in Europe, the **Atelier du Cuivre** (*open daily 9–12 and 1.30–5.30, Sun open one hour later; adm*) for copper working, and the **Maison de la Dentellerie et Musée de la Poeslerie** (*open Easter–11 Nov daily exc Tues am 10–12 and 2–6.30; adm*), combining the local women's lacemaking traditions with the men's copper working ones in a fine 18th-century copper workers' courtyard.

As if these weren't enough, the **Maison de l'Etain** (*open daily 9–12 and 1.30–5.30, Sun open one hour later; adm*) has a large pewter collection; **Le Royaume de l'Horloge** (*open daily exc Sun am outside July and Aug 9–12.30 and 2–6.30; adm*) is devoted to clockmaking; and the **Musée du Meuble Normand** (*open Easter–11 Nov exc Tues am outside July and Aug 10–12 and 2–6.30; adm*) presents Normandy furniture.

Back on the coast, gay old **Granville**, splendidly located on a natural fortification of a rock, sticks out dramatically into the sea, its port tucked away below. It would be a rival to St-Malo in the tourist stakes if its architecture had remained more homogenous, but it still has plenty of charm. The rock was first fortified by the English in the late 1430s, frustrated at not being able to wrest the nearby Mont-St-Michel from the French. English soldiers returned in the late 17th century to try and smoke out the irritating corsairs of Granville – they bombarded the place and the fortifications had to

Getting Around

For details on ferry services to Cherbourg, see **Travel**.

The fastest trains between Cherbourg and Paris take around 3hrs, via Carentan and Valognes, but many are much slower. Ferries leave for the Channel Islands from Goury, Diélette and Barneville-Carteret on the northwestern side of the Cotentin, but this area is surprisingly badly covered by public transport.

The southwestern coast of the peninsula has better bus and rail provisions, with train stations at Coutances, Foligny, Granville, Avranches and Pontorson-St-Michel.

Tourist Information

St-Vaast-la-Hougue: 1 Place Général de Gaulle, t 02 33 23 19 32, f 02 33 54 41 37.

Barfleur: 2 Quai Henri Chardon, t 02 33 54 02 48.

Cherbourg: Quai Alexandre III, t 02 33 93 52 02, f 02 33 53 66 97.

Barneville-Carteret: 10 Rue des Ecoles, t 02 33 04 90 58, f 02 33 04 93 24.

Coutances: Place Leclerc, t 02 33 19 08 10, f 02 33 19 08 19.

Granville: 4 Cours Jonville, t 02 33 91 30 03, f 02 33 91 30 19.

Where to Stay and Eat

Quinéville-Plage ✉ 50310

★★★Château de Quinéville, 18 Rue de l'Eglise, t 02 33 21 42 67, f 02 33 21 05 79 (*moderate*). Elegant, comfortable 18th-century château in its own park. 24 rooms. Restaurant (*menus 140–250F*). Closed Jan–Mar; and Oct–20 Dec Wed lunch.

St-Vaast-la-Hougue ✉ 50550

★★★La Granitière, 74 Rue Maréchal Foch, t 02 33 54 58 99, f 02 33 20 34 91 (*moderate–inexpensive*). Pleasant little manor of a hotel and garden in the middle of the village. Restaurant (*menus 85–220F*).

★★Hôtel de France et des Fuchsias, 18 Rue Maréchal Foch, t 02 33 54 42 26, f 02 33 43 46 79 (*inexpensive*). Charming hotel and excellent restaurant (*menus 125–300F*) with a lovely garden. Closed Jan and Feb; and mid-Sept–30 April Mon.

Chambre d'hôte of M et Mme Passenaud, La Dannevillerie, Route de Quettehou, ✉ 50630 Le Vast, t 02 33 44 50 45. Lovely, good-value B&B a short way inland.

Barfleur ✉ 50760

★★Le Conquérant, 16–18 Rue Thomas Becket, t 02 33 54 00 82, f 02 33 54 65 25

be rebuilt. Many of the old granite houses went up in the 17th and 18th centuries. Some people think that Granville has become a bit stuck in its bourgeois mud, but in recent years it has come out of its shell or perhaps more accurately its closet, thanks to two brilliant gay men who were born here.

The salmon-pink Villa Les Rhumbs, the delightful house in the posh residential area on the cliffs, was turned into the **Musée Christian Dior** (*open April–25 Oct daily exc Mon 10–12.30 and 2.30–7; adm*) in 1997, which produces an annual fashion exhibition. Dior's parents bought the villa around 1905, the year of Christian's birth. He started his career by making costumes for himself and his friends for the Granville carnival. The family moved to Paris, but Dior would often return for the summer, until his father went bankrupt in the early 1930s. Dior's rise in the fashion world began suddenly. He started designing clothes in 1935, and by 1947 had opened his own fashion house. Inspired by the Belle Epoque traditions, he clothed the likes of Marlene Dietrich and Olivia de Havilland. He died in 1957, not long after the young Yves St-Laurent became his assistant.

The bookshop owner and art collector Richard Anacréon is not as widely known as Dior, but through A l'Originale, the shop he opened in Paris during the war, he

(*inexpensive*). The most appealing hotel in the port, in a 17th-century house.

Le Moderne, 1 Place Charles de Gaulle, t 02 33 23 12 44, f 02 33 23 91 58 (*cheap*). Bargain rooms in a curious little building. Restaurant (*menus 90–245F*). *Closed Jan–mid-Mar; Tues and Wed exc mid-July–mid-Sept.*

Cherbourg ✉ 50100

★★Régence, 42 Quai de Caligny, t 02 33 43 05 16, f 02 33 43 98 37 (*inexpensive*). View of the port.

★★Ambassadeur, 22 Quai de Caligny, t 02 33 43 10 00, f 02 33 43 10 01. View of the port. 40 rooms, but no restaurant.

★★Croix de Malte, 5 Rue des Halles, t 02 33 43 19 16, f 02 33 43 65 66 (*inexpensive–cheap*). Comfortable rooms in the heart of town, in a convenient location for restaurants.

Goury ✉ 50440

Auberge de Goury, Port de Goury, t 02 33 52 77 01. Superlative grilled fish and superb views from the tip of the Cap de la Hague.

Bricquebec ✉ 50260

★★★Hôtel du Vieux Château, t 02 33 52 24 49, f 02 33 52 62 71 (*moderate*). The original owner took part in the Battle of Hastings, and Queen Victoria and Montgomery have counted among its famous guests.

Barneville-Carteret ✉ 50270

★★★La Marine, 11 Rue de Paris, t 02 33 53 83 31, f 02 33 53 39 60 (*moderate*). The best-known hotel, above all for its chic restaurant. (*menus 150–400F*). The rooms are sweet.

L'Hermitage, 4 Promenade Abbé Leouteiller, t 02 33 04 96 29, f 02 33 04 78 87 (*inexpensive*). A few delightful rooms above a restaurant looking on to the port.

★★Les Isles, 9 Bd Maritime, t 02 33 04 90 76, f 02 33 94 53 83 (*inexpensive*). Good value seaside hotel at Barneville-Plage.

Granville ✉ 50400

★★★Le Grand Large, 5 Rue de la Falaise, t 02 33 91 19 19, f 02 33 91 19 00 (*moderate–inexpensive*)). Grand, modern hotel with luxury thalassotherapy and beauty institute and well-equipped, smart rooms looking out to sea. Restaurant (*menus 120–150F*).

★★★Les Bains, 19 Georges Clemenceau, t 02 33 50 17 31, f 02 33 50 89 22 (*moderate–inexpensive*). Smart old Norman timber-frame exterior and old-fashioned rooms down by the casino. No restaurant.

★★Le Michelet, 5 bis Rue Jules Michelet, t 02 33 50 06 55, f 02 33 50 12 25 (*inexpensive–cheap*). Brightly, tastefully decorated little rooms. No restaurant.

fostered innumerable relations with significant writers and artists. Born in Granville in 1907, Anacréon died in his home town in 1992, leaving it his books and paintings, provided that it open a museum named after him. A 19th-century school in a commanding location above the sea was converted into the **Musée d'Art Moderne Richard Anacréon** (*open early April–mid-Sept daily exc Tues 10–12 and 2–6; adm*). Too plain-speaking for Granville's inhabitants in his lifetime, they can now thank him for Fauvist canvases by the likes of Vlaminck, Derain, Friesz and Chabaud, Pointillist works and others by Picabia, Van Dongen and Utrillo, and acrobatic ballet dancers by Rodin. One of Anacréon's closest literary friends was Colette, and one corner of the museum contains her bureau, pictures and rare personally signed editions. You can also see rare editions by Cocteau, Genet, Valéry, Claudel and Malraux.

The quirky rooms of the **Musée du Vieux Granville** (*open in season daily exc Tues 10–12 and 2–6; out of season Wed and weekends pms only; adm*) occupy an historic house just above the main gate into the old town. The days of pirate raids between Britain and France are recalled, and the issue of bathing is seriously treated. A poster from 1837 advertises the rules of the bathing police: men and women were segregated, women bathing on the north side of the rock, men on the south side. You might be surprised to learn that nude bathing was allowed in certain areas for men.

The ruined medieval **Abbaye de la Lucerne**, southeast of Granville (*open early Feb–Dec 10–12 and 2–6.30; Nov–Easter closes 1hr earlier; adm*) gained its subtitle 'd'Outremer' (from across the sea) by showing persistent loyalty to England. In 1204, when Philippe Auguste seized Normandy, the monks of La Lucerne remained stubbornly faithful to their previous master, King John of England. When the English reappeared during the Hundred Years' War, the abbey provided a chaplain for Edward III. This didn't prevent the abbey from becoming one of the largest religious houses in France, and remaining so right up until its dissolution in 1791. The main church (1164–78) was built in a simple, unadorned Norman Romanesque. Its very plainness gives it strength, and its crossing tower set the model for many churches in the region. A good deal of restoration has been undertaken, especially of the choir, with its superb 1780 organ now regularly used for concerts and services.

To Mont-St-Michel via Avranches

Mont-St-Michel, at the westernmost point of Normandy, is one of the very greatest sights in the Western world – a mesmerizing rock isolated in its vast bay and topped by its famous abbey.

South of Granville to Avranches

The coast road south from Granville offers breathtaking views of Mont-St-Michel. In fact, you may find a trip along this stretch of coast, especially at sunset, more moving than the tour of the abbey buildings themselves. At **Les Genêts**, the **Maison de la Baie** contains a mine of information on local wildlife and organizes walks across to the mount at low tide from May to October. Do not attempt this journey without a guide. Legends abound about the giant tides and quicksands of the bay, and real tragedies have occurred here when the foolhardy set out by themselves.

The city of **Avranches** sits atop a clutch of granite hills that fall precipitously to the great flat plain of the bay. Its history has been inextricably bound up with that of the mount since the apparitions to Bishop Aubert in the 8th century (*see* below). In Avranches' 19th-century **church of St-Gervais** the treasury (*adm*) contains as its greatest relic the skull of St Aubert, with the small hole in it supposedly left by the archangel Michael's finger. There are spectacular views of Mont St-Michel from Avranches' **Plate-forme**. Kneeling for a whole day dressed only in a shirt, Henry II did penance in front of the cathedral which once stood here for his part in the murder of Thomas à Becket. The king performed this act at the instigation of one of the greatest abbots of Mont St-Michel, also bishop of Avranches, Robert de Torigni.

Avranches' **Mairie** contains a matchless treasure in the form of the **Manuscrits du Mont-St-Michel** (*open June–Sept daily 10–12 and 2–6; adm*), saved at the Revolution from the library of the abbey. Some of them date from de Torigni's time, some from even earlier. They count among the finest illuminated pieces in the world, and a

Getting Around

Avranches has its own train station but for Mont-St-Michel you need to go to Pontorson-St-Michel and catch a bus; Mon–Sat *c.* 6 buses a day, Sun afternoons only.

Tourist Information

Avranches: 2 Rue Général de Gaulle, t 02 33 58 00 22, f 02 33 68 13 29, *avranches-tourisme @wanadoo.fr*.
Le Mont-St-Michel: t 02 33 60 14 30, f 02 33 60 06 75.
Pontorson: Place de l'Hôtel de Ville, t 02 33 60 20 65, f 02 33 60 85 67.

Where to Stay and Eat

Avranches ✉ 50300

★★La Croix d'Or, 83 Rue de la Constitution, t 02 33 58 04 88, f 02 33 58 06 95 (*inexpensive*). 27 rooms. Former coaching inn turned pleasing hotel. Restaurant (*menus 118–320F*). *Closed Jan and 15 Oct–25 Mar Sun eves.*

Ducey ✉ 50220

A small town with a couple of appealing, good-value riverside hotels.

★★★Moulin de Ducey, 1 Grande Rue, t 02 33 60 25 25, f 02 33 60 26 76 (*moderate–inexpensive*). 28 rooms in a converted mill. No restaurant.
★★Auberge de la Sélune, 2 Rue St-Germain, t 02 33 48 53 62, f 02 33 48 90 30 (*inexpensive*). Inventive cuisine and 20 smart rooms. Restaurant (*menus 84–208F*). *Closed mid-Nov–mid-Dec and 21 Jan–mid-Feb; Oct–Mar Mon.*

Le Mont-St-Michel ✉ 50116

It's expensive to stay on the mount and rooms tend to be cramped, but it greatly adds to the experience of a visit.

★★★Mère Poulard, t 02 33 60 14 01, f 02 33 48 52 31, *hotel.mere.poulard@wanadoo.fr* (*expensive–moderate*). The most famous name here, with some pretty rooms. The restaurant is best known for its omelettes.
St-Pierre, t 02 33 60 14 04, f 02 33 48 59 82. Looks suitably historical and its dining room (*menus 90–300F*) is even classified as an historic monument. Comfortable rooms. *Closed 20 Dec–2 Feb.*
★★★La Croix Blanche, t 02 33 60 14 04, f 02 33 48 59 82 (*moderate*). 9 comfortable rooms. *Closed 15 Nov–2 Feb Thurs.*
★★Hôtel du Mouton Blanc, t 02 33 60 14 08, f 02 33 60 05 62 (*inexpensive*). 9 rooms. A slightly less expensive option.

selection of them is put on show each summer. The more mundane **Musée Municipal** (*open Easter–Sept daily 9.30–12 and 2–6; adm*) displays religious sculpture, ethnographical bits and pieces from medieval times onwards, and a large collection of lithographs, inevitably with many views of Mont-St-Michel. The terraces of the town's **Jardin des Plantes** offer particularly wonderful views across the Bay of Mont St-Michel.

Mont-St-Michel

History

Mont-St-Michel is a glorious piece of Christian symbolism: its triangular shape from afar evokes the Holy Trinity; the narrow spit joining mainland to island seems to represent the straight and narrow path to God; and the church steeple pointing fiercely to the skies is a sharp reminder for visitors to turn their gaze towards heaven. The needle is topped by a gilded statue of St Michael, the weigher of souls at the Last Judgement.

Some kind of a Christian building was constructed on the rock before St Aubert founded the first shrine to St Michael, but it is Aubert who counts as the first significant figure in the mount's history. An early manuscript recounts the story of this 8th-century bishop of Avranches: in the year 708, so it is said, the Archangel Michael swooped down into Aubert's dreams and commanded the bishop to build a shrine to him on the rock in the middle of the bay. Aubert dismissed this dream twice, but the third time the archangel supposedly gave Aubert a vicious prod in the side of the head, prompting the bishop into action. Aubert first had a small oratory built, a grotto modelled on that at Mount Gargano in Italy where St Michael was said to have put in an earlier appearance. Monks were sent across the Alps to fetch relics of St Michael.

In 966 the mount became the site of the first Benedictine foundation in Lower Normandy. Later it was decided to replace the buildings with a more substantial Romanesque abbey, which went up roughly from the start of the 11th century to the mid-12th. Donations of land from nobles and of money from visiting pilgrims brought the abbey considerable wealth. It became a celebrated school of learning and was renowned for its illuminated manuscripts. Robert de Tombelaine and Anastase the Venetian were among the most revered scholars of the 11th century. In that period a first collection of stories of miracles connected with Mont-St-Michel was compiled, and a whole network of pilgrimage routes to the holy place developed, known as the *chemins montais*. However, it was under the abbot Robert de Torigni (1154–86) that the abbey knew its greatest period. The number of monks reached its peak of 60. Such was the prolific production of manuscripts in this period and such was the size of the abbey library that Mont-St-Michel became known as the 'City of Books'.

Mont-St-Michel also became a strategic and symbolic stronghold in the Middle Ages. At the start of the 13th century Breton soldiers fighting for Philippe Auguste set fire to part of the abbey, destroying much of it. The repentant Philippe Auguste, after his victory, donated an enormous sum to build a magnificent new monastic wing on the north side of the island. This Merveille, or Marvel, as it became known, counts as the greatest architectural achievement on Mont-St-Michel.

The ramparts around the bottom of the mount date mainly from the 15th century, built to defend the rock from the English in the Hundred Years' War. The English allowed pilgrims to reach the abbey through the warring, however, and in the course of fighting in 1421, the church choir collapsed. Once the war was over, many pilgrims came to thank St Michael for delivering them from the English, giving generously to help in the reconstruction of the choir and contributing to the abbey's coffers.

French kings too came to Mont-St-Michel on pilgrimage, but the nature of abbey life was radically altered in the early 16th century when the crown took control of the appointment of abbots across France under the system of *commende*. Some of the *abbés commendataires* scarcely visited the mount and were only interested in its revenue; inevitably the monastic life and scholarship suffered dramatically.

With the installation of the Maurist Benedictine order in 1622, religious life somewhat revived, but the place lay in a precarious state. Only some 10 monks lived in the abbey towards the end of the 18th century. During the Revolution the monks were replaced by prisoners. The abbey served this demeaning purpose until 1863. Then the 19th-century restorers moved in in force. The neo-Gothic spire, built in 1897, was the work of Victor Petigrand, a pupil of Viollet-le-Duc. The statue of St Michael that tops the spire, sparkling and golden, was executed by Frémiet.

Recently, Benedictine monks have been allowed back into the abbey. There are only a handful, but they do receive people coming to the abbey on religious retreats, keeping a little spiritual flame alive on the holy mount.

Touring Mont-St-Michel

Abbey open 2 May–Sept daily 9.30–5.30; rest of year daily 9.30–4.30.
Imaginaires mid-May–Aug 10pm–1am; last admission midnight.

This is the most visited site in France outside Paris – around three million people visit each year, and in summer the crush can be hellish. The picturesque, steep, narrow street up to the abbey panders to these modern-day pilgrims, crammed with shops selling tat. The bay itself is silting up fast, and a massive project is now under way to reestablish the natural setting. For the tourist, the most obvious change will come with the destruction of the causeway, to be replaced by a pedestrian and rail bridge. Mont-St-Michel is now on UNESCO's list of world heritage sites.

Such a gem from a distance, the **abbey** turns out to be austere and forbidding close up, designed to incite awe and reflection. The buildings were made from granite quarried locally and on the Iles Chausey, out in the bay. The work of heaving up great stones on such steep rock was an incredible achievement. A daunting number of steps leads up to the level of the abbey church. The reward is glorious views both of the abbey – its sheer stone faces plunging down the sides of the rock – and of the bay.

A classical façade was tacked on to one of the earliest Romanesque buildings in Normandy, built in plain style. Even the luminous late-Gothic choir has little decorative detail. The church was an extraordinary work of engineering: its crossing was placed on the very top of the rock. Most of the rest of the edifice rests on four supporting lower chapels or crypts.

The *tour-conférence* is a detailed guided tour – if you speak French, a more interesting experience than going round by yourself or on the guided tour in English, although it requires stamina and a head for heights. You are taken right up among the church's flying buttresses, an exhilarating but demanding climb, and definitely not for those who suffer from vertigo, then you plunge down to the four crypts, not all of which are accessible on an ordinary tour.

The brillliant **Merveille** (*open to all visitors*) was daringly built on the north side of the mount. It basically consists of two rooms on each of its three floors. On the top level the cloister garden stands open to the skies, while its galleries are held up on delicate double columns. Originally built as a peaceful retreat, nowadays it tends to be as calm as Paris in the rush hour. The refectory next to the cloister is beautifully lit, but there are no direct views out. With typical Christian self-denying perversity, many of the rooms in this magnificent site were deliberately deprived of views, with diagonal windows built to let the light in indirectly. On the middle level, the vast Salle des

Hôtes was where noble and prestigious pilgrims were received and camped out. The room next door, referred to as the Salle des Chevaliers, is thought to have served both as the abbey's chapterhouse and as its scriptorium, where manuscripts were prepared. A copy of Frémiet's statue of St Michael is displayed in the massive cellar on the lowest level of the Merveille, where mountains of provisions for the abbey and its pilgrims were stored. Close up, God's generalissimo looks mean and militant, dressed in armour, sword raised for action above his spiky head gear, only the wings adding a slightly softer touch.

At night the abbey is gloriously lit. In high season it hosts its own special son-et-lumière, the wonderfully atmospheric **Imaginaires**. In various spaces throughout the abbey, works of art and pieces of music, many of them contemporary, add greatly to the sense of occasion. You can take this tour at your own pace, and with fewer people around, the abbey is filled with an amazing and sometimes eerie Gothic grandeur.

Other attractions on the mount lie along the Grande Rue, the main street that snakes its way up to the abbey entrance. Down at the bottom, the simple **Musée Maritime** (*open daily exc Jan 9–6; adm*) climbs up four small floors filled with model ships and boats. A video on each level explains aspects of the bay and its natural habitat in a sensible manner – English-speaking visitors are provided with headphones.

Tucked into the rock to one side of the Grande Rue, the other serious religious stop on the mount besides the abbey is **St-Pierre**, a charming building from the 15th and 16th centuries. The **Archéoscope** (*open daily exc 15 Nov–Jan 9–6; adm*), almost opposite St-Pierre, offers a lively, contemporary introduction to the abbey. Smoke, lights and videos bombard the senses and, although the commentary is in French, the splendid film footage taken from a helicopter and the special effects are easy to appreciate.

By contrast, the **Musée Historique** (*open daily exc 15 Nov–Jan 9–6; adm*), close to the stairs at the entrance to the abbey, is amusingly archaic. Various torture instruments remind you of the abbey's secondary use as a prison. The **Maison de Tiphaine** (*open June–15 Sept daily 9–7; rest of period Feb–mid-Nov 9–6; adm*), close by, was built for the most famed Breton and French warrior of the Hundred Years' War, Bertrand du Guesclin and his wife.

Many tourists never get further than the Grande Rue and the abbey, but you can follow the old *chemin de ronde* from the entrance to enjoy spectacular views of the monastic buildings. The path winds down to the **Tour Gabriel** on the western side of the island, from where you can walk out to the old quay. Clamber along some rocks to see the little **chapel of St-Aubert** on the isolated northwestern corner of the mount.

Brittany

Brittany

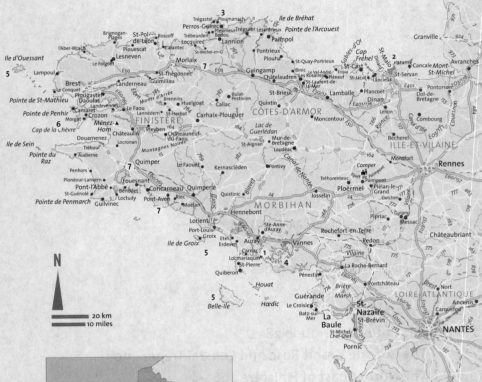

Highlights

1 Neolithic sites at Carnac and Locmariaquer
2 Corsair St-Malo
3 The wildly colourful Côte de Granit Rose
4 The inland sea of the Golfe du Morbihan
5 Boulder-strewn islands
6 The vicious cliffs of the Crozon peninsula
7 Estuary towns of Morlaix, Quimper and Pont-Aven

Food and Wine

A thin black buckwheat pancake is the national meal –
only the Bretons can comprehend its miserable culinary attractions.

Balzac, *Les Chouans*

The Breton crêpe (or the savoury *galette*) is considered the aristocrat of the pancake world these days. Delicate and thin, it comes with all sorts of fancy fillings and in Brittany crêperies are generally reliable and cheap places to eat.

Brittany is also known for its fish and seafood. Don't be surprised if shellfish is served in its shell, or if oysters and clams are served *cru* (raw). If you order a *plateau de fruits de mer* you will be faced with a sumptuous spread which will normally include certain types of crab, *langoustines* (Dublin Bay prawns), *crevettes* (shrimps), *palourdes* (clams), *coques* (cockles), *bigorneaux* (winkles) and *bulots* (whelks). Wash it down with a white Muscadet from the south of Brittany. *Cotriade* is the traditional Breton sailors' soup, made with a combination of whiting, cod, haddock, hake, mackerel, eel, and even mussels. Certain fish are particularly prized, such as St-Pierre (John Dory), *bar* (sea bass), *dorade* (sea bream), *rouget* (red mullet), turbot and sole. The marshes of Guérande in southern Brittany produce highly regarded salt, the *fleur de sel*. Crunchy little sprigs of *salicornes* (samphire) are another speciality from the salt-pans and are increasingly experimented with in Breton cuisine, as is algae.

Brittany is known for its pork, as well as for *saucissons* (salamis), *andouilles* (chitterlings) and *boudins* (black pudding). The town of Châteaubriant is renowned for the thick grilled fillet steak named after it. *Kig-ar-farz* (meat-and-pudding in Breton) is a traditional dish, now back in fashion in Breton restaurants, in which meat and vegetables are cooked together in a broth.

Gâteau Breton is a dense, dry Breton butter cake, while *kouign aman* is a cake that drips with butter. Various Breton towns, notably Pleyben and Pont-Aven, produce buttery biscuits known as *galettes. Far* is a heavy eggy pudding with dried fruit. Brittany, like neighbouring Normandy, is apple country, and makes good cider and delicious but relatively rare lambig, the Breton equivalent to calvados. Cervoise is a traditional beer, supposedly drunk by the most famous Breton of all, Astérix.

Along Brittany's ceaselessly dramatic coastline Neolithic monuments and ruined fortifications mingle with spectacular beaches, bays and ports. The north is rocky, the south gentler, with huge sweeps of sand, while the cliffs of the west create the most savage Breton scenery of all. A garland of islands encircles the Breton coast, each with its own personality; one in the sheltered Golfe du Morbihan conceals the finest Neolithic tomb in France. Morbihan was a happening place 5,000 years ago; one of its many sites is the great Carnac.

Brittany's place names, from St-Malo to the Pointe de St-Gildas, recall the holy men who crossed the Channel in the Dark Ages to set up communities, creating Brittany, little Britain. Arthurian legend also crossed the Channel, now most evident in the Forest of Brocéliande in the centre of the region.

Getting There and Around

By Air

Air France, **t** 0845 0845 111, *www.airfrance co.uk*, operates Brit Air services daily from London-Gatwick to Brest and Nantes, and from London-City to Rennes. Aer Lingus – Dublin **t** (01) 8444 777, Cork **t** (021) 327 15 – operates a service between Dublin and Rennes via Cork (*mid-May–early Oct*). Ryanair has low-cost flights from London-Stansted to Dinard.

By Rail

To travel from Britain, avoiding Paris, take Eurostar, **t** 0345 303 030, to Lille and change for Rennes, Nantes, Lorient, Quimper, etc.

From Paris, three main TGV lines leave for Brittany from the Gare Montparnasse: to Brest via Rennes; to Quimper via Rennes; and as far as Le Croisic via Nantes.

By Sea

For details on travelling to St-Malo and Roscoff, see pp.84, 274 and 294.

To find tranquil corners of Brittany in high summer, travel up the river estuaries or avens; the most renowned of these is Pont-Aven, where Paul Gauguin and Emile Bernard painted in the late 19th century. Up other estuaries stand picturesque historic towns – Morlaix, Dinan, Quimper and Vannes – tucked well out of sight from would-be invaders. The celebrated Breton calvaries are mainly a feature of the Finistère, France's Land's End in the west, the most traditional part of Brittany, where the Breton language (closely related to Welsh) was spoken as the first language by many children right up to the first half of the 20th century. Since then, thanks to the centralizing bureaucrats in Paris, Brittany's mother tongue has been almost wholly cut out. A small hard core keeps it alive, while a tiny minority fights for an independent Breton nation. Most Bretons are content merely to assert good-naturedly their cultural identity; Breton dance, music and the *pardons* – when local saints are taken out of their humid churches for an airing – are still going strong.

In recent decades, stretches of the Breton shore have fallen victim to appalling oil slicks caused by careless oil tankers. The beaches recover very fast, but sadly not the wildlife. Other portions of the coast have been polluted by farm fertilizers, but environmental issues are now starting to be taken much more seriously and most of Brittany's beaches are of a very high standard.

Around the Bay of Mont St-Michel

The daytime mirages and evening sunsets across the Bay of the Mont-St-Michel make for some of the most mesmerizing images of Brittany. Although the holy granite mount itself is in Normandy (*see* pp.263–6), much of the spectacular flat bay out of which it rises lies within the Breton border. A semi-submerged forest of wooden posts lies on this side of the bay, an amazing sea- and sandscape you can visit, where mussels really do grow on trees.

The **Mont-Dol** is another granite mount rising dramatically from the flats, this time surrounded by bucolic countryside. The tale goes that St Michael was called upon to fight Satan in this gorgeous spot, and the marks of their legendary struggle have supposedly been left in some of the rocks. **Dol-de-Bretagne** became the seat of one of the early Breton bishoprics in the Dark Ages and tradition has it that Nomenoë had himself crowned the first Breton king here in 850. Nomenoë certainly replaced the Frankish bishops with his own, securing some independence for the Breton Church.

The besieging of Dol by William the Conqueror is depicted on the Bayeux tapestry. The troops of his descendant King John burned down Dol's Romanesque **cathedral** in 1204, and it was almost completely rebuilt in the 13th century in the defensive, sober style you now see. The main façade has virtually no decoration, but one ugly male gargoyle does stand out – said by the townspeople to be a likeness of King John. Walking into the cathedral, dramatic 13th-century stained glass, some of the oldest in Brittany, gives colour to the distant apse – the building is 330ft long. Dol was an important halt on the Tro Breizh, the major pilgrimage route around the cathedrals of Brittany's seven founding saints. Unusually, some of the town houses on Dol's main shopping street date back to the Romanesque period and retain their carvings.

South of town the **Menhir de Champ-Dolent** is one of Brittany's most impressive standing stones. Legend says it fell from the skies to separate two feuding brothers. A cross was placed on top to Christianize it. The menhir is slowly sinking into the ground; it is said that when the stone disappears altogether, the world will end.

Getting Around

If you don't have a car, use the bus services from St-Malo.

Tourist Information

Dol-de-Bretagne: 3 Grande Rue, t 02 99 48 14 13, f 02 99 48 19 63.
Cancale: 44 Rue du Port, t 02 99 89 63 72, f 02 99 89 75 08.

Activities

Tractor tours of the mussel beds are available via the Centre d'Animation de la Baie du Mont-St-Michel, Le Vivier-sur-Mer, t 02 99 48 84 38, f 02 99 48 80 93.

Where to Stay and Eat

Roz-sur-Couesnon

There are some wonderful B&Bs scattered around the bay and the slope-side of this village.
Mme Gillet's B&B at Val-St-Revert, t 02 99 80 27 85.
M. Piel's B&B, La Poultière, La Bergerie, t 02 99 80 29 68.

Cherrueix

There are simpler B&Bs in this atmospheric village in splendid locations right down by the bay:
La Pichardière, t 02 99 48 83 82.
Lair Chambre d'Hôte, t 02 99 48 01 65.
Les Trois Cheminées, t 02 99 48 93 54.

Cancale and Around ✉ 35260

****Maison de Bricourt, t 02 99 89 64 76, f 02 99 89 88 47 (*expensive*). One of the best hotels in northern Brittany, in several delightful locations. Owned by one of the finest chefs in France, Olivier Roellinger, who has also opened a restaurant, **Le Bistrot Marin Le Coquillage** (*menus 460–690F*).
**Hotel de la Pointe du Grouin, t 02 99 89 60 55, f 02 99 89 92 22 (*moderate*). Headland location to die for. *Closed Oct–Mar; restaurant closed Tues* (*menus 120–315F*).
**Le Châtellier, t 02 99 89 81 84, f 02 99 89 61 69 (*inexpensive*). Modest converted farm, outside Cancale on the D355 to St-Malo – like staying with a charming French family.
Le St-Cast, t 02 99 89 66 08, f 02 99 89 89 20. Among the many restaurants looking on to the quays, serving particularly delicious seafood specialities in its conservatory dining room (*menus 120–220F*).

Houses climb up the steep cliffside of the delightful oyster port of **Cancale**, where tourists pack the quayside restaurants, looking across the vast bay to Mont-St-Michel. The rocky **Pointe du Grouin** closes off the western end of the bay, from where there are spectacular views in all directions. Just out to sea, l'Ile des Landes, with its scaly dragon's back, has been turned into a bird reserve. Colette particularly loved this stretch of coast, which she lovingly described in her scandalous novel of adolescent sexual awakening, *Le Blé en herbe* (*The Ripening Seed*).

St-Malo

In the Second World War, old St-Malo was almost entirely reduced to rubble, but it has since re-emerged as one of the great cities of France. Located on one corner of a stocky peninsula known as the Clos Poulet, irresistible sandy beaches stretch below the magnificent old walls.

The Walled City and the Islands

St-Malo has one of the most spectacular, fiery and controversial histories of any French city. A Celtic and then a Gallo-Roman settlement grew up west of the present city at Alet, and the first cathedral was possibly built there around 380. With the arrival of immigrants from across the Channel it thrived, and in the 6th century a man called Malo – or Maclou, or perhaps even Mac Low – came from Britain to work miracles. At the start of the Middle Ages, the bishop Jean de Chatillon saw to it that St-Malo was defended by solid ramparts and ordered the building of a much grander cathedral. St-Malo's fleet became active in both trade and war, and Philippe Auguste used it to assist him in chasing the English out of Normandy. But the city cultivated its independent streak down the centuries: '*Ni Français, ni Breton: Malouin suis* (I'm neither French nor Breton, but Malouin)' ran a popular motto. The Malouin merchants prospered, in part from backing corsairs sent out to pillage English ships.

Countless French explorers set out from St-Malo, most famously Jacques Cartier, who claimed Canada for France in the 1530s. The Iles Malouines (the Falklands) were discovered by its adventurers. St-Malo was glorious, and notorious. Merchants made fortunes from far-flung trade, including the slave trade; Malouin corsairs made a killing off British and Dutch merchants. France's greatest and most miserable Romantic writer, François-René de Chateaubriand is the city's most famous son, who wrote of his childhood in his *Mémoires d'Outre-Tombe*. In the 19th century time was up for the corsairs and slave-traders: cod-fishing took centre stage, and a radical change in Anglo-French relations brought a very different breed of invaders – tourists.

Touring St-Malo

To appreciate the location of the **ville intra-muros** (the historic walled city), take a bracing walk along the glorious ramparts, with their many gates and bastions, their watch-towers and statues of St-Malo's hot-headed heroes. Down below, the streets within the walls are dark with tall, tightly packed granite mansions. The **Demeure des**

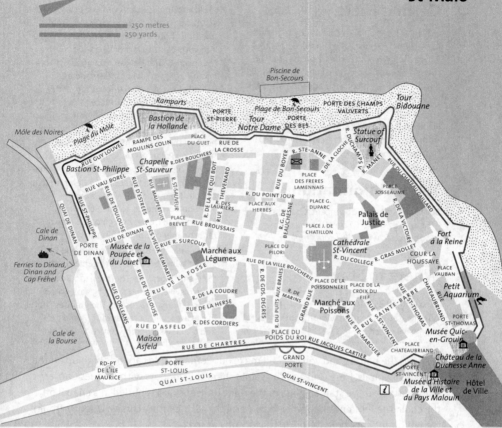

Magon de la Lande or Maison Asfeld (*open Mar–15 Nov 10–12 and 2–6.30; adm*) is one of the few great 18th-century merchant houses to have survived the Second World War intact. You'll get the best picture of the life of the wealthy merchants of the Ancien Régime: here deals were struck, voyages planned, exotic products stored while family life went on, thought the Magon family only spent around three months of the year in their town house. It's now flats, but one tenant has organized guided tours; not many of the original features have survived inside, but the guide's enthusiasm is infectious.

Dark and dismal by contrast, the **Musée d'Histoire de la Ville** (*open daily exc Mon 10–12 and 2–6; adm*), locked away in a grim part of the city's château, tells the story of St-Malo's past in rambling, chaotic fashion, and presents the main events of the town's history through set pieces with comical painted backdrops and stilted commentaries.

The cathedral's sharp spire is a landmark in the centre of town. Black and white photos in the side entrance show the extent of its devastation in the Second World War, although the nave, its vaulting and most of the 13th-century Gothic choir

Getting There

Ryanair, t 0870 156 9569, has cheap flights from London-Stansted to Dinard, across the Rance river. Brittany Ferries, t 08705 360 360, run ferries to St-Malo from the UK or Ireland. Condor Ferries, t 0845 345 2000, operate a fast service to and from Poole (*late May–end Sept*).

To reach St-Malo by train you need to travel via Rennes. St-Malo's station is a long way from the historic city. For local bus information call t 02 99 56 06 06.

Tourist Information

St-Malo: Esplanade St-Vincent, t 02 99 56 64 48, f 02 99 56 67 00; *office.de.tourisme@ wanadoo.fr, www.vilee-saint-malo.fr*.

Where to Stay

St-Malo ✉ 35400

Try to stay in the more vibrant, but relatively expensive old city.

***Elizabeth**, 2 Rue des Cordiers, t 02 99 56 24 98, f 02 99 56 39 24 (*moderate*). Small luxurious hotel within the ramparts, with a late-16th-century façade (*400–690F*).

***Central**, 6 Grande Rue, t 02 99 40 87 70, f 02 99 40 47 57 (*expensive–moderate*). Reliable Best Western (*menus 125–280F*).

****France/Chateaubriand**, Place Chateaubriand, t 02 99 56 66 52, f 02 99 40 10 04 (*inexpensive*). The most high-profile hotel in the walled city, with cafés below.

****Hotel du Palais**, 8 Rue Toullier, t 02 99 40 07 30, f 02 99 40 29 53 (*inexpensive*). A small hotel with character set in a quieter area up the hill. No restaurant. *Closed Jan*.

*****Hotel du Commerce**, 10 Rue St-Thomas, t 02 99 56 18 00, f 02 99 56 04 68 (*cheap*). A rare cheaper option within the walled city.

Many fine hotels are located outside the walled city, in St-Malo's more genteel suburbs.

*****Grand Hotel des Thermes**, 100 Bd Hébert, Courtoisville, t 02 99 40 75 75, f 02 99 40 76 00 (*luxury–expensive*). The grandest hotel in the area, with a restaurant (*menu 170F*) and a thalassotherapy centre. *Closed Jan*.

survived the bombs, and you can still make out Romanesque carvings high up on the columns' capitals. Here God and the saints share the honours with Jacques Cartier, who features in the stained glass in the right transept, and is buried in a chapel off the choir. The remains of another local 'hero', the 18th-century corsair, Duguay-Trouin, were brought back here from Paris as recently as 1973.

Down in the lower parts of the walled city you'll find the main shopping quarters; the favourite square is **Place Chateaubriand**, with its wonderful concentration of cafés below the castle.

When the tide goes out, ant trails of tourists head for the **islands** of the Grand-Bé and the Fort National (*open Easter–Sept at low tide during the day; adm*), from where the walled city looks stunning. Languishing Romantics visit the **Grand Bé** to see Chateaubriand's tomb. The **Island of Cézembre**, a boat ride away from St-Malo (boats leave from the Porte de Dinan, summer only), is a rocky island with little shade. You're not supposed to stray from the blindingly white sands as German mines may still be lurking under the surface.

Around St-Malo – the Clos Poulet

St-Malo's seaside resort, **Paramé**, stretching east of town behind a glorious arc of beach, is crammed with hotels. The **Musée Jacques Cartier** (*open July–Aug 10–11.30 and 2.30–6; June and Sept Mon–Fri 10–11.30 and 2.30–6; rest of year Mon–Fri tours at 10 and 3; adm*), further east in a small farm-cum-manor house, pays its respects to

***La Villefromoy**, 7 Bd Hébert, Rochebonne, t 02 99 40 92 20, f 02 99 56 79 49 (*expensive–moderate*). Smaller hotel in a 19th-century town house. Many sea views but no restaurant. *Closed 15 Nov–15 Mar.*

***Hotel Alba**, 17 Rue des Dunes, Courtoisville, t 02 99 40 37 18, f 02 99 40 96 40 (*moderate*). A delightful neat white villa with a few rooms with sea terraces.

***Le Beaufort**, 25 Chaussée du Sillon, t 02 99 40 99 99, f 02 99 40 99 62 (*moderate*). Stylish hotel closer to the old town. Some rooms have their own sea-facing terrace.

*****Les Charmettes**, 64 Bd Hébert, Courtoisville, t 02 99 56 07 31, f 02 99 56 85 96 (*cheap*). Good cheaper option in the area close to the big beach.

Eating Out

À La Duchesse Anne, Place Guy La Chambre, t 02 99 40 85 33, f 02 99 40 00 28. Classic, expensive Malouin restaurant, set within the thick town ramparts (*menus 250–320F*). *Closed high season Sun eve, Mon lunch and Wed.*

Brigitte et Didier Delaunay, 6 Rue Ste-Barbe, t 02 99 40 92 46, f 02 99 56 88 91. Very fresh regional dishes (*menus 180–240F*). *Closed 15 Nov–15 Dec, 15 Jan–15 Feb; Oct–April Sun and Mon.*

Le Chalut, 8 Rue de la Corne de Cerf, t 02 99 56 71 58. A posh fish restaurant with a good reputation (*menus 240–360F*). *Closed Sun eve and Mon.*

Le Chasse-Marée, 4 Rue du Grout St-Georges, t 02 99 40 85 10, f 02 99 56 49 52. A tempting little restaurant away from the crowds serving refined seafood dishes.

Le Borgnefesse, 10 Rue du Puits aux Braies, t 02 99 40 05 05. Run by a bit of a character, full of tales of St-Malo.

La Grève, St-Suliac, t 02 99 58 33 83, f 02 99 58 35 40. A few miles south of St-Malo up the Rance river in beautiful St-Suliac. By the port, with marine decor and fine seafood.

France's best-known explorer. There isn't a great deal to see inside, but the guided tour narrates the story of Cartier's life. Nearby, the **Rochers Sculptés de Rothéneuf** (*open daily exc in bad weather: Easter–Sept 9–9; rest of year 10–12 and 2–5.30; adm*) feature cartoonish figures hewn out of the rock as therapy by a sick priest, the abbé Fouré, in the late 19th century.

South of St-Malo, beyond the ferry port, you come to **Alet-cum-St-Servan**, St-Malo's older sibling, which has plenty of character of its own, and a divided opinion on its now much bigger brother. One side looks lovingly towards St-Malo, while the other side dominates the beautiful Rance estuary. The 14th-century Tour Solidor contains the old-fashioned **Musée International du Long-Cours Cap-Hornier** (*open April–Sept 10–12 and 2–6; Oct–Mar daily exc Mon 10–12 and 2–6; adm*) which tells the story of perilous voyages around Cape Horn. The new **Grand Aquarium** (*open July 9–8; Aug 9–10; Sept–June 10–6.30; adm*), south of town, contains eight impressive rooms.

The North Breton Marches

Brittany's eastern frontier is guarded by two of the mightiest medieval forts in France, built in the dark mottled stone of the region. **Fougères'** fort, unusually, doesn't dominate the town, but broods down in its valley; the best views of it are from the Bourg Neuf or upper town, or from the spectacular tower of the church of St-Léonard.

Getting Around

TGV high-speed trains from Paris to Rennes occasionally stop at Vitré.

Tourist Information

Fougères: 1 Place Aristide Briand, t 02 99 94 12 20, f 02 99 94 77 30.
Vitré: Place St-Yves, t 02 99 75 04 46, f 02 99 74 02 01.

Where to Stay and Eat

Fougères ✉ 35300

★★Le Balzac, 15 Rue Nationale, t 02 99 99 42 46, f 02 99 99 65 43 (*inexpensive*). Well positioned in the upper town, and the rooms are OK.

Les Vins et une Fourchette, t 02 99 94 55 88. By the castle, serving interesting dishes in the amusingly converted little rooms of a former butcher's shop.

Vitré ✉ 35500

★★Le Minotel, 47 Rue Poterie, t 02 99 75 11 11, f 02 99 75 81 26 (*inexpensive*). Well situated in the historic upper town; the rooms have been renovated but are unimaginative. No restaurant.

Fauchers', 2 Chemin des Tertres Noirs, t 02 99 75 08 69. B&B down the hill, set in an old house with plenty of character.

Auberge Le St-Louis, 31 Rue Notre-Dame, t 02 99 75 28 28. Charming restaurant, with a façade covered with fleurs de lys, a refined interior and an appealing terrace for the summer (*menus 74–142F*).

Taverne de l'Ecu, 12 Rue de la Baudrairie, t 02 99 75 11 09, f 02 99 75 82 97. A 15th-century tavern serving seafood specialities (*menus 90–240F*). *Closed Sun and Tues eve and Wed.*

Le Petit Pressoir, 20 Rue de Paris, t 02 99 74 79 79, f 02 99 74 07 00. Run, with passion, by chef Laurent Chauvin and wine expert Christophe Guihotel (*menus 89–300F*). *Closed Aug, Sun eve and Mon.*

Visitors sometimes miss Fougères' Bourg Neuf completely, but it has elegant 18th-century façades, the oldest free-standing merchants' belfry in Brittany, and the Musée Emmanuel de La Villéon (*open June–Sept daily; otherwise weekends and school hols; adm*), dedicated to the eponymous artist who painted sympathetic Impressionistic scenes of Brittany and the Breton poor.

The **Château de Fougères** (*open mid-June–mid-Sept daily 9–7; April–mid-June daily 9.30–12 and 2–6; other months exc Jan daily 10–12 and 2–5; adm*) turns out to be an immense empty shell, with virtually nothing to see in the surviving thirteen towers. But the great lengths of walls, the machicolations and loopholes, and the conical slate roofs make a perfect picture of medieval defence. Although often described as a Breton frontier castle, for much of the medieval period the Château de Fougères was a pawn in the much more complex local power games. Fougères also saw plenty of action in the Chouannerie, the violent anti-Revolutionary, pro-Catholic and pro-royalist uprising in which so many Bretons fought against the new French Republic in the 1790s. The bloody struggle in Fougères was romantically fictionalized by Balzac in his first bestseller, *Les Chouans*.

South of Fougères, **Vitré** boasts an outstandingly picturesque turreted triangular castle built in the same speckled stone as the town's 15th- and 16th-century houses. The château (*open July–Sept daily 10–12.30 and 2–6.15; April–June daily 10–12 and 2–5.30; Oct–Mar daily exc Tues 2–5.30; adm*) has been much tampered with, but while visiting the museum within you get to clamber up and down parts of the ramparts.

Rennes

Rennes, the capital of Brittany, is full of vitality – not surprisingly, with up to 50,000 students and researchers milling around the wonderful old streets and squares which are packed with masses of bars, *bistrots* and bookshops. Rennes also hosts a couple of major festivals. The city centre has both grand vistas leading to planned squares and secretive corners crammed with timberframe houses. Old Rennes lies north of the Vilaine, and the most interesting modern quarters have gone up on the southern side. To find a bit of calm in the centre, head up the hillside for genteel Jardin du Thabor.

The early Celtic settlement here was built at an obvious crossing of trading routes, where the Ille and Vilaine rivers meet. Armorica (ancient Brittany) was divided between five main tribes by the time the Romans arrived; the Riedones settled around Rennes. Now the Vilaine river is covered over by a road in the centre of town, and most of historic Rennes lies north of it. The oldest surviving part of the **cathedral** only goes back as far as 1560 when the messy but imposing façade was started, where symbols religious and temporal clash; glistening 19th-century decoration

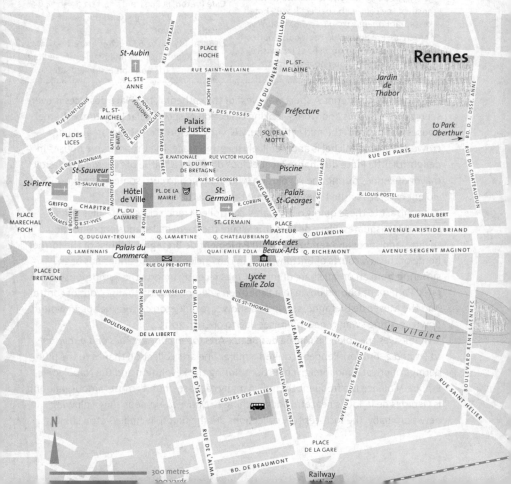

Getting Around

Air France, t 0845 0845 111, runs Brit Air flights from London-City to Rennes-St-Jacques-de-la-Lande.

You can hire boats on the Vilaine, particularly at Messac-Guipry.

Tourist Information

Rennes: 11 Rue St-Yves, t 02 99 67 11 11, f 02 99 67 11 10; info@tourisme.rennes.com, ww.ville-rennes.fr.

Where to Stay

Rennes ✉ 35000

****Le Coq-Gadby**, 156 Rue d'Antrain, t 02 99 38 05 55, f 02 99 38 53 40 (*expensive*). A bit north of the centre, the perfect luxury hotel . Restaurant (*menus 135–185F*). *Closed Sun eve.*

***Mercure Pré Botté**, Rue Paul Louis Courier, t 02 99 78 82 20, f 02 99 78 82 21 (*expensive*). Comfortable chain hotel; no restaurant.

****Hotel des Lices**, 7 Place des Lices, t 02 99 79 14 81, f 02 99 79 35 44 (*inexpensive*). A few rooms overlooking a spectacular square.

****Le Victor Hugo**, 14 Rue Victor Hugo, t 02 99 38 85 33, f 02 99 36 54 95 (*inexpensive*). Along a street full of antiques shops.

***Hotel de Léon**, 15 Rue de Léon, t 02 99 30 55 28, f 02 99 36 59 11 (*cheap*). A little address with character.

Eating Out

Le Rocher de Cancale, 10 Rue St-Michel, t 02 99 79 20 83. A few lovely rooms, but better known for its good restaurant.

L'Escu de Runfao, 11 Rue du Chapitre, t 02 99 79 13 10. Beautiful 16th-century house serving cuisine with daring touches (*menus 140–450F*). *Closed Sat lunch and Sun eve.*

Café Breton, 14 Rue Nantaise, t 02 99 30 74 95. Good, simple options, with the feel of a Parisian *bistrot*.

Le Bocal-Pty Resto, 6 Rue d'Argentré, t 02 99 30 42 55. Beautiful, Bohemian-style café serving unctuous tarts and home-smoked salmon.

overwhelms the interior. A short way west of the cathedral, the **Place des Lices** is overseen by a precarious and wonky-looking collection of spectacular lofty timberframe houses, dating from the mid-17th century. Nearby, the pretty restaurant- and bar-crowded **Place St-Michel** is another lively meeting place. The timberframe houses in delightful little **Place du Champ Jacquet** look down on a statue of Leperdit, the heroic mayor of Rennes during the Revolution who managed to curb some of the more violent excesses of the times with some timely rhetoric.

In contrast to these quirky old squares, controlled French classicism rules Rennes' other major squares: **Place de la Mairie** where the town hall stands opposite the theatre, and sober and serious **Place du Parlement de Bretagne**, address of the former home of the law courts of Brittany, built in the Ancien Régime. Rennes has been suffering from an unfair share of misfortunes recently. In 1994 the sumptuously decorated Parlement burned down in a fishermen's demonstration that got out of control. And the Musée de Bretagne, set up as a showcase of Breton culture, has been wound down awaiting swanky new premises due to open in 2003.

That leaves the splendid **Musée des Beaux-Arts** (*open daily exc Tues and public hols 10–12 and 2–6; adm*). Rennes acquired a major fine arts collection thanks to the plunderings of private and foreign collections during the Revolution and the Napoleonic Empire. Violence is a frequent theme on many canvasses, but its most famous painting is Georges de la Tour's peaceful and touching *Le Nouveau-né*, depicting a glowing new-born baby. The 19th-century collections are the first to include Breton subjects.

Among the post-Impressionists, look out for Paul Sérusier's melancholic *Solitude* and for Emile Bernard's striking *L'Arbre jaune*, which eclipse the Gauguins. Picasso's **Baigneuse**, painted on holiday in Brittany, looks like an outrageous pink monster wandering over a beach in search of her volley ball.

Around Rennes

Detours from Rennes take you south and west into the purple rocks of the Vilaine valley or the Forest of Paimpont, Merlin's legendary Forest of Brocéliande. To the north a 19th-century canal connects the rivers Rance and Ille, linking Rennes with Dinan, which boasts some of the most remarkably preserved ramparts in Brittany.

To the Purple Vilaine Valley and the Forest of Brocéliande

The many purple cobble stones you may have noticed in Rennes probably came from the **Vilaine Valley**. South of Guichen, along the west bank of the Vilaine, quarries have ripped great tears in the landscape, revealing the rich colours beneath. The village of **St-Malo-de-Phily** exudes charm from every pore, and is dominated by an oversized early 20th-century church in mixed neo-Byzantine-Gothic style. The combined ports of **Guipry** and **Messac**, with antiquated industrial areas by the river, form the main centre for hiring boats along the Vilaine. South past Pipriac, the monuments of **St-Just** are one of the most atmospheric and little-known Neolithic sites in Brittany, stretching across kilometres of heathland: you can go in search of curious menhirs, some in quartz, and all sorts of constructions in different styles.

To get your bearings in the forest head first for **Paimpont**, a purple village with a substantial abbey standing by a mirror-like lake. Around Brocéliande's much-reduced woodlands, **Comper** has been 'identified' as the place where Merlin built Viviane her invisible underwater palace, while the real château there has become the jumbled Centre de l'Imaginaire Arthurien, and the remnants of a Neolithic burial site have been turned into 'Merlin's tomb'. Morgane le Fay's secret valley, the **Val Sans Retour**,

The Legends of Brocéliande

Arthurian legend has triumphed over history in the purple **Forest of Paimpont** (30km west of Rennes – follow signs for Plélan-le-Grand). Arthurian aficionados call it Brocéliande, where the legends focus on Merlin and Viviane, with whom he falls passionately and fatefully in love. Merlin conjures up a beautiful castle for Viviane, hidden underwater, making her the Lady of the Lake. She takes in a baby boy she finds on the banks, who becomes Lancelot du Lac. Arthur's bitter and twisted half-sister Morgane le Fay also features large. She turns evil after her lover Guyomart is unfaithful to her, and in her secret valley in the Forest of Brocéliande she traps knights who have been unfaithful to their ladies. They are showered with all the pleasures they could wish for, but deprived of their freedom, and if they try to escape, terrifying visions stop them in their tracks. Lancelot eventually comes to their rescue.

Tourist Information

Guipry-Messac: 90 Av du Port, **t** 02 99 34 61 60.

Paimpont: t 02 99 07 84 23.

Tréhorenteuc: t 02 97 93 05 12.

Where to Stay and Eat

Bécherel and Around ✉ 35190

Château de Montmuran, t 02 99 45 88 88, **f** 02 99 45 84 90. Intriguing medieval château, with splendid views, for not outrageously expensive B&B.

Château de Léauville, Landujan, southwest of Bécherel, **t** 02 99 07 21 14. Another memorable address for B&B.

Hotel du Commerce, in Bécherel. No-frills, old-fashioned inn with cheap rooms and menus.

Paimpont ✉ 35380

★★Relais de Brocéliande, t 02 99 07 81 07 (*inexpensive*). A typical pretty country address by the main road.

Manoir du Tertre, Le Cannée (a few km due south of Paimpont), **t** 02 99 07 71 02, **f** 02 99 07 85 45. Charming hotel with a few luxurious rooms in a restored 17th-century home in peaceful surroundings.

Combourg ✉ 35270

★★Hôtel du Lac, 2 Place Chateaubriand, **t** 02 99 73 05 65, **f** 02 99 73 23 34 (*inexpensive*). Practical modern rooms overlooking the water, and a restaurant (*menus 70–190F*). *Closed Feb, and Oct–Mar Sun eve and Fri.*

★★Le Château, 1 Place Chateaubriand, **t** 02 99 73 00 38, **f** 02 99 73 25 79 (*inexpensive*). A grand house with lots of character, a restaurant (*menus 82–160F*), and a terrace overlooking the lake.

lies just south of Arthur-obsessed Tréhorenteuc, reached by a purple schist track. Today it is the best place to go and get lost on a long walk through the forest.

Romantic Châteaux from Rennes to Dinan

Bécherel, Brittany's answer to Hay-on-Wye, the Welsh capital of second-hand books, has had its ups and downs. Its hilltop long served as a fortified spot. The grand houses below are explained by the success of the linen made here, a trade which flourished in northern Brittany from the 16th to the 18th century. The second-hand book trade only took off at Bécherel in the late 20th century, and the town now champions Brittany and the Breton culture.

The medieval towers of the sinister **Château de Combourg** (*open Easter–Oct daily exc Tues 2–5.30; park also open daily 9–12; adm*) rise above the lake beside the little town of Combourg. Chateaubriand, who spent some of his unhappy childhood here, described it vividly in his memoirs. His father, who made his fortune from corsair and slave-trading expeditions from St-Malo, dominated this house with his terrifying moods and depressions.

The park of the **Château de la Bourbansais** (*open May–Sept daily 10–7; rest of year daily 2–6; adm*) west of Combourg looks elegant enough, but the château is more beautiful still, in its speckled schist, and built with a careful 16th-century regard for symmetry. On the tour you can visit a series of exquisitely panelled Louis XVI-style rooms, the masterpiece of the carpenter Mancelle whose son saved them from Revolutionary violence by plying the Republican troops who came to the château with wine. There is a little zoo attached to the château.

Dinan

The views from the Tour du Gouverneur take in much of the three kilometres of fortified walls and towers which still encircle upper Dinan. The **Château de Dinan** (*open June–15 Oct daily 10–5.45; March 16–May; Oct 16–Nov 15 10–12, 2–5.45; rest of the year daily exc Tues 1.30–5; closed Jan*) is a slightly misleading name for the soaring keep, built for Duke Jean IV of Brittany late in the 14th century. Exhibits on Dinan's history fill the different levels, while the dank basement of the Tour de Coëtquen contains evocative medieval tombs. The **Tour de l'Horloge**, Dinan's central belfry, dates from the 15th century. Belfries like this and the one at Fougères were symbols of civic pride and mercantile success. Kissing dromedaries, of all things, count among the decorations in Gothic **St-Sauveur** on its adorable square. The story goes that in the 12th century, the crusader Riwallon le Roux made a vow that he would build a church f he got back alive from Arab imprisonment, which he evidently did, with some vivid memories. The heart of the famous medieval Breton warlord, Bertrand du Guesclin, lies in a chest in the north transept. His famous joust with one Thomas of Canterbury took place in Dinan in 1357, as recalled in the triumphant early 20th-century equestrian statue of du Guesclin by Emmanuel Frémiet on the Place du Guesclin.

A winding street of timberframe houses descends to the lower town. You can head off on some delightful walks along the Rance or take a boat trip on the river. Its banks conceal some delightful spots, and none is prettier than Léhon, an old village near

Getting Around

Dinard airport lies not far to the north. Dinan itself is on a railway line between Dol and St-Brieuc.
There are boats for hire on the Rance.

Tourist Information

Dinan: 6 Rue de l'Horloge, **t** 02 96 87 69 76, **f** 02 96 87 69 77, *infos@dinan-tourisme.com*, *www.dinan-tourisme.com*.

Where to Stay

Dinan ✉ 22100
★★★**D'Avaugour**, 1 Place du Champ Clos, **t** 02 96 39 07 49, **f** 02 96 85 43 04 (*expensive*). Stylish, historic hotel on the largest of Dinan's squares, with tastefully decorated rooms. No restaurant.
★★**D'Arvor**, 5 Rue Auguste Pavie, **t** 02 96 39 21 22, **f** 02 96 39 83 09 (*inexpensive*). This hotel is built on the site of a former

Jacobin monastery, although the rooms are comfortably modern. No restaurant. *Closed 15–31 Jan.*
Au Vieux St-Sauveur, 19 Place St-Sauveur, **t** 02 96 85 30 20. Inexpensive rooms overlooking a wonderful square.
Le Logis du Jerzual, 25 Rue du Petit Four, **t** 02 96 85 46 54, **f** 02 96 39 46 94. Delightful, intimate B&B on the slope down to the port.

Eating Out

La Mère Pourcel, 3 Place des Merciers, **t** 02 96 39 03 80, **f** 02 96 39 49 91. Historic dining in a timberframe house, with an impressive 16th-century wooden staircase – the centrepiece of the dining room (*menus 280–450F*).
La Poudrière, attached to the d'Avaugour hotel. Restaurant set deep in one of Dinan's medieval rampart towers.
Relais des Corsaires, 3 Rue du Quai, **t** 02 96 39 40 17, **f** 02 96 39 34 75. A good seafood restaurant down at the portside, in one of the prettiest old houses of lower Dinan.

Dinan, where a palm tree grows in the middle of patterned hydrangeas in the enchanting cloister of the **abbey of Léhon** (*guided tours July–Aug 10–12, 3–6; adm, guided tours all year round by appointment*).

The Côte d'Emeraude

Delightful resorts with sandy beaches under the cliffs line the eastern half of the stretch of Breton shore known as the Côte d'Emeraude, the Emerald Coast. To the west, this coast becomes much more rugged and unspoilt, with few buildings standing out on the moors. One outstanding exception is the Fort La Latte.

From Dinard to Cap d'Erquy

We have one Mrs Faber, who settled on the almost virgin coast in the 1850s, to thank for still seductive if slightly jaded **Dinard**, St-Malo's spouse across the Rance estuary. By the turn of the century, it had become one of the liveliest and most chic resorts in France. Royalty swanned around the town and the wealthy built palatial villas. In the first half of the 20th century the place attracted artists too, including Picasso, who spent two summers here.

Sadly, several of the swanky buildings on the promenade behind the central Plage de l'Ecluse have been destroyed or truncated, but there is still action aplenty, with a casino, pools (indoor and outdoor) and of course the beach itself. However, the most exhilarating parts of Dinard are its coastal paths. Head east from the Plage de l'Ecluse round the Pointe du Moulinet for a stunning view of St-Malo. Beyond the landing stage for the ferry you come to the naffly romantic Promenade du Clair de Lune. By the landing stage, steps lead steeply up to Dinard's diminutive aquarium (*open mid-May–mid-Sept Mon–Sat 10.30–12.30 and 3.30–7.30, Sun and public hols 2.30–7.30; adm*), in a charming circular 1930s building. Heading west from the Plage de l'Ecluse, the coastal path past the Pointe de la Malouinet to St-Enogat is one of the most unforgettable walks in northern Brittany. It is rather civilized – the neat, narrow path taking you under rocks and grand villas to beautiful sandy beaches – and the views out to sea, the waters strewn with rocky reefs and sails, are superlative.

Debussy was apparently inspired to write *La Mer* at **St-Lunaire**, a resort just west of Dinard. The Belle Epoque Grand Hotel still dominates the main beach, but as the name of the place makes clear, a Celtic saint got here well before the property developers. The legend goes that dense fog greeted Lunaire and his companions as they arrived from Britain in the 6th century. Impatient to find land, Lunaire took out his sword and cut through the fog. With God's help, the horizon suddenly opened up before him. The coast all around **St-Briac** is cluttered with posh villas. Many late 19th-century artists paid homage to the place, among them Renoir, Signac, and Emile Bernard. The village itself looks out on to the Frémur estuary and its other-worldly rockscape, and the beaches have amusing beach huts.

The first part of the Côtes d'Armor shoreline across the Frémur estuary is littered with lovely holiday homes around the resort of **Lancieux**. Ruddy streaks of colour stain some of Lancieux's rocks – according to legend a Dark Ages saint returned to the area battered by pagans he had tried to convert to Christianity, and the blood he shed reddened the rocks.

The 19th century is well preserved in corners of **St-Jacut**, a resort on a thin finger of a promontory, although it has much older roots, and its many fine beaches have long made it a holiday destination. The now-ruined **Château du Guildo**, built for the lords of Dinan, once guarded the entrance to the Arguenon river. **St-Cast** boasts seven beaches, while its old fishermen's quarter, L'Isle, has been turned into a picturesque shopping area.

The Bay of La Fresnaye separates the St-Cast peninsula from that of Cap Fréhel and Fort La Latte. After all the beach-side villas, the wild heathery heaths come as a surprise. Isolated on its rocky promontory overlooking the sea, stung by winter storms, **Fort La Latte** (*open June–Sept and Easter hols daily 10–12.30 and 2.30–6.30; rest of year weekends and public hols only 2.30–5.30; adm*), the most sensational of Brittany's coastal castles, went up in the course of the 14th century, but significant parts date from the 17th century; you may recognize it from the film *Vikings* (1957) starring Kirk Douglas and Tony Curtis. The colours of the rocks are almost as sensational as the views as you approach **Cap Fréhel**. The corniche road round from the cape heads towards the failed utopian resort of **Sables-d'Or-les-Pins**, dreamed up by two developers in the 1920s. The Depression and mismanagement brought a swift halt to the plans. Never finished, it retains some of its period character by a glorious stretch of golden beach and pine-covered dunes.

The Bay of St-Brieuc

The views across the immense Bay of St-Brieuc almost match those across the Bay of the Mont-St-Michel. But whereas the coast along the latter bay is flat as a pancake, here cliffs line the shore where every fishing port-cum-beach resort has its own marina. The triangular **Ile Verdelet**, a bird reserve, is its answer to the Mont-St-Michel, drawing your attention magnetically across vast distances.

The Celts once guarded this coastline from the splendid vantage point of **Cap d'Erquy** above the port of **Erquy**. The local pink rocks have long been quarried – the stone of Erquy went into the building of the Arc de Triomphe. Cap d'Erquy has unfortunately been ravaged by tourists, but measures have now been taken to stop the worst excesses.

With the dramatic Ile Verdelet at one end of its long, broad sandy beach, **Le Val-André** was chosen as the site for a resort in the 1880s, with a promenade which stretches for some 2½ kilometres. **Dahouët** is the port with a glitzy new marina hidden away behind the western Pointe de la Guette. The Vikings hid here too during their 9th-century raids on the Breton coast, and Dahouët was one of the first French ports from which boats left for the gruelling cod-fishing expeditions off Newfoundland, at the start of the 16th century.

The coast down from Dahouët, with St-Brieuc coming into view at the bottom of the bay, is little known by Breton standards. Steep roads and paths lead down to sandy coves between the cliffs, and the **Dunes de Bon Abri** count among some of the

Getting Around

Ryanair, t 0870 156 9569, offers cheap flights from London-Stansted to Dinard-Pleurtuit. Plancoët, Yffiniac and St-Brieuc have railway stations, but otherwise public transport along this stretch of coast isn't good.

Tourist Information

Dinard: 2 Bd Féart, t 02 99 46 94 12, f 02 99 88 21 07.

St-Lunaire: Bd du Général de Gaulle, t 02 99 46 31 09.

St-Cast-le-Guildo: Place Charles de Gaulle, t 02 96 41 81 52, f 02 96 41 76 19.

Erquy: Bd de la Mer, t 02 96 72 30 12, f 02 96 72 02 88.

Pléneuf-Le Val-André: Cours Winston Churchill, t 02 96 72 20 55, f 02 96 63 00 34.

Where to Stay and Eat

Dinard ✉ 35800

★★★★Grand Hôtel, 46 Av George V, t 02 99 88 26 26, f 02 99 88 26 27 (*luxury–expensive*). Dinard's tip-top hotel, a distinguished, bulky establishment built high above the Rance promenade, overlooking St-Malo. *Closed Nov–Feb exc New Year.*

★★★Reine Hortense et Castel Eugénie, 19 Rue de la Malouine, t 02 99 46 54 31, f 02 99 88 15 88 (*expensive*). Another grand old Dinard address. No restaurant. *Closed Nov–Mar exc New Year.*

★★★Hotel Roche-Corneille, 4 Rue Georges Clemenceau, t 02 99 46 14 47, f 02 99 46 40 80 (*moderate*). Reasonably priced, but no direct sea-views. Good restaurant (*menus 125–250F*).

★★★Novotel Thalassa, Av Château Hébert, t 02 99 16 78 10, f 02 99 82 78 29 (*expensive*). A new monster of a health hotel at calmer St-Enogat, west of Dinard. *Closed Dec.*

★★Printania, 5 Av George V (*inexpensive*). An amusing Dinard institution. The rooms have fine views towards St-Malo. The restaurant is heavily kitsch Breton.

★★L'Hotel du Parc, 20 Av Edouard VII, t 02 99 46 11 39, f 02 99 88 10 58 (*inexpensive*). More basic, cheaper option.

La Salle à Manger, 25 Bd Féart, t 02 99 16 07 95. Well-regarded gastronomic restaurant (*menus 95–240F*). Reserve. *Closed Nov–Jan.*

Lancieux ✉ 22770

★★★Les Bains, 20 Rue du Poncel, t 02 96 86 31 33, f 02 96 86 22 85 (*moderate*). A little hotel with comfortable modern rooms.

Trégon ✉ 22650

Château de la Ville-Guérif, t 02 96 27 24 93, f 02 96 27 32 50. A joyous 19th-century villa for not outrageously expensive B&B.

Ferme du Breil, t/f 02 96 27 30 55. Reasonably priced B&B.

Plancoët ✉ 22130

★★★Hotel l'Ecrin, 20 Les Quais, t 02 96 84 10 24, f 02 96 84 01 93 (*expensive*). A luxury establishment, best-known for its Michelin-

most gorgeous in Brittany. At low tide, the mussel-farming tractors go in and out from these dunes; dogs race joyfully up and down; and trotters train on the sands, pulling their comical chariots.

Inland from St-Brieuc

Lamballe, Moncontour and Quintin are a trio of historic towns in the Penthièvre area around St-Brieuc, within easy enough reach of the coast, and also good bases for exploring inland, rural Côtes d'Armor. The artificial lake of Guerlédan lies at the very heart of Brittany.

Once capital of the quarrelsome county of Penthièvre, **Lamballe** is one of Brittany's most attractive, but also most overlooked, market towns. Its Musée Mathurin Méheut

starred restaurant, **Chez Crouzil** (*menus 400–610F*). Reserve at weekends.

Notre-Dame-du-Guildo ✉ 22380

Château du Val d'Arguenon, t 02 96 41 07 03, **f** 02 96 41 02 67. An aristocratic-looking B&B with the sea at the bottom of the garden.

St-Cast-le-Guildo ✉ 22380

★★★Les Arcades, 15 Rue du Duc d'Aiguillon, **t** 02 96 41 80 50, **f** 02 96 41 77 34 (*moderate*). Comfortable quiet rooms, some with sea views. Restaurant (*menus 79–158F*). *Closed Oct–Mar.*

★★Les Dunes, Rue Primauguet, **t** 02 96 41 80 31, **f** 02 96 41 85 34 (*inexpensive*). Old-fashioned, well-run hotel with a restaurant (*menus 110–380F*), near the beach. *Closed Oct–Mar.*

★★Hotel Les Mielles, 3 Rue du Duc d'Aiguillon, **t** 02 96 41 80 95, **f** 02 96 41 77 34 (*inexpensive*). Cheaper than the above.

★Crisflo, 19 Rue du Port, **t** 02 96 41 88 08 (*cheap*). Even some of the basic rooms have sea views.

Sables-d'Or-les-Pins ✉ 22240

★★Manoir St-Michel, Le Carquois, **t** 02 96 41 48 87, **f** 02 96 41 41 55 (*inexpensive*). North along the coast from the resort, an appealing hotel with a fine Breton exterior and spacious, well-furnished rooms.

★★Le Diane, **t** 02 96 41 42 07, **f** 02 96 41 42 67 9 (*inexpensive*). A hotel with plenty of period charm in the resort itself.

Erquy ✉ 22430

★★Le Relais, 60 Rue du Port, **t** 02 96 72 32 60, **f** 02 96 72 19 57 (*inexpensive*). Near the port, with lovely views across the bay and a popular seafood restaurant.

★★Beauséjour, 21 Rue de la Corniche, **t** 02 96 72 30 39, **f** 02 96 72 16 30 (*inexpensive*). A quiet, well-kept hotel a bit above the port.

L'Escurial, **t** 02 96 72 31 56. Imaginative dishes served on the seafront.

Le Nelumbo, 5 Rue de l'Eglise, **t** 02 96 72 31 31, **f** 02 96 72 38 12. Imaginative dishes in the centre of town.

Le Relais St-Aubin, Route de la Bouillie, St-Aubin. A refined restaurant 3km inland, with a blissfully calm setting, in a converted 17th-century priory with leafy garden.

Pléneuf/Le Val-André ✉ 22370

Domaine du Val, 22400 Planguenoual, **t** 02 96 32 75 40, **f** 02 96 32 71 50 (*expensive*). Luxury hotel, along the coast, with all mod cons in an exclusive castle and its outbuildings.

★★Grand Hôtel, 80 Rue Amiral Charner, **t** 02 96 72 20 56, **f** 02 96 63 00 24 (*inexpensive*). In the resort itself, with stylish façade and comfortable rooms.

★★Hotel Printania, 34 Rue Charles Cotard, **t** 02 96 72 20 51 (*inexpensive*). Another stylish choice, but the rooms are less comfortable.

La Cotriade, 1 Quai Célestin Bouglé, **t** 02 96 72 20 26. The best restaurant in the resort.

Au Biniou, 121 Rue Clemenceau, **t** 02 96 72 24 35, **f** 02 96 63 03 23. A good cheaper restaurant, with fish stews a speciality.

(*open June–Sept daily except Sun 10–12 and 2.30–6.30; adm*) shows the obsessive love Méheut (1882–1958) had for Brittany in simple paintings and drawings of everyday life. The museum occupies part of the grand old timberframe Maison du Bourreau, tucked in a corner off the sloping rectangle of the Place du Martray. Ironically, it is thanks to the French predilection for horse meat that the stocky breeds of Breton horses – *postiers* – have survived. Developed for strength, these are the rugbymen of the horse world, who served in the First World War pulling artillery. You can admire them in the magnificent 19th-century Lamballe Haras or Stud Farm (*open July and Aug daily 10.30–12.30 and 2–6; guided tours on the hour, some in English; rest of the year open Mon–Sat 2–5; adm*) surprisingly located in the centre of town.

Picture-postcard **Moncontour** looks like an escapee from the Dordogne. Long a stronghold of the lords of Penthièvre, the prosperity of its linen merchants explains the fine 17th- and 18th-century houses by the outsized Baroque façade of

Getting Around

St-Brieuc has an airport for internal flights. Lamballe is on the high-speed TGV line between Paris and Brest, but not all fast trains stop there. Local services are also available from Lamballe to other towns in the region.

Tourist Information

Lamballe: Maison du Bourreau, Place du Martray, t 02 96 31 05 38, f 02 96 50 01 96.
Moncontour: 4 Place de la Carrière, t 02 96 73 50 50.
Quintin: Place 1830, t 02 96 74 01 51, f 02 96 74 06 82.
Mur-de-Bretagne: Place de l'Eglise, t 02 96 28 51 41, f 02 96 28 59 44.

Where to Stay and Eat

Lamballe ✉ 22400
Le Tenos, 14 Rue Notre-Dame, t 02 96 31 00 41. In the centre of town. This was the birthplace of the artist Mathurin Méheut, and is now a good-value B&B full of character.

Plorec ✉ 22130
★★★Château Le Windsor, Le Bois Billy, t 02 96 83 04 83, f 02 96 83 05 36 (*moderate*). An upmarket, 18th-century castle hotel by the Arguenon river.

Quintin ✉ 22800
Le Clos du Prince, 10 Rue Croix-Jarrots, t 02 96 74 93 03. Unforgettable B&B, beautifully decorated by the present proprietor.

Mur-de-Bretagne ✉ 22530
★★★Auberge Grand'Maison, 1 Rue Léon le Cerf, t 02 96 28 51 10, f 02 96 28 52 30 (*moderate*). The best in the area, with charming rooms and superlative food (*menus 160–450F*).
★★Le Relais du Lac, t 02 96 67 11 00, f 02 96 26 04 25 (*inexpensive*). In a converted posting inn nearby, in the lakeside village of Caurel. Restaurant (*menus from 60F*).

St-Gelven and Abbaye de Bon Repos ✉ 22570
Hôtellerie de l'Abbaye de Bon Repos, t 02 96 24 98 38, f 02 96 24 97 80 (*inexpensive*). Old-beamed and wonderfully located by the abbey ruins. Restaurant (*menus 95–280F*).

St-Mathurin. Its pinnacled belfry was a quirky 20th-century addition; some of the splendid old stained-glass windows go back to the 1500s.

As at Moncontour, the hill at **Quintin** seemed an excellent site for the lords of Penthièvre to fortify in medieval times. A first castle went up at the start of the 13th century, guarding what was a major inland route through northern Brittany, and subsequent châteaux followed in the 15th, the 17th and the 18th centuries, each either devastated by war or left incomplete through lack of resources. The scrappy bits and pieces dominate one side of town. The displays inside are a bit scrappy too, but at least the Bagneux family that owns the **Château de Quintin** (*open July and Aug daily 10–7; June and Sept daily 10.30–12.30 and 2–6; April, May and Oct pm daily except Tues 2–6; adm*) runs it with bounding enthusiasm.

Quintin has more splendid old streets of linen merchants' mansions. The vast 19th-century neo-Gothic church with its soaring spire claims to own an exceptional piece of cloth: a fragment of the Virgin's girdle. Among Quintin's lovely squares, the **Place 1830** has all the timberframe charm you could wish for. The **Grand'Rue**, the principal shopping street, leads to the elegant cobbled **Place du Martray**, named after a horrifying event in medieval times when a group of English prisoners was savagely butchered here.

Heading further inland, the serpentine **Lac de Guerlédan** in the geographical heart of Brittany dates only from the 1920s, but some very picturesque historic sites stand around it. In the pretty town of **Mur-de-Bretagne** the main attraction is the Chapelle Ste-Suzanne, its ceiling covered with quirky 18th-century paintings. The lake's main resort, **Beaurivage**, offers boating and an artificial beach. **St-Aignan**, to the east, is an adorable village whose medieval church contains a few treasures. The delightful **Musée de l'Electricité** (*open 15 Jun–15 Sep daily 10–12 and 2–6.30; adm*) explains the creation of the hydroelectric dam and the artificial lake. At the western end of the lake, the ruins of the abbey of Bon Repos are eclipsed in beauty by **Les Forges-des-Salles**, an Ancien Régime iron-making village. Industrial sites don't come more enchanting than this.

The Goëlo Coast

The Goëlo coast forms the western side of the Bay of St-Brieuc from the city of St-Brieuc to Paimpol and the Ile de Bréhat. St-Brieuc doesn't lie on the classic tourist trail, but the amazing rock-strewn sites of Paimpol and Bréhat are among the most visited in the whole of Brittany.

St-Brieuc was founded by a Welshman, Brieuc or Briog, one of the seven saints credited with establishing the first Celtic bishoprics of Brittany. It may be the capital of the Côtes d'Armor but only the odd trace of its history survives, notably its forbidding medieval cathedral. From the west of town you can set off on a glorious roller-coaster of a ride up and down the cliffs of the Côte du Goëlo via the swanky villas and rough shacks of **St-Laurent-de-la-Mer**, and **Les Rosaires** where the elite do their dog-jog along the promenade on weekend mornings.

Head inland via Trégomeur with its valley zoo (lemurs the speciality) to arrive at **Châtelaudren**, where the **Chapelle Notre-Dame-du-Tertre** (*open July and Aug only Mon–Sat 10–12 and 4–7; adm*) is decorated with some 100 painted biblical scenes on its choir ceiling; others, in the side chapel, the Chapelle Ste-Marguerite, tell the stories of the much put-upon St Marguerite and St Fiacre. The paintings were executed between 1450 and 1480, some say by an Italian artist, although the figures look typically northern European.

Back on the Goëlo coast, the port of **Binic** boasted one of the most important long-distance cod-fishing fleets in 19th-century Brittany. A few old houses and streets recall those days, but Binic has long been converted to tourism – its port has been turned in good part into a yacht harbour. **St-Quay-Portrieux** is larger, part port, part resort. Out to sea, the smattering of islets known as the Rochers de St-Quay add character to the seascape.

The Breton-speaking frontier lies around Plouha, which at once feels more archetypally Breton. Some of the tallest cliffs in the region, 330ft in height, plunge down to the sea, and the clifftops have been left almost untouched. Roads shaded by tall trees run steeply down narrow valleys to flat stretches of sand or makeshift, tiny harbours: at **Gwin Zégal** the little boats are simply tied up to posts planted in the waters. The **Chapel of Kermaria-in-Isquit** (a few kilometres west of Plouha village) has a striking *Danse macabre* on its wall from c. 1490. Humans from various walks of life are in

Getting Around

St-Brieuc is the transport hub in these parts, with its rapid links with Paris and regional airport. There is a slow train from Guingamp to Paimpol, which is another TGV stop. The main bus station for the area stands beside St-Brieuc's train station. For details of local bus services, call t 02 96 33 36 60.

Book ferry tickets to the Ile de Bréhat in advance via Les Vedettes de Bréhat, t 02 96 55 86 99, f 02 96 55 73 96.

Tourist Information

St-Brieuc: 7 Rue St-Guéno, t 02 96 33 32 50, f 02 96 61 42 16.
Châtelaudren: 2 Rue des Sapeurs Pompiers, t 02 96 74 12 02, f 02 96 79 51 05.
Binic: Av du Gén-de-Gaulle, t 02 96 73 60 12, f 02 96 73 35 23.
St-Quay-Portrieux: 17 bis Rue Jeanne-d'Arc, t 02 96 70 40 64, f 02 96 70 39 99.
Paimpol: Place de la République, t 02 96 20 83 16, f 02 96 55 11 12.

Where to Stay and Eat

Plélo ✉ 22170
Ferme-Auberge Au Char à Bancs, t 02 96 74 13 63, f 02 96 74 13 03. Beautiful inn in its own picturesque valley 3km north of Châtelaudren. Traditional Breton fare and luxurious B&B.

St-Quay-Portrieux ✉ 22410
***Ker Moor**, 13 Rue du Président Le Sénécal, t 02 96 70 52 22, f 02 96 70 50 49 (*moderate*). Neo-Arabic, delightful folly of a villa-turned-hotel standing on its own headland.

Restaurant (*menus 135–345F*). *Closed Oct–Mar Sun eve.*

Pléhédel ✉ 22290
***Château Hotel de Coatguelen**, t 02 96 55 33 40, f 02 96 22 37 67 (*moderate*). A very pleasing little 19th-century château with golf course attached.

Paimpol ✉ 22500
***Le Repaire de Kerroc'h**, 29 Quai Morand, t 02 96 20 50 13, f 02 96 22 07 46 (*moderate*). Stands out as the really stylish address in the port, one of the few proud old buildings still standing on the quays.
**Hotel de la Marne, 30 Rue de la Marne, t 02 96 20 82 16, f 02 96 20 92 07 (*inexpensive*). Reasonable rooms and excellent food (*menus 105–450F*). *Closed Sun eve and Mon exc Jul–Aug and hols.*
La Vieille Tour, 13 Rue de l'Eglise, t 02 96 20 83 18. Excellent inventive Breton cuisine (*menus 118–350F*).

Pointe de l'Arcouest ✉ 22620
***Le Barbu**, t 02 96 55 86 98, f 02 96 55 73 87 (*moderate*). In poll position for the ferry to Bréhat, with great sea views. Restaurant (*menus 150–200F*). *Closed Jan–Feb and Mon in winter.*

Ile de Bréhat ✉ 22870
**Bellevue, Port Clos, t 02 96 20 00 05, f 02 96 20 06 06 (*moderate*). In a lovely location overlooking the port. Restaurant (*menus 130–195F*). *Closed Jan, Mon and Wed.*
**La Vieille Auberge, t 02 96 20 00 24, f 02 96 20 05 12 (*moderate*). A small hotel in the main village in the middle of the island. Restaurant (*menus 90–230F*). *Closed Nov–mid-April.*

period costume, stuck in static poses, while the boogying skeletons hold out their tentacular arms to trap them in a wild disco-style dance.

Back along the dramatic coast, at the **Pointe de Bilfot** Paimpol and its bay come into view. The rocky chaos looks as if a hail storm of meteorites has just rained down on the coast. **Paimpol** is known across France for its tough maritime past, its name synonymous with the demeaning life of the Breton fishermen exploited by the shipowners during centuries of long-distance cod fishing. However, despite expectations, Paimpol hides like a coward at the back of a bay. The shipowners' mansions on the quays have been replaced by a modern development with all the character of a shopping arcade. Swanky yachts fill the harbour. The national school of the merchant navy recently closed down – to be replaced by a catering college.

Yet a whiff of an atmosphere lingers in the air. Behind the quay you can find old squares and winding, cobbled streets, especially around the Place du Martray and the Place de l'Eglise. The **Musée de la Mer** (*open July–mid-Sept 10–12 and 3–7; Easter–June 3–6; adm*) pays its respects to Paimpol's maritime past in a former cod-drying building. Cod-fishing reached its zenith in the 19th century, during which the sailors switched their attention from Newfoundland to the seas off Iceland. This too came to an end in 1935, but it had been a squalid event all along. Lack of safety and hygiene and a heavy reliance on alcohol added to the perils.

The rocks of the **archipelago of Bréhat** with their many gradations of pinks and oranges are of a rare beauty. They look as if some clumsy god dropped a specimen in his rock collection on to the sea, shattering it into a thousand little pieces. Bréhat, the main island, is two large pieces of rock joined together by a diminutive bridge. The south island is more densely populated and much lusher than the north, bright with exotic flowers in season. The north island is more barren and tranquil, and more exposed to the wind. Bréhat only gradually turned so chic after the war, when posh outsiders bought properties and planted their semi-tropical flora. Up until then, potatoes had ruled. Some islanders pleaded with us to urge readers not to visit in high season. The whole ecosystem of the archipelago is in danger of being killed by tourism.

Inland Trégor

The region known as the Trégor straddles the *départements* of the Côtes d'Armor and the Finistère, stretching from the Trieux estuary in the east to the Morlaix river in the west. One of the four particular dialects of Breton language was traditionally spoken in the Trégor.

Pontrieux, stretching over both banks of the Trieux river, grew up to serve as a port for Guingamp much further inland. Its squares and streets almost mirror each other either side of the river. A large number of craftspeople have recently set up shop here. From the railway station nearby you can take the tourist train along a dramatic track above the Trieux river to Paimpol.

Perched above the river, the **Château de la Roche-Jagu** (*open July–Aug 10–7; otherwise 10.30–12.30 and 2–6; annual exhibition mid-June–11 Nov; adm; gardens free*) is the only survivor of some ten forts built along the Trieux in medieval times. An annual exhibition on a local theme is held in the otherwise empty chambers within, with their vast fireplaces and beams. The gardens are being carefully restored.

Guingamp is a traditional small market town whose main church is dedicated to the Black Virgin, or Notre-Dame du Bon Secours. Her *pardon* on the first Saturday in July is a major event for Catholics in this part of Brittany. The church looks darkly

Getting Around

Guingamp is the main transport hub for the area, with a railway station served by TGVs.

Tourist Information

Pontrieux: Maison Eiffel, t 02 96 95 14 03.
Guingamp: Place du Champ au Roy, t 02 96 43 73 89, f 02 96 40 01 95.

Where to Stay and Eat

Brélidy ✉ 22140

***Château de Brélidy, t 02 96 95 69 38, f 02 96 95 18 03 (*moderate*). Very comfort-able and much-restored 16th-century château, in its own gardens south of Pontrieux and just 15km north of Guingamp. Restaurant (*menus 150–190F*). *Closed lunch and Nov–mid April*.

Guingamp ✉ 22200

***Le Relais du Roy, 42 Place du Centre, t 02 96 43 76 62, f 02 96 44 08 01 (*inexpensive*). Exclusive little 16th-century hotel located on the smart square at the centre of town. The restaurant's star dish is *homard grillé* – grilled lobster; excellent wine list (*menus 130–300F*). *Closed Sun eve*.

La Roseraie, 90 Rue de l'Yser, t 02 96 21 06 35. The most characterful restaurant in town in its own picturesque grounds.

spectacular inside with its Gothic vaulting. Down from the church, the triangular **Place du Centre** is bordered by grand houses, some in stone, some in timberframe, its charm enhanced by the Renaissance Fontaine de la Plomée, in its finesse distinctly uncharacteristic of Brittany.

Pestivien and **Bulat-Pestivien**, westwards towards Callac, have an exceptional legacy. The Chapelle St-Blaise and its calvary at Pestivien are covered with grey lichen, and the elongated calvary figures looking down on the dead Christ are tenderly executed, conveying a rare sense of emotion for a Breton calvary. Notre-Dame de Bulat in Bulat-Pestivien became a particularly revered spot in Brittany because the saintly 13th-century Breton lawyer and defender of the poor, St Yves, often came to pray to the Virgin here. The church dates mainly from the 14th and 15th centuries. To the right of the main entrance, a mocking series of lively skeletons acts as a reminder of the frailty of human life. One of these figures of the grim reaper (called Ankou in Breton) is shown preaching vehemently, brandishing bones in one hand.

Christ has lost his arms at the top of the **calvary of Kergrist-Moëlou** south of Bulat-Pestivien. He stands dying in isolation on his column, while around the octagonal structure below, the story of his life unfolds. Inside the church, the painted ceiling is a clumsy record of the Vatican council in 1871, executed by a local artist.

The Côte de Granit Rose and Coastal Trégor

The capital of the Trégor is Tréguier, a delightful town dedicated to the great Breton defender of the poor, 13th-century St Yves. West of Tréguier, the Côte de Granit Rose, with its outrageous display of pink boulders, is probably the most famous stretch of shore in Brittany.

Tréguier and the Jaudy Estuary

Tréguier stands well back from the frivolous rocks of the Côte de Granit Rose, down the Jaudy estuary. The soaring steeple of its cathedral makes it very clear who was boss here in centuries past – Tréguier was one of the original seats of Christian power in Brittany. Tugdual or Tugwall, a Welsh monk, is reckoned to have been the first bishop of Tréguier in 540. Some eighty bishops of Tréguier followed him, but Tugdual's renown was eclipsed by that of local boy Yves Helory de Kermartin, who became a saint. A highly educated churchman and lawyer, he died on 19 May in 1303 after a life serving the poor, and was buried here. A cult grew up around his relics, and official recognition came from the pope in Avignon in 1347; since that time Yves' relics and his *pardon* have counted among the holiest in Brittany.

Tréguier is still renowned for its Gothic **cathedral** and cloister, the most quirky and charming in Brittany. From 1347 the tomb of St Yves was installed inside and for a small sum pilgrims were allowed to touch the saintly skull. The eccentric interior is described as a 'laboratory of medieval architecture', where each mason followed his own whim rather than aiming for a coherent plan. Off the nave, in the Chapelle au Duc, the tombs of St Yves and Duke Jean V of Brittany are modern replacements of the originals. Lawyers from around the world attend the annual Pardon de St-Yves: one of the stained-glass windows in St Yves' chapel was even donated by the US bar. The cloister, done in lacy Gothic tracery, serves as a museum of tomb effigies, collected from churches and abbeys that were destroyed in the Revolution. In the treasury you can still go and pay your respects to the skull of St Yves. Below the streets of the old town with their numerous monastic and timberframe buildings, fleets of yachts now moor.

Two extraordinary peninsulas stretch seawards either side of the beautiful Jaudy estuary. To the east, the **Presqu'île Sauvage** ends with the **Sillon de Talbert**, a fragile strip of sand and pebbles extending against the odds into the sea. On the peninsula northwest of Tréguier, make a special effort to visit the Chapelle St-Gonéry at **Plougrescant**, as crooked as a building from a fairy tale. The glory of the chapel is the striking series of biblical scenes on the vault.

The Côte de Granit Rose

The Côte de Granit Rose covers roughly 20km of gorgeously granity coast from the Pointe du Château west to Trégastel-Plage. It is not just that the rocks are pink; they have also been whipped by the elements into some bizarre shapes: the Die, the Bottle, Napoleon's Hat and even the Upturned Foot. People queue to see this coast in the busy holiday periods.

It is a relief for **Perros-Guirec** that in the 17th century the military engineer Vauban opted for Cherbourg as the site for a new military port. Perros-Guirec is now a beautiful, sprawling Breton resort with a modern marina. Grand villas and hotels climb its slopes, with a spectacular corniche road at the top. **St-Jacques** in the upper part of town is amazing for its colour; the dome looks like a sunburned breast. Down below,

Getting Around

Lannion (*see* below) has a train station, as well as a little airport with regular flights to and from Paris. For local bus services call **t** 02 96 20 59 50/**t** 02 96 37 02 40.

Tourist Information

Tréguier: Hôtel de Ville, **t/f** 02 96 92 22 33.
Perros-Guirec: 21 Place de l'Hotel de Ville, **t** 02 96 23 21 15, **f** 02 96 23 04 72.
Trégastel: Place Ste-Anne, **t** 02 96 15 38 38, **f** 02 96 23 85 97.

Where to Stay and Eat

Tréguier ✉ 22220
★★★Kastell Dinec'h, Route de Lannion, **t** 02 96 92 49 39, **f** 02 96 92 34 03 (*moderate*). Converted Breton manor hidden in the countryside a couple of km west of Tréguier, with ornately decorated, romantic little rooms. Restaurant (*menus 135–330F*). *Closed Tues eve and Wed out of season.*

★★★Aigue Marine, 5 Rue Marcellin Berthelot, **t** 02 96 92 97 00, **f** 02 96 92 44 48 (*moderate*). Large hotel down by the yacht harbour, with comfortable, traditional rooms and a restaurant (*menus 115–220F*).
★★Hôtel des Roches Douvres, 17 Rue Marcellin Berthelot, **t** 02 96 92 27 27 (*inexpensive*). Modern hotel looking on to the marina.
Château de Kermezen, 22450 Pommerit-Jaudy, **t/f** 02 96 91 35 75. Splendid little Breton castle in which to enjoy luxurious B&B.

Plougrescant and Around ✉ 22170
Manoir de Kergrec'h, **t** 02 96 92 59 13, **f** 02 96 92 51 27. 17th-century hotel with gorgeous rooms for B&B.
Mme Janvier's, Route du Gouffre, **t** 02 96 92 52 67. Simpler hotel with pleasant rooms.
Hôtel de la Plage, Hent-Pors, Pors-Hir, **t** 02 96 92 52 12. Basic rooms looking out over a delightful tiny port.

Port-Blanc ✉ 22710
★★Grand Hôtel, Bd de la Mer, **t** 02 96 92 66 52 (*inexpensive*). Overlooking the gorgeous rocky bay.

Trestraou beach has a thalassotherapy centre, the **Thermes Marins de Perros-Guirec** (**t** 02 96 23 28 97, **f** 02 96 91 20 75), and a casino. Boats leave for trips to the ornithological reserve of the Sept Iles, where rare sea birds call, including puffins and gannets in spring and early summer.

The coastal path from Perros-Guirec to Ploumanach becomes increasingly cluttered with the craziest rocks in Brittany. The **Plage St-Guirec** is one of the most dramatic beaches in the region, the little oratory perched on a rock dedicated to a saint who landed here in the 6th century. A wooden statue of him has stood here since the 12th century. Traditionally, young women anxious to get married would come to stick a hairpin in the statue's nose: his proboscis was pierced so many times that it eventually came off.

The walk around **Ploumanach**'s Parc Municipal takes you past absurd pink granite formations, which turn a fiery colour in the setting sun. Behind Ploumanach's lighthouse (pink too, of course), you come to the **Maison du Littoral**, where you can learn how all the pinkness derived from a vein of magma which remained open and active for an exceptionally long time. Postcards here show that not so long ago this coast was nowhere near as desirable as it is considered today; the very poor used to live in makeshift caves under the rocks.

Trégastel-Plage has the most melodramatic pink rocks of the lot. Its **Aquarium** (*open July–Aug 9–8; May, June and Sept 10–12 and 2–6; adm*) lies under a pile of

★★Le Rocher, Rue de la Sentinelle, **t** 02 96 92 64 97 (*inexpensive*). A simple, pleasant option, one street back from the seafront.

Perros-Guirec ✉ 22700

★★★Les Feux des Iles, 53 Bd Clemenceau, **t** 02 96 23 22 94, **f** 02 96 91 07 30 (*moderate*). Characterful rooms and wonderful views over to the Sept Iles. Restaurant (*menus 140–310F*). Closed Sun eve and Mon Oct–April.

★★★Le Manoir du Sphinx, 67 Chemin de la Messe, **t** 02 96 23 25 42, **f** 02 96 91 26 13 (*moderate*). A villa lording it over the Plage de Trestingnel, with a restaurant (*menus 185–300F*).

★★★Le Printania, 12 Rue des Bons Enfants, **t** 02 96 49 01 10, **f** 02 96 91 16 36 (*expensive*). A classic 1930s hotel among pine trees, with bright rooms. Restaurant (*menus 140–310F*).

★★Au Bon Accueil, 11 Rue de Landerval, **t** 02 96 23 25 77, **f** 02 96 23 12 66 (*inexpensive*). Most of the comfortable modern rooms have views over the port. Restaurant (*menus 90–250F*).

★★Ker Ys, 12 Rue du Maréchal Foch, **t** 02 96 23 22 16, **f** 02 96 23 28 36 (*inexpensive*). Slightly cheaper, and proudly run by a Breton family, the rooms decked out in Breton style, Breton food on the menu.

Le Gulf Stream, 26 Rue des Sept Iles, **t** 02 96 23 21 86, **f** 02 96 49 06 61. Wonderful set up on the Perros-Guirec hillside, facing the sea, warm, welcoming and not too expensive.

★Les Violettes, 19 Rue du Calvaire, **t** 02 96 23 21 33 (*cheap*). The best bargain choice.

Ploumanach ✉ 22700

★★Les Rochers, Chemin de la Pointe, **t** 02 96 91 44 49, **f** 02 96 91 43 64 (*inexpensive*). Has the distinction of being located by the beach, and its rooms are of a high standard.

★★Hotel du Parc, **t** 02 96 91 40 80 (*inexpensive*). A popular choice with a restaurant (*menus 78–158F*). Closed Sun eve and Oct–Mar Mon.

Trégastel-Plage ✉ 22730

★★★Armoric, Plage du Coz Pors, **t** 02 96 23 88 16, **f** 02 96 23 83 75 (*moderate*). Good old solid seaside hotel by this otherworldly stretch of coast.

★★Beau Séjour, Plage du Coz Pors, **t** 02 96 23 88 02, **f** 02 96 23 49 73 (*inexpensive*). A slightly cheaper alternative.

enormous pink boulders, resembling a daring feat of wacky modern architecture. Unfortunately, a naff white 19th-century figure of God the Father spoils the overall effect. The sea deserts the resort of Trégastel-Plage at low tide, when you can tramp past the rocky piles and isles. At any time, the walk on to the Ile Renote takes you to some spectacularly silly rock formations, including the Skull, the Great Chasm and, naturally enough in Brittany, the Pile of Crêpes.

Coastal Trégor

After Trégastel, the pinkness goes out of the rocks and the crowds gradually thin. The stretch around Trébeurden and the Léguer estuary is still resort territory, but beyond them the coast becomes much wilder as it enters the Finistère, the most Breton of Brittany's *départements*, which covers the whole western tip of the province. The outstanding monument along the coast of the Trégor Finistérien is the Neolithic Cairn of Barnenez.

From the Ile Grande to the Lieue de Grève

The **Ile Grande**, although no longer an island, stands slightly apart from the mainland. Among the little islands to the east of it, the wooded one puts in its claim to be

Getting Around

Lannion and Morlaix – at either end of this area – each have a train station and airport. Roscoff's ferry port lies just west of Morlaix. For local bus services, call t 02 96 37 02 40.

Tourist Information

Pleumeur-Bodou: t 02 96 23 91 47, f 02 96 23 91 48.
Trébeurden: Place de Crech-Héry, t 02 96 23 51 64, f 02 96 15 44 87.
Lannion: Quai d'Aiguillon, t 02 96 46 41 00, f 02 96 37 19 64.
St-Michel-en-Grève: t 02 96 35 74 87.
Locquirec: Place du Port, t 02 98 67 40 83, f 02 98 79 32 50.
Morlaix: Place des Otages, t 02 98 62 14 94, f 02 98 63 84 87.

Where to Stay and Eat

Trébeurden ✉ 22560
★★★**Manoir de Lan Kérellec**, t 02 96 23 50 09, f 02 96 23 66 88 (*luxury–expensive*). A 19th-century hotel with delightful rooms all of which have sea views. The dining room resembles the interior of a ship (*menus 140–370F*). *Closed Dec–Feb.*
★★★**Ti al-Lannec**, 14 Allée de Mezo Guen, t 02 96 15 01 01, f 02 96 23 62 14 (*expensive–moderate*). Overlooking the sea, with terraces among pretty gardens. The rooms are full of character, the food of the highest quality (*menus 195–395F*). *Closed Dec–Feb.*
★★**Ker An Nod**, 2 Rue de Pors Termen, t 02 96 23 50 21, f 02 96 23 63 30 (*inexpensive*). Down by the port, the place to enjoy perfect sunsets. Many of its small, neat rooms have sea views, and the restaurant has wide bay windows.

★★**Les Ajoncs d'Or**, 13 Rue Trozoul, t 02 96 23 50 40 (*inexpensive*). Small and peaceful, and only a few hundred metres from the beach.

Le Yaudet ✉ 22300
★★**Ar Vro**, t 02 96 46 48 80 (*inexpensive*). A simple, rural hotel: a wonderful place to stay.

St-Michel-en-Grève ✉ 22300
★★**Hôtel de la Plage**, Place de l'Eglise, t 02 96 35 74 43, f 02 96 35 72 74 (*inexpensive*). Views across the bay; some rooms have terraces.

Locquirec ✉ 29241
★★★**Le Grand Hôtel des Bains**, 15 bis Rue de l'Eglise, t 02 98 67 41 02, f 02 98 67 44 60 (*expensive*). A joy of a seaside hotel, with charming rooms and follies. *Closed Feb.*
L'Hôtel du Port, 5 Place du Port, t 02 98 67 42 10. A simple choice overlooking the port.
Les Sables Blancs, 15 Rue des Sables Blancs, t 02 98 67 42 07 (*moderate*). Another simple choice overlooking the sea from the slopes above the beach.
Café Caplan & Co., t 02 98 67 58 98. West of Locquirec at Poul-Rodou beach, a paradise for enthusiasts of second-hand books.

Morlaix ✉ 29600
★★**Hotel Europe**, 1 Rue d'Aiguillon, t 02 98 62 11 99, f 98 88 83 38 (*inexpensive*). The most stylish establishment in the centre. Restaurant (*menus 85–165F*).
Le St-Melaine, 75 Rue Ange de Guernisac, t 02 98 88 08 79. Small, basic and friendly family-run hotel with typically quirky French interior decoration.
Les Bains Douches, 45 Allée du Poan Ben, t 02 98 63 83 83. Eccentric restaurant in a former public baths. The food is typical French *bistrot* fare.
Brocéliande, 5 Rue des Bouchers, t 02 98 63 24 21. Looks a bit like a porcelain museum inside. The food is as refined as the decor.

the Avalon of Arthurian legend, where King Arthur went off to die, waiting to be brought back to life once more to fight for his British-Breton country and Celtic freedom. Inland from the Ile Grande by **Pleumeur-Bodou**, a vast satellite centre dominates the landscape, home to a telecommunications museum, planetarium and fake

Gaulish village. The charming but not especially Breton-looking resort of **Trébeurden** has half a dozen beaches. **Lannion**, a short way inland, has become more than a bit bloated in the past few decades thanks to the high-tech industries generated by Pleumeur-Bodou. The historic centre has a rich legacy of grand town houses, many turned into posh shops. Two beautiful churches are set in old outlying quarters, the church of Brélévenez on its hilltop, fortified by the Knights Templar, and the chapel of Loguivy-lès-Lannion with its delightful fountains on the west bank of the Léguer.

The name given to the coast south of the Léguer, La Côte de Bruyère (the Heather Coast), indicates that nature has the upper hand, the series of dramatic promontories proving unsuitable for holiday developments. **Le Yaudet**, set high above the southern bank of the estuary, would be delightful enough without the absurd theory that this might be the site of Astérix and Obélix's village. There is also talk of a pre-Celtic sacred site here on the hill. Le Yaudet's chapel contains some admirable kitsch, most absurdly a Virgin with her baby Jesus, tucked in a bed covered with lace. The bed is remade every May. To the west of Le Yaudet, the **Domaine du Dourven** is a magical estate on a pine-shaded, pine-scented spit of land where contemporary art exhibitions are often held.

At the **Pointe de Séhar** the rounded, barren, flat peninsula is made up almost entirely of pebbles and boulders. It has a messy charm, with its own little port, a fish market and a few shops and cafés. The coastal path heads due south from here along the cliffs of Trédrez, among the most unspoilt in Brittany. The point of land beyond is the glorious **Beg ar Forn**.

Extremely steep country roads lead down to **St-Michel-en-Grève**, on the eastern end of the protected bay of the **Lieue de Grève**. The seawaters withdraw some two kilometres at low tide. For centuries the Croix de Mi-Lieue, a cross planted in the middle of the bay, served as a marker for travellers and pilgrims: if, when you arrived at the bay, the cross's base was entirely clear of the water, it was safe to continue. Horror stories are still told of those who were caught out by the tide. Unfortunately since the 1970s the Lieue de Grève has periodically suffered from green algae that come to die on the beach with the most diabolical stench.

The Trégor Finistérien from Locquirec to Morlaix

Delightful **Locquirec** just in the Finistère takes up a whole little spit of land, with nine beaches to choose from. A few sandy creeks lie hidden below the coastal path taking you past the **Beg an Fry headland**, with the Chaises (Chairs) de Primel the rocks out to sea.

Neolithic builders appear to have had an aesthetic eye when it came to positioning their burial sites. The **Cairn of Barnenez** (*open daily for guided visits at 10.15 and 11.15 and 2.15–5.45; adm*) is possibly the largest Neolithic barrow built in Europe, a vast, step-layered, dry-stone structure constructed with infinite care. What you see is in fact two cairns stuck one against the other. On one side of the edifice, a staggering 230ft long, you will notice eleven separate tomb entrances. You are allowed to advance, crouching, into a couple of the chambers. According to the pottery found in the tombs, archaeologists date the earlier cairn to around 4500 BC. The later one, to the west, on more of a slope, and made of granite that had to be transported here, has been estimated to date from around 4000 BC.

Morlaix bridges the medieval counties of the Trégor and the Léon. Nature has provided a fine enough setting, but the extraordinary theatricality of the town comes from the massive arches of the 19th-century viaduct which dominate the centre. Tucked out of sight in its deep river estuary, Morlaix unsurprisingly became a haven for Breton corsairs in centuries past. English entanglements mark its history, but for many centuries the place also prospered thanks to the cloth trade. Commerce with the Iberian peninsula proved especially lucrative and it may possibly be that Morlaix's *maisons à lanterne* derived some of their features from the traditional Spanish house built around a patio. Cigarette-making became an important industry, only now coming to a painful end, although you can still admire the elegant 18th-century Manufacture de Tabac by the port, designed by the king's architect, Blondel. Central Morlaix appears so prosperously bourgeois now that it is hard to associate it with some of the most violent farmers' demonstrations in Brittany of recent decades.

The **Eglise et Musée des Jacobins** (*open July–Aug 10–12.30 and 2–6.30; Easter–June and Sept–Oct 10–12 and 2–6; rest of year daily exc Tues 10–12 and 2–5; adm*) evokes the history of Morlaix. The grimy **Maison de la Duchesse Anne** (*open April–Sept; closed Sun; t 02 98 88 23 26 to check times; adm*) is the best-known 'lantern house'; the architecture and carvings inside provide entertaining surprises.

The North Coast of Finistère

The charming ferry port of Roscoff has strong links with southern Britain, in recent times because of the Johnny onion sellers who set out from here to sell their produce door-to-door. To the west, the Pays des Abers is known for its strong Breton roots, its Breton legends, and its seaweed. Lighthouses warn ships off the many reefs, although they haven't always been successful. The Pays d'Iroise is best-known for the port of Le Conquet and the archipelago of Molène and Ouessant (Ushant). Brest is tucked out of the way of the wild coast in its beautiful bay.

Roscoff

Cross-Channel visitors may find that old Roscoff makes rather too much play of its pirating past, when shipowners, corsairs and smugglers were engaged in a centuries-long struggle with the English. Sailing vessels were so important that they were carved on the outside of the **Notre-Dame de Kroaz Batz** whose merry steeple looks like it has been built out of stone bells. Around the church, the grand granite houses reflect Roscoff's 16th- and 17th-century prosperity. Onion-selling to Britain began early in the 19th century. The **Musée des Johnnies** (*open June–15 Sept daily exc Tues 10–12 and 3–6; adm*), is situated at the entrance to the town centre, tells the story of the Breton salesmen who got on their bikes to sell onions to Britain. Other attractions in Roscoff include a slightly wilting aquarium and a flourishing semi-tropical garden.

From the old port you can take the short boat trip out to the unspoilt **Ile de Batz** with its palm oasis. The island has remained predominantly agricultural: on the southern coast there are excellent sandy beaches; the north coast takes you even further away from civilization.

St-Pol-de-Léon, south of Roscoff, was long the religious centre for this area of Brittany; in the Middle Ages the city became a major stop on the Tro Breizh pilgrimage route.

The little city's architecture still dominates the flat plain for miles, but the cathedral towers are well and truly beaten by the staggering spike of Notre-Dame du Kreisker. This is the tallest spire in Brittany, apparently commissioned out of pride by local merchants, not the Church, to see who could get closer to God. **Carentec**, the pretty resort down from St-Pol 'discovered' at the start of the 20th century, is still one of the area's most exclusive resorts.

Along the coast between Roscoff and Plouescat, vegetables grow almost to the edge of the sea – particularly artichokes. After Plouescat, wild sandy dunes stretch to the Grève de Goulven, strewn with huge dollops of granite. At the western end of the **Baie de Goulven**, sandyachts come out to play at low tide. Further west, granite blocks have been worn down by the elements into the Toad, the Sphinx, the Camel, and the Elephant. The resort of **Brignogan-Plages** curves round a great horseshoe bay full of wild rocks which make up for the characterless buildings of the town. To the north and west of Brignogan, seek out the boulder-strewn beaches at Les Chardons Bleus and Ménéham, the latter a hamlet of thatched cottages.

Inland, the incongruous **Basilique du Folgoët** lords it over a modest village close to Lesneven. This Flamboyant Gothic pilgrimage church was constructed in the 15th century in honour of the Virgin Mary and the piety of the village idiot obsessed by her – Folgoët means Madman of the Wood in Breton. Some of the sculpture is impressive and deeply moving, from the *Mater dolorosa* outside –her grief shown by the thick stone tears – to the rood screen within.

On your way to the built-up **St-Michel peninsula** and its popular beaches, stop to see the engraved tombstones of the **Iliz-Koz and the buried church of Tremenac'h** (*open 15 June–15 Sept daily exc Mon 2–6; rest of the year Sun only 2.30–5; adm*). The legend claims that the church was drowned by the sand as punishment for an evil

Pol the Dragon-Slayer

St-Pol-de-Léon is named after Pol, one of the seven founding saints of Brittany. According to legend he was born in Wales in the late 5th century and served King Marc'h at his Cornish court in Tintagel. He set sail for Armorica around 512 in the hope of converting non-believers. Landing first on Ouessant, he met with strong resistance from the locals and quickly left to found a monastery on the island of Batz, where he triumphed over an evil dragon. On the invitation of the local lord Withur, he then crossed to the mainland and was proclaimed bishop at Withur's castle which had just been devastated by raiders. Pol gave the community the impetus to rebuild and the place soon flourished.

Getting Around

Air France run Brit Air flights, t 0845 0845 111, www.airfrance.co.uk, from London-Gatwick to Brest-Guipavas. Brittany Ferries, t 08705 360 360, www.brittany-ferries.com, run ferries from Plymouth and Rosslare and Cork to Roscoff. Roscoff and St-Pol-de-Léon have railway stations and frequent connections with Morlaix for the TGV service between Paris and Brest. Buses from Brest serve the coast to the north.

Book ferry tickets to Ouessant in advance from the Compagnie Penn ar Bed, t 02 98 80 24 68, f 02 98 44 75 43, or Finist'Mer, t 02 98 89 16 61, f 02 98 89 16 78; or you can fly from Brest-Guipavas with Finist'Air, t 02 98 84 64 87.

Tourist Information

Roscoff: 46 Rue Gambetta, t 02 98 61 12 13, f 02 98 69 75 75.
St-Pol-de-Léon: Place de l'Evêché, t 02 98 69 05 69, f 02 98 69 01 20.
Carantec: 4 Rue Pasteur, t 02 98 67 00 43, f 02 98 67 90 51.
Le Conquet: Parc de Beauséjour, t 02 98 89 11 31, f 02 98 89 08 20.

Ouessant: Place de l'Eglise, Lampaul, t 02 98 48 85 83, f 02 98 48 87 09.
Brest: Place de la Liberté, t 02 98 44 24 96, f 02 98 44 53 73.

Where to Stay and Eat

Roscoff ✉ 29680

★★★**Brittany**, 22 Bd Ste-Barbe, t 02 98 69 70 78, f 02 98 61 13 29 (*expensive*). Wonderfully located by the old port. Make sure you stay in the old part. Restaurant (*menus 135–310F*).
★★★**Le Gulf Stream**, 7 Rue Marquise de Kergariou, t 02 98 69 73 19, f 02 98 61 11 89 (*moderate*). A modern hotel with the *institut marin* nearby for seawater treatments and restaurant serving excellent seafood (*menus 135–310F*). *Closed Nov–Feb.*
★★★**Talabardon**, Place de l'Eglise, t 02 98 61 24 95, f 02 98 61 10 54 (*moderate*). A comfortable Best Western. The restaurant has panoramic views (*menus 130–280F*).
★★**Le Tamaris**, 49 Rue Edouard Corbière, t 02 98 61 22 99, f 02 98 69 74 36 (*inexpensive*). A welcoming address by the sea, with some bright rooms looking out to the Ile de Batz. No restaurant. *Closed Dec–Feb.*

band of youths who captured the devil's cat. The church was only uncovered by accident by a bulldozer in the 1960s.

Continuing west, views open up on to the towering spectacle of the **Ile Vierge (Virgin Island) lighthouse**, the tallest in Europe (263 ft). Built at the end of the 19th century, the previous lighthouse looks childlike by its side. Round a further bay you come to Lilia and the magical rockscapes about its port, where you can often see seaweed being unloaded. **Portsall** had the misfortune of being all too closely linked with the environmental disaster of the *Amoco Cadiz*. It has kept the tanker's massive anchor as an ironic memorial.

Ouessant

The lethal rocks of *Ouessant* (Ushant) are notorious for shipwrecks. Tragedy has stalked the islanders too. Until recently it was the lot of many an Ouessant woman to become a widow before her time. The men being away fishing or in the navy, the women were left to tend their tiny walled allotments. These have been abandoned, but the other traditional mainstay, sheep, survive, although the tiny blackish brown breed peculiar to the island is now very rare.

Ferries arrive in the **Baie du Stiff**, where a lighthouse, the enormous Phare du Stiff (they've heard all the jokes), marks the highest point on Ouessant. Along the north

★★Les Chardons Bleus, 4 Rue de l'Amiral Réveillière, t 02 98 69 72 03, f 02 98 61 27 86 (*inexpensive*). A well-kept hotel with tasteful rooms, in a Renaissance house in the centre.
Hôtel des Arcades, 15 Rue de l'Amiral Réveillière, t 02 98 69 70 45, f 02 98 61 12 34. A good-value option, with recently refurbished rooms, some with sea views.
Le Temps de Vivre, Place de l'Eglise, t 02 98 61 27 28. A spectacularly good restaurant located in an old corsair's house (*menus 110–360F*).
L'Ecume des Jours, Quai d'Auxerre, t 02 98 61 22 83. Delightful restaurant looking out to sea (*menus 88–240F*).
Le Surcouf, 14 Rue de l'Amiral Réveillière, t 02 98 69 71 89. Good-value seafood (*menus 92–150F*).

St-Pol-de-Léon ✉ 29250
★★France, 29 Rue des Minimes, t 02 98 29 14 14 (*inexpensive*). Enjoyable hotel in an historic building. No restaurant.
La Pomme d'Api, 49 Rue Verderel, t 02 98 69 04 36. Restaurant in an old Breton house, with refined decor and excellent food (*menus 115–195F*). *Closed Sun eve and Mon exc Jul–Aug*.

Le Conquet and the Pointe St-Mathieu ✉ 29217
★★La Pointe Ste-Barbe, t 02 98 89 00 26, f 02 98 89 14 81 (*inexpensive*). Just up from the ferry jetty. The rooms have tremendous sea views. Restaurant (*menus 102–474F*).
★★★Hostellerie de la Pointe St-Mathieu, t 02 98 89 00 19, f 02 98 89 15 68 (*moderate*). Fine hotel and restaurant (*menus 98–420F*).
Le Relais du Vieux Port, 1 Quai du Drellach, t 02 98 89 15 91 (*inexpensive*). Beautiful rooms at a good price; crêperie downstairs.

Ouessant/Ushant ✉ 29242
All the hotels are in Lampaul – they're not luxurious, but they're pleasant enough.
★Le Fromveur, t 02 98 48 81 30, f 02 98 48 85 97 (*cheap*). Distinguishes itself from the crowd by having achieved one-star status.
Roch Ar Mor, t 02 98 48 80 19 (*inexpensive*). The most attractive of the hotels and well situated. Restaurant (*menus 98–270F*).
De l'Océan, t 02 98 48 80 03. Squeezed into a wedge of a building in the thick of the action.
La Duchesse Anne, t 02 98 48 80 25. A short distance from the major bustle, looking down on the port.

coast of the island you'll find the most fearsome rock formations, assaulted by the angry waves.

Bustling **Lampaul** (named after Pol, *see* above) in the west of the island opens out on to a surprisingly friendly bay with small beaches around it. Two museums stand nearby: the **Maison du Niou Uhella Ecomusée** (*open June–Sept daily 10.30–6.30; April–May daily exc Mon 2–6.30; rest of year daily exc Mon 2–6; adm*) crams information on the island's history and life into two charmingly claustrophobic cottages. The unusual **Phare de Créac'h Lighthouses Museum** (*open June–Sept 10.30–6.30; April–May daily exc Mon 1–6.30, but Sun 10.30–6.30; rest of year daily exc Mon 2–5; adm*) lies below the massive black and white Créac'h lighthouse. Lamps with some of the most powerful beams ever made on earth are displayed here, and the museum has explanations of lighthouses and other sea markers. Beyond the two museums are the bristling mounds of rocks of the **Pointe de Pern**, Ouessant's most westerly point, which have been classified as a national monument.

Brest

Dismissed by most guidebooks, Brest overlooks one of the most beautiful bays in France. For centuries the country's main naval port, Brest became the same for the Germans, and was smashed to smithereens by Allied bombing. So the architecture is mainly a postwar American-looking grid-plan of streets sloping down to a string of docks. Brest's main attraction, **Océanopolis** (*open June–Sept daily 9–7; rest of year 9–6; adm*), east of town, is a centre for the study of the world's oceans, and also one of the best aquariums in France, encouraging understanding of marine life and clarifying Brittany's sometimes murky waters. From the port by Océanopolis, you can take a boat tour of the Rade de Brest. The central **maritime museum** stands in the much-altered Château de Brest, built to guard the Penfeld estuary which divides the town in two. Some of the walls go back as far as Gallo-Roman times. The museum is devoted to ship-building traditions, but certain events in the history of the castle and the town are also portrayed. The **Museum of Fine Arts** (*open daily exc Tues and public hols 10–11.45 and 2–6, Sun pm only*) has some detailed old school paintings of Brest so you can see how the port looked in its heyday, although the place is best known for its works by the Pont-Aven School.

Inland Finistère

From the late 15th century, elaborate outdoor calvary platforms covered with sculptures in granite telling the story of Christ's life and in particular the Passion, became the rage in western Brittany. Occasionally, a local story or saint might creep in too. They were just one element in the distinctive *enclos paroissiaux* (parish church enclosures) which flourished in these parts in the 16th and 17th centuries.

Parish Churches and Calvaries

In war-damaged **Plougastel-Daoulas**, the church's famous calvary is covered with over 150 sculpted figures completed between 1602 and 1604, after the parish had suffered terribly from the plague in 1598. Some say that the bulbous protrusions on the crosses are symbols of the bubonic plague. The figures tend to share a rather stilted refinement, and the costumes, hats and hairstyles make for a fashionable display. The beautiful peninsula west of Plougastel-Daoulas is well-known for producing fine strawberries but relatively untouristy.

Landerneau was a prosperous river port in centuries past. The highlight of the historic town is the Rohan bridge, with a chaos of houses built on it that are still inhabited. East of Landerneau, the 16th-century church of St-Yves is best known for its rood screen on which twelve red-cheeked apostles line up underneath the figure of the crucified Christ. Outside in the parish enclosure, brutal reminders of death are stamped on the ossuary. Nearby, on a height close to the Elorn river, the **church of Pencran** is set in an *enclos paroissial* mostly dating from the 16th century and whose calvary has a particularly moving image of the grieving Mary Magdalene. Skulls are carved over the ossuary entrance, while elaborate carvings decorate the outside of the church steeple and some of the interior.

The well-known parish enclosures to the northeast of the Elorn valley around Landivisiau and St-Thégonnec don't stand in such picturesque locations as those along the river, but the church interior at **Lampaul-Guimiliau** shows off a rich series of

Getting Around

Local trains on the line between Brest and Morlaix stop at Landerneau, La Roche-Maurice, Landivisiau, Guimiliau and St-Thégonnec. Châteaulin, in the Aulne valley, also has a railway station.

Tourist Information

Plougastel-Daoulas: Place du Calvaire, t 02 98 40 34 98, f 02 98 40 68 85.
Landerneau: Pont de Rohan, t 02 98 85 13 09, f 02 98 21 39 27.
Huelgoat: Moulin du Chaos, t 02 98 99 72 32, f 02 98 99 75 72.
Châteaulin: Quai Cosmao, t 02 98 86 02 11, f 02 98 86 38 74.
Pleyben: Place Charles de Gaulle, t 02 98 26 71 05, f 02 98 26 38 99.

Where to Stay and Eat

Ty-Dreux ✉ 29410
B&B in a former weaver's village, south of Guimiliau along the D111. Contact Jean or Annie Martin, t 02 98 78 08 21.

St-Thégonnec ✉ 29410
★★★**Auberge St-Thégonnec**, 6 Place de la Mairie, t 02 98 79 61 18, f 02 98 62 71 10 (*moderate*). Old stone façade, comfortable rooms and a restaurant (*menus 110–230F*).
Ar Prospital Coz, 18 Rue Lividic, t 02 98 79 45 62, f 02 98 79 48 47. This former church presbytery is now a spacious B&B.

Commana ✉ 29450
Kerfornedic, close to the Lac du Drennec, t 02 98 78 06 26 (high-season minimum stay 3 nights). Gorgeous 17th-century B&B, 2km outside Commana in the Monts d'Arrée.

Brennilis ✉ 29690
Auberge du Youdig, t 02 98 99 62 36. Eccentric B&B and typical Breton meals.

Brasparts ✉ 29190
Domain de Rugornon Vras, t 02 98 81 46 27. Detached B&B accommodation in a stone house well placed for walks.

Huelgoat ✉ 29690
★★**Hôtel du Lac**, 12 Rue de Brest, t 02 98 99 71 14 (*inexpensive*). Small hotel and restaurant (*menus 100–150F*).

17th-century retables. The most famous one depicts stages in the life of St John the Baptist below tender 16th-century stained-glass figures caught in the tracery of a Gothic window. Looking down the nave you'll be struck by the organ perched on stilts and by the remarkable *poutre de gloire*, the main crossbeam with a polychrome crucifixion scene rising from it. The wild baldaquin-covered baptismal font is entertaining and the Entombment sculpture is famous. The ossuary, now converted into a shop, contains a retable covered with saints associated with the plague.

Two naive riders greet you at the arch into **Guimiliau**'s charming *enclos paroissial*. The figures are so blotched with lichen that it looks like they're afflicted by disease. However, their expressions show more vitality than the statues on any other Breton calvary. In the Last Supper, several apostles peer round from behind Christ's shoulder to see what's going on. One woman on the calvary is shown naked, her big breasts indicating the nature of her 'crime': she is a representation of Kat Golled, Lost Catherine, a local woman whose lover turned out to be none other than the devil himself. The interior of the church writhes with sculptural detail. One retable tells the story of St Miliau, a 6th-century Breton chieftain after whom the village is named.

St-Thégonnec boasts the most grandiose of all *enclos paroissiaux* from the second half of the 16th and early 17th centuries. The church itself was terribly damaged by a fire in the late 1990s, ruining its wildly elaborate interior. However, St-Thégonnec is also well-known for its calvary dating from 1610, one of the last to be made, which includes a statue of the saint Thégonnec who sailed across the sea to Ireland to become bishop of Armagh later in life.

The Monts d'Arrée and Aulne Valley

Other Bretons were long suspicious of the people of the Monts d'Arrée, a ridge of hills which in centuries past acted as a kind of no-man's-land between the county of Léon to the north and of Cornouaille to the south. The church and village of **Lannédern** lie on one of the most open slopes on the southern Monts d'Arrée. The *enclos paroissial* here is photogenic in the extreme, with carved deer featuring several times along with their protector, St Edern.

Northeast of Lannédern, **St-Herbot** has a gem of a Breton church in its small wooded valley. The charming decoration features a small calvary outside, where the crucified Christ has been given a caricature of a large Jewish nose and his ribs stick out painfully from his emaciated body. An angel hovers insect-like above him, while two robed figures are rather indifferently collecting drops of his blood. The two porches are wonderfully embellished. Over one stands a statue of St Herbot , protector of cattle and horses. In times past, local farmers would cut locks off the tails of their beasts and present them to him on the altar.

Some have said that the giant granite boulders at **Huelgoat** were brought together in a show of strength by the Celtic giant god Gawr; others blame a grumpy Gargantua for throwing down the rocks in a fit of pique at being served bad Breton gruel. The boulders, Huelgoat's natural wonder, lie by the river Argent. The town itself stands by a lake created in the 18th century to help exploit a silver-bearing lead mine down below in the valley. You can walk out of town to the **Camp d'Artus**, one of the few vestiges of the pre-Roman Armorican tribes in Brittany. Later legend claimed that this was one of Arthur's Breton camps, hence the name.

Heading up the beautiful Aulne valley from the Rade de Brest, **Pleyben** boasts just about the grandest of all the Breton *enclos paroissiaux*. The **calvary**, its most famous feature, resembles a massive triumphal arch. The ossuary, dating from the mid-16th century, has been converted into a tiny museum. Beyond its parish enclosure, Pleyben's other claim to fame is its Breton butter biscuits, the *galettes de Pleyben*, on sale here and all around Brittany.

The **Château de Trévarez** (*open daily July–Aug 11–6.30; April–June and Sept 1–6; rest of year, Wednesdays, weekends and school and public hols 2–6; adm*), below Châteauneuf-du-Faou, is nicknamed the Château Rose, although it's actually more ruddy orange than pink. It sticks out like a sore thumb on the slopes of the Montagnes Noires, a line of hills along the southern bank of the Aulne. It's quite rare to see brick at all in western Brittany, let alone employed for such a sumptuous dwelling. The castle only dates from the late 19th century, built for a Breton politician, the Marquis de Kerjégu, but it copies the style of the early 16th-century Loire châteaux. Exhibitions mainly centre around the special collections of plants in the grounds.

The Crozon Peninsula

If you can picture Brittany as a dragon's head stretching into the Atlantic, then the Crozon peninsula is its barbed tongue. Nowhere in Brittany does the coast look more viciously beautiful.

Le Faou is the northern gateway to the Crozon peninsula, a sweet old village set back in a typical Breton river estuary with 16th-century slate-covered houses. An exceptionally pretty corniche road leads to the **abbey of Landévennec** (*open May–Sept Mon–Sat 10–7, Sun and public hols 12–7; other school hols daily 2–6; rest of the year weekends 2–6; adm*), which celebrated its 1500th anniversary in 1985. Along with St-Sauveur in Redon, this abbey was the main centre for spiritual and literary endeavour in Dark Age Brittany. Archaeological digs have been going on here for years. Perhaps the most important outcome is that, for just about the first time in France, it has

Getting Around

There are no trains serving the peninsula, but there are buses from Brest or Quimper as far as Camaret.

Tourist Information

Le Faou: 10 Rue Gén-de-Gaulle, t 02 98 81 06 85.

Camaret-sur-Mer: Quai Kléber, t 02 98 27 93 60, f 02 98 27 87 22.

Crozon/Morgat: Bd de Pralognan-la-Vanoise, t 02 98 27 07 92, f 02 98 27 24 89.

Where to Stay and Eat

Le Faou ⊠ 29580
★★★La Vieille Renommée, 11 Place de la Mairie, t 02 98 81 90 31, f 02 98 81 92 93 (*moderate*). Hotel with a solid reputation.

Rosnoën ⊠ 29580
Ferme Apicole de Térénez, Route de Crozon, t 02 98 81 06 90. Beautiful B&B, which also produces honey.
Ferme Auberge du Seillou, t 02 98 81 92 21, f 02 98 81 07 14. A pretty stone farm with a few bright rooms for B&B.

Camaret-sur-Mer ⊠ 29570
★★★Thalassa, Quai du Styvel, t 02 98 27 86 44, f 02 98 27 88 14 (*moderate*). Modern and

comfortable bayside hotels. Restaurant (*menus 100–295F*). Closed Oct–Mar.
★★Le Styvel, Quai du Styvel, t 02 98 27 92 74, f 02 98 27 88 37 (*inexpensive*). A small traditional family establishment.
La Voilerie, 7 Quai Toudouze, t 02 98 27 99 55. A consistently good restaurant.

Morgat and Crozon ⊠ 29160
★★★Grand Hôtel de la Mer, 17 Rue d'Ys, t 02 98 27 02 09, f 02 98 27 02 39 (*moderate*). Large Belle Epoque hotel, redone in the 1990s. Restaurant (*menus 110–198F*).
★★Hôtel de la Ville d'Ys, t 02 98 27 06 49, f 02 98 26 21 88 (*inexpensive*). Large hotel; a number of its pleasant rooms have little balconies or sea views. Restaurant (*menus 88–240F*) Closed Oct–Easter.
★Hôtel Julia, 43 Rue de Tréflez, t 02 98 27 05 89, f 02 98 27 23 10 (*inexpensive*). A bright, white hotel with some pretty rooms, a garden and a restaurant (*menus 82–270F*).
Hôtel de la Baie, on the port, t 02 98 27 07 51. Simpler but also quite charming.
★★Le Moderne, 61 Rue Alsace-Lorraine, in Crozon, t 02 98 27 00 10, f 02 98 26 19 21 (*inexpensive*). One of the oldest hotels in the area, furnished with old-style Breton pieces.
Le Mutin Gourmand, Place de l'Eglise, Crozon, t/f 02 98 27 06 51. Draws in large numbers for its fine cuisine with exotic touches (*menus 100–350F*). Closed Nov.
La Pergola, 25 Rue de Poulpatré, Crozon, t 02 98 27 04 01. Refined cooking (*menus 78–210F*).

been possible to draw up a fairly complete picture of a Carolingian abbey. The funky **modern museum** displays some of the finds.

The north shore of the Crozon peninsula looks over the Rade de Brest. A large portion is reserved for the French military, but the views over to Brest are dramatic. You finally emerge from the military landscape around the **Plage de Trez Rouz**, named after the blood from dead English and Dutch sailors that stained its rocks after the naval battle of Camaret in 1694. The striking feature of picturesque **Camaret**, its pebbly jetty or *sillon*, curves out into its protected bay. The Tour Vauban, the thick-set, reddy-orange tower, built for the great French military engineer of that name, sits on this flat spit of land. Then comes the Chapelle Notre-Dame de Rocamadour, a squat, cleanly scrubbed Breton church. The wooden skeletons of several large abandoned fishing boats add a melancholic note to the scene.

A string of spectacular headlands lines the western side of the Crozon peninsula. Heading south, you pass some messy former Nazi fortifications, one turned into an ornithological and shell museum, another into a museum dedicated to the Battle of the Atlantic. Some 45,000 Allied merchant navy sailors lost their lives between 1939 and 1945 keeping supply convoys going between Britain and North America. Around 30,000 German submarine sailors also died in this atrocious Atlantic conflict – with an average age of just 20.

The Pointe du Toulinguet is breathtaking enough, but eclipsed by the Pointe de Penhir, the tourist-infested headland of the Crozon peninsula, where a huge cross of Lorraine commemorates Breton fighters in the Second World War. Its outstanding natural feature, the **Tas de Pois**, consists of a series of rocks ricocheting out to sea. The path from the Pointe de Penhir to the Cap de la Chèvre takes you along gloriously rugged coast. At the **Anse de Dinan** the bay changes with the tides; at low tide you can have a geology lesson just by walking below the cliffs as the beautiful beach is unveiled. Looking south you can see the **Pointe de Dinan**, where the rocks form what looks like a fort with a drawbridge in front of it, hence the nickname of the Château de Dinan.

At **Cap de la Chèvre**, the most southerly of the Crozon headlands, the views suddenly open up on to the enormous Bay of Douarnenez, and an alarming war memorial with the tail of an aeroplane sticking out of a hole in the ground, a moving reminder of French naval air pilots killed in action. **Morgat**, a better beach resort than Camaret, has a long stretch of sand reaching round its protected bay. To see the grottoes around Morgat take a boat trip to the **Grotte de l'Autel**, with its natural 'altarpiece'. The only way to appreciate the sensational coastline to Telgruc-sur-Mer and Trez Bellec Plage is to walk the six kilometres.

The Bay of Douarnenez and the Ile de Sein

Extremely long, spectacular stretches of beach run down the eastern side of this bay to the gutsy fishing port of Douarnenez. A precipitous coastal path leads west from Douarnenez to the two extraordinary headlands of the Pointe du Van and the

Pointe du Raz. For the French this is their true Land's End, even if the Pointe de Corsen west of Brest may be closer to North America by a neck.

Douarnenez has guts to match its beauty – it's a practical, political and poetic fishing town immersed in Breton legend. The fishing industry has been the mainstay of the people settled here since Gallo-Roman times, but it never made their fortunes. And in the early 20th century the workers exploited in the town's canning factories rose up against the squalid conditions of their existence. They also voted for France's first ever Communist mayor in 1921.

A whole stretch of river bank at **Port-Rhu**, just one of Douarnenez's ports, has been turned into an excellent boat museum, the **Musée du Bateau** (*open 15 June–Sept 10–7; Mar–June 14 daily exc Mon 10–12.30 and 2–6; closed in winter*), where you can admire real, not model boats. Colourful houses look down on to the separate **Port de Rosmeur**, which still counts among the dozen largest fishing ports in France. **Tréboul**, to the west, has a cute marina. Douarnenez' great legend is of the city of **Ys** whose ruins are supposed to lie under the waves.

You only have to take one look at **Locronan**'s central **Place de l'Eglise** to see how upmarket it was in centuries past. The substantial granite homes of sail merchants mostly date from the 18th century, their dormer windows sticking out of their silvery-slate roofs. There is still one weaver's shop, although the trade which made the place rich has long died out. Locronan has paid the price for being so pretty: virtually all the houses have been turned into restaurants, crêperies, or boutiques. The **Conservatoire de l'Affiche en Bretagne**, with stunning views up the hill from the village, houses collections of Breton posters.

Described by Chateaubriand as 'a masterpiece of humility', **Ronan's church** is the slightly unstable focal point of the town, named after a fervent Christian who came from Ireland in the early Dark Ages. The 15th-century building was funded by Breton

The Legend of Ys

King Gradlon built Ys to satisfy the desires of his wild daughter Dahut, whose mother had died at sea giving birth to her. The grieving Gradlon indulged his decadent girl's every whim, and no one except Bishop Corentin stood up to her. He warned Gradlon of Dahut's immodest clothing and her refusal to go to church, and tried to show Gradlon that his blind paternal love could lead to disaster. However, to fulfil his daughter's wishes, Gradlon built her a new city by the sea – without churches – designed to be so splendid that even the ocean would be dazzled. Dahut went to reign in Ys, where the people became increasingly wicked and the devil seduced the fallen princess. In the terrible finale, Gradlon escapes from the drowning city on his stallion Morvark, powerful and nimble enough to run over the waves, but the king tries to save his daughter too. Such is the weight of her sins that they drag the horse down. It looks as though all will be drowned. At the last moment Guénolé, a saintly monk, arrives to save Gradlon from the engulfing waves, but only by persuading him to let go of his daughter, who is swallowed by the sea and dashed to pieces on the rocks.

Getting Around

There are buses from Quimper to Camaret, Locronan and Douarnenez.

Boats to the Island of Sein leave from Ste-Evette, west of Audierne. Book tickets in advance from the Compagnie Penn Ar Bed, t 02 98 70 21 15, f 02 98 70 20 21.

Tourist Information

Douarnenez: 2 Rue du Docteur Mével, t 02 98 92 13 35, f 02 98 92 70 47, *tourisme.dournenez @wanadoo.fr*, *www.donarnez.com*
Locronan: Place de la Mairie, t 02 98 91 70 14, f 02 98 51 83 64.

Where to Stay and Eat

Ste-Anne-la-Palud ✉ 29550
****Hôtel de la Plage, t 02 98 92 50 12, f 02 98 92 56 54 (*expensive*). A very plush hotel, with the exclusive privilege of looking on to the broad beach. The restaurant serves fine cuisine, including Breton seafood at its most refined.

Plonévez-Porzay ✉ 29550
**Manoir de Moëllien, t 02 98 92 50 40, f 02 98 92 55 21 (*moderate*). Characterful hotel with rooms in the outbuildings of a sturdy little 17th-century manor; also has a well-regarded restaurant (*menus 126–215F*).

Locronan ✉ 29180
**Le Prieuré, 11 Rue du Prieuré, t 02 98 91 70 89, f 02 98 91 77 60 (*inexpensive*). On the tourist trail during the day, but staying here allows you to tour Locronan in peace. Restaurant (*menus 95–250F*).
Au Fer à Cheval, Place de l'Eglise, t 02 98 91 70 74. A good restaurant in the very heart of the village.

The handful of crêperies in Locronan are all exceptional.

---

dukes. Lovely Flamboyant Gothic tracery rails, some cut with the shapes of hearts, run around the outer sides. A 15th-century tomb effigy of Ronan lies inside the chapel. The Locronan *pardons* still count among the most celebrated local pilgrimages in Brittany.

The **Baie des Trépassés**, the Bay of the Dead, separates this headland from that of the Pointe du Van. The legends of death have piled up here like bits of wreckage, and this bay has often been cited as a point of departure for the afterlife. Another tradition says that the souls of drowned sailors congregate here in search of the loved ones they left behind.

La Pointe du Raz is the most famous of Breton headlands, and the most over-run by tourists (you even have to pay to park here). At the visitor centre you can find out about the local history, while a video tells the story of Ys. As you walk along to the end of the wild promontory you can see, straight out west, the famous Phare de la Vieille and Phare de la Plate. You may be able to make out the island of Sein, floating like a mirage in the distance.

Audierne, by the enormous exposed **Bay of Audierne**, still feels like a busy fishing port, with plenty of Breton atmosphere. Safely anchored up the Goyen estuary, the town's west bank is lined with shipping merchants' houses. Audierne boasts the largest lobster tanks in Europe, which you can visit. **Ste-Evette**, a very pretty spot just outside Audierne, has a long string of beaches. It is also the place from which boats leave for Sein.

It seems a miracle that the **island of Sein** has not been swallowed up by the ocean: its highest point doesn't reach 32ft above sea level, and is almost ceaselessly windswept. There are bars you can take refuge in if the weather turns nasty, but

Douarnenez and Tréboul ✉ 29100
★★Ty Mad, t 02 98 74 00 53, **f** 02 98 74 15 16 (*inexpensive*). Delightful hotel in quiet lanes up from the Plage St-Jean at Tréboul. Restaurant (*menus 72–192F*).

★★Hôtel de France, 4 Rue Jean Jaurès, **t** 02 98 92 00 02, **f** 02 98 92 27 05 (*inexpensive*). In the centre of Douarnenez, with simple but comfortable rooms and a restaurant (*menus 98–245F*).

Hôtel de la Rade, 31 Quai du Grand Port, **t** 02 98 92 01 81. Looks out on to the fishing port and the bay. The rooms are simple but well kept and cheap.

Le Tristan, 25 bis, Rue du Rosmeur, **t** 02 98 92 20 17. Among the best for local seafood.

Chez Fanch, 49 Rue Anatole France, **t** 02 98 92 31 77. Another good seafood restaurant.

Plogoff ✉ 29770
★★Ker-Moor, Plage du Loch, Route de la Pointe du Raz, **t** 02 98 70 62 06, **f** 02 98 70 32 69 (*inexpensive*). Probably the best of the hotels near the Pointe du Raz. The owner is also the chef here and can cook up a storm (*menus 82–330F*).

★★La Baie des Trépassés, t 02 98 70 61 34, **f** 02 98 70 35 20 (*inexpensive*). Down by the beach at the back of the bay, this large modern hotel is overrun during the day by the Pointe du Raz hordes.

Audierne ✉ 29770
★★★Le Goyen, Place Jean Simon, **t** 02 98 70 08 88, **f** 02 98 70 18 77 (*expensive–moderate*). Almost incongruously posh hotel with a smart conservatory, from where you can lap up the atmosphere of the port, and some of the finest seafood dishes in Brittany (*menus 165–450F*).

★★Au Roi Gradlon, 3 Bd Manu Brusq, **t** 02 98 70 04 51, **f** 02 98 70 14 73 (*inexpensive*). There's nothing ancient about this hotel, but it does stand right on the beach (*menus 300–380F*).

there's little to visit, apart from the village with its ugly church, two menhirs chatting to one another, and a little museum commemorating the heroes of World War II. While France capitulated in 1940, the men of the island took up General de Gaulle's call to join him across the Channel and fight for a free France. They made up such a large percentage of the first wave of volunteers to answer his call that the general is said to have exclaimed: 'So the island of Sein makes up a quarter of France, does it?'

The Pays Bigouden

The Pays Bigouden occupies the southwest corner of the Finistère, one of the wildest parts of the Breton peninsula. Pont-l'Abbé is its capital, where a uniquely tall coiffe was worn by women, a powerful image that to many has become a symbol for the whole of Brittany.

The Bay of Audierne
From Penhors one of the longest beaches in Brittany curves gently round the Bay of Audierne down to St-Guénolé, backed by a curious bank of ancient pebbles – not one of the friendliest of Breton beaches, but still ruggedly beautiful. The steeple of the **Chapelle de Tronoën** stands out of the melancholy countryside inland like a lichen-rusted trident. It possesses the most famous **calvary** in Brittany, and one of the oldest, dating from around 1450. The stone figures have been eaten away by the winds, but you can pick out some 20 scenes from Christ's life and Passion on the friezes. The three crosses rise up above them like bent masts.

Getting Around

There are no trains in this area, but there are reasonable bus services; there's a good bus service between Pont-l'Abbé and Quimper.

For cruises from Bénodet to Quimper or the Iles de Glénan, contact Les Vedettes de l'Odet, t 02 98 57 00 58.

Tourist Information

St-Guénolé and Penmarc'h: Place du Maréchal Davout, St-Pierre, t 02 98 58 81 44, f 02 98 58 86 62.

Loctudy: Place de la Mairie, t 02 98 87 53 78, f 02 98 87 57 07.

Pont-l'Abbé: Place de la République, t 02 98 82 37 99, f 02 98 66 10 82.

L'Ile-Tudy: 1 Rue des Roitelets, t 02 98 56 30 14, f 02 98 56 36 26.

Bénodet: 51 Av de la Plage, t 02 98 57 00 14, f 02 98 57 23 00.

Where to Stay and Eat

Landudec ✉ 29710
Château de Guilguiffin, t 02 98 91 52 11, f 02 98 91 52 52. Just southeast of Landudec

(midway between Audierne and Quimper), this is one of the most enchanting of 18th-century Breton castles, converted mostly into holiday flats, but with a handful of luxurious, very expensive B&B rooms as well.

Plonéour-Lanvern ✉ 29720
Manoir de Kerhuel, t 02 98 82 60 57, f 02 98 82 61 79. A comfortable hotel set in a splendid Breton manor in its own grounds.

St-Guénolé ✉ 29760
★★★**Le Sterenn,** Rue de la Joie, t 02 98 58 60 36, f 02 98 58 71 28 (*moderate*). Modern hotel right on the coast, with fine views of the rocks and reefs, and a restaurant (*menus 80–300F*). Closed Nov–Mar.
Hôtel de la Mer, t 02 98 58 62 22, f 02 98 58 53 86 (*inexpensive*). Rustic hotel in a typical port house. Restaurant (*menus 95–270F*). Closed Sun eve and Mon out of season.

Loctudy ✉ 29750
★★**Hôtel de Bretagne,** 19 Rue du Port, t 02 98 87 40 21 (*inexpensive*). Has just been charmingly done up.

Pont-l'Abbé ✉ 29120
★★**Château de Kernuz,** t 02 98 87 01 59, f 02 98 66 02 36 (*inexpensive*). The poshest hotel

At the southern end of the Baie d'Audierne, the rocks of the dramatic spit of the Pointe de la Torche are lashed by crashing waves. The four fishing ports of St-Guénolé/Penmarc'h, Le Guilvinec/Lechiagat, Lesconil and Loctudy on the southern side of the Pays Bigouden are '*ports de pêche artisanale*', craft fishing ports. Together they form the largest centre for this type of fishing in France. The harbour streets of these towns smell pungent, the screech of greedy gulls often filling the air.

Heading south from **St-Guénolé**, three lighthouses rise up in a row. The smell of rotting algae here can become overpowering. Dwarfing the older lighthouses beside it, the **Phare d'Eckmühl** (*open daily 10–12 and 2–6; adm*) is a landmark: its beam can reach over 40 miles out to sea. Climb up to enjoy the overview you can get of the Pays Bigouden.

Pont-l'Abbé and the Odet Estuary

Potatoes brought the port of **Loctudy** to life in the 19th century. Then sea-bathing became fashionable and rich families from Quimper and Pont-l'Abbé started building along its coast and river estuary. Loctudy has remained a chic resort ever since. Its beaches with their rock pools and slowly sloping sands are popular with young families. The **church of St-Tudy**, somewhat notorious for its little carving of a male

and restaurant in Pont-l'Abbé lies a little out of town, off the Route de Penmarc'h, its beautiful granite walls hidden behind curtains of chestnut and oak trees.

★★Hôtel de Bretagne, 24 Place de la République, **t** 02 98 87 17 22, **f** 02 98 82 39 31 (*inexpensive*). Well-kept 18th-century hotel in the centre of town, with an old Breton feel and a restaurant (*menus 130–260F*).

L'Ile-Tudy ✉ 29980

Hôtel Moderne, 9 Place de la Cale, **t** 02 98 56 43 34, **f** 02 98 51 90 70. Actually an old hotel, but it's in a great location and has plenty of atmosphere.

★★Euromer, 6 Av Téven, **t** 02 98 51 97 00, **f** 02 98 51 97 65. Large, well-run modern hotel in the newer part of the village close to the beach.

Ste-Marine v 29120

Hôtel de Ste-Marine, 19 Rue du Bac, **t** 02 98 56 34 79, **f** 02 98 51 94 09. Favoured by French celebrities, close to the old village chapel, with all rooms and the restaurant overlooking the delightful harbour.

L'Agape, 52 Route de la Plage, **t** 02 98 56 32 70. Restaurant away from the village centre, which serves the most refined cuisine.

Bénodet ✉ 29950

★★★Hostellerie Abbatiale, **t** 02 98 57 05 11, **f** 02 98 57 14 41 (*moderate*). At the centre of the action on the port, but the rooms are rather soberly decorated.

★★★Gwell-Kaër, 3 Av de la Plage, **t** 02 98 57 04 03, **f** 02 98 66 22 85 (*moderate*). Close to the beach; many rooms have terraces. Restaurant (*menus 98–325F*).

★★★Kastel Moor, **t** 02 98 57 05 01, **f** 02 98 57 17 96 (*moderate*). A stylish place.

★★★Ker Moor, **t** 02 98 57 04 48, **f** 02 98 57 17 96 (*moderate*). Shares various facilities with Kastel Moor. Restaurant (*menus 120–320F*).

★★Le Minaret, Corniche de l'Estuaire, **t** 02 98 57 03 13 (*moderate*). A jolly place to stay by the yachting harbour, with slightly kitsch rooms, a lovely garden, and views over the Odet. Attractive restaurant, the Alhambra (*menus 90–235F*). *Closed Nov–Mar.*

★★A l'Ancre de Marine (*inexpensive*). Comfortable rooms overlooking the port.

L'Hermitage, 11 Rue Laennec, **t** 02 98 57 00 37. A very simple but charming cheaper hotel, a few hundred metres up from the beach.

La Ferme du Letty, **t** 02 98 57 01 27, **f** 02 98 57 25 29. Outside the centre, for excellent cuisine in a converted Breton farm building (*menus 195–410F*). *Closed Nov–Jan and Wed.*

erection, lies just up from the port, surrounded by its sandy cemetery into which the grave stones appear to be sinking.

Pont-l'Abbé was once a thriving river port. Its castle houses the town hall, the tourist office and the **Musée Bigouden**. Even in the late 1990s you could still see the occasional old Bigoudène wandering around town in her towering coiffe, but most of those who stuck to this formal daily dress have now sadly passed away. The Bigoudène coiffe edged gradually skywards from the middle of the last century and reached its dizzying height around 1935.

L'Ile Tudy is not in fact an island, but a thin spit of land connected to the mainland by a sandy causeway, and an exceptionally picturesque old village, its houses huddled together. From here a great stretch of beach heads east to irresistible **Ste-Marine**, where the crescent of Breton houses around the port have mostly been converted into restaurants and cafés.

Bénodet, Ste-Marine's bigger brother, lies on the opposite side of the piney Odet river, its central beach well protected within the Odet estuary. Many regattas start out from the beautiful harbour, and tourist cruise boats leave from the quays in front of the church. They can either take you up the twisting wooded meanders of the Odet to Quimper or out to the tiny stepping-stone Iles de Glénan. Both trips are wonderful.

Quimper

The joyous twin spires of Quimper cathedral soar above the centre of this delightful historic city on the banks of the Odet river. Legend claims that Quimper became the seat of power of King Gradlon of Cornouaille some time in the Dark Ages, and that he appointed Corentin, a holy hermit he encountered while out hunting one day, as his bishop. The city is still devoted to Corentin, one of the major figures in the founding of Brittany after the fall of the Roman Empire. The **Cathédrale St-Corentin** is mainly Gothic, so it may come as a surprise to learn that the wonderful spires were only added in the 19th century. Much of the cathedral's interior decoration vanished with the Revolution.

The **Musée Départemental Breton** (*open daily 9–12 and 2–7; adm*) has taken over the bishops' palace and follows a chronological path through Armorican and Breton civilization. A stunning gold chain turns out to be one of the very oldest items, dating from many centuries before Christ. Upstairs are collections of Breton costume, furniture and pottery.

The **Musée des Beaux-Arts** (*open July–Aug daily 10–7; rest of year daily exc Tues 10–12 and 2–6, Oct–Mar also closed Sun am; adm*) is housed in the Place Laennec opposite the cathedral. It was purpose-built to display the collection of Jean-Marie de Silguy, who was particularly interested in fine Flemish art and French art from the 18th and 19th centuries. One of the most impressive Breton-inspired works is *Le Port de Quimper* by Boudin, painted in 1857. The Pont-Aven School is represented by some striking pieces by Emile Bernard, Charles Filiger and Paul Sérusier. One of the most famous illustrations of a Breton religious procession, by Alfred Guillou, depicts

Getting Around

Quimper is linked to Paris by high-speed TGV trains. You can also fly from Paris to Quimper-Pluguffan airport. For details of local bus services, call **t** 02 98 90 88 89.

Tourist Information

Quimper: Place de la Résistance, **t** 02 98 53 04 05, **f** 02 98 53 31 33.

Where to Stay and Eat

Quimper ✉ 29000

★★★La Tour d'Auvergne, 13 Rue de Réguaires, **t** 02 98 95 08 70, **f** 02 98 95 17 31 (*moderate*). Traditional old-fashioned French hotel and restaurant (*menus 105–310F*). *Closed Sun Oct–April and Sat lunch.*

★★★Gradlon, 30 Rue de Brest, **t** 02 98 95 04 39, **f** 02 98 95 61 25 (*moderate*). Pretty rooms and a little courtyard.

★★Le Dupleix, 34 Bd Dupleix, **t** 02 98 90 53 35, **f** 02 98 52 05 31 (*inexpensive*). Modern hotel looking out over the Odet to the cathedral.

★★Hôtel Mascotte, 6 Rue Théodore Le Hars, **t** 02 98 53 37 37, **f** 02 98 90 31 51 (*moderate*). Very central, well-kept hotel and restaurant (*menus 95–150F*).

Le Capucin Gourmand, 29 Rue des Réguaires, **t** 02 98 95 43 12. Refined cuisine (*menus 100–360F*). *Closed Mon lunch and Sun.*

L'Ambroisie, 49 Rue Elie Fréron, **t** 02 98 95 00 02. Restaurant with friendly 1950s feel and inventive cuisine (*menus 120–370F*).

Le Clos de la Tourbie, 43 Rue Elie Fréron, **t** 02 98 95 45 03. Excellent, slightly cheaper menus.

Le Jardin de l'Odet, 39 Bd de Kerguélen, by the Odet, **t** 02 98 95 76 76. Tasty dishes in a dining room which resembles an ocean liner (*menus 92–140F*).

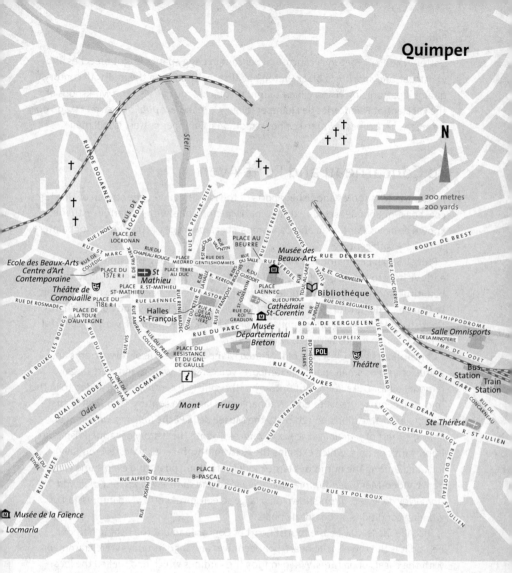

Quimper

N

200 metres
200 yards

Ecole des Beaux-Arts
Centre d'Art
Contemporaine

Théâtre de
Cornouaille

RUE DE ROSMADEC

Musée des
Beaux-Arts

Bibliothéque

Cathédrale
St-Corentin

Halles
St-François

Musée
Départemental
Breton

Mont   Frugy

Salle Omnisports

Théâtre

Bus
Station
Train
Station

Ste Thérèse

Odet

Musée de la Faïence
Locmaria

---

beautifully costumed women arriving by boat for a *pardon*. There are also melancholic pictures by Charles Cottet that convey how tough Breton life used to be. Breton legend isn't forgotten: Evariste Luminais interpretes the end of the city of Ys. One room is devoted to Max Jacob from Quimper, a gay Jew who converted to Catholicism. Better known as a writer than an artist, he lived with Picasso in their early years in Paris.

Quimper's best shopping streets lead off from the cathedral squares. **Rue Kéréon** has the poshest boutiques and finest old houses. A row of little pedestrian bridges spans the Odet river. The pottery quarters lie on the opposite bank of the river from the cathedral, in the shadow of the big Romanesque church of Locmaria. The **Musée de la Faïence** (*open mid-April–Oct Mon–Sat 10–6; adm*) tells the story of Quimper pottery. The 'Petit Breton', a caricatural peasant in baggy pants, bright breeches and waistcoat, and sporting a black Breton hat, first featured from the mid-19th century, a quaint if patronizing vision which caught on quickly. You can visit the workshops of the **HB Henriot Faïenceries de Quimper** (*open weekdays exc public hols; call t 02 98 90 09 36, to check times; adm*) to see how traditional Quimper pottery is still made.

To Concarneau and Pont-Aven

After the wild shores and fishing ports of the Pays Bigouden, the stretch of Finistère coast east of Bénodet seems extraordinarily picturesque, with its narrow estuaries known as *avens*. Pont-Aven and Concarneau became places of pilgrimage for painters in the late 19th century.

Proust, Sarah Bernhardt and a king of Egypt counted among the more illustrious early visitors to the resort of **Beg-Meil**, with its sandy coves looking out on to the beautiful Baie de la Forêt. A double row of pines forms the backdrop to the beach at **Le Cap Coz**, a delightful strip of land that crosses the bay. Cherry and apple orchards flourish, and the spring brings pink and white blossom; **Fouesnant**, with its cheerful centre, is synonymous with good Breton cider.

Concarneau's Ville Close, the old fortified island at the centre of town, crams an awful lot into its small space. The ramparts you can now walk round were largely remodelled for Duke Pierre II of Brittany in the mid-15th century, much added to in the mid-16th century, then altered by Vauban in the late 17th century. Through the first triangular fortifications, you come to the **Musée de la Pêche** (*open 15 June–15 Sept daily 9–8; rest of year daily 9.30–12.30 and 2–6; adm*). The history of canned fish is an important one here, which explains the rusty mid-19th-century tin, reverentially included among the numerous large models of fishing boats and even some whole boats. **Vidéo-Mer** (*open summer hols daily 10–6 and some evenings; rest of period April–Nov daily 2–6; adm*), shown on a large screen, gives you a vivid impression of working conditions on board the boats.

The Ville Close may be the tourist heart of Concarneau but the fishing harbour behind it is the town's true heart. Between 1870 and 1950 its quays were crammed with the easels of painters. When in 1905 the sardines which had fuelled the local economy suddenly moved on, the artists played a large part in organizing charitable assistance for the community.

Between Concarneau and Pont-Aven a slightly wilder stretch of coast leads down to the Pointe de Trévignon, then follows a delightful string of narrow little *avens*. Gorgeous sandy creeks replace the great stretches of beach. The beautiful village of **Pont-Aven** becomes a tourist black spot in high summer, all because of a certain Paul Gauguin who has taken on the role of a local deity. Thanks to him and a handful of other painters, European art took a great leap forward in this little Breton village in the 1880s and 1890s.

If today's tourist hordes come to worship Gauguin, they often find him rather absent, although you can always see him on the tins of Pont-Aven butter biscuits,

Getting Around

Concarneau has the only railway station in the area.

Tourist Information

Fouesnant: t 02 98 56 00 93, f 02 98 56 64 02.
Concarneau: Quai d'Aiguillon, t 02 98 97 01 44, f 02 98 50 88 81.
Pont-Aven: 5 Place de l'Hotel de Ville, t 02 98 06 04 70, f 02 98 06 17 25.

Where to Stay and Eat

La Forêt-Fouesnant ✉ 29940

****Manoir du Stang, t/f 02 98 56 97 37 (*expensive*). An immaculate Breton manor turned beautiful hotel, hidden in its own piece of wooded valley.

Concarneau ✉ 29900

***De L'Océan, Plage des Sables Blancs, t 02 98 50 53 50, f 02 98 50 84 16 (*moderate*). The only three-star hotel in town, with a restaurant (*menus 120–260F*).
**Ker Moor, Plage des Sables Blancs, t 02 98 97 02 96, f 02 98 97 84 04 (*inexpensive*). Nicely done rooms and direct access to the beach.
**Les Sables Blancs, t 02 98 97 01 39, f 02 98 50 65 88 (*inexpensive*). Also right on the beach.
Le Galion, 15 Rue St-Guénolé, t 02 98 97 30 16, f 02 98 50 67 88. Really posh restaurant, in one of the finest historic houses in the Ville Close. The rooms, in the Résidence des Iles opposite, are small and cosy.
L'Assiette du Pêcheur, 12 Rue St-Guénolé, t 02 98 50 75 84. A seafood restaurant run by the same man who directs Le Galion. Plenty of Breton atmosphere.

Pont-Aven and Around ✉ 29930

Le Moulin de Rosmadec, Venelle de Rosmadec, t 02 98 06 00 22, f 02 98 06 18 00 (*inexpensive*). Delightful little hotel in a converted 15th-century mill right in the centre of the village, beautifully shaded by its riverside trees, surrounded by water, and set somewhat apart from the tourist hordes. It also

serves excellent and expensive seafood (*menus 170–300F*). *Closed Feb.*
***Roz Aven, 11 Quai Théodore Botrel, t 02 98 06 13 06, f 02 98 06 03 89 (*moderate*). An especially charming hotel, divided between three different characterful buildings by the port, including the most beautiful of thatched houses. Many of the rooms overlook the port.
Hôtel Les Mimosas, 22 Square Botrel, t 02 98 06 00 30, f 02 98 06 18 40. At the southern end of the quays, with less immediate charm but a more peaceful location.
La Taupinière, c.4 km west of Pont-Aven, Route de Concarneau, St-André, t 02 98 06 03 12, f 02 98 06 16 46. The very high prices reflect the reputation of this restaurant serving extremely carefully prepared Breton fare; reservation recommended (*menus 265–465F*).
Ferme-Auberge de Kerambosser, t 02 98 06 07 43. East along the D4, the good-value and prettier auberge offers you Breton country cooking with farm rather than seafood specialities, which makes a change.

Riec-sur-Bélon ✉ 29340

***Domaine de Kerstinec, at the Pont-du-Guilly on the road towards Moëlan, 3km south, t 02 98 06 42 98, f 02 98 06 45 38 (*moderate*). Some of the smartest rooms in the area, in 19th-century farm buildings. The dining room overlooks the Bélon river.

Moëlan-sur-Mer ✉ 29350

****Manoir de Kertalg, t 02 98 39 77 77, f 02 98 39 72 07 (*expensive*). Luxury hotel overlooking the 15th-century manor and the Bélon estuary. *Closed Dec–Mar.*
***Les Moulins du Duc, t 02 98 39 60 73, f 02 98 39 75 56 (*expensive–moderate*). Lakes, the river itself and a swimming pool add their charms, and the characterful rooms are set out in various little Breton cottages and buildings along the river. The restaurant occupies the actual mill (*menus 185–360F*). *Closed Jan.*
**Hotel Kerfany, Blorimond-en-Moëlan, t 02 98 71 00 46, f 02 98 71 16 08 (*inexpensive*). More affordable, with peaceful rooms in a big new Breton house.

The Pont-Aven School

This innovative circle of artists, which included Gauguin and Emile Bernard, painted shockingly bold blocks of bright colour, separated by thick black cloisonné lines. Horizons were flattened and forms greatly simplified. People turned into statues. The style of their images harked back to more primitive forms and to a different conception of visual arts still familiar in Asia and Africa. It had a moving simplicity that must have alarmed many contemporaries, but today these canvases have an immediate emotional and aesthetic appeal. Many of the Pont-Aven painters stayed at the Pension Gloanec, run by Marie-Jeanne Gloanec. There are photographs of her surrounded by a posse of artists in the village museum.

and in the **Musée de Pont-Aven** (*open July–Aug daily 10–7; April, June, Sept, Oct daily 10–12.30 and 2–6.30; Feb, Mar, Nov and Dec daily 10–12.30 and 2–6; closed Jan; adm*), which has an excellent programme of temporary exhibitions.

Morbihan

Western Morbihan

Along the western coast of the Morbihan massive lengths of wild and bleak beaches stretch out in front of you. The marks of the Second World War and of the military past are still provocatively visible in these parts. Groix is the gritty island just out to sea.

Lorient is the Morbihan's answer to Brest, a naval port bombed to bits in the Second World War, but still grittily appealing. Some of the few things to have survived the war are the ugly concrete U-Boat covers to the west of town. The spiky citadel of **Port-Louis**, on the opposite side of the scrappy Rade de Lorient, guards memories of the past in the **Musée de la Compagnie des Indes** (*open April–Sept daily exc Tues 10–6.30; Oct–Mar daily 2–6 exc Tues; adm, closed Dec*) telling some of the history of France's 17th- and 18th-century colonial companies, and the bitter battles with the Dutch and British. Grand models of ships, maps and documents, and fine objects in glass cabinets give a notion of how colonial trade developed. But the tale told is only a partial one: the slave trade is only present if you read between the lines.

A low slice of island visible from much of the western Morbihan coastline, the **Ile-de-Groix** lies just beyond the mouth of the Rade de Lorient. Here gulls and rabbits rule, and in summer the whole island is scented with honeysuckle. The geology of the island sets it apart from the mainland, with a diversity of rocks that makes it a geologist's dream – to such an extent that Groix has had to protect itself against rock thieves. Some 2,500 people live on Groix; you can learn about their history and traditions at the **Ecomusée** (*open June–Sept daily 9.30–12.30 and 3–7; 15 April–May daily 10–12.30 and 2–5; rest of year Tues–Sun 10–12 and 2–5; adm*) at pretty Port Tudy, which used to be crammed with fishing boats. Groix grew successful through its fishing, and the islanders remain proud of this past, even if Lorient usurped its role in the

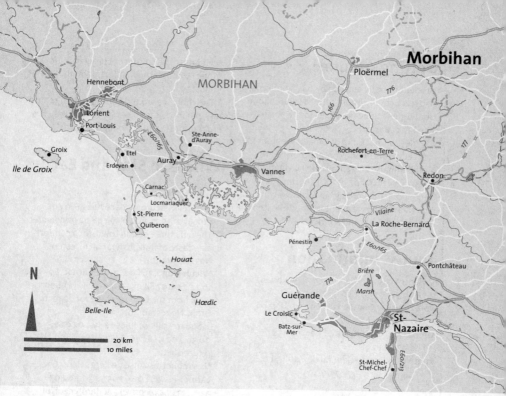

20th century. The main settlement is known as Le Bourg, a place with a quiet charm. Secretive covered fountains and Neolithic stones lie scattered over this scrub-covered island, and a pair of beautiful beaches line the eastern side.

Inland from the Rade de Lorient up the Scorff and Blavet Rivers

Inland along the river Scorff several exceptional Breton chapels are clustered around the village of Le Faouët. Between the lively towns of Hennebont and Pontivy in the pretty Blavet river valley, there are also some hidden churches which are worth seeking out.

The chapel in **Kernascléden** contains a splendid display of 15th-century wall paintings. The depiction of hell in the south transept shows devils, one with horns the size of antlers, come to pluck the condemned from a tree to be cooked in cauldrons. Other scenes, on the life of the Virgin and of Christ, adorn the choir. Just before Le Faouët, the church of **St-Fiacre** is a fine example of Breton architecture: awkward and appealing at the same time. The rood screen is a fantastic multicoloured piece, the wood as delicate as lace.

The great sloping roofs of the covered market dominate the central square of **Le Faouët**, its scale recalling important fairs, although now it tends to be a drowsy place. The **fine arts museum** (*open April and 11 June–2 Oct daily 10–12 and 2.30–6.30; adm*) in the former Ursuline convent holds a small permanent collection with works by the 19th- and 20th-century artists who came to paint here. The Flamboyant Gothic **chapel of Ste-Barbe** just north of Le Faouët was one of their favourite spots; the most

Getting Around

Lorient is easily reached by TGV from Paris. It also has a small airport, Lorient-Lann-Bihoué. From Lorient there are buses to the ports along the coast.

Ferries for the island of Groix leave from the very centre of Lorient; contact the **Société Morbihannaise et Nantaise de Navigation**, t 02 97 64 77 64, f 02 97 64 77 69. Inland, Hennebont and Pontivy have railway stations. A bus service from Lorient to St-Brieuc stops at Hennebont, Baud and Pontivy.

Tourist Information

Lorient: Maison de la Mer, Quai de Rohan, t 02 97 21 07 84, f 02 97 21 99 44.
Port-Louis: 47 Grande Rue, t 02 97 82 52 93, f 02 97 82 43 66.
Groix: Quai de Port-Tudy, t 02 97 86 54 96, f 02 97 86 81 98.
Pontivy: 61 Rue du Général de Gaulle, t 02 97 25 04 10, f 02 97 27 87 09.

Festivals

Tourists come in droves to Lorient for the enormous annual **Festival Interceltique** celebrating the culture of Europe's Celtic fringes through the first fortnight in August.

The churches around Pontivy put on temporary exhibitions in the Art dans les Chapelles programme (annually in high season).

Where to Stay and Eat

Lorient ✉ **56100**
★★★**Hôtel Mercure**, 31 Place Jules Ferry, t 02 97 21 35 73, f 02 97 64 48 62 (*moderate*). The only three-star in town, for a comfortable taste of dull postwar architecture. No restaurant.
★★**Victor Hugo**, 36 Rue Lazare Carnot, t 02 97 21 16 24, f 02 97 84 95 13 (*inexpensive*). Short walk from the landing stage for boats to Groix. No restaurant.
★**Le Square**, 5 Place Jules Ferry, t 02 97 21 06 36, f 02 91 84 76, (*cheap*). Recently refurbished.
★★**Les Mouettes**, Anse de Kerguelen, 56260 Larmor-Plage, t 02 97 65 50 30, f 02 97 33 65 33 (*inexpensive*). Modern, cheerful hotel well placed just behind the dunes at Larmor-Plage, on the coast southwest of Lorient.

beautiful feature of the church interior is the French Renaissance stained-glass windows of around 1520.

Heading up the Blavet river, the absurdly picturesque village of **Poul-Fétan** stands high above the valley near Quistinic. The hamlet had been virtually abandoned when the local community decided to buy and restore it in 1977. The restoration work is immaculate, and it has become a showpiece village for tourists (*adm*). Often at weekends enthusiasts in period costume busy themselves with spinning, millet-making and butter-churning.

Pontivy comprises a sober, imposing, straight-lined Napoleonic town tacked on to an eccentric, winding medieval one. Its château has two of the fattest, squattest towers in France. Once one of the mighty Rohan family's castles, it now hosts temporary exhibitions.

Quiberon Peninsula and Mega Megalith Country

The Etel estuary is the least known of the Morbihan's enormous river mouths – extraordinarily beautiful in parts, with very few modern additions. By contrast, the

Le Poisson d'Or, 1 Rue Maître Esvelin, beneath the Mercure, t 02 97 21 57 06, f 02 97 64 65 42. Central restaurant with startlingly bright dining room, and many colourful dishes (*menus 105–380F*).

Le Bistrot du Yachtman, 14 Rue Poissonnière, t 02 97 21 31 91. Close to the Bassin à Flot, serving good-value classic dishes.

Port-Louis ✉ 56290

Le Commerce, 1 Place du Marché, t 02 97 82 46 05, f 02 97 82 11 02. Well-kept, simple hotel on a shady square in the pleasant atmosphere of this walled town.

Avel Vor, 25 Rue de Locmalo, t 02 97 82 47 59. Elaborate seafood dishes.

Island of Groix ✉ 56590

**Hôtel Escale, on Port-Tudy's quay, t 02 97 86 80 04 (*inexpensive*). A very cheerful and loud welcome. The rooms are neatly done up, and have lovely views on to the harbour.

**La Jetée, 1 Quai de Port-Tudy, t 02 97 86 80 82, f 02 97 86 56 11 (*inexpensive*). Also down on the quays, with nicely presented rooms.

**La Marine, 7 Rue du Général de Gaulle, t 02 97 86 80 05, f 02 97 86 56 37 (*inexpensive*). A charming hotel up in the main village, with its appealing front courtyard

shaded by a mighty yew tree. Its restaurant has shell decorations attached to the old stone walls (*menus 85–150F*). *Closed Jan, Sun eve and Mon out of season*.

La Grek, 3 Place du Leurhé, t 02 97 86 89 95. Pleasing B&B on a square in the main village.

Berné and Meslan (near Le Faouët) ✉ 56240

Two picturesque B&B options just south of Le Faouët:

Mme Brigardis's, Marta, Berné, t 02 97 34 28 58.

Mme Jambou's, Roscalet, Meslan, t 02 97 34 24 13.

Hennebont ✉ 56700

****Château de Locguénolé, Route de Port-Louis en Kervignac, t 02 97 76 76 76, f 02 97 76 82 35 (*expensive*). Luxurious hotel in 120 hectares of grounds sloping down to the Blavet, south of town. Restaurant (*menus 190–520F*). *Closed Jan*.

Pontivy ✉ 56300

**Hôtel de l'Europe, t 02 97 25 11 14, f 02 97 25 48 04 (*inexpensive*). On a corner of a vast square-turned-car park. Some rooms have kept their 19th-century ambience.

nearby Quiberon peninsula is one of the most touristy stretches in Brittany. From the port of Quiberon, boats head out to a splendid trio of islands: Belle-Ile, Houat and Hoëdic.

A precariously narrow strip of sand known as a *tombolo* connects the **Quiberon peninsula** to the mainland. In the distant past, the landmass of Quiberon was cut off, and, with the continuing rise in sea levels, this may happen again. The western side is battered by the sea, its rocky shoreline known unreassuringly as the Côte Sauvage. The peninsula was one of the last Nazi strongholds to fall, on 8 May 1945. The most spectacular views are from the **Beg er Goalennec** headland, where the waves spit angry foam against the small cliffs.

Quiberon itself is a popular resort looking out to Belle-Ile but, apart from the odd row of fishermen's cottages, it doesn't look particularly Breton. In the course of the 19th century it became the largest sardine-fishing port in Brittany. The Grande Plage turns into a very busy family beach during the summer holidays; part of the area is dominated by a thalassotherapy centre, created in 1963, which set the trend for such establishments in Brittany.

It was Monet and Sarah Bernhardt who made a name for **Belle-Ile** at the turn of the 20th century. Although the mainland remains within view, the Bellilois are proud of

Getting Around

Book boat trips from Quiberon to the islands in advance from the Société Morbihanaise de Navigation, t 02 97 31 80 01 (Belle Ile), t 02 97 50 06 90 (Houat-Hoëdic).

Tourist Information

Quiberon: 14 Rue de Verdun, t 02 97 50 07 84, f 02 97 30 58 22.
Belle-Ile: Quai Bonnelle, B.P.30, Le Palais, t 02 97 31 81 93, f 02 97 31 56 17.
Erdeven: 7 Rue de l'Abbé Le Barth, B.P.27, t 02 97 55 64 60, f 02 97 55 66 75.
Carnac: 74 Av des Druides, B.P.65, t 02 97 52 13 52, f 02 97 52 86 10.
Locmariaquer: Place de la Mairie, t 02 97 57 33 05.

Where to Stay and Eat

St-Pierre-Quiberon ✉ 56510

★★★La Plage, 25 Quai d'Orange, t 02 97 30 92 10, f 02 97 30 99 61 (*moderate*). Modern hotel. Many of the rooms have balconies looking on to the bay. Restaurant (*menus 92–159F*).
★★St-Pierre, 34 Route de Quiberon, B.P.3, t 02 97 50 26 90, f 02 97 50 37 98 (*moderate*). Well-kept hotel and restaurant (*menus 89–195F*). *Closed Nov–Easter.*

Quiberon ✉ 56170

★★★★Sofitel Thalassa, Pointe du Goulvars, B.P.170, t 02 97 50 20 00, f 02 97 50 46 32 (*expensive*). Very large, uninspiring-looking luxury hotel known for its sea-water treatments. Restaurant (*menu 250F*).
★★★Bellevue, Rue de Tiviec, t 02 97 50 16 28, f 02 97 30 44 34 (*expensive–moderate*). Comfortable, modern and quite peaceful, but no beautiful views even though it's set back just behind the beach. Restaurant (*menus 100–160F*). *Closed Oct–Mar.*
★★La Petite Sirène, 15 Bd René Cassin, t 02 97 50 17 34, f 02 97 50 03 73 (*inexpensive*). Just next to the sea-water treatment centre, with restaurant (*menus 100–340F*). *Closed Nov–Mar.*

★Hôtel de l'Océan, 7 Quai de l'Océan, t 02 97 50 07 58 (*cheap*). A simple hotel with pretty views on to the fishing harbour.
Le Bon Accueil, 6 Quai de Houat, t 02 97 50 07 92, f 02 97 50 41 37. A basic friendly hotel handily located very close to the ferry terminal.
La Chaumine, 36 Place du Manémeur, t 02 97 50 17 67. A good restaurant with a rustic dining room in a fisherman's cottage (*menus 142–275F*).
Le Verger de la Mer, Boulevard du Goulvars, t 02 97 50 29 12. Another good restaurant with lots of charm (*menus 98–180F*).
La Belle Époque, 42 Rue de Port-Maria, t 02 97 50 17 68, and La Criée, 11 Quai de l'Océan, t 02 97 30 53 09. Among the best seafood restaurants that aren't too pricy.
Le Vivier, t 02 97 50 12 60. On the most spectacular of the Côte Sauvage headlands to the northwest of Quiberon, this restaurant is often packed out, and has a great view to accompany platters of mussels or langoustines.

Belle-Ile ✉ 56360

Hotels on Belle-Ile are expensive, sometimes outrageously, and many are modern.

★★★Le Clos Fleuri, Route de Sauzon, t 02 97 31 45 45, f 02 97 31 45 57 (*moderate*). Spacious and comfortable, and outside Le Palais, if you're in search of peace and quiet.
★★L'Atlantique, Quai de l'Acadie, t 02 97 31 80 11, f 02 97 31 81 46 (*moderate*). In Le Palais, right by the port, with extremely comfortable rooms with sea views.
★★Le Vauban, 1 Rue des Remparts, t 02 97 31 45 42, f 02 97 31 42 82 (*moderate*). Neat little hotel away from the quayside crowds, with some lovely views out to sea. Restaurant (*menu 150F*). *Closed Dec–Mar.*
★★Les Tamaris, 11 Allée des Peupliers, t 02 97 31 65 09, f 02 97 31 69 39 (*inexpensive*). Some cheaper, quite comfortable rooms in a modern house.
Le Frégate, Quai de l'Acadie, t 02 97 31 54 16. The best value for a sea view.
Annick Paulic, Port Hallan, t 02 97 31 85 20. Sweet B&B in a whitewashed hamlet.
Les Pougnots, t 02 97 31 61 03. Overlooking the port in Sauzon, an exclusive address with extremely charming B&B-style rooms.

La Saline, t 02 97 31 84 70. Restaurant worth seeking out, just inland along the quays.

Le Contre Quai, Rue St-Nicolas, **t** 02 97 31 60 60, **f** 02 97 31 60 70. A simple rustic decor, but its cuisine is highly reputed (*menus 220–340F*). *Closed Oct and Jan–Mar, Tues lunch and Mon.*

Le Roz Avel, Rue du Lieutenant Riou, **t** 02 97 31 61 48. Serves some very tasty dishes, including Belle-Ile lamb.

Port-Goulphar, on the rough southern side of the island, has some expensive hotels.

****Castel Clara, t 02 97 31 84 21, **f** 02 97 31 51 69 (*luxury–expensive*). Large, luxury hotel whose modern architecture might come as a shock. It has its own thalassotherapy and beauty centre, as well as excellent seafood cuisine (*menus 260–390F*). *Closed mid-Nov–mid-Feb.*

De Goulphar, t 02 97 31 80 10, **f** 02 97 31 80 05 (*moderate*). Near the Castel Clara. Residents have access to the Castel Clara's facilities.

Le Grand Large, t 02 97 31 80 92, **f 02 97 31 58 74 (*inexpensive*). Seems almost cheap by comparison, with sea views and a slightly neo-Gothic look on its barren plain.

Houat ✉ 56170

***La Sirène, Route du Port, **t** 02 97 30 66 73, **f** 02 97 30 66 94 (*moderate*). Cheerful restaurant on the outskirts of the village, where you're greeted by a tacky painting of a bare-breasted mermaid presenting a platter of fish (*menus 100–300F*). *Closed Nov–Mar.*

*Hotel des Iles, t 02 97 30 68 02, **f** 02 97 30 66 61 (*cheap*). In a field set back from the sea, with views to the Breton coast.

L'Ezenn Bar-Hôtel, t 02 97 30 69 73. On the way to the Plage de Treac'h Er Goured, this hotel has recently added some nice rooms.

Carnac ✉ 56340

****Le Diana, 21 Bd de la Plage, **t** 02 97 52 05 38, **f** 02 97 52 87 91 (*expensive*). The most luxurious of the modern seafront hotels at Carnac-Plage. Restaurant (*menus 260–350F*). *Closed Nov–Mar.*

***Le Bateau Ivre, 70 Bd de la Plage, **t** 02 97 52 19 55, **f** 02 97 52 84 94 (*moderate*). Set apart on the eastern edge of the beach, with extremely comfortable rooms.

Les Rochers, 6 Bd de la Base Nautique, **t 02 97 52 10 09, **f** 02 97 52 75 34 (*inexpensive*). Cheaper delightful option along Carnac beach, with balconies outside the larger rooms.

Carnac old town is much more traditionally Breton in style than Carnac-Plage and quite elegant.

Le Tumulus, 31 Rue du Tumulus, **t 02 97 52 08 21, **f** 02 97 52 81 88 (*inexpensive*). Set apart from the other hotels, on its height by the Tumulus de St-Michel.

Lann Roz, 36 Av de la Poste, **t 02 97 52 10 48, **f** 02 97 52 24 36 (*inexpensive*). Very pretty town house hotel with a garden right in the old centre, with flowers everywhere.

Auberge le Râtelier, 4 Chemin du Douët, **t 02 97 52 05 04 (*inexpensive*). Wonderful ivy-covered hotel hidden down a quiet side street. Restaurant (*menus 95–218F*).

Chez Nous, 5 Place de la Chapelle, **t 02 97 52 07 28 (*inexpensive*). Hotel with plenty of character.

Les Ajoncs d'Or, Kerbachique, between Carnac and Plouharnel, **t 02 97 52 32 02, **f** 02 97 52 40 36 (*inexpensive*). On the outskirts of Carnac, this is a joy: a characterful old stone family house turned hotel, set in a beautifully tended walled and shaded garden.

Le Passe-Mauve, 1 Rue Tumulus, **t** 02 97 52 04 14. Chic setting for good seafood.

La Calypso, t 02 97 52 06 14. Down by the Pô, with a fine reputation for its cuisine.

St-Philibert ✉ 56470

Les Algues Brunes, Route des Plages, **t 02 97 55 08 78, **f** 02 97 55 18 59 (*inexpensive*). A lovely, calm retreat well-shaded by pine trees, away from the summer madness and relatively cheap for this area.

Lann Kermané, t 02 97 55 03 75, **f** 02 97 30 02 79 (*inexpensive*). Charming little B&B rooms in a Breton stone house.

Locmariaquer ✉ 56740

L'Escale, 2 Place Dariorigum, **t 02 97 57 32 51, **f** 02 97 57 38 87 (*inexpensive*). Unpretentious hotel, beautifully situated on the waterfront.

Le Menhir, 7 Rue Wilson, **t/f** 02 97 57 31 41. Pleasant hotel-bar for the smaller budget.

their independence and energy. The largest Breton island – around 20km long and almost 10km across in parts– Belle-Ile has a magnificent coastal path that weaves its way all the way round the island. For centuries monks effectively ruled here, but as it acquired strategic importance in the 17th-century wars, the authorities called upon Vauban to put up serious defences. During the 19th century the citadel served as a prison of note; then Napoleon III decided to fortify the island on a grand scale. Many of these forts survive in a good state of repair. Even the beaches on the protected, northeastern side of the island (the '*dedans*', or 'inside') are fortified. The island's capital and main port, **Le Palais**, is dominated by the spectacular star-shaped structures of Vauban's citadel, which was bought in the 1960s by a wealthy couple who have been seeing to its slow and loving restoration. The citadel's museum (*open April–Oct 10–6, July–Aug 9–7, winter 10–12, 2–5; adm*) is crammed with bits and bobs on the island's history.

'Duck' and 'duckling' are the translations of the Breton names of the two little islands close to Belle-Ile, although it's the seagulls whose strident screams fill the air. **Houat** is a langoustine-shaped rock, 5km at its longest, whose beautiful beaches lie around the langoustine pincers. The deserted coastal path round the western parts of the island, with its sandy coves, has nothing to disturb the peace except the thousands of gulls reminding you to whom the place really belongs. **Hoëdic**, shaped a bit like a whelk, is smaller still: 2½km long and barely 1km at its widest, surrounded by reefs – an even more secretive paradise than Houat.

From Erdeven to Carnac and Locmariaquer

The most famous concentration of Neolithic monuments in France is crammed into the short stretch of Morbihan coast between Erdeven and Gavrinis. Such is the density of stone alignments and tumuli here that the authorities seem to be at a loss as to what to do with them all.

Although often ignored by tourists, there are important megaliths scattered south of the little town of **Erdeven**, along the main D781, and it is even possible to drive right through a section of them. While this relative neglect shows what happens when you have too much of a good thing, it at least means that you can still walk among many of the megaliths, unlike at Carnac. The **alignments of Kerzehro** look impressive, counting over 1,000 standing stones stretching over some 2 kilometres. Still more imposing than the alignments themselves are the **géants de Kerzehro** – massive raised granite blocks.

Carnac

Carnac is surely the densest Neolithic site in the world, with a concentration of dolmens, tumuli and, most famously, its four great alignments of standing stones: Le Ménec, Kermario, Kerlescan and Le Petit Ménec. The local map shows four tumuli, at least 16 dolmens and half a dozen menhirs beyond the thousands gathered in the alignments. There are effectively three Carnacs: Neolithic Carnac to the north; Carnac-Ville or Carnac-Bourg, the picturesque old town in the centre with its

Breton Neolithic People Had a Life

Although the precise meanings of the alignments and menhirs put up between 5000–2000 BC remain an enigma, they have inspired some very entertaining notions, from the legend of St Cornély which claims that Roman legionnaires who tried to persecute Christians were turned to stone, to the joke that American GIs who arrived to liberate this part of Brittany thought that the menhirs had been planted by the Nazis as anti-tank defences. The sensible lines of enquiry tend to focus on their possible religious function and their link to the solar and celestial calendar. Menhirs may well have symbolized fertility. Dolmens were burial chambers covered by mounds of rocks, the overall structures known as cairns or tumuli. The surviving buildings, finely wrought tools and engravings, reveal a complex civilization.

If megaliths get under your skin, seek out the more secretive monuments of the area, crawling down cramped muddy chambers, torch in hand, to find a Neolithic engraving into which you can read all sorts of fantastic meanings. The region's prehistory museums and the Archéoscope at Carnac may help get you started.

remarkable church dedicated to St Cornély; and Carnac-Plage, the modern seaside resort to the south.

The slick multimedia show of the **Archéoscope de Carnac** (*open Feb–Nov 15 and Christmas Holidays 10-12, 1.30–33.30; regular showings in English; adm*) successfully uses shock tactics to try to awaken visitors' interest in the subject of old stones. For a mine of information, visit the more sober **Musée de la Préhistoire Miln-Le Rouzic** (*open daily, May–Sept 10–6.30, closed weekend lunchtimes, Oct–April 10–12, 2–5; adm*), named after two of the most passionate archaeologists to have researched here: James Miln, a Scotsman who started his work on Carnac in 1874, and his helper Zacharie Le Rouzic. Although relatively new, this museum is old-fashioned. The displays contain interesting artefacts, but they are sometimes hard to decipher, and discoveries about the prehistoric societies around Carnac are advancing so fast that the museum has trouble keeping up to date. You would do well to pick up the English text you can borrow from reception, and watch the slide show with English commentary in the first room. The museum contains a number of engraved stones: the favourite Neolithic motifs of axes and horns reoccur, but other symbols aren't as easy to decipher. Crooks (*crosses* in French) have been described by experts as symbols of leadership, while certain shield-shaped, condom-teeted stylized engravings have been defined as female fertility symbols.

When you visit the 10,000 or so standing stones of Neolithic Carnac, consider the some 500,000 to one million days of work that one researcher estimated it would have taken to erect them. The alignments were probably put up c. 3000 BC. The four curving alignments stretch across some 4 kilometres. Most of the stones are lined up in roughly parallel rows, but at the ends of some of the rows there are some additional circular or four-sided enclosures. The individual stones are diverse in shape and size and tend to be much rougher than typical menhirs. Many have gone missing. The alignments might have been places of worship, concentrating on the important changes in the seasons, but because their complete structures aren't known, it is hard to prove definitively any astronomical use. The alignments might also have been connected with funeral rites and the concept of an afterworld, especially given the density of major tombs scattered in the vicinity.

The beautiful Carnac coast from the Pô in the west to the Plage du Men-Du in the east seems almost completely oblivious to its celebrated neighbours. At low tide, the flat sands of the Pô estuary can blind you in the sunshine; flat-bottomed oyster boats lie like beached whales on the firm bed. Past the picturesque village of St-Colomban you come to pine-backed beaches with lifeguards' ladders planted in the sands.

More Menhirs: Locmariaquer

Standing at the western entrance to the Golfe du Morbihan, **Locmariaquer's penin-sula** is another major megalithic site. Like Carnac, it is also a sprawling, highly popular summer resort. Three vast Neolithic monuments, **the Grand Menhir Brisé, the Tumulus Er-Grah and the Table des Marchands** (*open June–Sept daily 10–7; late Mar–May daily 10–1 and 2–6; Oct–Christmas and Jan–Mar daily 10–1 and 2–5; adm*), were excavated in the late 1980s and early 1990s; since then the three have been fenced in together and are explained at the adjoining Centre d'Informations Archéologiques. The connection between the great menhir and the two tumuli actually remains unclear, but their massive scale indicates the site's importance. This spot may have stood at a central or symbolic point in a whole network of megaliths along the Morbihan coast.

Weighing in at some 350 tonnes, the **Grand Menhir Brisé** (dating from between 5000 and 4000 BC) must have been awe-inspiring when it stood upright, some 60ft high. Even looking at it now, prostrate and split into four sections, you wonder how Neolithic people could possibly have erected such a mammoth piece of stone. Digs in 1989 discovered the roots of an alignment of menhirs stretching out from it, revealing that the menhir didn't always stand alone. It's thought that these menhirs were deliberately uprooted in the Neolithic period, and that the Grand Menhir was cut into pieces. Were the old gods or forces superseded or abandoned? And were later Neolithic peoples willing to put the massive menhirs to other building uses? The **Er-Grah tumulus**, much reduced from its original height, consists of a tomb covered by an enormous trapezoid barrow. Beautiful axeheads and beads were found during its excavation, suggesting that this was the burial chamber of an important figure. The building was extended to north and south, creating a stepped tumulus 558 ft long and between 50 and 90ft wide. The **Table des Marchands** was the latest of the three structures. After research had been carried out in the 1930s, this dolmen was covered up once again with a mass of stones to form a cairn. The roof slab of the Table des Marchands had a broken engraving of a horned cow on it; a matching piece of the engraved bull was later discovered in the tomb on the island of Gavrinis. The most remarkable carving left intact covers the ogival end stone, decorated with four rows of symmetrically positioned crooks.

From the village of **Locmariaquer**, the views on to the calm flat inland gulf of Morbihan, dotted with headlands and islands, are enchanting. South of

Locmariaquer, looking out on to the Bay of Quiberon and the ocean, the **dolmen of Les Pierres Plates** lies neglected on the beach. Several of its stones bear carvings, but most exciting of all is an illustration of what is described as a stylized boat with oars. For amateurs, the patterns look like stylized foliage.

Golfe du Morbihan and Eastern Morbihan

Measuring 25km from north to south and 20km from east to west, the magical Golfe du Morbihan is an inland sea peppered with islands and with just a narrow opening to the ocean. There may be just 40 islands, but it feels like there are many more. The two largest – the Ile aux Moines and the Ile d'Arz – are the only two not privately owned; both make wonderful days out. Major Neolithic sites lie scattered around the gulf, and some attractive historic towns, including Ste-Anne-d'Auray and Vannes, capital of the département, stand close by.

Ste-Anne-d'Auray draws large numbers of Catholic faithful away from the seductive coast. It is said that Anne, mother of the Virgin Mary, was born here, a legend that was probably derived from a muddle with Ana, mother goddess of the Celtic pantheon. The story of the major pilgrimage church begins in 1623, when one Yves Nicolazic, a local peasant, witnessed a recurring apparition of Ste Anne who repeatedly told him to build a chapel dedicated to her. After he 'unearthed' a supposedly miraculous statue of the saint, the Church took him seriously and acted on his words. The 17th-century building was replaced in the 19th century by the enormous neo-Renaissance church you now see. Inside, everything is very neat and labelled, a lesson in 19th-century religious teaching and Church propaganda. The *pardon* of Ste-Anne-d'Auray draws tens of thousands of people every year on 25 and 26 July; Pope John Paul II visited on his 1996 French tour. The biggest memorial to the Bretons who died in the First World War is also here, with tens of thousands of names engraved on the walls.

The **cairn of Gavrinis**, on its island, is the most mysterious Neolithic site in France, roughly reckoned to date from the 4th millennium BC. Many of the engraved patterns in the tomb look like magnified finger prints, semi-abstract forms that perhaps represent a goddess mother linking the world of the living with the world of the dead. Some researchers speculate that she is shown giving birth in some of the panels, although such imagery is hard to make out. Other patterns include spirals and a stylized human figure with an axe and a crook; serpentine shapes writhe below.

Apart from the crowds, **l'Ile aux Moines** is a little Breton paradise, with creeks and beaches, fishermen's cottages, walled gardens and heavenly views. The easiest way to discover the island in a day is by bike, although bikes aren't suitable for the coastal path that hugs the shore. **L'Ile d'Arz** is much flatter, less wooded and less popular than l'Ile aux Moines. It's not quite as easy to get to, but its thin strips of beach still fill up with families in summer.

A croissant of cafés curves out from the gateway from **Vannes**' marina into the old town. Some of the city fortifications date from the 14th century. The regional parliament was briefly moved to Vannes for 15 years to punish Rennes for its involvement in

Getting Around

Auray lies on the high-speed TGV rail line between Paris and Quimper. In summer there is a rail service from Auray down to Quiberon. At other times of the year you will have to rely on local bus services.

To take the boat from Larmor-Baden to the island of Gavrinis, call t 02 97 42 63 44. Book well in advance in high season.

Tourist Information

Auray: 20 Rue du Lait, B.P.403, t 02 97 24 09 75, f 02 97 50 80 75.

Ste-Anne-d'Auray: 12 Place Nicolazic, t 02 97 57 69 16.

L'Ile aux Moines: Le Port, t 02 97 26 32 45.

Vannes: 1 Rue Thiers, t 02 97 47 24 34, f 02 97 47 29 49.

Pénestin: Allée du Grand Pré, t 02 99 90 37 74.

La Roche-Bernard: Place du Pilori, t 02 99 90 67 98, f 02 99 90 88 28.

Where to Stay and Eat

Auray ✉ 56400

L'Abbaye, Place St-Sauveur, t 02 97 24 10 85. One of the restaurants at the port, with plenty of old Breton character and good simple Breton crêpes.

L'Eglantine, Place St-Sauveur, t 02 97 56 46 55. Another of the smarter addresses, a conservative-looking place with pictures of popular royalist Chouan leaders on the walls. The seafood is excellent.

Le Relais Franklin, 8 Quai Franklin, t 02 97 24 82 54, f 02 97 50 78 67. Nostalgic Americans may find it hard to resist the place where Franklin stayed when he landed here. Now it's one of Auray's most charming crêperies.

Le Bono ✉ 56400

★★★**Hostelleries Abbatiales**, Manoir de Kerdréan, t 02 97 57 84 00, f 02 97 57 83 00 (*moderate*). Has a great deal of style, a golf course and a restaurant (*menus 95–240F*).

Le Vieux Pont, 23 Rue Pasteur, t 02 97 57 87 71. A bar-cum-crêperie-cum-small hotel which is about as simple as they come, set on the delightful little port.

L'Ile aux Moines ✉ 56780

Le San Francisco, Le Port, B.P.7, t 02 97 26 31 52, f 02 97 26 35 59. A former Franciscan convent, with some much-sought-after cosy rooms and two dining rooms with views.

tax riots in 1675, bringing a period of prosperity to the town, as wealthy new politicians moved in. Up the posh parliamentarians' **Rue St-Vincent** from the port you come to a series of connecting, sloping squares with period buildings, some with timber frames. The Château-Gaillard, a smart 15th-century mansion, now houses the **Musée d'Archéologie du Morbihan** (*open July–Aug daily exc Sun and public hols 9.30–6; April–June and Sept daily exc Sun and public hols 9.30–12 and 2–6; rest of the year daily exc Sun and public hols 2–6; adm*). Inside are many of the finest finds from the Morbihan's Neolithic sites: polished axes whose design and finish seem almost contemporary; rougher necklaces, pendants and bangles; and fragments of tools, weapons and pottery.

The **Cathédrale St-Pierre** sits on the hill, hemmed in on all sides by pretty streets. The Act of Union between Brittany and France was signed behind the thick walls of **La Cohue**, opposite the cathedral, which now contains a collection of museums (*open 15 June–Sept daily exc public hols 10–6; rest of the year daily exc Tues, Sun am and public hols 10–12 and 2–6; adm*). The most famous work in the **Musée des Beaux-Arts** is Delacroix's *Crucifixion*, although it's not one of his best. Otherwise the museum is mostly devoted to Breton subjects. The **Musée du Golfe et de la Mer** covers the history

Vannes ✉ 56000

***Le Roof**, Presqu'île de Conleau, **t** 02 97 63 47 47, **f** 02 97 63 48 10 (*moderate*). The most exclusive hotel in Vannes, with wonderful views on to the Golfe du Morbihan.

****Marina**, 4 Place Gambetta, **t** 02 97 47 22 81, **f** 02 97 47 00 34 (*inexpensive*). Overlooking the port, which comes to life in the evenings.

Arnaud Lorgeoux, 17 Rue des Halles, **t** 02 97 47 15 96, **f** 02 97 47 86 39. A charming little restaurant in an old Vannes house.

La Table des Gourmets, 6 Rue Alexandre Le Pontois, **t** 02 97 47 52 44. Looking on to the ramparts from outside Vannes' walls, and specializing in gastronomic Breton cuisine (*menus 120–320F*). *Closed Sun eve out of season, Mon lunch and Wed.*

Arzon ✉ 56640

*****Miramar**, Port du Crouesty, **t** 02 97 67 68 00, **f** 02 97 67 68 99 (*luxury*). A fake luxury liner anchored in an artificial round pond by the sea, with mod cons galore and a restaurant (*menus 255–280F*). *Closed Dec.*

Hôtel de la Plage, Port-Navalo, **t** 02 97 53 75 92. Simple but clean hotel with a loud bar.

Le Grand Largue, 1 Rue du Phare, Port-Navalo, **t** 02 97 53 71 58, **f** 02 97 53 92 20. A fine reputation for the freshest of seafood (*menus 160–350F*).

Billiers ✉ 56190

*****Domaine de Rochevilaine**, Pointe de Pen-Lan, **t** 02 97 41 61 61, **f** 02 97 41 44 85 (*expensive*). Exclusive hotel which has bagged a headland for itself. You can try splendid seafood dishes in the dining room which makes the most of the panorama, like the rooms (*menus 270–500F*) .

La Roche-Bernard ✉ 56130

****Auberge Bretonne**, 2 Place Duguesclin, **t** 02 99 90 60 28, **f** 02 99 90 85 00 (*expensive*). Has one of the best restaurants in Brittany (*menus 210–630F*). The wine list is stupendous too, and there are eight very nice rooms.

****Auberges des Deux Magots**, 1 Place du Bouffay, **t** 02 99 90 60 75, **f** 02 99 90 87 87 (*moderate*). On a lovely square, distinguishing itself from the crowd by the two sculpted monkeys emerging from its walls. The rooms are comfortable in the old-fashioned French manner (darkish, with lots of wallpaper). Food is stock French (*menus 85–280F*).

Le Cardinal, Quai de la Douane, **t** 02 99 90 79 41. Down by the river, this popular restaurant overlooking the Vilaine is on the first floor, above the bar-cum-pizzeria on the ground floor.

and ethnography of the Golfe du Morbihan. Beyond the choir end of the cathedral, the Place Brûlée leads you down to the imposing **Porte Prison**, the best preserved of the medieval gates into town.

The **Presqu'île de Rhuys** is the long spit of land that forms the protective southern barrier to the Golfe du Morbihan and is best appreciated from the two Neolithic tumuli just outside Arzon, from where there are big views out to the gulf and ocean beyond. The **Petit Mont** (*open June–Sept daily 9–12 and 2–7; adm*) is one of the most surprising Neolithic sites in Brittany. The Nazis turned it into a bunker, which savage alteration has actually made it even more interesting to visit .

Heading east along the Atlantic coast, you may be surprised to come across a medieval castle plonked by itself on a beach. The **Château de Suscinio** (*open July–Aug daily 10–7; April–June and Sept daily 10–12 and 2–7; Oct–Mar Thurs, Sat and Sun 10–12 and 2–5, Mon, Wed and Fri 2–5; adm*) was built for hunting, as the peninsula was once covered with forests. Massive walls and towers aplenty survive from the 14th century, although some parts date from earlier still. The castle fell into decline in the 16th century. Don't miss the medieval flooring.

The **Pointe de Pen-Lan** marks the entrance to the beautiful **Vilaine estuary**, or Vilaine Maritime, visitable by boat from the marina by the dam. South of the Vilaine the beach at **Pénestin** is backed by high cliffs made of hardened sand, eroded into an arc. At sunset, the cliffs light up in a lustrous golden colour, and you can understand how the place got its nickname of La Mine d'Or, the Gold Mine. The comical **light-house at Tréhiguier** has been turned into a little museum (*open July and Aug daily 10–12 and 3–7; Easter–June and Sept–Oct weekends 3–6; adm*) explaining the mysteries of *mytiliculture* or mussel cultivation.

Heading up the Vilaine you arrive at the village of **La Roche-Bernard**, whose narrow streets tumble down steep hillsides to the river. Up in the flatter part of the village, good restaurants congregate in a series of adjoining squares. The **Musée de la Vilaine Maritime** (*open mid-June–mid-Sept daily 10.30–12.30 and 2.30–6.30; early June and late Sept daily 2.30–6.30; Mar–May and Oct–Dec weekends only 2.30–6.30; adm*) occupies the 16th-century **Maison des Basses-Fosses**, which looks unassuming from the upper town, but plunges dramatically down the hill. The museum pays particular homage to *La Couronne*, the first French ship to be built with three decks, which was constructed at La Roche-Bernard.

Inland Eastern Morbihan

Several attractive, prettified small towns lie scattered around the Oust valley above the Vilaine. Re-cobbled streets, for instance, have added to the atmosphere of beautiful **Rochefort-en-Terre**, although in summer you may find the tourists as numerous as the cobble stones. At the end of the 19th century a colony of artists came, saw, and fell in love with Rochefort-en-Terre.

Although not nearly as talented as the painters in Pont-Aven, they are remembered in the **museum** by the fake château (*both open July–Aug daily 10.30–6.30; June and Sept daily 10.30–12 and 2–6.30; April, May and Oct weekends and public hols only 10.30–12 and 2–6.30; adm*). At the beginning of the 20th century an American artist, Alfred Klots, bought what remained of the castle. By the end of the 1920s he had constructed a brand new historic manor by gathering bits of ruins from around the region. A few rooms are open, decorated in a unique Americano-Hispanic-Italiano-Breton style. Virtually every house in Rochefort-en-Terre has interesting details, but the Place du Puits is the most absurdly picturesque square.

A sturdy castle, built on a solid outcrop of rock, dominates the river Oust at **Josselin**. This is one of the rare great feudal Breton châteaux still owned by descendants of a great feudal family, the Rohans. Olivier de Clisson, one of the most power-hungry lords in medieval Brittany, fortified the **Château de Josselin** (*open July–Aug daily 10–6; June and Sept daily 2–6; April, May and Oct Wed, weekends and school hols 2–6; adm*). From the river it looks distinctly unwelcoming. By contrast, approaching from the town side, there is scarcely a hint of military architecture, and a fabulous riot of Gothic motifs and symbols covers the inner façade. The tour takes you around five extravagant neo-Gothic rooms.

Getting Around

There's a TGV from Paris to La Baule and Le Croisic (3hrs). Nantes airport is also convenient. For local bus services, call t 02 40 11 53 02.

Tourist Information

Redon: Place de la République, t 02 99 71 06 04, f 02 99 71 01 59.
Rochefort-en-Terre: Place des Halles, t 02 97 43 33 57.
Josselin: Place Congrégation, t 02 97 22 36 43.
St-Nazaire: Base Sous-Marine, t 02 40 22 40 65.

Where to Stay and Eat

Rochefort-en-Terre ✉ 56220
Au Vieux Logis, t 02 97 43 31 71, f 02 97 43 31 62. Pleasing restaurant in a picturesque old house on the eastern end of the main street.

Château de Talhouët (head briefly north towards Pleucadeuc then west for Talhouët), t 02 97 43 34 72, f 02 97 43 35 04 (*expensive*). Stunning 16th-century manor outside Rochefort, surrounded by greenery, with comfortable and well-furnished rooms.

Josselin ✉ 56120
La Carrière, 8 Rue de la Carrière, t 02 97 22 22 62. A refined townhouse near the château.
Les Cheminées, 117 Rue Glatinier, t 02 97 22 29 97. A good-value B&B run by a British couple should be your next choice after Le Carrière.
Le Manoir du Val aux Houx, 2km from Josselin towards St-Servan, t 02 97 22 24 32. Typical 17th-century Breton manor.
**Hôtel de France, Place Notre-Dame, t 02 97 22 23 06, f 02 97 22 35 78 (*inexpensive*). The best hotel in Josselin, set on a delightful little square. Restaurant (*menus 85–207F*). *Closed Jan, Sun eve and Mon Sept–Mar.*
Les Frères Blot, 9 Rue Glatinier, t 02 97 22 22 08. Fine dishes cooked up by two brothers.

From La Baule to St-Nazaire via Le Croisic Peninsula

The enormous safe sandy bay of La Baule welcomes throngs of people in summer. Beyond the beach, major attractions include the historic town of Guérande and the rocky finger of Le Croisic's peninsula. St-Nazaire, of ocean liner fame and German U-Boat infamy, is ignored by many tourists, but it lies in an extraordinarily dramatic position at the vast mouth of the Loire.

Guérande overlooks the vast salt marshes on which its wealth was built in times past. Solid protective granite ramparts still surround the streets with their fine granite houses. The most impressive entrance into town, the **Porte St-Michel**, was built in the second half of the 15th century. It was once home to the town governors, and has now been converted into the **town museum** (*open April–Sept daily 10–12.30 and 2.30–7; Oct daily 10–12 and 2–6; adm*). Inside, displays are devoted to local history, and you can walk out on to the ramparts. Below, the streets are packed with craft shops, gift shops, crêperies and restaurants. It's worth exploring the dour landscape of the **marais salants** below Guérande, with mounds of gourmet salt piled high in summer. Guided walking tours are run from the little **Maison du Sel** at Pradel (*open daily 10–1 and 3–7; adm*).

Charming and chic kitsch, the best of yachting facilities, and 9km of unbroken fine sand count among the attractions of **La Baule**, Brittany's poshest, most popular and busiest resort. The waterfront of the splendid sandy bay is lined with a curve of

Tourist Information

Guérande: 1 Place du Marché aux Bois, t 02 40 24 96 71, f 02 40 62 04 24.
La Baule: 8 Place de la Victoire, t 02 40 24 34 44, f 02 40 11 08 10.
Batz-sur-Mer: 25 Rue de la Plage, t 02 40 23 92 36, f 02 40 23 74 10.
Le Croisic: Place du 18 Juin 1940, t 02 40 23 00 70, f 02 40 62 96 60.
Pornic: Place de la Gare, t 02 40 82 04 40, f 02 40 82 90 12.
La Chapelle-des-Marais (Brière): 38 Rue de la Brière, t 02 40 66 85 01.

Where to Stay and Eat

Guérande ✉ 44350

**Les Remparts, 14–15 Bd du Nord, t 02 40 24 90 69, f 02 40 62 17 99 (*inexpensive*). Pleasant, comfortable rooms and good food (*menus 105–250F*). *Closed Jan, Sun eve and Mon exc July and Aug.*
**Roc Maria, 1 Rue des Halles, t 02 40 24 90 51, f 02 40 62 13 03 (*inexpensive*). Old-styled hotel in a charming old house.

La Baule ✉ 44500

La Baule is extremely popular, quite posh, and expensive by Breton standards.

****Hermitage, 5 Esplanade Lucien Barrière, t 02 40 11 46 46, f 02 40 11 46 45 (*luxury*). Luxury hotel offering sea-water treatments and refined cuisine (*menus 165–240F*). *Closed Nov–Feb.*
****Royal Thalasso, 6 Av Pierre Loti, t 02 40 11 48 48, f 02 40 11 48 45 (*luxury*). Luxury hotel offering all manner of sea-water treatments and refined cuisine (*menus 200–235F*).
****Castel Marie-Louise, 1 Av Andrieu, t 02 40 11 48 38, f 02 40 11 48 35 (*luxury*). More friendly neo-Gothic mansion with a large garden right in the heart of La Baule and a restaurant (*menus 260–460F*).
***Le St-Christophe, Place Notre-Dame, t 02 40 60 35 35, f 02 40 60 11 74 (*moderate*). Good example of of La Baule's early 20th-century architecture. Restaurant (*menus 145–195F*).
***Majestic, 14 Esplanade Lucien Barrière, t 02 40 60 24 86, f 02 40 42 03 13 (*moderate*). The rooms are luminous and modern, with excellent sea views. Restaurant (*menus 95–245F*). *Closed Jan–Mar.*
***La Concorde, 1 bis Av de la Concorde, t 02 40 60 23 09, f 02 40 42 72 14 (*moderate*). Looking out on to La Baule beach. No restaurant.
**Le Lutétia, 13 Av des Evens, t 02 40 60 25 81, f 02 40 42 73 52 (*moderate*). One of the smart addresses set among the chic streets behind the beach. Restaurant (*menus 120–250F*).

condominiums, but inland there are many older villas where fantasy flourished: Normandy beamed homes, Basque chalets, modern thatched villas, even the odd Arabic folly vie for your attention.

The peninsula of Le Croisic is much more exposed to the ocean than the bay of La Baule, although its coast doesn't look as wild as its nickname, the Côte Sauvage, would have you imagine. Every summer this thin peninsula is blighted by traffic. Batz-sur-Mer, straddling the peninsula, is a traditional village with its cluster of whitewashed houses, where you can still buy clogs at the **Maison du Sabot**. The **Batz Musée des Marais Salants** (*open June–Sept and school hols daily 10–12 and 3–7; rest of the year weekends only 3–7; adm*) counts among the oldest traditional museums in France, set up in 1887 by Adèle Pichon, a nun who was the daughter of a local salt farmer. The port of Le Croisic looks out across the peaceful inland sea of Le Traict to the salt flats of Guérande. Only a narrow channel of water allows the boats into the harbour. Beyond the port, the starfish-shaped **Océarium** (*open 10 July–20 Aug daily 10am–10pm; early July and late Aug daily 10–7; rest of year exc Jan 10–12 and 2–7; adm*) is the major attraction with its aquariums, set back in the rampant suburbs.

★★La Palmeraie, 7 Allée des Cormorans, **t** 02 40 60 24 41, **f** 02 40 42 73 71 (*moderate*). Lovely flower garden shaded by pines, and a restaurant (*menus 130–180F*). *Closed Nov–Mar.*

★★Hôtel Marini, 22 Av Georges Clémenceau, **t** 02 40 60 23 29, **f** 02 40 11 16 98 (*inexpensive*). Some rooms overlooking the bay. Restaurant (*menu 110F*).

★★Mariza, 22 Bd Hennecart, **t** 02 40 60 20 21, **f** 02 40 24 57 09 (*inexpensive*). A relatively cheap option for a seafront room.

La Marcanderie, 5 Av d'Agen, **t** 02 40 24 03 12, **f** 02 40 11 08 21. Excellent seafood (*menus 150–340F*).

Le Maréchal, 277 Av de Lattre-de-Tassigny, **t** 02 40 24 51 14. More rustic in look, and another good place for *fruits de mer* (*menus 99–350F*).

La Barbade, on the beach. Stylish and fun (*menu 160F*). *Closed Nov–Mar.*

Le Croisic ⊠ 44490

Port Lin, **t** 02 40 62 90 03, **f** 02 40 23 28 03 (*moderate*). Superbly located above the ocean, with charming rooms and an excellent seafood restaurant.

★★Castel Moor, Av du Castouillet, **t** 02 40 23 24 18, **f** 02 40 62 98 90 (*inexpensive*). A good cheaper option with a restaurant (*menus 125–200F*). *Closed Sun eve and Mon Oct–Mar.*

Le Pornic, **t** 02 40 23 18 56. Good seafood restaurant.

Bouillabaisse Bretonne, **t** 02 40 23 06 74. Good for seafood (*menu 100–220F*). *Closed Jan–Mar.*

Batz-sur-Mer ⊠ 44740

L'Atlantide, **t** 02 40 23 92 20. The restaurant with the best reputation for local seafood and an excellent view of the little bay of Port St-Michel.

L'Ecume de Mer, Route de la Grande Côte, **t** 02 40 23 91 40. Sensational sea views to accompany its fish.

In the Brière

★★Hôtel Les Chaumières du Lac, Route d'Herbignac, ⊠ 44410 St-Lyphard, **t** 02 40 91 32 32, **f** 02 40 91 30 33 (*inexpensive*). Modern cluster of upmarket, purpose-built thatched cottages connected to the **Auberge Les Typhas,** **t** 02 40 91 40 30, **f** 02 40 91 30 33, which serves refined food.

★★L'Auberge de Kerhinet, ⊠ 44410 Kerhinet, **t** 02 40 61 91 46, **f** 02 40 61 91 40 (*inexpensive*). Set in a perfect picture of thatched houses: the most touristy spot of all.

L'Auberge de Kerbourg, Kerbourg, **t** 02 40 61 95 15, **f** 02 40 61 98 64. Perhaps the most memorable Briély aloof in the upper old village.

Beau Rivage restaurant, Plage de la Birochère, **t** 02 40 82 03 08, **f** 02 51 74 04 24. Superb location and seafood cuisine to match.

The Brière Marsh, St-Nazaire and the South Side of the Loire Estuary

Inland, the secretive and reedy natural park of the Brière marsh stretches south from the Vilaine river to St-Nazaire. The best way to explore this peaty Pays Noir (Black Country) – the second-largest marsh in France – is in a punt, with a local guide. **Port des Fossés Blancs** and Bréca are good places from which to take a boat out on the waterways.

Kerhinet is the best known Briéron hamlet. The park authorities have taken it under their wing and made it into their main showcase, and it looks gorgeous, if slightly twee. The **Musée du Chaume** (*open 8 April–8 May and June–Sept daily 10–10 and 2.30–6.30; adm*) explains the principal features of the traditional Briéron home. The real heart of the Brière marsh is the posse of semi-islands around **St-Joachim** north of St-Nazaire. **L'Ile de Fédrun** is where the tourist action is concentrated. **Rozé** was once an important port. The **Parc Animalier** here (*open June–early Nov daily 9–6; adm*) gives you the chance to wander around and get a glimpse of the natural environment of the Brière.

Hard hit by war bombs, hard hit by the recent decline of shipbuilding in Europe, and hard hit by guidebooks, **St-Nazaire** still has bags of character. It was one of the major European ports to operate transatlantic services from the 1860s and many sailed off from here to seek a new life in the Americas. During the First World War, thousands of North American soldiers arrived at St-Nazaire before being sent out to the front in northeastern France. However, the port's most glorious period came between the two wars, when the most famous of France's ocean liners were built here, the *Paris*, the *Ile-de-France*, the *Champlain*, and most impressive of the lot, the *Normandie*, which was requisitioned by the US government during the Second World War, then spectacularly burnt and sank in New York harbour in 1942. In the past few years, the authorities have concentrated their energies on a massive redevelopment of the port area in an attempt to regenerate the historic heart of St-Nazaire. St-Nazaire also has an **Ecomusée** (*open June–15 Sept daily 9.30–6.30; 15 Sept–May daily exc Tues for the Ecomusée, Mon and Wed for the Espadon; adm*) which includes a tour of the *Espadon*, which in 1964 became the first French submarine to cross the North Pole under the ice. Among the new initiatives is the **Escal'Atlantic** (*open daily July–Aug 9.30–8 and twice a week till midnight; April–June Sept–Oct daily 9.30–12.30, 1.30–7; Nov–Dec Wed–Sun 10–12.30, 2–6, closed Jan; adm*); some 50 million francs were invested in this interactive ocean-liner universe, and this has bought them a fantastically sleek, high-tech exhibition. Although St-Nazaire was terribly smashed up by bombing, it still leaves a strong impression, especially with its giant serpent of a bridge arching over the mouth of the Loire to Mindin. When it was opened in 1975 this was the longest bridge in France.

South of the Loire estuary along the Côte de Jade, **St-Michel-Chef-Chef** and **St-Brévin-les-Pins** are very lively, but in style they fit in more with the long, flat Vendée beach resorts further south. However, the southern stretch of the Côte de Jade around Pornic puts in a strong claim to possessing the most southerly of truly Breton rocks. **Pornic** was good enough for Lenin: the Russian revolutionary stayed some time in this delightful bourgeois retreat. Take the coastal path to the new marina beyond Pornic's poshest houses, or to the north and south: secretive little beaches, the odd Neolithic chamber and Nazi blockhouses lie along the way.

The Loire Valley

11

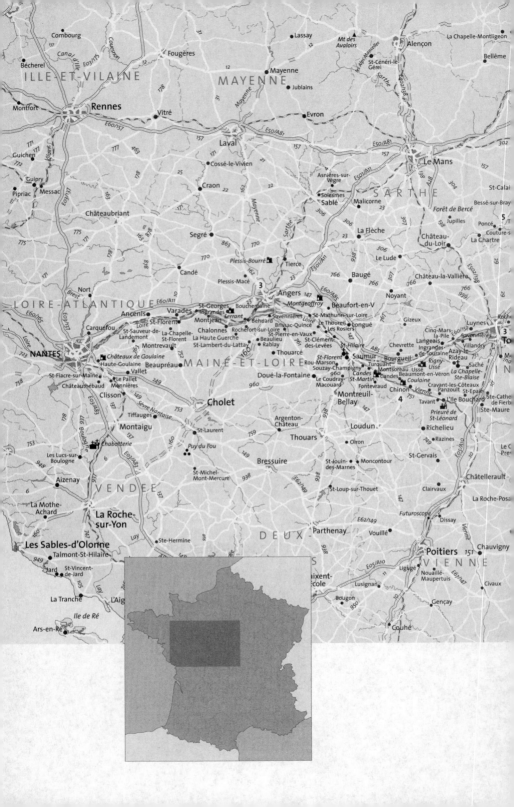

The Loire Valley

Highlights

1 Sensuous Sancerre wine hills
2 Rival cathedrals of Chartres and Bourges
3 The cosmopolitan Loire towns of Orléans, Blois, Tours and Angers
4 Gargantua's Chinonais
5 Troglodyte Troo on the Loir

In a roundabout way, you could consider the English responsible for the enchanting castles strewn along France's greatest river and its tributaries, since they forced Charles VII to flee from Paris in the second half of the Hundred Years' War. He came here, and his successors, Louis XI, Charles VIII and Louis XII, stayed. François I would move the monarchy back to Paris but hedged his bets by ordering Chambord, the biggest of all the Loire châteaux. Then, during sticky moments in the Wars of Religion, Catherine de' Medici and sons again sought refuge in the Loire Valley and lingered; their court left us the greatest architectural legacy of the region and arguably of provincial France.

But the truth is the Loire's credentials as France's Valley of the Kings predates Charles VII hotfooting it out of Paris. The Orléanais, in the east, was a stomping

Food and Wine

Signs signal wine estates and tastings (*dégustations*) at every turn in the greater Loire valley, home to a surprisingly wide variety of whites, reds and rosés. Among the fine white wines, Sancerre, Pouilly-Fumé, Vouvray and Montlouis count among the best, while the more popular Muscadet wine region spreads out from Nantes. The areas around Chinon, Bourgueil and Saumur produce the fruitiest reds, while Saumur also conjures up a creditable sparkling white. Tiny Anjou *appellations* produce the rare, deliciously dry Savennières and the splendid sweet Bonnezeaux and Quarts-de-Chaume, wines for connoisseurs.

Were you to follow the giants' diet as described by Rabelais, you'd expect to be served cartloads of tripe at every meal, washed down with a barrel or two of wine. And there is still one Rabelaisian food you can taste in Anjou – *fouaces* or *foués*, balls of dough that puff up when cooked in the oven.

Today the common features of Loire Valley cuisine are freshwater fish, vegetables and orchard fruits, goats' cheeses in a variety of building block shapes, and game in autumn. The Loire Valley fish is *sandre* (zander; often translated as pike-perch). Other fleshy freshwater fish include *brochet* (pike), *brème* (bream) and *alose* (shad). *Anguilles* (eels) are a speciality along the rivers, often served in a *matelote* (stew).

Meat dishes are often accompanied by regional wine sauces, or local fruit, for example pork served with apples, or better still, prunes. By French standards, Loire Valley restaurants tend to be generous with their vegetables – locally grown onions, leeks, asparagus, beans, cabbages, artichokes and lettuces. The majority of French *champignons de Paris* (button mushrooms) are actually produced in the region's vast underground caves. More exotic mushrooms such as *pleurotes* are also cultivated.

Pears and apples feature in delicious desserts, most famously in *tarte Tatin*, an apple tart with a caramelized top, invented by accident by an absent-minded woman from the Sologne. Good strawberries, raspberries, blackberries and even kiwis are produced in the valley. In the Blésois, Poulain chocolate (now owned by Cadbury's) is a well-known French brand, and the big towns each have their own chocolate speciality; horsey Saumur produces *crottins de cheval* – horse droppings! Bitter oranges from Haiti are imported to Angers to create Cointreau.

Getting There

By plane: For international flights, choose one of the Paris airports; there are also flights to Nantes from the UK.

By train: The city of Tours has by far the best rail links. Paris-Montparnasse is just 1hr away, London-Waterloo via Lille a mere 4hrs 15mins. There are slower trains to Orléans and Blois, and to Bourges in the Berry with a change of train at Vierzon. Vendôme in the Loir valley has a TGV stop, while Chartres nearby has regular trains to Paris. Angers and Nantes are easily reached from Paris by high-speed links via Le Mans; or from London-Waterloo via Lille. For French train information, **t** 08 36 35 35 35, *www.sncf.fr*.

By car: The A10 links Paris with the Loire Valley. The A11 branches off to Chartres, the Loir valley, Angers and Nantes. The soon-to-be-completed A85 joining the A10 and A11 between Tours and Angers will be a useful, fast route from east to west across the Loire Valley. The A71 branches off the A10 for the Berry and Bourges. From the A71, the A20 heads south via the Indre valley.

ground of the Capetians, while Anjou, to the west, was the cradle of the Plantagenets before the Blésois and Touraine became the haunts of the Valois kings. Their legacies can be seen in the splendid cities of Orléans, Blois, Amboise, Tours, Saumur, Angers, Bourges and Nantes. In the spaces between the cities and châteaux, charming villages lie scattered in famous vineyards, from Sancerre in the east to Muscadet in the west; others are built dramatically into the cliffs, notably around Saumur and in the Loir (without an 'e') valley.

The archetypical Loire Valley château fuses the exuberance of late Gothic with the controlled delicacy of the Renaissance, creating some of the most dreamy palaces on this planet – the Château d'Ussé is even claimed to have inspired Charles Perrault's *Sleeping Beauty*. Some have violent stories quite in contrast to their looks, marked by obscene extravagance, intrigue, and murder. The parties were legendary; Leonardo da Vinci arranged some humdingers for François I at Amboise.

This chapter heads down the greater Loire Valley from the rounded wine hills of Sancerre, and takes you as far west as Nantes. With fifty or more châteaux to visit on the way, you will be spoiled for choice. Chenonceaux, Chaumont, Chambord, Cheverny, Amboise, Blois, Azay-le-Rideau and Villandry may be the big draws, but don't neglect the older, larger fortifications, such as Sully-sur-Loire, Loches, Chinon, Angers and Saumur and the less well-known yet spectacular châteaux which often prove the best to visit: Montgeoffroy, Brissac and Serrant in Anjou; Valençay, Bourges, Ainay-le-Vieil and Meillant in the Berry.

Finally we head northeast to the great cathedral town of Chartres, from where we follow the course of the Loir valley southwest to Angers.

The Sancerrois

Sancerre wine and the magnificent vine-covered Sancerrois hills often divert attention from the beauty of Sancerre town. Since the 1950s, far more profitable vines have pushed the goats further westwards into the Pays Fort, but the area's goat's cheese is almost as celebrated locally as its wines.

Getting Around

There's a train from Cosne-Cours-sur-Loire to the station at the bottom of Sancerre's hill. There are also bus services to Sancerre and Henrichemont from Bourges.

Tourist Information

Sancerre: Nouvelle Place, t 02 48 78 03 58, f 02 48 54 24 52.
Henrichemont: t 02 48 26 74 13, f 02 48 26 96 12.

Where to Stay and Eat

Sancerre ✉ 18300
Le Panoramic, 18 Remparts des Augustins, t 02 48 54 22 44, f 02 48 54 39 55

(*inexpensive*). Spectacular views surpass the dull architecture of this very well located, comfortable hotel, with its restaurant, **La Tasse d'Argent**, t 02 48 54 01 44, f 02 48 54 39 55 (*menus from c. 100F*).
**Le St-Martin, 10 Rue St-Martin, t 02 48 54 21 11, f 02 48 54 17 50 (*inexpensive*). Central location with its own restaurant with cheap menus.
La Pomme d'Or, Nouvelle Place, t 02 48 54 13 54. The restaurant with the best reputation in town, serving good, traditional fare.
L'Esplanade, Place de la Halle, t 02 48 54 01 36. Restaurant in a good location on the lively central square.
La Tour, Nouvelle Place, t 02 48 54 00 81, f 02 48 78 01 54. Also located on the central square, and the dining room has lovely vineyard views.

Hilltop **Sancerre** rules the Berry bank of the Loire. Far to the north, you can sometimes make out the clouds of vapour of the nuclear power station of Belleville-sur-Loire, one of many built along the great river. During the Hundred Years' War Sancerre was an important frontier post of the shrivelled French kingdom and Jean de Bueil of Sancerre, the 'Scourge of the English', was a loyal companion to Joan of Arc. In the 1460s he recorded his experiences in *Le Jouvencel*, perhaps the first French historical novel. The main square is charming without being overprettified, and some of the steep streets that lead away from it have barn-door-size entrances awaiting the grape harvest. Other specialities are *croquets de Sancerre* (biscuits) and pottery. In the **Pays Fort**, just west of the Sancerrois, is the heavily restored **Château de Maupas**, with a huge collection of plates piled on its grand staircase walls. **La Borne** houses present-day potters as tightly packed together as pieces in a kiln. **Henrichemont**, by contrast, was a model new town of the early 17th century.

The Berry

Bourges

'The huge, rugged vessel of the church overhung me in very much the same way as the black hull of a ship at sea would overhang a solitary swimmer,' wrote Henry James of Bourges cathedral. 'It seemed colossal, stupendous, a dark leviathan.' UNESCO was just as impressed and made Bourges cathedral a World Heritage Site in 1992. The rest of the city is packed with fine historic streets and museums.

History

Avaricum, capital of the Bituriges tribe, was one of the glories of Gaul. Caesar destroyed it after a siege in 52 BC and chillingly described how his troops dealt with the Celts: 'None of our soldiers thought about making money by taking prisoners. They were exasperated by the massacre of Romans at Cenabum [Orléans] and the labour of the siege and spared neither old men, nor women, nor children. Of the whole popula-tion – about forty thousand – a bare eight hundred...got safely through to Vercingetorix.' Under the Romans, the town became for a time the capital of the vast Gallo-Roman province of Aquitania. The French crown took possession of the viscounty of Bourges in 1101, when Philippe I bought it, making eastern Berry one of the earliest possessions of the Capetian kings. Work began on the Cathedral of St-Etienne in 1195. In 1360 Jean, son of Jean le Bon, was made Duc de Berry and would later control the Auvergne and the Poitou. He was as ruthless, and fleeced his subjects to support his refined taste in the arts. In 1412 he tried to negotiate with the English, causing the French to besiege Bourges. The duke submitted.

After his death, the future Charles VII inherited the territories and Bourges became one of the bases of his peripatetic court. Charles was a weak, indecisive figure, often mockingly referred to as '*le petit roi de Bourges*' while Paris lay in English hands. Two vital figures came to his rescue. One was Joan of Arc. The other was Jacques Coeur, one of the most successful merchants in French history, grown fabulously wealthy from trade with the Orient and supplying the court with luxuries. As Charles VII's finance minister, Coeur worked the miracles economically which Joan of Arc had

Getting Around

There are trains to Bourges from Paris via Orléans and Vierzon. There are also trains from Bourges to and from Tours and the southern Berry.

Tourist Information

Bourges: 21 Rue Victor Hugo, t 02 48 23 02 60, f 02 48 23 02 69.

Where to Stay and Eat

Bourges ✉ 18000

Expensive

***Hôtel de Bourbon**, Bd de la République, t 02 48 70 70 00, f 02 48 70 21 22. The smartest hotel in Bourges, set in a converted 16th-century abbey, with a fine restaurant, **L'Abbaye St-Ambroix**, in a former chapel (*menus 250–420F*).

Moderate

***Hôtel d'Angleterre**, 1 Place des Quatre Piliers, t 02 48 24 68 51, f 02 48 65 21 41. Excellent location and elegant exterior, but the comfortable rooms turn out to be unimaginatively decorated. It has a stylish restaurant, **Le Windsor** (*menus 96–136F*).

Inexpensive

Le Christina, 5 Rue de la Halle, t 02 48 70 56 50, f 02 48 70 58 13. In a dull modern block, but in a pretty good central location with a few rooms furnished with character, and with views on to old Bourges rooftops.

Philippe Larmat, 62 Bis Bd Gambetta, t 02 48 70 79 00, f 02 48 69 88 87. Little restaurant named after its star of a chef, with some surprisingly good-value options for such sophisticated cuisine (*menus 130–250F*).

Jacques Coeur, 3 Place Jacques Coeur, t 02 48 70 12 72. Reasonably priced traditional French fare, in a grand neo-Gothic dining room (*menus 150–190F*).

inspired militarily. However, his influence earned him many enemies and in 1451 he was arrested on false charges of having poisoned the king's mistress. Just as Charles VII had done nothing to aid Joan of Arc, so he did nothing for Coeur. Coeur escaped to work for the pope while his money helped to finance the expulsion of the English from France. Charles VII is known in history as *'le bien servi'* (the well-served) but while his reign is often seen as weak, he nevertheless wrested control of the French Church from the papacy well before Henry VIII did the same for England.

Charles VII's son, Louis XI, was born in Bourges and saw to the founding of Bourges University in 1463. It became known for law and theology; German students brought with them the seeds of Luther's preaching and planted them in the brain of Jean Calvin, a student here in 1530. By the 17th century Catholicism was ascendant again, although more friction was inevitable, with the rebellious Condé family based at Bourges. When Louis XIV came to Bourges, he destroyed the Grosse Tour – a symbol of Condé power – and authority passed to the monarchy. Bourges declined, and would only really pick up with what might be described as the explosion in its arms industry under the Second Empire. Bourges boomed and, by the First World War, employed more than 20,000. It has remained the centre of the French arms industry, yet its population has been strongly left-wing since the war.

The Cathedral St-Etienne

The roughly almond-shaped old town boasts the first French Gothic cathedral built south of the Loire, begun in 1195 under Archbishop Henri de Sully. His brother was archbishop of Paris, and Bourges cathedral is just as large and grand as Notre-Dame. Consecrated in 1324, its five-portalled façade is unique. Below the arches stands a wealth of sculpture – almost all from the 13th century – depicting the Last Judgement, the lives of St Etienne, St Just, St Ursin, the Virgin, and St William, a Bourges archbishop. Between the portals, at the level of the niches, a series of bas-reliefs represents scenes from the life of Christ and from Genesis. The magnificent rose window above was added at the end of the 14th century by order of Jean Duc de Berry.

Unfortunately the ground wasn't strong enough to support the weight of the cathedral towers. On the south side, the *Tour Sourde* (Mute Tower – it has no bells) is propped up by an enormous pillar which was once a church prison. To the north, the Tour de Beurre (financed by patrons in return for a dispensation to eat butter and milk during Lent) fell down in 1506 and had to be restored. Like Chartres, St-Etienne demonstrates the engineering and visual possibilities of the flying buttress, which allow for much glass, and hence light, for the interior. The north and south side portals have Romanesque sculptures from an earlier cathedral. The north presents the story of the Virgin but was badly damaged by Protestants. Owls and monkeys add a lighter note. The south portal shows Old and New Testament figures.

The rows of Gothic lancet arches to the apse reach higher than the arches of Notre-Dame. Originally they would have been obscured by a *jubé* or rood screen but now the massive organ pipes – installed in 1663 and restored in 1985 – hide sections of the back window. Don't miss the complex astronomical clock from 1424. The famed 13th-century stained-glass windows in the ambulatory feature patterned settings which vary in each. You can only visit the crypt via a guided tour to see vestiges of the 13th-century rood screen, the Duc de Berry's tomb, a magnificent work by Jean de Cambrai, and several tall statues from the towers. After visiting the crypt, the ticket allows you to climb the Tour de Beurre for views of the old city.

Palais Jacques Cœur and the Bourges Museums

Although first impressions are that the **Palais Jacques Cœur** (*open Palm Sun–31 Oct daily 9–11.10 and 2–5.10; 2 Nov–Palm Sun daily 9–11.10 and 2–4.10; adm*) needs a good clean, this palatial town house is full of delights. Gothic sculpture adorns much of the building and above the entrance doorway look out for the false windows with stone people who – as Henry James wrote – 'appear to be watching for the return of their master, who left his beautiful house one morning and never came back'. Coeur had a finger in every pie: real estate, mining, banks and the arms trade. Appointed Charles VII's Minister of Finance in 1439 and ennobled in 1441, he became the king's councillor in 1442 and began this house in 1443. The bitter tale of Coeur's demise (legend has it that he was killed by the Turks, with a weapon he had sold to them) contrasts with the lightheartedness of the sculpture in his homes. In the 17th century the house was bought by the city to use as its town hall. Entertainingly carved fireplaces are high-lights of the interiors, while in the magnificent little chapel Jacques Coeur and his wife each had a private oratory.

The Hôtel Cujas housing the **Musée du Berry** (*open daily 10–12 and 2–6; closed Sun am and Tues; adm*) was built around 1515 for Durand Salvi, a Florentine trader. It contains two extraordinary exhibits: a re-created Gallo-Roman necropolis and some extremely moving marble *pleurants* (mourners) from Jean Duc de Berry's splendid tomb. Other rooms are given over to artefacts of Berrichon life in the 18th and 19th centuries.

A rich merchant family of German origin built the fine Hôtel Lallemant (1490–1518), now the elegant **Musée des Arts Décoratifs** (*open daily exc Sun am and Mon 10–12 and 2–6; adm*). Its fine Renaissance features include a loggia, frescoes and an oratory with an extraordinary coffered stone ceiling, each square decorated with an angel or symbol: a dove, a rose, a bee hive, and so on. Another joyous late-Gothic house, the Hôtel des Echevins, built as a new town hall in 1487, contains the riot of 20th-century colour of the **Musée Estève** (*open daily exc Sun am and Tues 10–12 and 2–6; adm*), with the abstract works of Maurice Estève, a native of the Berry. The **Musée des Meilleurs Ouvriers de France** (*open daily exc Mon and Jan 2–6; adm*), in the 17th-century clas-sical archbishops' palace, encourages modern craftsmenship.

Along the Cher Valley through the Berry

Several of the Berry's monuments lie south of Bourges, around the Cher Valley, including the châteaux of Meillant and Ainay-le-Vieil.

West of Bourges, on the west bank of the Cher, **Brinay's church of St-Aignan** stands by a quiet green. The choir contains some of the most moving Romanesque wall paintings in France. The east wall – normally the location for Christ in Majesty – is occupied by the Massacre of Innocents. On the south wall, Christ is shown overcoming the devil's temptations and turning water into wine at the feast of Cana. At St-Amand-Montrond, near the east bank of the Cher, the **Château de Meillant** (*open daily 9–11.45 and 2–6.45, or nightfall if earlier; closed 15 Dec–Jan; adm*) is mirrored in a crescent moat. It is mainly Gothic, constructed in three blocks: the first was erected for Etienne de Sancerre; the second was ordered by Charles I d'Amboise of the mighty Chaumont family. Charles held the highest posts in France and also became governor of Milan. Hence the saying; 'Milan made Meillant'. The château, however, is almost entirely Flamboyant Gothic. It was restored in 1842 and the interior reflects this. The highlights include the colourfully painted Salle de Justice, the dining room's patterned Córdoba leather, and the salon's fireplace, large enough to incorporate a minstrel's gallery. The chapel contains beautiful stained glass windows and fantastical sculpture.

West of the Cher at **Bruère-Allichamps**, a track leads you to the battered but remarkable Romanesque **Prieuré d'Allichamps** (*open July–Sept Mon–Sat 2–7; adm*) which the villagers claim stands at the exact centre of France.

The 12th-century **abbey of Noirlac** close to the Cher (*open April–Sept daily 9.45–12 and 1.45–6.30; July and Aug daily 9.45–6.30; Oct–Mar daily exc Tues 9.45–12 and 1.45–5; adm*) is one of the best examples of a Cistercian abbey still standing in France. The denuded buildings suggest states of uncluttered meditation, although the original asceticism of the life and architecture was gradually abandoned through time. By the Revolution, only six monks remained.

To the south lies the medieval **Château d'Ainay-le-Vieil**, over a moat teeming with water lilies and giant carp, while outside the walls lies a romantic rose garden, scattered with fragments of poems. The courtyard has suffered from unhistoric plastering, but the richly decorated octagonal tower, topped by a peculiarly curved roof, is still guarded by strange Gothic beasts. Mementoes abound of the Colberts, who bought the château in 1467. Three brothers served as Napoleonic generals so there are plenty of imperial souvenirs.

The Indre's Vallée Noire; the 'Pays de George Sand'

George Sand, who championed this 'eminently rustic' area, is the heroine of the Indre's Vallée Noire. Many of the leading artistic lights of the 19th century visited her at Nohant, including her most famous lover, Chopin. The picturesque Creuse valley also milks its one or two connections with Sand and with the Impressionists.

The Pays de George Sand centres around hillside La Châtre. A cobbled-together **Musée George Sand et de la Vallée Noire** (*open April–Sept daily 9–12 and 2–7; July and Aug daily 9–7; other months daily 9–12 and 2–5; closed Jan; adm*) is divided between a collection of stuffed birds, memorabilia of *la grande dame* and local traditions. Since 1992 the town has gained more of a reputation for its July festival, '*Chopin chez George*

Hey there, Georgie Girl

George Sand was born Amantine-Aurore-Lucille Dupin in 1804. Her father was a descendant of the Polish king Augustus II, her mother the daughter of a Parisian bird-seller. Early and disastrously married, she conducted a string of relationships with famous men of her day. Unfortunately her novels patronise the locals, and have none of the brilliant insight and finesse of that other literary woman she so admired, George Eliot. Sand was often writing desperately to stave off financial disaster. *La Mare au Diable*, the first of a series of novels set in the Berry, is a banal work written in four days. Her life as an early advocate of socialism and precursor of feminism is more interesting than her writings but she is caricatured as a trousered, cigar-smoking aristocrat with an insatiable appetite for socializing and brilliant lovers. Baudelaire once described her as a latrine, but she was loved by Flaubert.

Sand'. Sand spent much of her childhood and adult life at the **Château de Nohant** (*open July–Aug daily 9–7.30; April–June and Sept–15 Oct daily 9–12.15 and 2–6.30; rest of the year daily 10–12.15 and 2–4.30; adm*), moving from room to room as family (she had two children), work, and romantic whims dictated.

Just up the main road from Nohant, the frescoed Romanesque **church of Vic** has some wonderful early 12th-century paintings, uncovered in 1849 by the local priest. Sand sang their praises. The theme is Christ's crucifixion and resurrection, and the Last Judgement, enacted by figures with highly arched eyebrows, startled eyes and prominent red circles on the cheekbones. The **Château de Sarzay** (*open April–Oct daily 10–12 and 2–7; Nov–Mar weekends till 6; adm*), with its conical towers huddled together, is a superb remnant of a big medieval château built to keep the English at bay. It was bought in the 1980s for a *bouchée de pain*, and is filled with cobwebby bric-à-brac. Sand featured it in *Le Meunier d'Angibault*.

South of La Châtre lies the village of **Chassignolles**. Its story since the mid-19th century has been brought to life by the British writer Gillian Tindall, who bought a house there in the 1970s. She was galvanized into action by the discovery of a pile of love letters from the 1860s – 'the soft wads of paper delicate as old skin' – sent to the daughter of a village innkeeper, Célestine, after whom her book is named. George Sand and Gillian Tindall have taken the local Berrichons extremely seriously in their writing but the filmmaker Jacques Tati gently mocked them in the delightful '50s film, *Jour de Fête*.

The Creuse Valley in the Berry

The Creuse valley crosses the southwest corner of the *département* of the Indre. The romantic ruins of the castle of Crozant, the very sweet Gargilesse and the higgledy-piggledy housing on the waterfront at Argenton are reminiscent of a charming valley in the Dordogne.

The ruins of a great fortress mingle with the natural walls of rock at **Crozant**, on the southern end of the manmade lake of Chambon. In 1356, the Black Prince failed to take it. A Protestant fief in the Wars of Religion, it was partially destroyed by an earthquake in 1610. You can take an exciting walk through the remnants of its towers. The Crozant school of landscape painters flourished between 1850 and 1930. Most notable was Armand Guillaumin.

Claude Monet stayed in the area for nearly three months and, despite unpleasant spring weather, he completed 23 paintings around **Fresselines**. The village has turned a barn into a gallery displaying paintings of the Creuse by a host of other painters who have drawn inspiration from the area. None of Monet's canvases stayed at Fresselines but, at the confluence of the Petite Creuse and the Grande Creuse, you can visit the sites where he painted.

Picture-book **Gargilesse** stands above the Creuse north of Lac de Chambon. The village contains a little house George Sand's lover Manceau bought for them, which has been turned into a museum. The château, until recently in a bad state, has now been lovingly restored and the Romanesque church – although green with moss inside – has a wonderful array of capitals inspired by the Apocalypse and a lower church covered in wall paintings.

The old houses on **Argenton**'s banks, with their carelessly stacked levels of tumbling balconies, look like a hangover from the Middle Ages. However, the **shirt museum** (with contributions from Frank Sinatra and Richard Burton) shows that Argenton made it into the industrial age, and special numbers are still tailored here for Dior and Cardin. In neighbouring **St-Marcel**, however, you can see fashions going back into the recesses of prehistory at the **Musée archéologique d'Argentomagus** (*open daily exc Tues 9.30–12 and 2–6; adm*). Among the earliest displays are Magdalenian finds, with carved reindeer antlers – one with a human face – and prehistoric lamps. The Gallo-Roman collection includes a superb young Mercury, a splendid glass funerary vase, and a rare domestic altar. Christianity was introduced to the area in the mid-3rd century, but three centuries later the visiting St Yrieix wrote that the town was still 'a profane place devoted to the cult of the ancient religion of demons'.

The riverside town of **Le Blanc** is one of the gateways to the **Brenne** of 'a thousand lakes', designated a Regional Nature Park in 1989. The most characteristic part of the Brenne spreads north of the Creuse and is an ornithologist's paradise. The **Réserve de Chérine** has observatories open to the public and a second reserve has been established at **Massé**. The vast majority of the land and lakes, however, is in private hands.

The charming little town of **Mézières** has a museum devoted to regional traditions and west of the Brenne, the extensive **Parc de la Haute-Touche**, part of the French **Muséum National d'Histoire Naturelle**, allows you to observe an exceptional collection of deer among the many penned animals.

The Sologne

The heathery woods and lakes of the Sologne occupy the northern Berry and stretch into the Loiret *département*. This melancholic, mysterious-looking territory fills the big hunched back of the Loire below Orléans and descends as far as the Cher valley.

The magical party in Alain-Fournier's beloved pre-First World War classic *Le Grand Meaulnes* took place here, as did the shooting party in Jean Renoir's *La Règle du Jeu*: the Sologne teems with deer, wild boar, rabbits, birds, duck and fish, and is still regarded as something of a hunter's paradise.

Had Leonardo da Vinci's plans gone ahead, **Romorantin-Lanthenay** would no doubt be famous. François d'Angoulême spent some of his childhood in the town and, once crowned François I, he decided on a residence there. Leonardo, who had come to France at his behest, began drawing up the new château and town in 1517. The castle was to have, amongst other magnificent Renaissance features, a series of arcaded galleries giving on to the Sauldre river, on which courtly entertainments could be performed. As it was, a bout of the plague in 1518 devastated the town and the monarch decided to have his fabulous new hunting lodge built at Chambord. Romorantin-Lanthenay was left to play a bit-part as principal town of the Sologne and a symbol of *la France profonde*, backward, provincial France.

Lately, the town has become more prosperous, through the location of a car plant here in 1968. Now the Renault Espace model is built at Romorantin. The **Musée de Sologne** (*open April–Oct daily 10–6; rest of year daily exc Tues 10–12 and 2–6, Sun and hols 2–6; adm*) occupies old mill buildings and celebrates the area.

The **Château du Moulin** (*open April–Sept daily 9–11.30 and 2–6.30; Oct–15 Nov and Mar daily exc Wed 9–11.30 and 2–5.30; adm*) is the romantic star of the châteaux of the Sologne, a dreamy, hidden castle, due west of Romorantin-Lanthenay, its orange and purple patterned brick visible once you have walked down its avenue of old oaks. Swans glide along in the moat and branches dip their leaves into the water. The château is named after Philippe du Moulin, a loyal servant of Charles VIII, who rescued Charles from his first disastrous foray into Italy in 1495. The château was restored for an ancestor of the present châtelaine, who vacates her room every morning to let visitors through.

A Sologne lake-stopper made out of oak and said to be a staggering 800 years old is on display at **Aliotis** (*open Feb–Oct daily 11–10.30, Nov–Jan Wed and Sun 11–5; adm*), the Sologne aquarium by Villeherviers, east of Romorantin-Lanthenay. The development of the region's lakes for fishing dates back at least to early medieval times and now 3,000 of them cover some 12,000 hectares. Fish in the aquarium, however, are coyly introduced in the first person in an effort to give them more individuality.

Little **Nançay** (close to Neuvy-sur-Barangeon) appears thinly disguised as Vieux-Nançay in Alain-Fournier's *Le Grand Meaulnes*. It looks like the typical Sologne village, with its low brick houses in such contrast to the château to one side, only the houses have now been converted into a posse of chic boutiques. Antiques, fashion and jewellery have become specialities along with the *sablé de Nançay*, the local short-bread biscuit.

You cannot visit the château, but the superbly restored farm outbuildings house an art gallery-cum-museum, the **Galerie Capazza** or **Grenier de Villâtre** (*open mid-Mar–mid-Dec weekends and public hols only 9.30–12.30 and 2.30–7.30; adm*). The little museum pays homage to Alain-Fournier via the **Musée Imaginaire du Grand Meaulnes**.

Getting Around

A train line from Orléans leads down through the Sologne via St-Cyr-en-Val, La Ferté-St-Aubin, Lamotte-Beuvron and Salbris to Vierzon and then Bourges. A branch line from Salbris also serves Selles-St-Denis and Villeherviers in western Sologne. Various train lines from Bourges lead into southern Berry, the one to Montluçon serving St-Amand-Montrond, the one to Poitiers to Châteauroux via Argenton-sur-Creuse. You can reach La Châtre by bus from Châteauroux.

Tourist Information

St-Amand-Montrond: Place de la République, t 02 48 96 16 86, f 02 48 96 46 64.
La Châtre: Square George Sand, t 02 54 48 22 64, f 02 54 06 09 15.
Nohant: Place de Nohant, t/f 02 54 31 07 37.
Gargilesse: Le Pigeonnier, t 02 54 47 85 06, f 02 54 47 71 22.
Argenton-sur-Creuse: 13 Place de la République, t 02 54 24 05 30, f 02 54 24 28 13.
Le Blanc: Place de la Libération, t 02 54 37 05 13, f 02 54 37 31 93.
Mézières-en-Brenne: Le Moulin, 1 Rue du Nord, t 02 54 38 12 24, f 02 54 38 13 76.
Romorantin-Lanthenay: 32 Place de la Paix, t 02 54 76 43 89, f 02 54 76 96 24.
Aubigny-sur-Nère: 1 Rue de l'Eglise, t/f 02 54 00 00 42.

Where to Stay

St-Hilaire-de-Court ✉ 18100

Château de la Beuvrière, t 02 48 75 14 63, **f 02 48 75 47 62 (*inexpensive*). A real bargain of a simple little château on the south bank of the Cher from Vierzon, and well worth seeking out, although the route to it is awkward. Restaurant (*menus 95–200F*).

Bruère-Allichamps ✉ 18200

Auberge de l'Abbaye de Noirlac, t 02 48 96 22 58. Reliable restaurant opposite the abbey. In the Cistercian stone dining room you can sample all manner of Berry specialities (*menus 98–170F*).

Nohant ✉ 36400

Auberge de la Petite Fadette, Place du Château, **t 02 54 31 01 48, **f** 02 54 31 10 19 (*moderate–inexpensive*). Perfect, very comfortable stop for Sand pilgrims, with a good, if touristy restaurant (*menus 85–230F*) and outdoor seating.

St-Chartier ✉ 36400

***Hôtel La Vallée Bleue, Route de Verneuil, **t** 02 54 31 01 91, **f** 02 54 34 04 48 (*moderate*). Stay in period comfort at George Sand's doctor's house, a charming manor on the verge of being a château, with an elegant restaurant.

Aubigny-sur-Nère is proud of its links with Caledonia and could almost count as half-Scottish; its attractive carved timber-beamed houses were built under Robert Stuart, after a fire in 1512. Robert Stuart had inherited the town from an ancestor, John Stuart of Darnley. He arrived from Scotland to assist in fighting the English in the Hundred Years' War and provided the dispossessed Charles VII of France with Scottish troops, who were a crucial support at the Battle of Baugé in Anjou in 1421. John Stuart was given the town of Aubigny-sur-Nère in recognition, and the trusted *gendarmes écossais* became the French royal guard from then until the Revolution.

The Stuart family remained in charge of Aubigny until 1672. Louis XIV then donated it to the beautiful and ambitious Breton, Louise de Kérouaille, who was sent to England to gain support for alliance with France. Charles II of England was seduced and Louise became a favourite. He made her Duchess of Portsmouth, her son the Duke of Richmond. The Richmonds kept Aubigny until the 1840s and Diana, Princess of Wales, it seems, was a descendant.

Bouesse ✉ 36570

Château de Bouesse, t 02 54 25 12 20, f 02 54 25 12 30. Ten km west of Neuvy-St-Sépulchre along the pretty D927, this is a spectacular and good-value medieval castle. Run by a British couple to three-star standards.

Romorantin-Lanthenay ✉ 41200

****Le Lion d'Or, 69 Rue Georges Clemenceau, t 02 54 76 00 28, f 02 54 88 24 87 (*expensive*). Outrageously luxurious hotel in the town centre. Sublime cuisine.

**Le Colombier, 18 Place du Vieux Maré, t 02 54 76 12 76, f 02 54 76 39 40 (*inexpensive*). More down-to-earth hotel in an old coaching inn.

**Auberge de Lanthenay, Rue Notre-Dame-du-Lieu, t 02 54 76 09 19, f 02 54 76 72 91 (*inexpensive*). Tasty regional cuisine.

La Ferté-Imbault ✉ 41300

**La Tête de Lard, 13 Rue Nationale, t 02 54 96 22 32, f 02 54 96 06 22 (*inexpensive*). Friendly hotel, despite its name (which means 'pig-headed').

Nançay ✉ 18330

You pay a premium for staying or eating in posh Nançay.

***Auberge des Meaulnes, 2 Route de Vierzon, t 02 48 51 81 15, f 02 48 51 84 58 (*moderate*). Smart and cosy hotel in a triangle of land between the village's main streets.

Relais de Sologne, 1 Rue du Château, t 02 48 51 82 26. The best restaurant in the village, and it's covered in flowers.

Vouzeron pc 18330

***Relais de Vouzeron, Place de l'Eglise, t 02 48 51 61 38, f 02 48 51 63 71 (*moderate*). Charming former posting inn. A welcoming, smart stop amidst the large Sologne forests.

Aubigny-sur-Nère ✉ 18700

**La Chaumière, 2 Rue Paul Lasnier, t 02 48 58 04 01, f 02 48 58 10 31 (*inexpensive*). Neat hotel in thatched building.

Les Fermaillets d'Or, 6 Av Charles Lefèbvre, t 02 48 58 24 22. The best restaurant in town.

Around La Ferté-St-Aubin ✉ 45240

***Château des Muids, t 02 38 64 65 14, f 02 38 76 50 08 (*moderate*). An elegant late-18th-century brick château south of town, just off the N20. .

La Ferme de La Lande, just northeast of town, t 02 38 76 64 37, f 02 38 64 68 87. Very tempting little country restaurant in immaculate 18th-century farm which was attached to the Château de La Ferté-St-Aubin in times past.

The town's cross-channel history is charted in the **Château des Stuarts** and **Musée de la Vieille Alliance Franco-Ecossaise** (*open Mon–Sat 2.30–7; Sat and Sun 10–12 and 3–7; adm*).

La Ferté-St-Aubin, below Orléans, can claim to be the northern gateway into the Sologne. Its pale brick **château** (*open mid-Feb–mid-Mar daily 2–6; rest of Mar daily 10–6; April–Sept daily 10–7; Oct–mid-Nov daily 10–6; adm*) is among the most beautiful in the region. The entrance gate has comical bell-hatted pavilions flanking a curious classical arch (compared by one architectural historian to deerstalkers!). The two sections of the main logis were built in the 17th century. You can visit the two top floors unaccompanied, but the musty rooms are in a bad state of repair; the second floor is filled with bric-a-brac. A bell calls you to the guided tour of the ground floor, which takes you through some of the better preserved apartments and finishes with a little cookery demonstration in the basement kitchen.

The Loire Valley

From the Berry Border to Orléans

Briare's glory was created by one Gustave Eiffel; while his great Parisian erection sticks high into the air, this elegant bridge extends horizontally over 2,180ft. Briare's second glory is mosaics, best seen at the church of **St-Etienne**. This was commissioned by the heirs of Jean-Felix Bapterosses, the button and enamel industrialist who changed the face of the town. His commercial triumphs are retold through the exhibits at the **Musée de la Mosaïque et des Emaux** (*open Feb–May and Oct–Dec daily 2–6; June–Sept daily 10–6.30; adm*).

Gien, site of an ancient crossing over the Loire, was bombed to smithereens in the Second World War. It has been harmoniously restored using the typical regional patterned brick and stone. The **Château de Gien**, which somehow survived most of the destruction, was built in the 1480s for Anne de Beaujeu, daughter of Louis XI. At points during the Wars of Religion the royal family took refuge in the château, as did Louis XIV and Anne d'Autriche with the Fronde uprising. The **Musée International de la Chasse** (hunting; *open June–Sept daily 9–6; Jan–May and Oct–Dec daily 9–12 and 2–6; adm*) inside offers an insight into the outrageously refined art of its aristocratic practitioners. The **Musée de la Faïencerie** and **Factory** (*museum open Mon–Sat 9.30–12.15 and 2–6.15, Sun 10–12 and 2–6; adm; factory open Mon–Sat*), to the west, show how derivative Gien pottery styles were. The factory became best-known for its blue decorations. From the factory warehouse you can choose from the whole modern range and also get cut-price seconds.

The **Château de Sully** (*open Feb and Mar and Oct–Dec daily 10–12 and 2–5; April–Sept daily 10–6; adm*) makes one of the most beautiful pictures on the Loire. Its sturdy pepper-pot-topped towers are a model of their kind, although rebuilt in 1908. Three great families owned the château before 1602, when it became the property of Maximilien de Béthune, one of France's greatest ministers. He worked loyally for Henri IV and was rewarded with estates and the title of Duc de Sully. Often referred to as Le Grand Sully, his successes included the development of new roads (lined with trees, on his special order) and of the silk industry. His descendants lived in the château until they sold it to the *département* of the Loiret in 1962. Since then it has been considerably restored.

The **abbey church of St-Benoit-sur-Loire** or **Fleury** dominates the sweep of the Loire known as the Val d'Or. A massive structure in light stone topped by black slate, it dates from the 11th to 13th centuries, although its origins go back to the 7th century. Around 672, a band of monks set off to pilfer the bones of their founder, St Benedict, from Monte Cassino near Naples. A papal declaration accepted that the remains should stay at Fleury and it became a venerated pilgrimage site: 11 July, known as the day of the translation of Benedict's bones, is still celebrated. Towards the end of the 8th century, Théodulfe, a close adviser of Charlemagne, was made abbot of Fleury and it became of major importance for teaching and learning in Charlemagne's empire.

Getting Around

Gien has a railway station linked with Paris via Melun. To travel to Orléans by public transport you'll need to use the local bus services via Sully-sur-Loire and Châteauneuf-sur-Loire, **t** 02 38 61 90 00.

Tourist Information

Briare: 9 Place de la République, **t** 02 38 31 24 51, **f** 02 38 37 15 16.

Gien: Place Jean Jaurès, **t** 02 38 67 25 28, **f** 02 38 38 23 16.

Sully-sur-Loire: Place de Gaulle, **t** 02 38 36 23 70, **f** 02 38 36 38 62.

St-Benoît-sur-Loire: 44 Rue Orléanaise, **t** 02 38 35 79 00, **f** 02 38 35 79 35.

Châteauneuf-sur-Loire, 3 Place Briand, **t** 02 38 58 44 79, **f** 02 38 58 52 83.

Where to Stay and Eat

Gien ✉ **45500**

★★La Poularde, 13 Quai de Nice, **t** 02 38 67 36 05, **f** 02 38 38 18 78 (*inexpensive*). Discreet place that overlooks the plane trees by the Loire. It has simpler rooms but does fancy cooking.

★★★Sanotel on the south bank, 21 Quai de Sully, **t** 02 38 67 61 46, **f** 02 38 67 13 01 (*inexpensive*). The best views in town from the large rooms, typical modern boxes.

Les Bézards ✉ **45290 (Boismorand)**

★★★★Auberge des Templiers, entrance on the busy N7, **t** 02 38 31 80 01, **f** 02 38 31 84 51 (*expensive*). The height of luxury and expense in the area. The cuisine has a high reputation, for which you'll pay through the nose.

Sully-sur-Loire ✉ **45600**

★★Le Grand Sully, 10 Bd du Champ de Foire, **t** 02 38 36 27 56, **f** 02 38 36 44 54 (*inexpensive*). Doesn't look particularly grand but the food has a very solid reputation.

St-Benoît-sur-Loire ✉ **45110**

★★Hôtel du Labrador, 7 Place de l'Abbaye, **t** 02 38 35 74 38, **f** 02 38 35 72 99 (*inexpensive*). Near the abbey church, typical local architecture with brick surrounds, plus a more modern section. Not particularly attractive, it does have quite tasteful rooms, some with beams or with a view over the countryside.

Châteauneuf-sur-Loire ✉ **45110**

★★Hôtel du Parc and Restaurant de la Capitainerie, 1 Square du Général de Gaulle, **t** 02 38 58 42 16, **f** 02 38 58 46 81 (*inexpensive*). Very appealing hotel by the town flower garden within the gates of the former château's estate. The little rooms are rustically furnished, the cuisine classic French.

The Capetian kings became generous patrons in the 11th and 12th centuries, and the abbey church became one of the most important Romanesque churches in France. The narthex is decorated with powerful period sculpture; the Byzantine-style choir and transept have solid pillars and a mosaic floor.

The little **oratory at Germigny-des-Près**, which was built for Théodulfe, retains a very rare 9th-century mosaic in the style of Ravenna, made of glorious blue and gold pieces. The scene represents the Ark of the Covenant, above which hover two cherubs watched over by stern angels; the hand of God reaches out from a crack in the sky.

The Loire Valley around Orléans has been dubbed Cosmetics Valley after the many French perfume houses to have located there. Some 20 km northeast of Orléans, once you've passed through the dark Forest of Orléans, you emerge at the **Château de Chamerolles** (*open Feb and Mar daily 10–12 and 2–5; April–June daily 10–6; July–Sept daily 10–6; Oct–Dec daily 10–12 and 2–5; closed Tues; adm*), east of Chilleurs-aux-Bois. Recently given a major facelift, it is now dedicated to the history of perfume.

Orléans

At the crowning point of the Loire, Orléans could have been king of French cities. Under the Capetians it was a great seat of power until Paris seduced the sovereigns away. However, they periodically returned, at one point led by Orléans' uncrowned queen, Joan of Arc.

History

Orléans was an important Celtic settlement, Cenabum, that grew into a major Gallo-Roman town. In 451 it was the target of the Hunnish invaders under Attila, until St Aignan sent them from the city's doorstep and became Orleans' hero for almost a millennium before Joan came to outshine him. In 498 Clovis took the city. Converted to Christianity by his wife and a fortuitous victory, the council he assembled in Orléans in 511 cemented the all-too-close relationship between king and Church. On Clovis' death, Orléans became capital of one of the four smaller kingdoms of Gaul; its

Getting Around

Orléans has two main railway stations, Orléans-Centre and Orléans-Les Aubrais. Get off at Orléans-Centre for the historic part of the city. Orléans has good rail connections with Paris-Austerlitz, Blois and Tours, as well as a few trains a day to Chartres.

Tourist Information

Orléans: Place Albert Ier, t 02 38 24 05 05, f 02 38 54 49 84; and 6 Rue Jeanne d'Arc, t 02 38 53 33 44.

Where to Stay

Orléans ✉ 45000

Orléans caters better for businessmen than for tourists, with a mass of chain hotels. If you have a car, stay in Olivet in the southern suburbs, on the charming banks of the Loiret.

Moderate

***Les Cèdres, 17 Rue du Maréchal Foch, t 02 38 62 22 92, f 02 38 81 76 46. Just outside the busy broad avenues encircling the heart of town.

***Hôtel d'Arc, 37 Rue de la République, t 02 38 53 10 94, f 02 38 81 77 47. In an elaborate Belle Epoque building well situated on the main pedestrian shopping street.

***Quatre Saisons, 351 Rue de la Reine Blanche, Olivet, t 02 38 66 14 30, f 02 38 66 78 59. Looks like a classic beach house, with bright clapperboard sides, a smart restaurant, and a treehouse, but it stands on the banks of the Loiret.

***Le Rivage, 635 Rue de la Reine Blanche, Olivet, t 02 38 66 02 93, f 02 38 56 31 11. Stylish-to-chichi interiors, with swanky rooms and menus.

Inexpensive

**L'Abeille, 64 Rue Alsace Lorraine, t 02 38 53 54 87, f 02 38 62 65 84. On pedestrianized shopping street.

**Jackotel, 18 Cloître St-Aignan, t 02 38 54 48 48, f 02 38 77 17 59. Quiet hotel.

**St-Aignan, 3 Place Gambetta, t 02 38 53 15 35, f 02 38 77 02 36. Central town.

Cheap

Vieille Auberge, 2 Rue du Faubourg St-Vincent, t 02 38 53 55 81, f 02 38 77 16 63. One of the nicest cheaper options, occupying a pleasant 17th-century house.

Paris, 29 Rue du Faubourg Bannier, t 02 38 53 39 58. Very basic, popular in student circles, and run by a character who's familiar with the USA.

2

349

importance was confirmed when Charles le Chauve ('the Bald') was crowned king of the western Franks here in 848. Hugues Capet, founder of the Capetian dynasty, made the monarchy hereditary and indivisible at the crowning of his son Robert II le Pieux in Orléans cathedral in 987. Robert left his mark on the city in the infamous *Jour des Saints Innocents* in 1022 when he had a number of clerical intellectuals of the city branded heretics and burnt to death. Thereafter, the royal retinue alternated between Paris and Orléans until Louis VI preferred the Seine to the Loire. As Pope Honorius III banned the teaching of law in Paris in 1219, the majority of the 13th-century kings' lawyers were trained in Orléans. One student became Pope Clement V, who showed his gratitude by granting Orléans a university in 1306.

During the infamous English siege of 1428 to 1429, the townspeople endured months of starvation. On 29 April 1429 Joan of Arc broke through the English defences to enter the city, but the major French offensive began a week later. The French troops were actually under the command of Dunois, a royal bastard, but Joan gave them courage, spurring them on to victory when Dunois seemed prepared to give up. The

Eating Out

Les Antiquaires, 2–4 Rue du Lin, t 02 38 53 52 35. An upmarket choice in the centre, with a beamed, atmospheric dining room (*menus 200–320F*).

Florian, 70 Bd Alexandre Martin, t 02 38 53 08 15. Fine restaurant with a bright, cheerful dining room giving on to a garden (*menus 135–190F*).

La Chancellerie, 27 Place du Martroi, t 02 38 53 57 54. Has the good fortune to be located in a major building on Orléans' central square. The food is in uncomplicated brasserie style (*menus c. 150F*).

Promenade, Place du Martroi, t 02 38 81 12 12. Traditional cooking (*menus 90–190F*).

For international cuisine of all types, the Rue de Bourgogne is packed with choices.

L'Eldorado, 10 Rue Marcel Belot, Olivet, t 02 38 64 29 74. Inventive cuisine near the Loiret river (*menus 100–230F*).

Rivage, 635 Rue de la Reine Blanche, Olivet, t 02 38 66 02 93. Gastonomic restaurant near the Loiret river (*menus 130–200F*).

Shopping

Besides a tempting array of Joan of Arc tack, you may want to pick up culinary specialities of the Loiret in Orléans: goat's cheese from Olivet, pear liqueur from the Loire valley orchards and a quince jelly sweet, *cotignac*, made at St-Ay.

Orléans was once famous for its vinegar, a tradition which has almost died out, but you can still visit one house:

Martin Pourret vinegar cellar, 236 Faubourg Bannier, Fleury-les-Aubrais, north of Orléans. Produces vinegar in the old-fashioned way. *Open Mon–Fri 8–12 and 2–4.*

The most chic shops in the centre of Orléans are under the arcades of the Rue Royale.

Entertainment and Nightlife

You can pick from a wide choice of films at the UGC, in Place Jeanne d'Arc. There are plenty of bars in and around Place du Martroi.

Caveau des Trois Maries, 2 Rue des Trois Maries. Late-night spot to lounge in (*music eves Wed and Sat*).

Midnight Dreams, 66 Bd de Châteaudun. Cocktails, a billiards room and a laser karaoke show. *Open from 10pm.*

Gardel's Club, 20 Rue André Dessaux, t 02 38 43 56 57, at Saran, a car ride away due north of the city centre. Night club attracting a wide range of ages. *Closed Mon.*

Orléans

To Paris
Gare SNCF
AVENUE DE PARIS
RUE ALBERT 1ER
PLACE GAMBETTA
BOULEVARD DE VERDUN
RUE DU FAUBOURG ST JEAN
BOULEVARD ROCHEPLATTE
RUE GRANDS CHAMPS
RUE BOEUF ST-PATERNE
RUE DU POT DE FER
RUE DE LA BRETONNERIE
Palais de Justice
RUE DE LA BRE
RUE BANNIER
RUE DE VAUQUOIS
RUE DE LA LIONNE
RUE DE LA RÉPUBLIQUE
RUE STE-ANNE
RUE D'ES
RUE DU COLOMBIER
RUE DES
RUE D'ILLIERS
RUE DU GRENIER A SEL
RUE DES MINIMES
PLACE DU MARTROI
BOULEVARD JEAN JAURÈS
RUE PORTE ST-JEAN
PLACE CROIX MORIN
RUE DES CARMES
PLACE CHARLES DE GAULLE
RUE ROYALE
RUE JEANNE D
Musée Archéologique et Historique de l'Orléanai
PLACE DE LA RÉPUBLIQUE
RUE FAUBOURG MADELEINE
Centre Hospitalier
RUE D'ANGLETERRE
RUE DE RECOUVRANCE
RUE DU TABOUR
Maison de Jeanne d'Arc
Centre Charles Péguy
RUE DES TROIS
BOULEVARD JEAN JAURÈS
RUE CROIX DE BOIS
St-Paul
RUE DU CHEVAL ROUGE
RUE DE BOURGOGNE
RUE DU CERCEAU
To Blois and Tours
RUE NOTRE-DAME DE RECOUVRANCE
Notre-Dame de Recouvrance
Place du Vieux Marché
RUE ROYALE
Les Halles-Châtelet
QUAI ST-LAURENT
QUAI BARENTIN
QUAI CYPIERRE
PONT DU MARECHAL
PONT GEORGI
L o i r e

liberation, celebrated on 8 May, came to be seen as pivotal in securing the unity and independence of the nation, although historically it was one of many victories through which the French forces slowly ousted the English.

In 1560 a meeting of the Estates General was assembled in the city in a desperate effort to avoid civil war between the increasingly antagonistic religious factions. To add to the woes, the sickly young king François II died at the Hôtel Groslot. His widow was Mary, Queen of Scots. Orléans served as a shortlived headquarters for Protestants. A Protestant theology college was created at the university where Calvin had studied and Protestants attacked Orléans' churches, blowing up the cathedral. The St Bartholomew's Day massacres of August 1572 effectively silenced them. Once the religious wars had ended, Henri IV had Orléans cathedral rebuilt – an important gesture of reconciliation.

Economically, the mid-17th century to the mid-18th was a time of relative prosperity for Orléans, thriving on trade from the New World, especially the refining of sugar cane. The loss of French Caribbean and Canadian territories led to decline. Orléans' travails continued. Nazi attacks in June 1940 destroyed 17 hectares of the historic centre. Further devastation was wrought by American bombing in May 1943. The town was liberated on 16 August 1944 by US General Patton. In the 1960s Orléans became the administrative capital of the newly created region of the Centre-Val de Loire. A steady stream of business from the capital has been flowing Orléans' way for years and it remains one of the most important Loire-side cities.

Touring Orléans

The **cathedral of Ste-Croix** in the centre of Orléans is inescapable. Proust called it the ugliest church in France, complaining that the tops of its towers resembled a pompous strawberry gâteau. Only the radiating chapels around the choir and a couple of nave bays survived the Protestant destruction. The choir and transepts are 17th century, the rest is largely 18th. On the south transept Louis XIV's notably large conk forms the centrepiece of the rose window. Triumphalist 19th-century windows commemorate Joan of Arc.

By the cathedral stands the postwar **Musée des Beaux-Arts** (*open daily exc Mon 10–12 and 2–6; adm*). Despite its totalitarian sobriety, a riot of excess awaits within. A sculpture by Germain Pilon shows Monseigneur de Morvilliers, one-time bishop of Orléans, in sober reflection as if dejected by the extravagant works from Cardinal de Richelieu's fabulous collection which surround him. On panels by Martin Freminet, the evangelists and fathers of the Church look as vain as bodybuilders. The collections culled from churches and monasteries of the region during the Revolution show the Counter-Reformation led the French Church into a passionate Baroque fling. Other prizes are the *St Thomas* by Velásquez, an excellent Gauguin and the experimental scuptures of Orléans' own Henri Gaudier-Breska.

Opposite, the **Hôtel Groslot** (*open daily 9–6 exc if there's a reception; adm*) preserves its original Mannerist façade at the back of the courtyard. It was built for a high-ranking official called Groslot, under François I. The interior is 19th-century and sumptuously over the top. Close to Rue Jeanne d'Arc and Rue Royale, the Renaissance Hôtel Cabu contains the **Musée Archéologique et Historique de l'Orléanais** (*open Oct–April Wed, Sat and Sun 2–6; May, June and Sept Tues–Sun 2–6; July and Aug Tues–Sun 10–6; adm*), concealing a superb little collection of Gaulish bronzes. The horse, dedicated to the Celtic god Rudiobus, poses majestically on the ground floor and is thought to date from the 2nd century AD. Just west of the Hôtel Cabu is the **Rue Royale**, the poshest shopping street in Orléans. Joan of Arc inevitably triumphs on **Place du Martroi** with an equestrian statue by Foyatier (1855). Close by, on the mishmash of Place Charles de Gaulle, the fake **Maison de Jeanne d'Arc** (*open 2 May–Oct daily exc Mon 10–12 and 2–6; Nov–April daily exc Mon 2–6; adm*) is post-Second World War, and its models and mementoes do little for her memory.

Between Orléans and Blois

On the north bank of the Loire between Orléans and Blois, the little towns of Meung-sur-Loire and Beaugency are delightful havens off the commercially scarred N152. Their protected slopes have a legacy of châteaux often passed over by the hordes heading for Chambord.

The medieval bishops of Orléans kept their out-of-town residence at **Meung** and weren't ones to deprive themselves. The **Château de Meung** (*open Jan–mid-Feb Sat and Sun 10.30–12 and 2.30–4.30; mid-Feb–mid-April and Oct–mid-Nov daily 10–12 and 2–5.30; mid-April–Sept daily 10–6; adm*) has dilapidated charm as well as peeling wall-paper. It also boasts a huge ancient **abbey church**. Along with its trefoil choir end and its flying buttresses, this contains some older Romanesque features and ornate reli-quary boxes. Meung's north bank has a splendid avenue of plane trees and a prim

Getting Around

Meung and Beaugency have useful railway stations. You can also try bus services between Beaugency and Blois, **t** 02 54 58 55 55/**t** 02 38 86 26 21. By road, the south bank D951 is much prettier than the N152 along the north bank.

Tourist Information

St-Dyé-sur-Loire: 75 Rue Nationale, **t** 02 54 81 15 45, **f** 02 54 81 68 07.
Meung-sur-Loire: 42 Rue Jehan de Meung, **t** 02 38 44 32 28, **f** 02 38 44 72 22.
Beaugency: 3 Place de l'Hôtel de Ville, **t** 02 38 44 54 42, **f** 02 38 46 45 31.

Activities

Ride around the Chambord park in a horse and carriage, **t** 02 54 20 31 01.

Take a punt on the Cosson river, **t** 02 54 33 37 54, **f** 02 54 33 37 61 (*15 Mar–10 Nov daily 10–8*).

Le Cheval Roi presents a historical show about the French equestrian tradition (*May–Sept twice a day*). Contact the Ecuries du Maréchal de Saxe, **t** 02 54 20 31 01, **f** 02 54 20 38 52, for bookings.

Where to Stay and Eat

Beaugency ✉ 45190
***Hôtel de l'Abbaye**, 2 Quai de l'Abbaye, **t** 02 38 44 67 35, **f** 02 38 44 87 92 (*moderate*).

Hotel in a superb setting on the Loire. Many of the rooms have views of the river. The 17th-century monastic buildings are vast and the lodgings spacious. Restaurant (*menu 190F*).

Hôtel de la Sologne, 6 Place St-Firmin, **t 02 38 44 50 27, **f** 02 38 44 90 19 (*inexpensive*). Charming little hotel up the slope, surrounded by the town monuments.

Le Relais des Templiers, 68 Rue du Pont, **t 02 38 44 53 78 (*inexpensive*). Another pretty picture of a hotel, with a private garden and terrace.

Tavers ✉ 45190
****La Tonnellerie**, 12 Rue des Eaux-Bleues, **t** 02 38 44 68 15, **f** 02 38 44 10 01 (*expensive*). The most luxurious address in the area, with its many pleasures hidden behind an unassuming village façade.

Chambord ✉ 41250
Hôtel St-Michel, 103 Place St-Michel, **t 02 54 20 31 31, **f** 02 54 20 36 40 (*inexpensive*). In the thick of the tourist hordes during the day, but this hotel has the exclusive privilege of having many of its rooms looking out on to the château.

L'Orée de Chambord, 14 Route de Chambord, **t 02 54 81 42 42, **f** 02 54 81 66 76 (*inexpensive*). A few kilometres northwest at Maslives, a cheap and cheerful hotel-restaurant.

statue of Jean de Meun, principal author of the 13th-century *Roman de la Rose*, a best-seller with the French nobility for centuries. A second French poet has his place in Meung's history or, more precisely, in the prison of the bishops' palace. A notorious 15th-century wastrel, François Villon was admired for the puns and pathos of his poetry. In his mock wills, he left such delights as his hair clippings and egg shells.

South of the Loire, the land is flat as a pancake. From these fertile soils rises the **Basilique de Cléry-St-André**. In 1280 a local farmer supposedly ploughed up a statue of the Virgin and Child and miracles began to happen, hence this disproportionate Gothic church. The main impetus for reconstruction after the Hundred Years' War came from Louis XI, who attributed a difficult victory over the English at Dieppe to an act of intervention by the Virgin of Cléry. In repayment, he became involved in the

building work and elected to be buried there. His first tomb was destroyed by
Protestants and the replacement shows an ascetic king at prayer. Look out for the
secret peephole made for him to follow services undetected.

Cobbled quays, tall plane trees, low waterfront houses and, behind them, soaring
medieval monuments...seen from the south side of its bumpy, patched-up bridge, the
oldest on the Loire, **Beaugency** is one of its most beautiful towns. Two major councils
were held here in medieval times. The first, in 1092, examined the lifting of the
excommunication imposed by the pope on bigamous Philippe I. The second, more
momentous, decided in 1152 on the annulment of Louis VII's marriage to Eleanor of
Aquitaine. Eleanor took back her vast inheritance and promptly married Henri
Plantagenet of Anjou who became Henry II of England in 1154, triggering centuries of
conflict in France. The most imposing evidence of Beaugency's importance is the
massive 11th-century **Tour de César**. **Notre-Dame** next to it is from the same period,
and although badly damaged by fire and restored in 1642, it retains a strong
Romanesque feel, and massive columns with bold capital designs. One represents a
magnificently large nose. West of the disappointing Château Dunois, with the cluttered town museum, the other monumental tower is an impressive remnant of the
church of **St-Firmin**. Fleurs-de-lys are scattered on the Renaissance façade of
Beaugency's town hall. Inside, the eight exquisite embroideries remain a mystery.
Four of them appear to illustrate disturbing scenes of sacrifice.

The Château de Chambord

*Open Jan-Mar and Nov–Dec daily 9–5.15; April–June and
Sept–Oct daily 9–6.15; July and Aug daily 9–6.45; adm.*

Set in its glade, the Château de Chambord, François I's 'hunting lodge', is a truly
glorious and absurd monster. Work began in 1519 but the original architect remains a
mystery. Leonardo da Vinci is tantalizingly linked to the place, but a name more
concretely associated with it is that of Domenico da Cortona, who came to France from
Italy in Charles VIII's train and made models of various constructions for François as
early as 1517. One was of a version of Chambord. The king wasn't afraid of advancing his
own ideas too, so it's possible that he influenced the traditional French features.

Chambord's general forms are actually medieval. The solid round towers at the
corners, with their roofs like great upturned funnels, resemble copybook pictures of a
chivalric castle. But Chambord is obsessively ordered. Even the roof, which seems a
medieval riot, has a logic behind its wild visual fireworks. But why build so magnificently in the middle of a vast forest? The answer is that Chambord was not just a
hunting lodge but also a blatant statement of royal power during a blazing clash of
titanic European leaders. François I came to the throne when the young Henry VIII
ruled England. Soon after, Charles I of Spain outbid them both to become Emperor
Charles V. The three continued to compete with each other in an extravagant game of
power politics.

Chambord, largely complete by 1547, was a building site during François I's reign. It
was the pomp of Louis XIV's court which brought a spark of life to the château;

perhaps only a Sun King could appreciate its scale. He hunted, played, and was amused by Molière who staged the first performances of *Monsieur de Pourceaugnac* and *Le Bourgeois Gentilhomme* here. Louis XV was uninterested in the château and, in an act of dubious generosity, gave the palace to his father-in-law, the exiled king of Poland, Stanislas Leszcinski. After Leszcinski's death Louis XV gave it to the Maréchal de Saxe. This eccentric military man had delusions of grandeur. The Revolution saw most of the interiors stripped of their contents. In 1809 Napoleon donated Chambord to the Maréchal Berthier, for whom the title of Prince of Wagram was created. One of his ambitions was to replace the innumerable F motifs with Ws. Later, Chambord was bought by public subscription for Charles X's heir, Henri, Duc de Bordeaux, who took on the title of Comte de Chambord. With the 1830 revolution, the Orléans family fled and the Comte de Chambord stayed in Austria for 41 years, returning to spend his one and only night here in July 1871. Finally the State bought the property in 1930. It's reckoned that the château was lived in for only 20 years in its entire life.

The guides describe Chambord as one of the first apartment blocks in history and, between its Greek cross arms, hundreds of rooms repeat the same patterns. It has 14 major staircases, 70 lesser ones, and one considered a work of genius in itself, which ascends to the amazing roofs. As most of the interiors stand empty, the bare architecture is the main exhibit.

Blois

Charles VIII bumped his head on a door at the Château d'Amboise and died. Thus, in 1498 his cousin, Louis, count of Blois, became Louis XII and the town of Blois became the centre of French politics.

History

In the early Middle Ages, the powerful counts of Blois had their headquarters here until they also became counts of Champagne and were distracted by that region's riches. In the 12th century Etienne de Blois, a grandson of William the Conqueror, became the disastrous English king, Stephen. At the end of the 14th century the county of Blois was sold to Louis d'Orléans, brother of Charles VI. For several centuries it became the seat of a string of royals all confusingly carrying the title of duc d'Orléans. Louis d'Orléans was assassinated in 1407 and his wife, Valentine Visconti, from Milan, took refuge here. One of her sons was the famous duke Charles d'Orléans, captured by the English at Agincourt in 1415. He was held prisoner in England, and on his return settled back at Blois. His court brought prosperity and culture to the town. When he was nearly 70, Charles' wife bore him a son, Louis, who became Louis XII in 1498, when Charles VIII met his destiny with a door at Amboise. The new king divorced his crippled wife to marry Charles VIII's widow, Anne de Bretagne, as stipulated in the royal marriage contract and Blois became the centre of the royal court. Louis XII wished to claim his inheritance in Milan, via his Visconti grandmother Valentine, and followed the example of Charles VIII's forays into Italy. His daughter, Claude, would marry François d'Angoulême, the future François I.

The divide between the Catholics and the newly established Protestants or Huguenots led to outright civil war in France from 1562. In the meantime, the single-minded extremist Catholic League was asserting its power in Paris. Its leaders, the Duke and the Cardinal de Guise, had amassed enough support to provoke Henri III's desperate response. Forced to flee Paris, the king repaired to Blois. At the 1588 Estates General in Blois, he had the Duke and the Cardinal de Guise murdered in the château. The royal authorities declared an attempt had been made on the king's life and that a note had been found on Henri de Guise showing his collusion with the Spanish enemy. In Paris, the de Guises were accorded an almost saintly status. Henri III got his come-uppance when he was assassinated in Paris the following year. With him, the Valois dynasty, which had ruled France since 1328, came to its bloody end.

For years, the neglected royal château was virtually the only attraction in the town and contained most of Blois' museums. Everything changed in the 1990s, under the direction of the ultra-liberal mayor and minister, Jack Lang.

Touring Blois

The vortex of so much to do, the **Château de Blois** (*open July–Aug daily 9–7.30, Mar–June and Sept daily 9–6, Oct–Mar daily 9–12 and 2–5; adm*) has wings like an architectural game of Misfits, but the clashing styles are not unattractive. Each piece is a magnificent example of its own style. The exuberant late Gothic of the Louis XII brick façade leads into an inner courtyard with an arcaded gallery, significant because of the subtle inclusion of Italian Renaissance motifs in the bravura of late-Gothic detail; note on one stair tower the porcupines associated with Louis XII. The courtyard façade of the François I wing, begun in 1515, is a fusion of Gothic and Renaissance styles, this time decorated with salamanders, François I's emblem. The steep roof and dormers are traditionally French, but the outer façade of arcaded storeys is Italian. On the ground floor of this wing is the new **Musée Lapidaire** where you can admire the detail of the stone masons' decoration. There's also a new **archaeological museum** in the former kitchens.

The restored *apartements* are reached via the great staircase. In the François I wing one of the few authentic remnants are the ornate Renaissance fireplaces. One antechamber is named after Catherine de' Medici. She was forced by the Wars of Religion to stay at the castle with her sons from time to time and died immediately after the assassinations of the de Guises. The private little oratory has a rare painted ceiling. The Cabinet de Travail – the finest room in the wing – has retained its carved wood panelling. The **Salle des Etats Généraux** is the early 13th-century medieval hall squashed between the Louis XII and François I wings, supported on a row of alarmingly slender columns. Blois' **fine arts museum**, with mostly 19th-century paintings, items from the French Renaissance and the courtly crafts of Blois, occupies the first floor of the Louis XII wing. The most interesting room is the **salle des Guises**, with 19th-century works depicting their conflict with Henri III. The **Gaston d'Orléans wing** stands in stark, ordered contrast to the eccentric chaos of the other wings, although there is a great

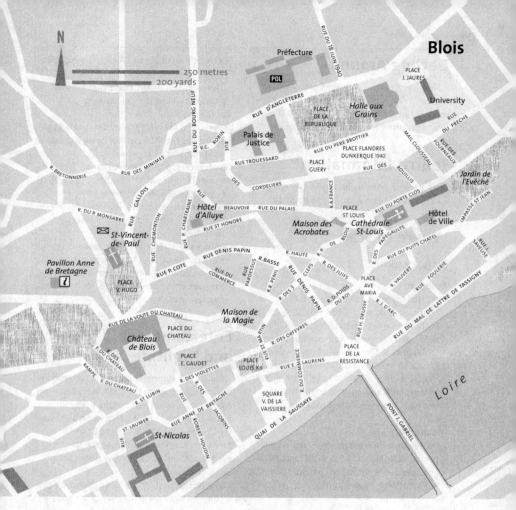

classical playfulness to Mansart's design. Much sillier, the ugly vast head of Gaston (the rogue brother of Louis XIII) – portrayed as some slimy Caesar – gloats above his coat of arms. The lobby has a sensational Baroque oval dome.

At the eastern end of the château's esplanade, dragons spit fire and words from the windows of a magnificent brick-patterned bourgeois house, the unique **Maison de la Magie** (*for opening hours, t 02 54 5 26 26; adm*), inspired by a highly respected Blois-born magician, Jean-Eugène Robert-Houdin. You can sit down in the underground theatre to watch a half-hour live magic show. Other spaces are devoted to the history of magic, techniques and elaborate demonstrations. While on the esplanade, look out for the **Maison du Vin** (11 Place du Château) and the grand stairways which descend into the main shopping quarters.

The massive spiky towers of **St-Nicolas** rise out of the lower town to puncture the Blois skyline. This church combines Romanesque and Gothic, with notes of grandeur inside; among the capitals are a few extremely bawdy carvings. The principal shopping street, the Haussmann-like **Rue Denis Papin**, leads to the main crossing over the

Getting Around

Blois has a central railway station with regular services to Orléans and Tours. Bus services radiate out from Blois around the whole *département* of the Loir-et-Cher.

Tourist Information

Blois: Pavillon Anne de Bretagne, 3 Av Jean Laigret, t 02 54 90 41 41, f 02 54 90 41 49.

Where to Stay

Blois ✉ **41000**

Moderate

***L'Holiday Inn Garden Court, 26 Av Maunoury, **t** 02 54 55 44 88, **f** 02 54 74 57 97. High-standard chain hotel, with a solid reputation and numerous well-equipped rooms.

***Mercure, 28 Quai St-Jean, **t** 02 54 56 66 66, **f** 02 54 56 67 00. You could do much worse than this other big chain hotel, done up with some style, standing close to the château and with some views over the Loire.

Inexpensive

Hôtel Anne de Bretagne, 31 Av Jean Laigret, **t 02 54 78 05 38, **f** 02 54 74 37 79. Only a few hundred metres from the château, with nice but somewhat noisy rooms.

Cheap

*Hôtel du Bellay, 12 Rue des Minimes, **t** 02 54 78 23 62, **f** 02 54 78 52 04. A pleasantly unpretentious little address, in a miniature 18th-century cottage, with bright rooms which are a bargain.

*A la Ville de Tours, 2 Place de la Grève, **t** 02 54 78 07 86, **f** 02 54 56 87 33. A hotel with character and very cheap rooms close to the river and the centre of town.

Eating Out

Au Rendez-Vous des Pêcheurs, 27 Rue du Foix, **t** 02 54 74 67 48, **f** 02 54 74 47 67. Very refined fish and seafood in a small town house close to the river.

L'Orangerie du Château, 1 Av Jean Laigret, **t** 02 54 78 05 36, **f** 02 54 78 22 78. An elegant, upmarket restaurant, occupying a much grander building behind the loggiaed façade of the château.

La Péniche, 3 Avenue Paul Reaulme, **t** 02 54 56 89 65. Has the attraction of being a good restaurant on a barge on the river.

L'Espérance, 189 Quai Ulysse Besnard (west along the river out of town), **t** 02 54 78 09 01, **f** 02 54 56 17 86. Behind the quirky architecture you can try inventive cuisine in the bright, raised dining room overlooking the Loire.

L'Embarcadère, 16 Quai Ulysse Besnard, **t** 02 54 78 31 41, **f** 02 54 74 54 59. A more crowded, lively restaurant, west of town and right by the river, which serves simpler food such as *moules-frites*.

Entertainment and Nightlife

Blois' main summer night-time attraction is the son et lumière at the château, called '*Ainsi Blois vous est conté*' – but mug up on your history beforehand. For information and bookings, **t** 02 54 78 72 76, **f** 02 54 74 82 61. *Shows take place June–first week in Sept virtually every night, and a couple of weekends in May; occasional English night.*

Scène Nationale, La Halle aux Grains, **t** 02 54 56 19 79. Blois' main theatre, dance and music venue.

You can choose from three cinemas in town:

Les Lobis, 12 Av Maunoury.
Les Trois Clefs, 12 Rue des Juifs.
Les Césars, 23 Av Wilson.

There are a couple of good nightclubs outside town.

Le Tango, St-Laurent-Nouan, **t** 02 54 87 57 20, over 20km east along the D951. For a good bop to classic disco stuff. *Open Thurs–Sun.*

Le Charleston, on Route de Nozieux, **t** 02 54 20 61 06, 10km out, again via the D951. With a barbecue and a pool. *Open Thurs–Sun.*

Pub Mancini, 1 Rue du Puits Chatel. For those desperate for a late-night drink in Blois. *Open till 4am.*

Loire, the refined **Pont Jacques V Gabriel**. An Egyptian-style needle, decorated with
cartouches by the great 18th-century sculptor Guillaume Coustou, adds grandeur. On
the north side of the Loire, a steep hillside east of Rue Denis Papin leads to the cathedral quarter. Here stand many of Blois' most atmospheric old residential streets,
where intimate courtyards have picturesque wells, stairtowers, galleries and Gothic
sculptures. Even the odd royalist symbol has survived the Revolution. The **Maison des
Acrobates** at the top of Rue Pierre de Blois is the most appealing of all Loire town
houses, covered with wooden beams carved with figures of jesters. The **cathedral**
façade is mostly 16th-century – a survivor of the freak weather that later destroyed
the rest of the edifice. The great bell tower is the old town's eastern landmark.

The **Musée de l'Objet** (*open Sept–May Sat and Sun 2–8, June–Aug daily exc Mon
1.30–6.30; adm*), the other new museum in Blois, is even more bewildering than the
Musée de la Magie. Set in the school of fine arts, it concentrates on, well, everyday
objects, but made into art and offering ironic, absurdist, or conceptual comments on
contemporary life.

Châteaux South of Blois

A whole clutch of châteaux hide in the woods south of Blois. The immaculate
Cheverny may be the best-known, but the others are worth seeking out if you want to
avoid the crowds.

The **Château de Beauregard** (*open Feb, Mar, Oct, Nov, 20 Dec–5 Jan daily exc Wed
9.30–12 and 2–5; April–June and Sept daily 9.30–12 and 2–6.30; July and Aug daily
9.30–6.30; adm*) hides down a wooded alley off the busy D765. The château is dull on
the outside, in part because it's covered with dull roughcast, in part because it dates
from the second French Renaissance. Its sober exterior, however, hides a 17th-century
Galerie des Illustres offering a lesson in history and fashion. The paintings may be
second-rate but 327 personalities feature, from the reign of the first Valois to Louis
XIII. The gallery is unique along the Loire, but not in France, for they were something
of a vogue at the time. A handful of other rooms present other extraordinary items,
notably the gilded Cabinet des Grelots. The re-creation of the Renaissance Jardin des
Portraits is a further attraction.

The 17th-century **Château de Cheverny** (*open Jan–Feb and Nov–Dec daily 9.30–12 and
2.15–5; May and Oct daily 9.30–12 and 2.15–5.30; April–June and Sept daily 9.15–6.15; July
and Aug daily 9.15–6.45; adm*) is the most refined Loire château of all, designed by
Jacques Bougier for a governor of Blois, Henri Hurault – for whom all vestiges of the
previous château on the site were wiped out. A generous lawn leads to the immaculate front which is so white and clean and seamless that many mistake it for
whitewashed clapboard. The building is only one room deep and pleasingly symmetrical. A pediment tops each window like a stylized eyebrow. On the first floor, busts of
12 Roman emperors cross the façade. Cheverny isn't vast but it is sumptuously
furnished and has the finest collection of paintings of any Loire chateaux, with its allegorical wall paintings by Jean Mosnier, three portraits of Hurault family members by
the great court painter Clouet, a portrait of Jeanne d'Aragon attributed to Raphael, a

Getting Around

Check in Blois for local bus services and excursions around the region.

Tourist Information

Cour-Cheverny: 12 Rue du Chéne des Darpes, t 02 54 79 95 63, f 02 54 79 23 90.

Where to Stay and Eat

Bracieux ✉ 41250

Bernard Robin/Le Relais de Bracieux, 1 Av de Chambord, t 02 54 46 41 22, f 02 54 46 03 69. The best-known name in the restaurant business in this area, named after its illustrious chef. From the roadside it looks deceptively normal, but all changes within (*menus 250–650F*).

Cheverny and Cour-Cheverny ✉ 41700

***Château du Breuil, Route de Fougéres-sur-Biévre, outside Cheverny, t 02 54 44 20 20, f 02 54 44 30 40 (*moderate*). The driveway through the densely wooded park puts you into a dreamlike state. This is a wonderful refuge, but there's no restaurant.

**Hôtel des Trois Marchands, Place de l'Eglise, t 02 54 79 96 44, f 02 54 79 25 60 (*inexpensive*). A bit of a tourist institution, with standard rooms and naff paintings, but also a large, comfortable dining room where reliably good meals are served up.

**St-Hubert, Rue Nationale, t 02 54 79 96 60, f 02 54 79 21 17 (*inexpensive*). Good hotel on a smaller, family scale.

Contres ✉ 41700

***Château de la Gondelaine, t 02 54 79 09 14, f 02 54 79 64 92 (*expensive–moderate*). A stylish 17th-century hunting lodge offering good rooms and inventive cuisine, and falconry training if you so desire.

***Hôtel de France, 37 Rue Pierre-Henri Mauger, t 02 54 79 50 14, f 02 54 79 02 95. Practical rooms with modern comforts in a typical local building.

La Botte d'Asperges, 52 Rue Pierre-Henri Mauger, t 02 54 79 50 49, f 02 54 79 08 74. Rustic regional cuisine.

Titian depicting the young Cosimo de' Medici and a tapestry cycle illustrating the Labours of Hercules.

A chip off the old block of Chambord is how the little **Château de Villesavin** (*open Feb–May daily 10–12 and 2–7; June –Sept daily 10–7; Oct–15 Nov daily 10–12 and 2–6; 16 Nov–Dec weekends and hols 10–12 and 2–6; adm*) is frequently described. It was built for Jean Le Breton, trusted friend of François I, who oversaw some of Chambord's construction and made use of its workmen to help build his relatively modest shack. The pyramidal-topped pavilions, the Renaissance fountain, and the exquisite dormer windows are its highlights. The tour inside is short but sweet and allows you to see the very worn but evocative Italianate wall paintings in the tiny chapel.

The **Château de Fougères-sur-Bièvre** (*open April–Sept daily 9.30–12 and 2–6; Oct–Mar daily exc Tues 10–12 and 2–4.30; adm*), southwest of Cour-Cheverny, is uncharacteristic of this region where châteaux are usually constructed of clean-cut white stone. Fougères looks pleasingly medieval, with its massed towers, small irregular stones and inner courtyard enclosed on all four sides. Despite the stern exterior, it was built in the last quarter of the 15th century and Renaissance influences are evident. Many rooms stand empty but the attics have fine rafters to admire and displays of château-building trades.

The Cher Valley from Selles to Chenonceaux

The Cher flows through the Berry to join the Loire near Tours and is celebrated for being spanned by arguably the most beautiful bridge in the world, the Château de Chenonceaux. The quiet, fertile, flat valley also has further châteaux, falconry and wines to offer.

'Shit in a silk stocking' is how Napoleon memorably described his brilliant minister Talleyrand, whom he allowed to abide in the splendid **Château de Valençay** (*open daily 9–12 and 2–6, or nightfall for the grounds; adm*), due south of Selles. The façades are 16th-century, and typical of the Loire Valley, mixing late-Gothic and French Renaissance forms. The guided tour focuses on Talleyrand, who married Catherine Worlée whose portrait by Le Brun shows her famous beauty. Her stupidity was as great as her looks. She was said to have *'pas plus d'esprit qu'une rose* (no more intellect than a rose)' and was easily supplanted in her husband's affections by the wife of his nephew, a driven, intelligent woman, who eventually came to reign with him at Valençay. The grounds are populated with a whole menagerie of animals and vintage cars.

The **Château de Bouges** (*open July and Aug daily 10–1 and 2–7; June daily exc Tues 10–12 and 2–7; April, May, June and Sept daily exc Tues 10–12 and 2–6; Mar and Nov weekends only 10–12 and 2–5; adm*) is a jewel box of a little château, similar to the Petit Trianon. It was built in 1762 for Count Charles Le Blanc de Marnaval, an owner of ironworks, and is furnished with the accoutrements of 18th- and 19th-century noble life: a man's dressing table for powdering his wig; a *voyeuse* chair for women in vast crinolines to watch the society games; a library ladder which converts into a leather-covered stool; and a 19th-century *fermage* – a farmer's table with a turning drawer to avoid the vulgarity of handling money.

The soaring tower of **St-Aignan** is a 19th-century addition to a large Romanesque church. Inside, the restorers have operated to give it an almost hospital-like white-ness. The dark, dank lower church contains fine vestiges of Romanesque wall paintings and capitals. The most original image is of St Gilles, who prays powerfully enough to save a ship from being wrecked. In the middle of the Cher, the **I'lle aux Trois Evêques** marks where the boundaries of the diocese of the Berry, the Orléanais and Touraine met. You can take a boat trip on the river or hire canoes and pedalos. The island is also the site of the town's **Maison du Vin**.

Not only the most glamorous Loire châteaux, the **Château de Chenonceaux** (*open mid-Mar–mid-Sept daily 9–7; rest of Sept daily 9–6.30; early Mar and first half of Oct daily 9–6; rest of Oct and mid–end Feb daily 9–5.30; first half Feb and Nov daily 9–5; mid-Nov–Jan daily 9–4.30; adm*) is the most visited in France after Versailles. One façade romantically fills the view at the end of an alley of vast plane trees as you arrive. There are two distinct parts to the château: this first square block with its splendid windows and corner turrets is the earlier of the two. It was built between 1515 and 1521 for Thomas Bohier, an inspector of finances for Louis XII and François I. While Bohier accompanied François on his expeditions, his wife Katherine oversaw the building. The initials TB and TK are evident in numerous locations. On the eastern

Getting Around

A railway line runs along the Cher Valley from Vierzon, with stations at Villefranche-sur-Cher, Gièvres, Selles-sur-Cher, St-Aignan, Montrichard and Chenonceaux.

A bus service from Amboise also serves Chenonceaux. For Valençay you need to change at Gièvres.

Buses from Selles-sur-Cher and St-Aignan serve the countryside north towards Blois, t 02 54 58 55 55.

Tourist Information

Valençay: 2 Av de la Résistance, t 02 54 00 04 42.
St-Aignan: 26 Av Wilson, t 02 54 75 22 85, f 02 54 75 20 26.
Montrichard: 1 Rue du Pont, t 02 54 32 05 10, f 02 54 32 28 80.
Chenonceaux: 13 Rue du Château, t 02 47 23 94 45.

Activities

Chenonceaux stages a *son-et-lumière*, t 02 47 23 90 97, for information and bookings.

A boat trip or gourmet cruise on board the *Bélandre* takes you under Chenonceaux's arches. Contact t 02 47 23 98 64, f 02 47 23 81 48, for details.

Where to Stay and Eat

Selles-sur-Cher ✉ 41130
**Hôtel du Lion d'Or, 14 Place de la Paix, t 02 54 97 40 83, f 02 54 97 72 36 (*inexpensive*). Joan of Arc is said to have stayed here. Inside it's quite bright and cheerful. Traditional regional food is served (*menus 85F and 129F*).

Noyers-sur-Cher ✉ 41140
***Clos du Cher, Route de St-Aignan, t 02 54 75 00 03, f 02 54 75 03 79 (*moderate*). On the north bank of the Cher outside St-Aignan, hiding coquettishly in its private park, with luxurious rooms furnished with antiques. The cuisine is stylish too.

side two prows of stone protrude over the river, the first containing the chapel, the second a delightful library. The pillars of the arch under the building have been ingeniously fitted with kitchens, with a little stairway leading down to a platform where boats could dock and unload provisions.

François I's financiers and many of the builders of the Loire's best châteaux were as often implicated in financial scandals as French politicians today. After Bohier's death, he was found guilty of embezzlement and his son was forced to give the château to the crown in 1535. So the profligate François I gained yet another beautiful building and Chenonceaux was reduced to serving the occasional royal hunt. Henri II succeeded François I in 1547 and gave away Chenonceaux as a love token to his mistress Diane de Poitiers. Although Diane had plans for Chenonceaux she rarely came, and Catherine de' Medici had her revenge on the death of her cheating husband in 1559, forcing Diane to give her Chenonceaux in exchange for the Château de Chaumont. Chenonceaux was transformed. Catherine ordered the second wing to be built over the Cher. Its probable architect was Jean Bullant. Dating from the 1570s, it looks soberly classical despite a wonderful rhythm to the bridge galleries.

In the 1560s, Catherine held a few '*triomphes de Chenonceaux*': the courtyards and gardens were decked out with architectural conceits; spectacular entertainments were laid on; one fountain spouted claret. The seductive powers of Catherine's

St-Aignan ✉ 41110

★★Grand Hôtel St-Aignan, 7-9 Quai J-J Delorme, **t** 02 54 75 18 04, **f** 02 54 75 12 59 (*inexpensive*). The archetypal, traditional old-fashioned French hotel, with large windows looking on to the banks of the Cher.

Hôtel-Restaurant du Moulin, 7 Rue de Novilliers, **t** 02 54 75 15 54 (*cheap*). Miniature hotel right by the river.

Chissay ✉ 41400 and La Ménaudière ✉ 41401

★★★Château de Chissay, **t** 02 54 32 32 01, **f** 02 54 32 43 80 (*moderate*). Stands out proudly pure and white among the woods above the valley road. The building has been mutilated in places for visitors' comfort and commercial expansion, but it has many attractions within. In the superb dining room you're served imaginative avant-garde cuisine on curiously shaped plates.

★★★Château de la Ménaudière, **t** 02 54 71 23 45, **f** 02 54 71 34 58 (*moderate*). Another quite luxurious option in the area. The 16th-century château's rooms are spacious and stylish, the setting peaceful, and the restaurant is of a high quality.

Chenonceaux ✉ 37150

★★★Bon Laboureur, 6 Rue du Dr Bretonneau, **t** 02 47 23 90 02, **f** 02 47 23 82 01 (*moderate*). The closest hotel to the château, a bulging, ivy-clad village inn which has pleasant rooms decked out with modern furniture.

★★La Renaudière, 24 Rue du Dr Bretonneau, **t** 02 47 23 90 04, **f** 02 47 23 90 51 (*inexpensive*). A chic brick façade and a pretty garden. 'Olde' recipes feature.

★★Hostel du Roy, 9 Rue du Dr Bretonneau, **t** 02 47 23 90 17, **f** 02 47 23 89 81 (*inexpensive*). A little turret marks the façade, and the rustic touch has been laid on a bit heavy-handedly, but the food is country-copious.

Civray de Touraine ✉ 37150

★★Hostellerie du Château de l'Isle, 1 Rue de l'Ecluse, **t** 02 47 23 863 60, **f** 02 47 23 63 62 (*inexpensive*). Away from Chenonceaux's bustle, this 18th-century home lies in private grounds which go down to the Cher. The cuisine is well prepared.

escadron volant, a 'flying squadron' of beautiful and intelligent aristocratic young women, entrapped leading nobles of the realm; the better to spy on them for the queen mother. François II's brother and successor, the flamboyant Henri III, had a devoted wife, Louise de Lorraine, and it was to her that Catherine left Chenonceaux. After her death, it was pretty well neglected for a century and more. Altered by restoration work, but spared revolutionary destruction, the château has been owned by the Menier chocolate family since 1913. During the Second World War, the Cher was the frontier between German-occupied France and Vichy France and the château gallery bridge is said to have been used by the Resistance.

On sunny days, the sparkling light reflecting off the Cher jumps around the rooms. Visitors are greeted by a surprising Mannerist conceit, an eccentric broken vault ceiling. The chapel retains its graffiti from the Scots guards who served the royal family (it was a captain of the Scots guard, Gabriel Montgomery, who accidentally killed Henri II in a jousting tournament). The room named Diane's bedroom has an extraordinary decorated fireplace by Jean Goujon, flanked by caryatids. Further rooms are extremely elegantly furnished. The gallery over the Cher, despite its magical light, would need an extravagant ball to bring it to life. The outbuildings contain a **waxworks museum** and a **tea-house**.

The Loire Valley from Blois to Tours

After passing the Château de Chaumont, standing so proudly above the Loire, we enter Touraine. Amboise is a great little town, once a centre of French royal life and the place where Leonardo da Vinci spent his last years.

Roads stick tightly to both banks of the Loire between Blois and Tours, giving wonderful views of its sandbanks and islands. From the north bank you can see the dramatically situated **Château de Chaumont-sur-Loire** (*open 15 Mar–Oct daily 9.30–6; Nov–14 Mar daily 10–4.30; adm*). It still has a strongly chivalric air, even though construction began at the start of the 1470s after the previous castle had been razed on Louis XI's orders as punishment for Pierre d'Amboise's part in a rebellion. He was subsequently pardoned, however, and had the north and west wings built before his death in 1473. His grandson Charles II d'Amboise inherited in 1481, but was so busy advancing his career abroad that it was only at the end of the century that the château was completed. On the imposing entrance towers, the Cs refer to Charles d'Amboise, and the Ds to Diane de Poitiers, who was forced to exchange Chenonceaux for Chaumont by Catherine de' Medici (*see above*). Catherine had

Getting Around

There are railway stations at Amboise and Montlouis.

Tourist Information

Chaumont-sur-Loire: 28 Rue du Maréchal Leclerc, t 02 54 20 91 73, f 02 54 20 90 34.
Vouvray: t 02 47 52 70 48, f 02 47 52 67 76.
Montlouis-sur-Loire: Place de la Mairie, t 02 47 45 00 16, f 02 47 45 10 87.

Activities

The excellent, often eccentric summer **Festival International des Jardins** takes place in the park of the Château de Chaumont-sur-Loire, t 02 54 20 99 22 (*2 June–21 Oct daily 9.30am–10pm; adm*).

Where to Stay and Eat

Chaumont-sur-Loire ✉ 41150
La Chancelière, 1 Rue de Bellevue, t 02 54 20 96 95, f 02 54 33 91 71. Restaurant tucked under the Loire cliffside, which serves refined cuisine in its two cosy dining rooms.

Noizay ✉ 37210
★★★★**Château de Noizay,** t 02 47 52 11 01, f 02 47 52 04 64 (*expensive*). This splendid little historic castle is a particular delight, set in a little village which boasts not one but two châteaux and strong connections with the great French 20th-century composer Poulenc. The chef cooks up memorable dishes (*menus 155–360F*).

Vouvray ✉ 37210
La Cave Martin. A wonderful Vouvray vineyard setting in which to enjoy simple menus on a summer evening.

Rochecorbon ✉ 37210
★★★★**Domaine des Hautes Roches,** 86 Quai de la Loire, t 02 47 52 88 88, f 02 47 52 81 30, hautesroches@relaischateaux.fr (*expensive*). This is a fabulous hotel which has some of the most extraordinary rooms you are likely to find along the Loire, luxuriously created out of troglodyte hillside caves. The dining room and salons are in the neat square-angled 18th-century pavilion alongside (*menus 165–370F*).
L'Oubliette, 34 Rue des Clouets, t 02 47 52 50 49. A regional restaurant with the great attraction of being set in a cave.

acquired this lucrative château in 1550 but rarely stayed. Legend has it that one of the famous astrologers of the day, either Ruggieri or Nostradamus, predicted a horrifying vision of the future at Chaumont, foretelling the untimely death of Catherine's husband and sons, and the downfall of the Valois dynasty. However, at the start of the 19th century wealthy new owners came to the rescue of the dilapidated château. Underfloor heating was added along with the collection of fine art pillaged from a pot-pourri of places. Visit, too, the extravagant 19th-century stables.

Amboise

French towns don't come more royal than Amboise. Its château was an important residence for a string of monarchs and remains in would-be royal hands today. A row of riverside houses crouches under its massive ramparts and, even though a large proportion of the vast complex has disappeared, it still makes a fine impression, flags flying from the battlements.

The **Château d'Amboise** was forfeited to the French crown in 1431 because of Louis d'Amboise's disloyal behaviour. Charles VII – the first royal proprietor of the castle – showed little interest in the place, but his son Louis XI and his family spent much time here. In 1469 Louis retired to Amboise to work out the terms of peace after his humiliating defeat by Burgundy. He then established the knightly order of St-Michel to support the French crown through flattery and favour. The château was a place of safety for Louis XI's wife to bring up the future Charles VIII, born here in 1470.

When Charles VIII acceded to the throne, the Château d'Amboise became *the* favoured royal residence and he ordered most of the building work above the massive ramparts, financed by raising a special levy on the salt tax, the *gabelle*. Work began in 1492. The two enormous towers above the riverside were extraordinary entrances, with wide spiralling ramps leading up from the valley to the plateau. The jewel box Chapelle St-Hubert is a glorious work of late Gothic but his main legacy is the wing over the Loire, on which he lavished magnificent furnishings and tapestries, with Joan of Arc's suit of armour and Lancelot's supposed sword holding pride of place. After his forays in Italy, he picked up much stolen booty and a taste for the Renaissance. Among the 20 or so Italians who came back with him were architects, a scholar of Greek, a sculptor, a gardener, and a Moor to pamper his parrots. After all the care that had been taken to protect him as a young man, and after his foolhardy Italian campaigns, Charles bumped his head in a dirty passageway where '*tout le monde pissait*', collapsed and died. Louis d'Orléans took the crown and Charles VIII's widow and moved to Blois.

However, the Château d'Amboise wasn't neglected. The Louis XII-François I wing was built for Louise de Savoie, who was brought up here and in 1488 married Charles d'Angoulême of the Orléans royal branch. He died in 1496. As Louis XII had no male heir, Louise's eldest son François d'Angoulême became king. In October 1534 François I was staying in his childhood home and woke to find a pamphlet stuck to his door. It contained a stinging attack on the meaning of the Catholic Mass. This irreverent

Affaire des Placards drove him into action against the Protestants and the persecution of the French Huguenots began.

With vast new châteaux at Chambord and Fontainebleau, the king neglected
Amboise more and more. So too did his successor, Henri II, but once again royal
children (he and Catherine de' Medici had ten of them) were sent here to be brought
up. In 1548 the six-year-old Mary Stuart had arrived from Scotland, her hand promised
to the future king of France. The beautiful governess, Diane de Poitiers, set Henri II
alight and their son, Henri d'Angoulême, joined the other royal children at Amboise.
But the troubles with the Protestants were growing, as was their persecution. By the
end of Henry II's rule France was ready to slide into civil war.

The bloody precursor occurred in and around Amboise. In 1558 the dauphin François
married Mary, Queen of Scots and a year later became François II. There were many
Protestant sympathizers in high places, the most powerful being the Bourbons of
royal blood, Antoine, King of Navarre, and his brother Louis, Prince de Condé. They
were outraged at the power Mary's Catholic uncles, the de Guises, were acquiring at
court. On their side stood Gaspard de Coligny, admiral of France and nephew of the
great constable Anne de Montmorency. In 1559 a plot was hatched by Condé to
capture the de Guises from the king's court. The Amboise Conspiracy is France's foreshadowing of England's Gunpowder Plot – but in reverse. In this case, Huguenots
plotted to overthrow the controlling ultra-Catholics with, it is said, the support of
Protestant England. Early in 1560 the court fled from Amboise. A Protestant defector
had revealed that an attack had been set for 15 March and many of the conspirators

Getting Around

Amboise has its own railway station.

Tourist Information

Amboise: Quai du Gén de Gaulle, t 02 47 57 09
28, f 02 47 57 14 35.

Where to Stay and Eat

Amboise ✉ 37400
****Le Choiseul, 36 Quai Charles Guinot,
t 02 47 30 45 45, f 02 47 30 46 10 (*expensive*).
Looks relatively modest for an exclusive
Relais et Châteaux hotel, but it's packed
with interesting features, including superb
former grain stores dug into the limestone
rock, the so-called **Greniers de César**, a site
in themselves. The restaurant is very highly
regarded.
****Château de Pray, t 02 47 57 23 67, f 02 47
57 32 50 (*expensive*). Just west of Amboise,

with a delightful mix of architectural styles,
very comfortable rooms and a splendid
dining room. The gardens are wonderful,
with terraces dominating the Loire.
**Hôtel du Lion d'Or, 17 Quai Charles Guinot,
t 02 47 57 00 23, f 02 47 23 22 49 (*inexpensive*). Back at the busy riverside road by the
Loire, a simpler, well-placed options.
***Belle Vue, 12 Quai Charles Guinot, t 02 47
57 02 26, f 02 47 30 51 23. Similar to the
above.
Manoir St-Thomas, 1 Mail St-Thomas, t 02 47 57
22 52, f 02 47 30 44 71. Renaissance manor
providing a fine setting for a highly regarded
restaurant.
L'Epicerie, 18 Rue Victor Hugo, t 02 47 57
08 94. Close to the intimidating ramp up
one side of the château, set in a lovely
timberframe house, it serves classic, reliably
good and relatively good-value dishes.
La Closerie, 2 Rue Paul-Louis Courier, t 02 47 23
10 76. Diminutive restaurant in a quiet little
setting for more traditional cooking.

were gathered at the Château de Noizay close to Amboise. That little château was duly surrounded and many of the conspirators captured, and the next day a failed attack was launched on Amboise by the couple of hundred remaining rebels. The king's response was to name François de Guise lieutenant-general of France and commission the conspirators' punishment. Some were tied up in sacks and thrown into the river, others were hung from the château's battlements overlooking the Loire. The scene was set for France's Wars of Religion. After this massacre, the Château d'Amboise was more or less abandoned by royalty. In Napoleonic times, most of it was dismantled. In 1821 the future king Louis-Philippe regained possession and work was carried out to turn it into a royal summer residence.

The château has been improved in recent years. Some interiors have been beautifully restored and embellished: the palm vaulting of the Salle des Gardes Nobles; the flooring in the Salle des Tambourineurs stamped with fleurs-de-lys; the superb council chamber with its vaulted bays. In the Louise de Savoie wing there is excellent 16th-century furniture but the style changes completely in the Louis-Philippe rooms. Rich red walls and drapery serve as the backdrop to elegant Restoration furniture and royal family portraits.

The **town of Amboise** grew fat and happy at the château's feet. It supplied the court with its vast needs and picked up the crumbs from its table. On the Quai du Général de Gaulle is the Max Ernst fountain, a comical piece by the surrealist who became a French citizen in 1958. Leonardo da Vinci's last home, the **Clos Lucé** (*adm*), was in Amboise and commercialization here is rampant now. Before experiencing Leonardo the Arms Maker, you're treated to Leonardo the Aphorist; Leonardo the Artist is present only in cheap copies. Outside Amboise, the **Pagode de Chanteloup** (*adm*) is the charming, slightly comical remnant of the great 18th-century Château de Chanteloup. The pagoda's seven decreasing circles end with a clownish hat of lead topped by a golden ball. The most popular attraction between Amboise and Tours is the **Aquarium de Touraine**. It looks like a modern conference centre, but within you can see all the fish you can eat along the Loire, only still alive.

Tours

Tours, a luminous, vibrant university city, is a break from châteaux. Its heart is divided in two by the north-south Rue Nationale. On the west side lies the frantically pumping Place Plumereau and the pedestrian streets around it, as well as the Quartier St-Martin. On the eastern side is the quieter cathedral district.

History

Tours has not just a major Gallo-Roman history, but also a very significant early-Christian one. Gatien is the first recorded bishop, at work before the Roman Emperor Constantine came to power. The most important bishop of Tours was a Hungarian who started his career as a Roman legion. Coming across a beggar in Amiens, he was apparently so moved by pity that he gave half his cloak to the suffering man. The

Tours

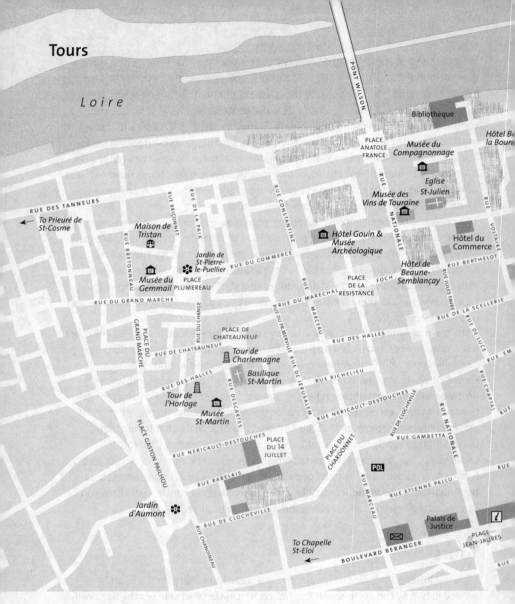

Loire

Bibliothèque

Hôtel B...
la Bour...

PLACE
ANATOLE
FRANCE

Musée du
Compagnonnage

Eglise
St-Julien

RUE DES TANNEURS

← To Prieuré de
St-Cosme

RUE BRICONNET

RUE DE LA PAIX

RUE CONSTANTINE

RUE NATIONALE

Musée des
Vins de Touraine

RUE VOLTAIRE

Maison de
Tristan

Hôtel Gouin &
Musée
Archéologique

Hôtel du
Commerce

RUE BRETONNEAU

Jardin de
St-Pierre-
le-Puellier

RUE DU COMMERCE

RUE BERTHELOT

Hôtel de
Beaune-
Semblançay

Musée du
Gemmail

PLACE
PLUMEREAU

PLACE
DE LA
RESISTANCE

FOCH

RUE JULES FAVRE

RUE DU GRAND MARCHE

RUE DU MARECHAL

RUE MARCEAU

RUE DE LA SCELLERIE

RUE DU CHANGE

PLACE DE
CHATEAUNEUF

RUE DU PR MERVILLE

RUE DE JÉRUSALEM

RUE DES HALLES

RUE DE LUCE

RUE EM...

PLACE DU
GRAND MARCHE

RUE DE CHATEAUNEUF

Tour de
Charlemagne

RUE RICHELIEU

RUE CHAPTAL

RUE EM...

RUE DES HALLES

Basilique
St-Martin

RUE NERICAULT-DESTOUCHES

RUE DE CLOCHEVILLE

RUE NATIONALE

RUE...

Tour de
l'Horloge

RUE DESCARTES

Musée
St-Martin

RUE NERICAULT-DESTOUCHES

PLACE
DU 14
JUILLET

PLACE GASTON PAILHOU

RUE RABELAIS

PLACE DU
CHARDONNET

RUE GAMBETTA

POL

RUE ETIENNE PALLU

RUE...

Jardin
d'Aumont

RUE DE CLOCHEVILLE

RUE CHANONEAU

RUE MARCEAU

Palais de
Justice

PLACE
JEAN-JAURES

i

To Chapelle
St-Eloi
←

BOULEVARD BERANGER

RUE...

night after, Martin had a vision of Christ dressed in the other half. He was duly
converted, and with Hilary, bishop of Poitiers, he created the first monastery in France,
at Ligugé in 360. He then travelled to Tours and founded a second monastery,
Marmoutier. He was made bishop around 371, and is considered one of the great
evangelizers of France. On his death, St Martin's cult spread from Tours. Miracles were
claimed and his tomb was moved to a specially designed chapel. Clovis, king of the
Franks, stopped at St Martin's shrine in 496 and vowed to convert to Christianity if he
defeated the Alamanni. He went on to be baptized at Reims. Among the pilgrims to
Tours was Gregory, a noble from the Auvergne, who stayed and became bishop in 573.

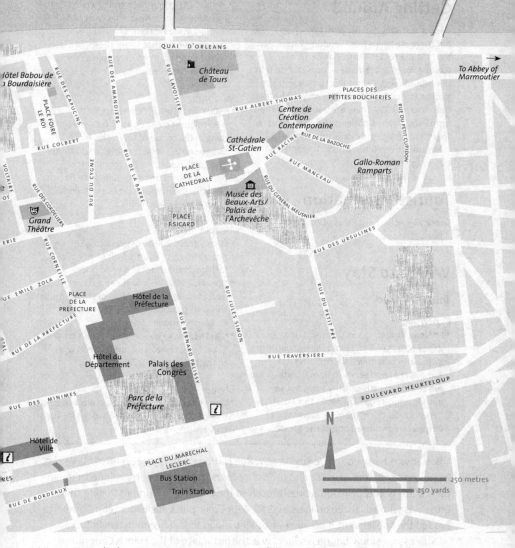

To Abbey of Marmoutier

His great work, the *Historia Francorum*, is one of the most important texts of the Dark Ages, crammed with the events, superstitions and biases of the period. The great Carolingian scholar Alcuin of York was named abbot in Tours in 796. He founded a brilliant school here and Tours became one of the intellectual centres of the West.

The counts of Anjou overran Touraine and controlled it by 1044. As part of the Plantagenet empire, it later fell to the French early in the 13th century. The paranoid Louis XI choose Tours as his capital after the Hundred Years' War ended in 1453. Trade and culture flourished, and even after Charles VIII moved to Amboise the city continued to enjoy great prosperity and administrative and trading importance.

Getting Around

Tours has a regional airport, t 02 47 49 37 00, but there are trains from London-Waterloo to Tours-St-Pierre-des-Corps via Lille (4hrs 15mins). Tours-St-Pierre-des-Corps station is in the suburbs, just a short link to the central station. Paris-Montparnasse is only 1hr by train from Tours by TGV. There are also direct trains from Paris' Roissy-Charles de Gaulle airport to Tours, avoiding central Paris (1hr 40mins).

For buses from Tours around Touraine, call t 02 47 47 17 18.

Tourist Information

Tours: 78 Rue Bernard Palissy, t 02 47 70 37 37, f 02 47 61 14 22.

Where to Stay

Tours ✉ 37000

Expensive

****Jean Bardet, 57 Rue Groison, t 02 47 41 41 11, f 02 47 51 68 72, bardet@relaischateaux .fr (luxury–expensive). Named after its famous chef and set in an immaculate white-stoned 19th-century town house with lovingly tended gardens, this hotel has luxurious-to-chichi rooms and what has long been considered one of the greatest restaurants in France (menus 250–850F). The cuisine is superlative, but recently the restaurant was rocked by scandal when it was discovered that some guests had been served ordinary plonk disguised as something supposedly better.

Moderate

***Clarion Hôtel de l'Univers, 5 Bd Heurteloup, t 02 47 05 37 12, f 02 47 61 51 80. Bang in the centre of town, this big Belle Epoque hotel was where the famous automatically used to stay in Tours, as the portrait gallery on the ground floor flaunts. Churchill counted among the number to grace one of its 85 rooms.

Inexpensive

**Du Cygne, 6 Rue du Cygne, t 02 47 66 66 41, f 02 47 66 05 13. Rooms with plenty of old-fashioned character at a good price.

**Balzac, 47 Rue de la Scellerie, t 02 47 05 40 87, f 02 47 05 67 93. Most of the rooms in this well-positioned hotel come with ensuite bathroom.

**Du Théâtre, 57 Rue de la Scellerie, t 02 47 05 31 29, f 02 47 61 20 78. Simpler hotel with character, in an older Tours house.

Cheap

*Mon Hôtel, 40 Rue de la Préfecture, t 02 47 05 67 53, f 02 47 05 21 88. Well situated for such bargain prices.

Balzac was born along Rue Royale, now Rue Nationale, in 1799. Several of his works, including Le Lys dans la vallée and Le Curé de Tours, expose the petty-minded shenanigans of his hometown. Tours briefly received the French government fleeing the Prussians who advanced on Paris in 1870. With Gallic pluck, its leader Léon Gambetta evaded the subsequent blockade by hot-air balloon to join his ministers in Tours .

Rather surprisingly, bourgeois Tours was the birthplace of the French Communist party in 1920. The Second World War brought terrible devastation to the old city – particularly its riverside quarters – but Tours was one of the first towns in France to benefit from renovation promoted by the Loi Malraux of 1962. The university is massive and attracts large numbers of foreign students. As Le Magazine de la Touraine puts it: Tours is only an hour away from Paris by train and only a month behind its fashions.

Touring Tours

The towers of the **Cathédrale St-Gatien** can be seen from afar, and up close the façade reveals a mass of Flamboyant Gothic detail topped by Renaissance domes.

Eating Out

Jean Bardet, *see above.*

Charles Barrier, 101 Av de la Tranchée, **t** 02 47 54 20 39, **f** 02 47 41 80 95. The next best known chef in Tours after Jean Bardet, who also has an eponymous restaurant.

Les Tuffeaux, 21 Rue Lavoisier, **t** 02 47 47 19 89. Opposite the château, this refined restaurant offers beams and limestone walls as well as warm traditional Touraine cuisine.

La Ciboulette, 25 Rue de la Paix, **t** 02 47 61 57 28. Stands out among the plethora of banal but well-located places to eat around the Place Plumereau, tucked away by the ruins of St-Pierre-le-Puellier, with plenty of charm.

Le Collet Royal, 37 Rue Etienne Marcel, west of the Place Plumereau, **t** 02 47 38 59 87. You'll be well looked after at this diminutive restaurant with such tasty dishes as eel and Vouvray rillettes among the interesting specialities.

Shopping

Tours is good for all kinds of shopping, from clothes to antiques. Among food specialities, the pork rillons are best tasted in a restaurant.

Charcuterie Lebeau, 34 Rue des Halles. The best-known address to buy rillons for a picnic.

Parfums de Beurre, 2 Rue Marceau. The place to buy Touraine goat's cheeses.

Le Calendos, 11 Rue Colbert. Another good fromagerie.

Pâtisserie Sabat, 76 Rue Nationale;

Pâtisserie Poirault, 31 Rue Nationale. Two sumptuous *pâtisseries* which produce old-fashioned *pruneaux fourrés* – harking back to the days when a lot of plums were grown in Touraine – and mountains of mouth-watering chocolate creations.

In mid-Oct there's an antiques festival, the **Jours de l'Antiquité.** Call, **t** 02 47 47 16 72, for more information.

Entertainment and Nightlife

Grand Théâtre, t 02 47 05 33 47. Tours main theatre puts on concerts and other events as well as plays.

Théâtre Louis Jouvet, 12 Rue Léonard de Vinci, **t** 02 47 64 50 50. The main venue for contemporary theatre.

Les Studios, east of the cathedral. A delight for cinema buffs, with an extensive programme of classic and contemporary films in their original versions.

The **Place Plumereau** area is the best for late-night bars.

Inside, the choir contains some truly superb 13th-century stained glass and the beautiful and moving tomb of the two shortlived sons of the ill-fated Anne de Bretagne and Charles VIII.

A triumphal arch by the cathedral leads into the grounds of the former archbishops' palace, now the **Musée des Beaux-Arts** (*open daily exc Tues 9–12.45 and 2–6; adm*), with an impressive collection of paintings, among them Rubens' *Ex-Voto of the Virgin Presenting the Child to the Donor Alexander Goubeau and his wife Anne Antoni* (1615) and the magnificent Mantegna panels, *Christ in the Olive Grove* and *The Resurrection.* Rembrandt is represented by *The Flight into Egypt* – a picture full of dark dread despite the sweet-eyed donkey. The Galerie de Diane houses Houdon's 1776 bronze of *Diana the Huntress.* The most fascinating Tourangeau artist represented here is Abraham Bosse, a 17th-century engraver who depicted all walks of life under the reign of Louis XIII. Balzac stands in thoughtful pose in a study commissioned by his great love, Madame Hanska, and there's a copy of Rodin's famous sculpture of Balzac, bound in a swirl of draped stone.

Rue de la Scellerie has some of Tours' best antiques shops and behind the cathedral hushed streets are watched by the well-buttressed religious buildings. This area was the oppressive setting for Balzac's tale of vicious religious rivalry, *Le Curé de Tours*. The curve of **Rue Meusnier**, with its high walls on either side, breathes the air of a different age. In the Logis du Gouverneur, the history of Tours is treated by the **Atelier Histoire de Tours** (*open mid-Mar–mid-Dec Wed, Sat and Sun 3–6.30*). A lovely pedestrian bridge crosses the river islands to the north bank of the Loire from the broken Château de Tours. The south bank is a good starting point for a walk along the great cobbled quays.

South of the château, **Rue Colbert** is one of Tours' finest streets, with some timber-framed fronts from the 15th and 16th centuries. At one end the church of **St-Julien**, behind the postwar precinct of Rue Nationale, looks grubby and neglected, yet for centuries it was one of Tours' great monasteries; the interior is pure Gothic style. The eccentric, old-fashioned **Musée du Compagnonnage** (*open mid-June–mid-Sept daily 9–12.30 and 2–6; rest of year daily exc Tues 9–12 and 2–6; adm*) is crammed with craftsmen's chef-d'oeuvres.

West of Rue Nationale, modern cafés line the way to the **Hôtel Gouin**. A riot of Renaissance detail has proliferated like brambles over its façade; it now houses the **Musée Archéologique** (*open mid-May–Sept daily 10–7; mid-Mar–mid-May daily 10–12.30 and 2–6.30; other months daily 10–12.30 and 2–5.30, but closed Fri; closed Dec; adm*). **Rue du Commerce** leads into the student quarter, and its bars and restaurants herald the superbly restored timberframe façades of Place Plumereau. The surrounding network of streets is filled with beamed houses. The **Musée du Gemmail** (*open July and Aug daily exc Mon 10–6.30; other months exc Dec daily 10–12 and 2–6.30; adm*), near Place Plumereau, celebrates 20th-century stained glass. The term *gemmail* was coined by Jean Cocteau for the superimposed layers of coloured glass invented by Jean Crotti and inspired by kaleidoscopes. The old religious **Quartier St-Martin** lies south of Place Plumereau. Two enormous towers standing in this prime shopping area offer a clue to the vastness of a Romanesque church that once stood here. The **Musée Martinien** (*open mid-Mar–mid-Nov Wed–Sun 9.30–12.30 and 2–5.30; adm*) occupies the former Chapelle St-Jean on Rue Rapin. Off it lie the beautiful remains of the **cloister of St-Martin**. St Martin's tomb was rediscovered during an archaeological dig in 1860 and gave rise to the **Nouvelle Basilique St-Martin**, a self-important white whale of a building. The crypt contains St Martin's tomb and his cult remains alive and well.

One site worth making a special detour for is the **Prieuré de St-Cosme** (*open June–Sept daily 9–7; mid-Mar–May and Oct daily 9–12.30 and 1.30–6; Feb–mid-Mar and Nov daily 9–12.30 and 1.30–5; adm*) – follow the south bank of the Loire towards La Riche. The Renaissance Pléiade poet Pierre de Ronsard, who wrote some of the most exquisitely lyrical verse in the French language, composed much of his epic *Franciade* here, singing the praises of France. Some of the priory remains date from the late 11th and 12th centuries. The Logis houses a museum in Ronsard's memory, with details on his life and loves. Roses recur time and again in Ronsard's verse, and his tomb lies amid the delightful **rose gardens** of the priory.

South from Tours to Loches

Following the Indre river from south of Tours to medieval Loches avoids the dull N143 and you can potter happily along the Vallée Verte. In its delightful mix of pastures and little woods stand shimmering plantations of poplars. Many villages along the way have a watermill and château.

Loches is named after the little fish which swims in the river and features on the town's coat of arms. A picturesque hill town, it is one of the most important medieval strongholds left in France. The counts of Anjou won Loches through marriage in the 10th century and it became an outpost in their conflict with the counts of Blois. The earliest remaining fortifications date from the 1030s. Royal connections start with Henri Plantagenet of Anjou (Henry II of England) who added ramparts and the enormous ditch. Philippe Auguste eventually wrested Loches back in 1205, after a one-year siege. The Loches fortifications were reinforced by beak-pointed towers, and further fortifications and royal lodgings were added during the 14th, 15th and 16th centuries.

Start the tour at the **Château et Donjon de Loches** (*combined ticket for the two visits. Times stated here are for the château; outside July–mid-Sept add half an hour for the keep closing times. Open July–mid-Sept daily 9–7; mid-Mar–June and mid–end Sept daily 9–12 and 2–6; Oct–Dec and Feb–mid-Mar daily 9–12 and 2–5; closed Jan; adm*). Its stunning keep – reached by an arrow-head barbacane and a drawbridge – is generally considered the finest medieval example in France. Black jackdaws circle the sheer walls and it has now become something of a museum of torture and imprisonment. The Martelet tower with its three levels of cells isn't as grim as might be expected. Its most famous prisoner was a duke of Milan. Known as 'the Moor', Ludovico Sforza was a pragmatic, ruthless and cultured politican who amassed great power in Italy at the end of the 15th century. He defended Naples against the assault of Charles VIII of France, held the most brilliant of courts, and was a patron of Leonardo da Vinci. In 1500, during Louis XII's Italian campaign to claim his inherited rights to Milan, Sforza was captured. He decorated his cells with insignia and inscriptions which can still be deciphered. The regime for such a high-ranking political prisoner wasn't harsh. He was allowed to receive certain guests and kept a servant. Even so the legend has persisted that, after years without daylight, when he was finally taken outside he died from the shock of seeing the sun.

Much play is made of Agnès Sorel at Loches; she of the single bared breast immortalized by the great 15th-century painter, Jean Fouquet. In 1444 she entered the royal court retinue as a lady-in-waiting to Charles VII's queen, Marie d'Anjou. Winning the king's affections, Agnès exercised political as well as emotional power over him. Charles treated her like a princess. She bore him three daughters and shocked many with her extravagant fashions and ways. The future Louis XI detested her, as did the Church, but when she died she was buried in a beautiful tomb in the church of St-Ours. It now rests in the royal lodgings. Joan of Arc, too, came to Loches and spurred on Charles VII to brave English-occupied territory. Anne de Bretagne, the pious wife of two French kings, Charles VIII and Louis XII, has a well-preserved oratory

Getting Around

The rail service between Tours and Châteauroux stops at Loches and other smaller stations along the Indre valley.

From Loches there are bus services into southern Touraine, t 02 47 47 17 18.

Tourist Information

Loches: Place de la Marne, t 02 47 91 82 82, f 02 47 91 61 50.

Montrésor: t 02 47 91 43 07, f 02 47 92 71 11.

Le Grand-Pressigny: Rue du Collège, t 02 47 94 96 82, f 02 47 94 96 82.

Where to Stay and Eat

Montbazon ✉ 37250

★★★★Château d'Artigny, Route de Monts, along the D17, t 02 47 34 30 30, f 02 47 34 30 39 (*expensive*). Standing above the Indre due south of Tours, this sumptuous, over-the-top château looks the image of an elegant French château of the Ancien Régime, although it was actually built at the start of the 20th century. The rooms, divided between the château and a number of outbuildings, have been immaculately to outrageously decorated.

La Chancelière, 1 Place des Marronniers, t 02 47 26 00 67, f 02 47 73 14 82. Tiny restaurant with one of the best reputations for cuisine in Touraine.

Le Jeu de Cartes. The sister establishment offering excellent simpler, cheaper dishes.

Loches ✉ 37600

★★★Hôtel George Sand, 37 Rue Quintefol, t 02 47 59 39 74, f 02 47 91 55 75 (*moderate*). In a house sandwiched between the river Indre and a narrow busy street, this hotel was once used by ground-breaking novelist George Sand as stables. It has been converted by the Fortins into an extremely attractive, well-kept hotel and is a lovely place for summer lunch, with its terrace overhanging the Indre river.

★★Hôtel de France, 6 Rue Picois, t 02 47 59 00 32, f 02 47 59 28 66 (*inexpensive*). Another hotel in a smart old town house, this one with a flowery inner garden, some rooms with views on to the medieval city and good food too.

Le Petit Pressigny ✉ 37350

La Promenade, t 02 47 94 93 52, f 02 47 91 06 03. Reason in itself for many

in Loches' royal lodgings. The one masterpiece among the paintings in the château is a superb late 15th-century triptych, perhaps by Bourdichon.

Montrésor exudes charm, the **Château de Montrésor** (*open April–Oct daily 10–12 and 2–6; adm*) overlooking its jumble of village houses. Robert le Diable had a keep built here in early-medieval times, but the buildings originate, in the main, from the 15th century and Imbert de Bastarnay, who served several French kings and was grandfather to Diane de Poitiers. At the Revolution much of the castle was burnt down. In the mid-19th century Count Xavier Branicki began its restoration. So many pieces of Poland transported to a Loire Valley château make it one of the most eccentric in the region. Montrésor's collegiate church of **St-Jean-Baptiste** (1541), again commissioned by Imbert de Bastarnay, is disproportionately splendid for such a small village. The Bastarnay tomb effigies look like a family tucked up in bed. The church contains other riches, including a 17th-century *Annunciation* painted by Philippe de Champaigne. Head on to the village of **Nouans-les-Fontaines** for one of the best 15th-century canvases in France. The mysterious depiction of Christ's deposition in the church of

Tourangeaux to come and discover southern Touraine, as visitors can taste gourmet cuisine at a bargain price in this former inn.

Le Grand-Pressigny ✉ 37350
L'Espérance, Place du Carroir des Robins, **t** 02 47 94 90 12. Well-known restaurant serving fine Touraine fare. The menus are excellent value. Also has basic rooms.

Villandry and Around ✉ 37510
La Grange aux Moines, Berthenay, **t** 02 47 50 06 91. In a traditional Touraine farmhouse on the delightful spit of land between Loire and Cher west of Tours, this has been very nicely converted to offer extremely comfortable B&B rooms.

Prieuré des Granges at Savonnières, **t** 02 47 50 09 67, **f** 02 47 50 06 43. Five fine B&B rooms run by an antiques dealer.

Domaine de la Giraudière, **t** 02 47 50 08 60, **f** 02 47 50 06 00. The ultimate goat meal experience, south out of Villandry towards Druye, in a good-value rustic farm restaurant.

Azay-le-Rideau and La Chapelle-Ste-Blaise ✉ 37190
★★★**Le Grand Monarque**, 3 Place de la République, **t** 02 47 45 40 08, **f** 02 47 45 46 25

(*inexpensive*). A former posting inn, offering good accommodation and food.

★★**Biencourt**, 7 Rue Balzac, **t** 02 47 45 20 75, **f** 02 47 45 91 93 (*inexpensive*). Charming accommodation, divided between an 18th-century town house and a 19th-century school.

★**Hôtel Balzac**, 4–6 Rue Adélaïde Richer, **t** 02 47 45 42 08, **f** 02 47 45 29 87 (*cheap*). A simpler, cheaper address in another old town house.

L'Aigle d'Or, 10 Av Adélaïde Riché, **t** 02 47 45 24 58, **f** 02 47 45 90 18. Comfortable restaurant with good food, which you can sample outside in summer.

Troglodyte Les Grottes, Rue Pineau, **t** 02 47 45 21 04, **f** 02 47 45 92 51. Refined cuisine, and a terrace for al fresco summer dining.

Saché ✉ 37190
Auberge du XIIe Siècle, Place de l'Eglise, **t** 02 47 26 88 77, **f** 02 47 65 76 83. Splendidly old, beamed restaurant which is a very inviting place to eat.

Rigny-Ussé ✉ 37420
Clos d'Ussé, **t** 02 47 95 55 47. In typical Touraine tufa, with a sweet little gravel terrace, close to the Château d'Ussé.

St-Martin – his body spread a ghostly white across the huge canvas – is attributed to the court painter Jean Fouquet.

The southern tip of Touraine is very attractive. The little villages have Romanesque churches, local museums and even the odd dolmen. The major site on the River Claise is the **Château du Grand-Pressigny** (*open June–Sept daily 9.30–6.30; mid-Mar–May daily 9–12 and 2–6; Oct–Nov and Feb–mid-Mar daily 9–12 and 2–5; adm*), a delight of impure Loire architecture. Much is medieval, but a confidently Italian Renaissance block divides the medieval parts. Its gallery contains a **Musée de la Préhistoire**. The objects most closely linked with Pressigny are silex or flint instruments, split from pieces now nicknamed '*livres de beurre*' because of their shiny, buttery appearance. Finds of Pressigny Neolithic exports have been unearthed in Belgium and Switzerland, indicating how extensive Neolithic commercial links were.

René Descartes didn't spend much of his childhood in his native Touraine, but the town near which he was born was nevertheless renamed **Descartes** and has a small museum on his life.

Along the Loire to the Anjou Border

North of the Loire River from Tours to the Anjou Border

Moving into western Touraine, traffic thunders along the main road where the medieval **Château de Luynes** (*open April–mid-Sept daily 10–6; adm*) looks down severely from its height, its towers spotted with large stone pimples. Inside the courtyard it's much more elegant. Charles d'Albret, later the Duc de Luynes, bought the château in 1619. Brought up with the future Louis XIII, the two were united by their love of falconry. In 1617 they conspired to have the Queen Mother Marie de' Medici's powerful Italian adviser-cum-lover Concini assassinated. Charles went on to become Connétable de France and the most important minister in the land. Richelieu succeeded him, although descendants of de Luynes still live here.

The château is finely furnished: the vast sunken Salle des Jeux has traditional ochre walls, the Grand Salon an elaborate fireplace thought to be the work of Jean Goujon. Fine medieval houses are the main attraction in the village at the château's feet.

A 100ft brick tower rises east of the village of Cinq-Mars-la-Pile, long thought to have been a lighthouse for boats on the Loire, or a marker for pilgrims. Actually, it was a mausoleum for a rich 2nd-century merchant. The ruined medieval **Château de Cinq-Mars-la-Pile** (*open daily exc non-public holiday Mondays, second half of Feb and second half of Nov–early Dec; adm*) was revived in the 19th century. It was decapitated in the 1640s along with its owner, the Marquis de Cinq-Mars, a political protégé of Cardinal Richelieu. He was given high rank and became a favourite of Louis XIII – possibly even his lover. The young upstart then conspired with Gaston d'Orléans to get rid of Richelieu; they were discovered and Cinq-Mars was executed at the age of 22.

A kitsch 1950s neo-Gothic bridge spans the river at Langeais but the **Château de Langeais** (*open mid-July–Aug daily 9am–9pm; April–mid-July and Sept daily 9–6.30; Oct daily 9–12.30 and 2–6.30; Nov–Mar daily 9–12 and 2–5; adm*) is the real thing – a villain of a Gothic Loire château. Louis XI ordered its building after the end of the Hundred Years' War, but there's none of the exuberance of so much late Gothic architecture. Here, the fate of Brittany's independence was effectively sealed when Anne de Bretagne went through with her enforced marriage to Charles VIII. Inside, the richness of the rooms counters the coldness of the exterior.

A trip into woods north of the Loire at Bourgueil takes you to the enormous **Château de Gizeux** (*open May–Sept Mon–Sat 10–6.30, Sun 2–6; adm*). The long driveway befits such a pile, but it is almost eclipsed by the extent and beauty of the stables, added in 1741. On the first floor your attention is drawn to splendid views down two long galleries. Both are elaborately decorated with scenes of courtly life and famous French châteaux. The village church has splendid kneeling effigies of two couples of du Bellays, cut from white marble.

South of the Loire River from Tours to the Anjou Border

Some of the most famous châteaux in France lie between Tours and the Anjou border. These fairy-tale castles overlook the Cher and the Indre, tributaries of the Loire. Cross the Cher at the gorgeous riverside village of **Savonnières** to reach the **Château de Villandry** (*open July–Aug daily 9–6.30; April–June and Sept daily 9–6; Oct–mid-Nov daily 9–5.30; mid-Feb–Mar daily 9.30–5; rest of winter open Christmas hols only; adm. Garden open July–Aug daily 8.30am–8pm; May, June and Sept daily 9–7.30; April daily 9–7; Mar and early Nov daily 9–6; mid-Nov–Feb daily 9–5; adm*). Here, the complex geometrical and symbolic forms of the gardens are a wonder and a delight. They reinvent the spirit of Renaissance design but were conceived by a Spanish-American couple, Dr Joachim Carvallo and Anne Coleman, who bought Villandry in 1906. The **potager** must be the most enviable kitchen garden in the world. Flowers and fruit trees have to bow to the beauty of beet, the charm of comely cabbages, the perfection of peppers. On the next level, the *jardin des simples*, or medicinal herb garden, hides behind vine-covered alleys. Several important elements date from the 18th century, including the pools of the water garden which provide irrigation.

You need to climb the hill to read the symbols drawn in the box hedges of the highest, ornamental gardens. Four boxes illustrate fickle love, love letters, tender love and maddened love. Beyond, the box hedges represent musical symbols, with stylized lyres, harps, musical notes and candelabra to light the sheet music.

It was at medieval Villandry on 4 July 1189 that Henry II of England, two days before he died, signed a peace treaty with Philippe Auguste. A minister of François I, Jean le Breton (*see* above, p.360, the Château de Villesavin), used the remains of the medieval castle to found three wings in the Italian Renaissance style with regular window openings, strong horizontal bands dividing up the façades and elegant colonnades. Certain French tastes remain, though, such as the splendid array of Loire windows in the slate roofs. The interiors were remodelled during the 18th century for the Castellane family. They are now characterized by the **Spanish art** that the Carvallos brought over, including some disturbing works from the school of Goya.

The beauty of the moated **Château d'Azay-le-Rideau** (*open July–Aug daily 9–7; mid-Mar–June and Sept–Oct daily 9.30–6; Nov–mid-Mar daily 9.30–12.30 and 2–5.30; adm*) was likened by Balzac to 'a diamond with its multiple facets set in the Indre'. The château was started in 1518 for Gilles Berthelot, a treasurer of France. The pepper-pot towers, the steepness of the roof and its finial tips give a Gothic twist to the whole. Italian influence can be seen in the château's symmetry and in typical medallions and candelabra. The famous staircase is renowned not just for its decoration but because it is among the first to have been incorporated into the main building rather than housed in a stair tower. Building work was still incomplete when Berthelot fled to avoid financial scandal in 1527, leaving François I to pick up yet another Loire château. You start the visit in the low kitchen, which has some hilarious Gothic touches. After that, you are treated to the hackneyed round of tapestries, chests, bad copies of paintings and a few good portraits. The gardens are used as the setting for an idiosyncratic *son-et-lumière*, **Les Imaginaires d'Azay-le-Rideau** (*contact the château, t 02 47 45 42 04, for further details*).

East from Azay-le-Rideau, the Château de Saché containing the **Musée Balzac** (*open July–Aug daily 9.30–6.30; mid-Mar–June and Sept daily 9–12 and 2–6; Feb–mid-Mar* *and Oct–Nov daily 9–12 and 2–5; adm*) is more a rugged manor. Balzac's mother had a liaison with the owner, Monsieur de Margonne, and a child by him. Balzac was always very well received by de Margonne, seeking refuge to write and to avoid his creditors in brief stays in the 1820s and 1830s. The museum 'pays homage to his excesses'. *Le Lys dans la vallée*, a melodramatic story of frustrated love, is mainly set in the Indre valley near Saché.

West from Azay-le-Rideau, the Indre draws closer to the Loire and flows past Rigny-Ussé, where another famous château nestles. The **Château d'Ussé** (*open mid-July–Aug daily 9–6.30; Easter–mid-July and first 3 weeks of Sept daily 9–12 and 2–6.45; mid-Mar–Easter daily 9–12 and 2–6; end Sept–mid-Nov daily 10–12 and 2–5.30; adm*) supposedly inspired the tale of *Sleeping Beauty* when its author Charles Perrault was an overnight guest. If you can't remember the story before the tour, you will have a job piecing it together from the waxwork scenes at the top of the greatest of the main towers. You can visit the chapel before the tour, a gem with the interlaced initials C and L referring to the couple for whom it was built, Charles d'Espinay and Lucrèce de Pons.

Chinon

With medieval houses close knit as chain mail fighting for space between the hillside and the Vienne river, Chinon is dominated by the ruins of its great Plantagenet castle. Distinctly provincial today, it retains more than a spark of courtly glory.

Chinon's first great courtly age came with Henri Plantagenet. The town wasn't part of his inheritance, but that of his brother Geoffroy, but Henri seized it anyway as it was excellently situated to administer his territories: Anjou, Maine, Normandy and Aquitaine, not forgetting England. He loved Chinon and enlarged the castle to become the greatest fortress of its time in Europe. He died at Chinon in 1189 and his son, Richard Coeur de Lion, may have died here too after being mortally wounded at the Battle of Châlus. As for son John, he was married to Isabelle d'Angoulême in Chinon, but Philippe Auguste's forces triumphed over his in a one-year siege here. From below, the **Château de Chinon** (*open July–Aug daily 9–7; mid-Mar–June and Sept daily 9–6; Oct daily 9–5; rest of year daily 9–12 and 2–5; adm*) seems little more than a string of battered towers which mark the boundaries of three castles that once stood here. The ruins of Charles VII's royal logis – where most of the exhibits are housed – was where Joan of Arc met the 'gentle dauphin' to convince him that she could rescue France. Her influential visit is recalled in the little museum in the Tour de l'Horloge. The royal apartments aren't very exciting, but from here Charles VII kept discreetly in touch with his mistress, Agnes Sorel. If Chinon's castle is ruined and quiet now, the **town** below is often bustling and crowded. There may not be many streets but they are crammed with splendid architecture.

The **Musée du Vieux Chinon et de la Batellerie** in the Maison des Etats Généraux (*open June–Sept daily 10–6; adm*) is situated in the house where it is claimed Richard Coeur de Lion died and where Charles VII called the Estates General of France to meet in 1428, after the English had laid siege to Orléans. Undoubtedly the most moving

Getting Around

An exclusive rail connection from Tours serves Chinon.

Tourist Information

Chinon: Place d'Hofheim, **t** 02 47 93 17 85, **f** 02 47 93 93 05.

Where to Stay and Eat

Chinon ✉ 37500

★★Hostellerie Gargantua, 73 Rue Voltaire, **t** 02 47 93 04 71, **f** 02 47 93 08 02 (*inexpensive*). Occupying one of Chinon's most famous historic houses, with some comfortable rooms and a medieval-style dining room serving quite modern cuisine.

★★Hôtel Diderot, 4 Rue Buffon, **t** 02 47 93 18 87, **f** 02 47 93 37 10 (*inexpensive*). A delightful 18th-century ivy-covered town house with its own courtyard.

★★La Boule d'Or, 66 Quai Jeanne d'Arc, **t** 02 47 93 03 13, **f** 02 47 93 24 25 (*inexpensive*). Hotel with some pleasant rooms overlooking the river, and an interior courtyard where you can dine on traditional Rabelaisian food in summer.

★★De France, 47 Place du Général De Gaulle, **t** 02 47 93 33 91, **f** 02 47 98 37 03 (*inexpensive*). Hotel calmly set back in a leafy corner of this square, with neat and comfortable rooms.

Hôtel de la Treille, 4 Place Jeanne d'Arc, **t** 02 47 93 07 71. A cheaper option, with simpler accommodation in what was once the 12th-century episcopal palace.

Au Plaisir Gourmand, 2 Rue Parmentier, **t** 02 47 93 20 48, **f** 02 47 93 05 66. This is Chinon's outstanding restaurant, reputed far and wide. Its greatest strength is producing traditional food to perfection.

exhibit is a copy of an 11th-century Crucifixion from the Chinon church of St-Mexme. The museum also displays St Mexme's cope, which turns out to be a piece of Arabian silk from the 11th century decorated with a pattern of stylized wild cats, that was probably originally intended for a horse. The undistinguished portrait of Rabelais is by Delacroix. Along Rue Voltaire, the **Musée Animé du Vin et de la Tonnellerie** (*open April–Sept daily 10.30–12.30 and 2–7.30; adm*) is set in a cave once quarried for stone and now devoted to Chinon's wines. Rue Voltaire ends in the very pleasant 19th-century **Place du Général de Gaulle**, complete with a crowd of cafés and a statue of Rabelais. Rue Jean-Jacques Rousseau takes you, eventually, to the troglodyte Chapelle Ste-Radegonde. Near St-Mexme, the streets lead to the big Place Jeanne d'Arc with its bellicose statue of the maid who is supposed not to have killed a single soul in battle. Southwest from Chinon, **La Devinière and the Musée Rabelais** (*open May–Sept daily 10–7; mid-Mar–April daily 9–12 and 2–6; rest of year daily 9–12 and 2–5; adm*) commemorate Rabelais, who was born on this farm and has become even more of a draw than Henri Plantagenet or Joan of Arc. At least he had a sense of humour. The museum paying homage to him, though, is relatively sober.

Around Chinon

The Vienne banks east from Chinon have so many Romanesque churches you get the impression the area must have been more populated in medieval times. Close to L'Ile-Bouchard, **Tavant** has the best church, or rather church crypt. **St-Nicolas** (*open by appointment, t 02 47 58 58 06; adm*) conceals an extraordinary Romanesque fresco cycle, among the most refined in France and Europe. It's as though characters in a

Getting Around

Bus services from Chinon serve L'Ile Bouchard and Richelieu, t 02 47 47 17 18.

Tourist Information

St-Epain: 33 Grand'rue, t 02 47 65 84 63.
Richelieu: 6 Grande-Rue, t 02 47 58 13 62, f 02 47 58 10 13.

Where to Stay and Eat

Beaumont-en-Véron ✉ 37420

Château de Danzay, off D749 on the way from Chinon to Avoine, along the route to Savigny, t 02 47 58 46 86, f 02 47 58 84 35. Appealing B&B with late medieval feel.
Château de Coulaine, t 02 47 98 44 51. Quirky, unsophisticated B&B rooms with bathrooms in the round towers, one of the enjoyable features among many eccentricities in this unkempt wine-making château.
Manoir de Montour, t 02 47 58 43 76. The B&B rooms here are much more elegant and beautifully decorated.

Richelieu ✉ 37120

Madame Couvrat Desvernes, 6 Rue Henri Proust, t 02 47 58 29 40. B&B with rooms set in a smart 19th-century building with a garden.
Madame Leplâtre, 1 Rue Jarry, t 02 47 58 10 42. Smart B&B with a garden. Mme Leplâtre can tell you a lot about the history of Richelieu.

Razines ✉ 37120

Château de Chargé, t 02 47 95 60 57. Once the country château of the governors of Chinon and Richelieu. You can stay here in one of three splendid B&B rooms.

passion play had been caught in their poses. Among them, Luxuria pierces her own breast in one of the Middle Ages' most favoured and disturbing visions of sin. On the south side at **L'Ile Bouchard**, the apse of the **Prieuré de St-Léonard** has retained some superb Romanesque carvings in its little semi-circular theatre of a church ruin. The grooved, parted, wave-like long-haired and finger-pointing characters are typical of the best of mid-12th-century sculpting.

The **Manse valley** is a well-kept secret, offering a delightful alternative route north of the Vienne valley. The name of **Ste-Maure** is synonymous to the French with goat's cheese, proliferated here in the Friday morning market. Another pleasant excursion from Chinon leads south to Richelieu, past the remnants of a 16th-century château at Champigny-sur-Verde. This is off limits, but you can visit the freestanding Renaissance **St-Louis chapel** (*open April–Sept daily exc Tues 10–12 and 2–6; adm*). Its stained glass counts as one of the great Renaissance works of the Loire and concentrates on the life of pious crusading Louis XI.

Louis XIII's great political fixer, Cardinal Richelieu, was a vandal of major proportions who had many provincial castles pulled down to assert the central authority of the royal state. But he commissioned two outrageously ambitious architectural projects to his own greater glory at **Richelieu**. With rough justice, his château has been almost entirely demolished, whereas the new town – built from scratch for courtiers and merchants – survives as a pretty unspoilt utopian 17th-century vision. Richelieu chose the location because a château belonging to his ancestors stood here. The future cardinal was in fact born into impoverished aristocracy and, intent on regaining the family honour, his swift rise to power enabled him to buy the château and lordship back for himself in 1621. In 1624 the architect Jacques Lemercier produced plans for Richelieu's château which eclipsed just about every previous Loire château and maybe even rivalled Chambord, filled with an art collection which included works by Michelangelo. The sole surviving tower still manages to impress. The park, with its towering avenue of planes, has a lingering scent of grandeur.

To accompany his château, Richelieu desired a **model town**, where courtiers would gather to enjoy his cultivated society. Lemercier planned an ideal classical city, and its symmetry gives a rhythm and a certain playfulness. The two outstanding buildings are on Place du Maré, with the splendid Halles on one side and the church of **Notre-Dame** on the other. The **Musée Municipal** in the town hall (*open July and Aug daily exc Tues 10–12 and 2–6; weekends only rest of year 10–12 and 2–4; adm*) contains drawings of the town and château and objects recovered before its destruction. None of the courtiers in Richelieu's time bought into his dream but by the start of the 18th century more than 3,000 people lived there. Which is more than do now.

The Loire from the Anjou Border to Saumur

Eastern Anjou begins after the Vienne joins the mighty Loire. Candes-St-Martin and Montsoreau, two beautiful villages on the south bank, are stuck together like Siamese twins but administratively, they lie in different regions. They're followed by a string of secretive villages built into the rockface, and by the famous abbey of Fontevraud.

Pretty **Candes-St-Martin** is steeped in Martin's memory. Climb the steep path to the top of the village for spectacular views of the confluence of the Loire and the Vienne as well as the chivalric plumes of steam rising from the Avoine-Chinon nuclear power station. St Martin had a church built here, dedicated to St Maurice, a martyred Roman knight. In November 397 he came to sort out a quarrel between clerks when he fell ill and died. Gregory of Tours, in his *History of the Franks*, tells of an unseemly argument over Martin's body between a group from Tours, where Martin had been bishop, and a group from Poitiers, where he founded the first monastery in France. The men of Tours settled it by stealing the body as the Poitevins slept. As the remains were carried up the Loire, the trees and shrubs on the banks flowered, and to this day an Indian summer is known in French as an *été de la St-Martin*. The squat **church** dedicated to St Martin dates from 1175. Inside, it appears somewhat unstable, with sloping floor and irregular bays. Extraordinary painted sculptures perch on the columns.

The medieval lords of **Montsoreau** once made a good living exacting tolls from those on the river crossing the border. Their bright Château de Montsoreau virtually bathed in the Loire itself in earlier times, the river waters supplying the moat. The castle was built for Jean de Chambes. One descendant married Françoise de Maridor, the famed Dame de Montsoreau, fictionalized by Alexandre Dumas in the novel of that name.

The **abbey of Fontevrault** (*open June–3rd Sun in Sept daily 9–7; rest of year daily 9.30–12.30 and 2–6; adm*) is truly exceptional. It was the first in a monastic order founded in the early 12th century by the charismatic Robert d'Arbrissel, a 'sower of the divine word' according to Pope Urban II who ordered him to extend his work. Women in particular were encouraged and their presence led to numerous scandals and

Getting Around

To cover this area by public transport use the local bus services from Saumur.

Tourist Information

Montsoreau: Av de la Loire, **t** 02 41 51 70 22, **f** 02 41 51 75 66.
Fontevraud-l'Abbaye: Chapelle Ste-Catherine, **t** 02 41 51 79 45, **f** 02 41 51 79 01.

Where to Stay and Eat

Candes-St-Martin ✉ 37500

La Route d'Or, Place de l'Eglise, **t** 02 47 95 81 10. It's worth making a pilgrimage to this tiny, simple but stylish restaurant tucked into the square by the great church to St Martin.

Montsoreau ✉ 49730

★★Hostellerie Le Bussy, 4 Rue Jeanne d'Arc, **t** 02 41 38 11 11, **f** 02 41 38 18 10 (*inexpensive*). Close to the château, a warm place to stay.
Le Saut aux Loups, Route de Saumur, **t** 02 41 51 70 30, **f** 02 41 38 15 30. In a sensational rock setting this restaurant specializes in *galipettes*, monster mushrooms which come with various fillings. Open lunchtime only.

Mestré ✉ 49590

Domaine de Mestré, t 02 41 51 75 87, **f** 02 41 51 71 90. Between Montsoreau and Fontevraud, you can now stay at this fine 17th- and 18th-century building in typical Loire tufa. It was once the property of the abbey and a place where pilgrims were put up.

Fontevrault ✉ 49590

★★La Croix Blanche, t 02 41 51 71 11, **f** 02 41 38 15 38 (*moderate*). Rooms round a courtyard at this well-established, traditional hotel, almost at the entrance to the abbey.
Hostellerie du Prieuré St-Lazare, t 02 41 51 73 16, **f** 02 41 51 75 50. Actually part of the old abbey, a slick conference-style adaptation of the lepers' monastery, the cells turned into quite nice rooms (although a friend has claimed to have scented the smell of old nuns in them). The cloister and church have been turned into delightful dining areas.
La Licorne, Allée Ste-Catherine, **t** 02 41 51 72 49, **f** 02 41 51 70 40. A highly reputed restaurant set in an 18th-century house close to the church.

rumours. After d'Arbrissel left Fontevrault it was ruled by a long line of forceful abbesses. The monks at Fontevrault would periodically protest at their treatment under their rule. One abbess, Mathilde d'Anjou, was the aunt of Henri Plantagenet, who stayed at Fontevrault before he set off for England to be crowned Henry II in 1154. The abbey became the burial place of the dynasty when Henry was buried at Fontevraud as his son Richard Cœur de Lion dictated. Four Plantagenet tombs remain in the vast void of the church, including that of Eleanor of Aquitaine.

In all, 149 Fontevrist monasteries were created, four in England. Come the Revolution, the nuns and monks were expelled and Napoleon transformed Fontevraud into a vast penitentiary. The criminal and homosexual author Jean Genet was imprisoned here and reveals its chilling side in *Le Miracle de la Rose*. The last inmates only left in 1985. The kitchen proves the most extraordinary feature of Fontevrault with its astounding fish-scaled roof. The huge fireplaces within give you a notion of the scale of cooking that took place.

A line of **troglodyte villages** built into the Loire's limestone cliff runs from Montsoreau to Saumur. There are no finer examples in the Loire Valley region. Look out for the particularly elegant troglodyte houses at **La Vignole** and **Turquant**. Continuing below the Loire cliff face, you arrive at Gratien et Meyer, one of the handful of wine houses with spectacular cliffside cave cellars which produce Saumur's sparkling wines. The others have gathered close together in St-Hilaire-St-Florent on the western side of Saumur: Bouvet-Ladubay, Ackerman, Veuve-Amiot and Langlois-Château.

Saumur

Two famous works depict the stunning Loire-side town of Saumur: the first is a page from the early 15th-century *Très Riches Heures du Duc de Berry*, showing a fantastic fairy-tale château with towers and pinnacles. The other is Balzac's great novel, *Eugénie Grandet*. The fictional inhabitants don't come out as idyllic as the château in the medieval manuscript. You won't see many profiles of self-sacrificing Eugénie adorning shop fronts, hotels and restaurants in the touristy Saumur of today. Nor are you likely to see beggars. The right-wing town council was one of the first in France to ban beggars at the start of the 1990s and '*la perle d'Anjou*' is the archetypal clean, white, bourgeois town. Its other nickname is the '*ville du cheval*'. Saumur has long been home to a famous cavalry regiment – and to the associated showmanship of the Cadre Noir. With changes in warfare, Saumur switched from horses to tanks. Yet in spite of all the women in Sloane Ranger gear wandering around with stiff men in military garb, it is a delightful town with a magnificent architectural heritage.

The **Château de Saumur** (*open June–Sept daily 9–6, with nocturnal visits possible in July and Aug; rest of the year daily 9.30–12 and 2–5.30; adm*) is more simply impressive than the version in the medieval manuscript. Its four towers stretch into the sky like thick upturned pencils. Most of it was built for Louis Duc d'Anjou in the 14th century. The low outer range of fortifications was added for Huguenot Duplessis-Mornay in the 1590s, who founded an Académie Protestante which caused Saumur to be nicknamed the Second Geneva. After the Protestant governor's enforced departure by order of Louis XIII in 1621, the glamorous building was neglected. It went on to serve as a barracks, then as a prison, housing the Marquis de Sade for a time. The town bought the château in 1906 to house its museums. The **Musée des Arts Décoratifs** (*guided tour; adm*) has a substantial collection of ceramics, one of the most important in France. The **Musée du Cheval** contains a mass of saddles, stirrups, bits and boots.

Below the château stand several grand churches. A couple are topped by vicious steeples resembling upturned tacks. On Place St-Pierre, a delightful sloping square with delicate trees, the church of **St-Pierre** has a misleading classical façade, added to a late 12th- and early 13th-century structure. Highlights inside include the mighty organ, tapestries and decorative choir stalls. Many houses around here are hidden behind grand gateways for carriages. A hearty walk will take you further out to two churches dedicated to the Virgin. **Notre-Dame de Nantilly** is a basic Romanesque block with a Gothic south aisle tacked on. The main surprise is the remarkable tapestry collection from the 16th and 17th centuries. Pilgrims pay homage to the 12th-century painted Virgin and Child. The hugely domed Counter-Reformation **Notre-Dame-des-Ardilliers**, built to combat the deep-rooted Protestantism of the

Getting Around

The occasional TGV stops at Saumur's railway station, otherwise there are slower local services.

Tourist Information

Saumur: Place de la Bilange, t 02 41 40 20 60, f 02 41 40 20 69.

Activities

The Ecole Nationale d'Equitation and the Cadre Noir (*open June, July and Aug Mon pm–Sat pm; April, May and Sept Mon pm–Sat am; note that visits start at 9.30 and 2.30 only*). For details on the weekends when the Cadre Noir puts on shows, t 02 41 53 50 60.

There are usually three dates in April, May and June, and one or two dates in July and Sept.

Where to Stay

Saumur ✉ 49400

Moderate

★★★Anne d'Anjou, 32 Quai Mayaud, t 02 41 67 30 30, f 02 41 67 51 00. The most elegant address in Saumur set in smart 18th-century premises on the Loire's southern bank.

★★★Loire Hôtel/Restaurant les Mariniers, Rue du Vieux Pont, t 02 41 67 22 42, f 02 41 67 88 80. Modern hotel on the Ile Offard which benefits from views on to the old town from its excellent riverside position.

Inexpensive

★★Central, 23 Rue Daillé, t 02 41 51 05 78, f 02 41 67 82 35. Neat, good-value hotel in the middle of town.

★★Le Volney, 1 Rue Volney, t 02 41 51 25 41, f 02 41 38 11 04. Smaller centrally located family-run hotel with homely touches.

★★Le Clos des Bénédictins, t 02 41 67 28 48, f 02 41 67 13 71. To get slightly out of town but still enjoy quite good views of Saumur's monuments in the distance, head up the hill from St-Hilaire-St-Florent, in a pleasant modern estate close to the renowned Ecole Nationale Equestre. The house is modern, but it has comfortable and well-kept rooms.

Eating Out

Les Délices du Château, t 02 41 67 65 60, f 02 41 67 74 60. Stylish restaurant which serves elaborate food, and has the privilege of being located in the outhouses of the castle, high on Saumur's hill.

L'Orangeraie, t 02 41 67 12 88, f 02 41 67 74 60. Attached to Les Délices, a less expensive restaurant with an equally fine setting with views on to the château.

Les Ménestrels, 11 Rue Raspail, t 02 41 67 71 10, f 02 41 67 51 00. An excellent restaurant adjoining the garden of the Hôtel Anne d'Anjou.

La Croquière, 42 Rue du Maréchal Leclerc, t 02 41 51 31 45. Warm, slightly rustic, with a good reputation, serving mainly traditional dishes, but also the odd experiment.

L'Escargot, 30 Rue du Maréchal Leclerc, t 02 41 51 20 88. As its name implies, it specializes in snail dishes but also offers a range of regional dishes at a reasonable price.

town, is reached through the Quartier de Fenet, wedged between the Loire cliff-side and the river.

You can cross the bridge from Place de la Bilange to appreciate the views of Saumur's **quays** and in summer you can take a river trip in an old-fashioned Loire boat. Outside the centre the **Musée des Blindés** (*open daily 9–12 and 2–6; adm*), the tank museum, presents something of a history of the major European wars of the 20th century. The prestigious **Ecole Nationale d'Equitation and the Cadre Noir** (*see* 'Activities', above) present the most glamorous side of French horseriding. Manure is plentiful in these parts, and in the cliff quarries there are dark, cool spaces; both essential elements for growing mushrooms. Saumurois production is on a vast scale.

At the **Musée du Champignon** (*open 15 Feb–15 Nov daily 10–7; follow the D751 out of St-Hilaire-St-Florent for Gennes; adm*) you can learn all you need to know.

Troglodyte Territories South of Saumur

To discover a land where people once lived in caves and where a hardy handful still do, head southwest from Saumur to Le Coudray-Macouard, Montreuil-Bellay and Doué-la-Fontaine.

In **Le Coudray-Macouard** the fine houses and troglodyte parts are often hidden behind stone walls. You can glimpse a typical underground house by visiting **La Magnanerie** (*open 15 May–15 Sept daily 10–6; Sept–All Saints' weekends 2–6; adm*) and also learn here about silk-making, a thriving local industry until an epidemic in 1855 killed the silkworms. The town of **Doué-la-Fontaine** has a couple of truly spectacular troglodyte sites. The first, **Les Caves-Cathédrales des Perrières**, consist of a series of interconnecting bottle-shaped chambers from the 18th century. So that agricultural land could be redeemed once a quarry was spent, the *caviers-cultivateurs* dug narrow trenches and then extracted the stone beneath to form an arch. The second site, the attractive **Zoo de Doué** (*open summer daily 9–7; winter daily 10–12 and 2–6; adm*), lies in the direction of Cholet. The visitors' trail leads through interconnecting caves and you quite forget you're in the middle of a dull Angevin plain by the time you reach the densely planted caverns where the great cats lounge.

Another troglodyte site has been opened in Doué; **La Cave aux Sarcophages** (*open April–Sept daily 10–12 and 2–7; adm*) speaks for itself. The soil in the Doué area is particularly suited to roses. Millions grow around the town and a **roseraie** has taken over the garden of a now vanished château, while a rose water distillery occupies the stables. A very large medieval crater known as **Les Arènes** now plays host to Doué's annual festival of roses.

Getting Around

There's a regular bus service from Angers to Doué-la-Fontaine but buses are rarer if you want to travel on to Montreuil-Bellay and Le Puy-Notre-Dame.

From Saumur there is also an occasional bus service to Doué-la-Fontaine and Montreuil-Bellay.

Tourist Information

Doué-la-Fontaine: 30 Place du Champ de Foire, t 02 41 59 20 49, f 02 41 59 93 85.
Montreuil-Bellay: Place du Concorde, t 02 41 52 32 39, f 02 41 52 32 35.
Le Puy-Notre-Dame: 16 Rue des Hôtels, t 02 41 38 87 30, f 02 41 38 89 99.

Where to Stay and Eat

Rou-Marson ✉ 49400
Les Caves de Marson, Rue Henri Fricotelle, t 02 41 50 50 05, f 02 41 50 94 01. Great troglodyte setting, where you can taste *fouaces*: dough balls cooked in the oven and stuffed with various fillings.

Rochemenier ✉ 49700
Les Caves de la Genevraie, 13 Rue du Musée, t 02 41 59 34 22, f 41 59 31 12. Another good troglodyte address serving *fouaces*.

Montreuil-Bellay ✉ 49260
★★Splendid Hôtel/Relais du Bellay, 96 Rue Nationale, t 02 41 53 10 00, f 02 41 52 45 17 (*moderate*). Two elegant hotels now joined together, a stone's throw from the château.

A dreamy cliché of a château, the **Château de Montreuil-Bellay** (*open April–Oct daily exc Tues 10–12 and 2–5.30; adm*), dominates its town, boasting 13 towers. Most of what you see dates from the 15th century. The **Château-Vieux**, begun in 1420, has two octagonal towers and big *lucarnes*. The small freestanding building with the curious roof is the 15th-century kitchen. Behind it, the **Petit-Château** was probably built to serve the collegiate church. In the painted 15th-century oratory, delightful angels sing on the ceiling. You can wander round the lovely *chemin de ronde* and garden. West of Montreuil-Bellay, **Le Puy-Notre-Dame**'s massive collegiate church owes its grandeur to a much-venerated piece of the girdle of the Virgin Mary brought back from the Crusades and long believed to promote fertility.

The Loire from Saumur to Angers

Two utterly splendid stretches of Loire-side road run between Saumur and Angers – try not to miss either the south or north route. The dazzling light limestone gives way to dark, earth-coloured schist and this has a striking effect on the area's architecture.

Along the north bank, the bare road rides on top of the Plantagenet **Grande Levée**, a protective wall built in the early Middle Ages to prevent flooding. In places, the great width of the meandering waters and the sandy shore create a coastal illusion. The major castle on the north side is the soberly symmetrical **Château de Montgeoffroy** (*open mid-June–mid-Sept daily 9.30–6.30; last week Mar–14 June and 16 Sept–Oct daily 9.30–12; adm*), an example of pure 18th-century Loire architecture built for the Maréchal de Contade, between 1773 and 1775. On entering, you're greeted by the man himself beaming from a painting. Still a family home, the household inventory drawn up before the end of the 18th century confirms it has retained the furniture of that time. On the south bank, **Cunault** had a port on the Loire to send off the local tufa, but its channel now becomes an expansive sandbank in summer. The village's Romanesque church of **Notre-Dame** has a vast tomb of a nave and extraordinarily imaginative sculpture on the exterior of the belfry. A mermaid who looks like a nun with a fish's tail appears to be fighting a man in a Loire boat. Off the beautiful ambulatory, a side-chapel contains the splendid polychrome reliquary chest of St Maxenceul who died on the spot. His memory was upstaged by the arrival of St Philibert's relics. Later, the community claimed to hold some real Christian whoppers: a ring belonging to the Virgin Mary and a phial of her milk.

Le Thoureil, the next village to the west, has 17th-century houses built for Dutch merchants trading along the Loire. Neolithic folks liked these parts too, judging by an extraordinary concentration of menhirs and dolmens in the hinterland. Also seek out the delightful Romanesque church at **St-Georges-des-Sept-Voies**. The nearby **Orbière** or **Hélice Terrestre** (*open May–Sept daily 11–8; rest of year daily 2–7; adm*) is a wacky troglodyte dwelling transformed by the late Jacques Warminski – a Gargantuan Balzac lookalike – into a work of art. A surprise awaits in the 'musical sphere': stamp around inside it to create a ringing musical note.

The Aubance and Layon Valleys

The big attraction of the Aubance is the curious **Château de Brissac**, a classical body trying to squeeze out of a medieval one (*open July–mid-Sept daily 10–5.45; April–June and 16 Sept–1 Nov daily exc Tues 10–12 and 2.15–5.15; adm*). The original was built for Pierre de Brézé, who served Charles VII and Louis XI. In 1502 Pierre's nephew sold the Gothic pile to René de Cossé, a minister under Charles VIII, whose family still owns it. At the end of the Wars of Religion Charles II de Cossé, the governor of Paris, opened the gates of the capital to the reconciling Henri IV. His reward was to be made a Maréchal de France and a duke. Charles marked his elevated rank on his château, for which he and his master mason, Jacques Corbineau, are to be blamed or congratulated. The main stairtower drips with stone garlands, heads, shells, coats of arms. Each window surround is like a grandiose gateway. A Mannerist slate roof rises with triumphant incompatibility. The guided tour takes you through some, but not all, of the 200 or so rooms, but it's more than enough. The beams of the Salle des Gardes are painted with miniature pastoral scenes, decorative motifs, gilded putti. In the rich atmosphere of a crimson bedroom, gold and blue tapestries depict the heroics of Alexander the Great.

The Layon river starts southwest of Doué-la-Fontaine, and around **Les Verchers-sur-Layon** the melting vineyard views suggest you might have been transported to a delightful corner of southwest France. After the Layon switches dramatically northeast, the architecture changes with the geology, schist and slate taking over from pale stones and southern tiles.

Getting Around

Bus services run between Saumur and Angers. To reach the villages of the Aubance and Layon valleys, take buses from Angers.

Tourist Information

St-Mathurin-sur-Loire: 20 Rue Roi René, t 02 41 57 01 82, f 02 41 57 08 02.
Cunault: t 02 41 67 92 70 or t 02 41 67 92 55, f 02 41 67 91 94.
Brissac-Quincé: 8 Place de la République, t 02 41 91 21 50, f 02 41 54 25 31.

Where to Stay and Eat

Chênehutte-les-Tuffeaux ✉ 49350
****L'Hostellerie du Prieuré, t 02 41 67 90 14, f 02 41 67 92 24 (*expensive*). The views on to the Loire valley are so spectacular from the luxurious terrace and dining-room, that it makes a very memorable stop. But if you're staying, be sure you avoid the hideous if comfortable maisonnettes in the grounds.

Les Rosiers ✉ 49350
***Auberge Jeanne de Laval/Les Ducs d'Anjou, 54 Rue Nationale, t 02 41 51 80 17, f 02 41 38 04 18 (*moderate*). Reputed for its cuisine. Most of the rooms are a very modestly slimming walk away in a grandiose house.
**Au Val de Loire, Place de l'Eglise, t 02 41 51 80 30, f 02 41 51 95 00 (*inexpensive*). Neat, smart little rooms and carefully prepared local food.

Thouarcé ✉ 49380
Relais de Bonnezeaux, Route d'Angers, t 02 41 54 08 33, f 02 41 54 00 63. Much appreciated restaurant which took over the railway station, and has views on to vineyards.

Angers

Apocalyptic Angers, black Angers...the titles for the historic capital of Anjou aren't reassuring. 'Black Angers' comes from its slate mines rather than filthy character; the apocalypse from two fabulous tapestry cycles. Angers doesn't lie along the Loire, but stretches across both banks of the Maine just north of it. On the plateau above sits the old city and its attractions.

History

Angers – the centre of a Celtic tribe, the Andes or Andecaves – became Juliomagus, the Gallo-Roman capital of a territory known as the Civitas Andecavorum. As the regional counts under the Carolingian kings became increasingly independent, the Ingelgérien family took power in Angers under Foulques le Roux in 898 – the first of a line of Angevin counts to go by the name of Foulques (or Falcon). The most famous Foulques was the formidable Foulques Nerra (Black Falcon) who took the Mauges southwest of Angers and then expanded to the east, taking over the Saumurois and most of Touraine. Foulques V had a son called Geoffroy – nicknamed Plantagenet because he habitually wore a piece of broom (*genêt*) in his helmet – who married Mathilda, daughter of Henry I of England, in 1128. Their son, Henri Plantagenet, famously became Henry II of England in 1154. This expansion of power meant that Angers was no longer at the centre of Plantagenet territories. Geoffroy had already shown a preference for Le Mans, while Chinon became Henri's main headquarters in these parts. He didn't neglect the family town, however, and had the elegant Hôpital St-Jean built in 1175. Even after the Plantagenets, Angers remained an important strategic position. Blanche de Castille, widow of Louis VIII and regent for her son Louis IX, took a great interest in the town, commissioning the building of a new castle around the 1230s and having the city protected by a great wall.

In the next century Jean le Bon offered Anjou as an appanage and dukedom to his son Louis. Louis vied with his brothers Charles V, Jean Duc de Berry and Philippe le Hardi to see who could lead the life of most sickening extravagance. But Louis' energetic administration also encouraged civic schemes, including the development of a university. Joan of Arc was supported by Yolande d'Aragon, wife of Louis II d'Anjou. These two produced a son called René, who is usually referred to as *le bon roi René* – he claimed the kingdom of Sicily – but was actually duke of Anjou and count of Provence and of Piedmont. René is often portrayed as a paragon of 15th-century chivalric culture, encouraging artists, composing poetry and music, speaking a handful of languages, and showing enough sensitivity to introduce new flowers to northern France. But he bled his subjects dry with grandiose dreams of kingship and with his extravagance. Louis XI forced him to return Anjou to the monarchy in 1474 and René left for Provence.

Granted a new royal charter and acquiring the first printing press on the Loire in 1476, Angers continued to grow commercially and academically. Trade was particularly prosperous through the 17th century. Anjou wines and fruit were exported to England and Holland. The anti-Revolutionary tide reached Angers in 1793, and a couple of thousand Vendéens were shot on what is now known as the Champs des

Angers

Martyrs. Catholicism reasserted itself in a big way and a Catholic university was set up in 1875 which still holds its own against the new lay university. Angers is now ranked as the 20th-largest city in France.

Touring Angers

Start at the **Château d'Angers** (open June–mid-Sept daily 9–7; end Mar–May daily 9–12.30 and 2–6.30; rest of year daily 9.30–12.30 and 2–6; adm). The rough medieval pentagon forms the most imposing military fortification in the greater Loire Valley. Seventeen towers rise from walls made of local black schist – repellent to invaders and the eye, although once through the fortified gateway you will find a château within a château, where lightness prevails. The main attraction is the fabulous

tapestry of the Apocalypse commissioned by Louis I d'Anjou. It tells the story of St John's revelation:

> *I saw a beast emerge from the sea: it had seven heads and ten horns, with a coronet on each of its ten horns, and its heads were marked with blasphemous titles.*
> *I saw that the beast was like a leopard, with paws like a bear and a mouth like a lion...*
> *I saw that one of its heads seemed to have had a fatal wound but that this deadly injury had healed and the whole world had marvelled and followed the beast.*
> *They prostrated themselves in front of the beast, saying, 'Who can compare with the beast? Who can fight against him?'*

A remarkable 76 of the original 84 tapestry scenes survived the Revolution. The biblical text and the order of events derive from an inaccurate manuscript. John stands by in all the scenes, often under a kind of sentry box, and his reactions reflect the scenes. Only two women feature: one symbolizing the virtuous Church, the other the Whore of Babylon, or the decadence of Rome. In one or two places the evil knights appear to bear the helmets of English soldiers, and the sea monster might be read at one level as a symbol of the English crossing the Channel. Elsewhere are Saracens. The tapestries demonstrate that evil can appear in many guises as well as emphasizing that divine rescue or salvation is at hand. The castle tour takes in the royal lodgings and the chapel, which once guarded a cross incorporating a fragment of the True Cross. With its two horizontal bars, rather than the usual one, it later became the symbol of the French Resistance. (You can still see this extraordinary relic in **Baugé** in northern Anjou, at the Chapelle de la Girouardière (*open daily exc Tues 2.30–4.15*)).

The cobbled quarter of Angers, north of the castle promenade, has quiet streets with late-medieval and Renaissance houses. Along Rue St-Aignan you can pop in to the **Logis de l'Estaigner** and **Musée de l'Etain**, to admire Anjou's pewterware. The streets to the north lead to the great stairway which comes up from the Maine to the **cathedral of St-Maurice** mostly dating from the 12th century. Below the eight formidable saints in battle gear on the façade, the single west portal is filled with sculpture reminiscent of Chartres. Inside is the graceful and much-vaunted Angevin vaulting that influenced church building in the west of France throughout the 13th century. Stained glass from the 12th to the 15th centuries embellishes the sombre interior, while frescoes from the 13th century depict the life of a local saint, Maurille. The 16th-century baldaquin and the 18th-century organ are held up by colossal atlantes so heavily loaded they look as though collapse is imminent. Behind the cathedral on **Place Ste-Croix** half-men-half-beasts, a mermaid and a three-balled man count among the weird cast who clamber over the beams of the remarkable half-timbered house known as the **Maison d'Adam**.

The ruined **Eglise de Toussaint** on Rue Toussaint was restored in the early 1980s and turned into the **Galerie David d'Angers**, cluttered with sculptures. They are all the work of David d'Angers – the grateful artist called the city his mother and took its name in 1828. He was given financial support by the city and, when he went to work in Paris, sent back plaster casts of his pieces to his home town by way of thanks. For Angers he made a statue of Good King René.

Getting Around

Angers has excellent train links with Paris (*1hr 30mins*), and with London-Waterloo via Lille (*c. 3hrs 30mins avoiding Paris*).

Tourist Information

Angers: Place Kennedy, **t** 02 41 23 51 11, **f** 02 41 23 51 10.

Sports and Activities

The main place for sports and summer water activities is a little way southwest of the centre at Lac du Maine.

Where to Stay

Angers ✉ 49000
***Hôtel d'Anjou/La Salamandre, 1 Bd Foch; hotel, **t** 02 41 88 24 82, **f** 02 41 87 22 21; restaurant, **t** 02 41 88 99 55, **f** 02 41 87 22 21 (*moderate*). Restored to a high standard. The restaurant serves accomplished cuisine in a neo-Gothic setting.
Hôtel du Mail, 8 Rue des Ursules, **t 02 41 88 56 22, **f** 02 41 86 91 20 (*inexpensive*). Characterful rooms set in a grand 17th-century town house in a quiet street.
St-Julien, 9 Place du Ralliement, **t 02 41 25 05 25, **f** 02 41 20 95 19 (*inexpensive*). Well-situated, very central, with simple, nicely done rooms giving on to a lively square.

Le Cavier, **t 02 41 42 30 45, **f** 02 41 42 40 32 (*inexpensive*). Atmospheric hotel in a traditional Anjou windmill, but in a commercial belt north of town, on the road to Laval.
****Château de Noirieux, 26 Route du Moulin, **t** 02 41 42 50 05, **f** 02 41 37 91 00 (*expensive*). Further north still, in the countryside and overlooking the Loir river, this is the height of luxury. The stylish rooms are set in a 15th-century manor house.

Eating Out

L'Entracte, 9 Rue Louis de Romain, **t** 02 41 87 71 82. Warm interior, including stained glass, in which to enjoy good food.
La Ferme, 2 Place Freppel, **t** 02 41 87 09 90, **f** 02 41 20 92 82. Popular restaurant with a terrace in the shadow of the cathedral where you can try dishes made with Anjou wines.
Les Trois Rivières, 62 Promenade de Reculée, **t** 02 41 73 31 88, **f** 02 41 36 28 20. A view on to the Main as well as good cuisine, on the Doutre side of the river. Fish a speciality.

Entertainment and Nightlife

Anger's main **theatre**, on Place du Ralliement, is a good venue for a variety of events. You'll find a choice of cinemas along the ever-lively Bd Foch, and a range of bars and nightclubs around Rue St-Laud.

Once a splendid 15th-century house, the Logis Barrault containing the **Musée des Beaux-Arts d'Angers** (*closed for renovation*) has suffered from neglect. When it reopens, look out for portraits of Agnès Sorel and Catherine de' Medici and her son Charles IX as a child. The 18th-century room is a drunken orgy of sweetness but the Chardin still lives offer relief. By the Logis Barrault, the **Tour St-Aubin**, a massive and isolated 12th-century tower, has some very fine Romanesque carvings. The **Hôtel de Pincé** and **Musée Turpin de Crissé** (*open mid-June–mid-Sept daily 9–6.30; rest of the year daily exc Mon 10–12 and 2–6; adm*), beyond Place du Ralliement, hide a collection of classical, Egyptian and oriental works behind an archetypal Renaissance façade.

In medieval times chains were placed across the western Maine to stop boat traffic slipping by without paying taxes, hence the Pont de la Haute Chaîne and the Pont de la Basse Chaîne. A great line of tall plane trees stretches down the Maine bank; behind them, the **Hôpital St-Jean** (*open mid-June–mid-Sept daily 9–6.30; rest of year daily exc Mon 10–12 and 2–6; adm*) is the oldest surviving hospital in France. It was founded in 1175, one of the institutions Henry II established in penance for Thomas à Becket's murder, with a charter stipulating it should be governed by laymen. In the Salle des Malades, two rows of slender sandstone columns hold up the parachute-like Angevin vaults. The walls have been hung with the second cycle of Apocalypse tapestries in Angers. Jean Lurçat came to the city at the end of the 1930s and embarked on his vast project using some of the techniques of medieval tapestry-making. Rather than being inspired by the Bible, he was moved by realities like the Hiroshima bomb. Woven at Aubusson, work commenced in 1957, but was incomplete at his death in 1966. Further tapestry works are displayed in the **Musée de la Tapisserie Contemporaine** (*same ticket as the Hôpital St-Jean*).

North of Angers

North of Angers, two contrasting châteaux carry the name of Plessis. The **Château du Plessis-Bourré** (*open July–Aug daily 10–5.45; Mar–June and Sept–Oct daily exc Wed and Thurs am 10–12 and 2–5.45; Feb and Nov daily exc Wed 2–5.45; adm*) is a pure delight, invitingly formal, white and moated on the outside, with the weirdest ceiling along the Loire inside. It was built from 1468 to 1473 for Jean Bourré, finance minister and general factotum to Louis XI. The outer forms have scarcely changed, although the outhouses beyond the moat are 17th-century additions. Wood carving, vaulting, floor tiling, and a monumental fireplace all take you back to Bourré's period. The astonishing painted ceiling of the Salle des Gardes upstairs includes pictures of a woman sewing up a magpie's arsehole and Venus standing up peeing into a bowl a man holds out below her.

In contrast to light Le Plessis-Bourré, you are confronted by dark, forbidding fortifications at the **Château du Plessis-Macé** (*open July–Aug daily 10–12 and 2–6.30; June and Sept same times, but closed Tues; Mar–May and Oct–Nov daily exc Tues 1.30–5.30; adm*). North of where the Mayenne and Sarthe become the Maine river, it stands not far from Anjou's frontier with Brittany. The keep survives from the medieval château. Once through the imposing walls, an appealing shambles of a courtyard opens up, mixing rugged schist with smooth tufa in almost comical fashion. Gothic accolades surmount some of the doors. One 15th-century lord, Louis de Beaumont, served Louis XI as chamberlain and as seneschal of Poitou; as a knight of the Order of St-Michael, his chapel is dedicated to the saint. The interiors were much altered by the 19th-century owners but the chapel preserves its original late-Gothic carved wood panelling, with the lords' box on the first floor an exceptional piece of work.

The Loire from Angers to Nantes

Follow signs to Bouchemaine and then the **Pointe de Bouchemaine**, south of Angers. Here are expansive views on to the merging rivers of the Maine and the Loire; in winter and spring the expanse of water can seem Amazonian. In summer it dwindles as riverbank flowers and *épis* emerge. *Epis* are the dykes built in the river from Bouchemaine to Nantes between 1900 and 1930, which secured the banks of the navigation channel.

The winding narrow rocky road along the north bank enters the prosperous and picturesque vineyards of **Savennières**. Down in the midst of the river, the lovely Ile Béhuard is regularly submerged and the houses are frequently *les pieds dans l'eau*. The more obvious but less attractive ways from Angers to Nantes are the busy N23 or the motorway.

The N23 takes you right past the gates of the autocratic **Château de Serrant**, east of St-Georges-sur-Loire (*open July–Aug daily 10–11.30 and 2–5.30; April–June and Sept–Oct same times exc Tues; visits on the hour; adm*). Within the courtyard the walls are pure tufa, blinding in the summer sunshine. Though begun in the middle of the 16th century, building work lasted more than 150 years; the great Philibert de l'Orme has been linked to the plans. Changes were made to the roof in the 19th century by the architect Lucien Magre, who added the lucarnes and the balustrade which runs right round to the two massive southern towers with their helmet-like slate roofs. The splendid **chapel** attributed to Hardouin Mansart serves as a mausoleum to the

Getting Around

Local buses serve both the north and south banks of the river.

Tourist Information

Bouchemaine: Mairie, Quai de la Noë, t 02 41 22 20 00.
Savennières: Mairie, 4 Rue de la Cure, t 02 41 72 85 00, or t 02 41 72 84 46.
Ingrandes-sur-Loire: Mairie, Rue de la Mairie, t 02 41 39 20 21, or t 02 41 39 29 06.
Rochefort-sur-Loire: 20 Av d'Angers, t 02 41 78 81 70.
Chalonnes-sur-Loire: Place de l'Hôtel de Ville, t 02 41 78 26 21, f 02 41 74 91 54.
St-Laurent-de-la-Plaine: t 02 41 78 24 08.
Montjean-sur-Loire: t 02 41 39 80 46, or t 02 41 80 26 32.
St-Florent-le-Vieil: Rue de Rénéville, t 02 41 72 62 32, f 02 41 72 62 95.

Where to Stay and Eat

L'Ile Béhuard ✉ 49170
Les Tonnelles, 12 Rue du Chevalier, t 02 41 72 21 50, f 02 41 72 81 10. An enchanting place to stop with its shady terrace on a secretive island in the Loire.

Rochefort-sur-Loire ✉ 49190
★★Le Grand Hôtel, 30 Rue René Gasnier, t 02 41 78 80 46, f 02 41 78 83 25 (*inexpensive*). Signposted by palm trees, signalling its presence along the village street. The rooms are rather basic, but the cuisine is lovingly prepared.

St-Florent-le-Vieil ✉ 49410
Hostellerie de la Gabelle, 12 Quai de la Loire, t 02 41 72 50 19, f 02 41 72 54 38. A traditional French provincial hotel in a lovely location on the Loire quayside. The cuisine is good.

La Chapelle-St-Florent ✉ 49410
Moulin de l'Epinay, t 02 41 72 70 70. *Crêperie* in a windmill, enjoying spectacular views over southern Anjou.

St-Sauveur-de-Landemont ✉ 49270
★★★★Château de la Colaissière, t 02 40 98 75 04, f 02 40 98 74 15 (*expensive*). Once a ducal home and now a luxurious hotel, with one wing from the 13th century and another from the 16th.

Marquis de Vaubrun who died at the battle of Altenheim in 1675 and, reclining semi-naked, is depicted in the laudatory sculpture by Antoine Coysevox, with Victory floating down to crown him.

An Irish family, the Walshes, became the next proprietors. They had moved to Nantes, faithful to the fleeing James II. Antoine, an arms dealer, acquired the home for his brother François. The castle entrance carries the family coat of arms, with three swans, one pierced by an arrow. It recalls a pretty story of an ancestor who, wounded in battle and left in the water to die, was rescued by two swans. François' son, also named Antoine, financed two ships for Bonnie Prince Charlie to sail across the Channel in the course of his 1745 rebellion. One of the elements that points most strongly to de l'Orme's involvement is the splendid central staircase. The sumptuous rooms are full of the extravagance of Ancien Régime living. Napoleon visited in 1808. He only stayed a few hours but his room has stayed, shrine-like, intact to this day.

Ingrandes marks the end of present-day Anjou on the north bank. It has a typical Angevin silhouette and a spire that resembles an obelisk. In the centre, the **Hôtel de la Gabelle** is a reminder of the much-resented salt tax of the Ancien Régime. Brittany was tax-free, but in Anjou the tax was often extortionate. To stop contraband, a separate police force made up of *gabelous* patrolled the border to catch salt-smugglers.

A string of picturesque hillside villages marks the Loire's southern bank from Angers to Nantes. The most spectacular stretch of road here is known as the Corniche Angevine; to reach it, cross the Loire at **Les Ponts-de-Cé**, due south of Angers. By **Rochefort-sur-Loire** you are in gorgeous Angevin countryside. Down at **Chalonnes**' old quays, *barques* (river boats) rest under the trees.

Loire navigation provides the main theme for **Montjean** today, with its great quays and a traditional boat, a *gabare*, that sails in the summer; book a trip from the scruffy Ecomusée or from the quayside. Tufa, flour, coal, lime, hemp, sails, wine, sugar, salt, were shipped from here for centuries. Boat timbers were used in local building work, and you can see their beams supporting older houses. A lower road from Montjean to St-Florent via Ingrandes' south bank reveals large sandbanks in summer in which people plant their parasols to picnic.

St-Florent-le-Vieil is another cliff-top village with spectacular views next to the neo-classical façade of its church. The church contains a statue of a local hero of the Guerre de Vendée, the Marquis de Bonchamp. As 150,000 Vendéens fled across the Loire from the oncoming Republican forces, Bonchamp, in a rare act of mercy, spared his Revolutionary prisoners, despite the bloody tactics of the Republican army. In the memorial by David d'Angers, he looks like a combination of classical virtue and a Christ of the Resurrection. Underneath him, on the slab on which his body lies, are quoted his words of restraint: '*Grâce aux prisonniers*'. The **Musée d'Histoire Locale et des Guerre de Vendée** (*open July–mid-Aug daily 2.30–6.30; rest of period Easter–Nov weekend afternoons only; adm*), set in a former 17th-century chapel, commemorates the wars, as well as Loire boats and Loire birds.

Nantes

Cosmopolitan Nantes feels oceanic even with the Atlantic some 50km away and the shipping trade long since moved seaward. Historic Nantes and its splendid 18th-century town houses were paid for in large part by the slave trade, although ironically Nantes is best known in history for the edict of tolerance, signed here by Henri IV in 1598 at the end of the Wars of Religion.

History

During much of the Dark Ages the county of Nantes was in the Frankish Marches, fought over by Franks and Bretons. Nomenoë, leader of Brittany, then made his bid for Breton independence, conquering Nantes and its territories. Soon the Vikings sailed up the Loire to wreak havoc, and one bishop of Nantes, Gohard, had his throat cut at the altar. At the end of the medieval period, under François II, the last duke of Brittany, Nantes thrived as the region's capital: a university was inaugurated in 1460 before his only child Anne was forced to wed Charles VIII and marry Brittany to France.

During the Wars of Religion, Nantes fell to the ultra-Catholic governor of Brittany before Henri IV signed the famous Edict of Nantes granting freedom of worship to Protestants. A century later, Louis XIV revoked it, rekindling the persecution of the Huguenots. By then Nantes had become a major port with France's acquisition of her Caribbean colonies in the 17th century; in the 18th it was one of the top European slaving centres. New industries grew up. Sugar was refined and cotton turned into printed calico, or *indiennes*, which went back to Africa to be bartered for more slaves. The Montaudoin family alone equipped 357 ships for the triangle trade between 1694 and 1791. During the 18th century Nantes' population doubled. Merchants used their sickly wealth to build grand town houses in the Louis XV and Louis XVI styles. In his book, *The Slave Trade*, Hugh Thomas writes of their way of life: 'Slave merchants, living in their fine town houses...would give such *"négrillons"* or *"négrittes"* to members of their household as tips. In 1754 an *ordonnance* provided that colonials could bring into France only one black apiece. But that rule was often forgotten.'

The Revolution banned the slave trade for a time. The terrifying Carrier was sent to Nantes by the Committee of Public Safety to make pig-headed royalists wed the cause of the Revolution. These 'Republican marriages' were enforced couplings. The offenders were tied in pairs, bundled on to a boat with a hole in the bottom, and drowned in the Loire. In the 1830s modern techniques of canning fish were developed and it became a big industry, replacing the slave trade. As part of the reparations after the First World War, the channels of the Loire flowing through the city centre were filled in by German workers. Allied bombing raids of the Second World War left scars and the great modern road through the centre known as the Cours des 50 Otages commemorates the execution of fifty hostages in 1942. The university, closed at the Revolution, was reinstated in 1962. High tech industries have replaced the shipbuilding industry, but sugar from the Caribbean still arrives, much of it going into Nantes' many biscuit factories, a last benign relic of its darker shipping past.

Touring Nantes

The massive **Château de Nantes** or **Château des Ducs de Bretagne** (*open July and Aug daily 10–12 and 2–6; rest of year same exc Tues; adm*) is just about the most westerly of the châteaux of the Loire. It's an architectural mess, but the dark outer walls enclose some more graceful wings within. Originally the Loire lapped at the château's walls. Now Nantais take their dogs for a walk in the dry moat. The château had several small museums but work is under way to create a single, grander one which will be ready around 2008.

Rue Rodier leads straight to the cathedral. To take a route there with something of Parisian proportions and elegance, opt instead for the wide mid-18th-century boulevard, **Cours St-Pierre**. While the exterior of the bulky, squat **Cathédrale St-Pierre** (begun in 1434) looks grey, inside it is the cleanest cathedral you are ever likely to see. It is also the emptiest as the interior had to be restored and cleaned after a fire in 1972. The major interest within lies in the tomb of François II Duc de Bretagne and his two wives, commissioned by Anne de Bretagne.

The splendid **Musée des Beaux-Arts** (*open daily exc Tues 10–6, Fri till 9, Sun 11–6; adm*) lies on the other side of Cours St-Pierre, in a beautiful building designed by Josso. It offers a crash course in the history of Western art from the 13th century to the present day. Of the three famous De la Tours it holds, two show his archetypal candlelit effects. The best 18th-century works include a Watteau inspired by the commedia dell'arte, several Greuzes, and a series of portraits by Tournières. Gros' *Le Combat de Nazareth* had a profound effect on Delacroix and is seen as a precursor of the Romantic movement. There are exceptional sculptures by Canova and Ceracchi. Ingres' *Mme de Senonnes* and Courbet's *Les Cribleuses de Blé* are highlights from the 19th century. Wildly over-the-top French Romanticism is there too, in *L'Esclave blanche* by Lecomte du Nouys, a pinky fleshed, doe-eyed European woman posing in the setting of a harem, opposite a statue of a black dancer. *Le Sorcier Noir* by Herbert Ward shows a European vision of the black man as sorcerer. On the ground floor, Monet takes you to Venice and the otherworldly visions of his *Nymphéas* (Waterlilies), Emile Bernard's *Le Gaulage des pommes* depicts a typically Breton landscape, and local arist Metzinger gives a Pointillist view of the Château de Clisson. A room is devoted to Kandinsky, while Chagall checks in with *Le Cheval Rouge*. Raymond Hains, a conceptual artist, pays homage to the Nantes biscuit industry via a barcode.

Rue du Roi Albert leads from the cathedral square to the **Préfecture**, the masterpiece of the architect Ceineray, begun in 1763, its façade sculpted with the arms of France and Brittany. Further west, beyond the Cours des 50 Otages tram route, lie elegant squares and streets from the 18th and 19th centuries. Aim for **Place Royale**, a sober square planned by the architect Crucy, and a wonderful array of cafés just south opposite the colonnaded **Bourse** on Place du Commerce, another work by Crucy. The dry quay was once reserved for the wine trade. Now it is the domain of students who come to forget about their studies.

The elegant shopping arcade, **Passage Pommeraye**, leads to Rue Crébillon from Rue de la Fosse; its mid-19th-century sweeps of stairs are romantically kitsch. Rue

Getting Around

Nantes has an international airport, with direct flights to and from the UK run by Air France and British Airways. There are also fantastic train links to Paris by TGV (*2hrs*). The links are also good with other train stations along the Loire Valey.

The city centre is well served by buses and trams; for details, **t** 02 40 29 39 39.

Tourist Information

Nantes: Maison du Tourisme, 7 Rue de Valmy, **t** 02 40 20 60 00, **f** 02 40 89 11 99.

Activities

To see the beautiful Erdre creeks and little châteaux north of Nantes, take a cruise from the Gare Fluviale de l'Erdre.

Bateaux Nantais, t 02 40 14 51 14. Run cruises April–Nov.

Where to Stay

Nantes ✉ 44000

Moderate

★★★La Pérouse, 3 Allée Duquesne, **t** 02 40 89 75 00, **f** 02 40 89 76 00. The most exciting hotel in central Nantes in ultra-modern style and well located.

★★★Hôtel de France, 24 Rue Crébillon, **t** 02 40 73 57 91, **f** 02 40 69 75 75. The smartest of the old-style hotels in town, and the rooms are quite cosy.

Inexpensive

★★Cholet, 10 Rue Gresset, **t** 02 40 73 31 04, **f** 02 40 73 78 82. Close to the theatre, with good-value, pleasantly renovated rooms.

★★Les Colonies, 5 Rue du Chapeau Rouge, **t** 02 40 48 79 76, **f** 02 40 12 49 25. Quiet rooms close to the central pedestrian area.

Cheap

★St-Daniel, 4 Rue du Bouffay, **t** 02 40 47 41 25, **f** 02 51 72 03 99. Good value and central.

Eating Out

La Cigale, 4 Place Graslin, **t** 02 40 69 76 41, **f** 02 40 73 75 37. Classic French brasserie with outstanding and extravagant Art Nouveau decor, a tourist sight in itself.

Auberge du Château, 5 Place de la Duchesse Anne, **t** 02 40 74 31 85, **f** 02 40 37 97 57. Intimate little restaurant opposite the castle, serving classic Nantes food.

Le Chiwawa, 6 Place Livette, **t** 02 40 69 01 65. Restaurant in the corner of a typically elegant Nantes square, presenting a range of inventive dishes.

La Découverte, 2 Rue Santeuil, **t** 02 40 73 27 40. Specializes in classic Loire dishes.

La Poissonnerie, 4 Rue Léon Maître, **t** 02 49 47 79 50. Good fish restaurant.

Le Carnivore, 7 Allée des Tanneurs, **t** 02 40 47 87 00, **f** 02 40 47 00 19. Traditional meat lovers might be surprised to see bison and ostrich on the menu.

Pommier Laprugne, 3 Allée de l'Ile Gloriette, **t** 02 40 47 78 08. One of many *crêperies* in Nantes. This one has the most interesting range of fillings.

Crébillon links Place Royale with Crucy's more serious **Place Graslin**, dominated by its theatre. **Cours Cambronne** could hardly be more perfect for promenading with your poodle. West of Place Graslin, the **Musée Thomas Dobrée** and **Musée Archéologique** in the Manoir de la Touche (*open daily exc Mon and public hols 10–12 and 1.30–5.30; adm*) stand on Rue Voltaire. The shining golden reliquary heart of Anne of Brittany lies here; the finest piece of craftsmanship in a museum crammed with such. Thomas Dobrée, a dedicated collector, amassed sculpture, paintings, furniture, art objects, manuscripts, and correspondence from the Great and the Good, building a grand neo-Romanesque house to contain them, all in brown bear-coloured stone with carved bears on the corners. He also restored the 15th-century Manoir de la Touche next door. Its ground floor is devoted to Nantes at the time of the Revolution while upstairs are Bronze Age, Celtic, Gallo-Roman and Merovingian finds.

In the Ste-Anne quarter, the little **Musée Jules Verne** (*3 Rue de l'Hermitage; open daily 10–12 and 2–5 exc Tues, Sun am and public hols; adm*), pays its respects to the 19th-century visionary from Nantes. Along the Quai de la Fosse is the **Maillé Brézé** (*open June–Sept daily 2–6; rest of year Wed, weekends and school hols 2–5; adm*), a decommissioned naval squadron escort vessel, now turned museum.

Around Nantes: Muscadet Country

The Loire Atlantique makes one extremely well-known wine, Muscadet. But although much good Muscadet is produced, the region has received a bit of a bashing in the press over recent years for failing to maintain quality across the board.

Between Nantes and Clisson at Le Pallet, the **Musée du Vignoble Nantais** (*open May–Sept daily exc Mon 10–12.30 and 2–6; Oct–April daily exc Mon 2.30–6; adm*) is a startlingly slick wine museum, exhibits placed neatly under glass. The museum is also devoted to the great scholar and theologian Peter Abélard, born into a noble family in Le Pallet in 1079, and his tragic love for Heloise, the brilliant and beautiful 17-year-old niece of the canon Fulbert with whom he lodged in Paris. A good place to start tasting Muscadet wines is the **Maison des Vins de Nantes** at La Haye-Fouassière (*open Mon–Fri 8.30–12.30 and 2–5.45; July–Aug also Sat and Sun 10.30–12.30 and 2.20–6; adm*), overlooking hectare upon hectare of vines.

Clisson is the town where Brittany and Italy meet, although the feudal **Château de Clisson** (*open daily exc Tues 9.30–12 and 2–6; adm*) looks French enough. Its ruins

Getting Around

There's a railway line down through the Muscadet area to Clisson, and there are bus services around this area from Nantes.

Tourist Information

Le Pallet: 26 Rue St-Vincent, t 02 40 80 40 24, f 02 40 80 42 48.
Clisson: 6 Place de la Trinité, t 02 40 54 02 95, f 02 40 54 07 77.

Where to Stay and Eat

St-Fiacre-sur-Maine, Châteauthébaud and Monnières ✉ 44690
Le Fiacre, 1 Rue des Echicheurs, St-Fiacre, t 02 40 54 83 92. You'll eat with loads of locals at this lively, simple village *bistrot-cum-bar*. The *patron* is passionate about Muscadet and has a list of over 100 different producers' wines.
Domaine de la Pénissière, t 02 40 06 51 22. At Châteauthébaud on the opposite bank of the Maine, offering smart B&B rooms in an atmospheric old house set on a wine estate with good views of the vineyards.
Le Petit Douet, t 02 40 06 53 59. Run by Thérèse Méchineau, a vinegrower's wife who provides wine books and wine conversation in her modern B&B.
Château de Plessis-Blézot, t 02 40 54 63 24, f 02 40 54 66 07. Little 17th-century property set above the Sèvre Nantaise at Monnières. A reputed wine domain and a luxury B&B.

Clisson ✉ 44190
La Bonne Auberge, 1 Rue Olivier de Clisson, t 02 40 54 01 90, f 02 40 54 08 48. Stylish gastronomic restaurant.

dominate the slopes of the valley where the Maine joins the Sèvre Nantaise. The church and town, however, look as though they've been shipped straight from Italy. Clisson was devastated by the Vendée uprising (*see* p.411) and what arose afterwards was the work of Pierre and François Cacault of Nantes and their friend, the sculptor Frédéric Lemot. All had travelled in Italy and they decided to build Roman-style homes. **Notre-Dame** is typical of Clisson's Italianate style, with a campanile. From the Pont de la Vallée bridge you get beautiful views.

The wonderful Italianate villa of **La Garenne Lemot** and its park (*park open April–Sept daily 9am–8pm; Oct–Mar daily 9.30–6.30; Maison du Jardinier open daily 10–1 and 2–6; adm; villa open during exhibitions; house and villa closed Mon; adm*) lie on the other bank of the Sèvre Nantaise. Frédéric Lemot, best known for his statue of Henri IV on the Pont-Neuf in Paris, bought La Garenne in 1805. The **Maison du Jardinier** is built in rustic Italian style and houses an exhibition that ranges widely over the Italian influence on French artistic circles in the 18th century. The **villa** is reached by a garden lined with statues, its front courtyard formed by a semi-circle of granite columns. The house contains Lemot's prize-winning sculpture of the Judgement of Solomon, while the grounds offer a treasure hunt of follies.

A Detour to Chartres and the Loir Valley

Chartres

Chartres lies at the edge of the Beauce, an enormous flat cereal plain that supplies Paris with much of its grain. But the famous photo view of the cathedral with its Gothic towers rising like a medieval skyscraper out of a field of wheat is becoming harder to find these days, as the town spreads over its countryside. The Romans found this part of Gaul inhabited by the Carnutii, after whom Chartres is named. The village, built around a sacred well, was an important religious site and as such it was a key target for the Christians. They substituted the worship of the Virgin Mary for that of the ancient mother goddess who always ruled over wells and underground springs – a primeval wooden statue of the goddess, recycled as Mary, was worshipped here as late as 1793. The first Christian basilica was built in the 4th century and rebuilt several times after fires.

Medieval Chartres, about the same size as the present version, was relatively much more important. In the 11th century its cathedral school was a rival to Paris itself. The current building took form after a fire in 1194 destroyed a brand new cathedral. Rebuilding commenced immediately and contributed much to the legend of pious community participation in constructing such edifices. Everyone pitched in with labour or funds to complete the inspired new design for the 'Palace of the Virgin' – even Philippe Auguste and Richard Coeur de Lion, who were then fighting over the area. By 1260 the building was nearly complete. The rapidity of the work allowed Chartres to have a stylistic unity seen in few other medieval cathedrals. **Chartres**

Cathedral perfects the concepts of roof vaulting and the flying buttress, enabling it to carry large expanses of glass-filled sides, with big windows in the clerestory and especially in the magnificent apse, nearly all of glass. Inside, carving the thick pillars into apparent bundles of slender columns accentuated the verticality and lightness.

In the words of art historian Emile Mâle, 'Chartres is medieval thought in visible form'. More than 10,000 figures in stone or glass make this cathedral an architectural encyclopedia. It would take a thorough knowledge of the Scriptures and medieval philosophy, and a lifetime's work, to decipher all the scenes. The west porch survived the 1194 fire. Besides the exquisite statues of saints that flank the doors, note the signs of the zodiac and labours of the months on the left door, the latter one of the loveliest of such Gothic stone calendars. While the tympanum of the central portal is dedicated to Christ those on the sides belong to Mary, with an Annunciation to the left and an Assumption to the right. The façade's south tower is original; the northern one was struck by lightning and rebuilt, more ornately, in the 14th century. The south porch honours Christian saints, with martyrs in the right door, apostles in the central door and confessors in the left door, surmounted by nine choirs of angels. The north porch, less extravagant, includes a tympanum showing the Adoration of the Magi.

Inside blaze the finest stained-glass windows in the world, 173 of them, mostly original. Here as in other cities, it was the custom for the different trade guilds to support the making of the stained glass. Look at the bottoms of the windows along the nave and in many you'll see scenes of goldsmiths, bakers, weavers, tavern-keepers, furriers, blacksmiths and others at work. Particularly outstanding are the tall windows in the

Getting Around

Chartres has good train links with Paris-Montparnasse (1hr). It's also fast by road from the capital, by the A10 and A11.

Tourist Information

Chartres: Place Cathédrale, t 02 37 18 26 26.

Where to Stay

Chartres ✉ 28000

★★★**Le Grand Monarque**, 22 Place des Epars, t 02 37 21 00 72, f 02 37 36 34 18 (*expensive*). The best hotel in Chartres, comfortable, appealing and central, with a large dining room where you can sample excellent French cuisine (*menus 160–300F*).

Hôtel de la Poste, 3 Rue du Général Koenig, t 02 37 21 04 27, f 02 37 36 42 17 (*inexpensive*). Quite good for the price and very close to the cathedral.

Le Chêne Fleuri, 14 Rue de la Porte Morard, t 02 37 35 25 70 (*cheap*). A bargain hotel in a charming part of town, with its own restaurant (*menus c. 100–200F*).

St-Prest ✉ 28300

Manoir des Prés du Roy, t 02 37 22 27 27, f 02 37 22 24 92 (*moderate*). Just 7km north of Chartres, by the Eure river, a delightfully restored manor house in a park. There is a mix of very comfortable and more modest rooms. Restaurant (*menus 145–180F*).

Eating Out

Rue au Lait by the cathedral has several interesting restaurants to choose from.

Le Buisson Ardent, 10 Rue au Lait, t 02 37 34 04 66, f 02 37 91 15 82. The pick of the bunch by the cathedral (*menus c. 100–218*).

La Truie qui File, Place de la Poissonnerie, t 02 37 21 53 90, f 02 37 36 62 65. The favourite for foodies in Chartres (*menus 180–360F*).

apse picturing the life of Christ and the great rose windows, especially the Rose de France in the north transept celebrating the Virgin.

On the floor of the nave, the famous labyrinth is now almost unique in France, although many other Gothic cathedrals once had similar ones. Most were destroyed in the vapid 18th century. A large exhibit off the nave attempts to explain the Christian meaning of the maze, but this attempt at Christian adoption is highly dubious. The symbolism of labyrinths since the remotest times has always had something to do with the passage of the soul and with astronomy. Here it possibly also reflects the patterns of a dance, a survival of pre-Christian times. Originally, there was a bronze relief of Theseus and the Minotaur at the centre. Below the choir, in the crypt, the ancient sacred wells still survive.

Just behind the cathedral, the **Musée des Beaux-Arts** (*open daily exc Tues 10–12 and 2–5; adm*) contains few artworks from the cathedral, but a fine collection of tapestries and Renaissance paintings. The oldest part of town, the Haute Ville, conserves a good many medieval buildings, although it seems a little over-restored. Some of the prettiest corners stand around Place de l'Etape du Vin and Place de la Poissonnerie.

The Loir Valley

The Loir (without an e) meanders through four French *départements*, its wide, flat valley often seeming to be too big for its slender size as it flows to join the Loire south of Angers. The names Loir and Loire suggest there's a connection between the two and similarities do exist: limestone in whites and beiges; troglodyte villages; Romanesque churches; and characteristic châteaux, from Poncé to Bazouges via the more famous Le Lude. The Renaissance touched this area too, and nowhere more than at La Possonnière, the house of the poet Ronsard. We concentrate here on the Loir's course from Vendôme in the Loir-et-Cher into Anjou.

The source of the Loir lies southwest of Chartres, close to **Illiers-Combray**, with its museum dedicated to Proust, whose family had a house there. The historic heart of **Vendôme**, some way south, is embraced by the Loir and guarded by remnants of a ruined castle. The massive abbey in the centre dates back to the 11th century when Geoffroy Martel of Anjou and his wife Agnès de Bourgogne witnessed what they took to be a divine sign. They set up the Abbaye de la Trinité with help from the bishop of Chartres and Geoffroy was granted some especially precious relics including an arm of St George and a tear of Christ. In the late 14th century Catherine de Vendôme married Jean de Bourbon and the Bourbon link with the town was established. The glove makers of Vendôme were highly regarded; Catherine de' Medici is said to have given her ladies-in-waiting Vendôme gloves so delicate that the gifts were presented in sewing thimbles. Vendôme also developed early as a printing centre. It fell into the hands of the Catholics in the Wars of Religion and the Bourbon Henri IV was forced to besiege his own town in 1589.

The **abbey church** is Romanesque, but its splendid façade is a last blaze of Gothic. The great window is alight with fiery tongues of stone tracery licking their way

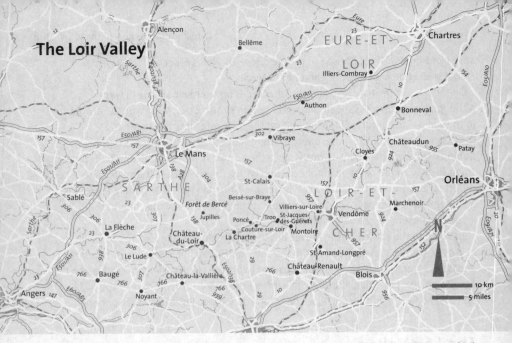

upward. Down the nave, you walk back in time from late Gothic to the transept which dates from 1040. Beyond, the choir and side chapels contain some of the oldest stained glass in France (from *c.* 1140) including an exceptional 14th-century scene showing Geoffroy Martel receiving the tear of Christ. The **abbey buildings** date from the 17th and 18th centuries, but some vivid Romanesque frescoes have survived from the old chapterhouse. At the **Musée du Cloître** (*open daily exc Tues 10–12 and 2–6; adm, free on Wed*) one floor has works by Louis Leygue, a 20th-century sculptor from the town. Spacious **Place St-Martin** is marked by a soaring tower to match that of the abbey, all that remains of a late 15th-century church. Cafés, bars and market stalls give the square plenty of life. The **Parc Ronsard** has a monumental statue of the poet by Louis Leygue.

Between Vendôme and Montoire you might seek out the wall paintings in the 15th-century church of **St-Hilaire** at **Villiers-sur-Loir** (*open daily 8–6*). The choir stalls have bawdy scenes which once graced Vendôme abbey. At **Montoire**, a pact with the devil was sealed with a handshake in the railway station. Here, Pétain met with Hitler in October 1940 to accept officially the German occupation of France and his collaborative role. The most charming part of town lies on the southern bank of the river where the tiny 11th-century **Chapelle St-Gilles** (*small charge; contact the tourist information office in Montoire*) crouches so low it is scarcely visible. Its truncated form cloaks three overwhelming Romanesque depictions of Christ. **Lavardin**'s ruined castle on a hillside is worthy of a Romantic painting. The village below has a church plastered with wall paintings, including a crucified Christ from a Passion cycle thought to be 15th-century and a queue of naked people waiting to enter paradise.

The secretive village of **Troo** climbs the steep bank of the Loir west of Montoire, its cliff punctured with troglodyte caverns turned into houses. In the valley, on the southern side of the Loir from Troo, the delightful **St-Jacques-des-Guérets** is a box-like space decorated with fine Romanesque art, including the familiar over-proud knight falling from his horse, the lustful woman piercing her breast, and even St Nicholas whose generosity we celebrate on 25 December. One utterly enchanting spot calls you north to Bessé-sur-Braye. On its outskirts, the **Château de Courtanvaux** is a story-book vision with late-Gothic silhouette, lovingly tended gardens and sweet courtyard.

The Renaissance poet Pierre de Ronsard was born just west of Troo, near Couture-sur-Loir, at the **Manoir de la Possonnière** (*open July–Aug daily exc Mon and Tues 3–7; April–June and Sept–15 Nov weekends and hols 3–6; adm*), and learning is literally written all over the house, as the windows are graced with Latin inscriptions. Many of these were ordered by Ronsard's father in celebration of his marriage. In the hillside opposite, seven cave entrances penetrate the rock, with inscriptions engraved over each. The manor was a stopping point on a pilgrimage route and many travellers rested beneath them.

Getting Around

Vendôme has fantastic high-speed train services to Paris, but the TGV station is some way outside the town centre. Slower trains serve Châteaudun.

Tourist Information

Vendôme: Hôtel du Saillant, 47 Rue Poterie, t 02 54 77 05 07, f 02 54 73 20 81.
Montoire-sur-le-Loir: 16 Place Clemenceau, t 02 54 85 23 30, f 02 54 85 23 87.
Troo: Rue Auguste Arnault, t 02 54 72 51 27, f 02 54 72 58 74.
Le Lude: Place François de Nicolay, t 02 43 94 62 20, f 02 43 94 48 46.
La Flèche: Bd de Montréal, t 02 43 94 02 53, f 02 43 94 43 15, *otxi-lafleche@libertysurf.fr*.

Activities

You can take boat trips around Vendôme (*May–Sept*). Call t 02 54 77 05 07, for details.

Where to Stay and Eat

Bonneval ✉ 28800
*Hostellerie du Bois Guibert, just off the N10 south of Bonneval, t 02 37 47 22 33, f 02 37 47 50 69 (*inexpensive*). A delightful, stylish manor with comfortable rooms and a good restaurant with a fireplace.

Cloyes-sur-le-Loir ✉ 28220
*Hostellerie St-Jacques, Place du Maré aux Oies, t 02 37 98 40 08, f 02 37 98 32 63 (*inexpensive*). Old timberframe building with some decent rooms and menus.

Vendôme ✉ 41100
Grand Hôtel St-Georges, 14 Rue Poterie, t 02 54 77 25 42, f 02 54 80 22 57 (*inexpensive*). Classic old-fashioned French hotel in the centre, with restaurant (*menus c. 100–150F*).

Troo ✉ 41800
Château de la Voûte, t 02 54 72 52 52 (*moderate*). A gem of a B&B on Troo's slope, with lovely rooms and splendid views.
Le Petit Relais, Place du Château, t 02 54 72 57 92. Adorable one-woman restaurant in the upper village.

Luché-Pringé ✉ 72800
Auberge du Port-des-Roches, t 02 43 45 44 48, f 02 43 45 39 61 (*inexpensive*). Sweet little roadside inn west of Le Lude. Lovely terrace by the river (*menus 115–195F*).

La Flèche 72200
Le Vert Galant, 70 Grand-Rue, t 02 43 94 00 51, f 02 43 45 11 24. Old-fashioned hotel with classic restaurant (*menus c. 100–200F*).

After Couture, the Loir passes by **Poncé**, colonized by craftspeople; jewellers, cabinet-makers, a hatter, a weaver and a candle-maker among them. The **Château de Poncé** (*open April–Sept daily exc Sun am 10–12 and 2–6; adm*) has known more elegant days and has been cruelly separated from the river by a busy road. But a great Renaissance staircase ascends in front of you as you enter, its coffered stone ceiling filled with sculptures – flowers, lions' heads, angels in foliage, salamanders, mythological creatures, flute-playing putti and another woman stabbing her own breast. A bust of Ronsard stands at the top of the stairs, accompanied by a poem he wrote dedicated to the Loir. From the pleasant little market town of La Chartre-sur-le-Loir, the **forest of Bercé** bends in a horseshoe around the village of Jupilles. It conceals mighty oaks such as the Chêne Boppe, the Nouveau Chêne Boppe and the Chêne Roulleau, the last two some 300 years old. Jupilles' **Maison du Sabot et de l'Artisanat du Bois** (*open Easter–1 Nov daily 2.30–6.30; closed Mon; adm*) is devoted to wood and, especially, clogmaking. Once Jupilles had 400 clogmakers producing more than 400,000 pairs a year – some for export to Holland. Ornaments and toys are now made here.

Beyond the orchards of Vaas, the **Château du Lude** (*open April–Sept gardens daily 10–12 and 2–6; château daily 2.30–6; adm*) competes in scale with some of the grandest Loire châteaux. Each corner is marked by a massive round tower covered with Renaissance decoration. It was substantially modified in the 18th century, and the classical façade and inner courtyard and interiors have the air of a great Parisian townhouse. In the library stands a bust of the Marquis de Talhouët-Roy, finance minister to Louis XVIII and Charles X, who initiated many of the internal modifications. From the spectacular ball-room, with its floral marquetry floor, you trip through a series of spacious salons. An intimate surprise awaits in a small jewel box of a room covered with paintings and grotesques in the Italian Mannerist style.

Take the prettier north bank from Le Lude to reach La Flèche. Here, the first Bourbon king, Henri IV, founded the elite Collège Royal run by Jesuits, now known as the **Prytanée National Militaire** (*open July and Aug daily 10.30–12 and 2–6.30; Easter hols daily 2–6; adm*). You can only visit outside term time. As well as an intellectual legacy – René Descartes was its star pupil – the Jesuits left their fine 17th-century building. Henri IV requested that his heart and that of his tempestuous wife Marie de' Medici be buried in the stunning Jesuit Chapelle St-Louis. They were ceremonially burnt in 1793. Napoleon turned the college into the élite military training school it remains to this day. Honours boards list pupils who became marshals and generals and the many more who have died in conflicts.

Atlantic Coast

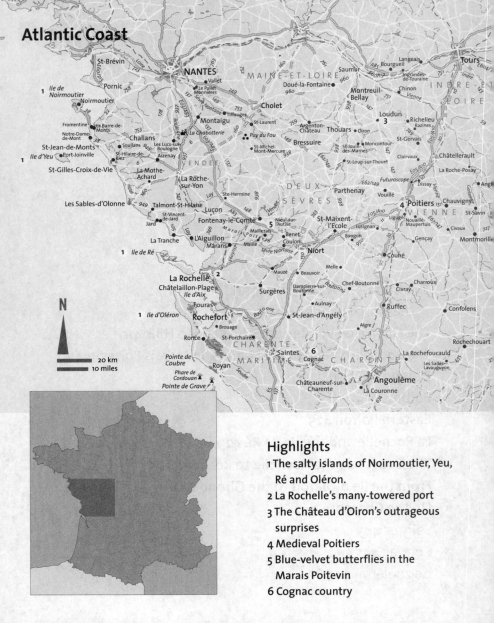

Atlantic Coast

Highlights

1 The salty islands of Noirmoutier, Yeu, Ré and Oléron.
2 La Rochelle's many-towered port
3 The Château d'Oiron's outrageous surprises
4 Medieval Poitiers
5 Blue-velvet butterflies in the Marais Poitevin
6 Cognac country

A hot Holland with hints of the Spanish costas, France's flat Atlantic coast from the Loire to the Gironde has sandy beaches stretching to the horizon. Here sunbaked terracotta roof tiles replace the slate. Whitewashed houses and white stones shine blindingly in the sun. The stretch of resorts includes a few old-world charmers, such as Les Sables-d'Olonne; blissful island resorts and oyster ports float just out to sea.

The coast's two great ports, La Rochelle and Rochefort, are now as busy with yachts and tourists as freighters and men-of-war. Just inland lie the *marais*, the marshes, many drained with the aid of Dutch experts. They turn out to be surprisingly beautiful, especially the dreamy Marais Poitevin. While the coastal flatness can be very painterly and picturesque, it becomes more monotonous inland, relieved by gentle river valleys, most importantly the Charente, the land of cognac.

One way of visiting the interior is to follow the Route d'Or, the medieval pilgrims' Golden Way to Compostela, stopping at the region's extraordinary and highly distinctive Romanesque churches – Aulnay, St-Savin, Saintes, and many others – dating from the time of Eleanor of Aquitaine. Poitiers, the city she chose for her court, has a church for every day of the week. Yet while the association between this region and the Middle Ages has given it an image of being stuck in the past, it is no stick in the mud; this is also the land of Futuroscope, said to be the largest high-tech movie centre in the world.

Food and Drink

Along stretches of this coastline enormous oyster and mussel parks emerge in the shallow waters as the tide goes out. They are particularly impressive around the islands. The coast's other great culinary asset is salt. Although production has declined radically in recent times, some salt is still produced, the Fleur de Sel being the best quality. On the islands, the patterning of the salt pans still marks the landscape.

Duck and other fowl are traditionally hunted in the band of marshlands which lies just inland, while the sheep reared on the salt marshes yield a succulent salty meat. White Charolais cows graze in vast numbers. Eels, frogs and snails thrive in the region; eels turn up in *matelote* (stew), snails often feature on menus under the aliases of *lumas* and *cagouilles*. Further inland, pork and geese are more popular, while goats give milk for some particularly tasty cheese known as *chabichou*.

Farci poitevin is another regional speciality: minced pork mixed with sorrel, garlic and lettuce and wrapped in cabbage leaves. Cabbage also features in regional soups, which may also incorporate ham, potato and *mojettes*, big white beans which are a particular speciality of the Vendée.

For the sweet-toothed, *brioche vendéenne* is a wonderfully light bread once made for special occasions and now often enjoyed at breakfast. *Tourteau fromagé* is another sweet bread-like speciality, made with *fromage blanc*.

Not much wine is produced in this region, and the little that is proves to be of mixed quality. But the wines of Les Fiefs Vendéens are very palatable, if a little pricey, and you can also find one or two surprises among the vineyards of the Haut-Poitou.

The region's alcoholic highlight, however, is of course cognac, a dash of which is often added to a sauce to add depth and flavour, or mixed with grape juice to make an apéritif, Pineau des Charente. Taste cognac by itself and you'll be hit by an extraordinarily rich array of flavours from caramels to violets (*see* p.407 for more details).

Getting There

By plane: Nearest airports are Nantes just to the north, or Bordeaux, just south; both have frequent direct flights from London. There are also smaller airports at Poitiers and La Rochelle which have internal flights from Paris.

By train: Using the TGV trains, Paris-Montparnasse and Poitiers are a mere 1hr 30mins apart, Paris-Montparnasse and Angoulême just 2hrs 15mins apart, and La Rochelle under 3hrs from the capital. There are also some amazingly fast direct TGV trains to Futuroscope just north of Poitiers. Coming from Britain to the region by fast train, you can avoid Paris altogether by changing at Lille.

By road: The A10 linking Paris and Bordeaux is the main fast road through the region. The A83 crosses Vendée from the A10 near Niort up to Nantes.

The Islands of Noirmoutier and Yeu and the North Vendée Coast

The adorable islands of Noirmoutier and Yeu beat the resorts of the northern Vendée mainland coast hands down.

Ile de Noirmoutier

Shaped like a sperm trying to break away into the Atlantic, the seductive island of Noirmoutier has now been chained to the mainland by a road bridge. This salty place is surprisingly fertile, renowned for the best spring potatoes in France. The east side of Noirmoutier's tail is oyster-farming territory; the west side has long beaches of soft sand and modest seaside villages. Barren salt marshes separate the northwest corner of the island from the villages of Noirmoutier-en-l'Ile and L'Herbaudière.

Noirmoutier-en-l'Ile, the cultural heart of the island, is bisected by a canalized waterway. On one side the medieval castle (*open high summer daily 10–7; rest of period 6 Feb–15 Nov daily exc Tues 10–12.30 and 2.30–6; adm*) contains a small historical museum with details on the island's past, exotica and scrimshaw brought back by sailors. The village church conceals a crypt of stunted columns. It is dedicated to St Philibert, who drained the island and rendered it fertile in the 7th century.

On the opposite side of the waterway, creosote-boarded buildings house an aquarium, a salt house and a museum on small-scale shipbuilding, the **Musée de la Construction Navale** (*open high summer daily 10–7; rest of period 3 April–7 Nov daily exc Mon 10–12.30 and 2.30–6; adm*). The best beaches on the island are to the northeast, lined with adorable beach huts in front of gnarled woods.

Ile d'Yeu

In old documents, the Ile d'Yeu was in fact referred to as God's Island, l'Ile Dieu. Its mix of Breton coastline and white Vendéen houses gives it a special charm, so although it is harder to reach than the neighbouring islands, don't expect to find a haven of peace. **Port Joinville**, the harbour, is busy and workaday. Vichy's Marshal Pétain was imprisoned here, in a curious sunken citadel hidden below the water

Getting Around

To get to l'Ile d'Yeu, leave your car on the mainland and take a boat, helicopter or plane. **Compagnie Yeu Continent, t** 02 51 49 59 69, **f** 02 51 49 59 70 *www.compagnie-yeu-continent.fr*. Boats from Fromentine. **V.I.I.V., t** 02 51 39 00 00. Boats from Fromentine or St-Gilles-Croix-de-Vie. **Oya Hélicoptères, t** 02 51 49 01 01. From La Barre-de-Monts, south of Fromentine. You can also fly from Nantes, **t** 02 40 84 95 30. There are train services to St-Gilles-Croix-de-Vie and Les Sables-d'Olonne.

Tourist Information

Ile de Noirmoutier: Noirmoutier-en-l'Ile, **t** 02 51 39 80 71, **f** 02 51 39 53 16.
Ile d'Yeu: Place du Marché, Port-Joinville, **t** 02 51 58 32 58.
St-Gilles-Croix-de-Vie: t 02 51 55 03 66, **f** 02 51 55 69 60.
Les Sables-d'Olonne: Centre de Congrès les Atlantes, **t** 02 51 96 85 85, **f** 02 51 96 85 71.

Where to Stay and Eat

Noirmoutier ✉ 85330
★★★**Hôtel du Général d'Elbée**, Place du Château, **t** 02 51 39 10 29, **f** 02 51 39 08 23 (*moderate*). Smart 18th-century house with a walled garden and pool.
★★★**Fleur de Sel**, Rue des Saulniers, **t** 02 51 39 21 59, **f** 02 51 39 75 66 (*moderate*). Easy-going, modern hotel with a pool. Restaurant (*menus 185–285F*). *Closed Sun eve, Mon lunch.*
★★**Les Douves**, 11 Rue des Douves, **t** 02 51 39 02 72, **f** 02 51 39 73 09 (*moderate–inexpensive*). Stylish modern building with a pool. An upmarket two-star. Tempting restaurant (*menus 99–180F*). *Closed Sun eve. Hotel closed Jan.*
★**Beau Rivage**, Plage des Dames, **t** 02 51 39 06 66 (*cheap*). Simple rooms overlooking a splendid beach in just about the best location on the island.
★★★**Punta Lara**, Route de la Noure, La Guérinière, **t** 02 51 39 11 58, **f** 02 51 39 69 12 (*moderate*). Stylish hotel among pines on the west of the island, by a soft sandy beach.

L'Ile d'Yeu ✉ 85350
★★★**Atlantic Hôtel**, 3 Quai Carnot, Port-Joinville, **t** 02 51 58 38 80, **f** 02 51 58 35 92 (*moderate*). Small, comfortable rooms overlooking the port. Book ahead for Aug.
★★**L'Escale**, 14 Rue de la Croix du Port, **t** 02 51 58 50 28, **f** 02 51 59 33 55 (*inexpensive*). Welcoming hotel with simple rooms.
Restaurant du Port-de-la-Meule. Tucked away down a lovely creek, and just about the only place to eat or drink on the south side of Yeu, with a very stylish terrace.

St-Jean-des-Monts ✉ 85160
★★**Le Robinson**, 28 Bd du Général Leclerc, **t** 02 51 59 20 20, **f** 02 51 58 88 03 (*inexpensive*). A sprawling hotel with a luxurious indoor pool. Restaurant (*menus 76–215F*). *Closed Dec and Jan.*

Challans ✉ 85300
★★★**Château de la Vérie**, Route de St-Gilles-Croix-de-Vie, **t** 02 51 35 33 44, **f** 02 51 35 14 84 (*moderate–inexpensive*). Small luxurious 16th-century château just outside Challans with refined cuisine (*menus 160–245F*).

St-Gilles-Croix-de-Vie ✉ 85800
★★**Les Embruns**, 16 Bd de la Mer, **t** 02 51 55 11 40, **f** 02 51 55 11 20 (*inexpensive*). A small, cheerful hotel; some of the rooms have sea views. The restaurant has a good reputation.

Les Sables-d'Olonne ✉ 85100
★★★**Les Roches Noires**, 12 Promenade Georges Clemenceau, **t** 02 51 32 01 71, **f** 02 51 21 61 00 (*moderate*). Wonderful sea views from the front rooms and a pleasant brasserie.
Atlantic Hôtel, 5 Promenade Georges Godet, **t** 02 51 95 37 71, **f** 02 51 95 37 30 (*expensive*). Luxury modern hotel on the seafront.
★★**Antoine**, 60 Rue Napoléon, **t** 02 51 95 08 36, **f** 02 51 23 92 78 (*inexpensive*). A peaceful, pleasant option in the centre.
Beau Rivage, 40 Promenade Georges Clemenceau, **t** 02 51 32 03 01. Special upmarket seafood restaurant (*menus 260–510F*).
Le Navarin, 18 Place Navarin, **t** 02 51 21 11 61. Well-located and elegant seafood restaurant (*menus 105–250F*). *Closed Sun eves and Mon.*

tower, when his death sentence was commuted after the Second World War. The house that Pétain's wife lived in has been converted into a little historical museum.

If you're on a day excursion, head for the sandy beaches east of Port Joinville. The beaches get better as you lose sight of the harbour, until they end around the Pointe des Corbeaux with a lighthouse and a pile of rocks that looks like a giant's pebble collection. If you have more time, hire a bike and cycle around the island, heading west from Port Joinville to the lighthouse (*open to the public*) and along picturesque rocky coasts. Port des Vieilles has the only sizeable and safe beach on the south coast.

The North Vendée Coast

Long strips of pine-backed beaches alternate with long strips of modern resorts and campsites along the north Vendée coast from Noirmoutier to Les Sables-d'Olonne; sand-yachting is popular. **Fromentine** bustles in summer with yachtsmen. **St-Jean-des-Monts** has some pleasant enough seafront apartments, and a few that look distinctly wacky, facing the generous beach. A rash of campsites stretches to **St-Gilles-Croix-de-Vie**, an older, popular resort which trumpets its **Corniche Vendéenne**, whose rocks bring to mind outsized dollops of elephant dung. The coast seems wilder and less friendly south of St-Gilles.

The huge beach north of **Les Sables-d'Olonne** is battered by waves, but the town's pride and joy is the lovely broad, central curve of flat, safe sands backed by the Remblai, the protected promenade. To the French Les Sables is synonymous with popular seaside holidays. The place appears a bit confusing at first sight, with a commercial port, a marina, a conference centre, a casino and several branches of water converging here. Along the seafront, modern apartment blocks have unfortunately shouldered out most of the grand old bourgeois buildings, although some of the streets inland have kept their character. When the beach begins to pall, seek out the **Musée de l'Abbaye Ste-Croix** with its challenging modern art.

The odd modest white house stands out like an egret in the marshy lands of the **Marais Breton and Marais de Challans**, peculiarly atmospheric strips of waterlands just behind the north Vendée coast. White Charolais cows graze among flat pastures divided up by little canals and dotted with *bourrines*, the typical thatched cottages.

The Guerre de Vendée and the Vendée Hills

If you squeezed the ground like a sponge, the blood of martyrs would gush out.
sign at a Vendéen memorial chapel

The bitter civil war known as the **Guerre de Vendée** takes you into the territory of Baroness Orczy's novel, *The Scarlet Pimpernel*. The swashbuckling hero may have cocked a snook at the French Revolutionary powers of the early 1790s, but the reality in the Vendée was far different, and the people suffered appallingly for their uprising against the Revolution. Even today, when locals mention the 'Grande Guerre' they may be referring to the Guerre de Vendée, not to the First World War.

The Guerre de Vendée

The Guerre de Vendée came about first and foremost through the local determination to defend the Catholic faith against radical Revolutionary policies. From 1792 uprisings multiplied as the Vendéens saw how harshly their priests were being treated. The Revolutionary national guard, referred to as *les Bleus* because of the colour of their uniforms, crushed these uprisings, at the same time destroying statues of saints and shutting churches. Resistance leaders, notably Cathelineau and Stofflet, rose from the ranks of the ordinary people. Independently, certain aristocrats also led actions against the Revolutionary guards. The execution of Louis XVI early in 1793 led to increased protests just as the European powers were threatening the French borders. The Republican authorities, desperate for new troops, attempted to enforce conscription by lottery to select 300,000 bachelors across France aged between 18 and 40 who hadn't already signed up. Riots broke out in many part of France and were quickly stamped out, except, through incompetence, in the Vendée. A couple of important army officers, notably d'Elbée and Bonchamp, even joined the Vendéen side.

The conflict escalated through June 1793, and the Vendéens experienced early victories, taking control of Cholet, and of Saumur and Angers along the Loire. Towards the end of June they attacked Nantes. By then Cathelineau had become virtual leader of the chaotically organized Vendéens, but with his death on 29 June fortunes were reversed. Kléber and Marceau were put at the head of the violent Republican troops sent to stifle the uprising, and at the battle of Cholet in October 1793 the Vendéens suffered a bruising defeat. They retreated, well over 50,000 in number, and crossed the Loire at St-Florent-le-Vieil. Their leader Bonchamp had been mortally wounded in action, but before he died, in a memorably rare act of mercy, he asked for the lives of 5,000 captive Republican soldiers to be spared.

The action then moved north of the Loire. In a campaign known as the Virée de Galerne, the Vendéens, under the hothead Henri de La Rochejacquelin, a general at the tender age of 21, swept into the province of Maine. Some 15,000 men may have been killed in the Vendéens' terrible defeat at Le Mans in December 1793. The Vendéens suffered a further massive loss at Savenay near Nantes. Early 1794 saw the thorough devastation of the Vendéens' territories by the *colonnes infernales*, vicious troops led by the Republican Turreau, who tortured, pillaged and burned as they went along. In Nantes, Carrier organized ritual drownings of Vendéens in the Loire.

The mass fighting at last died down, to be replaced by the actions of smaller bands such as the Chouans, particularly in Brittany. In 1795 peace was negotiated between the Vendéen leaders and the Republic, but guerrilla action continued; Stofflet and Charette were captured and shot in 1796. Eventually, in 1801, the Concordat passed laws guaranteeing Catholic freedoms, but the brutal, barbaric repression and devastation by the *colonnes infernales* left a deep scar across the Vendée and southwestern Anjou in particular. Some estimates put the numbers who died in the Guerre de Vendée between 200,000 and 300,000. Not surprisingly, the bicentennial of the French Revolution of 1989 wasn't seen as a cause for celebrations here.

Clustered together directly east of Challans are several modern museums recalling the Guerre de Vendée. **Les Lucs-sur-Boulogne** in particular is dedicated to its memory. A modern block of a memorial-cum-museum was built first, but more recently the main Vendéen museum was moved here from Le Puy du Fou. Through models, paintings and a good video, you can get a clear picture of the anti-Revolutionary struggle. Another Vendéen shrine, just northeast of Les Lucs, is the **Logis de la Chabotterie** (*open July–Aug daily 10–7; rest of year daily 9.30–6, exc Sun 10–7; adm*), a freckled little manor set in gardens. Effectively the anti-Revolutionary uprising came to an end here in 1796, when the wounded Vendéen hero Charette unsuccessfully sought refuge at the house before he was arrested. The interiors have been over-restored, but you can still pick up all sorts of details about Charette and the war.

The most moving and evocative homage to the Vendéens is the **Refuge de Grasla** (*open 15 June–14 Sept daily 11–1 and 2–6; rest of period 15 April–Sept daily 2–6; adm*), a refugee camp of makeshift huts reconstituted in the woods a little way east of La Chabotterie, where you can learn a little about what life might have been like for the terrorized but determined local population, forced into hiding and organizing itself against the Republican onslaught.

Tiffauges, a village southwest of Cholet, may be fairly unexciting, but the main figure associated with the **Château de Barbe Bleue** (*open July–Aug daily 11–7; rest of period Mar–19 Sept daily exc Wed outside June weekdays 10–12.30 and 2–6, weekends 2–7; adm*) is anything but dull. His story isn't a pretty one, yet the tour around the château doesn't shy away from telling it. Gilles de Rais lived in the same period as Joan of Arc, in the early 15th century. He suffered a cruel childhood, unlike Joan, but like her became a war hero fighting the English. However, he squandered his fortune, and had to sell his family châteaux in the Pays de Retz on the Breton border. Taken in by a so-called alchemist, he is supposed to have descended into the vilest depravity in an attempt to restore his fortune, and to have confessed to the violation and murder of around 150 children. How his confession was extracted isn't certain, but what is sure is that he was hanged and then burnt in Nantes for child murder on a vast scale. Bizarrely, it's said that the crowd at the execution pardoned him after he'd spoken on the virtues of a proper education. Even more strangely, after his death he came to be regarded as a protector of children, mothers travelling from afar to venerate his tomb. The château puts on entertainment for children: a shadow puppet show, a magic show and demonstrations of medieval war machines in action.

The **Puy du Fou** offers entertainment on a much vaster scale. A castle has stood here since 1540, with sober brick and granite galleries. In 1794 it was set on fire by the *colonnes infernales* and partially destroyed. The main show at the Puy du Fou, the **Cinéscénie** (*mid-June–1st weekend in Sept Fri and Sat only c. 10.30pm; adm*) brings together a large cast of enthusiastic locals and professional actors who perform against the backdrop of the ruined castle. They recount the history of the Vendée, and the Guerre de Vendée in particular, in dramatic style, with exciting lighting and water effects, cavalcades and fireworks. During the day, the **Grand Parcours** (*open June–mid-Sept daily 10–7; adm*) in the fake villages built around the grounds offers falconry, equestrian displays, and jousts, old-time craftspeople, and a show telling the story

Getting Around

A new motorway is being built to connect the A11 from near Angers to the big coastal resort of Les Sables-d'Olonne, passing via Cholet and the Puy-du-Fou.

There are bus services to these parts from Angers up close to the Loire.

Tourist Information

Puy du Fou: To book in advance contact Vendée Résa, **t** 02 51 62 76 82, **f** 02 51 62 02 51.
Cholet: Place Rougé, **t** 02 41 62 22 35, **f** 02 41 49 80 09

Where to Stay and Eat

Tiffauges ✉ 85130
★★**La Barbacane**, 2 Place de l'Eglise, **t** 02 51 65 75 59, **f** 02 51 65 71 91 (*moderate–inexpensive*). A welcoming, homely village hotel with 16 rooms and a garden. No restaurant.

The town of Les Herbiers caters to the Cinéscénie masses, but the hotels there get packed out with tour groups at weekends.

La Flocellière ✉ 85700
Château de la Flocellière, **t** 02 51 57 22 03, **f** 02 51 57 75 21, *erika.vignial@wanadoo.fr* (*moderate*). Just 7km south of Le Puy du Fou, a dramatic amalgam of bits of castle from

different periods, and surely the best choice if you're interested in a stylish B&B near Le Puy du Fou. The six rooms aren't outrageously expensive, and the owners are passionate about history.

St-Laurent-sur-Sèvre ✉ 85290
★★★**La Chaumière**, at La Trique, 1km north via the N149, **t** 02 51 67 88 12, **f** 02 51 67 82 87 (*moderate*). Midway between Le Puy du Fou and Cholet, this comfortable inn has an appropriately Vendéen atmosphere, and is a good place to stay after the Cinéscénie. Restaurant (*menus 150–300F*). Closed Oct–Mar Sat.

Cholet ✉ 49300
★★★**Château de la Tremblaye**, Route des Sables, **t** 02 41 58 40 17, **f** 02 41 58 20 67, *chateau.de.la.tremblaye@wanadoo.fr* (*moderate*). Stylish 19th-century pastiche of a Loire Valley château outside Cholet, built on the site of the Vendéen Battle of Cholet. Only moderately expensive given its standards.

Maulévrier ✉ 49360
★★**Château Colbert**, Place du Château, **t** 02 41 55 51 33, **f** 02 41 55 09 02, *guicheteau@nwt.fr* (*moderate–inexpensive*). A big, jolly, slightly tackily decorated but very good-value castle above a rather wonderful oriental park a dozen km southeast of Cholet. Restaurant (*menus 110–205F*).

of the saintly 7th-century Philibert (or Philbert) and his relics, which had to be shifted east time and again as the Vikings wrought havoc in western France.

Cholet in southwestern Anjou is an unassuming town, but the Guerre de Vendée is well presented in its swanky modern museum, the **Musée d'Art et d'Histoire** (*open Mon–Sat 10–12 and 2–5, Sun 3–6; closed Tues; adm*). Period items help recreate those turbulent times; the most striking room contains noble portraits of the main Vendéen leaders, commissioned by Louis XVIII after the restoration of the French monarchy, which obviously appreciated the Vendéen resistance to the Revolution. The **Musée du Textile** (*open daily 2–6, June–Sept daily 2–7; closed Tues; adm*) noisily recalls the textile trade responsible for Cholet's prosperity (it was especially renowned for handkerchiefs). East of town, the **Chapelle des Martyrs** in the Forest of Nuaillé-Vezins was originally built for a local lordly family, but it has been converted into a memorial for the Vendéens brutally massacred here in March 1794.

The Southern Vendée Coast and the Marais Poitevin

With their relative tranquillity and long beaches, the resorts between Les Sables-d'Olonne and La Rochelle offer a relaxing seaside holiday. Head east up the Sèvre Niortaise river from the Bay of Aiguillon and you come to what is without doubt the most beautiful marsh in France, the green, watery maze of the Marais Poitevin.

The South Vendée Coast

The sea once lapped the base of the castle of **Talmont-St-Hilaire**, although it is now 3kms away. The late 12th-century castle belonged to Richard Coeur de Lion. Some impressive if scrappy remnants of the ramparts and the keep survive just above the summer-busy town, and there is quite an amusing tour. In July and August visitors can dress up in medieval costume to be photographed looking ridiculous.

A tiger skin on the bed at **Belesbat** (the **Maison Clemenceau**), at St-Vincent-sur-Jard (*guided tours; open May–Sept daily 10–6; rest of year daily exc Tues 9.30–12.30 and 2–5; adm*), recalls the nickname of Georges Clemenceau, the early 20th-century French socialist prime minister, who was known as The Tiger. He was born in inland Vendée, and studied and practised medicine before becoming a politician. A man of passionately held beliefs, Clemenceau is perhaps best known for presiding over the Versailles Peace Conference at the end of the First World War. During his last years Clemenceau spent much of his time at this modest rented house on the beach, writing his memoirs at a plank of a desk looking out to sea. The combination of the house's architecture with objects and presents from around the world, including Japanese prints from Emperor Hirohito, give it a distinctly colonial atmosphere.

Peacefully old-fashioned and relatively unspoilt by modern developments, St-Vincent-sur-Jard and the little resort **Jard-sur-Mer** look across a wide wood-fringed bay. Further down the coast **La Tranche-sur-Mer** has been colonized by campers while **L'Aiguillon-sur-Mer** is divided in two by a large estuary. The sea recedes a long way from L'Aiguillon's sensational strand at low tide, turning it into a vast muddy plain. Oysters and mussels are cultivated nearby.

The Marais Poitevin

Frogs-a-croaking, blue-velvet dragonflies flitting past, white Charolais cows munching in neat, square-cut meadows divided up by countless canals...all in the shade of the most gorgeous giant poplars you have ever seen. At the height of the season the wonderful bucolic canals of the Marais Poitevin clog up with boats, just as the water itself becomes clogged up with a peasoup layer of duckweed. But even in summer the marsh is the loveliest waterland in France. To do it justice, take to the water in a *plate* or *batai*, the local names for a punt (it is probably a good idea to get a guide for your first trip). The delightful but crowded village of Coulon might be considered the Marais Poitevin's little tourist capital, Maillezais its spiritual capital, but another half a dozen villages hire out punts.

Getting Around

Not an easy area to reach by public transport. Look for excursion possibilities from the major towns nearby, including Les Sables-d'Olonne, Fontenay-le-Comte, Niort and La Rochelle.

Tourist Information

St-Vincent-sur-Jard: Place de l'Eglise, t 02 51 33 62 06, f 02 51 33 01 23.
La Tranche-sur-Mer: Place de la Liberté, t 02 51 30 33 96, f 02 51 27 78 71.
L'Aiguillon-sur-Mer: t 02 51 56 43 87, f 02 51 97 18 99.
Fontenay-le-Comte: Quai Poey d'Avant, t 02 51 69 44 99, f 02 51 50 00 90.
Maillezais: Rue du Docteur Daroux, t 02 51 87 23 01, f 02 51 00 72 51.
Coulon: Place de l'Eglise, t 05 49 35 99 29, f 05 49 35 84 31.

Where to Stay and Eat

St-Vincent-sur-Jard ✉ 85520
★★L'Océan, Rue Georges Clemenceau, t 02 51 33 40 45, f 02 51 33 98 15 (*inexpensive*). A charming, relaxed hotel just inland from the Clemenceau museum. Restaurant (*menus 80–240F*). *Closed 20 Nov–20 Feb and Wed out of season.*

Jard-sur-Mer ✉ 85520
★★★Le Parc de la Grange, Route de l'Abbaye, t 02 51 33 44 88, f 02 51 33 40 58 (*moderate*). Very close to the sea in this charming old-fashioned seaside spot, a comfortable

modern hotel lost in the midst of fragrant thick pine woods.

La Tranche-sur-Mer ✉ 85360
★★L'Océan, 49 Rue Anatole France, t 02 51 30 30 09, f 02 51 27 70 10 (*inexpensive*). By a great big beach excellent for all types of watersports. Restaurant for residents only (*menus 98–270F*). *Closed Oct–Mar.*

Velluire ✉ 85770
★★Auberge de la Rivière, t 02 51 52 32 15, f 02 51 52 37 42 (*moderate*). An inn which hogs an exceptional spot on the edge of the marshes. You feel that if you leave your door open you might get a wild boar popping in. Good restaurant (*menus 120–240F*).

Maillezais ✉ 85420
Mme Bonnet, 69 Rue de l'Abbaye, t 02 51 87 23 00, f 02 51 00 72 44. Thoroughly delightful village B&B run by a true professional.
Le Collibert, Rue Principale, t 02 51 87 25 07, f 02 51 87 25 24. This is a restaurant where they will go out of their way to tempt you with local specialities, including dark eels in wine and cabbage leaves, snails, and some surprising local Mareuil wines.

Coulon ✉ 79510
★★★Au Marais, 46–48 Quai Louis Tardy, t 05 49 35 90 43, f 05 49 35 81 98 (*moderate*). In poll position by the punting quay, a bright and attractive little hotel. *Closed 25 Dec–4 Feb.*
La Passerelle, 86 Quai Louis Tardy, t 05 49 35 80 03. Charming restaurant by the river, with a pretty little garden (*menus 60–150F*).
Le Central, t 05 49 35 90 20. Another charming restaurant.

The Marais Poitevin's network of waterways flows into the Sèvre Niortaise river. You can still see the little cliffs that marked the northern and southern edges of the Marais, dividing the Vendée or Bas Poitou from the old Aunis region. Limestone hillocks among the marshes were colonized by religious communities from the Dark Ages on, when they may have started draining some of the territory. Through the Middle Ages monks did a great deal to conquer the marshlands: five abbeys co-operated to dig the Canal des Cinq-Abbés, helping clear much of the northern Marais. In the 16th century, under Henri IV, Dutch Protestant engineers were called in to undertake further major drainage projects, building the Aigullion dyke and the so-called Ceinture des Hollandais (Dutch Belt). A major achievement in the 19th century was the drying of the western marshes, hence the division today between the Marais Désséché, which stretches from as far west as La Tranche-sur-Mer and the Bay of Aiguillon to beyond Marans, and the Marais Mouillé, which is where to go boating.

Once capital of the Bas Poitou, but now somewhat isolated on the southern fringes of the Vendée region, old **Fontenay-le-Comte** is the northern gateway to the Marais Poitevin. A few old streets have 16th-century houses with elegant entrances, built when Fontenay flourished. The mostly medieval church of Notre-Dame with its towering steeple has an entrance decorated with the Wise and Foolish virgins, a popular theme of medieval Poitevin churches. Beside the church, the earnest **Musée Vendéen** (*open mid-June–mid-Sept daily exc Mon and weekend mornings 10–12 and 2–6; rest of year daily exc Mon and Tues 2–6; adm*) has, among other exhibits, a large-scale model of the town where you can listen to a commentary on Fontenay's history and learn that Rabelais came here to learn Greek in 1520 before retreating to the more discreet abbey of Maillezais. The 16th-century poet Nicolas Rapin left a much more concrete mark on Fontenay with his **Château de Terre-Neuve** (*guided tour only; open June–Sept daily 9–12 and 3–6; May daily 2–6.30; adm*), built on the outskirts of town. In the Wars of Religion, when Fontenay was a Protestant stronghold, Rapin helped to pen the *Satire Ménipée*, a highly influential political attack on the fanatical Catholics of the Ligue. His château, although much restored, shows the influence of Italian style on French architecture in his time. The interior is filled with disparate collections, and decorations such as a ceiling covered with alchemical symbols, elaborate fireplaces and panels recovered from the Château de Chambord (*see pp.354–5*).

Heading into the heart of the Marais Poitevin, it now seems improbable that rural **Maillezais** was once the seat of a bishopric. But go to one end of the village and you can visit the ruins of a vast medieval **abbey** (*open July–Aug daily 9–8; April–June and Sept daily 9–12.30 and 2–7; Feb–Mar and Oct daily 9–12 and 2–6; Nov–Jan daily 9–12 and 2–5.30; adm*). Founded in the 10th century by a count of Poitou, it became such an important religious centre that three dukes of Aquitaine, including Eleanor of Aquitaine's great-grandfather, were buried here. From the mid-14th century to the mid-17th, Maillezais' abbey church was turned into a cathedral. The sweet little **punting port** lies just down from the abbey.

The bright village of **Coulon** is the major punting port of the Marais Mouillé, radiating out from its cleanly scrubbed church, but be warned that it gets packed out in high summer. Many houses have been turned into restaurants and shops. The local specialities include angelica, derived from a plant that thrives in these parts, and *myocastor* (i.e. coypu) pâté. In summer it takes some time to get in and out of the boating scrum along Coulon's quays, and you need a good few hours to explore the quieter reaches of the wide network of canals.

Three Romanesque churches in the vicinity are worth a look: **Maillé** with its entertainingly eccentric portal; **Benet**, with its delightful floating angels; and **Nieul-sur-l'Autise**, the most substantial, located in the supposed birthplace of Eleanor of Aquitaine. **Niort** is the bustling main town on the eastern edge of the Marais Poitevin. Two enormous medieval keeps have been joined into one to oversee its vibrant centre and contain the main historical museum.

Down the Thouet

A little-sung but delightful tributary of the Loire, the Thouet flows up through the *département* of Deux-Sèvres. The route here takes you in the opposite direction, down from Thouars to Parthenay, where pilgrims once padded their way to Santiago de Compostela, well away from the motorways rushing through western France.

Below Montreuil-Bellay in the Loire (*see* p.386), follow the Thouet up to the little towns of Thouars and Loudun, both of which have picturesque historic centres. **Thouars** has several grand buildings, including a church with an intriguing Romanesque façade full of carved figures, although the town is now encased in a dull working-class quarter. **Loudun** seems by contrast hardly to have grown since the Ancien Régime, with fields coming up to encircle its gentle old centre. A 17th-century scandal that shook the place – a local priest was accused of bringing demons into the Ursuline convent – was taken up by Aldous Huxley in his book *The Devils of Loudun*.

The **Château d'Oiron** (*open July–mid-Sept daily 10–7; rest of year daily 9.30–12.30 and 2–5; adm*) is visible from afar, rising out of the flat cereal plains like a mirage. Its French Renaissance parts were built for the Gouffier family, and it was greatly added to in the 17th century when it briefly became the property of Mme de Montespan, Louis XIV's powerful mistress. The beautiful collegiate chapel, a mix of late-Gothic architecture and Renaissance embellishments, contains a couple of finely executed 16th-century family tomb effigies as well as a couple of really gruesome ones. The decaying cayman hanging on one wall of the church is said also to date from the 16th century. Claude Gouffier, a follower of Henri II, was caught up in the excitement at the discovery of the new worlds, and followed the trend among the very wealthy to gather objects from around the globe in cabinets of curiosities. Hence the cayman, and the inspiration for the works you can see in the château.

Although the château has some remarkable period rooms, it also contains some wacky contemporary curiosities. In the 1990s the decision was taken not to refurnish the then neglected château according to Ancien Régime tastes, but to commission modern artists to create pieces, playing on the theme of the cabinet of curiosities. It was also decided that these new commissions should say something about the people who live in the village today.

Of the few Ancien Régime salons, don't miss the Chambre du Roi, with its garlands and mottoes, some alluding to the bitterness of Louis Gouffier, who was exiled from court after being accused of plotting against Richelieu. The Cabinet des Muses drips with gold, but best of all is the breathtaking gallery with its murals of the Trojan War. The large, splendid horses of various colours, the teeming scenes and detailed backgrounds count among the most powerful images of the French Renaissance.

Heading south from Oiron, **St-Jouin**'s fort of a church and Moncontour's dilapidated hilltop keep peer suspiciously at each other across the shallow Dive valley. St Jouin himself, an influential 4th-century abbot, is said to figure among the statues ranged on the Poitevin-style façade, but a wild Eve entwined by a snake is much the most striking character of the bunch. The church's long nave descends in levels to a

Tourist Information

Thouars: 3 bis Bd Pierre-Curie, t 05 49 66 17 65, f 05 49 67 87 58.
Loudun: Rue des Marchands, t 05 49 98 15 96, f 05 49 98 12 88.
St-Loup-Lamairé: 6 Grand-Rue Théophane Vénard, t 05 49 64 82 45.
Parthenay: 8 Rue de la Vau St-Jacques, t 05 49 64 24 24, f 05 49 94 61 94.

Where to Stay and Eat

Oiron ✉ 79100

*Le Relais du Château, Place des Marronniers, t 05 49 96 54 96, f 05 49 96 54 45 (*cheap*). A simple rustic inn with 14 rooms and hearty regional food (*menus 80–235F*). *Closed Sun eves and Mon lunch.*

Thouars ✉ 79100

**Le Clocher St-Médard, 14 Place St-Médard, t 05 49 66 66 00, f 05 49 96 15 01 (*inexpensive*). 5 rooms in an historic town house that might even tempt you to stay in Thouars. Restaurant (*menus 130–400F*). *Closed Aug; Feb hols; Mon, Sat lunch and Sun eves.*

Ternay ✉ 86120

Château de Ternay, t 05 49 22 92 82, f 05 49 22 97 54. A splendidly restored Loire Valley-style château in delightful countryside between Thouars and Loudun, whose bed and breakfast rooms aren't outrageously expensive. Admiral Ternay, who led Rochambeau's men in the American War of Independence and died in Newport in 1781, was born here.

St-Loup-Lamairé ✉ 79600

Château de St-Loup, t 05 49 64 81 73, f 05 49 64 82 06 (*expensive*). In splendid grounds, with B&B rooms in the medieval keep where the French king Jean le Bon was apparently briefly kept as a prisoner of the English after the medieval Battle of Poitiers.

Amailloux ✉ 79350

Château de Tennessus, t 05 49 95 50 60, f 05 49 95 50 62 (*moderate*). Surrounded by a moat, reached by a drawbridge, this splendid 14th-century fortress, c. 7km north of Parthenay off the N149 towards Bressuire, is owned by a British couple, and makes another exceptional B&B stop. Wonderful characterful bedrooms.

---

mesmerizing choir and ambulatory bathed in a greeny-white light. Look up to see the capitals and keystones carved with action scenes.

Back on the banks of the Thouet, **Airvault** boasts the impressive Romanesque abbey church of St-Pierre, where the Poitevin style once again comes to the fore. As well as a ring of elders carved round the door, you can see the remains of one of those mysterious equestrian statues found on so many Poitou churches – thought to represent the first Christian Roman emperor, Constantine. The interior details are good, too, simple saints standing on beasts above the chunky capitals of the nave, ribs and keystones decorating the ceiling.

A medieval keep stands guard at the gates to the pure 17th-century **Château de St-Loup** (*open May–Sept daily 2–7; rest of year weekends and public hols daily 2–7; adm*), a delightfully airy building in brick and stone, with so many windows that the walls of its salons seem almost transparent. The much older keep briefly served as a prison for French royalty in the Hundred Years' War, when the French king Jean le Bon was captured by the Black Prince. You can only see a few rooms on the ground floor, but the place still has charm. The château is surrounded by elegant gardens, recently recreated in mid-18th-century style.

Pretty bridges and a riverbank bordered by a curve of weeping willows make the Thouet particularly attractive at **Parthenay**. One bridge leads to a medieval gateway into the old town where you'll find the little town museum. To reach the old upper town, climb the slope of the Rue de la Vaux St Jacques, lined with picturesque timber-frame and thin brick façades. On the way to the castle you may notice the remnants of a church façade with another fragment of a Poitou equestrian figure, just the horse's rump bizarrely protruding. The ruined medieval castle stands on a rocky outcrop, overlooking a bucolic bend in the Thouet river.

Poitiers

The provincial capital of Poitou has known successive periods of greatnesss, even if it has very much declined in size and importance since medieval times when it was the third largest city in France, a golden period reflected in its superb Romanesque churches. The hill town still retains its historic atmosphere and, as a university town, is fairly lively most of the time. With the opening of showy Futuroscope north of town, Poitiers has been put firmly back on the modern map. This cinema park looks obscenely kitsch rising out of its flat plain, but it offers the finest array of large screens anywhere in Europe, and possibly even the world.

History

Poitiers lies on one of those French hilltop sites (here almost encircled by the Clain and Boivre rivers) that must have seemed an obvious base for the local Celtic tribe, in this case the Pictones or Pictavi. The Romans called the Gallo-Roman town which they then developed on the spot Limonum. The city became one of the most important early-Christian centres in Gaul – thanks to St Hilaire and his great protégé, St Martin, who in the 4th century founded one of the first monasteries in France, Ligugé, just south of Poitiers, and thanks also to the Merovingian saint Radegonde, the wife of Clothaire I. She sought refuge from her husband's violence and his taunts at her childlessness by founding a convent in Poitiers where she encouraged learning. She was considered a saint for her charitable works even before she died.

Poitiers became one of the seats of power of the Visigoth Alaric II. In 507 at the battle of Vouillé (northwest of town) the Frankish king Clovis succeeded in driving him out. The results of a second battle resounded beyond the frontiers of France. The Moors had swept through Spain and were advancing northwards. In 732 they arrived in Poitiers and burnt down the church of St-Hilaire, only to be defeated so decisively by Charles Martel, grandfather of Charlemagne, that they retreated back to Spain.

The battle of Poitiers in the Hundred Years' War (in fact fought beside Nouaillé-Maupertuis to the southeast) saw the French nobility crushed and the French king himself captured by the Black Prince. Poitiers and the Poitou would in fact be held by English royalty for several periods during the Middle Ages. Poitiers first became part of the Anglo-French Angevin empire when Eleanor of Aquitaine married Henry II Plantagenet in 1152. Eleanor made Poitiers her court of love and chivalry, drawing the greatest troubadours of the day. Pilgrims poured into its splendid churches. Trade boomed and the population soared.

Du Guesclin won back Poitiers and Poitou for the French monarchy in the early 1370s and the province then became an appanage of the extravagant Jean Duc de Berry. When the future king Charles VII of France was chased out of Paris, he took refuge with his court in the Berry, Loire and Poitou. It was in Poitiers that he was declared king in 1422. Joan of Arc, when she arrived on the scene to help him, was sent here to have her credentials and her virginity tested by the French Church before her wild claims were accepted.

Poitiers' glory days were cut short by the Wars of Religion, despite an important gathering during the conflict – known as the Grands Jours de Poitiers – at which an effort was made to try to find solutions to the religious strife. The city's subsequent stagnation was to last for centuries. Since the Second World War, the lively university, the motorway, the TGV and Futuroscope have at last made the Poitevins look forwards instead of backwards.

Notre-Dame-la-Grande and the Upper City

The heart and soul of Poitiers, Notre-Dame-la-Grande has one of the best Romanesque façades in France. At the top of the great front, Christ sits in majesty although, as with most of the other human figures on the façade, his face has been hacked off. Below his mandorla stand statues of the apostles and St Hilaire (in the top left arch) and St Martin (with his shield in front of him in the right). The best carving runs along the band above the ground floor arches. To the left you can make out Old Testament figures, from Adam trying to hide his private parts, via Nebuchadnezzar seated legs apart, to various prophets holding scrolls as if they were advertisements. Then come New Testament scenes: the Annunciation, a Tree of Jesse, the Visitation and the Nativity, Mary depicted in bed, exhausted, baby Jesus being bathed and Joseph meditating. A wealth of Romanesque creatures crammed in here and there adds to the medieval excitement. The interior has fared less well; according to Henry James, the geometrical patterns added inside the church in the 19th century were 'the most hideous decorative painting that was ever inflicted upon passive pillars and indifferent vaults'. Cafés spill out over the large pedestrian square surrounding the church, and to one side of it you will find the busy covered market.

The **Palais de Justice**, or law courts, now a confusing amalgam of buildings, has a core that dates back to the Plantagenets when this was the palace of Poitiers. Gothic alterations were made for Jean Duc de Berry, and much later, after the buildings had been converted into courts, a grand classical façade was added on one side. You can enter via the majestic staircase to see the enormous early 13th-century Grande Salle or Salle des Pas Perdus. Measuring almost 160ft in length, and without any central columns to help hold up the ceiling, it is of impressive size even by today's standards. Jean Duc de Berry had the splendid Gothic end done in grand style: angels hold coats of arms above the massive triple fireplace, and much higher up, four idealized lords stand aloof, looking down on the hoi polloi. These days, when the courts are in session, you can see lawyers in black and white garb flitting in and out of the doorways of the massive room as though engaged in some theatrical farce.

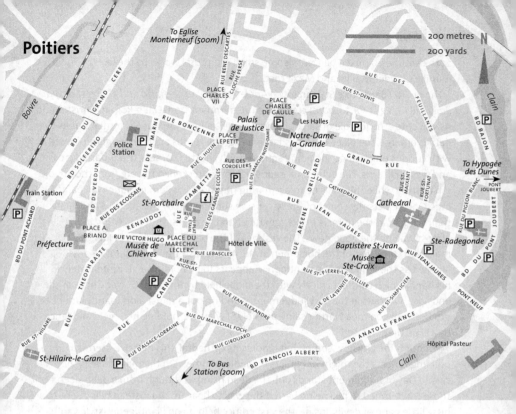

Head south along the busy Rue Gambetta from the law courts and you pass by **St-Porchaire**, with its Romanesque heads on the outside and its refined Gothic interior. The town hall presides over **Place du Maréchal Leclerc**, the second hub of the upper city.

Wide Rue Victor Hugo leads off the square to the **Musée de Chièvres** (*open Tues–Fri 10–12 and 1–5, Sat and Sun 2–6; closed Mon; adm*), set in a grand town house, but backed by a modern department store. Rupert de Chièvres was a wealthy 19th-century traveller and bachelor who left his splendid and varied art collections to the town. Some of the furniture is outstanding.

The Historic Quarter Down the Hill

Take the **Grand Rue**, with its old-style shops, down to Poitiers' still older historic quarter towards the Clain river. The area of the cathedral, the Musée Ste-Croix and the Baptistère now consists of a chaotic mishmash of buildings. The modern **Musée Ste-Croix** (*open Tues–Fri 10–12 and 1–5, Sat and Sun 2–6; closed Mon; adm*) conceals a wide display of Poitou culture down the ages, including Gallo-Roman statues and funerary stelae, exquisite and weird Romanesque carvings, among which are comical flattened elephants and vestiges of the vanished 12th-century church of Ste-Croix – Poitiers once had many, many more churches than it does today. An astonishing blue glass reliquary vase is thought to have come from eastern Europe, and there are beautiful pieces of medieval Limoges work. Most of the art dates from the 19th and

20th centuries, a mixed bag, with some small sculptural works by the likes of Rodin, Camille Claudel, Maillol and Max Ernst.

The nearby **Baptistère St-Jean** (*open April–Oct daily 10.30–12.30 and 3–6; rest of year daily exc Tues 2.30–4.30; adm*) contains a rare remnant from Gallo-Roman Christianity. As you enter, the jumble of sarcophagi resembles a junk yard for old tombs, but as the details emerge, the place becomes fascinating. The tombs are Merovingian, covered with curious engravings, including squares with knotted corners, three-barred crosses and wavy patterns. The octagonal baptismal font is reckoned to date from the 4th or 5th century while the walls bear fascinating fragments of Romanesque wall paintings. One depicts the Christ of the Ascension surrounded by the apostles showing their wonder at the miracle in exaggerated hand gestures, angels floating along almost waving the good news. The vestiges of the painted cavaliers below might make you think first of the horsemen of the Apocalypse, but one rider is clearly labelled as the Emperor Constantine. He appears to be holding a globe delicately in his hand, which contrasts nicely with the globe held by the large Gothic Christ of the end apse, who sits in the Last Judgement, standing out against a dramatic black background. Look too for a warrior saint, possibly St Maurice, holding his shield and lance by a slain dragon.

Although the city now somewhat ignores its **cathedral**, this massive, stern-faced building reflects the might of Poitiers in medieval times. On the main façade, the carved Day of Judgement stands out, the dead rising as though from a deep sleep, those condemned to hell being barred the way to heaven, and instead being sent to a busy little gang of devils. Inside, the vast edifice held up on Plantagenet-style vaults contains many delightful decorative details. These include the odd panel of very old stained glass, the entertaining, awkwardly seated stone figures carved along the cornice, and the wood carvings on the 13th-century choir stalls, perhaps the oldest in France. Kings holding a crown in each hand are a recurring motif.

Don't miss the atmosphere-charged **Ste-Radegonde**, tucked out of sight below the cathedral. Radegonde founded the church here as a funerary chapel for the nuns of the abbey of Ste-Croix in the 6th century, and was herself buried here in 587. The entrance tower is Romanesque, as is the apse, but the Gothic remainder very much resembles the cathedral, only on a more human scale. A Flamboyant Gothic portal from the 15th century is decorated with statues representing the saints of Poitiers. The superb rounded Romanesque apse is held up on chunky columns with chunky decoration. The wall paintings were added in the 13th century, but much restored in the 19th. In the crypt, the sarcophagus of Ste Radegonde dates from the 8th or 9th century. Then there's the monument to a footstep; legend has it that Christ appeared to Radegonde to announce her death and to tell her of the special place that awaited her in heaven – as he went off, he left an imprint of his right foot in the stone.

Ste-Radegonde lies close to the pretty banks of the Clain. Cross the river and climb the opposite hillside to find the **Hypogée des Dunes** (*open June–mid-Sept daily exc Mon 10–12 and 1–5, weekends 2–6; rest of year daily exc Mon 2–4; adm*). The outer building is a 20th-century pastiche of a Gallo-Roman structure. It covers an underground chapel from around the 7th century, decorated with very rare pieces of

Getting Around

Poitiers has excellent train connections, as does Futuroscope; both have TGV stops. Paris-Montparnasse is a mere 1hr 30mins away. The A10 passes close to Poitiers city centre.

Tourist Information

Poitiers: 8 Rue des Grandes Ecoles, t 05 49 41 21 24, f 05 49 88 65 84.

Where to Stay and Eat

Poitiers ✉ 86000

***Le Grand Hôtel**, 28 Rue Carnot, t 05 49 60 90 60, f 05 49 62 81 89 (*moderate*). A slightly impersonal swish modern number, discreetly positioned in a small modern precinct off one of the major old streets. The 41 rooms are very comfortable.

****Le Grand Hôtel de l'Europe**, 39 Rue Carnot, t 05 49 88 12 00, f 05 49 88 97 30 (*inexpensive*). A still bigger hotel which makes a grand impression set back in its own courtyard, and is quite swanky for a two-star.

****Le Plat d'Etain**, 7–9 Rue du Plat d'Etain, t 05 49 41 04 80, f 05 49 52 25 84 (*inexpensive*). A former posting inn tucked away in a great central position behind the Place du Maréchal Leclerc.

****Le Central**, 35 Place du Maréchal Leclerc, t 05 49 01 79 79, f 05 49 60 27 56 (*inexpensive*). Which is indeed very central.

****Le Chapon Fin**, 11 Rue Lebascles, t 05 49 88 02 97, f 05 49 88 91 63 (*inexpensive*). Also very central.

Cheaper hotels crowd around the railway station below the centre.

Maxime, 4 Rue St-Nicolas, t 05 49 41 09 55. Very fine restaurant where the chef does magic tricks with regional cuisine (*menus 100–260F*). *Closed Oct–Feb Sat eves and Sun.*

Le St-Hilaire, 65 Rue Théophraste Renaudot, t 05 49 41 15 45. Don't be put off by the entrance in a modern building: the restaurant itself is hidden in 12th-century cellars. The chef uses spices to good effect. The waiters dress in medieval style (*menus 99–280F*). *Closed Mon in summer and Sun.*

Les Bons Enfants, 11 Bis Rue Cloche Perce. An appealing tiny restaurant.

Le Pavé de la Villette, 21 Rue Carnot, t 05 49 60 49 49. Meats are the speciality, including the likes of local kid with garlic (*menus 100–130F*). *Closed Sat lunch and Sun.*

Chasseneuil-du-Poitou ✉ 86360

***Le Clos de la Ribaudière**, 10 Place du Champ de Foire, t 05 49 52 86 66, f 05 49 52 86 32, www.ribaudiere.com (*moderate*). The best hotel near Futuroscope, but away from the mayhem in delightful grounds on the side of the Clain river. Some of the more glamorous rooms are in a grandiose little 19th-century château, others in a comfortable modern block close to the pool. The dining room is over the top, but the food and local wines are good (*menus 160–295F*).

Mignaloux ✉ 86550

***Manoir de Beauvoir**, 635 Route de Beauvoir, t 05 49 55 47 47, f 05 49 55 31 95 (*moderate*). A luxurious, Victorian golfing hotel 8km southeast of Poitiers.

Vouillé ✉ 86190

***Château de Périgny**, La Chapelle, t 05 49 51 80 43, f 05 49 51 90 09 (*moderate*). 15km west of Poitiers and Futuroscope, some rooms are set in the sweet little restored château, others in villas alongside. Swimming pool and tennis court too.

Merovingian carvings. A dolmen, the Pierre Levée, stands nearby, and there are excellent views over the roofscape of Poitiers from this quarter, best appreciated from beside the vast gilded Virgin and Child.

Back in the historic centre, two major churches wait on either end of the old heart of town. **St-Hilaire-le-Grand** to the south is much the more spectacular, another great early-medieval pilgrimage church on the route to Santiago de Compostela. The 19th-century restorers got carried away, in particular ruining the façade, but the series of

Romanesque apses decorated with animal panels and other figures is truly beautiful. Enter the church and you get a splendid view down to the raised choir with its thin Romanesque arcade. The nave is more striking still, and extraordinarily wide with its six side aisles. Three curious octagonal cupolas hold up the main nave bays. In the choir, one capital shows St Hilaire being placed in his tomb, while some of the faded ochre wall paintings depict dignified bishops of Poitiers. Other more lively frescoes tell the stories of St Quentin and St Martin. Beyond St-Hilaire, the picturesque public garden, the **Parc de Blossac**, has views down on to the Clain from its shaded walks behind the remaining portions of the city's ramparts. The severe **Mortierneuf** church stands to the north, in a neglected part of town, the most sidelined of the city's plethora of churches, even though Pope Urban II no less consecrated it in 1096.

Futuroscope Film Park

Springing up in the midst of the Poitou farmland north of Poitiers, Futuroscope film park is at the cutting edge of world cinema. It has its own TGV train station and takes just one and a half hours to reach from central Paris. There is no harmony to the buildings, although they were all created by the same Belgian group: the Pavillon du Futuroscope has a ball caught in glass sides; organ barrels hold the Tapis Magique (Flying Carpet); the Kinémax is the dark crystal-like structure. Futuroscope claims to offer the best large-scale screens anywhere in the world, and they deliver some unforgettable visuals, even if the contents of the films themselves are a mixed bag. Entrance is expensive, but you are unlikely to regret it. To do the place justice takes two days. For English-speaking visitors, dubbing earphones are provided at the Maison de la Vienne by the main entrance.

Futuroscope was conceived and built by the Poitou-Charente regional council, and three of the films are devoted to the region. Le Pavillon de la Vienne presents two: after you have sat quietly through the bureaucratic one, you are treated to a wild ride across Poitou-Charentes, shaken around so violently in your seat that anyone with a wobbly heart should give it a miss. The new Atlantis building with its hemispheric screen showing 3-D presentations also has alarmingly unstable seats. The vast Imax films are stunning, the Kinémax screen, the size of two tennis courts, stupendous. Other screens have their good and bad points: the circular screen is liable to cause neck ache; the Tapis Magique underfloor screen is a bit awkward to appreciate. There are a few simpler spaces with quieter interactive presentations and games geared towards younger children. Evenings end with a vulgar but vibrant fireworks shows around the artificial central lake with its shooting fountains.

Historic Spots around Poitiers

North of Futuroscope, the **châteaux of Dissay and Clairvaux** provide more traditional French fare, the first a heavily restored pile in the Loire Valley style, with pea-soup moat, the second hidden from any prying villagers by substantial walls, and now devoted to the history of chess, a passion of the present owner.

South of Poitiers by the Clain, **Ligugé** claims to have been the site of the first monastery in Western Europe, founded by Hilaire and Martin in 361; Martin spent almost ten years here. The badly cemented crypt contains tombs from the Dark Ages. Following the Revolution, monks returned in the mid-19th century. The messy buildings contain a scrappy museum on monasticism and a display of enamel works produced here. More charming **Nouaillé-Maupertuis**, a short way east, has medieval fortifications around its towering abbey church. The church encloses a large stone tomb said to be that of St Junien, painted with striking birds from the 8th or 9th century. The site of the battle of Poitiers that so marked the course of the Hundred Years' War is just a modest little field nearby, but an explanatory panel and memorial recall the significance of the clash between the Black Prince and Jean le Bon.

Eastern Poitou

East of Poitiers, the Vienne and Gartempe valleys run up through quiet eastern Poitou. However, Chauvigny, with vestiges of five forts packed together on its hilltop, picturesque Angles-sur-l'Anglin with its gutted castle, and St-Savin, its church nicknamed the Sistine chapel of Romanesque art, certainly offer some excellent reasons for heading this way. St-Savin has been declared a UNESCO World Heritage Site.

For such a small place **Chauvigny** has a mighty medieval centre, with the remnants of five forts crammed into its upper village, all topped by the Romanesque church of **St-Pierre**. Inside, the columns are sculpted with memorable bold figures, some representing biblical characters, others monsters, including winged sphinxes wearing what look like jester hats. Very rarely for medieval church carving, one is signed: '*Gofridus me fecit*'. Chauvigny's main keep, the **Donjon de Gouzon** (*open 15 June– 15 Sept daily 10–12.30 and 2.30–6.30, exc Sun 11–6.30; 16 Sept–Oct weekends and public hols; rest of year daily 2–6; adm*), has been turned into a slick little museum. A funky lift takes you up to the terrace with views over the roofs and vegetable gardens in town, and as far as the nuclear power station on the Vienne. In the floors below, the beautiful spaces are more impressive than the exhibits. One floor is dedicated to local pottery, from Neolithic times to the present day. Chauvigny still produces dinner services, several of which feature here, ordered for the Ritz or embellished with Astérix and Obélix (available from La Boutique du Planty on Route de Montmorillon in town).

Chauvigny's biggest tourist draw takes place in another of the five castles, the massively walled **Château Baronnial**, which holds regular displays of falconry. This château was built for the bishops of Poitiers in the early Middle Ages when they were lords of the land. The few remaining rooms in the courtyard of the neighbouring **Château d'Harcourt**, built a little later in the Middle Ages for the viscounts of Châtellerault, are devoted to seasonal displays by contemporary artists. The remnants of the fifth château have in part been turned into a B&B. Lower Chauvigny has its own attractions, including a Romanesque church with more carvings, and a bathhouse turned into a centre for contemporary art.

Just south of Chauvigny, big lime trees shade the beautifully located **St-Pierre-les-Eglises** and its cemetery. The waters of the Vienne shimmer close by. The superb faded frescoes in the apse are claimed to date back to Carolingian times, and reflect a rare sense of movement for such early paintings, from the three kings travelling to offer their gifts to Mary and Jesus, to St Michael battling it out with a dragon. Despite the menacing towers of two nuclear power plants, **Civaux**, south along the Vienne, merits a brief halt for the most curious cemetery walls in France, constructed from Merovingian sarcophagi, carved with bold, multi-barred crosses. A little museum gives more details.

Due east of Chauvigny, the vast abbey church of **St-Savin** contains nothing less than the finest cycle of Romanesque art in France (*open April–Sept daily am and pm; Feb–Mar and Oct–Nov daily pm only; Dec–Jan weekends only; bring binoculars; guided tours or taped commentary available; adm*). Four bands along the nave ceiling depict Old Testament scenes drawn from Genesis and Exodus. God's greatness is subtly indicated by presenting him as much taller and nimbler than the mere mortals. Eve memorably dances with a snake which is taller than she is. Noah's ark is a simple ship with a comical dog's head of a prow, on which one deck is reserved for mammals, one for birds and one for humans. Noah is shown drunk in bed, cape open to reveal his inebriated erection. Not much survives of Abraham's story, but Joseph's tribulations in Egypt remain in place. The last series, telling the story of Moses, includes memorable scenes of the horses of the Egyptian charioteers jumping up as the Red Sea closes in, while the commandments are trumpeted in by angels. On the guided tour you can see further murals in the entrance porch. Unfortunately, the most interesting paintings, those in the crypt depicting the legend of Savin and Cyprien, have been so badly attacked by fungi that they are no longer

Getting Around

Too delightfully a secretive rural area to benefit from much public transport.

Tourist Information

Chauvigny: 5 Rue St-Pierre, **t** 05 49 46 39 01.
St-Savin: 15 Rue St-Louis, **t** 05 49 48 11 00.
Angles-sur-l'Anglin: La Place, **t** 05 49 48 86 87.

Where to Stay and Eat

Chauvigny ✉ 86300
Château de Montléon, 8 Plan St-Pierre, **t** 05 49 46 88 96 (*inexpensive*). A characterful B&B with its own little courtyard in the vestiges of one of old Chauvigny's five forts.
✷✷Le Lion d'Or, 8 Rue du Marché, **t** 05 49 46 30 28, **f** 05 49 47 74 28 (*inexpensive*).

Traditional type of provincial French hotel in the lower village. Restaurant (*menus 90–200F*).

St-Savin-sur-Gartempe ✉ 86310
✷✷Hôtel du Midi, N151, **t** 05 49 48 00 40 (*inexpensive*). A cheap former coaching inn with a restaurant, in this pleasant village.
✷La Grange, Route d'Antigny, **t** 05 49 48 07 07, **f** 05 49 48 21 04 (*cheap*). A converted barn very close to the abbey with simple roooms and a restaurant.

Angles-sur-l'Anglin ✉ 86260
✷Relais du Lyon d'Or, Route de Vicq, **t** 05 49 48 32 53, **f** 05 49 84 02 28 (*inexpensive*). A perfect fit in this adorable village, this hotel with 10 rooms is set back in its own courtyard in the upper village. Restaurant (*menus 110–190F*). *Closed Tues lunch and Mon*.

shown. Instead, a reasonably good photographic copy is on display in the 17th-century chapterhouse.

Angles-sur-l'Anglin, north of St-Savin, is a gorgeous village set above meanders in the Anglin river, in a corner where the Poitou meets the Touraine and Berry. Its name is supposed to derive from 5th-century Angles who settled here. The medieval **château** (*open July–Aug daily exc Tues 10–12 and 2.30–6.30; adm*) has romantically crumbling towers and lodges rising out of the limestone cliff above the river. Above the ruins, steps hewn into the rock lead up to a Romanesque chapel converted into a showroom for the local cutlery and embroidery, the latter known as Les Jours d'Angles because of its openwork effects.

Pilgrimage Churches between Poitiers and the Charente

The millions of visitors rushing down the A10 between Poitiers and Bordeaux each year may think the countryside rather dull and flat. But off the motorway, or more precisely just off the D950 between Poitiers and St-Jean-d'Angély, you can go in search of some of the most exuberant pilgrimage churches in France and the cutest donkeys in the world.

The stepped tumuli grouped together near **Bougon** (south of St-Maixent-l'Ecole) form one of the finest Neolithic burial sites in France. The tombs stand among small oaks in the midst of large Poitevin fields, well distanced from the modern glass and metal explanatory **museum** (*open Feb–Dec daily, but Wed pm only; summer daily 10–7; rest of year daily 10–6; adm*). Built in a variety of shapes, the Neolithic ensemble was added to at different periods, the oldest dating as far back as the 5th millennium BC. The largest, a trapezoid, measures 236ft in length. In summer, you'll find craftspeople practising supposed Neolithic stone-moving techniques, silex cutting, pottery, weaving and other trades which created the Neolithic revolution.

Melle (a good way southeast of Niort) boasts the finest equestrian statue of the emperor Constantine in Poitou, in the church of St-Hilaire down in the valley. Here, for once, you get an almost complete picture of a scene which elsewhere in the region survives only in fragments. With his straight back, long flowing hair, slim figure and stern face, he looks not only dignified, but close to divine. His horse with its long tail, large penis and funny face would be lifting a leg to pass over a little cowering figure if the leg hadn't disappeared. Knights holding shields stand in the portal below. Inside, the capitals with curvaceous monsters are superb. Two other Romanesque churches are worth seeking out in Melle: St-Pierre, on the edge of the hill, with more remarkable and sometimes earthy carvings; and in the centre of the upper town, recently restored St-Savinien. Melle produced silver coins from local mines during the medieval period – in fact the town's name apparently derives from *metallum*. You can learn more about local silver-mining at the **Mines d'argent** (*open June–Sept daily 10–12 and 2.30–7.30; rest of year weekends and public hols only 2.30–6.30; adm*) outside town.

Getting Around

You'd do as well to hire your own gorgeous Poitou donkey to get around this area as to rely on public transport.

Tourist Information

Celles: t 05 49 32 92 28.
Melle: t 05 49 29 15 10, f 05 49 29 19 83.

Where to Stay and Eat

St-Maixent-l'Ecole ✉ 79400

***Le Logis St-Martin, Chemin de Pissot, t 05 49 05 58 68, f 05 49 76 19 93 (*expensive–moderate*). In woods on the banks of the Sèvre Niortaise, a couple of kilometres south of town and just north of the A10, a very pretty little hotel in a cleanly renovated 17th-century house with the additional delight of a round tower. Restaurant (*menus 250–395F*). *Closed Jan; Nov–April Mon lunch; May–Oct Wed lunch and Sat lunch; Sun eves.*

Melle ✉ 79500

**Les Glycines, 5 Place René Groussard, t 05 49 27 01 11, f 05 49 27 93 45 (*inexpensive*). Set up in the old town in a characterful medieval house, this is a pleasant place to eat or just stop. Restaurant (*menus 80–240F*). *Closed Sun eves; Nov–Mar Mon.*

Gript ✉ 79360

***Domaine du Griffier, t 05 49 32 62 62, f 05 49 32 62 63 (*moderate–inexpensive*). This sprawling, rustic château has been turned into a very bright, appealing hotel with a good restaurant (*menus 150–200F*). It's 8km due south of Niort and very close to the A10, above the Forêt de Chizé.

Enclosed in its cypress-bound cemetery, St-Pierre at **Aulnay** is one of the most famous Romanesque churches in France. On the façade, the equestrian statue of Constantine has disappeared, but the decoration of the three lower arches has survived. St Peter is hanged upside down on the left side; Christ in majesty is on the right. Four layers of figures embellish the central arch: angels hold the holy Lamb, then come knights with long shields, then virgins, then symbols of the zodiac and seasonal labours. Even better is the virtuoso display of carving on the south transept where the most fabulous medieval creatures are crammed into the outer ring of the arch. They're followed by an extraordinary row of seated elders of the Apocalypse, arms raised, holding musical instruments and phials, while curious kneeling men have been squeezed in below them, made to look as though they are straining to keep the elders up. An inner semicircle of mythical creatures stands caught in an embroidery of stone. Further up the outside of the south transept, in the upper window, note the amazing split-shield row of folded knights. Inside, around the capitals and the apse, details cry out for attention. Just nearby, in a much prettier setting, the church of **St-Mandé** has its own intriguing portal; its makers clearly had an obsession with serpents.

Adorably dopey donkeys are the main reason for heading to **Dampierre-sur-Boutonne**, although the village also has a charming little run-down Renaissance château. Signposted a few kilometres outside the village, the **Maison de l'Ane du Poitou** houses Poitou donkeys. With their heavy, tatty coats and muddy dreadlocks, they look like a cross between a yak and a cutely naive grunge victim knocked out by a week of spliffs at Woodstock. For more animals, visit the **Zoorama Européen**, an animal park set in the Forêt de Chizé not far north of Dampierre.

La Rochelle and the Ile de Ré

La Rochelle is a wonderfully cheerful town, so when you are sipping an apéritif by the historic quays of the old harbour it is hard to think of the terrible squalor suffered by the British sailors once locked up in one of the sturdy medieval towers at the entrance to the port. And if you are eating at a quayside table it is hard to think of the besieged Protestants of La Rochelle who in 1628, in the most infamous time in La Rochelle's history, were reduced to such desperation that they ate not just rats, but leather too.

History

A little fishing village before the 12th century, La Rochelle developed rapidly under Duke Guillaume d'Aquitaine with its excellent, naturally protected opening to the sea. In 1199 his daughter Eleanor granted La Rochelle special status as a *commune*, with its first mayor, one Robert de Montmirail, first of a long tradition of powerful mayors of which La Rochelle is proud. The town grew rich, in particular through the export of salt and wine.

The seeds of La Rochelle's terrible entanglement with the French monarchy were sown in the 16th century, when the city became the major centre of French Protestantism. Its merchants had grown still richer by then, some of them counting among the first French to benefit from trade with Africa and the New World. As Protestantism grew militant, the mayor of La Rochelle had the Catholic churches razed to the ground in 1568. The authority of the *intendant*, the regional representative of the king, was no longer accepted. In 1573 the crown decided to intervene, sending troops led by the Duc d'Anjou, the future Henri III, but La Rochelle successfully resisted the siege which lasted about six months.

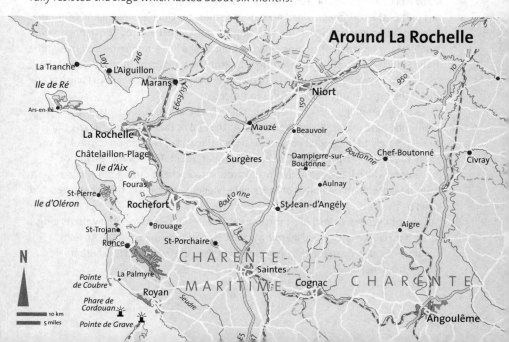

As Protestants were so well protected within La Rochelle's walls, many rich and powerful Huguenots found refuge here, including a future king of France, the young Henri de Navarre, who arrived with his formidable mother, Jeanne d'Albret. La Rochelle had become a quasi-independent Protestant state in a Catholic nation, and when Richelieu and Louis XIII decided to extract the thorn, La Rochelle called on England for protection. The Duke of Buckingham landed on Ré with his fleet in 1627, but was easily defeated. The French monarchy then resorted to heavy-handed means. On land, a 14km perimeter wall was erected around the town, manned by tens of thousands of soldiers to stop any produce getting in or out. More dramatically still, Richelieu had an elaborate mile-long sea barrage built across the entrance to the port, made from sunken wooden boats filled with rubble and topped by sharp wooden stakes. The Rochelais didn't believe it would withstand the power of the sea, and the mayor at the time, Jean Guiton, called on the citizens never to give in. But the barrage held and the stranglehold proved too strong. Eventually, in late October 1628, the town surrendered after 13 months of terrible isolation. Only 5,000 out of a population of 28,000 survived.

However, La Rochelle revived, and although much is made of the town's sufferings for its Protestantism, not quite so much mention is made of its eager participation in the slave trade: its wine and brandy went to African traders who in turn sold it for slaves which they exchanged for American goods. From 1670 to 1692, 45 slaving expeditions headed out from port. In the 18th century, La Rochelle was one of the top slaving ports in France, with 400 ships recorded heading out on slaving expeditions, many owned by the Rasteau family; much of the glorious 18th-century architecture of La Rochelle was derived from slave-trading profits. Canadian fur was also important to La Rochelle's merchants until 1763 and the French colonial losses in North America. Many North Americans of French descent can trace their roots back to La Rochelle, as this part of the country provided numerous settlers for Quebec, Acadia and Louisiana.

Slave trading was banned in the 19th century, and La Rochelle took on a much lower profile. Many prisoners, including Dreyfus, bound for a life sentence on Devil's Island in the French colony of Guyana, left from La Rochelle right up to the outbreak of the Second World War. The creation of a deep-water port north of town at La Pallice at the end of the 19th century helped revive commerce.

Like the other major French Atlantic ports, La Rochelle was turned into a Nazi submarine base in the Second World War. At the end of the conflict the Nazis clung on desperately to these vital ports, and La Rochelle was only given up to the Allies on 7 May 1945. Luckily the city avoided heavy bombardment. The strong Resistance movement which had been active in and around La Rochelle during the war was honoured afterwards. A mayor of La Rochelle, Vieljeux, was one of those deported and killed by the Nazis.

In recent decades, La Rochelle's fortunes have been closely associated with its long-serving socialist mayor, the dynamic Michel Crépeau, who died in 1999. An early environmentalist, he made the preservation of the old town a model of urban conservation in France.

La Rochelle

All three of the medieval towers of the Vieux Port are open to the public (*open April–Sept daily 10–7; rest of year daily exc Tues 10–12.30 and 2–5.30; adm*). The **Tour de la Lanterne**, by far the tallest with its crocketed Gothic spire, served not just as a seamark for centuries, but also as a prison, and inside is covered with centuries-old graffiti of British and Dutch sailors. During the Wars of Religion, 13 priests were held here before having their throats cut and being thrown into the sea below. Nowadays they'd land in a car park. From the top of the tower you can see a cordon of trees a short way north, a well-laid out park where the ramparts once stood. These elegant gardens, much appreciated by the Rochelais, end with the Plage de la Concurrence, although the estuary outside La Rochelle is hardly an ideal spot for a swim.

At the narrow neck of the entrance to the inner port, the Tour de la Chaîne and the Tour St-Nicolas stand guard opposite each other, divided only by a thin channel. A chain used to be strung between them in centuries past to regulate trade and to stop illicit traffic passing through at night. The interior of the **Tour de la Chaîne** is a bit of a disappointment, with its panels in French recalling the town's history. Restaurants line the historic quay, the **Cour des Dames**, which leads to the chubby statue of Victor-Guy Duperré, twenty-second child of a Rochelais family who grew up to become a scourge to the British on the seas in the early 1800s. He wasn't popular with the Algerians either, after commanding the fleet which captured Algiers in 1830, leading to the founding of France's North African colonies. Beyond Duperré's statue the gateway through the mighty **Grosse Horloge tower** beckons. This tower is another landmark of the Vieux Port. The original building dates from the 14th century, part of the city's formidable medieval ramparts, but in the 18th century the tower was embellished with its elaborate top, including two great stone globes, the one terrestrial, the other celestial.

On the other side of the Vieux Port, the **Tour St-Nicolas** was constructed as a residence for the port governors in the 14th century. Worn Gothic figures and devices look over the intriguing labyrinth of little rooms and stairways, where it's easy to become disoriented.

A short walk into town from the Quai Duperré at the back of the Vieux Port takes you to the grand **Place de l'Hôtel de Ville**. The statue in the centre represents a defiant Jean Guiton, mayor at the time of Richelieu's siege. Although Guiton failed to withstand the siege, although he failed to live up to his promise to kill himself rather than surrender, and although he even went on to join the French navy after the siege had ended, he has gone down in La Rochelle as a hero, a symbol of the city's proud defiance. Behind the crenellated Gothic walls of the town hall courtyard, you can just see a colourful ceramic statue of Henri IV high up under a canopy, sporting caramel leggings and a purple top. Walk into the courtyard to see the rich Baroque decoration of the main façade. The caryatids above represent Prudence, Justice, Fortitude and Temperance; in their company Henri IV looks a comical Dapper Dan.

Many of La Rochelle's arcaded streets lie around the town hall and behind the Grosse Horloge. Here two great civic buildings, the **Bourse** or exchange (now the chamber of commerce) and the **Palais de Justice** stand side by side on Rue du Palais. Stone prows of vessels and naval trophies stick out of the ornate façade of the Bourse, while the decorations of the Palais de Justice are more discreet. One curiosity among the tempting shops here is the **Musée du Flacon à Parfum** (*open Tues–Sat 10.30–7, Mon 3–7; closed Sun; adm*), along the Rue du Temple, with its extensive collection of scent bottles.

The town's best museum, the **Musée du Nouveau Monde** (*open daily exc Tues 10.30–12.30 and 1.30–6; adm*) is one of the few in France to confront the subject of slavery seriously. The story is told in good part by showing the luxuries purchased with the proceeds of the trade, including the sumptuous mansion itself which houses the museum – the Hôtel Fleuriau – named after a shipowning family who had a flourishing plantation on Santo Domingo. One room has pompous allegorical paintings of America, while the office of a Rochelais shipowner has been recreated in one corner. A series of 19th-century clocks in the form of busts of black figures stands out. Upstairs, the attention focuses on the slave trade; it is estimated that in the 18th century La Rochelle ships alone transported some 140,000 slaves from West Africa to the West Indies, principally to Santo Domingo. The paintings and engravings offer an insight into the often disturbing mentality of the period. The revolutionary mementoes of the anti-slavery movement are much more heartwarming. Napoleon then reinstated slavery, but the trade declined after him. The museum also has an exceptional series of photos of Indian chiefs by Edward S. Curtis.

Although the **Musée des Beaux-Arts** (*open daily exc Tues 2–7; adm*) is housed in the Hôtel de Crussol d'Uzès, a grand mansion from the 1770s, the collections have been shoved unceremoniously to the top of the building, reached by a shoddy staircase. At the entrance, the black and white representations of Christ's story by Rouault are striking, but they're followed by a chaotic display of cloying, overblown canvases. Bouguereau, born in La Rochelle and a great salon favourite (not to mention a saloon favourite for his titillating nudes) comes out comparatively well here with a touching portrait of Mme Deseilligny. You can compare some classic maritime scenes with a vibrant Signac pointilliste view of La Rochelle.

A short walk from these two museums, the **cathedral** occupies one corner on the massive and barren **Place de Verdun**. The cathedral itself is vacuous behind its grand, wide, 18th-century classical façade, and contains some truly sickly 19th-century decoration, both in the stained glass and the paintings. Blame Bouguereau for the worst excesses in the choir end.

The **Musée d'Orbigny-Bernon** (*open daily exc Tues and Sun am 10–12 and 2–6; adm*) has more charm than the fine arts museum. Ceramics from around France are the forte. Some striking engravings illustrate the siege of La Rochelle and the persecution of Protestants. Further sections are devoted to Oriental miscellany and to the Second World War. Around the corner stone heads pop out from the **Maison Vennette**, an elaborate mansion built for a doctor who decorated his home with busts of famous medical figures through the ages.

La Rochelle

Musée d'Histoire Naturelle

Jardin des Plantes

RUE ALBERT 1ER
RUE DELAYANT
RUE ALCIDE D'ORBIGNY
AV DES CORDELIERS

RUE RAMBAUD
RUE DU COLLEGE
RUE DU CORDOUAN
PLACE DES CORDELIERS

Parc Charruyer

RUE CHAUDRIER
RUE DU MINAGE
POL
PLACE DE VERDUN
Musée des Beaux-Arts
RUE DES GOUTTIERS
P

AV DU GENERAL LECLERC
Musée du Nouveau Monde
RUE GARGOULLEAU
RUE GAMBETTA
RUE GAMBETTA

RUE FLEURIAU
Les Halles
RUE THIERS
RUE ST-LOUIS
RUE THIERS

RUE ST-COME
Cathedral
RUE BAZOGES
RUE ST-YON
RUE THIERS

Musée d'Orbigny-Bernon
RUE AUFREDY
RUE DES AUGUSTINS
RUE MERCIERS
RUE AMELOT
VILLENEUVE

RUE DE L'ABREUVOIR
Maison Vennette
RUE ST-MICHEL
PLACE BAPTISTE MARCET

Palais de Justice
RUE DUPATY
Hôtel de Ville
RUE ST-LOUIS
P

REMPARTS
RUE REAUMUR
RUE ADMYRAULT
RUE DU PALAIS
Bourse
PLACE DE LA CAILLE
RUE DU TEMPLE
Musée Protestant
PLACE DE L'ARSENAL
P

DELMAS
RUE CHEF DE VILLE
RUE ST-SAUVEUR
QUAI MAUBEC
QUAI LOUIS DURAND

AV JEAN GUITON
Grosse Horloge
RUE VIELJEUX
PLACE BARENTIN
Musée du Flacon à Parfum
QUAI DUPERRE
RUE ST-NICOLAS
RUE DU DUC
Bassin de Retenue

CHEMIN DES
RUE REAUMUR
Musée Grevin
COUR DES DAMES
VIEUX PORT
QUAI CARENAGE
QUAI VALIN
RUE ST-CLAUDE

AV MAURICE
RUE DES STS-PERES
RUE DES CARMES
PLACE MARECHAL FOCH
RUE DE REMPART-ST-CLAUDE

RUE DE LA MONNAIE
RUE ST-JEAN DU PEROT
PLACE DE LA CHAINE
Tour St-Nicolas
Bassin à Flot
RUE DE L'OUVRAGE A CORNE

Tour de la Lanterne
RUE SUR LES MURS
Tour de la Chaîne
P
RUE DE L'ARMIDE
LE GABUT
QUAI DU GABUT
P
AV DU GENERAL DE GAULLE

PLACE DE LA CONCURRENCE
P
ESPLANADE ST-JEAN D'ACRE
i

Hôpital St-Louis

QUAI GEORGES SIMENON

Le Bout Blanc
Bassin des Grands Yachts
P
QUAI DE LA GEORGETTE
AV DU 123EME R.I.
BD JOFFRE
Train Station
P

RUE DU LOUP MARIN
Musée des Modèles Reduits
SENNAC DE MEILLAN
P

AV MARILLAC
LA VILLE EN BOIS
RUE DU CERF VOLANT
Musée des Automates
QUAI LOUIS PRUNIER
P

AV MARILLAC
Musée Maritime Neptunéa

N

200 metres
200 yards

Getting Around

There are two daily return flights between La Rochelle and Paris, run by Air Liberté, t 0803 805 805 (toll free in France).

La Rochelle has good train links with Paris-Montparnasse (under 3hrs).

For bus information around La Rochelle, t 05 46 34 02 22.

For taxis around town, t 05 46 41 22 22, t 05 46 34 02 22, or t 05 46 41 22 22.

Tourist Information

La Rochelle: Place de la Petite Sirène, t 05 46 41 14 68, f 05 46 41 99 85.

Where to Stay

La Rochelle ✉ 17000

****Hôtel du Nouveau Monde, 43 Rue du Minage, t 05 46 28 06 00, f 05 46 28 06 03 (*expensive*). The loveliest hotel in town in an old building with a new tower: calm and decorated with great taste.

***Le St-Jean-d'Acre, 4 Place de la Chaîne, t 05 46 41 73 33, f 05 46 41 10 01 (*moderate*). A characterful old building on the old port, in a great position for crowd-gazing. Get a room high up to appreciate the views of the port.

***France-Angleterre et Champlain, 20 Rue Rambaud, t 05 46 41 23 99, f 05 46 41 15 19 (*moderate*). Central, with plenty of charm, traditional furnishings and a garden.

***Hôtel de la Monnaie, 3 Rue de la Monnaie, t 05 46 50 65 65, f 05 46 50 63 19 (*moderate*). Central hotel around an old cobbled court-yard, with very comfortable, modern rooms.

**Ibis Grosse Horloge, 4 Rue Vieljeux et Chef-de-Ville, t 05 46 50 68 68, 05 46 41 34 94 (*inexpensive*). Chain hotel in one of the very finest buildings, right in the centre.

**Trianon, 6 Rue de la Monnaie, t 05 46 41 21 35, f 05 46 41 95 78 (*inexpensive*). Charming hotel close to the little town beach and town gardens. Restaurant (*menus 98–200F*). *Closed 15 Oct–15 Mar Sun; Sat lunch. Hotel closed Jan.*

**Hôtel du Commerce, 6 Place de Verdun, t 05 46 41 08 22, f 05 46 41 74 85

(*inexpensive*). Slightly swanky hotel with some large if rather vacuous rooms on this large square. Restaurant (*menus 98–200F*). *Closed Sat lunch, Sun Oct 15–15 Mar. Hotel closed 23 Dec–1 Feb.*

*Henri IV, 31 Rue des Gentilshommes, t 05 46 41 25 79, f 05 46 41 78 64 (*inexpensive–cheap*). A really sweet find right in the historic centre, by the Grosse Horloge.

*Bordeaux, 43 Rue St-Nicolas, t 05 46 41 31 22, f 05 46 41 24 43 (*inexpensive–cheap*). A very decent option, tucked away in a pretty little quarter just behind the eastern side of the Vieux Port.

Eating Out

La Rochelle is packed with restaurants. A whole lot of indifferent ones stretch out across the pavements along the quays: head elsewhere for finer cuisine.

Richard Coutanceau, Plage de la Concurrence, t 05 46 41 48 19, f 05 46 41 99 45. By far the most highly regarded restaurant in town, with fabulous cooking. The chef is renowned for producing some of the best seafood dishes on the French coast, particularly scampi (*menus 235–450F*). *Closed Sun.*

Les Flots, 1 Rue Chaîne, by the Tour de la Chaîne. Richard Coutanceau's son cooks up inventive and refined dishes (*menus 195–360F*). *Closed Oct–April Mon; Sun eves.*

André, 5 Rue St-Jean du Pérot, t 05 46 41 28 24, f 05 46 41 64 22. An institution in La Rochelle, with its long front made to resemble a ship, split into smaller dining rooms within (*menus 130–300F*).

Côté Sud, Rue Chef de Ville. With its white walls and fishermen's decoration, this is a jolly, good-value restaurant, and serves excellent seafood (*menus under 100F*).

A Côté de Chez Fred, 30–32 Rue St-Nicolas, t 02 46 41 65 76. Surprising little fish restaurant attached to the adjoining fishmonger's (*menus 150–220F*). *Closed 25 Oct–15 Nov; Mon exc April–Oct eves; Sun.*

Café du Nord. A good bet among the plethora of restaurants on the south quay of the Vieux Port, with simple cookery served either on the quayside terrace or in one of the few old houses in the Gabut area.

The **Muséum d'Histoire Naturelle** (*open Tues–Fri 10–12.30 and 1.30–5.30; Sat and Sun 2–6; closed Mon; adm*), east of the other museums, has for its highlight an 18th-century cabinet of curiosities collected by a civil servant and natural scientist, Clément de Lafaille, displayed in elaborate wood panelling. If you're interested in the history of Protestantism in France and in La Rochelle in particular, make a special effort to see the little **Musée Protestant** (*open July–15 Sept daily exc Sun 2.30–6; adm*) back near the Vieux Port behind Quai Duperré. The museum stands next to the large Protestant church, with the wonkily arcaded **Cloître des Dames Blanches** an oasis of peace on the other side.

On the south side of the Vieux Port, quayside cafés and restaurants front the attractive modern village of the **Gabut quarter.** La Rochelle's modern museums lie beyond its new, ultra-modern and impressive aquarium opened here at the end of 2000. The most famous exhibit at the **Musée Maritime Neptunéa** (*open April–Sept daily 10–8; rest of year daily 2–6.30; adm*) is Jacques Cousteau's *Calypso*, in the process of being restored, which sits in the Bassin des Grands Yachts alongside other real ships, several of which you can board. The rest of the museum occupies the former fish market. One of the latest areas to be created takes you on an undersea adventure fantasy, from Jules Vernes' fictional Captain Nemo to the *Calypso*. On the other side of the dock, the **Musée des Automates** has amusing automata with complex moving parts, while the **Musée des Modèles Réduits** next door is for those who like making scale models; some of the models here are pretty impressive, including a whole naval battle scene.

The Ile de Ré

Ré's similarity in name to the Egyptian sun god Ra doesn't do its image any harm as a highly prized destination for French sun worshippers, who bask in its special microclimate. Vines and villages dominate the eastern half of Ré. The western half has salt marshes and oyster beds. The opening in 1988 of a road bridge (*expensive toll*) connecting it with the mainland has made the island somewhat less exclusive, and the two main island roads, one running roughly along the north side, the other roughly along the south side, rapidly clog up with traffic.

Rivedoux, closest to the bridge, is too close to the industrial quarters of La Rochelle for comfort, but its sandy beach is popular. Heading along the southern side of the island, **Ste-Marie-de-la-Mer**, though lacking a proper beach, has old streets full of charm, with shutters painted various shades of green. You can visit the fish *écluses* here, the old fish farms cleverly constructed on the low rocks by the shore. **Le Bois-Plage** is located close to the long stretches of sand west of Ste-Marie, and is also the island's wine centre. The southern road continues to **La Couarde**, a purpose-built resort, popular because of its good beaches.

The road north from the bridge leads past the roofless Cistercian Abbaye des Châteliers and round **La Flotte**, a stylish village, home to Ré's new thalassotherapy centre and a delightful strip of beach backed by pines which dwindles to nothing at high tide. **St-Martin-en-Ré** is Poitou-Charente's answer to St-Tropez. Even if the yachts are smaller here, it certainly has the right to boast about its gorgeous circular harbour, a perfect stage for Côte d'Azur-style posing. Even the penitentiary set among the pointed Ancien Régime fortifications is almost picturesque.

Heading towards the western part of the island, a road branches off north to **Loix**, past the isolated whitewashed building of the **Maison des Marais Salants**, which recalls the strong salt-making tradition of Ré, now much reduced. The black and white spiky Gothic spire of the church of **Ars-en-Ré** serves a second purpose, as a seamarker.

Heading north beyond **St-Clément-des-Baleines**, with its centre on Ré flora and fauna, the lighthouse, the **Phare des Baleines**, stands out, open to visitors for its great views across Ré, along the coast, and out to sea. The **Arche de Noé** zoo close by contains a collection of both living and stuffed animals from around the world. An enormous turtle that landed on Ré in 1978 is honoured. **Les Portes-en-Ré** is tucked away in the least accessible corner of Ré and lies close to some of the best beaches, those which suffer less from the receding tides.

Tourist Information

Ile de Ré: 5 Rue de la Blanche, Le Bois-Plage-en-Ré, **t** 05 46 09 00 55, **f** 05 46 09 00 54.
St-Martin-en-Ré: 15 Av Victor Bouthillier, **t** 05 46 09 20 06.

Where to Stay and Eat

La Flotte-en-Ré ✉ 17630

★★★★Le Richelieu, 44 Av de la Plage, **t** 05 46 09 60 70, **f** 05 46 09 50 59 (*expensive*). The most exclusive address on Ré: a beautiful, luxurious hotel in a wonderful village, with a thalassotherapy centre and a fantastic restaurant; speciality – grilled lobster (*menus 300–400F*). *Closed Jan.*

St-Martin-en-Ré ✉ 17410

If you like to be in the midst of the glamour get a room on the port, but you need to book well ahead.
★★★La Jetée, 23 Quai Georges Clemenceau, **t** 05 46 09 36 36, **f** 05 46 09 36 06 (*moderate*). Exclusive hotel with 31 rooms.
★★Les Colonnes, 19 Quai Job Foran, **t** 05 46 09 21 58, **f** 05 46 09 21 49 (*inexpensive*). 30 rooms in the heart of the action with a bar spilling out below it. Restaurant (*menus 139–239F*). *Closed Wed. Hotel closed 15 Dec–1 Feb.*

★★Le Port, 29 Quai de la Poithevinière, **t** 05 46 09 21 21, **f** 05 46 09 06 85 (*inexpensive*). Simple hotel with 35 spacious modern rooms.
★Le Sully, 19 Rue Jean Jaurès, **t** 05 46 09 26 94, **f** 05 46 09 06 85. For a cheaper option, try this pleasant little hotel in the shopping streets up from the port.
La Baleine Bleue, Quai Launay Razilly, **t** 05 46 03 30, **f** 05 46 09 30 86. Irresistible restaurant on the port's central island, attracting the smart set.

Ars-en-Ré ✉ 17580

Le Bistrot de Bernard, 1 Quai de la Criée, **t** 05 46 29 40 26, **f** 05 46 29 28 99. Immediately eye-catching among the sweet restaurants at the port, and serving excellent seafood (*menus 130–400F*). *Closed 11 Nov–20 Dec; 4 Jan–15 Feb; Oct–Mar Tues; Mon eves.*

Bois-Plage ✉ 17580

★★L'Océan, 4 Rue St-Martin, **t** 05 46 09 23 07 (*moderate–inexpensive*). Delightful relaxing hotel in a relatively unspoilt part of the island, with a typical regional design and a maritime feel. This place takes you just about as far as you can get from the main crowds on Ré. Restaurant (*menus 130–180F*). *Closed Wed exc school hols. Hotel closed 5 Jan–10 Feb.*

The Coast from La Rochelle to Rochefort

This coastal stretch offers many surprises for English-speaking visitors. The resorts of Châtelaillon-Plage and Fouras contrast in style, the first modern, the second old-fashioned and historic. Out to sea from Fouras lie the island of Aix and the TV star Fort Boyard. Rochefort has a major naval past, blinding architecture and some great places to visit. As it grew up it eclipsed the fortified port of Brouage to the south, now stranded among wide marshes.

Châtelaillon-Plage was once the medieval capital of the Aunis region, but now has the cheerful look of a small, modern seaside resort with lots of hotels behind the mimosas of the promenade. **Fouras** has by contrast kept a strong historical atmosphere. A splendid solid medieval **keep** sticks out from a high prow of land above the beaches. Fortifications here have long guarded the northern entrance to the Charente river. The main building you now see dates from the 15th century, while Vauban had further layers of defence added in the 17th. The museum in the keep contains a miscellany of sea shells, maps and models – navies often fought off the waters of Fouras, most notably in 1809, when much of the French fleet of Brest was destroyed by the British in the *Journée des Brûlots*, the Day of the Fire Ships.

A spit of land, the Pointe de la Fumée, tapers off to the north of Fouras. From its tip packed with oyster farms you can take a ferry out to the **Ile d'Aix**, a tiny crescent of an island that conceals a concentration of Napoleonic memorabilia in its **Musée Napoléon**. The house containing the museum was ordered by the megalomaniac himself in 1808 and was where he spent his last days on French soil in July 1815 before being shipped off to St Helena. The man who left this fascinating collection to the nation, one Baron Gourgaud, was a great-grandson of an *aide-de-camp* to the emperor. The island itself produces exotica in mother-of-pearl. The impenetrable smooth-rounded oval of the **Fort Boyard** (*not open to visits*) lurks out to sea, a massive 19th-century defence started under Napoleon I, completed under Napoleon III. In 1871 it was turned into the Alcatraz of the Atlantic, receiving Communards from the failed uprising in Paris. It has gained fame recently thanks to the TV challenge programme.

Rochefort

Rochefort, an extremely handsome, muscular town, was born a child of war. In the 1660s it grew rapidly into a square-shouldered worker to construct a fleet for the Sun King capable of taking on the great seapowers of the time, England and Holland. La Rochelle was considered too exposed for the purpose, while the old port at Brouage was already silting up. But Rochefort seemed ideal: it lay up the Charente estuary, 15km from the sea, protected from the weather and easy to defend. Vast war vessels were put together here. A grand grid of streets up the slope from the river was constructed under Michel Bégon, the royal naval *intendant* at the end of the 17th century, now best known for giving his name to the begonia plant. Between 1690 and 1800, 300 vessels were launched at Rochefort. Shortly before the Revolution, in 1780,

Lafayette sailed from here on his second expedition to America, on board the *Hermione*. In the first half of the 19th century the *Sphinx* was the first major naval steam ship built in France. The *Mogador* was celebrated in its time as the largest naval paddle vessel made in the country. But orders dried up at the start of the 20th century, and in 1944 the Nazis torched some of the great old riverside buildings before leaving. Depressed, bruised and blackened, Rochefort waned.

Getting Around

There is a local rail llink between La Rochelle and Rochefort.

Tourist Information

Châtelaillon-Plage: 5 Av de Strasbourg, t 05 46 56 26 97.

Fouras: Fort Vauban, B.P.32, t 05 46 84 60 69.

Rochefort: Av Sadi Carnot, t 05 46 99 08 60, f 05 46 99 52 64, *www.tourisme.fr/rochefort*.

Where to Stay and Eat

Châtelaillon-Plage ✉ 17340

Le Rivage/Le St-Victor, 35 et 36 Bd de la Mer, t 05 46 56 25 79/t 05 46 56 25 13, f 05 46 56 19 03/f 05 46 30 01 92. These small modern blocks share pleasant plain rooms with fine sea views.

**La Pergola, 2 Rue de Chassiron, t 05 46 56 27 86 (*inexpensive*). With its awnings close to the 'port', this is a pleasant, simple option with 14 rooms. Restaurant (*menus 95–195F*). *Closed Nov–mid-March.*

**Le Majestic, Place St-Marsault, t 05 46 56 20 53, f 05 46 56 29 24 (*inexpensive*). On a lovely avenue lined by plane trees, this grandiose hotel may not be on the seafront, but it has some style and the beach isn't far away. Restaurant (*menus 115–220F*). *Closed 21 Dec–25 Jan; Fri exc restaurant; Oct–Mar Sat and Sun.*

Fouras ✉ 17450

**Grand Hôtel des Bains, 15 Rue du Général Brüncher, t 05 46 84 03 44, f 05 46 84 58 26 (*inexpensive*). Set around a large, summery courtyard, this well-run, clean and charming hotel was once a posting inn. Restaurant for residents only (*dinner only*). *Closed Nov–Easter.*

**La Roseraie, 2 Av du Port-Nord, t 05 46 84 64 89 (*inexpensive*). An equally delightful hotel, outside the centre at the base of the Pointe de la Fumée. It looks like a large friendly family villa.

Hélène Chognot, 35 Rue du Général Brüncher, t 05 46 84 21 78. Good for a central B&B room with sea view just by the fort.

La Jetée, Pointe de la Fumée, t 05 46 84 60 43. Probably the best place for fresh seafood.

Rochefort ✉ 17300

****La Corderie Royale, Rue Audebert, B.P.275, t 05 46 99 35 35, f 05 46 99 78 72, *hotel@corderieroyale.com* (*expensive–moderate*). In an excellent location, this hotel occupies a wonderful 17th-century building which offers peace away from the crowds by the Charente. The swimming pool is set in a wonderful courtyard. Rooms are very comfortable, the cuisine is of a high standard (*menus 150–320F*). *Closed Feb; Nov–Easter Sun eves and Mon.*

**Roca Fortis, 14 Rue de la République, t 05 46 99 26 32, f 05 46 87 49 48 (*inexpensive*). In a bright old-stone town house. The rooms may be a bit worn, but they are spacious and full of character, and the place is well run.

**Le Paris, 27–29 Rue La Fayette, t 05 46 99 33 11, f 05 46 99 77 34 (*inexpensive*). Better known for its cheerful restaurant (*menus 129–210F*) than its rooms. *Closed Mar–May Fri eves; Oct–Feb Sun.*

L'Escale de Bougainville, Quai de la Louisiane, t 05 46 99 54 99, f 05 46 99 54 99. The most reputed cuisine in town, opposite the marina (*menus 160–230F*). *Closed 10–31 Jan. Sun evenings, Mon.*

Brouage

Le Brouage, Rue du Québec, t 05 46 85 03 06. A good restaurant to incite you to linger a bit longer in this time-warped town.

Things began to look up when Jacques Demy shot a successful musical here in the 1960s: *Les Demoiselles de Rochefort* starring Catherine Deneuve. The grid of streets, now scrubbed bright, are lined with palms. Down by the Charente, the **Corderie Royale** is a stunning building, supported on one side by scrolled buttresses; it goes on and on – ships' ropes were laid out, twisted and treated here. Part of the interior holds the **Centre International de la Mer** (*open summer daily 9–7; rest of year daily 9–6; adm*), with a permanent exhibition on ropemaking and a programme of changing temporary exhibitions. Beyond one end of the Corderie Royale and the provisions building which could churn out 20,000 kilos of bread a day, you come to the dock, now Rochefort's yacht marina. Beyond the other end, a copy of Lafayette's *Hermione* (*guided tour only; open July–Aug daily 10–7; rest of year daily 10–1 and 2–6; adm*) is being put together, the site wrapped in protective materials. The name is a bit of a cheat, as the new ship is actually modelled on the old frigate *Concorde*, whose plans ended up in Greenwich when the vessel was seized by the British. This is a long-term project; in the old days, some 1,500 workers might have taken a year to complete such a vessel; the new *Hermione* was started in 1997 and is due to be completed by 2007. Its size out of water is deeply impressive. On weekday tours you can often see specialist craftsmen going about their work.

Further splendid vessels are the glory of the **Musée de la Marine** (*open April–Sept daily 10–6; rest of year daily exc Tues 10–12 and 2–5; adm*), set in an elegant building just up from the *Hermione* dock, only this time they are scale models. The setting is appropriate; the Hôtel des Chausses served as the residence of the commander of the royal navy based at Rochefort, and some of France's most famous fleet commanders stayed here. The beautiful scale models include a replica of the original *Hermione*. You can also examine elaborately engraved coconuts turned into powder containers, carved by the prisoners who also did much of the shipbuilding work. A magnificent model of 19th-century Fort Boyard is the closest you'll get to seeing it in any detail.

The Musée de la Marine lies by the imposing **Porte du Soleil**, erected in 1831 as the new entrance to the arsenal. Beyond the gate, an elegant building serves as a covered market. Head for central **Place Colbert**, with the intimidating classical church of **St-Louis** off one corner. Some of Rochefort's straight streets are paved with blue-tinged stone shipped back from Quebec. Lost in the grid plan, the **Maison Pierre Loti** (*guided tour only; open July–15 Sept daily 10–6, tours every half-hour; rest of year daily exc Tues and whole of Jan, tours at 11, 12, 2, 3 and 4; adm*) may not stand out on the outside, but a riot of decoration awaits within, created by a man whose 'life was one long carnival,' according to one of the Goncourt brothers. Loti was born here in 1850 and was baptized Julien Viaud. He became a sailor and writer of exquisite romantic fiction. He combined a lust for fancy dress with grand political aspirations, but at heart was a restless, troubled soul. He found his pen name on a trip to Tahiti in 1872. The entertaining if rather-too-reverent tour takes you past family portraits and the odd photo of Loti in fancy dress. He also dressed up the family home. There's a richly decorated Renaissance hall and a medieval room with Gothic tracery and amusing heads. By contrast, Loti's bedroom has something of the simplicity of a monastic cell (his wife wasn't allowed in). Much play is made of Loti falling in love with a young

Turkish woman on his first journey to Istanbul at the age of 26, although no mention is made of the fact, revealed by his serious biographers, that he also had quite an appetite for having sex with men. On his trips around the world he picked up a lot of exotica and half-digested ideas: hence the Arab room, the Turkish salon and the travesty of a mosque. But Loti was a dedicated defender of many of the foreign peoples he visited. Although Loti's novels are now somewhat neglected, in 1891 he was elected to the Académie Française, beating one Emile Zola for the honour.

The nearby **Musée d'Art et d'Histoire** (*open July–Aug daily exc public hols 1.30–7; rest of year daily exc Sun, Mon and public hols 1.30–5.30; adm*) contains a splendidly detailed scale model of Rochefort from 1835 and the town's art collections. The **Musée des Commerces d'Autrefois** (*open 15 Mar–15 Nov daily 10–12 and 2–7; rest of year daily 10–12 and 2–6; adm*) pays homage to the shops of yesteryear.

South of Rochefort, the **Conservatoire du Bégonia** is devoted to the plant in all its hundreds of varieties (*guided visits only; book via tourist office: tours Tues–Sat at 2, 3, 4 and 5; adm*). Here too is the **Pont Transbordeur de Martrou**, the transporter bridge built in 1900 which marks the flat landscape south of Rochefort almost as sensationally as the modern toll bridge over the Charente river. It is now open for pedestrians and cyclists.

Fantastically preserved in a time warp, the old harbour of **Brouage** south of the Charente was going downhill as Rochefort rose. Brouage lies in the flattest of landscapes, and since its first life as a port, it has long lived totally isolated in the midst of wide green marshland. The most famous sailor Brouage produced, Protestant Samuel de Champlain, founded Quebec, and is still celebrated in his home port. During the siege of La Rochelle, Richelieu had the place turned into a heavily defended arsenal. The main pleasure of going to Brouage today is to walk round the top of these splendid ramparts so bizarrely abandoned among the marshes.

From the Ile d'Oléron to the Gironde

Oystery Oléron has a couple of truly memorable beaches. Cross the deep, wide estuary of the Seudre and you come to the pine-backed Côte Sauvage, or Wild Coast, which lives up to its name. When you reach the vast mouth of the Gironde estuary the coast becomes a good deal calmer, hence the row of very popular resorts: La Palmyre, St-Palais and Royan.

L'Ile d'Oléron is linked to the mainland by one of the longest bridges in France, more precisely, a viaduct on pillars. At high tide the channel between mainland and island is full of seawater, but at low tide, extensive mudflats and oyster beds lie exposed. **St-Trojan**, at the southern end of the island, is the best place to stay. To find the nearest beach, head south for the glorious wide **Plage de Gatseau**, backed by woods and with just a couple of beach bars sinking into its powdery sands. Unfortunately, it's not made for bathing due to the tidal squeeze; for that try the **Grande Plage** on the southwestern tip of Oléron, with a black mussel-clad wreck stranded in the sands. **Le Château** is the most important historic village on the island, although it in fact has a substantial citadel rather than a castle, commissioned by Richelieu. The very modest port below is strung along the channel coming in from the sea. From Le Château you can follow meandering lanes through the attractively shabby territory of the oyster farms to **St-Pierre-d'Oléron**, the island's bright little capital. In the small **Musée de l'Ile d'Oléron Aliénor d'Aquitaine**, Pierre Loti (*see* 'Rochefort', above), whose family had a holiday home in this Oléron village, is better remembered than the great Eleanor.

Back by the coast Boyardville was the base for the 19th-century builders of Fort Boyard and has now become a popular tourist port for ferries around the islands. Continue north above Boyardville and you come upon a truly splendid curve of pale sandy beach, the **Plage de la Gautrelle**. The island becomes drabber as you reach the northern tip with its big black and white striped lighthouse and poxy cliffs. Much of the west coast is marred for beach-lovers by rocks between the sand and the sea, and the plastic rubbish brought in by the tides. Rather than searching for shells, you can go along picking up a plethora of plastic containers and then arrange them by country of provenance – an educational game for the children.

Moving back to the mainland, **Ronce-les-Bains** is a plainish resort protected by Oléron's tail. The piny hillocks of the **Forêt de la Coubre** bobble up and down south of town to the tall thin phallus of the lighthouse of la Coubre. The exposed Atlantic coast beyond is highly dangerous, with strong undercurrents and shifting sandbanks. The deafening roar of the waves should put you off taking a dip, but the vast stretches of untouched dunes are impressive.

Things calm down beyond the Pointe de la Coubre, where a row of popular resorts looks across the vast mouth of the Gironde estuary. In the midst of the estuary, the **Phare de Cordouan** (*see* p.508–9) sticks up like a little tongue. Modern **La Palmyre** has purpose-built, Spanish style villas under the pines, a marina, and an absurdly packed zoo in summer. Beaches lead on down to St-Palais, one nudist, one wildly popular with gay men. **St-Palais-sur-Mer** has a genteel charm. By far the most stylish resort along this stretch, it offers a string of little rocky creeks, while large fishing nets hang picturesquely in readiness for action.

Much of central **Royan** was destroyed by bombing in the Second World War, but it is hugely popular as a summer resort, thanks to a large, well-protected curve of sand which appeals to those who don't pay too much attention to the architecture. The enormous cement silo of a church is hard to avoid. Step into it and you feel as if you have been swallowed by Jonah's whale. Once it has spat you out again, wander to the covered market in the shape of a clam. However, the landmark which unfortunately stands out most is the watertower on the horizon, a giant cement ice-cream cone.

You'll find more traditional architecture south down the Gironde estuary. **Talmont** could scarcely have a better-located church, standing out over the water. The village too is charming; in summer the hollyhocks grow as high as the cottages, but the streets are packed with visitors. Things quieten towards **Mortagne-sur-Gironde**. In the low cliff face here you can visit a hermitage and chapel dug into the rock. In the Middle Ages the local hermits helped pilgrims to cross the Gironde on their journey to Santiago de Compostela.

Getting Around

You can get to Royan by train via Saintes, inland on the Charente.

Tourist Information

Ile d'Oléron: Route du Viaduc, Bourcefranc-le-Chapus, t 05 46 85 65 23.

St-Trojan-les-Bains: Av du Port, t 05 46 76 00 86.

Le Château-d'Oléron: Place de la République, t 05 46 47 60 51.

St-Palais-sur-Mer: 1 Av de la République, t 05 46 23 22 58.

Royan: 1 Bd Grandière, t 05 46 05 04 71.

Where to Stay and Eat

L'Ile d'Oléron
St-Trojan-les-Bains ⊠ **17370**

**L'Albatros, 11 Bd du Dr. Pineau, t 05 46 76 00 08, f 05 46 76 03 58 (*inexpensive*). In a delightful location right by the southern coastal path, unspoilt by roads, with a terrace right by the sea – a special little place even if the rooms aren't that exciting.

**La Forêt, 16 Bd Pierre Wiehn, t 05 46 76 00 15, f 05 46 76 14 67 (*inexpensive*). A big modern block set among shady trees. Some of the natty rooms and the restaurant look out to the vastly long viaduct to the island.

**Le Homard Bleu, 10 Bd Félix Faure, t 05 46 76 00 22, f 05 46 76 14 95 (*inexpensive*). A diminutive roadside hotel with a good seafood restaurant (*menus 95–310F*). *Closed 3 Jan–15 Feb; 1 Nov–Easter; Tues eves and Wed.*

La Belle Cordière, 76 Rue de la République, t 05 46 76 12 87. Attractive restaurant serving inventive cuisine.

Le Grand Large, Baie de la Rémigeasse, ⊠ 17550 Dolus d'Oléron, t 05 46 75 37 89, f 05 46 75 49 15, *grandlarge@relaischateaux .fr* (*expensive*). The most luxurious hotel on the island, right by a west-coast beach, with a smart restaurant looking on to the sea, but the boxy modern architecture is a bit of a shocker, even with all the ivy draped over it. *Closed 1 Oct–30 April.*

Up the Charente

The gentle vine-clad banks of the Charente offer an alternative to the busy rollers and cars on the Atlantic coast. Heading upriver from splendid naval Rochefort (*see* pp.437–40), you pass through a series of historic towns pickled in the past – Saintes, Cognac, Jarnac and Angoulême. East of Angoulême, the area's major sight is the massive Château de la Rochefoucauld.

Introduced by balustraded gardens, the lovely **Château de la Roche-Courbon** (*gardens open daily 9–12 and 2–6.30, winter till 5.30; guided tours of the château daily exc Thurs outside summer 10 and 2.30, but times otherwise the same; adm*) is lost in woodland close to St-Pourchaire between Rochefort and Saintes. Most of the castle dates from the 15th century, but it was considerably embellished in the 17th century. In the early 20th century Pierre Loti launched a campaign to save it from ruin, describing it as a true Sleeping Beauty castle, and it turns out that he, Rochefort's prince of camp, gave it the kiss of life. On the short guided tour you can admire some rustic 17th- and 18th-century panel paintings. The Cabinet de Peintures, also now known as the bathroom, has the labours of Hercules competing with the life of Christ.

Le Gua ✉ 17680
★★★Moulin de Châlons, 2 Rue du Bassin, **t** 05 46 22 82 72, **f** 05 46 22 91 07 (*moderate–inexpensive*). This transformed tidal mill on the eastern end of the extraordinary inland oyster sea of the Seudre river gives you an excellent flavour of the watery landscapes typical of this coastal strip. Restaurant (*menus 120–390F*). *Closed Oct–April and Mon–Fri lunch.*

St-Palais ✉ 17640
★★★Résidence de Rohan, Parc des Fées, Route de St-Palais, Vaux-sur-Mer, **t** 05 46 39 00 75, **f** 05 46 38 29 99 (*moderate– inexpensive*). Appealing rooms split between a charmingly messy 19th-century villa and a modern block. The place has the odd palm tree and direct access to the beach south of St-Palais, plus a tennis court.
★★Le Frivole, 10 Av du Platin, **t** 05 46 23 25 00, **f** 05 46 23 20 25 (*inexpensive*). Peaceful bourgeois house with character, well run and definitely a cut above your normal two-star.
★★Téthys, 60 Av de la Corniche, **t** 05 46 23 33 61 (*inexpensive*). Very well located.

23 rooms, some of which have sea views, as does the dining room (*menus 100–200F*). *Hotel closed Oct–April; restaurant closed Oct–May.*

St-Georges-de-Didonne ✉ 17110
★★★Suzac, 17–26 Chemin du Fort de Suzac, **t** 05 46 06 26 46, **f** 05 46 06 26 13 (*expensive–moderate*). On the cliffs at the dramatic mouth of the Gironde. Comfortable rooms above a gorgeous beach.

Meschers-sur-Gironde ✉ 17132
★★Les Grottes de Matata, Bd de la Falaise, **t** 05 46 02 70 02, **f** 05 46 02 78 00 (*inexpensive*). Hotel in a modern building with majestic views over the Gironde estuary.

St-Fort-sur-Gironde ✉ 17240
Château des Salles, **t** 05 46 49 95 10, **f** 04 46 49 02 81 (*moderate*). A light, restored late-medieval manor house set a bit back from the Gironde estuary, this B&B is run lovingly and with panache by the family that owns it. *Closed 30 Sept–1 April.*

Saintes

Arriving in riverside Saintes, it makes chronological sense to look at the Gallo-Roman sites first. Saintes was named from the Celtic tribe of the Santons, and it grew into an extremely important Gallo-Roman city: with 30,000 inhabitants it was the capital for a time of the Roman province of Aquitaine. The early 1st-century AD **Arch of Germanicus**, moved to a picturesque location by the Charente, pays tribute to Tiberius and his family, including his brother Drusus and the latter's popular warrior son Germanicus.

The **Musée Archéologique** (*open summer daily exc Mon 10–12 and 2–6; winter daily exc Mon and Sun am 10–12 and 2–5.30; adm*) near the arch is a confusing little thing in two buildings, that turns out to be disappointing given the scale of the Gallo-Roman city. There's a bit of glass and pottery, oil lamps with animal designs, dice, and fragments of a chariot unearthed from a 1st-century tomb. The second building, a former abattoir, appropriately holds offcuts from Gallo-Roman buildings incorporated into the 4th-century walls. The explanatory sheet in English helps make sense of it all. The most remarkable sculpture stares out from the far end, a row of stocky cows' heads.

The ruined amphitheatre, or **Arènes** (*open April–Oct daily 9–7; rest of year daily 10–12.30 and 2–4.30; adm*), stands outside the historic centre. Built around 40 AD under the reign of Claudius, it could seat 15,000. The ribs of its stairways plunge down the grassy slopes through which some rows of stone seats poke out.

While there, visit the church of **St-Eutrope** nearby, named after the first bishop of Saintes, founded in the 11th century by Cluniac monks. The main façade may be dull, but the interior contains some entertaining carving. In the choir, the apostles are grouped two by two under elegant Gothic canopies. Below this church you can visit a surprising semi-subterranean church, with a tomb reckoned to be that of St Eutrope.

Saintes' main medieval attractions are in the centre of town. The **Abbaye aux Dames** (*open mid-April–Sept daily 10–12.30 and 2–9; rest of year daily 2–6, but Wed and Sat also 10–12.30; adm*), consecrated in 1047 and later something of a finishing school for noble ladies, lies on the east bank of the Charente beyond the Roman arch. The badly damaged façade is notable for its exuberant and disturbing sculpture, especially in the central portal with eight tightly packed rows, including brutal martyrdoms, the horrid image of little figures pierced by swords repeated again and again. Inside, the extra wide nave was topped by Saintonge cupolas and has wonderful acoustics, perfect for the concerts held here. A pedestrian bridge leads across the Charente to the main centre of town. A lead skullcap of a roof covers the cathedral tower, resembling a rocket, only in stone. The original idea was to end with a soaring spire, but this was never carried out, hence the cap.

Not far away in a residential area, the **Musée Dupuy-Mestreau** (*guided tours dailly 2.30, 3.30 and 4.30, July and Aug also 11; adm*) occupies a grand 18th-century house, with collections on local arts and crafts, including painted panelling from Madame de Montespan's family château, costumes, jewellery, fans, cards, miniatures, and a pair of Louis XVI's slippers. In the 16th century the ground-breaking potter Bernard Palissy set up his workshop in Saintes where he elaborated his wild glazed enamel designs; there are seemingly no originals left in town, but you can see copies of his style here. A certain Joseph Guillotin, a surgeon from Saintes, is also recalled. He was *not* pleased that the Revolution's killing machine, which he *did not* invent, was named after him. What he did say at the National Assembly in 1789 was that the form of capital punishment should be the same for all strata of society and he recommended a specific machine, originally known as a Louisette, as the least painful.

The **Musée du Présidial** and the **Musée de l'Echevinage** (*both open summer daily exc Mon 10–12 and 2–6; winter daily exc Mon and Sun am 10–12 and 2–5.30; adm*) are really sister museums set in the thick of the main shopping streets. The first presents the fine arts collections from the 15th to the 18th centuries. A couple of surprisingly good Flemish works stand out, along with a portrait of a magistrate by Rigaud. The Musée de l'Echevinage, set back from the shops in a posh courtyard, has an 18th-century façade with a protruding 16th-century stairtower. Inside, run-of-the-mill 19th- and 20th-century art is on display.

Cognac

To many in the English-speaking world, Cognac is synonymous with brandy, a word derived from the Dutch *brandwijn* or burnt wine. Cognac is distilled from the grape of the ugni blanc vines planted in a wide radius around the town of Cognac on the Charente. The vineyards are divided up into six areas: the most famous, the Grande Champagne and the Petite Champagne, stretch south from the Charente valley below Cognac and Jarnac. They produce a light white wine which is then 'burned' or distilled, twice. The resulting spirit is then aged for many years in oak barrels. A surprising percentage evaporates in time, 'the angels' share'. *Bouilleurs de cru*, the colourful term for home distillers, don't blend eaux de vie from the different areas of the Cognac region. But the bigger cognac houses do. This blending is the last crucial step before the ageing process to give a distinctive flavour to the famous cognac brands, the job of the trusted cellar master or *maître de chai*.

The big cognac houses are household names: Hennessy, Martell, Courvoisier, Rémy Martin, Hine, and so on. Most of these big companies are based in the two riverside towns of Cognac and Jarnac, many with their cellars on the quays, as in centuries past the barrels would be transported by water. Six are well set up for visitors, with slick tours in which the making of cognac and the history of the individual house are well explained (*see* below). Five of the six are in or around Cognac town, the sixth in Jarnac. But there are in fact some 250 cognac houses in all, as well as many smaller local producers from whom you can buy direct. If you buy from them, then the cognac will be much more marked by local characteristics.

The labelling of cognac is complex. Three-star cognac is actually ordinary cognac which has been aged for five to nine years. V.O. (Very Old) and V.S.O.P. (Very Superior Old Pale) are considered a level up, having aged between 12 and 20 years (the use of English hints who used to buy the most brandy). Then come the special blends which will have been left to mature 20 to 40 years, or sometimes longer, such as X.O., Vieille Réserve, Grande Réserve, Royal and Napoléon. The term Fine Champagne means that the cognac is made from blends only from the Petite and Grande Champagne areas. The inner sanctum of the cellars goes by the name of *le paradis*, the place where the very oldest matured cognac is kept. This paradise is generally protected by solid bars and only opened to a very select few. The age of some of the cognacs is staggering – Hennessy's very finest blend, the Richard Hennessy, might contain a drop or two of the same vat of brandy that Napoleon tasted.

Although it seems sacrilegious, concerns about alcohol consumption have led to cognac being served increasingly as a long drink, with tonic and so on. Another refreshing apéritif from these parts, **pineau des Charentes**, mixes grape juice with a hint of cognac, a combination which was accidentally discovered in the 16th century when a grower left some pressed juice in a cognac barrel which still contained a small amount of the liqueur.

Cognac is a town as well as a spirit, but of course the spirit dominates the town. The buildings of massive cognac houses loom over the Charente. The future François I was born here in 1494, in a riverside château taken over by the Otard cognac house at the

Getting Around

A railway line links Saintes, Cognac and Angoulême along the Charente river.

Tourist Information

Saintes: Villa Musso, 62 Cours National, t 05 46 74 23 82, f 05 46 92 17 01.
Cognac: 16 Rue du 14 Juillet, t 05 45 82 10 71.
Jarnac: Place du Château, t 05 45 81 09 30.
Angoulême: Place des Halles, t 05 45 95 16 84.
La Rochefoucauld: 1 Rue des Tanneurs, t 05 45 63 07 45.

Where to Stay and Eat

Crazannes ✉ 17350
Château de Crazannes B&B, t 05 46 90 15 94, f 05 46 91 34 46 (*expensive–moderate*). The fairy-tale Flamboyant Gothic façade of this little white-stoned château makes it an unforgettable place to stay, in a delightful spot along the Charente valley north of Saintes. *Closed Nov–Feb.*

St-Georges-des-Coteaux ✉ 17810
B&B Chez M et Mme Trouvé, 5 Rue de l'Eglise, t 05 46 92 96 66, f 05 46 92 96 66. Amusingly decorated, tasteful, good-value rooms off a dramatic converted farm building owned by charming gentle people

in this village a few km northwest of Saintes off the N137.

Saintes
****Le Relais du Bois St-Georges,** Rue de Royan, t 05 46 93 50 99, f 05 46 93 34 93 (*expensive*). A big, vibrant, quite beautiful and excessive establishment on the edges of town, with indoor pool, tennis courts, croquet lawn and piano bar, as well as a first-class restaurant (*menus 205–590F*). Speciality – octopus.
**Hôtel des Messageries, Rue des Messageries, t 05 46 93 64 99, f 05 46 92 14 34 (*inexpensive*). Central, calm and simple.
**Hôtel St-Pallais, 1 Place St-Pallais, t 05 46 92 51 03, f 05 46 92 83 81 (*inexpensive*). In a very attractive, atmospheric location on the square in front of the church of St-Pallais and the Abbaye aux Dames.

Cognac ✉ 16100
Hostellerie Les Pigeons Blancs, 110 Rue Jules Brisson, t 05 45 82 16 36, f 05 45 82 29 29 (*moderate*). Looks the part of a 17th-century posting inn, close to the centre of Cognac. The place is still family-run. The 6 rooms are kept to the highest standards, while the cuisine is expertly executed (*menus 120–280F*). *Closed Jan and Sun eves.*
**Domaine du Breuil, 104 Rue Robert Daugas, t 05 45 35 32 06, f 05 45 35 48 06 (*inexpensive*). Set apart in elegant grounds on the outskirts of town, this is a grand

Revolution. The guided tour plays on the royal history, although the historic parts of the château are a bit of a mess, encased in later commercial structures.

Hennessy makes its presence most felt in Cognac through sheer size. As well as visiting its glamorous shop, you can go on a guided tour of its cellars, crossing the river in a little boat. The house was founded by an Irishman who fought for Louis XV but after 12 years changed from warring to spirit-making. **Martell** claims to be the oldest cognac house, set up by Jean Martell from the Channel Islands. Among other attractions on the tour, you can see a copy of a *gabare*, the traditional river boat. The other two major cognac houses you can easily visit are **Camus**, still family run, and **Rémy Martin**. A visit to the latter actually takes you out to see some of the vines; they also claim to have the largest barrel-making plant in Europe. At the entrance to the town's public gardens, the **Musée de Cognac** (*open June–Sept daily exc Tues 10–12 and 2–6; Oct–May daily exc Tues 2–5.30; adm*) mixes displays on the art of cognac-making with art art – Flemish and Mannerist works, and local Impressionists.

place indeed for a two-star hotel.
The big bourgeois house has 24 bright
comfortable rooms reached through dull
institutional doors. You can enjoy dreamy
summer dining on the superb terrace at the
back, even if the food is only average
(*menus 120–170F*).
★★La Résidence 25 Av Victor Hugo, **t** 05 45 32
16 09, **f** 05 45 35 34 65 (*inexpensive*). Right in
the centre, this is a good cheaper option
with plenty of character.

Jarnac ✉ 16200

Restaurant du Château, 15 Place du Château,
t 05 45 81 07 17, **f** 05 45 35 35 71. An
extremely cheerful and appealing address
on Jarnac's main square, serving excellent
fresh seasonal dishes (*menus 155–236F*).
*Closed 1–15 Mar; Aug; Sun eve, Wed eve
and Mon.*

Bassac ✉ 16120

★★L'Essille, t 05 45 81 94 13, **f** 05 45 81 97 26
(*inexpensive*). A quietly charming simple
little hotel on the Charente.

Asnières-sur-Nouère ✉ 16290

★★★ Moulin du Maine Brun, some 12km
northwest of Angoulême, off the D939,
t 05 45 90 83 00, **f** 05 45 96 91 14
(*moderate*). A seductive riverside mill in old
stone, converted into a stylish country
hotel with well-furnished rooms and a
fine restaurant.

Angoulême ✉ 16000

★★Le Palais, 4 Place Francis Louvel, **t** 05 45 92
54 11, **f** 05 45 92 01 83 (*inexpensive*). An
appealing old-style address on an attractive
small square.
La Ruelle, 6 Rue des Trois Notre Dame, **t** 05 45
95 15 19. This restaurant's setting is almost
as impressive as the cuisine, the first
boldly historical, the second delicately
subtle (*menus 180–280F*). *Closed Sat lunch
and Sun.*

Verteuil-sur-Charente ✉ 18510

★La Paloma, Rue Fontaine, **t** 05 45 31 41 32
(*cheap*). A basic, cheap rustic inn with a
pretty terrace for dining.

Suaux ✉ 16260

Relais de L'Age, t 05 45 71 19 36. Lost in really
tranquil countryside some 15 km northeast
of La Rochefoucauld south off the N141, this
appealing, well-run B&B has simple, practical rooms in a converted speckled-stoned
farm building.

Nieuil ✉ 16270

★★★★Château de Nieuil, Route de Fontafie,
t 05 45 71 36 38, **f** 05 45 71 46 45,
nieuil@relaischateaux.fr (*expensive*). Historic
style, superb regional cuisine (*menus
200–350F*) and modern comforts in 11
splendid rooms, this enchanting little 16th-
century castle has it all. Restaurant. *Closed
Sun eves and Mon exc July and Aug.*

Cognac to Angoulême

The centre of **Jarnac** looks ugly at first sight, thanks to the brutish buildings which
have muscled in along its quays. The **Courvoisier brick château**, with its fussy
windows and Napoleon hat logo, dominates the main square. Several other famous
cognac houses are also based in Jarnac, including Louis Royer and the upmarket Hine.
On a **river cruise** you can see the façades of some of these cognac houses, as well as
the prettier side of town.

Along the quays, the bizarre **Donation Mitterrand** (*open July–Aug daily 10–12 and
2–7; April–June and Sept daily exc Tues 2–6; adm*) was the gift of François Mitterrand
who was born at Jarnac, the son of a station master, the grandson of a vinegar-maker.
Although Mitterrand remained sour about his home town, he did make sure it benefited from his fame, donating many extravagant presents given to him as president
of France.

The most delightful stretch of the Charente lies between Cognac and Angoulême. *'On vit au rythme du vieillissement du Cognac'* ('We live at the speed that Cognac ages') is what the locals like to say. Along the north bank you might take some time to discover a string of pretty villages. Penetrate the walls of **Bassac**'s quiet abbey to see the Gothic church with its tall Romanesque tower. However, be aware that monks still live here. Inside the church, the 18th-century embellishments turn out to be surprisingly excessive, even erotic, as in the exquisite carved torsos of the atlantes.

The village of **St-Simon** has recently been given a new lease of life by the revival of its boating past. Many villagers once worked as boatmen: one house has a river boat carved on it, and in the cemetery some of the tombs have anchors engraved on them. A diminutive **Maison des Gabariers** (*open June–Sept daily exc Tues 10–12 and 2–6; rest of year daily exc Tues 2–6; adm*) recalls the local craft of boat building.

At **Vibrac**, delightful bridges cross a confusing number of arms of water. To the south a big cross of Lorraine pays tribute to heroes of the Resistance, including a New Zealander and an RAF pilot, but focuses in particular on Claude Bonnier, alias Hypoténuse, a brilliant associate of De Gaulle who was flown into the area in 1943 to set up sabotage groups. Betrayed, he committed suicide in early 1944 rather than divulge any secrets to the Nazis.

On the south bank of the river, the church of St Pierre at **Châteauneuf-sur-Charente** has a lively façade of acrobats, men kicking monsters, and what looks like a cow flying up towards a Paschal lamb (which looks a bit like a cow itself). It also has a near-complete equestrian statue of Constantine, an evocative figure with robes flying, albeit minus head and arms.

For a detour into particularly delightful Charente countryside, head down from Châteauneuf-sur-Charente towards Plassac-Rouffiac. The pine-cone dome of **Plassac-Rouffiac**'s church gives this village a special character. Entwined naked men holding each other by the foot count among the more bizarre of the carvings inside. **Le Maine Giraud** (*open daily 9–12 and 2–6; English audioguide; adm*), a pretty 15th-century manor house, is still a working farm where cognac is produced. It was also the ivory tower of the much-loved 19th-century Romantic writer with liberal political ambitions, Alfred de Vigny, an Anglophile who married a well-connected Englishwoman and made Shakespeare popular in France with his adaptations.

Blanzac church boasts Gothic figures and wall paintings, but to see the wonderful 12th-century crusading frescoes hidden in the **Chapelle des Templiers de Cressac** nearby, you must telephone in advance (*t 05 45 64 08 74, after 6pm, to arrange a tour*). **Pérignac** church, though roughly restored, has some delightful Romanesque carvings, including little men sprouting from various parts. The hilltop **church of Puypéroux** looks plain and badly restored, standing at the end of dull abbey buildings, but this church contains one of the most disturbing little collections of Romanesque sculpture in France. The capitals around the crossing show beasts with two bodies or two heads, some of the heads clearly human. Rarely does Romanesque art show man and beast more clearly merged and, symbolically, the bestiality within mankind.

Angoulême

Historic Angoulême stands proud on its hill above the Charente, surrounded by ancient walls, but there is another Angoulême, a sprawling industrial town in the valley below. Balzac described the divide in his *Illusions perdues*, much of which takes place in Angoulême:

Up above the Nobility and Power, below, Commerce and Money.
Two social zones that can't stop viewing each other as enemies.
It's hard to know which of the two rival towns hates the other more.

Angoulême may lie a bit off the beaten track these days, but it is a bit more friendly than Balzac's narrator may suggest. The city has known more important times. In 1200 King John of England came here to marry Isabelle d'Angoulême. Much fought over in the Hundred Years' War, Angoulême became the possession of a junior branch of the Valois dynasty, until in 1515 François d'Angoulême was crowned king of France as François I. His sister, Marguerite d'Angoulême (better known perhaps as Marguerite de Navarre), was born here and went on to write the Boccaccio-like tales of the *Heptaméron*.

Angoulême's early 12th-century **cathedral**, with its tall Italianate north tower, its enormous cupola and its façade covered with a Last Judgement, looks extremely impressive at first sight, but close up you can see how it suffered from a heavy-handed restoration by Paul Abadie. The bishops' palace has been turned into the town's **Musée des Beaux-Arts** (*open Mon–Fri 12–6; Sat and Sun 2–6; adm*), featuring a 6th-century sarcophagus, Romanesque capitals, a splendid collection of African carvings, and an amazing elaborate Celtic helmet from the 4th century BC, made of gold and discovered in 1981 in a cave north of Angoulême.

One nice thing to do in town is to wander along the ramparts, where a plaque recalls the first motorless flight in France, in 1806. General Resnier, a native of the city, launched himself into the air on a machine he had invented – to help in a possible Napoleonic invasion of Britain. He survived the landing with just a broken leg. A steep public garden leads down to the Charente.

Against the hillside, the bold form of a funkily converted paper mill holds the **Musée de la Bande Dessinée** (*open May–Sept Tues–Fri 10–7, Sat and Sun 2–7; rest of year Tues–Fri 10–6, Sat and Sun 2–6; adm*). This comic book centre, one of the few Grands Projets built outside Paris under Mitterrand, itself looks unreal, with the sides of its vertiginous glass curve joined together by a perilously perched red bridge. If you are interested in French cartoons, you will love the place. Opposite and by the Charente you can also visit a more prosaic paper-making museum, the **Atelier-Musée du Papier** (*open Tues–Sun 2–6; adm*), where cigarette paper was made until 1970.

More interesting, though, is the **Musée du Papier d'Angoumois** (*open April–Oct Mon and Wed–Fri 10–12 and 2–7, Sat and Sun 11–12 and 3–7; rest of year Mon and Wed–Fri 2–6, Sat and Sun 3–6; adm*) in the restored Moulin de Fleurac west of Angoulême, where specialist paper is still made by hand.

Beyond Angoulême

East beyond Angoulême the Charente forms a last big loop, where the famous **Château de La Rochefoucauld** (*open Easter–Nov daily 10–7; rest of year Sun and public hols 2–7; adm*) dominates its little town. Over the centuries the de La Rochefoucauld family, who still live here, produced powerful and talented men. One, godfather to François I, introduced the French king to Leonardo da Vinci – which is how Leonardo came to draw the Château de la Rochefoucauld. However, the most celebrated De la Rochefoucauld was the 17th-century razor-sharp wit François, who led a colourful political and love life and exposed the shallow values of 17th-century courtiers, most tellingly in his viciously revealing *Maximes*.

From the splendid courtyard, wander along the ground-floor gallery where the saucy sculptures might make you chuckle. Otherwise the decoration of the galleries is decorously Renaissance. The chapel was heavily restored in the early 20th century. You can go down into the kitchens, and even further down into the grottoes under the castle. The main staircase was built to a splendid grand design around a twisting cord of stone. Disaster struck the château in 1960 when the medieval keep collapsed. Much money has gone into its restoration, and an exciting project is in the pipeline for its transformation into a virtual library by I.M. Pei.

Following the loop in the Charente northeast of Angoulême, **Verteuil-sur-Charente** straddles the river, dominated by the château where La Rochefoucauld wrote many of his maxims. The church conceals a life-size Entombment scene attributed to the masterly 16th-century sculptor Germain Pilon. Unassuming **Civray** boasts one of the most startling of all Poitevin Romanesque churches, **St-Nicolas**, its façade enlivened by richly carved arcades. The top level proves the most engrossing: above the entrance with its enthroned Jesus, wise and foolish virgins, and symbols of the Zodiac, the saints Peter and Paul calmly hold up their scrolls. But around them Virtues and Vices fight it out. Look out in particular for the elongated knights with shields crammed into the arch. Little remains of the equestrian statue of Constantine except mutilated parts of the horse's body. Inside, late-medieval frescoes illustrate the 8th-century hermit St Gilles absolving a king of his sins.

Christ's prepuce, or a piece of his foreskin, coyly termed the 'Sainte Vertu', helped give the **abbey of St-Sauveur** at Charroux its preeminence. Charlemagne donated it, and it was given to Charles VII at his sacred crowning at Reims as good juju against the English, after which it vanishes from sight. Following the Revolution, much of the abbey's stone was cannibalized, but the skeleton of an octagonal tower, the Tour Charlemagne, gives an indication of its scale. Ruined statues are displayed in the chapterhouse and the treasury has a few medieval bits, while a model in the tourist office shows the abbey at its apogee in the 11th century.

The Southwest

13

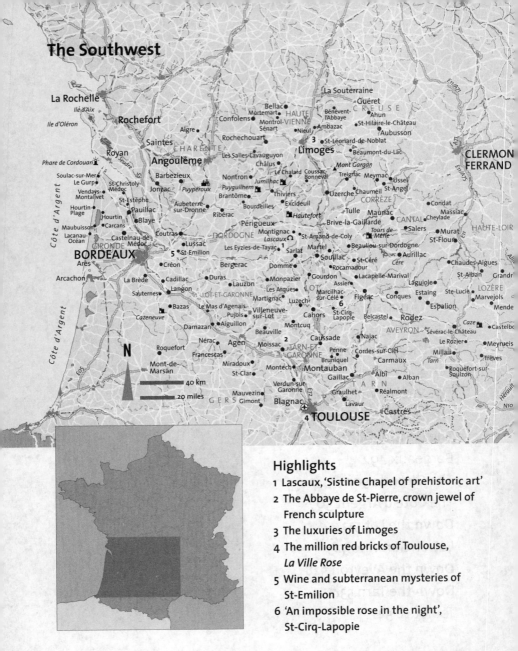

The Southwest

Highlights
1 Lascaux, 'Sistine Chapel of prehistoric art'
2 The Abbaye de St-Pierre, crown jewel of French sculpture
3 The luxuries of Limoges
4 The million red bricks of Toulouse, *La Ville Rose*
5 Wine and subterranean mysteries of St-Emilion
6 'An impossible rose in the night', St-Cirq-Lapopie

This part of France, with Bordeaux at one end and Toulouse at the other, is defined by rivers of exceptional beauty: the Dordogne, Lot, Aveyron and Tarn, all of which meander down through dramatic gorges into sunny valleys of vines and orchards to join the big one – the Garonne – and the Atlantic. Although battered by the Albigensian Crusade, the Hundred Years' War, and the Wars of Religion, much of the southwest has since kept clear of history (and what passes for progress) leaving it a remarkably intact architectural legacy of medieval châteaux, villages, 13th-century new towns (*bastides*) and Romanesque and Gothic churches, including some of the greatest ones, in Conques, Moissac, Albi and Toulouse. The southwest has other superlatives as well: the world's greatest concentration of Palaeolithic art, beginning with Lascaux; the spectacular wines of Bordeaux; the biggest sand dune in Europe by Arcachon; the immense subterranean fantasies of the Gouffre de Padirac and the

Food and Wine

Although it may not seem like it at first glance, the southwest diet, with an emphasis on duck and goose fat, garlic and red wine, is good for you; the native rate of heart disease is half that of the United States. Besides foie gras (studded with a black truffle) and various pâtés, look for succulent *maigrets* (fillet of duck breast) and *confits* (duck preserved in its own fat) or even duck sausage. In autumn mushrooms and truffles are prized ingredients in local omelettes and sauces. Around Bordeaux, look for beef steaks with shallots cooked over vine cuttings, oysters and other seafood, with stewed lamprey (*lamproie*) the region's favourite.

The sunny southwest produces more fine wines than any other region. Bordeaux, of course, holds pride of place, covering four regions, which together produce 500 million litres a year: the Libournais along the north of the Dordogne (St-Émilion, Pomerol, Fronsac); the Entre-Deux-Mers, between the Dordogne and Garonne; the Graves, south of the Garonne (Sauternes, Barsac, etc.); and the Médoc, along the south bank of the Gironde estuary north of Bordeaux (Margaux, Pauillac). The English acquired a taste for Bordeaux and claret in the time of Eleanor of Aquitaine, and after 1853, with the construction of the railway to Paris, the market began to expand in France as well. Bankers and investors, both French and foreign, bought up estates. New technologies revolutionized Bordeaux in the 1960s and '70s – the use of sprays against rot, adjustments in the temperature of fermentation to an even coolness, and mechanical harvesters that gather all the grapes in at their peak. And once again international investors have moved in to buy up the vineyards. An ideal introduction to all Bordeaux wines is offered at La Maison de la Qualité, halfway between Bordeaux and Libourne on the N89, near Beychac-et-Caillau (*t 05 56 72 90 99, open Mon–Fri 8.30–12.30 and 1.30–5, also Sat in the summer*); there's a film, free tastings of select wines, commentaries and advice on visiting the châteaux. You can study the subject before leaving home at *www.vins-Bordeaux.fr*. The Haut Pays is the general term for all of the wine-producing region up river. Bordeaux's location at the mouth of the Garonne allowed it to give priority to its own wines at the expense of other growers for centuries, but many of these smaller AOC areas are riding high again, and offer excellent buys. Sweet Monbazillac and red Pécharmant of Bergerac, and the powerful reds – Cahors, Côtes de Duras, Buzet, Côtes de Frontonnais, and Gaillac are the best known, but only the tip of the iceberg. Estates here tend to be family concerns rather than bankers' investments, and nearly all welcome visitors who just pop in for a taste or a tub of loose wine.

Getting Around

By plane: The Limousin has three airports for internal flights to Paris and eastern France, including Strasbourg, Dijon, Clermont-Ferrand, Lyon, Toulon, Marseille and Nice: Limoges-Bellegarde, t 05 55 43 30 30; Brive-Laroche, t 05 55 86 88 36; Lépaud-Montluçon, t 05 55 65 73 30.

By train: Limoges and Brive-la-Gaillarde are on the Paris–Toulouse line. The fastest trains from Paris-Austerlitz to Limoges take just 3 hours.

By road: Limoges is around 400km from Paris. By motorway, take the A10 to Orléans, the A71 to Vierzon, and the A20 towards Toulouse (toll-free) which passes by La Souterraine, Limoges, Uzerche and Brive-la-Gaillarde.

Aven Armand; the breathtaking Gorges du Tarn, and pink Toulouse, the effervescent fourth city of France.

The Limousin might be considered a missing link in southwest France, a quieter version of Périgord, only in granite rather than honey-coloured stone; the Parc Naturel Régional Périgord-Limousin has recently been created on their frontier. Beyond the capital of Limoges, however, most of the Limousin feels lost in the past.

The Limousin

Even the French have trouble telling you much about what lies in the three shy, retiring and rural *départements* of the Limousin. Limoges, famous for pottery, springs first to mind, while many can name Oradour-sur-Glane, a town martyred by the Nazis. Aubusson may ring a bell for its tapestries, while the Corrèze has a cluster of gorgeous villages south of its main town, the cheerfully named Brive-la-Gaillarde.

So how did a type of car come to be named after such a seriously unindustrial region? Some claim that the limousine was named after the wide cloak of the Limousin shepherds, as the early limousines had wide covers that extended over the driver's seat. More sober books say that cartwrights from the Limousin helped produce the first automobiles; hence the name.

Into the Eastern Limousin or the Creuse

The Creuse river cuts diagonally through the eastern Limousin and the *département* named after it, passing Guéret, a town which could put in a strong claim to being the least-known *départemental* capital in France, and the historic tapestry towns of Aubusson and Felletin.

A Detour into the Northeastern Creuse

If you're desperately seeking out-of-the-way corners in France, try the northeastern Creuse. Aim for pretty **Boussac**, which shares the same gorgeous brown roofs with its freckled Gothic château. One lord, Jean I de Brosse, fought alongside Joan of Arc. Tapestries are the theme of the visit inside: the château long held France's most beautiful cycle of tapestries, those of the Lady with the Unicorn, now in the Musée de Cluny in Paris.

Getting Around

The little Lépaud-Montluçon airport, t 04 55 65 73 30, lies just east of this area. The main train station is Guéret, on the Bordeaux–Lyon line. Public transport to towns such as Boussac, Aubusson and Felletin is much more limited. For details on bus services from Guéret, t 05 55 52 46 44.

Tourist Information

Boussac: Place de l'Hôtel de Ville, t 05 55 65 05 95.

Guéret: 1 Av Charles de Gaulle, t 05 55 52 14 29.

Aubusson: 67 Rue Vieille, t 05 55 66 32 12.

Felletin: 2 Petite Rue du Clocher, t 05 55 66 54 60.

Where to Stay and Eat

Boussac ✉ 23600

Le Relais Creusois, t 05 55 65 02 20. One of the main gastronomic stops in the Creuse, which also has pretty views on to the Petite Creuse valley.

Guéret ✉ 23000

**Hôtel Auclair, 19 Av de la Sénatorerie, t 05 55 41 22 00, f 05 55 52 86 89 (*inexpensive*). A clean, basic hotel.

St-Hilaire-le-Château ✉ 23250

Château de la Chassagne, t 05 55 64 50 12/ t 05 55 64 55 75, f 05 55 64 90 92 (*moderate*). Superlative luxury, spacious B&B rooms in this adorable little château just south of St-Hilaire, with pastures in front and woods behind.

**Hôtel du Thaurion, t 05 55 64 50 12, f 05 55 64 90 92 (*inexpensive*). A renovated roadside inn run with the same cheerful enthusiasm by the same family as the château above. The rooms are comfortable and the regional cuisine, reputed to be the best in the Creuse, is served in a plush dining room (*menus 99–320F*).

Aubusson ✉ 23200

**Hôtel de France, 6 Rue des Déportés, t 05 55 66 10 22, f 05 55 66 88 64 (*inexpensive*). A pleasant central hotel which is the best option in Aubusson.

South of Boussac, bizarre twisted granite boulders, the **Pierres Jaunâtres**, have great views over the Auvergne, but nearby **Toulx-Ste-Croix** has even better: on clear days, the views over the Puys de Dôme are staggering. The main street splits its Romanesque church in two, where a couple of worn lions guard the entrance to the nave and a curious round porch tower is roofed with the chestnut tiles typical of the region. A lighthouse of a tower on the north end of Toulx-Ste-Croix has the best views of all.

Generally the Limousin's pleasures are more secretive. Two soporifically charming places lie tucked away in Les Combrailles, an undulating plateau spanning the Limousin and Auvergne. When Vikings were threatening, monks from Limoges carried the relics of St Valérie to well-hidden **Chambon-sur-Voueize**. But the massive Romanesque church **Ste-Valérie** can scarcely be called discreet, and boasts a remarkable array of apse chapels that cluster round the choir like pups feeding greedily off their mother. **Evaux-les-Bains**, Chambon's rival, is proud of its decorative and naturally colourful church of St Peter and St Paul.

The Creuse Valley South from Guéret

Backed by wooded hills, **Guéret** was the capital of the miniature province of La Marche, before it became capital of the Creuse. Steeped in provincial atmosphere,

Guéret also has a pair of creditable museums: one on local history and traditions, and the larger devoted to fine arts, with brutish, naked Roman gods carved in granite, medieval enamel works, a trio of startling medieval reliquary arms, and Impressionist views of the Creuse by Armand Guillaumin.

Back down the Creuse, **Moutier-Ahun** lies prettily by the river, its landmark a stub of a church, entered by way of a Flamboyant Gothic gateway teeming with tonsured monks. Inside (*adm*) are virtuoso Baroque late 17th-century wooden stalls by Simon Bauer, where sphinxes, dogs and grotesques with Carmen Miranda headgear keep company with saints. Linden trees trace the nave, destroyed in the Wars of Religion.

At **Masgot** south of Ahun, houses are decorated with late 19th-century **naive carvings** by François Michaud, one of many stone carvers who found work in the restoration of medieval buildings. A **Neolithic trail** leads through the delightful **Gorges du Péry** from Masgot to St-Hilaire-le-Château: signs indicate the way to the dolmens and a Roman bridge.

Aubusson, with its granite houses, would look Breton were it not for its brown roof tiles. The remains of a medieval castle stand on the rocks above town, and the attractive main street has several shops selling tapestries. The **Musée Départemental de la Tapisserie** (*open July–Aug daily 10–6, Tues 2–6; rest of year daily exc Tues 9.30–12 and 2–6; adm*) explains the techniques and has changing exhibitions of tapestries from down the centuries. To see old looms in a historic atmosphere, go to the **Maison du Vieux Tapissier** in the old town.

Felletin, down the Creuse, is more attractive than its competitor. Of its two old churches, the Eglise du Moutier contains charming old frescoes and naive statues and retables, while the other one, the Eglise du Château, is often used for temporary tapestry exhibitions. Tapestry-making continues here at the Manufacture Pinson; ask at the tourist office about visits.

The Tapestry Tradition: Aubusson and Felletin

It may have been Flemish weavers who first established tapestry weaving in Aubusson and Felletin in the 14th century, creating Gothic scenes of warriors and verdant landscapes, then moving on to complex historical and mythological subjects. In 1665 Aubusson was declared a *Manufacture royale*, a privilege Felletin received in 1689, a time when cartoons were by court artists such as Charles Le Brun. But with the Revocation of the Edict of Nantes, many of the Aubusson Protestant manufacturers went into exile. Fortunes revived under Louis XV, and although the Gobelins and Beauvais by then produced more refined tapestries, the fashion spread to these parts for pastoral scenes *à la* Watteau. The lack of demand for luxury goods after the Revolution spelled a sharp decline for tapestry-making, but the need for copies and replacements for older works preserved the art. Aubusson owes much of its 20th-century revival to Jean Lurçat, who introduced more striking colours and bolder textures, and encouraged artists such as Picasso and Rouault to draw cartoons. One of the most famous postwar commissions was the massive Apocalypse cycle for the cathedral of Coventry, executed in Felletin from cartoons by Graham Sutherland.

Dead quiet and dead pretty, the village of **Crocq**, east of Felletin, is dominated by the twin towers of a ruined castle. The sweet granite **Chapelle de la Visitation** has a stepped gable front and contains a delightful 16th-century altarpiece on the life of the Limousin saint Eloi, from his mother in bed seemingly with a migraine after giving birth to him, via the story in which he managed to make two thrones for the price of one for King Clotaire II, to his funeral. A dramatic grisaille Last Supper has figures in rich costumes with severe Flemish faces in an elaborate architectural setting, although the artist's control of perspective was clearly shaky.

The Central Limousin

Eight villages in the centre of the Limousin vanished with the creation of beautiful Lac de Vassivière, its waters now a popular resort and surprising art centre. The red-tinged Limousin race of cows hail from the surrounding hills, while the Monts d'Ambazac northeast of Limoges form a tough granite barrier between the northern Marches and the rest of the region.

Woods surround the many arms of the **Lac de Vassivière**. Lost in the heart of one of the quietest regions in France, it comes surprisingly to life in summer, teeming with bathers, boaters and windsurfers. One island, reached via the south side, is the site of the **Centre d'Art Contemporain** (*open June–15 Oct daily 11–1 and 2–7; rest of year exc Jan daily 11–1 and 2–6; adm*), a 1.5km walk from the car park, but well worth the hike. Conceptual pieces dot the island's woods, many of which are integrated into the natural setting. Exhibitions are held in the clean granite and brick building designed by Aldo Rossi, matched by a large chimney of a tower with an impressive snailing staircase inside.

St-Léonard-de-Noblat surrounds a quirky pilgrimage church. Born into an aristo-cratic Frankish family in the 6th century, Léonard became a hermit and one day saved the life of a queen who came into labour while hunting with her husband. To thank Léonard, the king offered him a *noble lieu* – as much land as his donkey could walk round in 24 hours – on which Léonard founded a religious community to reform former captives and criminals through Christian labour. An eccentric tower rises from his church, and there are some entertaining stone sculptures down below; an extraordinary crowd of Gothic and Romanesque columns cluster in the choir. The statue on the next square is of Gay-Lussac, the great physicist and chemist born here, and a little museum is devoted to his discoveries. The town is also proud of its marzipan, the secret recipe held by Massepains Petitjean.

The **Monts d'Ambazac** reach as high as 2,296ft and the climate can be harsh. Etienne Muret, a hermit from Auvergne, settled here in 1076 and led an exemplary life of spirituality and poverty. His followers, the order of Bons Hommes, founded Grandmont and acquired massive riches. The order was closed down before the Revolution and its treasures dispersed, although one fabulous reliquary chest (1190) remains in the **church of Ambazac**. This is one of the most ostentatious pieces of Limoges enamel work ever made, a true little treasure house topped by a curious

Getting Around

St-Léonard-de-Noblat has a railway station, but this area isn't well-served by public transport.

Tourist Information

Ile de Vassivière: Beaumont-du-Lac, **t** 05 55 69 76 70, **f** 05 55 69 23 98.
St-Léonard-de-Noblat: Place du Champ de Mars, **t** 05 55 56 25 06.
Ambazac: Av de la Libération, **t** 05 55 56 85 76.

Where to Stay and Eat

Pallier ✉ 23340

Commanderie de Pallier, Gentioux, **t/f** 05 55 67 91 73 (*inexpensive*). The past centuries seem to have been cleaned up, pickled and beautifully preserved at this superbly characterful B&B, which is excellent value for such high standards.

Lac de Vassivière and Peyrat-le-Château ✉ 87470

★★★La Caravelle, **t** 05 55 69 40 97, **f** 05 55 69 49 51 (*moderate*). A comfortable modern hotel, right by the water, the beach and a major campsite on the western side of the lake, a lively corner in summer. Rooms have lake views.
★★Le Bellerive, 29 Av de la Tour, **t** 05 55 69 40 96, **f** 05 55 69 47 96 (*inexpensive*).

Attractive option near the lake, with charming rooms.
★★Auberge du Bois de l'Etang, 38 Av de la Tour, **t** 05 55 69 40 19, **f** 05 55 69 42 93 (*inexpensive*). Another good option, with innovative cuisine (*menus 75–195F*).

St-Léonard-de-Noblat ✉ 87400

★★Le Grand St-Léonard, 23 Av du Champ de Mars, **t** 05 55 56 18 18, **f** 05 55 56 98 32 (*inexpensive*). Wide-fronted, updated posting inn, which seems an appropriate enough place to stay in this venerable old town. The food is worth stopping for too (*menus 130–320F*).
Le Gay-Lussac, 18 Bd Victor Hugo, **t** 05 55 56 98 45. Another popular eating place in town, serving less refined country cooking (*menus 105–140F*).

In the Monts d'Ambazac

A few really interesting B&Bs with excellent hosts add to the gentle attractions of the Monts d'Ambazac.
Château de Chambon, Bersac-sur-Rivalier, 87370, **t** 05 55 71 47 04/**t** 05 55 71 42 90, **f** 05 55 71 51 41 (*inexpensive*). A little taste of rustic château life, with very spacious rooms. Amazing value.
Les Chênes, Les Sauvages, 87240 St-Sylvestre, **t/f** 05 55 71 33 12 (*inexpensive*). Experience an environmentally friendly night with the Rappellis, who have built their green-conscious retreat in a peaceful corner of the local hills. M. Rappelli's paintings hang on the walls.

statue of a bird, its beady eye focused on the bright cabochons sticking out of the enamel work. A bit further north, the church of St-Sylvestre contains a late-Gothic silver reliquary bust of Etienne Muret. In the neighbouring hamlet of Grandmont, a few sad vestiges of the mighty monastery have been incorporated into the houses.

Limoges

Limoges is a lively university city synonymous with luxury; even one of its 6th-century saints, Eloi, was a goldsmith. Later, the city was renowned for its exquisite *émaillerie champlevée*, first made in the abbey of St-Martial around 1185 and exported across Western Europe. Porcelain took off after the discovery of all-important kaolin in the 1760s at St-Yrieix; Auguste Renoir, born in Limoges, started off as a porcelain painter. To produce such luxuries meant exploiting local labour, which responded by founding France's powerful trade union, the Confédération Générale du Travail, or CGT. So for all its delicate designer goods, Limoges remains a militant and progressive force in a sleepy rural region.

High above the Vienne river, the **Musée Municipal de l'Evêché** (*open July–Sept daily 10–11.45 and 2–6; rest of year daily exc Tues 10–11.45 and 2–5*) has taken over the 18th-century bishops' palace. It throws up some surprises: fragments of Gallo-Roman frescoes depicting birds and wild cats, a figure of a decapitated Gaulish god holding a torque, and two plates with childlike graffiti that turn out to be rare examples of Celtic writing. There are fine Romanesque capitals and tombs, and two heads with groomed moustaches and curled hair. Sadly, the best early-medieval enamels were stolen in the 1980s, but there are still a few good pieces and a large collection of painted enamels inspired by German and Italian engravings. The paintings aren't up to much, beyond Renoir's *Portrait de Jean*. A separate building by the gardens is devoted to the Resistance; although Limoges of course honours its Resistance fighters, it is embarrassed that it celebrated Pétain's visit in 1941 so enthusiastically.

Getting Around

Limoges-Bellegarde airport lies 10km west of the city. The railway station, the Gare des Bénédictins, is a splendid, ornate neo-Byzantine and Art Deco building, covered in proud symbols of the Limousin. The main bus station on Rue Charles Gide is slightly closer to the centre, a short walk from Place Jourdan; some services leave from Place des Charentes at the opposite end of town.

Tourist Information

4 Place Denis Dussoubs, t 05 55 79 04 44; or 27 Bd de la Corderie, t 05 55 45 18 80.

Where to Stay and Eat

Limoges ✉ 87000

Moderate

Castel Marie, 43 Route de Nexon, t 05 55 31 11 34, f 05 55 31 30 17. Relatively exclusive and not too far from the centre; just six lovely rooms in this wealthy family mansion from the start of the 20th century, set in a large garden with a splendid glass house. Restaurant (*menus 150–400F*).

***Le Richelieu, 40 Av Baudin, t 05 55 34 22 82, f 05 55 32 48 73. Opposite the town hall just outside the main ring of boulevards, with good rooms and service.

Royal Limousin, Place de la République, t 05 55 34 65 30, f 05 55 34 55 21. A comfortable central modern hotel.

Inexpensive

**Orléans Lion d'Or, 9–11 Cours Jourdan, t 05 55 77 49 71, f 05 55 77 33 41. An OK choice near the railway station.

Cheap

*Beaux-Arts, 28 Bd Victor Hugo, t 05 55 79 42 20, f 05 55 79 29 13. Central, if noisy, and most of the rooms are basic.

L'Amphitryon, 26 Rue de la Boucherie, t 05 55 33 36 39, f 05 5532 98 50. An attractive timberframe front in the old butchers' quarter, with fine porcelain on the tables and refined cuisine, the best-known restaurant in Limoges.

There are a few interesting restaurants around the main covered market:

Philippe Redon, 3 Rue d'Aguesseau, t 05 55 34 66 22. Interesting dishes combining Limousin meats with seafood (*menus 160–290F*).

Chez Alphonse, 5 Place de la Motte, t 05 55 34 34 14. For a lively, good-value lunch or à la carte dinner with pork specialities.

Le Paris, 7 Place Denis Dussoubs, t 05 55 77 48 31. A buzzing *bistrot*, specializing in beer, mussels and chips.

You can enter the **cathedral** via an enormous telescoping porch tower that resembles an industrial chimney, or through the fine Flamboyant portal of St-Jean on the north side. The interior is splendid and simple, influenced by the Gothic of the north. An elaborate Renaissance roodscreen has been moved to the back of the church. In the choir, monumental tombs stand out, as does the 19th-century imitation medieval stained glass. The **Haute Cité** quarter surrounding the cathedral has grand houses but not a lot of life.

The nearby **Boulevard Louis Blanc**, by contrast, is far too busy – a major artery for cars, and porcelain and enamel shops. Head into the historic butchers' quarter, **La Boucherie**, where one shop on the Rue de la Boucherie has been turned into an Ecomusée showing how the butchers' families lived, basically surrounded by slaughtered beasts. Nowadays people come to shop and eat in the restaurants. The Gothic **Chapelle St-Aurélien** was saved from Revolutionary vandals by the butchers' fraternity which still owns it. It has an amusing belltower and a collection of statues, furniture, and the relics of the second bishop of Limoges.

Most visitors ignore all this and head straight for the porcelain. You're unlikely to find more beautiful vases, pots and plates in one place than at the **Musée National de la Céramique Adrien-Dubouché** (*open July–Aug daily exc Tues 10–5.45; rest of year daily exc Tues 10–12.30 and 2–5.45; adm*). The building alone, a mishmash of Italianate, neo-Gothic and arts and craft, is an arresting sight. A video explains the stages in making porcelain, using a mixture that includes kaolin, the secret of its translucent finesse discovered in China in the 8th or 9th century, but only worked out by Europeans in the 18th. Meissen in Saxony was the first to produce European porcelain in 1710; Limoges followed in the 1770s. The first European manufacturers obsessively made fake Chinese pieces, with silly, coarsely copied scenes of Chinese decoration. And funnier still are the pieces made in China during the Ancien Régime showing Europeans with long noses. Limoges is best known for its refined, elegantly bordered dinner services, but here too are some funkier modern creations.

You can see the different stages of production and decoration in making Limoges porcelain at the **Bernardaud**. A more unusual but engrossing visit is to the very old-fashioned **Four des Casseaux** in the labyrinthine GDA factory; contact the Limoges tourist office for details.

Western Limousin

West of Limoges, a slice of charming country has been incorporated into the Parc Naturel Régional Périgord-Limousin, where the Richard Cœur de Lion tourist trail is dedicated to that overromanticized Anglo-French king. On a different plane altogether, the atrocities committed by the Nazis are kept painfully alive at Oradour-sur-Glane.

Getting Around

Limoges is the hub of the train service through this area, which stops at many of the little towns along the way, although there are only a few each day.

Tourist Information

Oradour-sur-Glane: Place du Champ de Foire, t 05 55 03 13 73.
Mortemart: Château des Ducs, t 05 55 68 98 98, or t 05 55 68 12 09.
Rochechouart: 6 Rue Victor Hugo, t 05 55 03 72 73.
Châlus: 22 bis Av de Flaury, t 05 55 78 51 13.

Where to Stay and Eat

Nieul ✉ 87510
****La Chapelle St-Martin**, St-Martin-Fault, c. 10km northwest of Limoges towards Oradour-sur-Glane, t 05 55 75 80 17, f 05 55 75 89 50, chapelle@relaischateaux.fr (*expensive*). A really luxurious, exclusive little hotel in a 19th-century bourgeois house which has been converted to offer spacious rooms and has an excellent restaurant (*menus from 180F*).

In the Monts de Blond
Les Hauts de Boscartus, 87520 Cieux, t 05 55 03 30 63 (*inexpensive*). A peaceful B&B in a slope-side hamlet in a typical corner of these hills – the home of a delightfully welcoming couple.

Mortemart ✉ 87330
*****Le Relais**, t 05 55 68 12 09, f 05 55 68 12 09 (*cheap*). By the quaint covered market, this is a delightful stop both for a good meal and a simple room.

Champagnac-la-Rivière ✉ 87150
Château de Brie, closer to Châlus than Rochechouart, t 05 55 78 17 52, f 05 55 78 14 02 (*moderate*). With so many châteaux tantalizingly set along the local tourist route it seems only fair that one should offer B&B rooms for the night. A stay doesn't come cheap, but the rooms in this stocky little 15th-century castle are memorably decorated in various styles.

La Roche-l'Abeille ✉ 87800
******Au Moulin de la Gorce**, t 05 55 00 70 66, f 05 55 00 76 57, moulingorce@relais chateaux.fr (*expensive–moderate*). An oasis of luxury off the beaten track (off the D704 some 12km north of St-Yrieix), this has grown charmingly from its origins as a 16th-century watermill into a waterside inn with extremely refined rooms and restaurant (*menus 250–400F*).

Coussac-Bonneval ✉ 87500
****Les Voyageurs**, t 05 55 75 20 24, f 05 55 75 28 90 (*inexpensive*). Some decent rooms in a modern building and a restaurant in a charming old inn serving traditional country fare (*menus 70–250F*).
Moulin de Marsaguet, t 05 55 75 28 29 (*inexpensive*). Lakeside setting and picturesquely rustic millhouse make this a charming simple B&B.

Oradour-sur-Glane and the Monts de Blond

Oradour-sur-Glane is perhaps *the* most painful symbol to the French of the German atrocities of the Second World War. The Das Reich division descended on the old village on 10 June 1944, just a few days after D-Day. They rounded up everyone they could find, divided the men into groups and shot them in buildings around the village, before pillaging them and setting them alight. Just five men hiding in a barn managed to get away. As to the women and children, they were herded into the church, where they thought they would be safe. Instead the Nazis gassed them, threw grenades into the church, then set it alight . Only one woman escaped the hellish turmoil, managing to smash her way out through a stained-glass window.

In all, there were 642 victims that day at Oradour-sur-Glane, 205 of whom were children. Most had been mutilated beyond recognition and were laid unidentified in mass graves.

Why Oradour? Not special in any way, nor a centre of the Resistance, it was a random scapegoat which happened to lie on the division's route; the Nazis were looking to make examples to scare the French away from participating in the Resistance and in sabotage.

The burnt-out ruins of the 328 buildings of Oradour are heartrending to visit. Old sewing machines and coffee grinders lie among the rubble. There are still pots in the fireplaces. There's a bike here, a car there. The metal rings are all that remain of the barrels in the wine shop. The memorial in the **cemetery** has family photos of the victims, which in some minuscule but vital way brings them back to life. A terrible bunker contains their mangled possessions.

In 1999 a new **memorial museum** was opened to offer a wider historical context. Emphasis is put on the way the SS were trained in savagery and terror, but special mention is also made of Germans who resisted the Nazis back home. French collaboration isn't ignored, with details on the creation of the feared Milice in 1943. The film's slightly clinical virtual reconstruction of events seems an inappropriate use of new technology. The trial after the war and the building of the new Oradour are also covered.

Bad feelings remain towards the people of Alsace who fought with the Nazis; 14 members of the Das Reich division came from there. To the horror of the people of Oradour, they were amnestied after their trial in 1953; Oradour responded by cutting its links with the French state. In 1983 one of the Germans responsible for the massacre, Lieutenant Barth, was tracked down. He confirmed that the place was not destroyed by mistake, but on orders, but showed no regret. Sentenced to life imprisonment, he was released in the late 1990s on grounds of ill health. General Lammerding, who was in charge of the division (although he didn't play a direct role at Oradour-sur-Glane), escaped justice altogether, became a businessman and died of natural causes in 1971. On a more positive note, in 1999 some Alsatians, including the mayor of Strasbourg, were invited to attend the inaugural ceremony for the new museum.

The tranquil **Monts de Blond** to the north offer some relief after Oradour-sur-Glane. This thin strip of granite heights once separated the *langue d'oïl*-speakers of northern France from the *langue d'oc* speakers of the south. But the look here is more Breton or Scottish, or even Arthurian. A local map pinpoints the dolmens; other 'Arthurian' features, the black lakes and thick forests, date from recent times as agriculture has waned.

Two delightful villages wait on the northern side of the Monts de Blond. **Montrol-Sénart** has huge views and rustic art – a crucifixion by the Romanesque church, and the stoup and the statuary within. **Mortemart** has remnants of two monasteries and a château; don't miss the carved choir stalls in the big airy church. As well as the monkeying around under the seats, there is a hilarious end piece showing a lord and a monk, one of them mooning.

Parc Naturel Régional Périgord-Limousin

Although hit by a massive meteorite 200 million years ago, **Rochechouart** doesn't look different from its neighbours, except perhaps that things are a bit twisted – the slate spire of its church and the remarkable columns in its speckled late-Gothic château. This now serves as the Haute-Vienne's **Musée d'Art Contemporain** (*open summer daily exc Tues 10–12.30 and 1.30–6; spring and autumn daily exc Mon and Tues 2–6; adm*), strong on modern British and Italian artists. The **Espace Météorite** (*open summer daily 9.30–12.30 and 2–6, weekends pm only; spring and autumn daily 2–6; adm*) tells the story of the rock from space that hit with a force 14 million times stronger than the Hiroshima bomb.

The gruesome martyrdoms at **Les Salles-Lavauguyon** were only found under the whitewash in 1986. These extraordinarily rich Romanesque frescoes are painted against sumptuous bands of colour, the costly blue particularly surprising. A proud dogged saint is shown being stoned and then laid out dead on a bed – not the usual St Stephen but the story of St Eutrope, who survived his stoning, so his persecutors took an axe to finish him off. In the first bay to the left you can make out Ste Valérie being decapitated, but then carrying her head to the first bishop of Limoges, St Martial. Other gorey martyrdoms include that of St Laurent being grilled and the giant St Christopher resisting the archers' arrows only to be executed by axe as well.

The château with its big tubular keep is being restored by a Limousin industrialist, but at the time of writing, the tour is a mixed bag of the tatty interiors; some sections are devoted to modern art, others to the *feuillardiers*, who made their livings from the chestnut woods.

The cemetery by the time-battered church in **Le Chalard** contains a rare collection of carved and curiously uplifting Romanesque tombs. **St-Yrieix-la-Perche** is worth a halt just to see the 15th-century reliquary bust of St Yrieix in the Gothic church. The beaten silver head is rendered down to the beard stubble, added as gold points.

The **Château de Coussac**, aloof on the edge of the village of Coussac, has been the home of the Bonneval family for over ten centuries. The square multi-towered castle derives mainly from the 14th century; the tour takes in family portraits and objects, and splendid tapestries from Aubusson. One Bonneval died heroically defending

The Entrails of Richard Cœur de Lion

Duke of Aquitaine in 1169, Richard Cœur de Lion was crowned king of England in 1189. Ten years later he was mortally wounded while besieging the **Château de Châlus**, intent on punishing the treacherous Aimar V, Viscount of Limoges. One day as Richard was overseeing the siege, Pierre Basile, a dexterous soldier defending the castle, stood at the top of the keep using a pan to deflect the arrows of the enemy. Richard, impressed, got up and applauded. The sharp-eyed Basile spotted him, drew his crossbow and shot him, and Richard died 10 days later in Chinon on the Loire. It serves as a reminder of how extensive the Plantagenet possessions were that Richard's entrails ended up in the Limousin, his body in the abbey of Fontevraud by the Loire, and his heart in Rouen. As for Pierre Basile, he was flayed alive.

François I at the Italian battle of Marignan. The most eccentric was Claude-Alexandre, born in 1675: exiled from France, he converted to Islam, reorganized the Turkish army and was honoured with the title of a three-tailed pasha. The present Brazilian marquise has added an exotic touch.

The meanders of the Auvézère river shaded by sycamores create the enchanting setting for **Ségur-le-Château**, where the ruined schist castle was besieged by Richard the Lionheart in 1177. **Arnac-Pompadour** is home to a national stud farm, created for Louis XV, who bought the castle (*brief tour of the exteriors possible*) for his mistress Jeanne Poisson (Joan Fish), who understandably preferred to be known as the Marquise de Pompadour.

Southern Limousin and Upper Vézère, Corrèze and Dordogne Valleys

Dark stone and slate dominate the little-explored upper valleys of the Vézère and the Corrèze. Five dams have effectively tamed the mighty Dordogne into a series of well-regulated lakes. Further downstream, a swathe of the southern Limousin and northern Périgord and Quercy once formed the territory of the Viscounty of Turenne, one of the most stubbornly independent of fiefdoms in France, embellished with a clutch of gorgeous red villages.

The Upper Vézère and Corrèze Valleys

Treignac on the Vézère was lucky to have been included in the Plus Beaux Villages club: it's more a small town than a village, and doesn't really make the grade in the beauty stakes. But it is often lively, and from the Gothic bridge you get a good view of the ruined castle walls. Old houses with sculpted entrances lie between Place de la République and Place du Collège.

From Treignac, a magnificent alley of beeches takes you up to panoramic **Mont Gargan**. Its name has led to stories of connections with Gargantua, or perhaps the Gargano in Italy associated with the cult of St Michael. In the midst of the pudding-shaped **Monédières hills** between the Vézère and the Corrèze, the easily reached Suc-au-May offers more great views. Here **Chaumeil** has a tough but likable huddle of stone houses.

Northeast of Chaumeil, the **Corrèze river** starts off on its path to join the Vézère. **Gimel-les-Cascades**, with its waterfalls (*adm*), is tucked down a valley with dramatic wooded views. As for **Tulle**, the capital of the Corrèze, beyond the cathedral and Musée du Cloître most of its charm has been destroyed. The museum, in a Benedictine monastery, has 13th-century chapterhouse frescoes, a collection of tulle – the net fabric named after the town – arms and accordions, a local passion.

Back north along the Vézère, **Uzerche** is much more appealing than Tulle, its towers rising on a narrow promontory above a hairpin bend in the river. A prehistoric precious metals route from Britain and Brittany to the Mediterranean may have passed this way, and the relics of two Breton saints, Léon and Coronat, ended up in the former abbey church of **St-Pierre**, decorated with Moorish-Gothic arches and archaic carvings. But much earlier traces of civilization have been found here; find out more at the **Centre Régional de Documentation sur l'Archéologie du Paysage en Limousin** (*open daily 10.30–12.30 and 2.30–6.30; adm*).

Down the Dordogne River in the Limousin

Bort, the Limousin town furthest up the Dordogne, may be ugly, but it is overseen by the extraordinary **Orgues de Bort**, massive tubes of rock, some over 300ft high. The plateau above affords spectacular views of the Dordogne valley and Cantal mountains. Just north of Bort rises the picture perfect mid-15th-century **Château du Val**, with superb pepperpot roofs that narrowly escaped disappearing under the waters with the first plan for the Bort dam.

Intrepid art-lovers might make a detour west through the sleepy towns of **Ussel** and **St-Angel** to **Meymac**, which has been given a somewhat alarming shot in the arm with the establishment of a contemporary art centre in the former abbey. Continuing down the Dordogne from Bort, beyond the grim dams at L'Aigle and Le Chastang, **Argentat** originally marked the highpoint of the Dordogne's navigability. For centuries Argentat's boatmen would load timber, cheese, leather, pelts and wine on to their flat-bottomed *gabares* and sail down to Bordeaux, where the boats themselves would be sold for firewood. The town itself, under its *lauze* roofs, has the air of a cheerful, prosperous pensioner.

The **Tours de Merle** may be lost up the Maronne river from Argentat, but ruined castles don't come much more romantic than this massive complex. But what was it doing in a meander in a minor river, like an armoured knight hiding in the woods? Why, collecting tolls. As as alternative to the busy roads to Beaulieu, seek out the country roads south to the Cère valley, taking in superb views of its tight wooded gorges around Camps.

Lovely riverside **Beaulieu-sur-Dordogne** still looks credibly medieval, built around the 12th-century abbey of St-Pierre, with its magnificent tympanum of the Last Judgement. Christ has his arms outstretched in triumph while a carnival of monsters rolls across the lintel, supported by a figure Freda White described as 'flowing upward like a flame of prayer' (to continue down the Dordogne, *see* p.479).

The Old Viscounty of Turenne Between Beaulieu and Brive

Just four families succeeded each other across ten centuries as the Viscounts of Turenne, who commanded a remarkable degree of autonomy from other overlords. Established by the Comborns, who obtained privileges from the kings for the part they played in the crusades, they were followed by Comminges from the Pyrenees in the 14th century and the Rogers, who gave Rome two popes, Clement VI and Gregory XI. But the best known viscounts were the La Tour d'Auvergnes (1444–1738). The Protestant Henri I de la Tour d'Auvergne supported the future Henri IV of France, while his son, another Henri, became known as Le Grand Turenne for his battle prowess. But by this time the little village of Turenne had lost its importance; the La Tour d'Auvergnes spent most of their time at court, or in their seat at Sedan in the Ardennes. Gambling brought their downfall. In 1738 Charles-Godefroy of Turenne gave up his possessions in exchange for the monarchy wiping out his debts.

Three castles are crammed on the narrow ridge of **Curemonte**. None is open to visitors, but one holds memories of Colette, who spent the early days of the Second World War here. Just south, tiny **La Chapelle-aux-Saints** caused a stir in the early 1900s when the Homme de La Chapelle-aux-Saints was found in a cave; the excitement was caused by evidence that this Neanderthal had been given a ritual burial back in 45,000 BC. Although he was moved to the Musée de l'Homme in Paris, a **museum** here explains his importance.

The extraordinary measled stones of **Meyssac** affect, or rather infect, its whole appearance, from its Gothic church and the pillars of its covered market to the turrets of its picturesque old houses. Whereas Meyssac looks slightly alarming, **Collonges-la-Rouge** is utterly irresistible. And knows it. It was here that the Association des Plus Beaux Villages de France was born in 1982, preserving lovely villages while perhaps inevitably turning them into tourist traps. Collonges is one. It owes its wealth of fine houses with turrets sticking out left, right and centre, to the administrators of the Viscounty of Turenne, who based themselves here in the 16th century. The Romanesque Gothic **church** has the fanciest towers in town; remarkably, during the bitter Wars of Religion, Protestants and Catholics reached some kind of agreement to share it. The entrance has curious lobed arches, and figures of the Christ of the Ascension above the Virgin and two posses of apostles, strikingly carved in white limestone against the red sandstone. Inside, the church is full of quirky corners and statues.

After Collonges' vivid tints, most of the blood seems drained out of **Turenne**, which looks a much tougher nut, although it too is a Beau Village. Once the tiny capital of the viscounty, its streets strain to make it up to the dramatic castle ruin. On the way up you might stop for a breather at the grand but cold classical church, with a defensive tower topped by a spiked slate roof. Begun in the late 16th century when Turenne was a Protestant stronghold, its gilded retable with its cluster of putti adds a note of Catholic excess. Further up, remnants of three rings of walls surround the ruined castle, marooned like an ark on its hilltop; its watch tower sticking up like a figurehead on the prow. Fantastic views open out from a formal garden to a network of high castles.

Old **Brive-la-Gaillarde** is an attractive onion of a town, its layers encased in the outer skin of the busy boulevard. Built on the Corrèze just before it joins the Vézère, Brive stands in contrast to ugly Tulle and plays better rugby too, winning the European Cup in 1997. A row of indiscreetly protruding busts marks the Renaissance façade of the **Musée Labenche** (*open April–Oct daily exc Tues 10–6.30; rest of year daily exc Tues 1.30–6; adm*) where, among relics and portraits of the leading lights of Brive, the surprise is a series of fine classical tapestries made at Mortlake, south of London.

Getting Around

Brive-la-Gaillarde is the main transport hub, with the Corrèze's airport and main train station. For reservations for Brive-Laroche airport, t 05 55 86 88 36. A fair number of trains using the Paris-Toulouse line stop at Brive. Local railway lines run from here along the Vézère and Dordogne valleys.

Tourist Information

Uzerche: Place de la Lunade, t 05 55 73 15 71.
Meymac: Place de la Fontaine, t 05 55 95 18 43.
Beaulieu-sur-Dordogne: Place Marbot, t 05 55 91 09 94.
Collonges-la-Rouge: Place de l'Ancienne Gare, t 05 55 25 47 57.
Turenne: Place du Foirail, t 05 55 85 94 38.
Brive-la-Gaillarde: Place du 14 Juillet, t 05 55 24 08 80.

Where to Stay and Eat

Uzerche ✉ 19140
**Hôtel Teyssier, Rue du Pont Turgot, t 05 55 73 10 05, f 05 55 98 43 31 (*inexpensive*). An old-fashioned provincial hotel, but one of the few places to stay in the upper Vézère. The flowers on the front terrace may be well loved but the old rooms are neglected. The food is copious.

Confolent-Port-Dieu
Presbytère de Port-Dieu, t/f 05 55 94 39 56. Good-value B&B hideaway in a wonderful location by the Dordogne north of Bort-les-Orgues, tucked away behind a rural church and run by an engaging, easy-going young couple.

Neuvic ✉ 19160
**Château de Mialaret, Route d'Egletons, t 05 55 46 02 50, f 05 55 46 02 65 (*inexpensive*). An appealing little rustic château, offering simple country pleasures in a wooded, hilly setting.

Beaulieu-sur-Dordogne ✉ 19120
**Le Turenne, 1 Bd St-Rodolphe-de-Turenne, t 05 55 91 10 16, f 05 55 91 22 42 (*inexpensive*). Turreted old hotel in a medieval house with bags of atmosphere, and a charming restaurant to match, with duck specialities.

Collonges-la-Rouge ✉ 19500
**Le Relais St-Jacques, La Porte Plate, t 05 55 25 41 02, f 05 55 84 08 51. An utterly delightful simple hotel in an adorable house; the only drawback is the tourist crowds outside.
Le Prieuré, Place de l'Eglise, t 05 55 25 41 00 (*inexpensive*). A very cosy restaurant with a few rooms attached in a great central location by the church.

Turenne ✉ 19500
La Maison des Chanoines, Route de l'Eglise, t 05 55 85 93 43 (*moderate–inexpensive*). With its lovely stone front covered with ivy, this used to be the home of church canons, but is now an extremely attractive stop for tourists. The food's good, served in a vaulted cellar (*menus 150–200F*).

Brive-la-Gaillarde ✉ 19100
***La Truffe Noire, 22 Bd Anatole France, t 05 55 92 45 00, f 05 55 92 45 13, *www.hotelvision.com/brive.la-truffe-noire* (*moderate*). On the outer layer of the historic onion, by the big central avenues encircling the old town. A generous terrace separates the rooms from the road, and it's soberly comfortable and friendly with a solid restaurant (*menus 150–300F*).
Chez Francis, 61 Av de Paris, t 05 55 74 41 72. Lively *bistrot* with the odd eccentric touch of regional cuisine.

Varetz ✉ 19240
****Château de Castel-Novel, 5km northwest of Brive, t 05 55 85 00 01, f 05 55 85 09 03, *novel@relaischateaux.fr* (*expensive*). Arguably the grandest hotel in the Limousin, and once home to Colette. The towers date back to the 15th century; rooms are sumptuously furnished. Restaurant (*menus 220–400F*).

Northern Dordogne and Périgueux

Cross into the *département* of the Dordogne (or Périgord, as it is still known in France), and a warm sun gilds the limestone and a distinct twang flavours the local accent. Ironically, what so delights visitors today – idyllic landscapes, a thousand castles, fortified churches, and medieval villages with *lauze* roofs – were born of long centuries of war, poverty and neglect; basically, after the Middle Ages, no one ever had the wherewithal to improve them. This, of course, has changed dramatically in the past thirty years as the English, after ruling the roost before the Hundred Years' War, have moved back in a big way to their 'Dordogne-shire.'

The *département*, one of the largest in France, divides itself into four quarters, each with its own colour. Jules Verne dubbed northernmost Périgord 'Green' for its forests and rivers that remain lush even in midsummer. 'White Périgord' of the pale stone is the home of the Dordogne's capital Périgueux. 'Black Périgord' is named for the dense forests around Sarlat, while 'Purple' has been stuck on the wine area around Bergerac.

Northern Périgord

Brantôme is a charming town of medieval and Renaissance houses built on an island in the Dronne. A 16th-century doglegged bridge crosses to its white **abbey** built against a steep bank (*open Feb–Dec daily 10–12 and 2–5 exc Tues; July and Aug daily 10–2; closed Jan; adm*), founded by Charlemagne in 769, sacked by the Normans in the 11th century, when the **bell tower** (the oldest in France) was rebuilt on its Merovingian base. A bas-relief of the *Massacre of the Innocents* under the porch and a carved capital, used as a font, survive from the original church. The best bits are the curious *grottes et fontaines sacrées* in the cliff behind the abbey, including a grotto where the 15th-century monks carved reliefs of the *Last Judgement* and *Crucifixion*. It survived the Wars of Religion thanks to *abbé* Pierre de Bourdeilles (1540–1614), known in French literature simply as Brantôme. Brantôme used the abbey's revenues to finance his escapades as a soldier of fortune and lover of court ladies. Injured in battle, he settled here and wrote spicy accounts of the people of his time, all so true that he left instructions for his heirs to wait 50 years before publishing them.

Of the 1,001 châteaux of Périgord, the most splendid is the **Château de Puyguilhem** (*open Mar–June and Sept–Dec daily 10–12.30 and 2–5.30 exc Mon; July and Aug 10–7; adm*), northeast of Brantôme near Villars. Built in 1524, its rooftop forest of richly carved dormers and chimneys is as impressive within – it resembles the hull of a ship. Saved from collapse in the 1930s, Puyguilhem has been refurnished with period pieces and Renaissance tapestries. The nearby **Grotte de Villars** (*open April–Oct daily 2–6.30; May, June and Sept daily 10–11.30 and 2–6.30 and July–Aug daily 10–6.30; adm*) combines natural art – brilliant white, translucent stalactites and draperies – with prehistoric drawings in magnesium oxide from the Aurignacian era (30,000 BC).

From Brantôme, follow the Dronne 7km southwest to **Bourdeilles**, seat of the oldest of Périgord's four baronies. High over the river, their **Château** (*open daily exc Tues 10–12.30 and 1.30–5.30, April–June and Sept and Oct till 7; July and Aug daily 10–7; closed Jan; adm*) guarded the frontier between English Guyenne and France. Naughty

Getting Around

Two bus lines cross this area, one run by CFTA (t 05 53 08 43 12) linking Angoulême, Mareuil, Brantôme and Périgueux twice a day, once on Sunday, and the other run by Citram running twice a day between Angoulême, Mareuil and Ribérac. If you're taking the Bordeaux train from Paris, Angoulême is the stop nearest the Dordogne.

Tourist Information

Brantôme: Pavillon Renaissance, t/f 05 53 05 80 52.

Ribérac: Place de Charles de Gaulle, t 05 53 90 03 10, f 05 53 91 35 13.

Where to Stay and Eat

Brantôme ✉ 24310

★★★Moulin de l'Abbaye, 1 Rte de Bourdeilles, t 05 53 05 80 22, f 05 53 05 75 27 (*moderate*). Dreamy, ivy-covered hotel-restaurant in a delightful garden, just outside the centre on the Dronne. Exquisite dishes, based on local ingredients (*menus from 240F*). *Closed Nov–April. Restaurant closed Sept–June lunch exc weekends; July and Aug Mon lunch.*

★★★Hôtel Chabrol, 57 Rue Gambetta, t 05 53 05 70 15, f 05 53 05 71 85 (*moderate*). Excellent, elegant restaurant in handsome old white building on the river Dronne, serving generous portions of favourites such as *millefeuille de ris de veau au foie de canard et truffe*, and wonderful hot desserts (*menus 165–500F*). *Closed Sun eve, Mon, 15 Nov–15 Dec and most of Feb.*

★★★Domaine de la Roseraie, t 05 53 05 84 74, f 05 53 05 77 94 (*moderate*). A Relais du Silence hotel, outside the centre on the Angoulême road at Les Courrières. Set in the middle of a rose garden with seven old-style

but well-equipped rooms, a pool, and tennis and riding nearby, as well as a restaurant (*menus from 169F*). *Closed mid-Dec–mid-Mar.*

★★Périgord Vert, 6 Av de Thiviers, t 05 53 05 70 58, f 05 53 46 71 18 (*inexpensive*). Reliable Logis de France hotel in ivy-swathed building (*menus from 95F*).

Chez Mérillou, Rue A.-Maurois, t 05 53 05 74 04 (*cheap*). Very pleasant B&B.

Au Fil de l'Eau, 21 Quai Bertin, t 05 53 05 73 65. A good 115F menu; choose *filets de perche rôtis au ris crémeux et aux amandes* if they're on the menu. *Closed Jan and Feb, Mon eve and Tues exc July and Aug.*

Bourdeilles ✉ 24310

★★★Château de la Côte, at Biras, southwest of the centre on the D106, t 05 53 03 70 11, f 05 53 03 42 84 (*moderate*). 15th-century château lost in an immense park; 14 beautiful rooms furnished with antiques, pool, billiards, tennis and helipad, golf, riding, and canoeing nearby (*menus from 170F*). *Closed mid-Nov–mid-Mar.*

Ribérac ✉ 24600

★★Hôtel de France, 3 Rue Marc-Dufraisse, t 05 53 90 00 61, f 05 53 91 06 05 (*inexpensive*). Family-run hotel in a 16th-century post house – the best and biggest hotel in town, with an old-fashioned dining room and a garden courtyard. A wide choice of fish and duck dishes (*menus from 85F*). *Restaurant closed Mon and Tues midday out of season; hotel closed mid-Nov–mid-Dec.*

Hôtel de l'Univers, 2 Av de Verdun, t 05 53 90 04 38, f 05 53 90 98 39 (*cheap*). Central small and simple, with a small pool.

La Charouffie, 10 Chemin des Tilleuls, t 05 53 91 63 29. Just 1km from the centre of town, a popular small *chambres d'hôte* in an attractive house with a shaded garden and pool (*250F for two with breakfast; supper possible at 80F*).

writer Brântome was born here, in 1540, and the adjacent Renaissance château was built by his sister-in-law, Jacquette de Montbron, to impress Catherine de' Medici (who in fact never visited). She even designed it herself – a rare and perhaps unique feat for a woman in the 16th century. The interior is richly appointed with 16th- and 17th-century furniture from Spain and Burgundy.

Peaceful and full of happy cows, this corner of Périgord manages to stay relatively aloof from the tourist madness. It does have a picture postcard village, **St-Jean-de-Côle**, with a Gothic humpback bridge and steep tile roofs on the houses, and a church tower with delightful carvings, especially one of God modelling Adam out of clay. In summer you can get inside the 15th-century **Château de la Marthonie** (*open July and Aug daily 10–12 and 2–6.30; adm*).

More Romanesque awaits 7km west in the 12th-century church of **Thiviers**, built over Merovingian foundations, with a Renaissance porch and sculpted capitals. A plaque opposite the Maison de la Presse commemorates the town's link with Jean-Paul Sartre, who spent much of his (predictably) miserable childhood here. Northeast of Thiviers, lost on the ferny forested frontier of the Limousin like Sleeping Beauty's castle, is the enchanting **Château de Jumilhac** (*guided tours June to end of Sept daily 10–7; Oct–mid-Nov and mid-Mar–end of April daily 2–6.30; adm*). Antoine Chapelle, the brain behind it, converted a former Templar stronghold into a fantasia of towers, turrets and chimneys coiffed with blue slate pepperpots, topped in turn by an equally fantastic array of forged-iron froufrous.

West of Jumilhac, the river Isle loops down to pick up the waters of the Auvézère just before Périgueux. The busiest market town in the area, **Excideuil** once belonged to the Viscounts of Limoges, who built a vertiginous fortress on a butte of Jurassic limestone. The best scenery in the area is along the Auvézère, beginning at **Cherveix-Cubas**, from where you can drive, ride, or trek along the delicious **Gorges de l'Auvézère** as far as the waterfalls.

South of Cherveix stand the striking high-domed towers of the **Château de Hautefort**, the 12th-century fortress of the battling troubadour, Bertran de Born, which was rebuilt in 1640 by a famous miser, Jacques-François de Hautefort (the model for Harpagon in Molière's *L'Avare*). You can visit the immaculate French **gardens** (*open April–early Oct daily 10–12 and 2–6; July and Aug daily 9.30–7; early Oct–early Nov daily 2–6; otherwise Sun only 2–6; closed mid-Dec–mid-Jan; adm*).

Périgueux

Set in a fertile valley on the river Isle, the capital of the Dordogne is a cheerful city of 35,000 people who produce and market truffles, foie gras and fat strawberries, and print all the postage stamps in France. The old streets around the famous five-domed cathedral of St-Front have been intelligently restored over the past decades to give the city a lively and lovely heart; another plus is its museum, with its exceptional prehistoric and Roman sections.

Set back from the river, the **Cité**, the oldest part of Périgueux, has a handful of Gallo-Roman and medieval souvenirs tucked between the modern buildings, including the 65ft **Tour de Vésone**, the central *cella* of a circular 1st-century AD Gallo-Roman temple. Just west in Rue des Bouquets are the ruins of the **Villa de Pompeïus** (*ask about guided tours run by the tourist office*). Pompeïus, whoever he was, wallowed in a de luxe set of heated Roman baths; frescoes and mosaics survive as well. The impressive

Getting Around

Périgueux's train station, in Rue Denis-Papin, is 4 hours from Paris (change in Limoges), 75 minutes from Bordeaux, 3 hours from Agen or Toulouse; Citram buses from the station also link Périgueux to the Paris–Bordeaux TGV in Angoulême, by way of Ribérac. Buses depart from Place Francheville and the station to Sarlat, Montignac, Ribérac, Bergerac, and Brantôme. The biggest car park in the city is up at Place Montaigne, near the Musée du Périgord.

Tourist Information

Périgueux: 26 Place Francheville, t 05 53 53 10 63, f 05 53 09 02 50.

Where to Stay

Périgueux ✉ 24000

Moderate

*** Bristol, 37–39 Rue Antoine Gadaud, t 05 53 08 75 90, f 05 53 07 00 49, www.bristolfrance .com. Modern hotel near the centre of town, with spacious rooms and the usual facilities. Parking, but no restaurant.

Inexpensive

****Hôtel du Périgord, 74 Rue Victor Hugo, t 05 53 53 33 63, f 05 53 08 19 74. Comfortable Logis de France rooms in the centre of town, with an inner garden.

****L'Universe, 18 Cours Montaigne, t 05 53 34 79. Near the museum, with dining under the arbour in summer (menus from 90F).

Eating Out

Expensive

Le Roi Bleu, 2 Rue Montaigne, t 05 53 09 43 77. Smart restaurant with chic selections such as tartare de saumon fumé aux chips de légumes et langoustines rôties (menus 170–450F). Closed Sat lunch and Sun and third week in Aug.

Le 8, 8 Rue de la Clarté, t 05 53 35 15 15, near the cathedral. Very good reputation for imaginative regional dishes in small and lively dining room (menus 165–400F). Closed Sun, Mon, early July and a week or two in Feb, reserve.

Le Rocher de l'Arsault, 15 Rue de l'Arsault, t 05 53 53 54 06. Tasty tatin de foie gras and other regional delicacies in a Louis XIII dining room (menus 155–450F). Closed Sun, half of July and start of Aug.

Moderate

Hercule Poireau, 2 Rue de la Nation, t 05 53 08 90 76. Vaulted Renaissance cellar restaurant, serving Rossini de canard and other treats at very reasonable prices (menus 99–220F). Closed Sat lunch, Sun and most of Aug.

Aux Berges de l'Isle, 2 Rue Pierre-Magne, t 05 53 09 51 50. Terrace overlooking the river and St-Front. Try the refined pavé de bœuf au foie gras and one of the luscious desserts (menus from 98F). Closed Sun eve and Mon.

if now mutilated church of **St-Etienne-de-la-Cité** stands on the site of a Temple of Mars. In the 11th century it was rebuilt by a Crusader who took notes, becoming the prototype of the Périgourdin domed Romanesque church, with wide Byzantine domes not only over the crossing but cupping the length of the nave.

The compact medieval quarter of **Puy-St-Front** has been beautifully restored; you can peep inside some of the courtyards, and around the last remnant of Puy's walls, the **Tour Mataguerre**. If St-Etienne was the prototype, the **Cathedral of St-Front** was the ultimate expression of medieval Périgord's particular romance with domes. It's especially breathtaking from a distance, and especially so at night when it is illuminated. Close up, it is much harder to overlook the fact that most of what you see was rebuilt at the end of the 19th century, when additions were added to the 11th-century original, including the pinnacles on the domes. Inside the most lingering impression

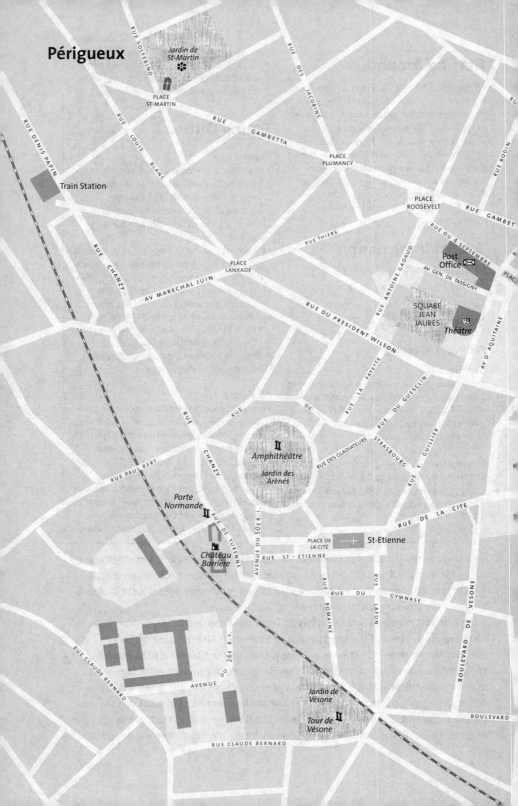

Périgueux

Jardin de St-Martin

PLACE ST-MARTIN

RUE SOLFERINO

RUE DES JACOBINS

RUE GAMBETTA

RUE LOUIS BLANC

PLACE PLUMANCY

Train Station

RUE DENIS PAPIN

RUE BODIN

PLACE ROOSEVELT

RUE GAMBET

RUE DU 4 SEPTEMBRE

RUE CHANZY

RUE THIERS

RUE ANTOINE GADAUD

Post Office ✉

AV GEN. DE TASSIGNY

PLAC

PLACE LANXADE

AV MARECHAL JUIN

RUE DU PRESIDENT WILSON

SQUARE JEAN JAURES

Théâtre 🎭

AV D' AQUITAINE

RUE

DE

RUE LA FAYETTE

RUE DU GUESCLIN

RUE

RUE DES GLADIATEURS

STRASBOURG

RUE E. GUILLIER

Amphithéâtre Ⅱ

Jardin des Arènes

RUE PAUL BERT

CHANZY

Porte Normande Ⅱ

RUE DE TURENNE

Château Barrière

AVENUE DU SOER. I.

RUE DE LA CITÉ

PLACE DE LA CITÉ ✝ **St-Etienne**

RUE ST - ETIENNE

RUE DU GYMNASE

BOULEVARD DE VESONE

RUE CLAUDE BERNARD

AVENUE DU 26E R.I.

AVENUE

RUE ROMAINE

RUE LAFON

Jardin de Vésone

Tour de Vésone Ⅱ

BOULEVARD

RUE CLAUDE BERNARD

RUE VICTOR HUGO

RUE PAUL LOUIS COURIER

NEMER

RUE FOURNIER LACHARMIE

LOUIS MIE

RUE DE L'ARSAULT

PLACE DU
GENERAL
LECLERC

Palais de
Justice

ALLEES DE TOURNY

RUE MALEVILLE

PLACE
MONTAIGNE

L'Isle

BOULEVARD MICHEL MONTAIGNE

RUE MONTAIGNE

COURS DE TOURNY

Musée du
Périgord

MICHEL

RUE VOLTAIRE

PLACE
DU MUSEE

RUE FENELON

RUE AUGUSTINS

PLANTIER

MONTAIGNE

RUE EGUILLERIE

PLACE
ST-LOUIS

RUE ST-FRONT

LIMOGEANNE

PLACE DU
MARCHE
AU BOIS

RUE DES

Maison
Tenant

MAUROIS

COURS

RUE DE LA SAGESSE

RUE LAN MARY

RUE BARBECANE

RUE NOTRE-DAME

PLACE
GENERAL
DE GAULLE

PLACE
ST-SILAIN

RUE DES CHAINES

RUE MISERICORDE

RUE DES DE PECHES

RUE DE LA REPUBLIQUE

RUE DE LA NATION

Maison Estignard
Galeries
Daumesnil

SAUMANDE

RUE DES PRES

COURS BUGEAUD

PLACE DU
CODERC

PLACE
DAUMESNIL

AV DAUMESNIL

RUE DU PORT DE GRAULE

RUE AUBAREDE

PLACE
BUGEAUD

RUE A. SAIGNE

PLACE DE
L'HOTEL
DE VILLE

Hôtel
de Ville

PLACE DE
LA CLARTE

RUE DE
LA CLARTE

AV DAUMESNIL

Maison des Consuls
Maison Lambert

PLACE
BUGEAUD

PT DES
BARRIS

RUE TAILLEFER

PLACE DE
LA CLAUTRE

Musée
Militaire

RUE TOURVILLE

RUE PIERRE MAGNE

ACE
HEVILLE

Tourist
Information

RUE CONDE

RUE DES FARGES

Cathédrale
St-Front

Vieux
Moulin

ST GEORGES

RUE DE LA BRIDE

Maison
des Dames
de la Foi

RUE DU CALVAIRE

RUE MAUVARD

Tour
Mataguerre

RUE AUBERGERIE

PLACE
MAUVARD

RUE DES TANNERIES

tation

RUE SEGUIER

RUE LACOMBE

RUE LITTRE

COURS FENELON

BOULEVARD

RUE W. ROUSSEAU

PONT
ST-GEORGES

BOULEVARD LAKANAL

L'Isle

COURS ST-GEORGES

RAN DE BORN

N

200 metres
200 yards

is one of vastness (it's one and a half times as long as a football pitch); in its minimal decoration it looks more like a mosque.

Place Daumesnil, next to St-Front, is the centre of a fascinating web of 15th- and 16th-century pedestrian lanes. Steep, stepped streets descend to the river; houses in Rue du Plantier have terraced gardens, while medieval Rue du Port-de-Graule is lined with tiny boutiques. The pedestrian **Rue Limogeanne** has been Périgueux's busiest shopping street since the Middle Ages; most of the houses here, and on Rue de la Sagesse, date from the 16th century.

The **Musée du Périgord** (*22 Cours Tourny; open April–Sept Mon–Fri 11–6, weekends 1–6; Oct–Mar Mon–Fri 10–5, weekends 1–6; closed Tues and hols; adm*) is a cut above the average provincial museum. Ethnographic collections, devoted to stone-age cultures, form a comparative introduction to the prehistoric section, which includes three of the oldest complete skeletons ever found. The Gallo-Roman rooms are filled with jewellery, frescoes, mosaics, and a 2nd-century BC altar dedicated to the Eastern cult of Cybele and Attis. The Beaux-Arts section has ceramics and enamels from Limoges, followed by paintings and sculptures.

West of Périgueux: the Dronne and Forêt de la Double

The Dronne is a charmingly bucolic river by the gentle rolling hills of the **Double forest**, crisscrossed by streams that feed moody marshes, created by medieval monks to farm fish for Lent. The big town here, with nearly 5,000 souls, **Ribérac** has the Romanesque Notre-Dame, with a handsome apse and dome; in fact this entire area bubbles with multi-domed Romanesque churches: to see them all, pick up the tourist office's map of *églises romanes à coupoles*.

The most fascinating churches in the area, however, have no domes and lie 2km into the Charente at the ivory-tinted hill town of **Aubeterre-sur-Dronne**. The uncanny **Eglise Monolithique** (*open 15 June–15 Oct daily 9.30–12.30 and 2–7; other times till 6; adm*) was founded in a cave in the 5th century. In the 11th century Benedictines enlarged the holy precinct, quarrying into the limestone to create the tallest rock-cut church in the world, rising 65ft from the ground and supported by two blackened columns as thick as sequoias. A stairway cut in the rock leads to the upper galleries with windows peering down into the shadowy depths. The floor is pitted with the graves of medieval monks, and below these an ancient **mithraeum** was found, where adherents of Mithras would be baptized in a rain of hot blood from a bull sacrificed above. Rampaging Protestants smashed up Aubeterre's other gem, the 11th-century **St-Jacques**, although they spared the magnificent three-arched Romano-Hispano-Moorish façade, decorated with signs of the zodiac, monsters and abstract patterns.

The Vézère Valley

Some 400,000 years ago, people settled on the fair banks of the Vézère. It was a Palaeolithic paradise: bulging cliffs pocked with caves, fresh water, river pebbles, abundant flint, and herds of bison and reindeer to hunt. Long forgotten, the existence of these early settlers was first hinted at in 1862 when a deposit of carved flints and bones was uncovered at La Madeleine. This set off a quest for signs of 'antediluvian man', leading to a torrent of discoveries. In 1895 the first Magdalenian paintings in France were noted at Les Eyzies' Grotte de la Mouthe, but it was the finding of Lascaux in 1940 that really put it on the map. To date, 200 Palaeolithic sites have been discovered along the Vézère, now designated a World Heritage site by Unesco.

Montignac

Once a busy river port, Montignac sits pretty on the Vézère, its wooden balconies reflected peacefully in the waters, belying a violent past when the ruined **Château de Montignac** was the chief citadel of the Taillefer, the Counts of Périgord, who of all the vassals of the king of France stood apart for having no redeeming virtues whatsoever, although by the 18th century their hot blood had cooled enough to produce the wily diplomat Talleyrand.

Lascaux I and II

Guided tours (t 05 53 51 96 23 for schedule of English tours); open April–Sept daily 9–7; tickets (which include Le Thot Centre de Préhistoire) from the booth near the Montignac tourist office from 9am. Other times tickets purchased at Lascaux II; open daily 10–12.30 and 1.30–5.30; closed Mon.

Montignac remained pensioned off from history until one morning in September 1940, when two local lads and two young war refugees from Paris went in search of treasure in a pit above Montignac used as a dead donkey dump and stumbled across the **Grotte de Lascaux**, which had been virtually vacuum-sealed when the original entrance was blocked by an ancient landslide. Within 15 years of its discovery, however, the fabulous 'Sistine Chapel of Prehistoric Art' was fading under a film of white calcite deposits caused by carbonic acid from the breath of a million visitors, and on 20 April 1963 Lascaux was closed forever to the public; although the deterioration has stopped, admission is limited to five prehistorians twice a week.

Disappointment at the closure was so universal that the *département* financed the 15-year-long construction of **Lascaux II**, 650ft below the original. This incredibly painstaking reproduction of the Hall of the Bulls and the long narrow *Diverticule axiale* was painted with the same colours and techniques used 17,000 years ago. Far better than any photograph ever could, it reproduces the ravishing exuberant life, movement and the clever use of natural protuberances, faults and shadows of the original paintings, although it hardly explains how an artist limited to a lamp of animal fat and juniper twigs could get the proportions of a 16ft bull so perfectly. Scattered among the animals is a vocabulary of mysterious symbols and a Dr Seuss-ish beast dubbed the 'unicorn', the only known 'imaginary' creature yet discovered in prehistoric art.

Around Montignac

Six km southeast of Montignac, the golden *lauze*-topped **Château de La Grande Filolie** (14th–15th century) (*open July and Aug daily 10–7; other times your odds are about 50–50; ring ahead, t 05 53 51 67 50, to make sure*) is one of the Dordogne's dreamiest châteaux. Just as striking, the fortified **church of St-Amand-de-Coly** (6km east) has a massive *clocher-mur* and a superb roof of *lauzes*, looming like a skyscraper over its narrow valley and hamlet. It is stirring, wholesome Romanesque, unusually built on a slope (the walls of the nave converge slightly, to create a curious perspective). The dome hovers 66ft over the nave: stand under it and sing, and like all true Romanesque churches it rings like a bell.

Down the Vézère from Montignac to Les Eyzies

Le Thot Centre de Préhistoire (*same hours, same ticket as Lascaux II*) features audio-visuals on Palaeolithic art and on the creation of Lascaux II; there's a replica of the tiny chamber at the back of Lascaux with its stick man 'sorcerer'; and living (or mechanical) examples of the animals that once roamed the Vézère valley.

In 1944, in reprisal for Resistance activity, the retreating Nazis burned the village of **Rouffignac**. Only the church of St-Germain remained; under the bell tower a doorway of 1530 survives, its lintel carved with mermaids. If it's open, don't miss the Flamboyant Gothic interior, with elaborate vaulting and twisted columns. Five km south is the **Grotte de Rouffignac**, 'the Cave of a Hundred Mammoths' (*open April–Oct daily 10–11.30 and 2–5; July and Aug daily 9–11.30 and 2–6; adm*). A little electric train takes you 4km down into the bowels of the earth as the guide illuminates the vivid etchings, drawings of mammoths and woolly rhinoceroses, and niches in the clay floor formed by generations of hibernating bears. The ceiling of the innermost chamber is an excellent pastiche of horses, mammoths, bison, and an ibex.

Down the river from the idyllic hamlet of **St-Léon-sur-Vézère** is the curved prow of **La Roque St-Christophe**, a cliff half a mile long, sliced into five shelves, one of which is the largest natural terrace in Europe (*open Oct–Feb daily 11–4.30; Mar–Sept daily 10–6.30; adm*). Inhabited from Mousterian times, the caves along the tiers sheltered up to 3,000 people, who had their own church, cemetery, monastery and, after the 900s, a fort, thrown up against the Vikings.

Les Eyzies-de-Tayac, the 'World Capital of Prehistory'

The Vézère and Beune rivers meet at Les Eyzies, where the first known bones of *Homo sapiens sapiens* were discovered in 1888 at a place called Cro-Magnon. As the valley's chief crossroads, with major prehistoric sites in every direction, Les Eyzies is swamped with summer visitors. A good place to start is the **Musée National de Préhistoire** (*open daily 9.30–12 and 2–5, July and Aug daily 9.30–7; adm*), tucked under the overhanging cliffs that dominate Les Eyzies, in a 16th-century castle. Level II is a Louvre of prehistory, with the largest collection anywhere of Palaeolithic reliefs and sculpture in stone, bone and ivory, while Level III stars the very first prehistoric sculptures – buxom, balloon-bottomed beauties known as the 'Venuses'.

Getting Around

Public transport is thin on the ground in the Vézère valley. There are daily bus connections to **Montignac** (Lascaux) from **Périgueux** and Sarlat run by CFTA (**t** 05 53 43 13 08). Les Eyzies station has one train a day linking it to Sarlat, Périgueux, and Agen. Parking in Les Eyzies in season is notoriously frustrating. The bus company Rey operates routes around the region (**t** 05 53 07 27 22).

Tourist Information

Montignac: Place Bertran-de-Born, **t** 05 53 51 82 60, **f** 05 53 50 49 72.
Les Eyzies-de-Tayac: in the centre, **t** 05 53 06 97 05, **f** 05 53 06 90 79. The hours for the caves are prone to change: pick up the latest schedules here.

Where to Stay and Eat

Montignac ✉ **24290**
★★★★Château de Puy Robert, 2km from Lascaux on the D65, **t** 05 53 51 92 13, **f** 05 53 51 80 11 (*expensive*). Bijou turreted 19th-century château in a 20-acre park with a pool; luxurious rooms in the Relais et Châteaux tradition. *Closed mid-Oct–May*.
The restaurant uses local ingredients to concoct innovative, exquisite dishes (*menus 215–445F*).
★★★Le Relais du Soleil d'Or, 16 Rue du Quatre-Septembre, **t** 05 53 51 80 22, **f** 05 53 50 27 54, in the centre of Montignac (*moderate*). Old inn surrounded by a shady park, with a heated pool, tennis and riding. *Closed mid-Jan–mid-Feb*. In the restaurant traditional southwestern cuisine is given a modern, lighter touch (*110–275F*). *Closed Mon lunch and Nov–Mar Sun eve*).

★★★La Roserai, Place d'Armes, **t** 05 53 50 53 92, **f** 05 53 51 02 23 (*moderate*). Charming 19th-century house with lovely rooms, attractive gardens, pool and good restaurant (*menus 145–215F*). *Closed Nov–Mar*.
De la Grotte, 63 Rue du Quatre-Septembre, **t** 05 53 51 80 48, **f** 05 53 51 05 96 (*inexpensive*). Little hotel with riverside terrace, canoeing and playground. Good restaurant, with lovely asparagus in season (*menus 60–195F*).

Les Eyzies-de-Tayac ✉ **24620**
★★★Du Centenaire, **t** 05 53 06 68 68, **f** 05 53 06 92 41 (*expensive–moderate*). Plush Relais et Châteaux in the centre yet far from the brouhaha. Outdoor heated pool, sauna and gym. Its crowd-puller is the rather pompous dining room, where chef Roland Mazère concocts the most exquisite meals in the entire region, based on the freshest local ingredients, accompanied with an *embarass du choix* from one of the best wine cellars in the Dordogne (*lunch menus at 185F exc Sun, others – excellent value – from 325F*). *Closed Tues and Wed lunch, and Nov–Mar*.
★★★Hôtel Cro-Magnon, **t** 05 53 06 97 06, **f** 05 53 06 95 45 (*moderate*). Creeper-covered family-run hotel with friendly atmosphere; the garden annexe near the pool has the nicer rooms. Charming restaurant serving traditional cuisine; try the *lotte aux morilles* or *truffe en croustade* (*menus from 140F*). *Closed Wed lunch, and mid-Oct–April*.
★★Hôtel du Centre, **t** 05 53 06 97 13, **f** 05 53 06 91 63 (*inexpensive*). Family-run hotel with comfortable rooms bang in the middle of town, but maintains a modicum of seclusion. The restaurant serves regional specialities, indoors or out under the parasols (*menus from 120F*). *Closed Nov–Mar*.
Les Falaises, **t** 05 53 06 97 35 (*inexpensive–cheap*). A good budget choice with parking and a little garden.

Close by, a second overhang protects the **Abri Pataud** (*open July–Aug daily 10–7; adm*) where Upper Palaeolithic hunters lived over a span of 20,000 years. A museum in the nearby shelter contains the finds, including one of the oldest known reliefs, an ibex dated 18,000 BC.

Grotte de Font-de-Gaume

Tours daily exc Wed 10–12 and 2–5; April–Sept daily 9–12 and 2–6; adm. Reservations essential in summer and can be made days in advance: t 05 53 06 86 00.

The Grotte de Font-de-Gaume, a 10-minute walk east of Les Eyzies, has nothing less than the finest prehistoric art open to the public in France. The paintings and engravings in remarkable flowing lines from *c.* 12,000 BC were created with the same drawing and colour-blowing techniques used at Lascaux, and similarly employ natural relief to lend volume to the figures. Some of the paintings are damaged, others look as if they were made yesterday, as in the magnificent friezes of bison, reindeer and horses. The partially painted, partially engraved black stag and kneeling red doe are unique in the canon of Upper Palaeolithic art, and only become visible after the guide traces the lines with a light. The stag is leaning over delicately to lick the doe's brow, an image of tenderness as sublime as it is startling.

More sites around Les Eyzies

The Beune valley is especially rich in cave art. Some 800 engravings dated 12,000–10,000 BC have been distinguished in the last 400ft of the **Grotte des Combarelles** (*reserve, t 05 53 06 86 00; same hours as Font-de-Gaume exc closed Wed; adm*), including 140 horses and 48 rare human representations – hands, masks, women and a seated person. Many are incomplete, most are superimposed in wild abandon, and others only appear when lit from various angles. Most beautiful of all is the reindeer leaning forward to drink from a black cavity suggesting water. Three km down the road, 100 paintings and engravings decorate the **Grotte de Bernifal** in Meyrals (*t 05 53 29 66 39; open June and Sept daily 9.30–12.30 and 2.30–6; July and Aug daily 9.30–7; otherwise by appointment; adm*). The dominant animal is the mammoth, similar to the ones in Rouffignac, but the star of the show is a rare ancestor of the ass.

The **Abri du Cap Blanc** (*open April–Oct daily 10–12 and 2–6; July and Aug daily 10–7; adm*) has a vigorous, 42ft frieze of nearly life-size horses in high relief, following the natural contours of the limestone cliff; the shelter also yielded a Cro-Magnon tomb and tools. Just beyond rise the romantic ruins of the 13th-century **Château de Commarque**, ruined by the English in the Hundred Years' War; the elegant keep was added in the 16th century.

The Dordogne Quercynois

By the time the Dordogne makes its appearance here, the river's queenly character has been formed: from here on it meanders dreamily past the castles that made it a medieval Loire. Before gracing the *département* that bears its name, the Dordogne flows through the Lot, or Quercy – rugged country, shot with velvet-green valleys between dramatic cliffs and caves.

Down the Dordogne

The Dordogne bristles with castles, but the oldest, the burnished red **Château de Castelnau** (*guided tours daily 10–12.15 and 2–5.15; summer till 6.15; July and Aug daily 9.30–6.45; closed Tues; adm*) is still the most redoubtable, set on a conical, 750ft outcropping where the river flows into the *département* of the Lot. Begun in the year 1000 and rated the second military castle in France after Pierrefonds in the Oise, it was restored by Jean Mouliéret, tenor at the Opéra Comique, who refurnished one wing with *objets d'art*.

The main base for the area is **St-Céré**, on the banks of the Bave, or 'dribbler', which tumbles down into the Dordogne. The town reached its peak in the 15th century and has barely changed since, espeically Place du Mercadial, the market square, surrounded by half-timbered buildings. St-Céré has been an art colony since 1945, when Jean Lurçat, the tapestry master of Aubusson (*see* p.456) based himself here: his symbol, the Coq Arlequin was designed to restore Gallic pluck after the war. Lurçat is not everyone's cup of tea, but his work in the Galerie du Casino is worth a look (*open daily 9–12 and 2–7*).

Only 2km west of St-Céré, the golden **Château de Montal** (*open Palm Sun–Oct daily 9.30–12 and 2.30–6; closed Sat; adm*) was built by Jeanne de Balzac, who was enraptured by the Italian Renaissance and decided to replant some of it in this corner of *la France profonde*. At the end of the 19th century the château was stripped of all its finery, but in 1908, oil tycoon Maurice Fénaille stepped in, repurchased as many of its original works as he could, and had copies made of the bits the Americans wouldn't sell back, and donated the château and all its fittings to the state. From the exterior, Montal looks like a typical medieval castle, but step inside the rough walls and a magical courtyard opens up, decorated with ornate dormers and an imaginative frieze over 100ft long. The interior is just as beautiful with a meticulous grand stair carved in golden cream stone, the rooms furnished with Renaissance furnishings.

Further west, a belvedere overlooks the 100ft-high falls of the river Autoire; across the bridge and up the path is a tremendous view stretching from the natural amphitheatre of the **Cirque d'Autoire** to the little village of **Autoire** and all the way to the Dordogne valley. Autoire's steep brown-tiled roofs form an exquisite ensemble; even back in the 1700s, Parisians chose it to build summer homes. Another exceptionally lovely village, 15th-century **Loubressac**, has sloping brown-tiled roofs overlooking the confluence of the Bave, the Cère and the Dordogne.

The Gouffre de Padirac

Open April–mid-Oct daily 9–12 and 2–6; first half of July daily 8.30–12 and 2–6.30; second half same hours uninterrupted; Aug daily 8am–7pm; adm exp.

The chasm at Padirac plunges down 296ft through the limestone of the Causse de Gramat before forming 13 miles of galleries – or at least that's the length that's been explored so far. It is spectacularly beautiful, and spectacularly popular: be prepared to queue (and bring a sweater – down below the temperature is a constant 13°C/55°F).

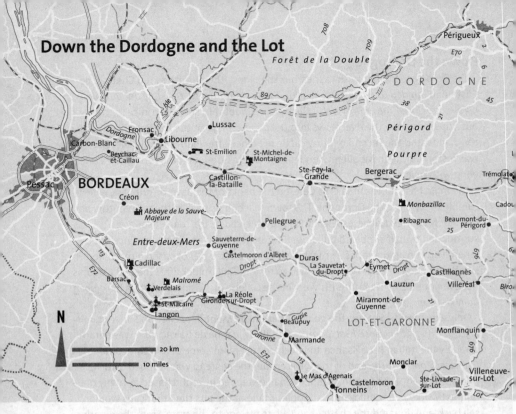

The 90-minute **guided tour** takes you through chambers and along an underground canyon to the river Plane, where gondoliers wait to row you past the Grande Pendeloque, an enormous stalactite that almost touches the water. On foot once more, the tour contines into the Salle des Grands Gours, a fascinating series of basins, flowing one into the other, with a 20ft waterfall and a green lake at the bottom. And then, after all that, comes the breathtaking grand finale: the Salle du Grand Dôme, a vaulted space soaring up to 305ft, capable of containing two Notre-Dames.

West of Padirac

From the river, **Carennac** presents an enchanting cluster of roofs, walls and turrets around its famous honey-coloured **Prieuré St-Pierre**. Founded in 932 and fortified in the 16th century, it managed to repulse Protestant attacks to preserve some of the finest Romanesque art in the area: the beautiful 12th-century tympanum, sculpted by the school of Toulouse. The frieze below is decorated with an unusual zigzag pattern of animals; in the shadowy interior, capitals carved with primitive birds, animals and monsters add to its atmosphere of archaic mystery. The **cloister** (*open June–mid-Sept daily 10–7; other times phone t 05 65 10 97 01; adm*) houses a 15th-century *Mise en Tombeau*, a poignant composition of eight intricately detailed figures. The Virgin's arms reach out stiffly in grief; Nicodemus and Joseph of Arimathea, in Renaissance costumes, hold the shroud, while John and women in biblical draperies mourn.

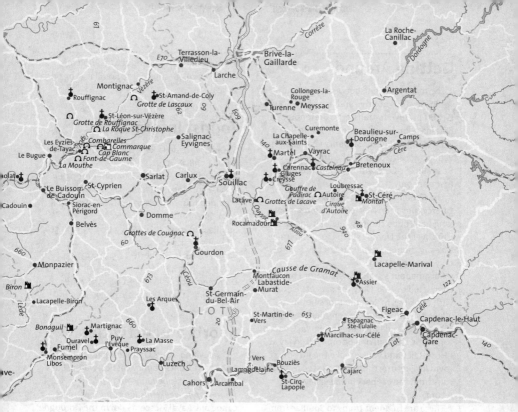

Proud, staunchly medieval **Martel**, the 'City of Seven Towers', resolves under the microscope to a rustic village of 1,400 souls. Severely depopulated over the last century, despite its beauty it wears a melancholy air. In Place des Consuls you'll find the covered market and the huge Palais de la Raymondie (*c.* 1300), now the **Musée d'Uxellodunum** (*open July–Aug Mon–Sat 10–12 and 3–6*), with prehistoric and Gallo-Roman finds. Its *beffroi* is the first of the 'seven towers'. Another is the bell tower of **St-Maur**, a fortified but exquisite Gothic church built into the walls with excellent 16th-century stained glass.

The Dordogne is at its scenic best between Martel and Souillac, meandering cheerfully through dramatic countryside. The riverside village of **Gluges** fairly cowers beneath a steep riverside cliff, with a church half cut into the rock, and a cave, converted to a fortress in the Middle Ages. Continue along the river to **Creysse**, an exquisite village built around a Romanesque church. Further down, **Lacave** is named after a spectacular subterranean wonder (*open Mar–11 Nov daily 10–12 and 2–5; July and Aug daily 9.30–6.30; adm*) – a mile of caverns where the reflections of stalactites in the water give the illusion of an underwater city.

Rocamadour

From neighbouring **L'Hospitalet**, you can get the picture-postcard view of Rocamadour, wedged tight under its overhanging cliff. You can also meet, probably more intimately than you might wish, the 150 Barbary apes and macaques at liberty

Getting Around

The main SNCF line between Paris and Toulouse stops at Brive and usually at Souillac. Get off at Brive to transfer to Bretenoux, or Bétaille (4km from Carennac) on the Brive–Aurillac line, or St-Denis-lès-Martel and Padirac-Rocamadour on the Brive–Figeac line. Buses link St-Céré with the Gare Bretenoux (summer only).

The **Chemin de Fer Touristique du Haut Quercy runs** from Martel to St-Denis – not a long haul, but a thrilling one, skirting 240ft cliffs over the Dordogne: the return journey takes 1½ hours; 2 departures a day summer only, t 05 65 37 35 81.

Rocamadour's station is 4km from town and connected by taxi. Only the cars of visitors with bookings in Rocamadour's hotels are allowed in the village. In summer, when the car parks outside the gates fill up fast, park on top at the château or a 600m walk away at L'Hospitalet and walk or take the lifts into town (23F return; there are 223 steps). A train runs from the car park in the valley (20F return).

There are frequent trains to **Souillac** from Paris, Brive, Cahors and Toulouse, and bus services to Sarlat (t 05 65 53 27 50) and Martel (SNCF buses, t 05 65 32 78 21).

Direct trains from **Sarlat** go to Bordeaux, Les Eyzies, Bergerac, and Souillac from Av de la Gare; July and Aug there are daily links to Bergerac known as *Autorail Espérance* – a guided tour, with tastings of local products along the way (tickets and info from the train station, t 05 53 59 00 21). There's one bus each morning exc Sun to Périgueux (Laribière, t 05 53 59 01 48), another to Souillac (t 05 65 53 27 50).

Tourist Information

St-Céré: Place de la République, t 05 65 38 11 85, f 05 65 38 38 71.

Rocamadour: Rue de la Couronnerie, t 05 65 33 62 59. Stop here for the hours of the guided tour of the shrines (*June–Sept daily exc Sun am*).

Souillac: Bd Louis Jean Malvy, t 05 65 37 81 56, f 05 65 27 11 45.

Sarlat: Place de la Liberté, t 05 53 59 31 45, f 05 53 59 19 44.

Domme: Place de la Halle, t 05 53 31 71 00, f 05 53 31 71 09 (*winter am only*).

Sports and Activities

Quercyland at Les Ondines near Souillac, t 05 65 37 33 51, offers bouncy castles, water slides and mini-golf (*open July–Aug daily 10am–10pm, weekends June and Sept*); plus canoe and kayak descents down the Dordogne from an hour to a week in length; also try Safraraid, t 05 65 30 74 47, for canoes/kayaks, from Lanzac or St-Sozy.

Where to Stay and Eat

St-Céré ✉ 46400

★★★France, 181 Av F. de-Maynard, t 05 65 38 02 16, f 05 65 38 02 98 (*moderate*). Cosy

in the **Forêt des Singes** (*open April–mid-Oct Wed and Sun pm only; July–early Sept daily 11–7*), only one of a dozen roadside attractions cashing in on the fame of Rocamadour. There's no place quite like it, a vertical cliff-dwellers' town where golden stone houses and chapels are piled on top of one another, while far, far below the little Alzou continues its work of aeons, cutting even deeper into the gorge. Thanks to its cult of the Black Virgin, Rocamadour has been one of France's top pilgrimage shrines since the 12th century. After falling into decay, it was given a Disney-style restoration, and the pilgrims have been replaced by tourists – arrive early to avoid the crowds.

The holy road from L'Hospitalet enters Rocamadour by way of the 13th-century **Porte du Figuier**, one of four gates that defended the village's one real road; you'll find the lift near the second gate, **Porte Salmon**. Beyond, the 15th-century Palais de la Couronnerie is now the **Hôtel de Ville** and tourist office. The street continues through another gate

modern rooms, a garden and pool, plus an elegant restaurant with delicious *marmite Quercynoise en croûte* (*menus 120–260F*). *Closed Nov–Easter.*

★★★Ric, 2km south in St-Vincent-du-Pendit, **t** 05 65 38 04 08, **f** 05 65 38 00 14 (*moderate*). Five rooms with marvellous views over St-Céré, and a beautiful pool. The pretty restaurant serves classic southwest cuisine with a creative touch (*menus 130–350F*). *Closed Mon out of season, Sat lunch, and Dec–Mar.*

★★Victor Hugo, 7 Av du Maquis, **t** 05 65 38 16 15, **f** 05 65 38 39 91 (*inexpensive*). Nine pretty rooms in a 16th-century inn in the centre of town, run by a transplanted Irishman, Monsieur Tom. Lovely *cuisine recherchée* (*menus 90–200F*). *Closed Mon, also Sun eve in winter.*

Rocamadour ✉ 46500

One advantage of staying in Rocamadour is seeing it without the coaches, but book.

★★★★Château de Roumégouse, **t** 05 65 33 63 81, **f** 05 65 33 71 18 (*expensive*). Six km east in Rignac, romantic Relais et Chateaux in a pretty park with a terrace and a well-known restaurant featuring traditional Quercy foie gras, truffles and seasonal dishes (*menus from 185F*). *Closed Tues out of season, and Dec–mid-April.*

★★★Beau Site, Rue R.-le-Preux, **t** 05 65 33 63 08, **f** 05 65 33 65 23 (*moderate*). The fanciest place in town, in the same family for five generations, in a medieval house. Its dining room, Jehan de Valon, serves exquisite food (*menus 115–320F*). *Closed mid-Nov–mid-Feb.*

★★Ste-Marie, Place des Senhals, **t** 05 65 33 63 07, **f** 05 65 33 69 08 (*inexpensive*). A simple family place in the heart of things; the restaurant is one of the best in town – leave room for dessert (*menus 76–200F*). *Closed mid-Oct–Easter.*

★★Lion d'Or, just beyond the Porte du Figuier, **t** 05 65 33 62 04, **f** 05 65 33 72 54 (*inexpensive*). About as old fashioned and traditional as it comes, with comfortable rooms and solid Périgord cuisine overlooking the Alzou gorge; *tartin de foie gras, foie gras frais, magret sauce aux crèpes...* (*menus 65–210F*).

Souillac ✉ 46200

★★★La Vieille Auberge, 1 Rue de la Recège, **t** 05 65 32 79 43, **f** 05 65 32 65 19 (*moderate*). A whiff of Louis XV by the river; and a pool, sauna, hammam and jacuzzi. The excellent restaurant serves dishes based on the recipes of a century ago, including mountains of foie gras but with a lighter touch (*menus 120–350F*).*Closed Jan–Mar Sun eve and Mon.*

★★★Les Granges Vieilles, **t** 05 65 37 80 92, **f** 05 65 37 08 18 (*moderate*). Large country house in a shaded park just outside town, on the D703 from Sarlat. Some of the rooms are elegant and spacious; all have views on to the park and there is a pool. Menus tending towards the regional, and you can eat on the patio (*menus 85–270F*).

★★Les Ambassadeurs, 12 Av de Général-de-Gaulle, **t** 05 65 32 78 36, **f** 05 65 32 72 70 (*inexpensive*). Elderly hotel with simple rooms, some en suite, and simply prepared

into the **Quartier du Coustalou**, the least restored part of the village, with jumbly houses and a fortified mill.

The Grand Escalier leads up via Place des Senhals, and Rocamadour's oldest street, Rue de la Mercerie, to a small square, the **Parvis de St-Amadour**, the centre of the holy city, where the pilgrim could visit seven churches just as in Rome, but in a much abbreviated space. These days only four are open all year; for the others you need to take the guided tour (*see* 'Tourist Information', above). Rocamadour's holy of holies, the Flamboyant Gothic **Chapelle Notre-Dame**, dates only from 1479, after a rock crashed off the cliff through the original sanctuary. Inside, darkened by candle smoke, the miraculous Black Virgin still holds court, the proof of her mystic power in the *ex-votos* and chains from pilgrim petitioners which fill the chapel. Above, the rusty sword in the stone cliff is the legendary Durandel, entrusted by Roland as he died at

but very good local dishes. Popular with the locals (*menus 85–195F*).

★★Auberge du Puits, Place du Puits, t 05 65 37 80 32, f 05 65 37 07 16. Wide choice of entrées, from tripe to trout, prepared in an old-fashioned way (*menus 85–275F*). *Closed Sun eve and Mon out of season.*

Sarlat ✉ 24200

★★★Relais de Moussidière, t 05 53 28 28 74, f 05 53 28 25 11 (*moderate*). Traditional stone manor house set on a cliff with simple, modern rooms, 40-acre landscaped park, a pool and duck ponds. Riding, golf and tennis nearby. *Closed Nov–Mar.*

★★★La Madeleine, 1 Place de la Petite Rigaudie, t 05 53 59 10 41, f 05 53 31 03 62 (*moderate*). Near the medieval centre, converted from a 19th-century town house; rooms are air-conditioned and soundproof and there's a private garage. Owned by a chef, the restaurant serves regional specialities – *civet d'oie* in vin de Cahors – and lighter, more modern dishes (*menus 115–215F*). *Closed Mon lunch except in July and Aug, and Jan–mid-Feb.*

★★★De Selves, 93 Av de Selves, t 05 53 31 50 00, f 05 53 31 23 53, *www.selves-sarlat.com* (*moderate*). Classy modern hotel with airy rooms in pastel colours, some with a terrace. Relaxing gardens and a pool. *Closed Jan.*

★★La Couleuvrine, 1 Place de la Bouquerie, t 05 53 59 27 80, f 05 53 31 26 83 (*inexpensive*). Unusual antique-furnished rooms in a tower in the 14th–18th-century ramparts. The restaurant prides itself on its market-fresh produce (*menus from 98F*). *Closed part of Jan.*

Pierre Henri Toulemon, 4 Rue Magnanat, t 05 53 31 26 60 (*inexpensive*). Up the steps through big oak doors, this *chambres d'hôte* bang in the middle of the old town is classified a historical monument. Very atmospheric.

Le Présidial, near the Place de la Liberté, t 05 53 28 92 47. Elegant dining room and large patio. Extravagant regional dishes such as *suprême de pigeonneau en croûte sauce aux truffes*, with a choice of French wines (*menus 115–195F*).

Chez Marc, 4 Rue Tourny, t 05 53 59 02 71. So covered in ivy you might not spot the name. Small and popular, serving regional food plus a little something: *civet de canard au vin de noix* and *magret de canard aux fruits rouges* (*menus 55–135F*). *Closed Sun.*

Domme ✉ 24250

★★★L'Esplanade, t 05 53 28 31 41, f 05 53 28 49 92 (*moderate*). Tranquil hotel with cosy rooms, some overlooking the Dordogne. Half-board is mandatory in season – but the restaurant, with a terrace, serves some of the richest food in Périgord, especially when asparagus is in season (*menus from 165F*; much more if you splurge with the truffles). *Closed Mon, and Nov–Feb.*

★★Relais du Chevalier, Grand Rue, t 05 53 28 33 88 (*inexpensive*). Eight comfortable rooms with exposed beams in 15th-century town house. *Closed Nov–Feb.*

La Porte del Bos, t 05 53 28 58 55 (*inexpensive*). B&B in the medieval centre, with en suite rooms, garden, pool and view. *Closed early Nov–Easter.*

Roncevalles to the Archangel Michael, who flung it here from the Pyrenees. A hairpin walk (or lift from the Parvis de St-Amadour) takes you up to the 14th-century **château** (*open April–Oct daily 8.30am–9pm; otherwise daily 9–6.30; adm*), offering a vertiginous view over Rocamadour.

Souillac: Dancing Isaiah and Banjo-strumming Automats

Back on the Dordogne, Souillac doesn't look like much, but its church of **Ste-Marie** makes it a mandatory stop to see one of the true jewels of the Midi. Ste-Marie is Romanesque at its most Roman, striving above all for monumental presence – best seen outside in the majestic apse. The interior is even better: a single, domed nave, graceful and strong. The surviving fragments of the portal have been reconstructed inside the main door. The wild scene on top, showing a fellow with some serious devil

Creamy Cabécou

When it comes to dining, Rocamadour is famous throughout the southwest for its creamy, flat cylinders of goat cheese, so special that they've been classified like wine: AOC *cabécou de Rocamadour*. Connoisseurs like them ripe, pungent, and coated with a tawny crust – the perfect accompaniment to a well-aged Cahors, at their very best between June and November. If you and French goat's cheese haven't been previously introduced, you may want to try a mild fresh white *cabécou* to start with, or have it grilled – somehow heat takes away some of the immediately goaty impact and leaves a warm, soft, distinct taste, delicious as a starter with salad.

troubles, represents *St Theophilus the Penitent*. Flanking the relief are the two figures without which no French portal would be complete: St Peter (with the keys) and St Paul (with the book). Outstanding as these reliefs are, the eye is inevitably drawn below to the **'dancing' Isaiah**. Poised on one foot, with stone draperies flowing, the composition is unlike anything else produced in the Middle Ages; a virtuoso display of careful precision and extreme stylization: studied and consistent, a vision of form that is the work of a true artist – one of the greatest between the Greeks and Donatello.

Souillac has acquired another attraction, the ambitious **Musée de l'Automate**, run in collaboration with the robotic experts of the Cité des Sciences de La Villette in Paris (*open Nov–Mar Wed–Sun 2–5; April–June and Sept–Oct daily 10–12 and 3–6 (exc Mon in April and May); July and Aug daily 10–7; adm*). Scores of mechanical dolls haunt the premises, and they have some modern robots to keep them company.

Sarlat-la-Canéda

Cocooned inside a clinking ring of 20th-century sprawl, this noble and golden Renaissance town is architecturally the foie gras of southwest France and a favourite location for filming swashbucklers. One architectural gem, the 16th-century **Hôtel de Maleville** (now the tourist office) has two distinct Renaissance façades – one French, one Italian. The French one overlooks elongated **Place de la Liberté**, Sarlat's favoured café stop; its northern extension is the **Place du Marché**, venue for Sarlat's prestigious late July–early August theatre festival, starring the Comédie Française. The narrow **Rue des Consuls** contains many magnificent hôtels; the **Hôtel Selve de Plamon** (Nos. 8–10) stands out – it's early Gothic on the ground floor, Flamboyant Gothic on the first and Renaissance on the second.

Sarlat's great oddity is the **Lanterne des Morts**, a stubby stone rocket built at the end of the 12th century; its original use has been forgotten. Below stretch the flying buttresses and bulb-topped steeple (locally known as the 'scarecrow') of the **Cathédrale St-Sacerdos**, completed in the dull 17th century; there's nothing particularly to recommend it apart from its spaciousness. Opposite the cathedral stands the most ornate town house in Sarlat, the **Hôtel de La Boétie** (1525), built by the father of the precocious Etienne de La Boétie, who was born here in 1530. La Boétie is principally remembered as Montaigne's perfect pal in the latter's beautiful *Essay on Friendship*. Richly ornamented mullioned windows dominate the upper three floors, squeezed

Les Mai

One last thing that may or may not be in Domme when you visit is a tall pine pole in Place des Halles, decorated with hoops and tricolores and a sign reading *Honneur à Notre Maire*; you may well spot similar poles in other villages or towns, or even next to private homes, honouring a boss, a newly married couple, or a newborn baby. They are called *les Mai*, or maypoles, and are erected at boozy confabs known as *la Plantation de Mai*. They are meant to rot away rather than ever be taken down. The Périgourdins have been planting *les Mai* ever since Gallo-Roman times, when a newly elected official would be honoured with a similar pole crowned with a garland. Since the Liberty Trees of the Revolution, they have taken on an added republican virtue.

between a vertiginously steep gable. The decoration reaches a curlicue frenzy in the dormer window, in frilly contrast with the sombre *lauzes* of the roof.

A 19th-century street, the **Traverse** cuts the wealthy Sarlat of aristocratic town houses from the steeper, popular neighbourhood to the west, where some alleys are scarcely wide enough to walk arm in arm. On the outskirts, the **Musée de l'Automobile** (*open Nov–early July and late Aug–Oct daily 2–6.30, Nov–Mar weekends only; most of July and Aug daily 10–7; adm*) has an accumulation of cars up to 1940, including the 1926 Le Mans winner, a Lorraine-Dietrich.

Domme: the 'Acropolis of Périgord'

Founded by Philippe the Bold in 1281, lovely, honey-hued Domme is a typical *bastide* – but one that totters on a steep cliff over the Dordogne. The **Porte des Tours** is the best preserved of its three gates, framed by two fat guard towers, but as with any *bastide*, the focal point is its market square, **Place de la Halle**. One side gives on to the **Belvedere de la Barre**, with panoramic views from Monfort to Beynac. The turreted, asymmetrical Governor's House (from the 1500s) is now the tourist office, where you can buy tickets for the **Grottes de Domme** (*open Mar–Oct daily 2–6; April–June and Sept daily 9.30–12 and 2–6, July and Aug daily 9.30–7; adm*) entered through the market in the middle of the square. Although the lower part of the cave was used as a refuge during the Hundred Years' War, the upper part, where fossilized bison and deer bones were found, was discovered only in 1954; beyond is a well-lit stalactite phantasmagoria that ends with a ride in a glass lift up the cliff.

The Central Dordogne

This pretty region has always been a major crossroads, once for merchants and armies, now for tourists; few of its fairytale castles were built for decoration.

La Roque-Gageac and a flurry of châteaux

Often called *the* most beautiful village in France, the warm stone houses and brown roofs of **La Roque-Gageac** are piled against the overhanging cliff so harmoniously that they hardly seem real. Facing the sunny south (the colours are especially intense at sunset), the village is sheltered enough to grow an exotic garden of cacti by the little church, set on a throne of rock. A few minutes away in **Vézac**, you can wander through some of the prettiest French gardens in the region, by the 17th-century riverside **Château Marqueyssac**, with over 150,000 ancient box trees in hedges on panoramic terraces (*park open mid-Nov–Jan daily 2–5; Feb–April and Oct–mid-Nov daily 10–6; May, June, and Sept daily 10–7; July and Aug daily 9–8*).

The overpowering **Château de Beynac** at Beynac-et-Cazenac soars high over the Dordogne (*open Dec–Feb daily 12–dusk; Mar–Sept daily 10–6; Oct–Nov daily 10–dusk; adm*). Partially wrecked when it was taken by Simon de Montfort in 1214, a monumental 17th-century stairway, a Grand Siècle salon and late 15th-century frescoes in the Oratory survive inside. Opposite Beynac, the powerful hulk of its longtime English nemesis, the **Château de Castelnaud** stands arrogantly on the cliffs at the confluence of the Dordogne and Céou. Its **Musée de la Guerre au Moyen Age** (*guided tours in French and English; open mid-Nov–Feb daily exc Sat 2–5; Mar, April and Oct–mid-Nov*

Getting Around

Trains on the Sarlat–Bordeaux line stop at Le Buisson, Bergerac and St-Émilion; Le Buisson is also on the main Périgueux–Agen line.

Activities

Flat-bottomed *gabares* in La Roque-Gageac offer hour-long tours of the cliffs and châteaux of the Dordogne, t 05 53 29 40 44 (*Easter–early Nov daily 10–6*); others depart from Beynac, t 05 53 28 51 15 (*in April, May and Oct only by reservation*). You can also float down the river in a canoe and get a bus lift back: contact Canoë-Dordogne, t 05 53 29 58 50, f 05 53 29 38 92. Or rise above it all in a balloon from La Roque-Gageac, with Mongolfière du Périgord, t 05 53 28 18 58, f 05 53 28 89 34.

Where to Stay and Eat

La Roque-Gageac ✉ 24250
**La Belle Etoile, t 05 53 29 51 44, f 05 53 29 45 63 (*inexpensive*). Modest but welcoming family hotel with a terrace and views of the river and village. Great food: *tatin de foie gras au jus d'agrumes* (*menus 125–200F*). Closed Mon and Nov–Easter.
** Périgord, t 05 53 28 36 55, f 05 53 28 38 73 (*inexpensive*). Huge house in large grounds outside the village in peaceful surroundings

with a pool, tennis and restaurant (*menus 90–250F*). *Closed mid-Dec–mid-Feb*.
La Ferme Fleurie, t 05 53 28 33 39 (*cheap*). Good B&B near the village, with a room sleeping three (*270F, with breakfast*). Open Easter–early Nov.
La Plume d'Oie, t 05 53 29 57 05, f 05 53 31 04 81. Modern, attractive restaurant overlooking the Dordogne, serving excellent, light renditions of Périgourdin specialities (*menus 195–295F*). There are also four pretty rooms to rent (*inexpensive*). Closed Mon, Sept–June Tues lunch, July and Aug Sat lunch, and mid-Jan–Feb.
Le Pres Gaillardou, t 05 53 59 67 89. Highly recommended, with a superb five-course menu, beginning with *amuse-gueules*, in a charming stone building, partially furnished with antiques (*menus from 110F*).

Trémolat ✉ 24510
**Le Vieux Logis, by the church, t 05 53 22 80 06, f 05 53 22 84 89 (*expensive*). Utterly sybaritic 17th-century manor with a stunning garden and pool. To quote a reader: 'This is the place that everyone should be compelled to go for at least one night and day before they say anything about France.' So there! The restaurant serves the best meals for miles around: heavenly *salade du terroir* and *langoustes*, with an excellent wine list (*menus 210–430F; reserve*). Closed Tues and Wed lunch.

daily 10–6; May, June and Sept daily 10–7; July and Aug daily 9–8; joint ticket available with Marqueyssac) fills the castle once again with catapults and crossbows, along with audio-visuals on warfare nearly a thousand years ago.

A wooded lane north of Castelnaud follows the river past the privately owned **Château de Fayrac**, built between the 14th and 17th centuries and romantically restored in the 19th. Further on, in its own hamlet, is Castelnaud's third château, **Les Milandes** (*open Jan–Mar and Oct–Dec daily 10–12 and 2–5; April, May and Sept daily 10–6; June–Aug daily 10–7; adm*), a Renaissance beauty which captured the imagination of the cabaret star Josephine Baker in the 1930s. At time the highest paid performer in Europe, she purchased Les Milandes and 600 acres, and used it to hide people wanted by the Nazis, earning a medal for her work in the Resistance. After the war she spent millions on its restoration, filled it with 13 adopted children of every race and creed, and hosted anti-racism conferences until she fell so deeply into debt that she had to sell Les Milandes in 1964. Today it is a shrine to her memory; if you're lucky, the Flamboyant Gothic Chapel where Josephine married may just be open.

Cadouin and Christ's Turban

In the 12th century, the **abbey** at Cadouin got hold of a precious relic that put it square on the pilgrimage map of France – the St Suaire, the cloth used to wrap the head of Christ, a lesser Shroud of Turin. In 1100 Hugues, brother of King Louis the Fat of France, purchased the cloth, and when he died he gave it to his confessor, who passed it on to a priest from Périgord, who returned home with it hidden in a vat of Communion wine. He could not help blabbing his secret, however, and it wasn't long before the monks at Cadouin got it off him. Pilgrims to Compostela poured in until the Hundred Years' War, when the monks deposited the holy relic in Toulouse's Eglise du Taur for safekeeping; it didn't return to Cadouin until 1456. In 1935 a scientific examination of the cloth showed it to be an 11th-century Egyptian weaving.

The **abbey church** (*open Mar, April and Oct–Dec daily 10–12.30 and 2–5.30, May, June and Sept till 6.30; July and Aug daily 10–7; Sept–April closed Tues*) was consecrated in 1154. The interior, with its three naves and domes, has been stripped naked to reveal the vigorous architecture in all its purity. The reliquary holding the St Suaire originally hung behind the altar; only the dangling chains remain. The Flamboyant Gothic **cloister** took so long to build that the west gallery is entirely Renaissance, with a hearty mix of sacred and profane sculpture.

Bergerac

Bergerac is a fine little city where swans swim in the Dordogne and a cluster of medieval, half-timbered houses basks by the old river port. In the 12th century it became a majoar crossroads, thanks to a bridge – at that time the only one on the river – and naturally evolved into a commercial city. The Bergeracois converted to Protestantism with gusto, and by the end of the 17th century, an estimated 40,000 inhabitants had emigrated to England and Holland. The city only revived at the end of the 19th century thanks to wine and the national gunpowder works.

And tobacco, which grows as well in southwest France as in Virginia. Bergerac is the home of the national Institut du Tabac and celebrates the much-maligned weed, first popularized in France by Catherine de' Medici who used it to cure her migraines, in the **National Tobacco Museum** (*open daily 10–12 and 2–6 exc Sun am and Mon; adm – but no smoking!*), in the handsome, turreted Maison Peyrarède in Place du Feu. It's full of curiosities that trace the evolution of snuff, pipes, cigars and cigarettes in Europe.

The picturesque 16th-century Cloître des Récollets serves as the **Maison des Vins** (*open Easter–mid-Oct daily 10.30–12.30 and 2–6, closed Sun; July and Aug daily 10–7*), headquarters of the regional wine council, stocking a wide selection of Bergerac vintages and other regional products. Tree-filled Place de La Myrpe contains the town's photo opportunity: a suitably nosed statue of swashbuckling **Cyrano de Bergerac**, although Rostand's poet cavalier never set foot in the town, and neither did his real-life inspiration, Savien Cyrano.

Getting Around

Bergerac's airport, Roumanières, lies 10km to the south (**t** 05 53 57 76 03) with three flights a day to Paris on Air Liberté. The station is on the Bordeaux–Sarlat line; to get on the Périgueux–Agen line change at Le Buisson.

Tourist Information

Bergerac: 97 Rue Neuve d'Argenson, **t** 05 53 57 03 11, **f** 05 53 61 11 04.

Where to Stay

Bergerac ✉ 24100

Moderate

***Le Bordeaux**, 38 Place Gambetta, **t** 05 53 57 12 83, **f** 05 53 57 72 14. Modern hotel in the centre, with a garden and pool; its restaurant serves unusual delicacies – the most upriver version of *lamproie à la bordelaise*, and *aiguillettes de canard au miel* (*menus 110–260F*).

***La Flambée**, 153 Av Pasteur, **t** 05 53 57 52 33, **f** 05 53 61 07 57. Welcoming family-run hotel outside the centre on the Périgueux road, with pool and tennis in a panoramic park. Kitchen noted for its delicious southwest specialities (*excellent menus 100–300F*). Closed Sun eve, Mon out of season, and Jan.

Inexpensive

****Le Family**, 3 Rue du Dragon, near Place du Marché Couvert, **t** 05 53 57 80 90. Central and friendly; parking available.

Eating Out

Moderate

Côté Dordogne, 17 Rue du Château, **t** 05 53 57 17 57. Probably the restaurant of the moment: beautiful 17th-century house with a wisteria-covered terrace and superb food: *morue fraîche à l'ail et olives* or *pigeonneau au foie poêlé* (*menus 100–160F*). Closed Sun pm and Mon.

L'Imparfait, 8 Rue des Fontaines, **t** 05 53 57 47 92. In the historic centre, serving fresh cuisine (*menus 90–190F*). Closed Sun and Mon out of season.

Le Poivre et Sel, 11 Rue de l'Ancien Port, **t** 05 53 27 02 30. Old, timbered and elegant restaurant with a pretty patio under huge parasols. Culinary delights include *gambas flambés au pastis* and a good choice of salads (*menus 78–195F*).

Château de Monbazillac, **t** 05 53 58 38 93. Outside the centre, a restaurant in the former *chais* of this château – a favourite for its fine classic cuisine, with a long wine list and summer dining on the terrace (*menus from 145F*). Closed Mon out of season.

Michel de Montaigne

The eldest of eight children raised by a Catholic father and Jewish mother, Montaigne learnt Latin as his first language and Greek as a child's game. He followed a legal career as a court counsellor in Périgueux and Bordeaux until 1572, when he despaired over the hypocrisy of the law and the horror of the St Bartholomew's Day Massacre, and retreated from the world (helped by a sizeable dowry from his wife) to his château above the Dordogne. He was 39 at the time, and vowed to spend the rest of his life doing nothing at all; instead, he wrote three volumes of *Essays*. The freest French thinker of the 16th century, Montaigne was also the most sceptical. The only sane response to the world, he reasoned, was to accept constant mutability and chaos with a smile. 'Que sais-je?' ('What do I know?') was his motto, and he had it inscribed over the château door.

High on a ridge, 6km south of Bergerac, the **Château de Monbazillac** (*open June–Sept daily 10–7; other times daily 10–12 and 2–5; closed Jan, and Mon in Nov–Mar, adm*) was erected in 1550 and – miraculously – essentially remains the same as the day it was built, undamaged and unimproved: a nice compromise between the necessities of defence and beauty. The grounds and two lower floors are open to the public, with displays on the château's famous golden wine and the noble rot that makes it so good.

The Château de Montaigne

Further down the Dordogne, swathed in vineyards next to the hamlet of St-Michel-de-Montaigne, stands the Château de Montaigne, where Michel Eyquem de Montaigne was born in 1533. In 1885 the château went up in flames, but the round tower where Montaigne wrote his celebrated *Essays* survived (*guided tours daily exc Mon and Tues 10–12 and 2–5.30; July and Aug daily 10–6.30; closed Jan and early Feb; adm*). On the top floor is the philosopher's famous inner sanctum, a library, where he could sit at his desk surrounded by bookshelves and windows; the beams still bear the Greek and Latin maxims Montaigne liked to ponder.

St-Emilion

Set in a natural amphitheatre surrounded by vines, St-Emilion is a gem, a lovely town mellowed to the colour of old piano keys. Its lanes, called *tetres*, are so steep that handrails have been installed down their centres. The town's greatest secrets are kept underground – not only the ruby nectar in its cellars, but Europe's largest subterranean church. Four of these secrets can only be seen on the tourist office's guided tour (*see* box, right). If you're staying the night, save the tour of the town walls for dusk, when the views are at their most romantic.

The ruined Romanesque **Cloître des Cordeliers** (*open daily 10–12 and 2–6.30*) was built in 1383 by the Franciscans. Note the carving of two snakes entering a jar in the adjacent chapel – a symbol that goes back to the ancient Greeks and which the friars must have copied from the Eglise Monolithe, where it appears twice. Further up, **Place du Marché** is a magnificent urbane stage set, where cafés are shaded by a Liberty Tree planted in 1848.

Getting Around

There are two railway stations near St-Émilion, 2km away in the countryside, on the Bordeaux–Bergerac–Sarlat line, and Libourne, 7km away, on the Bordeaux–Paris TGV line. Several Citram buses link it daily to Bordeaux and Libourne, t 05 56 43 68 43.

Tourist Information

St-Emilion: Place des Créneaux, t 05 57 55 28 28, f 05 57 55 28 29, *www.st-emilion-tourism.com*. The place to book a tour of the Église Monolithe, the Chapelle de la Trinité, the catacombs and the Grotte de l'Ermitage *Open daily 9.30–12.30 and 1.45–6; July and Aug 9.30–8.*

Where to Stay

St-Émilion ✉ 33330
Don't expect to find any bargains.

Luxury
★★★★**Château Grand-Barrail**, Route de Libourne, t 05 57 55 37 00, f 05 57 55 37 49 (950–3200F). Very exclusive, with attitudes to match. Good restaurant (*lunch menu 180F; eves more*). *Closed Feb.*

Expensive
★★★★**Hostellerie de Plaisance**, Place du Clocher, t 05 57 55 07 55, f 05 57 74 41 11. Handsome stone building housing the most luxurious hotel in town, and the only one with facilities for the disabled; it has an elegant gourmet restaurant and terrace featuring the likes of *langoustines royales* and *mignons de bœuf aux girolles* (*good-value menus from 150F*). *Closed Jan.*

Moderate
★★★**Palais Cardinal**, Place du 11 Novembre 1918, t 05 57 24 72 39, f 05 57 74 47 54. Stately family-run hotel with small but handsome rooms, and a heated pool; ask for a room overlooking the lovely garden terrace. *Closed Dec–Feb.*

★★★**Le Logis des Remparts**, 18 Rue Guadet, t 05 57 24 70 43, f 05 57 74 47 44. Sweet and pretty, with a little inner courtyard and hospitable staff.

Château de Roques, in Lussac, t 05 57 74 55 69, f 05 57 74 58 80. On the D21 on the road to St-Médard. B&B amid the vineyards with copious country cooking (*around 110F*), bikes to rent and free wine-tasting. *Closed Jan.*

Inexpensive
★★**Auberge de la Commanderie**, Rue des Cordeliers, t 05 57 24 70 19, f 05 57 74 44 53. 18 rooms on a pretty street, the best overlooking the garden and heated pool.

Eating Out

Expensive–Moderate
Francis Goullée, 27 Rue Guadet, t 05 57 24 70 49. Taste-packed Rabelaisian cuisine (*menus 90–240F*). *Closed Sun eve and Mon and late Nov–mid-Dec.*

Le Tertre, on Tertre de la Tente, t 05 57 74 46 33. Broad range of regional dishes (*menus 115–260F*). *Closed Tues in summer, Mon and Tues out of season.*

Cheap
L'Envers du Décor, Rue du Clocher, t 05 57 74 48 31. Excellent value wine bar with a terrace, where you can try a wide variety of local labels by the glass, with a snack or light meal (*c. 100F*). *Closed weekends out of season.*

La Ferme Auberge du Cros Figeac, t 05 57 24 76 32. In a lovely vineyard setting on the road to Libourne: exquisite meats grilled over vines, and a memorable warm foie gras with apple (*menus from 80F*). Book.

Built into the flank of the cliff here is the strange **Eglise Monolithe**, started by the Benedictines in the 8th century; when they had excavated a cavity measuring 124 by 66ft in the 11th century, they gave it up to construct the Collégiale. It is a primitive, sombre and uncanny place, its nave supported by ten rough, ill-aligned pillars. The only decoration that remains are bas-reliefs: four winged angels, signs of the zodiac, and a dedicatory inscription. Bell ropes from the original bell tower hung through the hole in the ceiling.

Next door is the round **Chapelle de la Trinité**, built in the 13th century by Augustinian monks and converted into a coopery during the Revolution; wall paintings between the ribs of the apse have recently been restored. In the adjacent 8th-century **catacombs** you can make out the engraved figures of three corpses with upraised arms, weird zombies symbolic of the Resurrection. Bones were deposited through the funnel-like cupola connecting the catacombs with the cemetery. The **Grotte de l'Ermitage**, the cave of the hermit Emilion, was reshaped over the centuries into a chapel. The cave's spring has been worshipped since pagan times, and is especially good for afflictions of the eye; the story also goes that any young woman who can drop two hairpins into the water in the form of a cross will surely be married within the year.

St-Emilion's landmark 11th–15th-century **bell tower** rises up 173ft from Place des Créneaux; for a small fee you can climb up for a superb view of the entire town (if it's closed, the tourist office has the key). Here, too, is the entrance to the **Collégiale**, a hotchpotch begun in 1110; in the choir are 15th-century stalls and the treasure, and Emilion's saintly relics. From the tourist office you can enter the pretty twin-columned Gothic **Cloître de la Collégiale**. There are more grand views from the top of the austere Norman **Tour du Roi** (*open June–Sept daily 10.30–12.45 and 2.15–8.30; adm*), all that remains of the castle built by Henry III (*c.* 1237).

Then there's the **wine**. No one can really explain why St-Emilion is so good, except that it has been subject to the strictest quality control in France for centuries. The **Maison du Vin**, Place Pierre-Meyrat (*t 05 57 55 50 55*), and the tourist office have booklets on the *chais* open for visits – and how much you'll pay for a tasting. Another alternative is to take one of the tourist office's tours (*June–Sept; English translation available*).

Bordeaux

Bordeaux is both terribly grand and terribly shabby and monotonous, a mercantile city that has lost its port, a city of long flat vistas tinted in a thousand nuances of white, from golden cream to unwashed tennis socks. Bordeaux is Gothic and 18th-century, splenetic, nostalgic and funky. Most of the city as you see it today was begun in the 18th century, when Bordeaux's *intendants* started demolishing its poky, crowded medieval streets to replace them with the Place Royale (now Place de la Bourse) and other new squares, wide *cours* or *allées* planted with trees to link them, and the first public gardens; to adorn them, 5,000 new buildings went up, including the riverfront Grande Façade. By the beginning of the Revolution, Bordeaux was the third city in France, and one of the most cosmopolitan, with a population of over 100,000 and close trading contacts with the new United States.

During and immediately after Napoleon, Bordeaux hit one of its low ebbs and – although its first-ever bridge over the Garonne was built in 1822, its quays were modernized and it had one of the first railways in France (1841) – little new industry came its way. However, Bordeaux still managed to spread; these days the 220,000 Bordelais have the dubious honour of taking up more room per capita than any other city dwellers in France. Even the vineyards fell victim – today you'll find some of the most august wine châteaux totally immersed in sprawl.

The South Side of Town: Ste-Croix and St-Michel

The first monuments that beckon in this once busy medieval but now genteelly dilapidated neighbourhood are in the vicinity of the former monastery church of **Ste-Croix**. Built in the 12th century, this once had a remarkably exuberant Old Curiosity Shop of a façade that was sadly entrusted in 1860 to Paul Abadie who, full of the destructive self-confidence of his time, completely dismantled it and put it back together all wrong. The south tower, portal, figures of Avarice and Luxury, and some carved capitals in the transept survived the Abadie touch; the relics in the parish chapel were reputed in the Middle Ages to cure madness.

Since Charlemagne's day, a church has stood at the site of **St-Michel**, in what is now a lively Portuguese–North African neighbourhood. A morning flea market takes place under its 15th-century detached bell tower, the 'arrow' or **Flêche**, at 377ft the highest monument in southwest France. Grimy, Flamboyant Gothic St-Michel was a product of Bordeaux's medieval prosperity, largely built by the city's guilds. It is missing one of its best features – the stained glass, blasted away by Allied bombers in the last war. The chapels furnished by the guilds contain the best art, most of it from the 15th century. On the river near St-Michel, the **Porte des Salinières**, the 'salt' gate (1755), overlooks the **Pont de Pierre**, the oldest of Bordeaux's bridges, built in 1842 and prettily lit at night by a necklace of street lamps.

From here busy Cours Victor Hugo will take you to the bustling heart of Bordeaux, past the 14th-century belled gate built under the reign of the Black Prince, the **Grosse Cloche** to pedestrian-only **Rue Ste-Catherine**, the city's main shopping street since Roman times, and often swarming with bargain-hunters; if you continue along Cours Victor Hugo you'll come to the Musée d'Aquitaine.

Musée d'Aquitaine

20 Cours Pasteur; open daily exc Mon and hols 11–6; adm.

One of the most compelling museums in southwest France, its subject is the history of Aquitaine, and one of its first works is the mysterious 25,000-year-old bas-relief of the *Venus with a Horn* from Laussel in the Dordogne. The excellent Gallo-Roman section has coins, mosaics, sculptures (note the fragment of a highly stylized relief of horses pounding through water) and a fascinating set of reliefs from everyday life in ancient Burdigala. Further on is a legless but still impressive bronze

Bordeaux

RUE CROIX DE SEGUEY

RUE DE SEGUEY

RUE DE FONDAUDEGE

Jardin Botanique

Musée d'Histoire Naturelle

Jardin Public

PLACE DU CH. DE MARS

Cité Mondiale du Vin

Temple

Hôtel Fenwick

RUE NOTRE DAME

X. ARNOZAN

COURS

Entrepôt Lainé (Musée d'Art Contemporain)

RUE FERRERE

ALLEES DE CHARTRES

QUAI DES CHARTRONS

to C Col

Palais Gallien

RUE E.

RUE DOCTEUR BARRAUD

FOURCAND

RUE DE L'ABBE DE L'EPEE

RUE R. PEREIRE

RUE TURENNE

RUE DU PALAIS GALLIEN

RUE THIAC

RUE CASTEJA

St-Seurin

PLACE DES MARTYRS DE LA RESISTANCE

Colonnes

Rostrales

ALLEES DE BRISTOL

Esplanade des Quinconces

Monument aux Girondins

QUAI LOUIS XVIII

QUAI

COURS DE VERDUN

COURS MAR. FOCH

Bus Station

PLACE DE TOURNY

COURS DE TOURNON

RUE HUGUERIE

PLACE DES QUINCONCES

RUE SEZE

ALLEES DE TOURNY

ALLEES D'ORLEANS

Tourist Information

RUE ESPRIT DES LOIS

Grand Théâtre

COURS DU 30 JUILLET

Maison du Vin de Bordeaux

MARCHE DES GRANDS HOMMES

R. BUFFON

RUE CLEMENCEAU

PLACE DU CHAPELET

PLACE DE LA COMEDIE

COURS DU CHAPEAU-ROUGE

Notre Dame

COURS DE L'INTENDANCE

DAURADE

R. M. RUE

Palais de la Bourse

PLACE DE LA BOURSE

Musée des Douanes

QUAI DE LA DOUANE

RUE JUDAIQUE

RUE MONTESQUIEU

PLACE GAMBETTA

Porte Dijeaux

PORTE DE GRASSI

RUE DE GRASSI

RUE DES PILLIERS DE TUTELLE

RUE ST-REMI

RUE PARL.

RUE P. MARGAUX

PLACE DU PARLEMENT

PLACE ST PIERRE

RUE DE LA DEVISE

RUE BAHUTIERS

RICHELIEU

St-Pierre

Porte de Cailhau

PLACE DU PALAIS

RUE GEORGES BONNAC

RUE DU CHATEAU D'EAU

Post Office

PLACE DU COL. RAYNAL

RUE ST-SERNIN

RUE BOUFFARD

Musée des Arts Décoratifs

RUE VITAL - CARLES

R. MOLIERE

Centre National Jean Moulin

RUE DES 3 CONILS

RUE MAUCOUDINAT

PLACE C. JULLIAN

RUE DU PAS-ST-GEORGES

Galerie des Beaux-Arts

RUE CLAUDE BONNIER

Musée des Beaux-Arts

RUE MONTBAZON

Hôtel de Ville

Palais Rohan

PLACE PEY. BERLAND

Tower

RUE DU LOUP

COURS D'ALSACE ET LORRAINE

Nouveau Quartier Mériadeck

RUE JEAN FLEURET

PLACE ROHAN

Cathédrale St-André

RUE DUBERGIER

RUE DES AYRES

RUE STE-CATHERINE

RUE ST-JAMES

COURS MARECHAL JUIN

RUE BELLEVILLE

RUE DE BELFORT

COURS D'ALBRET

RUE DES FRERES BONIE

RUE MAR. JOFFRE

Palais de Justice

RUE DU CDT

RUE DE CURSOL

Musée d'Aquitaine

Grande Cloche

St-Eloi

COURS VICTOR HUGO

RUE DU MIRAIL

RUE ST-FRA

RUE DE BELFORT

RUE JEAN FLEURET

RUE DE ST-GENES

RUE J. BURGUET

RUE ARNOULD

Ste-Eulalie

RUE P.-L. LANDE

RUE PASTEUR

RUE STE-CATHERINE

RUE LEYTEIRE

RUE BERG

RUE FRANCOIS DE SOURDIS

COURS ARISTIDE BRIAND

Bourse du Travail

Porte d'Aquitaine

PLACE DE LA VICTOIRE

Musée Ethnographique

COURS DE L'ARGONNE

RUE KLEBER

RUE DE PESSAC

N

250 metres
250 yards

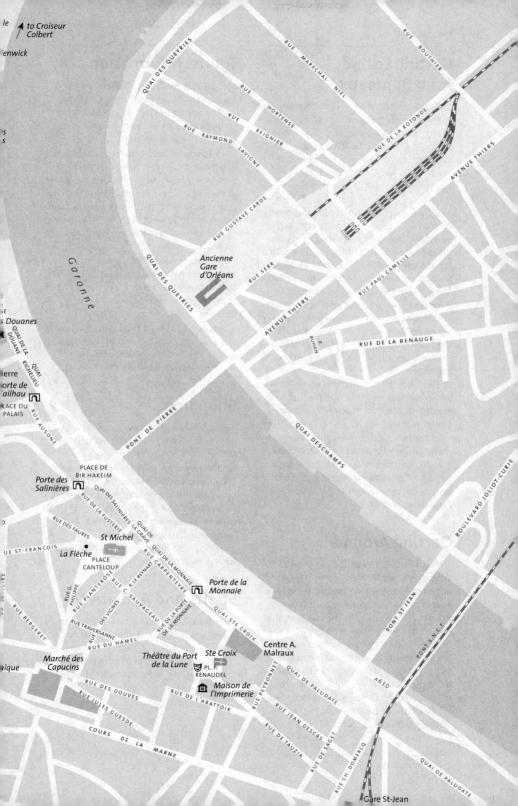

Getting to and from Bordeaux

Bordeaux International Airport is 12km west of the centre at Mérignac, t 05 56 34 50 50. A shuttle bus links the airport to the railway station, the tourist office (Place Gambetta: stop M13), and the Barrière Judaïque approximately every half-hour from 5.25am, weekends 8.45am. A taxi into the centre costs 100–180F.

All trains use Bordeaux St-Jean station in Rue Charles-Domerq, t 08 36 35 35 35. TGVs from Paris-Montparnasse take 3hrs; regular trains from Paris-Austerlitz take 4½hrs. Other connections are Périgueux; Sarlat by way of St-Emilion and Bergerac; Tarbes by way of Orthez, Pau and Lourdes; TGVs or regular trains to Hendaye by way of Dax, Bayonne, Biarritz and St-Jean-de-Luz, or to Toulouse (2hrs) by way of Agen and Montauban, or 3hrs by way of Moissac. Local lines run to Mont-de-Marsan, Pointe de Grave and, roughly once an hour, to Arcachon.

The station for Citram buses serving most towns and villages in the Gironde is at Allée des Chartres, just off Place des Quinconces, t 05 56 81 16 82.

Bordeaux has a ring road called the *rocade*, making it sometimes easier to circumvent it than to penetrate to its centre. There are a number of carparks in the centre, and near the station; the easiest place to find a spot is in Place des Quinconces.

Getting Around

The city's CGFTE buses (t 05 57 57 88 88 for information) are frequent, convenient and huge, prowling the long straight streets like links of metal sausages. Buy blocks of 10 tickets at kiosks or pay on the bus; from the station, bus no.7 will take you to Place Gambetta and the Chartrons; bus no.1 follows the river. Bus maps are free at the tourist office or railway station. You can hire bikes at the station. Cabbies are not allowed to cruise in Bordeaux, but there are taxi ranks in key locations, and 24-hour ranks at the railway station and Place Gambetta.

Tourist Information

Bordeaux: 12 Cours du 30-Juillet, t 05 56 00 66 00, f 05 56 00 66 01; there's a branch office open June–Sept in Gare St-Jean, t 05 56 91 64 70; www.bordeaux-tourisme.com.

The tourist office organises an introduction to wine tasting at the Maison du Vin de Bordeaux, 3 Cours du 30 Juillet, on the corner of Place de la Comédie (2hrs, cheese and charcuterie included, 125F); they also run regular excursions to some of the most famous vineyards with tastings – the only way to get into most of them.

If you plan to do lots of sightseeing, you can save money with their Bordeaux Découverte card, entitling the bearer to discounts in the city's museums, excursions and some theatres.

If you spend at least two nights in a two- to four-star hotel, you can also get a discount, as well as a guided tour of Bordeaux and the vineyards (Forfait Bordeaux Découverte).

Shopping

Bordeaux is a great town for antiques, with a bric-a-brac antiques market in Place St-Michel (daily exc Sat) and shops on Rue Bouffard, by the Musée des Arts Décoratifs, and Rue Notre-Dame in the Chartrons; English books are available at Bradley's Bookshop, 8 Cours Albret. One of the last remaining shops of its kind in France, founded in 1814, Au Sanglier de Russie, 67 Cours d'Alsace et Lorraine, sells a huge range of exotic brushes for any imaginable use.

Sports and Activities

Bordeaux's beloved rugby team plays in Bègles just to the south, in the Stade André Moga, t 05 56 85 94 01; the first division Girondins football team plays in the Art Deco Stade Municipal, in Bd du Maréchal Leclerc, t 05 56 93 25 83.

Where to Stay

Expensive

★★★Ste Catherine, 27 Rue du Parlement, **t** 05 56 81 95 12, **f** 05 56 44 50 51. In a handsomely restored 18th-century *hôtel* near the Grand Théâtre, the most comfortable hotel in its class, with exceptionally nice rooms.

★★★★Burdigala, 115 Rue Georges-Bonnac, **t** 05 56 90 16 16, **f** 05 56 93 15 06. Luxury and personality in the heart of town, with elegant, air-conditioned rooms individually styled with wood, stone and marble.

★★★Le Majestic, between the Grand Théâtre and Place des Quinconces, **t** 05 56 52 60 44, **f** 05 56 79 26 70. Dead central with comfortable air-conditioned rooms, an inner garden and garage, but no restaurant.

Moderate

★★★Le Bayonne Etche-Ona, 4 and 11 Rue Martignac, **t** 05 56 48 00 88, **f** 05 56 48 41 60. 18th-century hotel on the corner of the Allées de Tourny. Contemporary décor.

★★★Royal Médoc, 3 Rue Sèze (just off Place Tourny), **t** 05 56 81 72 42, **f** 05 56 48 98 00. Comfortable modern rooms and a garage.

★★★De la Presse, 6–8 Rue Porte-Dijeaux, **t** 05 56 48 53 88, **f** 05 56 01 05 82. Very central, with good sound proofing and parking nearby. Simply decorated, well-equipped rooms.

Inexpensive

★★Les Quatre Sœurs, 6 Cours 30-Juillet (near the Quinconces), **t** 05 57 81 19 20, **f** 05 56 01 04 28. Where Richard Wagner slept, before he was run out of town for dallying with the wife of a local politician; cosy rooms, overlooking the street or courtyard.

★★Le Continental, 10 Rue Montesquieu, **t** 05 56 52 66 00, **f** 05 56 52 77 97, *www.hotel-le-continental.com*. Elegant hotel on a central pedestrianized street.

★★Notre Dame, 36 Rue Notre-Dame, **t** 05 56 52 88 24, **f** 05 56 79 12 67. Pretty little hotel in a 19th-century building in the Chartrons.

★★La Tour Intendance, 16 Rue Vieille-Tour, **t** 05 56 81 46 27, **f** 05 56 81 60 90. Centrally located, on a pedestrian-only lane off Cours de l'Intendance; simple and sweet and run by two friendly women; parking available.

Cheap

★Studio, 26 Rue Huguerie, near the bus depot off Place du Tourny, **t** 05 56 48 00 14, **f** 05 56 81 25 71. Larger rooms (with ensuite shower).

Amboise, 22 Rue Vieille-Tour (near Place Gambetta), **t** 05 56 81 62 67. One of the best of the cheaper options.

Boulan, 28 Rue Boulan, **t** 05 56 52 23 62, **f** 05 56 44 91 65. Another good cheap option, near the cathedral.

Eating Out

Unlike most folks, who pick a bottle to go with their meal, the Bordelais tend to choose a vintage first, then create a menu that will enhance the wine. The wide choice of Bordeaux specialities range from the famous *entrecôte à la bordelaise* to the more rarefied pleasures of lamprey, which is 'in season' in April and May. Prices here have remained reasonable; to dine as well in Paris or along the Côte d'Azur would cost an arm and a leg. Note that you could starve in August or on Sundays, when the city's beaneries shut down as tight as a clam.

Luxury–Expensive

Le Chapon Fin, 5 Rue Montesquieu, **t** 05 56 79 10 10. The oldest restaurant in Bordeaux (since 1800) and one of the best. Sarah Bernhardt and Edward VII stopped in whenever they were in town. Its sumptuous rococo décor and inner garden are a perfect match for the *marbès de ris de veau et foie gras*, *marmite* of fish and crustaceans with *pistou* – Provençal pesto – or the celebrated lobster gazpacho; long lists of *grands crus* (*lunch menu 170F, others up to 440F*). *Closed Sun and Mon.*

Expensive

Jean Ramet, 7 Place Jean-Jaurès, **t** 05 56 44 12 51. One of Bordeaux's classiest restaurants where chef Ramet prepares both old-fashioned (braised veal knuckle) and original dishes (*gratin de figues*) to the delight of his fashionable customers (*menus 170–350F*). *Closed Sat lunch, Sun and mid-Aug.*

Expensive–Moderate

La Chamade, 20 Rue des Piliers de Tutelle, **t** 05 56 48 13 74. Large restaurant in a 17th-century hôtel – downstairs under the vaulted ceiling or on an open balcony. Emphasis on seasonal products, and traditional and regional fare; foie gras all year. Large wine selection (*menus 100–350F*).

La Tupina, 6 Rue Porte-de-la-Monnaie, near St-Michel, **t** 05 56 91 56 37. Bailiwick of Jean-Pierre Xiradakis, master of bringing out the true tastes of ingredients, and a good place to fill up on hearty delights like *émincé de canard* with shallots (*lunch menu 100F, dinner up to 280F*).

Didier Gelineau, 26 Rue du Pas St-Georges, **t** 05 56 52 84 25. Charming restaurant offering haute cuisine at affordable prices: try the breaded lamb chops with truffles (*menus 130–300F*). *Closed Sat lunch and Sun, and two weeks in Aug.*

Moderate

L'Alhambra, 111 bis Rue Judaïque, **t** 05 56 96 06 91. For a delicious beef fillet with a creamy mustard sauce or poached pineapple with kirsch sorbet (*menus lunch 110F, dinner 100 and 220F*). *Closed Sat lunch and Sun.*

Chez Philippe, 1 Place du Parlement, **t** 05 56 81 83 15. Fish-lovers come to worship here (*menus lunch 100F, dinner 180F*). *Closed Sun, Mon and Aug.*

Gravelier, 114 Cours Verdun, in the Chartrons, **t** 05 56 48 17 15. Very toothsome cuisine, especially seafood, prepared with an exotic touch: couscous with tuna and spices, or St-Pierre with ginger (*110F lunch menu, others 145 and 195F*). *Closed Sat lunch and Sun and half of Aug.*

Restaurant de Fromages Baud et Millet, 19 Rue Huguerie, **t** 05 56 79 05 77. Offers 950 wines from around the world to go with its 200 types of farm cheese and *raclettes* (*menus from 110F*). *Closed Sun.*

Moderate–Cheap

Le Bistro du Sommelier, 163 Rue Georges-Bonnac, **t** 05 56 96 71 78. Simple meals and a wide array of bottles (*menus 80–128F*). *Closed Sat lunch and Sun.*

Le Café Gourmand, 3 Rue Buffon, **t** 05 56 79 23 85. Elegant *bistrot* with a menu for midday and evening: *aiguillettes de canard aux pêches* and *moussaka d'agneau à la coriande fraîche*. The desserts are yummy (*lunch menus from 90F, dinner from 140F*). *Closed Sun.*

Le Bistrot de la Port de la Lune, 59 Quai Paludate, **t** 05 56 49 15 55. A haven for jazz lovers near the train station, with simple but tasty fare and it swings until 2am (*menus 106F, 150F with wine*).

Cheap

La Boite á Huîtres, 36 Cours du Chapeau Rouge, **t** 05 56 81 64 97. Oysters by the 6, 9 or dozen, from Brittany, Ile d'Oléron or locally raised. (Mostly à la carte, about 50F for 6; there are a few other things to choose from too).

La Rital, 3 Rue des Faussets, **t** 05 56 48 16 69. Delicious fresh pasta and home-made desserts (*menus 50–98F*). *Closed weekends and the first two weeks in Sept.*

Entertainment and Nightlife

The premier stage remains Victor Louis' Grand Théâtre, Place de la Comédie, box office **t** 05 56 48 58 54 (*open 11–6; closed Sun and hols*), followed by the Théâtre Femina, 8 Rue de Grassi, box office **t** 05 56 52 58 84. The Orchestre National Bordeaux Aquitaine frequently performs in the Palais des Sports, Place de la Ferme Richemont, **t** 05 56 79 39 61. The ultramodern Espace Culturel du Pin Galant, out at Mérignac due west of Bordeaux, **t** 05 56 97 82 82, puts on a full calendar of performances. Of Bordeaux's cinemas, the Trianon Jean Vigo, Rue Franklin, **t** 05 56 44 35 17, is the most likely to show something good in VO; also try UGC, 20 Rue Judaïque, **t** 05 56 44 02 60.

To top off a late night in Bordeaux, finish up at the Marché des Capuchins near St-Michel for a bowl of onion soup with the workers unloading the produce. Bars here open from 1 to 5am; try Le P'tit Déj, 8 Place des Capucins.

Hercules, and a room dedicated to finds from a mithraeum discovered in 1982 during the construction of a car park in Cours Victor-Hugo: in the 2nd and 3rd century, Mithraism, an all-male, monotheistic religion from the east, posed serious competition to Christianity. A statue shows the birth of Mithras, rising from earth with the cosmic globe in one hand and a knife to slay bulls in the other; there are statues of Cautes and Cautopatès, his two companions in Persian costumes, and a rare *Leontocéphale*, a lion-headed man holding keys, his legs entwined with chicken-headed snakes.

Cathédrale St-André

Bordeaux's great Gothic cathedral was built under English rule between the 13th and 15th centuries. Like St-Michel, it has a lofty detached bell tower, the **Tour Pey-Berland** (*open June–Sept daily 10–6.30, otherwise daily 10–12.30 and 2–5.30; closed Mon and public hols; adm*), which was used as a lead ball factory from 1793 until 1850, when it was repurchased by the archbishop, truncated and crowned with a shiny Notre-Dame-de-Aquitaine. The views over Bordeaux are superb. The cathedral itself is supported by an intricate web of buttresses; its west front, originally part of the city wall, is strikingly bare. A fine 14th-century tympanum with the *Last Supper* crowns the north transept door; the nearby Porte Royale (used by visiting kings and dignitaries) has another, with a rhythmic *Last Judgement*. The south portal, dedicated to the Virgin, lost its tympanum to make room for carts when the church was converted into a feed store during the Revolution. As in the Middle Ages, the doors are usually left wide open, as a pedestrian shortcut; the single nave is nearly as long and wide as Notre-Dame (410 by 145ft).

Just north of the cathedral, the **Centre National Jean Moulin** (*open Tues–Fri 11–6, weekends 2–6*) contains a collection devoted to the Occupation, Resistance and Deportation, from posters to an ingenious folding motorcycle (part of a parachute drop to the Resistance). Upstairs, the office of the courageous resistance leader Jean Moulin has been reconstructed.

Musée des Beaux-Arts and Musée des Arts Décoratifs

20 Cours d'Albret; open daily exc Tues and hols 11–6; adm, free the first Sun of each month.

Most of the large and luxurious **Palais Rohan** (1770s) holds Bordeaux city hall (*guided tours Wed 2.30*), but one wing contains paintings by artists rarely seen in French provincial museums – Titian, Perugino, Van Dyck, Rubens, Reynolds, Ruysdael, Chardin, Delacroix, Boudin, Magnasco, and Bordeaux native Odilon Redon (1840–1916), introspective precursor of the Surrealists. Two other native sons are also represented: Albert Marquet (1875–1947), a fellow student of Matisse and co-founder of Fauvism who went on to paint simple landscapes, and André Lhote (1885–1962), represented by his hallmark colourful, geometric compositions on various planes. There is also a selection of minor paintings by major 20th-century artists – Matisse, Bonnard, Renoir and Seurat.

Behind the museum is the **Nouveau Quartier Mériadeck**, the largest single urban renovation scheme in France. Seven hectares were set aside for greenery and fountains, and the buildings facing this central mall were designed in cruciforms to spare pedestrians the sight of the plain-jane skyscraper. Most of Mériadeck is occupied by government bureaucracies, and it shrivels to a desert after dark. It did, however, earn an environmental gold star as the first major project in Europe to make large-scale use of geothermal heating (1981).

Nearby the excellent **Musée des Arts Décoratifs** (*39 Rue Bouffard; open daily exc Tues and hols 11–6, weekends 2–6; adm, free the first Sun of each month*) has a perfect home in a neoclassical *hôtel particulier* (1779), with fine furniture, wallpaper, ceramics, paintings, gold and silverwork, glass, jewellery, and costumes. In summer, breakfast, brunch and lunch are served in the elegant courtyard.

St-Seurin

Bordeaux's oldest church, founded by the city's 5th-century bishop Severinus, still stands, although in an often remodelled state (*open daily 8–12 and 2–6.30*). The 14th-century porch with lavish sculptures survives, as does, rather unusually, an 11th-century porch, hidden behind the undistinguished façade of 1828. Inside, a 7th-century sarcophagus does duty as an altar in the Chapelle St-Etienne, and there is a beautiful 15th-century alabaster retable in the Chapelle of Notre-Dame-de-la Rose and 14 alabaster panels in the choir. Note, too, the magnificent 15th-century episcopal throne, curiously made of stone imitating wood, and the sculpted choir stalls. The **crypt** (you may have to ask the sacristan to open it) holds a collection of 6th- and 7th-century treasures; excavations have revealed the 4th-century **Palaeo-Christian crypt** underneath, with sarcophogi and frescoes (*guided tours June–Sept daily 3–7; adm*).

Quartier St-Pierre

From the 3rd to the 12th century, St-Pierre was a separate walled quarter outside Bordeaux, built around the Palais de l'Ombrière, home of the dukes of Aquitaine and kings of England, of which only the **Porte Cailhau** (*open June–Sept daily 3–7; adm*) survives, overlooking the river with its asymmetrical turrets and tower. From here, you can see the 18th-century **Grande Façade** project that created a kilometre of homogenous architecture from Cours du Chapeau Rouge to Porte de la Monnaie, a row of pale stone houses, with arcades and *mascarons*, topped by two floors of large windows and mansard roofs with dormers.

The presence of the Parlement from the 15th century on led to the construction of stately 18th-century *hôtels particuliers*. You can see the best of them by walking straight through Porte Cailhau to Rue du Loup, crossing Rue Ste-Catherine, and turning right into Rue de Cheverus. From here turn up Rue Poquelin-Molière, find Rue Grassi, and turn right into Rue St-Rémi, which leads into Bordeaux's neoclassical showcase, the **Place de la Bourse**. In the centre a fountain of the Three Graces (1864) holds court between the Palais de la Bourse (now the Chamber of Commerce) and the Hôtel des Douanes, which must be the most grandiose customs house in the world, now home to the **Musée des Douanes** (*open daily 10–6, closed Mon; adm*).

The Golden Triangle

Bordeaux's Golden Triangle of good taste and luxury shops is formed by Cours de l'Intendance, Cours Georges-Clemenceau and Allées de Tourny. Setting the tone is the lavishly Baroque **Notre-Dame** (1684–1707), in Place du Chapelet, modelled after the Gesù in Rome. Behind it, in the centre of the Golden Triangle, is the shopping mall, the **Marché des Grands-Hommes**, perhaps better known as the *bouchon de carafe* (the 'carafe stopper').

Bordeaux's **Grand Théâtre,** designed by Victor Louis (1773), is its proudest showcase, resembling a Greek temple fronted by a row of mighty Corinthian columns and crowned with statues of goddesses and muses. If it looks fairly restrained from the outside, all sumptuous hell breaks loose within. The vestibule has more columns, supporting a magnificent coffered ceiling, lit by a 62ft cupola; the bold grand stair was copied by Garnier for the Paris Opéra; the auditorium has golden columns and a domed ceiling hung with a massive crystal chandelier weighing 2,860 lbs.

The Esplanade des Quinconces and Around

Just down the Cours 30 Juillet rises the irresistibly overblown 19th-century **Monument aux Girondins**, a lofty column crowned by Liberty over a fountain mobbed by Happiness, Eloquence, Security, a crowing cockerel and a host of other attractive allegories. The Nazis stripped the fountain of its bronzes in 1943; to everyone's surprise they weren't melted down, but later found squirrelled away in Angoulême. Stretching out endlessly from here is Europe's largest, and one of its least interesting, squares-cum-car parks, the **Place des Quinconces**.

In contrast, the **Jardin Public** (*open summer daily till 9pm; winter till 6pm*), Bordeaux's first patch of greenery (1756), redesigned a century later in the romantic *style anglaise*, makes for a delightful wander; it contains the **Jardin Botanique** and the **Musée d'Histoire Naturelle** (*open daily exc Tues 11–6, weekends 2–6; adm, free the first Sun of each month*). Behind the museum, a monumental entrance and a few arches known as the **Palais Gallien** are all that remains of the 15,000-seat Roman amphitheatre of Burdigala (3rd century AD).

The Chartrons

The Chartrons quarter prospered in the 17th century when Flemish wine merchants set up shop here, followed by the German, Irish and English, who founded fabulously wealthy wine dynasties. The area declined during the Revolution when many Chartrons merchants were guillotined and most of the others moved abroad. Its commerce revived into the 20th century, but since the 1960s Bordeaux has sought a new role for the quarter while maintaining as much of its original wine trade as possible. There's the new (and utterly sterile) **Cité Mondiale du Vin** on the Quai des Chartrons, as well as hotels and a conference centre, with exhibitions and shops open to the general public. The vast neoclassical Entrepôt Lainé, where spices and other goods imported from France's colonies were unloaded, now hosts the giant installations of the **Musée d'Art Contemporain** (*open daily 11–6, Wed until 8; closed Mon and hols; adm, free the first Sun of each month*), as well as a charming café.

The old wine trade is remembered in the **Musée des Chartrons**, 41 Rue Borie (*open Mon–Fri 2–6; adm*), with a collection of lithographed wine labels and bottles going back to the 1600s. Then there's **Vinorama**, 12 Cours Medoc (*open Tues–Sat 2–6.30; adm*), a cheesy museum of talking wax figures who explain the history of Bordeaux wine, complete with a tasting of wines made in the Roman style, in the 19th-century style, and so on.

The Gironde

Bordeaux's *département*, the Gironde, is full of superlatives. It is the largest in France, contains 2,170 miles of rivers and 72 miles of Atlantic coast, the whole lined with fine silver sand. In the Gironde you'll find France's largest two lakes, Europe's largest estuary, its oldest lighthouse, its highest sand dune and the northern fringes of Les Landes, its largest forest. Not to mention the largest and, by most criteria, the best wine region in the whole wide world.

Entre-Deux-Mers

This is one of France's best-kept secrets: a lovely undulating plateau of soft lime-stone (the name comes from *inter duo maria*, 'between two estuaries': the Dordogne and the Garonne), occasionally reaching over 320ft in altitude, pocked with natural cavities. Its fine, blond stone was quarried to build Bordeaux, leaving behind tunnels converted into mushroom farms.

The Abbaye de La Sauve-Majeure

Créon, a *bastide* of 1316, is one of the chief towns in the region. Three kilometres to the east stand the remarkable ruins of the Benedictine **Abbaye de La Sauve-Majeure**, founded in 1079 (*open June–Sept daily 10–6.30; otherwise daily 10–12.30 and 2.30–5.30; adm*). The great Romanesque church dates from the golden age of the 1200s, although only the skeleton survives. Few skeletons, however, command such presence: three of the twelve massive pillars that supported the triple nave still stand, culminating in a row of five 'bread oven' apses, while the lofty hexagonal bell tower still rises with panache from the fourth bay, fitted with a viewing platform on top. The most spectacular capitals are in the choir and apses: there are scenes of drinking griffons, fighting centaurs, scenes from Genesis, Daniel in the Lion's Den and Samson; more relics are in the **museum** in the former monastery.

Along the Garonne

The most dramatic scenery in the Entre-Deux-Mers overlooks the Garonne, where the vineyards produce AOC Premières Côtes de Bordeaux instead of white wine. Here you'll find **Cadillac**, a riverside *bastide* of 1280, which gave birth to a local boy named Antoine Laumet, who went off to seek his fortune in America, where he adopted the grander alias of Lamothe-Cadillac. In 1702 he founded Detroit, and in 1902 a Detroit car-maker in turn adopted his name, and the rest is history. The village also boasts something even bigger than its eponymous car: the **Château de Cadillac** (1620), built by Henri III's favourite *mignon*, the fabulously wealthy Nogaret de La Valette, Duc d'Epernon (*open Oct–Mar daily 10–12 and 2–5.30, closed Mon; July and Aug daily 9.30–1 and 2–7; adm*). After serving duty as a women's prison, the château has lost some of its original sparkle, but is still worth a visit: with great vaulted guard rooms below and painted ceilings above, tapestries from the 13th and 17th centuries and, best of all, eight monumental chimneypieces, beautifully sculpted in part by Jean Langlois and decorated with rare marbles, cascades of flowers and fruits, cupids and armour.

Perched on its rock over the Garonne, **St-Macaire** is one of the Gironde's medieval gems. In the 18th century, when the Garonne slightly altered its course, the Macariens woke up one morning to find their quays left high and dry – in effect taking away any economic impulse to modernize, and leaving St-Macaire a village of considerable charm. Three fortified gates still defend the town, including the Porte de l'Horloge, equipped with a tower, bell and clock. Best of all is the irresistible Place du Mercadiou, or 'God's marketplace', lined with Gothic arcades and houses in a picturesque variety of styles from the 13th to the 16th centuries. Sitting atop the village ramparts, St-Sauveur, part of a 12th-century Benedictine priory, has an interesting carved portal and tympanum, and a curious plan, ending in a choir shaped like a cloverleaf.

The 14th-century **Château de Malromé**, 6km northeast of St-Macaire in St-André-du-Bois (*open Easter–Oct Sun and hols 2–6; July and Aug daily 10–12 and 2–7; adm*), was completed in the 18th and 19th centuries by the Counts of Toulouse-Lautrec. The famous artist often spent summers here with his mother, and died here in 1901 aged 37, burnt out from syphilis and alcoholism. Reproductions of his works are displayed in a plush Second Empire setting. Toulouse-Lautrec is buried nearby in the prim and proper Basilique de Notre-Dame at **Verdelais**, a pilgrimage church with a medieval miracle-working statue of the Virgin; a collection of ex-votos testify to her powers of intervention (*open daily summer 3–7; winter Sun only 9.30–12.30 and 3–7*).

La Réole presents a stately river façade, especially with the mass of the 18th-century Prieuré des Bénédictins on its riverside terrace. In nearby Place Rigoulet, the old priory church of St-Pierre has a pair of pretty Gothic chapels, a painting of the *Marriage of the Virgin* (1666), and mermaids carved on the capitals in the nave. Among the old boutiques and houses in medieval La Réole is the oldest Hôtel de Ville still standing in France, built in the early 1200s by order of Richard the Lionheart, pierced with irregularly placed mullioned windows, and below, a *halle* on Romanesque columns with capitals naively imitating antique models. Rue Peysseguin is a charming street, with La Réole's synagogue and medieval houses.

South of the Garonne: the Graves and the Bazadais

Graves isn't so sombre when you remember that it has more to do with gravel than boneyards; the greatest vineyards in the *appellation* look as if they're growing out of gravel pits. The most famous Graves vintner was the great Enlightenment philosopher Montesquieu, whose *De l'Espirit des Lois* (1748) was the basis of the United States

Getting Around

Trains from Bordeaux on the Soulac line stop in many of the Médoc villages, including Pauillac; the area is also served by Citram buses from Bordeaux.

If you're driving from the north, there's a ferry across the Gironde between Blaye and Lamarque near Fort Médoc, sailing roughly every 1½ hours in July and Aug, much less other times; call **t** 05 57 42 04 49, for schedules.

Tourist Information

Villandraut: Place de la Mairie, **t** 05 56 25 31 39, **f** 05 56 25 89 33.
Bazas: 1 Place de la Cathédrale, **t** 05 56 25 25 84.
Pauillac: the Maison du Tourisme et du Vin du Médoc, La Verrerie, **t** 05 56 59 23 38, **f** 05 56 59 03 08, hires out bikes, offers a guide to the châteaux and tasting courses, and sells over 300 wines from all the Médoc *appellations*, at châteaux prices.

Where to Stay and Eat

Cadillac ✉ 33410
★★★Château de la Tour, D10, **t** 05 65 76 92 00, **f** 05 56 62 11 59 (*moderate*). Plush place to stay, overlooking the château, with a pool and tennis, and a good restaurant – lobster ravioli and elegant desserts (*menus 95–320F*). *Closed Fri eve, Sun eve and Nov–Mar Sat.*
L'Entrée Jardin, 22 Rue de l'Oeuille, opposite the castle, **t** 05 56 76 96 96. Old stone building with blue and white décor, and a patio. Refined, local cuisine: *le marbre de foie gras et pruneau à la vinaigrette de truffes* and *filet d'espadon* (*menus 62–150F*). *Closed Sun and Mon and the first half of Aug.*
Au Fin Gourmet, 6 Place République, **t** 05 56 62 90 80. Platefuls of standard regional fare. Buzzing with happy locals at lunch time (*menus 65–260F*).

Sauternes ✉ 33210
Le Saprien, in the village centre, **t** 05 56 76 60 87. Well-prepared fish and other dishes according to the market, topped off with

Constitution. His delightful ivory tower (and still flourishing vineyard) was the moated **Château de La Brède**, off the N113 (*open July–Sept daily exc Tues 2–5.15; Easter–June and Oct–early Nov weekends only; adm*); it has a lovely park of ancient cedars, and his library and bedroom, preserved as it was when he died.

The Barsac-Sauternes Circuit

The world's finest dessert wines are grown here in a microclimate of special autumnal mists that promotes, better than any, the essential *Botrytis cinerea*, or noble rot, that makes grapes look like brown turds before they're turned into golden nectar. **Barsac**'s two *premiers grands crus classés* come from Château Coutet, a *gentil-hommière* built around a medieval tower; and a former charterhouse, the Château Climens, which many oenophiles rate as second after Yquem (*visits Mon–Fri 8–12 and 2–5; closed Aug*). The neighbouring village of **Sauternes** snoozes away without a care in the world, with its disdainful Maison de Vin and a couple of friendly wine shops in the centre. The spectacular 17th-century Château de Lafaurie-Peyraguey has a *premier cru classé* vineyard set in 13th-century walls; equally exalted are the adjacent Château Rabaut-Promis and the 19th-century Italianate Château Filhot, in a stunning park (*visits daily 8.30–12.30 and 2–7*).

Sauternes by the glass (*menus 119–250F*). *Closed Sun eve and Mon.*

Les Vignes, Place de l'Eglise, **t** 05 56 76 60 06. Charming little country inn for an entrecôte, omelettes with cèpes and other bordelais treats (*lunch menu 65F, also 100F and 160F*). *Closed Mon and Feb.*

Broquet chambres d'hôtes, in the centre, **t** 05 56 76 60 17 (*inexpensive*). The only place to stay, with three rooms and a pool (*250F with shower*).

Bazas ✉ 33430

★★★Domaine de Fompeyre, Route de Pau, **t** 05 56 25 98 00, **f** 05 56 25 16 25 (*moderate*). Modern hotel with 35 rooms in a delightful four-acre park overlooking Bazas, with a tropical garden, pools, tennis and billiards; the lovely restaurant serves lovely food (*menus 185–250F*). Closed Sun eve in winter.

Château d'Arbieu, just east of Bazas on the D655, **t** 05 56 25 11 18, **f** 05 56 25 90 52 (*moderate*). Four comfortable B&B rooms, plus a pool and billiards.

Les Remparts, Place de la Cathédrale, overlooking the Jardin de Sultan in the Espace Mauvezin, **t** 05 56 25 95 24. For the most succulent entrecôte in town, delicious Grignols capon with cèpes, game or fish specialities (*menus 70–210F*). *Closed Sun eve out of season, and Mon.*

Houn Barrade, **t** 05 56 25 44 55, at Cudos, on the D932, 4km south of Bazas. *Fermeauberge* with home cooking; be sure to leave room for the *tourtière bazadaise* (*menus 80 and 115F, menu gastronomique 140F*). Open year-round weekends; July–Aug daily; reserve.

Pauillac ✉ 33250

★★★★Château de Cordeillan-Bages, Rte des Châteaux, **t** 05 56 59 24 24, **f** 05 56 59 01 89 (*expensive*). Lovely little hotel in a sea of vineyards, with 25 charming rooms in the Relais et Châteaux tradition and the best restaurant in Médoc, using the best local ingredients: the *ragoût* of asparagus and morels is heavenly. Astounding wine selection (*dinner menus 190–390F*). *Closed Mon and Sat lunch, and 15 Dec–Jan.*

★★De France et d'Angleterre, 3 Quai Albert de Pichon, **t** 05 56 59 01 20, **f** 05 56 59 02 31 (*moderate*). Half the price (but still dear for two stars), with pleasant riverside rooms in a pretty building.

The famous and magnificently positioned **Château d'Yquem** is just north of Sauternes, but you can only ogle it from the road. The château dates from the 15th to the 17th centuries. The pale gold wines produced on its 250 acres have been the quintessence of Sauternes since the 18th century, a position confirmed since the 1855 classification that put it in a class all of its own. One place you can visit is the elegant 17th-century **Château de Malle** in nearby Preignac (*open April–Oct daily 10–12 and 2–6.30; visits to the chais by appointment, t 05 56 62 36 86; adm*), with its distinctive breast-shaped towers; it is one of the few châteaux in France never to have fallen into ruin, and still has most of its original furnishings

Langon

The port at Langon, the capital of the southern Graves, is the highest on the Garonne to feel the tide; note the flood markers posted on the corner of Rue Laffargue. Its Gothic church of **St-Gervais** contains a surprise: a Zurbarán (the *Immaculate Conception*), long forgotten and discovered by the local curé by accident in 1966. In the **Maison du Paysan**, at 1 Allées Jean-Jaurès, are some remains of the 12th-century church of Notre-Dame-du-Bourg, but the most beautiful capitals are now in the Cloisters Museum in New York.

South of Sauternes: a Detour into the Landes

Landes in French means moors, sand and maritime pines, and once they begin south of the Garonne they don't stop until the foothills of the Pyrenees, constituting the largest single forest in Europe. There is already a definite Landaise air about **Villandraut**, the birthplace of Pope Clement V, who built the strong, moat-belted **Château de Villandraut**, on a plain instead of on a hill, and without a keep; it became a model for other 'clementine' castles in the area (*open June–Sept daily 10–12.30 and 2.30–7; July and Aug daily 10–7; otherwise 2–5 only*).

Southwest of Villandraut, **Bourideys** is a perfect and utterly tranquil example of a Landes village. Further east, overlooking the gorge of the river Ciron, sits the irregular polygonal **Château de Cazeneuve** (*open Easter–Oct Sat, Sun and hols 2–6; June–mid-Sept daily 2–6; adm*). Built in the 11th century by the d'Albrets, the family of Henri IV, the castle was turned into a pleasure palace in the 17th century. Their descendant, the Duke of Sabran-Pontevès, owns it to this day. Of special note are the *salles troglodytes* cut into the central court, a Greek nymphaeum (the *Grotte de la Reine*), furnished royal apartments, and sculpted chimneypieces, as well as a mill, lake, bamboo garden and lovely park along the river.

The little town of **Uzeste** has a small but dignified collegiate church, paid for by Clement V, who was buried here when he died from indigestion after eating a plate of ground emeralds, prescribed by his doctor. His once bejewelled tomb (1315–59) took some mighty whacks from the local protestants, but what survives shows a great attention to detail. These days Uzeste is especially zesty around 15 August, when a four-day music festival fills its streets.

Bazas and its Cathedral

For the past 2,500 years, Bazas has been the capital of a little cattle-rearing region south of the Garonne, and home to a unique relic – the blood spilled at the beheading of St John the Baptist, supposedly wiped up in a cloth by a local woman. To shelter the precious relic, a triple church was built on the town's most prominent site; in 1233 when this threatened to fall over, the present **cathedral** was begun in its magnificent setting, atop the vast, gently sloping Place de la Cathédrale. A flamboyant rose window, pinnacles, buttresses and a gallery were added *c.* 1500 to set off the three great 13th-century Gothic doorways. The central portal is devoted to the Last Judgment; along the lintel are scenes from the life of Bazas' patron saint, John the Baptist; the north portal is dedicated to the Mission of the Apostles; the south portal belongs to the Virgin, showing her Coronation and Assumption. All survived the Huguenots in 1578 when the bishop ransomed the façade for 10,000 écus; the interior was completely wrecked.

North of Bordeaux: the Gironde Estuary and Médoc

Freighters and tankers promenade along Europe's largest estuary, along with dainty fishing smacks. From March to September the prize catch is elvers (*pibales*), only two inches long, a delicacy that can demand as much as 1,000F a kilo on the market and must be eaten with wooden forks. **Pauillac** started off an important port here, and was home to one of the oldest sailing clubs in France, long predating the views over the estuary to the Braud nuclear power plant. But Pauillac is best known for the purest gravelly ridges which produce the mightiest Médocs of all, full-bodied, presumably non-radioactive wines laced with a distinctive blackcurrant bouquet. Here you'll find the legendary **Château Latour** (*visits by appointment only, t 05 56 73 19 80*), which introduced stainless-steel vats to Bordeaux in the 1960s, and the **Château Mouton-Rothschild**, which owes much of its current fame to Baron Philippe de Rothschild. One of his first moves, in the 1920s, was to bottle all the wine at the château, an idea that seemed eccentric at the time. The tour (*open Mon–Thurs 9.30–11 and 2–4, Fri till 3; April–Oct also weekends with visits at 9.30, 11, 2 and 3.30; ring ahead, t 05 56 73 21 29; adm 30F*) takes in the *grand chai*, with its immaculate blond wood barrels, a collection of wine labels by famous artists (Dalí, Picasso, Warhol, etc), a museum of art devoted to wine, and finishes with a descent into the cellar, where bottles worth as much as your house and car put together do their silent alchemical work. Mouton's eternal rival, the **Château Lafite-Rothschild** (owned by the Baron's cousins), broods over the Pauillac-Lesparre road (*visits by appointment only, t 01 53 89 78 00; Mon–Thurs 1.30–3.30, Fri 1.30–2.30; closed Aug–Oct*). Lafite's cellars, designed by Ricardo Bofill, have bottles as old as 1797.

To the north lies **St-Estèphe**, an *appellation* that produces vigorous, deeply coloured wines that differ from other Médocs in their need for extra-long periods of bottle-ageing. The leading producer is **Château Cos d'Estournel** (*open Mon–Fri 10–12 and 2–4, ring ahead, t 05 56 73 15 55; tastings for a fee*), which is also the most striking landmark along the *route des châteaux*, with its *chais* designed as a replica of the palace of the Sultan of Zanzibar.

The Côte d'Argent

From Médoc's Pointe de Grave to the Basque lands in the south runs a nearly straight, wide 228km ribbon of silver sand, 'the Silver Coast', with the giant rolling waves of the Atlantic on one side and deep green pine forests on the other. Such broad sweeping vistas of empty space are rare in Europe, and just on the other side of the dunes is a score of lakes and ponds for calmer water sports, which also happen to lie on a major flyway for migratory birds.

Soulac-sur-Mer and the Phare de Cordouan

The current resort, **Soulac-sur-Mer**, 'the Pearl of the Côte d'Argent', replaced an older Soulac that was methodically swallowed up by sand in the 18th century. All that remains of the medieval port where English pilgrims to Compostela disembarked is the Basilique de Notre-Dame de la Fin des Terres, always the first shrine that pilgrims visited in France. Even this was buried twice by the voracious dunes, but now sits tidily in a sand-lined hollow. It has a remarkable 13th-century apse: the statue of the Virgin worshipped by the pilgrims is still in place, and there are good carved capitals of St Peter in prison and Daniel in the lions' den.

Getting Around

Frequent trains link Bordeaux to Soulac-sur-Mer, Le Verdon-sur-Mer and Pointe de Grave; there are bus links from Lesparre station direct to Vendays-Montalivet and Hourtin in July and Aug. Some trains are replaced by SNCF bus from Pauillac (**t** 05 58 59 00 63).

In summer, the little PGV train runs along the ocean from Pointe de Grave to Verdon and Soulac (*June and Sept weekends, July and Aug daily*).

There are trains nearly every hour from Bordeaux to Arcachon, and in the summer, TGVs direct from Paris Montparnasse. Several Citram buses a day run from Bordeaux (8 Rue Corneille, **t** 05 56 43 68 43) or from the station coinciding with the TGVs serving Pyla, Andernos, Arès and Cap Ferret. There are frequent half-hour boat crossings from Arcachon to Cap Ferret and to Andernos (**t** 05 56 54 92 78, or **t** 05 56 54 83 01).

Tourist Information

Soulac-sur-Mer: 68 Rue de la Plage, **t** 05 56 09 86 61, **f** 05 56 73 63 76.
Lacanau-Océan: Place de l'Europe, **t** 05 56 03 21 01, **f** 05 56 03 11 89.
Arcachon: Esplanade Georges-Pompidou, **t/f** 05 57 52 97 97.

Where to Stay and Eat

Soulac-sur-Mer ✉ 33780

★★Des Pins, **t** 05 56 73 27 27, **f** 05 56 73 60 39 (*inexpensive*). Simple Logis de France: nothing fancy, but pines and sea views and a beach 100m away; one of the best restaurants in the area, for good reliable food (*menus from 100F*). *Closed mid-Jan–mid-Mar.*

★★Michelet, 1 Rue Bernard Baguenard, **t** 05 56 09 84 18, **f** 05 56 73 65 25 (*inexpensive*). Popular seaside villa near the beach, with 20 pleasant rooms and a warm welcome. *Closed Jan.*

Lacanau-Océan ✉ 33680

★★★Du Golf, **t** 05 56 03 92 92, **f** 05 56 26 30 57 (*moderate*). Perfect for golfers, with a discount on green fees and a heated pool.
★★★Aplus, Route du Baganais, **t** 05 56 03 91 00, **f** 05 56 03 91 10 (*moderate*). Lovely hotel with gym and equestrian centre, among the pines. All rooms have balconies. Quality restaurant (*menus 75–145F*).
★★L'Oyat, Front de Mer Ortal, **t** 05 56 03 11 11, **f** 05 56 03 12 29 (*inexpensive*). On the seashore; half-board – the restaurant has some of the best food in town. *Closed Nov–Mar.*

Arcachon ✉ 33120

Fashionable Arcachon is usually more expensive than the rest of the region. Book months in advance for July or August.
★★★★Arc-Hôtel sur Mer, 89 Bd de la Plage, **t** 05 56 83 06 85, **f** 05 56 83 53 72 (*expensive–moderate*). Medium-sized, modern but stylish hotel where the rooms all have balconies and overlook the water or the garden; heated pool, sauna and Jacuzzi.
★★★Semiramis, 4 Allées Rebsomen, **t** 05 56 83 25 87, **f** 05 57 52 22 41 (*expensive–moderate*). Charming 19th-century villa in the Ville d'Hiver. No two of the 20 rooms are alike. The pool is set in a garden of palms, mimosas and acanthus.
★★Marinette, 15 Allée José Maria de Hérédia, **t** 05 56 83 06 67, **f** 05 56 83 09 59 (*expensive–moderate*). Large white house in the Ville d'Hiver, with comfortable rooms. Breakfast on a flowered terrace, but no restaurant. *Open mid-Mar to end Oct.*

From June to September, *La Bohème II* sails out from Le Verdon-sur-Mer (just south of Soulac) to an islet in the Gironde's shipping lanes and Europe's oldest surviving lighthouse, the **Phare de Cordouan** (*for times and bookings in English, call* **t** 05 56 09 62 93). It was the Black Prince who first settled a hermit here to feed a fire on top of an 11th-century tower, and in the 16th century the whole was rebuilt as a monument to the

Le Patio, 10 Bd de la Plage, t 05 56 83 02 72.
Surrounded by bright clutter, a waterfall and
delicious aromas, try the lobster salad,
oysters in flaky pastry, hot stuffed crab and
bouillabaisse océane (*menu 165F inc wine*).
Closed Tues in winter, and Mon lunch.
L'Ombrière, 79 Cours Héricart-de-Thury, t 05 56
83 86 20. Garden terrace and delicious
seafood platters, as well as duck and veal
dishes, and a good selection of wine (*menus
from 127F*).
Chez Yvette, 59 Bd du Général-Leclerc, t 05 56
83 05 11. Fresh seafood immaculately
prepared; try the fish soup (*menus 98F*).

Pyla-sur-Mer ✉ 33115
★★★Haitza, Place Louis-Gaume, t 05 57 52 79 27,
f 05 56 22 10 23 (*moderate*). Simple quiet
rooms set in the pine woods, a stone's throw
from the beach. *Open April–Sept.*
★★La Guitoune, 95 Bd de l'Océan, t 05 56 22
70 10, f 05 56 22 14 39 (*inexpensive*). A
favourite weekend retreat of the Bordelais,
with comfortable rooms and an excellent
seafood restaurant (*menus from 145F*).
★★Côte Sud, 4 Av de Figuier, t 05 56 83 25 00,
f 05 56 83 24 13 (*inexpensive*). Delightful,
intimate 1940s villa in the pines, a 5min walk
from the beach, with an excellent little
restaurant; for something unusual try the
civet d'esturgeon aux huîtres pochées (*menus
108–165F*). *Closed mid-Nov–Jan.*

Lège-Cap-Ferret ✉ 33970
The trendiest spot on the Bassin these days.
★De la Plage Chez Magne, in the Port de
l'Herbe, t 05 56 60 50 15 (*cheap*). Delightful
simple eight-room wooden hotel by the
beach, with a good restaurant (*menus –
rarely committed to paper – from 90F*).
Rond-Point, 2 Bd de la Plage, t 05 56 60 51 32.
Simple décor but more pretensions in the
kitchen: abundant portions of sea and land

food, served inside or out on the terrace
(*menus from 100F*). *Closed Mon and Tues out
of season.*
Chez Irène, Rue Ste-Catherine, t 05 56 60 81 92.
The best restaurant in this corner: an institution decorated with paintings by local
artists, and excellent food, especially
seafood (*menu 180F*). Book. *Open Sun lunch
and eves only; closed Oct–May.*
Pat-à-Chou, in Le Grand Piquey, t 05 56 60
51 38. The best ice cream on the Bassin.

Sports and Activities

Soulac's tourist office can tell you where to
parachute, land yacht (*char à voile*), surf, kayak
surf, body board, speed sail, canoe, gallop, play
Paintball, or tennis; at night, you can leave
what money you have left at the Casino de la
Plage, t 05 56 09 82 74.

In Lacanau you can rent surfboards and
learn how to use them, even in the off season:
try Lacanau Surf Club, t 05 56 26 38 84, or
Surf Sans Frontiers, t 05 56 26 22 80, or if you
know how, hire a board and wetsuit at Surf
City, Bd de la Plage, t 05 56 03 12 56. Sail,
windsurf or kayak at Voile Lacanau Guyenne,
t 05 56 03 05 11.

In Arcachon, the UBA (t 05 56 54 60 32) and
Arcachon Croisiere Ocean (t 05 56 54 36 70)
make 2-hour excursions every afternoon to
the Ile aux Oiseaux, which is given over to sea
birds, oyster farms and sailing boats. The Ile's
landmarks are its picturesque *cabanes tchan-
quées*, huts perched on stilts. In July and
August both companies also offer days on
the sandy Banc d'Arguin, a wildfowl refuge at
the entrance of the Bassin. UBA also offers
tours of the oyster beds, and 4-hour trips up
the cool, forested river Leyre; both companies,
and the Arcachon Bateau Croisieres, t 05 56 83
39 39, also offer cruises up the coast, including
sunset cruises with shellfish platters.

glory of Henri IV. This extraordinary confection was truncated in 1788, when a 130ft, no-
frills utilitarian white cone was added. Inside, the first floor houses royal apartments
just in case the king came to call; and the second has a chapel. Another 250 steps lead to
the lantern for a bird's-eye view of the estuary.

The Lakes

More pines, more sand, more water...one of the selling points of the Côte d'Argent is the proximity of its calm lakes to the Atlantic breakers, popular with windsurfers and sailors who don't want to get too wet. **Etang d'Hourtin** and its contiguous twin **Etang de Carcans** stretch 16km from north to south, making the longest lake in France. A cycle track runs between the Atlantic and the lake, between **Hourtin-Plage**, a small family resort in the north, and **Carcans-Maubuisson**, a sports-orientated resort to the south, with a 15km sandy beach. Otters, rare in France, are occasionally sighted here. South of the big lake, dunes and trees encompass the lovely **Etang de Cousseau**, with 13km of paths for cyclists and walkers, who may sight a wide variety of migratory waterfowl along the way, along with boar, deer, aquatic tortoises, genets, European mink and otters. Further south, **Lac de Lacanau** has been a favourite escape of the Bordelais since the early 1900s. They built summer villas at **Lacanau-Océan**, now a big resort famous for Europe's surfing championships in mid-August.

Arcachon and its Bassin

The straight line of the Côte d'Argent is broken by the Bassin d'Arcachon, which in the mid-19th century discovered its double destiny as a nursery for oysters and a resort for the Bordelais; the Dune du Pilat alone attracts a million visitors a year. Yet mass tourism has left corners untouched: if you squint, the little villages in the back Bassin could be part of a 17th-century Dutch landscape painting, sheltering their distinctive shallow-keeled sailboats called *pinasses*, painted the colour of the owner's house, usually green, light pink or straw yellow.

Arcachon was similarly a fishing village, until 1852 when two brothers, Emile and Isaac Pereire, extended the railway from Bordeaux and laid out a new resort with winding lanes and four residential sections, each named after a season. The sheltered **Ville d'Hiver**, always 3°C warmer than the rest of Arcachon, attained full fashion status by the 1860s – Gounod, Debussy, Alexandre Dumas and Napoleon III were all habitués of its gingerbread villas, some 200 of which survive. The **Ville d'Eté**, facing the Bassin and cooler in the summer, has most of Arcachon's tourist facilities, seaside promenades and sheltered beaches. Its most notorious resident was Toulouse-Lautrec, who had a house by the ocean and liked to swim in the nude; when his neighbours complained, he surrounded the house with a high fence – but covered it with obscene drawings just to annoy them. The neighbours banded together to buy the house and, much to their descendants' chagrin, gleefully burned the fence.

The Dune du Pilat

Eight km south of Arcachon, the white Dune du Pilat rises between the sea and trees like Moby Dick: at 347ft it's the highest pile of sand in Europe, at a mile and a half, the longest, and at 550yds the widest. It began to form 8,000 years ago with the merging of two sets of dunes, and more or less grew to its present dimensions in the 18th century, when a huge sandbank offshore was destroyed and all the sand was blown here. Like all dunes, it's in a constant state of flux, and every year it inches inland at the rate of 17ft a year. A wooden stair helps you get to the top of the behemoth for an unforgettable view – especially at sunset.

Around the Bassin d'Arcachon

East of Arcachon, pines line the Bassin at **La Teste de Buch**, which has houses dating back to the 18th century, and includes in its boundaries the **Lac de Cazaux**, the second largest lake in France. The Bassin's oyster capital is **Gujan-Mestras**, where *oustaous* (oyster huts) provide the perfect backdrop for ordering a plate of oysters or attending the oyster fair in early August (you can eat them in non-R months now); there's even a **Maison de l'Huitre**, at the Port de Larros, where you can learn their oyster secrets (*open Mar–Sept daily 10–12 and 2.30–6.30*).

The **Parc Ornithologique du Teich** (*open daily 10–6; July and Aug daily 10–8; adm; bring binoculars, or rent them on the site*) is the kind of marshy delta beloved of migratory waterfowl, who stop off en route between Africa and Scandinavia. It is also a nesting ground for grey herons, black cormorants, white storks, black and white oystercatchers, egrets, kingfishers, dabbling garganeys and spoon-billed shovelers. There's an information centre, the **Maison de la Nature du Bassin d'Arcachon**, and a fine viewpoint over the delta from the **Observatoire du Delta de Leyre**.

The northwestern curve of the Bassin is sprinkled with little oyster port-resorts set between the calm waters and rough Atlantic, all part of **Lège-Cap-Ferret**. The prettiest port is **L'Herbe**, an intimate hamlet of wooden houses on tiny lanes, founded in the 17th century. The miles of ocean beaches culminate in the sandy tail of Cap Ferret, which in the past 200 years has grown 4km and gobbled up several fashionable villas in its wake. A path leads around to the tip of the cape, with splendid views of the Dune du Pilat, most breathlessly from the top of the 255 steps of the lighthouse (*open June and Sept weekends 10–12 and 3–6; July and Aug daily 10–12 and 3–6*). The cute **Tramway du Cap-Ferret** (*t 05 56 60 62 57; 15 June–15 Sept daily frequent journeys*) covers the 2km from the end of the road at the Bassin to the ocean beaches, where surfers ride the big rollers.

The Oyster's their World

The **Bassin d'Arcachon** is the fourth-largest oyster producer in France, and the first in Europe in trapping microscopic oyster embryos and larvae swishing about the sea in search of a home – they simply can't resist stacks of canal roof tiles, bleached in a mix of lime and sand. After eight months clinging to a tile, the baby oysters are moved into calm nurseries in flat cages; the next year, they are moved once more to oyster parks, in fresh plankton-rich waters, where the oyster farmers defend them against greedy starfish, crabs and other crustaceans, who will nevertheless devour 15 to 20 per cent of the crop. In the parks for three years, the oysters are constantly turned, to encourage them to develop a nice shape and a hard shell. When they're ready to go on the market, they are placed for up to four days in special pools that trick them into no longer trusting the tide, so that they remain sealed tight while they are shipped and sold by size, from 6 (the smallest) to 0 (the largest and best).

Down the Lot

Outsiders often lump it together with the Dordogne to the north, but in fact the noodling Lot's heartstrings have always pulled it in the other direction – to the south. Its landscapes are more rugged, tossed up in wild limestone plateaux called *causses*, and what soil it has, especially in Quercy, is said to be the worst in France (the vines that produce black *vin de Cahors* don't seem to mind). Besides the river's beauty, high points are the great Romanesque abbey and medieval village at Conques, the prehistoric paintings at Pech Merle, the handsome medieval cities of Figeac and Cahors, and medieval villages of Espalion, Estaing, and St-Cirq-Lapopie.

Down the Lot: from the Lozère

The Lot (and the Tarn) both have their sources on either side of big bald **Mont Lozère** (5,574ft), the tallest non-volcanic peak of the Massif Centrale. It lent its name to the Lozère, the altogether loftiest and least populated *département* in France, with all of 74,000 souls, known as Gévaudan in the Ancien Régime. In the 1960s and '70s the Lozère was a favourite spot for setting up hippie communes, and as neighbours here are still pretty rare it remains a great place for anyone suffering from *mal de civilisation*. Of the two rivers, the Lot takes the easier, northerly route, passing by the Lozère's midget capital, **Mende**, an overgrown village gathered around the skirts of its cathedral. This was built in 1369 by Urban V, who was born in nearby Pont-de-Montvert, but in 1579 the cruel but efficient Protestant Captain Merle blew up most of it and wrecked along the way the town's pride and joy, *la Non-Pareille*, the biggest bell in all Christendom; all that remains is the 7-foot clapper, stashed under the pretty organ. Its crypt of St-Privat, dating from the 3rd century, is one of the oldest in France

The north bank of the Lot is closed off by a lonely basalt and granite plateau called the **Aubrac**, dotted here and there with stone huts or *burons* where shepherds slept and made their cheese. The chief town is **Marvejols**, a medieval *ville royale* which supported Henri de Navarre in the Wars of Religion, attracting the attentions of the Duc de Joyeuse, who massacred three-quarters of the population. When Henri became king, he made amends by rebuilding the lofty fortified gates that are the glory of Marvejols today.

The climate here is rough and ready, but it's one that wolves from Mongolia, Canada and Europe find amenable enough; over 100 are bred and kept in semi-liberty in the **Parc du Gévaudan**, 9km north of Marvejols at Ste-Lucie (*open daily 10–4.30, till 6 in summer; adm*). A museum compares lupine folklore to reality; wolves, for instance, are good family beasts, who regurgitate to feed their mate and cubs, and rarely, if ever, attack man. This point is emphasized, as the Lozère is famous for the Bête du Gévaudan, who over a three-year period in the 1760s killed 99 people (mostly children and women). Louis XV sent his best hunters to shoot the beast, and although wolves were bagged the killings continued, then suddenly stopped. The mystery has inspired a number of theories: current ones have it that the Bête was a sex maniac and serial killer, back before there were words for such things (also *see* Saugues, p.814).

Getting Around

Mende and Marvejols are linked by train to Paris, Marseille and Béziers. At least one bus a day links Mende and the upper Lot to Rodez. From Rodez (on the rail line from Toulouse) there are one or two buses weekdays to Espalion, Laguiole and Conques.

Tourist Information

Mende: 14 Bd Henri-Bourrillon, **t** 04 66 48 48 48, **f** 04 66 65 03 55.

Where to Stay and Eat

Mende ✉ 48000

Note that Mende is also a convenient base for visiting the Gorges du Tarn (*see* pp.534–5).
★★★Lion d'Or, 12 Bd Britexte, **t** 04 66 49 16 46, **f** 04 66 49 23 31 (*moderate*). Fanciest in town, with comfortable recently modernized rooms, a pool, garden and nearby riding stables. Good *cuisine de terroir* in the restaurant.

★★★Pont Roupt, 2 Av du 11 Novembre, **t** 04 66 65 01 43, **f** 04 66 65 22 96 (*inexpensive*). Modern, unfussy, agreeable hotel, just outside of town on the Lot, with an indoor pool and brasserie (*menus from 90F*).
Auberge La Boulène, outside of town at Aspres, **t** 04 66 49 23 37, **f** 04 66 49 34 43 (*inexpensive*). A *ferme-auberge* attached to a riding stable with rooms overlooking the *causse* and fine restaurant. Book.

Laguiole ✉ 12210

★★★★Michel Bras, 6km from Laguiole on the Rte de l'Aubrac, **t** 05 65 51 18 20, **f** 05 65 48 47 02 (*expensive*). Chic, formal rooms in a small hotel attached to one of the most famous restaurants in southwest France. Michel Bras is an individualist and a perfectionist: all is top notch (*menus from 480F*). Book. *Closed Nov–Mar.*
★★Régis, 3 Place de la Patte-d'Oie, **t** 05 65 44 30 05, **f** 05 65 48 46 44 (*inexpensive*). Long-standing family hotel with a pool and renovated rooms, and a good traditional restaurant (*menus from 90F*). *Closed Sun eve, Mon in winter.*

The Uplands of the Rouergue and the Gorges du Lot

West of the Lozère, the Lot cuts into the uplands of the Rouergue, or *département* of the Aveyron. A series of quaint villages decorate its upper stretches; **Ste-Eulalie-d'Olt**, with an 11th-century church, and fortified **St-Côme-d'Olt** are both members of the Beaux Villages club; *Olt* was the river's Celtic name. Further down at **Espalion**, a 13th-century bridge, medieval houses and Renaissance château are reflected in the river's waters. Espalion has two museums: the **Musée de Rouergue**, with exhibits on music, costume, and folkways housed in the cells of a prison of 1838 (**t** 05 65 44 19 91) and the **Musée Joseph Vaylet** (*open July–Aug daily 10–12 and 2–7; May, June, Sept and Oct daily exc Tues 2–6; other times Wed and Sat 2–5 only*) on local arts and, rather surprisingly, diving, in honour of the two locals who invented the diving suit. Best of all are two churches: Romanesque **St-Hilarion de Perse** with an unusual *Last Judgement* on the tympanum and carved capitals within, and 4km south of Espalion, 16th-century **St-Pierre de Bessuéjouls**, where the tower hides an 11th-century chapel, its capitals inspired by Conques, its altar covered with interlacing.

Cheese, knife and food fanciers in general may be tempted by a detour to **Laguiole**, 24km north of Espalion, the capital of the lofty Aubrac. Laguiole cheese comes from cows grazed above 2,600ft, while the knife-making tradition originated with a local who in 1829 came up with the idea of a folding blade so shepherds could carry knives in their pockets. Napoléon III granted the firm the permission to mark each knife handle with a bee, but by the 1950s the local industry had died out completely. But in

1981, Laguiole was revived with panache – with a new range of knives designed by Philippe Starck, who is also behind the avant garde factory, topped by a 60ft knife. Now the 50 employees can hardly keep up with the demand; you can visit the forge and watch them in action (*Mon–Fri 8.15–12 and 1.30–5.30*).

Below Espalion, the **Gorges du Lot** offers ravishing scenery between the picture postcard village of Estaing and Entraygues-sur-Truyère. **Estaing** was the cradle of the counts of the same name, one of whom saved the life of Philippe Auguste, and another, Charles-Hector, a great admiral and Republican, who tried out of a sense of humanity to do the same for Louis XVI and Marie Antoinette and was guillotined for his trouble. At the end of the gorge, **Entraygues-sur-Truyère** stands at the confluence of the Lot and Truyère. In its descent from the Auvergne, the Truyère has carved an even narrower and more dramatic gorge in the granite. You can catch glimpses of it, and its big dams, from the road to Sarrans.

Conques

Further down the Lot, but tucked away in a steep wooded valley of the Dourdou, hides one of the blazing stars of French Romanesque. Conques abbey was set up by the hermit Dadon in the late 8th century and financed by Charlemagne, but it soon became apparent that after this notable start, the abbey's only resources were water and birdsong. Conques needed a miracle to prosper, and its abbot decided that if none was in the offing, he'd steal one in the form of relics, the cash cows of the medieval church economy. After several aborted attempts at body snatching, the abbot in 873 sent his most trusted monk to Agen, where the abbey had grown sleek from the miracle-working bones of a 3rd-century girl martyr, St Foy. The monk from Conques, disguised as a layman, enrolled as a novice, and spent ten years gaining the trust of the brothers until they left him alone guarding the relics. He tossed them in a bag and ran for it. The Agenais followed in hot pursuit, but St Foy's bones enveloped her kidnapper in a mist. No sooner were the relics installed than the miracles began; the donations rolled in and Conques became a stop on the pilgrimage route from Le Puy-en-Velay to Compostela.

Many of the pilgrims' gifts went into a fabulous golden reliquary for St Foy's bones. The fact that you can still see this and the rest of Conques' medieval treasure is due to the prescience of the mayor during the Revolution. The pilgrims and miracles had dried up, and the abbey was in a bad way, having been burnt by the Huguenots. But learning that government officials were on their way to 'liberate' its treasure and melt it into coins, the mayor called a town meeting, announced the Revolution, and distributed the treasure among the people, adding: 'I shall remember which family has which gem.' When the officials arrived, the mayor confessed that Conques in its Revolutionary enthusiasm had already re-distributed the abbey's wealth. Faced with the stubborn peasantry of the Rouergue, there wasn't much the officials could do. When the Terror was over, every single bit of the treasure was returned.

Tourist Information

Conques: By the abbey, **t** 05 65 72 85 00, **f** 05 65 72 87 03.

Where to Stay and Eat

Conques ✉ 12320
***Le Moulin de Cambelong, **t** 05 65 72 84 22, **f** 05 65 72 83 91 (*expensive–moderate*).

Delightful watermill on the Dourdou, converted into a hotel with nine charming rooms and a fine restaurant to match; try the roast lamb *en croûte* (*menus 170–250F*). ****L'Auberge Saint-Jacques**, **t** 05 65 72 86 35, **f** 05 65 72 82 47 (*inexpensive*). In the medieval centre facing the basilica, with comfy quiet rooms, restaurant and free morning wake-up calls provided by the good fathers and their bells. *Closed Jan*.

The **Abbatiale Ste-Foy** (*open daily 9am–8pm*) was salvaged in the 19th century by the tireless Prosper Mérimée and the Beaux Arts, and now shelters 24 monks who once again make it their business to take care of pilgrims. The basilica was completed c. 1140 and served as a model for St-Sernin in Toulouse; its tympanum is sculpted with an extraordinary *Last Judgement* of 124 figures, which startlingly have kept most of their original paint, watched from the edge by 14 '*Observers*' – the first known Kilroys in art. The interior is lofty, majestic, pure and harmonious, designed to 'process' large crowds of pilgrims in a processional path around the central altar. Lit by translucent windows by Pierre Soulages that replace the jarring imitation medieval stained glass, decoration is limited to a 12th-century wrought iron grille in the choir that once protected the holy of holies (Conques, understandably, was obsessed about security) and the lavish, vigorously sculpted capitals. The master of the tympanum sculpted the bas relief of the *Annunciation* in the north transept. The Romanesque cloister, with a lovely serpentine basin in the centre, was long used as a quarry.

Conques has two **treasures** (*open daily 9–12 and 2–6; July and Aug daily 9–1 and 2–7; adm*). **Trésor I** in the cloister has remarkable reliquaries donated by Pepin and Charlemagne (the latter in the form of the letter A), and the **Majesté de Ste Foy**, the only surviving reliquary of its kind in the world – a magnificent, awful, compelling golden idol, studded with gems and ancient cameos. The head with staring gaze dates from the 5th century, and formed part of the original heist from Agen, while the body, with hands outstretched to hold flowers, and the throne are from the 9th century. **Trésor II**, in the tourist office, has Renaissance and later works. On top of the exceedingly picturesque village, the mostly underground **Centre Européen d'Art et de Civilisation Médiéval** (*open Mon–Fri 9–12 and 2–6*) opened in 1993; it puts on exhibitions and sponsors concerts of medieval music.

Figeac

Figeac, just north of the Lot on its pretty tributary, the Célé, gave the world Champollion, who cracked Egyptian hieroglyphics, and Charles Boyer, the archetypical French lover of the silver screen (and the inspiration for the cartoon skunk, Pepe le Pew). But for the unsuspecting visitor, it's Figeac's medieval heart of golden sandstone that comes as the most charming surprise of all, its curving lanes packed with

Getting Around

Figeac's railway station is on the Brive–Toulouse branch line, with direct connections to Gramat, Rocamadour and Capdenac. The SNCF runs regular buses from Figeac to St-Cirq-Lapopie, St-Géry and Cahors; private companies also link Figeac to Toulouse, St-Céré, and Lacapelle-Marival.

Tourist Information

Figeac: Hôtel de la Monnaie, Place Vival, t 05 65 34 06 25, f 05 65 50 04 58.

Where to Stay and Eat

Figeac ✉ 46100

★★★★Château du Viguier du Roy, Rue Droite, t 05 65 50 05 05, f 05 65 50 06 06 (*expensive*). Renovated 14th-century building with cloister, plus 18th-century houses, enclosed courtyard and terrace with a pool. 17 rooms and 3 suites, individually furnished with appropriate antiques. *Closed Nov–early April.* Its restaurant, **La Dinée du Viguier**, is Figeac's gourmet shrine (*menus 140–360F*). *Closed May–Sept Mon lunch; Oct–April Sun eve and Mon.*

★★Hostellerie de l'Europe, 51 Allées Victor-Hugo, t 05 65 34 10 16, f 05 65 50 04 57 (*inexpensive*). Stylish, Art Deco-kitsch hotel with garden, pool, garage. Its restaurant, Chez Marinette, does wonderful things with mushrooms and other traditional Quercy ingredients (*menus 78–190F*).

★★Hotel–Bar Le Champollion, 4 Place Champollion, t 05 65 34 04 37, f 05 65 34 61 69 (*inexpensive*). Small and modern with friendly staff and a bright bar where locals come to have their *café*.

★★Le Terminus St-Jacques, 27 Av Georges-Clémenceau, by the station, t 05 65 34 00 43, f 05 65 50 00 94 (*inexpensive*). Nicest of the cheaper options, with a bit of garden; the restaurant serves a tender slice of beef with Roquefort sauce (*menus 115–200F*).

La Puce à l'Oreille, 5–7 Rue St-Thomas, t 05 65 34 33 08. Restaurant in a 15th-century mansion; traditional menus – snails in flaky pastry and duck *confits* – and unusual dishes – duck with *sabayon* (syllabub) and honey (*menus 75–190F*). Book. *Closed Sun eve and Mon, exc July and Aug.*

tall houses crowned with covered terraces, which offered city dwellers a breath of fresh air and came in handy for drying textiles for sale. A dozen small piazzas form focal points; on one, **Place Vival**, is the 13th-century Hôtel de la Monnaie, one of the most beautiful medieval secular buildings in France, now home to the tourist office and the little eclectic **Musée du Vieux Figeac** (*open daily 10–12 and 2.30–6; closed Sun; adm*).

Just west of Place Vival, **Rue Caviale** is one of Figeac's prettiest streets, leading into Place Carnot, the ancient market square. In Rue Séguier, the **Musée Champollion** (*open July and Aug daily 10–12 and 2.30–6.30, other times closed Mon; Nov–Feb daily 2–6; adm*) is in the 14th-century house where Jean François Champollion was born in 1790. A precocious linguist, he was fascinated with hieroglyphics as a teenager and suspected they might be a form of writing. The discovery in 1799 by French soldiers of the Rosetta Stone, with inscriptions in hieroglyphics, Greek and a demotic script, proved the key: in 1822 Champollion worked out that the hieroglyphics were not only phonetic ideograms, but figurative and symbolic. A copy of the Rosetta Stone is engraved in the pavement outside the museum; inside there's a small Egyptian collection and audio-visuals on how he cracked the code.

The much-tampered-with 12th-century **Notre-Dame-du-Puy**, at the top of the hill, retains a carved 14th-century portal and capitals inside, and affords wonderful views over Figeac's medieval roofscape. From here descend by way of picturesque Rue

Delzhens, past the **Hôtel du Viguier** (1300s, now a superb hotel, *see* 'Where to Stay and Eat', above), to Rue Roquefort and **St-Sauveur**, once Figeac's greatest medieval church. The chapterhouse was given its remarkable ogival vaulting in the 15th century, and in the 17th century, to cover up some of the damage caused in the Wars of Religion, a local sculptor added the naïve painted reliefs of the Passion.

The classic Figeac excursion is to its mysterious 26ft obelisk-needles or *Aiguilles*, erected in the 12th century on the summit of two nearby hills – the **Aiguille de Lissac** to the west and the **Aiguille du Pressoir** to the south. Their original purpose has long been forgotten, but they may well have been set up by the abbey of St-Sauveur either to lift the spirits of pilgrims, or perhaps to set the limits within which fugitives were guaranteed the abbey's asylum.

The Limargue, the Château d'Assier and Gramat

Northwest of Figeac runs a long broad swathe of land known as the Limargue – a lush micro-region of chestnut forests and meadows of wildflowers. It has some charming villages on either side of the N140 around **Lacapelle-Marival**, and one of the most blustering castles ever built by man, the once enormous **Château d'Assier** (*open daily exc Tues 10–12.15 and 2–5.15; adm*), straddling the divide between the Limargue and the Causse de Gramat.

Built in the 16th century by Galiot de Genouillac, François I's Captain General of Artillery, only the relatively simple west wing of the quadrangle – the guards' quarters – remains intact after centuries of cannibalizing by the locals, framed by two of the château's original four towers. The interior façade is a handsome Renaissance work: large stone windows and walls bear medallions of Roman emperors, while a frieze shows swords and cannons relating to Galiot's deeds or those of Hercules, to whom Galiot fancied a resemblance. The interior, once the best furnished in France, now contains only one of its grand stairways. A pendant in the vault is inscribed with Galiot's motto: *J'aime fort une* ('I love fortune' or 'I love one very much') – the declaration of a lifelong affair with himself. Galiot also built the **church** in Assier (1540s) as a personal shrine to himself and his weapons. Although Gothic in form, the decoration is Renaissance: devoted to cannons, battles, and artillery, with nary a Christian symbol in sight. Inside, under the star vaulting, is Galiot's tomb, topped with a statue of you-know-who in battle gear, leaning nonchalantly against a cannon.

The Célé Valley and Grotte du Pech Merle

Once past Figeac, the Célé splashes through gentle valleys and steep gorges protected by cliff forts, the *châteaux des Anglais* left over from the Hundred Years' War. **Espagnac-Ste-Eulalie** is the beauty spot: a tiny hamlet watched over by a striking *clocher* belonging to a 12th-century convent fittingly named Notre-Dame-du-Val-Paradis, the whole almost too quaint to be real. With a population of 240, **Marcilhac-sur-Célé** is one of the valley's larger villages, with more ducks than people. The ruins of the abbey's Romanesque church form a courtyard around what is now the parish church, decorated with 15th-century frescoes; the original Romanesque church's south portal has a rare Carolingian tympanum.

Four km above the Célé village of Cabrerets, the **Grotte du Pech Merle** is one of the finest prehistoric caves open to the public (*open mid-April–1 Nov; guided tours 9.30–12 and 1.30–5: buy a time-stamped ticket when you arrive; adm*). Its entrance was rediscovered in 1922 by two teenage boys, who were inspired by the cave finds in the Dordogne. They wormed their way through a narrow 400ft passage and found just what they were looking for: a magnificent decorated cave. The 80 drawings and hundreds of symbols date from three distinct periods, from the Solutrean to the Magdalenian (20,000–15,000 BC).

The tour begins with the **Chapel of the Mammoths**, a gallery carved by an underground river, with a great spiral frieze of mammoths, horses and bison outlined in black. The **Ceiling of Hieroglyphs** is covered with finger drawings of female and animal figures and mysterious circular signs. Beyond is the **Hall of Discs**, where water dripping slowing through hairline fissures in rock left rare concentrations in concentric circles. Even more extraordinary are the footprints left by a woman and her 12-year-old child in the muddy clay at least 12,000 years ago. The **Bear's Gallery**, with claw marks and a bear's head carved faintly in the wall, leads to the two beautiful **spotted horses**, fat yet graceful beasts reminiscent of ancient Chinese figures. Six feminine 'negative hands' (made by blowing paint over hands) seem to be yearning to stroke or hold the horses. Over the horses is a rare picture of a fish – a large pike.

St-Cirq-Lapopie

St-Cirq appeared to me, embraced by Bengal fires –
like an impossible rose in the night...
I no longer have any desire to be anywhere else.
                                        André Breton

Back on the Lot, close to Pech Merle, waits Breton's Surrealist dream village, St-Cirq-Lapopie. Built of harmonious golden stone and topped by high-pitched brown tile roofs, St-Cirq hovers in its spectacular setting 330ft above the river Lot just before it meets the Célé. In season parking is difficult (there's a car park just west of St-Cirq,

Tourist Information

St-Cirq-Lapopie: Place du Sombral, t 05 65 31 29 06, f 05 65 31 29 06.

Where to Stay and Eat

St-Cirq-Lapopie ✉ 46330

★★★**La Pélissaria**, t 05 65 31 25 14, f 05 65 30 25 52 (*moderate*). Intimate hotel run by charming couple in a 13th-century house, with ten wonderful rooms.

★★**Auberge du Sombral**, t 05 65 31 26 08 f 05 65 30 26 37 (*inexpensive*). Medieval house in the centre, with eight charming rooms under its steep-pitched roof. *Closed mid-Nov–Mar*. The restaurant serves a delicious *gratin aux cèpes* and trout in old Cahors wine (*menus 110–220F*). *Closed Tues eve and Wed, exc July and Aug*.

Lou Bolat, on the side of the road as you start to climb out of the village, t 05 65 30 29 04. A pretty café-bar-restaurant-crêperie with a terrace, serving regional dishes such as *truite au vin de Cahors*, a range of savoury and sweet pancakes and ice-cream desserts (*menus 60–170F*). *Open mid-Feb to mid-Nov; closed winter eve*.

next to the belvedere), but in winter you may well have it all to yourself. Only a few crumbling but panoramic walls survive above the **church** (1522–40), now the most prominent building, its buttressed apse high on the bluff, its turreted watchtower running up the side of the stout bell tower. Many of the cut Gothic stones from the walls were reused in the houses.

South of St-Cirq rises the dry, sparsely populated Causse de Limogne. More woodsy than the Causse de Gramat, its rocky emptiness is dotted with dolmens, magnificent *pigeonniers*, abandoned walls and stone huts. Lavender is grown commercially here, and most of the Lot's truffles hide out near the roots of its twisted dwarf oaks. What is modestly claimed to be 'the world's biggest truffle market' is held at **Lalbenque** (*Dec–Mar Tues at 2pm sharp*).

Cahors

The anomic clutter of the newer parts of Cahors matches its immediate surroundings – some of the most discouraging landscapes in France – but in the heart of the town you'll find a medieval city of surprising subtlety and character. Its star attraction is the Pont Valentré which, as any Frenchman will tell you, is the most beautiful bridge on this planet. Cahors' golden age, funded by merchant finance and money-lending, lasted from the 13th century until the Hundred Years' War, giving it impressive palaces, a new set of fortifications, a university and the completion of the cathedral. The disruption of trade meant a strangling of its business affairs, but the refined little city made a modest living off its rents and wine trade and, during the Renaissance, had a reputation as a cultured place, full of academies and libraries.

Cahors' charms are discreet, but a careful eye can make this well-preserved and genteel medieval town come alive. The broad, leafy **Boulevard Gambetta** follows the course of the old walls, but old Cahors' high street was **Rue du Château-du-Roi**, north of the cathedral, and **Rue Nationale**, south of it. Along this are most of the merchants' palaces; to each side, the ranks of alleys crowded with tall houses give an idea of how dense the medieval town was.

Inspired by St-Etienne in Périgueux, the domed **cathedral of St-Etienne** was begun in the 10th century, but not completed until the 1400s, when its western and eastern ends were completely rebuilt. The original entrance, moved around to become the **north portal** in the 14th century, is one of the finest in southern France. Christ in a mandorla is flanked by angels tumbling down out of the heavens and scenes of the martyrdom of St Stephen; below are the Virgin Mary and 10 apostles (there wasn't room for 12). The borders and *modillons* have a full complement of monsters, scenes of war and violence, and motifs of roses. Inside, fine frescoes from Genesis (*c.* 1320) are high above the west door, and others are under the first of the two domes in the nave, including eight *prophets*, and the '14 *lapidateurs*' with their stones, ready to ensure Stephen's status as the first Christian martyr. The Gothic **apse** (1330) is an odd pentagonal structure; its chapels contain fine sculptural work (1484–91). More of the same can be seen in the **cloister** (1509), spread with flowing flamboyant decoration,

Getting Around

Cahors has frequent rail connections north to Gourdon, Souillac and Paris, and south to Montauban and Toulouse; from here SNCF buses go towards Fumel and Figeac.

Tourist Information

Cahors: Place François Mitterrand, t 05 65 53 20 65, f 05 65 53 20 74.

Sports and Activities

Summer Quercyrail excursions in a 1950s omnibus, Micheline, chug along the river Lot from Capdenac or Cahors several times a week in the summer; information and tickets from the Figeac or Cahors tourist offices.

Safaraid, t 05 65 35 98 88. River excursions from Bouziès and Cahors as far as St-Cirq-Lapopie and Vers (*April–Oct daily*). Also hire of canoes, kayaks and *gabares*.

Babou Marine, in Cahors, t 05 65 30 08 99. Houseboats for up to 9 people, and motor-boats by the day or half-day.

Where to Stay and Eat

Cahors ✉ 46000

****Château de Mercuès, Mercuès, ✉ 46090, t 05 65 20 00 01, f 05 65 20 05 72 (*expensive*). Sumptuously renovated Relais et Châteaux on a spur high above the valley – the last word in luxury with hanging gardens, a pool and tennis. *Closed Nov–Easter*. The restaurant is equally classy, and the vast cellars feature owner Georges Vigouroux's famous wines (*menus 280–450F*). *Closed Mon and Tues lunch out of season, and Nov–Easter*.

***Le Terminus, 5 Charles de Freycinet, t 05 65 53 32 00, f 05 65 53 32 26 (*moderate*). Charming, resolutely retro, ivy-covered hotel opposite the station. Garage, disabled access, TV and Cahors' best restaurant, **Le Balandre**, which serves delectable Quercy dishes with a twist, accompanied by some great wines (*menus 175–450F, à la carte much more*). *Closed Sun eve and Mon in winter, Mon lunch only mid-July–end of Aug*.

**L'Escargot, 5 Bd Gambetta, t 05 65 35 07 66, f 05 65 53 92 38 (*inexpensive*). Simple comfortable rooms in the big stone walls of the old palais Duèze, including two family rooms. The restaurant is popular with locals and serves regional favourites (*menus 62–168F*). *Closed Sun eve and Mon. Hotel closed Dec*.

Le Rendez-Vous, 49 Rue Clément Marot, t 05 65 22 65 10. Popular place in the heart of old Cahors; for a splurge try the ravioli filled with foie gras in truffle juice (*menus 130–150F*). *Closed Sun and Mon, exc July and Aug Mon eve*.

Au Fil des Douceurs, anchored off Quai Verrerie, t 05 65 22 13 04 (*menus from 75F*). For a romantic evening on the Lot (literally), try the well-prepared regional and fish dishes. *Closed Sun eve and Mon*.

Marie Colline, 173 Rue Georges-Clemenceau, t 05 65 35 59 96. A rare proper vegetarian restaurant: *cannelloni aux carottes* or *gratin au chèvre* followed by *chocolat aux noix-moelleux au chocolat* (*entrées 20F, plat du jour 42F, desserts 22F*). In summer you can sit outside on the pavement. *Open Mon–Fri lunch only; closed Aug*.

Le Bistrot du Cahors, 46 Rue Daurade, t 05 65 53 10 55. Extensive list of local wines by the bottle or the glass (*10–30F*) plus light meals. *Closed Mon eve and Tues*.

which leads you to the handsome Renaissance **Archidiaconé**. Through here, in Rue de la Chantrerie, Cahors' wine-growers have restored **La Chantrerie** (13th-century) and made it into a wine museum (*open July and Aug daily 10–12 and 3–7; closed Tues; free*).

North of the cathedral extends the **Quartier des Soubirous**, the wealthy merchants' quarter in medieval times; *soubirous* means superior, for the way the area climbs uphill towards the citadel. Neglected for centuries, the Cadurciens have recently begun to restore some of its old mansions. **Rue du Château-du-Roi** is an elegant street reminiscent of Siena or Perugia. Its most impressive façade is at No.102, the 13th-century **Hôpital de Grossia**. The alley to the right of it will bring you to a tiny courtyard decorated with modern murals and a musical fountain that works about half the time. Now Rue des Soubirous, the street continues to the austere church of **St-Barthélemy** and the adjacent **Palais Duèze**. The best surviving parts of it can be seen from Boulevard Gambetta, including the graceful **Tour de Jean XXII**, and, further north, the *barbacane* with its massive **Tour des Pendus**.

The **Pont Valentré**, the only remaining of Cahors' three bridges, survived because it was out of the way and carried little traffic. Begun in 1308, and financed with the help of Pope John XXII (a native of Cahors), the bridge took nearly a century to complete. With the Hundred Years' War in full swing, it isn't surprising that defence became the major consideration: the three towers that look so picturesque are three rings of defences designed to keep the English out; each had its portcullis, and slits for archers and boiling oil.

Down the Lot

Abruptly leaving the cliffs and *causse* behind, after Cahors the Lot winds around in big lazy loops through the heart of the Cahors wine region, dotted with modest attractions, as well as plenty of wine châteaux and country inns. **Luzech** enjoys the most striking setting of the river villages, on a narrow isthmus where two loops of the Lot nearly meet. Some remains of a Gallo-Roman citadel survive on the steep hill above the town at the Oppidum d'Impernal. Below, what remains of medieval Luzech gathers itself under the stout *donjon épiscopal* (or Tour Impernal) and around the 13th-century Maison des Consuls, now the small Musée Municipal (*open all year by appointment, t 05 65 20 17 27*) with finds from the oppidum. Luzech's Flamboyant Gothic church, Notre-Dame-de-l'Isle, was begun in 1505, in the same style as the Cahors cathedral cloister, with a flamboyant portal.

Prayssac started out as a round *bastide*, a mere circle of houses around a market-place. Now the biggest producer of vin de Cahors, Prayssac is also worth a mention for its addiction to marble statuary, starting with the unforgettable nude Venus on Venus Square. Signs point the way up the ridge to the *circuit des dolmens*: there are two, along with *garriotes* (corbelled stone huts) and three huge menhirs amid the rocks known as Chaos. The oldest of the Cahors wine dynasties is headquartered here at the **Clos de Gamot**; the family also owns the elegant, 17th-century **Château de Cayrou**, by the river in Puy-l'Evêque.

The hills close in on the river again at **Puy-l'Evêque**, giving the village its exceptional setting, best seen from the bridge. A 13th-century donjon, similar to Luzech's, sits at the highest point of the town. Not long after, many of the local nobles added their houses in its shadow, creating a lovely ensemble. Take a look around its medieval streets, the battered Flamboyant Gothic portal of St-Sauveur (near the top of the town), and views over the valley. Two hamlets in the environs have churches frescoed with the *Seven Deadly Sins* – **La Masse** and **Martignac**, while **Duravel**, on the main road, has a good 11th-century church.

North of the Lot: La Bouriane

In this most Périgordian corner of Quercy, *borie* means a 'farmhouse', especially a fortifed medieval retreat of Cahors's merchant élite; scattered farmhouses amid lush landscapes of chestnuts, pines and meadows are the order of the day. The star attraction is **Les Arques**, a sleepy village that's always had an artist or two ever since the Cubist sculptor Ossip Zadkine of Smolensk bought a home here in 1934; a little Musée Zadkine has a collection of his work (*open June–Sept school hols and weekends 10–1 and 2–7; otherwise 2–5; adm*). Next to the museum is the superb 11th-century church of St-Laurent; Zadkine loved it and initiated its restoration. The interior has been stripped to reveal its essentials: a single nave ending in three tiny apses, divided by columns with primitive carvings and little Mozarabic horseshoe arches.

Harmoniously piled on a bluff, rose-coloured **Gourdon**, the capital of the Bouriane, is easily spotted from miles around. In the 18th century the city walls went down to form a circular boulevard. The massive church of St-Pierre, begun in 1302, is flanked by two 100ft towers, linked by a gallery over the rose window. For a view from Gourdon equal to the view of Gourdon, climb the stairs here to the site of the old castle. Below, the famous Rue Zigzag is lined with medieval houses. Near the church, the 13th-century consulate was converted in the 1700s into the Hôtel de Ville, with graceful arcades on the ground floor. Main Rue du Majou is lined with more medieval relics: handsome houses, a fortified gate and chapel.

North of Gourdon are the **Grottes de Cougnac** (*open Palm Sun–Nov 1 daily 9.30–11 and 2–5; July and Aug daily 9.30–6; adm*). One is full of stalactites. The second, 300yds away, preserves the *département*'s second most important collection of prehistoric paintings: black and red outlines of goats, deer, mammoths, symbols and humans, some pierced by lances. Amongst them, palaeontological detectives have found fingerprints believed to be 20,000 years old.

Getting Around

There are frequent trains from Gourdon to Cahors, which has good connections with other parts of the region.

Tourist Information

Gourdon: Rue du Majou, t 05 65 27 52 50, f 05 65 27 52 52.

Where to Stay and Eat

Gourdon ✉ 46300

***Hostellerie de la Bouriane**, Place du Foirail, t 05 65 41 16 37, f 05 65 41 04 92 (*moderate*). Large country inn that has long been the place to stay in Gourdon; lovely rooms and delicious food – including some fish (*menus 85–250F*). Closed mid-Jan–mid-Mar, Mon lunch, Sat lunch and Sun eve out of season.

***Domaine du Berthiol**, on the D704 towards Cahors, t 05 65 41 33 33, f 05 65 41 14 52 (*moderate*). Large stone Quercy manor house in the woods, with a pool and tennis and games for the kids; the restaurant has a delectable seasonal menu (*menus 100–275F*). Closed Nov–Mar; restaurant also closed Thurs lunch.

Bissonnier La Bonne Auberge, 51 Bd Martyrs, t 05 65 41 02 48, f 05 65 41 44 67 (*inexpensive*). Nicest of the cheaper places, in the medieval town and run by the same family since the early 18th century. Rooms can be noisy (*menus 85–240F*). Closed Dec and Jan, and Fri eve.

Lot-et-Garonne

The Lot next flows into the rolling and fertile Lot-et-Garonne, famous for high-class prunes, *pruneaux d'Agen*, although it produces masses of other fruit as well, notably grapes; as Bordeaux's neighbour it has excellent wine regions that get better all the time. The east is dotted with castles and *bastides* similar to the Dordogne; the southern *département* is part of Gascony. Throughout, rugby is taken as seriously as prunes, especially in Villeneuve and Agen.

The Château de Bonaguil

It's so perfect that it seems ridiculous to call it a ruin.
Lawrence of Arabia, 1908

At the east end of the Lot-et-Garonne, tucked in the wooded hills where no one can ever find it, is one of the most useless but photogenic castles in France, as stunning as a Hollywood set, espeically on summer nights when it's illuminated until midnight. Begun in the 13th century by the knights of Fumel, in the 1460s it passed to the hunchback baddie Brengon de Rocquefeuil. Brengon surrounded it with a moat and a surging prow of walls and towers – just as all the other French nobles were abandoning their medieval castles. By the 18th century Brengon's lair was such a white elephant that it changed hands for 100 francs and a bag of walnuts and was partially demolished in the Revolution. The **interior** (*open Feb–end of Nov daily 10.30–12 and 2–4.30; June daily 10–12 and 2–5; July and Aug daily 10–5.45; closed Jan and Dec, exc school hols*), however, can't begin to match the exterior: there are fireplaces in the void, graffiti and views from the walls.

Bastide Country

Bonaguil stands on the edge of the rolling hills and woodlands that Stendhal called the 'Tuscany of France', planted with a superb collection of castles and *bastides* – planned towns from the Hundred Years' War, when this peaceful region was on the front lines. One of the most strategic, set on a high hill with views for miles around, is **Monflanquin**, founded in 1256. It has preserved most of its original *bastide* elements: the central square bordered with wide arcades, or *cornières*, a fortified church, its grid plan and blocks of medieval houses; the exhibitions in the new Espace Bastides will tell you all about them. Others include **Villeréal**, 13 km north, founded in 1269 on the Dropt; the shop-filled arcades of the main square overlook the 14th-century *halle*; the façade of the church is framed by two towers and retains the loopholes in the apse from where the citizens shot at the rampaging English. Another, **Monpazier**, 'the most perfect *bastide*', is 15km further up the river Dropt. Founded by Edward I in 1284, its 16th-century *halle* still has its original grain measures. Note that the regulation arcades, or *cornières*, around the square are irregular, and that narrow spaces were left between the houses – not to give the residents air or light as much as a place to throw their rubbish.

The vast **Château de Biron** (*open Mar, April and Sept–Dec daily 10–12.30 and 2–5.30; Mar and Oct–Dec closed Mon; May–June daily 10–12.30 and 2–6.30; July and Aug daily*

10–7; closed Jan and Feb; adm) was founded in the 11th century to command the northern approaches to the Agenais. In 1189 Gaston de Gontaut (an ancestor of Lord Byron) got his hands on it, and the family remained in charge for 24 generations, creating along the way one of the more eclectic castles in France, beginning with a 12th-century *Tour Anglaise*, 13th-century Romanesque walls and the *Tour du Concierge* (with Renaissance dormers). In the 15th century Pons de Gontaut-Biron added the delicate Pavillon de la Recette and a two-storey chapel – the ground floor for the villagers, and the upstairs for the nabobs, although its two 14th-century master-pieces, a *Pietà* and *Mise au Tombeau*, were sold to the Metropolitan Museum in New York. The moat was filled in under Richelieu, who didn't like the great lords of France feeling safe or secure. The tools were laid down at last with the Revolution.

Villeneuve-sur-Lot and Pujols

The bustling market city of Villeneuve-sur-Lot likes its rugby *à treize* so much that it needs three stadiums to contain all the action. Although now spread every which way,

Getting Around

Monsempron-Libos (nearest station to Bonaguil) has a few trains to Les Eyzies and Périgueux, and Agen. More frequent buses run up the Lot valley as far as Cahors.

Agen's airport La Garenne is to the south-west, **t** 05 53 96 22 50, and is served by three flights a day to Paris on Air Liberté, **t** 0803 805 805. There are several trains a day to Monsempron-Libos, Villeneuve, Penne, Périgueux, Les Eyzies, and TGVs to Bordeaux, Toulouse and Paris.

t 05 53 89 50 80, by the canal lock at Le Mas d'Agenais, or from Aquitaine Navigation, **t** 05 53 84 72 50, at Le Coustet in Buzet. For a trip on the river, try Garonne Evasion, Quai de La Barre, in Tonneins, **t** 05 53 88 28 58. Locaboat Plaisance run boat trips lasting 1½ hours leave from the Port de Plaisance in Agen, **t** 05 53 87 51 95.

Parc Walibi, at Roquefort near Agen, is one of the biggest amusement/water parks in southwest France (*open late April–late Sept; June–Aug daily 10–6*; **t** 05 53 96 58 32).

Tourist Information

Monflanquin: Place des Arcades, **t** 05 53 36 40 19, **f** 05 53 36 42 91.
Villeneuve-sur-Lot: 1 Bd de la République, **t** 05 53 36 17 30, **f** 05 53 49 42 98.
Agen: 107 Bd Carnot, **t** 05 53 47 36 09, **f** 05 53 47 29 98.
Nérac: 7 Av Mondenard, **t** 05 53 65 27 75, **f** 05 53 65 97 48.

Activities

Bateaux Promenades Electriques, **t** 05 53 36 17 30, organise excursions on the water from Ponton de l'Aviron, in Villeneuve. You can also hire canoes and kayaks, **t** 05 53 49 18 27.
Rent a houseboat in summer to sail along the Canal Latéral from the Crown Blue Line,

Where to Stay and Eat

Pujols ✉ 47300
★★★★**La Toque Blanche**, **t** 05 53 49 00 30, **f** 05 53 70 49 79. Classic, intimate and elegant restaurant which attracts gastronomes from across France. Panoramic views are accompanied by some of the most delicious duck dishes you've ever had (especially the *magret* grilled with preserved pears); extensive wine list (*menus 145–450F*). *Closed Sun night and Mon.*
Auberge Lou Calel, **t** 05 53 70 46 14. Annexe to La Toque Blanche, in a handsome medieval house with a big fireplace and terraces overlooking the valley and Villeneuve; delicious food (*menus 85–210F*). *Closed Tues eve and Wed exc Aug.*

it grew out of yet another *bastide*, founded in 1264 by Alphonse de Poitiers, St Louis' brother and Count of Toulouse. The central market square, **Place Lafayette**, is still framed in its *cornières*, rebuilt in the 17th century after the riots of the Fronde. Near by, the brick **Ste-Catherine** was completed in the 1930s, replacing a Gothic church in danger of collapse. The magnificent Gothic and Renaissance stained glass of the latter was incorporated in the new church. St James the Greater appears three times, recalling the Compostela pilgrims who passed through Villeneuve; it was one of the few places on the Lot with a bridge, the **Pont Vieux**.

Walled, medieval antique-dealing **Pujols**, 2km from the Pont Vieux, was originally a Celtic oppidum. To enter its ancient square, pass under the arch of the tower of the Flamboyant Gothic St-Nicolas. Inside, the church has star vaulting and curious tribunes with little fireplaces so the local barons could attend Mass more snugly. A second church in Pujols, Ste-Foy la Jeune, dates from the 1400s and contains some excellent frescoes, one showing St Foy of Agen (and now of Conques), a 3rd-century maiden whom the Romans roasted on a gridiron.

★★★Les Chênes, at Bel-Air, t 05 53 49 04 55, f 05 53 49 22 74 (*moderate*). Charming hotel with refined rooms, warm family atmosphere and heated pool.

Agen ✉ 47000
★★★★Château St-Marcel, 3km south on the N113 towards Toulouse, at Boé ✉ 47550, t 05 53 96 61 30, f 05 53 96 94 33 (*expensive*). 17th-century castle which belonged to Montesquieu. Sumptuous suites furnished with antiques, or more modern (and far less pricey) rooms in the annexe; a pool and tennis. The restaurant serves imaginative, delicate combinations of local ingredients (*menus 120–250F*). *Closed Sun eve and Mon.*
★★★★Hôtel-Château des Jacobins, Place des Jacobins, t 05 53 47 03 31, f 05 53 47 02 80 (*expensive*). Very comfortable, beautifully restored, ivy-covered *hôtel particulier* in the centre, with parking and a pretty garden.
★★★Le Provence, 22 Cours du 14-Juillet, t 05 53 47 39 11, f 05 53 68 26 24 (*moderate*). A pleasant little hotel in the centre, with spruce, soundproofed rooms.
★★★Mariottat, 25 Rue Louis Vivent, t 05 53 77 89 77, f 05 53 77 99 79. Handsome townhouse in the centre; the chef-owner works wonders with the best the daily market provides (*menus 110–295F*). *Closed Sat lunch, Sun eve and Mon.*

★Les Ambans, 59 Rue des Ambans, t 05 53 66 28 60, f 05 53 87 94 01 (*cheap*). One of the nicest cheap hotels (showers in every room).
Fleur de Sel, 66 Rue C Desmoulins, t 05 53 66 63 70. Charming restaurant with expert menus leaning towards regional fare (*menus 110–210F*). *Closed Sat lunch, Sun and mid-Aug.*
Le Grillée, 14 Rue des Cornières, t 05 53 66 60 24. Lively, local favourite under the arcades – mostly regional food but also kangaroo and ostrich; (*menus 63–160F*). *Closed Tues and Wed eve, Sun and bank hols.*

Nérac ✉ 47600
★★Du Château, on Av Mondenard, t 05 53 65 09 05, f 05 53 65 89 78 (*inexpensive*). Not an *hôtel* of note, but a memorable restaurant, for salmon in millefeuille and roast duck with strawberry vinegar (*menus 68–240F*). *Closed Fri, Sat and Sun eve out of season.*
★★Hôtel d'Albret, 40 Allées d'Albret, t 05 53 97 41 10, f 05 53 65 20 26 (*inexpensive*). Simple family-run hotel, with a much-loved restaurant with an outside terrace (*menus 68–240F*). *Closed Sun eve.*
Le Relais de la Hire, 11 Rue Porte-Neuve, t 05 53 65 41 59. One of the best places to dine in the area, south of Nérac in Francescas, in an 18th-century house, where the freshest ingredients appear in creations such as *artichaut de l'Albret soufflé au foie gras* (*menus 140–350F*). *Closed Sun eve and Mon.*

Agen

Agen owes much of its current prosperity to its location between Bordeaux and Toulouse; transport depots, fruit-packing and bureaucracy are the things that keep the money coming in. Admittedly these aren't big tourist magnets, but this shapeless, rather staid departmental capital does have an ace up its sleeve: one of the finest provincial art museums in France. Or come when the Agenais show their wild and crazy side, when their beloved rugby squad is thumping some hapless opponent. You'll know if they're doing well: all the shops will have team photos and banners in their windows, next to all the displays of chocolate-filled prunes.

The **Musée Municipal des Beaux Arts** (*open Oct–April daily 10–5; May–Sept daily 10–6; closed Tues; adm*) occupies four beautifully restored 16th- and 17th-century *hôtels particuliers* in Place du Docteur-Esquirol. The star of the Gallo-Roman section is the *Vénus du Mas*, a 1st-century Greek marble who, despite her lack of a head, is still quite a tomato. The medieval collection includes tombstones and effigies, goldwork, and Romanesque and Gothic capitals. A beautiful spiral stair leads up to the 16th- and 17th-century paintings and ceramics. Beyond minor works by Tiepolo and Greuze are five Goyas, including a powerful *Self Portrait*. The last rooms move on to the 19th century – Corot, Sisley and Boudin. Agen's cathedral, **St-Caprais** (north of the museum in Rue Raspail), is named after a local boy who was beheaded for declaring his faith. There isn't much to see inside, but the Romanesque tri-lobe apse has good *modillons* sculpted with heads of humans and animals. In the northwest corner of Agen an impressive 23-arch aqueduct, the **Pont Canal** (1839) carries the Canal Latéral over the Garonne, not far from the favourite promenade, the **Esplanade du Gravier**.

The Néracais

This pleasant *pays* is often called the 'Pays d'Albret'; its long history as the feudal domain of the d'Albrets has given it an identity that endures to this day. Its capital, fat **Nérac**, counts scarcely more than 7,000 inhabitants, but its association with the family in the 1500s has given it some fine monuments and the air of a little capital, if you see it from the right angle.

Pruneaux d'Agen

The first plums in the area were brought from Damascus by the Crusaders in 1148, and took so well that today some 65 per cent of all French plums, or 30,000 metric tons a year, come from the Lot-et-Garonne. Most are dried as *pruneaux d'Agen* which, as every French gourmet knows, are the finest in the universe. Most of them don't come from Agen at all, but from the rich Lot valley between Villeneuve and Aiguillon, a businesslike agricultural paradise, packed with not only plum orchards but strawberries, asparagus and all the other *primeurs* that decorate France's markets. In Granges-sur-Lot, one plum farm has created the Prune Museum (*open daily 8–12 and 2–6, Sun 3–7; adm*) for the curious and the constipated; it offers a 35min prune video, drying ovens, costumes, a jammery and chocolaterie, free tastings and the plummiest shop in the hemisphere.

The Marguerite of Marguerites

The d'Albret family came into spectacular prominence in the 15th and 16th centuries: the French kings showered every sort of prize on the family, and with their help Henri d'Albret became king of Navarre, at which point François I found him a fitting match for his sister, Marguerite d'Angoulême, better known as Marguerite de Navarre. Already a widow at 35, she was the most eligible lady of France – not just for being the king's sister, but for a wit, charm and intelligence that stood out even in Renaissance courts. Marguerite turned their favoured residence of Nérac into a brilliant court where poetry and humanistic learning were the order of the day. She also had literary ambitions of her own. Best known among her works is the *Heptaméron*, a collection of stories inspired by Boccaccio's *Decameron*.

South of Nérac, around **Mézin**, the countryside is lush and delightful. On the D656, along the valley of the Gélise, you'll pass *pigeonniers* on stilts, and farmers hanging signs out to sell you asparagus and *cèpes*, foie gras, armagnac and *Floc de Gascogne*, the 'Flower of Gascony' – the apéritif wine, made since the 1500s and revived, uniquely for France, almost exclusively by women.

The **Moulin de Henri IV** (*open May–Sept daily 10.30–12.30 and 2.30–7.30*), north of Nérac, is one of the famous sites of the southwest. If it looks more like a castle, it is that too; fortified mills are not uncommon, built in feudal times when grain was precious and there were plenty of enemies ready to try to grab it. The story has it that the nobleman who built it had four daughters of different ages, and made the mill's four towers different heights in their honour. In later times the mill belonged to the d'Albrets, and it passed from them to Henri IV.

Western Lot-et-Garonne: Down the Garonne

In fact, it isn't just the Garonne; you have a choice of following the river or the **Canal Latéral Garonne**, the 19th-century waterway that parallels the river, providing a complement to the Canal du Midi, and providing boats with a passage from the Mediterranean to the Atlantic.

Le Mas-d'Agenais

An elegant modern suspension bridge crosses both the Garonne and the canal, and although the customary sign announces the village, not a house is to be seen. Mas is up in the clouds, closed into itself; it is special, and it knows it. It isn't large, just a few lovely streets and squares, a brick medieval gateway, a wooden market *halle* from the 1600s, and a beautiful view over the Garonne from its park. It also has one of the region's best churches, **St-Vincent**, begun in 1085, replacing a church of *c.* 440 built on the site of a Roman temple. The interior contains a wealth of sculptural decoration and two relics: an early Christian sarcophagus, said to be that of the obscure martyr Vincent, and a Roman *cippus* with a confusing inscription, maybe the base for the statue of a pagan god. Mas' claim to fame, a Rembrandt, was donated to the church in 1873. Originally, *The Face of Christ on the Cross* was part of a series of seven on the

Passion; all the rest are now in Munich. These are intense paintings, where Jesus goes up on the cross a man and comes down a god.

Down the Aveyron

South of the Lot, the next major river is the Aveyron, flowing down the *département* of the same name to join the Tarn. This area, known as the Rouergue after the Rutène Celts, is famous for its wide open spaces pierced by deep ravines, its clear skies and environmental purity – why the award-winning insect film, *Microcosmos,* was filmed here. The Aveyron twists down to the Tarn north of Montauban, capital of the Tarn-et-Garonne, a *département* that contains enough fruit to have kept Carmen Miranda in hats forever, producing melons, greengages (*reine-claude* plums), table grapes, hazelnuts, pears, apples, peaches, kiwis, cherries and nectarines, a dazzling richness echoed in the stone of one of France's finest medieval monuments: Moissac.

Rodez and Villefranche-de-Rouergue

Rodez was a major Gallo-Roman city on a breast-shaped hill that thrived in the Middle Ages, when the locals felt flush enough to build a cathedral on top of town. It was the 13th century, and what is surprising about **Notre-Dame** is that they chose northern Gothic for their model, and stuck with it over the next three centuries. Was it an aftershock of the Albigensian crusade that made Rodez march in step with the conquerors, or did they just prefer the style? No one knows. The west front, part of the city wall, resembles a red cliff pierced by a large rose window. The 16th-century **bell-tower**, however, steals the show, a Flamboyant Gothic masterpiece of pinnacles and stone lace standing 288ft tall and crowned by a statue of the Virgin. Inside, the tall pillars have no capitals, as if emphasizing the height. The lively 15th-century choir stalls are by the local sculptor André Sulpice, and there are other things to seek out – the rococo organ cabinet, the remarkable tomb of Bishop Jean-François Croizier, the Flamboyant choir screen, and a painted stone *Deposition*.

Following the Aveyron west, **Belcastel** is one of those medieval towns hanging over the river, so picturesque that they resemble a stage set, complete with a medieval bridge and 15th-century château. It lies midway between Rodez and the *bastide* of **Villefranche-de-Rouergue**, founded in 1252 by Alphonse de Poitiers at the confluence of the Aveyron and the Alzou. Although one of the larger towns in the area, Villefranche has preserved its medieval essence, with a dense grid of pale limestone houses built by merchants who made fortunes from wool and the local silver mines. The central arcaded *place* is perfect, with the church of **Notre Dame** protruding in one corner, a Gothic arch yawning under a massive tower. Inside, take time to examine the ravishing choir stalls by André Sulpice, who spent 15 years on the project (sadly the sanctimonious Huguenots and their saws had a go at it as well).

Villefranche was still a going concern in 1642, the date of the octagonal Baroque **Chapelle des Pénitents-Noirs** on Boulevard de la Haute Guyenne (the very next year, however, 10,000 starving peasants, squeezed to the limit by the town, revolted; many

Getting Around

Rodez's airport has two flights a day from Paris and several times a week to Lyon. There are trains to Paris, Toulouse, and Montpellier; buses from Place du Foirail, **t** 05 65 68 11 13, go to Millau, Villefranche-de-Rouergue, Cahors, Albi, and Montauban. Cordes is a 6km taxi ride (**t** 05 63 56 14 80) from the train station at Vindrac, coming from Villefranche or Toulouse.

Tourist Information

Rodez: Place du Maréchel-Foch, **t** 05 65 68 02 27, **f** 05 65 68 78 15.

Villefranche-de-Rouergue: Promenade du Guiraudet, **t** 05 65 45 13 18.

Cordes: Maison Fontperyrouse, on top of town, **t** 05 63 56 00 52, **f** 05 63 56 19 52.

St-Antonin-Noble-Val: at the mairie, **t** 05 63 30 63 47.

Bruniquel: Rue d'Albi, **t** 05 63 67 29 84.

Where to Stay and Eat

Rodez ✉ 12000

★★★Hostellerie de Fontanges, 2km north of Rodez at Onet-le-Château, **t** 05 65 77 76 00, **f** 05 65 42 82 29 (*inexpensive*). A handsome 16th-century château with stylish rooms, pool, tennis and golf nearby, and imaginative cooking in the restaurant.

Goûts et Coleurs, 38 Rue de Bonald, **t** 05 65 42 75 10. The best restaurant in Rodez: a pretty, cosy place, where chef Jean-Luc Fau adds a light, exotic sparkle to his delicious specialities, such as salmon marinated in a soy mousse, with asparagus and grilled sesame seeds (*menus 140–290F*). Book. *Closed Sun and Mon.*

Belcastel ✉ 12390

★★★Le Vieux Pont, **t** 05 65 64 52 29, **f** 05 65 64 44 32 (*moderate*). Two sisters have converted their family home by the 15th-century bridge

into a hotel restaurant, with seven well-equipped rooms and rich, flavourful cuisine based on local ingredients, served on a riverside terrace in summer (*menus 140–350F*). *Closed Sun eve, Mon eve, Jan and Feb.*

Najac ✉ 12270

★★Miquel, Place du Bourg, **t** 05 65 29 74 32, **f** 05 65 29 75 32 (*inexpensive*). Century-old family hotel in the centre with trendy-rustic rooms and an excellent restaurant, serving seasonal dishes; try the *astet najacois*, roast pork with *filet mignon* inside (*menus 100–260F*). *Closed Mon. Hotel closed Jan–Mar.*

Cordes-sur-Ciel ✉ 81170

★★★★Le Grand Écuyer, Rue Voltaire, **t** 05 63 53 79 50, **f** 05 63 53 79 51 (*expensive–moderate*). On top of Cordes, 13 elegant rooms in a medieval setting, and Yves Thuriès' cuisine – famed for delicacy, finesse and *savoir faire*, with lots of seafood specialities; save room for the classy desserts. *Closed Mon and weekday lunch, also mid-Oct–Palm Sun.*

★★★Le Vieux Cordes, Rue St-Michel, **t** 05 65 63 79 20, **f** 05 63 56 02 47 (*inexpensive*). In a 13th-century building with charm and mod cons, including modems. Parking nearby. Run by the tireless Yves Thuriès (twice honoured as the Best Worker in France), with fine dining on salmon or duck under a massive wisteria.

St-Antonin-Noble-Val ✉ 82140

★★Le Lys Bleu de Payrols, 29 Place de la Halle, **t** 05 63 68 21 00, **f** 05 63 30 62 27 (*inexpensive*). Several medieval houses in the heart of town, the rooms furnished with antiques and minibars. The little restaurant serves good pizza for dinner.

Bès de Quercy, on the D926 towards Caylus, **t** 05 63 31 97 61 (*inexpensive*). *Ferme-auberge* with four comfortable B&B rooms; meals based on chicken, duck or guinea fowl (*menus 90–190F*).

were executed in Place Notre-Dame for their presumption). The Counter-Reformation decoration reaches its apogee in the wooden retable on the *Adoration of the Cross* (*open July–mid-Sept daily 10–12 and 2–6*). Just outside of town, the **Chartreuse St-Sauveur** (*same hours*) is a rare Charterhouse of 1450 that survived the Revolution intact. André Sulpice carved the choir stalls, and the smaller cloister is a masterpiece of Flamboyant Gothic.

Najac, Cordes, St-Antonin-Noble-Val and Bruniquel

Beyond Villefranche, the Aveyron retreats into a wooded gorge, its twists and turns lassoing along the way the promontory of **Najac** and one of the most theatrical castles in France, hovering on the tip of an old volcanic cone. Built in 1269 by Alphonse de Poitiers, it gave its master control over the entire valley, although by the time of the Revolution it was so damaged it was sold for 12 francs (*open April–Sept daily 10–12 and 2.30–5, till 7 in July and Aug; adm*). Najac's Gothic church was built in the same century; the Inquisition ordered the locals to pay for it as punishment for supporting the Cathars. Halfway up the hill, another local has succumbed to an even more curious passion: building ships out of matchsticks, on show in the **Musée de l'Art de l'Allumette** (*open April–June daily 2–6; July–Sept daily 10–7*).

At Laguepie the Aveyron makes a sharp turn to the west: at this point it's only 13km to one of the loftiest and most famous of all *bastides*, **Cordes-sur-Ciel** ('in the sky'), founded and heavily fortified in 1222 by Count Raymond VII of Toulouse. Although friendly to the Cathars, it was never captured in the Albigensian crusade (hence its fine state of preservation), although the Inquisitors were certainly on hand to mop up the heretics after the fact. In later years its most famous resident was Albert Camus. 'All is beautiful there, even regret,' he once wrote; the superb Gothic houses and lanes are especially atmospheric if you can manage to see them out of season or at night. The huge *halle* in the main square dates from the 14th century; the medieval wells here go down 370ft through the rock. The 13th-century Maison Prunet is now the **Féerie de l'Art du Sucre**, packed full of sugary sculptures by Cordes' renowned chef, Yves Thuriès (*open daily 10–12 and 2.30–6; closed Jan; adm*). The **Musée d'Art et d'Histoire** at the Portail Peint (*open July and Aug daily 11–12 and 2–6; April–Oct Sun and hols only 3–6; adm*) keeps the charter of 1222 and the illuminated city code, as well as other odds and ends. The terraces of the lower town have been converted into an updated oriental dream garden, the **Jardin des Paradis** (*open June–Oct daily 10–7; adm*).

To the west, the Aveyron then snakes below **St-Antonin-Noble-Val**. The Romans named it *Nobilis Vallis*; the St Antonin was tacked on when the saint's body floated downstream and a monastery was founded to hold it. St-Antonin has an exceptional assortment of medieval houses. Foremost is the lovely Gothic **Place des Halles** and its **Maison des Consuls** (1120) – unfortunately Disneyfied by Viollet-le-Duc. On the first floor, note the pillar sculpted with Byzantine Emperor Justinian holding his code of law. Along the Promenade des Moines are the remains of the tanneries which once made St-Antonin's fortune. The paths around St-Antonin make for fine walking, especially up to the 660ft **Rocher des Anglars** with its belvedere over the gorge; for more big scenery, take the narrow corniche road, the D173 past medieval **Penne**, with its astonishing castle hanging over the cliffs.

Next down the river is picturesque **Bruniquel**, former Protestant stronghold and current artists' colony, overlooking the cliffs at the confluence of the Aveyron and

Vère. Rising 300ft over the rivers, the **château** (*open April–Oct Sun and public hols 10–12.30 and 2–6; April, June and Sept Mon–Sat 10–12.30 and 2–7*) dates back to the 12th century – the tour includes the keep, the knights' room and chapel, and an elegant Renaissance gallery. The nearby **Maison des Comtes Payrol** is a fine example of 13th-century civic architecture, with its original windows and a coffered ceiling (*open April–Sept daily 10–6; Mar and Oct weekends only 10–6; adm*).

Montauban

Originally covered with silvery willows, hence *Mons Albanus* ('white hill'), Montauban prefers to be known as 'the pinkest of the three pink cities' (ie pinker than Toulouse and Albi). Founded by the Counts of Toulouse in 1144, Montauban was such a successful experiment in city planning that it spawned dozens of baby Montaubans, known as the *bastides*, in the 13th and 14th centuries. Not many of the others, however, have evolved into such pleasant medium-sized cities, or can claim a collection of art as prestigious as the Musée Ingres.

The finest gift bestowed on Montauban was its central square, the **Place Nationale**. Although the prototype for the *bastide* market square, none can match its urbane sophistication; first off, it isn't even a square at all, but a subtle, irregular trapezoid with covered chamfered corners. Its unique 'double cloister' arcades date from 1144

Getting Around

Montauban's train station on Rue Solengro is well served by trains between Paris and Toulouse via Angoulême, and Toulouse and Bordeaux via Moissac and Agen. Chauderon Jardel (**t** 05 63 22 55 00) and Barrière & Gau (**t** 05 63 30 44 45) run buses serving most of the *département* and the big towns beyond.

Tourist Information

L'Ancien Collège, Place Praux–Paris, **t** 05 63 63 60 60, **f** 05 63 63 65 12.

Where to Stay and Eat

Montauban ✉ 82000
★★★Hostellerie Les Coulandrières, on the D958 at Montbeton, **t** 05 63 67 47 47, **f** 05 63 67 46 45 (*moderate*). The prettiest place to stay, 3km west of the city. A modern inn under a superb cedar tree, with a pool and park and bright rooms; the restaurant is one of the best, featuring delicious seafood (*menus from 110F*). *Closed Sun eve and Jan.*

★★★Ingres, 10 Av de Mayenne, **t** 05 63 63 36 01, **f** 05 63 66 02 90 (*moderate*). A fine modern hotel near the station, with garden and pool.

★★D'Orsay, Rue Salengro, **t** 05 63 66 06 66, **f** 05 63 66 19 39 (*inexpensive*). Opposite the station, with very comfortable rooms, and the best food in town at the welcoming **La Cuisine d'Alain**, which takes local traditions and gives them an original slant (*menus 130–320F*); the *à la carte* includes Montalbanais *cassoulet*. Fabulous desserts. *Closed Sun, Mon lunch and mid-Aug*

Ambrosie, 41 Rue Comédie, **t** 05 63 66 27 40. A fair name for the delicious dishes served in this up-to-date restaurant (tiny, so get there early for lunch) – try the duck in an onion fondue (*menus from 80F*).

Au Chapon Fin, Place St-Orens, **t** 05 63 63 12 10, **f** 05 63 20 47 43. Just off the roundabout after crossing Pont Neuf, this is a local favourite serving traditional food: *cote d'agneau grillées* and *entrecôte au roquefort*, and some fish (*menus 85–260F*). *Closed end July to mid-Aug, Fri eve and Sat.*

and were originally built in wood; after a fire in 1614 they were rebuilt exactly as they were in warm brick. On this stage the Montaubanais bought their food, hanged their thieves and issued their proclamations.

In Place Victor-Hugo, **St-Jacques**, is a combination church and assembly hall built by the city's consuls in the 13th century. During the repairs following the Hundred Years' War, it was given an octagonal bell tower; the neo-Roman portal with its tile decoration dates from the 19th century; the interior is typically southern Gothic, with a large single nave. Down from St-Jacques, **Place Bourdelle** is named after Bourdelle's dramatic 1895 *Monument to the War Dead of 1870,* an early major work, showing the influence of his master Rodin. The Tarn here is spanned by the **Pont Vieux**, a 677ft structure begun in 1311 – a technological *tour de force*, with seven uneven arches and, originally, three fortified towers, which were demolished in the early 1900s to let more traffic through.

The **Musée Ingres** (*19 Rue de l'Hôtel de Ville; open all year daily 10–12 and 2–6; mid-Oct–Easter closed Mon and Sun am; adm*), housed in the bishops' palace at the eastern end of the bridge, is a monument to the city's favourite son, Jean-Auguste-Dominique Ingres (1780–1867). The painter's donations make up the core of the collection, including thousands of drawings, portraits, and mythologies such as the *Dream of Ossian*. He also gave the museum a Masolino predella panel, a *Nativity* by Carpaccio, and a striking *St Jerome* attributed to Ribera. Montalbanais sculptor **Antoine Bourdelle** (1861–1929) gets a room to himself; his most acclaimed work, the *Last Centaur Dying*, stands out in front of the museum.

The **Cathédrale Notre-Dame** was rebuilt between 1692 and 1739 by Louis XIV's own architects. Its white stone and frostily perfect classicism betrays its Parisian origins, in a city of warm brick. The vast interior is full of equally frigid furnishings, and one of Ingres' major works, the enormous *Vow of Louis XIII*, commissioned for the cathedral (1820–1824).

In 1679 Montauban's *intendant* Foucault initiated the greening of the pink city by planting thousands of elms on the banks of the Tarn, along the broad street that now bears his name, **Cours Foucault**. Popular ever since, its focal point, closing the view between the long alleys of trees, is Bourdelle's *La France veillant sur ses morts*, a First World War monument inspired by the temples and sculpture of ancient Greece, typical of the sculptor's later career.

Moissac

There's only one reason to visit Moissac, but it's hard to beat: the **Abbaye de St-Pierre**, founded by Clovis in 506 and one of the crown jewels of French sculpture. Sheltered by a 12th-century tower, the sublime **porch** is one of the most powerful and beautiful works of the Middle Ages. The **tympanum** rests on a lintel recycled from a Gallo-Roman building, decorated with eight large thistle flowers and enclosed in a cable or vine, spat out by a monster at one end and swallowed by another monster at the other. In the centre, Christ sits in the Judgement of Nations. You might notice that

Moissac Abbey Cloister

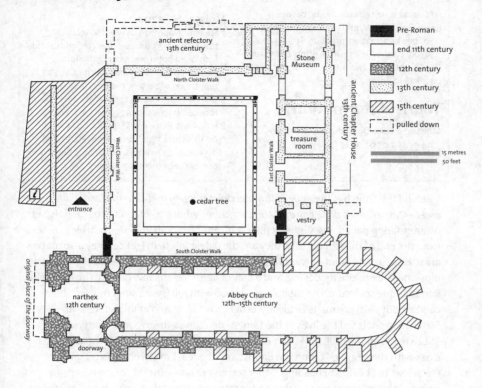

ancient refectory
13th century

Stone
Museum

North Cloister Walk

West Cloister Walk

East Cloister Walk

ancient Chapter House
13th century

treasure
room

● cedar tree

entrance

vestry

South Cloister Walk

original place of the doorway

narthex
12th century

Abbey Church
12th–15th century

doorway

Pre-Roman
end 11th century
12th century
13th century
15th century
pulled down

15 metres
50 feet

he has three arms, one on the Book of Life, one raised in blessing, and another on his heart; no one knows why. The four symbols of the Evangelists twist to surround him, and two seraphim carrying scrolls are squeezed under the rainbow. The rest of the tympanum is occupied by the 24 Elders, each gazing up from their thrones at Christ. The whole wonderfully rhythmic composition could just as easily be an old-timers' band raising their glasses in an intermission toast to a stern, but respected and beloved bandleader.

But that's not all. The door's central pillar, the **trumeau**, is sculpted with pairs of lions in the form of Xs symbolically guarding the church. On either side are *Peter*, *Isaiah*, *Paul* and *Jeremiah*, elongated, supple figures that sway and almost dance. To the right are scenes from the life of the Virgin; to the left, poor Lazarus' soul is taken into the bosom of Abraham, while below the soul of the feasting Dives is carried off to hell. Look for the miser with demons on his shoulder, refusing alms to a beggar, and Lust, serpents sucking at her breasts.

The **interior** of the church had to be rebuilt in 1430 and can't compete with the fireworks on the portal. Only one chapel retains its 15th-century geometrical murals, which inspired the restoration on the other walls; some excellent polychrome sculpture survives as well.

Getting Around

Moissac is on the railway line between Bordeaux, Agen, Montauban and Toulouse. For bus information, ring **t** 05 63 04 92 30.

An old barge, *Le Grain d'Or*, offers cruises on the Canal Latéral and the river Tarn, call **t** 05 63 04 48 28 for information.

Tourist Information

Moissac: 6 Place Durand-de-Bredons, **t** 05 63 04 01 85, **f** 05 63 04 27 10.

Where to Stay and Eat

Moissac ✉ 82200

★★Le Pont Napoléon, 2 Allées Montebello, **t** 05 63 04 01 55 (*inexpensive*). Delightful old-fashioned hotel overlooking the Tarn. Purchased by master chef Michel Dussau, its reputation of serving the best food in Moissac on its lovely terrace will only increase (*menus from 139F*). *Closed Wed.*

Bar de Paris, Place des Récollets, **t** 05 63 04 00 61, across from the market. Pizzas and brasserie-style dishes, including a fine plate of frogs' legs (*menus 70–150F*).

Behind the church is the abbey's famous **cloister** (*open mid-Oct–mid-Mar daily 9–12 and 2–5; other times till 6; July and Aug till 7; adm*), whose 76 magnificent capitals, set on alternating paired and single slender columns of various coloured marbles, come from the end of the 11th century; they are the oldest *in situ* in France. They also mark an artistic turning point, towards more fluid, stylized poses with a sense of movement, exquisite modelling, and a play of light and shadow hitherto unknown in Romanesque sculpture. The capitals are carved with foliage inspired by Corinthian capitals, but with luxuriant virtuosity; others have birds and animals intertwined. Some 46 capitals tell the lives of the saints – don't miss the dynamic martyrdoms: St Lawrence on the grill, while two Romans blow on the flames; St Martin dividing his cloak with the beggar; St John the Baptist and the feast of Herod; St Peter on his cross next to St Paul's beheading. Other scenes are rare – the city of Jerusalem vs. unholy Babylon, the story of Nebuchadnezzar, and Shadrach, Meshach and Abednego in the furnace.

Down the Tarn

Dordogne, Lot, Aveyron – heading south, the next of the Garonne's great tributaries is the Tarn. Like the Lot, it has its origins at Mont Lozère, but the scenic drama begins when it meets the soft limestone plateaux of the Grands Causses, where it cuts through a spectacular canyon on its way to Millau and Roquefort country, past Albi of the great red cathedral, sweeping down to Toulouse only to change its mind and head up to Montauban and Moissac (*see* above) and join the Garonne there.

The Grands Causses and the Gorges du Tarn

Some of France's emptiest and most monotonous spaces are the four grey limestone plateaux of the **Grands Causses** south of the Massif Central. Although it certainly rains here, the *causses* are arid – they soak up water like a sponge, and are fit only for grazing sheep, half a million strong, who find enough to drink in water holes called *lavognes*. For all the emptiness, however, the region is extraordinarily rich in flora and fauna; the Grands Causses, Mont Lozère and much of the southern half of the Lozère and western Gard fall into the confines of the **Parc National des Cévennes** (*see* pp.976–7).

For most visitors, the fascination with the Grands Causses has everything to do with what water has wrought here, the great subterranean cavities, the peculiar forma-tions, the cliffs and magnificent gorges.The most famous of these, the spectacular 53km **Gorges du Tarn**, runs through a fault between the **Causse de Sauveterre** and **Causse Méjean**. Time your visit carefully, if possible – the canyon is too crowded (and hot) in July and August, but if it's cloudy, you'll miss the beautiful colours of the gorge's stone. May and September are ideal. November to March are deserted.

The Tarn's bed changes from granite to limestone in **Florac**. Beyond here, the 40 or so streams that feed the crystal-clear river are subterranean resurgences that spill down the cliffs. The canyon begins in earnest at **Ispagnac**. **Quézac** has a Gothic bridge built by Pope Urban V to permit pilgrims to visit the church he built here, to house a statue of the Virgin discovered in 1050.

The next village, **Castelbouc**, built into the cliff under a ruined castle, is just as famous for its impiety: while the local men were off at the Crusades, the local lord, as the only male, took it upon himself to solace their women. His exertions eventually killed him in the arms of a lover, and his soul flew out of the castle in the form of a giant billy goat (or *bouc*). Further down, you can visit the (intact) **Château de Prades** on its rocky perch, built in the 13th–15th centuries by the priors at Ste-Enimie to defend the gorge.

Ste-Enimie itself is set under steep cliffs; the descent by the D986 from Mende is wonderfully scenic and offers a splendid view over the village and its site. It owes its lushness to generations of peasants who brought the soil in, basket by basket. It owes its name to a beautiful Merovingian princess (d. 628) who came down with leprosy when her father, Clotaire II, engaged her to be married against her will. An angel advised her to come here to be cured in a local spring, and it worked, but when-ever she tried to leave the area the leprosy returned. So she stayed with her followers and built a convent, which the devil kept knocking down until she gave chase (*see* below). From the D986 it's a 30-minute walk to her Grotte-Ermitage, with fine views. There are even better ones from a belvedere 6km south, on the same D986.

The main river road, the D907, carries on to **St-Chély** and **Pougandoires**, both villages set in striking *cirques* or curls in the river. The most beautiful of the gorge's castles, the 15th-century fairytale **Château de la Caze** (now a hotel, *see* p.537) was built by Soubeyrane Alamand, who was famous for his eight lovely daughters, the Nymphs of the Tarn, whose portraits can be seen.

At **La Malène**, the 'Bad hole' boatman waits to take you through the **Détroits**, the narrowest part of the gorge, where rock walls (at their best in the morning) rise over 1300ft above the river and into the magnificent burnished red **Cirque des Baumes**. By road, the best view of the narrows is from the **Roc des Hourtous** on the south bank of the river, reached by way of the D43 from La Malène.

At the lower part of the Cirque des Baumes is a jumble of massive rocks called the **Pas du Souci**. While chasing Satan, St Enimie realized that she could never catch him up and asked the Roque Sourde to help her. The cliff dutifully gave way and fell on top of him and only a small hole in the pile allowed him to slip out and return to hell. Geologists prefer to date the rock slide to an earthquake in 580. The valley then widens at **Les Vignes**, from where a road winds up to the **Point Sublime**, a viewpoint over the gorge that lives up to its name. From Les Vignes the river funnels down its canyon with a few rapids to **Le Rozier**, built at the junction of the Gorges du Tarn and the steep **Gorges de la Jonte**. There are magnificent excursions possible by car or foot in all directions; the day-long walk along the **Corniches du Causse Méjean** is one of the most breathtaking, but bring plenty of water (and avoid the by-ways with iron ladders, if you're subject to vertigo).

A drive up the Gorges de la Jonte will take you to the remarkable pit of the **Aven Armand** north of **Meyrueis**, discovered in 1887 and now reached by way of a subter-ranean funicular (*open April, May, Sept and Oct daily 9.30–12 and 1.30–5.30; June–Aug daily 9.30–7; adm*): this consists of a massive chamber, with a wonderland of 400 stalagmites known as the Virgin Forest – its discoverers, not inaccurately, compared it to something out of the Arabian Nights.

Millau and Roquefort-sur-Soulzon

After squeezing through its gorge, the Tarn flows past **Millau**, a bustling city in the valley between the Causse Noir and the Causse du Larzac. By the 12th century Millau discovered its vocation, making fine gloves from the skins of young lambs slaugh-tered so that the maximum amount of their dam's milk is available for cheese. After booming in the 19th century, the glove business nearly died in the 1930s: the old tanning techniques, which took two months, couldn't compete with faster methods and cheap imitations. In recent times, however, the fashion houses in Paris realized that the old ways are still best, and Millau is back in business.

The city has erected plaques in the historic centre that explain what's what; the atmosphere already hints of the Mediterranean. Handsome arcaded **Place du Foch**, the heart of town, is the address of the **Musée de Millau** (*open April–Sept daily 10–12 and 2–6; closed Sun out of season*), with artefacts of the Rutènes Celts and Millau's predecessor, the large Gallo-Roman city of Contatomagos, which was famous for red stamped or *sigillum* vases, which were mass produced, so to speak, by 500 potters. Examples have been discovered as far away as Scotland and India. The museum's great pride and joy, however, is the skeleton of a plesiosaurus, a marine dinosaur who swam around here 180 million years ago. Another section tells the story of glove-making.

You can visit the **excavations of Contatomagos** at La Grafesenque, 1km south of Millau (*open daily 9–12 and 2–6.30*) or take the scenic D110 16km east to **Montpellier-le-Vieux** – not an earlier version of Montpellier, but a fantastic chaos of boulders and rocks that hauntingly resembles a ruined city (*open mid-Mar–Nov daily 9–6; adm*). The largest of the Grands Causses, the **Causse du Larzac**, begins at Millau and

Getting Around

Millau is served by trains from Paris, Toulouse, Rodez, Montpellier, Perpignan and Béziers.

Buses, **t** 05 65 60 28 63, from the train station make a circuit to Meyrueis, Aven Armand, Ste-Énimie, and down the Gorges du Tarn back to Millau; others travel to Albi and Rodez.

Tourist Information

Ste-Énimie: at the Mairie, **t** 04 66 48 53 44, **f** 04 66 48 52 28.
Millau: 1 Av Alfred-Merle, **t** 05 65 60 02 42, **f** 05 65 61 36 08.

Sports and Activities

Canoes and kayaks can be hired at most ports in the Gorges du Tarn, especially at Ste-Énimie.
Bateliers de La Malène, t 04 66 48 51 10. Boat rides for four or five people at a time down the most scenic sections of the Gorges du Tarn and minibus rides back to La Malène (*several times daily April–Oct; 100F*).

Where to Stay and Eat

For all hotels in the Gorges du Tarn, book well in advance. Mende (*see* p.513) is also close by.

Ste-Enimie/La Malène ✉ 48210
****Château de la Caze, towards La Malène, **t** 04 66 48 51 01, **f** 04 66 48 55 75 *chateau.de.la.caze@wandadoo.fr* (*luxury–expensive*). The prettiest castle along the Tarn (*see* above) is also the most fashionable place to stay, with elegant rooms and apartments individually styled with charm and antiques, a pool, terrace and lovely restaurant with a Gothic fireplace, serving the likes of saddle of lamb with baby artichokes (*menus from 130F*). *Closed Wed and Thurs lunch out of season, and mid-Nov–mid-Mar.*

***Manoir de Montesquiou, La Malène, **t** 04 66 48 51 12, **f** 04 66 48 50 47 (*expensive–moderate*). Ivy-covered 15th-century manor house, with romantic rooms furnished with antiques, and a restaurant where the chef does delicious things with morels and free range chickens (*menus from 140F*). *Closed Nov–Mar.*
Auberge du Moulin, Ste-Énimie, **t 04 66 48 53 08. **f** 04 66 48 58 16. Rooms in a restored stone mill (*inexpensive*). *Closed 15 Nov–20 Mar.*
*Auberge de la Cascade, t 04 66 48 52 82, **f** 04 66 48 52 45 (*inexpensive*). In the centre of charming St-Chély, rooms in an older building or new annexe, with a pool overlooking the Tarn and simple restaurant. *Closed 15 Oct–15 Mar.*

Millau ✉ 12100
***International, 1 Place de la Tiné, **t** 05 65 59 29 00, **f** 05 65 59 29 01 (*moderate–inexpensive*). A large modern family-run hotel disguised as a chain, with comfortable air-conditioned rooms; restaurant has a view and dishes such as *civet de canard* and plenty of freshwater fish (*menus from 130F*). *Closed Mon and Sun eve in winter.*
***Château de Creissels, 2km southwest of Millau, **t** 05 65 60 16 59, **f** 05 65 61 24 63 (*inexpensive*). Big rooms furnished in an antique style in a 12th-century château and a modern addition. *Closed Jan and Feb.*
*Grand Hôtel Moderne, 11 Rue Jean-Jaurès, **t** 05 65 60 59 23, **f** 05 65 59 29 01 (*cheap*). Neither grand nor modern, but full of old-fashioned charm. *Open May–Sept only.* Book.
Capion, 3 Rue J-F Alméras, **t** 05 65 60 00 91. A local culinary institution off Rue Jean-Jaurès, featuring a surprising array of dishes from the most traditional to exotic. Excellent value (*menus 65–185F*). *Closed Wed out of season.*

continues all the way to Lodève in Languedoc. A route to Compostela passed through here, and the pilgrims, prone to attack in the empty wilderness, were given succour by the Knights Templar, whose greatest survival is **La Couvertoirade**, a walled commandary similar to Middle Eastern *caravanserai* and one of the most striking of the *beaux villages de France*.

Another *causse*, du Combalou, stands above **Roquefort-sur-Soulzon**. In prehistoric times part of it collapsed, forming a maze of caverns. The story goes that one day in the early Middle Ages a young shepherd left his bread and cheese in one of them and lost track of it; when he found it, it was mouldy but surprisingly delicious – and well-preserved under its crust.

Originally known as *ruppefortis*, Roquefort cheese owes its unique qualities to the high rate of cool natural humidity in the caves, and the *penicillium roqueforti* that grows on bread. You can learn all about it, in French and in great detail at the cellars of **Roquefort Société** (*open daily 9–11.30 and 2–5; July and Aug daily 9.30–6.30; adm; bring a pullover*) complete with *son et lumière* and tastings, or a bit more modestly at family-run **Roquefort Papillon** (open *Mon–Fri 9.30–11.30 and 1.30–4.30; July–Sept daily 9.30–6*).

South of Roquefort, the 12th-century Cistercian **Abbaye de Sylvanès** was founded by a brigand who got religion. The typically severe church is exceptionally wide, and after falling into near total ruin was restored over a 15-year period. It has a national reputation for its July festival of religious music and summer courses on illumination, Byzantine painting, and bookbinding (*t 05 65 98 20 20*).

Albi

'Red Albi', the brick capital of the Tarn, has often been compared to a Tuscan hill-town piled under its church, in this case, the extraordinary **Cathédrale de Ste-Cécile**, a huge red fortress. This show of ecclesiastical force psychologically goes beyond the fact that the cathedral was part of the city's defences; it was to remind Albi who was boss. After all, in the early 12th century when the austere St Bernard came to tell the Albigeois to repent, they laughed him out of town. They sympathized with the Cathars and gave them refuge, and the Cathars in turn made Albi the seat of a bishop – hence, the word 'Albigensians'. Albi itself was never taken in the Crusade that took its name, but was made to pay afterwards by the Inquisition. Horrified by its cruelties, the people in 1234 rescued several heretics condemned to the stake and chased the bishop into the cathedral, from where he excommunicated the entire town.

Subsequent bishop-inquisitors, determined to protect the episcopal person, used their position to accuse anyone with money of lapsing in the faith, in order to expropriate their wealth. This they used to build themselves a castle, the Palais de la Berbie, and then in 1280 began a new cathedral in the purest southern Gothic style, with a single nave 100ft high and as long as a football pitch. It was no sooner consecrated in 1480 when an arty string of bishops began embellishing it. Biggest of these decorations is the exotic 256ft bell tower that wouldn't look too out of place in Central Asia.

Getting Around

Albi's train station is a 10-minute walk from the centre in Place Stalingrad and is linked by the Occitan night train with Paris, and frequently by train with Toulouse. The bus station is in Place Jean-Jaurès, t 05 63 54 58 61.

Tourist Information

Albi: Place Ste-Cécile, t 05 63 49 48 80, f 05 63 49 48 98.

Where to Stay and Eat

Albi ✉ 81000

****La Réserve**, Rte de Cordes, t 05 63 60 80 80, f 05 63 47 63 60 (*expensive*). An elegant Relais et Châteaux on the banks of the Tarn in a French colonial style mansion, with 20 rooms, a pool, tennis and topnotch restaurant. *Closed Nov–April*.

****Grand St-Antoine**, 17 Rue St-Antoine, t 05 63 54 04 04, f 04 63 47 10 47 (*expensive*). Soignée, central, and family-run (they also own La Réserve, and guests can use the tennis courts and pool). Big quiet comfortable rooms, and a restaurant to match.

****Chiffre**, 50 Rue Séré-de-Rivières, t 05 63 48 58 48, f 05 63 47 20 61 (*moderate–inexpensive*). In the heart of town, air-conditioned rooms in a traditional hotel full of mod cons, with a pretty garden terrace.

****Georges V**, 29 Av Maréchal Joffre, t 05 63 54 24 16, f 05 63 49 90 78 (*inexpensive*). Opposite the train station, formerly the house of an apothecary, with delightful rooms and a very warm welcome. Big breakfasts in the garden. Book.

****Vieil Alby**, 23 Rue Toulouse-Lautrec, t 05 63 54 14 69, f 05 63 54 96 75 (*inexpensive*). In the historic centre, friendly and well kept Logis de France hotel, with nine rooms and a good restaurant featuring well-prepared *cuisine de terroir*, with plenty of lamb and duck dishes. *Demi-pension obligatory in July and Aug*.

Moulin de la Mothe, Rue de Lamothe, t 05 63 60 38 15. Wonderful, refined regional cusine by chef Michel Pellaprat on the banks of the Tarn in a charming brick-walled garden or indoors by the fire (*menus 150–170F*). *Closed Sun eve, Wed, and Nov*.

Auberge Rabelaisienne, 22 Av de Colonel-Teyssier, t 05 63 47 97 19 (*inexpensive*). Cosy bourgeoise house specializing in classics like foie gras, free range pigeon, and *gigot de lotte* (*menus from 80F*). *Closed Sun eve, Mon lunch*. They have a few pleasantly old fashioned rooms.

Le Tournesol, Rue de l'Ort-en-Salvy (off Place du Vigan), t 05 63 38 44 60. Best vegetarian restaurant in the Tarn, with apple crumble for the homesick and organic beer (*menus around 80F*). *Open Tues–Sat for lunch, and Fri and Sat eve*.

Another is the finely carved stone porch at the top of the stairs, a preview of the richness of the **interior** (*open daily 9–12 and 2.30–6.30; June–Sept daily 8.30–7*). This positively glows with colour, the vaults completely covered with 16th-century frescoes by painters from Bologna. On the west wall, an enormous, harrowing 15th-century fresco of the *Last Judgement*, by an unknown French or Flemish painter, was mutilated to provide an entrance to the tower chapel; now a magnificent 18th-century organ replaces the central figure of Christ the Judge (perhaps appropriate for a church dedicated to Cecilia, who invented the instrument). The Flamboyant *jubé* or choir screen, carved by Burgundians, is a masterpiece of delicate tracery in stone, inspite of being deprived of its many figures in the Revolution. Behind, the choir itself (*adm*) is decorated with a full quorum of biblical figures and saints, natural, very human figures sculpted at the very tail end of Gothic, including a lovely sensuous Cecilia and charming child angels.

The **Musée Toulouse-Lautrec** (*open June–Sept daily 9–12 and 2–6; April and May from 10; other times daily 10–12 and 2–5; closed Tues; adm*) is next door in the Palais de la Berbie, or bishop's palace. This castle was stripped of most of its towers and walls after the Edict of Nantes, and in 1922 found a new role as an art museum, housing the world's largest collection of works by Henri de Toulouse-Lautrec (born in Albi in 1864), donated by his mother and relatives. Here are his first childhood efforts and pictures of his aristocratic family before he left for Montmartre aged 18, where he charted the depths and exhilaration of the other side of life with a keen eye, compassion and superb draughtsmanship. One of the rare paintings is the famous *Au Salon de la rue des Moulins* (1894). Most of the other works are drawings, including remarkable portraits and caricatures, as well as the famous posters. His famous hollow walking stick is here too, the one he filled with cognac when supposedly detoxing. There are other paintings, including fine ones by Matisse and the Fauves.

You can easily spend a day poking around the rest of Albi; the tourist office has set up three different walks, marked with explanatory panels. The old quarter below the Cathedral, **Vieil Alby**, has handsome *hôtel particuliers*, including the artist's birthplace (at 14 Rue de Toulouse-Lautrec) where he had the two accidents that stunted the growth in his legs; also look for the charming, decrepit 11th–13th-century **Collégiale St-Salvy** and its cloister.

The centre of life in modern Albi is **Place du Vigan**; from here the Lices Pompidou (named after the president, who as a young man taught in Albi) leads to the river and its two bridges; from the Pont du 22-Août there are fine views of the city, its mills and the 13th-century **Pont-Vieux**.

Gaillac

Down the Tarn from Albi, Gaillac is a merry town under its red tile roofs, in the midst of one of France's oldest wine regions. Grapes were first grown here under the aegis of the **Abbaye St-Michel**, founded in the 10th century; rebuilt after the Wars of Religion, it preserves a 13th-century polychrome Virgin among its treasures, some of which have been moved into the adjacent museum.

The oldest part of Gaillac is behind the abbey, and there are 17th-century gardens to visit, as well as a wonderfully old-fashioned **Musée d'Histoire Naturelle**, in 2 Place Philadelphe-Thomas (*open mid-June–mid-Sept daily 10–12 and 2–6; other times 2–6 only*). Gaillac's vineyards stretch as far north as Cordes, and produce fine red, rosé and white wines in three distinct areas; for something different, try Gaillac AOC Fraîcheur Perlée, lightly sparkling with 'pearls', drunk as an apéritif or with seafood.

Castres

South of Albi, Castres is famous for its colourful old houses of tanners, weavers and dyers overhanging the Agout, and the historic centre on either side of the river, chock-a-block with buildings from every period. The grandest of these is the 17th-century episcopal palace designed by Mansart, a building now shared by the Hôtel de Ville and the **Musée Goya** (*open daily 9–12 and 2–5; closed Mon exc in July and Aug; adm*).

Tourist Information

Gaillac: Abbaye St-Michel, **t** 05 63 57 14 65, **f** 05 63 57 61 37.

Castres: Rue Milhau-Ducommun, **t** 05 63 62 63 62, **f** 05 63 62 63 60.

Where to Stay and Eat

Castres ✉ 81199
***Renaissance, 17 Rue Victor-Hugo, **t** 05 63 59 30 42, **f** 05 63 72 11 57 (*moderate–inexpensive*). Pretty 17th-century half-timbered building in the historic centre with antiques and mod cons.

***Europe, 5 Rue Victor-Hugo, **t** 05 63 59 00 33, **f** 05 63 59 21 38 (*inexpensive*). A charmingly restored 18th-century house, with delightful rooms and modern baths.

Le Périgord, 22 Rue Émile-Zola, **t** 05 63 59 04 74 (*cheap*). Little old-fashioned hotel in the centre, offering simple en suite rooms.

Le Victoria, 24 Place du 8 Mai 45, **t** 05 63 59 14 68. In a vaulted cellar, delicious classics served with a southwestern twist: *gibolotte du lapin à l'ancienne* (*menus 98–250F*). *Closed Sat lunch, Sun, and part of Aug.*

La Mandragore, 1 Rue Malpas, **t** 05 63 59 51 27. Contemporary décor, run by an award winning sommelier, with a massive wine list and tasty dishes (*menus from 80F*). *Closed Sun and Mon lunch.*

Castres has nothing less than the second most important collection of Spanish painting in France after the Louvre, thanks to the art-loving native, who moved to Barcelona and donated his three Goyas to the town, including a *Self-portrait with glasses* and the *Assembly of the Philipines Company*. The museum has nearly all Goya's engraved works, including the famous anti-war *Los Caprichos*. Other paintings, spanning the 15th to 20th century, are by Macip, Pacheco, Velázquez (*Portrait of Philip IV*), Ribera, Valdés Real, and Cano. Other nationalities are represented as well, the English with George II's fancy-dress ivory helmet, topped by a winged dragon. Next to the palace along the river bank stretches a beautifully kept **garden** *à la française* by Le Nôtre.

Castres is also famous for the great progressive politician Jean Jaurès (b. 1859), whose life is the subject of the **Musée Jaurès** in Place Pélisson (*same hours as Goya*). A brilliant journalist as well as France's youngest deputy (elected aged 26) Jaurès fought successfully for the re-trial of Dreyfus and co-founded the French Socialist party with Aristide Briand; his arguments against colonialism, nationalism and the death penalty were so convincing that he had scores of enemies, one of whom, appropriately named Villain, assassinated him in 1914. The museum has memorabilia and photos, but concentrates on his writings and ideas.

Toulouse

One thing that keeps southwest France from nodding off in its goose fat and wine is this big pink dynamo, *La Ville Rose*, built of millions of pink bricks. Toulouse has 650,000 lively inhabitants, counting 110,000 university students, and 70 per cent of the industry in the Midi-Pyrénées region. It should have been the rosy capital of a nation called Languedoc, but it was knocked out of the big leagues in the 1220s by the popes and kings of France and their henchman Simon de Montfort. Nearly eight centuries later, it is finally getting its rhythm back.

Toulouse

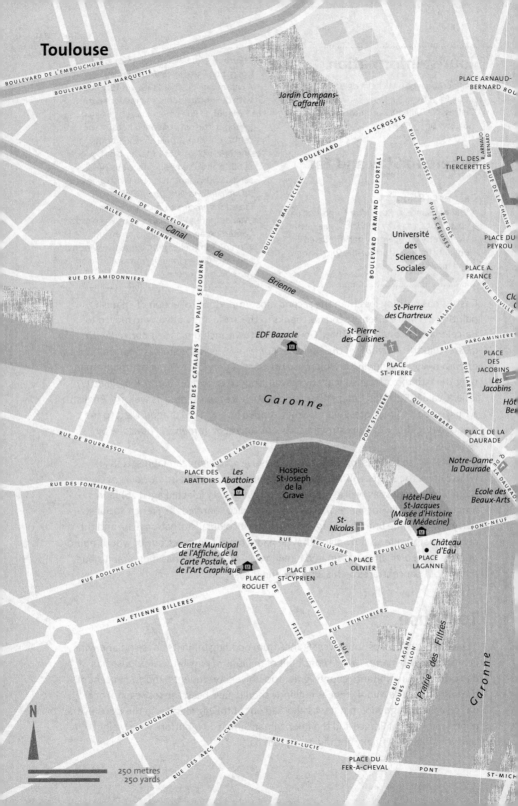

BOULEVARD DE L'EMBOUCHURE

BOULEVARD DE LA MARQUETTE

Jardin Compans-Caffarelli

PLACE ARNAUD-BERNARD BOU

LASCROSSES

RUE LASCROSSES

PL. DES TIERCERETTES

R. ARNAUD BERNARD

RUE DE LA CHAINE

BOULEVARD

ALLEE DE BARCELONE

ALLEE DE BRIENNE

Canal

de

Brienne

BOULEVARD MAL. LECLERC

BOULEVARD ARMAND DUPORTAL

RUE DES PUITS CREUSES

Université des Sciences Sociales

PLACE DU PEYROU

PLACE A. FRANCE

RUE DEVILLE

Clo C

RUE DES AMIDONNIERS

AV. PAUL SEJOURNE

St-Pierre des Chartreux

RUE VALADE

RUE PARGAMINIERES

EDF Bazacle

St-Pierre-des-Cuisines

PLACE ST-PIERRE

PLACE DES JACOBINS

Les Jacobins

PONT DES CATALANS

Garonne

PONT ST-PIERRE

QUAI LOMBARD

RUE LARREY

Hôt Ber

RUE DE BOURRASSOL

RUE DE L'ABATTOIR

PLACE DE LA DAURADE

PLACE DES ABATTOIRS

Les Abattoirs

Hospice St-Joseph de la Grave

Notre-Dame la Daurade

RUE DE LA DAURADE

RUE DES FONTAINES

ALLEE

CHARLES

Ecole des Beaux-Arts

St-Nicolas

Hôtel-Dieu St-Jacques (Musée d'Histoire de la Médecine)

PONT-NEUF

RUE ADOLPHE COLL

Centre Municipal de l'Affiche, de la Carte Postale, et de l'Art Graphique

PLACE ROGUET

RUE

RECLUSANE

DE

PLACE ST-CYPRIEN

RUE DE LA PLACE OLIVIER

REPUBLIQUE

Château d'Eau

PLACE LAGANNE

AV. ETIENNE BILLERES

FITTE

RUE VIE

RUE COUPEFER

RUE TEINTURIERS

RUE LAGANNE

COURS DILLON

Prairie des Filtres

Garonne

N

RUE DE CUGNAUX

RUE DES ARCS ST-CYPRIEN

RUE STE-LUCIE

PLACE DU FER-A-CHEVAL

PONT

ST-MICH

250 metres
250 yards

Bus station
(buses to airport)

Train
Station

PLACE ARNAUD-
BERNARD

BOULEVARD D'ARCOLE

RUE DE LA CONCORDE

RUE DES
RETTES

RUE MATABIAU

Lycée
St-Sernin

Basilique du
St-Sernin

PLACE
ST-SERNIN

RUE ST-BERNARD

BOULEVARD DE STRASBOURG

PLACE
JEANNE
D'ARC

RUE DE BAYARD

PLACE
DE BELFORT

PLACE
DE BELFORT

BOULEVARD RAYMOND IV

RUE DE LA CHAINE

Musée
St-Raymond

RUE DE PERIGORD

RUE DU TAUR

LORRAINE

PLACE DU
PEYROU

Chapelle des
Carmélites

PLACE
VICTOR
HUGO

R. PORT
SALDANE

RUE DE CAFFARELLI

PLACE CASTELLANE

RUE GABRIEL PERI

BOULEVARD

ACE A.
RANCE

RUE DES LOIS

Nôtre-Dame
du Taur

RUE RIVALS

R.
AUSTERLITZ

RUE DE L'INDUSTRIE

RUE MAURY

BOULEVARD

Clocher des
Cordeliers

RUE DE
DEVILLE

Post
Office

RUE DE LA COLOMBETTE

RGAMINIERES

RUE
ROMIGUIERES

Hôtel
de Ville

RUE LA FAYETTE

SQ CH
DE GAULLE

PLACE
WILSON

BOULEVARD LAZARE CARNOT

RUE D'AUBUISSON

RIQUET

PLACE
DES
JACOBINS

RUE MIREPOIX

PLACE DU
CAPITOLE

Tourist
Information

RUE D'ALSACE

RUE M. FONVIELLE

RUE DE LA GARE

Les
Jacobins

LAKANAL

Théâtre du
Capitole

R. DES
GESTES

RUE DE LA POMME

PLACE
OCCITANE

RUE DU REMPART ST-ETIENNE

Hôtel de
Bernuy

PEYROLIERES

GAMBETTA

Musée du
Vieux
Toulouse

RUE DU MAY

RUE
ROME

PLACE DES
PUITS-CLOS

PLACE
ST-GEORGES

RUE
CANTEGNI

RUE RIQUET

ACE DE LA
AURADE

PLACE DE
LA BOURSE

R. PEYRAS

Musée des
Augustins

RUE DES ARTS

RUE DES

PLACE
DUPUY

Dame
rade

Fondation
Bemberg/
Hôtel d'Assézat

RUE DE METZ

PLACE ESQUIROL

RUE DE METZ

FR. LION

RUE DES
POTIERS

Ecole des
Beaux-Arts

PLACE DU
PONT NEUF

PLACE
DE
LA TRINITE

RUE CROIX BARAGNON

PLACE
ST-ETIENNE

Cathédrale
St-Etienne

PLACE
DUPUY

ONT-NEUF

RUE DES COUTELIERS

RUE DE METZ

R. DE LA TRINITE

RUE TOLOSANE

RUE FERMAT

Préfecture

Halle aux
Grains

AV. DE
TOUNIS

RUE DU
COQ D'INDE

RUE DES FILATIERS

PLACE
MAGE

ALLEE F. VERDIER

QUAI

Nôtre-
Dame

PLACE DES
CARMES

RUE DU LANGUEDOC

RUE PERCHEPINTE

Hôtel
d'Ulmo

GARONNE

GARONNETTE

Halles

Musée
Paul Dupuy

R. PLEAU

RUE NAZARETH

RUE NINAU

RUE DES MARTYRS

Hôtel
de Pierre

RUE ST ROMESY

Hôtel
de Malte

PHARAON

Hôtel du
Vieux Raisin

RUE OZENNE

Grand
Rond

ALLEE P. SABATIER

PORT SAINTE

Canal du Midi

AVENUE M. HAURIOU

RUE DE LA FONDERIE

PLACE
DU SALIN

Jardin
Royal

ALLEE DES SOUPIRS

RUE DE LA DALBADE

PLACE DU
PARLEMENT

Palais de
Justice

ALLEES J. GUESDE

Théâtre
Sorano

ALLEE F. MISTRAL

ST-MICHEL

RUE ALFRED DUMERIL

Musée
d'Histoire
Naturelle

Jardin
des
Plantes

RUE MONPLAISIR

Musée
Labit

ALLEE P. FEUGA

Monument à la Gloire
de la Résistance

Getting There and Around

By plane: Toulouse's airport is at Blagnac, 10km from the centre, t 05 61 42 44 00. The airport bus, t 05 34 60 64 00, departs from the bus station (next to the train station) every 20mins or so (*weekdays 5.20am–8.20pm, weekends shorter hours*). Tickets 36F; get them at the counter just inside the airport door.

By train: Trains run from Paris–Austerlitz through Gourdon, Souillac, Cahors and Montauban to Toulouse in 6½hrs; TGVs from Paris-Montparnasse do the same in around 5hrs – by way of Bordeaux.

The slow trains to Bordeaux take 2½hrs and stop in Montauban, Moissac and Agen. Other connections include Albi (1hr) and Castres (1½hrs), Auch, Carcassonne and Marseille.

By coach: The coach station is next to the railway station at 68 Bd Pierre Semard, t 05 61 61 67 67; there are buses to Foix, Albi, Gaillac, Auch and Montauban.

By métro: The métro runs northeast to southwest from Joliment, the railway station and the Capitole to the Mirail.

The metro and city buses are run by SEMVAT, which has an information office at 7 Place Esquirol, t 05 62 11 26 11, but you'll hardly ever need either: all the sites are within walking distance in the compact centre.

By car: The most convenient pay car parks are at Place du Capitole, Place Wilson and Place St-Etienne; closest free parking is at Place St-Sernin and Allées Jules Guesde.

Tourist Information

Donjon du Capitole, Rue Lafayette, t 05 61 11 02 22, f 05 61 22 03 63, *www.mairie-toulouse.fr/*.

Markets and Shopping

On Wednesday, Thursday, Friday and Sunday mornings, **Place du Capitole** has a lively food and flea market. Sunday morning sees a huge flea market around St-Sernin and along the length of the boulevards.

The Pink City is the shopping mecca of the southwest, although specifically local products, besides Airbuses, are mostly violet – soaps, eau-de-cologne or sweets – and rubbery aniseed or mint-flavoured *cachou* pellets, invented here a century ago.

Librairie Etrangère, 16 Rue des Lois, t 05 61 21 67 21. For books in English.

The Bookshop, 17 Rue Lakanal, t 05 61 22 99 92. Also for books in English.

Sports and Activities

The Toulouse Football Club (T.F.C., pronounced 'tayfessay') plays in France's first division, but the city's heart lies with its rugby team, the Stade. They play on Sunday afternoons at the stadium, either *rugby à XV* or *rugby à XIII* (heretical 'Cathar rugby').

Where to Stay

Expensive

★★★★**Grand Hôtel de l'Opéra**, 1 Place du Capitole, t 05 61 21 82 66, f 05 61 23 41 04. The most beautiful hotel in Toulouse, with 50 sumptuous Italianate rooms and three suites in a former convent, with indoor pool, fitness room and a magnificent restaurant (*see* below).

★★★**Grand Hôtel Capoul**, 13 Place Wilson, t 05 61 10 70 70, f 05 61 21 96 70. Large,

The city is home to Aérospatiale, the birthplace of Ariane rockets and Hermès, the European space shuttle, as well as Caravelle, Concorde and Airbus jets, and to CNES, the French space agency, and the national weather service. The air and space industries have attracted research centres, 600 related high-tech firms and élite schools of engineering and aviation. Since 1964 Toulouse, the fourth city in France, has been capital of its largest region, the Midi-Pyrénées, encompassing the western half of its old realm of Languedoc.

luminous air-conditioned rooms, a Jacuzzi and an excellent *bistrot*.

***Des Beaux Arts**, 1 Place Pont-Neuf, t 05 34 45 42 42, f 05 34 45 42 43. Charming, welcoming hotel in an 18th-century *hôtel* with pleasant, soundproofed rooms overlooking the Garonne.

Moderate

***Mermoz**, 50 Rue Matabiau, t 05 61 63 04 04, f 05 61 63 15 64. Near the station, with delightful air-conditioned rooms overlooking inner courtyards and perhaps the best breakfast in Toulouse.

***De Diane**, 3 Route de St-Simon, t 05 61 07 59 52, f 05 61 86 38 94. In a country setting, yet close to the centre, with a pool and tennis, and an excellent restaurant serving a mean *cassoulet* (*menus 105–190F*).

Inexpensive

Park Hotel, 2 Rue Porte-Sardane, t 05 61 21 25 97, f 05 61 23 96 27. Modern rooms with most creature comforts, including a sauna and Jacuzzi.

Hôtel du Grand Balcon, 8 Rue Romiquières, at the corner of Place du Capitole, t 05 61 21 48 08. One of Toulouse's best-loved institutions, where St-Exupéry and friends stayed. The current owners have run it for some 40 years, preserving the rooms as they were, along with a fascinating collection of memorabilia from France's early days of aviation.

Castellane, 17 Rue Castellane, t 05 61 62 18 82, f 05 61 62 58 04. Down a quiet side street off Bd Carnot, and if you are willing to pay more has quite spacious and light rooms with the usual facilities. Private parking for a price (*40F a night*).

Cheap

*****Anatole France**, 46 Place Anatole France, t 05 61 23 19 96. Some of the nicest cheap rooms in Toulouse, near the Capitole, all with showers and phones.

*****Des Arts**, 1 bis Rue Cantegril, t 05 61 23 36 21, f 05 61 12 22 37. Friendly place near Place St-Georges in a lively part of town.

Eating Out

Toulouse claims to make a *cassoulet* that walks all over the cassoulets of rivals Carcassonne and Castelnaudry. To the base recipe of white beans, garlic, herbs, goose fat, salt bacon, fat pork, and *confits* of goose or duck, the Toulousains like to chuck in a foot or two of their renowned sausage (*saucisse de Toulouse*), shoulder of mutton, and perhaps some ham. The final touch: sprinkle with breadcrumbs and bake in the oven.

Expensive

Les Jardins de l'Opéra, in the Grand Hôtel de l'Opéra, t 05 61 23 07 76 (*see* above). Toulouse's finest gastronomic experience, and one of the most beautiful restaurants in the southwest: a glass-covered oasis overlooking a garden pool. The food matches the setting: aromatic mushroom dishes (morels stuffed with foie gras, when available), seafood cooked to perfection, a classic *cassoulet*, topped off by delicate desserts (*lunch menu 220F with wine, other menus up to 540F*). *Closed Sun, Mon lunch, hols and most of Aug*.

Place du Capitole

Big Place du Capitole is the heart of Toulouse, emblazoned with the Cross of Languedoc, the arms devised in 1095 by the city's greatest Count, Raymond IV, when he led the first Crusade. Rimmed with neoclassical brick façades, the square is dominated by the city hall, or **Capitole**, named after the *capitouls*, who were first appointed by the Counts to run the city in the 12th century and who transformed their medieval digs into this splended brick building in 1750. Pedestrians cut through

Michel Sarran, 21 Bd Armand-Duportal, **t** 05 61 12 32 32. For a wonderful synthesis of sun-soaked southwest and Provençal cusines: superb food in an elegant town house, and charming service too. *Closed Sat, Sun, and Aug.*

Le Pastel, 237 Rue de St-Simon, in a villa at Mirail, **t** 05 62 87 84 30. Make the extra effort to book for some of the finest, most imaginative gourmet food in Toulouse at some of the kindest prices; the 155F lunch menu is exquisite (*menus up to 370F*). *Closed Sun and Mon.*

Moderate

Le Cantou, 98 Rue Vélasquez, **t** 05 61 49 20 21. A lovely ivy-covered house in a beautiful garden, in the suburb of St-Martin-du-Touch, for some of the very best regional cuisine in Toulouse, with an enormous southwest wine list (*menus 98F and 198F*). *Closed Sat and Sun.*

Chez Emile, 13 Place St-Georges, **t** 05 61 21 05 56. An institution serving some of the finest seafood in Toulouse or a *confit de canard*; in warm weather, there are worse things to do than sit out on the terrace (*menus 105–250F*). *Closed Sun and Mon, just Mon lunch in summer.*

Le Bibent, 5 Place du Capitole, **t** 05 61 23 89 03. One of the most beautiful brasseries in Toulouse, with a grand dining room last remodelled in the Roaring '20s, and a terrace; excellent shellfish selection (*menus around 200F*).

Le Colombier, 14 Rue Bayard, **t** 05 61 62 40 05. A contestant in the best *cassoulet* in Toulouse contest, with all the other southwest treats as well (*menus 75–185F*). *Closed Sat lunch, Sun and July.*

Sept Place St Sernin, address as the name, **t** 05 62 30 05 30. Large ivy-covered house in a perfect spot opposite the cathedral, just as pretty inside. The menus are delightful and varied: *tournedos d'espadon lardée sur sa lasagne de courgette* or *foie gras de canard aux figues et salade d'herbes* (*menus 95F (petit sacristan du midi) –200F (du vicaire)*). *Closed Mon lunch, Sat lunch and Sun.*

Inexpensive

Les Beaux-Arts-Flo, 1 Quai Daurade, **t** 05 61 21 12 12. Well-prepared brasserie favourites in a handsome Belle Epoque brasserie on the Garonne: seafood platters, salmon and sorrel, *cassoulet*, good desserts (*menus 119F and 159F*).

Grand Café de l'Opéra, 1 Place du Capitole, **t** 05 61 21 37 03. Excellent versions of the classics in a cosy brasserie atmosphere (*menus 129–200F*).

Benjamin, 7 Rue des Gestes (off Rue St-Rome), **t** 05 61 22 92 66. In the centre of old Toulouse, serving up the likes of fennel and courgette terrine, or steak with *cèpes*, for some of the friendliest prices in town (*menus 65–134F*).

La Daurade, anchored at the Quai de la Daurade, **t** 05 61 22 10 33. Dine on a barge (*péniche*) in a magnificent setting; the food is just as lovely (*menus 60–160F*). Book. *Closed Sat lunch and Sun.*

Cheap

Marché Victor-Hugo. The first floor is chock-a-block with cheap little beaneries that daily attract Toulousains of every ilk for lunch. *Closed Mon.*

its **Cour Henri IV** to Square Charles de Gaulle, defended by the **Donjon** of 1525, where the *capitouls* kept the city archives; it's now the city tourist office.

Running north from Place du Capitole, narrow **Rue de Taur** commemorates the bull which dragged the body of Toulouse's first saint, Sernin, through the city streets to his death in *c.* 240. An oratory was built over Sernin's tomb, replaced in the 14th century with **Notre-Dame-du-Taur**, with a *clocher-mur* that looks like a false front in a Wild West town.

A la Truffe du Quercy, 17 Rue Croix-Baragnon, **t** 05 61 53 34 24. The same family for three generations has been dishing out delicious southwestern home-cooking (*formule menu 55F*). *Closed Sun and hols.*

Cafés, Bars and Wine Bars

Le Père Louis, 45 Place des Tourneurs, between Rue Peyras and Rue de Metz, **t** 05 61 21 33 45. The most resolutely traditional bar in Toulouse which has drawn Toulouse's quinquina drinkers for over a century; in fact, it's so traditional it's been declared a historical landmark. *Open daily 9–3 and 5–10; closed Sun and Aug.*

Le Mangevins, 46 Rue Pharaon, **t** 05 61 52 79 16. Has a wide variety of wines accompanied by fancy snacks or light meals. *Open till 11.30pm; closed Sat, Sun and Aug.*

Le Why not Café, 5 Rue Pargaminières, near Place St Pierre, **t** 05 61 21 89 08. A good place to have a beer. Be sure not to miss its inconspicuous entrance and unexpected shaded courtyard filled with locals who also know the secret. *Open 11am–2pm.*

Entertainment and Nightlife

The weekly *Flash*, available at any newsstand, will tell you what's on in Toulouse; and thanks to its students, its Spanish blood and the do-re-mi provided by the city's high-tech jobs, there's plenty. The Orchestre Nationale du Capitole is now one of the top symphony orchestras in France. They often play in the acoustically excellent La Halle aux Grains, Place Dupuy, just east of Cathédrale St-Etienne (**t** 05 61 62 02 70).

In July and August, the city puts on a music festival; in September the cloister of the Jacobins is the site of the Festival International Piano aux Jacobins (book early, **t** 05 61 23 32 00). From October to June, the prestigious Théâtre du Capitole, Place du Capitole, **t** 05 61 22 31 31, presents a series of opera and dance.

Théâtre National de Toulouse Midi-Pyrénées, 1 Rue Pierre-Baudis, **t** 05 34 45 05 05, probably puts on the finest plays in Toulouse.

Zenith, Av Raymond Badiou, **t** 05 62 74 49 49. The biggest stage and performance venue in the area and hosts a range of events from displays of Basque sport to pop concerts, and more besides.

Toulouse likes its movies as well.

Cinémathèque, 69 Rue du Taur, **t** 05 62 30 30 10. Newly refurbished, and the second most important in France. Often shows films in V.O. (*version originale*).

Le Cratère, 95 Grand Rue St-Michel, **t** 05 61 53 50 53. Films in V.O.

ABC, 13 Rue St-Bernard, **t** 05 61 29 81 99. Films in V.O

Toulouse stays up later than any other city in the southwest, but places open and close like flowers in the night – check posters. Favourite music bars include:

Rag Time, 14 Place Arnaud-Bernard, **t** 05 61 22 73 01. Jazz and Latin music as well as drinks. *Open until 2am, 5am on Sat. Closed Sun and Mon.*

Puerto Habana, 12 Port St-Etienne, **t** 05 61 54 45 61. For a lively night out à la cubana, with live salsa and great dance floor. *Closed Sun.*

El Barrio Latino, 144 Av de Muret, **t** 05 61 59 00 58. Another good Latin music venue. Also a restaurant. *Closed Sun–Wed.*

The Basilique du St-Sernin

Sernin's tomb had attracted so many pilgrims that in 403 he was moved 300 yards to the north, and when earlier churches failed to hold the crowds, this basilica was begun in 1075. Completed in 1220, it's the largest surviving Romanesque church in the world (only the abbey church of Cluny, destroyed in the Revolution, was bigger). Modelled after Conques, its plan is identical to the basilica of St James at Compostela, begun at the same time: a cross, ending in a semi-circular apse with five radiating chapels. Seen from Rue St-Bernard, this apse is a fascinating play of white stone and red brick, a crescendo culminating in the octagonal **bell tower** that is Toulouse's landmark; St-Sernin's original three storeys of arcades were increased to five for the sole purpose of upstaging the campanile of the Jacobins across town. The odd, asymmetrical **Porte Miège-ville** on the south side, has a tympanum carved by the 11th-century master Bernard Gilduin, showing the *Ascension of Christ*, a rare scene in medieval art. On the brackets are figures of David and others riding on lions; the magnificent capitals tell the story of the Redemption. The eight capitals on the south transept door, the **Porte des Comtes**, also by Gilduin, show the torments of hell, most alarmingly a man having his testicles crushed and a woman whose breasts are being devoured by serpents.

Begun in 1969, the 'de-restoration' of the **interior** stripped the majestic brick and stone of Viollet-le-Duc's ham-handed murals and fiddly neo-Gothic bits. In the process some 12th-century frescoes have been found; note the serene angel in the third bay of the north transept, which also has the best capitals. For a small fee you can enter the **ambulatory** (*open daily 10–11.30 and 2–5; July and Aug daily 10–6; closed Sun am*) to see the 17th-century bas-reliefs and panels on the lives of the saints whose relics are housed here. Opposite the central chapel are seven marble bas-reliefs (1096) by Bernard Gilduin. The Christ in Majesty set in a mandorla is as serene and pot-bellied as a Buddha, surrounded by the Evangelists.

On the south side of Place St-Sernin, the rich archaeological collections of the **Musée St-Raymond** (*open daily 10–6; June–Aug daily 10–7*) include gold torques from the legendary swamp treasure of the Tectosages, the remarkable Celtic tribe who founded Toulouse, a superb set of busts of Roman emperors and fine marbles depicting the *Labours of Hercules*. The surrounding neighbourhood has been the city's Latin Quarter ever since 1229 when the **University of Toulouse** was founded in Rue des Lois.

Les Jacobins

The Spanish priest Domingo de Guzmán tried hard to re-convert Languedoc's heretical Cathars before the Albigensian Crusade, and in 1215 founded a preaching order in Toulouse, just west of Place du Capitole. The Dominicans soon became so popular that in 1230 they built a great mother church, **Les Jacobins** (*open daily 10–12 and 2–6; July–Sept daily 10–6.30; closed Sun and hols am; adm for the cloister*), a masterpiece of southern French Gothic that so impressed the popes that they sent it the relics of the greatest Dominican of them all, St Thomas Aquinas (d. 1274). One aspect of the Order's appeal was their reaction to Rome's love of luxury, which they expressed so successfully here that Les Jacobins became the prototype for all Dominican churches. Gargoyles are the only exterior sculpture in the harmonious pile of buttresses, alternating with flamboyant windows; its octagonal bell tower of brick and stone crowned with baby towers is a landmark on the city skyline. The interior is breathtakingly light and spacious, consisting of twin naves, crisscrossed by a fantastic interweaving of ribs in the vault, reaching an epiphany in the flamboyant *palmier* in the apse. A small door leads out into the lovely **cloister** (1309), with brick arcades and twinned marble columns.

Just south of Les Jacobins, at the end of Rue Gambetta, is one of the city's most splendid residences, the **Hôtel de Bernuy**, built in 1504 by Don Juan de Bernuy, a Spanish Jew who fled the Inquisition and became a citizen – and *capitoul* – of Toulouse. The Gothic exterior hides an eclectic fantasy courtyard, a mix of Gothic, Plateresque and Loire château, topped by a lofty tower, now enjoyed by students; the *hôtel* is now the prestigious **Lycée Pierre de Fermat**.

The elaborate **Hôtel d'Assézat** (1555) is just west, off Rue de Metz, a wide street rammed through medieval Toulouse in the 19th century. Built by a magnate of the *pastel* trade (dyer's woad – the source of Toulouse's wealth in the Renaissance), its rhythmic decoration of columns is similar to the old Louvre. Inside, the **Fondation Bemberg** (*open daily 10–6; closed Mon; night visits Thurs at 9pm; themed visits Thurs at 7pm and Sat at 11am; adm*) has a fine collection of Renaissance and modern French paintings, including over 30 by Bonnard. Rue de Metz continues to Toulouse's oldest bridge, the **Pont Neuf** (1544–1632), with its seven unequal arches. One of the finest views of the Pont Neuf and riverfront is to the south along the **Quai de Tounis**. Rue du Pont de Tounis leads back to Rue de la Dalbade, the favourite address for the nobility; the sooty **Hôtel de Pierre** at No.25 is, extravagantly for the *ville rose*, made of stone, with a grandiose Baroque façade.

The Quartier du Jardin

South of the Place du Parlement, Allées Jules-Guesde replaces the walls torn down in 1752. Here, by the Théâtre Sorano, a plaque marks the exact spot where the hated Simon de Montfort was brained (by a woman with a homemade catapult). The Grand Rond at the end of Allée Jules-Guesde was planned as a garden in the midst of six wide radiating promenades, or *allées*, of which only four were laid out: the old **Jardin Royal** and the 19th-century **Jardin des Plantes** are delightful refuges from the big city. If you're fond of Egyptian, Indian and Far Eastern art, don't miss the **Musée Georges Labit** (*43 Rue des Martyrs-de-la-Libération, off Allée Frédéric-Mistral; open daily 10–5; summer daily 10–6; closed Tues and hols*) – considered the best oriental museum in France after the Musée Guimet in Paris.

Around the Cathedral of St-Etienne

In the mesh of quiet lanes between the old *parlement* and the cathedral are distinguished houses, all uniform pink brick, with grey shutters and wrought-iron balconies, such as the ornate **Hôtel du Vieux Raisin** (1515), 36 Rue du Languedoc. The **Musée Paul-Dupuy** (*13 Rue de la Pleau; open daily 10–5; summer daily 10–6; closed Tues and hols*) is named after the collector who left Toulouse his watches, automata, fans, faïence and ivories.

The **cathedral of St-Etienne** was begun in the 11th century and only completed in the 17th, resulting in a church that seems a bit drunk. In the centre of the façade rises a massive brick bell tower with a clock, over the Romanesque base. To the right is a worn, asymmetrical stone Gothic façade, where the portal and rose window are off-centre; to the left extends the bulge of the chapel of Notre-Dame, a small church in itself stuck on the north end.

It's even tipsier inside, but many of its best decorations are stowed away in the **Musée des Augustins** at the corner of Rue de Metz and Rue d'Alsace (*open daily 10–6; winter daily 10–5; closed Tues and hols; Wed night until 9pm*). The museum, one of the oldest in France, is housed in a 14th-century Augustinian convent. Gothic sculptures occupy the flamboyant chapterhouse, and the church holds religious paintings by Van Dyck, Rubens and Murillo. Best of all are the Romanesque works from St-Etienne – the delicate, fluid scene of the dancing Salome and the beheading of the Baptist. The first floor has paintings by Guido Reni, Simon Vouet, Guardi, Delacroix, Ingres, Manet, Morisot, Vuillard, Maurice Denis and Toulouse-Lautrec.

Toulouse's Left Bank

Just over the Pont Neuf, the round brick tower of a pumping station, built in 1817 to provide drinking water to the city, has found a new use as the **Galerie Municipale du Château-d'Eau** (*open daily 1–7; closed Tues and hols; adm*). The hydraulic machinery is still intact, while upstairs you can visit one of Europe's top photographic galleries; an annexe has been installed in an arch of the Pont Neuf. Opposite, a medieval pilgrimage hospital houses a **Musée d'Histoire de la Médecine** (*open daily 9–5; closed Tues*).

Gascony, the Basque Lands and the Pyrenees

14

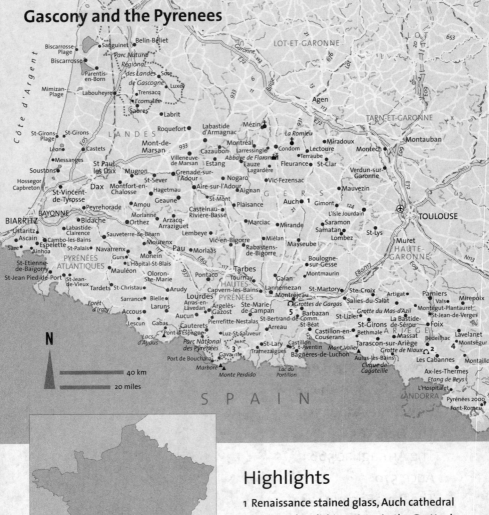

Gascony and the Pyrenees

Highlights

1 Renaissance stained glass, Auch cathedral
2 Upper Palaeolithic artistry in the Grotte de Niaux
3 The vertiginous Cirque de Gavarnie
4 The Château de Montségur, the Alamo of the Cathars
5 Gothic beauty and Roman Lugdunum Convenarum, at St-Bertrand-de-Comminges

This far southwest corner of France is a land of strong character and panache, of garlicky, twanging, Armagnac-swigging Gascons like Henri IV and D'Artagnan, *pelote* players and old Basque whale ports, the majestic *cirques* and romantic peaks of the Pyrenees, the endless pine forest of the Landes and the endless ocean beaches of the Côte d'Argent. This is not one of France's wealthy arty areas; besides a few Palaeolithic

Food and Wine

A good part of the finer things in life appear on the table: the Gascons and Basques are probably the biggest eaters in France. Gascony is France's top producer of foie gras, *confits*, and other ducky delights, as well as the home of the classic *poule au pot*, the favourite of Henri IV (stuffed with ham and breadcrumbs, then boiled with vegetables), and *garbure*, a hearty soup based on goose, salt pork, sausage and cabbage. Game, especially pigeon, is very popular.

Marseille has its *bouillabaisse*, but the Basques maintain that their version, *ttoro* (pronounced tioro), is the king of them all; the cooks of St-Jean-de-Luz make the best ones. Another icon is the red pepper, the *piment d'Espelette*; Basque housewives still hang them on the walls of their houses for drying (and for decoration). Some go into *piperade*, the relish that can accompany almost any Basque dish. Other treats include the sheep cheese from the Pyrenees, the best in France, and the famous Bayonne ham, which is hung for over a year.

The region is famous for golden Jurançon, the Gascon version of Sauternes, which is often served with foie gras (there's also a dry version); Pacherenc, the wines of Tursan and Chalosse, and the inimitable Madiran, the most tannic wine in France, perfect with rich duck dishes, red meat and cheese. The Basques use mountain herbs to make Izarra liqueur. Then there's armagnac (*see* p.567) – older than cognac and somehow quintessential to the Gascon soul.

painted caves, and some great medieval churches (especially St-Bertrand-de-Comminges), the one five-star man-made attraction, Auch cathedral, was something of a fluke. Pau and Biarritz and a score of mountain spas were favourite if now forgotten Victorian retreats; today the region's natural beauty, its open space, its serenity, and the Gascon and Basque flair for the finer, simpler things of life are powerful reminders of something many of us have forgotten in the 21st century.

Parc Naturel des Landes de Gascogne

'Landes' means moors, but the moors that take up most of this second-largest *département* in France have never had a Thomas Hardy to evoke their strangeness. Rather they were a territory outside the pale, swept by storms off the Bay of Biscay, winds powerful enough to lift hay wagons off the ground and stop up the rivers with sand, creating insalubrious marshlands. The only inhabitants were 'Tartars', who walked about on stilts, raising sheep for their manure to grow their miserable crops of rye, as the land was too poor for wheat.

Then one day in 1856, as Napoleon III changed trains at Labouheyre, he had a flash of inspiration; he would promote business in the Landes, first through drainage, followed by 'scientific exploitation' – not of timber, but of resin. Maritime pines were planted over an area a third the size of Belgium, and although the invention of new solvents has since cut into the resin trade, the pines still supply much of France's lumber, paper and the '*pâte fluff*' for disposable nappies. The dunes have been

Tourist Information

Belin-Béliet: the main information office for the Parc Régional is at 22 Av d'Alienor, **t** 05 57 71 99 99, **f** 05 57 88 12 72.

Activities

Few rivers are as ideal for rowing gently down the stream as the Grande Leyre. The season runs from May to September. The seven bases along the river hire canoes and can arrange to pick you up downstream: details from the Parc Information office.

Where to Stay and Eat

Moustey ✉ 40410
Some of the best cooking in the area comes from **La Haut Landaise**, Place du Bourg, a 17th-century *auberge* in the middle of Moustey, **t** 05 58 07 77 85; the name is a play on words: the owners are from Holland but they serve up fine southwestern family fare (*menus ranging from 95 to 189F*). Closed Mon.

Sabres ✉ 40630
★★The Auberge des Pins, Route de la Piscine, **t** 05 58 08 30 00, **f** 05 58 07 56 74 (*moderate*), offers the complete Landais experience: renovated rooms in a typical country house, set in a pretty park, with an excellent restaurant serving delicious dishes involving *cèpes*, *langoustines*, roast pigeon, *magrets* (try the salad of foie gras and asparagus tips) and a chance to try a variety of southwest wines, as well as a superb *tourtière*; English spoken (*menus 100–400F*). Closed January and Sun eve and Mon outside of season.

converted into a playground, the Côte d'Argent. The farmhouses, made of beams and white plaster, with a large sloping roof on the west side (as protection from the winds), are being converted into *gîtes*.

The **Parc Naturel des Landes de Gascogne** stretches from the Bassin d'Arcachon in the north (*see* p.510) to Brocas in the south. The park encompasses the Grand and Petite Leyre rivers, immersed in greenery. Paths and rural roads will get you into the pines, passing by villages and churches from the days when most visitors were pilgrims en route to Compostela.

Into the Park: Up the Grande and Petite Leyre

Located on the Leyre and the N10 from Bordeaux, modest **Belin-Béliet** was, until the 11th century, a fierce rival of Bordeaux; it was the birthplace of Eleanor of Aquitaine in 1122, and (some say) of her favourite son, Richard Cœur de Lion. The castle she was born in is now a low mound, marked by a stele. The church of **St-Pierre-de-Mons** was built during Eleanor's reign, although its bell tower was only fortified during the Hundred Years' War – that time bomb she left behind by her marriages. Inside are archaic capitals carved with mysterious scenes.

Moustey stands at the confluence of the Grande Leyre and the Petite Leyre. Unusually, its square has two churches from the 1200s, side by side: one, Notre-Dame, the chapel of a pilgrims' hospital, houses the Parc Régional's **Musée de Patrimoine Religieux et des Croyances Populaires** (*open June, July and Aug 10–12 and 2–7; Sept 2–6; April, May and Oct, weekends and hols only, 2–6; adm*), with exhibits on popular beliefs and superstitions.

Tchanquayres: Why the Landais Wore Stilts

If pines are synonymous with the Landes today, in the past the region's symbol was something straight out of Monty Python: shepherds on stilts, dressed in sheepskin coats and boots and black berets. Introduced only in the 16th century, the stilts, or *tchanques*, are about a yard high, are strapped around the calves and end in points made of horn or hard wood. They were handy for walking through marshy land, and the extra altitude was all a shepherd required to keep track of his flock while he concentrated on his knitting, a favourite pastime. Once they had mastered stilts, the Landais took to dancing on them as well. Some twenty societies keep up the lofty tradition, dancing at local fêtes, or running races like drunken flamingos. No one has yet topped the feat of Sylvain Dornon, who climbed up to the second platform of the Eiffel Tower on stilts, then ran on his *tchanques* from Paris to Moscow and back again in 1891.

From Moustey the D120 follows the valley of the Petite Leyre, a favourite with otters. **Luxey**, a sweet little village, is the site of the **Atelier de Produits Résineaux**, in an old resin distillery (*guided tours at 10, 11, 3, 4, 5 and 6; adm*), where you can learn all about the sticky stuff. In the early 1900s, 30,000 *gemmeurs*, or tappers, worked the forest; today there are a mere 50. Since 1960, new techniques using sulphuric acid have doubled the yield; now instead of 1000, the *gemmeur* only has to visit 500 trees in five days to fill a 200-litre barrel.

The lush Grande Leyre is kept clear for canoes. **Sabres** on its banks attracts plenty of tourists on their way to the Eco-musée, but don't neglect its 11th-century church, with a triangular *clocher-mur* and carved portal. Sabres was so cut off from the rest of the world that when the first German soldiers in their long black coats marched through the village in 1940, some old women were heard to cry in terror that the Huguenots were back in town.

Marquèze and the Eco-musée de la Grande Lande

The only access to Marquèze is by a steam train that chugs 5km from Sabres. From June–Sept there are departures at 10.10, 10.50, 11.30, 12.10, 2, 2.50, 3.20, 4, 4.40 and 5.20. The last return from Marquèze is at 7. In April, May and Nov, there are four departures Mon–Sat between 2 and 4 while on Sun all 10 trains run. Adm. Brochure in English. For reservations, call t 05 58 07 50 47.

Until the 1940s, the Landes were divided into *quartiers*. Each *commune* had between six and twelve *quartiers*; the most important had the church, school, *mairie* and shops. The other *quartiers* were all more or less alike: in the centre, a *maison du maître*, or landowner's house, along with the servants' house, the shepherds' houses, the miller's house, and the *maisons des mètayers*, or farm labourers' houses. Other houses belonged to the *brassiers*, who lived only from the strength of their *bras*, or arms. Around the houses were barns, pig sties, mills, ovens, sheepfolds, hives and chicken coops (on stilts, because of the foxes). Marquèze was an abandoned *quartier*

Getting Around

Public transport is thin on the ground. Buses link Arcachon to Biscarrosse in the summer; contact Autobus d'Arcachon, t 05 56 83 07 60; others go down to Mimizan, ring t 05 58 09 10 89. For the southern Côte d'Argent, the nearest stations are in Dax and Bayonne, and from there buses travel to the main points.

Tourist Information

Biscarrosse-Plage: 55 Place de la Fontaine, t 05 58 78 20 96, f 05 58 78 23 65.
Mimizan-Plage: 38 Av Maurice-Martin, t 05 58 09 11 20, f 05 58 09 40 31.
Léon: Place Jean-Baptiste Courtiau, t 05 58 48 76 03, f 05 58 48 76 03.
Hossegor: Place des Halles, t 05 58 41 79 00, f 05 58 41 79 09.
Capbreton: Av Georges Pompidou, t 05 58 72 12 11, f 05 58 41 00 29.

Where to Stay and Eat

Biscarrosse ✉ 40600
**Atlantide, in Place Marsan, t 05 58 78 08 86, f 05 58 78 75 98 (*inexpensive*); is a new establishment with 33 pleasant, modern rooms.
**La Caravelle, at Ispe (5314 Route des Lacs), t 05 58 09 82 67, f 05 58 09 82 18 (*inexpensive*). Near the golf course, this is a lovely, quiet place, right on the Etang de Cazaux et de Sanguinet; but the food is so good that many non-guests drop in for a meal (*menus around 90F*).

***La Forestière, Av du Pyla, t 05 58 78 24 14, f 05 58 78 26 40 (*expensive–inexpensive*). At Bicarrosse-Plage, this is the nicest place on the sea, and also has a pool.

Mimizan ✉ 40200
***Au Bon Coin du Lac, 34 Av du Lac, t 05 58 09 01 55, f 05 58 09 40 84 (*expensive–moderate*). If your pockets are deep enough, this wonderful hotel right on the lake is hands down the most delightful place to sleep and eat in Mimizan. There are only 4 luminous, elegant rooms and 4 apartments; tables from the equally attractive restaurant spill out along the lakeside terrace, where you won't go wrong trying one of the house specialities, small crabs stuffed with tiny vegetables and shrimp. The desserts, prepared by a special pastry chef, are out of this world, and the cellar offers a magnificent array of wines and armagnacs (*menus from 160 to 350F*). *Closed Sun eve, Mon and Feb.*
***Côte d'Argent, 6 Av M-Martin, t 05 58 09 15 22, f 05 58 09 06 92 (*inexpensive*). Best of the options by the beach, this hotel is only 5 minutes from the sea; the restaurant enjoys a huge view of the coast.
**L'Emeraude des Bois, 68 Av du Courant, t 05 58 09 05 28 (*inexpensive*). Set among lofty old trees a few minutes from the centre of Mimizan, this is an attractive old house, with a range of rooms in a range of prices; the restaurant is excellent and serves many old French favourites.

of Sabres, rescued in 1978 by the Parc Naturel to become the first *eco-musée* in France. Its surroundings have been meticulously maintained, including the orchard and stream, the fields and Landais sheep; one goal of all *eco-musées* is to conserve old varieties of seeds, trees, and domestic animals in danger of being lost forever.

Down the Côte d'Argent

Three million visitors a year descend on the 'Silver Coast,' as it was dubbed by a Bordeaux newspaperman in 1905. There's room: this is the biggest beach in Europe, 228km of pale sand between the forest and the bracing Bay of Biscay, which sends big rollers ideal for surfing. Just on the other side of the dunes are lakes formed by the

Soustons ✉ 40140

***Relais de la Poste**, t 05 58 47 70 25, f 05 58 47 76 17 (*expensive*). The very best place to eat and stay is 10km east of Soustons, at Magescq, with comfortable rooms set in a park with huge pines, a heated pool and tennis court. But it's the exquisite Landais cuisine, prepared by Bernard and Jean Coussau, that has made it renowned: the pigeon with *girolle* mushrooms, the foie gras, duck fillets, and potatoes sautéed in goose fat that melt in your mouth, accompanied by warm, crisp bread made in the Relais' special oven, a superb list of wines from Bordeaux and Burgundy as well as the finest armagnacs, not to mention perfect desserts as full of rich flavours as all the other courses (*menus are at 280 and 390F; ring ahead to book*).

Hossegor ✉ 40150

Of the two towns, Hossegor has the nicer places to stay, many set back in the trees.

***Beauséjour**, a stone's throw from the saltwater lake at Av du Touring Club, t 05 58 43 51 07, f 05 58 43 70 13 (*moderate*), is the classiest, surrounded by trees and a garden with a heated pool, and with prettily furnished rooms and a restauarant (*menus 190–400F*). *Closed Jan–mid-April.*

Les Huîtrières du Lac, 1187 Av du Touring Club, t 05 58 43 51 48, f 05 58 41 73 11 (*inexpensive*). Owned by a family of oystermen,, this lovely place is on the main lake road. Rooms are pleasant and immaculate; be sure to reserve one with a view. The restaurant naturally features oysters and other seafood is also good (*lunch menu 95F*).

Les Hélianthes, Av de la Côte d'Argent, t 05 58 43 52 19, f 05 58 43 95 19 (*moderate*). A welcoming, family-run Logis de France hotel with a pool, a km from the beach. *Closed mid-Oct–Mar.*

Dégustation du Lac, 1830 Av du Touring Club, t 05 58 43 54 95. Besides the hotel restaurants, try Marianne Lamoliate's fine establishment for exquisite seafood platters and fish soup at very reasonable prices, served on a charming terrace (*usually under 100F*).

Capbreton ✉ 40130

***L'Océan**, a big white hotel near the port at 85 Av G-Pompidou, t 05 58 72 10 22, f 05 58 72 08 43 (*moderate*). The nicest place here, with large, comfortable, soundproofed rooms and a restaurant (*menus 75 and 130F*). *Closed mid-Oct–Mar.*

Bellevue, Av G-Pompidou, t 05 58 72 10 30, f 05 58 72 11 12 (*inexpensive*). Twelve recently refurbished rooms and a delightful restaurant, serving good seafood but lots of other dishes as well if you hate fish (*menus 99–160F*). *Closed Sun eve and Mon.*

Pêcheries Ducamp, 4 Rue du Port d'Albret, t 05 58 72 11 33. This delightful place is a fishmonger's converted into a restaurant, where waitresses in plastic boots and aprons serve nothing but the freshest of fish and shellfish, beautifully prepared (*menus from 175F*). *Closed Mon.*

streams that crisscross the Landes, ideal for calmer sports and for birdwatching: they lie on one of the continent's major flyways.

Biscarrosse to Mimizan

Biscarrosse is a big town but a dull one, and owes what panache it has to its land-of-lakes setting. In the early days of aviation it was an important seaplane port, a past remembered at the **Musée Historique de l'Hydraviation**, 332 Av Louis Bréguet (*open July and Aug, daily 10–7; the rest of the summer 3–7, winter 2–6; adm*), with models, mementoes of great aviators, photos and a video. Now rockets occasionally blast off from the Centre d'Essai des Landes, which keeps the coast between Biscarrosse-Plage and Mimizan-Plage strictly off limits. **Biscarrosse-Plage** is a rather characterless resort that sprouted up in the 1970s; one of the best things to do is take the coastal road north towards Arcachon for the magnificent views of coast and dunes. If the Atlantic is too rough, the lakes, especially the Etangs de Cazaux et de Sanguinet, have sandy beaches as well. **Sanguinet** itself stands over a Gallo-Roman village; its submerged stone temple can be seen some 12ft under the surface of the lake.

If Biscarrosse feels put out by the adjacent rocket-testing area, **Parentis-en-Born** and its lake have been undermined, since 1955, by petroleum derricks – the first lake platforms in Europe, sucking up the contents of France's biggest oil field. And with all these pine trees, there has to be a paper mill somewhere, and **Mimizan** won the prize. But don't let it put you off: Mimizan, the 'Pearl of the Côte d'Argent', has character. Once a Roman port, it had a 12th-century abbey, of which only the *clocher-mur* and Gothic portal have survived the usual vicissitudes, not the least of which was being buried in sand along with the rest of the town, in 1342. In the old days, the abbey and town enjoyed salvage rights that made them the dread of sailors; whenever a ship floundered, the abbey bell would toll, and Mimizan would pounce.

North of Mimizan, the lovely **Etang d'Aureilhan** enchanted the Duke of Westminster, who in 1910 built himself a Tudor-style manor; today only the façade and two wings are intact. South of Mimizan the coast is empty; small villages sometimes have road access to the beaches.

The Southern Côte d'Argent

Things pick up again around **Léon**. Traditional houses give the town its tone, while the most beautiful river in the Landes, the **Courant d'Huchet**, brings visitors from far and wide. The Huchet flows 12km down to the sea, in a lush African Queen setting, passing under a canopy of trees hung with garlands of ivy and creeper, through majestic ferns, hibiscus and water lilies. Throughout April to the end of October, the flat-bottomed boats of Les Bateliers du Courant d'Huchet make the trip, lasting up to four hours (*2hr trips daily at 8am; 3–4hr trips daily at 2.30pm; book ahead – up to two weeks ahead in August – on* t *05 58 48 75 39*).

The biggest holiday centre between Arcachon and Biarritz is **Capbreton-Hossegor**, two *communes* with a warm, sandy tidal lake, two rivers and a canal and the Pyrenees hovering on the horizon. In the early 1900s, artists and writers from Biarritz set up a colony around the Lac d'Hossegor, and in the 1930s the property developers followed. Capbreton too has been filled with much new building; its marina – the only one between Arcachon and Bayonne – named Mille Sabords (translated as 'Blistering Barnacles!' whenever Capt. Haddock says it in *Tintin*). Along the ocean beach, only swim in the designated areas with lifeguards; the big rollers that bring champion surfers to Capbreton hit the coast just to the north.

Mont-de-Marsan

Mont-de-Marsan isn't exactly cosmopolitan – except for six days in July when it explodes in honour of the Magdalene, with *corridas*, *courses landaises*, and a megaton

Getting Around

A few trains on the Bordeaux–Tarbes line stop. For information on the *département*'s bus network contact **RDTL**, 99 Rue Pierre Benoit, **t** 05 58 05 66 00.

Tourist Information

Mont-de-Marsan: 6 Place du Général-Leclerc, **t** 05 58 05 87 37.

Where to Stay and Eat

Mont-de-Marsan ✉ **40000**

***Abor, on the Grenade road, **t** 05 58 51 58 00, **f** 05 58 75 78 78 (*moderate–inexpensive*). Set in the forest, this air-conditioned hotel has a pool and a good restaurant with a garden terrace and generous regional cuisine (*menus at 88–150F*).

***Le Renaissance, Rte de Villeneuve, **t** 05 58 51 51 51, **f** 05 58 75 29 07. Actually neoclassical in spite of its name, a handsome manor house set amid verdant lawns, with a pool; rooms are large and comfortable and the bathrooms luxurious. The restaurant draws in hungry clients from all over the area with delicate dishes based on regional products; try the *magret de canard* with peas (*menus 135–245F*). *Closed Sat lunch.*

Richelieu, Rue Wlérick, **t 05 58 06 10 20, **f** 05 58 06 00 68 (*inexpensive*). A typical old-fashioned hotel in the medieval centre, quiet, and comfortable; the restaurant serves good, hearty Landais dishes (try the *pavé de saumon au Madiran*) at reasonable prices (*menus 88 to 220F*).

of fireworks. Made departmental capital, what character it has is in its neoclassical administrative buildings.

Around Town

To create a harmonious neoclassic ensemble, even the Gothic church of the Magdalene was destroyed in the early 19th century and replaced with the current bland model. What Mont-de-Marsan is proudest of is the only museum in France solely devoted to modern figurative sculpture, the **Musée Despiau-Wlérick**, in a medieval keep at 6 Place Marguerite-de-Navarre (*open daily exc Tues and hols, 10–12 and 2–6; adm*). Two native sons dominate here: Charles Despiau (1874–1946), Rodin's assistant, and Robert Wlérick (1882–1944) who sculpted half of the Monuments aux Morts in the Landes. In May some of the museum's inhabitants are taken out for a breath of air, standing around the streets, as if waiting for something to happen.

During the Feria de Ste Madeleine, the action takes place down by the train station at the venerable **Arènes du Plumaçon**, built in 1889. Children love the **Parc de Nahuques**; part of it is home to free-range swans, donkeys, Tibetan goats and other small animals (*open Mon–Fri 9–12 and 2–7, Sat, Sun and holidays 3–7, 2–6 in the winter; adm*).

Down the Adour

South of Mont-de-Marsan the very first toes of the Pyrenees embrace the green-blue Adour, an important river and one so prone to flooding that it has made itself an extra wide bed to lie in, a swampy muddy prairie of islets and canals known as the *barthes*. The *barthes* are a special environment, host to 130 species of bird, terrapins, and 50 or so little *poneys barthais*, the last members of a native species living in semi-liberty. The fertile hills south of the Adour offer a striking contrast to the dream-like infinity of flat pine forests to the north. Here the main tree is oak, standing amid rolling fields of grain, vineyards, and pastures.

Aire-sur-l'Adour and the Tursan

Aire-sur-l'Adour

Aire is a hoary old town that went on to become the occasional capital of the Visigothic kings of Aquitaine in the 5th century, who were Arian Christians. Their most memorable deed in Aire involved a young Catholic princess named Quitterie who refused to marry a local Visigoth lord, who took it bad and cut off her head. She picked it up and walked up the hill; a miraculous fountain at once gushed forth. In the obtuse associative logic of religion, Quitterie and her fountain were soon performing miraculous cures of headaches and mental illness. She is the patron saint of Gascony, and her cult is widespread on both sides of the Pyrenees.

The church of **Ste-Quitterie** still presides over upper Aire. In the old days, a constant stream of pilgrims assured that it was always open; nowadays you have to arrange for a tour (*M. Labadie*, **t** 05 58 71 79 78). The façade was much chewed by Huguenots, Revolutionaries and the weather. However, the portal under the bell tower is still intact and decorated with an impressive Gothic Last Judgement. The interior was reworked in reheated Baroque, but the sculpted Romanesque capitals are good. The crypt was originally part of a temple to Mars and the miraculous spring flowed where the baptistry is now. In the old days, the mentally ill were locked in cells here in hope of a cure. The magnificent 3rd- or 4th-century marble sarcophagus of Ste-Quitterie shows a great scene of God, dressed in a Roman toga, creating man. A sacrificial altar, probably from the Roman temple, is opposite; test its bizarre acoustics.

Grenade-sur-l'Adour

The first town of importance down river, Grenade-sur-l'Adour is a *bastide* town founded in 1322; its *cornières* are still intact, and the church conserves a pretty Flamboyant Gothic retable. Better known, however, is the chapel just across the river, **Notre-Dame-du-Rugby**, hung with rugger jerseys. But the stained glass and other art is what stays with you, especially the statue made by an old captain of a young Jesus handing off the ball to his Mother.

The Tursan: Eugénie-les-Bains and Samadet

A region of broken valleys south of Aire and Grenade, the Tursan is the source of most of the Landes' geese and ducks, as well as good wine. It also has a spa, **Eugénie-les-Bains**, named after its godmother, the Empress Eugénie, although by rights it should be renamed Michel-Guérard-les-Bains after the chef who put it on the map when he transformed it into a healthy *nouvelle cuisine* pleasure dome (*see* box opposite). Eugénie's waters are used for treating obesity and digestive troubles – hence its slogan, 'France's Top Slimming Village'.

Tourist Information

Aire-sur-l'Adour: Place Charles-de-Gaulle, B.P. 155, t/f 05 58 71 64 70.

Grenade-sur-l'Adour: 1 Place des Déportés, t 05 58 45 45 98, f 05 58 43 45 55.

Eugénie-les-Bains: Rue René Vielle, t 05 58 51 13 16, f 05 58 51 12 02.

Saint-Sever: Place du Tour-du-Sol, t 05 58 76 34 64, f 05 58 76 43 55.

Where to Stay and Eat

Aire-sur-l'Adour ✉ 40800

Chez l'Ahumat, 2 Rue Pierre-Mendes-France, t 05 58 71 82 61 (*cheap*). Set on a quiet lane near the centre of Aire, has some of the nicest low-price rooms around. The restaurant features delicious Landaise cuisine at exceptional prices as well, served with local wines (*menus from 55F*). *Closed Wed.*

★★★Domaine de Bassibé, at Segos (✉ 32400), 8km south of Aire on the N134, and then east on the road to Madiran, t 05 62 09 46 71, f 05 62 08 40 15 (*expensive*). Considerably more opulent, this a lovely place, a venerable farm set in a park with century-old trees and a pool, and cosy, comfortable rooms; member of the prestigious Relais et Châteaux chain. The restaurant, in a renovated *chais*, is excellent as well, serving a delightful *poule au pot farcie* and other good things (*menus from 245F*). *Closed Jan and Feb.*

Grenade-sur-l'Adour ✉ 40270

★★★Pain Adour et Fantaisie, Place des Tilleuls, t 05 58 45 18 80, f 05 58 45 16 57 (*expensive–moderate*). Set in a handsome old house in the arcaded heart of the *bastide*, has comfortable rooms overlooking the river and a celebrated restaurant, where Philippe Garret prepares excellent, aromatic dishes prepared from a wide variety of ingredients, many local (home-smoked salmon from the Adour, asparagus from the Landes), followed by luscious desserts; the 175F menu is tremendously delicious good value (*there's another menu for 360F*). *Closed Sun eve and Mon, exc in July and Aug; it's a good idea to reserve.*

Eugénie-les-Bains ✉ 40320

Eugénie-les-Bains is the fief, or rather little paradise, created by Christine and Michel Guérard. Set in a beautiful 30-acre wooded park full of rare trees and flower gardens, **★★★Les Prés d'Eugénie**, t 05 58 05 06 07, f 05 58 51 10 10 (*luxury*). One of the dreamiest small hotels in all France; romantic rooms with wrought-iron balconies occupy the main neoclassical wing, while others, exquisitely furnished with antiques, are in a 19th-century convent near the herb garden. A gymnasium, billiards hall, sauna, beauty centre, tennis courts, heated pool and thermal slimming centre are on the grounds, and guests can join in courses on *nouvelle cuisine. Closed Jan.*

★★La Maison Rose, t 05 58 05 06 07, f 05 58 51 10 10 (*expensive–moderate*). This charming country inn was also refurbished and redecorated by Christine Guérard. Most rooms come with kitchenettes. The restaurant, the one which attracts visitors from around the world to this remote corner of the Landes, is best known by the name of the legendary sorcerer of saucepans, Michel Guérard. After installing himself in Eugénie-les-Bains in the early 1970s, Guérard hit the world of *haute cuisine* like a comet, earning a constellation

Hilltop **Samadet** is synonymous with the Manufacture Royale de Fayance de Samadet (1732–1840), remembered in the **Musée de la Faïencerie** (*open May-Sept daily 10–6; rest of the year 2–6, closed Tues; weekends only in Jan, 10–6; adm*). After Louis XIV bought his first faïence (after having had to melt his gold and silver plates to pay for his wars), it became fashionable on the tables of aristocrats. Samadet is characterized by delicate, highly stylized animal and floral motives, painted in rich pure colours. Pieces sell for small fortunes today.

of stars and toques from the guides. He has remained firmly at the summit ever since, continuously improving and adding new imaginative dishes to his repertoire, based on the finest natural ingredients and especially products from the Landes – many of them, like the herbs, picked fresh the same day. The Baroque dining room provides an exquisite stage setting for each exquisite dish, as beautiful to look upon as to taste, with Guérard's flawless combination of flavours and textures. The wine list covers most of the great vineyards of the southwest, and includes the excellent white Baron de Bachen vin de Tursan that Guérard produces in his own vineyard (*lunch menus at 390, 600 and 820F; for a table, book as far in advance as possible*, **t** 05 58 05 06 07, **f** 05 58 51 13 59). *Closed Thurs lunch and Wed, except in high season; also closed Christmas–Feb.*

Les Charmilles, t 05 58 51 19 08. La Ferme aux Grives, a recent Guérard acquisition, is an old Landais farm and specializes in the kind of food the original owners may have dined on – wonderful country hams, melt-in-your-mouth roast suckling pig, and big desserts that will send you trotting over to make an appointment at the slimming centre (*195F menu*). *Closed Mon eve and Tues in season, and Jan–Feb.*

St-Sever ✉ 40500

★★Le Relais du Pavillon, Quartier Péré (at the crossroads of the D 924 and D 933), **t** 05 58 76 20 22, **f** 05 58 76 25 81 (*inexpensive*). A peaceful modern haven in a garden with pool, where the chef prepares a tasty *pot-au-feu de canard* and other tasty delights from the regional repertory (*menus at 150–280F,*

with lots of foie gras). *Closed Sun eve out of season.*

Relais de la Chalosse, t 05 58 76 10 47 (ring ahead). Northwest of Saint-Sever at Cauna, this highly recommended restaurant prepares exquisite versions of some of the more difficult Landais dishes, such as *cou de canard farci*, duck's necks stuffed with *foie gras* and also fish dishes; there's a lovely dining terrace for lingering the afternoon away (*menus from 90 to 200F*). *Closed Sun eve and Mon.*

In Toulouzette, 7km west of St-Sever on the D352, the **Maison Salis, t** 05 58 97 76 04, is a *ferme-auberge* specializing in many of the usual Gascon delights – *garbure*, foie gras and *confits*, although in the summer, if you order ahead, they'll cook you up a shad or *sandre* (pike) fresh from the Adour (*menus 70–165F*).*Open daily, booking essential.*

Montfort-en-Chalosse ✉ 40380

★★Aux Tauzins, on the D2 towards Hagetmau, **t** 05 58 98 60 22, **f** 05 58 98 45 79 (*inexpensive*). This family-run place has been open for decades, a cosy old country inn with comfortable rooms, set in a garden with a pool. The restaurant makes excellent use of the good things from the Chalosse, as in *foie frais aux raisins* or *tournedos landais* (*menus 100–200F*). *Closed Sun eve and Mon out of season, Jan, and first 2 weeks Oct.*

Domaine Testilin, t 05 58 98 61 21 (*inexpensive*). At Baights, this warm and friendly hotel offers 12 lovely rooms in a magnificent *maison de maître*, set in a park; the food is equally lovely, featuring succulent *magrets* and other regional specialities, washed down with *vin du Tursan* (*menus 130 and 190F*).

The Chalosse and St-Sever

The Chalosse is the 'Secret Garden of the Landes'. One of the best views of it is from **St-Sever**, which enjoys a superb setting on a balcony between the Chalosse and the endless sea of pine forests to the north. The lofty plateau of Morlanne was the site of the Roman castrum, where St Severus converted the 5th-century Roman governor. Not a stone remains of this, but you can drive up for the view. Below stretches the town, the goose-feather capital of France, stuffing the by-product of the foie gras industry into duvets, sleeping bags and jackets.

The town grew up around the **abbey of St Sever** founded in 988 by the Count of Gascony. It reached its golden age under Abbot Grégoire de Montaner of Cluny (1028–72) who rebuilt the church with seven staggered apses. Heavily damaged in the Hundred Years' War, the nave was rebuilt in the 1300s. Worse was yet to come: Protestants, Revolutionaries, and 19th-century restorers whose leaden neo-Romanesque touch destroyed much of the abbey's charm. Fortunately, they left the capitals alone. Those from the 11th century have simple designs. Later sculptors added figures amid the leaves: birds and Daniel in the lions' den. The finest capitals of all, in the north tribune, are attributed to the vigorous School of Toulouse.

In 1280 Eleanor of Castile, wife of Edward I, founded another monastery in St-Sever, the **Couvent des Jacobins**. The cloister now houses the **Musée des Jacobins** with Gallo-Roman artefacts, items relating to the pilgrimage route and the celebrated illuminated 11th-century Apocalypse of St-Sever (now in the Bibliothèque National).

The Adour is at its most scenic between St-Sever and **Mugron**, the 'Belvedere of the Chalosse'. West of Mugron, the pretty 13th-century *bastide* of **Montfort-en-Chalosse** was founded by the king of England. The **Musée de la Chalosse** (*open 21 Mar–21 Dec daily 2–7pm; adm*) is contained in a well preserved master's house from the 1890s, and concentrates on wine. The church of Montfort is equally worth a look, a charming combination of Romanesque and Gothic; but as with many villages in the Chalosse, many people come to Montfort just to eat.

Dax

With five wells pouring out over 7 million litres of hot mineral water every day, Dax easily makes its living as France's top thermal spa, full of flowers, mimosas and mini-vans transferring patients to and fro. The story goes that an old Roman soldier stationed here had a dog so stiff with rheumatism that he left it behind when his legion went to Spain. When he returned, he was amazed to see Fido frisking about like a pup. Curious, he followed the dog to a pool of hot mud on the Adour. The soldier joined his dog in the mud and quickly spread word of a cure. Word reached Julia, the daughter of Augustus, who was afflicted with rheumatism. She became the first celebrity to take the cure, and renamed the place Aqua Augustus after her dad, a name that contracted on Gascon tongues to Dax. Its current career as a full-time spa took off after the construction of the railway from Bordeaux in 1854.

A Walk Through Old Dax

From the 4th century to the mid-1800s, Dax was corseted in its walls on the left bank of the Adour; eight of the original 49 towers have survived near the river. It has the perfect centrepiece for a spa, the arcaded Fontaine Chaude, built in 1818 around the most generous of hot springs in France. In Gascon it's called *Lou Bagn Bourren*, the Boiling Bath; housewives found it handy for cooking hardboiled eggs, dipping chickens for plucking and washing the sheets.

Getting Around

A special bus service links Dax to Biarritz and Bordeaux airports; ring the Dax tourist office to reserve a place. The train station is on the TGV Atlantique route from Paris. For regional bus information, call **t** 05 58 56 80 80. For a taxi, call **t** 05 58 74 74 06 or **t** 05 58 91 20 60.

Tourist Information

By the river in Place Thiers, t 05 58 56 86 86, **f** 05 58 56 86 80.

Where to Stay

Dax ✉ 40100

In Dax 16 out of 58 hotels are connected to thermal establishments. High season is Sepember and October, when it can be hard to find a place that will take you for just one or two nights. Note that at least half-pension is obligatory in nearly every hotel.

- ★★★**Hôtel Splendid**, 2 Cours Verdun, **t** 05 58 56 70 70, **f** 05 58 74 76 33 (*expensive*). This was built in 1928, and has an enormous lobby, Art Deco furnishings and grand old bathrooms intact; along with a spa cure there's a health centre on the premises, and lounging about in white bathrobes is *de rigueur. Closed Dec–Feb.*
- ★★**Auberge des Pins**, 86 Av Francis-Planté, **t** 05 57 74 22 46, **f** 05 58 56 05 62 (*inexpensive*). A charming little inn with a large garden just outside the centre, country family-style meals (but they will adapt to any diet; *lunch menu 65F, dinner 100–165F*) and free minibus service to the baths.
- ★★**Beausoleil**, near the centre at 38 Rue du Tuc-d'Eauze, **t** 05 58 74 18 32, **f** 05 58 56 03 81 (*inexpensive*). This white, old-fashioned hotel oozes charm and comfort, peace and quiet and offers lots of personal attention.
- ★★**Le Richelieu**, 13 Av Victor-Hugo, **t** 05 58 90 49 49, **f** 05 58 90 80 86 (*inexpensive*). Centrally located and recently renovated, with a pleasant patio for sunny days and a restaurant that tries harder than most; the owners have recently opened a '**Club**

Rétro' on Rue St Eutrope where for a 30F cover charge you can dance and sing to French golden oldies.

- ★**Au Fin Gourmet**, 3 Rue des Pénitents, **t** 05 58 74 04 26 (*moderate–inexpensive*). Right in the centre by the Fontaine Chaude, with rooms ranging from the very basic to others with private bathrooms and TVs as well as studios. Half- or full *pension* is mandatory, but the food is very good with many Landais recipes on the menu (try the delicate *cèpe omelette*) served in a choice of pretty little rooms (*menus range from 70 to 130F*).
- **Hôtel Loustalot**, 60 Place Joffre, **t** 05 58 74 04 13 (*cheap*). Just over the bridge; the décor inside is more modern than the exterior suggests, and there's a chance of finding a room with a bathroom for only one or two nights.

Eating Out

As most guests dine in their hotels, Dax has relatively few restaurants.

- **L'Amphitryon**, 38 Cours Gallieni, **t** 05 58 74 58 05, is a friendly place with constantly changing menus that feature plenty of delights from Amphitryon's watery realm (*menus range from 110 to 220F*). *Closed Sun dinner, Mon, and last fortnight in Aug.*
- **Restaurant du Bois de Boulogne**, Allée du Bois-de-Boulogne, **t** 05 58 74 23 32. With a shady summer terrace, overlooking the Adour, this is another good bet for seafood lovers, but the chef also does good regional meat dishes (*menus from 110 to 170F*).
- **Le Moulin de Poustagnacq**, Saint-Paul-lès-Dax, **t** 05 58 91 31 03, **f** 05 58 91 37 97. When the Dacquois do dine out, they usually get in their cars and head out of the centre. This popular place overlooks a forest and pond; the kitchen uses local ingredients to create imaginative dishes such as crayfish tempura seldom seen in the Landes, served with a wide choice of wines (*menus from 140 to 300F*). *Closed Sun eve and Mon.*

Dax Facts

Dax calls itself 'La Première Station de Pélothérapie' or 'First in Hot Mud Pie Cures'. Originally pits were dug along the river, oozing with the mud from the *barthes* where everyone could wallow to their heart's content. These days, the mud is scientifically gathered, mixed with hot water from the fountain and ripened in large solar basins. Here algae and bacteria incubate in the mud mix which contribute in some mysterious way to the anti-inflammatory, soothing effect when the plasticky grey mud is heated and applied to aching joints and bad backs. The spas apply 1,000 cubic metres of the stuff every year, by prescription only; if you'd like to try a bath, however, the **Thermes Borda**, 30 Rue des Lazaristes, t 05 58 74 86 13, is *open daily exc Sun from 2 to 6.*

From the Fontaine Chaude, Rue Cazade leads to the **Musée de Borda** (*open 2.30–6.30, closed Tues and Sun*). This houses a bit of this and that: Upper Palaeolithic ivories, Roman bronzes, mosaics and a statue of Sleeping Eros. In the medieval section are a pair of Merovingian sarcophagi, and a stone where debtors who couldn't pay were made to sit in Rue du Mirailh; every time someone passed by they had to receive three smacks on the bottom. The coin collection ranges from the ancient Greek to ceramic pennies minted by the Weimar Republic.

The ponderous **Cathédrale Notre-Dame** is the third church on the site. Its mongrel Baroque-Classical interior is morose, but contains two features from the Gothic cathedral: 80 choir stalls from the mid-1500s, carved with a lunatic asylum of figures twisting about the seats, and the early 13th-century Portal of the Apostles installed in the left transept to protect it from the elements. Its tympanum depicts the Weighing of Souls. Christ holds the book of the Seven Seals; along the lintel, the dead rise from their graves, the blessed from smart tombs on the right, while on the left the repro-bates are chewed by devils, monsters and Deadly Sins.

Behind the cathedral, pedestrian-only Rue Neuve leads to Cours de Verdun with the handsome Atrium Casino, built in 1929 and scarcely touched since. Up the Adour, in the riverside **Parc Théodore Denis**, the rather elegant white Arènes with its domed towers is the busiest arena in the Landes, with both *courses landaises* and Spanish *corridas* from June to October.

The Gers

You've seen the Eiffel Tower and Mont Blanc, but have you been to the *département* that produces more garlic than any in France? No doubt everyone knows the Gers as home of the World Championship Snail Races (in Lagardère) and the World Championship Melon Eating Contest (in Lectoure), but beyond these, *département* 32 may seem a bit obscure. Most of the Gers, in fact, is serious farmland, a stronghold of Coordination Rurale, the group that is always dumping tons of manure on some poor *préfecture* and capable of sticking a sharp Gascon rapier into anybody's political

Getting Around

You aren't going to get very far here without a car. From Auch, there are bus connections (ring t 05 62 05 76 37) to Condom and some of the larger villages.

Tourist Information

Condom: Place Bossuet, t 05 62 28 00 80, f 05 62 28 45 46, www.condom.org.

Eauze: Rue Félix Soulès, next to the church, t 05 62 09 85 62, f 05 62 08 11 22.

Marciac: Place du Chevalier, t 05 62 09 30 55, f 05 62 09 31 88.

Where to Stay and Eat

Condom ✉ 32100

***Hôtel des Trois Lys, right in the centre on Rue Gambetta, t 05 62 28 44 06, f 05 62 28 41 85 (*moderate*). Occupying an 18th-century mansion, this hotel is welcoming and well kept. It has just enough room at the back for a small swimming pool.

**Logis des Cordeliers, Rue de la Paix, t 05 62 28 03 68, f 05 62 68 29 03 (*inexpensive*). This choice has a pool but no restaurant.

Table des Cordeliers, Rue Cordeliers, t 05 62 68 28 36. Condom's best restaurant, housed in a beautiful 14th-century chapel with a terrace in summer. Regional cuisine and foie gras *de la maison* are as good as it gets (*menus 140–345F*).

Montréal ✉ 32250

Chez Simone (opposite the church), t 05 62 29 44 40. This old building decorated with frescoes shelters a superb restaurant known for its duck and foie gras, truffle omelettes and old armagnacs (*the 70F lunch menu is a bargain, otherwise menus 80F–120F*).

Fourcès ✉ 32250

Chateau de Forcès, t 05 62 29 49 53, f 05 62 29 50 59 (*expensive–moderate*). This is a superbly restored château on the edge of this *bastide* village, with fine spacious rooms, a ravishing garden and a swimming pool. The food is also a treat, professional and inventive, and service is friendly (*menus 175–230F*).

L'Auberge, t 05 62 29 40 10. This restaurant on Fourcès' circular square offers simple, good-value local food such as *cassoulet* and duck breasts. There's a terrace in summer and roaring fire in winter (*menus 65F–105F*).

Eauze ✉ 32800

Henri IV, round the corner from the church, t 05 62 09 75 90 (*inexpensive*). This place will provide a quiet night's sleep.

Auberge du Moulin de Pouy, Moulin de Pouy, t 05 62 09 82 58. Home cooking on *menus of 85–150F*.

Marciac ✉ 32230

La Petite Auberge, on the arcaded square, t 05 62 09 31 33. This is a popular spot for lunch, with a simple and filling four-course meal for 63F. Go for the 115–200F menus if you want the duck.

career; it will come as no surprise that the Gers is very well taken care of. It's probably the only *département* with more geese than people, not to mention the ducks, and a few million free-range chickens. It's the perfect place to dip into *la France profonde* at its best, and home to one great unmissable sight: the cathedral of Auch.

The Armagnac

'Armagnac' can mean the old territories of the counts of Armagnac, the big bosses in Gascony before the French rubbed them out in 1473. But to people today it is more likely to mean the area that produces the finest French brandy (cognac? they've never heard of it). This roughly includes everything west and north of Auch, and armagnac is still its name and its fame.

Condom and La Romieu

With such a name, what's a town to do? The natural instinct of the Gascon, of course, would be to flaunt it. There are plans to open a Musée des Préservatifs, and they stage an exhibition of prophylactics in the summer. Nobody knows where the name came from. Ask any of the farm boys, slouching in the bars on Saturday night, and they may well tell you that the name is entirely deserved; one senses they feel the bright lights of Auch or Agen calling them away. **Condom**'s one sight is its

All For One and One For The Road: Armagnac and Floc

The vines in the Gers date back at least 1,000, if not 2,000 years, but until the Middle Ages the 10° white wine they produced could barely travel across the table; the main variety of grape, folle blanche, was nicknamed *picquepoul*, 'tingle-lips'. Turning tingle-lips into a fine amber brandy was an idea introduced in 1285 by Arnaud de Villeneuve, a medical student at the University of Salerno, who joined the University of Montpellier and went on to become the personal doctor of Clement V. In Salerno, the Arab-Italian faculty had perfected the ancient Egyptian art of distilling essences, and the first record of the Gascons applying this fine art to grapes dates from 1411. As far as anyone knows, armagnac is the oldest eau de vie distilled from grapes in the world.

What all armagnac has in common is the use of acidic, low-alcohol white wine, which makes it perfect for distillation. The essential technique for making armagnac hasn't changed since 1818, when the Marquis de Bonas patented an armagnac still that permitted a single-pass distillation process as opposed to the two-step process formerly used, and still used to make cognac. Fresh from the still, armagnac is rough 58 to 63° brandy; it is then put in a oak cask in a darkened store room. In the first ten years of ageing some 6 per cent of the brandy is lost every year through evaporation ('the angels' share') and is carefully replenished by distilled water; meanwhile the brandy receives its distinctive burnished hues by dissolving the tannins of the wood. After ten years it is transferred into old casks with no tannin. The finest brandies are aged for up to 40 years. When the *maître de chai* decides that the armagnac has at last reached its apogee of finesse, further evolution is stopped by transferring it to glass vats or bottles. Everywhere that armagnac is produced, you'll also find floc de Gascogne, the 'Flower of Gascony', an aperitif that has been made here since the 1500s and has recently started to become popular once more. Essentially, floc is grape juice mixed with armagnac, but don't sniff – it has been strictly AOC since 1989. Fresh and fruity, it goes down quite well chilled in summer. Uniquely in France, floc owes its revival and success almost exclusively to women, who in 1980 formed the only French female wine confraternity (perhaps consorority is the proper word), the Dames du Floc de Gascogne. Their symbol is a bouquet of violets, roses and plum flowers – the traditional perfumes of armagnac.

Cathédrale de St-Pierre, begun in 1507, a magnificent building, but one that has taken its lumps. The interior is an excellent example of the southern approach to Flamboyant Gothic, featuring complex vaulting and big gallery windows.

The nearby abbey of Flaran (*see* below) gets most of the tour buses, but **La Romieu**, east of Condom, is more rewarding if you only have time for one. Its monastery was founded in 1082. It hit the jackpot in the 14th century, when a local, Arnaud d'Aux, had a cousin who became pope – Clement V, the Gascon elected with the connivance of the king of France. Arnaud became a cardinal, and presided over the trial of the Templars in 1307, and must have picked up considerable loot from them. In 1312, he began spending on the **abbey** (*open Oct–May daily 10–12 and 2–6; July and Aug 10–12.30 and 2–7.30; June and Sept 10–12 and 2–7; closed Jan and Sun mornings*). The church's interior is a delight, but the real treasure is the so-called **sacristy**, an octagonal hall intended as a tomb for Arnaud d'Aux. Frescoes of beautiful angel musicians look down from the ceiling, and portraits of family members and biblical personalities line the walls – along with a set of completely mysterious painted designs. If someone is around with the keys, ask to see the unusual double-spiral staircase.

The Abbaye de Flaran

Open July–Aug daily 9.30–7; Feb–June and Sept–first week in Jan daily 10–12.30 and 2–6; closed last 3 weeks Jan and hols; guided tours; adm.

Just south of Condom on the outskirts of Valence, the Abbaye de Flaran was founded by the Cistercians in 1151. Although the Cistercians did not care to dress up their buildings, they were hardly otherworldly mystics. Following the lead of Bernard, one of the most mean-spirited ayatollahs in history, they did have two little weaknesses: money and power. In the order's golden age, the 12th century, they acquired vast lands, and used the most up-to-date agricultural methods to exploit them, while their leaders meddled in politics. Bernard was the great enemy of Abelard and the universities, and Cistercians dedicated themselves to stamping out free-thinking wherever they could find it. As such, they weren't warmly welcomed in the south; this is one of their very few colonies here. The church, begun in 1180, shows the restrained elegance common in the best Cistercian buildings; there's an equally austere cloister, a lovely chapter house, built with Roman columns, the refectory and library.

West of Condom: the Bas-Armagnac

The countryside is green and delicious, and signs for armagnac pop up at every crossroads. The main route west, the D15, passes **Larressingle**, the 'Carcassonne of the Gers' – a wonderful specimen of Gersian hyperbole, but just the same this medieval fortified village (the smallest one in France) makes a striking sight. East of here, **Montréal** is an English *bastide* of 1289, snoozing on its balcony, while its Roman ancestor lies down on the plain at **Séviac**. One of the mega-villas of Roman Gaul, it was built on the usual peristyle plan; highlighs are the baths and pool, and the well-preserved mosaics, especially the one with a goldfinch among vines. More finds can be seen in the **museum** on the site (*open Mar–Nov daily 10–7; adm*).

North of Montréal, **Fourcès** was one of the few medieval *bastides* laid out in the form of a circle. **Mézin**, beyond, was the home of Armand Fallières, president of France from 1906 to 1913. His presidency caused no embarrassment, so the villagers named their main square after him. There is a **museum** with exhibits on Fallières' life, and on corks, too (*open July and Aug daily 10–12 and 2.30–6.30; April–June and Sept–Oct Tues–Sun 2.30–5.30*). Mézin grew up around a Cluniac abbey, and it retains the church – Romanesque in the apse while the rest is graceful Gothic. Over the altar, note the carving of a grimacing giant and a pot of flowers.

Everyone in the Bas-Armagnac comes to the Thursday morning market at **Eauze**, the centre of the armagnac trade. The Vikings trashed it in the 840s, and nothing but eau de vie has come out of it since. The market takes place on the edge of the old town, in a delightful open place where the branches of the plane trees have been tied together to make a roof. The convivial **Café Commercial**, centre of all Eauze's comings and goings, has a rugby mural on the wall. The only other noteworthy thing about Eauze is its war memorial, which won fourth prize in a contest in the 1920s, back when every town and village in France was erecting one.

Nogaro to Marciac: the Pays d'Artagnan

The biggest village in the eastern Armagnac, **Nogaro** has plenty of brandy and foie gras, but likes better to dress up in racing colours and expound on the joys of speed at its race track – heady stuff, for a place where every day seems like Sunday and dogs sleep in the middle of the street. The town's sedentary church, begun in the 11th century, it has some lively capitals, and a window of the Coronation of the Virgin, claimed to be a work of Arnaut de Moles.

Termes-d'Armagnac takes its name from the Latin terminus; this village was the boundary between the Dukes of Armagnac and Viscounts of Béarn. What remains of its strong castle, built by Thibaut de Termes, who fought with Joan of Arc, is now the **Musée du Panache Gascon**, with dioramas of historical scenes (*open May–mid-Sept daily 10.30–12.30 and 3–8; mid–end Sept daily 10–12 and 2–7; Oct–April Wed–Mon 2–6*). **Aignan**, in the middle of delicious country east of Termes, is one of the most attractive villages in the Gers. The original seat of the counts of Armagnac, it was wrecked by the Black Prince in 1355, but retains its arcaded square and 12th-century church. Charles de Batz – D'Artagnan – was born at the Château de Castelmaure north of nearby **Lupiac**.

Plaisance-du-Gers, little capital of the 'Pays d'Artagnan', hasn't done much for itself since the Black Prince burned it down on his 1355 tour. Just south of Plaisance, the beautiful D946 branches east for Auch, with views of the Pyrenees; further south is the busy village of **Marciac**, a late 13th-century *bastide* that now stands the Gers on its ear each August with one of France's biggest jazz festivals (ring the tourist office for details). Marciac is also known for furniture-making, and for the tallest tower in the Gers, the 293ft steeple of its church, a glorious 14th-century building with some good sculptural work inside.

Auch

Auch with its 23,000 people could be a lovely little town, if it wanted to. It has all the ingredients: a pretty setting over the River Gers, and a core of monuments inherited from the days when its archbishops were in control. But Auch seems to have no ambitions to be anything more than an overgrown farmers' market. The centre is dowdy, and every open space has been pressed into service as a car park. Visitors will just have to settle for two of the greatest artistic achievements France has ever produced: Arnaut de Moles' stained-glass windows, and a set of choir stalls that have to be seen to be believed. Both are in the cathedral.

Cathédrale de Ste-Marie

At first sight this building is a bit disconcerting, with its strange façade looming over Place de la République. This is one of the last cathedrals in France to be completed and the west front was not added until the 1600s. The French would call it *classique*, which means lots of bits and pieces from Italian Renaissance style books pasted together.

Walking around the sides, you can see the Flamboyant Gothic intent of the first architects. Work, however, didn't really get rolling until 1463, when France was awakening to the Renaissance. In the early 1500s, Auch had an archbishop who had travelled in Italy and had access to serious money; Cardinal Clement-Lodève was the brother of Georges d'Amboise, sometime chief minister to Louis XII.

The Stained Glass

Nobody knows much about Arnaut de Moles, except that he came from St-Sever in the Landes, and that he started work here in 1507. If he hadn't chosen the obscure medium of stained glass, and to leave his life's work in the middle of the Gers, he might have gained the renown he deserves; his brilliant High Renaissance draughtsmanship has much in common with his contemporary, Albrecht Dürer. New advances in technique helped him achieve incredible colour effects. In all, Arnaut's work, in which he engraved details on the glass with acid, is an art that seems much closer to painting, born of an age obsessed with all the tricks of light, colour and composition it could create.

The eighteen windows in the ambulatory chapels make a complete account of the Christian story. Old and New Testament figures are mixed together according to the medieval idea of typology, in which everything in the Old prefigures something in the New. Their complex symbolism makes a progression from Genesis, through the Crucixion, to the Resurrection. At the end, the artist signs off: 'On the 25 June 1513 these present works were completed for the honour of God and Our Lady. *Noli me tangere*. Arnaut de Moles.'

The Choir Stalls

The choir is completely enclosed as in a Spanish cathedral, and it's usually locked, but someone is sure to be around with the key. The entire space is filled with a set of

Getting Around

Auch has rail connections to Agen (via Fleurance and Lectoure), and to Toulouse. Auch is also the centre of what bus service there is (**t** 05 62 05 76 37): to Tarbes, Bordeaux, Toulouse and Mont-de-Marsan; slightly more frequently to Condom, Vic-Fézensac, Fleurance, Lectoure and nearby villages.

Tourist Information

1 Rue Dessoles, **t** 05 62 05 22 89, **f** 05 62 05 92 04.

Where to Stay

Auch ✉ 32000

★★★★**Hôtel de France**, Place de la Libération, **t** 05 62 61 71 84, **f** 05 62 61 71 81 (*expensive–inexpensive*). Few hotels in all of France have as many stories to tell as this place. As the Armes de France it was a noted establishment 200 years ago. The Auscitains claim that no less a personage than the son of Louis XVI, the poor Dauphin Louis, was smuggled out of Paris during the terror and ended up here, working as a stable boy (until recently, his descendants still lived in the area, though no one took their claim to the throne very seriously outside the Gers). For all that, it is a thoroughly modern hotel, with luxurious rooms and amenities including a sauna. No pool, but they will arrange sports such as riding and golf out in the nearby countryside.

★★★**Le Robinson**, just south of Auch, **t** 05 62 05 02 83, **f** 05 62 05 94 54 (*inexpensive*). In a beautiful forest setting, this hotel has cleanly stylish modern rooms with balconies and television.

★**Hôtel de Paris**, Av de la Marne near the train station, **t** 05 62 63 26 22, **f** 05 62 60 04 27 (*inexpensive*). This is a family-run, well-cared-for hotel and restaurant.

Eating Out

Jardin des Saveurs, in the Hotel de France (*see above*), **t** 05 62 61 71 84. This famous hotel also claims the highest-rated restaurant of the *département*, with new chef Roland Garreau as accomplished as his legendary predecessor, André Daguin. The lunch menu goes for 180F with wine; otherwise you'll find *menus for 79–100F* in the brasserie, and *166–506F* in the restaurant. And for that, they lay it on thick: the very best foie gras, perhaps with a hint of truffles, along with all the other natural delights of the southwest. Some of the dishes on offer are traditional favourites (it's a surprise to find *cassoulet* on the menu in such a place), others inspired flights of fancy. For accompaniment, they have probably the best cellar in the southwest.

Claude Lafitte, Rue Desoules, **t** 05 62 05 04 18. Here is a champion of regional cooking and fresh local ingredients. For 75F you will get charcuterie and a Gascon favourite such as Henri IV's *poule au pot*; there are also formidable menus of 150, 250 and 350F which are not to be entered into lightly.

★★**Relais de Gascogne**, 5 Av de la Marne, **t** 05 62 05 26 81. This hotel-restaurant delivers good local cuisine such as *daube à l'armagnac, cassoulet*, duck and fish (*menus 100–165F*).

113 stalls, made of heart of oak, soaked in water for fifty years to harden and permit the carving of the tiniest of details. Two centuries ago, a monk of Auch tried to count all the figures on the stalls, and came up with over 1500. At first glance, expending so much time and talent on a locked-up place for monks to plant their bums might seem a mad obsession. But take this rather as a glorious example of that Renaissance innovation: art for art's sake, the first great work executed for the Church in France where religious symbolism takes a back seat to pure artistic expression. These stalls took over fifty years to make and many hands assisted, but unlike Arnaut's windows,

there is no grand scheme; rather, within limits each artist seems to have done as he pleased. Some mirror the figures in the glass, which was under way at the same time; others represent other biblical personages or vignettes. Hercules makes an appearance, slaying Antaeus; others are pure flights of fancy, concealed among the Gothic traceries, on the arms or under the seats. It's great fun and takes two hours to look over carefully.

The Rest of Auch

Auch turns its back towards the River Gers; just the same, this is its best face, with a quiet riverfront boulevard and the monumental stair, built in the 1860s, leading down from the apse of the cathedral. There are 370 steps if you're going that way, and landings with a statue of D'Artagnan and a modern work that consists of the story of Noah, in Latin, engraved in the pavement. Also behind the cathedral is the striking 14th-century Tour d'Armagnac, a landmark and a proud monument for all Gascons. Unfortunately, the tower and its building never belonged to the Armagnacs but they served as the offices of the archbishops and their prisons.

South of the stair and the cathedral is the old **Quartier du Caillou**, a forbidding tangle of narrow alleys that often turn into stairways. The locals call these old streets the '*pousteries*', a fittingly strange setting for a place that briefly was the home of Nostradamus. The wizard spent some time in Auch in the 1540s, and taught at the old Jesuit College on Rue de la Convention.

There's more life north of the cathedral. Just off Place de la République stands the lovely **Maison Fedel** from the 15th century, which now houses the tourist office; it leans in so many directions at once it seems to be made of pastry. Rue Dessoles is the main street; at its opposite end are relics of the **Priory of St-Orens**, once one of the most powerful monasteries in Gascony.

From here, find your way to Rue Daumesnil and the **Musée des Jacobins**, housed in a 17th-century monastery (*open Tues–Sun 10–12 and 2–6, till 5 Oct–April; adm*). Founded in the middle of the French Revolution, in 1793, this is one of the best-run little provincial museums in France. There are 1st-century frescoes from a Roman villa near Auch, a big statue of Emperor Trajan with a big Roman nose, a fine Renaissance *gisant* of Cardinal Jean d'Armagnac, and some beautifully made musical instruments. Holding pride of place among the paintings are the works of a local boy named Jean-Marie Roumeguère, who specialized in sunrises, sunsets, and burning houses.

The upstairs is devoted to Gascon crafts, an exhibit on D'Artagnan, and a room of lovely 18th-century faïence from Auch and Samadet. Best and last is a collection of pre-Colombian and colonial Latin-American art – pottery, figures and fabrics from Teotihuacan, Peru (including a statue of Manco-Capac, founder of the Inca dynasty) and the Caribbean. Some of the best of these works are 19th-century fakes, proudly given a display case of their own. From after the Spanish conquest there is mostly naive religious art and crafts, including wonderful carved stirrups and a bolo from Argentina.

The Valley of the Gers

This *pays*, called the Lomagne, is a country of knobby hills where both the roads and the rivers meander around, not in much of a hurry to get anywhere. The Lomagne is known for wheat and garlic (a third of all the garlic in France!) and not much else.

Lectoure

High on its hill, Lectoure was the military key to Gascony from Celtic times to the Middle Ages, when it became the capital of the counts of Armagnac. In 1473, as France was beginning to recover from the Hundred Years' War, Louis XI decided to assert greater control over the south. His army attacked Lectoure, defended by Count Jean V in person; after a long siege, the two sides agreed on a peace. But the French were just joking. When Jean V opened the gates they sacked and burned the town, murdered the count, and most of the population. That put an end to the Armagnacs once and for all, and to the independence of Gascony.

Louis XI rebuilt the city, and in the Wars of Religion Lectoure had the good sense to side with the future Henri IV. Henri and his son Louis XIII favoured Lectoure, but with the dividing of France into *départements*, Lectoure lost out to Auch, and now has an aristocratic and somewhat forlorn air about it, sitting up on its cliff with its memories. Some of these are kept in the excellent **Musée Lapidaire** (*open daily 10–12 and 2–6; closed Tues from Oct to Feb, and hols; adm*). From under its cathedral came a score of Gallo-Roman tauroboles, funeral monuments decorated with bulls' heads dedicated to Cybele, the Great Goddess of Asia Minor whose cult became widespread in the western Empire. Translations of the inscriptions (into French) give a fascinating insight into life in ancient Lectora. Along with them is an early Christian marble sarcophagus, jewellery from Roman and Merovingian times, and bits of mosaics found around the town, including one labelled Ocianus – a very strange face, full of foreboding.

Tourist Information

Lectoure: Place de la Cathédrale, t 05 62 68 76 98, f 05 62 68 79 30.

Fleurance: 112 bis Rue de la République, t 05 62 64 00 00, f 05 62 06 27 80.

Where to Stay and Eat

Lectoure ⊠ 32700

**Hôtel de Bastard, Rue Lagrange in the centre, t 05 62 68 82 44, f 05 62 68 76 81 (*inexpensive*). The best thing about staying here is of course sending a card home from it. The nobleman who built this stately town mansion in the 1700s may have been a real bastard, but the current owners are actually quite amiable. The atmosphere is conservative French provincial, the rooms airy and tasteful; there's a terrace with a pool looking out over the rooftops of Lectoure and even room for a small garden. In the restaurant, along with traditional Gascon fare, the cooking takes some welcome detours, usually in the direction of Italy, with dishes such as *carpaccio* and lasagne with lobster (*menus 90, 160 and 250F*).

Bellevue, 55 Rue Nationale, t 05 62 68 80 06 (*inexpensive*). This place does indeed offer a belle vue from some of its rooms.

Auberge des Bouviers, Rue Montebello. Happy place where the windows are full of flowers and the cooking first class (*menus 79–125F*).

Lectoure cathedral's present incarnation was begun in 1488, as part of Louis XI's rebuilding programme. There is little of note inside, but if the sacristan is around, ask if you can go up the bell tower, for a view that takes in half the Gers, and on a clear day, the Pyrenees. Failing that, the view from the Bastion on the east edge of the town is almost as good.

Into the Lomagne

There are quite a few châteaux that can be visited in this out-of-the-way region (*ask at the Lectoure tourist office*). One of them, at **Terraube**, once belonged to a renowned warrior of the Hundred Years' War, Hector de Galard, who lives on as the Jack of Diamonds in the French pack of cards (in France, all the face cards are historical personages). Terraube also has a famous well, into which Blaise de Montluc's men stuffed all the local Protestants.

Here too is another *bastide* (1272), **Fleurance**, one of the few in Gascony to grow into a real town, with an elegant ensemble of 18th-century buildings around the central Place de la Halle. The real reason for stopping is Notre-Dame, with three stained-glass windows by Arnaut de Moles, as good as the ones in Auch and perhaps even more colourful.

The Pays Basque

You'll know you've crossed into the pays Basque or Euzkadi when you find a village with a *fronton* (*pelote* court), where the shop signs are full of z's and x's, and everything except the dogs is painted red, white and green. Those are the colour of the Basque flag, which waves proudly over the autonomous Basque provinces in Spain, but is discouraged by authorities in the three of the seven traditional provinces of Euzkadi that are in France. Sights, frankly, are few and far between. The real attraction is the Basques themselves, a taciturn though likeable lot, and their distinctive culture, language (a Kafkaesque product from the Stone Age) and their way of life. The setting also helps: tidy emerald landscapes that have been well tended by the oldest people in Europe for millennia.

Basques love to play outlandish games. Many are based on pure brute strength, the celebrated *force basque*. One can imagine them, in the mists of time, impressing each other by carrying around boulders – because that's what they do today, in the *harri altxatzea*. Related to this is the *untziketariak*, in which we see how fast a Basque can run with 100lb weights in each hand. They probably invented tug-of-war. At the same time they developed *pelote*, the fastest ball game in the world. Every Basque village has a *fronton*, usually right in the centre. *Pelote* may be played with another wall on the left side, *a jaï-alaï*, the fastest and most furious form.

Modern Basque nationalism started in the 18th century in Bilbao. The development of Basque culture proceeded apace in Spain, while at least on the political side it ran into a stone wall in France. Franco's rule was a catastrophe for the Basques; the ETA (*Euzkadi ta Askatasuna*, or Basque Homeland and Liberty) was founded in 1959. Its

Getting Around

Bayonne and Biarritz are on the main line from Paris and Bordeaux to Spain, with daily TGVs (SNCF information in Bayonne **t** 05 59 55 20 45, Biarritz **t** 05 59 50 83 07). Other lines from Bayonne go to Orthez and Pau, and to St-Jean-Pied-de-Port. There is a parallel bus service down the coast run by **ATCRB**, **t** 05 5926 0699 – about a dozen a day from Bayonne and Biarritz to St-Jean-de-Luz and Hendaye.

Public transportation in the Bayonne-Biarritz area is run by an aggressive-sounding **STAB**; Infobus provides information on all services, **t** 05 59 52 59 52. Regular buses connect the two cities, from the Hôtel de Ville in Bayonne to the Hôtel de Ville in Biarritz – line 1 or 2, or faster, the Express BAB. Biarritz's SNCF station is far from the city centre; the no.2 bus terminates here. The no.6 bus from Biarritz goes to the airport, the Aérogare de Parme, **t** 05 59 43 83 83, with four or five flights a day from Paris Orly with Air France, **t** 08 02 80 28 02, and three a day from Charles de Gaulle. Ryanair, **t** 05 59 43 83 93, flies daily from London-Stansted.

bombing campaign near the end of Franco's reign was singularly effective – notably when they blew up his successor, Carrero Blanco. In the new Spain the Basques got full autonomy and the right to their language and culture; this left the ETA out in the cold as a band of die-hards demanding total independence. It does not keep them from continuing their terror tactics in Spain up until the present day.

Although most French Basques decided long ago that being French wasn't so bad, there are plenty of nationalists, who are sure to grow more vocal with the recent autonomy gains of the Corsicans. One supporter told us: 'They'll never let the Basque lands unite, because together we would be stronger than either France or Spain.' A marvellous people, bless them.

Bayonne

Arthur Young, in the 1780s, called it the prettiest town he'd seen in France. Young had a good eye; even today, Bayonne is as attractive and lively an urban setting as you'll find. From the beginning, it was predominantly a Gascon town rather than Basque, but the two have always got along. English from 1151 to 1452, Bayonne gave the Plantagenets a strong base in the south, and in return enjoyed considerable privileges, not to mention a busy trade with Britain. All that ended when Charles VII marched in at the end of the Hundred Years' War.

Not long after, an even bigger disaster hit – the River Adour suddenly moved, leaving the port high and dry. But Bayonne, close to Spain, was important to Paris; in 1578 they sent down engineers to dig a canal and redirect the Adour, and the port was back in business.

A century later, Louis XIV dispatched Vauban to make Bayonne impregnable (it took Wellington two goes to capture it). An armaments industry gave us the word 'bayonet'. The city's other passion was chocolate. Jewish refugees from Spain introduced it to Bayonne in the 1600s, and Louis XIV and his courtiers spread it across France. Some of Bayonne's *chocolatiers* are still in business.

Grand Bayonne and the Cathedral

Bayonne's main street is a river, the little Nive, and it is one of the most delightful centrepieces a city could ask for, lined on both sides with busy quays and tall houses with trim painted in bright colours. The Nive also marks the division between the two old quarters, Grand Bayonne and Petit Bayonne. The former is the business end, jammed with shopping streets.

Tourist Information

Bayonne: Place des Basques, **t** 59 46 01 46, **f** 59 59 37 55.
Biarritz: Square d'Ixelles, **t** 05 59 22 37 00, **f** 05 59 44 14 19.

Where to Stay

Biarritz ✉ 64200

Luxury

★★★★Hôtel du Palais, 1 Av de l'Impératrice, **t** 05 59 41 64 00, **f** 05 59 41 67 99 (*rooms 1,500–3,000F*), is probably the most prestigious address on France's west coast. Built in Biarritz's glory days on the site of Napoleon and Eugénie's villa, this compound on the beach, where the amenities even include a private putting green, has a circuit of old wrought-iron fences to separate you from the rest of the world. For a while in the 1950s, the Palais was closed, but the city got it fixed up and reopened, under a determined mayor who had campaigned under the simple slogan: 'No Palace, No Millionaires'. Some of the rooms are palatial, many with period furnishings.

Expensive

★★★★Café de Paris, 5 Place Bellevue, **t** 05 59 24 19 53, **f** 05 59 24 18 20, is a chic alternative close to the sea. It is one of Biarritz's best restaurants but also has rooms above, all with magnificent sea views, some with huge terraces.
★★★Plaza, Av Edward VII, **t** 05 59 24 74 00, **f** 05 59 22 22 01 (*rooms 600–900F*), built in 1928, has a touch of restrained Art Deco elegance. It has retained much of its original decoration, with a quiet sense of decorum to match.

Moderate

★★★Maison Garnier, 29 Rue Gambetta, **t** 05 59 01 60 70, **f** 05 59 01 60 80. This place is currently fashionable, set in a 19th-century Basque house. There are seven exquisitely restored rooms, all with antique furniture.
★★★Château de Clair de Lune, 48 Av Alan Seeger, **t** 05 59 41 53 20, **f** 05 59 41 53 29. An alternative far from the centre. It's in a Belle Epoque villa in a delicious park, with tranquillity assured, and lovely rooms, though it's a bit expensive.
★★Hostellerie Victoria, 11 Av Reine Victoria, **t** 05 59 24 08 21, is in a delightful villa from the old days, close to Grande Plage.

Inexpensive

★★★Palacito Hotel, 1 Rue Gambetta, **t** 05 59 24 04 89, **f** 05 59 24 33 43. A traditional small hotel in the middle of town.
★Palym, 7 Rue du Port-Vieux, **t** 05 59 24 16 56, **f** 05 59 24 96 12 (*inexpensive*). A family-run, old-style place popular with surfers.

Bayonne ✉ 64100

If you're not too concerned about proximity to a beach, the animated streets of Bayonne might make a nice, cheaper, alternative to staying in Biarritz.

★★Hotel Ibis, 44–50 Bd Alsace-Lorraine, Quartier St-Esprit, **t** 05 59 50 38 38, **f** 05 59 50 38 00. A functonal chain hotel with a small garden and a restaurant.
★Des Arceaux, 26 Rue Port-Neuf, **t** 05 59 59 15 53. One of the best options, near the cathedral.
★Monbar, 24 Rue Pannecau, **t** 59 59 26 80. On a lively street in Petit Bayonne, across the Nive, and well kept.

One of these, narrow Rue Argenterie, will take you to the Northern Gothic **Cathédrale Ste-Marie**, a work largely financed by Bayonne's whalers. The bishops exacted a tenth of their profits, and the most prized parts of each whale for themselves – the tongue and the fat. Despite all the loot from cetaceans, the cathedral still wasn't finished until the 1800s. So far from the Ile-de-France, and so long in building – what is surprising is how well it all fits together. Best of all, it still enjoys the setting

Eating Out

Biarritz ✉ 64200

La Rotonde, Hôtel du Palais, t 05 59 41 64 00. This may be the southwest's ultimate trip in luxurious dining: a magnificent domed room with its original decoration, and views over the beach and sea. They've just changed chefs and the personality of the cuisine is yet unclear – only expect it to remain first rate. There is a formidable wine list (*menus start at 290F for lunch; the full treatment will set you back 350–600F*).

Les Jardins de l'Océan, Hôtel Régina et Golf, 52 Av de l'Impératrice, t 05 59 41 33 00. Good for a slightly more modest seafood extravaganza. Menus cost 200F (lunch) and 250F, but you may be tempted to an *à la carte* splurge for the grand *plateau de fruits de mer*, including lobster.

Le Clos Basque, 12 Rue Louis Barthou, t 05 59 24 24 96. An authentic little bistro with stone walls and Spanish tiles inside, and a charming terrace outside. Local specialities such as squid with peppers are served (*menu 140F*).

Cafe de la Grand Plage, 1 Av Edouard VII, t 05 59 22 77 88. Facing the ocean and overlooking the Grand Plage. It's a 1930s-style brasserie-café, with a wide range of drinks, snacks and meals.

Bar Jean, 5 Rue des Halles, t 05 59 24 80 38, is a Biarritz classic. It's the place to go for superb fresh tapas, oysters and a good choice of wines in a traditional Spanish tiled *bodega*.

Bistrot des Halles, Rue du Centre, t 05 59 24 21 22. Usually crowded for both lunch and dinner. As in any French town, you won't go wrong looking around the market, and for 75F you won't do better than the daily special (usually a grilled fish or steak) here (*menu 160F*).

Bayonne ✉ 64100

Le Cheval Blanc, Rue Bourg Neuf, just round the corner from the Musée Bonnat, t 05 59 59 01 33, f 05 59 59 52 26 (*expensive*). At the top of the heap, by popular acclaim. Even though the Tellechea family has been running this place for a long time, they never get tired of finding innovative twists to traditional Basque cooking: from stuffed squid crab dishes to a *poulet basquaise* with *cèpes* (*menus 128–290F*).

Francois Miura, 24 Rue Marengo, t 05 59 59 49 89 (*moderate*). A stylish small restaurant with modern furniture and contemporary paintings, specializing in fish dishes (*menus 115–190F*).

The Bayonnais, 38 Quai Corsaires, t 05 59 25 61 19 (*moderate–cheap*). A traditional Basque restaurant in the old town, with décor dedicated to local sporting heroes (*menus start at 98F*).

Sports and Activities

If you should feel a sudden desire to take up surfing, there are five schools in Biarritz, and plenty of places to rent equipment. Thalassotherapy – the use of sea water for aiding stress, fitness or recovery from diseases – is big business; Biarritz has two of the most up-to-date establishments, the **Institut Thalassa**, 11 Rue Louisson Bobet, t 05 59 24 20 82, and **Les Thermes Marine**, 80 Rue de Madrid, t 05 59 23 01 22. Golf thrives in Biarritz, with 10 courses and several more in St-Jean-de-Luz. Or else, you can fritter away francs on the *tiercé, quarté* and *quinté* at the **Hippodrome de la Cité des Fleurs** on Avenue du Lac Marion, still one of France's premier racing venues.

a Gothic cathedral should have – among tightly packed tall buildings, where its verticality makes the impression its designers intended. No church in the southwest save the Jacobins in Toulouse can match its lofty interior. The sacristy shelters the only sculptures that survived the Revolution: one tympanum of the Last Judgement, and another of the Virgin Mary, surrounded by angel musicians. Just behind the cathedral, the **Château-Vieux** was the seat of Bayonne's English, and then French governors.

Tours by the Syndicat d'Initiative will take you here, and also through the amazing expanses of subterranean chambers under Bayonne. In medieval times they were used for storing wine.

Petit Bayonne

Petit Bayonne, the livelier side of the Nive, is an old, unspoiled city neighbourhood crowded with popular bars and restaurants. Right in the middle is the **Musée Basque**, the largest collection of Basque artefacts anywhere, slated to reopen in 2001 after a 12-year restoration. Then there's the **Musée Bonnat** at 5 Rue Jacques Laffite (*open Wed–Mon 10–12 and 2.30–6.30, Fri until 8.30, closed Mon and hols; adm*), bequeathed by Bayonne's Léon Bonnat, a famous salon painter of the late 19th century: there's his philistine fluff, but also works by quattrocento masters Domenico Veneziano and Maso di Banco, and highly stylizied Catalan-Aragonese paintings from the same age. There is a late Madonna by Botticelli; plus two El Grecos, plenty by Rubens, and works by Murillo, Ribera, and Goya. Ingres was a favourite of Bonnat's; among his works here is an unspeakable portrait of the unspeakable last Bourbon, Charles X.

The **Château-Neuf**, begun in 1460 by the French (*open Tues–Fri 2–6, Sat 9–1, closed Sun–Mon*), looms over the town with the Remparts de Mousserolles. Baroque fortifications are notable for the space they take up; to defend a city, it was usually necessary to destroy at least half of it, as Vauban did here; today the ramparts are a city park.

Biarritz

For their 1959 season, the designers at Cadillac came up with something special: a convertible, nearly 25ft long, with the highest tailfins in automotive history (22 inches). They called it the Biarritz, a tribute to the Basque village that was chosen by fortune at the end of the 19th century to become the most glittering resort in Europe. Now freed from the burden of being the cynosure of fashion, the resort has become a pleasantly laid-back place. Come in the off season, and you'll notice the other Biarritz – the retirement capital of France. Already 34 per cent of the population are retirees. After September, it declines into an overgrown village.

In the 1860s, Biarritz was a simple fishing village, with memories of a great whaling past, when it began to make part of its living from a new phenomenon, the desire of northerners to spend a holiday beside the sea. It owes its present status to Empress Eugénie. As a girl, she and her mother had summered at Biarritz. As Empress, she dragged Napoleon III down with her and established the summer court, in a palace built on the most prominent spot along the beach in 1854. Everybody who was anybody in Paris soon followed, along with dukes and factory owners with marriageable daughters. Queen Victoria came; the Prince of Wales left so much money in the casino they named two streets after him. The Belle Epoque brought grand hotels, the casino, a salt-water spa and acres of villas. The First World War started Biarritz's fall from fashion; in the 1920s everybody started shifting to Nice and Cannes.

Biarritz

Rocher de
la Vierge

Plateau de
l'Atalaya

Port des
Pêcheurs

Musée
de la Mer

Plage de
Port-Vieux

ESPL. DU PORT-VIEUX

RUE DU PORT-VIEUX

LA PERSPECTIVE

Atlantic
Ocean

Côte des Basques

BOULEVARD DU PRINCE DE GALLES

N

Grand Plage

Casino
Municipal

To Bayonne

AVENUE EDOUARD VII

AV DE LA MARNE

i

Casino
Bellevue

BD MARECHAL LECLERC

RUE MAZAGRAN

PLACE
BELLEVUE

PLACE
CLEMENCEAU

AV DE VERDUN

Musée de
Vieux Biarritz

RUE BROQUEDIS

AVENUE VICTOR HUGO

Post
Office

AVENUE DU MARECHAL FOCH

RUE GAMBETTA

AVENUE VICTOR HUGO

Jardin
Public

Palais des
Festivals

AVENUE CARNOT

AVENUE DE LONDRES

AVENUE DE LA REPUBLIQUE

RUE JEAN JAURES

200 metres
200 yards

↓ To St-Jean-de-Luz

Biarritz has begun to shake off the dust with the dramatic refurbishment of its hotels and the splendid Municipal Casino on the Grand Plage, with its entertainment centres and grand café. France Telecom has made it the experimental city for the communications of the future. Plenty of young people come, for surfing; stuck in its odd angle of coast, Biarritz provides what many claim are the Atlantic's only perfect waves, making it the modest Malibu of Europe.

The Atalaya

Here, on the tip of Biarritz's little peninsula, is the height where the watch would send up smoke signals when whales were sighted. To the right, the Port des Pêcheurs now holds only pleasure craft; to the left is the old port, now the beach of Port-Vieux, and the best place in Biarritz for a stroll. Napoleon III and Eugénie built the causeways and tunnels, connecting crags and tiny islands into a memorable walk above the surf. Up on top of the Atalaya, the **Musée de la Mer**, t 05 59 22 33 34 (*open daily 9.30–12.30 and 2–6, plus evenings in summer; adm; the seals are fed at 10.30 and 5*), in an Art Deco building, contains an imaginatively decorated old aquarium for a look at what's below the surface of the Bay of Biscay.

Descending eastwards from the Atalaya, the Bd Maréchal Leclerc takes you to the church of Ste-Eugénie, another contribution of the Empress's; the organ inside won a prize at the 1900 Paris World's Fair. It faces the beautiful **Casino Bellevue**, now used for exhibitions.

Below this, the shore straightens out into the long, luscious **Grande Plage**, which before Eugénie was called (for reasons not entirely clear) the Plage des Fous. Farther up the beach, behind the wrought-iron fences, is Biarritz's landmark, the sumptuous **Hôtel du Palais**. This is the spot where Eugénie built her palace, destroyed by fire in 1881. The present hotel, begun in 1905, is the successor to an even grander one that also burned down. Across the street, the Russian aristocrats built their onion-domed church of **St-Alexandre-Nevsky** (1908). Avenue Edward VII, which becomes Avenue de l'Impératrice further on, was the status address of Belle Epoque Biarritz, lined with ornate hotels and residences now largely converted to other uses. In the shady streets behind them, scores of villas still survive, in a crazy quilt of styles.

As for beaches, there is a wide choice of places to plant your towel. At Biarritz' southern limits is the broad expanse of the Plage de la Milady, Plage Marbella and the Côte des Basques, a favourite of the surfing set. Under the old town is the tiny Plage du Port Vieux. The Grande Plage and Plage Miramar, the centre of the action, are lovely if often cramped, but further out, stretching miles along the northern coast in Anglet, there are plenty more.

St-Jean-de-Luz to Hendaye

For those who do not naturally gravitate towards the beach, a seaside resort needs a certain intangible quality that allows one to suspend one's disbelief. In all of southern France, there are very few places that can do this: one is St-Jean-de-Luz. The name is perfect. Light and colour can be extraordinary here, illuminating an immaculately white Basque town and the acres of glistening rose-silver seafood its restaurants roll out to lure in customers. Best of all, the fishermen on the quay still strut around like they own the place.

Unfortunately, the name really has nothing to do with light (*luz* in Spanish); etymologists have traced it back to a Celtic or Latin word meaning mud. St-Jean grew up in a swampy nowhere that had a good harbour. It started thriving when the Adour started silting up the harbour of Bayonne in the Middle Ages.

A casual visitor could walk around St-Jean and never notice it had a beach, but it's a good one, tucked away on the northern side of town, protected by a jetty, and very safe for swimming. At its centre is the lavish **casino**, built in 1924. St-Jean naturally turns its face to the port and France's largest tuna fleet. Behind the port is the town hall and the adjacent **Maison de Louis XIV**, where the Roi-Soleil stayed for his wedding to the Spanish Infanta.

From the port, Rue Gambetta takes you to **St-Jean Baptiste**, largest of all Basque churches in France, where Louis XIV and Maria Teresa were married. It is a lesson in Basque subtlety, plain and bright outside, and plain and bright within. The aesthetic is in the detail, especially the wooden ceiling formed like the hull of a ship, and the three levels of wooden galleries, carved with all the art and sincerity the local artisans could manage. Another feature, also typical of Basque churches, is the altarpiece, dripping with Baroque detail. The main door of the church was sealed up after Louis and Maria Teresa passed through on their wedding day.

Tourist Information

St-Jean-de-Luz: Place Maréchal Foch, **t** 05 59 26 03 16, **f** 05 59 26 21 47.

Hendaye: 12 Rue des Aubépines, **t** 05 59 20 00 34, **f** 05 59 20 79 17.

Where to Stay and Eat

St-Jean-de-Luz ✉ 64500

★★★★**Chantaco**, Route d'Ascain, **t** 05 59 26 14 76, **f** 05 59 26 35 97 (*rooms 950–1,900F*). The emphasis is on golf, with the area's most famous course next door. The hotel, in a 1930s-style Andalucían villa, with a patio covered in vines, is set in a lovely park, and offers tennis courts and a pool in addition to golf. Here you'll find de luxe rooms and service, with prices to match. *Closed Dec–April.*

★★★★**Parc Victoria**, 5 Rue Cèpe, **t** 05 59 26 78 78, **f** 05 59 26 78 08. Set in a gracious mansion on the outskirts of town. It's a beautifully decorated, intimate place (only eight rooms and four suites). It has its own park with a pool.

★★**Hôtel de la Plage**, 33 Rue Garat, **t** 05 59 51 03 44, **f** 05 59 51 03 48 (*rooms 400–500F*). A comfortable hotel.

Bakea, 9 Place Camille Julian, across the harbour in Ciboure, **t** 05 59 47 34 40 (*rooms 180–250F*). Twelve inexpensive rooms.

Auberge Kaiku, 17 Rue de la République, **t** 05 59 26 13 20 (*expensive*). The oldest house in St-Jean (1540), rolls out one of the most sumptuous tables; no fixed menus here, but you can negotiate your way to a fine marine repast between 200 and 300F. *Closed Mon lunchtimes year round, 12 Nov–22 Dec, and Wed 15 Sept–15 June.*

Pasaka, 11 Rue de la République, **t** 05 59 26 05 17 (*moderate*). Has a cosy interior and two terraces, where you can feast on local grilled sardines, or *ttoro* (a satisfying Basque fish soup with potatoes and saffron). *Menus cost upwards of 120F.*

Chez Pantxua, Port de Soccoa, **t** 05 59 47 13 73. A long-established local favourite decorated with Basque paintings, serving *fruits de mer* and fish according to the catch of the day (*menu 140F*)

Le Patio, Rue de l'Abbé-Onaïndia, **t** 05 59 26 99 11. A place with a Spanish accent that serves up a very gratifying *parillada* (seafood mixed grill) with just about everything you can imagine, including lobster (*menus 130–200F*).

Hendaye ✉ 64700

★★★**Hotel Serge Blanco**, Bd Mer, **t** 05 59 51 35 35, **f** 05 59 51 36 00 (*rooms 595–1,190F*). Named after the famous Basque rugby star who is the proprietor and whose empire features a thalassotherapy centre and restaurant on the beach.

★★**Santiago**, 29 Rue Santiago, **t** 05 59 20 00 94, **f** 05 59 20 83 26. One of the least expensive hotels around. *Open all year.*

Urrugne and Hendaye

To get to Hendaye, you have a choice of the scenic Corniche Basque (the D912), or else the inland N10 or the motorway; these two pass through **Urrugne**, where the church of St-Vincent has a Renaissance portal with excellent reliefs, damaged by English artillery in 1814. Note the inscription on the sundial: *vulnerant omnes, ultima necat*, referring to the hours – each one wounds, the last one kills. Just outside Urrugne, garden lovers won't want to miss the 30,000 trees and million flowers of **Parc Floral Florenia** (*open 5 Feb–5 Mar and Oct–5 Nov Tues–Sun 2–6; April–Sept Tues–Sun 10–7; closed Mon except hols; adm*). It will seem hard to believe, but it opened only in 1993. A local official, after visiting Vancouver's Butchert Gardens, was inspired to create something like it back home. Girard got everyone else in the area involved with the project, and young as the plantings are they're already impressive.

Hendaye is divided into the old town and Hendaye-Plage with a long and broad beach where old villas are gradually replaced by concrete hotels. Hendaye's border location puts it in the news every century or so; an uninhabited island in the river belongs to neither country, and is under joint administration – Spanish from February to July, French the rest of the year. In 1659, the Treaty of the Pyrenees was signed here, and the following year representatives returned to plan the marriage of Louis XIV and Maria Teresa. A pavilion was erected for the occasion and decorated by Velázquez – who died from the bad cold he caught here. In October 1940, Hendaye's station was the scene of the famous meeting between Hitler and Franco. Hitler had come down to bluster the Caudillo into joining the war; later he said he would rather have his teeth pulled out than talk to such a stubborn character again.

Into the Pays Basque

In the green hills (it rains as much as Ireland), there's nothing as pretty, simple and functional as a traditional Basque cottage, with its distinctive long, low gable along the façade, and half-timbering and shutters, inevitably painted deep red or green. Older houses have carved lintels over the main door, with the year and name of the builder, accompanied by odd symbols.

La Rhune and Around

La Rhune, westernmost monument of the Pyrenean chain, is full of cows and sheep, crossed by tracks used by Basque smugglers for centuries. The summit had a reputation as an *akelarre*, a ritual ground for sorcery; up until the 18th century the villages around it always paid a monk to live on top as a hermit for four years, to keep the witches away and to pray for good winds.

Coming in from Hendaye or St-Jean, the first of the villages below La Rhune is **Ascain**, with its landmark bridge over the Nivelle and a 16th-century church on its lovely square. From here you can take the D4 up to the Col de St-Ignace and take an old, open tramway to the top, the **Petit Train de la Rhune** (*mid-March–mid-Nov daily every half-hour from 9am, 8.30am in summer, plus night runs in July and Aug*). In Neolithic times, La Rhune was a holy mountain, as evidenced by the wealth of stone circles, dolmens and circular tumuli on its slopes.

Just beyond the pass lies **Sare**, one of the capitals of the Basque soul. For its independent ways, people jokingly call it the 'Republic of Sare'. Since the 1400s, it was a centre for 'night work' – smuggling. Folks on both sides of the border never saw the logic of paying duty to French and Spanish foreigners. In 1938 and '39, Sare's night workers helped their countrymen escape Franco's troops; a few years later, they smuggled Allied pilots and spies back the other way.

East of Sare, the D4 gives you a choice of destinations: east to **Ainhoa** or north to **St-Pée-sur-Nivelle**, where there is another attractive church, with a spectacular Baroque altarpiece, and a ruined feudal castle, burned by the villagers in 1793. They weren't just angry with the local baron; this castle had long been known as the

'Château des Sorciers'. The trouble with 'witches' began in 1609. A lawyer named de Lancre was sent from Bordeaux and like most witch-hunters revealed himself as a murderous psychotic. On the testimony of children and tortured women, he had

Tourist Information

Sare: Mairie, **t** 05 59 54 20 14, **f** 05 59 54 29 15.

St-Pée-sur-Nivelle: Place de la Poste, **t** 05 59 54 11 69, **f** 05 59 54 17 81.

Ustaritz: Centre Lapurdi, **t** 05 59 93 20 81, **f** 05 59 70 32 80.

Cambo-les-Bains: Parc Publique, **t** 05 59 29 70 25, **f** 05 59 29 90 77.

Where to Stay and Eat

Ascain ✉ 64310

Du Pont, Route de St-Jean-de-Luz, **t 05 59 54 00 40 (*moderate–cheap*). Rooms overlooking the Nivelle and its bridge and a delightful restaurant with a garden terrace: *feuilleté de langoustines* and other delicate dishes appear on menus costing 70–130F. *Open March–Oct.*

Sare ✉ 64310

***Arraya, Place du Village, **t** 05 59 54 20 46, **f** 05 59 54 27 04, (*moderate*), is fanciest. It's quite expensive for the area, but with a memorable restaurant. Menus cost 130–200F, but you might want to surrender a few francs more for specialities such as the *mesclange*, veal stuffed with foie gras, artichoke hearts and morels.

Ainhoa ✉ 64250

Itthurria, Place du Fronton, **t** 05 59 29 92 11, **f** 05 59 29 81 28 (*moderate*). A large traditional Basque house with a celebrated restaurant, featuring dishes such as pigeon with garlic, and local foie gras (*menus 170 and 260F*).

Oppoca, Place du Fronton, **t 05 59 29 90 72, **f** 05 59 29 81 03 (*moderate*). On the main street of this pretty village, in a restored 17th-century post house. Despite lovely rooms, some furnished with antiques, it still seems a bit dear. There is also a fine restaurant with a terrace, serving seafood and *confits*.

Espelette ✉ 64250

Euzkadi, Rue Principle, **t 05 59 93 91 88, **f** 05 59 93 90 19 (*moderate*). Worth travelling out of your way for, even in an area rich in good restaurants. There are nice rooms with a small pool and tennis, and a remarkable restaurant where the chef is passionate about traditional Basque country recipes and traditions. Some of the house specialities are things you won't see elsewhere, such as *axoa*, a stew of veal and peppers, and *tripoxa*, a black pudding in a pepper and tomato sauce (*menus 90–175F*).

Cambo-les-Bains ✉ 64250

Bellevue, Rue des Terrasses, **t 05 59 93 75 75, **f** 05 59 93 75 85 (*moderate*). An old, pleasant establishment with a view, near the top of town. The restaurant serves *menus costing 103–175F.*

***Relais de la Poste, Place de la Mairie, **t** 05 59 29 73 03 (*moderate*). In the lower part of town, with 10 pretty rooms, a little garden, and a restaurant that turns out some truly refined dishes: roast pigeon with *cèpes* and salmon *roulés* with foie gras inside (*menus 160 and 290F*). There is outside dining in summer.

Chez Tante Ursule, Bas Cambo, **t 05 59 29 78 23, **f** 05 59 29 28 57. A small rustic hotel with a modern annexe. There is also an excellent restaurant (*moderate*). Try the pimentoes stuffed with *morue* or salads with foie gras or *boudin noir* (*menus 90–200F*).

Domaine de Xixtaberri, **t** 05 59 29 85 36 (*moderate)*, up in the hills at Quartier Hegala. A *ferme-auberge* that is simpler but equally special. There is a restaurant with 98–160F menus full of duck and foie gras. *The hotel opens year round, but the restaurant opens May–Sept only.*

The *Pottok*

It has a face that would make you suspect there was a camel somewhere in the family tree – but a sweet face just the same, with big soft eyes and a wild shaggy mane. It is quite shy, hiding out on the remotest slopes of the western Pyrenees, but it's not afraid of you; come too close and you'll get a bite to remember. The *pottok* is the wild native pony of the Basque country. They've been around for a while; drawings of *pottoks* have been found in the prehistoric caves up in the Dordogne.

Though they're hard to catch, people have been molesting the poor *pottoks* for centuries. A century ago, they were shipping them to Italy to make salami, or to Britain to pull mine cars, a dismal task for which their strength and small size made them perfectly adapted. Annual horse fairs took place in the villages of Espelette and Hélette. Business was so good that the *pottoks* were on the road to extinction a few decades ago. A famous mayor of Sare, the late Paul Dutournier, stepped in, and got the government to set up a reserve for them on the slopes of La Rhune.

several hundred people condemned to the stake over the next three years. When he started barbecuing priests, the Bishop of Bayonne put an end to it.

Ainhoa, one of the southernmost of all *bastides*, was founded in the 13th-century. A Navarrese baron started it, not only to keep the English out, but with the intention of charging tolls and making money off pilgrims to Compostela. Ainhoa is a lovely village with many old houses – note the lintel over the door of the Maison Gorritia on the main street, telling how a mother built it in 1662 with money sent home by her son in the West Indies. From either St-Pée or Ainhoa, the next step is **Espelette**, the charming village of old houses famous for red peppers; in the late summer you'll see them hanging everywhere.

Cambo-les-Bains

From Bayonne, one road into the heart of the Basque country is the D22, the beautiful **Route Impériale des Cimes**, built in the time of Napoleon over the hilltops. Otherwise, there's the main D932 up the Nivelle valley leads to Cambo-les-Bains, a genteel spa that became briefly fashionable when Napoleon III, Eugénie and the Prince of Wales visited from Biarritz, the latter to see a legendary *pelote* star named Chiquito de Cambo play. Cambo's attraction is the **Villa Arnaga**, the home of dramatist Edmund Rostand, who came here to treat his pleurisy (*open Feb school hols–March Sat–Sun 2.30–6.30; April–Sept daily 10–12.30 and 2.30–6.30; Oct daily 2.30–6.30*). The house contains mementoes from his life and the Paris of the turn of the last century; the real attraction is the splendid 18th-century-style French gardens.

St-Jean-Pied-de-Port

This town's real name in Basque is *Donibane Garazi*. The French name is even more curious, but port is an old mountain word for a pass, and St-Jean stands at the foot of

Tourist Information

St-Jean-Pied-de-Port: Place Charles-de-Gaulle,
   t 05 59 37 03 57, f 05 59 37 34 91.

Where to Stay and Eat

St-Jean-Pied-de-Port ✉ 64220

Les Pyrénées, Place Général de Gaulle, t 05 59
   73 01 01, f 05 59 37 18 97 (*expensive*), With a
   restaurant that is one of the most esteemed
   culinary temples in all the Basque country.
   People come from miles around for cooking
   that, while not notably innovative, brings
   the typical Basque-Gascon repertoire of
   duck, foie gras and game dishes to perfection; they're especially noted for their
desserts. A gratifying 250F menu (exc Sun)
puts Les Pyrénées within the reach of most
(*other menus are 300–550F*).

Hotel Central, Place Charles de Gaulle, t 05 59
   37 00 22, f 05 59 37 27 79 (*moderate*), is an old
   family hotel and restaurant with views over
   the River Nive, which according to the
   fishing season yields such delights as
   salmon and eels for the table (*menus
   110–230F*).

**Ramuntcho, 1 Rue France, t 05 59 37 03 91,
   f 05 59 37 35 17 (*moderate–cheap*). One of the
   nicest places to stay in the old town, just
   inside the Porte de France. Rooms have
   balconies and a view. The restaurant serves
   good simple dishes (*menus 66–102F; the
   Sunday menu costs 155F*).

the pass of Roncevaux, the 'Gate of Spain' of medieval legend. From the 8th century,
Arab armies passed this way to raid France; Charlemagne and Roland came back the
other way to raid Spain, and pass into legend along the way. Pilgrims from all over
Europe came through on their way to Compostela, and another visitor, Richard the
Lionheart, put the original town – now nearby St-Jean-le-Vieux – to siege in 1177.
When he took it, that most pitiless of warriors razed it to the ground; the kings of
Navarre refounded St-Jean on its present site soon after.

St-Jean today makes more of its living from visitors; it's the main centre for mountain tourism in the Basque lands. Old houses with wooden balconies hang over the
little river, and facing the bridge stands the church of Notre-Dame, founded by
Sancho the Strong of Navarre in commemoration of the battle of Navas de Tolosa
(1212), where the Christian Spaniards finally put an end to Muslim dominance of
the peninsula.

The streets climb up from here to the so-called **Prison des Evêques** (*open 22 April–
21 Oct daily 10–12.15 and 3–4.15*). The house in fact seems to have belonged to a
merchant. The bishops who lived in the mansion above it *c.* 1400 weren't exactly
kosher – supporters of the Antipope at Avignon during the great Schism – and the
chains and shackles in the cellar wall were probably used by local authorities in the
18th century to lock up poor peasants who didn't pay their salt tax.

Just east stands St-Jean's original, **St-Jean-le-Vieux**. The town destroyed by the
Lionheart has only the Romanesque tympanum of its church to remind it of its
former importance. North of St-Jean-le-Vieux on a height above the D933, a venerable
stone pillar with a cross is known as the Croix de Ganelon, supposedly the spot where
Roland's treacherous stepfather was pulled apart by wild horses on Charlemagne's
command. South of St-Jean, the D933 leads down to the Spanish border and 16km
beyond that, the cold, misty pass of Roncevaux itself.

Roland the Rotter

All over the south of France, the very mountains and rocks carry the memory of Roland. His fame spread across Europe, remembered in everything from Ariosto's epic *Orlando Furioso* to the mysterious statue of 'Roland the Giant' in front of Bremen city hall. But who is this Roland really? Outside the *Chanson de Roland*, information is scarce. The chronicler Eginhardt, writing *c.* 830, mentions a Roland, Duke of the Marches of Brittany, who perished in the famous ambush in the Pyrenees in the year 778. Two hundred years later, this obscure incident had blossomed into one of the great epics of medieval Europe. Here is the mighty hero, with his wise companion in arms Oliver. He is the most puissant knight in the army of his uncle Charlemagne, come down from the north to crusade against the heathen Muslims of Spain. Charlemagne swept all before him, burning Pamplona to the ground before coming to grief at an unsuccessful siege of Zaragoza. On their return, Roland and Oliver, with the rearguard, are trapped at the pass of Roncevaux, thanks to a tip from Roland's jealous stepfather Ganelon. Though outnumbered, the French cut down Saracens like General Custer or John Wayne against the savage Injuns. Finally Roland, cut with a hundred wounds, sounds his horn Oliphant to warn Charlemagne and the main army, alas too far away to rescue them.

History says it wasn't a Muslim horde at all, but rather the Basques who did Roland in. And why shouldn't they get their revenge on these uncouth Franks who were devastating their lands, trying to force this democratic nation to kneel before some crowned foreign thug? We might excuse a people who did not even have a word for 'king', if they were not impressed with Charlemagne or his duke. How this affair metamorphosed into an epic will never be known, but tales and songs must have spread and refined themselves, until the caterpillar Roland of history re-emerged into the written word as the mythological butterfly of the *Chanson*. A modicum of propaganda is involved. For the French, up in Paris, glorification of Carolingian imperialism provided poetic justification for the expansionist dreams of the medieval Capetian kings. And replacing the embattled Basque farmers with bejewelled infidel knights makes perfect sense: the time of the *Chanson* also witnessed the beginning of the Crusades.

Béarn

The Béarn, once an independent state, is a stalwart Ruritania, an isolated region known for its grazing land. The scenery is terrific, not only in the Pyrenees, but looking at them from the intensely green rolling foothills. Most of Béarn is contained in the valleys of two impetuous rivers, the Gave d'Oloron and the Gave de Pau; there is the thoroughly delightful spa town of Salies-de-Béarn; fine medieval monuments at Sorde, l'Hôpital-St-Blaise, Lescar, and Oloron-Ste-Marie. Pau, the resort of the Victorian British, has grown into one of the liveliest cities of the southwest. From Pau's famous balcony, you can see Béarn's choice stretch of mountains, with wonders like the Cirque de Lescun and the lakes and gorges around the Pic du Midi.

Along the Gaves de Pau and d'Oloron

Peyrehorade and Around

For centuries, this river town was Béarn's window on the world. Now it's a time capsule, with a pretty riverfront boulevard, and the ruined 13th-century Château d'Aspromonte on a hill. To the south is **Bidache**, which by some quirk owed no allegiance to the viscount nor the king of France, and remained practically independent up to the Revolution. Today, it offers the visitor the romantically ruined **Château de Gramont**, home of trained eagles, vultures, falcons and kites (*open April–Nov, daily 2.30–6.30; the birds fly at 3.30 and 5pm; adm*). For a surprise, take the D29 east to **Sorde**, where a Roman villa metamorphosed into a Benedictine abbey during the Dark Ages: the abbot's residence occupies the central part of the ancient Roman villa. Its mosaics are excellently preserved, with fresh colours and original designs, little known but among the very best ever found in France.

Salies-de-Béarn

Salies may be the loveliest town in Béarn, a vision of steep-gabled houses overlooking the River Saleys. 'Salt City', they call it, and ever since Roman times an endless supply of the ever-popular NaCl has made its fortune. A mighty underground source, seven times saltier than the sea, once poured out enough water to make the area a saline swamp. Nearly everyone lived from salt, collecting the water, boiling it down, and carting the precious mineral off to the warehouse. Undercut by competition in the 19th century, Salies found new life by becoming a spa. It still does good business, and the boosters have come up with a slogan that might have been penned by Gertrude Stein: 'It's here; it's there … it isn't anywhere else!'

A walk through the old town is a delight. By Place du Bayaa, with the bronze boar's head fountain, are two small museums: a **Musée des Arts et Traditions Locales**, and on Rue des Puits-Salants, a **Musée du Sel**, where you can learn everything you wanted to know about salt in the old days. Many of the old half-timber houses still have the outdoor basins called *coulédés*, where they kept their salt. The spa area is set in a park on the north edge of town. Besides the parfait-striped Moorish bathhouse, there is the old casino, now a library, a Victorian bandstand, and the Hotel du Parc, worth a look for its spectacular lobby.

Sauveterre-de-Béarn

A *sauveterre* was supposed to be a place of peace, exempt from all the terrors of feudal warfare; all the local barons, counts and dukes would promise to leave it alone. To show just how successfully this worked in practice, here is Sauveterre-de-Béarn, with the most imposing fortifications of any town in the region. Viscount Centulle IV gave this *sauveterre* its charter in 1080, and for the next two centuries it prospered, as evidenced by the ambitious Romanesque church of **St-André**. But the real attraction of Sauveterre is its lovely setting on the wooded banks of the Gave d'Oloron, where you can see the town's landmark, a fortified, half-demolished medieval bridge called the **Pont de la Légende**.

L'Hôpital-St-Blaise and its Moorish Church

L'Hôpital-St-Blaise may be little more than a few houses in a clearing south of Gurs, but do stop for the unusual and beautiful 12th-century church of St-Blaise. Its Greek plan with its central dome is enough of a surprise, but so is the delicate stone lattice-work that fills some of the windows, an art that was popular in Islamic Spain. Doubtless the architects came from Spain, and they skilfully wove Andalucian elements into the Byzantine plan: lobed arches in the apse, and a dome made of four pairs of round arches, interlaced to form an eight-pointed star. Among the few carved decorations, note one very un-Christian symbol, the Pythagorean pentagram on the left transept. The village has cobbled together an endearingly screwy home-made *son et lumière* to entertain you; just drop a coin in the box by the door.

Orthez

After seeing half a medieval bridge in Sauveterre, you might like to have a look at a whole one. Orthez, capital of Béarn when Pau was still a village, is the place to go. Gaston Fébus spent much of his time here; Froissart, the chronicler of the Hundred

Tourist Information

Peyrehorade: *mairie*, 147 Quai du Sablot, t 05 58 73 00 52, f 05 58 73 16 53.
Salies-de-Béarn: Rue des Bains, t 05 59 38 00 33, f 05 59 38 02 95.
Sauveterre-de-Béarn: Place Royale, t 05 59 38 58 65.
Orthez: Rue du Bourg Vieux, t 05 59 69 02 75/ t 05 59 69 37 50, f 05 59 69 12 60.

Where to Stay and Eat

Salies ✉ **64270**
**Hôtel du Golf, t 05 59 65 02 10, f 05 59 38 16 41 (*inexpensive*). A posh-looking place with reasonable rates, a golf course and a good restaurant (*menus 90–185F*). *Open July–Sept.*
*Hélios, Domaine d'Hélios, t 05 59 38 37 59, f 05 59 38 16 41 (*inexpensive–cheap*). In the same complex as the Hôtel du Golf, but less expensive, with a garden setting and use of the golf course. *Open all year.*
La Terrasse, Rue Saley, across from the church on Rue l'Oumé, t 05 59 38 09 83. For confits and suchlike, on a pleasant terrace overlooking the Saleys (*menus 80–120F*).

Sauveterre-de-Béarn ✉ **64390**
*Hostellerie du Château, Rue Bérard, t 05 59 38 52 10, f 05 59 38 96 49 (*cheap*). An excellent-value hotel; the pretty rooms have a view over the valley and it has an equally good restaurant (*menus 80–160F*).

Orthez ✉ **64300**
**La Reine Jeanne, behind the tourist office on Rue du Bourg-Vieux, t 05 59 67 00 76, f 05 59 69 09 73 (*inexpensive*). Pleasant, simple rooms; the same can be said of the restaurant, where you can have *truite saumonée* and braised duck on an 85F menu (*also 130 and 180F*).
Auberge St-Loup, 20 Rue du Pont Vieux, t 05 59 69 15 40. Orthez's longtime favourite restaurant has had its cuisine revitalized by a new young chef; duck is the star of the menu – as *confits*, *aiguillettes*, in pies and everything else you could do to a quacker; also interesting seafood dishes. Summer dining is in a pretty garden courtyard; it's just across the river near the medieval bridge (*menus 98F; lunch 160F*).
**Auberge du Relais, just west of Orthez, on the D933 at Berenxin, t 05 59 65 30 56, f 05 59 65 36 39 (*inexpensive*). In a rustic setting with a park and swimming pool; the restaurant has an outdoor terrace (*menus 55–140F*).

Years' War, wrote of Fébus's sophisticated court, with 'knights and squires coming and going, talking of arms and love', and where all the news from Scotland to Spain passed over the dinner table. Orthez was wakened from its dream with a start in 1569, when Protestant soldiers burned the place to the ground.

Orthez's centre having moved away from the river, this beautiful fortified bridge is now hard to find – go to the end of Rue du Bourg-Vieux, and take a right into Rue des Aiguilletiers. Gaston Fébus built it, c. 1370, but it was heavily restored after damage by Wellington's army in 1814. Note the little window in the central tower; this was medieval Orthez's garbage disposal – everything was simply tossed out into the Gave de Pau. The Protestants of 1569 expanded on the concept, using the window to dispose of all the town's priests and nuns.

In the centre, the tourist office is in the **Maison de Jeanne d'Albret**, a restored 15th–18th-century mansion. Beyond this, in Rue Moncade is the charming **Hôtel de la Lune**, where Froissart stayed when he visited Gaston Fébus's court in 1388. Further out, Rue Moncade becomes the spine of a medieval bourg that grew up around the castle of the Béarn viscounts. Only the tall, five-sided keep, the **Tour Moncade** survives, and the great hall of Gaston Fébus, who unintentionally killed his only son and heir here, in one of Froissart's more chilling stories from the Hundred Years' War.

Pau

Pau has something of the air of a Ruritanian capital, from the 14th century when Gaston Fébus made it his chief seat in Béarn. Henri IV was born there, but after Louis XIII seized Béarn in 1640, Pau dwindled into a medieval relic. In the hotels and shops, however, you may see old Victorian hunting prints, a reminder of Pau's days as the Gascon outpost of the British Empire. The trend started with some of Wellington's veterans, who retired here, but the real impetus came with a Scottish doctor named Taylor, who in 1869 wrote a book called *The Climate of Pau*. Pau became one of the star resorts of Europe. The British built the first golf course on the continent, along with a race track and a casino; they established cricket and hunt clubs, fancy milliners' shops and tea rooms. Then fashion moved to Biarritz. For a while, Pau struggled on, as Parisians replaced the Anglo-Saxons; a few even learned to play cricket and drink tea.

King Henri's Castle

Pau's old centre is a delightful place, a lively pedestrian zone of restaurants and cafés around **Nouste Henric's castle**, a vision of Renaissance turrets and gables, like a château on the Loire (*guided tours 9.30–11.45 and 2–4.15, till 5.45 mid-Jun–mid-Sept; adm*). It is entered through a beautifully carved marble triple arch; beyond this is the elegant courtyard, the heart of the residential palace. In 1620, after the conquest of Béarn, Louis XIII took its contents to Paris and made the castle a prison. Restored by Viollet-le-Duc in the 1830s, enough of the original furnishings have been reassembled to make the tour worth the trouble. The highlight is **King Henri's Cradle**: in 1553, Jeanne d'Albret had rushed back home from the north so the heir to Gascony could be

Getting Around

The rail station, with connections to Bordeaux, Tarbes and Lourdes, is by the river, underneath the Boulevard des Pyrénées on Av Jean Biray. For the coast and the mountain villages, buses leave from Place Clemenceau. The **TPR** line (**t** 05 59 82 95 85) has frequent services (four or five a day) to Salies-de-Béarn-Bayonne-Biarritz, Nay-Lourdes, Mauléon, Monein, Mourenx and Orthez (via Lescar). There are also services to Tarbes, Mont-de-Marsan, Oloron and up the Gave d'Ossau to Laruns and Gourette.

Tourist Information

Place Royale, **t** 05 59 27 27 08, **f** 05 59 27 03 21, *www.ville-pau.fr*

Where to Stay

Pau ✉ 64000

★★★**Bristol**, 3 Rue Gambetta, **t** 05 59 27 72 98, **f** 05 59 27 87 80 (*inexpensive*). On the posher end of the scale, the Bristol is as old-fashioned as its name, but comfortable, quiet and reasonably priced.

★★★**Roncevaux**, 25 Rue Louis-Barthou, just off Place Royale, **t** 05 59 27 08 44, **f** 05 59 27 08 01 (*inexpensive*). Similar to the Bristol (above).

★★**Grand Hôtel du Commerce**, 9 Rue Maréchal Joffre, **t** 05 59 27 24 40, **f** 05 59 83 81 74

(*inexpensive*). A traditional hotel close to the castle with a decent restaurant.

★★★**Hotel Montpensier**, 36 Rue Monpensier, **t** 05 59 27 42 42, **f** 05 59 27 70 95 (*inexpensive*). A charming, old-fashioned place; although there is no restaurant, meals are available to order.

★**Hôtel Matisse**, 17 Rue Mathieu-Lalanne, near the Musée des Beaux-Arts, **t** 05 59 27 73 80 (*cheap*). A simple place, but a good choice in this price range.

Eating Out

Restaurant La Brochetterie, 16 Rue Henri-IV, **t** 05 59 27 40 33. Very popular for its grilled duck and spit roasted pig and lamb (*menus 59–105F*)

Le Viking, 33 Bd Tourasse, **t** 05 59 84 02 91. A rustic and intimate little restaurant, treating local produce with style; try their stuffed courgette flowers with *cèpes* or *poires williams* with Jurançon wine for dessert (*menus 130–200F*).

Chez Pierre, 16 Rue Louis-Barthou, **t** 05 59 27 76 86. A firm favourite, considered 'très British' with its golf clubs over the bar, but serving firmly southwest French cuisine, notably foie gras and Bearnais *cassoulet* (*menus 200F*).

Au Fin Gourmet, 24 Av. Gaston-Lacoste, down below the Boulevard des Pyrénées, **t** 05 59 27 47 71. For more ambitious dining (*menus 95–170F*). Fried crayfish tails with orange come specially recommended.

born in Pau, and the affair was so hurried that no one could find a proper cradle – so Jeanne used a big tortoise's shell, now displayed here in a charming shrine. The guides will mention how Henri's grandfather rubbed the newborn's lips with garlic and Jurançon wine to make him a proper Gascon from the very start.

The cliffs above the Gave de Pau give the city its most memorable embellishment, the **Boulevard des Pyrénées**, providing a dreamy panorama over a 50-mile stretch of mountains and the wooded foothills. But beware: its charms can be dangerous. Charles Maurras, the writer and politician, had a kind of mystic experience here in the 1880s, when he first realized 'the natural necessity of submission for the order and beauty of the world'. He went on to found the fascist Action Française, and he ended his life in prison as a Vichy collaborator.

The **Musée des Beaux Arts**, 10 Rue Mathieu Lalanne (*open 10–12 and 2–6, closed Tues; adm*), is a surprisingly good collection. The majority of the paintings are 18th- and 19th-century French, with Pyrenean landscapes well represented, but there is also an odd night scene by Luca Giordano, an equally unexpected *Last Judgement* from Rubens, even an El Greco, the *Ecstasy of St Francis*. Perhaps the best-known work is a classic of Degas, the *Cotton Brokers' Office in New Orleans*, displayed at the Second Impressionist Exhibition in 1876.

There isn't much else in Pau. The city's churches were wrecked by Protestant fanatic Jeanne d'Albret, but there is another museum, dedicated to Jean-Baptiste Bernadotte. A soldier who worked himself up through the ranks to become a confidant of Napoleon, Bernadotte fell out with the emperor over his warmongering. The heirless king of Sweden made him an adopted son, and Bernadotte wound up leading troops against Napoleon in the Russian campaign. In 1826 he assumed the Swedish throne, and ruled for 26 years as Charles XIV, ancestor of the kings who rule today. The **Musée Bernadotte** (*open 10–12 and 2–6 pm, closed Tues; adm*) contains personal relics and period furniture. In the same neighbourhood, some of the villas of the English survive on the streets off Rue Montpensier.

North of Pau: the Vic-Bilh

Looking at a relief map, you'll see how the tremendous run-off from the Pyrenees creates wild landscapes of narrow, closely packed parallel valleys. Nowhere is this more pronounced than in the area between Pau and Aire-sur-l'Adour, the tract of deepest Gascony people call the Vic-Bilh, the 'old country'. There are no trains, few buses, and no main routes through it. Trying to get across its tangle of winding back roads is utterly exasperating – so very few ever try.

Oloron-Ste-Marie, the Vallée d'Aspe and the Vallée d'Ossau

Oloron-Ste-Marie

Oloron, the gateway to the Béarnais Pyrenees, was burnt by the Normans, then reappeared as twin towns, Oloron on its high hill and Ste-Marie, a medieval bourg across the river. This has a typically bastard French **cathedral**: Romanesque in front, Gothic behind and a little of everything else mixed in. But the portal is a remarkable flight of medieval fantasy in the style of Moissac. It has two remarkable *voussures*, one carved with the 24 Elders of the Apocalypse; the other recalls the parable from Matthew:22 about the preparations for a wedding feast. The joys of heaven are described in Gascon terms: they're hunting the boar, fishing for salmon, bringing in the wine and cheeses. At the top of the arch, a demon underlines the point that 'many are called but few are chosen'. On the tympanum, by a different artist, is the Descent from the Cross. On the right, the statue on horseback is Constantine, representing the true faith (some say he's really Gaston IV of Béarn). The trumeau between

Tourist Information

Oloron-Ste-Marie: Place de la Résistance,
t 05 59 39 98 00, f 05 59 39 43 97.

Accous: Moulin Bladé, on the N 134, t 05 59 34
71 48.

Laruns: Maison de la Vallée d'Ossau, t 05 59 05
31 41/t 05 59 05 35 49.

Where to Stay and Eat

Oloron-Ste-Marie ✉ 64400

***Darroze, Place de la Mairie, t 05 59 39 00
99, f 05 59 39 17 88 (*inexpensive*). The
Darroze doesn't look very promising at first
sight, but they lay on the best table in this
town. Salmon, trout and foie gras figure
prominently on *menus of 120 and 185F*;
the rooms and public areas are decorated
with taste and style (and there's a
snooker table).

Château de Boués, just outside town on the
D919, t 05 59 39 95 49 (*inexpensive*). A lovely
château with a few guest rooms.

St-Christau ✉ 64660

***Au Bon Coin, on the D 918 (Route des
Thermes), t 05 59 34 40 12, f 05 59 34 46 40
(*inexpensive*). A modern hotel in a lovely
forest setting. In this perfect isolation, there
are pretty rooms at reasonable rates, a pool,
gardens and an excellent restaurant serving
both simple Béarnais favourites and some

surprising seafood dishes – from peppers
stuffed with crabmeat to lobster lasagne
(*menus 90–300F*).

The Upper Aspe Valley

Maison de l'Ours, Etsaut, t 05 59 34 86 38
(*cheap*). Rooms (*50–75F*) and meals are
offered, along with nature walks and other
activities.

**Pas d'Aspe, on the N 134 between Urdos, the
last village before the Spanish border, and
the Col de Somport, t 05 59 34 88 93. A little
more conventional.

Laruns and Environs ✉ 64440

**Hôtel de la Poste, Eaux-Bonnes, t 05 59 05
33 06, f 05 59 05 43 03 (*inexpensive*). Ten nice
rooms and a restaurant with a delicious 98F
menu: soup, salmon terrine and grilled lamb
persillade (*others 72 and 175F*). *Closed
Jan–mid-May.*

*Le Glacier, t 05 59 05 10 18, f 05 59 05 15 14
(*inexpensive*). The ski station at Gourette,
high up at the Col d'Aubisque, can be a pain
to reach but it promises some memorable
scenery. The hotels up there are modern
and all of a piece; Le Glacier is the least
expensive.

Auberge Bellevue, Rue de Bourguet, Laruns,
t 05 59 05 31 58. One of the best places in the
mountains, where you can have a fine
Béarnais garbure or a *confit* at very reasonable prices (*a choice of five menus for
78–180F*).

the doors shows two Saracen captives, perhaps an allusion to Gaston IV's successes in
the Crusades. Inside, the choir and apses are impressive Flamboyant Gothic work. If
it's near Christmas, you can see the cathedral's elaborate crêche, carved in about 1700;
some of the figures wear Gascon berets.

Modern Oloron spreads along three valleys, where the Gave d'Aspe and Gave
d'Ossau come together to make the **Gave d'Oloron**. The Gave d'Ossau bridge is a 13th-
century original, while the Pont de Ste-Claire over the Gave d'Aspe was an early iron
work of Gustave Eiffel. Between the two bridges, you can take the formidably steep
Rue Dalmais up to the **Quartier Ste-Croix**, the acropolis of medieval Oloron. The
square around the church was the site of the important fair in the Middle Ages; parts
of the market hall survive. Restorations disfigured Ste-Croix's exterior, but there is
some good Romanesque carving on the apses. The interior rises to a splendid Moorish
dome in the form of an eight-pointed star, like the one in l'Hôpital-St-Blaise. Carvings
on the capitals are a full illustrated Bible, including Salome's Dance.

The Vallée d'Aspe

From here the N134 follows the Gave d'Aspe to the pass, the Col du Somport, from the Latin Summus Portus, the highest gate. The first place of interest is **St-Christau**, its waters a sure cure for skin diseases; it was one of the first spas of France, and the first to be forgotten. What's left of it stands in a quiet clearing around a stately building called the Rotonde built over the source in the 1630s. From here the serious mountains begin; the N134 continues south through a dramatic gorge, the **Défilé d'Escot**, and then skirts the charming village of **Sarrance** with its chapel, a place of pilgrimage since the 1400s. Kings have visited, and Marguerite d'Angoulême set the frame story here for her collection of tales, the Heptaméron.

Around **Bedous**, the green hills give way to stark grey cliffs, and there may be a chill in the air even in summer; Bedous isn't much, but it's proud to be the birthplace of the explorer Pierre Laclede, founder of St Louis, Missouri. **Lescun**, high above the valley, offers the greatest natural attraction of the area, the spectacular **Cirque de Lescun**. Back on the N134, at the tiny village of **Etsaut** is the **Maison du Parc**, information centre for this part of the Parc National des Pyrénées. Etsaut also has another nature centre, the **Museum of the Bear** (*open mid-May–mid-Nov 9.30–12.30 and 2–6.30*). Just across the road from Etsaut, **Borce** is the one hamlet in this part of the Pyrenees that never suffered from fires or wars. It is also the home of a celebrity: Jojo, a bear found by local children in 1985, when he was a lost cub.

The Vallée d'Ossau

Closer to the heart of the Pyrenees, this valley is a little wilder than the Aspe. The people who live here, a self-governing community of shepherds, claim to be a race apart, and some have speculated that they are direct descendants of the Celtiberians. Coming from the direction of either Oloron or Pau, you'll first pass **Arudy**, centre of the Pyrenean marble trade. Here the **Maison d'Ossau** provides an introduction to the valley, including exhibits on nature and traditions of the area (*open July and Aug 10–12 and 3–6; Jan–June, Sept and school hols Tues–Fri 2–6 and Sun 3–6; adm*).

At **Béon** and **Aste**, steep winding roads lead up to the marble quarries; here you can also visit **La Falaise aux Vautours** (*open daily July and August 10–1 and 2–7; adm*), an observation centre (with cameras hidden on the cliffs and interactive computers) for the many birds of prey that live around the mountaintops: kites, eagles, buzzard, and the rarer lammergeyer, and since 1998, Egyptian vultures. **Laruns**, the little capital of the Ossau, won't detain you, unless you come on 15 August when everyone's in traditional costume for the valley's big festival.

Seven km south of Laruns, a narrow dead-end road to the right leads into the Gorges du Bitet, a narrow defile full of waterfalls. **Gabas** is the usual base for ascending the Pic du Midi; here too is the **Centre d'Ecologie Montagnarde** with a conservatory of rare Pyrenean plants (*open in summer, daily 9–12 and 2–6*).

The **Little Train of Artouste** begins at Artouste, a ski resort south of Gabas; built for dam workers, the train with its open carriages has become a tourist attraction in its

This Valley is Doomed

While you're here, take a minute to think the unthinkable. Imagine a four-lane highway, lined with heavy trucks, running up the middle of the Vallée d'Aspe, and then through a 5-mile tunnel under the Col de Somport into Spain. Imagine also that your EU tax money is going to help pay for it. This plan has been in the works for a long time, and has proved hard to stop – the road on the Spanish side is nearly done. The plan has become the one of the biggest environmental issues in France. The Aspois themselves are divided; many businessmen and landowners just can't wait, while most people are bitterly opposed to what they see as the total destruction of their home and their way of life. Almost nowhere is the valley wide enough to take a major road; the highway would have to pass literally next to most of the villages, if not through them; between the smog and the noise they would all become uninhabitable.

The anti-road campaign found an unexpected ally – the Pyrenean brown bear. Only two decades ago, villages paid bounties for bears; now the government has banned all hunting, and reimburses herdsmen for any sheep the bears nab at double their value. It is probably too late. The handful of surviving bears (a dozen or so) may not be enough to breed successfully. They are the last in France. As a symbol of something wild and free, in a Europe that is becoming increasingly flattened into suburbia, the bears have caught the public's fancy. Still, road work is due to start at the end of 2000.

The most curious stretch of the GR 10, the Chemin de la Mâture, meets the highway a little further south. Pyrenean pines made the longest and straightest masts France could get. The Chemin, built at tremendous expense in the 1860s, was nothing more than a long steep slide, down which the trunks would go to the valley on rollers. Following the GR 10 this way will bring you to the striking mountain lakes, the Lacs d'Ayous, all under the 9,573ft Pic du Midi d'Ossau, the pyramidal landmark of the western Pyrenees.

own right, and makes its scenic 11km run year-round (*book*, *t* 05 59 05 34 00). To reach it, take the *téléphérique* near the Lac de Fabrèges up to the rail terminal.

Lourdes

Even a century ago, honest souls like Emile Zola were disgusted by the holy circus of Lourdes. But in our times, when vulgarity and commercialism crasser than Lourdes are on the television any night of the week, being shocked isn't so easy. And it's hard to be dismissive about a place that means so much to so many sincere people – millions of them. The pilgrims in fact upstage Lourdes itself: coachloads of chattering Italian housewives, youngsters with guitars who have walked or hitched from Ireland; youth groups from Missouri. It's not uncommon to hear them singing in the streets – and where else in Europe can you see that?

Apparitions of the Virgin are common in the Pyrenees, and Bernadette's visions in 1858 would probably not have made much of a stir but for two factors. First, the spring soon developed a reputation for curing hopeless cases. Second, anti-clericalism and free thinking were in the ascendant everywhere, and such a simple country miracle proved a tonic for the faith. Massive promotion of the pilgrimage began in the 1870s, after the Paris Commune and the end of papal rule in Rome. The Church saw itself and society in crisis, and Lourdes was the response. Within a few years, Lourdes had become what it is now: the biggest (if not the most dignified) Christian pilgrimage site in the world, drawing over five million a year.

The Cité Religieuse

When the pilgrims are in town, the Boulevard de la Grotte is the closest thing the Pyrenees can offer to a North African souk – jam packed with people babbling in every imaginable tongue, and vast heaps of sea-shell shrines, medallions, Virgin Mary toaster covers, gargantuan rhinestone rosaries, and gilt plastic-framed magic pictures that show Bernadette in the grotto when you look one way, and a smirking pope when you look the other.

Bernadette

Bernadette Soubirous was 14 years old, a sickly, asthmatic girl in a religious family that had come down in the world, reduced to living in a hovel that had once been a prison cell. On 11 February 1858, Bernadette, her sister, and a friend went out to the 'old cave', Massabielle, to gather scraps of wood. To reach the spot, a shallow canal had to be crossed. Bernadette, worried about her asthma, stayed behind. There, at about 1pm, she felt a warm breeze that seemed to caress her face. Then the vision manifested itself. A 'girl', as Bernadette first described her, spoke kindly in Gascon, telling her 'three secrets', and directing her to dig in the cave, where the miraculous spring came forth.

Bernadette's talkative sister soon spread the word around. Crowds began gathering around the spring. The Virgin appeared three more times to Bernadette, and to many others as well. By April a kind of hysteria had taken over Lourdes, and miracles could not be far behind. The first was bestowed on Louis Bouriette; blind in one eye, he procured some mud from around the spring and made a compress of it, and regained his sight. Newspapers picked up on the story, and Lourdes became a very busy place. Throughout the carnival that followed, Bernadette seemed to be the only one to keep her head. She continued to have her visions, and described them politely to anyone who troubled to ask; that was all.

Bernadette entered a convent up north in Nevers in 1866, where she led a secluded life. Always subject to ill health, she died there in 1879, at the age of only 35. A movement for canonization sprang up immediately, and in 1933 Bernadette was made a saint. As for her role in history and religion, her own wishes sum it up best: 'The less people say about me,' she once said, 'the better.'

Getting Around

Come on a religious holiday, and your introduction to Lourdes will be the sight of cars parked along the main roads for miles before you reach the town limits. At other times, it will always be hard to park around the central hotels (try around the market and *mairie*). The No. 1 city bus shuttles between the rail station and the Grotte. Lourdes also has good bus connections to the Pyrenean valleys: there are at least eight buses a day up the valley to Argelès and Cauterets, slightly fewer to Luz and Barèges.

Tourist Information

Place Peyramale, t 05 62 42 77 40, **f** 05 62 94 60 95, *www.lourdes.france.com*.

Where to Stay

Lourdes ⊠ 65100

In France, only Paris has more rooms. Nearly all close in winter and require half-board.

★★★Grand Hotel de la Grotte, 66 Rue Grotte, **t** 05 62 94 58 87, **f** 05 62 94 20 50 (*moderate*). A traditional grand hotel just below the château, with ring-side rooms overlooking the basilica.

★★★Moderne, Av Bernadette Soubirous, **t** 05 62 94 12 32, **f** 05 62 42 10 07 (*moderate*). Another real palace of the Belle Epoque. The restaurant has a *menu for 135F*.

St-Savin, Rue des Pyrénées, **t** 05 62 94 06 07, **f** 05 62 94 75 51 (*inexpensive*). Neat rooms on a street where you might even find parking, a major consideration in Lourdes.

★★Hotel Majestic, 9 Av Maransin, **t** 05 62 94 27 23, **f** 05 62 94 64 91 (*inexpensive*). A good option not far from the shrines, with comfortable rooms, a terrace and simple restaurant (*menus 50–150F*).

★★Le Montaigu, 5km south of Lourdes on a hill above the N 21, **t** 05 62 94 44 65, **f** 05 62 94 75 44 (*inexpensive*). Great views from most rooms (with balconies) and a garden.

★★Le Virginia, Adé, 5km north of Lourdes on the N 21, **t** 05 62 94 66 18, **f** 05 62 94 61 32 (*inexpensive*). A motel outside the centre with separate cottages and a restaurant (*menus 95–160F*).

Eating Out

Le Magret, 10 Rue des 4 Frères-Soulas, **t** 05 62 94 20 55. Worth a visit for good unpretentious local cuisine and southwest wines (*menus 80–350F*).

Pizzeria da Marco, Rue de la Grotte. An inexpensive oasis for Italian pilgrims (most of whom are convinced that French food is inedible, though they say the wine isn't bad), with a 68F menu, Italian pasta and wines.

La Bodega, Rue Basse. A popular and chaotic self-service with a Spanish touch, offering paellas and *zarzuela*, but also *confits* (*average dishes about 80F*).

A La Petite Bergère, Bartrès, **t** 05 62 94 04 28. It's worth travelling out to Bartrès for the food at La Petite Bergère. On the garden terrace, you can try lamb and chicken dishes, shad and salmon, prepared in often surprising ways (*good value menus at 65–200F*).

After running the gauntlet, you'll cross the little bridge over the Gave de Pau and enter the '**Domaine de la Grotte**' – no shorts or beach clothes, no dogs, no smoking. Everything is impeccably organized, as it has to be, and there are guides, maps and signposts everywhere, along with visitors' centres that speak every language known to Catholicism. The Domaine begins with the pretty **Esplanade des Processions**, with room for 40,000 people – and it's often full in the evening when groups from all over the world parade up and down with their home-town banners. At the end of this stands the **Basilique du Rosaire**, built in 1883. Unlike the souvenirs, this bit of kitsch fails to amuse. The 'Romanesque-Byzantine' style, invented in 19th-century France, undoubtedly marks the low point of Christian sacred architecture, a degenerate parody of the medieval Age of Faith; Emile Zola found it 'ugly enough to make one cry'. The frescoes and mosaics within match the architecture perfectly.

Even when it was new the Basilica often proved too small to accommodate the crowds, but not until the '50s was a larger facility built. The chilly **Underground Basilica Pius X**, to the left of the Esplanade, seats 20,000. Walk around the back of the Basilique du Rosaire to see where it all started, the little **Grotte de Massabielle**, and the adjoining spring, where the water that doesn't get packed into little bottles is channelled into pools to bathe the sick. Up above on the hillside, pilgrims trek a **Calvaire** made of giant bronze statues.

Roadside Attractions and More Mysteries

Beyond the *cité religieuse* Lourdes has a formidable array of holy sites and dubious 'museums' to entertains its pilgrims. Among many others, there's the **Musée de Lourdes**, at the car park l'Egalité (**t** 05 62 94 28 00; *open April–Oct daily 9–11.45 and 1.30–6.45; to 6.15pm the rest of the year; adm*), with dioramas of little Bernadette's vision and village life in the 1850s. Of course there's also a branch of the **Musée Grévin** (87 Rue de la Grotte, **t** 05 62 94 33 74; *open April–Oct daily 9–11.30 and 1.30–6.30; also July and Aug evenings 8.30–10pm; adm*), with more of the same, along with Jesus and 12 pasty-faced Apostles reproducing Leonardo's *Last Supper*. And if you can stand any more, there's the **Musée de la Nativité** (21 Quai St-Jean; *open Easter–Nov daily 9–12 and 1.30–7; adm*), and the **Musée du Petit Lourdes** (67 Av Peyramale, **t** 05 62 94 24 36; *open April–Oct daily 9am–7pm; adm*), with the village of Bernadette's time in miniature and some toy trains. On Rue des Petits-Fosses, a building that was once a prison and later the home of Bernadette's family can be visited: **Le Cachot**, 'the cell' (*open daily in summer 9–12 and 2–7; in winter 3–7*).

Visitors also like to take trips up the mountains that fringe the town; you can ride to the top of the 3,081ft Pic du Jer on a **funicular railway**; there is a grand view, and **caves** to explore near the summit (*open April and Sept–Oct 1.30–6.30; May–June 9.30–6.30, July–Aug 9.30–12.30 and 1.30–6.30; Nov–Mar closed; adm includes fare and cave visit*).

Tarbes

Almost half the 220,000 people of the Hautes-Pyrénées live in or around this grey, unfathomable toadstool of a departmental capital. Among all the cities of southern France Tarbes is the one most sadly wanting in personality (Salon-de-Provence comes in a close second). It has long been a military town (like Salon), and do not doubt there is a connection.

For all its industry and bureaucrats, Tarbes is really just a big market town, and its liveliest corner is Place Marcadieu, with metal halles built in 1880. The Place got its centrepiece at the same time: the Fontaine Duvignau, with an allegory representing the four valleys that stretch up to the mountains from here, dripping with cute allegorical maidens, bears, and izards.

Tourist Information

Tarbes: 3 Cours Gambetta, t 05 62 51 30 31, f 05 62 44 17 63.

Getting There and Around

Tarbes-Lourdes airport, halfway between the two cities, has a daily flight to Paris on Air France; t 05 62 32 92 22.

Another easy way to get into the region is the TGV from Paris. Tarbes is also the hub for buses; most start from Place du Forail near the market (t 05 62 34 76 69). There are at least a dozen a day to Lourdes, and many to Argelès, Arrens and Pierrefitte; others go to Bagnères and a few to Pau.

Where to Stay and Eat

Tarbes ✉ 65000

***Henri IV, 7 Av Betrand Barère, between the rail station and Place de Verdun, t 05 62 34 01 68, f 05 62 93 71 32 (*moderate–inexpensive*). A good bargain, with helpful staff and very comfortable rooms.

**Hôtel de l'Avenue, Av Bertrand Barère, t/f 05 62 93 06 36 (*cheap*). Basic, with the cheapest rooms in town.

***Hôtel l'Aragon, Juillan, on the D921 towards Lourdes, t 05 62 32 07 07, f 05 62 32 92 50 (*inexpensive*). A modern but gracious establishment set in spacious gardens. Even if you don't stay you should try to drop in for dinner. The restaurant, t 05 62 32 07 07, is run by the Cazaux brothers (one cooks, one looks after the wine); it's quite popular, with a reputation for the best food around; ring ahead for their famous salads with quail or foie gras, game dishes, and unusual concoctions including a seafood *cassoulet*; garden terrace (*menus 250 and 340F*). There is also a *bistrot* with a 75F menu.

L'Isard, Av Maréchal-Joffre, near the rail station, t 05 62 93 06 60. Usually crowded at lunchtime, with filling *menus for 65–190F*.

L'Ambroisie, 48 Rue Abbé, t 05 62 93 09 34. A popular local restaurant in an old presbytery, with a terrace and garden. Tuna steak and beef roasted with Madiran wine are especially recommended (*menus 100–290F*).

Besides the market, Tarbes is also an army town. On Cours de Reffye is the Haras Nationaux, a cavalry stud farm founded by Napoleon, a compound of Empire-style buildings with a **Maison du Cheval** to explain what it's all about (*open July–Feb Mon–Fri 10–12 and 2–5*). Just north of the Haras is the heart of the old town, with the cathedral, an ungainly thing full of Baroque fripperies. Nearby, on Rue de la Victoire, you might visit the **Birthplace of Marshal Foch**, the Hero of the Marne (*open daily except Tues and Wed 10–12 and 2–6, till 5pm Oct–April*).

The real reason for stopping at Tarbes is the **Jardin Massey**, a remarkable, wrought-iron-fenced island of civility, with trees and plants from around the world, including palms in the beautiful Orangerie. The entire 14th-century **cloister** from St-Sever-de-Rustan is here as well; the carving is first-rate, and strange: birds pull a woman's toes, swans kill a bear, and a fellow chases a lady with a long knife. A neo-Moorish villa houses the **Musée Massey** (*open July–Aug daily 10–12 and 2–6.30; the rest of the year daily except Mon and Tues 10–12 and 2–6; adm*). There's a bronze mask of about the 3rd century BC, said to represent the Pyrenean god Ergé, possibly an equivalent of Mars. There's also a picture gallery, with a view of Tarbes by Utrillo, a work attributed to Pontormo, and some ripe Dutch paintings of the 1600s. Most of the space, however, is taken up with the **Musée Internationale des Hussards**.

High Pyrenean Valleys: the Lavedan

It wasn't just after Franco's death that Spain wanted to become part of Europe. On the contrary, the island that is now Iberia began snuggling desperately up to the continent a few million years ago, and as it threw up the Pyrenees, the highest points naturally grew up near the northern edge, as if on the crest of a wave. A trio of the chain's giants, Balaïtous, Vignemale and Monte Perdido, look down on a host of smaller fry – mere 7,500-footers – as well as the most astounding sight the mountains have to offer, the great natural wall of the Cirque de Gavarnie. The mountain views are never short of spectacular, a paradise for skiers and hikers, though beyond sports and activities there isn't a lot to do. Cauterets and Gavarnie were the first fashionable resorts in the Pyrenees, back in the early 19th century when mountain-touring first became popular, and tourism remains the sum total of the Lavedan economy.

Tourist Information

Argelès-Gazost: Grande Terrace, t 05 62 97 00 25, f 05 62 97 50 60.
Pierrefitte-Nestalas: Av Jean-Moulin, t/f 05 62 92 71 31.
Cauterets: Place du Maréchal Foch, t 05 62 92 50 27, f 05 62 92 59 12.
Gavarnie: Route Nationale, t 05 62 92 49 10, f 05 62 92 41 00.
Barèges: t 05 62 92 16 00, f 05 62 92 69 13.
Luz-St-Sauveur: t 05 62 92 81 60/30 30, f 05 62 92 87 19.

Besides these, you can find out everything about the natural wonders, hiking and sport at the Maisons du Parc of the Parc National des Pyrénées. There is one at Cauterets, t 05 62 92 52 56, at Luz, t 05 62 92 38 38, and at Gavarnie, t 05 62 92 49 10.

Where to Stay and Eat

Argelès-Gazost ✉ 65400

Bon Repos, Av des Stades, t 05 62 97 01 49, f 05 62 97 03 97 (*inexpensive*). Sometimes we take France for granted, but it's gratifying to think that nearly always, when you find a hotel with a name like this, the establishment is likely to provide just that. There are 18 rooms, a pool, a welcoming family and very reasonable rates.
Le Relais, Rue Maréchal Foch, t 05 62 97 01 27, f 05 62 97 90 00 (*inexpensive*). This choice is an unremarkable village inn, but a good bargain demi-pension makes it attractive.

The restaurant is one of the better ones in town, the kitchen giving a new spin on classic mountain dishes such as *civet de brebis*, a thick mutton stew. There's a garden terrace (*menus 70–200F*).

St-Savin ✉ 65400

Le Viscos, t 05 62 97 02 28, f 05 62 97 04 95 (*inexpensive*). On the edge of the village, with beautiful views over this exceptional corner of the valley, this hotel has functional rooms, but a restaurant you'll remember. M. Saint-Martin presents innovative dishes that are never over the top; everything seems just right, as in the *lotte* (monkfish) in a casserole with ham. Also wonderful are simple desserts such as tarts made with wild strawberries (*menus 120–310F*).
Panoramic, a block from the church, t 05 62 97 08 22 (*inexpensive–cheap*). The hotel alternative is this venerable village inn with grand mountain views.

Cauterets ✉ 65110

Hotel Club Aladin, t 05 62 92 60 00, f 05 62 92 63 30 (*expensive*). Such luxury as the town can provide is limited to this modern hotel, with a pool, in-room TVs and gym.
Bellevue et George V, Place de la Gare, t 05 62 92 50 21, f 05 62 92 62 54 (*inexpensive*). This is one of the many hotels still in business from the days when Cauterets was fashionable, though they have come down in the world a bit. It's a wonderful, rambling old place; some rooms have balconies.

Argelès and St-Savin

Heading south from Lourdes on the N21, the big mountain on your left is the **Pic du Pibeste**. **Argelès-Gazost**, one of the centres of mountain tourism, is here: an attractive medieval centre of stone houses, and below that a spacious spa resort laid out in the 1890s. From here, there is a choice of roads: either down the D921 into the heart of the mountains, or a detour west into the **Val d'Azun**, passing through medieval villages with Romanesque churches such as Arras, Aucun, and Arrens to the glacier-covered face of **Balaïtous** on the Spanish border,.

South of Argelès, the D921 passes through one of the most densely inhabited valleys of the Pyrenees. Beautifully sited on a shelf, **St-Savin** once had a Benedictine abbey. Of this only the church remains, but it's a good one. The austere exterior is punctuated by buttresses representing the 12 Apostles. Some odd Renaissance paintings can be seen around the altar: mythological figures and allegories of the liberal arts. The

Hôtel César, 3 Rue César, **t** 05 62 92 52 57 (*inexpensive*). Conveniently situated for the *thermes* and ski lift alike, this hotel has a good traditional restaurant (*menus 80–160F*).

Gèdre ✉ 65120

★★Brêche de Roland, **t** 05 62 92 48 54, **f** 05 62 92 46 05 (*inexpensive*). One of the famous old hotels of the Pyrenees, this is an old mansion, all mountain austerity outside but retaining many of its original furnishings and walnut panelling within. There is a garden and a restaurant with outdoor terrace, and the management helps arrange winter sports, and helicopter rides.

Gavarnie ✉ 65120

★★★Hôtel-Club Vignemale, **t** 05 62 92 40 00 (*expensive*). This hotel has little to justify its rates, but its restaurant is the best in the valley: mountain trout and *écrevisses*, and good desserts on a pretty outdoor terrace (*menus 130F and up*).
★★Le Marboré, **t** 05 62 92 40 40, **f** 05 62 92 40 30 (*inexpensive*). Set in a distinctive 19th-century building, this place has a sauna and gym.
Hotel des Voyageurs, **t** 05 62 92 48 01, **f** 05 62 92 40 89 (*inexpensive*). The hotel provides plain rooms today, but this was once the place to go for visiting the cirques. All the famous Pyrenean explorers are in the guest book, along with many 19th-century notables. According to legend, Hortense de

Beaumarchais conceived the future Napoleon III here, with the assistance of a local shepherd. If you're interested in fishing, this is definitely the place to go, the only Relais St-Pierre hotel in the region (this *relais* is an association of French hotels that cater specially for fishermen).

Luz-St-Sauveur ✉ 65120

★★★Le Montaigu, on the D 172 to Vizos, **t** 05 62 92 81 71, **f** 05 62 92 94 11 (*moderate–inexpensive*). A beautiful hotel in a beautiful setting, this is a modern building in a traditional style. Rooms are spacious and comfortable, some with balconies and all with a great view.
Les Cimes, in the centre of Luz, **t** 05 62 92 82 03 (*cheap*). This is a good choice at the lower end of the scale.

Barèges ✉ 65120

★★Le Richelieu, Rue Ramond, **t** 05 62 92 68 11, **f** 05 62 92 66 00 (*moderate–inexpensive*). Barèges has something rare in this part of the Hautes-Pyrénées, a modern and rather swish hotel with a sauna; some rooms have TV and balcony. *Closed April–May.*
★★Hôtel de l'Europe, **t** 05 62 92 68 04, **f** 05 62 92 65 29 (*inexpensive*). This is more traditional than the Richelieu and with comparable amenities. *Closed April–May.*
Auberge du Lienz, just east, near the cable car up the Pic de l'Ayre, **t** 05 62 92 67 17. This restaurant provides home-cooking in a lovely setting (*menus 95, 135 and 155F*).

abbot who commissioned them in 1546, François de Foix-Candale, translated the mystic books of Hermes Trismegistus. Among the paintings are three grimacing '*barabouts*' – representing the three men it took to work the organ. Note the Crucifixion; Christ seen from one side seems to be dead, while alive from the other.

The beautifully forested slopes around St-Savin are one of the most delightful corners of the valley. Further south, **Pierrefitte** is the crossroads for Cauterets or Luz-St-Sauveur.

Cauterets

In the 18th century, Cauterets became fashionable among French aristocrats, and with the rediscovery of the beauties of nature in the Romantic era, the elite poured in from all over Europe, drawing crowned heads and several presidents of France. Cauterets is still a major tourist centre, comfortably down at heel. Among the relics of the old days is the rail station, an 1890s wooden confection now used as a coach station. Another remarkable feature is the **Gave de Cauterets** and its rapids, flowing right through the centre with houses closely built up along both sides. Cauterets has also become a ski resort, with a *téléphérique* up to the slopes on the Cirque du Lys, tucked under 8,853ft **Moun Né**; it runs in summer too.

The Route to the Cirques

The other road from Pierrefitte, the D921, will be a little busier. This leads up to the cirques, the most obviously spectacular and most-visited sites in the Pyrenees. These mountains may be good granite, but there are layers of mostly limestone to either side. In places like the Gavarnie, these strata were pushed up to form the highest peaks of the chain. In geological periods when the climate was much warmer, rainfall on the northern face started to erode the limestone, and the Ice Age glaciers finished the job, leaving landforms that seem to have been gouged out by an ice-cream scoop, one several miles wide.

First, though, the road passes through the long Gorge de Luz, and arrives at **Luz**. This is a medieval-looking place of not much interest, except for its 14th-century church, St-André, built by the Knights Hospitallers. Across the Gave de Gavarnie from Luz stands another spa: **St-Sauveur**. Here you can find sulphurous waters to fix up your aches, and an impressive arched bridge embellished with imperial eagles, the gift of satisfied customer Napoleon III.

Continuing south, the D921 traverses more gorges, and then passes the hydro-electric plant, at Pragnères. From any high ground at **Gèdre**, the next village, you can glimpse the Cirque de Gavarnie. **Gavarnie**, the highest village in the Pyrenees , is the traditional base for the area.

Cirque de Gavarnie

There are two ways to see the Cirque de Gavarnie: either walking (about 4hrs) or on the back of a donkey. (The families with the donkeys usually only take you one way; if you want them to wait for the trip back make arrangements in advance.) On the way, you will pass the lovely **Jardin Botanique**, part of the Parc National, with hundreds of Pyrenean species.

The spectacular panorama of the cirque takes in the 7,547ft Pic des Tantes on the right, then fragments of the tremendous glacier that once covered all of Gavarnie. Near the centre is the huge gash in the wall, the Brèche de Roland. In local legend, the hero (*see* p.587) smote at the mountain with his sword Durendal in futile rage when he was surrounded by the Saracens. One of the most spectacular sights (if you can get close enough to it), the **Grande Cascade** is the highest waterfall in Europe; the water drains out of semi-frozen marshes, high above on the Spanish side. On the eastern edge loom two formidable mountains: Marboré ('marble' in Gascon) and behind it, visible from some angles, the second-tallest peak of the entire chain, 10,904ft Monte Perdido, entirely on the Spanish side of the border.

For another view, there is a steep motor road (the D923) from Gavarnie village up to **Port de Boucharo**, where it peters out into a hiking trail; this is the only reliable path into Spain in a stretch of some 40 km, and a long-favoured route of smugglers. Along the way, you can get out and climb to the top of Pic des Tantes, for a grandstand seat that takes in the entire area.

Anywhere else, the **Cirque de Troumouse** would be a star attraction, but next to the awesome Gavarnie it gets stuck with the role of little sister. It's just as broad, but much lower, with neither a waterfall nor a brèche – but it may afford more peace and quiet in July and August when all the trails around Gavarnie are packed. To get there, take the D922 from Gèdre up the Gave de Héas. The last part of the route is a toll road, but it leads up to a 6,500ft peak for a grand view of the cirque. Even less visited is the Cirque d'Estaubé, smallest of the three. A trail from the Lac des Gloriettes is the only way in.

On the way back, you can take a convenient short-cut into the next valley, the **Vallée d'Aure**, by means of the D918 from Luz. This is big skiing country, beginning with **Barèges**, an old thermal resort that has successfully made the transition to concentrating on winter sports. Barèges and La Mongie, just down the road, have between them the greatest number of pistes in the Pyrenees. A *téléphérique* from La Mongie (*June–Sept 9.30–4.30; reservations t 05 62 40 21 00, www.picdumidi.com*) goes to the top of the Pic du Midi de Bigorre to a magnificent observatory, built by the University of Toulouse in 1881, with one of the biggest telescopes in Europe. It is now open to the public as a **Musée des Etoiles**, with splendid viewing platforms and observatories and a restaurant. Farther east, another cable car leads up to the Lac de Greziolles; beyond the hairpin turn there's a favourite postcard subject, the Cascade de Garet.

The Vallée d'Aure and Vallée de Louron

These sunny mountains are 'the Pyrenees of the Nestes of the Garonne' – the mighty Garonne, in fact, hatches out of *nestes*, the Gascon word for river. During the Spanish Civil War, the population picked up a bit, and during the Second World War, the traffic went the other way, as local shepherds and woodcutters helped Jews,

Getting Around

All trains between Pau, Tarbes and Toulouse stop at Lannemezan, and from there buses continue to Sarrancolin, Arreau, and St-Lary. Once a day there's a direct connection between Tarbes and St-Lary. For information, call t 05 62 98 00 49.

Tourist Information

Arreau: Place du Monument, t 05 62 98 63 15, f 05 62 40 12 32.
St-Lary: Rue Principale, t 05 62 39 50 81, f 05 62 39 50 06.
Piau-Engaly: Maison du Tourisme, t 05 62 39 61 69, f 05 62 39 61 19.
Bordères-Louron: Maison du Tourism, t 05 62 99 92 00, f 05 62 99 92 09.

Where to Stay and Eat

Arreau ⊠ 65240
★★Hôtel d'Angleterre, on the edge of town, t 05 62 98 63 30, f 05 62 98 69 66

(*moderate–inexpensive*). This is a big comfortable country inn, with a garden terrace to sit out on; the owners arrange rafting or hang-gliding excursions. The restaurant serves good hearty food – *garbure, confits* and regional dishes – perfect for high-altitude appetites (*menus 70–200F*).

★Hôtel de l'Arbizon, in the centre, t 05 62 39 90 08, f 05 62 39 92 42 (*inexpensive*). This hotel-restaurant is a tidy little place; some rooms have balconies over the river (*menus 65–120F*).

★★Hostellerie du Val d'Aure, just south of Arreau in Cadéac, t 05 62 98 60 63, f 05 62 98 68 99 (*inexpensive*). The *hostellerie* offers quiet, well-furnished rooms on the banks of the Aure (*menus 65F and up*).

St-Lary-Soulan ⊠ 65170
In the town that helped inaugurate package ski holidays in the Pyrenees, there are no bargains. The restaurants in St-Lary, such as they are, are notoriously mediocre: most people eat in their hotels.

German dissidents and escapees from French political prisons flee over the mountains; in the Aure Valley alone, an estimated 1500 of the 2000 who made the attempt survived to make it to Spain.

The Vallée d'Aure: Sarrancolin to St-Lary

Moulded by ancient glaciers into a giant fishhook, the Vallée d'Aure receives more sunshine than most French valleys and is blessed by a warm Spanish wind which sweeps the surrounding peaks clear of clouds and mists. Perhaps because of its sunny disposition, the Vallée d'Aure was one of the first, back in the 1950s, to reverse its decline by attracting tourists and skiers. Another feather in its cap is the recent opening of the Aragnouet-Bielsa tunnel, confirming the Aure's age-old links with Spain that began with a Neolithic track linking the Garonne valley and the Atlantic with those of the Ebro and the Mediterranean.

South of **Lannemezan** and the A64, the D929 follows this old trail through dismal scenery to **Sarrancolin**, famous for red marble with grey veins used in Versailles and for the grand stair of the Paris Opéra. The medieval town has picturesque lanes, especially Rue Noire, but the pride of Sarrancolin is the church of St-Ebons, begun in the 12th century. Inside, the relics of St Ebons (d. 1104) are preserved in a magnificent 13th-century gold and copper enamel casket made in Limoges. Carefully preserved through the centuries, the casket was stolen in 1911, and given up for lost – until one dry year,

Hôtel de la Neste, 5 minutes north of Saint-Lary in Vigneac, **t 05 62 39 42 79, **f** 05 62 39 58 77 (*moderate–inexpensive*). By the river, the hotel enjoys a grand view of the mountains; all rooms have bath, TV and mini-bar. The restaurant serves meals from 72 to 110F. *Hotel and restaurant closed May and Oct–mid-Dec.*

Andredena, near the centre just off Chemin de Sailhan, **t 05 62 39 43 59, **f** 05 62 40 04 12 (*inexpensive*). This family-orientated up-to-date chalet-hotel overlooks a heated pool and is set in a small, tranquil park. *Closed Oct–mid-Dec.*

La Terrasse Fleurie, 21 Rue Principale, **t 05 62 40 76 00, **f** 05 62 39 50 10 (*inexpensive*). This is the nicest choice, with wooden balconies and comfortable rooms.

*Pons 'Le Dahu', Rue de Couderes, **t** 05 62 39 43 66, **f** 05 62 40 00 86 (*inexpensive*). This is an inexpensive and sunny choice.

Le Barbajou, in Fabian, at the beginning of the Route des Lacs, **t** 05 62 39 61 34 (*cheap*). Five comfortable *chambres d'hôte*.

Chez Lulu, in Sailhan, **t** 05 62 39 40 89. Here you can dine pleasantly on the summer terrace. There are Gascon favourites on menus at 55 and 130F.

Vallée de Louron ✉ 65590

Le Peyresourde, Bordères-Louron, **t 05 62 98 62 87 (*inexpensive*). This is the fanciest hotel in the valley (*menus 70–120F*).

Auberge des Isclots, overlooking the Lac de Loudenvielle at Aranvielle, **t** 05 62 99 66 21 (*inexpensive–cheap*). This *auberge* is utterly pleasant, with doubles, or cheaper *gîte d'étape* rooms in a dormitory. There are good-value menus from 99–160F, with *magret* or *confit de canard*.

Le Relais d'Avajan, Avajan, **t** 05 62 99 67 08 (*moderate*). The *relais* has a handful of reasonably priced rooms and a stout 75F menu.

Accueil sans Frontière Pyrénées, Germ, **t** 05 62 99 65 27, **f** 05 62 99 63 22 (*cheap*). The favourite place to stay in the region is this complex of well-furnished *gîtes* and hostel accommodation, with a camp site, good food, swimming pool and loads of information and equipment for summer and winter sports in the area.

---

when the waters in the Neste d'Aure were exceptionally low and it was spotted in the middle of the river where the thief had dropped it.

The main valley road continues 7km south to **Arreau**, the pretty, slate-roofed capital of the Quatre Vallées, located at the meeting of the Aure and Louron rivers and various roads. A popular base for walks, rafting, hang-gliding and skiing, Arreau has a 17th-century *halles* and pretty 16th-century Maison des Lys; the diminutive Château des Nestes contains the tourist office and a **Musée des Cagots** (*open Tues–Sat*), dedicated to the pariahs of the Pyrenees, a people whose origins were as mysterious as the elaborate ways in which they were segregated.

The best church around is 3km east of Arreau at **Jézeau**, beautifully set on the mountain flank. Ask at the *mairie* for the key before setting out: when it was enlarged in the 16th century, the church was given a magnificent Renaissance retable, polychrome statues, and on the wooden ceiling, vigorous, imaginative paintings by an unknown hand, including a remarkable *Last Judgment* that has inspired Jézeau's enthusiasts to call it 'The Sistine Chapel of the Pyrenees'.

St-Lary and Around

St-Lary claims to be nothing less than the biggest sports resort in the Pyrenees. It certainly had a head start. By 1957 the town had built its first aerial cableway, at the time the largest in the world, to the ski slopes of Pla d'Adet (these days it looks quite puny); most recently it built a deluxe modern spa at Soulan, to treat rheumatism and nose-ear-throat troubles in the hopes of attracting tourists in May, October and November. Another recent project has been the restoration of the old core of St-Lary, including the 16th-century Maison Fornier in Place de la Mairie, now home to the **Musée du Parc National** (*open Jan–Sept daily 9–12 and 2–6.30*). But it's the great outdoors that brings people to St-Lary – in the winter, ice skating and skiing; in the summer, paragliding, riding, rock climbing, canyoning and walking.

Continuing up from St-Lary, the village, sheer rock and ruined **castle of Tramezaïgues** stands like an exclamation mark at the beginning of the arcadian 12km-long **Vallée du Rioumajou**. Daniel Defoe came this way in 1689, during one of the worst winters in history; he fictionalized the experience in *Robinson Crusoe*. The D929 continues to **Fabian**, the crossroads for the Réserve Naturelle de Néouvielle, and then to **Le Plan d'Aragnouet**, with a photogenic Templars' chapel. At Le Plan a road branches off for **Piau-Engaly**, the highest and snowiest ski resort in the Pyrenees, with illuminated night skiing to prolong the thrills.

In 1935, the great south-facing granite massif of **Néouvielle** became the first national reserve in France. Golden eagles soar high overhead, and the reserve has the highest growth of pines in Europe. Thank the power monopoly, EDF, for the road up from Fabian, which for a few months in the summer allows you (and half the population of St-Lary) to motor as far as the **Lac d'Orédon** and **Lac de Cap-de-Long**, both within easy striking distance of other lovely lakes.

The Vallée de Louron: the Valley of Romanesque Churches

Arreau stands at the foot of the 25km-long Vallée de Louron, green and tranquil compared to its neighbours. It has a pair of ski resorts, at **Val-Louron** (7,415ft) and **Peyresourde** (7,352ft), and is increasingly a popular base for hang-gliding and paragliding daredevils.

By the 16th century, the wool and cloth business in the Vallée de Louron was good enough for the inhabitants of its villages to pool their money to hire painters to decorate their churches. Unfortunately they are often locked; the afternoon tours offered on Thursdays by the Maison du Tourisme at **Bordères** is the easiest way to get into them (**t** 05 62 99 92 00; *ring ahead and book if possible*). Heading up the valley, **Lançon** (take the D219 from Arreau) has a Romanesque church, not with murals but an unusual bell tower topped with a pepperpot roof; **Ilhan** just south has fine views of the valley. South of Bordères-Louron, **Vielle-Louron**'s church has both walls and ceilings covered with 16th-century paintings. **Loudenvielle**, south of its large man-made lake, and the power station at **Tramezaygues** 8km further south, are the bases for walks in the upper Vallée de Louron. Other good Romanesque churches are just to the east: one at **Cazaux-Fréchet** and another at **Armenteule**, isolated and decorated with a curious carved frieze. **Mont** has the finest frescoes in the whole valley, painted in 1573 by one Melchior Rodiguis of St-Bertrand-de-Comminges. Lastly, tucked off the main route, is a clean and pleasant little hamlet lost in nature called **Germ** (yes, really), named after a saint so obscure that he never made it out of the valley.

Into the Haute Garonne: the Comminges

East of the Vallée de Louron extends the southernmost bit of the *département* of the Haute Garonne, formerly known as the Gascon province of the Comminges. Located exactly midway between the Atlantic and Mediterranean, the Comminges encompasses the upper valley of one of France's four great rivers, the Garonne, and as its relics show, has been inhabited since the cows (and bison and woolly mammoths) came home in the last Ice Age.

Up the Garonne: Montréjeau and the Grotte de Gargas

At the confluence of the Neste and Garonne, **Montréjeau** stands on a natural terrace, where it was founded as a *bastide* in 1272. It has lovely views over to the Pyrenees from its two main squares, arcaded Place Valentin Abeille and Place Verdun, with the market and public garden; on Boulevard de Lassus, skirting the edge of the plateau, an orientation table has been set up.

There's always an ineffable quality to prehistoric caves, but the **Grotte de Gargas**, south of Montréjeau is more uncanny than most (*open spring and summer school*

Tourist Information

Montréjeau: Place Valentin Abeille, t 05 61 95 80 22, f 05 61 95 37 39.
St-Bertrand-de-Comminges: by the cathedral, t 05 61 95 44 44, f 05 61 95 44 95.
St-Béat: t 05 61 79 45 98, f 05 61 79 57 07.

Where to Stay and Eat

St-Bertrand-de-Comminges ✉ 31510
**L'Oppidum, up in the medieval town, t 05 61 88 33 50, f 05 61 95 94 04 (*inexpensive*). This pretty place has 15 comfortable rooms, some sleeping as many as six. *Closed Dec–mid-Feb.* The restaurant serves local specialities: stuffed trout and veal (*menus 80–180F*).
*Hôtel du Comminges, facing the cathedral, t 05 61 88 31 43, f 05 61 94 98 22. An old ivy-covered building that was once a private house, with nicely furnished large rooms, and an interior garden to sit in as well as the terrace in front. *Closed Nov–March.*
Chez Simone, a street back from the cathedral, t 05 61 94 91 05. If you crave a good old stuffed Gascon chicken, ring Simone and have her cook one up to go with the home-made desserts and pretty views from the terrace (*meals cost around 90F*).

Le Lugdunum, Valcabrère, t 05 61 94 52 05. For something unique in France, book a table here and dine like Pompey himself. Here chef Renzo Pedrazzini (born locally of Italian parents) bases his dishes on the recipes compiled in the *Ten Books of Cooking* by the gastronome Apicius in the 1st century. No Caesar salads or hummingbirds' tongues, but dishes such as partridge in cold sauce and young boar, served with spiced wines; a local herbalist supplies the authentic ingredients (*menus 90–175F*). The restaurant terrace has an equally delicious view of St-Bertrand. *Closed Tues out of season.*

Barbazan ✉ 31510
***Hostellerie des Sept Molles, on the D9 just east of Barbazan, in Sauveterre-de-Comminges, t 05 61 88 30 87, f 05 61 88 36 42 (*expensive–moderate*). The all-white Relais et Château hotel is perched on a high hill and offers luminous rooms, spread out in several buildings, with a heated pool, tennis, and bubbling stream in the grounds. The restaurant has a lovely terrace for summer dining, or a roaring fire in the winter, and specializes in baby lamb with *mounjetado*, the local version of *cassoulet* (*menus 195–310F*). *Restaurant closed mid-Feb–mid-March.*

hols daily 2.30–5.30; July–Aug daily 10–11.30 and 2–6; Sept–10 Oct daily 2.30–4; winter school hols daily 2.30–4). Gargas is one of the oldest-known decorated caves known, from the Aurignacian era (*c.* 33,000 BC), and its oldest paintings and engravings of animals (and unusually, two birds) are still rather awkward, compared to the more graceful works of the Magdalenian era (*c.* 12,000 BC). But what sets Gargas apart are its bizarre, mutilated hands – 231 pictures, made by blowing paint through a tube around a hand. Nearly all are somehow deformed. Fingerprints suggest that both living and amputated hands were used for models, and guesses are that they were damaged either through frostbite, disease, accidents or ritual mutilation.

St-Bertrand-de-Comminges

Before Lourdes, the religious centre of the Pyrenees was St-Bertrand-de-Comminges. Magnificently set on a promontory over the Garonne, the massive Gothic church of **Ste-Marie** makes an unforgettable sight, a kind of inland Mont-St-Michel, with its nearly windowless walls, tower and butresses rising up like an ocean liner, dwarfing the village below.

St-Bertrand was settled by Iberians, and their Celtic cousins gave it its name, Lugdunum, the 'Citadel of the Rising Sun'. By 76 BC, the region was empty except for guerrilla tribes holding out against the joys of Roman rule, known as the Convenii, the 'robbers of souls'. Even Pompey thought twice about going after them, and decided to win them over by kindness by declaring them to be Roman colonists. The ferocious Convenii turned out to be excellent citizens, and their Lugdunum Convenarum grew by leaps and bounds. When Caligula exiled the Tetrarch Herod, Salome and family in 39 AD from Palestine, this is where they came.

After the Dark Ages, the town next appears in the 11th century, in the biography of Bertrand de l'Isle-Jourdain, a cousin of the remarkable count of Toulouse, Raymond IV, who fought with El Cid and led the First Crusade. Bertrand shared much of Raymond's energy; when appointed bishop of Comminges he rebuilt the church and the town, and performed enough miracles to be canonized by popular demanded in 1175. In the late 13th century, another Bertrand, Bertrand de Got of Bordeaux, was named bishop and built a grand Gothic church.

The Ste-Marie Cathedral

Open July–Aug daily 9–7; April–June and Sept daily 9–12 and 2–7; March and Oct daily 9–12 and 2–6; Nov–Feb daily 9–12 and 2–5; closed Sun morning; adm to cloister, treasury and choir.

When Bertrand de Got rebuilt St Bertrand's cathedral, he left the 100ft bell tower and the rather severe façade intact. The richly decorated portal also dates from the 12th century, its tympanum carved with the Three Magi (and the future St Bertrand) paying their respects to the Virgin, an image known in the Pyrenees as 'the Seat of Wisdom'. As you enter, don't miss the embalmed crocodile; no one knows who left it here, but guesses tend towards a passing Crusader. On the left, columns support one of the most lavish **Renaissance organs** in France, known as 'the Third Wonder of Gascony', decorated with finely carved wooden panels representing the labours of Hercules. Although its 3000 pipes were purloined in the Revolution, the organ was restored in the 1970s and works a treat, as you can hear every Sunday at 10.30am.

The nave is closed off from the choir by an opulently carved Renaissance rood screen, but to continue any further down the nave you have to buy a ticket. It's worth it: the superb **choir stalls** were carved between 1523 and 1551 by sculptors from Toulouse. Inspired perhaps by the great choir stalls then underway at Auch, they expressed a large part of their humanistic view of the universe on the 66 stalls: wicked sins and somberly elegant religious and secular scenes intermingle with an imaginary bestiary. Along the top of the choir are sibyls, prophets, Christian virtues, and Roland and Oliver, and over the screen an intricate Tree of Jesse. Behind the high altar, a chapel holds the tomb of St Bertrand, decorated with folksy 15th-century paintings, showing Bertrand de Got (Pope Clement V) as big as the Jolly Green Giant.

The delightful **cloister** is another legacy of St Bertrand d'Isle-Jourdain. The west gallery is the oldest; in the centre you'll find one of the **Pillar of the Evangelists**, carved with four column-like figures, topped with the Labours of the Months and signs of the Zodiac. Upstairs, the treasury has two exquisite medieval copes that belonged to Clement V, who also donated the alicorne, a horn from a unicorn (really a narwhal). Water that passed through the alicorne was considered a sure-fire antidote for poison. Catherine de' Medici tried all she could to get her son Charles IX to get it, without success; in 1594 a band of Huguenots under Corbeyran d'Aure stole it, but even Corbeyran feared the vengeance of St Bertrand, and he returned the alicorne in exchange for a complete amnesty. And it's still in the treasury.

Lugdunum Convenarum and Valcabrère

To visit the excavations of Lugdunum Convenarum, first check the opening hours with the tourist office, and then follow the road for Valcabrère. In the centre the Forum temple with its big podium is believed to have been dedicated to the cult of Rome and the Emperor. The baths, or **Thermes du Forum**, were built about the same period; you can make out the hot and cold rooms (*caldaria* and *frigidaria*) and much of the plumbing. Across the D26 stood the commercial heart of Lugdunum, the *macellum*, with 26 boutiques paved with black and white mosaics – a 1st-century AD covered shopping mall. Measuring over 500 square metres, it is among the largest and most opulent covered markets ever discovered in the western Roman empire. Towards the car park, a raised circular sanctuary of uncertain import has recently been unearthed. The large **Thermes du Nord** were run by the city; they included an early version of the sauna, as well as an open-air pool, a *palaestra* (an open-air exercise area), and a row of small shops. South of the *macellum*, Lugdunum's Palaeo-Christian **basilica** dates from the mid-5th century, has a pretty green, red and white mosaic floor and was used at least into the 8th century. The little **theatre** in the hillside was damaged when a road was run through in the 18th century. A **museum** near the site houses the numerous finds, including the handsome sculptural groups from an Augustan trophy discovered near the temple.

On the edge of Lugdunum, in the rural hamlet of **Valcabrère**, the 11th or 12th century **Basilique St-Just** (*open Easter–June, Oct and school hols daily 9–12 and 2–6; July–Sept daily 9–7*) is one of the most beautiful churches in the Pyrenees, isolated in a field, with the cathedral at St-Bertrand looming behind its shoulder. The square apse with radiating polygonal chapels is a unique essay in medieval geometry, as well as a collage of Roman bits and bobs; note the theatre mask embedded in the wall, and a relief of a supper party. The portal was inspired by Roman models, crowned with a tympanum showing Christ in majesty while on the sides are marble column statues of saints; the capitals over their heads show various forms of martyrdom with relish. The interior, beautiful in its simplicity, has fine acoustics; note the reuse of antique columns and Roman and Merovingian capitals.

South of St-Bertrand: St-Béat

Further south, squeezed in between the Cap det Mount and the Cap d'Ayre mountains, **St-Béat** has long been known as the 'Key to France'; any army from Spain would have to beat its way past its citadel, so naturally well defended that it could be held with only a handful of men. It was the home of the Garunni, the tribe who gave their name to the River Garonne; in 75 BC Pompey founded a fort here. While in the area, he might have noticed that the two mountains that enclose St-Béat were made of white marble. One massive vertical excavation is said to have been carried off to Rome to become Trajan's column; an altar discovered nearby, dedicated by two quarrymen, thanked the gods for allowing them to extract such a chunk without accident. Not surprisingly, much of St-Béat is built of marble, including the clock tower, all that remains of its 11th-century castle. Elsewhere in St-Béat, the **Maison Consulaire** in Rue Galliéni dates from 1553; it inspired the balcony scene in Rostand's *Cyrano de Bergerac*. The street is named after Maréchal Joseph-Simon Galliéni, who was born here in 1849 and who, as his last great act for the *patrie* in 1914, rounded up Paris taxis to transport troops to the Battle of the Marne; his statue stands on the right bank.

The Upper Comminges

Set in a sunny amphitheatre, surrounded by the highest peaks of the Pyrenees and a web of luscious valleys, the 'Queen of the Pyrenees', **Bagnères-de-Luchon**, or just Luchon as everyone calls it, wears two different hats: as France's fourth (some say fifth) largest spa and as a base for the mountains. It attracted rheumatic Romans: 'The Best After Naples' reads the old Latin slogan on the baths. In the mid-18th century it underwent a revival: an entire *Who's Who* descended upon Luchon, from Flaubert and Louis Napoleon to Bismarck and Mata Hari.

Bagnères-de-Luchon and its Valleys

Luchon (Lootch-ON) is a bustling modern town, but the gilded days of its spa have left a burnished glow, especially along the elegant **Allée d'Etigny**. Lined with lime trees, grand old hotels, restaurants and cafés, it culminates in the lovely **Parc des**

Getting Around

Both trains and buses pull in at the *gare*. All come by way of Montréjeau, with connections to Lourdes, Tarbes and Toulouse. For information, **t** 05 61 79 03 36.

Tourist Information

Bagnères-de-Luchon: 18 Allée d'Etigny, **t** 05 61 79 21 21, **f** 05 61 79 11 23.

Where to Stay and Eat

Luchon ✉ **31110**

★★★Corneille, 5 Av A. Dumas, **t** 05 61 79 36 22, **f** 05 61 79 81 11 (*expensive–moderate*). Handsome 19th-century hotel set in a lovely garden on the edge of Luchon, with tranquil rooms and a restaurant (*menus 120–198F*). *Closed Nov–mid-Dec.*

★★Hotel d'Etigny, 3 Av Paul Bonnemasion, **t** 05 61 79 01 42, **f** 05 61 79 80 64 (*expensive–moderate*). Opposite the baths, an atmospheric, old-fashioned place with a restaurant (*menus 99–220F*). *Closed Nov–March.*

★★Grand Hôtel des Bains, 75 Allée d'Etigny, **t** 05 61 79 00 58, **f** 05 61 79 18 18 (*inexpensive*). An atmospheric turn-of-the-20th-century hotel. *Closed Nov–Dec.*

Jardin des Cascades, near the church of Montauban-de-Luchon, east of Luchon,

t 05 61 79 83 09 (*inexpensive*). A few double rooms, enchanting views from the dining terrace and excellent preparations of *pistache* and other traditional dishes, although they don't come cheap: the average is around 200F per person. The restaurant's always packed, so book. *Closed mid-Oct–mid-March.*

★Des Deux Nations, 5 Rue Victor-Hugo, **t** 05 61 79 01 71, **f** 05 61 79 27 89 (*inexpensive–cheap*). Quiet, yet central and an old favourite, this hotel-restaurant is run by a friendly family, who are also more than competent in the kitchen (*three good menus for under 100F*).

Around Luchon ✉ **31110**

★★L'Esquerade, Castillon-de-Larboust, **t** 05 61 79 19 64, **f** 05 61 79 26 29 (*inexpensive*). A favourite of *les sportifs* and lazybones alike, this is a handsome old mountain inn, set in the lush green valley. Opt for the demi-pension scheme, or just stop by to eat – the *magret de canard* with crayfish and other local dishes are superb and reasonably priced (*menus 120–165F*).

★★Le Sapin Fleuri, Bourg d'Ouell, **t** 05 61 79 21 90, **f** 05 61 79 85 87 (*inexpensive*). At 4,620ft, this comfortable little Logis de France chalet hotel is in a magnificent setting. Regional cuisine is served on a summer terrace (*menus from 110 to 250F*). *Closed Nov–24 Dec.*

Quinconces, with its catalpas and tulip trees, and Luchon's **Thermes** (1849). Since 1973, these have had a natural cave sauna and 'Vaporarium', good for respiratory ailments; singers, preachers and lawyers form a large part of the clientele. The **Musée du Vieux Luchon**, 18 Allée d'Etigny (*open Dec–Oct daily 9–12 and 2–6; Nov Wed, Fri and Sat 9–12 and 2–6*), has displays on the early days of mountaineering and memorabilia of celebrity visitors, and tools used (and invented) by the legendary Norbert Casteret (1897–1987), a father of French speleology.

Exploring the majestic high altitude scenery around Luchon can take up an entire holiday. The classic excursion is to the **Port de Venasque**, at the top of the superb **Vallée de la Pique**, lined with silver firs and beeches – unfortunately, many ill from the worst acid rain in the Pyrenees. To make it to the 8,078ft Port de Venasque and back, start early in the morning and count on at least a 6hr march past forests, waterfalls and pastures. The reward: an unforgettable view of the Maladetta massif, the 'accursed mountains', a jagged, 6km-long, glacier-crowned spine, reaching 11,233ft at Aneto, the highest peak in the Pyrenees.

Other excursions include the D46 into the **Vallée du Lys**, carved by glaciers with a rare symmetry. Along the way you can peer down an abyss, the Gouffre Richard, then take the road up to the ski resort, **Superbagnères**, with superb views. Best of all, continue up the main road to the Cirque de Lys and its **Cascade d'Enfer**, a waterfall splashing through a cleft in the rocks that could pass for the gate of hell. Another excursion is up the **Vallée d'Oô**, by way of **St-Aventin**, a 12th-century gem of a church 5km from Luchon. Perched high on its promontory, it has a tympanum carved with a Christ in Majesty and fine capitals, one with a bear; according to the story, bears would come to Aventin, a hermit, to have thorns removed from their paws. Inside, the stoup is a remarkable pre-Romanesque work. Around Aventin's tomb are more sculpted capitals; murals show him with St Sernin, patron of Toulouse.

At Castillon, the road forks; take the left along the Neste d'Oô, which is driveable as far as the **Granges d'Astau**. There you can pick up the GR 10, passing the silvery waterfall known as the **Chevelure de Madeleine** to the stunningly azure **Lac d'Oô**, the loveliest of a pocket of glacier lakes, set in nearly lunar surroundings, near a 900ft waterfall.

West of Luchon, the **Vallée de Larboust** leads up to the **Col de Peyresourde**, one of the highest passes in the Pyrenees. Just after the turn-off for the Vallée d'Oô, on the D618, **Cazaux** has a church with a remarkable late medieval mural of the Last Judgement. The iconography is unique: the Christ is shown sitting atop a rainbow, not in majesty, but with the bleeding wounds of the Passion. On his right, the Virgin pleads for mercy, but intercedes in a most unusual way: she bares her breasts and squirts milk on her son's wounds. Unfortunately, the church is usually locked, but the Luchon tourist office may help locate the key.

St-Gaudens and the Petites Pyrénées

For 90 per cent of people travelling in the region, bedazzled by the beauty of the Pyrenees, the area north and west of the Garonne of the baby mountains, or 'Petites Pyrénées', is *terra incognita*. Yet these rolling hills of the Comminges were beloved in antiquity and have seemingly changed little since: remarkably intact landscapes, unspoiled by billboards, subdivisions, and all the other detritus of our times. The departmental roads are still lined on either side with ancient plane trees, rare in the rest of France, where one or both sides are sacrificed to road-widening schemes. Here there's not enough traffic to bother.

St-Gaudens

St-Gaudens, with a population of 13,000, is the metropolis in these parts. It is named after a 12-year-old shepherd boy who met a band of Moorish cavalrymen who demanded that he convert to Islam. Gaudens asked his mother if it was all right, but she said no. The Moors then chopped off his head, but his body had the panache to pick it up, and with the Moors in hot pursuit, he ran with it to the nearest church. No wonder Gascons make such good rugbymen.

Getting Around

St-Gaudens is the transport centre for the region, with trains to Toulouse and Luchon, and TER busess to Montréjeau, Lannemezan, Tarbes, Lourdes, and Luchon.

Tourist Information

St-Gaudens: 2 Rue Thiers, **t** 05 61 94 77 61, **f** 05 61 94 77 50.

Where to Stay and Eat

St-Gaudens ✉ 31800
***Hostellerie des Cèdres**, just outside St-Gaudens in Villeneuve de Rivière, **t** 05 61 89 36 00, **f** 05 61 88 31 04 (*moderate*). Set in a large park, the building formerly belonged

to the Marquise de Montespan, Louis XIV's mistress. Rooms are elegantly furnished with antiques, and there is a pool, tennis courts, and a fitness room. The restaurant specializes in various veal dishes the marquise would have approved of (*menus 130–220F*).

Pedussaut, 9 Av de Boulogne, **t 05 61 89 15 70, **f** 05 61 89 11 26 (*inexpensive–cheap*). Recently renovated, this hotel has an excellent restaurant, serving good-value menus chock full of regional ingredients (*menus 70–180F*).

Montmaurin ✉ 31350
Caso Nuosto, in the woods not far from the Roman villa, **t** 05 61 88 25 50 (*inexpensive*). This place offers three *chambres d'hôte* rooms in a restored old farmhouse, with a pool and garden.

The most important church, however, is the **Collégiale**, with a great square bell tower. Along the nave, 18th-century tapestries from Aubusson illustrate the Martyrdom of St Gaudens. Best of all are the capitals by the choir, by sculptors from Aragon: bears fight, monkeys make faces, Adam seems to gag on the forbidden fruit. Just east of the Collégiale, the **Musée du Comminges** (*open Tues–Sat 9–12 and 2–6; closed Sun–Mon and hols*) has tools, costumes, and memorabilia related to the army heroes from the Pyrenees: Foch, Joffre and Galliéni.

Montmaurin, and the Biggest Gallo-Roman Villa of Them All

North of St-Gaudens on the River Save, the **Gallo-Roman Villa** at Montmaurin (*open April–Sept daily 9.30–12 and 2–6; Oct–March daily 9.30–12 and 2–5; adm*) stands in bucolic splendour. In the 1st century a certain Nepotianus, owner of the surrounding 7,000 hectares, built himself a country estate. The Save flooded and covered it in muck, but by the 4th century Nepotianus' heirs were ready to rebuild: nothing would do but a white marble palace with 200 rooms, the largest and most luxurious villa ever discovered in France. In the centre of Montmaurin, a **museum** (*same hours and tickets*) in the *mairie* contains a model of the villa and Roman and prehistoric finds.

The Ariège

Once the proud and independent Comté de Foix, the Ariège occupies several frontiers: obviously Spain and Andorra, but also the more subtle division between Gascony and Languedoc. The difference was most acute when the medieval Cathar heresy thrived on the Languedoc side of the Ariège, and Montségur became the Cathars' Alamo.

The Western Ariège: the Couserans

The Couserans, once a vassal of the Comminges, is the emptiest corner of the Ariège, but it also has the most beautiful: two rivers, the Lez and the Salat, and their tributaries literally cascading down from the tremendous frontier range form its heart. Its valleys, especially the Biros and Bethmale, are renowned among students of folklore for their costumes.

St-Lizier

Piled on its hill, St-Lizier is the age-old capital of the Couserans. Begun in the 11th century, its **cathedral** looks fairly normal, but step inside: the nave and choir are built on different axes, the left wall is tilted, the columns don't match up, the transepts are uneven. Rare 12th-century frescoes decorate the arches, while in the apse there's a 14th-century Christ Pantocrator with a stern, but startled expression (a comment on

Getting Around

Buses link St-Girons to Toulouse; others descend daily to Seix and Aulus-les-Bains (t 05 61 66 08 87).

Tourist Information

St-Lizier: Rue Neuve, t 05 61 96 77 77. They have daily tours in season, 10–12 and 2–6, the only way you can get in to see the cathedral treasure and hospital pharmacy.
Aulus-les-Bains: t 05 61 96 01 79.

Where to Stay and Eat

St-Girons (by St-Lizier) ✉ 09200
★★★**Eychenne**, 8 Av Paul-Laffont, t 05 61 04 04 50, f 05 61 96 07 20, was built as St-Girons' posthouse and has been in the same family for six generations. Over the decades they have made it into a wonderfully comfortable inn with a heated pool and garden. The vast old-fashioned dining room (*moderate*) has a menu of classic French specialities, including home-made foie gras, and one of the Ariège's best wine lists (*lunch menu 95F; others 130–320F*). *Closed Sun eve and Mon Nov–March, and 22 Dec–31 Jan.*
★★**La Clairiere**, Av de la Rèsistance, t 05 61 66 66 66, is a modern wood-shingled hotel and restaurant (*moderate*) just outside St-Girons, with a garden and swimming pool. The

restaurant offers such delights as *papillote de truites*, *magret de canard*, or veal with *mousserons*, tiny local mushrooms (*menus 70–220F*).
Le Relais d'Encausse, t 05 61 66 05 80, mornings t 05 61 96 21 03 (*rooms 230F with breakfast*), is just 1.5km outside St-Girons, at Saudech, in an old country house full of character. It has been beautifully restored by the Kawczynskis (who speak English). There are four rooms, and a salon with a fireplace.

Aulus-les-Bains ✉ 09140
★★★**Hostellerie La Terrasse**, t 05 61 96 00 98, in the main street, is the most delightful place to stay and eat (*moderate*) in Aulus, with a terrace over the Garbet and an interior furnished with antiques. Try one of the delicious specialities of the house, *capeline de veau mijotée aux herbes* or salmon with foie gras *en papillotes* (*menus 85–160F*).
★★**Hotel Beausejour**, t 05 61 06 00 06, is a classic old hotel saved from extinction and with much of its original decor, the 1960s overlay currently being peeled back to return to 30s style. There are small, pleasant bedrooms, though not all have adequate bathrooms yet.
★★**Les Oussaillès**, t 05 61 96 03 68, has mock Gothic turrets and balconied rooms. You can feast on delicious salads, trout or veal, or ask for a picnic basket to take away. Even vegetarians are catered for (*menus 40F (child) to 160F*).

the architecture). The pretty two-storey 12th-century cloister is to the right, and the treasure with a 14th-century reliquary bust of St Lizier. The tour includes a perfect 18th-century pharmacy, with its armillary sphere that doctors would consult for the most auspicious time for an operation.

The road from the cathedral leads to the massive **Palais des Evêques** (1660) (*open April–June and Sept–Oct daily 2–5.30; July–Aug daily 10–12.30 and 2–6.30*), that incorporates three Roman towers and has excellent views over the Couserans. Housed in the palace is the **Musée Départemental**, with the ethnographic collections, particularly on the Vallée de Bethmale.

The Valleys of the Couserans

Francis Bacon's 'One triumphs over nature only by obeying its rules,' is the slogan of the **Biros valley**, one of the finest places for walks in the Pyrenees, with the majestic backdrop of **Mont Valier** (9,369ft), once thought to be the highest of the Pyrenees; its abrupt east flank, rising 5,577ft is the loftiest rock face in the range. The classic route up Valier is to drive up the Riberot valley (south of Bordes-sur-Lez) to the car park, then walk 4 hours to the Refuge des Estagnous (**t** 05 61 96 76 22), leaving the remaining ascent until morning.

Bordes-sur-Lez stands at the entrance of the **Vallée de Bethmale**, celebrated for both its beauty and its delightful traditional red and black costumes and scimitar-shaped clogs decorated with copper nails and hearts. The most traditional village, **Ayet-en-Bethmale**, is the starting point for the valley's prettiest walk, to the romantic Lac de Bethmale (about 2 hours, there and back).

At the top of the valley, the D17 continues east over the beautiful Col de la Core to the **Vallée de Salat**. The main centre is **Seix**, a convivial old cheese-making village, with houses overlooking the Salat and places to hire canoes or kayaks for thrills and spills.

From the north, the equally beautiful **Vallée du Garbet** (take the D32 between Soueix and Seix) leads to **Aulus-les-Bains**, the spa of the Couserans, in a cirque of wild rocky walls and waterfalls – one of the most spectacular settings in the Pyrenees. A brand-new glass and wood *thermes* is worthy of its surroundings, with a pool open to the general public. The most popular walk from Aulus is to the gorgeous triple waterfall with an irresistible name, the **Cascade d'Arse**. Another beauty spot is the **Col d'Escot**, overlooking the **Cirque de Cagateille**.

The Lower Ariège

The northwest corner of the Ariège has for its centrepiece the Grotte du Mas-d'Azil, a cave with a record-breaking occupancy rate for more millennia than tongue can tell. It occupies the green hilly piedmont area where the mountains meet the plain, where far too often the traditional free spirit of the mountains collided head on with less tolerant central powers.

Tourist Information

Le Mas-d'Azil: opposite the church, t 05 61 69 97 22.
La Bastide-de-Sérou: t 05 61 64 53 53.

Where to Stay and Eat

Le Mas-d'Azil ✉ 09290
**Hôtel Gardel, on the main square, t 05 6169 90 05, is pleasantly old-fashioned. The restaurant (*cheap*) features freshwater fish and Ariègeois cheeses (*menus 55–100F*).
La Plagne, t 61 69 99 52/61 69 95 23 (*inexpensive*). A manor house with six *chambre d'hôte* rooms.

Le Jardin de Cadettou, St-Ferréol, t 05 61 69 95 23 (*inexpensive*), is just outside the centre and serves the best food in Le Mas-d'Azil in its cosy dining room. The restaurant (*moderate*) specializes in an unusual variety of *confits* – potted duck, pork, lamb, rabbit and pigeon; the pork served with an onion confiture is especially good (*menus 80–190F*). *Closed Oct, Mon, Wed eves and Sun eves.*

Lanoux/Artigat ✉ 09130
Thibaut, 1km from Artigat, t 05 61 68 58 45 (*inexpensive*). Handy if you want to spend time in the *pays de Martin Guerre*. There is a restaurant (*menu 80F*). *Closed Dec–March.*

Le Mas-d'Azil

It sounds like something you'd expect in California: a drive-through prehistoric cave. But there it is – the D119 winds right into the 214ft mouth of the Grotte du Mas d'Azil. People were here by c. 30,000 BC and they stuck around until the end of the Ice Age (8000 BC), an epoch called Azilian after this cave. Even after that it was rarely empty. Christians were here in the 3rd century; in the 9th century there was an abbey; Moors, Cathars, and Protestants all took refuge here. Their traces can be seen in the **galleries** (*open March, Oct and Nov Sun and hols only 2–6; April–May Mon–Fri 2–6, Sun and hols 10–12 and 2–6; June–Sept daily 10–12 and 2–6*). Tools from the Azilian technological revolution are in the **museum** (*same hours*) in Le Mas-d'Azil, a *bastide* and Protestant stronghold; they say Calvin himself preached here.

The region around Le Mas-d'Azil is called the **Montagnes du Plantaurel** – mountains that are really gentle hills. At **Montégut-Plantaurel**, you can visit the **Sculpture Monumentale d'Amnesty International**, by Christian Lovis; northeast, **Artigat** was the scene of one of the most haunting stories to come out of the 16th century, when a man returning from war convinced most of the village and his 'wife' that he was who he said he was, even if he bore only a faint resemblance to Martin Guerre. When the real Guerre returned, there was trouble. The imposter's trial in Toulouse was the basis for *The Return of Martin Guerre* – the book by Natalie Zemon Davis and the film with Gérard Depardieu, filmed in the lushest Ariège.

Foix

Foix may be among the tiniest departmental capitals in France, but it's one of the most striking, a wing of a town tucked between the Arget and Ariège rivers, crowned with a triple tiara of towers on its immense rock. This was once the base of the Counts of Foix, who, with the Counts of Toulouse and Carcassonne, protected the

Cathars and fought for their independence in the Albigensian Crusade. Later their power spread over the Pyrenees, especially under Gaston Fébus (d. 1391). His grandson, another Gaston de Foix, made his reputation as the Renaissance's 'perfect knight', before he was killed in the Battle of Ravenna.

Ringed by 19th-century development, old Foix is still intact, closed in by its rivers and the mighty rock of the castle. Down at the bottom of Rue des Marchandes you'll find the market square and its church, **St-Volusien**, begun in the 11th century by the Counts, but mostly rebuilt; don't miss the 16th-century terracotta *Deposition*.

The **Château des Comtes de Foix** (*open June and Sept daily 9.30–12 and 2–6; July–Aug daily 9.30–6.30; Oct–May 10.30–12 and 2–5.30; closed Mon and Thurs Oct–April; adm*) has seen its share of action, especially under its Cathar Count Raymond Roger. His arch-enemy Simon de Montfort vowed to 'make the Rock of Foix melt like fat and grill its master in it'. When he failed after four tries, Montfort burned the rest of Foix to the ground, and Raymond Roger surrendered – but got his castle back a few years later when Montfort was killed. The château houses the Musée Départemental with a complete mammoth skeleton, pre-Roman and Roman altars, and Romanesque capitals from St-Volusien, one showing the siege of Toulouse in 507.

Getting Around

Foix is on the Toulouse–Barcelona line, with connections to Pamiers, Tarascon-sur-Ariège, Ax-les-Thermes and L'Hospitalet (with bus connections to Pas de la Casa and Andorra). The station is on Av Pierre Semard, t 05 61 02 03 60.

Several runs are taken by SNCF buses; all depart from the station at the north end of town off Cours I.-Cros. SALT buses, t 05 61 65 08 40, link Pas-de la Casa and Toulouse; Denamiel buses, t 05 61 65 06 06, run from Foix to St-Girons; and Sovitours, t 05 61 01 02 35, link Foix, Lavelanet, Mirepoix and Perpignan.

Tourist Information

45 Cours Gabriel-Fauré, next to the *mairie*, t 05 61 65 12 12.

Where to Stay and Eat

Foix ✉ 09000

★★★**Audoye-Lons**, Place Duthil, t 05 61 65 52 44, f 05 61 02 68 18 (*moderate–inexpensive*), is in a former posthouse near the Ariège River. It is a comfortable place to stay, with renovated rooms and a terrace restaurant (*menus 75–145F*) overlooking the river. . Closed mid-Dec–mid-Jan.

★★★**Hôtel Pyrène**, Rue Serge-Denis, Le Vignoble (2km north on the N20), t 05 61 65 48 66/05 61 65 51 12, f 05 61 65 46 69 (*inexpensive*), has up-to-date furnishings, a pool and garden. Closed mid-Dec–mid-Jan.

★★**Barbacane**, Av de Lérida, t 05 61 65 50 44, is one of the nicer places to stay in the centre of town, in a grand bourgeois mansion. Closed Nov–Mar.

Le Phoebus, 3 Cours I.-Cros, t 05 61 65 10 42, is a popular local restaurant (*moderate*) with a balcony facing the château. They serve local produce with a rich twist; try duck liver with caramelized apples, or duck with armagnac. There's a good wine list (*menus 65–200F*). Closed Sat lunchtimes and Mon.

Le Sainte-Marthe, 21 Rue Noel Peyrévidal, t 05 61 02 87 87, is a restaurant (*moderate*) serving classics such as *cassoulet*, but also inventive dishes such as a tart of *boudin noir* with *champignons*, salmon with vanilla (*menus 95–220F*).

Around Foix

Six km northwest of Foix on the D1 you can take a fantastic 75-minute boat ride down the **Rivière Souterraine de Labouiche**, nothing less than 'Europe's Longest Subterranean River Open to the Public' (*open either 1 April or Easter to Pentecost, 2–6 and Sun and school holidays 10–12 and 2–6; Pentecost–Sept 10–12 and 2–6; July–Aug 9.30–6; Oct to 11 Nov Sun only 10–12 and 2–6; adm. In season go in the morning to avoid the crowds*).

The Castle of Montségur

Open Sept–June daily 9–6, July–Aug 9–7; guided visits July–Aug at 11am and 1, 3, 4.30 and 5.30pm; adm. It takes about 20 minutes to walk up to the chateau.

The castle of Montségur on its rocky outcrop is a magnet for anyone fascinated by the virtuous heretics. But for many southerners, Montségur symbolizes the lost soul of an aborted nation, symbolized by the 'Occitania Indépendante!' scrawled under the castle (*see* p.74).

At the beginning of the path to the fortress, a stone memorial marks the **Camp des Crémats**, where a stockade full of wood was set alight as the archbishop of Narbonne arrived to take possession of Montségur and the souls who converted to Catholicism. Not a single one took up the offer; all 225 preferred to jump into the flames. In the castle itself there's not much to see, but a curious feature are two lateral openings in its triangular walls, aligned to the rising of the sun on the summer solstice; celebrations are held every 21 June.

Getting Around

Public transport is pretty thin on the ground here, although there are bus connections from Toulouse to Lavelanet and Mirepoix (Pouplain **t** 05 61 01 54 00; SALT buses **t** 05 61 65 08 40) and from Foix to Lavelanet on Sovitour buses, **t** 05 61 01 02 35.

Tourist Information

Montségur: **t** 05 61 03 03 03 (*open June–Aug*).
Mirepoix: **t** 05 61 68 83 76.

Where to Stay and Eat

Montségur and Environs ✉ 09300

★★Costes, **t** 05 61 01 10 24, **f** 05 61 03 06 28, is a pleasant creeper-covered old hotel with a garden in the middle of town. It has an excellent restaurant (*moderate*), serving omelettes with *cèpes* and other south-western delicacies (*menus 85–190F*). *Closed mid-Nov–March, and Mon Sept–June.*
L'Occitadelle, **t** 05 61 01 21 77, serves well-prepared dishes (*cheap*), such as perch in sorrel sauce (*menus 85–110F*).
★★Hôtel d'Espagne, 20 Rue Jean-Jaurès, Lavelanet, **t** 05 61 01 00 78 (*cheap*). With a pool and good restaurant (*menus from 60F*).

Mirepoix ✉ 09500

★★★La Maison des Consuls, 6 Place Couvert, **t** 05 61 68 81 81, **f** 05 61 68 81 15, is a stylishly decorated hotel in the Maison des Consuls, an arcaded building with wonderful carved beams. Antique-furnished rooms overlook the medieval streets.
★★Commerce, Cours Docteur-Chabaud, **t** 05 61 68 10 29, **f** 05 61 68 20 99, is the nicest place in town, with a shady garden and good restaurant, with a menu based on seasonal ingredients. *Closed Jan and early Oct.*

The Cathars, the Inquisition, and the Fall of Montségur

Few beliefs have had the staying power of dualism, a doctine first expounded by the Greek Gnostics. Good and Evil were explained as eternal opposing forces, Good residing somewhere beyond the stars, while Evil was here and now – in fact all of creation was Evil, the work of a fallen spirit, identifiable with Satan. Although condemned by the Church, dualism made an organized revival in the 9th century with the 'Bogomils' in the Balkans. By the 11th century it had spread through much of Europe. The Church burned as many as it could catch, but in southern France, the faith attracted many merchants, craftsmen, poor people and members of the nobility.

The Cathars believed that their faith was a return to the virtue and simplicity of the early Church. Their teaching encouraged separation from the Devil's world; feudal oaths were forbidden, and believers solved differences by arbitration of in courts of law. They promoted vegetarianism and non-violence; marriages were by simple agreement and enhanced the freedom of women. They also had a more mature atti-tude towards capitalism than the Roman church, with no condemnation of loans as usury, and no church tithes, and no big church organization, making a favourable contrast with the corrupt machinery of the Church of Rome. There was also a very forgiving attitude towards sinners; if creation itself was the Devil's work, how could people not err? Cathars were divided into the mass of believers, upon whom the religion was a light yoke indeed, and the few *perfecti*, those who had received a sacrament called the *consolament*, and were required to lead a life devoted to faith and prayer. Most Cathars conveniently took the *consolament* on their deathbeds.

In 1203, a Spanish monk, Domingo Guzman embarked on a mission to save the souls of the heretics, founding the Order that would become the Dominicans. But by 1209, the papacy saw enough of a threat to prefer a policy of genocide. When the terror, enforced by French arms and promises of southern land to good Catholic crusaders, failed to kill enough Cathars, the Church turned to specialists – the followers of Dominic. The first Inquisitors, based in Toulouse, torched so many people that the Toulousains rioted and expelled them in 1235. But they were back the next year, more murderous than ever. In May 1242, knights from Montségur killed the 12 top Inquisitors. The next year 6000 men under Hugues des Arcis began their siege of Montségur, where some 350 Cathars lived, protected by a garrison of 150 men.

Montségur held out for ten months, into the difficult winter; impatiently, Hugues des Arcis hired mercenaries from the surrounding villages, who in the dead of night led the Crusaders up to the east end of the hill, where they killed the defenders and captured a tower within catapult range of the castle. The Cathars held out another two months in the snow, but on 2 March, as all chances of relief were eliminated, the commander, Pierre Roger de Mirepoix, opened talks. The Cathars were given two weeks' grace. If they became Catholics they would be free, if not, they would be burnt alive.

Montségur

A steep road winds down to the small village of Montségur, a cute little place built in tiers on the hillside with more footpaths than streets. Here **L'Occitadelle** offers an audio-visual on the history of the Cathars and the Albigensian Crusade. Montségur's little **Musée Archéologique** (t 05 61 01 06 94; *open Feb daily 2–5.30; Mar–April daily 11–5.30; May–Aug daily 10–12.30 and 2–7.30; Sept daily 10–12 and 2–5.30; Oct–Nov daily 1.30–5; Dec Wed–Sun 2–5.30; closed Jan; adm; March–Dec ticket also valid for Montségur Castle*) has finds from excavations and a model of the château.

Mirepoix and the Vertical Church of Vals

Mirepoix, a major Cathar stronghold, is one of the prettiest villages in the Ariège. It looks very much as it did in the 14th century, with its half-timber houses and arcaded square. In 1317, Pope John XXII elevated Mirepoix to a bishropic as part of a scheme to bring danger zones of heresy back into the fold. The Lévis, the rulers installed by Simon de Montfort, began to enlarge the church of St-Maurice into a cathedral. They went for broke: the bell tower stands 190ft high, and behind the handsome Gothic portal it measures 73ft across, making it the second widest single nave in Europe, only a tad smaller than the cathedral of Gerona in Spain.

Towards Pamiers are a pair of Romanesque churches well worth a detour. The one at **Teilhet** is fortified with a *clocher-mur*, sculpted with a knight; the portal has beautifully capitals and a frieze of grotesques. Two km further on, the unique church at **Vals** (if locked, the key is available from Mme Andrieu, who lives in the last house on the right, with brown shutters) stands on a huge rock that supported a temple to the Celtic god Rahus. An uncanny tunnel and stair follow a natural fault to the 8th-century church, excavated in the living rock. To this, a vaguely Mozarab apse was added in the 11th century; in the 1100s it was beautifully frescoed by Catalan artists. A second, upper nave was added, dedicated to the Virgin Mary; above that, orientated sideways is a 12th-century chapel of St-Michel, built into a *clocher-mur*.

Tarascon-sur-Ariège and the Upper Ariège Valley

Up the Ariège from Foix, Tarascon-sur-Ariège is one of the main crossroads of the *département*. It held a similar status in the dawn of time: today it's the capital of prehistory in the Pyrenees.

Tarascon-sur-Ariège and its Caves

Tarascon-sur-Ariège was settled by the Tarusques, a Ligurian tribe mentioned by Pliny. It has an isolated baby mountain for a landmark, crowned by a round clock-tower. But most of all Tarascon is famous for its caves; its new **Parc Pyrénéen de l'Art Préhistorique** (*open Sept–June daily 10–6; July–Aug daily 10–7; adm exp*) was opened to console the many hopefuls turned away from the Grotte de Niaux; it has perfect replicas of the art, 'the biggest facsimile in the world' and a 'sonar labyrinth', too.

Getting Around

The railroad between Tarascon-sur-Ariège, Ax-les-Thermes and L'Hospitalet is the highest in Europe and was a great engineering feat when it opened in 1888. For train information in Ax, ring t 05 61 64 20 72.

Tourist Information

Tarascon-sur-Ariège: Place du 19 Mars 1962, t 05 61 05 94 94.
Ax-les-Thermes: Place du Breilh, t 05 61 64 60 60.

Where to Stay and Eat

Tarascon-sur-Ariège ✉ 09400
★★Hostellerie de la Poste, 16 Av V. Pilhes, t 05 61 05 60 41, has a terrace over the river and a restaurant (*menus 65–185F*).
★★Le Confort, 3 Quai A. Sylvestre, t 05 61 05 61 90, is small and nice, overlooking the Ariège.

Hotel-Restaurant Le Bellevue, 7 Place Jean-Jaurès, t 05 61 05 52 06 (*cheap*), is an adequate small hotel with a decent restaurant (*moderate*), serving local specialities such as *azinat*, Ariège's famous filling cabbage soup (*menus 89–160F*).

Ax-les-Thermes ✉ 09110
★★Le Grillon, Rue St-Udaut, t 05 61 64 31 64, f 05 61 64 25 48, has lovely views, a garden and pretty panelled rooms, making it the nicest place to stay in Ax. The excellent restaurant (*moderate*) serves Ariègeois specialities, such as *confit de canard* with apples (*menus 98–168F*). *Closed Tues eves and Wed out of season.*
★★L'Orry Le Saquet, t 05 61 64 31 30, f 05 61 64 00 31, just south of Ax, has nice rooms, a garden, a terrace, and a fireplace in winter. They also have a refined kitchen (*expensive–moderate*) that keeps travellers coming back year after year. Inventive cuisine combines, for example, fish with *cèpes* and foie gras (*menus 45F (child)–390F*).

From Tarascon it's 5km up to the **Grotte de Bédeilhac** and its huge porch (*open April–June and Sept daily 2.15–5; July–Aug daily 10–5.30; Oct–March Sun and school hols only 3–4.30; bring something warm*). A large stalactite cave, it was only in 1906 that the Abbé Breuil, the 'father of prehistory' discovered its Palaeolithic art: deer, horses, bison, goats, and mysterious symbols, and four bison modelled out of clay with a pubic triangle inscribed above them. A Neolithic skeleton of a man measuring only 4ft 6in tall was found near the entrance.

If you think Bédeilhac is a monster of a cave, a few kilometres south of Tarascon on the N20 is the **Grotte de Lombrives**, the biggest cave in Europe open to the public, so vast that even though visits are by a little train, you'll still only see a fraction of the whole (*departures July and Aug daily every 15mins 10–7; during school holidays, in June and Sept, and Sat–Sun between Palm Sunday and 11 Nov, at 10am and 2, 3.30 and 5pm; afternoons only in May; adm*). Among the stalactite and stalagmite formations is the remarkable *Mammoth*, the *throne of King Bébrix*, and the *sepulchre of Pyrène*, his daughter, the lover of Hercules and namesake of the mountains that became her funerary monument. Lombrives goes on and on – it's said to have subterranean links to Niaux – and has upper galleries, 150ft up, accessible only by ladders. Numerous skeletons, nearly all women and children, were found up there; in his *Gallic Wars*, Caesar wrote how the Romans snuffed out many Pyrenean tribes by walling them up in their cave refuges, but in Lombrives all the legionnaires had to do was take away the ladders.

Another cave nearby, the **Grotte de Bethléem**, was apparently used by the Cathars for initiation ceremonies of the *consolament*; no one knows what kind of mumbo-jumbo they got up to, but there's a very Pythagorean pentangle deeply engraved in the wall.

The Grotte de Niaux

Open July–Sept, visits every 45mins 8.30–11.30 and 1.30–5.15; Oct–June, three tours daily at 11, 3, and 4.30; only 20 people admitted at a time; reservations essential, t 05 61 05 88 37. Arrive 15mins before your departure time. The walk in the cave is nearly 2km and not advised for anyone who has difficulty walking. Bring something warm.

The most beautiful prehistoric art in the Pyrenees, and according to many, the best after Lascaux and Spain's Altamira, is in Niaux, discovered in 1906 in the cliffs. A winding road leads up to its gaping mouth, marked by a metal prow-like structure extending into space. Mysterious signs are painted in red and black near the entrance, reminiscent of the private symbols of Joan Miró, and appear to direct visitors to the superb **Salle Noir**, decorated with an immensely powerful and poetic composition of charcoal line drawings from *c.* 10,500 BC. Bison, horses and mountain goats are beautifully rendered, a few superimposed but all wonderfully clear, making expert use of the natural contours and formations of the walls.

Up the Ariège to Ax-les-Thermes and Montaillou

There are two ways to continue southeast of Tarascon to **Ax-les-Thermes**. The N20 or 'Route du Pastis', is often saturated with traffic trundling to Spain by way of the duty-free republic of Andorra. The alternative is the far more scenic D20/D2 or Route des Corniches. Ax has a long history, but a long record of fires to go with it. Its name may come from the Iberian word *ats*, meaning 'stinker', after its sulphurous waters. One of the first people to exploit Stinker-les-Thermes was St Louis, who built a hospital for Crusaders who caught leprosy. Beisdes the spa, Ax is also the best base for exploring the highest mountains of the Ariège.

Northeast of Ax, **Montaillou** is synonymous with Emmanuel LeRoy Ladurie's now classic study of a 14th-century village. Even after the fall of Montségur, Catharism continued to exist in pockets, especially in the mountains of the Ariège and Catalunya; in spite of the threat of the Inquisition, there was even a heresy revival in 1300 until 1326, when the last Cathars were all rounded up, burned at the stake, imprisoned, or made to wear a big yellow cross sewn on their backs. Ladurie owed the amazing detail in his *Montaillou: The Promised Land of Error* to the zeal of the head Inquisitor, Jacques Fournier, Bishop of Pamiers, who painstakingly had every word of his inquiries recorded. The incorruptable, ascetic Fournier so distinguished himself for his diligence in catching heretics that in 1334 he was elected Pope Benedict XII. Only a handful of souls live in Montaillou now, but in the 1970s Ladurie looked through the telephone directory and found the same surnames common 650 years ago.

The North

15

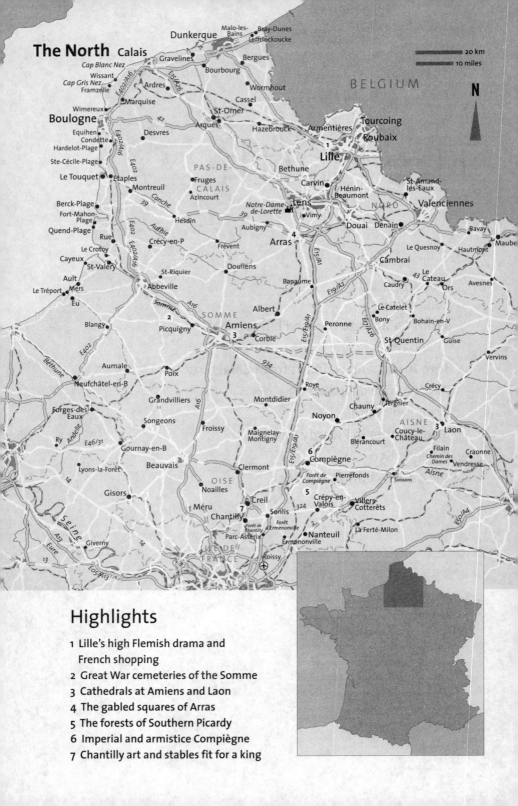

The North

Calais

Cap Blanc Nez
Wissant
Cap Gris Nez
Framzelle
Marquise

Wimereux
Boulogne
Equihen
Condette
Hardelot-Plage
Ste-Cécile-Plage
Le Touquet
Etaples
Montreuil
Berck-Plage
Fort-Mahon-Plage
Quend-Plage
Rue
Le Crotoy
Cayeux
St-Valery
Ault
Le Tréport
Mers
Eu
Blangy

Aumale
Neufchâtel-en-B
Forges-des-Eaux
Songeons
Ry
Andelle
Gournay-en-B
Lyons-la-Forêt
Gisors
Giverny

Dunkerque
Malo-les-Bains
Bray-Dunes
Leffrinckoucke
Gravelines
Bergues
Bourbourg
Wormhout
Cassel
Ardres
St-Omer
Arques
Hazebrouck
Armentières
Tourcoing
Roubaix
Lille

BELGIUM

Desvres

PAS-DE-
Fruges
CALAIS
Azincourt
Canche
Hesdin
Aubigny
Crécy-en-P
Frévent
Doullens

Bapaume

St-Riquier
Abbeville

Somme
Picquigny
Amiens
Corbie

Poix
Grandvilliers
Froissy
Maignelay-Montigny
Beauvais
Clermont
OISE
Noailles
Méru
Creil
Chantilly
Senlis
Forêt de Chantilly
Parc-Astérix
Forêt d'Ermenonville
Ermenonville
ÎLE-DE-FRANCE
Roissy

Bethune
Carvin
Hénin-Beaumont
St-Amand-les-Eaux
Lens
Vimy
NORD
Valenciennes
Notre-Dame-de-Lorette
Douai
Denain
Bavay
Maube
Arras
Le Quesnoy
Hautmont
Cambrai
Le Cateau
Ors
Avesnes
Caudry
Le Catelet
Bony
Bohain-en-V
Peronne
St-Quentin
Guise
Roye
Vervins
Montdidier
Chauny
Tergnier
Crécy
Noyon
AISNE
Coucy-le-Château
Laon
Blérancourt
Filain
Craonne
Compiègne
Chemin des Dames
Vendresse
Pierrefonds
Forêt de Compiègne
Soissons
Aisne
Crépy-en-Valois
Villers-Cotterêts
La Ferté-Milon
Nanteuil

20 km
10 miles

N

Highlights

1 Lille's high Flemish drama and French shopping
2 Great War cemeteries of the Somme
3 Cathedrals at Amiens and Laon
4 The gabled squares of Arras
5 The forests of Southern Picardy
6 Imperial and armistice Compiègne
7 Chantilly art and stables fit for a king

Food and Drink

All sorts of stews feature on northern French menus – this is a part of France where much of the traditional cooking is warming and copious. Rabbit stews are popular, as are stews with mixed meats, known as hochepot, and stews with beer. Soups are another favourite, from vegetable soups to broths with tripe and frogs. Maroilles is much the best-known cheese, pungent and powerful, melting slowly in the mouth; its origins date back to Maroilles abbey in the 10th century.

There are a lot of similarities with Flemish or Belgian cuisine, including a delight in sweet things and chocolate in particular. In the autumn, hillocks of white sugar beet are gathered on the edge of fields. Beer is a popular local tipple, as well as chicory coffee and locally produced gin.

Getting There

By ferry: For details on arriving in one of the three Channel ports of Calais, Boulogne or Dunkerque, *see* **Travel**.

By plane: Paris-Charles de Gaulle aiport lies just south of the region (*see* **Travel**). Lille, Beauvais and Reims are smaller airports to consider.

Ryanair operates a useful service from Glasgow-Prestwick to Beauvais, a little way north of Paris.

By train: Lille-Europe is just 2hrs from London-Waterloo by Eurostar, with 12 return services a day Mon–Sat (*from 6am*) and 8 return services on Sun (*from 8.30am*). The TGV high-speed train from Paris-Gare du Nord to Lille-Europe takes 1hr, the TGV train from Paris-Charles de Gaulle to Lille-Europe between 50 mins and 1hr.

By car: Northern France is well served by motorways, some of them free. The A16 runs down the coast from Dunkerque to Abbeville and then inland to Paris via Amiens and Beauvais. The A26 cuts diagonally across Northern France from Calais to Reims. The A1 links Lille and Paris.

Tourist Information

For information on Picardy in the UK, contact: **t** (020) 7836 2232, **f** (020) 7240 8999, *marie-stella@thehatfactory.com*.

So much muscle and blood in the earth.
Sebastian Faulks, *Birdsong*

Killing fields, Gothic cathedrals, Flemish art and cross-Channel shopping are among the contrasting attractions of northern France, which in this book means the modern regions of Nord Pas-de-Calais and Picardy, embracing historical French Flanders and Hainaut along the frontier with Belgium, and Artois.

The name of the Somme is inevitably linked with the First World War. From time to time, the bodies of war victims are still unearthed, and bombs are still found every year by the thousand. So much of northern France was bombed to bits in the two world wars that it may come as a surprise to find glorious cities in these parts. In Nord Pas-de-Calais head for St-Omer and Montreuil, Arras and Lille. In Picardy, the cathedral cities of Laon and Senlis stand out, as do the castle towns of Coucy, Compiègne and Chantilly.

Northern France to most French people is bleak industrial mining country, its name justifiably blackened by the likes of Zola, who in *Germinal* revealed the horrors of miners' lives. Coal mining ceased here in the 1990s, but its reputation lives on, as well as the slag heaps. However, most of northern France consists of gently undulating fields, and in southern Picardy large swathes of forests have been preserved, once the reserve of royal hunts. The rough, high-duned coast that runs down from Belgium to Normandy has been nicknamed the Côte d'Opale after the colour of the seawater.

Calais

It would take a drug-crazed advertising copywriter to describe Calais as a Venice of the north, but at least this all too put-upon town does not look too hideous viewed from a ferry a safe distance out to sea. However ugly it may be, Calais remains close to many an Englishman's heart – mainly, it has to be admitted, for cheap beer, wine and cigarettes these days, but its historic symbolism as an outpost of England hasn't been entirely forgotten. Unless you are here to shop, Calais really is no place to linger.

Getting Around

Calais has two railway stations, the central Calais-Ville and the station serving the Channel Tunnel, Calais-Fréthun. Calais-Fréthun is linked by regular high-speed services to Paris-Gare du Nord (*c. 1hr 30mins*). Calais is also linked to Lille by fast trains (*c. 30 mins*). Trains between the two Calais stations are not that regular, and nor is the *navette* (shuttle bus service; Ligne 7 between Gare SNCF and Cité d'Europe-Coquelles).

To order a taxi in Calais, **t** 03 21 97 89 89/ **t** 03 21 97 35 35/**t** 03 21 97 05 22/**t** 03 21 97 13 14.

Tourist Information

Calais: 12 Bd Clemenceau, **t** 03 21 96 62 40, **f** 03 21 96 01 92, *www.OT-calais.fr*.

Where to Stay

Calais ✉ 62100

There are a few decent hotels in Calais, but many more charming places to stay not far away, *see* p.629.

Moderate

***Holiday Inn**, 6 Bd des Alliés, **t** 03 21 34 69 69, **f** 03 21 97 09 15. A big chain hotel in an unremarkable tall building between the port and the main shopping street. Some rooms look out to sea (*menus 45–130F*). *Restaurant-grill closed Sat and Sun lunch.*

***George V**, 36 Rue Royale, **t** 03 21 97 68 00, **f** 03 21 97 34 73. Set in the thick of the action on the main shopping street. *Restaurant closed 22 Dec–14 Jan, Sat lunch and Sun* (*menus 95–285F*).

Cheap

*Bristol**, 13 Rue du Duc de Guise, **t**/**f** 03 21 34 53 24. A cheap hotel with a cheerful front, well situated off Rue Royale.

Eating Out

L'Aquar'aile, Plage de Calais, 255 Rue Jean Moulin, **t** 03 21 34 00 00, **f** 03 21 34 15 00. One of the best restaurants in town, looking out over the busy shipping lanes (*menus 130–230F*). *Closed 16–31 Aug, 15–29 Feb, Sun eve and Mon.*

Le Channel, 3 Bd de la Résistance, **t** 03 21 34 42 30, **f** 03 21 97 42 43. Popular for fish, with views on to the marina (*menus 120–200F*). *Closed Dec, Sun eve and Tues.*

La Sole Meunière, 1 Bd de la Résistance, **t** 03 21 34 43 01, **f** 03 21 97 65 62. Neighbour of Le Channel, with similar features.

You can find many more restaurants around the Place d'Armes, fish almost always the speciality.

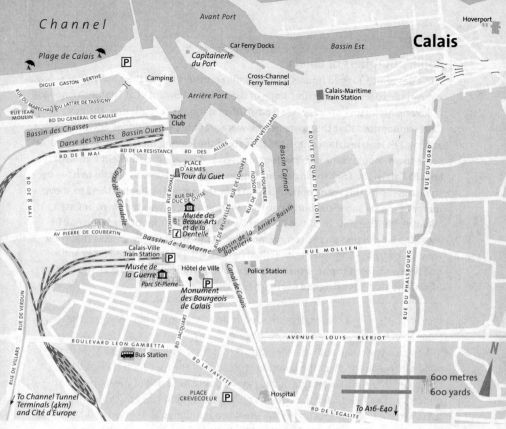

It is one of the most depressing towns in France, and also one of the most depressed, with unemployment almost as evident as the factories on the horizon.

So long fought over by the English and French crowns, now the tensions in town are likely to be between fellow Brits fighting over their place in a shopping queue. In the centre of Calais, the main shopping artery of the **Rue Royale** heads down from the busy **Place d'Armes** close to the port, marked out by an unfriendly-looking 13th-century watch tower – a rare vestige of the old town. Heading south across the canal, **Boulevard Jacquart** continues where Rue Royale left off. **Boulevard La Fayette** beyond also has major shops, while **Place Crèvecoeur**, the large square just off it, hosts a major market on Thursdays and Saturdays. Beyond the shopping streets, the town has become a no-man's-land. Large numbers of visitors make straight for the Cité d'Europe close to the Chunnel terminal, where, among other shops, there is an enormous Carrefour and Auchan, the latter generally regarded as having a slightly better quality of goods. Wine and beer warehouses are dotted around Calais and its outskirts.

If you get stuck in the centre of Calais, you could visit the **Musée des Beaux-Arts et de la Dentelle** (*open daily exc Tues and Sun am 10–12 and 2–5.30; adm*), close to what is described as the only Tudor church in France. Housed in a typically characterless 1960s building, it has displays on the industrial but beautiful lace-making for which Calais was long renowned and an introduction to Flemish art. The good sculpture

Rodin's Burghers of Calais

The desperate, ragged figures, some dignified, others lost in their individual agony, were made to recall the terrible siege of the town by Edward III of England (1346–47), following his victory at Crécy (*see* p.649). After 11 months of suffering, the governor of Calais announced that the townspeople were prepared to surrender. Edward, furious at the city's long resistance, insisted that six of the leading merchants of the troublesome town should come out barefoot, noosed and begging, to present him with the keys to Calais. The English king's wife, Queen Philippa of Hainaut, is said to have been so distressed by this scene of humiliation that she entreated her husband to show mercy to the six sacrificial burghers. They were spared, as was the town of Calais.

Rodin's life-size statues of the burghers were put up in front of the town hall in 1895. The French text on the commemorative plaque mistakenly implies that they were killed by the English. The wretched figures, with their hollowed faces and hollow eyes turned copper-green like their robes, symbolize all too well the horrors of warfare that have plagued northern France.

section starts with a provocative small equestrian statue of Napoleon, but the main focus is on Rodin's studies for *The Burghers of Calais*.

The 1920s town hall with its soaring belfry copies the typical Flemish style of such buildings, made to reflect the power and prestige of the merchant classes. Well concealed in the unremarkable public park opposite lurks one of the longest Nazi bunkers you will ever have the dubious pleasure of seeing. Cleverly camouflaged by ruins when it was built, it survived all the Allied bombings and served as a Nazi naval headquarters. Now converted into the **Musée de la Guerre** (*open April–Sept daily 10–5.15; rest of year daily exc Tues 11–5; adm*), one room is devoted to the First World War, when Calais was in British hands and already received its first pasting from bombs. But the museum concentrates on the German occupation of Calais from May 1940 to autumn 1944. A clutter of cuttings, posters, uniforms, weapons and other war paraphernalia fills the room. At one point the Germans deliberately flooded the plain around Calais, so that the town had to be rebuilt after the war; for a long time afterwards the fields were so badly affected by the sea salt that nothing grew.

The long **suburban beaches** lie west of the port, backed by cheap apartment blocks and graffiti-covered shacks that watch the ferries and seacats ploughing into and out of town. At **Blériot-Plage** a little further west you can pay homage to Louis Blériot, the Frenchman who made the first flight across the Channel, in July 1909.

From Calais into French Flanders

The best-known of France's Channel ports is also a good gateway to fortified French Flanders, passing via Gravelines and Dunkerque on the coast before heading down to Lille. Cassel was for some time the headquarters of the French military in the First World War. You can easily pick up Flemish programmes on the car radio.

Gravelines and the Aa Estuary

East of Calais, the canalized estuary of the Aa river is guarded by Gravelines and its two coastal outposts, Grand-Fort-Philippe and Petit-Fort-Philippe. The Philippe referred to was none other than Philip II of Spain, whose soldiers took French Flanders for the Emperor in the late 1580s. After the failure of the Spanish Armada in 1588, some of the same Philip's fleet was scattered in disarray along this coast.

Gravelines's moated ramparts date back in part to the late 17th century, when Louis XIV's great military architect, Vauban, was called upon to fortify strategic points along France's frontiers. His arsenal now houses the **Musée du Dessin et de l'Estampe Originale** (*open daily exc Tues 2–5; adm*), with exhibitions on the graphic arts. The lighthouse at the end of the canal stands out like a stick of liquorice. The large

Getting Around

Dunkerque has regular train connections with Paris-Gare du Nord (1hr 30mins–2hrs 30mins, and with Lille.

Tourist Information

Gravelines: 11 Rue de République, t 03 28 51 94 00, f 03 28 65 58 19.
Dunkerque: 4 Place Charles Valentin, t 03 28 66 79 21, f 03 28 63 38 34.
Bray-Dunes: Place J. Rubben, B.P.9, t 03 28 26 61 09, f 03 28 26 64 09.
Bergues: Place de la République, t 03 28 68 71 06, f 03 28 68 71 25.
Cassel: Grand'Place, t 03 28 40 52 55, f 03 28 40 59 17.

Where to Stay and Eat

Gravelines ✉ 59820

Gravelines is far preferable to Calais as a place to stay, despite the nuclear power station east of town.
***Hostellerie du Beffroi, Pl Ch. Valentin, t 03 28 23 24 25, f 03 28 6 5 59 71. Neat, smart and clean brick hotel which looks on to the main square, in the shadow of the towering belfry.
Hôtel de l'Univers, 8 Av du Calvaire, 59153 Grand Fort-Philippe, t 03 28 65 35 07 (*cheap*). On the western side of the Aa, an unpretentious hotel with a flat dramatic view east along the coast. 40 rooms. Restaurant (*menus 99–195F*). *Closed Sat lunch, Sun eve.*

Bergues ✉ 59380

A lovely unspoilt town just south of Dunkerque: a good place to stay or eat.
**Le Commerce, Contour de l'Eglise, t 03 28 68 60 37, f 03 28 68 70 76 (*inexpensive*). Surprisingly unpretentious hotel in the centre, with bright rooms.
**Au Tonnelier, 4 Rue du Mont de Piété, t 03 28 68 70 05, f 03 28 68 21 87 (*inexpensive*). Central hotel in a lovely location, with a quiet charm (*menus 130–160F*). *Restaurant closed Sun eve and Fri.*
Le Cornet d'Or. 26 Rue Espagnol, t 03 28 68 60 37. The poshest restaurant, by the water, with décor of tapestries, beams and heavy curtains and chairs. Expect hefty prices for grand-style cuisine (*menus 168–326F*).
Taverne Bruegel. The most picturesque restaurant, in an excellent spot by the water, serving simple regional platters.
Le Berguenard, 1 Rue Faidherbe, t 03 28 68 65 00. More discreet and cosy, this tempting street-corner restaurant offers refined cuisine even if the menus are limited. (*menus 125–260F*). *Closed Sun eve and Mon.*

Cassel ✉ 59670

You'll realize just how Flemish Cassel still is by eating here.
Estaminet T'Kasteel Hof, t 03 28 40 59 29, f 03 28 42 43 23. Up at the top of the Mont Cassel, a slightly messy but charming restaurant serving local Flemish dishes and speciality Flemish beers.
La Taverne Flamande, t 03 28 42 42 59, f 03 28 40 51 84. Flemish specialities down in the grandiose main square.

beaches are enticing, although the enormous casserole pots of a nuclear power station will deter you from walking too far east.

Dunkerque

Given its relatively small population, Dunkerque (or Dunkirk in English) has massive industrial outskirts. Comparable to Calais, this war-torn port is hardly an obvious tourist destination, but it does have slightly more charm than Calais. The harbour attracts plenty of yachts, while the tall ship, the *Duchesse Anne*, is moored there by the **Musée Portuaire** (*open daily exc Tues 10–12.15 and 2–6; adm*), put together by dockers and telling the story of Dunkerque's fishing port. The **Musée des Beaux-Arts** (*open daily exc Tues 10–12 and 2–6; adm*) is housed in a supermarket of a building. You have to sift through the paintings hung on cheap-looking panels, but there are some fine still lives, portraits by Pourbus and Reyn, and a noble head of a young turbaned black man by Rigaud, his neck collar a sign of his exploitation.

Enthusiasts maintain a small **Musée de la Guerre** (*check opening times with tourist office*) east of the centre, for anyone interested in the war-time history of Dunkerque, when the the town witnessed the devastating retreat of British and French troops at the outset of the Second World War. In Operation Dynamo, in May 1940, British naval command gathered a fleet of destroyers and private vessels to sail across the Channel and pick up the desperate fleeing Allied troops. Hundreds of thousands of Allies were saved by the skin of their teeth: between 27 May and 4 June, 340,000 or so British and French troops were evacuated, along with 16,000 Belgian and other men.

On Dunkerque's eastern shore, a monument put up in the 1960s recalls some 250 boats lost in the evacuation as well as the airmen, seamen and soldiers who died. Beyond the seaside resort of Malo-les-Bains, at Leffrinckoucke, there is a French national war cemetery with panels describing the events in sober tone. The resort of **Bray-Dunes**, the last town before the Belgian border, has retained some of its old-fashioned villas, and has a basic memorial on its beach-front promenade – to an infantry division which put up a brave resistance to the Germans here.

Bergues

Surrounded by moated ramparts, the atmosphere of old Bergues has been well preserved. It developed around an abbey dedicated to St Winoc, who came to these parts from Brittany. On the Groenberg, the town's highest point, a couple of striking towers stand out, one sharply pointed, the other looking like a caricature of a giant in stone – virtually all that remains of abbey, brought down at the Revolution. A proud Flemish belfry dominates the town centre, decorated with bartizan towers, copper-meringue ornaments and 50 bells. Several houses here boast high-scrolled Flemish gables. The grandiose classical building with its balustraded roof and small obelisks is the town hall. Homage is paid on it to Alphonse Lamartine, generally considered France's greatest Romantic poet, but also a significant mid-19th-century political figure. The main claim to fame of the **Musée Municipal** (*open daily exc Tues and Jan 10–12 and 3–5; adm*) is a work by Georges de La Tour, *The Nightwatchman with a Dog*.

First World War Memories

A more sacred place for the British race does not exist in the whole world.
Winston Churchill, referring to Ypres (1919)

For views over French Flanders, head up one of the winding routes to **Cassel**, some 20 kilometres south of Bergues. Cassel's hilltop may only reach 176 metres/577 ft in height, but it commands vast panoramas over the flat countryside around. Local legend has it that the hill was formed by a clod of earth that fell from the giant boots of Reuze Papa and Reuze Maman. Flanders is full of tales of such Gargantuan figures, effigies of whom are still brought out for local festivals. Real armies have fought over Cassel's strategic site for centuries, and it was even immortalized in a nursery rhyme: the Grand Old Duke of York led forces against the French Revolutionary army here. During the First World War, General Foch, leader of the French army, had his head-quarters at Cassel, and is remembered with an equestrian statue by the windmill – French Flanders once had thousands of windmills, and this is one of the few to survive and still grind flour. Down below, the small town stretches around a sloping cobbled main square. By far the grandest building, La Chatellainie, has been reno-vated and is used for temporary exhibitions. Many of the other buildings had to be rebuilt after the war. The brick church stands out, a typical Flemish Hallekerque (in which the side aisles are as tall and wide as the central nave) with triangular gables.

East of Cassel, the main road leads across the Belgian border to **Poperinge** and **Ypres** (Ieper in Flemish), an area which saw some of the most appalling fighting in the First World War. It became the infamous place where gas was first put to use by the Germans. Some 100,000 soldiers from the British Empire lost their lives here. On the Menin Gate, the number of dead soldiers' names listed is overwhelming – almost 55,000 British and Commonwealth men died in these parts without a known grave. Every night two buglers still sound the *Last Post* here. There are several exhibitions on the First World War, as well as sites which lay on the front line. British war cemeteries are dotted around Ypres, and some way south, by Mesen, at **Messines Ridge** a new Peace Tower was recently erected as the first joint memorial to the Great War dead of Ireland, North and South – some 200,000 Irishmen were enlisted during the conflict.

Lille

Hidden in layers of industry, Lille, the capital of French Flanders, has a glamorous old centre of outrageous Flemish Baroque buildings, towering belfries and elegant shop-ping streets that used to be something of a secret. The arrival of the Eurostar, and the tourists who pour out of it, has changed all that, and Lille, centre of the fourth largest conurbation in France, seems set to grow into one of the most vibrant cities in France.

A bone of contention for much of its history, Lille survived its frequent changes of overlord as a market town and textile centre. By the time Charles de Gaulle was born here in 1890 it had developed into an industrial powerhouse. It was occupied by German forces in both World Wars; bombs rained down on the city in the Second World War, and after the war Lille's industrial base declined. Like its southern

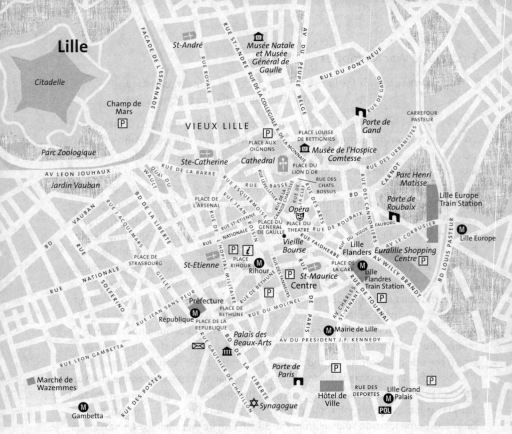

counterpart, Marseille, it suffered from a bad press, fuelled by images of gross industrialization and racism. Now a banking, administrative and university town, with some 100,000 students, Lille is an extremely lively place.

Vieux Lille

Rue Faidherbe leads from the central Lille-Flandres station to Place du Théâtre. Hemmed in by houses off the Rue Faidherbe, the **Eglise St-Maurice** is a rare vestige of the city's medieval prosperity. In the form of a Flemish Hallekerque, the church has recently been scrubbed clean to reveal its white stone, but the interior still looks on the lugubrious side. The spacious five aisles are held up by a forest of columns; heavy 17th-century religious paintings line the walls.

The very heart of Lille is split in two, Place du Théâtre to the right, Place du Général de Gaulle (also known as the Grand' Place) to the left, with the Vieille Bourse in between. Two outrageous buildings from the early 20th century flaunt themselves on **Place du Théâtre**. The sparklingly white **opera house** is crowned by the *Triumph of Apollo* by Hippolyte Lefebvre, a sculpture that's more than a match for the most ludicrous of opera plots. The architect was Louis-Marie Cordonnier, who was also responsible for the **Palais de la Bourse** with its rocketing Flemish belfry on one corner. The **Vieille Bourse**, although on a smaller scale, also smacks of excess, Baroque this time, with weighty, decadent garlands of fruit drooping from the caryatids and atlantes on the façades. Designed by Julien Destrée in the 1650s, the recently restored inner courtyard shelters market stalls. Plaques on the walls behind sing the praises of leading men of commerce and science. Above the colonnade, the stones have been squeezed and twisted like Plasticine to create grotesque animal faces.

In the centre of **Place du Général de Gaulle**, Lille's dominatrix of a **Déesse** (Goddess) holds court, a symbol of the city's success in repulsing the Austrian forces in 1792. The object in her hand, which looks like a whip from a distance, is described as a *boutefeu*, used to light cannons. This square has many grand façades, and looks predominantly Flemish, particularly the massive stepped gable of the *La Voix du Nord* building, headquarters of the largest newspaper in the region. The bronze figures on high stand for the historic provinces of Flanders, Hainaut and Artois.

A third grand square connects with Place du Général de Gaulle. However, **Place Rihour** has none of the architectural swagger of the other two: it's a bit of a 20th-century mess. A mausoleum-like war memorial dominates one corner. Behind it hides the tourist office, in the sorry remnants of the Palais Rihour, the Lille palace of the dukes of Burgundy. The chapel above the tourist office is used for exhibitions. Just a little west of the Place Rihour, **St-Etienne**, on Rue de l'Hôpital Militaire, is one of several grand Baroque churches tucked into Lille's residential streets. Rue Nationale and Rue de Béthune, respectively north and south of Place Rihour, are major shopping arteries.

Immense **Place de la République** looks overblown and vacuous at the same time. Two stupendously pompous buildings stare across at each other, both from the second half of the 19th century: the **Préfecture** and the Palais des Beaux-Arts.

Palais des Beaux-Arts

Open Mon 2–6, Wed–Sun 10–6, Fri 10–7; closed Tues; adm.

Recently cleaned, and reopened by the French president in 1997, this is your most obvious cultural call in Lille. Don't miss the excellent medieval and Renaissance galleries of the first basement level, which include Donatello's bas-relief *Feast of Herod*. Still further down you can go in search of the excellent archaeological section and amazingly detailed large-scale 18th-century models of some of the fortified towns of northern France. In the sculpture gallery you'll find Rodin's extraordinary caramelized figure of *L'Ombre*, the Shadow, and pieces by Camille Claudel, Rodin's put-upon lover. Rubens' powerful depiction of the deposition of Christ opens proceedings among the paintings, superbly displayed on the first floor. Interiors by De Witte and De Hooch and landscapes by Van Ruysdael and Siberecht stand out as does Courbet's *Après dîner à Ornans*, a manifesto of Realism in painting.

Boudin and Sisley also feature, but perhaps the highlight of the 19th-century collection is Emile Bernard's cloisonné *Les Cueilleuses de pommes*. Born in Lille, Bernard was the man who along with Gauguin developed the synthetist style of the School of Pont-Aven in Brittany (*see* p.314). There are works by Picasso and Léger, but for other 20th-century art you must visit the museum at Villeneuve-d'Ascq, east of the town (*see* below, p.637).

Getting Around

Lille-Lesquin **airport** is less than 10km from the centre, for internal flights only, **t** 08 36 35 35 35. A coach shuttle service links the airport with Lille-Europe railway station, **t** 03 20 66 26 66.

Lille-Europe **railway station** is where Eurostar trains arrive from London. It has fantastic train links with other parts of France, and is only a 10–15min walk from the city centre. Coming from Paris-Gare du Nord, trains arrive at the more central Lille-Flandres station.

Toll-free **motorways** from the Channel ports of Calais and Dunkerque will bring you swiftly to Lille.

To book a taxi in Lille, **t** 03 20 06 06 06/ **t** 03 20 06 64 00/**t** 03 20 55 20 56.

Tourist Information

Lille: Palais Rihour, Place Rihour, **t** 03 20 21 94 21, **f** 03 20 21 94 20.

Shopping

Coming from Lille-Europe railway station, don't be diverted by the vast Euralille commercial centre: it has about as much atmosphere as an airport terminal. Just ten minutes' walk away, many of the same shopping names and many better ones besides are to be found along enchanting streets in Vieux Lille. The perfect starting point is the Grand Place, surrounded by restaurants and cafés, at the heart of the pedestrianised area.
La Vieille Bourse has ground floor arcades, and a bustling flower and second-hand book market within its cloisters.

Wazemmes flea market, Place de Wazemmes. Everything from clothes to crockery to local fruit and veg (*Sun 10–1, Tues and Thurs 7–2*). There is a smaller **market** at Place du Concert (*Wed, Fri and Sun 7–2*).

The **Braderie de Lille** is the biggest flea market in Europe – two days of madness on the first weekend in September, attracting over a million visitors.

Where to Stay

Lille ✉ 59800

Luxury–Expensive

****Carlton, 3 Rue de Paris, **t** 03 20 13 33 13, **f** 03 20 51 48 17. The plushest address in town, extremely well located opposite the opulent opera building (which eclipses it). It has two restaurants and two bars although the Hippopotamus Grill beneath the hotel isn't connected.
****Alliance, 17 Quai du Wault, **t** 03 20 30 62 62, **f** 03 20 42 94 25. The other posh hotel in the centre, in a converted 17th-century convent. 80 rooms. Restaurant (*menus 95–165F*). *Closed Mon 15 July–30 Aug.*
***Grand Hôtel Bellevue, 5 Rue Jean Roisin, **t** 03 20 57 45 64, **f** 03 20 40 07 93. In the very heart of town. Insist on a room overlooking the Grand' Place.

Moderate

***Hôtel de la Treille, 7–9 Place Louise de Bettignies, **t** 03 20 55 45 46, **f** 03 20 51 51 69. Appealingly located and comfortable.

Inexpensive

Brueghel, 5 Parvis St-Maurice, **t 03 20 06 06 69, **f** 03 20 63 25 27. Well located and well

Then I saw the Goyas at Lille. That was when I understood that painting could be a language: I thought that I could become a painter.

Matisse

The most talked-about works in the Spanish collection are typically disturbing fruits of Goya's imagination. *Le Temps, dit Les Vieilles* shows two caricatures of decrepit society women who look like coquettish grimacing cadavers dressed up for their walk. A separate room is devoted to drawings, notably Italian Old Masters.

run, overlooking the grand Eglise St-Maurice. It has an appealing lobby and tasteful corridors, an hilarious little lift and comfortable smallish rooms.

★★Hôtel de la Paix, 46 bis Rue de Paris, **t** 03 20 54 63 93, **f** 03 20 63 98 97. Nearby and not quite as appealing, but the rooms are well kept.

★★Ibis Opéra, 21 Rue Lepelletier, **t** 03 20 06 21 95, **f** 03 2074 91 30. Centrally located chain hotel rather surprisingly in the midst of luxury shopping streets.

Mister Bed, 57 Rue de Béthune, **t** 03 20 12 96 96, **f** 03 20 40 25 87. A cheap chain option, in an excellent position in the most popular shopping street in the centre.

The cheapish hotels in the arc of buildings outside the Lille-Flandres railway station are conveniently close to the centre of town, and vie for your attention with their flashing neon signs.

★★Flandre-Angleterre, 13 Place de la Gare, **t** 03 20 06 04 12, **f** 03 20 06 37 76. One of the best and one of the most expensive by this station.

Cheap

★Les Voyageurs, 10 Place de la Gare, **t** 03 20 06 43 14, **f** 03 20 74 19 01. Amusing and cheap hotel.

Eating Out

A l'Huîtrière, 3 Rue des Chats Bossus, **t** 03 20 55 43 41, **f** 03 20 55 23 10. Among the most highly rated of Lille's restaurants and very expensive. As the name implies, seafood is the speciality (*menus 260–600F*). *Closed 22 July–25 Aug and Sun eve.*

Le Compostelle, 4 Rue St-Etienne, **t** 03 28 38 08 30, **f** 03 28 38 08 39. The finest setting for a smart traditional Flanders dinner, in the only Renaissance mansion in Lille, with a courtyard with a pretty olive tree and separate *salons (menus 110–200F).*

Le Porthos, 53 Rue de la Monnaie, **t** 03 20 06 44 06, **f** 03 20 21 04 15. Opposite the Hospice Comtesse. Filled with lively lawyers during the week (*menu 175F*).

Paul is both the name of a chain of splendid *pâtisseries* in Lille and of a good-value restaurant, overlooking the Place de l'Opéra.

Les Compagnons de la Grappe, 26 Rue Lepelletier, **t** 03 20 21 02 79 (*cheap*). Set back in its own gravelled courtyard off this prime shopping street, the interior has a striking modern art décor and the food and wine are as interesting as the setting.

Bistrot de Pierrot, 6 Place de Béthune, **t** 03 20 57 14 09, **f** 03 20 30 93 13. Down by the Palais des Beaux-Arts, this very well-known *bistrot* is run by a bit of a TV star, Pierrot. He's a big character, and although his *bistrot* is small it is packed with masses of atmosphere.

Nightlife

Cinéma Metropole, 26 Rue des Ponts des Comines, **t** 03 20 15 92 23. Daily screenings of films in their original language; there are usually a few showing in English.

L'Illustration Café, 18 Rue Royale, **t** 03 20 12 00 90. Trendy Art Nouveau-style bar. *Open daily until 2am.*

L'Angle Saxo, 36 Rue d'Angleterre, **t** 03 20 06 15 06. Relaxed bar with good live jazz every day, although the drinks are a little expensive. *Open 9pm–2am.*

Shopping Streets

A short walk southeast from the Musée des Beaux-Arts brings you to the **Porte de Paris**, the most imposing of Lille's surviving gates, now isolated by traffic. This homage to Louis XIV was designed by Simon Vollant and shows Victory crowning the Sun King. In a square to one side stands the **Hôtel de Ville**, completed in 1932. Another flabbergasting Flemish belfry blasts up over 300ft into the sky from here. The legendary giant founders of Lille, Phinaert and Lydéric, are portrayed on the belfry but dwarfed by it. You can climb up (*open first Sun in April–last Sun in Sept daily exc Sat; adm*) for views over the whole of Lille. At night, the belfry turns into a great lighthouse, with its lamp revolving over the city.

Back up by the Grand' Place, head up Rue Esquermoise or Rue de la Bourse and the Grande Chaussée, the glamorous shopping streets of Vieux Lille, strung with delightful squares. Pretty **Rue Esquermoise** is followed by Rue de la Barre, off which lies another neglected old church, Ste-Catherine. Rue Lepelletier and Rue Basse are further elegant streets south of the cathedral. Rue des Chats Bossus (the Hunchbacked Cats), the continuation of Rue Basse, ends in the charming triangular Place du Lion d'Or; off here is Rue de la Monnaie, another shopping street. The vast, incomplete and hideous 19th-century cathedral lurks in this quarter, but thankfully surprisingly well hidden.

Musée de l'Hospice Comtesse

Rue de la Monnaie; open daily exc Tues 10–12.30 and 2–6; adm.

Lille's second most important museum contains Flemish collections set within what was formerly a hospital, founded in 1237, and rebuilt in 1468 after a fire, and much altered again after another fire in the 17th century. Its long medieval ward is used for temporary exhibitions. Beyond a screening wall at one end you can make out the ceiling of the chapel, adorned in the mid-19th century with 66 coats of arms representing the hospital's principal benefactors. The community building in the main courtyard contains fine Flemish art, ceramics and furniture, including a couple of rooms covered with Delft tiles showing windmills, men fishing in canals, and shepherds and shepherdesses among typical Flemish scenes. Look out also for the paintings of Flemish interiors and urban scenes, including processions and the **Lille Braderie**, an annual great market that still exists as a massive antiques fair.

Outside the Centre

To the north of the centre, in a quiet corner of town, the **Maison Natale et Musée Général de Gaulle** (*9 Rue Princesse; open daily exc Mon and Tues 10–12 and 2–5; adm*) is most easily reached by heading up Rue de la Collégiale and Rue de St-André; it is signalled by the French flag waving above the door. This is where Charles de Gaulle was born on 22 November 1890 in his grandmother's house, a bourgeois Lille property with a pretty little courtyard. Charles only lived here for the three months following his birth, but he visited his maternal grandmother regularly. Inside, the overwhelming feeling is of bourgeois piety preserved in aspic. A bust of the general stands in the small garden beyond the charming conservatory. In the former workshops the general's life story is told in indigestible fashion with panels, texts and photos, the emphasis on the military writings which he penned throughout his extraordinary career.

West from the museum, beyond the massive, free Champ de Mars car park, the Lille **citadel** lurks concealed behind woods within the loop of the river Deule. The French army still owns this startling star-shaped fortification, a well-preserved example of Vauban's defensive architecture (*tours arranged by the tourist office Sun pm; adm*).

Major roads speed round the **Musée d'Art Moderne at Villeneuve d'Ascq** (*open daily exc Tues 10–6; adm*), in the Lille suburbs, and the architecture looks like something lifted out of a 1960s university campus. Within, however, the museum contains a good collection by some of the great names of 20th-century art. The selection of Modigliani's elongated, almond-eyed portraits outshines a run-of-the-mill selection of Picassos. Braque, Rouault and Léger are well represented, as well as the intriguingly flattened forms of Henri Laurens' sculptures. The museum also puts on excellent temporary exhibitions.

Into Artois and Hainaut from Calais

As well as preserving terrible memories of the First World War, this area boasts two splendid small cities, St-Omer and Arras. Such Hainaut towns as Douai and Cambrai are for the more culturally experimental traveller, but boast splendid museums.

St-Omer

St-Omer, once within Flemish territory, has been an outpost of Artois since 1678. To many British visitors nowadays it counts as 'the first real French town' after leaving Calais. The place was founded in 637 by Audomar (later known as St Omer), a monk sent to evangelize this area of bogs and swamps. He founded an abbey, St-Bertin, which remained a powerful influence in the town until its dissolution during the Revolution. In the early Middle Ages, St-Omer stood alongside the likes of Bruges as one of the richest cities in Flanders. However, its location also put it squarely in the middle of the area chosen by France, England and, later, Spain as a battleground for four centuries. When the town was finally secured for Louis XIV after a long siege in 1677, Vauban encased it in a massive set of walls; a giant screen of plain brick is all that remains, in the attractively landscaped Jardin Public. St-Omer served as British General Headquarters from 1914 to 1916. It suffered from bombing in both World Wars.

At the top of the town, **Place Foch** is still very much St-Omer's hub, and, like many town squares in Flanders and Artois, its scale is startling. The little streets that run down from the cafés on the south side will take you into the charming old town, mostly built in the 18th century. Next to Place Victor Hugo stands the grandest Gothic church in the Pas-de-Calais, the **Basilique Notre-Dame**, which served as a cathedral from 1559 to 1801. The most impressive entrance, the south transept's Portail Royal, is flanked by two massive towers. Inside, the transepts are nearly as big as the nave. Perhaps the most striking of the basilica's many treasures is the magnificent organ, a superb piece of Baroque wood carving from 1717 that manages to fit in perfectly with its medieval surroundings. In the north transept stands a wonderful and rare 16th-century astrological clock.

Getting Around

The A26 from Calais races past St-Omer and Arras, not far from Douai and Cambrai. Arras is easy to reach by train, on the Dunkerque–Paris-Gare du Nord line (*c.* 50mins). Change at Arras for trains to St-Omer. Douai is on the Paris-Gare du Nord–Valenciennes line. Change at Douai for trains to Cambrai.

Tourist Information

St-Omer: Bd Pierre Guillair, t 03 21 98 08 51, f 03 21 98 22 82.
Arras: Place des Héros, t 03 21 51 26 95, f 03 21 71 07 34.
Douai: 70 Place d'Armes, t 03 27 88 26 79, f 03 27 99 38 78.
Cambrai: 48 Rue de Noyon, t 03 27 78 36 15, f 03 27 74 82 82.

Sports and Activities

Just east of St-Omer you can discover an atmospheric, silent web of canalized marshes in the **Marais Audomarois**, rich in wildlife, reed beds and prolific vegetable gardens. Between spring and autumn you can take a boat trip through the *watergangs*. Three companies run tours. Most accessible to casual travellers without bookings is Isnor, based in Clairmarais.

Shopping

If you take a shine to the traditional **Arras blue porcelain**, you should know that Cotellerie Caudron on Place de la Vacquerie in Arras has recreated the techniques for making it and sells it exclusively.

Where to Stay and Eat

Recques-sur-Hem ✉ 62890
★★★★**Château de Cocove**, Av de Cocoves, t 03 21 82 68 29, f 03 21 82 72 59 (*moderate*). A rural idyll in an 18th-century country house southeast of Ardres with spacious rooms and fine menus which delight the traveller on a bigger budget. You can buy fine wines from the cellars, while the restaurant is set in former stables (*menus 150–380F*).

Tilques ✉ 62500
★★★★**Château de Tilques**, t 03 21 8899 99, f 03 21 38 34 23 (*expensive*). A large, luxurious 19th-century home set in its park off the N43 some 6km northwest of St-Omer. Restaurant (*menus 220–350F*).

St-Omer ✉ 62500
★★**St-Louis**, 25 Rue d'Arras, t 03 21 38 35 21, f 03 21 38 57 26 (*inexpensive*). Welcoming hotel just below the centre of town. The restaurant goes by the name of Le Flaubert (*menus

Between Place Foch and Notre-Dame, down Rue Carnot, the **Musée Sandelin** (*open daily exc Mon and Tues 10–12 and 2–5; adm*) is set in a very elegant Louis XVI townhouse. The interiors are one of the prime attractions, especially the delicate turquoise dining room laid out with the fine blue local china for which St-Omer was reputed in the 18th century. Equally pretty in their chocolate-box way are the 18th-century paintings, and there is an extensive display of other fine porcelain and ceramics. The museum's greatest possessions, however, are relics of the area's medieval abbeys . A joint ticket allows you to visit the stuffed birds etc. in the natural history collection of the nearby **Musée Henri Dupuis** (*open same times; adm*).

A plaque outside the **Ancien Collège des Jésuites** on Rue St-Bertin records that it was built as an English College, at a time when to be found in England on 'a mission from St-Omer' was much like being discovered with KGB credentials in the Cold War. In 1592, as measures against Catholics in England became ever more restrictive, English Jesuits sought help to found a new college on safe soil to educate the sons of Catholic families. Lavishly endowed by Philip II of Spain, the school at St-Omer

75–155F). 30 rooms. *Closed Christmas, Sat lunch and Sun lunch.*

Ibis, 2–4 Rue Henri Dupuis, **t 03 21 93 11 11, **f** 03 21 88 80 20 (*inexpensive*). Part of a chain, but exceptionally well-located at the top of the old town, close to the cathedral and the main square. Restaurant (*menus under 100F*).

La Belle Epoque, Place Paul Painlevé, **t** 03 21 38 22 93. Admirably energetic, Mme Dacheville, the female chef, serves comforting local dishes in this small and popular restaurant at the top of the town.

Arras ✉ 62000

***L'Univers, 5 Place de Croix Rouge, **t** 03 21 71 34 01, **f** 03 21 71 41 42 (*moderate*). Hotel in a 16th-century monastery; many of the rooms set around a plush courtyard have a great deal of character. 37 rooms. *Restaurant closed Jan–Feb Sun eve (menus 120–260F).*

***Les Trois Luppars, 49 Grand-Place, **t** 03 21 07 41 41, **f** 03 21 24 24 80 (*inexpensive*). Overlooking the most fabulous square in Arras, in the oldest house in town, this wonderful-looking Gothic building stands out from the others with its big step-gabled roof and watchtower.

Le Beffroi, 28 Place de la Vacquerie, **t** 03 21 23 13 78, **f** 03 21 23 03 08. A really well located and appealing-looking basic option above a lively café.

La Faisanderie, 45 Grand-Place, **t** 03 21 48 20 76. Highly reputed restaurant, the finest in Arras, where innovative, ebullient Jean-Pierre Dargent cooks up spectacular versions of traditional northern French dishes. You usually eat in an elegant airy barrel-roofed cellar, one of the many caves beneath the square (*menus 145–315F*). *Closed 1–21 Aug, 4–10 Jan, Feb hols, Sun eve and Mon.*

Le Victor Hugo, 11 Place Victor Hugo, **t** 03 21 71 84 00, **f** 03 21 71 84 00. The other top restaurant in the centre of town, a posh address serving classic French cuisine.

Douai ✉ 59500

****La Terrasse, 36 Terrasse St-Pierre, **t** 03 27 88 70 04, **f** 03 27 88 36 05 (*expensive*). Hotel-restaurant unfortunately located opposite the old public toilets, but it is elegant within and well known for its refined cuisine.

Cambrai ✉ 59403

***Château de la Motte Fénelon, Allée St-Roch, **t** 03 27 83 61 38, **f** 03 27 83 71 61 (*moderate*). Separated from the town by its own gardens, this is a smart 19th-century house in classical style, around 1km from the centre. The posh restaurant is located in the vaulted cellar (*menus 145–240F*). *Closed Sat lunch Nov–Mar and Sun eve.*

became the most important of several English colleges in Spanish-ruled territory. To English ministers it was a den of subversion, and indeed the Gunpowder Plot and diverse other Catholic conspiracies were almost certainly discussed within its walls. It remained an English college until 1762, when all Jesuits were expelled from France.

Towards Arras

Two First World War memorials lie along the so-called Crêtes du Sacrifice, between Lens and Arras: the French national cemetery of Notre-Dame de Lorette and the Canadian memorial at Vimy. Tall crosses form part of the white lantern tower at **Notre-Dame de Lorette**, where the Battle of Lorette raged for a year from October 1914 to October 1915. French losses were heavy: the vast cemetery is dedicated to over 40,000 dead, half of whom have individual graves.

On 9 April 1917 the Canadians managed to win the strategic heights at Vimy, and **Vimy Ridge** was chosen after the war as the site for a **Canadian National Memorial and Park**. Some 3,600 Canadians lost their lives here; they are remembered along with the 11,285 Canadians who went missing in action in other parts of the front during the First World War. The monument is noble, its two wings symbolizing the British and French origins of so many Canadians. Canadian students conduct the free guided tours (*April–Nov daily 10–6; adm*). The park is well known for its preserved trenches and underground tunnels. Above ground, a Canadian tree has been planted for each of the Canadian soldiers who went missing in the war.

Arras

Arras is a superlative northern French city, long celebrated for its production of cloth and tapestries, prized luxuries as far away as Byzantium. In *Hamlet*, Polonius is hiding behind such an 'arras' when he is stabbed. Arras often looked towards Flanders for its political and cultural links, and its grandest squares have a distinctly Flemish air.

The spectacular scale of the **Grand-Place**, one of the largest squares in a European city, indicates just how important Arras was during its Golden Age in the 14th and 15th centuries. Merchants from all over the continent came to buy and sell here in great markets, occasionally replaced by jousts. The Flemish-style houses have gorgeously curly gables. Many had to be rebuilt after both World Wars.

The **Petit-Place or Place des Héros** is scarcely more intimate than the Grand-Place, but here the mansions are eclipsed on one side by the a roaring Gothic **town hall**, the grandest piece of post-war reconstruction in Arras. The Flamboyant Gothic central section was built in the early 16th century, its elaborate tracery displayed below a peppering of tiny dormer windows in the roof. You can climb to the top of the **belfry** (*open Mon–Sat 10–12 and 2–6; Sun and hols 10–12 and 3–6.30; adm*) for panoramic views of the town, or visit the 1920s interiors if meetings aren't in progress. The Salle des Mariages has murals with Isadora Duncanesque Grecian maidens, while the main hall is decorated with murals by the artist Hoffbauer imagining life in Arras in the 1400s.

Beneath Arras' squares lies a **labyrinth** of cellars and tunnels, known as Boves (*same opening times as the belfry*), used over the centuries as chalk mines, wine stores, refuse dumps or refuges. Tours leave from the basement of the Hôtel de Ville. Some of the tunnels existed back in Gallo-Roman times, and many more were opened up during the Middle Ages. The caverns were greatly extended in 1916 and 1917 by British troops who used them as a safe means of getting to the trenches just outside town.

Vaast by name, vast by nature, the neoclassical **Abbaye de St-Vaast**, next to the cathedral, contains the **Musée des Beaux-Arts** (*open April–Sept Mon and Wed–Sat 10–12 and 2–6; Oct–Mar Mon and Wed–Sat 10–12 and 2–5; Sun 10–12 and 3–6; adm*). The abbey's roots go back to a saintly 7th-century bishop called Vaast, but in the 1740s it was decided to knock down the early-medieval abbey buildings and replace them with new ones. Inside, many of the paintings are little better than wall paper, but there's a beautiful collection of 18th-century Arras and Tournai porcelain and several landscapes by Corot, who often painted in the area. The medieval sculptures are the best bit, including an extraordinary 1446 tomb sculpture of Guillaume Lefranchois, a canon of Béthune with a decomposing skeleton. In contrast, the 14th-century *Head of a Woman* has a serenely beautiful face. The museum has only one Arras tapestry (there are very few still in existence), *St Vaast and the Bear*, with a delightful, almost abstract background. One of the most colourful inhabitants of the abbey was a notorious cardinal, Edouard de Rohan, who ordered the **cathedral** next door – a colossal, overwhelming building.

Just off Place du Théâtre stands the former home of Maximilien Robespierre, who lived here in the late 1780s while he was establishing his reputation as a ferocious lawyer before going off to display his talents on a wider stage in the French Revolution. This street is named after him, although Arras has never known quite what to do with him: being the home town of a man widely credited with the invention of modern totalitarianism isn't all that easy to handle.

Arras was on the front during the First World War, and it suffered terribly from bombardments. Its **First World War British cemetery** is one of the largest of so many in the area, containing over 2,600 graves with the names of nearly 40,000 men with no known grave around the walls.

The Towns and Countryside of Hainaut

To the east of Arras, the historic towns of Hainaut (or Hainault), Douai, Cambrai and Valenciennes are all incorporated into French Flanders. Too war-scarred to be obvious tourist stops, the towns have surprisingly strong artistic legacies.

Douai was once a major religious and intellectual centre. Its origins go back to Roman times. Philip II of Spain endowed the town with a university in 1562. Its religious houses promoted the Counter-Reformation with zeal, and Douai became an important gathering place for English, Irish and Scottish Catholics hounded out of their home countries. A handful of institutions for English-speaking Catholics were even set up in town. William, later Cardinal, Allen, was particularly active here, founding the English seminary in Douai in 1568. He also organized the translation of the Bible into English – the so-called Douay Bible, which was published in town in 1610. Kennedy, the first Catholic president of the United States, took his presidential oath on the Douay Bible. Hundreds of foreign priests were trained here. A large number went back to England to preach, many coming to a sticky end as martyrs. Through most of the 18th century the Parlement of French Flanders was also based here, taking over a former abbey on the River Scarpe. Its wide Gothic arches have survived.

Douai no longer retains a cohesive historic core, but several buildings have survived dull postwar reconstruction. You can climb the big fat medieval **Flemish belfry** to get a bird's eye view over the town. It contains what's said to be the largest collection of bells in Europe, 62 in all; on Saturday mornings you can hear them in full swing. The town hall below looks very Gothic. Some of it is original 15th century, some 19th-century restoration work.

The main attraction over the river is the **Musée de la Chartreuse** (*open daily exc Tues 10–12 and 2–5, Sun 3–6; adm*). The brick and stone façades from the 16th and 17th centuries look inviting, and some of the art within is outstanding. The *Polyptique d'Anchin* by the late 15th century Douai artist Jean Bellegambe stands out as the most remarkable of his works, for the richly coloured main panels and the staggering grisaille work on the back. The other highlight is Veronese's *Portrait of a Venetian Woman*, an arrogant young thing in gorgeous autumnal brown velvet and pearls. The few 19th-century pieces include works by Boudin, Jongkind, Sisley, Renoir and Pissarro. Douai's post-Impressionist, Henri Edmond Cross, puts on a good show too.

For centuries an important fortified frontier post, **Cambrai** is a bit like Douai in that it still looks battered and bruised, with some dreary postwar reconstruction, but, as with Douai, it's hard not to feel a certain liking for the place. The massive **cathedral** dates from the 18th century. At the end of its apse stands a splendid statue of Cambrai's most illustrious archbishop, the great François de Salignac de la Mothe Fénelon, nicknamed le Cygne de Cambrai, the Swan of Cambrai. He has come down through history as one of the most attractive courtiers from Louis XIV's reign. A supremely successful establishment figure, he wasn't afraid to criticize the establishment. He served for ten years as tutor to Louis XIV's grandson, the then duke of Burgundy, writing for him the popular *Les Aventures de Télémaque* (1699) which the king would later construe as criticism of his warped priorities. Fénelon also showed sympathy towards mystical religion. He fell from grace, and no longer welcome at court, he saw one of his books condemned by the pope. David d'Angers' 19th-century Romantic rendition of the man makes him look like an heroic dandy of an archbishop-cum-salon intellectual, so at ease on his chaise longue, with his flowing hair and flowing robes, one arm resting on tassled pillows, one hand clasped to his bosom.

A surprising bold mix of new and old architecture houses the **Musée de Cambrai** (*open daily exc Mon and Tues 10–12 and 2–6; adm*). French speakers might appreciate the half-hour film on the history of Cambrai, but everyone can marvel at the craftsmanship of the medieval masons and sculptors. Of the Romanesque pieces, the most moving shows the tragic couple of Pyramus and Thisbe lying on top of each other impaled by the same sword. The museum also boasts an exceptional collection of carved alabaster figures from the late 16th and early 17th centuries. Most of these were rescued from Cambrai's vanished Gothic cathedral, built on the same vast scale as the cathedral at Reims. Paintings give an idea of the old Cambrai; one outstanding work from the 19th century is Ingres' *Head of the Grand Odalisque*.

The Baroque **church of St-Géri**, near the ugly main square, contains a superlative Rubens *Entombment*, infuriatingly hard to make out in any detail, but close-up photos show Christ's body like a carcass, and St John in a blood-red robe held by Mary.

Le Cateau-Cambrésis is a drab town, and the only good reason for visiting is the **Musée Matisse** (*closed until 2002*). The artist was born in Le Cateau in 1869, and spent his childhood nearby, at Bohain-en-Vermandois. He escaped just about as quickly as he could from what he considered a bleak part of France, but kindly donated a reasonable number of works to his birthplace. East of Le Cateau-Cambrésis, on the Canal de la Sambre à l'Oise, lies **Ors**, where Wilfred Owen, the most famous of all the British Great War poets, died.

Bavay, close to the Belgian border, is a modest town with a surprise. At first you might be forgiven for thinking that you have come upon a World War bomb site, but a closer look reveals the groundplan of Gallo-Roman Bagacum, the capital of the Nervii. The modern bunker of a **museum** (*open July–Aug daily 10–12 and 2–6; rest of year daily exc Tues 9–12 and 2–5; adm*) doesn't look inviting, but it contains some **Gallo-Roman treasures**. A video in French gives some helpful background notes on the local tribe based in this corner of a region known to Caesar as Belgica. Set at major crossroads, the city of the Nervii thrived for several centuries.

Artois' Côte d'Opale

Dramatic windblown headlands, dunes and long beaches stretch down from Calais to Normandy. Known as the Côte d'Opale because of the sometimes iridescent, milky-green colour of its waters, some of this coast resembles that of southeast England – not surprisingly, as they are both chips off the same geological block. The historically minded might care to visit the sites of Crécy and Agincourt, scenes of two crucial English victories during the Hundred Years' War, while keen ornithologists will head for the Parc du Marquenterre in the Somme estuary.

Côte d'Opale Resorts from Calais to Boulogne

West of Calais, France and England come as close as they get to rubbing noses with each other. From the headland of **Cap Blanc-Nez** (Cape White Nose), spectacular views open up on to the beach, the dunes and rural Artois behind. England lies on the horizon. The ugly grey obelisk is a First World War memorial dedicated to the Dover Patrol which guarded the British Expeditionary Forces sent across the Channel to fight the Germans. Up on Mont d'Hubert, the hill behind the cape, the **Musée du Transmanche** (*in the basement of the restaurant with a panoramic view – open April–Sept daily 10–6; adm*) catalogues great Channel crossings and celebrates all the attempts to dig a tunnel between France and England, beginning with Napoleon's .

Down below Cap Blanc-Nez, old **Wissant** (old Flemish for 'White Sand') sits seemingly half-swallowed up by the stuff. Its big beautiful beach is a magnet for sand-yachters and windsurfers. Wissant can claim to be almost as old a Channel port as Boulogne: Caesar probably used it for his second invasion of Britain in 54 BC. It was an important port in the Middle Ages, and Thomas à Becket passed through here in 1170 on his last, fateful journey back to Canterbury. By the 16th century, though, the harbour had silted up. Since then, the fishermen have had to drag their distinctive little boats, called *flobarts*, back and forth across the beach. A few still do so.

From Wissant, there's a great walk west to **Cap Gris-Nez** (Cape Grey Nose). This has been colonized by tourists, the village of Framzelle set back from the point turned

Getting Around

For details on ferries to Boulogne-sur-Mer see **Travel**.

Le Touquet has a little airport used by the jet-set. The A16 runs from Calais past Boulogne and along the coast to the Somme estuary and beyond. There is a local railway line along the coast, leaving from Calais-Ville station rather than Calais-Fréthun, but there isn't much choice of trains beyond Boulogne.

Tourist Information

Wissant: Place de la Mairie, t 03 21 85 15 62, f 03 21 85 50 44.

Wimereux: Quai Alfred Girard, B.P.33, t 03 21 88 27 17, f 03 21 32 76 91.

Etaples: Le Clos St-Victor, Bd Bigot Descelers, B.P.102, t 03 21 09 56 94, f 03 21 09 76 96.

Montreuil-sur-Mer: 21 Rue Carnot, t/f 03 21 06 04 27.

Hesdin: Place d'Armes, t 03 21 86 19 19, f 03 21 86 04 05.

Where to Stay and Eat

Wissant ✉ 62179

Several well-established hotels are found in this lively village, behind the beach.

★★Le Vivier, t 03 21 35 93 61, f 03 21 82 10 99 (*inexpensive*). The modern part stands above the coast road south and has rooms with balconies and wonderful views. The sweet old stone part lies on the church square in the village, with a traditional boat outside. There are a few pleasant rooms above the seafood restaurant.

Hôtel de la Plage, Place Edouard Houssin, t 03 21 35 91 87, f 03 21 85 48 10. A large, plain, rambling old-style French hotel, a bit misleadingly named as it's not right on the beach, but it's not far away, by a pond.

Marquise ✉ 62250

Le Grand Cerf, 34 Av Ferber, t 03 21 87 55 05. A meal here justifies a trip across the Channel by itself even if this converted coaching inn stands in an unremarkable village just off the A16 towards Calais from Boulogne (*menus 165–330F*). *Closed Sun eve and Mon.*

Wimereux ✉ 62930

A better place to stay than nearby Boulogne.

★★★Atlantic, Digue de Mer, t 03 21 32 41 01, f 03 21 87 46 17 (*moderate*). Six pricey rooms with good views out to sea shared by the restaurant, the Liègeoise, and the tea room.

★★Spéranza, 43 Rue du Général de Gaulle, t 03 21 32 46 09, f 03 21 87 52 09 (*inexpensive*). Tucked in a street just behind the Atlantic. Its timber gables conceal some cheerfully painted, good-value rooms.

Echinghen ✉ 62360

Boussemaere's B&B, Rue de l'Eglise, t 03 21 91 14 34 (*inexpensive*). Tucked away in a peaceful village just east of Boulogne, the comfortable rooms here are good-value. Mme is a helpful whirlwind of activity.

Hesdin-l'Abbé ✉ 62360

★★★Château de Cléry, 62360 Hesdin-l'Abbé (not to be confused with Hesdin), t 03 21 83 19 83, f 03 21 87 52 59 (*expensive–moderate*). A gorgeous gem of a miniature château set in elegant grounds around 10km southeast of Boulogne. Restaurant (*menus 145–185F*).

into aggressive B&B territory. Hordes wander across the grassy headland to get the best views of England available from France; the Kent coast by Folkestone lies just under 30 kilometres away. The remnants of concrete bunkers recall how the Nazis could fire rockets at England from such close quarters. The shipping flow into and out of the Channel is regulated from the cape, while millions of migrating birds apparently use the headland as a useful marker on their seasonal flights.

Wimereux has one of the most attractive seafronts on the Côte d'Opale, with some older mansions with turrets and timbered gables holding their own among the modern blocks. Waves crash in close to the promenade. In the north part of town, the

Le Touquet ✉ 62650

★★★★Westminster, 5 Av du Verger, t 03 21 05
48 48, f 03 21 05 45 45 (*expensive*). The image
of a palatial 1930s hotel. Its luxurious, high-
ceilinged rooms have marble bathrooms.
Restaurant for dinner only. *Restaurant closed
5 Jan–1 Mar, and Tues exc July and Aug*
(*menus 250–380F*). *Hotel closed Feb.*
★★★★Park Plaza Grand Hôtel, 4 Bd de la
Canche, t 03 21 06 88 88, f 03 21 06 87 87
(*expensive*). Large and luxurious, in a modern
building, with indoor pool and health centre.
Restaurant (*menus 170F*).
Novotel Thalassa, t 03 21 09 85 00, f 03 21 09
85 10 (*expensive*). Luxury sea treatments on
the sea front. Restaurant (*menus from
c. 100F*).
★★Le Nouveau Caddy, 130 Rue de Metz, t 03 21
05 83 95, f 03 21 05 85 23 (*inexpensive*). A
central cheerful place near the beach.
★★Le Chalet, 15 Rue de la Paix, t 03 21 05 87 65,
f 03 21 05 47 49 (*inexpensive*). A few rooms
have balconies with sea views.
Flavio, 1–2 Av du Verger, t 03 21 05 10 22, f 03 21
05 91 55. The top restaurant in town, for fine
cuisine (*menus 130–750F*). *Closed 10 Jan–10
Feb. Mon (exc July and Aug, and bank hols*).

Montreuil-sur-Mer ✉ 62170

An excellent place in which to stay.
★★★★Château de Montreuil, 4 Chaussée des
Capucins, t 03 21 81 53 04, f 03 21 81 36 43,
montreuil@relaischateaux.fr (*expensive*).
Arguably the poshest hotel, a luxurious
modern manor set exclusively in the
grounds of the town's citadel. The restaurant serves superlative cuisine (*menus
200–400F*). *Closed 17 Dec–3 Feb Mon,
Oct–April and Thurs lunch.*

★★★Les Hauts de Montreuil, 21-23 Rue Pierre
Ledent, t 03 21 81 95 92, f 03 21 86 28 83
(*moderate*). A comfortable hotel set around
a charming old timberframe town house,
with a modern annexe, restaurant and
terrace (*menus 160–270F*).
★★Les Remparts, Place du Général de Gaulle,
t 03 21 06 08 65, f 03 21 81 20 45 (*inexpensive*). A cheerful, bright little stop with a
good restaurant.
Le Darnétal, Place Darnétal, t 03 21 06 04 87,
f 03 21 86 64 67 (*inexpensive*). On a delightful
square, with a few spacious if spartan rooms
which contrast with the merry clutter of
objects in the enjoyable restaurant (*menus
100–190F*).
Le Relais du Roy, 58 Rue Pierre Ledent, t 03 21
81 53 44. Excellent restaurant in a picturesque restored 18th-century coaching inn.
Auberge de la Grenouillère, t 03 21 06 07 22.
Just below Montreuil, at La Madeleine, a
superb restaurant in a restored farmhouse
by the river Canche, set amid woods and
lush meadows and with a good view
up to Montreuil's remarkable ramparts.
A combination of pure gastronomic
pleasure, comfort and rural calm, with a
few rooms.

Argoules ✉ 80120

★★★Auberge du Gros Tilleul, Place du Château,
t 03 22 29 91 00, f 03 22 23 91 64
(*inexpensive*). A very welcoming-looking inn
in a pretty, quirky village. The rooms are
charming if a bit cramped, the ones under
the eaves better than the tight modern
ones. You can sit out on the terrace under
the fine lime tree after which the place is
named (*menus around 100F*).

parish cemetery contains the grave of the Canadian doctor, Lieutenant-Colonel John
McCrae, author of 'In Flanders Fields', one of the most famous of Great War poems:

*In Flanders fields the poppies blow
Between the crosses, row on row...*

On the north side of Boulogne, the **Colonne de la Grande Armée** stands out, surely
one of the greatest monuments ever raised to a non-event. In the early 1800s
Napoleon kept an army of some 200,000 encamped at Boulogne while he and his
commanders tried to work out a way of invading England. They finally gave up on the

idea and marched them off to greater glory in Germany. Curiously, the troops waiting at Boulogne so enjoyed themselves that they elected to erect a memorial to their stay, with the statue of the emperor on top. The monument (*open April–Sept Mon and Thurs–Sun 9–12 and 2–6; Oct–Mar Mon and Thurs–Sun 9–12 and 2–5; adm*) was only completed under King Louis-Philippe in 1841. The war cemetery of **Terlincthun** down the hillside from the column contains graves of soldiers who died in both World Wars.

Boulogne

Boulogne claims to be the oldest cross-Channel port. On his first invasion of England in 55 BC Caesar sailed from here, and in the following century the Romans built a fortress-town as their base for communications with the new colony. After the fall of Rome, Boulogne was semi-abandoned, but revived in the early Middle Ages as the seat of a line of independent counts. In 1214 the French king Philippe Auguste succeeded in establishing his authority, and from that time on Boulogne was the main bastion of French royal power in the north. The world wars would be disastrous. Through the First, the town served as the main port for ferrying over British soldiers and was heavily bombarded. The Second left 85 per cent of Boulogne in ruins – hence the ranks of postwar blocks below the historic upper town.

Nausicaa (*open June–14 Sept 10–8; 15 Sept–May Mon–Fri 10–6, Sun and hols 10–7; closed 2 weeks in Jan; adm*), on the waterfront by the beach, is Boulogne's biggest attraction for children. Behind the unmissable modernistic exterior, it provides a wealth of ecological information about the sea through dynamic multi-media

Tourist Information

Boulogne-sur-Mer: Quai de la Poste, **t** 03 21 10 88 10, **f** 03 21 10 88 11.

Shopping

If you arrive in Boulogne on a Wednesday or a Saturday morning, make straight for the Place Dalton off the Grande Rue (in the lower town) and site of one of the best traditional markets in this part of France. Boulogne of course has its hypermarkets, mostly near the motorway or the N42 towards St-Omer, but the main town-centre shopping area lies just across the Grande Rue from the market, around Rue Thiers and Rue Victor Hugo. The little **Fromagerie** of Philippe Olivier, 43 Rue Thiers, is a foodie institution, but there are many other cheese, wine and cake shops of quality in town. Rue de Lille contains some tempting food shops and restaurants.

Where to Stay

Boulogne ✉ 62200
★★★Métropole, 51 Rue Thiers, **t** 03 21 31 54 30, **f** 03 21 30 45 72. Comfortable central hotel with some rooms giving on to a garden. 35 rooms. No restaurant. *Closed 22 Dec–2 June.*
★★Ibis, **t** 03 21 31 21 01, **f** 03 21 31 48 25. Just by the Porte Neuve, in a good location up by the walled city.

Eating Out

La Matelote, 80 Bd Ste-Beuve, **t** 03 21 30 17 97, **f** 03 21 83 29 24. A cheerful restaurant looking out to sea, serving excellent seafood (*menu 25F*). *Closed 24 Dec–20 Jan, Sun eve (exc July and Aug).*
There's a wide choice of restaurants along Rue de Lille up in the old walled city.

displays, with good provision for English speakers. It has a few theme-park-style attractions like the deck of a trawler in a storm, and a sealed 'tropical environment'.

The tight ring of walls creates an enclosed, hushed, atmosphere in Boulogne's **Haute Ville**. Steps at various points allow you to go walking up on the 13th-century ramparts. Beneath the Haute Ville's ramparts, on the broad esplanade to the left of the Porte des Dunes, is an odd monument of a man in a fez on top of a pyramid. This is Auguste Mariette, distinguished Boulonnais and father of French Egyptology.

Standing out in the eastern corner of the walls is the well-preserved 13th-century castle, now the **Château-Musée** (*open 15 May–14 Sept Mon, Wed–Sat 9.30–12.30 and 1.30–6, Sun 2.30–6; 15 Sept–14 May Mon, Wed–Sun 10–12.30 and 2.30–5; adm*). The collections are a hotch-potch of donations from private collectors and *savants*: mummies and other Egyptian relics from Mariette feature alongside some very fine classic 18th-century porcelain and a remarkable collection of Inuit and Native American masks aquired by a local anthropologist, Alphonse Pinart, in Alaska in 1871.

The undulating dunes along the coast south of Boulogne are impressive and the beaches attractive, but the resorts themselves – **Equihen**, **Hardelot-Plage**, **Condette** (where Dickens stayed on cross-Channel trips), **Ste-Cécile-Plage** and **St-Gabriel-Plage** – are monotonous and modern.

Etaples

A **war cemetery** with its pinnacled entrance tower designed by Sir Edwin Lutyens greets you as you arrive at the port of Etaples, a place with traumatic memories from the Great War. The cemetery contains almost 11,000 graves, making it the largest British and Commonwealth cemetery in France. Officers were accorded single graves, other ranks being placed in pairs, while Chinese and other minority troops were buried on the periphery.

Etaples had the main war hospital, at one stage dealing with over 20,000 casualties. One nurse here was Vera Brittain, who lost her brothers and her fiancé in the fighting and wrote moving accounts of her war experience. Etaples was also one of the main centres for training reinforcements. A few trainees rebelled, notably in the so-called case of the Monocled Mutineer of 1917. Now Etaples is a rough-and-ready fishing port with a fishermen's quarter and a maritime museum, but it is rather spoilt by the busy road cutting through it.

Le Touquet-Paris Plage

Le Touquet is an artificial town, created in the 1890s to rival Deauville in Normandy. It was long popular with British high society, some of whom got into the habit of hopping over the Channel by plane, so putting Le Touquet's airfield on the map. The **Aqualud water park** (*open mid-Feb–early Nov 10–6; 8 July–20 Aug also open Fri and Sat 8pm–midnight*) stands out among the endless seafront car parks and wall of tower blocks.

But a grander Le Touquet still exists, and the surviving Art Deco architecture, casino and grand hotels give the part of town behind the seafront a vaguely Noel Coward air. There is a race course, and golf courses are scattered beyond the rather naff, pine-shaded pastiches of Norman villas on the outskirts of town. Just north of the resort, the mouth of the Canche river remains beautifully unspoilt.

South of Le Touquet modern resorts line up like clones. **Quend-Plage** distinguishes itself from the othes as it has so far avoided the temptation of building big modern blocks on the seafront. It seems a little friendlier and more down to earth, with pines covering the dunes around it, and a comical little cinema in the centre.

Inland from Boulogne to Montreuil and Hesdin

Set on a rock above the wooded valley of the Canche, **Montreuil** is still contained within its walls as it was in the 16th century, and shows no inclination to outgrow them. During the 13th century it had a thriving port, apparently one of the wealthiest in northern France, trading in grains, wines and wool, but the Canche had already begun to silt up and by 1400 was virtually impassable. Today the sea lies a full 15 kilometres away, although the town is still sometimes called Montreuil-sur-Mer.

In 1537 the army of Emperor Charles V besieged and virtually destroyed the town. Afterwards, François I ordered it to be rebuilt in a radically different manner. In the 16th century, as the French frontier moved east and the sea receded further west, Montreuil became a backwater, but continued to serve as a stop for the Paris-Calais mail coaches. Victor Hugo passed through, and set part of his novel *Les Misérables* here – this is where Jean Valjean briefly achieves peace and prosperity as mayor.

The spectacular walls form an unbroken loop around the town. In the northwest corner of the ramparts a little bridge leads to the **Citadelle** (*open Mon and Wed–Sun 9–12 and 2–6; closed Oct; adm*). Parts of it vary enormously in age, from the first fortifications of the 9th century and two massive towers built for Philippe Auguste, to the 17th-century additions with an entrance designed by the ever-present Vauban. The Tour de la Reine Berthe is where one of France's least distinguished kings, Philippe I, is supposed to have confined his Dutch queen in 1091 after he had repudiated her in order to marry another woman, Bertrade de Montfort.

During the second half of the First World War Montreuil was the headquarters of the British Army in France. The **Grande-Place** or **Place Général de Gaulle** is overlooked from one corner by Field Marshal Haig on horseback. Haig became a familiar figure in the countryside around Montreuil, going riding every morning, preceded by another horseman carrying a Union Jack. North of the Grande-Place, the intertwining streets are small; the little white cottages in the older streets almost look as if they have been washed up from a fishing village. Montreuil has a curious range of churches. St-Saulve on Place Gambetta is the largest, a fine Gothic pile, but only half of it survived the sack of 1537. The mock Flamboyant Chapelle de l'Hôtel-Dieu across the square was built in the 1870s by Clovis Normand, a revivalist of the school of Viollet-le-Duc. Go down the street to the right of the Hôtel-Dieu and you come to a quiet little square, with the whitewashed Chapelle de Ste-Austreberthe. From there, the Rue Porte Becquerelle and the Rue de Paon will take you to the most picturesque area of all, with the little cobbled alleys of Clape-en-Bas and Clape-en-Haut. The remains of open sewers still run down the middle of them (*clape* translates roughly as drain).

Hesdin and Its Famous Battlegrounds

The main town of Artois' Sept Vallées, **Hesdin** lies up the pretty Canche valley from Montreuil. The main Place d'Armes seems almost too big for the town, with its grand, very Flemish-looking town hall fronted by a magnificent Baroque porch. The French fleur-de-lys at the top was added in the 18th century, but the coat of arms in the centre of the balcony is Spanish. Nearby, the large church of Notre-Dame was built between 1565 and 1585 on the Flemish Hallekerk model. Its brick façade is mainly Gothic, but it has an impressive Renaissance-style stone porch, surmounted, again, by the Spanish Habsburg arms. Next to the church is the river, which playfully runs through the middle of the town under little hump-backed bridges, sometimes disappearing under buildings. In Rue Daniel Lereuil, you can locate the birthplace in 1697 of that notoriously naughty priest, l'Abbé Prévost, author of *Manon Lescaut*.

To the north of Hesdin lies the site of the **Battle of Agincourt** (or Azincourt), where Henry V of England's troops famously defeated a French force five times larger in one rain-soaked day in 1415, largely thanks to the English longbowmen. Among the most important prisoners taken was Charles d'Orléans, father of a future king of France, Louis XII, and inspiration to Joan of Arc, whose part in French victories 15 years later would help reverse the English triumph. In Azincourt a small **museum** (*open April–Oct daily 9–6; Nov–Mar daily 2–6; adm*) helps make sense of the battleground.

The little town of **Crécy-en-Ponthieu** tumbles down the hillside below the Crécy battle site. The obelisk opposite the town hall is dedicated to Jean de Luxembourg and his '*vaillants compagnons d'armes morts pour la France à Crécy le 26 août 1346*'. In 1346 Edward III of England and his army went on a highly successful rampage through northern France, landing on the Cotentin peninsula in Normandy, carrying on via Rouen to the edges of Paris before heading up to Artois. Panels at the battlefield car park explain the action. It is said that Edward's men defeated the French army of King Philippe VI that was three times its size. Again, the English archers wrought the most terrible damage. Edward III's warrior son who came to be known as the Black Prince won his spurs here. Legend has it that he adopted his motto, the Germanic '*Ich dien* (I serve)', at Crécy as well as his insignia of the so-called Prince of Wales' feathers, taken from the badge of King John of Bohemia.

The Somme in Picardy

First World War battlefields still draw large numbers of visitors to the *département* of the Somme in Picardy. Its capital, Amiens, a fascinating cathedral city, straddles the River Somme. East of it lies the major arena of the 1916 Battle of the Somme. A dreadful density of war cemeteries covers the area radiating out from Albert, while numerous moving war memorials pay homage to those who died and recall the hellish events.

The Bay of the Somme

In the giant landscape of the Bay of the Somme, borders between earth, sea and sky often become hard to distinguish. The light has an opaque quality celebrated by such writers as Jules Verne and Colette and by painters like Degas and Seurat. At low tide the sea recedes for miles and the placid channels, sandbanks and expanses of coarse grass, rushes and marsh lavender present an ever-changing mix of subtle colours fading into the horizon. Birds love it too. One of its most beautiful parts has become the **Wildlife Reserve of Marquenterre** (*open April–Sept daily 9.30–7; Oct–11 Nov daily 10–5; 12 Nov–Mar Sat, Sun and hols 10–5; adm*), a 2,300-hectare stretch of marsh, lake and dunes, all well-organized for visitors.

The little towns around the Bay of the Somme seem lost in the immensity of the landscape and left behind by history in the rarely broken stillness. **Le Crotoy** is one of the places where Joan of Arc was briefly held prisoner after her capture by the Burgundians in 1430. It also enjoyed a certain vogue at the end of the 19th century as a resort. When Jules Verne stayed, he spent a lot of time with the inventor and experimenter in submarine technology, Jacques-François Conseil, who provided inspiration for *Vingt Mille Lieues sous les mers* (*Twenty Thousand Leagues Under the Sea*). Atmospheric **St-Valéry-sur-Somme**, on the south side of the Bay, is where William, Duke of Normandy, sailed from to conquer England in 1066.

Amiens

Presiding over central Amiens is France's largest cathedral, described by John Ruskin as the most perfect creation of medieval Christianity in northern Europe. The city was badly scarred in both world wars, but within its modern sprawl it has an attractive old heart, thanks in part to its river setting. The Somme flows around narrow islands connected by footbridges and lined by old, leaning, steep-roofed houses with many-coloured façades.

St-Martin

A shining example of Christian charity radiated out from Amiens across Western Europe in the 4th century. A certain Martin, born in what is now Hungary, was serving as an officer in the Roman army. The story goes that he was passing through the city gate into Amiens on a bitter winter's day when he was moved by the sight of a poor naked man begging for help. Martin drew out his sword and cut his officer's cloak in two, offering the poor man one half to protect himself. That night, Martin had a revelation and saw Jesus coming to him dressed in the other half of his cape. Martin went on to become one of the main Christian evangelists in France. He helped to found the first monastery in the country, near Poitiers. He also became a celebrated bishop of Tours on the Loire, and innumerable places in the French provinces are named after him.

Tourist Information

Amiens: Rue Jean Catelas, t 03 22 91 79 28, f 03 22 71 60 51, www.amiens.com.

Where to Stay

Amiens ✉ 80000

★★★**Grand Hôtel de l'Univers**, 2 Rue de Noyon, t 03 22 91 52 51, f 03 22 92 81 66 (*moderate*). Good hotel near the cathedral; 41 rooms, but no restaurant.

★★**Le Prieuré**, 17 Rue Porion, t 03 22 92 27 67, f 03 22 92 46 16 (*inexpensive*). Charming hotel in part of a 17th-century priory.

★★**Le Victor Hugo**, 2 Rue de l'Oratoire, t 03 22 91 57 91, f 03 22 92 74 02 (*inexpensive*). The romantically cheap option by the cathedral.

Eating Out

La Couronne, 64 Rue St-Leu, t 03 22 91 88 57. The best place to find classic French cuisine in town (*menus 92–170F*). Closed 15 July–14 Aug, 2–11 Jan, Sun eve and Sat.

Les Marissons, 68 Rue des Marissons, Pont de la Dodane, t 03 22 92 96 66, f 03 22 91 50 50. In the picturesque canal quarter, a pretty dining room where you can enjoy really refined cooking.

As the Gallo-Roman city of Samarobriva, it was, in the 2nd century AD, the most important city in northern Gaul, twice the size of Paris' predecessor Lutetia. For centuries the city's rich merchants thrived. In the First World War Amiens served as a vital Allied communications centre, but it was the Second World War that hurt old Amiens the most, much of it destroyed in only two days, 18 and 19 May 1940, when German incendiary bombs rained down on the city.

The **cathedral** fortunately survived. It was begun in 1220, after Amiens had acquired no less a prize of a Christian relic than the supposed head of John the Baptist, brought here in dubious circumstances after the Fourth Crusade. Much of the cathedral was completed within 50 years, giving it an unusual unity of style. Also, unusually for a medieval building, it has a known first architect, Robert de Luzarches, whose name has been preserved in the centre of the great 'labyrinth' in the cathedral's intricate tiled floor. From the outside, the whole structure seems too tall for its length. The strange slender spire was only added in 1529. But the exterior detail is totally absorbing.

Ruskin called the staggering west façade 'the Bible in stone', with its hundreds of scenes and figures of saints and apostles. In the small roundels around the base of the portals are vignettes of 13th-century life: scenes of men working in the fields or cooking fish over an open fire. The central statue of Jesus, the *Beau Dieu*, was, legend has it, sculpted directly from a vision of Christ, and is extremely beautiful.

Inside, the cathedral soars like few others. Vaults and columns seem to reach for the sky and high windows give the nave a rare luminosity. If the façade is the Bible in stone, the stalls of the choir might well be described as the Bible in wood, carved by Amiens craftsmen between 1508 and 1522. In the ambulatory, the outer walls of the choir are just as impressive. Two series of scenes in polychrome stone from the early 16th century depict, on one side, the life of John the Baptist, on the other the life of St Firmin, credited with having brought Christianity to Amiens. As to the three great rose windows, although much of their glass is no longer original, they are breathtaking nonetheless, made more of light than of stone.

On the way to the riverside district, stop at **Place du Don**, a cobbled square with 16th-century houses, some original and some restored. Virtually every house contains an antiques shop, a restaurant or a bar, with pavement tables outside. Just off the square at 67 Rue du Don is the tiny shop of Jean-Pierre Facquier, the only remaining maker of the traditional Amiens puppets, the *Cabotans*. At the centre of each story is Lafleur, a roguish Mr Punch character, considered the archetypal Amiens and Picard character. Across the river, the engaging **canalside quarter of St-Leu** was formerly the weavers' and dyers' district. The houses are endlessly varied, with original half-timbered, stucco or plain brick façades.

Back in the centre of town, the large Hôtel de Ville, rebuilt after the war, stands in front of a square recently remodelled to an innovative, locally controversial design by the Catalan architect Joan Roig, with intriguing inclined fountains. Walk around the town hall and you come to a solid 15th-century belfry, once a prison.

The **Musée de Picardie** (*open Tues–Sun 10–12.30 and 2–6; adm*) is housed in a Second Empire wedding cake, comparable to the Paris Opera. It was opened by Napoleon III in 1867 and the large 'N' stamped on the front stands for him, the 'E' for his Empress Eugénie. Inside, it is still more imposing, with a giant main staircase and a vast Grand Salon with murals by Puvis de Chavannes. They present a fanciful vision of the prehistoric Picards, in the artist's monumental style based on Italian trecento frescoes.

The museum contains a great many fine Roman artefacts, a good number from excavations of Samarobriva, and rooms of medieval sculptures in wood and stone, including an exquisitely modelled series of bas-reliefs of the life of Christ, from around 1500. Most extraordinary and unique, though, are the *Puys*, paintings offered to the cathedral during the 16th century by the Fraternity of Notre-Dame, an association of local merchants. It was the custom for each master of the fraternity to commission a painting, and the results are a fascinating panorama of Amiens and its burghers over more than a century. Beyond the *Puys* you can discover several fine works by famous artists such as El Greco, Salvator Rosa, Frans Hals, Fragonard and Boucher. The more modern sections aren't so eye-catching, but the museum does have one great recent addition in *Wall Drawing 711*, a rotunda on the ground floor painted in 1992 by the American artist Sol LeWitt who used a whole spectrum of colours in a series of complex geometrical patterns.

One particularly striking curiosity near the museum is the **Cirque Municipal**, an odd, drum-like building with many ornate 19th-century details, which is invariably associated with Jules Verne. He was actually born in Nantes, but his wife Honorine was from Amiens, and after they moved here in 1871 he became an institution in the city for over thirty years. Verne busied himself with every aspect of local life, serving on the city council and in 1889 badgering his fellow councillors into giving Amiens one of the world's few permanent circus halls. Just east of here you can visit the **Centre de Documentation Jules Verne** (*open Tues–Sat 9.30–12 and 2–6; adm*), where the great author lived, which is crammed with information.

The most eccentric trip to take in Amiens is in a punt along the **Hortillonages**, the water gardens by the Somme east of the cathedral. Vegetable plots existed on the drained marshes as far back as Gallo-Roman times. The network of canals was much extended down the centuries, and at the start of the 20th century nearly a thousand people lived on the Hortillonages, a separate community. Only a handful do so now, but many people work the plots, or just use them as a weekend retreat. The association of allotment holders runs tours of some of the over 50 kilometres of channels (*April–Oct from 2pm, depending on demand; call t 03 22 92 18; adm*).

Into the Somme Battlefields

For at least ten years I dreamt that I was crawling through
ruined houses or corridors where there was scarcely room to pass.
The ruins were always present in my mind.
Otto Dix

In roughly a third of the *département* of the Somme virtually every house was reduced to rubble in the Great War. East of Amiens, vast areas still look remarkably empty. The scattering of war cemeteries is extremely dense in parts, particularly around Albert.

More than half a dozen British cemeteries lie along the N29 road or south of it. The biggest Commonwealth cemetery between Villers-Bretonneux and Corbie includes the **Australian National War Memorial**, commemorating the 1,200 Australians who died in the 1918 action at Villers-Bretonneux and the 10,797 Australians who died on the Western Front but were left without a known grave. Villers-Bretonneux itself was totally destroyed in the conflict and was rebuilt with Australian aid. The remains from

The Outbreak of the First World War

The First World War was caused by a number of festering wounds. A split had formed early in the 20th century between the major European powers, the Triple Alliance of Austro-Hungary, Germany and Italy on the one side, the Triple Entente of France, Great Britain and Russia on the other. The spark for the war was lit in Serbia, a reluctant part of the Austro-Hungarian Empire. When Serbian nationalists assassinated the Archduke Franz Ferdinand, heir apparent to the Austro-Hungarian throne, on 28 June 1914, the Austrian powers saw red. A month later they decided to declare war on Serbia. Russia, seeing itself as the protector of the Serbs, mobilized its troops on 30 July. On 1 August Germany declared war on Russia and used the situation as an excuse to attack France. On 2 August it began its invasion of Belgium; on 3 August it declared war on France. The Germans' Schlieffen plan, devised as far back as 1895, was to storm through Belgium, taking the French army by surprise. The operation to conquer France was to last just six weeks. Once achieved, the Germans would then concentrate on taking Russia. They were only prevented from pulling off this plan thanks to desperate French actions in 1914, so they decided to dig in. The appalling years of atrocious trench warfare followed. Britain entered the war on 4 August 1914, honouring its agreement to defend Belgium should its neutrality be violated.

Getting Around

Amiens is the main hub for public transport in this area. Amiens railway station lies on the Paris-Gare du Nord–Calais line; trains also stop at Abbeville, Noyelles-sur-Mer and Rue. You can reach a few of the towns near the First World War battlefields on the Amiens–Arras and Amiens–St-Quentin/Laon lines, in particular Albert and Villers-Bretonneux. To reach Péronne by public transport, take the TGV Haute-Picardie railway station on the Lille-Paris Gare du Nord line and catch a bus.

Tourist Information

Le Crotoy: 1 Rue Carnot, **t** 03 22 27 05 25, **f** 03 22 27 90 58.
Péronne: 31 Rue St-Fursy, **t** 03 22 84 42 38.
Albert: 9 Rue Gambetta, **t** 03 22 75 16 42, **f** 03 22 75 11 72.
St-Quentin: 27 Rue Victor Basch, **t** 03 23 67 05 00.

Where to Stay and Eat

Remaisnil ✉ **80600**
Château de Remaisnil, 80600 Doullens, **t** 03 22 77 07 47, **f** 03 22 77 41 23, *www.chateau-de-*

remaisnil.com (*luxury*). A very grand, beautifully decorated 18th-century country château 35km north of Amiens, once the home of Laura Ashley. Luxury meals available.

Albert ✉ **80300**
★★★**Royal Picardie,** Av du Général Leclerc, **t** 03 22 75 37 00, **f** 03 22 75 60 19 (*inexpensive*). Curious grandiose modern stone building with comfortable rooms and a good restaurant (*menus 78–300F*). *Closed Sun eve.*

Rancourt ✉ **80360**
★★**Le Prieuré,** RN17, **t** 03 22 85 04 43, **f** 03 22 85 06 69 (*inexpensive*). A large, clean-lined, modern stone hotel close to the A1 and A2 motorway junction above Péronne, this place has comfortable rooms from which to set out to visit the war sites. Restaurant (*menus 78–260F*). *Closed Sun eve.*

Bapaume ✉ **62450**
★★**La Paix,** 11 Av Abel Guidet, **t** 03 21 07 11 03, **f** 03 21 07 43 66 (*inexpensive*). A friendly hotel off the A1 north of Péronne, with its own restaurant (*menus 78–225F*). *Closed Sun.*

one of the graves were removed in November 1993 to be taken to rest in the Tomb of the Unknown Australian Soldier at the Australian War Memorial in Canberra.

Péronne has an important modern museum on the First World War, the **Historial de la Grande Guerre** (*open May–Sept daily 10–6; rest of year daily exc Mon 10–5.30; adm*), the best introduction in the area to the historical context and the campaigns of the Great War. English speakers are well catered for.

The museum pays particular homage to the part played by the British Isles in the First World War. The response by some one million British and Irish men to Kitchener's call for voluntary enlistment is described as one of the miracles of the First World War. The main film tells the story of the Battle of the Somme through the memories of a British soldier, Harry Fellows, with Benjamin Britten's *War Requiem* playing. Like so many naive volunteers, he left for France with a feeling of excitement, pleased at the thought of getting in some free foreign travel, little realizing the hell he was heading for. The postwar period isn't forgotten. In particular, reference is made to the Zone Rouge, the vast swath of land between Albert, Péronne, Villers-Cotterêts and Soissons where 80 per cent to 100 per cent of buildings were destroyed. One plan was to leave woodland to grow across the whole area, as at Verdun, but the idea was abandoned.

The concentration of cemeteries and memorials close to Albert indicates the crucial importance this stretch of territory assumed in the years of relentless trench warfare. The vast triple-arched **Thiepval British memorial** can be seen rising above woods for miles around. Its inhuman scale helps recall the number of British men who went missing – almost 75,000. The great majority died between July and November 1916. The only non-British remembered here are 858 South Africans and one West Indian.

The monument, designed by Sir Edwin Lutyens, is apparently the largest British war memorial in the world. The inauguration ceremony took place in 1932, while back in Britain some criticized the money spent on the monument rather than on the large number of unemployed, war-shattered men back in Britain. It is a depressing, coldly grandiose structure, the individual names lost in huge long lists. Registers scattered around the monument indicate where to find specific soldiers. Among the names are several men awarded the Victoria Cross, several war poets, and the writer H. H. Munro, better known as Saki. Below the memorial, 300 French gravestones were added alongside 300 British ones as a symbol of the unified effort of the two armies.

The **Ulster memorial** stands out on the high ridge nearby, the tower a copy of Helen's Tower at Clandeboyne outside Belfast. From the top, you get a vantage point over the wider battle area. A two-room museum recalls the Ulstermen's heroism here.

The **Beaumont-Hamel Parc Terre-Neuvien** is dedicated above all to troops of the 1st Newfoundland Regiment. The park is basically a very large field sloping gently down to 'Y' Ravine. On the first day of the Battle of the Somme, some Allied troops made it as far as the ravine, where the regiment distinguished itself in brutal action. Scottish soldiers are also remembered here. You can walk round a few remnants of trenches, the ground all around still puckered with craters.

The town of St-Quentin lay in German hands through the First World War. The so-called Second Battle of the Somme of 1918, when the Germans captured tens of thousands of British prisoners, took place west of the town. Some way north, up the N44, an important **American war memorial** stands at the panoramic site at Bellicourt. Nearby is the **American Somme Cemetery** at Bony. Around 1,200 Americans broke through the German line here at the end of September 1918 only to find themselves tragically cut off.

Picardy East and South

Geographically and administratively part of Picardy, emotionally part of the Ile de France – the areas around Soissons, Compiègne, Senlis and Beauvais in southern Picardy merge with the Paris bassin, and their magnificent churches vie with the Gothic giants of the Ile de France. Compiègne and Senlis escaped the wars relatively unscathed. The awe-inspiring medieval sights of Coucy-le-Château and Laon and the picture-book restored Château de Pierrefonds are further highlights. Although Paris lurks close by, most of this thickly forested area still feels rural and provincial, and it is something of a surprise that the showy Château de Chantilly and the amusement parks of Parc Astérix and La Mer des Sables lie within the Picardy border.

Laon

Laon's colossal Gothic cathedral calls out to passers-by from high on its vantage point, even visible to motorists some distance away on the A26 motorway to Reims. Laon's elevated position 100 steep metres above the plains of Champagne made it an obvious place of fortification, back at least to Gallo-Roman times. St Remigius, the famous Rémi who became bishop of Reims, founded a bishopric here in the 5th century. During a stormy period in 1111, a bishop was murdered and the cathedral burnt down, to be replaced by the gloriously grand Gothic edifice you see today.

Most of the vast **cathedral** was finished by 1230, although only four of the seven towers planned were included in the final construction. Unfortunately the treatment of the sculptures of the west front was particularly heavy-handed during the 19th-century restoration. Strain your eyes to make out the carved oxen high on the towers. They serve as a reminder of a legend associated with the construction of the building: one of the exhausted beasts being used to transport the building blocks from the Chemin des Dames up to Laon was replaced by an unusually energetic animal, sent down from heaven no less, to make the sure the job got done. Inside, the view down the nave is through a vast tunnel of masonry in the shape of a Gothic lanced arch, the choir end with its three lancet windows surmounted by a large rose window glowing purple, blue and red. The architecture has a rare clarity and purity: the four levels follow the same pattern all the way round. Off the aisles and ambulatory, the side chapels look like monastic cells divided by Renaissance openings. When you reach the choir end, take a closer look at the stained glass: to the right and in the middle are scenes from Christ's life, while to the left scenes show the stoning of St Etienne and Théophile's pact with the devil.

Nearby, the **Musée de Laon** (*open April–Sept daily exc Tues 10–12 and 2–6; rest of year daily exc Tues 10–12 and 2–5; adm*) contains items from ancient Mediterranean cultures amassed by a 19th-century collector, some of extraordinarily high quality. The three Le Nain brothers were born in Laon in the 17th century, and the highlight of the painting collection is *Le Concert* by Mathieu Le Nain.

In the museum garden, the diminutive **Romanesque Templars' chapel** contains a sickening-looking corpse effigy, the skeletal figure made all the more shocking by the thin flowing hair it still sports. The streets of old Laon are crammed with former religious houses, some hiding behind gateways, some visible to you as you pass by. The tourist trail indicates them clearly. Out on the city walls, splendid views open out on to the plains and the forests around. Just avoid looking at the ugly modern town below.

The Chemin des Dames

The charming name of this tragic ridge south of Laon refers to the fact that this spectacular way was specially cleared and paved for the passage of the royal daughters of Louis XV, back in the 18th century. Its strategic importance is evident, lording it over the vast flat plain of Champagne to the east and rising sharply up in front of the Aisne river to the south.

The military history of the ridge probably goes back to the Dark Ages, but in the First World War it became the target of repeated disastrous French campaigns on a sickening scale. In fact, it was along the Aisne valley from Compiègne to here that the terrible trench warfare of the First World War began. After the German military planners' failure to pull off the Schlieffen Plan in 1914, they retreated to strong positions that could be easily defended. One of the very first places where they dug themselves in was along the Chemin des Dames. The infamous Western Front was established, running hundreds of miles from near the Belgian border with France, through French Flanders, Picardy, Lorraine, down to the border with Switzerland.

The Germans turned the Chemin des Dames into one of the strongest points along the front, making the most of the superb natural defences and the underground caverns. The most absurd campaign here was overseen by the French commander Nivelle in 1917. Madly ambitious, Nivelle wanted the French army to storm the German positions between Soissons and Reims from the spring of 1917. A great deal of hope was pinned on this new offensive. Over 1 million men and half a million horses were massed at the foot of the Chemin des Dames. Wave after wave of French soldiers were sent to their deaths on the slopes of the impregnable ridge. The failure to take the Chemin des Dames plunged the French army into depression. Finally a number of the common soldiers put up what now seems like a reasonable protest, but because of the social and political implications, the French leadership called it a mutiny and came down hard on those they considered the troublemakers. A small number were shot. They have never been pardoned. The French leadership are still divided on the subject: in a bitter debate in November 1998, Socialist Prime Minister Lionel Jospin argued that it was time that these men were forgiven, while President Jacques Chirac insisted that the matter should rest as it stands.

Heading along the Chemin des Dames from its western end below Filain, there is a **French war cemetery and memorial chapel** at the crossroads with the D967. Further south on the D967 a beautiful **British war cemetery** graces the slope at Vendresse. The brash modern museum on stilts at the **Caverne du Dragon**, midway along the Chemin des Dames, recalls the dreadful disasters of the Great War in these parts.

The most stunning section of the Chemin des Dames lies at its eastern end. From the **Plateau de Californie** you look down on to an immense, dreamy view of the plains where Picardy and Champagne meet. As you walk along, discreet panels give details of the fighting and the dreadful conditions for the soldiers who took part in the trench warfare. A disturbing monument has recently been erected at the start of the walk, showing repeated copies of a bald head trapped in mesh.

Down from the Plateau de Californie, the spire of modern **Craonne** sticks out in the foreground. The old village was one of many places obliterated in the war. The substantial pits in the ground of the modern arboretum above the modern village are reminders of the brutal shelling.

Most of the graveyards lie down below the Chemin des Dames in the Aisne valley – some sixteen French cemeteries, nine British, thirteen German and one Italian. At

The *Chanson de Craonne*

In the modern church at Craonne, pinned to the inside of the door, you should find a copy of the *Chanson de Craonne*. This protest song written from the perspective of ordinary soldiers circulated among the troops during the 1917 unrest, and was banned for a long time after.

Adieu la vie, adieu l'amour
Adieu toutes les femmes
C'est bien fini, c'est pour toujours
De cette guerre infâme
C'est à Craon sur le plateau
Qu'on doit laisser sa peau
Car nous sommes tous condamnés
Nous sommes les sacrifiées

Ceux qu'ont le pognon, ceux-là reviendront
Car c'est pour eux qu'on crève
Mais c'est fini car les troufions
Vont tous se mettre en grève.

Ce s'ra votre tour, messieurs les grands
De monter sur le plateau
Car si vous voulez faire la guerre
Payez-la d'votre peau.

(Farewell to life, to love farewell,
Farewell to all our girls and women
For we can hear our own death knell
In this infamy for common men.
It's high on the Craon plain
That we'll know our final agonizing pain
For we are all condemned
We are the sacrificed.

Those with dosh, they'll come out alright
For them we die by bomb and shell and pike
But that'll change, we ordinary men will show our might
We'll all go out on strike.

Your turn will come, you men who make the law,
To climb the ridge in war's defeaning din
You men who make the rules, if you want to make war
Pay for it with your own skin.)

Craonnelle you will find one of the most moving, the slope covered by white crosses and distinguished by two ossuaries. Although the vast majority of the 2,000 tombs are marked by classic French crosses, they are interspersed not just with British and Belgian graves, but also with Muslim and Jewish ones, a moving example of the joint efforts of different nations and religions during the First World War.

Coucy-le-Château

Open April–Sept daily exc Tues 9–12 and 2–6; rest of year daily
exc Tues 10–12 and 1.30–4; adm.

Southwest of Laon, set on its defensive hilltop, are the still splendidly walled ruins of Coucy-le-Château, so well evoked in Barbara Tuchmann's *A Distant Mirror*, which tells the story of one of the most notable lords of Coucy, Enguerrand VII. This 14th-century heart-throb apparently so impressed Edward III of England that he offered the Frenchman his daughter Isabelle's hand in marriage.

Once twice the size of the Louvre in Paris, the massive castle at first seems rather forlorn, but on the far side among the ruins you stumble upon bits and pieces that give an idea of its grandeur in medieval times. The vaguely rounded pile of rubble was the keep, described as the largest ever built in the Christian world, dating back to 1240. It originally stood almost 200ft high.

The occupying Germans dynamited the keep in 1917 along with the whole village outside the bailey. Much of the castle had been destroyed earlier, in 1652, by order of France's chief minister Mazarin. However, the forms of two of the castle's major halls, the Salle des Preuses and the Salle des Preux, can still be made out clearly. The latter, measuring roughly 200 by 50ft, was one of the largest medieval rooms ever built in France. Four powerful but savaged stone lions with splendid manes stand among the ruins. They formed part of the Banc d'Allégeance, a 13th-century stone table where the vassals of Coucy came to pay homage and taxes. The vast vaulted cellars below give perhaps the best notion of the building's scale.

Soissons

South of Coucy, in the Aisne valley, the city of Soissons played an important part in French history a long time ago. In 752 Pepin le Bref, the first of the so-called Carolingian monarchs and father of Charlemagne, was declared king here, putting an end to the 'do-nothing' Merovingian dynasty. For most of the First World War, the city lay in Allied hands, although unfortunately the Germans succeeded in destroying much of it. The Gothic **cathedral** looks a bit grubby on the outside and is surrounded by a large car park. The medieval **Abbey of St-Léger** has been turned into the town's **museum** (*open daily exc Tues 10–12 and 2–5; adm*), with the *Head of a Negress* by Houdon, a bust showing a tenderly sad face, that was used at the Revolution as a symbol of the abolition of slavery in France. The former abbey church contains beautiful pieces ofmedieval scupture from Soissons and around.

The most spectacular building left in Soissons is in fact a ruin aloof outside the centre. The stunning, soaring façade of the **Abbaye St-Jean-des-Vignes** (*open*

Getting Around

Paris-Charles-de-Gaulle airport lies just south of this area, Reims airport just east of it. A couple of train lines cross the area, between Paris-Gare du Nord and Compiègne/St-Quentin, and Paris-Gare du Nord and Soissons/Laon.

Tourist Information

Laon: Parvis de la Cathédrale, t 03 23 20 28 62, f 03 23 20 68 11, www.ville-laon.fr.

Coucy-le-Château: 8 Rue des Vivants, t 03 23 52 44 55, f 03 23 52 44 55.

Blérancourt: Maison de St-Just, 2 Rue de la Chouette, t 03 23 39 72 17.

Noyon: Place de l'Hôtel de Ville, t 03 44 44 21 88.

Soissons: B.P.216, 16 Place F. Marquigny, t 03 23 53 17 37.

Pierrefonds: Place de l'Hôtel de Ville, t 03 44 42 81 44.

Compiègne: B.P.9, Place de l'Hôtel de Ville, t 03 44 40 01 00, f 03 44 40 23 28.

Senlis: B.P.24, Place du Parvis Notre-Dame, t 03 44 53 06 40, f 03 44 53 29 80.

Ermenonville: 1 Rue de Girardin, Parc Jean-Jacques Rousseau, t 03 44 54 01 58.

Chantilly: B.P.233, 60 Av du Maréchal Joffre, t 03 44 57 08 58.

Beauvais: 1 Rue Beauregard, 60000, t 03 44 15 30 30.

Where to Stay and Eat

Laon ✉ 02000

***La Bannière de France, 11 Rue Franklin Roosevelt, t 03 23 23 21 44, f 03 23 23 31 56 (*moderate*). Up in the old town, this hotel has a pretty front section, a former coaching inn, but also a duller modern wing. The rooms are comfortable, the food good (*menus 123–320F*). 18 rooms. *Closed 22 Dec–21 Jan.*

**Les Chevaliers, 3–5 Rue Sérurier, t 03 23 27 17 50, f 03 23 23 40 71 (*inexpensive*). By the town hall square up on the hilltop, the façade in the row of townhouses may be modern, the rooms in standard style, but the place is very well located. 14 rooms. *Closed 1 Jan–15 April.*

Courcelles-sur-Vesle ✉ 02220

**Château de Courcelles, 8 Rue du Château, t 03 23 74 13 53, f 03 23 74 06 41, courcelles@relaischateaux.fr. Racine, La Fontaine, the Dumas and Jean Cocteau all stayed in this very clean-lined 17th-century white-stoned château by the Vesle river some 20km east of Soissons towards Reims. It now provides one of the most refined stops in northern France.

Fère-en-Tardenois ✉ 02130

****Château de Fère, Route de Fismes, t 03 23 82 21 13. A very luxurious stop 26km southeast of Soissons near the Oise-Aisne American war cemetery and opposite the ruins of a medieval castle, with a fabulous restaurant (*menus 290–480F*). *Closed Jan.*

Léchelle ✉ 02200

La Ferme de Léchelle, Hameau de Léchelle, t 03 23 74 83 29, f 03 23 74 82 47. South of the picturesque village of Berzy-le-Sec, this has good-value B&B rooms with a family feel, set off the large farmyard. A choir of farm animals will sing to you in the morning. A train line passes discreetly through the wooded valley opposite the village.

Noyon ✉ 60400

**Le Cèdre, 8 Rue de l'Evêché, t 03 44 44 23 24, f 03 44 09 53 79 (*inexpensive*). This may be a modern brick hotel with standard modern bedrooms, but it stands in a really good location, built on an historic site, most of the rooms with views onto the side of the cathedral and a little brick Renaissance manor. Restaurant (*menus 80–159F*).

Elincourt Ste-Marguerite ✉ 60157

****Château de Bellinglise, Route de Lassigny, t 03 44 96 00 33, f 03 44 96 03 00 (*expensive*). A stylish 16th-century brick château not far off the A1 motorway and southwest of Noyon. The rooms in the outhouses are much cheaper than those in the château itself. Stylish restaurant too (*menus 195–395F*).

Longpont ✉ 02600

★★Hôtel de l'Abbaye, 8 Rue des Tourelles, t/f 03 23 96 02 44 (*inexpensive*). An adorable inn in an adorable village with adorable abbey ruins which you can visit at weekends, this is a bit of a forest idyll. But it won't necessarily be quiet, with the village bar and restaurant (*menus 100–200F*) below the rooms. The people who run it are charming.

Pierrefonds ✉ 60350

This village is well used to dealing with the tourist hordes. There are several hotels within walking distance of the picture-book castle, and numerous places to eat.

★★Hôtel des Etrangers, 10 Rue de Baudon, t 03 44 42 80 18, f 03 44 42 86 74 (*inexpensive*). A popular hotel with a restaurant in a pretty location by the lake.

Auberge Aux Blés d'Or, 8 Rue J. Michelet, t 03 44 42 85 91, f 03 44 42 98 94 (*inexpensive*). Lakeside neighbour to the above, a reasonable slightly cheaper option.

Hôtel-Crêperie Château Gaillard, 20 Rue Viollet-le-Duc, t 03 44 42 80 96 (*inexpensive*). Sweet and simple, closest to the castle.

St-Jean-aux-Bois ✉ 60350

This village in the forest just west of Pierrefonds absorbs the overspill of tourists going to enjoy Viollet-le-Duc's great restoration work.

★★★A La Bonne Idée, 3 Rue des Meuniers, t 03 44 42 84 09, f 03 44 42 80 45. A charming if slightly expensive option in this modestly pretty village, the restaurant serving good traditional fare.

Compiègne ✉ 60200

★★Hôtel de France, 17 Rue Eugène Floquet, t 03 44 40 02 74, f 03 44 40 48 37 (*inexpensive*). Characterful, concave-fronted, timber-framed hotel tucked down a side street right by the central square. Creaking corridors decorated with tasteful art and furnishings lead to somewhat less tasteful rooms, but these cram a lot in for the good price. Really this is an excellent moderately priced, old-style place to stay, with a restaurant.

★★Les Flandres, 16 Quai de la République, t 03 44 83 24 40, f 03 44 90 02 75

(*inexpensive*). Another good option, in vast neoclassical rather than medieval style.

Senlis ✉ 60300

★★Hostellerie de la Porte Bellon, 51 Rue Bellon, t 03 44 53 03 05, f 03 44 53 29 94 (*inexpensive*). Much the best place to stay in Senlis, just outside the historic centre. This is a characterful and good-value hotel set well back from the main road in a 400-year-old house. *Closed 20 Dec–6 Jan.*

Ermenonville ✉ 60950

Good choices here, so close to Paris.

★★★Château d'Ermenoville, Rue René Girardin, t 03 44 54 00 26, f 03 44 54 01 00 (*moderate–expensive*). A luxury hotel in a stunning-looking moated castle where Jean-Jacques Rousseau spent his last days. There are one or two cheap rooms. 49 rooms. There's also a fine restaurant (*menus 195–450F*).

★★Auberge de la Croix d'Or, 2 Rue Radziwill, t 03 44 54 00 04, f 03 44 45 05 44 (*inexpensive*). A characterful rustic, cheaper option.

Gouvieux ✉ 60270

Two vast, luxurious hotels just west of Chantilly stand out. (Paris's main airport, Roissy Charles de Gaulle, lies *c.* 30 mins' drive away.)

★★★★Château de Montvillargenne, Av François Mathet, t 03 44 62 37 37, f 03 44 57 28 97, *montvillargenne@wanadoo.fr* (*luxury*). You'll find a large number of rooms and facilities in this bulky 19th-century château. There are some slightly cheaper rooms as well as the more expensive Jacuzzi suites. Restaurant (*menus 210–410F*).

★★★Château de la Tour, Chemin de la Chaussée, t 03 44 62 38 38, f 03 44 57 31 97, *le.chateau.de.la.tour@wanadoo.fr* (*expensive*). More like two 20th-century pastiche manicured manors joined together, with a large terrace and good sporting facilities in the well-kept grounds. Restaurant (*menus 210–340F*).

St-Leu-d'Esserent ✉ 60340

★Hôtel de l'Oise, 25 Quai d'Amont, t 03 44 56 60 24, f 03 44 56 05 11 (*inexpensive*). A riverside bargain just northwest of Chantilly.

Mon–Sat 9–12.30 and 1.30–6, Sun 10–12.30 and 1.30–7; adm) has two towers over 230ft in height, but like a theatre backdrop, there is nothing behind them. You can, however, wander round the beautiful Gothic emptiness of the abbey refectory, the cellars and the two remaining sides of the cloister with their curious hybrid Gothic beasts.

Around the Oise Valley to Compiègne

Over 20 kilometres up the Oise from Compiègne lies the little-known cathedral town of **Noyon**, with a history quite out of proportion to its size today. St Médard and St Eloi were two of its famous Merovingian bishops. In 768 Charlemagne came here to be crowned King of Neustria, meaning most of France and large portions of Germany. In 1509, Noyon was the birthplace of the reformer Calvin, who from the safer havens of Geneva made life so hard for the Catholic Church. Many people think of him as a Swiss, but his native town pays its respects to him at the **Musée Jean Calvin**, on the site of the house of his birth. In the First World War, Noyon was in the unfortunate position, until 1917, of being the closest German-occupied town to Paris. It was largely destroyed at the end of the war, and again in the Second World War, but some pleasant quarters survive.

The **cathedral** is the centre of attention. Completed around 1220, all the statuary in the deep western porches was ripped out at the Revolution. Inside, it is built up on four levels as at Laon cathedral, the Gothic arches surmounted by a wide, light tribune, followed by the triforium and the clerestory. On the right side of the nave you can enter two ornate chapels. The first has angels suspended in the bosses of the ceiling, the second refined wood panelling. At the back of the cathedral, the 16th-century library stands out with its wooden-pillared colonnade.

Between Noyon and Compiègne, what remains of the **Château de Blérancourt** designed by Salomon de Brosse (*open daily exc Tues 10–12.30 and 2–5; adm*) are two modest but gracious wings. Anne Morgan, daughter of the fabulously wealthy American banker John Pierpoint Morgan, bought the castle and in 1917 set up an American women's volunteer service to offer humanitarian aid to the French in the First World War. Her efforts are recalled here along with memorabilia and documents, but the place has been turned into a much larger **National Museum of French–American Friendship and Cooperation** (*open Mon, Wed–Sun 10–12.30 and 2–5; adm*). The modern extension displays paintings by American artists in France, John Singer Sargent among them, and French artists in America.

Compiègne and the Forest of Compiègne

At the **Clairière de l'Armistice** in the Forest of Compiègne, you can visit a replica of the railway carriage in which Marshal Foch of France agreed to the armistice on 11 November 1918, marking the end of the First World War. On 22 June 1940 Hitler insisted that the French sign the armistice signalling their swift defeat at the hands of the Germans in the very same place. The original carriage was taken to Berlin during the war and destroyed by bombing.

The town of **Compiègne** isn't simply royal, it's positively imperial, and is surprisingly little known. Its enormous, pompous **château** (*open April–Sept daily exc Tues 9.15–6.15; rest of year daily exc Tues 9.15–4.30; adm*) dominates the centre. It was built for Louis XV, but Compiègne had been a firm favourite with French royals as far back as Carolingian times. Its abbey of St-Cornelius, now vanished, was the royal necropolis until St-Denis took over the role. Building work began on the vast new palace of Compiègne in 1738 under Louis XV, and construction would continue into Louis XVI's reign. Marie-Antoinette met the future Louis XVI here for the first time in 1770. Her great-niece, Marie-Louise of Austria, was brought to the château in 1810 to be married to Napoleon, and Empress Eugénie and Napoleon III of Second Empire France entertained here with wild extravagance in the mid-19th century.

With well over 1,000 rooms, this is one of the largest castles in France. The interiors mainly recall the two French imperial periods of the 19th century. After Napoleon I had divorced Josephine de Beauharnais, he rapidly married Marie-Louise of Austria. By 1811 they had a son, François. Many of the apartments evoke the little family. The boy became known as the Roi de Rome, and enjoyed five days as Napoleon II in 1815. He spent most of his short life in Vienna, dying of tuberculosis in 1832.

The triangular château encases several rectangular courtyards and three museums. On the long guided tour of the imperial apartments, you will be regaled with trompe-l'oeils by Sauvage, heroic wall paintings by Girodet, Bohemian crystal chandeliers, ravishing parquet floors, and the finest tapestries, some from Beauvais. The Museum of the Second Empire contains an absurd number of portraits and family objects of outrageous extravagance. In the **Musée de la Voiture** you can admire a wide range of old carriages, early cars and bicycles, and if it all gets too much, you can go for a walk in the splendid **grounds** much loved by the town's inhabitants.

It was in Compiègne in May 1430 that Joan of Arc was captured by Burgundian troops as she tried to storm the town. (A typically melodramatic 19th-century statue of Joan by Frémiet stands on Place du 54ème Régiment d'Infanterie.) On one side of the impressive Hôtel de Ville, the **Musée de la Figurine Historique** contains an innumerable collection of toy soldiers set in historical scenes. Surprisingly, Napoleon's defeat at the Battle of Waterloo counts among them. At the **Musée Vivenel** (*open Mar–Oct daily exc Sun am and Mon 9–12 and 2–6; rest of year same days 9–12 and 2–5; adm*), the artefacts from Egypt and ancient Greece collected together by a certain Antoine Vivenel eclipse the local archaeological finds.

The Château de Pierrefonds

Open May–Aug daily 10–6; Mar–April and Sept–Oct daily 10–12.30 and 2–6; rest of year daily 10–12.30 and 2–5.

The Château de Pierrefonds, on the eastern side of the forest of Compiègne, presents a picture-book vision of a medieval castle. The original went up for the brother of Charles VI of France in the late 14th century, the main fortification in a whole line built for Louis d'Orléans to protect his Valois duchy. In the 16th century, Antoine d'Estrées, father of the beautiful Gabrielle d'Estrées whom Henri IV took as his mistress, owned the castle, which was destroyed after he opted for the wrong side under Henri IV's son Louis XIII. Napoleon I bought Pierrefonds' ruins for a pittance early in the 19th century, but it was Napoleon III in 1858 who ordered Viollet-le-Duc to reconstruct the massive pile as a Second Empire imperial residence. Viollet-le-Duc set forth his ideas in *Les Entretiens sur l'architecture*, and here you can see them put into action.

The 19th-century decorations, and in particular the sculptures, prove absorbing from the moment you enter the courtyard with its enormous lizard gargoyle. Some of the carving is sickly sweet – twee squirrels hold up coats of arms – but some is weird and wonderful. Most of the rooms lack furniture, but all their walls are decorated. The most impressive room in the place, the long Salle des Preuses, is dedicated to heroic women. From the sentry walk you can look down on the village and lake.

Senlis

A delectable, pale little cathedral town, Senlis' cobbled streets are like onion rings encased in the batter of Gallo-Roman walls. Senlis prospered under the early Capetians. Philippe Auguste ordered a second set of ramparts for the city, and his close friend Guérin was elected bishop of Senlis and set up the Abbaye de la Victoire. In the Wars of Religion, the Huguenot contingent supported Henri IV, but after him the town's royal links ceased, and it sank into a torpor.

The **cathedral** was begun in 1155, one of the first batch of French Gothic cathedrals. Two stern towers rise from the west front, only one of which was completed with a spiky Gothic spire. The sculptures on the west front are superb, and unlike most of the other cathedrals of northern France, this one has preserved many of its originals. The large figures represent eight prophets, with 19th-century restored heads. Among those easiest to identify are Abraham grasping his son by the hair and David, his legs crossed. Note the importance given to the Virgin, placed on the same footing as Christ. This cathedral was in fact the first to devote a portal to the Virgin. In a slide show in the **Hôtel Vermandois** next door, you can appreciate the carved figures on the west front of the cathedral close up. Inside, the Flamboyant south transept features pendant bosses and a stylized window with tracery in the form of teardrops and flames. The nave is very short for a Gothic cathedral and its arches look tentative, but for such an imposing structure it has a rare, warm feeling.

The bishops' palace has been transformed into the **Musée d'Art et d'Archéologie** (*open Mon and Thurs–Sun 10–12 and 2–6; Nov–Jan until 5pm; closed Tues, and Wed am; adm*), which is packed with interest. The Gallo-Roman collection includes the base of a grand monument to the Emperor Claudius and two extraordinary bronze crayfish. Down in the basements, you can admire some of the city's Gallo-Roman walls, and an alarming display of Gallo-Roman ex-votos from a shrine near Senlis, including countless hands, feet and heads, and male genitalia under raised tunics – seemingly venereal diseases were common. The Gothic gallery contains medieval statuary, none finer than the so-called 13th-century *Tête de Senlis*, in which the sculptor conveyed exceptional maturity and wisdom.

On Picardy's Border with the Ile de France

The **Abbaye de Chaalis** contains the **Musée Jacquemart-André** (*museum open Mar–11 Nov daily 10.30–12.30 and 2–6; rest of the year open Sun only 10.30–12.30 and 1.30–5.30; park open same days 10–7; adm*), an art collection founded by the same Nélie Jacquemart-André as the Musée Jacquemart-André in Paris (*see p.160*). The elegant 18th-century Abbaye de Chaalis, adopted as her country home a decent period after the religious community had left, doesn't contain the same wealth of masterpieces, but in the grounds pay a visit to the small Gothic chapel containing some delicate ceiling frescoes of angels, apostles and evangelists by the 16th-century Italian artist Niccolo dell'Abbate, who had come over to France to help Primaticcio decorate the château of Fontainebleau.

Opposite the abbey, **La Mer de Sable** (*open April–Sept, but not every day, and times vary: t 03 44 54 00 96, f 03 44 54 01 75; adm*) consists of an exotic barren landscape of dunes caused by deforestation in the 19th century. It has now been turned into a popular theme park, even if it's not all that well known to English-speaking tourists .

Just off the A1 a short way south of Senlis, the **Parc Astérix** (*open April–Sept most days at least 10–6, but times are complex: t 01 60 77 04 04; adm*) has one of Europe's most terrifying roller-coasters, and will please all children who love the feisty moustachioed cartoon character.

The Château de Chantilly

The Château de Chantilly looks as rich and luscious as the whipped cream invented here. The Romans were the first to build a fort on what was then an island in a bog, replaced with a feudal castle by the Montmorencys. This was rebuilt in the French Renaissance by the Grand Connétable, Anne de Montmorency, under kings François I and Henri II. His granddaughter Charlotte caught the roving eye of Henri IV who thought the best way to have his evil way with her would be to marry her off to an obliging husband, Henri de Bourbon-Condé. The plan backfired when the groom refused to recognize the king's *droit de seigneur*, and the king showed his displeasure by exiling the young couple. They were able to return to Chantilly after the king's death and left the estate to their son, best known as the Grand Condé, who brought the château its greatest fame, commissioning gardens and fountains from Le Nôtre.

The Renaissance château, however, was destroyed at the Revolution, then rebuilt, only to be destroyed again in 1848. The elegant mess you see today is the fifth edition, the former bog turned into a delightful mirror of a lake.

The castle contains the **Musée Condé** (*open daily exc Tues 10–6; adm*), which boasts one of the best art collections in France outside the Louvre. The splendid Italian Renaissance selection includes works by Annibale Carracci, Palma Vecchio, Raphael, Andrea del Sarto, Filippino Lippi, Masolino and Sassetta. Perugino is represented by a sad-sweet Virgin, Botticelli by a very linear *Autumn*, Piero di Cosimo by a *Portrait of Simonetta Vespucci* wearing a viper around her neck. There are exceptional French works too, by the likes of François Clouet, Watteau and Poussin. Ingres's *Antioches et Stratonice* is a startling piece of kitsch. Among some exceptional portraits, you can admire Talleyrand; Molière rendered by Mignard; Louis XIV shown by Rigaud daintily lifting his fleur-de-lys skirts; and the Gérard portrait of Bonaparte as First Consul. The château harbours some of the finest illuminated works of the Middle Ages, and the jewel of the whole collection is the *Très Riches Heures du Duc de Berry*, the unparalleled masterpiece of early 15th-century illumination. You're only permitted to see a well-made facsimile, but you can still admire the detail of their fairytale interpretations of 15th-century French châteaux.

The grandson of the Grand Condé, convinced that he would be reincarnated as a horse, gave Chantilly one of the most palatial stables in the world, the **Grandes Ecuries**, now the **Musée Vivant du Cheval** (*open daily 10.30–5.30, April–Oct daily 10.30–6.30; adm*), where you can admire beautifully groomed steeds of nearly every conceivable breed. There are also three dressage demonstrations daily, and over 30 rooms packed full of horsey artefacts and toys.

Beauvais

Beauvais lies a bit out on a limb among the cereal plains on the western side of the Oise *département*. The little city was devastated by Second World War bombing, but it is of particular interest if you are hunting down all the great cathedrals in northern France. You actually only get half a cathedral here, but what it lacks in length it makes up for in height. Beauvais' **Cathedral St-Pierre** was a work of staggering vanity – it is the cathedral with the tallest Gothic vaulting in the world, over 150ft in height. Walk inside and you may well get vertigo from looking *up*. Begun in 1227, work continued until the end of the 16th century. Unfortunately the pillars and buttresses proved inadequate to support the huge weight of the towering masonry; the nave kept collapsing, and what remains is usually clad in scaffolding. There are outstanding stained glass windows around the choir, especially those with backgrounds of cobalt blue and purple, and one of the most elaborate of mechanical clocks.

The Musée Départemental de l'Oise, housed in the late-Gothic bishops' palace, contains the **Musée des Beaux-Arts** (*open daily 10–12 and 2–6; closed Tues and public hols*). From a beautiful 1st-century Gaulish warrior via the comical late 15th-century ceramic knight, on past the grandiose Italian works to those of the French Romantics, this museum reserves plenty of surprises. The **Galerie Nationale de la Tapisserie** (*open daily 10–12 and 2–6; closed Tues and public hols*), at the opposite end of the cathedral, recalls the fact that Beauvais became a highly reputed tapestry-making town back in Louis XIV's reign.

The Northeast

16

The Northeast

Highlights

1 The Champagne Wine Routes
2 Troyes and its artistic treasures
3 Verdun's First World War memorials
4 Nancy's Ancien Régime and
   Art Nouveau glamour
5 Strasbourg's splendours
6 The absurdly cute Alsace wine route
7 The stained glass in Metz cathedral

Food and Wine

Champagne is synonymous with its sparkling wine, but also produces some fine cheeses, notably soft and creamy Chaource and Langres from the south of the region, while the **Ardennes** has become almost synonymous with pâtés made from game such as wild boar, venison or hare.

Lorraine is famous for its creamy egg and bacon flan, quiche Lorraine. Its pork specialities include potée Lorraine, which features all manner of pork cuts. Damsons, cherries and blueberries are widely grown, as well as *mirabelles*, little yellow plums which go into the region's best-known liqueur, Mirabelle de Lorraine. The vineyards around Toul produce some decent wines, including a rosé, Vin Gris. For those with a sweet tooth, there are buttery madeleines from Commercy and the alcohol-soaked baba au rhum.

Alsace offers choucroute, beer and some great white wines from riesling and gewürztraminer grapes. Neighbouring Germany influences much of the cuisine, with overgenerous portions of pork in many a dish; bäeckoffe is a copious, aromatic stew of pork, mutton and beef combined with large potatoes, onions and garlic marinated in Riesling. Foie gras is also closely associated with Alsace. Extremely smelly Munster is the tastiest Alsace cheese.

Among sweet specialities, gingerbread is popular, while Alsace's fruit brandies, sometimes known as *alcools blancs*, are used to flavour puddings or drunk as a *digéstif*.

Travel east from Paris and the landscapes unroll like a three-act play. The action opens with Champagne and its glamorous vineyards, where the dramatis personae include three rival sisters: jewel-like Troyes, bustling Reims and businesslike Epernay, the latter the best place to visit the big champagne houses.

Act Two is the surprisingly pretty countryside of Lorraine, one of the French regions least known to English-speaking tourists, but packed with historical resonance for the French thanks to Joan of Arc, Verdun, General de Gaulle and the Cross of Lorraine. World famous crystal Baccarat and Lalique is produced here. Lorraine also boasts several surprising cities that deserve to be better known, starting with Nancy and her Art Nouveau finery, but not forgetting Metz, Bar-le-Duc and Lunéville.

The Vosges, the red sandstone range that divides Alsace from Lorraine and the Rhine valley from the rest of France, add a theatrical backdrop to Act III: gorgeous little Alsace, a French curiosity – so full of Kaffee and Kuchen culture, and yet the Alsatians would be offended to be considered German nowadays. Strasbourg, Alsace's capital and now one of the capitals of the European Union, has one of the most uplifting of all Gothic cathedrals; Colmar holds the most devastating Crucifixion in Western art. Around them, absurdly picturesque timberframe and geranium-crazed wine villages lie below the forested Vosges slopes with their romantic ruined red castles.

Getting There

By plane: From Britain, there are direct flights from London-Gatwick to Strasbourg via Air France, t 0845 0845 111, www.airfrance.co.uk. Mulhouse in southern Alsace also has an important international airport which it shares with Basel in Switzerland. There are direct flights to Basel-Mulhouse from Edinburgh and New York (Newark). There are smaller airports at Reims, Troyes, Nancy and Belfort. Luxembourg is just over the region's northern frontier.

By train: This region doesn't have the best train links with Paris. Trains from Paris-Gare de l'Est stop at Epernay, Châlons-en-Champagne, Bar-le-Duc, Toul, Nancy, Lunéville, Saverne and Strasbourg. Trains from Paris-Gare de l'Est stop at Troyes, Chaumont, Belfort and Mulhouse.

By road: Coming from the Channel ports, the A26 links Calais with Reims. The A4 links Paris with Reims, Châlons-en-Champagne, Verdun and Metz before heading down to Strasbourg. The A5 links Paris with Troyes. Motorways also link the main towns within each region.

Reims

Closely linked with the bubbly stuff, Reims (sometimes spelt Rheims in English) lies in the flat Vesle valley below some of Champagne's prettiest slopes. The cathedral has been declared a UNESCO World Heritage sight, and the wide shopping streets around make up in bustle what they lack in beauty.

History

Settled by the Remi tribe in Celtic times, and an important city on the Roman Empire's eastern border, Reims' Christian history began in 496 (or 498 – historians aren't sure) when the king of the Franks, Clovis, was baptized by Bishop Rémi, who at the same time granted the divine right of the French kings to rule. Down the centuries, French monarchs would come to be crowned in Reims in the *sacre* or coronation ceremony.

Reims continued to grow in importance in the Middle Ages. The local sheep brought a thriving textile trade, and Reims cathedral would count as one of the greatest building enterprises of the 13th century. The drapers' city became a university town in 1547. In Napoleon's last desperate bid to regain power in 1814, Reims saw a late if futile victory, on 13 March. Through the 19th century the champagne and textiles made the city fat and prosperous.

Much of Reims' historic centre was reduced to rubble in the First World War. Taken briefly by the Germans in 1914, the French then managed to hold on to the city, but it was so close to the front that it inevitably suffered. During one week around Easter 1917, it was pounded by 25,000 shells. A large percentage of houses disappeared, and the cathedral was reduced to a skeleton. More destruction followed in the Second World War, if on a smaller scale. At least Reims had the honour of witnessing the signing of the Germans' unconditional surrender at Eisenhower's headquarters on 7 May 1945. In 1962 President Charles de Gaulle and the Chancellor Konrad Adenauer officially celebrated French and German reconciliation at Reims cathedral. In 1991 the cathedral, the adjoining Palais du Tau and the basilica of St-Rémi were placed on UNESCO's World Heritage list.

Touring Reims

Known as the cathedral of angels, **Reims Cathedral** (1221–1311) is a staggering achievement, one of the most vertical and successful Gothic cathedrals ever built and covered with dazzling sculpture. The central portal is dedicated to the Virgin, the left one to local Christian martyrs and to angels – including the much-photographed *Ange au Sourire*, with its sickly smile – while the right one shows the Christ of the Last Judgement. The statuary on the higher level is even more exceptional. The central scene of David and Goliath is still extraordinary, and up above, the row of kings has a truly splendid dignity. These figures, over 15ft in height, represent the kings of France; the baptism of Clovis takes centre stage. High up in the niches on the buttresses you can make out a row of massive open-winged angels, hence the cathedral's nickname.

Most unusually, the brilliant carving continues on the inner side of the west façade. As you enter, look back to see a wall of niches filled with remarkable statues. Some of the most arresting are knights in chain mail. Unfortunately much of the Gothic stained glass was destroyed in the First World War, but much has been restored, and Chagall produced the striking stained-glass window in the end chapel of the choir.

Many of the figures on the cathedral façade turn out to be copies. The originals, superlative pieces of Gothic sculpting, are the glory of the museum in the former archbishops' palace, the **Palais du Tau** (*open July–Aug daily 9.30–6.30; mid-Mar–June and Sept–mid-Nov daily 9.30–12.30 and 2–6; mid-Nov–mid-Mar daily 10–12 and 2–5; adm*). The museum also houses beautiful tapestries and a splendid treasure that includes a 12th-century chalice used for royal coronations.

The **Musée des Beaux-Arts** (*open daily exc Tues 10–12 and 2–6; adm*) contains a rich collection in the drab surroundings of an 18th-century building that could do with a clean. Look for Cranach's studies of princes and dukes of the Holy Roman Empire, a splendid collection of Flemish masters, and 17th-century works by Philippe de Champaigne, Simon Vouet and Le Nain, who painted scenes of common, everyday life. The 19th century is well represented by Boudin, Jongkind and Pissarro along with numerous paintings of trees by water by Courbet.

Reims' **shopping boulevards** lie at the northern end of town, with **Cours J-B Langlet** as the major artery, where countless cafés, brasseries and shops stand shoulder to shoulder. East of here you will find the set-piece squares that more or less survived the bombardments: **Place Royale** is the most ordered, with a statue of Louis XV at its centre. Scrappier **Place du Forum** contains the vestiges of the Roman city, including the underground vaulted **cryptoporticus** (*open 15 June–15 Sept daily exc Mon 2–5*).

Be prepared to devote a couple of hours to **Hôtel Le Vergeur** (*guided tours in English; open daily exc Mon 2–6; adm*). Heavily restored, the house dates from the Gothic period, and was built in what was once the rich bourgeois quarter of Reims. Nicolas Le Vergeur altered it to Renaissance tastes in the 16th century. In the 19th it belonged to the Veuve Clicquot-Ponsardin clan, but at the start of the 20th century it was bought by a German champagne heir, Hugues Krafft, who travelled around the world building up his art collection. He recovered fragments of historic churches and homes in Reims destroyed in the First World War – numerous depictions and models of the city show how it once looked.

Getting Around

From Britain, the most practical way to get to Reims is to drive from Calais down the A26. Reims' airport (**t** 03 26 07 15 15) is for internal flights only. The train between Paris-Gare de l'Est and Reims takes 1hr 30mins. The A4 links the two cities. For bus information in Reims, **t** 03 26 88 25 38.

Tourist Information

Reims: 2 Rue Guillaume de Machault, **t** 03 26 77 45 25, **f** 03 26 77 45 17, *www.tourisme.fr/reims.*

Shopping

Reims main commercial centre covers Rue Carnot, Rue de Vesle, Rue Condorcet and Rue de Talleyrand. Food markets take place on Av Jean Jaurès (*Sun until 1pm*), and Place du Boulingrin (*Wed and Sat until 2pm*). There is a flea market the first Sun of every month.

Where to Stay

Reims ✉ 51100

Luxury–Expensive

****Boyers' Les Crayères**, 64 Bd Henry Vasnier, **t** 03 26 82 80 80, **f** 03 26 82 65 52. Outrageously expensive, but the height of sophistication and luxury, both for the cuisine and the rooms, set in a grand little château built for the Pommery family early in the 20th century.

****Grand Hôtel des Templiers**, 22 Rue des Templiers, **t** 03 26 88 55 08, **f** 03 26 47 80 60. At roughly half the price of Les Crayères, this neo-Gothic hotel is still expensive, but full of style. It even manages to fit in a pool.

****L'Assiette Champenoise**, 40 Av Paul Vaillant-Couturier, 51430 Tinqueux, **t** 03 26 84 64 64, **f** 03 26 04 15 69, *infos@chateau-muire.com*. On the western edge of town, expanded from a 19th-century neo-Gothic mansion. It has 62 reasonably priced rooms and prides itself on its indoor pool and its high-quality cuisine.

Moderate

****Hôtel de la Paix**, 9 Rue Buirette, **t** 03 26 40 04 08, **f** 03 26 47 75 04. Large Best Western hotel down a few notches, with comfortable rooms in the heart of the action.

Inexpensive

***Le Crystal**, 86 Place Drouet-d'Erlon, **t** 03 26 88 44 44, **f** 03 26 47 49 28. Well-located, relatively peaceful hotel with a flowery courtyard, but no restaurant.

***Azur Hotel**, 9 Rue des Ecrvées, **t** 03 26 47 43 39, **f** 03 26 88 57 19. Central, cheap and well run.

Cheap

Hôtel Linguet, 14 Rue Linguet, **t** 03 26 47 31 89. Family-run and cheaper still.

Eating Out

There are innumerable brasseries and cafés along the main boulevards.

Au Petit Comptoir, 17 Rue de Mars, **t** 03 26 40 58 58, **f** 03 26 58 26 19. Distinguished *bistrot* serving old-fashioned dishes and good-value champagne. *Closed Sat lunch*.

Le Drouet, **t** 03 26 88 56 39. Also has a good reputation.

Entertainment and Nightlife

Opéra Cinema, 3 Rue T-Dubois, **t** 03 26 7 29 36. Shows non-dubbed films.

Cinéma Gaumont, 72 Place Drouet d'Erlon, **t** 03 26 47 32 02. Non-dubbed films every Tues. Place Drouet d'Erlon is lined with brasseries and cafés.

Cactus Café, 47 Rue des Capuchins, **t** 03 26 88 16 99. Mellow Tex-Mex bar. *Open daily 11am–12.30am, Fri 11am–1.30am, Sat 4pm–1.30am; closed Sun*.

Le Gaulois, 2–4 Place Drouet d'Erlon. Cocktails and ice cream.

In the summer, as part of **Les Flâneries Musicales d'Été**, there are over 120 classical music concerts, many of which are free. Contact Reims Tourist Board (**t** 03 26 77 45 25, **f** 03 26 77 45 27) for more information.

Among the outer boulevards stands the substantial Gallo-Roman **Porte de Mars**, sadly isolated by traffic at the end of the Boulevard Foch. Beyond, the neo-Romanesque **Chapelle Foujita** (*open 2 May–Oct daily exc Wed 2–6; adm*) is covered with wall paintings and stained glass by the Japanese artist Foujita, who converted to Christianity after a mystical experience in St-Rémi, and only began work on his chapel in 1965, at the age of 80.

Tucked away behind the station, the **Musée de la Reddition** (*open daily exc Tues 10–12 and 2–6; adm*) contains the room in which the Second World War officially came to an end. On 7 May 1945, in a technical college serving as Allied headquarters, General Eisenhower had the commanders of the German army, navy and air force sign their surrender. The news was announced simultaneously in the Allied capitals on 8 May 1945. The adjoining museum concentrates on the events that led up to the German capitulation.

The main focus in the southern half of the centre is the **Basilique St-Rémi**, a massive Romanesque church consecrated in 1049 by Pope Leo IX, that has just about managed to preserve its dignity among the apartment blocks. Supported by later Gothic buttresses, the interior is darkly atmospheric, cavernous even, with only a few small openings. Other Gothic additions are clearly visible in the ceiling vaults and in the choir, but the Romanesque carved capitals are harder to make out. Some rare Romanesque stained glass has been preserved in the choir, where you can see the grand tomb for St Rémi, who figures along with Clovis and the 12 peers witnessing the coronation. These ornate statues only date from the 17th century and the tomb had to be put back together again after the Revolution.

The **Musée St-Rémi** (*open daily 2–6.30; adm*), the region's archaeological and historical museum, occupies large parts of the monastery next door. Just one or two rooms

The Making of Champagne – A Fragile and Explosive Affair

Between 25,000 and 30,000 hectares are devoted to true champagne vines, the majority of which lie around Reims and Epernay. Makers use three varieties of grapes, pinot noir, meunier and chardonnay: pinot noir is considered the backbone of most champagne, imparting force and character; pinot meunier is known to give a faster maturing wine, and tends to feature in cheaper champagne; when a champagne is made using just chardonnay, the crisp, widely known white grape variety, it is known as *blanc de blancs*.

Up until the first fermentation champagne is made like an ordinary white wine. At the vital second fermentation (the *méthode champenoise*) sugar is added, and the yeast that eats it up creates carbon dioxide – bubbles. For weeks, each bottle is turned a little each day (now mostly by machine) to coax the dead yeast up to the top. When the residue reaches the top, it is frozen, the bottle is opened and the dead yeast pops out (a process known as *dégorgement*). The bottle is topped up with a *liqueur d'expédition*, a little extra champagne mixed with sugar, the level of sweetness dictating whether the champagne will be *brut* (dry), *sec* (sweeter), or *demi-sec* (sweeter still). Tradition has it that we should thank the monk Dom

were saved from the medieval monastery, including the chapterhouse, paved with beautiful period tiles. Gallo-Roman finds feature mosaics and a 4th-century sarcophagus. The cycle of tapestries of scenes from the life of St Rémi is a Gothic delight, with devils dancing in the gardens.

Not far from St-Rémi, the **Ancien Collège des Jésuites** (*guided tours daily exc Tues am and weekend am at 10, 11, 2.15, 3.30 and 4.45; adm*) has retained a good degree of its 17th-century grandeur, including the library and its extravagant Baroque woodwork. The former college also hosts contemporary art exhibitions, and its own **Planétarium** (*shows at weekends and school hols at 2.45, 3.30 and 4.45; adm*).

Champagne Routes Between Reims and Troyes

The champagne vineyards are more attractive than the champagne towns, and there are hundreds of small champagne producers you can call on in the countryside. Epernay, however, has the densest concentration of major houses to visit, while the small town of Ay is packed with even more.

Reims to Epernay

The **Montagne de Reims** natural park encompasses the hills southwest of Reims, its northern and eastern sides densely planted with vines. Tucked away at **Pourcy** you'll find the Maison du Parc, with details on its geology and wildlife in particular. Scattered to the north of Pourcy lie First World War cemeteries. Near Marfaux British and German cemeteries have been quite shockingly laid back to back – white crosses contrasting startlingly with the black ones next to them.

Pérignon, buried at the abbey church of Hautvillers near Epernay, for mastering this tricky process.

Most champagne is left to age for two or three years before coming on the market, but the most prestigious champagnes are kept back still longer. Vintage champagne is made using grapes from a single year. Champagne connoisseurs go for lesser-known names such as Bollinger and Billecart-Salmon, two of the superlative producers. Dom Pérignon is much the best-known top-quality champagne, the top blend of Moët et Chandon.

Many champagne houses have their headquarters in Reims, but only a few are open to the public. The tours tend to be better in Epernay (*see p.678*).

Taittinger, 9 Place St-Nicaise. No need to book. *Open Mar–Nov weekdays 9.30–12 and 2–4.30, weekends and hols 9–11 and 2–5; rest of year weekdays only; adm.*

Piper-Heidsieck, 51 Bd Henry Vasnier. No need to book in advance. *Open daily 9–11.45 and 2–5.15; closed Tues and Wed Dec–Feb; adm.*

Charles Heidsieck, 4 Bd Henry Vasnier, t 03 26 84 43 50. Book in advance.

Pommery, 5 Place du Général Gouraud, **t** 03 26 61 62 55. Book in advance.

Veuve Clicquot, 1 Place des Droits de l'Homme, **t** 03 26 89 54 41. Book in advance.

Tourist Information

Epernay: 7 Av de Champagne, B.P.28, t 03 26 53 33 00, f 03 26 51 95 22.

Châlons-en-Champagne: 3 Quai des Arts, t 03 26 65 17 89, f 03 26 21 72 92.

Château-Thierry: 11 Rue Vallée, t 03 23 83 10 14, f 03 23 83 14 74.

Sézanne: Place de la République, B.P.21, t 03 26 80 51 43, f 03 26 80 54 13.

Where to Stay and Eat

Beaumont-sur-Vesle ✉ 51360

**La Maison du Champagne, t 03 26 03 92 45, f 03 26 03 97 59 (*inexpensive*). A simple little hotel, although some rooms are a bit rough. The food draws in the locals, and the wine list represents many smaller champagne producers (*menus 85–230F*). *Closed 1st half Dec; Feb hols; Sun eve; Tues lunch and Mon.*

Sept-Saulx ✉ 51400

****Le Cheval Blanc, Rue du Moulin, t 03 26 03 90 27, f 03 26 03 97 09 (*expensive*). The 22 well-equipped rooms are in an annexe to this family-run inn. Excellent classic French cuisine in the restaurant (*menus 180–540F*).

Ambonnay ✉ 51150

**Auberge St-Vincent, 1 Rue St-Vincent, t 03 26 57 01 98, f 03 26 57 81 48

(*inexpensive*). Inn with a few comfortable rooms and a chef who has revived and modernized traditional regional dishes (*menus 140–360F*). *Closed Sun eve and Mon.*

Champillon ✉ 51160

***Royal Champagne, t 03 26 52 87 11, f 03 26 52 89 69, *royalchampagne@relaischateaux.fr* (*moderate*). Old inns don't come much more luxuriously done up than this one, with its intoxicating views above this village just north of Epernay. The restaurant has a very high reputation, the wine list a fabulous array of champagnes (*menus 300–500F*).

Cumières ✉ 51480

Le Caveau, Rue de la Coopérative, t 03 26 54 83 23, f 03 26 54 24 56. Atmospheric restaurant in a cave in a village just west of Hautvillers.

Epernay ✉ 51200

***Le Clos Raymi, 3 Rue Joseph de Venoge, t 03 26 51 00 58, f 03 26 51 18 98. At last in the Champagne wine capital a refined, stylish hotel, set back in its own courtyard in one of the typical brick mansions built for wealthy Epernay merchants, in this case the Chandons. Just seven rooms.

Vinay ✉ 51530

****La Briqueterie, 4 Route de Sézanne, t 03 26 59 99 99, f 03 26 59 92 10 (*expensive*).

Verzenay's landmark is a comical lighthouse sticking out of a sea of steep vine slopes. Built in 1909 and long abandoned, it was given a barrel-shaped annex and reopened in 1999 as an attractive new **wine museum**. It focuses on the vinegrowers with films and commentaries (in French) while the views down the champagne slopes are utterly delightful.

Ay on the north side of the Marne looks rather friendlier than burly Epernay on the south side, and although it is less well known, it's also packed with champagne houses. These include Gosset, which claims to be the oldest, with credentials going back to 1584, and the very exclusive Bollinger, whose headquarters stand by vine-covered slopes on the edge of the town. Unfortunately the only place you can easily visit without an introduction is the **Ay Wine Museum**, with its traditional display on local wine-making.

Epernay's saving grace is the cluster of world-famous champagne houses, pompously seated around big courtyards on the Avenue de Champagne. **Hautvillers**, a short way northwest, is probably the prettiest and best kept of all the champagne

A very smart hotel among the vineyards 7km south of Epernay, with modern comfortable rooms, a splendid stylish restaurant (*menus 250–420F*) and a covered pool with a view.

Châlons-en-Champagne ✉ 51000

Well away from the vines, but it has some cheaper options.

★★Le Pot d'Etain, 18 Place de la République, **t** 03 26 68 09 09, **f** 03 26 68 58 18 (*inexpensive*). A pleasant old town house hotel. Restaurant (*menus 180–470F*). *Closed 16 Jul–8 Aug; Christmas; Sat lunch and Sun.*

★★Le Renard, 24 Place de la République, **t** 03 26 68 03 78, **f** 03 26 64 50 07 (*inexpensive*). Modern rooms and a restaurant which spills out into the main square. *Closed Christmas. Restaurant closed Sat lunch and Sun eve* (*menus 98–350F*).

Le Mesnil-sur-Oger ✉ 51190

Le Mesnil, 2 Rue Pasteur, **t** 03 26 57 95 57, **f** 03 26 57 78 57. A popular restaurant in a village among the vines, with a superb choice of champagnes (*menus 105–360F*). *Closed 15 Aug–8 Sept, 23 Jan–8 Feb, Mon and Tues eve, and Wed.*

Bergères-les-Vertus ✉ 51130

★★★Hostellerie du Mont-Aimé, 4–6 Rue de Vertus, **t** 03 26 52 21 31, **f** 03 26 52 21 39 (*moderate*). On the outside it just looks like a modest roadside village house that's been

tarted up a bit, but inside the atmosphere is comfortable, the 30 rooms are sweet – set around the garden – and the cooking's bright too (*menus 120–360F*). *Closed Feb hols and Sun eve.*

Etoges ✉ 51270

★★★Château d'Etoges, **t** 03 26 59 30 08, **f** 03 26 59 35 57, *etoges1@wanadoo.fr* (*moderate*). This gloriously moated little castle is a classified historic monument, gorgeous to look at behind its walls, with its own smart gardens and own natural springs.

Montmort ✉ 51270

★★Le Cheval Blanc, Rue de la Libération, **t** 03 26 59 10 03, **f** 03 26 59 15 88 (*inexpensive*). Neatly kept by the roadside, an old-fashioned style provincial hotel with reasonable prices. 19 rooms. Restaurant (*menus 98–450F*).

Sézanne ✉ 51120

★★Le Relais Champenois, 157 Rue Notre-Dame, **t** 03 26 80 58 03, **f** 03 26 81 35 32 (*inexpensive*). Doesn't look much, but the welcome and the decoration in the rooms is very bright, and the cuisine makes the most of local produce (*menus 115–250F*).

★★La Croix d'Or, 53 Rue Notre-Dame, **t** 03 26 80 61 10, **f** 03 26 80 65 20 (*inexpensive*). 13 rooms. Reasonable option, with good food (*menus 85–295F*). *Closed 2–17 Jan and Tues.*

villages. Its abbey, now owned by Moët et Chandon, was once home to the celebrated monk Dom Pérignon. His tombstone is by the altar in the well-restored **abbey church**. The epitaph recalls his death in 1715 and his charitable work rather than his winemaking ingenuity.

Around Epernay

Château-Thierry, some way west of Epernay along the Marne but still in champagne-producing territory, was the birthplace of the witty 17th-century poet La Fontaine, best known for his poems based on the classical animal fables of Aesop. He gained the rather wonderful reputation for being 'the least serious man in France'. The town has a museum devoted to his life, his works and time.

The main champagne route leads south from Epernay. Take the famed **Côte des Blancs** along the D10 to Vertus, with busy wine villages along the way. South of Vertus, climb the **Mont-Aimé** for the finest views of the Côte des Blancs and the Marne valley. Head for the further Champagne vine slopes around Sézanne following

Champagne Houses between Reims and Epernay

Moët et Chandon, Epernay (*open throughout the year weekdays 9.30–11.45 and 2–4.45; open April–mid-Nov weekends only; adm*). Informative tour around the enormous cellars, plus a tasting of Napoleon's favourite champagne. Good shop.

Mercier, Epernay, **t** 03 26 51 22 22 (*open all year exc Dec, Jan and Feb Tues and Wed; visits 9.30–11.30 and 2–4.30; adm*). A more relaxing house to visit.

A couple of small family properties are also recommended:

Leclerc-Briant, 67 Rue Chaude Ruelle, Epernay, **t** 03 26 54 45 33. Call in advance to organize a tour down into the deep cellars, or to visit on weekends or public hols.

Achille Princier, 9 Rue Jean Chandon Moët, Epernay, **t** 03 26 54 04 06. 18th-century cellars and one of the oldest presses in Champagne.

Champagne Houses West and South of Epernay

G. Tribaut, 88 Rue d'Eguisheim, Hautvillers, **t** 03 26 59 40 57. A good family-run estate.

Jean-Marie Rigot, in Binson-et-Orquigny, **t** 03 26 58 33 38. Call ahead to make an appointment at this well-established family estate.

Charlier et Fils Aux Foudres de Chêne, 4 Rue des Pervenches, in Montigny-sur-Châtillon, **t** 03 26 58 35 18 (*open daily exc Sun pm and harvest time; adm*). Interesting estate where the family produces champagne using traditional methods.

The Tarlants, in Oeuilly, **t** 03 26 58 30 60. Family estate (since 1687) on the south side of the river, which runs a B&B as well.

Château de Pierry, at Pierry, **t** 03 26 54 05 11. *Dégustations* and visits to the castle. Call to arrange a visit.

Launois Père et Fils, 2 Av Eugène Guillaume, Le Mesnil-sur-Oger, **t** 03 26 57 50 15. Atmospheric family estate. Call to confirm a good time to visit.

a detour west round the marshes of St-Gond. Close to sleepy **Sézanne**, an enormous First World War memorial marks the hillside of **Mondemont-Montgivroux**, a dramatic spot recalling the first French victory of the Marne in September 1914. It was one of the bloodiest confrontations of the war. The French managed to hold the line – at a pivotal moment, thanks to the taxis of Paris transporting troops to the front – causing the Germans to retreat and start digging their trenches.

Troyes

Troyes' splendid historic centre, shaped like a champagne cork, contains a clutch of glorious late-Gothic to Renaissance churches and picturesque streets of timberframed or chequered brick façades. For centuries Troyes was known for its fine textiles production, although it is now famous for its cheap outlet stores. It also has an astounding fine arts collection, one of the major surprises of eastern France.

History

Troyes' history goes back to Gallo-Roman times, but the first man to stand out was Bishop Loup in the 5th century, who offered himself up as a hostage to Attila and his Huns in return for the sparing of his city. Bishops kept power until the counts of Champagne took over in the 10th century, making Troyes their capital; their refined court produced one of the most celebrated poets of medieval Europe, Chrétien de Troyes. The importance of the Champagne counts dwindled when the last heir to the county, Jeanne, was married to the French king in 1284 and the region became part of the French royal domains.

The Treaty of Troyes was signed in the city in 1420, by which the French royal heir, Charles, was stripped of his rights and Henry V of England, married to Charles' sister Catherine, was accepted as heir to the French crown. Henry V died in 1422. Joan of Arc would help stop Henry VI from ruling both sides of the Channel by her support for the young Charles VII of France and she played her part in freeing Troyes from the English. Troyes remained an important commercial and cultural city for centuries to follow, especially in the Renaissance. Bonnet-making took off at the start of the 16th century, and Troyes is still one of France's most important textiles centres.

Getting Around

Troyes has quite good links with Paris via the A5, or by rail; trains from Paris-Gare de l'Est take c. 1 hr 20mins. The A26 from Calais is also convenient.

Tourist Information

Troyes: 16 Bd Carnot, 10000, t 03 25 82 62 70, f 03 25 73 06 81.

Where to Stay

Troyes ✉ 10000
****Hôtel de la Poste, 35 Rue Emile Zola, t 03 25 73 05 05, f 03 25 73 80 76 (expensive). This Best Western hotel has the most stars in town, is the most central of the lot and boasts three restaurants.
***Le Relais St-Jean, 51 Rue Paillot de Montabert, t 03 25 73 89 90, f 03 25 73 88 60. Wonderfully located, delightfully beamed building, tucked away down a narrow street in the centre of the best part of town. No restaurant.

***Le Champ des Oiseaux, 20 Rue Linard Gonthier, t 03 25 80 58 50, f 03 25 80 98 34 (moderate). Stylish timberframed hotel not far from the cathedral, with 12 nicely converted rooms.
**Les Comtes de Champagne, 54–56 Rue de la Monnaie, t 03 25 73 11 70, f 03 25 73 06 02 (inexpensive). A lovely hotel with a warm welcome and a strong sense of history, set in an historic building around an inner courtyard.

Eating Out

Le Valentino, 35 Rue Paillot-de-Montabert, t 03 25 73 14 14. Refined restaurant next to Le Relais St-Jean, which shares the same picturesque charm and also has a lovely courtyard (menus 110–270F). Closed 21 Aug–4 Sept; Jan; Oct–Easter Sat lunch, Sun eve and Mon.
Le Cheval de 3, 31 Rue de la Cité, t 03 25 80 58 23. An appealing small restaurant near the cathedral which offers well-prepared regional dishes in a pleasant dining room.

Touring Troyes

The compact old city is divided in two by the canalized line of the Seine. Northeast of the canal lies the quarter around the **Cathédrale St-Pierre-et-St-Paul**, a broad shouldered Gothic giant that took centuries to complete. It was begun in the 13th century, when the choir and parts of the transepts went up, but the intricate façade shows all the signs of the Flamboyant late Gothic with its decorative pinnacles, buttresses and gargoyles. Joan of Arc is supposed to have witnessed the consecration of the cathedral with King Charles VII in 1429. Much of the fine detail and statuary were destroyed at the Revolution, leaving the Gothic niches empty. The interior is vast, grey and empty, relieved only by the stained glass.

Next door, the former bishops' palace contains the **Musée d'Art Moderne** (*open daily exc Tues and public hols 11–6; adm*), a superb repository of works from 1850 to 1950, gathered by textile tycoon Pierre Lévy: there are portraits by Millet and Courbet, Fauvist canvases, especially by André Derain (a friend of Lévy); a disturbing portrait of the prostitute Yvette by the lesser known Chabaud; works by Soutine and Vuillard, and the Cubist Gris and Metzinger, after which Robert Delaunay's *The Runners* returns to the brilliance of colour and movement. Sculpture is well represented as well, especially with figures from Africa.

On the opposite side of the cathedral, the **Musée des Beaux-Arts** (*open daily exc Tues and public hols 10–12 and 2–6; adm*) occupies the enormous former **abbey of St-Loup**. By comparison with the modern art museum it looks dowdy, but it contains its share of treasures: beautiful Neolithic polished axe heads, the Gallo-Roman bronze Apollon de Vaupoisson, and some of the finest Merovingian jewellery and weapons in the country – the *Trésor de Pouan*, recovered from a 5th-century princess's tomb. The library claims to be one of the oldest public libraries in France (1651), and at the Revolution it received 50,000 works from the abbey of Clairvaux – some unique manuscripts dating back to the 7th century; now the precious books seem imprisoned here and are only reluctantly shown. The fine arts section contains some interesting works, especially by the 17th-century maestro of realism, Philippe de Champaigne; there are also two sweet works by Watteau.

The church of **St-Nizier**, north of the cathedral, is hard to miss with its gaudy tiles. Largely reconstructed, it's a fusion of Gothic and Renaissance, and contains a fine carved Entombment scene typical of the Troyes School. A short way south of the cathedral, the enormous former hospital or **Hôtel-Dieu** houses a splendidly preserved Ancien Régime pharmacy, now the **Musée de la Pharmacie** (*open daily exc Tues and public hols 10–12 and 2–6; adm*).

The star attractions of the lively southern section of historic Troyes are the sculptures and stained glass of a cluster of brilliant late-Gothic churches. Check their opening hours with the tourist office or at the doors, as they vary bizarrely from one church to the next.

The most prominent, **St-Urbain**, cuts quite a dash with its gables and gargoyles in the centre of its own renovated square – it has the rare privilege in Troyes of not being hemmed in by houses. Commissioned by Pope Urban IV on the spot where his father had a cobbler's shop, the church was built in the second half of the 13th century, although it has been heavily restored and added to, and the main façade is a late-19th-century recreation. The interior is rather disappointing, with just a few bits of old stained glass, and some of Pope Urban's remains buried in the choir.

South of St-Urbain, **Rue Emile Zola** is the city's main commercial artery, but just a short walk west, by the **covered market**, the soaring twisting slate-covered spire of **St-Rémy** stands out. Like St-Urbain it has recently been scrubbed clean. Inside, the grisaille painted wood panels add 16th-century decoration to the Gothic forms. Beyond St-Rémi is **Ste-Madeleine** which, although the original was built late in the 12th century, was so redone in the early 16th century that it looks a typical late-Gothic work, with a few Renaissance touches added, and much heavy 19th-century reworking. A truly staggering Flamboyant Gothic rood screen dripping with stone decoration dominates the interior. By contrast, the larger figures of the Crucifixion on top of the rood screen balustrade have a powerful simplicity to them. The whole work is attributed to the sculptor Jean Gailde and dated to between 1508 and 1517. There are also fine stained-glass windows.

In the main shopping area, squeeze along the Ruelle des Chats where the gables either side of the street virtually touch each other. In the thick of the action, the church of **St-Jean** is where the marriage of Catherine of France to the future King Henry V of England was celebrated on 2 June 1420. Long neglected, the battered Gothic edifice has been recently restored inside. It contains splendid stained-glass windows, some attributed to the local master craftsman Linard Gontier.

The church of **St-Pantaléon** is full of virtuoso pieces, and its fine architecture is Gothic bent to Renaissance shapes. The interior has been turned into something of a sculpture museum, with some of the statues made specially for the church, such as the theatrical stone pair peering down from one gallery, while others were recovered from local churches destroyed at the Revolution. The grisaille and gold stained-glass windows attributed to Macadré contain some memorable scenes, such as the sacrifice of the Christians to the lions.

Opposite, the **Musée Historique de Troyes et de la Champagne et Musée de la Bonneterie** (*open daily exc Tues and public hols 10–12 and 2–6; adm*) occupies the Hôtel de Vauluisant, one of the finest stone-fronted houses in Troyes, set around a courtyard hidden behind high walls and a massive gateway. Splendid old statues and medieval decorated tiles feature, while a whole section is devoted to Troyes' bonnet- and sock-making traditions.

The elegant **Musée de l'Outil et de la Pensée Ouvrière** (*open daily 9–12 and 2–6; adm*) extends around the lovely chequered brick and limestone courtyard of the Hôtel de Mauroy. Once an orphanage, where orphans made bonnets and stockings, in 1746 it became the first place in Troyes to be mechanized. The museum is dedicated to the tools of craftsmen. Some of the most appealing displays are those of the glove-makers, with an amusing collection of wooden hands, and of the farriers, who liked their tools decorated with horses.

The Côte des Bars

Chaource, south of Troyes, has probably the greatest masterpiece of the Champagne's school of sculptors: a remarkable Entombment group hidden in a little corner chapel of its church. Rarely does art plunge so directly into the drama of Christ's death – two guards stand menacingly on either side of the door, and the figures around the laid-out body show an intense, pale grief, their eyes fixed on the corpse. Two patrons kneel miserably to one side. This group was made around 1515 by the anonymous Master of Chaource, sometimes known as the Master of the Sad Faces. The gilded 16th-century carved Nativity in an extravagant Renaissance side chapel is also beautifully executed, including a comical dromedary with a serpent's neck. In addition, the church has exceptional stained glass.

In wine terms, the area around Bar-sur-Seine and Les Riceys is perhaps better known for the curiosity of its exclusive rosé wine than for champagne, but the champagne vineyards extend down the valley just into northern Burgundy around **Châtillon-sur-Seine**.

The little town of **Essoyes** on the River Ource became home to Renoir, as this was where Aline Charigot was born – one of Renoir's most important models and his wife. The couple bought a property here in 1885 and came frequently. Renoir painted many works around these parts, and Aline and Auguste are both buried in the cemetery. So too are their three sons, including Jean Renoir, the great French film director who emigrated to the United States during the Second World War. The workshop at the end of the garden has been turned into a small museum, the **Atelier Renoir** (*open July–Aug daily 2.30–6.30; rest of period Easter–1 Nov, weekends and public hols only 2.30–6.30; adm*), run by enthusiastic locals, although don't expect to see any of Renoir's art. An annual prize supports a young artist, who is given the studio above the museum. Essoyes itself is quite a cheerful little place, proud of its champagne-making tradition. A pyramid of barrels stands in the middle of the river running through town, and there is a rather dull **Maison de la Vigne** (*open Easter–All Saints' daily 2.30–6.30; adm*).

Continuing south along the Seine valley, the area of champagne production stretches a finger into northern Burgundy, but the main attraction here is the most fabulous of Iron Age treasures, found in tombs on the **Mont Lassois** above Vix. This was clearly an important strategic site at the end of the first Iron Age, or Hallstatt, period. A citadel was erected here, protected by a complex system of defences, and a number of major tombs dating from the end of the 6th century BC and start of the 5th century BC have been excavated.

The treasures are now in the **Musée du Châtillonnais** in nearby **Châtillon-sur-Seine**, (*open mid-June–mid-Sept daily 9–12 and 1.30–6; April–mid-June and mid-Sept–mid-Nov daily exc Tues 9–12 and 2–6; rest of year daily exc Tues 10–12 and 2–5; adm*). The **Vix bronze vase** is the highlight, discovered in 1953, and it's as tall as a human being. Tongues stick out from the two fantastic handles, belonging to two scary figures with plaited hair. They are said to represent two of the three snakey-haired Gorgons, who here have serpents for legs, while serpents coil around their biceps. A frieze of

Getting Around

To get to the Côte des Bars by public transport, you'll have to take a bus from Troyes.

Tourist Information

Bar-sur-Seine: 33 Rue Gambetta, t 03 25 29 94 43, f 03 25 29 75 43.
Les Riceys: Rue du Pont, Riceys Haut, t/f 03 25 29 15 38.
Chaource: 20 Rue du Pont de Pierre, t 03 25 40 10 67, f 03 25 40 00 22.

Where to Stay and Eat

Chaource ✉ 10210

Les Fontaines, 1 Rue des Fontaines, t 03 25 40 00 85, f 03 25 40 01 80. For a good, cheap country lunch (*menus 58–140F*).

Fouchères ✉ 10260

B&B Le Prieuré, Place de l'Eglise, t/f 03 25 40 98 09 (*inexpensive*). Full of history and life, a priory turned farm with some simple, but characterful, excellent value rooms in a village on the west bank of the Seine between Troyes and Bar-sur-Seine.

Bourguignons ✉ 10110

Gradelets' B&B, t 03 25 29 84 43. Flowers everywhere in the small rooms of this house set just towards the Seine outside a village 2 km north of Bar-sur-Seine. The array of teapots in the breakfast room is staggering, and Mme can provide you with advice on good local champagne estates.

Les Riceys ✉ 10340

**Le Magny, Route de Tonnerre, t 03 25 29 38 39, f 03 25 29 11 72 (*inexpensive*). A pleasant cheap option.

Bar-sur-Aube ✉ 10200

Hôtel St-Pierre, 5 Rue St-Pierre, t 03 25 27 13 58. Likeable, cheap and basic. 12 rooms. Restaurant (*menus 70–21F*). *Closed most of Jan and Feb; Oct–April Tues eve and Wed; May–Sept Wed lunch.*

charioteers runs round the edge. The vase was probably made in Etruria in northern Italy, possibly to contain wine, and possibly to be given as a gift to the princess controlling the tin trade route in the late Hallstatt era: her death mask shows a long thin face, graceful apart from her funny teeth. Other treasures from the tomb include a diadem torque, a unique work of Celtic jewellery with two tiny winged horses carved at either end. The Tumulus de la Garenne, discovered in 1846, also yielded some startling treasures, not least of which was a chariot. There are also some fine Gallo-Roman objects in the museum, such as an elegant if headless Venus and fragments of a scene showing Europa being whisked away by Zeus disguised as a bull.

'The abbey is now a prison,' explains the sign at the entrance to **Clairvaux** just south of Bar-sur-Aube, a sad fate for one of the most powerful and influential monasteries of medieval Europe. This was the most important of the four daughters of Cîteaux and the strict reforming Cistercians, founded in 1115 by the austere and sour Bernard de Clairvaux, confidant of popes, tub thumper for the Second Crusade and archenemy of Peter Abelard. Because of him, the place gained the highest reputation for imposing Christian rigour, often as opposed to learning and art, both of which Bernard disdained. Ransacked by Huguenots in the 16th century, the monastery was turned into a glassworks at the Revolution. In 1808 the State decided to turn it into a prison, although it is still possible to visit to learn about the exceptional power the abbey and its founder once enjoyed.

La Boisserie at Colombey-les-Deux-Eglises (*open year round exc Jan daily exc Tues 10–12 and 2–5.30; adm*), 16 km due east of Bar-sur-Aube, is haunted by the spirit of arguably the most important Frenchman of the 20th century, Charles de Gaulle, who bought this property in 1933, and would retire here after losing power both in 1946 and in 1969. He died here on 9 November 1970 and was buried in the village cemetery. He wrote in his memoirs of his attraction towards the calm, sad, wide horizons of the Champagne region and its unchanging, unpretentious villages, of which Colombey-les-Deux-Eglises is so typical. You only see a few rooms on the guided tour, the salon with plenty of photographs, the dining room, and the study where de Gaulle worked. A large Cross of Lorraine on the hill honours his importance in the fight to liberate France from the Nazis.

The Upper Marne

If you follow the Marne back to its source from St-Dizier up into the most south-easterly corner of the Champagne region, one or two little surprises lie along the way, notably the historic towns of Chaumont and Langres. Other little pleasures include the Château de Cirey-sur-Blaise, closely associated with Voltaire, and even the odd patch of vineyard.

The **Château de Cirey-sur-Blaise** (*open 15 June–15 Sept daily 2.30–6.30; adm*), in the Blaise valley, may be intimately linked with Voltaire, the brightest flame of the French Enlightenment, but he shares star billing with the exceptional Marquise du Châtelet who was attracted to some of the most brilliant minds of her age and seduced them, mind and body. She offered Voltaire refuge at her husband's pretty little Louis XIII-style brick château after his *Lettres anglaises* caused a furore at the French court. The marquise and Voltaire began their stormy relationship in 1733, and Voltaire was to stay here for long periods until 1749. Together the lovers translated Newton's major work on gravity from Latin into French, and Voltaire wrote plays, having them performed up in the tiny theatre in the château's eaves (now being restored). Much of the time Voltaire spent with the marquise was happy: he called her his '*divine Emilie*', and they entertained society figures. However, all ended sadly when the marquise died in childbirth at the age of 42. (The father was Voltaire's friend, the now-forgotten poet St-Lambert.)

Old **Chaumont** on its hill is built in blindingly grey-white stone, with an enormous 19th-century railway viaduct (*you can walk along one level*) spanning the Suize valley to one side. The old centre may be small, but it has character, despite the modern blocks pressing in round it. Many houses have a distinctive hanging half-stair tower, and the grand 18th-century hôtels also have splendid carriage gateways leading into their little courtyards. The town developed from a keep built by the counts of Champagne; below this, a small **museum** contains a mixed bag of archaeological bits, paintings, and a room devoted to the Bouchardon family of sculptors from Chaumont. However, the most intriguing art is hidden in the **Basilique St-Jean**, which develops from Gothic to Flamboyant Gothic as you walk from nave to choir, with a

Tourist Information

Chaumont: Place du Général de Gaulle, t 03 25 03 80 80, f 03 25 32 00 99.

Langres: Square Olivier Lahalle, t 03 25 87 67 67, f 03 25 87 73 33.

Where to Stay and Eat

Arc-en-Barrois ✉ 52210

A delightful little village to stop in close to the A5 motorway, with two appealing hotels and a small golf course.

***Château d'Arc-en-Barrois, t 03 25 02 29 20, f 03 25 02 73 00 (*moderate*). Built for French royalty in the 19th century, walled off from the interesting village church, this is a very posh, clean-stoned château. The rooms are comfortable and stylish, the naff pictures an aberration. The large dining rooms are decorated with some striking paintings of naval battles.

Hôtel du Parc, 1 Place Moreau, t 03 25 02 53 07, f 03 25 02 42 84. In the centre of the village as well, this former hunting lodge looks stylish too. Inside, it's a rustic, cheap inn. You can eat out on the terrace on warm sunny days (*menus 100–160F*). Closed Feb; 7 Mar–31 May Sun eve and Mon; Sept–Jan Tues eve and Wed.

Chaumont and Chamarandes ✉ 52000

**Au Rendez-Vous des Amis, 4 Place du Tilleul, Chamarandes, t 03 25 32 20 20, f 03 2502 60 90 (*inexpensive*). By the church in this quiet village by the Marne just below Chaumont town, this well-flowered hotel looks simple on the outside but has 19 brightly redone rooms and serves good local cuisine (*menus 95–280F*). Closed most of Aug; Christmas; Fri eve and Sat.

**Hôtel de France, 25 Rue Toupot de Beveaux, t 03 25 03 01 11, f 03 25 32 35 80 (*inexpensive*). Comfortable modern option in the centre of Chaumont. Restaurant (*menus 125–185F*). Closed Mon lunch and Sun.

Langres ✉ 52200

**Le Cheval Blanc, 4 Rue de l'Estres, t 03 25 87 07 00, f 03 25 87 23 13, cblangres@aol.com (*inexpensive*). With its medieval abbey buildings turned auberge at the Revolution, this lovely central hotel has five delightful little vaulted rooms, plus more conventional ones. The restaurant, named after Diderot, serves inventive cuisine (*menus 140–180F*). Closed Tues eves exc July and Aug; and Wed lunch.

---

touch of Renaissance thrown in. Carved stone setpieces stand out, including a dramatic late 15th-century Entombment scene, a hilarious Tree of Jesse in stone, the kings perched on branches, and wildly pendant keystones in the choir. Other Chaumont curiosities are its collections of *crèches* (nativity scenes) and of old posters.

Fortified **Langres**, dramatically situated on a hilltop near the source of the Marne, wasn't always such a backwater. St Benignus is said to have established a church here way back in the 2nd century. One of the earliest bishops, 4th-century St Didier, was martyred defending his city, but retained his dignity even after having his head chopped off – legend has it that he simply picked up his severed bonce and rode off. Located on the frontier with Lorraine, Franche-Comté and Burgundy, Langres long served as an important outpost of the French kingdom; hence the substantial fortifications. One of the best ways to appreciate Langres is by walking around its **ramparts**. The recorded tour (in French or English) from the tourist office takes about two hours. Langres is also immensely proud of having been the birthplace, in 1713, of that great Enlightenment figure and author of the Encyclopédie, Denis Diderot, the son of a cutlery maker, although after his schooling in Langres, he rarely returned.

Into Lorraine via the French Ardennes

The Meuse River to Verdun

The Meuse, the major river of western Lorraine, flows in a gentle valley from the Langres plateau north. Here we follow its course from the Belgium border south through the French Ardennes towards its source. The sleepy, shabby towns along the way are slowly being restored to life. Joan of Arc was born here, at Domrémy.

The French Ardennes, tucked between Champagne and Belgium, has known hard times more recently: the Germans invaded France here not once, not twice, but three times between 1870 and 1940. A little horn of French territory sticks up into Belgium north of Charleville. This is by far the most dramatic stretch of the Meuse in France, the river having to dig its way through tough rock. This is slate-mining country, and you can't fail to notice one enormous wall of slate just south of **Givet**, the prettiest French town along the Meuse, near the Belgian border. Many of the houses in the old centre were built in an attractive mix of brick and local blue-grey stone. As well as walking along the quays, you might visit the **Centre Européen des Métiers d'Art** (*open daily exc Mon and Sun am 10–12 and 2.30–6; adm*), a substantial craft centre.

Heading south, the little towns of Haybes, Fumay, Revin and Monthermé were all built in meanders in the Meuse and are linked by the road along the densely wooded high banks of the valley. **Fumay**'s small **Musée de l'Ardoise** (*open April–Oct daily 10–6; Nov–Mar daily 2–6; adm*) pays homage to the slate mines which closed in 1971.

The best way to appreciate the impressive star-shaped fortifications of **Rocroi**, west of Revin, is from the sky but should you fail to arrive by helicopter, a tour of the ramparts on foot is the next best thing. The streets of this model of a military town head out like the spokes of a wheel from the central square with its classical church, blue-tinted stone well and recently rebuilt covered market. The **Museé de la Bataille de Rocroi** (*open April–Oct daily 10–12 and 2–6; Nov–Mar daily 2–5; commentary in English; adm*), in a late 17th-century guard house, presents a short recorded show on the terrible Battle of Rocroi fought outside the town in 1643, a pivotal moment in the long power struggle between the Hapsburgs and the Bourbons. In seven dreadful hours of fighting, some 10,000 men died; 8,000 out of 18,000 troops on the Spanish side were killed, another 7,000 taken prisoner. The French victory, which secured the kingdom, came in the year that Louis XIV inherited the throne.

Charleville's central Place Ducale has wonderfully grand 17th-century brick façades topped by tall sloping slate roofs – more than a match for Paris' Place des Vosges (and designed by Clément Métezeau, brother of Louis credited with the great Parisian square). In one corner, the gorgeously presented **Musée de l'Ardenne** (*open daily exc Mon 10–12 and 2–6; adm*) has little to retain your attention, except for the workings of the marionette scenes that appear on the hour below the large clock on another grand square connected to Place Ducale and a collection of marionettes. Charleville has an international reputation for its puppet gatherings.

Getting Around

A good railway line passes through the French Ardennes from Lille, via Charleville-Mézières and Sedan.

Tourist Information

Givet: Place de la Tour, t 03 24 42 03 54, f 03 24 40 10 70.
Rocroi: 14 Place d'Armes, B.P.50, t 03 24 54 20 06.
Charleville-Mézières: 4 Place Ducale, t 03 24 32 44 80.
Sedan: Place du Château Fort, B.P.322, t 03 24 27 73 73, f 03 24 29 03 28.
Mouzon: Place de l'Hôtel de Ville, t 03 24 26 10 63, f 03 24 26 27 73.
Stenay: 5 Place Raymond Poincaré, t 03 29 80 64 22, f 03 29 80 62 59.

Where to Stay and Eat

Givet ✉ 08600
★★Le Roosevelt, 76 Av Roosevelt, t 03 24 42 14 14, f 03 24 42 15 15 (*inexpensive*). One of the most attractive choices overlooking the river, with a terrace. 12 rooms. No restaurant.
★★Le Val St-Hilaire, 7 Quai des Fours, t 03 24 42 38 50, f 03 24 42 07 36 (*inexpensive*). 20 rooms. A lot of charm too to this 18th-century riverside house. Restaurant (*menus 90–250F*).

Charleville-Mézières ✉ 08000
★★Hôtel de Paris, 24 Av Corneau, t 03 24 33 34 38, f 03 24 59 11 21 (*inexpensive*). Decent option near the station. No restaurant.
★★Le Relais du Square, 3 Place de la Gare, t 03 24 33 38 76, f 03 24 33 56 66 (*inexpensive*). Also near the station.

Le Sautoy ✉ 08350
B&B Domaine du Sautoy, t/f 03 24 52 70 08. Delightful little fudge-coloured stone hunting lodge with towers, lost in dense woods north of Vrigne-aux-Bois between Charleville and Sedan, along a long, rough track and surrounded by the silence of a pine forest. The interiors have been lovingly redone by its new proprietors. The rooms are tastefully decorated and two have the added delight of a little round tower room.

Bazeilles ✉ 08140
Château de Bazeilles, t 03 24 27 09 68, f 03 24 27 64 20, *bazeilles@chateaubazeilles.com* (*moderate*). The rooms in this smart hotel just east of Sedan are set in the outbuildings of a Louis XV château. Stylish restaurant, L'Orangerie (*menus 148–350F*). *Closed Sat lunch, Sun eve and Mon lunch.*

Stenay ✉ 55700
Les Tilleuls, 10 Rue Jeanne d'Arc, t 03 29 80 35 72. Beer sometimes features in special dishes at this very satisfying restaurant in its agricultural setting.

Along the main artery leading down to the Meuse, the grandiose 17th-century mill, built in a similar style to Place Ducale, hosts temporary art exhibitions and houses the scrappy **Musée Rimbaud** (*open daily 10–12 and 2–6; adm*). The precocious 19th-century literary bad boy ran away from Charleville at an early age to liberate himself and his poetry. He was none too complimentary about his home town, but it did inspire him, if only by representing so finely the values that he wanted to reject. He had a notorious homosexual affair with his mentor, the married poet Verlaine, who shot and wounded him when Rimbaud tried to end their relationship. His poetry delved into the chaos of human emotions through a startling display of fireworks of the French language, but he stopped writing at the age of 19, and died young.

The historic centre of **Sedan** has suffered from war damage and economic depression. The grand old buildings in brass-coloured stone look tarnished and in need of a good polish. For the French, however, Sedan is still associated with one of the major disasters of the 19th century, when the Franco-Prussian War was lost, Napoleon III's Second Empire ended, and Alsace and part of Lorraine were annexed to Germany. The intimidating **fort**, one of the largest in Europe, was built mainly in the late 15th and mid-16th centuries. The **museum** (*open daily 10–6; adm*) clearly explains the fort's architecture, its history and that of the town.

The Meuse valley looks more rustic as you head south, with an understated charm, the old stone buildings a particularly appealing fudge colour. **Mouzon** is a quiet and attractive port on the Meuse, although much damaged in the world wars. Its powerful 13th-century **Notre-Dame** has large twin spires added at a later date, while the interior resembles a copy of Laon cathedral with its four levels of architecture. The early Gothic lines are pleasing, and the lightness of the gallery arches contrasts nicely with the solid ones of the nave. The splendid 18th-century organ was saved at the Revolution and has recently been restored to working order. On the tour, you're taken up to the wide gallery where pilgrims were allowed to sleep – one chapel on this level is dedicated to Thomas à Beckett who is said to have stayed here.

Slipping into Lorraine, sleepy **Stenay** tempts beer-lovers with its sprawling **Musée Européen de la Bière** (*open Mar–Nov daily 10–12 and 2–6; adm*), set in part of a 16th-century citadel. Beer-making has long been an important activity in northern France and you are given the chance to taste the local brews at the end of your visit.

Verdun, the First World War Battle Sites and Joan of Arc's Meuse

Verdun, c'est une guerre entière insérée dans la Grande Guerre...
(Verdun is a whole war in the midst of the Great War.)
Paul Valéry

I arrived there with 175 men, I returned with 34, several half mad...not replying any more when I spoke to them.
French officer Augustin Cochin during the April 1916 artillery combat

Touring the Sites In and Around Verdun

Most of the war sites of Verdun lie north of the city. It makes sense to start a visit to the battlefields at the **Mémorial de Verdun** (*open mid-Mar–mid-Dec daily 9–6; mid-Jan–mid-Mar daily 9–12 and 2–6; adm*), a modern block of a museum on the site of Fleury-Devant-Douaumont, a village pounded into oblivion by artillery fire. Objects are displayed on two floors in a daunting clutter, around a mound of rubble recalling the destruction of the area. The big-screen film in the main hall clarifies the phases of the battles, with moving footage and sober subtitles in English as well as French. The Mémorial also has information on war walks.

There is no more potent symbol to the French of the Great War's destruction than the **Ossuaire de Douaumont** (*open daily 9–12 and 2–5, sometimes later; adm*), its big tower, the Tour des Morts, marked by large crosses. It symbolizes an enormous shell.

Verdun in the First World War

Verdun has become the greatest symbol of French resistance in the First World War, a place of national mourning and national pride. The long-drawn-out battles over Verdun preceded those of the Somme through 1916 and were one of the very worst follies of the Great War. Before the First World War, Verdun lay in a key position close to the French border with Germany. Following the disaster of the 1870 war with Prussia, a line of up-to-date forts was built between Givet and Belfort.

In the German army's 1914 advance, it failed to take Verdun, although it gained a strong position around it on three sides. In the course of 1915 the German commander von Falkenhayn decided that a major offensive was needed on the Western front to break the spirit of the enemy once and for all. He believed that the German army would be able to bleed the French army dry at Verdun. The initial part of Falkenhayn's appalling plan worked. As the 1916 Battle of Verdun began, large numbers of French soldiers were rushed to the area. Verdun was to be defended at all costs: *'Ils ne passeront pas'* ('They will not pass'). A ceaseless chain of truck supplies was brought along from Bar-le-Duc via the road which became known as the **Voie Sacrée**; it's still marked with milestones carrying the hats of French soldiers.

Because of the terrible German offensive, the territory north of the city became one of the worst killing fields in the whole war. Around 175,000 French soldiers and 165,000 German soldiers died, and roughly one million soldiers were wounded in action, most of them suffering permanent disabilities. In the deluge of artillery fire, over 200,000 hectares of land were decimated. Villages disappeared, wiped off the map, and even today you can wander round areas cratered by shellfire. The arrival of two million American soldiers was crucial to the Allied success in ending the 'War to end all wars', and the American cemetery at Romagne is the largest in Europe.

The Ossuaire was where the remains of 130,000 men were brought after the war, French and German. The names of French dead stretch down the long main gallery, well over 100 yards long. There's a large chapel. The tower contains a small museum and orientation tables to identify where the main campaigns took place. In the fields of cemeteries that stretch down the slope below, a little rose is planted in front of each dirty gravestone. A whole section of sickle-shaped tombstones is a reminder of all the North African fighters who fought for the Allies. The **Tranchée des Baïonnettes** nearby is a monument to one specific incident, when on 10 June 1916 two companies of men were buried in their trenches by an enormous artillery bombardment.

The dank **Fort de Douaumont** (*open daily 10–6; adm*) a bit further north looks dismal when you wander through its echoing, dripping, underground darkness. There isn't much to see inside, but the ghosts of the First World War lurk here, in rooms with metal bed frames or basic washing facilities. This was the largest of 38 forts constructed after the Franco-Prussian war to protect Verdun. The guided tour describes the atrocious conditions experienced by the soldiers during the Great War. Built to take up to 800 soldiers, sometimes more than 3,000 were holed up here. At certain times it was hit by around 1,000 shells a day.

America and the Great War

Two areas recall the American contribution to the Great War with beautiful monuments and cemeteries. North of Verdun, and just north of Le Mort Homme and Cote 304, a fat white column rises out of the woods on the **Butte de Montfaucon**, honouring the victory of the 1st American Army here in the Meuse-Argonne campaign of autumn 1918. They took this height on 27 September 1918. The village of Montfaucon vanished almost completely in 1918 except for the ruins of a medieval church. The hundreds of rows of pure white grave stones –14,246 all told – spilling down from the neo-Romanesque chapel at the immaculately kept **US war cemetery of Romagne** just north of the Butte de Montfaucon make a terrible sight, although under half of the Americans who died in the Meuse-Argonne campaign are buried here.

Verdun

The city of Verdun understandably looks rather scrappy, although the quays and upper cathedral quarter have been considerably restored. In 843 the Treaty of Verdun carved the massive Western European empire which Charlemagne had brought together into three, and it was not until the mid-16th century that the French regained the three bishoprics of Verdun, Metz and Toul. The Prussians briefly occupied Verdun during the Revolution, and the Germans took the citadel in the Franco-Prussian War, after a long siege. However, it was the massive German attack during the First War World which left the enormous scars which are still felt today.

The **Centre Mondial de la Paix** (*open June–15 Sept daily 9.30–7; Feb–May and mid-Sept–Nov daily exc Mon 10–1 and 2–6; adm*) is located in the recently renovated, oversplendid bishops' palace. As you look at the thought-provoking objects on display, disturbing tapes play in the background – the sound of groaning or extracts from war-time letters. Next door, the interior of the cathedral is a mix of styles: Gothic side-aisles, a Renaissance nave, a wild Baroque baldaquin in the choir, and an impressive Romanesque crypt. Many of the capitals in the crypt illustrate scenes from the Great War. During the lurching half-hour tour of the **Citadelle Souterraine** (*open daily 9–12.30 and 1.30–6; adm*) the filmed scenarios tends to skim over difficult First World War issues. The tour ends with an evocation of the choosing of France's unknown soldier, which took place in 1920. The body was buried at the Arc de Triomphe in Paris.

St-Mihiel

St-Mihiel really needs a clean up if it is to be truly appreciated, but several fine Renaissance houses stand out along the town's streets, while the main historic building is the massive abbey founded in the 8th century, and much rebuilt in the 17th. Its library has, unusually for France, preserved an extraordinarily rich collection of manuscripts and old books. The oldest manuscripts date back to the 9th century. The virtuoso sculptor Ligier Richier was born in St-Mihiel at the start of the 16th century, when the town's merchants experienced a period of prosperity. One of his finest works, carved in walnut, stands in the abbey church. It represents the Virgin fainting, overcome with grief at the crucifixion – his head from this group is now in the Louvre in Paris. The weight of the Virgin's body falling into the arms of St John is very real, and her flaccid hands are interpreted with striking realism. The church of **St-Etienne** contains an astounding Entombment by Ligier Richier. This time Christ figures at the centre, but all 12 other characters are sculpted with extraordinary individuality.

The Battle of St-Mihiel in September 1918 was an extremely important victory for the American troops. Between 12 and 16 September 15,000 prisoners and 700 square kilometres were captured. The battle monument stands in perhaps the most beautiful spot in the Lorraine, east of St-Mihiel, on the **Butte de Montsec**.

Hattonchâtel, one of the prettiest villages in the whole region, stands on a rocky promontory a short way north. At one end a château, a copy of a 15th-century original, looks out over the plain below. The church, flanked by a tiny cloister, contains a retable of dramatic polychrome figures attributed to Ligier Richier, showing Christ carrying the cross, his crucifixion, and his entombment. The faces reflect the pain and grief of

Getting Around

To reach Verdun by train from Paris, change at Châlons-en-Champagne (*c.* 2hrs 30mins). To get to the battlefields without a car join a guided bus tour from the tourist office (*May–Sept daily 2pm; c. 150F*), or take a taxi: **t** 03 29 86 05 22/**t** 03 29 84 53 59/**t** 03 29 86 47 30/**t** 03 29 86 00 16.

Tourist Information

Verdun: Place de la Nation, B.P.232, **t** 03 29 86 14 18, **f** 03 29 84 22 42.
St-Mihiel: Rue du Palais de Justice, **t/f** 03 29 89 06 47.
Bar-le-Duc: 5 Rue Jeanne d'Arc, **t** 03 29 79 11 13, **f** 03 29 79 21 95.

Where to Stay and Eat

Vilosnes ✉ 55110
★★Le Vieux Moulin, **t** 03 29 85 81 52, **f** 03 29 85 88 19 (*inexpensive*). A simple converted mill by the Meuse north of Verdun.

Verdun ✉ 55100
★★★Le Coq Hardi, 8 Av de la Victoire, **t** 03 29 86 36 36, **f** 03 29 86 09 21 (*moderate*). The main hotel in the centre, plush behind its timber-frame façade and slightly pricey, with a mix of styles. The smart restaurant serves classic

cuisine (*menus 215–450F; bistro menus 98–150F*). Restaurant closed Fri exc bank hols.
★★Le St-Paul, 12 Place St-Paul, **t/f** 03 29 86 02 16 (*inexpensive*). A less ostentatious but popular option with a restaurant serving solid French cooking.
L'Estaminet, 45 Rue des Rouyers, **t** 03 29 86 07 86. Café on the quays which serves some interesting local specialities.

Buzancy ✉ 08240
★★Le Saumon, Place Chanzy, **t** 03 24 30 00 42 (*inexpensive*). Lost in a typical downbeat village of the Ardennes *département*, north of the US Verdun memorials and cemeteries, this bright new hotel is run with verve and has surprisingly nice rooms and restaurant.

Les Montahairons ✉ 55320
★★★Château des Monthairons, **t** 03 29 87 78 55, **f** 03 29 87 73 49 (*expensive–moderate*). A very grand 19th-century château in its walled grounds 12 km south of Verdun (on the west bank D34), this hotel even has its private 'beach' on the Meuse riverbank. The place is stylish, the food excellent (*menus 185–450F*).

St-Mihiel ✉ 55300
★★Hôtel Rive Gauche, Place de la Gare, **t** 03 29 89 15 83, **f** 03 29 89 15 35 (*inexpensive*). The disused railway station well converted to new use, with a restaurant attached (*menus 105–155F*).

Joan of Arc

Joan of Arc was born in or around 1412 in the quaint little village of **Domrémy-la-Pucelle** (Domrémy-the-Virgin), in one of the prettiest spots along the Meuse. Her parents' house survives – quite comfortable for its day. The coats of arms over the door were added by Joan's great-grand-nephew, but for several centuries the house was used simply as a storehouse, until the *département* bought it in 1818.

Joan lived at Domrémy for the first 18 years of her short life, and started hearing the voices of SS Catherine, Marguerite and Michael here. Although abandoned by the French monarchs, who didn't lift a finger to help her in her hour of need (*see* Rouen), she was rehabilitated by the crown at the end of Charles VII's reign and a cult grew up around her. By the end of the 16th century the village had become celebrated as Domrémy-la-Pucelle. Joan was canonized in 1920.

The **Centre Johannique** opened in 1999 to set her story in its historical context. Dense panels of earnest visuals and text are devoted to the power politics of late-medieval France. However, Joan's character is rather surprisingly neglected. Her exceptional will and her passions come across clearly in the trial records which still exist, but these are passed over cursorily. No concessions have been made to English-speaking visitors for the moment.

The **Basilique du Bois-Chenu**, 2km south of Domrémy, was built between 1881 and 1926 in striking black and white bands of stone, in one of the spots where Joan is said to have heard her saintly voices. The interior is richly decorated, notably with mosaics and with large colourful wall paintings depicting major episodes in Joan's life.

the events, except for St Veronica's – she looks calmly at the image of Christ's face she has captured on her veil. East of Hattonchâtel, at **Beney-en-Woëvre** by Thiaucourt-Regniéville, a beautifully manicured US cemetery contains the graves of over 4,000 soldiers killed in the action at St-Mihiel.

Bar-le-Duc is known in French history as the supply centre for Verdun during the First World War, at the other end of the Voie Sacrée (*see* box, p. 689). Its **Ville Haute**, sitting dramatically atop a high rock, was the seat of the local lords, who remained semi-independent of the rest of Lorraine for centuries. Beyond the vestiges of its castle lie streets crammed full of Renaissance mansions built from the beautiful local limestone. The church of **St-Etienne** contains more than one staggering work by Ligier Richier. His magnificent horror, *Le Transi*, was commissioned by Anne de Lorraine in memory of her husband René de Chalon, who died while besieging French troops at the town of St-Dizier. He is shown as a semi-decomposed figure, yet in defiant pose, one leg forward, one arm raised, proudly upright and grinning. Richier's Crucifixion scene shows Christ and the two thieves, the characters fantastically executed with an amazing sense of the flesh of their disturbingly beautiful bodies.

The **Musée Barrois** in the castle, although recently reorganized, retains a 19th-century cluttered feel. The archaeological collections include a superb 2nd-century mother goddess and an intriguing stela representing a Gallo-Roman eye doctor. The variable collection of paintings features the *Temptation of St Anthony* by David

Teniers the Younger, and Jan Steen's *Beer Drinker*. In the attractive Ville Basse, or lower town, which spreads out either side of the Ornain river, a statue recalls the Michaux brothers who invented the pedal bicycle. Nowadays the town's absurd speciality is redcurrant jam made from currants whose pips are removed using a goose's feather.

Over 20km southwest of Domrémy, the Gallo-Roman site at **Grand** long lay forgotten. Dedicated to Apollo, this was once one of the most important spa towns of Roman Gaul; emperors Caracalla and Constantine are claimed to have visited. The amphitheatre on the edge of town has been modernized for modern shows. Better still is a sumptuous carpet of a mosaic from a Roman basilica, one of the largest to have survived in France, displayed in a charming little museum. It is similar to one at the Baths of Caracalla in Rome. You can admire the play of geometrical patterns from the raised walkway, although only one complete man remains, a grotesque figure, thought possibly to represent either a shepherd or a pilgrim coming to pay homage to Apollo. At the corners of the central panel four animals stand out – two wild cats, a boar, and a bear-dog. Finds from archaeological digs at Grand are nicely displayed in cabinets around the gallery, but the most famous discovery, of small wood-carved astrological tablets from Egypt, has been transferred to Epinal (*see* pp.699–700).

Metz

Metz, modern capital of Lorraine, feels Gallic and Germanic at the same time. When Caesar came here he described it as one of the oldest settlements in Gaul. Up until the mid-16th century Metz was an important bishopric on the western edge of the Holy Roman Empire, the main centre of a semi-autonomous region known as the Trois Evêchés, including the areas of Toul and Verdun, which only fell to the French in 1552. The Germans reclaimed it as their own after the Franco-Prussian War and during the Second World War, and the American troops fought a courageous and difficult campaign to liberate Metz in late 1944.

One of the tallest in France, Metz's **cathedral** only lacks soaring spires to allow its silhouette to compete with the very greatest. The outside stone looks very yellow, while the green copper roofing dates from after a fire of 1877. The two pinnacled towers, the Tour de Mutte with its massive bell, and the Tour du Chapitre with its big carving of Christ, started going up in the 13th century, with the bulk of the nave. The west front rose window is a beautiful 14th-century design, the portals are neo-Gothic, and much of the choir was only completed in the early 16th century.

The scale of the massively and darkly Gothic interior is daunting; two churches used to stand on this site, and the view down to the altar offers an unbroken perspective framed by sharply pointed vaults. The **stained glass** is phenomenal, covering all three levels, aisles, gallery and top windows. Much of it features individual figures rather than more complex stories; the most stunning examples are in the two transepts, where you're confronted by sheer walls of stained glass. Chagall contributed some striking modern windows in the 1960s, the intense figures seeming to jump against the coloured backgrounds.

Getting Around

Metz has a small airport, but Luxembourg's airport is more useful for international flights. There are train links from Metz to Lille (and on to London-Waterloo), and Strasbourg.

Tourist Information

Metz: Place d'Armes, t 03 87 55 53 76, f 03 87 36 59 43.

Where to Stay and Eat

★★★**Du Théâtre**, 3 Rue du Pont St-Marcel, t 03 87 31 10 10, f 03 87 30 04 66 (*moderate*). Modern hotel giving on to the central marina, with spacious, comfortable, well-equipped rooms.

★★★**Le Royal Bleu Marine**, 23 Av Foch, t 03 87 66 81 11, f 03 87 56 13 16 (*moderate*). Comfortable hotel in a typical building near the station. Restaurant (*menus 95–145F*).

★★**Grand Hôtel de Metz**, 3 Rue des Clercs, t 03 87 36 16 33, f 03 87 60 40 38 (*inexpensive*). Stylish two-star on a pedestrianized street in the heart of town.

★★**Cecil**, 14 Rue Pasteur, t 03 87 66 66 13, f 03 87 56 96 02 (*inexpensive*) A cheaper option near the station, in an elegant house with 39 rather dull rooms. No restaurant.

La Dinanderie, 2 Rue de Paris, t 03 87 30 14 40. The best restaurant in town, by the Moselle, serving classic cuisine (*menus 160–240F*).

Le Pont St-Marcel, 1 Rue du Pont St-Marcel, t 03 87 30 12 29. Next to the Hôtel du Théâtre, but in an historic house right by the river, this restaurant offers more touristy regional cuisine and costume.

Metz's main museum, **La Cour d'Or** (*open daily 10–12 and 2–6; adm*) has taken over a former 17th-century Carmelite monastery, under which excavations in the 1930s revealed Gallo-Roman baths. The collections are extensive, but the Gallo-Roman rooms are not to be missed. The translucent amber-coloured onyx funerary vase stands out – the stone came from Egypt but the vase was fashioned by a master Roman craftsman – but the best Gallo-Roman item of all is the patched-up shrine to Mithra, a Persian god of light who gained great popularity as Christianity was emerging. This shrine, found at Sarrebourg, depicted Mithra slaying the primordial bull with whose blood the world, according to Mithraism, was fertilized and regenerated. The fine arts are another highlight – the Dutch 17th-century portraits are particularly strong, including an amazing teary, red-eyed *St Jude* by Van Dyck.

The lively shopping quarters of Metz march southwards from the cathedral. Head along the Rue Tête d'Or to reach the Place St-Louis, a stocky arcade running down one side. Up the hill the streets become quieter and more atmospheric. The Moyen Pont, down on the Moselle, offers the best views on to the river banks and its monuments. On the other side of the water lies the surprising enclosed marina surrounded by slickly converted industrial buildings, now a chic place to live. A separate section of town, the **Esplanade** with its green spaces above the Moselle bank, stands on the site of Metz's former citadel. Here **St-Pierre-aux-Nonnains** puts in a claim to being one of the oldest surviving churches in France. Heavily restored, its roots go back to the 4th century, although it was greatly modified in the Romanesque and Gothic periods. The big arsenal building has been spruced up and turned into a bright arts centre. Walks out from the centre of Metz take you to the medieval Porte des Allemands; to the grandiose imperial Germanic quarter around an impressive neo-Renaissance monster of a railway station; or to St-Maximin, with its stylized Afro-exotic stained-glass windows by Jean Cocteau.

Nancy

Bang in the middle of Lorraine, the region's historic capital bursts with life and culture. The city centre is made up of grand gilded squares which scream of 18th-century excess, creating a wonderful urban ensemble which has been placed on the UNESCO list of World Heritage Sites. Nancy's museums have superb collections, and the city blossomed in the early 20th century, when it became the main centre of Art Nouveau in France.

History

Nancy began when Gérard d'Alsace, founder of the line of Lorraine dukes, chose this curious spot for a new castle, set between two marshes against the bank of the Meurthe river. A fire in 1228 destroyed much of the settlement, but it was reconstructed, and a wall was built around the burgeoning town in the 14th century, recalled now only by the Porte de la Craffe.

After the destruction of the Thirty Years' War in the 17th century came more prosperous times. Stanislas Leczinski was appointed as last duke of Lorraine by his son-in-law, the French king, and from 1738 he had his magnificent capital at Nancy. Stanislas enjoyed the good life, with perhaps too much of an appetite for women and food, but he also loved sumptuous architecture. Over a 30-year period he summoned fine architects and artists to create one of the great towns of 18th-century France. Although the ducal palace and the ducal tombs were vandalized at the Revolution, much of the town survives relatively unscathed.

After France's humiliating defeat in the Franco-Prussian War Nancy remained French. Many leading families from annexed territories moved here, bringing a new wave of wealth. At the same time Emile Gallé, Daum and others introduced a new, splendidly langorous style, Art Nouveau. Although the town suffered somewhat from bombing in the First World War, it escaped relatively unscathed in the Second. Since then, major new quarters have been built on the Meurthe hillside, while a plethora of research and higher education institutes have created a centre of learning. Set in relatively sleepy Lorraine, Nancy appears all the more vibrant.

Rococo Nancy

Place Stanislas is wonderfully extravagant. French 18th-century architecture doesn't come much more ornate or striking than this. Stone urns and putti wrapped in protective nets top the balustraded façades of the square, which play second fiddle to the elaborate wrought-iron gates on the corners, framing sculptural scenes.

Looking on to the square you will find the superb **Musée des Beaux-Arts** (*open daily exc Tues 10–6; adm*). A spectacular curving Baroque stair leads up from the beautiful entrance hall to the 18th-century French paintings, hung against boldly coloured backgrounds. The basement contains stunning Art Nouveau glass. The pre-Revolutionary collections are divided according to Italian, Flemish and French schools, each well represented. The most striking Italian works include Perugino's beautifully composed *Virgin with children* and Caravaggio's *Annunciation*. Rubens' enormous and

Getting Around

Nancy has a small airport, and is connected by trains to Paris-Gare de l'Est (the fastest take under 3hrs).

Tourist Information

Nancy: Place Stanislas, t 03 83 35 22 41, f 03 83 35 90 10.

Where to Stay

Nancy ✉ 54000

***Le Grand Hôtel de la Reine, 2 Place Stanislas, t 03 83 35 03 01, f 03 83 32 86 04 (*expensive*). In a superb location, this the most luxurious hotel in Nancy looks on to the finest square in town. The rooms are in Ancien Régime style, as is the restaurant Le Stanislas, which serves refined cuisine (*menus 180–370F*).

***Le Crystal, 5 Place Maginot, t 03 83 17 54 00, f 03 83 17 54 30 (*moderate*). Recently upgraded to a three-star, a surprisingly comfortable hotel not far from the centre towards the railway station. No restaurant.

***Le Résidence, 30 Bd Jean Jaurès, t 03 83 40 33 56, f 03 83 90 16 28 (*moderate*). A bit out of the centre south of the station and run by someone mad about trains. Good value.

**De Guise, 18 Rue de Guise, t 03 83 32 24 68, f 03 83 35 75 63 (*inexpensive*). On a wonderfully atmospheric street in a great location close to the Musée Lorrain, packed full of old-fashioned, worn style.

**Le New York, 63–65 Rue St-Nicolas, t 03 83 32 92 74, f 03 83 32 52 12 (*inexpensive*). Unexciting rooms, but a good two-star option close to the heart of town.

Eating Out

Le Capucin Gourmand, 31 Rue Gambetta, t 03 83 35 26 98, f 03 83 35 99 29. A classic high-class exclusive restaurant (*menus 220–320F*). Closed most of Aug; Feb hols; Sun, exc Sept–June lunch; and Mon.

Mirabelle, 24 Rue Héré, t 03 83 30 49 69, f 03 83 32 78 93. Charming restaurant, in a fantastic location between the two greatest squares in Nancy, with a superb value lunch. (*menus lunch 105F, eves 145–330F*). Closed Aug, Sat lunch, Sun eves and Mon.

Le Comptoir du Petit Gastrolâtre, 1 Place de Vaudémont, t 03 83 35 51 94, f 03 83 32 96 79. The friendly *patron* helps make this *bistrot* one of the most popular in town, though not the cheapest. Traditional local food.

Les Bacchanales, 16 Rue de la Primatiale, t 03 83 37 37 77, f 03 83 55 24 71. You can eat very well at this restaurant behind the cathedral.

Méréville ✉ 54850

***Maison Carrée 12 Rue du Bac, t 03 83 47 09 23, f 03 83 47 50 75 (*moderate*). A good modern option on the edge of the Moselle river a short way south of Nancy, but set in greenery and quite spacious and luxurious. 22 rooms. Closed Dec–Feb Sun eves. Restaurant (*menus 145–480F*). Closed Feb hols; Sun eves and Mon.

gloriously melodramatic Transfiguration is the star of the Flemish collection, showing Christ heading up to heaven on a swirl of cloud. The French rooms are all in danger of being eclipsed by the views on to Place Stanislas. This museum was the first to display a Manet, his *Automne*, and there are gorgeous works by Signac and Sérusier as well as others by Bonnard, Modigliano, Utrillo, Vlaminck and Valloton.

Splendid **Place de la Carrière** links Place Stanislas with the ducal palace – its shape recalls its role as a medieval jousting ground. Stanislas had it remodelled by Héré, turning it into Nancy's second most glamorous square. Its southern entrance is through a blindingly white classical arch, a copy of an imperial Roman arch, erected in honour of Louis XV. At the other end, a row of dignified imperial busts add decorative delight to the hemicycle. There are more outrageous wrought-iron gateways by Lamour, and the lamps drip off their gilded brackets like outsized earrings.

The great Gothic gargoyled façade of the ducal palace conceals the **Musée Lorrain** (*open May–Sept daily 10–6; rest of year daily 10–12 and 2–5; adm*), a huge rambling historical museum. Its trump card is a collection of dramatic works by France's 17th-century master of chiaroscuro, Georges de La Tour. Also seek out the fine Gallo-Roman glass, the Merovingian jewellery, and the portraits of Lorraine dukes and dignitaries. A large late-medieval tapestry cycle made in Tournai is a violent morality tale against gluttony. The Callot engravings show more disturbing violence and poverty, while in the candle-lit night of the canvases of Georges de La Tour the figures seem silently absorbed in their tasks: St Jerome reads a page made translucent by the candelight; a boy blows on embers to light a pipe; a woman concentrates on squashing a flea between her nails. De La Tour spent the last 30 or so years of his life at nearby Lunéville, where he died in 1652. Smaller rooms are devoted to the Revolution, Napoleon, the First World War and a collection of Jewish ceremonial objects.

As if all this were not enough, the museum has an annexe, the **Musée d'Art et Traditions** in the former cloister of the Cordeliers, a celebration of Lorraine crafts and rural life. The church incorporated into the museum has some fine statues, but its most amazing feature is the **ducal mausoleum**, modelled on the Medici Chapel in Florence, with a dazzling coffered ceiling above the black tombs, decorated with angels, putti heads, ducal initials and stars.

Art Nouveau Nancy

Characterful old streets run between the Palais Ducal and the Cours Léopold, another imposing square. At its northern end waits a first taste of the city's Art Nouveau architecture. The main **Art Nouveau quarter** occupies a grid plan in the southwest corner of the centre, where the houses went up in the boom of the Belle Epoque, after French society had recovered from the trauma of the Franco-Prussian War. Emile Gallé, the founder of the Ecole de Nancy, was inspired by the Arts and Crafts movement in Britain, by oriental styles, and by his studies in botany. The flourishing of Art Nouveau in Nancy involved the close cooperation and cross-fertilization of ideas of a large number of committed architects and artists. The tourist office's Art Nouveau itinerary locates individual addresses to look at. The architects of the school were Henri Gutton, George Biet, Lucien Weissenburger, Fernand César, Paul Charbonnier and Joseph Hornecker. In furniture Louis Majorelle and Eugène Vallin stand out; the latter commissioned the first Art Nouveau house in Nancy, in 1896. Another figure, Victor Prouvé, applied himself to marquetry, sculpting, engraving, jewellery and bookbinding. Antonin Daum, like Gallé, produced exquisite glass.

The excellent **Musée de l'Ecole de Nancy** (*open daily exc Mon am and Tues 10.30–6; adm*) is in an early 20th-century house crammed full of Art Nouveau delights. The woodwork by Majorelle and Vallin steals the show, with amazing pieces such as the Meuble à Blé, which uses 58 different woods. Beautiful lamps and vases from Gallé and Daum decorate many a corner, while Gallé's Dawn and Dusk bed, with a butterfly and moth at either end, has to be seen to be believed.

South of Nancy

Except for the occasional industrial blip, the Meurthe and Moselle valleys become increasingly rustic as you head up towards their sources in the southwestern Vosges. The towns along the way each have something of interest. Lunéville boasts a huge château, Baccarat its famous crystal, and Epinal its old-fashioned images and brand new museum. West of here lie the spa lands, where Vittel and Contrexéville are the two best-known resorts.

The Upper Meurthe and Moselle Valleys

Soaring up to match the factory chimneys southeast of Nancy, the bright white **Basilique St-Nicolas-de-Port** is an uplifting Gothic building, and all the more so for holding its own in such an industrial landscape. This pilgrimage church, built to house one of St Nicholas' fingers, dates from the late 15th and early 16th centuries. During the last war the church suffered from heavy bombardments, and it took the fortune of Camille Croue-Friedman, a native girl who married a wealthy American, to restore the building from the 1980s onwards. It now looks immaculate. The two magnificent towers, over 260ft tall, are topped by slate helmets. The scene in the central portal, of St Nicholas performing a miracle, is attributed to Claude Richier, brother of the more celebrated Ligier. The cleaned interior could scarcely look purer, but the building has a kink in it. The vertiginous tubular columns are decorated not with traditional capitals, but with ornamental rings. Two spectacular columns rise above the rest, stupendous palm trees of stone, 92ft high, and said to be the tallest church columns in France. Faded wall paintings curve round the lower parts of some of the columns. Surprisingly, some fine Renaissance stained-glass windows have survived in the left side chapels.

The modest town of **Lunéville** doesn't know quite what to do with the vast, overblown, 18th-century **château** it inherited from the Ancien Régime, sometimes nicknamed the Versailles of Lorraine. Through the dramatic open colonnade of the façade there are views out to the lovingly tended gardens at the back, with their pools and fountains, which are open to the public. The **Musée du Château** (*open April–Sept daily 10–12 and 2–6; rest of year daily exc Tues 10–12 and 2–5; adm*) displays portraits of the exiled King of Poland, Stanislas Leczinski, who died here in 1766, and of his daughter Maria and her husband, Louis XV of France. You are only allowed a distant glimpse of the château's theatrical Baroque chapel and old pharmacy full of ceramic pots. Lunéville has long been an important producer of high-quality pottery; the tourist office has a list of the pottery houses open to the public. The château is so large that it is also home to local government offices and the fire station. The ornate church of **St-Jacques** near the château would look like it had been lifted straight out of Baroque Rome were it not built from dried-red Vosges stone. Putti play around the central clockface, flanked on either side by soaring temple fronts. The visual tricks of Baroque continue inside, with columns suffering from midriff bulges leading up to garlanded capitals. An amazing nave balcony of curving and broken arches is backed by a trompe-l'œil scene.

Getting Around

You can get a train from Nancy to Lunéville, Epinal and Baccarat.

Tourist Information

St-Nicolas-de-Port: 13 bis Rue Anatole France, t 03 83 48 58 75, f 03 83 46 80 01.
Lunéville: Le Château, t 03 83 74 06 55, f 03 83 73 57 95.
Baccarat: Place du Général Leclerc, t 03 83 75 13 37, f 03 83 75 36 76.
Epinal: 13 Rue de la Comédie, B.P.304, t 03 29 82 53 32, f 03 29 35 26 16.

Where to Stay and Eat

Lunéville and Rehainviller ✉ 54300
***Château d'Adoménil**, Rehainviller, t 03 83 74 04 81, f 03 83 74 21 78, *adomenil@relais-chateaux.fr* (*moderate*). Tucked away on the north bank of the Meurthe a few km southwest of Lunéville, this is more a glorified manor than a château, with 7 spacious rooms and an inventive restaurant (*menus 250–475F*). *Restaurant closed 16 April–31 Oct Mon lunch; Sun eve and Tues lunch. Hotel closed Jan; Nov–mid-April Sun and Mon.*

***Des Pages**, 5 Quai Petits Bosquets, t 03 83 74 11 42, f 03 83 73 46 63 (*moderate*). Quiet, comfortable and quite central, but modern and on the wrong side of the river from the Château de Lunéville. Petit Comptoir restaurant (*menus 98–130F*). *Closed Sun eve.*

Senones ✉ 88210
***Au Bon Gîte**, 3 Place Vaultrin, t 03 29 57 92 46, f 03 29 57 93 92 (*inexpensive*). Friendly, small hotel between Baccarat and St-Dié. Restaurant (*menus 99–160F*). *Closed 22 July–6 Aug; Feb hols; Sun eve and Mon.*

Fougerolles ✉ 70220
Au Père Rota, 8 Grande Rue, t 03 84 49 12 11, f 03 84 49 14 51. A remarkable restaurant in cherry country north of Luxeuil-les-Bains, the local Kirsch liqueur of course featuring in some of the wonderful puddings served in this bright restaurant with modern decor (*menus 175–340F*). *Closed Jan; Sun eve and Mon exc bank hols.*

Luxeuil-les-Bains ✉ 70300
***Beau Site**, 18 Rue Georges Moulimard, t 03 84 40 14 67, f 03 84 40 50 25 (*moderate*). A bit of a suburban feel to this large house of a hotel with a mix of styles. But it's comfortable, serves good food (*menus 175–340F*) and has quite a lot of facilities. *Closed Nov–Feb Fri; Sat lunch and Sun eve.*

Southwest of Lunéville, the village of Haroué boasts the beautiful **Château d'Haroué** (*open July–Aug daily 10–12 and 2–6; rest of period April–1 Nov daily 2–6; adm*), reflected in its moats. The magnificent wrought-iron gate was made by Lamour of Nancy fame, and the delightful putti were originally sculpted for Nancy's Place de la Carrière. Mainly built in 1720, Haroué has great style, with its colonnaded side wings topped by human and lion heads. Inside are the portraits of the Beauvau-Craon family who built it; splendid tapestries depicting the triumphs of Alexander the Great, made from cartoons by Le Brun; and delightfully decorated apartments, including a charming water closet and the Chinese tower room.

Epinal was devastated in the Second World War, and little remains of its mighty medieval castle and walls, but in the modern **Musée Départemental d'Art Ancien et Contemporain** (*open Mon–Sat 8.30–12 and 2–6.30, Sun and public hols 2–6.30; adm*) – one of the best museums in Lorraine – you can at least see them in a charming 17th-century fantasy bird's-eye view by Nicolas Bellot. *Job* by Georges de La Tour intrigues, and seek out too *L'Embarquement de St Paul à Ostia*, one of the few works in the region by perhaps the greatest artist Lorraine ever produced, Claude Gelée, nicknamed Le Lorrain. Rembrandt's dark *Mater Dolorosa* looks surprisingly modern, and Jan Breughel's *L'Hiver* is full of caricatures. The archaeological collection includes two tablets showing signs of the Zodiac from Egypt. The top floor is taken up by contemporary art, including Gilbert and George's mock stained-glass window, and a whole section of the museum is devoted to the *images d'Epinal*, simple prints with saturated colours produced in town since the late 18th century. The term *images d'Epinal* has now come to signify a hackneyed cliché. You can take a guided tour at **L'Imagerie d'Epinal** up river to see how the images are made and coloured.

Stop at **Baccarat** if you want to take home some beautiful crystal. A large shop near the museum sells top-quality pieces, even the smallest costing a small fortune, while there are other cheaper (but tackier) shops in town.

The Spa Towns of Southern Lorraine and Northern Franche-Comté

Vittel and Contrexéville are well known because of their widely marketed mineral waters, but this swathe of specialist spa resorts includes many others, such as Bourbonne-les-Bains, Plombières-les-Bains, Luxeuil-les-Bains and even Bains-les-Bains. These towns enjoyed a glamorous period through the 19th century, and they are still very busy – mainly with patients of the generous French National Health Service, who are sent here on *cures*. **Luxeuil-les-Bains** has more atmosphere than the others. The local stone has a tinge of Vosges red to it, while many of the old windows date back to Gothic and Renaissance times. The Irish saint Columbanus set up a monastery here way back in the early 7th century, and the abbey dedicated to him still occupies the centre of town. Track-suited **Contrexéville** has retained the most glamorous feel of these spas, with a splendid old central building held up on mosaic columns; its neo-Byzantine forms date from 1912. Its highlight is the circular room where you can taste the waters, a mosaic of flowers cascading down the dome above you.

The Northern Vosges: from Lorraine into Alsace

The densely wooded, red-stoned hills and mountains of the Vosges boast two regional parks, the Parc Naturel Régional des Ballons des Vosges in the south, the Parc Naturel Régional des Vosges du Nord in the north. After gruffly fortified north-eastern Lorraine, the timberframe towns and villages of nothern Alsace appear merry and seductive.

Much of the northern *département* of Moselle is grimly industrial, but **Sarreguemines**, on the Sarre, has an artistic legacy worth stopping for, centered on the ceramics industry, which flourished here in the 19th century. The star of the **Musée de la Faïence** (*open daily exc Tues 10–12 and 2–6; adm*) is the so-called winter garden decorated with large ceramic panels, smothered with decoration, commissioned in the early 1880s and looking like a precursor of the Art Nouveau movement. To buy ceramics, visit **La Maison de Vaisselle**.

The fortified town of **Bitche** came under siege in the Franco-Prussian War from 1870 to 1871 – those 200 days and more of desperate defence are considered to have been its finest hour, and the story is well told on a tour inside the massive hill fort. Most of the fort is atmospherically empty, cold and dark, but the commentary evokes the dreadful conditions during the siege and explains the significance of the Franco-Prussian War. The most vivid and moving testimony comes from an officer who kept a diary through the dark days of the siege.

Much of the finest crystal and glass in France is produced in the Vosges woods south of Bitche. **Meisenthal** was the village where Emile Gallé worked for over 25 years and perfected his new techniques, bringing the curvaceous forms of Art Nouveau to France in the last decades of the 19th century. The **Maison du Verre** (*open July–Aug daily exc Tues 2–6; rest of period Easter–1 Nov daily exc Tues 2–4; adm*) holds regular exhibitions, and contains one of Gallé's first designs – with flowers and luminous *clair de lune* blue – and some later works employing sophisticated enamel layering. You can also learn how glass and crystal are made.

Picturesque **La Petite-Pierre**, a favoured tourist spot, is home to the Maison du Parc which explains the fauna and flora of the Parc Régional des Vosges du Nord. The northern Vosges are more secretive than the more sensational southern Vosges, but hikers enjoy the wooded surrounds of La Petite Pierre. A short way south of town, a delightful row of troglodyte houses with bright blue fronts are wedged into the rock-face above the village of **Graufthal** (*open Sunday afternoons*). Heading east of Bitche, the **Lac du Hanau** has many walking trails and red ruined castles on spurs, including the **Château de Falkenstein** – not to be confused with the even more sensational **Château de Fleckenstein**, nearby.

A walk up around the old ramparts of **Wissembourg** offers a delightful overview of this characterful border town with its steep-roofed timberframe buildings. Some church towers stick out, in particular two belonging to the enormous church of St-Pierre and St-Paul, the second largest Gothic church in Alsace. Gorgeous old stained-glass windows illuminate the choir, the oldest dating as far back as the 12th century. **Hunspach** is a delightful farmers' village – all the immaculate black and white houses set around spotless courtyards.

Haguenau suffered wholesale destruction on a couple of occasions, first in Louis XIV's campaign to take Alsace, then in the Second World War. After the Sun King's troops had done their worst, a new 18th-century town went up, parts of which still stand today. The **Musée Historique** contains some splendid Celtic artefacts as well as more common Gallo-Roman finds. On the ground floor are pieces of medieval statuary rescued from the earlier ruined Haguenau. The **Musée Alsacien**, devoted to crafts and traditions, has good displays of Alsace pottery. If you're tempted, you could head off through the enormous **forest of Haguenau** in search of more contemporary stuff: **Betschdorf**, an amalgam of old villages on the northern side of the forest below Hunspach, specializes in grey and blue salt-fired stoneware; **Soufflenheim**, on the east side of the forest, deals in less exclusive tableware.

The surprisingly grand small town of **Saverne** has as its centrepiece a building that might be dubbed the Buckingham Palace of the Vosges – a vast red-stoned castle

Getting Around

Wissembourg, Hunspach and Haguenau have good train links with Strasbourg. Saverne lies on the line between Lille and Strasbourg.

Tourist Information

Sarreguemines: Rue du Maire Massing, t 03 87 98 80 81, f 03 87 98 25 77.
Bitche: Hôtel de Ville, B.P.47, t 03 87 06 16 16, f 03 87 06 16 17.
Wissembourg: 9 Place de la République, t 03 88 94 10 11, f 03 88 94 18 82.
Saverne: 37 Grand'Rue, t 03 88 91 80 47, f 03 88 71 02 90.

Where to Stay and Eat

La Petite-Pierre ✉ 67290

A seriously touristy village in the northern Vosges.
**Au Lion d'Or, 15 Rue Principale, t 03 88 70 45 06, f 03 88 70 45 56 (*inexpensive*). Really quite luxurious with 40 rooms, forest views and serious cuisine (*menus 120–290F*). *Closed 25 June–4 July and Feb.*
***Aux Trois Roses, 19 Rue Principale, t 03 88 70 45 02, f 03 88 70 41 28. Another smart option. Restaurant (*menus 98–265F*). *Closed Sun eve and Mon.*

Obersteinbach ✉ 67510

**Chez Anthon, 40 Rue Principale, t 03 88 09 55 01 (*inexpensive*). With its lovely welcoming courtyard, a tasteful place to stay (just 9 rooms) and to eat; the dining room has views on to the woods too (*menus 155–380F*). *Closed Jan; Tues and Wed.*

Lembach ✉ 67510

Auberge du Cheval Blanc, 4 Route de Wissembourg, t 03 88 94 41 86, f 03 88 94 20 74. A splendid, highly reputed restaurant, one of the best in northern Alsace, and a pretty timberframe picture in pink.

Wissembourg ✉ 67160

Hostellerie du Cygne, 3 Rue du Sel, t 03 88 94 00 16, f 03 88 54 38 28. In beautiful old timberframe houses in the historic centre (*menus 195–470F*). *Closed July; Feb; Mon and Tues.*
Le Châtelet, 65 Faubourg de Bitche, t 03 88 94 16 11. A pretty little gastronomic restaurant in a picturesque spot by a weir on the edge of the old town.

Saverne ✉ 67700

**L'Europe, 7 Rue de la Gare, t 03 88 71 12 07, f 03 88 71 11 43 (*inexpensive*). 28 stylish modern rooms. No restaurant.
Taverne Katz, 80 Grand'Rue, t 03 88 71 16 56. Excellent traditional restaurant with elaborate, carved façade.

built for the Rohans of Strasbourg fame. The staggering 460ft façades went up for Louis de Rohan after a fire had gutted the previous château in 1779. Work stopped at the Revolution, before the interiors had been completed, and the town bought it in the 1950s, filling it with amenities, including the archaeological, historical and art museums. The Donation Louise Weiss, the gift of the pioneering feminist journalist, includes drawings by Vlaminck and Van Dongen, and objects collected on her travels. Lovely old houses line the streets parallel to the palace.

On the heights above Saverne, the dramatic remains of the **Château du Haut-Barr**, built in the 12th century and transformed in the 16th, overlook the Rhine plain and the Zorn valley. French troops brought most of the place down in 1648. The red architectural ruins merge with the fissured rocks on which they stand, and there's not much to see beyond a restored Romanesque chapel, a restaurant in the ruins, and, best of all, the magnificent views.

Strasbourg

Alsace's answer to Paris, its gorgeous historic centre set on an island on the Ill, its cathedral one of the glories of European Gothic, Strasbourg of course has 'its' own little parliament, that of the European Union, as well as being the seat of the Council of Europe, which includes the European Court of Human Rights. When the EU parliament is sitting, Members move into town with their retinues, adding to the flocks of businessmen, students and tourists. Strasbourg still has one of the largest ports in France, along the Rhine, but the historic centre is so packed with riches – including three splendid art museums – that visitors rarely notice.

History

Strasbourg grew up as a port on the west bank of the Rhine. Through the Dark Ages it lay on the path of invaders from the east, suffering destruction after destruction, and from the 9th to the 17th centuries lay within the boundaries of the Holy Roman Empire. However, the city leaders retained a great degree of independence, first through a line of powerful bishops, then from the 14th century through the control of powerful trade guilds. Strasbourg was also a place where culture and intellectual advances often thrived. A lot is made of Gutenberg's years here working on the invention of the printing press, and the city drew some of the major figures of the Reformation: von Kaysersberg, Bucer and Calvin. The university opened in 1566; one of its most famous students was Goethe, who studied here from 1770 to 1771.

In the late 17th century, Strasbourg became part of France along with the rest of Alsace, and it was an aristocratic French family, the Rohans, that most marked the city in the 18th century. Four Rohan cardinals succeeded each other as bishops of Strasbourg. In late April 1792, as the Army of the Rhine waited here to head into action, Rouget de Lisle composed a stirring song for the departing troops. The result was soon adopted by volunteers from Marseille, and henceforth became known as the **Marseillaise**, now the French national anthem.

The Prussian bombardments during the Franco-Prussian War caused great damage to the centre and fires destroyed many houses. Once France had lost the war Strasbourg became capital of the annexed territory of Elsass-Lothringen, and only reverted to France at the end of the First World War. The town suffered badly from more bombing during the Second World War, but this time the historic centre emerged relatively unscathed.

The Cathedral

What an overwhelming skyscraper of a medieval building Strasbourg's **cathedral** is. It was mainly built through the 13th and 14th centuries; the massive Romanesque choir went up first, followed in the mid-13th century by the Gothic nave. The soaring 466ft spire, one of the landmarks of the Rhine Valley, was completed in 1439. The fabulous west façade, designed by Erwin de Steinbach, is one of the greatest in the world. Work began around 1280 but it was not completed until well into the middle of the 14th century, after Erwin's death. The tiny-looking green wings of a row of high-perched angels stand out against the almost uniformly red standstone façade; the central rose windows are stunning; the gabled doorways are filled with sculpture. Prophets feature in the arches of the central door, with Christ's life told in the tympanum. The right-hand portal contrasts the wise and the foolish virgins above signs of the zodiac. The women of the left-hand portal, representations of the virtues, lance the vices at their feet. Those cavaliers much higher up represent Merovingian, Carolingian and later kings. Apostles stand even higher above the rose window. Climb up to the spire to admire views of Strasbourg's roofs and the Rhine valley.

Inside, splendid stained-glass windows spread their mysterious light down the long nave. In contrast, the choir is lit by a single, small central opening. A startling nest of an organloft, elaborately gilded, hangs precariously in the nave; while the pulpit is richly carved. The Chapelle Ste-Catherine is lit by gem-like 14th-century glass. The transept beyond is held up by a fabulous central pillar known as the Angels' Pillar or Pillar of the Last Judgement, an exceptional piece of Gothic art with expressive figures of the evangelists, musical angels, and the Christ of the Last Judgement, his foot on a globe.

The **Musée de l'Oeuvre Notre-Dame** (*open daily exc Mon 10–12 and 1.30–6; Sun 10–5; adm*) has dozens of rooms devoted to medieval and Renaissance art, and religious art in particular, including the Romanesque cloister from Eschau just south of Strasbourg. The museum lays claim to the oldest known piece of figurative stained glass, the Wissembourg head of Christ, dated to around 1070.

Museums in the Palais Rohan

The outrageous bishops' residence, the **Palais Rohan** was badly damaged in 1944, and the restoration of the ground-floor apartments was only completed in 1980. A trio of major museums is housed within (*all open daily exc Tues 10–12 and 1.30–6; Sun 10–5; adm*). The **Musée Archéologique** down in the basement covers Alsace culture from 600,000 BC to AD 800. There are some interesting Neolithic engravings, but the Gallo-Roman section is the best, with a monumental 3rd-century head of a cross-eyed emperor and fine carved stelae. An early-Christian engraved glass depicts the sacrifice of Isaac with startling sophistication; some of the Dark Age weapons share the high standard of craftsmanship.

Poverty and meekness were not words in a Rohan's vocabulary. On the ground floor the formal apartments of the **Musée des Art Décoratifs** count among the most ostentatious anywhere, with gilded, stuccoed ceilings and painted allegories. The Salle du Synode treated visiting bishops to a trompe-l'oeil painting of the goddess Ceres, a bust of Caesar, and putti riding dolphins. The Salon des Evêques, decorated with images of the virtues, was the games room under the Rohans. The Chambre du Roi, exquisitely gilded, is where Louis XV stayed in 1744, and Marie-Antoinette in 1770. Copies of works by Raphael adorn this room and the Salon d'Assemblée. A whole series of rooms display ceramics, of which Strasbourg became a major producer from the late 17th century. At first decorated with simple blue patterns, big purple and pink flowers soon came to dominate.

Strasbourg

To European Parliament
and Parc de l'Orangerie (1km)

250 metres
250 yards

PLACE
DE LA
REPUBLIQUE

Palais de
Justice

Hôtel de Ville

Eglise St-
Etienne

PLACE
ST-ETIENNE

QUAI ST-ETIENNE

RUE DE LA KRUTENAU

RUE DE ZURICH

PLACE DE
ZURICH

PLACE DE
ZURICH

RUE DU JEU-DE-PAUME

RUE DES BATELIERS

PLACE
D'AUSTERLITZ

RUE DE LA CROIX

PLACE DU
MARCHE DU
GUYOT

RUE DES FRERES

RUE DES SOEURS

RUE DES VEAUX

PLACE DES
FRERES

RUE DES ECRIVAINS

Cathedral

Palais de
Rohan

Musée de
l'Oeuvre
Notre-Dame

Musée du
CHATEAU

RUE DU MAROQUIN

RUE DU DOME

RUE DU SANGLIER

RUE DE L'OUTRE

RUE DES ORFEVRES

PLACE
DU CORBEAU

Musée
Alsacien

PLACE
D'AUSTERLITZ

1 ERE ARMEE

RUE DE LA

RUE DES BOUCHERS

RUE DU VIEUX MARCHE AUX POISSONS

RUE DES ARCADES

PLACE
GUTENBERG

RUE DE LA DIVISION LECLERC

RUE DES FRANCS-BOURGEOIS

Eglise St-Thomas

PLACE
ST-THOMAS

Eglise St-Louis

RUE DE LA MONNAIE

Eglise St-
Pierre-le-Jeune

QUAI STURM

QUAI SCHOEFFLESIM

QUAI FINKMATT

RUE DU FAUBOURG DE PIERRE

RUE DE LA FONDERIE

RUE DE LA NUEE BLEUE

PLACE DE
BROGLIE

PLACE DE L'HOMME-DE-FER

PLACE
KLEBER

RUE STE-HELENE

RUE DU BOUCLIER

Hôpital Civil

RUE HUMANN

QUAI FINKWILLER

FOSSE DES TANNEURS

RUE DES
DENTELLES

GRAND RUE

Les Halles

RUE DE SEBASTOPOL

QUAI KLEBER

QUAI DE PARIS

RUE DU 22 NOVEMBRE

RUE DES MOULINS

Eglise St-Pierre-
le-Vieux

QUAI DE TURKHEIM

PETITE
FRANCE

PONTS COUVERTS

QUAI DE LA PETITE FRANCE

Barrage
Vauban

Musée d'Art Moderne
et Contemporain

Hôtel du
Département

RUE DU FAUBOURG DE SAVERNE

QUAI ST-JEAN

QUAI ALTORFFER

RUE DU FAUBOURG NATIONAL

RUE DE TURKHEIM

RUE STE-MARGUERITE

RUE DE MOLSHEIM

RUE DE WASSELONNE

RUE DE MOLSHEIM

BD DU PRESIDENT WILSON

RUE DU MAIRE-KUSS

Train Station

PLACE DE
LA GARE

BD DE METZ

AV DE LA LIBERTE

AV DE LA MARSEILLAISE

RUE DES JUIFS

RUE BRULEE

PLACE DE
TEMPLE NEUF

BD DE LA VICTOIRE

QUAI DES PECHEURS

RUE DE L'ABREUVOIR

RUE DE ZURICH

RUE DES ORPHELINS

QUAI DES BATELIERS

Getting Around

There are direct flights daily to Strasbourg from London-Gatwick, operated by Canadair Regional Jet Aircraft, a franchise partner of Air France, t 0845 0845 111, www.airfrance.co.uk. You can also fly in from Paris and other French airports. The Strasbourg-Entzheim airport lies 15km southwest of the city centre; buses into the centre run Mon–Fri roughly every 30mins. There are trains from Paris-Gare de l'Est to Strasbourg city centre (at least 4hrs).

Tourist Information

Strasbourg: 17 Pl de la Cathédrale, t 03 88 52 28 28, f 03 88 52 28 29, www.strasbourg.com. There are also offices at Pl de la Gare, t 03 88 32 51 49, and Pont de l'Europe, t 03 88 61 39 23.

Shopping

There is a food market on Bd de la Marne (*Tues and Sat am*) and a flea market on Rue du Vieux-Hôpital (*Wed and Sat*).
The Bookworm, 3 Rue de Pâques. English-language bookshop,
Christian Maître Chocolat, 12 Rue de l'Outre. Traditional-style chocolates, such as pralines, marzipan, liqueur chocolates, flavoured truffles and the Alsatian speciality chocolate 'chestnuts'.

Activities

Take a relaxing *vedette* or riverboat cruise around central Strasbourg from the terraces on the riverside of the Palais Rohan.

Where to Stay

Strasbourg ✉ 67000

You should book well ahead if you want to stay in Strasbourg, which is very popular and packed out when the European Union Parliament is sitting.

Expensive
****Régent Contades, 8 Av de la Liberté, t 03 88 15 05 05, f 03 88 15 05 15. Spacious, luxurious hotel with old-fashioned style in an imposing building in the Prussian quarter just east of the central island, constructed in the late 19th-century.
****Régent Petite France, 5 Rue des Moulins, t 03 88 76 43 43, f 03 88 76 43 76. Sister hotel with a contemporary feel in big converted old buildings in the delightful Petite France district. Dull exterior but exciting and recently done up hotel, if still more outrageously expensive than its older relative. Restaurant (*menus 160–300F*). *Closed June–Sept Mon; Oct–May weekends.*

Moderate
***Maison Kammerzell, 16 Place de la Cathédrale, t 03 88 32 42 14, f 03 88 23 03 92. Near the cathedral, a fabulous many-storeyed timberframe house built in the 15th and 16th centuries, with sumptuous interior decoration. A small number of lovely rooms, but known above all for its restaurant and the reputed *choucroute Baumann*, named after the proud proprietor (*menus 177–295F*) *Closed Feb hols*.
***Beaucour, 5 Rue des Bouchers, t 03 88 76 72 00, f 03 88 76 72 60. Appealing group of timberframe façades just on the south side of the Ill close to the Pont du Corbeau, also owned by Baumann. A bit overdone for some tastes and very pricey, but the rooms are extremely comfortable and really luxurious for a three-star.
***Hôtel des Rohans, 17–19 Rue du Maroquin, B.P.39, Cathédrale, t 03 88 32 85 11, f 03 88 75 65 37, info@hotel-rohan.com. A charming, comfortable hotel in a prime location close to the cathedral, but perhaps just a tad too close to the major tourist path.
***Maison Rouge, 4 Rue des Francs-Bourgeois, t 03 88 32 08 60, f 03 88 22 43 73, Maison.Rouge@wanadoo.fr. Large, but the rooms have individual style.
**Suisse, 24 Rue de la Rape, t 03 88 35 22 11, f 03 88 25 74 23. In a great location opposite the cathedral, with a stylish blue façade behind the pavement terraces.

Inexpensive

Hôtel de l'Ill, 8 Rue des Bateliers, **t 03 88 36 20 01, **f** 03 88 35 30 03. In a great location just south of the main island, close to the church of Ste-Madeleine.

Couvent du Franciscain, 18 Rue du Faubourg de Pierre, **t 03 88 32 93 93, **f** 03 88 75 68 46. Just north of the main island, good value and reasonable rooms.

Eating Out

Buerehiesel, 4 Parc de l'Orangerie, **t** 03 88 45 56 65, **f** 03 88 61 32 00. Absolutely fabulous cuisine in a ridiculously pretty old Alsatian house (*menus 320–790F*).

Au Crocodile, 10 Rue de l'Outre, **t** 03 88 32 13 02, **f** 03 88 75 72 01. Another starry reputation for superlative light but classic cuisine (*menus lunch 295F, dinner 450–700F*). *Closed 16 July–7 Aug; Christmas; Sun and Mon.*

L'Arsenal, 11 Rue de l'Abreuvoir, **t** 03 88 35 03 69, **f** 03 88 35 03 69. Refined, light and modern Alsatian cuisine in an interesting interior in a timberframe building in the Krutenau quarter (*menus 240F*). *Closed Aug; Sat exc Sept–June eve.*

L'Ami Schutz, 1 Ponts-Couverts, **t** 03 88 32 76 98, **f** 03 88 32 38 40. Strasbourg institution in a medieval setting in Petite France, with a well-located terrace and Alsatian specialities (*menus 165–225F*).

La Choucrouterie, 20 Rue St-Louis (just south of the main island, opposite the church of St-Thomas), **t** 03 88 36 52 87. An extremely popular and lively place to try *choucroute*, in a converted 18th-century posting inn. Musical evenings, especially gypsy bands.

Chez Yvonne, 10 Rue du Sanglier, **t** 03 88 32 84 15. Excellent *winstub* on the main island with great cuisine and atmosphere.

Le Festin de Lucullus, 18 Rue Ste-Hélène, **t** 03 88 22 40 78. Fine fresh cooking at a reasonable price near the centre of the main island. *Closed Aug; Sun and Mon exc Dec.*

There's an appealing choice of places to eat on the Place du Marché Guyot, the delightful, cobbled square at the back of the cathedral.

Ostwald ✉ 67540

****Château de l'Ile, 4 Quai Heydt, **t** 03 88 66 85 00, **f** 03 88 66 85 49, *ile@wanadoo.fr* (*expensive*). Highly reputed hotel southwest of the centre, midway to the airport, in a meander of the Ill river. All mod cons and sumptuous cuisine (*menus 230–420F*). *Closed Sat lunch, Sun eve and Mon.*

Entertainment and Nightlife

There are often free concerts in Parc des Contades and Parc de l'Orangerie.

Le Bateau Ivre, Quai des Alpes. A spacious, elegant boat, moored on the quaynear the city centre, a popular spot for the trendy and fashionable. *Open Thurs–Sat 10.30pm–4am.*

Chez Yvonne, 10 Rue du Sanglier, **t** 03 88 32 84 15. Famous *winstub* near the cathedral, where regional fare is prepared with perfection. Reservations recommended. *Open for lunch and 5.30–midnight. Closed Sun and Mon afternoon.*

Café P'tit Max, 4 Place de l'Homme de Fer, **t** 03 88 23 05 00. A pillar of Strasbourg nightlife, with singers and dinner concerts (*Tues, Thurs and Fri nights*). *Open all day until 1/1.30am.*

Bar du 7e Art, 18 Rue du 22 Novembre. The movie-lover's bar, linked to the Etoile Cinema, a relaxed place where movie buffs can read newspapers and sip coffee. *Open daily 8am–1.30am, Sun 2.30pm–11.30pm.*

Le Café du TNS, 1 Av de la Marseillaise. The National Theatre of Strasbourg café with a striped ceiling and stylish, subdued designer furniture, all black and white. Brunch-type breakfasts, fresh sandwiches and exquisite regional dishes. *Open daily 8am–1am.*

Opéra Café, Place Broglie. Attractive baroque-style café in the beautiful Opera House. Attracts a fashionable, artsy crowd. Limited menu available at lunch time. *Open daily 11am–3am, Sun from 2pm.*

Les Aviateurs, 12 Rue des Soeurs. Stronghold of the eternally attractive Michèle Noth, Strasbourg's night queen. Great atmosphere, great place to meet. *Open daily 6pm–4am.*

The **Musée des Beaux-Arts** is one of France's great provincial museums. The major European schools are covered, and the Italian, Flemish and 17th-century French paintings are exceptionally rich. One of the oldest works is a small Giotto Crucifixion. Botticelli, Piero di Cosimo, Del Sarto and Correggio are all here, but look out too for lesser-known artists such as Barocci and Negretti. The Flemish masterpieces include Rubens' Resurrected Christ, and some delicious still lives.

Elsewhere around Strasbourg

The **Musée Alsacien** (*open daily exc Tues 10–12 and 1.30–6; adm*) lies on the southern quay of the Ill. Three substantial houses have been knocked into one to make a rambling museum of popular arts and crafts, a good introduction to traditional life in Alsace. Don't miss the fantastical prophylactic masks.

The major shopping streets lie on the central island, west of the cathedral quarter. In the centre of **Place Gutenberg**, the green statue, a 19th-century work by David d'Angers, honours the inventor of the printing press. The Rue des Arcades leads up to **Place Kléber** which comemmorates a more controversial figure. Born in Strasbourg, Jean Baptist Kléber is remembered above all as a ruthlessly determined general who fought for the Revolution and then for Napoleon, notably in Egypt, where he was eventually assassinated.

Tourists flock to the line of smaller islands, and the quarter which goes by the curious title of **Petite France**. The waterways here reflect some splendid timberframe houses, where millers, tanners and fishermen once lived. The **Barrage Vauban** is a covered walkway, a remnant of the fortifications Vauban planned for the city. From its roof there are great views over Petite France to the cathedral. On the opposite side you also get an excellent view of Strasbourg's slick new modern art museum, a sculpture of a horse calmly perched on its roof. This, the **Musée d'Art Moderne et Contemporain** (*open daily exc Tues 10–12 and 1.30–6; Sun 10–5; adm*), opened in November 1998 as the focal point of a whole new quarter. The collection starts in the last decades of the 19th century: there are paintings by Monet, Renoir, Boudin, Emile Bernard, Burne-Jones and Klimt, followed by Vlaminck, Gris and Picasso. A special place is reserved for Jean Arp, born in Strasbourg and a founding figure of the Dada movement, and there's space too for contemporary installations and exhibitions.

East and north of the cathedral, **Place du Marché Gayot** is a popular haven of restaurants and cafés. Cross the northern branch of water embracing Strasbourg's central island and the **Place de la République** is dominated by the imposingly pompous German structures of the late 19th century. The Prussian architecture extends outwards to the university and the Orangerie, a park originally designed by Le Nôtre at the end of the 17th century.

The **new European Union Parliament building** opened in 1999, and has been something of an architectural fiasco. Many important features of the state-of-the-art building would not function at the inauguration, and the colours inside were considered so repellent by those who were going to work there that a great deal of the interior has had to be redecorated. Check with the tourist office if you want to visit the parliament building and see the latest colour scheme.

The Alsace Wine Route, Part 1

The enchanting Alsace wine route runs almost straight south along the bottom slopes of the Vosges from Strasbourg down to the Thann area. It's an easy route to follow, but at certain times of year it can become frustratingly busy with tour buses. The wine villages are almost all as beautiful as each other, often with round ramparts and old gateways embracing colourful timberframe, orange-roofed houses. Among the Vosges woods, crumbling medieval castles peer down across the Rhine plain. The one château to have been restored is Haut-Koenigsberg, rebuilt for Kaiser Wilhelm II in the early 20th century, a symbol of Germany's authority over Alsace at that time. Traces of the two world wars remain in Le Linge's First World War trenches and in the Nazi concentration camp of Le Struthof, the only one on French territory.

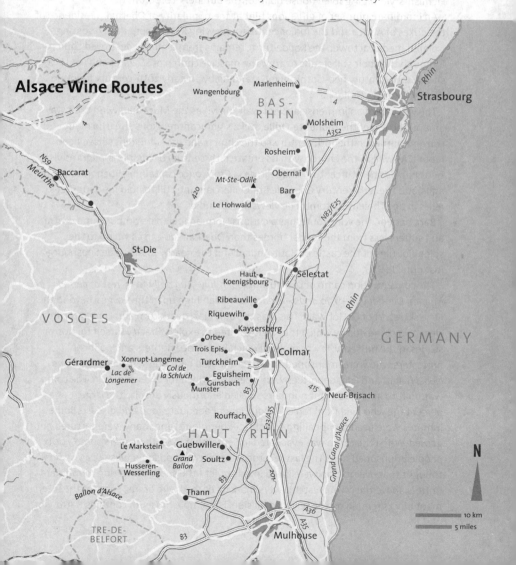

Alsace Wine Routes

The main Alsace wine route starts due west of Strasbourg, at the base of the Vosges. **Marlenheim** counts as the first northerly stop, a well-known wine-producing parish. Next, **Molsheim** is a wealthy town which has sprawled out beyond its red walls. During the 17th century it became perhaps the most important religious centre in Alsace, when the Archduke Leopold of Austria, also bishop of Strasbourg, founded the Jesuit University here in 1618, which lasted until 1702, when a Rohan cardinal transferred it to Strasbourg to counteract the Protestant influences there. The **Musée de la Chartreuse**, in the priory of what was an enormous charterhouse, is the local history museum. In 1909 the Italian Ettore Bugatti set up his celebrated car factory at Molsheim. The museum contains a few old models, and Bugattis are still built on the outskirts of town. The **Metzig** is the most celebrated of the old houses in town – a Flemish-style, high-gabled house built for the butchers' corporation.

An inordinate number of gift shops hint at the popularity of **Obernai**, a residence of the dukes of Alsace and the major centre for brewing Kronenberg beer. A soaring, isolated medieval tower, the Kappelturm, remains from a mostly destroyed church, although the choir still stands nearby. The massive church of SS. Peter and Paul is a showy 19th-century neo-Gothic giant, standing by an early 20th-century fountain dedicated to Ste Odile.

The vestiges of an immense ancient wall known as the **Mur Païen** wind their way around the top of the **Mont Ste-Odile**, still a significant religious site. The main convent burned in the 16th century, so the church and other buildings have been rebuilt. As well as the church with its ornate 18th-century decorations, pilgrims visit two chapels, the 11th-century Chapelle de la Croix, once containing Etichon's sarcophagus, and the 12th-century Chapelle Ste-Odile, claiming still to hold his daughter's relics in an 8th-century tomb. The views are splendid .

Barr, back on the wine route, has a curious Norman feel to its timberframe centre and suffers less from the tourist hordes than Obernai. You can climb up to the splendid ruins of the castle of Haut-Andlau and the nearby Château de Spesbourg just outside Barr.

The concentration camp of **Le Struthof** (*open July–Aug daily 10–5, rest of period Mar–24 Dec daily 10–11.30 and 2–4; adm*) is hidden high up in the Vosges, beyond the little ski resort of Le Hohwald. This was the only Nazi death camp on French territory, close to a stone quarry which the Nazis wanted to exploit. Brace yourself for horror stories in the museum. It was mainly French Resistance fighters and political protesters who were imprisoned and exterminated here. The so-called *Nacht und Nebel* (Night and Fog) deportees were openly destined for extermination. The camp was built to hold 2,000, but numbers swelled enormously despite the large percentage who died from forced labour, lack of adequate food and disease. Some inmates were used for appalling scientific experiments, and many were tortured and gassed. When the camp was evacuated in September 1944, there were some 7,000 people imprisoned here. The last recorded number for a prisoner was 17,045, so it is thought that over 10,000 were killed in this quiet little spot. A towering monument unfurls above the camp. Watchtowers mark its barbed wire limits. Some of the internment blocks remain on the terraced hillside. The simple museum contains harrowing

Ste Odile

Obernai was the birthplace of Ste Odile. She was born blind, much to the anger of her father, Duke Etichon of Alsace, and he ordered her to be killed. Rescued by her wetnurse, she was brought up religiously, and when Bishop Erard baptized her she recovered her sight. Eventually her mother and brother revealed her existence to Etichon, but on finding out the violent man murdered his son with his own hands. Filled with remorse, he tried to make up for his sins by offering Odile in marriage to a fine knight, but she refused, wanting to lead a religious life. Infuriated beyond reason yet again, the duke chased after Odile to kill her, but miraculously a rockface opened up between them and saved her. Her father finally gave in and offered her the Hohenbourg, now the **Mont Ste-Odile**, on which she built two convents. The mountain became a major pilgrimage site, visited by Holy Roman Emperors from Charlemagne on. Odile was made patron saint of Alsace at the start of the 19th century; she is also patron saint of the blind.

photos and displays. At the bottom of the camp lies the pit where the remains of the dead were incinerated. A gas chamber still stands down the road opposite an inn.

Preserving several fortified gateways, its picturesque houses laden with flowers, **Dambach-la-Ville** is a prosperous wine village, one of the largest producers of riesling. Legend has it that a bear enjoying grapes from a wild vine nearby showed the locals the way to proceed, as is recalled on a Renaissance fountain in the centre of town. A path through the vines leads to the Chapelle St-Sébastien. Outside, the ossuary is still packed with bones, while inside you can hardly miss the twisted columned, wildly carved wooden altarpiece. It's a more demanding walk up to the ruins of the **castle of Bernstein**, destroyed in the Thirty Years' War.

An irritating row of towering red and white masts dominates the Rhine plain by **Sélestat**, which may have lost most of its medieval fortifications, but remains an attractive old town. Vying for attention, the churches of **Ste-Foy** and **St-Georges** stand close to each other. The first, with its twin towers and pyramidal structure over the crossing, has been much played about with since it originally went up in the 12th century as a dependency of Conques in southwest France. The nave looks surprisingly small behind the bold exterior. A few statues adorn the mysterious crypt, while a Baroque pulpit recalls the times when Jesuits took over. The second church has a massive central entrance tower and long, long, Gothic nave; the splendid flat choir end has kept some original windows. The **Bibliothèque Humaniste** (*open Mon–Fri 9–12 and 2–6, Sat 9–12; adm*) recalls the time when the town boasted one of the finest schools in Europe. Books were rare and precious, but various masters, former pupils and locals donated their volumes to the school. Some were so valued that they were chained up to stop thieving. The greatest bequest of all came from Beatus Rhenanus of Sélestat, who studied for some time in Paris and was a close friend of Erasmus. This is one of the few great collections of humanist works to have survived in Europe and is well-explained to English-speaking visitors.

The most spectacular castle in Alsace, visible across the Rhine plain at the top of its precipitous wooded mountain, the **Château du Haut-Koenigsbourg** (*open July–Aug*

Getting Around

Sélestat is well served by trains, on the Strasbourg-Colmar-Mulhouse line. A branch line from Strasbourg also stops at Molsheim, Rosheim, Obernai, Barr and Dambach.

Tourist Information

Molsheim: 17 Place de l'Hôtel de Ville, t 03 88 38 11 61, f 03 88 49 80 40.
Obernai: Place du Beffroi, t 03 88 95 64 13, f 03 88 49 90 84.
Dambach-la-Ville: Place du Maré, t 03 88 92 61 00.
Sélestat: Commanderie St-Jean, Bd du Général Leclerc, t 03 88 58 87 20, f 03 88 92 88 63.
Ribeauvillé-Riquewihr: 1 Grand'rue, t 03 89 73 62 22, f 03 89 73 23 62.
Kaysersberg: 31 Rue Geisbourg, t 03 89 78 22 78, f 03 89 78 11 12.

Where to Stay and Eat

Itterswiller ✉ 67140

***Arnold**, 98 Route des Vins, t 03 88 85 50 58, f 03 88 85 55 54 (*moderate*). Very attractively located among the vines, a large, comfortable hotel and restaurant serving copious Alsace dishes (*menus 130–365F*). *Closed 1st half Feb; Nov–May Sun eve and Mon.*

Dambach-la-Ville and Blienschwiller ✉ 67650

**Le Vignoble, 1 Rue de l'Eglise, Dambach-la-Ville, t 03 88 92 43 75 (*inexpensive*). Very sweet converted timberframe barn. *Closed Christmas–16 Mar and Sun eve out of season.*
**Winzenberg, 46 Route du Vin, Blienschwiller, t 03 88 92 62 77, f 03 88 92 45 22 (*inexpensive*). Appealing hotel with 13 modern rooms, a lovely little courtyard and outrageous blackberry colour in a wine village just north of Dambach. *Closed Jan and Feb.*

Sélestat ✉ 67600

***Abbaye La Pommeraie**, 8 Av du Maréchal Foch, t 03 88 92 07 84, f 03 88 92 08 71, *pommeraie@relaischateaux.fr*, *www.relais-chateaux.fr/pommeraie* (*expensive*). No asceticism these days in this luxurious hotel which has grown out from the buildings of a Cistercian abbey. It even has two restaurants (*menus from 290F including wine*).

Thannenkirch ✉ 68590

**Auberge de la Meunière, 30 Rue Ste-Anne, t 03 89 73 10 47, f 03 89 73 12 31 (*inexpensive*). A delightful small hotel with 23 rooms in this village close to but tucked away from the overtouristy wine route. Restaurant (*menus 100–195F*). *Closed Christmas–24 Mar.*

daily 9–6.30; May, June and Sept daily 9–6; Mar, April and Oct daily 9–12 and 1–5.30; other months daily 9.30–12 and 1–4.30; adm) was rebuilt as a pastiche of a medieval castle with much assistance from Kaiser Wilhelm II at the very start of the 20th century, when Alsace was annexed to Germany. A grandson of Queen Victoria, Kaiser Bill, as the British nicknamed him, is the man popularly linked with the outbreak of the First World War. This is not strictly accurate – although he had supported putting pressure on Serbia after the Archduke Franz Ferdinand was assassinated in Sarajevo in 1914, once he realized it was a mistake and that a war might break out, he made diplomatic efforts for peace, but too little, too late.

Bodo Ebhardt, a young German architect, was called upon to recreate the late medieval fort. The sheer verticality of its walls and towers and the dramatic location make it an exciting place (but come early to avoid the crowds). A CD-audioguide (available in English) comments on the architecture and on the pomp-loving Wilhelm II and Ebhardt. The mock medieval reaches the height of absurdity in the Salle du

Ribeauvillé

La Tour, 1 Rue de la Mairie, **t 03 89 73 72 73, **f** 03 89 73 38 74 (*inexpensive*). 35 rooms in a typical house in the midst of the old village. *Closed Jan–15 Mar.*

Riquewihr ✉ 68340

Riquewihr is an excellent place to stay, despite the crowds, with a half-dozen good hotels, although you may feel like you're in a fake tourist tinsel village rather than a genuine traditional wine-making community. However, prices are surprisingly reasonable for Alsace.

La Couronne, 5 Rue de la Couronne, **t 03 89 49 03 03, **f** 03 89 49 01 01 (*inexpensive*). A charming hotel with splendid 16th-century timberframe walls and beamed rooms.

***A l'Oriel, 3 Rue des Ecuries Seigneuriales, **t** 03 89 49 03 13, **f** 03 89 47 92 87 (*moderate*). 19 rooms in a 16th-century building inside the walls.

Le Sarment d'Or, 4 Rue du Cerf, **t 03 89 47 92 85, **f** 03 89 47 99 23 (*inexpensive*). A rival in cuteness to the above, also set along the ramparts, with 17th-century interiors, cosy rooms. *Closed Jan.* Quite inventive Alsace food in the restaurant (*menus 120–320F*). *Closed Jan; Sun eve, Tues lunch and Mon.*

St-Nicolas, 2 Rue St-Nicolas, **t 03 89 49 01 51, **f** 03 89 49 04 36 (*inexpensive*). Right by the Sarment d'Or inside the walls.

Au Moulin, 3 Rue du Général de Gaulle, **t 03 89 47 93 13, **f** 03 89 47 87 50 (*inexpensive*). Advertises itself with a bright blue façade inside the walls.

***Le Schoenenbourg, Rue du Schoenenbourg, **t** 03 89 49 01 11, **f** 03 89 47 95 88 (*moderate*). Just outside the village walls, close to the naff pond but right next to vineyards, not as charming as the others, but a comfortable modern hotel with modern facilities. Restaurant (*menus 190–420F*). *Closed Jan; May–Oct lunch: Nov–April Wed eve.*

Illhaeusern ✉ 68970

****Auberge de l'Ill and Hôtel des Berges, Rue de Collonges du Mont d'Or, **t** 03 89 71 89 00, **f** 03 89 71 82 83 (*expensive*). The most fabled restaurant in Alsace in a village by the Ill river east of Riquewihr. The regional cuisine and the wine list are absolutely stunning (*menus lunch 550F, dinner 760F*). Impeccable rooms too. *Closed Feb; Tues and Wed.*

Kaysersberg ✉ 68240

*Du Château, 38 Rue du Général de Gaulle, **t** 03 89 78 24 33, **f** 03 89 47 37 82 (*cheap*). A simple option, but one where you can sample an Alsace wine village on a budget.

Kaiser, smothered in ornate woodwork and coats of arms. On the clearest days the views from the château reach the Alps.

Three ruined medieval castles built by the Ribeaupierre family, one of the most powerful in Alsace, survey the wine village of **Ribeauvillé**. Although the village was bombed in the Second World War it has recovered remarkably well. The hike to see all three castles takes a good three hours. The **castle of St-Ulrich** was once the Ribeaupierres' magnificent seat; the form of a splendid Romanesque hall can be made out and you can climb a couple of formidable towers that have survived. From the heights you will spot the picturesque ruins of the former **castle of Girsberg**. The name has been adopted by one of Ribeauvillé's wines, a highly reputed *grand cru* riesling. There are also views from the **Château du Haut-Ribeaupierre**.

The archetypal Alsace picture-book wine village, **Riquewihr** often gets totally overrun by its admirers. Behind the fortifications, the 16th- and 17th-century vintners' houses are immaculate. In summer, a *son-et-lumière* show telling the history of

The Wines of Alsace

Alsace wines are like very opinionated guests around a dinner table: they have powerful, challenging, competitive characters. Single grape varieties give distinctive qualities to the different wines. Almost all the production is of dry and white, and most of the bottles contain wine from just one of the eight or nine grape varieties grown across the region. The very best wine-making regions are in the Haut-Rhin or southern half of Alsace. *Grand cru* Alsace wines can be made from riesling, the most typical Alsace variety, gewürztraminer, pinot gris and muscat. The other common varieties are sylvaner, pinot blanc, auxerrois and chasselas. Riesling tends to taste dry and clean, wine experts talking of steel and gunflint, minerals and masculinity. Gewürztraminer is sweeter, but spiciness is its essential quality, from smoky frankfurters to perfumed lychees. More fragile muscat produces dry, crisp, but delicately fruity wines.

Riquewihr takes place around the château. Head down the Rue des Juifs to the former Jewish quarter and you come to the ramparts and the Musée de la Tour des Voleurs, the former village prison. Riquewihr is home to many celebrated wine houses, its slopes producing some of the finest riesling in Alsace.

Kientzheim, an open little village peering over simple red walls, occupies an inordinately large place in the Alsace wine world. The Confrérie St-Etienne, which oversees the control of the quality of the wines, meets at its château. Its museum in the outhouses of the castle is devoted to wine-making in the region, with lots of old tools enjoying a pleasant retirement.

Birthplace of the 1952 Nobel Peace Prize winner Albert Schweitzer, **Kaysersberg** is a self-important town full of splendid old houses. An exceptional timberframe collection runs alongside the boulder-strewn river Weiss. The name of the place, the Emperor's Hill, derives from Gallo-Roman times, when a major route between Gaul and the Rhine valley passed this way. In the 13th century, Emperor Frederick II bought the village and paid for fortifications to keep out the dukes of Lorraine. The **Centre Culturel Albert Schweitzer** occupies a house next to the one in which he was born. In 1896, at the age of 21, the precocious student of philosophy, theology and the organ decided that he would devote himself to science and art until he was 30, and that after that he would serve humanity. (*See also* p.718.)

Colmar

For the very best timberframe show in Alsace, head for Colmar, Strasbourg's rival as tourist capital of the region. Red-tinged Gothic churches and stupendous Gothic paintings are the main attractions, the Musée d'Unterlinden famously housing Grünewald's harrowing Issenheim altarpiece. One museum is devoted to Bartholdi, the creator of the Statue of Liberty.

Set in the Rhine plain by the Lauch river, Colmar grew up around a Carolingian villa which Charlemagne and his sons visited several times. The prosperous place became a free imperial city in 1226. In the mid-15th century the emperor's representative in Alsace, the Archduke Sigismond, temporarily gave up part of his province to Charles the Bold of Burgundy in exchange for much needed funds. The Burgundian appointed Pierre de Hagenbach to rule Colmar. His cruelty towards the locals was eventually repaid when he had his head chopped off. After Swedish troops briefly took Colmar in the Thirty Years' War, French forces stepped in from 1635, but Germany took back Alsace in 1871. In the last war, the Germans held on fiercely to Colmar, but luckily the centre survived relatively unscathed.

Touring Colmar

As you wander round the **Musée d'Unterlinden** (*open April–Oct daily 9–6; rest of year daily exc Tues 10–5; adm*) the fountain splashes in the the unkempt cloister garden. The convent was founded in the 13th century and up to the Revolution was renowned for its strict rule and a strain of Christian mysticism. It now contains one of the finest collections of Rhenish art in the world, a whole series of north European masterpieces, including Hans Holbein's portrait of a sour woman and Lucas Cranach's study of Melancholy.

It is impossible to avoid being shocked into reflection by the greatest piece in the museum, Grünewald's **Issenheim altarpiece**, a complex work, brilliantly displayed in the former convent church. A model shows how the layers of panels were meant to be put together. The outer panels depict a gruesome crucifixion scene. Christ's body is covered with gaping bleeding sores, his fingers are contorted, rigid with suffering, while a disturbing growth emerges from one of his feet. He wears a heavy crown of thorns and hangs, mutilated and dead, against a black backdrop. The figure of St Sebastian is reckoned by some to be a portrait of the artist. The second layer of painted panels depicts the Annunciation to the Virgin and the resurrected Christ. The temptations of St Anthony, the most disturbing scenes of all, are saved until last.

The **Eglise des Dominicains** (*small fee*), topped by a patterned roof of green diamond tiles, is home to the most famous Virgin in Alsace, Schongauer's *Virgin in the Rose Bower*, which is utterly dwarfed by the vast Gothic edifice. The church is held up by some of the tallest Gothic columns in France, soaring uninterrupted by capitals to pointed vaults. The first stone was laid in 1283, but the building is essentially 14th and 15th century. Schongauer's Mary and Jesus appear against a background trellis of roses teeming with birds. The depiction of the Virgin in a garden was a popular theme, but no artist produced a more intense version than this. It is also rare for such a figure to have been painted slightly larger than life-size.

Don't miss the concentration of superlative historic houses along the **Rue des Marands** just off the Place de la Cathédrale, especially where it meets Rue Mercière and Rue Schongauer. The **Maison Pfister** boasts wonderful wooden galleries with Renaissance paintings below Old Testament figures, evangelists and symbols of Christian virtues.

The beautiful naked buttocks of Patriotism may entice you into the courtyard of the **Musée Bartholdi** (*open Mar–Nov daily exc Tues 10–12 and 2–6; adm*) at 30 Rue des Marands. This museum occupies the opulent 18th-century house where the sculptor

Getting Around

Colmar's airport is for special business services only, **t** 03 89 20 22 90, **f** 03 89 20 22 99. Colmar is on the train line through Alsace from Strasbourg to Mulhouse and Basel. The train from Strasbourg takes *c.* 30mins.

Tourist Information

Colmar: 4 Rue des Unterlinden, **t** 03 89 20 68 92, **f** 03 89 41 34 13.

Where to Stay

Colmar ✉ 68000

Expensive

★★★★Les Têtes, 19 Rue des Têtes, **t** 03 89 24 43 43, **f** 03 89 24 58 34, *Les-tetes@rmcnet.fr.* An unforgettable hotel in an unmissable 17th-century house covered in little figures in the busy centre of town; once a wine exchange. The 18 rooms and restaurant (*menus 170–360F*) are luxurious. *Restaurant closed Feb hols; Sun eve and Mon. Hotel closed Feb hols.*

★★★★Romantik Hôtel Le Maréchal, 4–6 Place des Six-Montagnes-Noires, **t** 03 89 41 60 32, **f** 03 89 24 59 40. Occupying a fabulous timberframe house in the Little Venice district, a luxurious hotel set back in its own courtyard. The restaurant with its dining room giving on to the water serves exciting updated regional cuisine.

Moderate

★★★St-Martin, 38 Grand'Rue, **t** 03 89 24 11 51, **f** 03 89 23 47 78. By the Schwendi fountain, the appealing old façade of this hotel looks over one of the most central spots in Colmar.

★★★Le Colombier, 7 Rue de Turenne, **t** 03 89 23 96 00, **f** 03 89 23 97 27. Very charming, cleanly restored and historic timberframe hotel with 24 rooms in the quieter quarter of the Little Venice district. No restaurant. *Closed Christmas.*

Inexpensive

★★Colbert, 2 Rue des Trois-Epis, **t** 03 89 41 31 05, **f** 03 89 23 66 75. Near the station, lively, friendly and comfortable.

Eating Out

Au Fer Rouge, 52 Grand'Rue, **t** 03 89 41 37 24, **f** 03 89 23 82 24. The finest address for classic regional cuisine (*menus 295–510F*). *Closed Mon exc May–Oct eve; Jan and 25 June–7 July Sun.*

Le Caveau St-Pierre, 24 Rue de la Herse, **t** 03 89 41 99 33. Characterful Little Venice restaurant with a terrace by the water, serving good-value Alsatian dishes (*menus 115–180F*). *Closed Sun lunch and Mon.*

Les Tanneurs, 12 Rue des Tanneurs, **t** 03 89 23 72 12. In the same area, also with a terrace; try trout in riesling sauce (*menus 109–185F*).

S'Parisser Stewwele, 4 Place Jeanne d'Arc, **t** 03 89 41 42 43, **f** 03 89 41 37 99. In a house with a typical timberframe façade.

was born in 1834. Many of his works celebrated leading lights in the history of Colmar and Alsace, including General Rapp, a firm-headed Colmarien who served as aide-de-camp to Napoleon. Bartholdi is particularly known as the sculptor of the Statue of Liberty, and the second floor concentrates on its making. A room on the ground floor is devoted to Jewish history in Colmar.

In **Place de l'Ancienne Douane**, the imposing **Koifhus** was Colmar's late 15th-century customs house and warehouse. The delightful **Place du Marché aux Fruits** is overseen on one side by the 18th-century **Palais de Justice**, where the Conseil Souverain d'Alsace, a regional parliament, sat before the Revolution. The enormous Gothic **St-Mathieu**, now Protestant, originally served a Franciscan monastery. A masonry screen divides the nave and choir, and the gallery running round the nave is decorated with panels depicting the miracles of Christ.

South of the Place du Marché aux Fruits, the stunning timberframe houses lead you to the ravishing waterways of Colmar's **Petite Venise**. Take a punt out on the water and watch the façades and the tourists peeping between the railings, hung with colourful hanging baskets.

The Alsace Wine Route, Part 2

Gorgeous wine villages lie along the slopes from Colmar down to Thann. Haughty but tattered medieval castle towers peer down from the Vosges heights above. The small towns along the way tend to be quiet, despite their rich religious legacies. Roads west of these towns and villages lead rapidly up into the Ballons des Vosges, the big pudding-shaped mountains of southern Alsace, with tiny ski stations dotted here and there.

For the benefit of the tourists, triangular old **Turckheim** is still 'patrolled' by a loud nightwatchman every evening between May and October. Within its three gateways, central Place Turenne is named after the French general who masterminded a tough winter campaign in these parts between 1674 and 1675 against the imperial army trying to win back Alsace for Louis XIV. Beyond the Flemish-gabled Hôtel de Ville rises the church spire, as colourful as the village houses with its green diamond patterning. Even the hospital looks utterly enchanting. The village museum is devoted to the battle for the Colmar pocket in the Second World War.

Delightful circular old timberframe streets surround the centre of **Eguisheim**, disputed birthplace of Pope Leo IX, alias Bruno d'Eguisheim. His statue stands above a fountain. Painted medallions on the ceiling of a neo-Romanesque chapel nearby tell events in his life. He was elected in 1048, and is said to have tried hard to encourage peace in Europe. The soaring 13th-century Gothic tower of the main church is regularly graced by a nesting stork.

More lovely wine villages lie south. A single red stone tower stands out at **Gueberschwihr**, the remnants of the Romanesque church. Surrounded by tall hedges of vines, **Pfaffenheim** has delightfully powdery coloured houses. **Rouffach** makes a more substantial stop and is less overrun by tourists. Its architectural legacy is of dignified Rhenish Renaissance buildings, and with its array of scrolled gables, the centre looks Flemish.

Up into the Ballons des Vosges Mountains Southwest of Colmar

Popular routes head up steeply into the Vosges west of Colmar. From Turckheim, one road quickly rises to **Les Trois-Epis**. In the late 15th century, a travelling smith was halted here by a figure of the Virgin, who warned him that unless the locals mended their wicked ways, they would be struck by the plague. If they repented, then they would know prosperous times, symbolized by three ears of corn she preferred in her right hand. The locals chose to change. The corny story has made Les Trois-Epis surprisingly popular, although the resort itself is dull. Walkers use it as a base for hikes up to the glacial lakes, the Lac Noir and the Lac Blanc.

The trenches of **Le Linge** seem lost in the most unlikely of locations high up in the Vosges, where bitter fighting raged in 1915 and 1916. A war museum recalls the campaign, and the trenches are remarkably preserved with their stone walls – white crosses rising out of the ground between them. Even today some areas are still out of bounds, marked as danger zones.

Munster carries its Irish name because monks came here from the Emerald Isle in the 7th century to evangelize the region. The abbey closed at the Revolution, and much of the village was destroyed in the First World War. Its fame now rests on smelly cheese. A wing of the abbey holds the headquarters of the **Parc Naturel Régional des Ballons des Vosges**. **Gunsbach** just down from Munster was where Albert Schweitzer (*see* p.714) spent his childhood and had a house built for himself in 1928. Although he worked so much in Africa, he returned here regularly, and his study has been left more or less as it was when he died.

Heading higher into the Vosges, a little south of the **Col de la Schlucht** pass you come to **Hohneck**, one of the very highest peaks in the Vosges at 4,467 ft. Cars wind up to the simple hotel-restaurant close to the summit, which means it's hardly tranquil, but massive views open up in all directions from the mountain's bald pate.

The popular resorts of Gérardmer, just in Lorraine, and **Xonrupt-Longemer**, lie next to the prettiest lake in the Vosges, Lac de Longemer, a pretty spot, pines coming right down to the water's edge. This glacial 'sea' is the venue for all sorts of water sports, and you can take a boat cruise or a *pédalo* to enjoy it at a gentle pace.

The Alsace Wine Route from Guebwiller to Thann

Back on the Rhine side of the Vosges, along the Alsace wine route, a trio of splendidly different churches in red Vosges stone mark **Guebwiller**. It may not be the prettiest town in the region, but it isn't swamped by tourists, and has plenty of character, overseen on one side by extremely steep terraced vineyards. The three churches all lie on the flat just off the Rue de la République. **St-Léger** is the oldest, its Romanesque-Gothic façade flanked by twin towers, with striking criss-cross patterning decorating its gable. A simple trinity of figures, Jesus' hands raised in blessing, greets you in the porch. Inside, the style turns clearly Gothic, with a dimly lit row of perfect squat little arches and striking stained glass.

The long Gothic **SS Peter and Paul** formed part of a Dominican abbey. Now a cultural centre, the choir features an exhibition on the Dominicans in Alsace and the nave is a concert venue. Most startling of Guebwiller's churches is the giant neoclassical **Notre-Dame**. Built from 1760 to 1785 for the last prince-cum-abbot of Murbach abbey above Guebwiller, the architecture may look sober, but the interior looks like a vast terracotta masterpiece ready for firing in the kiln. Stunning Corinthian columns hold up the vast nave, and the choir has a Baroque cascade of a centrepiece illustrating the Assumption of the Virgin.

Up to the Grand Ballon and the Ballon d'Alsace

The **Grand Ballon** is the highest mountain in the French Vosges, at 4,671ft, and is a sensational viewing point. The *grand ballon* on the top is used for radar. You can climb

Getting Around

Some trains between Colmar and Mulhouse stop at Rouffach. Take the local line west from Colmar to Turckheim, Gunsbach and Munster. Another local line from Mulhouse heads west to Thann and various other little stations.

Tourist Information

Turckheim: Corps de Garde, t 03 89 27 38 44, f 03 89 80 83 22.

Eguisheim: 22A Grand'rue, t 03 89 23 40 33, f 03 89 41 86 20.

Les Trois-Epis: Rue Thierry Schoerl, t 03 89 49 80 56, f 03 89 49 80 68.

Munster: 1 Rue du Couvent, t 03 89 77 31 80, f 03 89 77 07 17.

Guebwiller: 5 Place St-Léger, t 03 89 76 10 63, f 03 89 76 52 72.

Where to Stay and Eat

Eguisheim ✉ 68420

★★★Hostellerie du Château, 2 Rue du Château, t 03 89 23 72 00, f 03 89 23 79 99 (*moderate*). 12 rooms. Smart and expensive, by fountain and chapel. *Closed Jan.* Restaurant (*menus 175–375F*). *Closed Thurs lunch and Wed.*

★★Hostellerie du Pape, 10 Grand-Rue, t 03 89 41 41 21, f 03 89 41 41 31 (*inexpensive*). A bit special for a two-star. The restaurant is atmospheric too (*menus 280–700F*). *Closed Jan; Tues lunch and Mon.*

Rouffach ✉ 68250

★★★★Château d'Isenbourg, t 03 89 78 58 50, f 03 89 78 53 70 (*expensive*). Dominating the vineyards, flanked by a curious tower, this place once belonged to those decadent bishops of Strasbourg. Now its posh 19th-century frame offers 40 luxurious rooms and two fine restaurants, one set in a vaulted cellar (*menus 280–700F*). *Closed 16 Jan–10 Mar.*

Guebwiller ✉ 68500

★★★★Château de la Prairie, Allée des Marronniers, t 03 89 74 28 57, f 03 89 74 71 88. Elegant and good-value little 19th-century château, with 20 luxurious rooms. More French than Alsatian.

Buhl-Murbach ✉ 68530

★★★★Hostellerie St-Barnabé, 53 Rue de Murbach, t 03 89 62 14 14, f 03 89 62 14 15, *www.oda.fr/aa/saint-barnabe* (*expensive*). Excellent hotel on the quiet road between Guebwiller and Murbach. Fine cuisine too (*menus 158–398F*). *Closed Feb; Nov–April Sun eve; Mon lunch and Wed lunch.*

Soultz/Jungholtz-Thierenbach ✉ 68500

★★★Résidence Les Violettes, Jungholtz-Thierenbach, t 03 89 76 91 19, f 03 89 74 29 12 (*moderate*). 25 rooms. Set against a backdrop of trees above Soultz, this well-run hotel is immaculately kept inside and out. Restaurant (*menus 170–420F*). *Closed Mon eve and Tues.*

Thann ✉ 68800

★★★Du Parc, 23 Rue Kléber, t 03 89 37 37 47, f 03 89 37 56 23, *www.alsanet.com/parc-thann* (*moderate*). The bright yellow façade of this romantic hotel hides Italian touches inside. Restaurant (*menus 155–280F*).

up to its base and walk round the open-air gallery with viewing tables. On clear days you can supposedly see as far as the Alps, and on most days the views down over the last black edges of the Vosges to the vast plain from Belfort to the Rhine are breathtaking.

Flanked by vine slopes and a fragment of old castle, **Thann** has a Gothic church teeming with statuary and carved figures. Even the high buttresses are embellished.

The best place to appreciate the romantically wooded Thur valley is **Husseren-Weserling**, a pretty village in which a large textiles factory still produces high-quality fabric which you can buy from the factory shop. The textiles tradition goes back to the Ancien Régime, when the village had the only textile factory in Alsace given the French royal seal of approval. A new, slickly presented **textiles museum** has been opened alongside the factory.

One Marquis de Pezay, in 1770, summed up the spot you'll find yourself in by climbing to the top of the **Ballon d'Alsace**: one foot in Alsace, the other in Lorraine, with Franche-Comté just an arm's length away. A belligerent equestrian statue of Joan of Arc indicates that officially at least the Ballon d'Alsace lies just in Lorraine. The views from here are stupendous.

The combination of beautiful houses gathered from across Alsace, well-tended gardens, farm animals and traditional craftsmen is a recipe for mass tourist success at the **Ecomusée d'Alsace** outside Pulversheim. This artificial village was deliberately put up in a deserted area, which it has successfully revived. From the tallest old building, a stocky timberframe tower, you can see the Vosges in the distance as well as the storks 'encouraged' to settle on the chimneys. You are free to wander, but the explanatory panels and the demonstrations are only in French and German.

Below the Southern Vosges

Mulhouse, Belfort and Montbéliard tend to be overlooked by tourists, but all three cities have surprises. The area covered here also boasts two of the best churches built in France since the war, the Audincourt church with stained-glass windows by Fernand Léger, and Ronchamp's Notre-Dame-du-Haut, a wonderful flight of fancy by Le Corbusier.

Mulhouse

Historically, **Mulhouse** long lay out on a limb. While the rest of Alsace became French in the 17th century, the Republic of Mulhouse joined the Swiss Confederation, and only in 1798 decided to join the French Republic. This was the town that the Jewish army officer **Alfred Dreyfus**, who was framed and persecuted at the close of the 19th century, came from, although it was of course annexed to Germany for most of his troubled life. These days what Mulhouse has the most of is museums.

Outside the centre, the best known is the massive **Musée National de l'Automobile (Collection Schlumpf)** (*open daily exc Tues 10–6; adm*) which gives pride of place to its Bugatti collection. Train-lovers might prefer the equally large **Musée Français du Chemin de Fer** (*open April–Sept daily 9–6, otherwise till 5; adm*). A state-of-the-art electricity museum, the **Musée Electropolis** (*open July–Aug daily 10–6; rest of year closed Mon; adm*) stands next door. The **Musée du Papier-Peint at Rixheim** (*open June–mid-Sept daily 9–12 and 2–6; otherwise daily exc Tues 10–12 and 2–6; adm*) is a charming museum, dedicated to the French people's long love affair with wallpaper.

Mulhouse has a lively old heart too. The Protestant **Temple St-Etienne** contains a stunning collection of 14th-century stained-glass windows, with a gallery that enables you to admire it close up. In the town hall, a wildly decorated 16th-century piece of Rhine architecture, the **Musée Historique** (*open May–Sept daily exc Tues 10–12*

Getting Around

There are direct flights to Basel-Mulhouse, t 03 89 90 25 77, from Edinburgh and New York (Newark). Mulhouse and Belfort are on the train line from Paris-Gare de l'Est to Basel in Switzerland. Belfort is *c.* 5hrs from Paris, Mulhouse another 45mins.

Tourist Information

Belfort: Av Clemenceau, t 03 84 55 90 90, f 03 84 55 90 99.

Mulhouse: 9 Av Foch, t 03 89 35 48 48, f 03 89 45 66 16.

Montbéliard: 1 Rue Henri Mouhot, t 03 81 94 45 60, f 03 81 32 12 07.

Where to Stay and Eat

Belfort ✉ 90000

***Grand Hôtel du Tonneau d'Or**, 1 Rue Reiset, t 03 84 58 57 56, f 03 84 58 57 50 (*moderate*). A luxurious mix of Belle Epoque and modern styles. Restaurant (*menus 135–230F*). Closed Jan; Aug; Mon lunch and Sun.

***Hostellerie du Château Servin**, 9 Rue Général Négrier, t 03 84 21 41 85, f 03 84 57 05 57 (*inexpensive*). Stylish old house with pleasant garden below the fort, just 8 comfortable rooms and a reputable restaurant (*menus 120–450F*). Closed Aug; Sun eve, Mon lunch and Fri.

St-Christophe, Place d'Armes, t 03 84 55 88 88, f 03 84 54 08 77 (*inexpensive*). Overlooking one of the central squares, with a terrace where you can eat out on good days, a comfortable and characterful dining choice.

Montbéliard ✉ 25200

***La Balance**, 40 Rue de Belfort, t 03 81 96 77 41, f 03 81 91 47 16 (*moderate*). Suiting the new image of this town, in a soft-coloured historic house in a street just below the castle, a very comfortable hotel, 42 rooms renovated in style, using wood.

Chez Joseph, 17 Rue de Belfort, t 03 81 91 20 02, f 03 81 91 88 99. A neat little restaurant nearby in the old heart of town, serving pleasant cuisine (*menus 175–270F*). Closed Christmas; Aug lunch; Sat lunch and Sun.

---

and 2–6; rest of year till 5; adm) offers a ramble through local history. The **Musée des Beaux-Arts** (open mid-June–Sept daily exc Tues 10–12 and 2–6; rest of year till 5; adm) has sections on local painters. When you're all museumed out, escape into Mulhouse's pretty orchardy countryside, the **Sundgau**.

Belfort

The town of **Belfort** spreads out in a vulnerable gap, the Trouée de Belfort, between the Vosges and the Jura mountains, an all too tempting natural corridor for armies invading from the east. Part of the Prussian army advanced this way in 1870, and at Belfort the French soldiers under Colonel Denfert-Rochereau put up a brave defence despite being subjected to one of the first major deluges of artillery fire in modern warfare. They survived a siege of just over 100 days and only emerged from the citadel once the armistice had been signed.

Belfort still resists any connection with Alsace, but much of the centre – including the castle, the citadel within which it stands, the town's basilica and even the famous lion – is built in red Vosges sandstone, so it does *look* a chip off the Alsatian block even if its historical spirit aims elsewhere. The **citadel** is Belfort's major feature, and it contains the large **lion of Belfort**, sculpted by Bartholdi. Symbol of Belfort pride, it sits alert and menacing, backed up against the hillside. Below, engraved in Roman letters, the inscription reads: To the Defenders of Belfort, 1870–1871.

The French flag flies prominently from the top of the château at the top of the citadel. Its **museum** houses archaeological finds as well as photos of the appalling destruction caused by the Prussian bombardments. A copy of Vauban's 1687 model of the new Belfort citadel shows how the more complete fortifications once looked. The fine arts sections have Dürer prints, a school of Rubens Resurrection, ghostly works by Carrère, and Rodin sculptures. You can climb up on to the castle's flat roof to appreciate Belfort's strategic location.

Below, the red sandstone mass of the neoclassical 18th-century **cathedral** calls out for the most attention. In the grand squares beyond you will find statues to victory, including the theatrical setpiece of Bartholdi's group of defenders of Belfort.

Le Corbusier's Chapelle Notre-Dame du Haut

Like a giant single-winged bird that has landed on the steep slope above the village of **Ronchamp**, Le Corbusier's great **Chapelle Notre-Dame du Haut** is surely his best-loved and best-lasting work in France. Built in 1955, it contains elements that you would expect to find in medieval French architecture: three rounded castle-like towers and a tight array of window openings as if for bows, crossbows and small cannon. The most remarkable element is perhaps the grey concrete roof curving over the whitewashed walls like the flat cap of an enormous eccentric mushroom. An outdoor altar and pulpit stand below a single window featuring a statue of the Virgin and Child. From inside, set against the single source of light along the end wall, your attention is brilliantly concentrated on this group. In each of the secretive towers a Bible is left open for visitors to read. Close by a memorial pays homage to Resistance fighters killed on this spot.

Montbéliard

This industrial town, 16 km south of Belfort (and also in the very north of the Franche-Comté), sprawls around the banks of the Doubs. Ruled by the Württemberg family between 1397 and 1793, it still feels rather Germanic: from the time of the Reformation it was strongly marked by their Protestantism and claims the oldest Protestant church still standing in France. At the start of the 17th century the architect Schickhardt was taken round Italy by Friedrich I of Württemberg to prepare him for beautifying Montbéliard, and several of his efforts still add style to the town. Montbéliard's recent rejuvenation has included a refurbishment of the fine arts museum in the castle. The streets below the castle have also been spruced up and given news soft coloured façades.

East of the centre, industrial **Sochaux** is best known as the home of Peugeot cars; its museum tells the story of car-making through the 20th century. South of Sochaux, in the quiet residential quarters of **Audincourt**, the unmistakable tubular forms of Fernand Léger's figures decorate the glowing stained-glass windows of the Eglise du Sacré-Coeur. The baptistry is a sheer delight – it's like walking inside a bag of giant, vibrantly coloured boiled sweets.

Burgundy

17

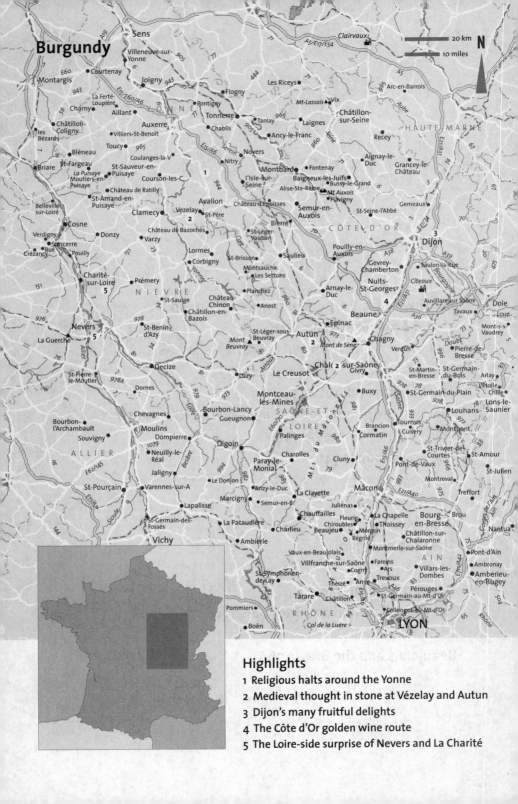

Burgundy

20 km
10 miles

N

Highlights

1 Religious halts around the Yonne
2 Medieval thought in stone at Vézelay and Autun
3 Dijon's many fruitful delights
4 The Côte d'Or golden wine route
5 The Loire-side surprise of Nevers and La Charité

Food and Wine

The Burgundians are very proud of their culinary traditions, which often combine alcohol with food. *Boeuf bourguignon* and *coq au vin* are famed regional dishes, while wine sauces are a great favourite, with beef, chicken, pork or hare. *Oeufs en meurette* is a delicious recipe in which wine is combined with eggs. Bacon, pork, onions and mushrooms are often thrown into traditional Burgundian sauces. Mushrooms are still quite easy to find in season in the region's many woods. Snails too are a regular feature on local menus. White Charolais cattle graze across large parts of southern Burgundy – the town of Charollais (with its extra 'l') has even opened a rather bizarre museum devoted to its cattle. The flatlands of the Bresse produce the white-plumed blue-stockinged *poulets de Bresse*, chickens with a formidable culinary reputation.

Dijon is of course reputed for mustard, but also for its gingerbread and blackcurrants, which go into making the intense liqueur, Crème de Cassis. One of Burgundy's finest cheeses, Epoisses, is matured in a marc, or liqueur.

Most burgundy wines grow on the eastern side of the region, along the slopes of the Saône valley. Heading south from Dijon past Beaune, the Côte de Nuits and the Côte de Beaune combine to make the legendary Côte d'Or which produces the most famous wines of all. Continuing southwards beside the Saône, the Côte Chalonnaise and the Mâconnais also yield splendid wines, sold at more reasonable prices. Then comes brash Beaujolais of the famous young fresh wines. Chablis, in the northwest of Burgundy, produces a popular white wine.

Lush Burgundy (Bourgogne to the French) is synonymous with wine, and remains surprisingly rural. But there were three periods when Burgundian doings profoundly changed the history not just of France but also of Western Europe. First, as the Astérix comics remind their readers, this is where the Gauls met with their decisive defeat against Caesar, at Alésia in 52 BC. The second important period came in early medieval times, when powerful monastic orders took root at Cluny and Cîteaux and then spread their influence across the continent, while leaving Burgundy a feast of great Romanesque architecture, at Vézelay, Autun, and golden stone churches of the Brionnais and Charlieu.

The third period, in the 14th and 15th centuries, saw the proud Dukes of Burgundy, difficult and dangerous cousins of the kings of France, swallow up Flanders and Holland as well as portions of northern France. Dijon flourished as their capital. Beaune, the historic capital of the earlier Capetian dukes, now has the distinction of being capital of the Burgundian wine trade. Later castles decorate the land: Tanlay, Ancy-le-Franc, Cormatin and Bussy-Rabutin are outstanding.

South of diminutive modern-day Burgundy are lands strongly linked to it: the Bourbonnais, home of the notorious spa town of Vichy, and bibulous Beaujolais. On the opposite side of the Saône, the flat, watery Bresse is the last area that has sneaked into this chapter, best known for its culinary specialities, notably the poulets de Bresse, the only AOC chickens in France.

Getting There

By plane: Dijon has an airport, but no helpful international links. For international flights, Paris-Orly isn't far from northern Burgundy, while Lyon-Satolas airport is a good option for southern Burgundy and even better for Beaujolais and the Bresse.

Clermont-Ferrand is linked to the UK by direct flights to and from London-City Airport.

By train: Dijon has a TGV link with Paris-Charles de Gaulle and Lille (and on to London-Waterloo), but it only goes once a day. Mâcon in southern Burgundy actually has better, faster connections with Paris.

By road: From Paris, the motorway into Burgundy is the A6. From Calais, you can easily avoid Paris by taking the A26 via Reims to Troyes, then the A5 and A31 down to Dijon. A new motorway, the A77, is being built down the western side of Burgundy.

Northwestern Burgundy: the Yonne, Serein and Armançon Valleys

The Yonne river starts in the wooded hills of the Morvan and flows northwest to join the Seine near Fontainebleau. Along the way stand two mighty cathedral cities, Sens and Auxerre, although they have been somewhat eclipsed by much smaller Vézelay and Avallon. Pontigny and vinous Chablis make popular stops along the Serein river. A couple of the finest châteaux in Burgundy, Tanlay and Ancy-le-Franc, lie by the Armançon river.

Sens

Sens, sandwiched between the Ile de France and Champagne, was a major Gallo-Roman town called Agedincum. The first bishops established themselves here in the 4th century, and by the 8th century they styled themselves archbishop of the Gauls and the Germans. Up to the 12th century they reserved the right to crown new kings of France. One medieval chronicler referred to the archbishop of Sens, who governed ecclesiastically over Paris and Chartres and five other major bishoprics, as 'a second pope', and briefly (1163–4), the real Pope Alexander III resided here. Thomas à Becket spent several years in exile at Sens, and the city has retained some of his wardrobe. It wasn't until the 1620s that Paris was finally granted its own archbishopric.

The **Musée de Sens** (*open June–Sept daily 10–12 and 2–6; rest of year daily 2–6, also Wed am and weekends 10–12; adm*) occupies the truly palatial archbishops' palace adjoining the cathedral. On one side stands the long Gothic hall where the bishops would meet, its roofs covered in multicoloured patterned tiles, something of a Burgundy trademark. Justice was meted out here, and the prison area contains centuries-old prisoners' graffiti. The brick and limestone façades of the other two sides of the courtyard are decorated with rich Renaissance motifs. Downstairs you can discover one of the best the Gallo-Roman collections in France. On the finest mosaic, a deer sticks out its long tongue.

The main treasures of the museum were acquired by medieval bishops of Sens, carved and bejewelled reliquaries which are only upstaged by saintly vestments probably woven in Persia or Byzantium. One is decorated with stylized lions, another with griffins, and the best with a moustachioed hero holding a lion by the throat in each hand. But the most famous cloth of all belonged to Thomas à Becket. His ceremonial garb, including an enormous alb, or linen piece, and his rather worn liturgical slippers, were considered relics after his assassination in Canterbury cathedral.

The **cathedral of St Stephen** has formidable credentials. Work began on it in the 1130s in Romanesque style, but from as early as the 1140s new Gothic forms were adopted, as at St-Denis in Paris. The architect, William of Sens, went on to remodel the choir end of Canterbury cathedral, helping export Gothic to England. The imposing west front is dedicated to St Stephen, shown in a dour statue, and the central portal tympanum is also devoted to him. The other portals show scenes from the lives of John the Baptist and the Virgin. Inside, the vast Gothic nave is grimly grey, but some of the stained-glass panels are the finest in Burgundy. The most famous concentrates on Thomas à Becket and was produced surprisingly soon after his death.

Along the Yonne from Sens to Auxerre

The old streets of **Joigny** rise sharply above the Yonne south of Sens. Some extraordinary carved timberframe houses stand out along the close-packed streets, one decorated with a Tree of Jesse, another with an equestrian figure who also features on the Gothic church of St-Thibault, dedicated to St Theobald of Provins, who went a-wandering all round Europe. It contains naive Renaissance touches: carved medallions and grotesques and a choir dripping with pendant bosses. The remarkable Smiling Virgin was carved in the 14th century. The nearby Renaissance church of St André has an ornate entrance lintel with a striking figure of St Andrew on his skewed cross. From the Renaissance Château de Gondi above, you get extensive views along the Yonne valley. Vines grow on the still higher slopes, the Côte St-Jacques, known above all for producing a Vin Gris. Down on the water, you'll find Joigny's river port. (For the route southwest into the Puisaye and the Loire-side Nivernais, *see* pp.739–41.)

Auxerre

The cathedral of Auxerre rises like a great Gothic vessel moored on the Yonne. A second enormous church, dedicated to St Germain, rises like another medieval ocean-liner docked by the river. Auxerre (Gallo-Roman Autessiodurum), long an important centre, lay on one of the main routes through Gaul linking Lyon with Boulogne, and the Mediterranean with the Channel.

The **Cathédrale St-Etienne** provides a splendid example of the Rayonnant Gothic style: sophisticated, yet simple in its sense of order. There is a fine view of it from the Pont de Bert. Between the flying buttresses, each bay finishes with a rose window. The cathedral dominates the roofscape of the town, harmoniously covered with the same earthen tiles as the buildings around it. Only one tower rises from the west front; the other one fell down in 1217, just two years after construction. At the west front you are greeted by superb portals full of sculptures, even if many were cruelly hacked at the Revolution. A striking central typanum scene shows Christ enthroned, above the Last Judgement. Carved panels around the doorways depict a wealth of

Getting Around

This is the area of Burgundy closest to Paris-Orly airport, from where the A6 or A5 swiftly bring you here.

Sens has a railway station on the TGV line from Melun, southeast of Paris, heading for Marseille. Auxerre, Avallon and Tonnerre also have useful railway stations.

Tourist Information

Sens: Place Jean Jaurès, **t** 03 86 65 19 49, **f** 03 86 64 24 18.
Auxerre: 1–2 Quai de la République, **t** 03 86 52 06 19, **f** 03 86 51 23 27.
Vézelay: Rue St-Pierre, **t** 03 86 33 23 69, **f** 03 86 33 34 00.
Avallon: 4 Rue Bocquillot, **t** 03 86 34 14 19, **f** 03 86 34 28 29.
Chablis: 1 Quai du Biez, **t** 03 86 42 80 80, **f** 03 86 42 49 71.
Tonnerre: 12 Rue François Mitterrand, **t** 03 86 55 14 48, **f** 03 86 54 41 82.

Where to Stay and Eat

Joigny ✉ 89300

****La Côte St-Jacques**, 14 Fbg de Paris, **t** 03 86 62 09 70, **f** 03 86 91 49 70, *lorain@relaischateaux.fr* (*luxury–expensive*). Overlooking the Yonne river, one of the most sumptuous hotels in Burgundy with 25 rooms and some of the finest cuisine in France (*menus 350–780F*).
***Le Rive Gauche**, Rue du Port au Bois, **t** 03 86 91 46 66, **f** 03 86 91 46 93 (*moderate*). Less exciting, but run by the same family and very comfortable. Restaurant (*menus 160–220F*).

Aillant-sur-Tholon ✉ 89110

****Domaine du Roncemay**, **t** 03 86 73 50 50, **f** 03 86 73 69 46, *roncemay@aol.com* (*expensive*). A relatively luxurious hotel by a golf course in a beautiful wooded setting. 16 tasteful rooms. Club House Restaurant (*menus 220–250F*).

Auxerre ✉ 89000

***Le Parc des Maréchaux**, 6 Av Foch, **t** 03 86 51 43 77, **f** 03 86 51 31 72 (*moderate*). Elegant 19th-century property, tucked away just outside the historic centre. A wonderful and not too pricey hotel. 25 stylish, relaxing rooms named after Napoleonic marshals.
***Le Maxime**, 2 Quai de la Marine, **t** 03 86 52 14 19, **f** 03 86 52 21 70 (*moderate*). The posh option on the busy but picturesque road down beside the river Yonne.
Le Maxime, 6 Quai de la Marine, **t** 03 86 52 04 41. There's also a separate, swanky beamed restaurant with the same name (*menus 180–270F*).
Le Seignelay, 2 Rue du Pont, **t** 03 86 52 03 48, **f** 03 86 52 32 39 (*inexpensive*). Sweet-looking hotel in the historic centre, with timberframe front, courtyard and restaurant (*menus 70–295F*).
Le Normandie, 41 Bd Vauban, **t** 03 86 52 57 80, **f** 03 86 51 54 33 (*inexpensive*). Larger and not as well located as the last, but well run, and comfortable in an old-fashioned kind of way.
Jean-Luc Barnabet, 14 Quai de la République, **t** 03 86 51 68 88, **f** 03 86 52 96 85. A 17th-century coach inn with delightful cuisine (*menus 235–305F*). *Closed Sun eve and Mon.*
Le Jardin Gourmand, 56 Bd Vauban, **t** 03 86 51 53 52, **f** 03 86 52 33 82. An artist of a chef serving experimental but still refined fare (*menus 150–280F*). *Closed Tues and Wed.*

Vincelottes ✉ 89290

Auberge Les Tilleuls, 12 Quai de l'Yonne, **t** 03 86 42 22 13, **f** 03 86 42 23 51. A riverside inn with plain rooms and a popular restaurant which has a curious terrace by the water (*menus 140–350F*). *Closed 20 Dec–20 Feb, Wed eve, and Thurs out of season.*

Vézelay ✉ 89450

***Le Pontot**, Place du Pontot, **t** 03 86 33 24 40, **f** 03 86 33 30 05 (*expensive*). With its secret garden and protecting fortified walls, the kind of delightful and exclusive place where even if you aren't staying you'll wish you could have a good look round. Very comfortable and very close to the church. *Closed 16 Oct–19 April.*

Cabalus, Rue St-Pierre, **t** 03 86 33 20 66, **f** 03 86 33 38 03. Atmospheric B&B in the former medieval hostelry of the abbey. The rooms are artistically sparse and charitably cheap. The café downstairs is charming.

***La Poste et le Lion d'Or, Place du Champ de Foire, **t** 03 86 33 21 23, **f** 03 86 32 30 92 (*moderate*). Most comfortable option in the busy lower part of the village, with a lovely terrace. Restaurant (*menus 126–240F*). *Closed Tues lunch, Thurs lunch and Mon. Hotel closed 12 Nov–31 Mar.*

Le Compostelle, Place du Champ de Foire, **t 03 86 33 28 63, **f** 03 86 33 34 34 (*inexpensive*). Popular, with 18 modern rooms, many with good views of the countryside.

Le Relais du Morvan, Place du Champ de Foire, **t 03 86 33 25 33, **f** 03 86 33 36 98 (*inexpensive*). The other obvious option at the entrance to Vézelay. Restaurant (*menus 86–195F*).

St-Père-sous-Vézelay ✉ 89450

***L'Espérance, **t** 03 86 33 39 10, **f** 03 86 33 26 15 (*expensive*). You can't get a more luxurious place to stay around Vézelay. The conservatory dining room is a Mecca for food lovers (*menus 380–690F*). *Closed 15 Jun–15 Oct Tues lunch, Wed lunch. Hotel closed Feb.*

***Le Crispol, Hameau de Fontette, **t** 03 86 33 26 25, **f** 03 86 33 33 10 (*inexpensive*). A smart, small modern hotel, well located on a small hill with views of Vézelay. Restaurant (*menus 110–280F*). *Closed 10 Jan–20 Feb, and 12–Nov–Mar Mon.*

Avallon ✉ 89200

****Hostellerie de la Poste, 13 Place Vauban, **t** 03 86 34 16 16, **f** 03 86 34 19 19, *www .hostelleriedelaposte.com* (*expensive*). A central 18th-century posting inn, with its own cobbled courtyard and modern interiors. Restaurant (*menus 155–430F*). *Closed Feb, Mar, Sun eve, and Mon out of season.*

***Hostellerie du Moulin des Ruats, Vallée du Cousin, **t** 03 86 34 97 00, **f** 03 86 31 65 47 (*moderate*). Former flour mill by the river in the delightful valley south of Avallon. Well converted too, with a very pleasant restaurant (*menus 155–235F*). *Closed Tues lunch and Mon. Hotel closed 21 Feb–10 Nov.*

Le Moulin des Templiers, Vallée du Cousin, **t 03 86 34 10 80 (*inexpensive*). Des Ruat's smaller neighbour: another comfortable mill with 12 rooms. Breakfast in the garden by the river. *Closed 1 Feb–1 April.*

Avallon Vauban, 53 Rue de Paris, **t 03 86 34 36 99, **f** 03 86 31 66 31 (*inexpensive*). Nicely done-up old coaching inn in the centre of town, with good restaurant and garden.

Vault-de-Lugny ✉ 89200

****Château de Vault de Lugny, 11 Rue du Château, **t** 03 86 34 07 86, **f** 03 86 34 16 36, *www.vault-de-lugny-chateau.com* (*luxury–expensive*). A splendid place with a medieval look, surrounded by a moat. A dozen superbly comfortable rooms with antique furnishings and four-posters. Restaurant for residents only (*dinner only; menus 290–480F*). *Closed mid-Nov–mid-Mar.*

Chablis ✉ 89800

***Hostellerie des Clos, 18 Rue Jules Rathier, **t** 03 86 42 10 63, **f** 03 86 42 17 11 (*moderate*). The posh option, with 26 spacious and modern rooms. Fine restaurant reputed for its Burgundian dishes (*menus 200–450F*).

L'Etoile, 4 Rue des Moulins, **t 03 86 42 10 50, **f** 03 86 42 81 21 (*inexpensive*). Very attractive building in the historic centre, offering old-fashioned rooms.

Le Vieux Moulin, 18 Rue des Moulins, **t** 03 86 42 47 30. Attractive restaurant down by the river (*menus 99–240F*).

Ligny-le-Châtel ✉ 89144

Relais St-Vincent, 14 Grande Rue, **t 03 86 47 53 38, **f** 03 86 47 54 16 (*inexpensive*). Appealing timberframe old house with hearty country cooking (*menus 78–160F*).

Ancy-le-Franc ✉ 89160

Hostellerie du Centre, 34 Grande Rue, **t 03 86 75 15 11, **f** 03 86 75 14 13 (*inexpensive*). A comfortable traditional option with 22 rooms. Restaurant (*menus 88–250F*).

Noyers ✉ 89310

La Vieille Tour, Place du Grenier à Sel, **t** 03 86 82 87 69, **f** 02 86 82 66 04 (*cheap*). A relaxing, and atmospheric cheap hotel in an historic house in the village.

biblical stories. Wonderful scenes around the north portal start with the story of Creation and end with a Noah's ark crammed full of animals.

Inside, the rhythm of the plain Gothic bays is impressive; the huge vaults of the crossing look slightly bowed by the pressure of their role. Each transept is embellished by a rose window containing Renaissance glass. In the ambulatory, the deep blue stained-glass windows are dense with biblical and saintly scenes separated by wonderful blood-red rings. The crypt, from an earlier Romanesque cathedral, is a wonky structure resting on simple rounded arches. The end chapel contains a couple of remarkable frescoes based on the Book of Revelations: Christ riding a white horse, accompanied by four angels on horseback, and a Christ in Majesty.

Just a short walk from the cathedral stands the **abbey of St-Germain**. Germain was born in Auxerre in 378, and took up the torch from St Martin in the race to convert Gaul to Christianity. As bishop of Auxerre he greatly encouraged Christian learning in the city, and is said to have overseen St Patrick before he sailed off on his mission to Ireland. Germain also travelled extensively: he probably studied for a time in Rome, and made it as far west as Wales, and as far east as Ravenna in Italy, where he died in 448. The empress there had his body sent back to Auxerre, where it was placed in a small oratory which the bishop had had prepared for himself. Clothilde, wife of Clovis, founded the abbey some time around the beginning of the 6th century. In the 9th century Count Conrad of Auxerre had a new edifice constructed, including what is now the best-preserved Carolingian crypt in France. A later Romanesque abbey built around this burned down in the 13th century, except for the Tour St-Jean. The whole messy complex is now the **Musée d'Art et d'Histoire d'Auxerre** (*open June–Sept daily 10–6.30; rest of year daily 10–12 and 2–6; adm*).

There are regular guided tours of the crypt. The *confessio* at the centre, held up on columns taken from a Gallo-Roman building, contains a decoy sarcophagus of St Germain; a hole shows where the real one could be hidden in times of emergency. The north side of the crypt is decorated with 9th-century frescoes, the oldest Christian ones in France, but the scenes are very faded. The rest of the museum is spread out around the chalky-white, classical 17th-century cloisters.

St-Pierre, also rising haughtily above the Yonne river and city roofs, has a lovely square Flamboyant Gothic tower, but inside the style is sober round-arched classicism. The rest of Auxerre's historic centre, with its densely packed, winding streets, is a delight to wander round. It has the second largest area of protected old streets in Burgundy after Dijon, tightly bound by boulevards which follow the lines of the former fortifications.

Vézelay

Vézelay, with its violent past, is a very pretty but overhyped fortified hilltop village dominated by a famed church, **La Madeleine**, which grew into a great pilgrimage centre on the back of a big Christian fib. The first abbey of Vézelay was founded in the 9th century. The story goes that an early abbot sent a monk to Provence to save the relics of Mary Magdalene (*see* Stes Maries de Mer, pp. 885–7) from Saracen raids. Around the year 1000 the rumour spread that Mary Magdalene's bones now rested in

Vézelay, a story sanctioned by the papacy in 1058. The overexcited abbots also put in claims to having relics of Martha and Lazarus. Work on the splendid abbey church began around 1096, and most of it was built in the 12th century. The best sculptors carved the capitals and tympanum. Important figures visited the abbey, exploiting its renown for their own advancement; most notoriously, St Bernard set the Western Christian world alight in 1146 with his preaching here in favour of a Second Crusade.

As well as serving as a crusading centre, Vézelay became one of the four major starting points in France for the pilgrimage to Santiago de Compostela. In 1217 St Francis also sent a couple of trusted friars to set up the first Franciscan monastery in France here. Louis IX, known as St Louis, came on several occasions to Vézelay as a pilgrim. But before the end of the 13th century the abbey of Vézelay would be discredited. The monks at St-Maximin in Provence had been instructed to try to find Mary Magdalene's remains in their abbey, which they duly did. During the Revolution most of Vézelay's abbey buildings were brought down, and a fire in 1819 saw the church fall into ruin. Its restoration by Viollet-le-Duc began in 1840.

After the disappointment of the stilted carving on the outer façade, the interior is very striking. In the celebrated tympanum, energy emanates from the massive, confident Pentecostal Christ surrounded by his apostles, chatting in animated fashion, and spreading the Good Word to a curious representation of the peoples of the world: Jews, Arabs, Byzantines, Ethiopians, Phrygians, Armenians and Scythians can all be identified in the cavalcade, along with giants, pygmies and 'the ones with big ears'.

The vast Romanesque nave appears to have been transported from Moorish Spain. Different coloured stone makes a decorative patterning, and there is a fabulous array of capitals on the columns, among the greatest in France. Violence is a main theme: try counting the number of swords and daggers drawn. Beheadings feature, as does an angel slicing an armoured man in two, and disturbing wild creatures also put in appearances – strange birds, serpents and monsters adding to the general feeling of menace; pick up the detailed guide to the capitals. The mix of scenes include Old and New Testament stories, classical tales and early Christian saintly lives – all jumbled up. Surprisingly, there are no scenes from Christ's life.

Along Vézelay's main village street, art exhibitions, wine shops and other tourist boutiques occupy the magnificent cellars below many of the houses. A walk around the medieval ramparts offers splendid views all round, with the beautiful hills of the Morvan to the south.

Around Vézelay

Down in the valley below Vézelay, **St-Père** makes a quieter stop. An abbey existed here first, but its destruction by Viking raiders led to the establishment of the other one on its more easily defended hilltop. But St-Père has a delightful church of its own, **Notre-Dame**, with an elaborate screen of a Gothic façade decorated with statues. The three main ones represent Christ and the two Marys like Olympic medal winners. A lovely three-tiered tower rises from the church. The interior is luminous, the vaults finished by charming decorated key stones. Set back in a little courtyard, the **archaeological museum** (*open April–Oct daily 10–12.30 and 1.30–6.30; adm*) contains a few remarkable finds from the nearby Fontaines Salées, which were being exploited at least 2,500 years ago and remain as salty as ever.

Hilltop **Avallon**, 15km east of Vézelay, is relatively peaceful thanks to its neighbour's fame. Its old streets are still contained in remnants of medieval walls, looking dramatically over the narrow Cousin valley. On this side stand intriguing vestiges of the Romanesque church of **St-Lazare** which was supposed to contain a relic of Lazarus. In a section of town wall nearby, the collections of the **Musée de l'Avallonnais** (*open May–Oct daily exc Tues 10–12 and 2–6; adm*) reveal that civilization on this rocky outcrop dates back to Gallo-Roman times and beyond. The **Musée du Costume** (*open early April–Oct daily 10.30–12.30 and 1.30–5.30; adm*) in the historic centre reconstructs the inside of a well-to-do bourgeois townhouse from the Ancien Régime.

The splendid 12th-century **Château de Bazoches** (*open Easter–early Nov daily 9.30–12 and 2.15–6; Oct–early Nov till 5; adm*) surveys an unspoilt valley on the northern edge of the Morvan and commands views up to hilltop Vézelay. The castle dates in large part from the second half of the 12th century. Richard Coeur de Lion and Philippe Auguste are said to have stayed here before heading out on the Third Crusade, but the man most associated with Bazoches is Sébastien Le Prestre de Vauban, the great military strategist. Vauban was born in modest circumstances in nearby St-Léger-de-Forcheret. Through brilliance and hard work he rose to become one of the key figures in the reign of Louis XIV, devoting most of his life to planning meticulous sieges and new fortifications. The successful siege of Maastricht in 1672 was one of his finest military achievements. In reward, Louis XIV gave Vauban a grant of 80,000 livres, with which the Morvan boy was able to buy the local château and see to its refurbishment. Although the original medieval forms had lasted well, he added elements for the needs of his family and his work.

The castle has been lovingly restored in recent decades. The tour takes you round elegant rooms, where the 17th-century Aubusson tapestry with peacocks and the Chinese lacquer work stand out. Splendid portraits depict royalty: Queen Henrietta of England, sister of Louis XIII of France and later wife of Charles I of England, is shown pale-faced, wearing a magnificent shimmering robe. A collection of remarkable earlier portraits by Clouet and Quesnel represent a string of Valois kings. Vauban had the long gallery constructed specially to serve as an office to draw up plans for his fortifications. Among the models, the largest one shows Neuf-Brisach in Alsace, built to his specifications between 1698 and 1709. Explanations include his theories on defence. Vauban died in Paris, but was buried in Bazoches church.

East of Bazoches, the unremarkable village where Vauban was born also honours its most famous son. For a start it has changed its name from St-Léger-de-Forcheret to **St-Léger-Vauban**. It has also recently created a small museum, the **Maison Vauban** (*open late Mar–early Nov daily 9.30–12.30 and 2.30–6.30; adm*), whose tone is pleasingly didactic. Vauban was a bold political thinker as well as a military strategist, who wrote on economics, taxation, social questions, land management and the French colonies. While an ardent royalist, he argued against the abuse of privileges and for a lessening of the tax burden on the poor – he was a kind and caring patriot, and a man ahead of his times.

The Serein and Armançon Valleys

Chardonnay has brought success to the lovely little wine town of **Chablis**, which sits prettily below the sensuous hills of the Serein valley east of Auxerre. A few swanky estates lie behind gates on the outskirts, but the vats belonging to the cooperative don't look too pretty.

Along the Serein north of Chablis, Cistercian **Pontigny** was founded in 1114, the second of the four so-called daughters of Cîteaux. Thomas à Becket found refuge here in 1164, and Edmund Rich, an intriguing figure who fought with Henry III for the independence of the English Church, was buried here. Known as St Edmund in English, in these parts he is known by the name of St Edme. Pontigny witnessed a 20th-century intellectual flowering when the philosopher Paul Desjardins drew literary figures here for his Décades meetings between the wars.

For a Cistercian building, Pontigny's church façade has a certain stylishness. Inside, however, is all sobriety – Romanesque moving towards Gothic, on a vast scale, uncluttered and pure. The Baroque additions come as a bit of a surprise: a screen with paintings of a stormy *Annunciation* and a *Flight into Egypt*. Feathery-looking putti float on the ornately carved choir stalls. An extraordinary stone baldaquin at the end of the choir serves as a melodramatic setting for St Edmund's gilded reliquary chest, held up by muscular, sky-gazing angels.

East of Chablis in the Armançon valley, **Tonnerre** boasts one of the oldest and largest medieval hospitals in France, as well as arguably the finest washhouse. With its mysterious watery pool emerging straight out of the ground, the Fosse Dionne is tucked away in a quiet corner of the old town. The covered colonnade adds to the feeling that this is a place of devotion, rather than somewhere to clean dirty linen.

The massive **Hôtel-Dieu** (*open June–Sept daily exc Tues 10–12 and 1.30–6.30; rest of period early April–Oct weekends and public hols 10–12 and 1.30–6.30; adm*) was built at the end of the 13th century, thanks to generous donations from Marguerite of Burgundy, the young widow of Charles d'Anjou, King of Sicily and Naples, who withdrew to Tonnerre when her husband died. A splendid timberframe ceiling covers the length of the building, in which the sick would have been looked after in beds, placed in alcoves along the walls. The hospital museum preserves some of its founding documents, and displays gruesome old surgical instruments, vying for attention along with treasured possessions of Marguerite and Charles.

Chablis

Chablis is only a small wine-producing area: under 3,000 hectares of land have been designated as suitable for producing the Chablis *appellations*, of which there are four: Petit Chablis, Chablis, Chablis Premier Cru and Chablis Grand Cru, in ascending order of merit. A mere 100 or so hectares are deemed capable of producing the best quality Grand Cru Chablis – the very finest vineyards lie on exclusive terrain northeast of town. Chablis is generally considered to produce a very crisp Chardonnay (the variety is sometimes known in the area as Beaunois). The better ones have delicate and complex flavours to accompany the clean taste.

The **Château de Tanlay** (*open April–15 Nov daily exc Tues, visits at 9.30, 10.30, 11.30, 2.15, 3, 3.45, 4.30 and 5.15, plus one at 5.45 in July and Aug; adm*), a short way east of Tonnerre, oozes style and excess. Built in light local limestone, topped by black slate roofs, this innovative château was begun in the middle of the 16th century. The two side wings end with big-breasted cupolas, and the central section is flanked by two striking, pilaster-decorated towers. Not surprisingly, the interiors have their excesses and eccentricities too, including some magnificently grotesque fireplaces. The high-point is the so-called Tour de la Ligue, whose ceiling is covered with nude figures painted in the 16th-century Fontainebleau style. Catherine de' Medici features as Juno, Diane de Poitiers, her rival in Henri II's affections, as Venus, while the king himself appears, appropriately enough, as a two-faced Janus.

Along the Armançon from Tanlay, the sober **Château d'Ancy-le-Franc** (*open Easter–11 Nov, visits at 10, 11, 2, 3, 4 and 5, Easter–15 Sept till 6; adm*) was built according to the plans of Sebastiano Serlio in the mid-16th century for Antoine III de Clermont, Diane de Poitiers' brother-in-law. The plainish frame hides a riot of wall paintings within, by the likes of Primaticcio, Nicolo dell'Abbate and the Burgundians André Meynassier and Philippe Quantin. In the Chamber of Judith and Holofernes, the biblical scenes take place against superb backgrounds; the Cabinet du Pasteur Fido features original wood panelling, and shepherds and shepherdesses by Philippe Quantin; and the Salon Louvois has superb gilded Renaissance grotesques on its coffered ceiling. The highlight is the splendid battle scene between Pompey and Caesar by dell'Abbate, full of terrible action, the horses menacingly forceful, the naked men fighting viciously. The Chambre des Fleurs, with its beautiful floral panels, and the Chambre des Muses, in which Primaticcio represents the liberal arts, introduce a calmer note. In recent times there has been a legal wrangle over ownership, which may affect visits.

The Morvan and Autun

Land of lakes, logging and, above all, endless wooded hills, the Morvan might be the geographical heart of Burgundy, but in tourist terms it lies off the beaten track. Château-Chinon is its main town, where the late President Mitterrand (nicknamed *Tonton* (uncle) or simply *Dieu* (God)) was long-time mayor, with a finger in every pie. The creation of the Parc Régional du Morvan in the 1970s has also helped tourism to develop, and a few little museums or *maisons* now highlight the park's main features.

The Maison du Parc at **St-Brisson** is a good place to pick up information on the area. The **Musée de la Résistance en Morvan** (*open June–mid-Sept daily exc Fri 10–12.30 and 2–6; early April–May and mid-Sept–early Oct Sat, Sun and hols 10–12.30 and 2–6; adm*) keeps alive the wretched stories of the wartime deportees, the martyred villages of the area, and the Resistance cells in the hills.

Saulieu, somewhat spoilt by the busy road passing through it, is an eastern gateway into the park. The medieval **Basilique St-Andoche** is dedicated to an evangelizer from the Middle East martyred here in early Christian times. It has been messed about with down the centuries, but the nave's Romanesque capitals, carved by the Cluny

Getting Around

This area is not easily accessible by public transport, but Autun has a railway station.

Tourist Information

St-Brisson: Maison du Parc, t 03 86 78 79 00, f 03 86 78 74 22.
Saulieu: 24 Rue d'Argentine, t 03 80 64 00 21, f 03 80 64 21 96.
Château-Chinon: Place Notre Dame, t/f 03 86 85 05 58.
Autun: 2 Av Charles de Gaulle, t 03 85 86 80 38, f 03 85 86 10 17.
Le Creusot: Château de la Verrerie, t 03 85 55 02 46, f 03 85 80 11 03.

Where to Stay and Eat

Saulieu ✉ 21210
★★★★**La Côte d'Or/Bernard Loiseau**, 2 Rue d'Argentine (N6), t 03 80 90 53 53, f 03 80 64 08 92, *loiseau@relaischateaux.fr* (*expensive*). Swanky hotel run by a celebrity chef. Awful location by the busy N6, but the dining areas give on to a pleasant garden; the cuisine is pure theatre (*menus 490–980F*). A few luxury and a few more modest rooms.

Anost ✉ 71550
★★**Village Fortin**, t 03 85 82 71 11, f 03 85 82 79 62 (*inexpensive*). In the Morvan hills east

of Château-Chinon, a basic, cheap and cheerful stop, with a bar below.

St-Léger-sous-Beuvray ✉ 71990
★**Hôtel du Morvan**, t 03 85 82 51 06, f 03 85 82 45 07 (*cheap*). A pleasant, basic little country hotel at the foot of Mont Beuvray, run by a welcoming Irish woman.

Autun ✉ 71400
★★★★**Hôtel St-Louis et de la Poste**, 6 Rue de l'Arbalète, t 03 85 52 01 01, f 03 85 86 32 54 (*expensive*). Extremely nicely done rooms, not outrageously expensive, set around a courtyard where you can eat in summer (*menus 90–320F*). Napoleon stayed here.
★★★**Les Ursulines**, 14 Rue de Rivault, t 03 85 86 58 58, f 03 85 86 23 07 (*moderate*). Once a convent, the 17th-century buildings have been transformed into a very comfortable hotel, just within the Gallo-Roman city walls at the top of the old town. The restaurant has character too (*menus 160–395F*).
★★**La Tête Noire**, 3 Rue de l'Arquebuse, t 03 85 86 59 99, f 03 85 86 33 90 (*inexpensive*). Characterful building, but there's a supermarket below it. Some pleasant rooms and the restaurant isn't bad (*menus 70–270F*).
★★★**Hostellerie du Vieux Moulin**, t 03 85 52 10 90, f 03 85 86 32 15 (*inexpensive*). Delicious food and wine at this quiet riverside address just out of town, surrounded by trees: lentils in truffle juice, the tenderest Burgundy *escargots* with mushrooms. But the rooms are badly in need of renovation.

school, still make for an impressive show . Among the best scenes look out for the Flight into Egypt and the false prophet Balaam riding on his donkey. The **Musée Pompon** (*open April–Sept daily exc Tues 10–12.30 and 2–6; rest of year daily exc Tues 10–12 and 2–5; adm*), adjoining the church, is named after a 19th-century animal sculptor of some repute born here, François Pompon, whose ultra-polished creations are a far cry from the sculptures of his teacher, Rodin.

South of St-Brisson, above the popular artificial **Lac de Settons**, several villages, notably Montsauche and Planchez, were completely destroyed by the Nazis in 1944 and have been rebuilt since the war. The town of **Château-Chinon** stands in a fine location, but it is not an attractive place. Mayor Mitterrand helped establish two big museums: the stylish **Musée du Costume** (*open July–Aug daily 10–1 and 2–7; May–June and Sept daily exc Tues 10–1 and 2–6; mid-Feb–April and Oct–Dec daily exc Tues 10–12 and 2–6; adm*), covering French fashion down the centuries; and the **Musée du Septennat** (*open same times; adm*), an hilarious absurdity, showing off ostentatious and outrageous gifts from around the world donated to Mitterrand during his time as president of France.

Bibracte, on the Mont Beuvray, has officially been designated a site of national importance. It was the main fortified oppidum of the Aedui, the local Celtic tribe, and is one of the rare pre-Roman towns of which any vestiges remain in France. In recent times Mitterrand came, saw and inaugurated. A slick modern museum, the **Musée de Bibracte** (*open July–Aug daily 10–7; rest of period mid-April–mid-Sept daily 10–6; mid-Mar–mid-April and mid-Sept–mid-Nov daily exc Tues 10–6; adm*), explains the oppidum and puts it in the wider context of its Celtic times. Disappointingly few of the objects unearthed here are on display, but you can visit the archaeological digs for free. Sections of ramparts and a gateway have been reconstructed; the location of the main street has also been identified. You'll need to use a great deal of imagination to recreate the oppidum; confusingly, the most substantial ruins up here formed part of a 15th-century Franciscan monastery. But the setting is majestic, and beyond a splendid beech wood, spectacular views open out over southern Burgundy and down on to the city of Autun.

Autun

Sloping up from the river Arroux, this city was one of the great cities of Roman Gaul. Two well-preserved monumental gateways stand strangely isolated on the edge of town, along with the more subdued remnants of a large theatre and a tower of the so-called Temple de Janus, now thought to have been dedicated to Mars. Built in the 1st century AD to control the territory of the Aedui tribe, the city lay along the Roman road between Lyon and Boulogne. It grew into an important centre of learning, renowned for its school of rhetoric. In medieval times the bishopric managed to secure what were claimed to be the relics of Lazarus, a major pull for pilgrims. The town would be greatly altered by the wealthy Rolin family in the 15th century.

It makes chronological sense to first visit the archaeological, historical and art collections of the **Musée Rolin** (*open June–Aug daily exc Mon and Tues 10–12 and 2–6; rest of year daily exc Mon and Tues 2–5; adm*) to get some inkling of the grand Gallo-Roman city that once stood here. After the impressive classical pieces, go on to admire the Romanesque section, including the renowned and powerful depiction of Eve's temptation, a work attributed to the great Gislebertus, generally regarded as the finest French Romanesque sculptor, and one of the few whose name has survived. The museum also contains some excellent paintings from the late 15th and early 16th centuries. The most famous features Cardinal Jean Rolin – baggy eyes, wrinkles and all – thought to be by the Master of Moulins (*see* p.741).

The cathedral of **St-Lazare**, built to hold the relics of Lazarus, has a mainly Romanesque body wearing a Flamboyant Gothic coat. The latter was commissioned by Cardinal Rolin. The soaring spire, the side chapels and the choir are all elaborate Gothic. Viollet-le-Duc's team got their hands on the west front in the 19th century and it shows. The tympanum, although spoilt by all the plaster around it, is decorated with one of the most celebrated works of Romanesque sculpture in France, signed by

Gislebertus. The elongated figures play out their parts in the Last Judgement as St Michael and Satan weigh souls.

The cathedral's capitals are superb, but you need a torch to illuminate them. You can appreciate some of the best from close up by climbing from the choir to the chapter-house. The most delightful one depicts the dream of the Magi, the three kings tucked up cosily together in bed, an angel coming to touch one on the hand to wake him up with the good news.

Western Burgundy: the Puisaye and the Nivernais

West of the Yonne and the Morvan hills, the quiet wooded countryside of the Puisaye and the Nivernais rolls down from below the A6 to the Loire. Colette spent her childhood in the Puisaye, while the obstreperous Grande Mademoiselle, head-strong cousin of Louis XIV, was expelled to the backwater of the Château de St-Fargeau where she called in the architect Le Vau to make things more to her liking. A few churches conceal wonderful wall paintings. Many of the villages dream away in the past, but the number of tourist attractions has grown rapidly in the last two decades. The Loire forms the frontier between Burgundy and the Berry in the Nivernais. Nevers is a great find, famed for its fine pottery traditions, but also for its historic centre, and for the preserved body of Bernadette of Lourdes, who died there.

Through the Puisaye

Heading down from the busy Yonne river and Joigny into the Puisaye, try to make a detour to see the late-medieval wall paintings of skeletons in the church at **La Ferté-Loupière**: flesh-coloured and big-eyed, one eyes a baby in a cot while some of his colleagues play musical instruments and others adopt saucy poses. A short way south, the church of **Villiers-St-Benoît** contains a depiction of three lords meeting three skeletons from a medieval fable, a reminder that death may pounce at any time. Here the **Musée d'Art et d'Histoire de Puisaye** (*open Feb–15 Dec daily exc Tues 10–12 and 2–6; adm*) is set in a pretty 18th-century Puisaye home, resembling an elegant but cluttered roadside antiques shop. Numerous objects reflect the crafts-manship of the area, especially the local pottery.

The **Château de St-Fargeau** (*open April–early Nov daily 10–12 and 2–7; adm*), in little St-Fargeau, capital of the Puisaye, looks old-fashioned and messy while boasting possibly the largest towers of any château in France, thick and dumpy. Most of what you see today dates back to the 15th century, ordered for Antoine de Chabannes, favourite of Charles VII. When Louis XIV's awkward cousin Anne-Marie-Louise d'Orléans, alias La Grande Mademoiselle, was exiled here, she ordered Louis Le Vau to give the pile some poise and panache. The inner castle therefore looks more stately, but the displays inside are amateurish, and many of the rooms stand in a state of disrepair. You can wander freely around some rooms, but on the guided tour you are shown a few restored chambers – the dining room is the *pièce de résistance* with its

Getting Around

Cosne and Nevers have railway stations.

Tourist Information

St-Fargeau: Maison de la Puisaye, 3 Place de la République, **t** 03 86 74 15 72, **f** 03 86 74 15 82.
St-Sauveur-en-Puisaye: Parking du Château, **t** 03 86 45 61 31.
La Charité-sur-Loire: Place Ste-Croix, **t** 03 86 70 15 06, **f** 03 86 70 21 55.
Nevers: Palais Ducal, **t** 03 86 68 46 00, **f** 03 86 68 45 98.

Where to Stay and Eat

Villiers-St-Benoît ✉ 89130

Relais St-Benoit, Rue Paul Huillard, **t 03 86 45 73 42, **f** 03 86 45 77 90 (*inexpensive*). Small inn with 6 rooms and a restaurant (*menus 98–158F*). *Closed Feb, Sun eve, and Mon.*

Donzy ✉ 58220

Le Grand Monarque, 10 Rue de l'Etape, **t 03 86 39 35 44, **f** 03 86 39 37 09 (*inexpensive*). Pleasing golden stone building with a slightly run-down charm but up-to-date décor. Restaurant (*menus 89–220F*). *Closed Sun eve and Mon exc hols.*

La Charité-sur-Loire ✉ 58400

***Le Grand Monarque, 33 Quai Clémenceau, **t** 03 86 70 21 73, **f** 03 86 69 62 32 (*moderate*). Small hotel with good view of the Loire and excellent food (*menus 138–238F*). *Restaurant closed Sun eve.*

Tintury

Guény, Fleury La Tour, **t** 03 86 84 12 42. Big, tranquil lakeside farmhouse with simple large B&B rooms in the quiet Nièvre countryside between Nevers and Château-Chinon. A really restful retreat. The retired farmer and his wife are very jolly.

curved corners, caramel wood panelling and marble fireplace. Restoration work began at the end of the 1970s, after the passionate M. Guyot acquired the property. It is partly financed by the spectacular summer evening shows which tell the story of the castle. Don't miss the tour of the attics, on a path measuring half a kilometre taking you around the impressive oak timbers beneath the castle roofs. The grounds were landscaped in English style before the Revolution.

In **St-Sauveur-en-Puisaye**, the wonderfully evocative new **Musée Colette** (*open April–Oct daily exc Tues 11–7; Mar, Nov and Dec, weekends and public hols 2–6; adm*) is housed in the village château and pays homage to the taboo-breaking author, drama queen and animal lover. (Her bisexuality, sometimes shockingly right-wing views and neglect of her daughter go unmentioned.) Inside, the spaces are covered with photos. Several rooms from her flat in Paris have been recreated. At the top of the stairs a slide show concentrates on Colette's eyes, making you feel as if the author's spirit watches over the museum. In the library each of the specially created cardboard books contains just one short, sweet, pithy quote.

In 1982 a dry spell made the whitewash peel off the walls of the church in sleepy little **Moutiers-en-Puisaye**, revealing the traces of a series of excellent medieval wall paintings. For 10 years work was carried out to bring the paintings back to life. Scenes from Christ's life and the Old Testament feature down the nave; in the choir two big figures carry a rock in each hand, ready to stone St Stephen as if in a fairground game.

M. Guyot, the restorer of the Château de St-Fargeau, is also responsible for an extraordinary building enterprise at **Guédelon** (*open July–Aug daily 10–7; April–June daily exc Wed 10–6; Sept–mid-Nov daily exc Wed 10–5.30; adm*) just below St-Sauveur-en-Puisaye, where he and his team are recreating a 13th-century fort from scratch, using 13th-century techniques. The project, started in 1996, will take 25 years to complete. Perhaps the most fascinating aspect is watching the masons painstakingly preparing the individual stones. You can also see the wood being prepared, specialist craftsmen such as ironmongers and potters at work, and peripheral activities including the copying of illuminated manuscripts, all the workers in period costume.

Below Guédelon, the charming, turreted **Château de Ratilly** (*open 15 June–15 Sept daily 10–6; Easter–15 June and 15 Sept–Oct daily 10–12 and 3–6; rest of year daily exc Sun 2–5; adm*) – a real 13th-century castle – lies hidden in the woods. It is now a pottery centre with potters at work, a permanent collection, exhibitions and concerts in summer. The simple château in nearby **St-Amand-en-Puisaye** also houses a pottery museum, and there are plenty of opportunities to buy a pot to take home.

The Nivernais or Nièvre

La Charité-sur-Loire

Historic La Charité-sur-Loire has remained virtually unspoilt, except for the odd old 20th-century advertisement fading on the wall by the priory. Large numbers of pilgrims crossed the Loire here on the long trail to Santiago de Compostela, and the *bons pères* gave them free room and board. This charity helped the town to develop, as the merchants outside the priory walls did a roaring trade. In the past two centuries, however, the priory have been terribly neglected. Parts of the once-sumptuous 18th-century buildings were even used for storing wine.

The church of Notre-Dame (1059–1135), built by monks from Cluny, was one of the most splendid of medieval France, and although now truncated and battered, it remains a unique, atmospheric place, best visited on a guided tour. The scale of the enterprise was awesome. The soaring entrance tower survives, with a tympanum showing Christ seated a bit precariously in his mandorla, blessing the Cluniac foundation. Delightful New Testament scenes appear below. Further scenes feature in another energetic tympanum inside the church, the main episode devoted to Christ's Transfiguration. A courtyard now lies between the tower and the nave, large parts of which fell down in a 16th-century fire. This much-reduced plain nave in the Cluniac style is held up by large rounded Romanesque arches. It leads on to exceptionally lofty transepts and a crossing supported on huge Gothic vaults. The crossing is topped by a tower, on the outside of which stand couples of curious statues whose exact significance has yet to be fathomed (you need binoculars to pick them out in detail). The choir end has a host of carvings of beasts and the end chapels are also richly carved.

Recent excavations beyond the choir seem to indicate that an enormous second church once stood next to Notre-Dame. The sorry remnants of the medieval chapterhouse and two later courtyards lie forlornly to the side, all in dire need of restoration. One large space is given over to the Cellier du Goût, on the history of taste. The separate Musée Municipal holds interesting finds from the priory excavations, as well as works from various 19th- and 20th-century art movements.

Nevers

The charming old centre of Nevers is still relatively undiscovered, although it has been known for some time for its pottery and as a place of pilgrimage to see the body of St Bernadette. The elegant centrepieces of the city stand on a broad, flat plateau, the château somewhat stealing the show from the cathedral, which appears to turn its back rather petulantly on its rival.

The beautiful **Palais Ducal** – the castle – is made of light beige stone, with large expanses of slate covering its roof and pointed towers. Round towers from the medieval castle survive on the north side, but the bulk of the building dates from the second half of the 16th century, when the Clèves family lived here and, through marriage, the son of the duke of Mantua became lord of Nevers. He encouraged the pottery manufacturers to settle in the city, and today a few still follow Italian traditions. The swan, the symbol of the Clèves family, appears in several carvings, and is also one of the most popular motifs painted on Nevers pottery.

One end of the **cathedral of St-Cyr and Ste-Juliette** is defensively Romanesque, the other openly Gothic: two churches facing in different directions were joined to form one massive whole. Walk round the outside to appreciate the rich decoration. Inside, a vast, black-eyed, rosy-cheeked and youthful Christ in Majesty looks down from the Romanesque apse. The perspective of this extraordinary painting creates unexpected effects, while the abundant drapery unfortunately makes it look as if Christ is trying to hide his flab. From a distance the almond-shaped mandorla takes on the shape of a globe, with Jesus appearing like a single huge continent upon it. Close up, you can also make out symbols of the evangelists and apostles. The nave is Gothic: comical straining figures are carved at the base of the pillars of the triforium arcade. The carved angels have a much easier time floating happily above. The bulk of the stained glass is modern, replaced after Second World War bombing. Out on the interconnecting squares, further golden buildings vie for attention.

The blue line on the pavements indicates a trail through the **pottery quarter** just down from the plateau. The Fayencerie Gonzague, 8 Rue des Récollets, is one of the outstanding pottery shops in this area. Some more tempting shops can be found on Rue du 14 Juillet and Rue de la Porte du Croux. Gerard Montagnon is one of the rare *maîtres-faïencier* still using traditional methods. Look out too for the names of Leatitia Welsch and Christine Girande.

The **Porte du Croux** holds the **Musée de la Porte du Croux** (*open daily exc Mon am and Tues 10–12 and 2–7; adm*), which includes local Gallo-Roman pieces and Romanesque fragments saved from an all-but-vanished the church, St-Sauveur. Outside the ramparts, the **Musée Frédéric Blandin** (*open daily exc Tues May–Sept 10–6.30; rest of year 1–5.30, but Sun 10–12 and 2–5.30; adm*) is mainly devoted to the development of Nevers pottery from the late 16th century on, but it also serves as the fine arts museum. Some rooms occupy the former medieval abbey of Notre-Dame. A wonderful array of Nevers pottery is displayed in the restored vaulted chapterhouse. The diversity is striking. The main distinguishing feature of Nevers-ware is its use of blue; few other colours were employed, except for yellow.

Cross the pleasant municipal garden beyond Place Carnot to reach the **convent of St-Gildard**, and the body of St Bernadette. She arrived here in 1866, some eight years after her visions at Lourdes (*see* p.596) and lived at the convent under the name of Sister Marie-Bernard until her death in 1879. Up to half a million pilgrims a year come to see her body, laid out in a see-through box. The crowds come to pray to her or simply stare. Her face and hands glisten with a kind of wax coating.

The Bourbonnais

The Bourbonnais was roughly converted into the *département* of the Allier at the Revolution, and although now officially part of the Auvergne, it is much more akin to Burgundy. The Bourbon dukes were renowned for their semi-independence in the late-Gothic period. Moulins, their capital, deserves to be better known. Vichy is an extraordinarily chic spa town which infamously became the headquarters of the collaborationist French government.

Moulins, the capital of the dukes of Bourbon between the early 14th century and the early 16th century, held one of the most sumptuous courts of any of the semi-independent provinces of that time. The town now has an attractive mix of architectural styles: grand buildings in stone, patterned ones in brick, timberframe ones, and some covered in colourful plaster. The **cathedral**, rebuilt in striking white stone with black decorative additions from the 19th century, contains one of the great masterpieces of late-Gothic painting, a superlative triptych by an artist known simply as the Maître de Moulins.

Groups are only allowed into the sacristy to see the **triptych** every 20 minutes. In the grisaille Annunciation on the exterior, two angels hover over the Virgin, anxious to present her to the archangel, but it is the sumptuously coloured paintings inside the triptych that people come to see. The donor couple and their sickly daughter are depicted with piercing reality. They look wearied by mortal life, while their patron saints radiate calm assurance. However, the reason for all the fuss – floating on a chair in the midst of a spectacular rainbow – is the gorgeous slip of a Virgin: a girl suddenly faced with the serious responsibility of motherhood who looks down with maternal concern at her beautiful new-born son.

The magnificent **stained-glass windows** in the choir end of the cathedral seriously rival the triptych. Along with their wealthy donors, they feature a collection of gruelling martyrdoms, and some of the most painful episodes in Christ's life.

The daunting and dilapidated **medieval castle** (*open June–mid-Oct; adm*) of the Bourbon dukes stands opposite the cathedral. It served as a prison until 1983, and the Nazis used it as an internment centre during the Second World War. Some 10,000 Jews passed through here on their way to deportation and death. Before heading down the slope to the town's shopping district, walk up **Rue de Paris**, which features some remarkably fine courtyards along its way. Below the cathedral, the sloping **Place de l'Hôtel de Ville** is surrounded by a charming hotchpotch of architectural styles, an orangey-red stone belfry rising above the mêlée. The major shopping artery,

Getting Around

Moulins and Vichy both have railway stations. Clermont-Ferrand not far south of the Bourbonnais is linked to the UK by direct flights to and from London-City Airport (*2 flights weekdays, and a couple at weekends*). Air France in the UK, t 0845 0845 111.

Tourist Information

Moulins: 11 Rue F.-Peron, t 04 70 44 14 14, f 04 70 34 00 21.
St-Pourçain-sur-Sioule: Place Mar. Foch, t 04 70 45 32 73, f 04 70 45 60 27.
Vichy: 19 Rue du Parc, t 04 70 98 71 94, f 04 70 31 06 00.

Where to Stay and Eat

Moulins ✉ 03000
**Grand Hôtel du Dauphin, t 04 70 44 33 05, f 04 70 34 05 75 (*inexpensive*). Coaching inn turned modern hotel right in the centre, with comfortable rooms.

St-Pourçain-sur-Sioule ✉ 03500
**Le Chêne Vert, Bd Ledru-Rollin, t 04 70 45 40 65, f 04 70 45 68 50 (*inexpensive*). Traditional provincial hotel with reasonable rooms and excellent regional food (*menus 95–200F*). Closed June and Mon exc July–15 Sept eve. Hotel closed 15 Sept–30 June.

Vichy ✉ 03200
****Aletti Palace, 3 Place Joseph Aletti, t 04 70 31 78 77, f 04 70 98 13 82 (*expensive–moderate*). By the casino and seat of the Vichy government, a big Belle Epoque posh hotel with a restaurant (*menus 130–200F*).
***Magenta, 21 Av Walter Stucki, t 04 70 31 80 99, f 04 70 31 83 40 (*inexpensive*). Chic hotel among a select group of houses close to the Allier river-cum-lake. Restaurant (*menus 110–140F*). Closed Oct–May.
**Hôtel du Louvre, Rue des Intendants, t 04 70 98 27 71, f 04 70 98 86 85 (*inexpensive*). Reasonable middle-of-the-range option.

Rue d'Allier, leads to lively Place d'Allier, where you can drink at the stylish Belle Epoque Grand Café.

The beige stones and brown roofs typical of the Bourbonnais look at their best in the small town of **Souvigny**, just south of Moulins. The former abbey church of St Peter and the monastic gateways dominate the centre. Their grandeur seems quite out of keeping with the little place, but Souvigny was an *haut lieu* of the Cluniac Benedictine order and of the lordly Bourbon family. Two of Cluny's greatest and longest-serving abbots, Mayeul and Odilon, died and were buried here, and much later, the great Bourbon dukes chose it as their burial place.

The great **abbey** is a startling five-aisled mix of Romanesque and Gothic, teeming with architectural and decorative curiosities. The long nave has a kink, said to have been built deliberately to reflect the bend of Christ's head on the cross. The windows in the choir end are in Gothic style, as are those of the first storey, but the aisles have rounded Romanesque arches, with carved capitals featuring bearded figures. Many of the heads of the tomb effigies have been chopped off, but the finely draped bodies remain. The two grand Bourbon tombs lie behind lacy Gothic stone bars. The adjoining museum fills you in on many more details.

Vichy

Vichy is a town of two sides. One side of the Allier river you have Belle Epoque Vichy, the Vichy of palatial hotels and grand town houses. This is the chic Vichy of the elderly and the sickly *curistes* who come to drink the hot eggy waters for their health. This is also the Vichy where Pétain installed his government under the Nazis. The other side of the river is young and sports-mad Vichy, where all manner of events take place and France's future gym teachers are put through their paces. The Allier here resembles a lake, and is good for rowing.

There may not be much to do in Vichy besides drinking the waters or playing sports, but the place has a mesmerizing quality. Virtually every building in the centre holds some interest, with every possible pastiche present – mock Gothic, mock Arabic, mock Venetian, mock Spanish, and plenty of Art Nouveau and Art Deco. Grand set pieces include the mock Mannerist Palais des Congrès, which opened as the first grand casino in France in 1865, and the Centre Thermal des Dômes, with its gilded Arabic-style cupola.

Between the two stretches the Parc des Sources, a civilized public garden with a delightful tree-lined covered walkway. The park's Hall des Sources is the best-known centre for taking the waters. Six thermal springs bubble up here like mini Jacuzzis; you can try them for a small fee.

South of the thermal establishments and shops, the little quarter around St-Blaise is more historic. St-Blaise itself is a curious hybrid: a showy 20th-century church with rounded nave and choir, containing glittering mosaics and big panels of gaudy stained glass, was added on to the medieval church sheltering Notre-Dame des Malades, a dark wood Virgin venerated by the sick. The Parc des Célestins nearby is fronted by an ostentatious oval pavilion. The thermal spring water is free here.

The Auxois

A sober Cistercian abbey, Fontenay has been declared a UNESCO World Heritage Site. A short way southeast, the Mont Auxois was the site of Alésia, where in 52 BC the Gauls under Vercingétorix met with their final defeat against Caesar.

Getting Around

The Paris train to Dijon stops at Montbard, from where there's a bus to Semur-en-Auxois.

Tourist Information

Flavigny-sur-Ozerain: t 03 80 75 81 21, or t 03 80 75 83 32.
Semur-en-Auxois: 2 Place Gaveau, t 03 80 97 05 96, f 03 80 97 08 85.

Where to Stay and Eat

Fain-les-Montbard ✉ 21500
***Château de Malaisy, t 03 80 89 46 54, f 03 80 92 30 16 (expensive–moderate).

A clean-lined and neatly restored 17th-century manor with 24 rooms, 6km southeast of Montbard. Impeccably kept, with a good restaurant (menus 150–320F).

Semur-en-Auxois ✉ 21140
A charming place in which to stay, with a good choice of delightful but modestly priced hotels.

**Les Cymaises, 7 Rue de Renaudot, t 03 80 97 21 44, f 03 80 97 18 23 (inexpensive). Adorable hotel with 18 rooms in an 18th-century town house. Closed Nov and 15 Feb–5 Mar.
**La Côte d'Or, 3 Place Gaveau, t 03 80 97 03 13, f 03 80 97 29 83 (inexpensive). A traditional converted coaching inn which is also a lovely place to stay. .

The **abbey of Fontenay** (*guided tours 15 Mar–15 Nov daily 9–12 and 2–6; rest of year daily 9–12 and 2–5; adm*), hidden in its shallow valley, is one of the best-preserved and earliest Cistercian monasteries in Europe. In 1118 the future St Bernard of Clairvaux sent out his cousin Godefroy de la Roche-Vanneau to found a new Cistercian community. When it became established a new monastery was commissioned and work began on the church in the 1130s. Pope Eugenius III, a former protégé of Bernard's, came to consecrate the church in 1147. The rest of the complex, including the forge, was completed by the end of the century.

At its height, the abbey had 300 monks, but it waned after the 16th century. Sold off at the Revolution, it was turned into a paper works, which it remained through the 19th century. Yet from its inception Fontenay was an industrial centre, iron-working its speciality. The rigorous Cistercian rule of prayer and work was strictly adhered to. Well restored, of the original complex the only major building missing is the refectory.

The church is the very model of Cistercian simplicity and severity. There is, however, a superb view down the nave to the straight-ended apse. A few decorative items were allowed in as the order became more relaxed. The chapterhouse was one of the few places where the monks would talk, discussing matters affecting the abbey. The work room and warming room would normally indicate that manuscripts were copied here, but there's no evidence for this, and the work may simply have been shoe-making instead. Fontenay – rare because of its state of preservation – was in fact a relatively modest monastery.

Vercingétorix the Gaul

As Caesar conquered Gaul to further his political career back home, the Celtic settlement on this hilltop became the fatal hideout for the Gaulish troops united in rebellion under Vercingétorix. Vercingétorix had carried off a memorable victory over the Romans at Gergovie in his home territory of the Auvergne earlier in the year. Caesar had then headed up north to join forces with troops under his second in command, Labienus. Vercingétorix decided to surprise the Romans and attacked them near Dijon. Unfortunately for the Gauls, Caesar turned the situation round. His legions not only survived the surprise attack, but emerged victorious. Vercingétorix and his men sought refuge on the height of Alésia. Caesar pursued them and had his men build a double line of fortifications round the base of the Mont Auxois. The Romans, who included Mark Anthony and Brutus among their number, then laid siege through August and September. The Gauls' allies found it impossible to get past the Roman lines to provide the besieged men with provisions. Vercingétorix and his troops made a desperate last bid to break out themselves, but, unable to escape, they were forced to surrender after six weeks. Vercingétorix would be sent to Rome to be paraded in front of the crowds before being strangled, and in Gaul serious resistance to Rome would come to an end. A large 19th-century statue on top of the Mont Auxois pays homage to Vercingétorix, as does the quote from Caesar admitting that a unified Gaul could take on the universe.

Roger the Rogue

The lovable but uncontrollable courtier and scandalmonger Roger de Rabutin was François de Rabutin's grandson. The paintings in the castle reflect his colourful life with their mordant wit. Born in 1618, Roger was destined for a military career, and he served in the Thirty Years' War. He married in 1643 and had children, but his wife died after just four years. He quickly gained a reputation for his scurrillous verse, while his actions were invariably excessive too. He had already spent a brief spell imprisoned in the Bastille for an affair with a married woman before his first marriage.

Roger's pen would be his downfall. He sank deeper and deeper into trouble from the middle of the 17th century, angering the great military leaders of the period, Turenne and Condé. When he insulted Louis XIV he was exiled to his estates in Burgundy where he whiled away the months writing naughty and thinly disguised sketches of Louis XIV's courtiers, *L'Histoire Amoureuse des Gaules*.

Bitterness mixed with his wit, Roger commissioned local artists to illustrate the goings-on in court at the Château de Bussy. Many are allegorical, containing period allusions, but the indomitable, saucy spirit of the great rogue can't fail to emerge.

The unpretentious old village of **Alise-Ste-Reine** clings to the steep slope below the flat summit of the Mont Auxois. This hill, known to the Romans as Alésia, witnessed the last great stand of the Gauls against Caesar.

Some still dispute whether the Mont Auxois was the place where Vercingétorix was defeated, but what is beyond doubt is that the remains of an important **Gallo-Roman settlement** (*open July–Aug daily 9–7; late Mar–June and Sept–Oct daily 10–6; adm*) have been discovered around the hilltop. This settlement grew here after the infamous siege, with all the trappings you would expect, including basilica, forum, temples and a theatre capable of seating some 5,000 spectators. The remains are hard to make out on the ground, but the old-fashioned-looking **museum** (*open same times; adm*) in the village contains some revealing finds – the latest excavations took place through the 1990s. In particular, Gallo-Roman Alésia became an important place for bronze craftsmen, praised by Pliny the Elder, and some impressive bronze pieces were recovered from the digs, including some beautiful heads.

The name of Alise-Ste-Reine indicates the importance in these parts of the early Christian saint, Reine or Regina, martyred here in 262 AD after espousing Christianity and refusing to marry the Roman governor Olibrius. Her relics were kept on the hill for many centuries after her death, but were moved to the nearby hilltop site of **Flavigny-sur-Ozerain** in the 860s. The smell of aniseed often wafts across the fortified village – the tradition of making aniseed sweets here also goes back as far as the 9th century. Flavigny has a potentially fine array of old gateways and houses in need of restoration. The former abbey of St-Pierre looks particularly battered, and the ugly aniseed sweet factory has taken over many of its 17th-century buildings. Among the fragments of the abbey cower the dingy remnants of the Carolingian crypt.

The charmingly acerbic **Château de Bussy-Rabutin** (*open April–Sept daily 9.30–11.30 and 2–5, plus daily visit June–Aug at 6; Oct–Mar daily exc Tues and Wed 10–11 and 2–3;*

adm), hidden in a little valley northeast of Alise-Ste-Reine, deserves a detour for the very lively guided tour. The castle is surrounded by pretty gardens, and substantial late-Gothic round towers mark the corners of the moated building. The wings were redone in Renaissance style for the Comte de Rochefort in the 16th century. Having lost his fortune, his principal creditor, François de Rabutin, acquired the castle and commissioned the redesign of the central section in the first half of the 17th century.

Four sturdy round towers rise above the river at **Semur-en-Auxois**, a small town set on its spur above a meander in the Armançon, 12km west of Alise-Ste-Reine. This served as an important fortress for the dukes of Burgundy. The church of Notre-Dame is the town's focal point. Much of the statuary on the main Gothic portal was hacked away at the Revolution, but the north doorway has retained its touching scenes of the life of Doubting Thomas. Side chapels in Flamboyant Gothic and Renaissance styles lie off the surprisingly tall and slender nave. The restored Gothic stained-glass windows show drapers and butchers at work – engaging pieces of a rare clarity. The **Musée Municipal** (*open daily exc Tues April–Sept 2–6; rest of year 2–5; adm*) has extensive collections of sculpture. The 19th-century plaster casts by Augustin Dumont are classic stuff – he is best known for the Spirit of Liberty on the Place de la Bastille in Paris. The Gallo-Roman ex votos of body parts were left at shrines dedicated to healing gods.

Surrounded by a dry moat, the **Château d'Epoisses** (*grounds open daily 9–7; interior open July–Aug daily exc Tues 10–12 and 3–6; adm*) west of Semur is cut off from its village by a double line of fortifications. In the medieval outer bailey stand a solid dovecote and a simple, atmospheric church containing a 16th-century pietà and a Christ attributed to the great 16th-century sculptor Germain Pilon. What remains of the castle is still substantial, with various towers. One is named after a 6th-century queen of Burgundy, Brunehaut, who frequently stayed around Epoisses, another, the most remarkable with its layering of different-coloured stone, after the Grand Condé, who owned the château for a time.

Lovely valleys of oaks, with Charolais cows grazing in the meadows, lead to the **source of the Seine** which has been turned into what looks like a 19th-century city park in the middle of nowhere, ordered by Napoleon III and Haussmann. The site is owned by the city of Paris. In a grotto around where the first waters of the Seine emerge from the ground, the recumbent statue represents Sequana, the residing Gallo-Roman goddess.

Dijon

Most people will be familiar with the culinary Dijon, its mustard and its Crème de Cassis, the intense blackcurrant liqueur mixed with white wine to create a drink known as a Kir (named after a one-time mayor of Dijon), not to mention the fabulous local wines. But first-time visitors will be surprised by this splendid Burgundian city, where the culinary even extends to the architecture, the finest façades weighed down with stone garlands of fruit.

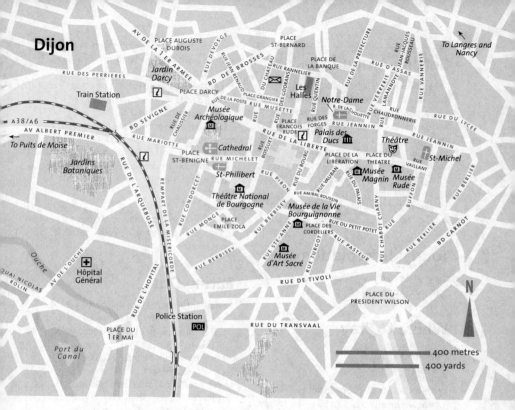

There was a Gallo-Roman settlement here, Divio, and early Christian activity is traced to a misty figure known as St Bénigne or Benignus. In 989, Mayeul, the great abbot of Cluny, sent a brilliant Italian protégé, William of Volpiano, to the abbey of St-Bénigne to restore the Benedictine rule there. The first Capetian duke of Burgundy, Robert I, chose Dijon as his capital in the first half of the 11th century. A terrible fire ravaged much of the town in 1137, causing it to be rebuilt.

The powerful Valois line of Burgundy dukes – Philippe le Hardi and his three successors – came to an end in 1477, and from 1482 Burgundy remained a possession of the French monarchy. Louis XI created a regional Parlement here; the great houses were built for its members. In more recent times the area's vinous and culinary specialities have brought this city – now with a thriving university – a great deal of attention.

Touring Dijon

The **Musée Archéologique** (*open June–Sept daily exc Tues 10–8; rest of year daily exc Tues 9–12 and 2–6; adm*) is housed in an impressive wing of the medieval abbey next to the cathedral. The prehistoric finds include some glittering pieces of bronze and gold jewellery, most spectacularly the Blanot treasure. The Gallo-Roman collections feature votive offerings left to Sequana, the goddess of the Seine. The medieval carvings are the most beautiful artefacts on display, with some wonderful representations of St Bénigne.

Getting Around

The Dijon-Bourgogne airport, t 03 80 67 67 67, f 03 80 63 02 99, *www.dijon.aeroport.fr*, lies 6km southeast of town, but most flights are routed via Clermont-Ferrand in the Auvergne.

By train there is a TGV from Paris-Charles de Gaulle airport (*c.* 1hr 55 mins) or from Lille (2hrs 50mins), but there is only one service a day on each line.

Trains from central Paris to Dijon leave from the Gare de Lyon.

Tourist Information

Dijon: Place Darcy or 34 Rue des Forges, t 03 80 44 11 44, f 03 80 30 90 02.

Where to Stay

Dijon ✉ 21000

Expensive

★★★★Hostellerie du Chapeau Rouge, 5 Rue Michelet, t 03 80 50 88 88, f 03 80 50 88 89. Good hotel with old stone façade on the edge of the historic heart of Dijon. Actually quite reasonably priced, with 30 rooms and exquisite cuisine (*menus 250–400F*).

Moderate

★★★Hôtel Wilson, Place Wilson, t 03 80 66 82 50, f 03 80 36 41 54. 27 comfortable rooms set around a charming little courtyard. No restaurant.

★★★Hôtel du Nord, Place Darcy, t 03 80 50 80 50, f 03 80 30 61 26. Central, with well-equipped rooms, a fine restaurant and a cellar for Burgundy wine tastings (*menus 100–200F*).

Inexpensive

★★Le Jacquemart, 32 Rue Verrerie, t 03 80 60 09 60, f 03 80 60 09 69. Delightful, well-run, old-style but stylish hotel in the centre of town. A real bargain.

★★Le Sauvage, 64 Rue Monge, t 03 80 41 31 21, f 03 80 42 06 07. Lovely hotel with timber-frame walls and courtyard; practical for parking.

★★Le Palais, 23 Rue du Palais, t 03 80 67 16 26, f 03 80 65 12 16. Appealing hotel in an 18th-century limestone building, well located in the centre of the city.

★★Le Chambellan, 92 Rue de la Vannerie, t 03 80 67 12 67, f 03 80 38 00 39. Hotel in an historic house close to the theatre and the church of St-Michel.

Cheap

Hôtel Lamartine, 12 Rue Jules Mercier, t 03 80 30 37 47, f 03 80 30 04 43. Well located but basic.

Eating Out

Restaurant Thibert, Place Wilson, t 03 80 67 74 64, f 03 80 63 87 72. Connected to the Hôtel Wilson, with a top-class reputation thanks to Monsieur Thibert's inventive Burgundian cuisine (*menus 140–450F*). *Closed Feb and Aug.*

Le Pré aux Clercs/Jean-Pierre Billoux, 13 Place de la Libération, t 03 80 38 05 05, f 03 80 38 16 16. Splendid restaurant, set in the semi-circle of architecture in front of the ducal palace. Renowned in particular for poultry dishes (*menus 260–500F*). *Closed 2nd half Aug, Sun eve and Mon.*

Au Moulin à Vent, 8 Place François Rude, t 03 80 30 81 43, f 03 80 30 30 83. Typical Burgundian cuisine served in a friendly and lively atmosphere.

Le Cézanne, 40 Rue Amiral Roussin, t 03 80 58 921 92. Charming small-scale restaurant in an old house in an old street, with a small terrace (*menus 99–250F*). Book in advance. *Closed 2nd half Aug, Mon lunch and Sun.*

Coum'Chez Eux, 68 Rue Jean-Jacques Rousseau, t 03 80 73 56 87, f 03 80 73 34 45. Run by a chatty man from the Morvan; generally serves an excellent dish of the day.

Le Passé Simple, 18 Rue Pasteur, t 03 80 67 22 00. Cosy, hearty traditional bistro, a bit further out towards Place du Président Wilson.

The great medieval church dedicated to St Bénigne has only been a **cathedral** since 1731. Virtually nothing remains of the 11th-century original, except the crypt (*small fee*) which is damp and badly restored, but more impressive than the building above. Among the underground chapels stands the base of a rotunda, said to have originally had three storeys. Some of the capitals show fascinating primitive Carolingian figures. The vast Gothic building above was begun around 1280. After the colourful roofs outside, the wide interior looks extremely sober, although the shift from the pink-tinged stone of the nave to the golden-orange stone of the choir is striking. A few embellishments from the Ancien Régime add a bit of interest, including statues on the columns, some elaborate tombs in the side aisles, and a wild baptismal font.

The pompous **Palais des Ducs** was reshaped in the late 17th century at the same time as the charming semi-circular Place de la Libération. It now holds the town hall and the enormous **Musée des Beaux-Arts** (*open daily exc Tues 10–6; adm*). The chapterhouse contains some fabulous Burgundian statuary and precious religious items. But the most famous pieces in the museum lie in the **Salle des Gardes** on the first floor: the famed tombs of the dukes of Burgundy, especially Claus Sluter's magnificent tomb of Philippe le Hardi. One the finest of all medieval sculptors, he also trained his nephew Claus de Werve to succeed him. Sluter carved most of the mourning monks, known as *pleurants*, around the base of the tomb; de Werve completed the collection. The tomb of Jean sans Peur and his wife Marguerite of Bavaria by Spaniard Juan de la Huerta and Antoine Le Moiturier of Avignon more or less copied the style of the first tomb. The retables made for the ducal charterhouse by the Flemish artists Melchior Broederlam of Ypres and Jacques de Baerze are also stupendous.

The room devoted to Flemish painters is another delight, with a famed Nativity scene by Robert Campin or the Master of Flémalle. The riches continue in the Dutch, German, Swiss, Italian and French late-Gothic and Ancien Régime collections, but the 19th- and 20th-century collections prove a bit disappointing beyond some Delacroix drawings; many of the 20th century works are execrable. The smooth animal sculptor Pompon has a room of his own, and a few pieces by the monumental 19th-century sculptor François Rude stand out here and there.

Rude has also been given his own museum, the **Musée Rude** (*open June–Sept daily exc Tues 10–12 and 2–5.45; adm*), in the converted church of St-Etienne east of the Palais des Ducs, on the same square as the classical theatre. Beyond, the virtuoso façade of the church of **St-Michel** makes a grand Renaissance song and dance at the end of Rue Vaillant. In the centre, the Christ of the Last Judgement appears like an overenthusiastic conductor who has turned up for a last night of the Proms in a toga.

Dijon's grand quarter just north of the Palais des Ducs contains truly spectacular mansions. **Rue des Forges** boasts some of the very finest. The **Maison Maillard** built from the second half of the 16th century for one of Dijon's mayors, Jean Maillard, wins the prize for most overdressed house of all, the façade groaning under a bumper crop of garlands. Nearby, three rows of hefty gargoyles, with floral decoration stuffed between their contorted figures, decorate the Gothic church of **Notre-Dame** which more than holds its own amongst all the neighbourhood's excesses. The portal sculptures were unfortunately hacked to bits, but the plethora of stone carvings above remain. Green *jacquemarts*, or bell strikers, add a carnival touch to the bell tower. Inside, the church has been greyly restored.

The streets north and east of Notre-Dame have more fabulous town houses: along Rue de la Chouette, the **Hôtel de Vogüé** vies with the Maison Maillard for the accolade of finest in town. It exudes refinement, its pink-stoned arch leading into an exquisite courtyard embellished with enchanting carvings. Rue Jeannin, Rue Verrerie, Rue Chaudronnerie, Rue Lamannoye, Rue Jean-Jacques Rousseau and Rue Vannerie contain more wonderful buildings.

To the south of the Palais des Ducs, semi-circular **Place de la Libération** is the most elegant place to shop. Hidden away down Rue des Bons Enfants, the **Musée Magnin** (*open daily exc Mon 10–12 and 2–6; adm*) allows you into one of Dijon's great houses without an invitation to dinner. It is crammed full of small works of art collected in the late 19th century and early 20th century by Maurice Magnin and his sister Jeanne.

Two lesser-known museums stand next to each other on Rue Ste-Anne. The **Musée d'Art Sacré** (*open daily exc Tues 9–12 and 2–6; adm*) occupies the domed circular church of the Bernardines, a dramatic setting for some absorbing religious works. The **Musée de la Vie Bourguignonne** (*open daily exc Tues 9–12 and 2–6; adm*) has taken over other buildings of the former convent, set around a classical cloister. The rambling collection includes 19th-century Burgundian costumes and interiors, recreated old shops and builders' crafts. Some way west, the **Musée Amora or Musée de la Moutarde** (*48 Quai Nicolas Rolin; guided tours mid-June–mid-Sept daily exc Sun at 3pm only; adm*) will fill you in on the story of mustard-making in Dijon; the recipe was apparently invented by the son of a Roman Prefect of Gaul in the 4th century.

Among the sprawling buildings of the **psychiatric hospital** a kilometre west of Place Darcy, you can go in search of some of the finest statues to be have survived from the great 14th-century ducal period, on the so-called **Puits de Moïse** (the Moses Well). Six life-size statues were carved round the base of what must once have been a superlative calvary made to sit in the cloisters of the **Chartreuse de Champmol**, built for the dukes of Burgundy. The ducal tombs have been moved to the central Musée des Beaux-Arts (*see* above), but the vestiges of the calvary have stayed put. The work of Claus Sluter of Haarlem, executed between 1395 and 1405, they are regarded as one of the very finest groups of Gothic sculpture ever made. The Old Testament figures are reality in stone: forceful old men with wrinkled faces worn with care as well as age. Moses stands out, with his horned brow and his firm gaze. The other statues represent David, Jeremiah (wearing spectacles), Zachariah, Daniel and Isaiah. The drapery too carried realism in sculpture to new heights, way ahead of its times.

The Côte d'Or

This is one of the most famous stretches of vineyards in the world, running for some 56km south from Dijon, past Beaune, to Santenay (near Chagny). Many of the best wines in the world are made here and rival the top Bordeauxs for the position of the most absurdly prized and priced wines on the planet.

The wine route along the Côte d'Or sticks to the middle section of the slopes. We also slip across the valley to Cîteaux, birthplace of the Cistercian order. Beaune, capital of Burgundy's wine trade, demands a stop with an underground town of cellars existing under street level.

The Côte de Nuits

This section of the Côte d'Or has been dubbed the Champs Elysées of Burgundy. Along the D122 or **Route des Grands Crus**, lies a string of villages which produce arguably the most envied red wines in the world, Gevrey-Chambertin followed by Chambolle-Musigny, Clos de Vougeot and Vosne-Romanée. The most celebrated estate around **Gevrey-Chambertin** is the Clos de Bèze, which produced Napoleon's favourite wine. You can go on an entertaining tour of the **Château de Gevrey-Chambertin** (*open daily 10–12 and 2–6; adm*), with a tempting range of wines on offer. A pretty road leads up into the **Hautes-Côtes de Nuits** from Gevrey-Chambertin. Head for the **Vergy hilltop** for extensive views of the area.

The **Château du Clos de Vougeot** (*open April–Sept daily 9–6.30 – but Sat closes at 5; Oct–Mar daily 9–11.30 and 2–5.30 – but Sat closes at 5; adm*) stands as a stately symbol for the whole Côte de Nuits, in the midst of the world renowned Clos Vougeot. The solid, square castle was built for the monks of Cîteaux, who planted vines here and made wine on the spot until the Revolution. Clos Vougeot wine hasn't been made at the château since 1913, but since the war the castle has been the headquarters of the Confrérie des Chevaliers du Tastevin which promotes Burgundy wines. The regular tourist tour is a little disappointing, despite the hulking great wooden wine presses. Through inheritance, the 51 hectares of the walled estate have been divided into little plots, yielding 90 differently labelled wines, making the Clos Vougeot vintages yet more precious and yet more absurdly priced.

Nuits-St-Georges is packed with cellars selling fine wines. A good address at which to pick up relatively reasonably priced bottles is **Le Cavon de Bacchus** (*t 03 80 61 15 32, f 03 80 61 28 20*). The local community shows its devotion to the god of wine with regular wine festivities, including a celebrated wine auction on the Sunday before Palm Sunday. Nuits-St-Georges has strong connections with Cîteaux, and the **local history museum** (*open 2 May–Oct daily exc Tues 10–12 and 2–6; adm*) contains an 18th-century model of the famous abbey.

The Wines

The great red wine is made using Pinot Noir, the great white wine using Chardonnay. A little red is produced using Gamay, a little white using Aligoté. The Côte de Nuits production is almost entirely of the finest possible reds; the Côte de Beaune yields both fabulous reds and whites. The very top wines carry the *appellation* Grand Cru; there are 33 Grand Cru appellations in all, producing a tiny 2 per cent of Burgundian wine. Next come the Premier Cru *appellations*, of which there are some 561. Some way below follow the village *appellations*, and lastly the regional *appellations*, which make up roughly half of all Burgundy's wine each year.

Burgundy Wine Routes

Saulieu

Pouilly-en-Auxois

Dijon

Gevrey-Chamberton

Saulon-la-Rue

Morey-St-Denis

Chambolle-Musigny · Vougeot

Vosne-Romanée · Gilly-les-Cîteaux

Arnay-le-Duc

Nuits-St-Georges

Cîteaux

Bouilland

Château de Savigny-les-Beaune

Auvillars-sur-Saône

Aloxe-Corton

Dole

Beaune

Tavaux

Epinac

Pommard

Volnay

Mont-s-s-Vaudrey

Autun

Mersault

Nolay La Rochepot

Puligny-Montrachet

Chassagne-Montrachet

Mont de Sène

Santenay

Verdun

Pierre-de-Bresse

Dezize-les-Maranges

Chagny

Bouzeron

Rully

St-Germain-du-Bois

Couches

Chalon-sur-Saône

St-Martin-en-Bresse

Arlay

Le Creusot

Givry

St-Germain-du-Plain

Lons-le-Saunier

Montceau-les-Mines

Buxy

SAÔNE-ET-LOIRE

Palinges

Brancion

Louhans

Cormatin

Montpont

Tournus

Paray-le-Monial

Cuisery

Charolles

Cluny

Pont-de-Vaux

St-Trivier-de-Courtes

St-Julien

Berzé-le-Châtel

Berzé-la-Ville

Montreval

La Clayette

Sologny

Milly-Lamartine

St-Point

Château de Pierreclos

Solutré

Pouilly Fuissé

Mâcon

Treffort

Chauffailles

Juliénas

Brou

Chénas

Fleurie

La Chapelle

Romanèche-Thorins

Bourg-en-Bresse

Charlieu

Chiroubles

Villié Morgon

Thoissey

Vonnas

Beaujeu

Morgon

Régnié

Belleville

Châtillon-sur-Chalaronne

AIN

Vaux-en-Beaujolais

Montmerle-sur-Saône

Villars-les-Dombes

Ambronay

Amberieu-en-Bugey

Villefranche-sur-Saône

Fareins

Cogny

Ville-sur-Jarnioux

Jarnioux

Ars

Trevoux

St-Symphorien-de-Lay

Oignt

Theizé

Anse

Pérouges

Tarare

Châtillon

St-Germain-au-Mt-d'Or

Feurs

Collonges-au-Mt-d'Or

RHÔNE

Champagne-au-Mt-d'Or

Col de la Lüere

LYON

N

10 km

5 miles

Take a good look, because little remains of **Cîteaux**, the birthplace of that most austere of religious orders, the Cistercians. The **revived abbey** (*open mid-May–mid-Oct daily exc Tues 9–6, guided tours at 9.15, 11, 1.45 and 4.15; adm*) was in fact also largely responsible for giving birth to the great vineyards which were tended for so many centuries by the monks. The guided visit around the sad remnants of Cîteaux is one of the most intelligently conceived tours in Burgundy. Most of the great abbey was destroyed after the Revolution, but a few scattered old buildings remained standing and, after a long period of neglect, some of these have been restored. It is once again a living community, the monks provided with one old wing and a modern church. Other parts have now been opened for guided visits.

The first abbey was founded in 1098 by Robert, a monk from the Benedictine abbey of Molesme, who would be succeeded almost immediately by his right-hand man Alberic. An English religious man, Stephen (Etienne to the French) Harding, became the third abbot after Alberic's death in 1109. Harding was responsible for developing the vibrant intellectual and cultural aspects of the monks' religious life at the parent abbey, encouraging the highest standards in copying texts and illuminating manuscripts, as well as in music. The future St Bernard joined the abbey in 1113; he would be sent out from Cîteaux by Stephen to found Clairvaux (*see* p.683). The Cistercian order reached its height in the 13th century, becoming the largest in Europe. Texts give glimpses of Cistercian thinking, and the rules of the order along with its five pillars are clearly explained; you are even asked to observe a degree of silence.

The Côte de Beaune

This is one of the top white wine territories in the world, although the estates of **Aloxe-Corton** have the distinction of producing both red and white wines of supreme quality. The village château has an outrageous colourfully tiled roof. Charlemagne is said to have owned vineyards here, hence the magical name Corton-Charlemagne in white wines. The *appellation* stretches into neighbouring Pernand-Vergelesses whose church dates from the Romanesque period. The grand **Château de Savigny-lès-Beaune** contains the **Musée de la Moto, de l'Aviation et de la Voiture de Course** (*open 15 Jan–Dec daily 9–12 and 2–6, but 5 in winter; adm*), a large collection of vintage cars, motorbikes and planes gathered together by a vinegrower. The fighter planes make a curious sight parked next to vines in the noble grounds. The village of Savigny-lès-Beaune has plenty of delightful old wineries.

A detour not far from busy Beaunes takes you up the gorgeous and quiet wooded Rhoin valley from Savigny-lès-Beaune to **Bouilland**, the limestone clifftop of a Burgundian *combe* (a steep indented valley) sticking out above the trees. Not far from Bouilland, the ruins of the **abbey of Ste-Catherine** rise as high as the tall trees which surround it. The Romanesque to Gothic abbey church stands open to the elements, romantically roofless.

The Côte de Beaune vineyards continue south of Beaune. Pommard and Volnay both produce top quality red wines. In Pommard, the **Domaine Coste Caumartin** (*Rue du Parc, t 03 80 22 45 04, f 03 80 22 65 22*) in the same family since the Revolution, is a down-to-earth but serious wine-making estate run by charming people. The villages

Getting Around

Gevrey-Chambertin, Vougeot and Nuits-St-Georges have railways stations on the Dijon–Beaune line, and there are regular services to Chagny on the Dijon-Mâcon line. Otherwise to reach the villages along the Côte you can take a bus from Dijon or Beaune.

Tourist Information

Gevrey-Chambertin: Place de la Mairie, t 03 80 34 38 40, f 03 80 34 30 35.

Nuits-St-Georges: Rue Sonoys, t 03 80 62 01 38, f 03 80 61 30 98.

Meursault: Place de l'Hôtel de Ville, t 03 80 21 25 90, f 03 80 21 26 00.

Chagny: 2 Rue des Halles, t 03 85 87 25 95, f 03 85 87 14 44.

Nolay: Maison des Halles, t/f 03 80 21 80 73.

Where to Stay and Eat

Gevrey-Chambertin ✉ 21220

★★★**Arts et Terroirs**, 28 Route de Dijon, t 03 80 34 30 76, f 03 80 34 11 79 (*moderate*). Painting and culture on the agenda at this hotel in an old home done out with panache.

★★★**Les Grands Crus**, Route des Grands Crus, t 03 80 34 34 15, f 03 80 51 89 07 (*moderate*). Modern-looking but very comfortable, set among the vineyards. *Closed Dec–Feb.*

★★**Aux Vendanges de Bourgogne**, 47 Route de Beaune, t 03 80 34 30 24, f 03 80 58 55 44 (*inexpensive*). The 14 rooms aren't much, but the restaurant is down-to-earth, with well-chosen wines and good fare (*menus 115–145F*). *Restaurant closed Sun.*

Les Millésimes, 25 Rue de l'Eglise, t 03 80 51 84 24, f 03 80 34 12 73. One of Burgundy's legendary restaurants with what's regarded as just about the best wine list in the region and delicious seafood (*menus 355–655F*). *Closed 12 Dec–25 Jan, Wed lunch and Tues.*

Rôtisserie du Chambertin, Rue du Chambertin, t 03 80 34 33 20, f 03 80 34 12 30. Splendid food and staggering wines at staggering prices (*menus 210–330F*). *Closed 1st half Aug, Feb, Sun eve and Mon exc bank hols.*

Saulon-la-Rue ✉ 21910

★★**Château de Saulon-la-Rue**, t 03 80 79 25 25, f 03 80 79 25 26 (*inexpensive*). Appealing 17th-century château in large grounds with comfortable sitting rooms and a stylish pool and terrace. Restaurant (*menus 100–200F*).

Morey-St-Denis ✉ 21220

★★★**Castel de Très Girard**, 7 Rue Très Girard, t 03 80 34 33 09, f 03 80 51 81 92 (*moderate*). Walled 18th-century manor offering a calm retreat, set among vineyards, with a pool. Wide selection of wines in the gastronomic restaurant (*menus 180–250F*). *Closed Wed.*

Caveau St-Nicolas, 13 Rue Haute, t 03 80 58 51 83. Run by a former travelling salesman who likes a good joke, a simple but sweet B&B tucked away in a cul-de-sac.

Chambolle-Musigny ✉ 21220

★★★★**Château-Hôtel André Ziltener**, Rue de la Fontaine, t 03 80 62 41 62, f 03 80 62 83 75 (*luxury–expensive*). Splendid, exclusive little

of **Meursault**, **Puligny-Montrachet** and **Chassagne-Montrachet** are synonymous with superlative white wines. The famous estates are discreet here. In Puligny-Montrachet, **Le Caveau de Monsieur Wallerand**, Rue de Pouisseuil, is a good little wine shop.

Get away from the main Côte de Beaune wine route by heading into the delightful hills of the **Hautes-Côtes de Beaune** west of Puligny and Chassagne-Montrachet. The **Château de la Rochepot** (*open April–Oct daily exc Tues 10–11.30 and 2–5.30; adm*) offers the most dramatic silhouette in the area, its towers with coloured Burgundian tiles rising above a rather dull village. The original fort dated from the 12th century, but was completely transformed by the Pot family in the 15th century. Much of the castle was brought down at the Revolution, and rebuilt in the 19th century. Full of mock-

hotel hidden behind walls. 10 rooms and its own wine cellars. *Closed 1 Dec–14 Mar.*

Gilly-lès-Citeaux ✉ 21640

****Château de Gilly**, t 03 80 62 89 98, f 03 80 62 82 34 (*expensive*). High-class luxury combined at this former abbots' country pile. Excellent cuisine (*menus 210–415F*). *Closed Feb.*

Auvillars-sur-Saône ✉ 21250

Auberge de l'Abbaye, Route de Seurre, t 03 80 26 97 37. Good food in an appealing setting (*menus 118–245F*). *Closed Sun eve, Tues eve and Wed.*

Châteauneuf-en-Auxois ✉ 21320

***Hostellerie du Château**, t 03 80 49 22 00, f 03 80 49 21 27 (*inexpensive*). Some of the 17 rooms have a brilliant valley view by the spectacular castle. Dining à la carte (*menus 140–220F*). *Closed 22 Nov–10 Feb, Mon and Tues exc July and Aug.*

Aloxe-Corton ✉ 21420

*****Villa Louise**, t 03 80 26 46 70, f 03 80 26 47 16 (*expensive*). Charming and understated in the shadow of the village castle.

Levernois ✉ 21200

*****Hostellerie de Levernois**, Route de Combertault, t 03 80 24 73 58, f 03 80 22 78 00 (*expensive*). A haven of tranquillity overlooking large gardens and a river. Enormous wine list to go with the ultra-refined cuisine (*menus 345–680F*). *Restaurant April–Oct closed lunch exc Sun.*

Meursault ✉ 21190

Les Magnolias, 8 Rue Pierre Joigneaux, t 03 80 21 23 23, f 03 80 21 29 10 (*moderate*). Lovely 18th-century manor with its own courtyard and charming rooms. *Closed 15 Mar–30 Nov.*

Le Chevreuil, Place de l'Hôtel de Ville, t 03 80 21 23 25, f 03 80 21 65 51. A good restaurant serving well-prepared Burgundian classics.

Puligny-Montrachet ✉ 21190

*****Le Montrachet**, 10 Place des Marronniers, t 03 80 21 30 06, f 03 80 21 39 06 (*moderate*). Slightly unexciting hotel, but a special restaurant (*menus 215–435F*). *Restaurant closed Wed lunch. Hotel closed 30 Nov–10 Jan.*

Chagny ✉ 71150

*****Lameloise**, 36 Place d'Armes, t 03 85 87 65 65, f 03 85 87 03 57 (*expensive*). Traditional hotel with the highest reputation for its cuisine, but it's expensive and standards have been known to slip (*menus 410–630F*). *Closed 20 Dec–25 Jan, Thurs lunch and Wed.*

***Château de Bellecroix**, RN6, t 03 85 87 13 86, f 03 85 91 28 62 (*expensive–moderate*). Pleasing 12th-century château with 18th-century additions, 21 rooms and restaurant (*menus 270–360F*). *Restaurant closed 21 Dec–13 Feb, Thurs lunch and Wed June–Sept.*

Bouilland ✉ 21420

***Hostellerie du Vieux Moulin**, t 03 80 21 51 16, f 03 80 21 59 90 (*expensive*). Delightful address well away from the crowds. Cuisine of the highest quality (*menus 210–490F*), the rooms more modest. *Closed Wed exc May–Oct eve, and Thurs lunch exc hols.*

medieval charm inside, with period furniture and weapons on display, the Pot family stories are thoroughly explained by the guides.

Seek out the picturesque vineyards route via the **Vallon de la Tournée** from La Rochepot to reach **Nolay**, a village with a tatty appeal set in a bowl of flat-topped hills. The central square with its wooden market place, big church and timberframe houses is charmingly unrestored. A short way south, below the Mont de Sène, **Dezize-lès-Maranges** benefits from an enviably picturesque location, with some approachable wine estates. The vineyards rise high up the sides of the dramatic **Mont de Sène**, also known as the Montagne des Trois Croix because of the three crosses at the top. Climb its height for dramatic views over Burgundy and across to the Jura.

Beaune

Chock-a-block with wine cellars, wine-lovers and hotels and restaurants, you might think that Beaune had sold its soul not to the devil but to Bacchus. It is the main centre for marketing the great wines of Burgundy. These have benefited from rich US and Japanese buyers who have pushed the prices to obscene levels. But Beaune also has the famous charitable foundation of the Hospices de Beaune which has become the proprietor of a large number of the best vineyards, the produce of which is auctioned off at vast prices each November.

The **Hospices de Beaune** (*open late Mar–late Nov daily 9–6.30; rest of year daily 9–11.30 and 2–5.30; adm*) buildings were commissioned by the massively wealthy Nicolas Rolin and his wife after the local population had suffered poverty, famine and disease in the wake of the Hundred Years' War. It was meant initially to accommodate the poor, who were to be cared for by religious sisters. Begun in 1443, it was probably designed by a Flemish architect, Jehan Wiescrère. Its reputation was such that merchants and nobles also came to be treated here. It served as a hospital right up until 1971 when it was turned into a museum, devoted mainly to hospitals in medieval times. These were as much involved with treating the soul as the body. Wondrous works of art were often commissioned.

Inside the courtyard, the building is highly decorated: the famed coloured tiles form complex diamond patterns on the roofs; ornate pinnacles rise from the dormers; carved angels glide down from the gables, their feet hanging comically in the air. Inside, the enormous paupers' ward is extremely impressive with its neat, crimson-covered beds. The carvings on the ceiling may represent leading figures in 15th-century Beaune. The chapel area at one end was always an integral part of the paupers' ward, where **Van der Weyden's polyptych** originally stood.

This sublime work now takes pride of place in a separate room. On the outer panels the donors look miserable; Nicolas Rolin holds his helmet, a red-faced angel blowing its trumpet by his side. An Annuciation scene is depicted above, the text of the Virgin's book beautifully illustrated – just one example of the artist's amazing attention to detail. The great main scene depicts the Christ of the Last Judgement sitting on a rainbow like a poised gymnast, holding the lily, symbol of purity, and the sword, symbol of punishment. Magnificent purple-clad angels blow their trumpets to either side. Below, the androgynous St Michael with his intense gaze and brilliant peacock-coloured wings weighs souls. To the left of him, the Virgin, apostles and saints pray to Christ. To the right John the Baptist is accompanied by further apostles and three female saints. A magnifying glass has been set up for you to appreciate the detail.

The Romanesque **Notre-Dame** contains some great late-Gothic art treasures including a series of tapestries depicting the life of the Virgin. The **Musée des Beaux Arts** (*open April–Oct daily 2–6; adm*) presents lesser Flemish works of art and scenes by the local 19th-century painter Félix Ziem. The **Musée du Vin de Bourgogne** (*open daily 9.30–6; Dec–Mar closed Tues; adm*) occupies a property once owned by the dukes of Burgundy.

Getting Around

Beaune is a little over 2hrs from Paris-Gare de Lyon by train. There are also regular train services to and from Dijon.

Tourist Information

Beaune: 1 Rue de l'Hôtel Dieu, **t** 03 80 26 21 30, **f** 03 80 26 21 39.
Safari-Tours, run via the Beaune tourist office, offer a good if pricey introduction (in English) to selected vineyards.

Shopping

There are numerous specialized wine merchants' houses or *négociants* you can visit in Beaune, invariably with impressive cellars under their houses. Expect to pay an entrance fee.

Caves Patriache Père et Fils, 7 Rue du Collège, **t** 03 80 24 53 78. Boasts the largest medieval cellars in town, where you can see some of the company's millions of bottles at temporary rest and try a dozen or so wines.

For a more exclusive tasting, you could arrange a visit to a more small-scale merchant house who will expect you to be serious about buying. Ask about possibilities at the tourist office.

Maison Champy, 5 Rue du Grenier à Sel, **t** 03 80 24 97 30. Claims to be the oldest of the great Burgundy wine companies, founded back in 1720. It has recently been taken over by a dynamic new team of experts headed by Henri and Pierre Meurgey. The house has seven hectares of its own vines and buys in other wines to sell.

Denis Perret, on Place Carnot. An excellent wine shop that represents some of the really top-class Burgundy *négociants* at quite competitive prices.

Le Tast' Fromage. Sells superlative Epoisses, Chambertin and Cîteaux cheeses, among others.

Védrenne. With its cassis-coloured façade, specializes in Crème de Cassis.

Where to Stay

Beaune ✉ 21200

Expensive

****Le Cep**, 27 Rue Maufoux, **t** 03 80 22 35 48, **f** 03 80 22 76 80. A Renaissance town house in an arcaded courtyard. Attached to it, **Bernard Morillon**, **t** 03 80 24 12 06, has a splendid old dining room for classic Burgundian cuisine (*menus 180–480F*). *Closed Jan, Tues lunch and Mon.*

****Hôtel de la Poste**, 5 Bd Clemenceau, **t** 03 80 22 08 11, **f** 03 80 24 19 71. Big hotel with relatively small rooms with views of the ramparts or some vines. Wine-tasting cellar and restaurant (*menus 145–349F*). *Closed Mon lunch and Sun.*

Moderate

***Central**, 2 Victor Millot, **t** 03 80 24 77 24, **f** 03 80 22 30 40. A satisfying address, both for its central location, its good-value, comfortable rooms and its original cuisine in the **Cheval Blanc**, **t** 03 80 24 69 70 (*menus 135–220F*). *Closed Nov–Mar Wed. Hotel closed 22 Nov–19 Dec.*

Inexpensive

***Grillon**, 21 Rte de Seurre, **t** 03 80 22 44 25, **f** 03 80 24 94 89. Substantial town house with a garden; reasonably priced and charming. Cellars below. *Closed Feb.*

Eating Out

Le Verger, 21 Route de Seurre, **t** 03 80 24 28 05. In the Grillon hotel's garden, in a striking building, a restaurant run with love (*menus 120–250F*). *Closed Feb, Wed lunch and Tues.*

La Ciboulette, 69 Rue Lorraine, **t** 03 80 24 70 72. The decor may be basic, but the food is satisfyingly tasty and not overpriced by Burgundy standards.

Ma Cuisine, Passage Ste-Hélène, **t** 03 80 22 30 22. A husband and wife team run this bright little restaurant. From your table you may be able see the wife cooking up Burgundy favourites with great dexterity in the kitchen (*menu 90F*). Book in advance. *Closed school hols, Aug, Sat and Sun.*

Down the Saône

The Côte Chalonnaise, west of Chalon-sur-Saône, is a natural extension of the Côte d'Or. Its 4,000 hectares of vines produce some delightful Burgundies, most of which are much cheaper than their northern cousins. The Mâconnais is planted with more hectares of vines than any of the other wine areas in Burgundy, some 6,500, although that still pales into insignificance when compared with the vast extent of the vine-yards of Beaujolais to the south (*see* p.767). Mâcon whites use the great Burgundy grape variety, Chardonnay, while the Mâcon reds are made from Gamay, like Beaujolais. The Saône riverside towns of Tournus and Mâcon are good starting points for trips westwards into lovely countryside marked by the legacy of Cluny.

The Côte Chalonnaise and the Mâconnais

The Côte Chalonnaise begins where the Côte de Beaune left off. A winding route along little roads will lead you along the vine slopes from Chagny to Châlon. **Bouzeron** offers an Aligoté white wine surprise. Over **Rully**, a medieval **château** is the most spectacular wine-making property of the Côte Chalonnaise, still owned by descendants of its 13th-century builders. Wine-lovers should then wend their way to little **Mercurey**, with five Premier Cru vineyards. **Givry** boasts a late-18th-century church by Emiland Gauthey with extravagant domes. Tatraux-Juillet is a wine domaine to look out for at Poncey, west of town.

Chalon-sur-Saône may be fairly industrial, with drab quaysides, but the old town has dashes of colour and the odd fancy façade, particularly on Rue du Châtelet. The **Musée Niepce** (*open July–Aug daily exc Tues 10–6; rest of year daily exc Tues 9.30–11.30 and 2.30–5.30; adm*) on the quays is devoted to the pioneering photographer born here, and to the history of photography. The presentation is quite technical, but the museum holds the oldest machine for taking photography in the world as well as high-tech equipment used for the Apollo moon landing. Sadly, the first photograph ever taken has now flown to Texas. On Place St-Vincent, the main square in the old town, timberframe houses look on to the cathedral with its sharp-edged rectangular towers. Romanesque faces peer out of the odd capital, but the style of the interior is three-storey Gothic. The **Musée Denon** (*open daily exc Tues 9.30–12 and 2–5.30; adm*) stands across the square from the cathedral, old-fashioned behind its classical façade. The chaotic displays include wonderful Celtic bronzes and some surprising Gallo-Roman objects. There are some splendid portraits too, hung all crammed together as though for sale.

Around Tournus, Roman-style terracotta tiles start to put in an appearance on the roofs, a sign that you are approaching southern France. **Tournus** is a little town sand-wiched between a busy main road and a dull bank of the Saône river. However, its **abbey church** was at the centre of a melodramatic tale. Running away from the Vikings with the relics of the influential Philibert (*see* Noirmoutier, p.408, and Jumièges, pp.213–14), a religious community eventually joined an existing monastery here with some inevitable clashes. The church dates from the Romanesque recon-struction. You can still make out the form of the oval defensive enclosure, fortified

Getting Around

There's actually a faster train service from Paris-Gare de Lyon to Mâcon (c. 1hr 40mins) than to Châlon-sur-Saône further north (2hrs 30mins). Mâcon has two separate train stations, the TGV station Mâcon-Loché and the central Mâcon-Ville. Regular trains between Dijon and Mâcon serve Chalon-sur-Saône and Tournus.

Tourist Information

Chalon-sur-Saône: Square Chabas, Bd de la République, t 03 85 48 37 97, f 03 85 48 63 55.
Tournus: 2 Place Carnot, t 03 85 51 13 10, f 03 85 32 18 21.
Mâcon: 1 Place St-Pierre, t 03 85 21 07 07, f 03 85 40 96 00.

Where to Stay and Eat

Rully ✉ 71150
**Le Vendangerot, 6 Place Ste Marie, t 03 85 87 20 09, f 03 85 91 27 18 (*inexpensive*). A simple but satisfying hotel-restaurant in the centre, with good wines to appreciate with your food (*menus 98–240F*). *Closed 4–20 Jan, 15 Feb–9 Mar, Thurs lunch, and Wed.*

Mercurey ✉ 71640
***Le Val d'Or, Grande Rue, t 03 85 45 13 70, f 03 85 45 18 45 (*inexpensive*). A 19th-century coaching inn with a dozen comfortable rooms and serious Burgundian fare (*menus 120–365F*). *Closed Dec, Nov–Mar Sun eve, April–Nov Tues lunch, and Mon.*

Chalon-sur-Saône ✉ 71100
***St-Georges, 32 Av Jean Jaurès, t 03 85 48 27 05, f 03 85 93 23 88 (*moderate*). The best place in Chalon, set in an appealing old building. There's a cheaper *bistrot* (*menus 85–120F*) as well as the reputed restaurant (*menus 115–400F*). *Bistrot closed Sat lunch.*
**Hôtel St-Jean, 24 Quai Gambetta, t 03 85 48 45 65, f 03 85 93 62 69 (*inexpensive*).Restful rooms overlook the calm river. Good value.

Buxy ✉ 71390
**Hôtel Fontaine de Baranges, t 03 85 94 10 70, f 03 85 94 10 79 (*moderate–inexpensive*). Nicely done up 19th-century house with terraces and balconies to the rooms.
Aux Années Vins, Place du Carcabot, t 03 85 92 15 76. A well-run restaurant with tempting menus. Doubles as an interesting wine shop.

Tournus ✉ 71700
****Hôtel Greuze, 5 Place de l'Abbaye, t 03 85 51 77 77, f 03 85 51 77 23 (*expensive*). Beautifully restored old house near the abbey with 21 rooms . *Closed 22 Nov–10 Dec.*
***Le Domaine de Trémont, Route de Plottes, t 03 85 51 00 10, f 03 85 32 12 28 (*moderate*). A restful and exclusive address south of town.
**Hôtel de Saône, Rive Gauche, Quai Georges Bardin, t 03 85 51 20 65, f 03 85 51 05 45 (*inexpensive*). Quietly set by the river, with a terrace looking on to it.
Greuze, Rue Albert Thibaudet, t 03 85 51 13 52, f 03 85 51 75 42. A bastion of the finest traditional Burgundian cuisine and wine (*menus 285–560F*). *Closed 20 Nov–8 Dec.*

Mâcon ✉ 71000
***Bellevue, 416 Quai Lamartine, t 03 85 21 04 04, f 03 85 21 04 02 (*moderate*). Good, solid, respectable old hotel with satisfying cuisine (*menus 140–295F*). *Closed winter Sun lunch, and Tues lunch.*
Inter Hôtel de Bourgogne, 6 Rue Victor Hugo, t 03 85 38 36 57, f 03 85 38 65 92 (*moderate*). Central address by a nice square, with a restaurant, **La Perdrix, t 03 85 39 07 05 (*menus 90–150F*). *Closed 22 Nov–12 Dec, Sat lunch, Mon lunch, and Sun.*

gates and all, within which the monks built their new abbey. The west front openings look like loopholes. Some patterning in the Lombard tradition adds meagre visual relief to the front. The narthex is flanked by two bodyguards of towers. Walk inside and you will see that the narthex has the dimensions of a separate church, held up on enormous columns. Further staggeringly high columns hold up the nave. Actually made of pink stone, they have been set out so as to resemble brick. The choir, the last part of the church to be built, in contrasting white stone, seems dwarfed by the scale of the nave. The dank crypt takes you back to earlier days, with some ancient capitals. St Valerian's relics lie down here, St Philibert's up in the choir.

In the pretty houses encircling the church, craft and tourist shops sell wicker baskets and pottery, but the black coiffes with veritable chimney tops steal the show in the local history museum. The town's most famous son is that tear-jerker of a pre-Revolutionary painter, Greuze. At the time of writing, his museum is being revamped (*due to reopen in 2002*).

Macho **Mâcon** has been expanding along the flat west bank of the Saône for some time now. It was the home of the Romantic poet-cum-politician Alphonse Lamartine, whose statue stands on the central quayside. The **Musée Lamartine** (*open daily exc Tues 10–12 and 2–6, Sun pm only; adm*), in a splendid pre-Revolutionary stone mansion tells his story. Having enjoyed a fairly happy childhood in the idyllic countryside west of town, Lamartine went on to lead a dissolute student life. After his first passionate fling with an Italian mistress, he then fell madly in love with a sickly married woman he met in Aix-les-Bains, but she soon died. He then married an English woman, Mary Ann Birch. The tragedy of their daughter's death haunted him for the rest of his life. His first volume of poetry, **Méditations**, was published in 1820; a decade later *Harmonies poétiques et religieuses* caused him to be elected to the Académie Française. A liberal thinker and politician (he served in parliament) he believed that politics should mainly be concerned with trying to solve the problem of poverty, and championed the separation of Church and state as well as press freedom.

The **Musée des Ursulines** (*open same hours; adm*) occupies a former convent and offers an extensive introduction to the Mâconnais from prehistory to the present (a new museum up at the dramatic nearby hill of Solutré is devoted to the important prehistoric finds made there). Not much remains of Mâcon's medieval **cathedral**, but you can make out some of the fine detail of the Last Judgement scenes on the tympanum of the 12th-century narthex. The sober replacement cathedral went up in the early 19th century. The unmissable Hôtel-Dieu opposite, still a hospital, was the work of Soufflot, he who designed the Panthéon in Paris.

The wines of the Mâconnais are of course on sale in town, but the Maison Mâconnaise des Vins is a short drive north of the centre, on the busy N6. This large establishment represents the wines of some 20 *appellations*, and the prices aren't exorbitant by Burgundy standards. But to appreciate the beauty of the Mâconnais vineyards, head west into the rolling countryside.

The Charollais and the Brionnais

Among the splendid hills of this most southerly section of Burgundy lie the sad but significant vestiges of what was once the greatest early medieval abbey in France – Cluny. For a touch of Ancien Régime decadence, head for the Château de Cormatin, and for sheer indulgence don't miss the gorgeous wine villages of the charming Mâconnais countryside.

To Cluny

Two routes from the Saône-side vineyards to Cluny offer many distractions along the way. The northerly one goes west from Tournus past delightful wooded hilltops villages, including **Brancion** (*small fee to enter the village*), the prettiest one in Burgundy, which has done well in protecting itself from the tourist hordes. While a good number of houses remain from the 15th century, the medieval castle has fallen into picturesque disrepair. For a small fee you can wander round its mostly empty chambers and climb to the top of its keep. From here you get a lovely view of the village church at the top of the hill which contains some of the gentlest of medieval frescoes. One scene shows sweet-faced pilgrims kneeling as they arrive at Jerusalem; others emerge calmly from their stone tombs for the Last Judgement.

Bears and lions once favoured the **Grottes d'Azé** (*open April–Sept daily 10–12 and 2–7; adm*). Now tourists come to cool down in these caves in summer, the largest in Burgundy. Azé lies south of Brancion, reached via picturesque winding roads. The archaeological finds displayed at the caves also show the traces of many humans from down the millennia. The guided tour includes a long stretch of underground river and pretty pools.

The recently restored **Château de Cormatin** (*open May–Sept daily 10–12 and 2–6.30; rest of period Easter–11 Nov daily 10–12 and 2–5.30; adm*) is surrounded by playful Baroque-style gardens, with a labyrinth, chequerboard effects, and the odd folly. It was built for Antoine du Blé d'Huxelles, between 1605 and 1616. His son ordered the extravagant banquet of 17th-century interiors, with Mannerist paintings, gold-leaf, painted flowers and putti, and garlands and grotesques carved on the ceiling. The *pièce de résistance* is the small study, a gem of a blue and gold room, especially made to glitter by candlelight.

The second route to Cluny takes you west from Mâcon, into the irresistible country-side of the Mâconnais with its vineyards. The orange-stained Roche de Solutré, a massive outcrop of limestone watching over the Mâconnais on its border with Beaujolais, commands the landscape. In the 19th century, the remains of thousands of wild horses were found at the base of the Roche; these Solutré finds gave their name to the Upper Paleolithic Solutrean era (20,000–16,000 BC). The **Musée de la Préhistoire** (*open June–Sept daily 10–7; Feb–May and Oct–Nov daily exc Tues 10–12 and 2–5; adm*) just below the outcrop explains the technicalities.

The Solutré rock overlooks the orange-stone villages of Mâconnais wine country. Two of these, **Pouilly** and **Fuissé** have given their name to a highly regarded white wine produced in a handful of parishes here. Goyon at Solutré is one Pouilly-Fuissé producer who is worth seeking out. It is hard to find a prettier wine village than nearby **Chasselas**, which shares its name with a well-known sweet table grape, but also produces good Mâconnais wines.

North from Solutré a clutch of utterly charming Mâconnais villages have strong connections with Lamartine (*see* Mâcon, above), hence its tourist label – the Val Lamartinien. The irresistible **Château de Pierreclos** (*open daily 9.30–6; adm, you may need to shout to draw the attention of the feisty Mme Pidault – she's often serving* *customers in the wine cellars*) dominates its village. The medieval structure was brought up to date in the 16th century. You can visit the vaulted cellars and one or two rooms reception rooms which serve for local events. You can also buy Mâcon wines – Madame makes the white, her son the red – and liqueurs.

Milly-Lamartine has changed its name to reflect the fact that the poet spent his childhood here. The Lamartine home is a wine property dating back to the 17th century, set around an enchanting courtyard; if you arrive at the right moment the courteous owner will let you try his wines and show you around. The chapel at **Berzé-la-Ville** is famous as one of the rare places to have preserved Cluniac wall paintings, dating from no later than the 12th century. The colours and size of the 15ft high Christ in Majesty are striking. He has a middle-aged wise face, with wide eyes, inspired by Byzantine art. The medieval château at **Berzé-le-Châtel**, just north, is a superb structure in earth-brown stone, surveying the southern approaches to Cluny. Now an elegant residence, you can wander around its terraces. Lamartine and his wife had a fine property in **St-Point** and lie in a mausoleum nearby.

Cluny

With the largest church in Europe through the Middle Ages, and for a time home to the most powerful abbey in Europe, Cluny saw its sublime abbey church hammered to bits at the French Revolution. Begun in 1085, completed about 1130, it was at 613 ft long the largest church in Europe until St Peter's in Rome went up in the 16th century.

The **Musée Ochier** (*open July–Aug daily 9–7; Sept daily 9–6; April–June daily 9.30–12 and 2–6; mid-Feb–Mar plus Oct daily 10–12 and 2–5; Nov–mid-Feb daily 10–12 and 2–4; adm*) will help you visualize the scale of the medieval abbey. It also has a wonderful collection of carved stone sculptures. From the museum you can take a 1½ hour-guided tour of the abbey vestiges; or you can visit them at your own pace. Traces of the narthex and the nave are well below street level. The narthex by itself would have been the size of a mighty church. Head to the granary building for the highlight of the tour, beautifully carved and beautifully displayed capitals rescued from Cluny III's choir end on display. The most striking one depicts Adam and Eve desperately trying to hide from God behind big leaves.

Paray-le-Monial

To see a small-scale model of Cluny III, visit Paray-le-Monial. The exterior decoration is concentrated on the two transept doors, with their chevrons and chequered effects, their Romanesque beasts and vines in stone. The church was planned under the great Cluniac abbot Hugues de Semur, who was overseeing the construction of the mighty Cluny III at exactly the same time. The entrance to the nave lies curiously off centre. The nave itself is tall and dark, the main arches in Gothic style with egg-patterned borders, the two levels of arcades above have round Romanesque arches. The architecture is divided up along its length by Roman-style channeled pilasters and columns. Experts say that this interior reflects the plan of Cluny III the most clearly of any church in France. A Christ in Majesty was painted in the apse, one of the few additions made to the medieval structure, although the whole has been much restored.

The Story of Cluny

The abbey was founded in 910 after Bernon, abbot of Baume-les-Messieurs in the Franche-Comté, was given land here. Bernon wanted to encourage the strict observance of the Benedictine Rule, but most importantly, the Cluny abbey charter gave it total independence from all authorities except for the papacy. The abbots turned into powerful feudal landowners and ran an immense network of learning in well over 1,000 Cluniac foundations, including 50 in England and almost 100 in Germany, although most were in France.

Maieul of Avignon became abbot in 965. Admired and respected, Maieul emphasized the importance of charity and commissioned the church known as Cluny II. His successor, Odilo, ruled the order for 55 years, from 994 to 1049, when Cluny grew into the most important abbey in Europe. Odilo insisted on the rigorous spirit of monasticism, fought against abuses and forged very close ties with the papacy in Rome. He forwarded the importance of Mary in medieval theology and also instituted All Souls' Day on 1 November to commemorate all the dead. By the end of his time, there were around 60 monasteries under Cluny's control.

Hugues de Semur, later St Hugues de Cluny, held the post of abbot of Cluny for a record 60 years, from 1049 to 1109, and ordered the building of the vast Cluny III and a new monastic ensemble as the headquarters of the order. Under him the number of Cluniac dependencies exploded perhaps to as many as 2,000 institutions. Kings, emperors and even popes came to Cluny to seek advice. In the 12th century Cluny was starting to go downhill. St Bernard railed against the decadence of the Cluniac order in this period; he would develop the much stricter Cistercian order in response.

Paray's abbey church was dedicated to the Virgin Mary, but the visions of an extraordinary woman in the 17th century eventually changed that. Marguerite-Marie Alacoque was the daughter of a Charollais lawyer who felt a strong religious calling. In 1671 she entered a convent where she received several visitations from Christ exhorting her to encourage a cult devoted to his Sacred Heart, a symbol of his love for mankind. Her fellow nuns and Louis XIV pooh-poohed her 'delusions', and it was only after the French Revolution that the need for religious fervour encouraged a wider interest in the cult she had started. The first important pilgrimage to Paray-le-Monial in honour of the Sacred Heart took place in 1873 and the annual event has been going strong ever since. Marguerite-Marie was canonized in 1920. A good number of religious orders now have communities in town, and the pilgrimage to Paray now ranks second in importance in France after Lourdes. You can visit the 17th-century **Chapelle de la Visitation** where Marguerite-Marie experienced her major visions.

The Brionnais

The southwest section of Burgundy, the triangular Brionnais, rolls down east of the Loire below Paray-le-Monial, from Charolles to Charlieu. This is the closest Burgundy comes to the Massif Central, the Monts de la Madeleine on the opposite side of the Loire forming a distant deep-blue backdrop. Set in a lovely countryside of rural

Getting Around

A local railway line from Le Creusot, which is linked to Paris by TGV, serves Paray-le-Monial, Marcigny, Pouilly-sous-Charlieu and Roanne.

Tourist Information

Cluny: 6 Rue Mercière, t 03 85 59 05 34,
f 03 85 59 06 95.
Charolles: Rue Baudinot, t/f 03 85 24 05 95.
Paray-le-Monial: Av Jean-Paul II, t 03 85 81
10 92, f 03 85 81 36 61.
Charlieu: Place St-Philibert, t 04 77 60 12 42,
f 04 77 60 16 91.

Where to Stay and Eat

Salornay-sur-Guye
M Forestier et M Berclaz, t 03 85 59 91 56.
A couple of young Swiss guys have done up this large B&B – in a quiet village 12km north of Cluny – thoughtfully and stylishly. They'll also provide lively and intelligent conversation over dinner.

St-Vérand ✉ 71570
*****Auberge du St-Véran**, La Roche, t 03 85 37 16 50, f 03 85 37 49 27 (*inexpensive*). Utterly enchanting small, simple wine village hotel with 11 rooms and a restaurant to match serving good local wine (*menus 105–230F*). *Closed Jan, Mon, and Sept–June Tues.*

Berzé-la-Ville ✉ 71960
******Le Relais du Mâconnais**, La Croix Blanche, t 03 85 36 60 72, f 03 85 36 65 47 (*inexpensive*). Some sweet rooms and a sensational restaurant in this ever-so-peaceful spot.

Igé ✉ 71960
*******Château d'Igé**, t 03 85 33 33 99, f 03 85 33 41 41 (*expensive*). Just east of Cluny, some vaulted rooms, a beamed dining room, and a history going back to medieval times. Good cuisine (*menus 200–380F*). *Closed Tues lunch exc hols. Hotel closed Dec–Feb.*

Bourgvilain ✉ 71520
Auberge La Rochette, t 03 85 50 81 73. Traditional inn serving the best of regional produce in a village just south of Cluny.

Cluny ✉ 71250
*******De Bourgogne**, Place de l'Abbaye, t 03 85 59 00 58, f 03 85 59 03 73 (*moderate*). Right by the former abbey, with new owners. Check to see your room's been renovated. The restaurant is plush and old-fashioned, with pleasing, traditional cuisine (*menus 130–220F*). *Closed Wed lunch and Tues. Hotel closed Dec–Feb.*
******St-Odilon**, Rue Belle-Croix, t 03 85 59 25 00, f 03 85 59 06 18 (*inexpensive*). A reasonable modern option by the racecourse on the D15. *Closed 17 Dec–15 Jan.*
*****Hôtel du Commerce**, 8 Place du Commerce, t 03 85 59 03 09, f 03 85 59 00 87 (*cheap*). Basic and central hotel.

Paray-le-Monial ✉ 71600
*******Terminus**, 27 Av de la Gare, t 03 85 81 59 31, f 03 85 81 38 31 (*inexpensive*). Comfortable rooms and restaurant (*dinner only; menus 79–120F*). *Closed Sat and Sun out of season.*
******Grand Hôtel de la Basilique**, 18 Rue de la Visitation, t 03 85 81 11 13, f 03 85 88 83 70 (*inexpensive*). More characterful. A few rooms have views of the basilica. Restaurant (*menus 75–230F*). *Closed 1 Nov–14 Mar.*

Sermaize near Poisson ✉ 71600
Mathieu, t/f 03 85 81 06 10. Among gorgeous pastures dotted with Charolais cows, due south of Paray-le-Monial, a gentle, retired farming couple greet you at the round stairtower to their adorable medieval stone farmhouse. Charming rooms with old stone features.

Roanne ✉ 42300
********Troisgros**, Place de la Gare, t 04 77 71 66 97, f 04 77 70 39 77 (*expensive*). One of the greatest, most exciting French restaurants, and the main reason to come to Roanne – if you can afford the endlessly inventive cuisine (*menus 340–830F*) and the 13 stylish modern rooms. Book in advance. *Closed 1–16 Aug, Feb hols, Tues and Wed.*

hedgerows, these quiet parts are known above all for their Romanesque churches from the late 11th and early 12th centuries, from the time the abbey of Cluny was at the height of its powers.

Rarely will you see so much elation portrayed in Christian art as on the tympanum of the golden-tinged stone church of **Montceaux-l'Etoile**. Christ seems to be stepping out of his mandorla like a showbiz queen making her entrance on stage. His shapely front leg is scarcely disguised by drapery. Below, the crowded apostles join in, lifting their hands high with wild excitement. Inside, second-rate 18th-century decorators were let in and added sickly paintings of putti on the ceiling.

Anzy-le-Duc, a short way south, has one of the most important churches of the Brionnais, part of a former priory. It was built in the 11th century, but instead of adopting the model of Cluny, this church, like the splendid one in Charlieu (*see* below), was constructed in a form that would be adopted at Vézelay. In the carvings on a gate in the priory walls, the style is wonky and naive, although probably from the middle of the 12th century. Adam and Eve's fall is presented next to three kings come to see the Virgin on her throne. Scenes of sacrifice and jousting add to the sense of threat and turmoil.

A lovely octagonal tower with twin arcaded layers rises from the church itself. On the outside, the carved figures on the main tympanum have had their faces hacked off, but the Virgin and apostles along the lintel still stand in expressive poses, hands raised high. From the priory courtyard you can admire a row of *modillons*, offering a great display of medieval creatures and faces. Inside some truly weird and wonder-fully monstrous capitals line up along the nave columns. St Michael, carrying a big shield, fights a hideously deformed creature. Two men pull each other's beards. A musician plays the flute, his wild hair like unkempt foliage. One strange couple are joined at the hip.

Once a sturdy fortified hill village, **Semur-en-Brionnais** has now been reduced to a bucolic tourist one. The remnants of a medieval castle stand in the centre, and you can squeeze through its tight corridors and staircases on a self-guided tour. Hugues de Semur, the great abbot of Cluny, was born to a lord of the village. Not surprisingly, the centre boasts a church on the lines of Cluny III, but the 12th-century building looks a bit of a shambles and has been heavily restored. The lovely crossing tower is its finest feature. The tympanum represents Christ in Majesty, but the lintel scene is less familiar, representing the life of St Hilaire, the Poitevin saint to whom the church was dedicated. Crude carvings decorate the apse. The chapterhouse has been turned into a centre explaining the roots of Romanesque sculpture.

Charlieu

Charlieu at the southern tip of the Brionnais triangle has a magnificent golden-stoned legacy – despite the fact that most of its once-splendid abbey church, St-Fortunat, was destroyed at the Revolution. But its narthex or entrance porch survives, covered with some of the finest Romanesque stone-carving produced in France in the 12th century.

The ornate detail of the two north doorways is absorbing. A fleecy Paschal lamb in high relief peers down, half-wise, half-dumb, from the highest point of the main portal. Bands of floral and geometrical patterns like finely designed cloth, only wrought in stone, embellish the arch. Below, many of the figures have been decapitated, but they are still impressive. In the tympanum, Christ sits in Majesty in his mandorla held by angels, the four animals symbolizing the evangelists crammed into the spaces around them. Below, on the lintel, the Virgin and apostles feature. On the smaller portal, many confuse the event of the wedding scene at Cana, when Christ performed his first miracle, with the Last Supper. The other main scene represents the Transfiguration, with Moses, Elijah, Peter, James and John as witnesses. Bits and pieces of the rest of the abbey have been transformed into museum spaces.

Charlieu has a splendid Gothic church that survived the Revolution, on the main square. The 13th-century **St-Philibert**, with three tympanum reliefs on the façade, contains remarkable decoration within, especially the painted late-Gothic stalls depicting beautifully robed saints carrying banners, set against floral backgrounds – like the finest wallpaper.

Charlieu has a long reputation for silk. The **Musée de la Soierie** (*open July–Aug daily 2–6; rest of year daily exc Mon 2–6; closed Jan; adm*) has taken over the 18th-century Hôtel-Dieu – the last patients were only evacuated in 1981. A good video in French explains silk weaving, and there is a corridor of haute couture silk dresses made in Charlieu, including a leopard-silk number cut by Yves St-Laurent for Catherine Deneuve.

If you're not sated by St-Fortunat and St-Philibert, you can visit, with a guide, the late 14th-century **Couvent des Cordeliers** in the drab western outskirts of town. The church is typically Franciscan, big and plain, but decorated with worn fragments of Gothic paintings. More ornate images were added in the 15th and 16th centuries, some of which have been rediscovered – although they are hard to decipher. Most of the capitals in the cloisters have simple floral motifs, but one side is enlivened by comical scenes, such as a squirrel and hen, a chained monkey, and a thief caught with his hand in a chest.

Beaujolais and the Bresse

The massed ranks of vines rising above the west bank of the Saône between Mâcon and Lyon produce the wines of Beaujolais, outside the region of Burgundy. This area, a mere 60 by 20 kilometres, makes almost as much wine as all of Burgundy put together. Beaujolais is meant to be drunk young, but the rush to produce the Beaujolais Nouveau each November is a marketing coup that cuts both ways.

The best wines come from the northern Beaujolais, where the fragrant *crus* (St-Amour, Juliénas, Chénas, Moulin-à-Vent, Fleurie, Chiroubles, Morgon, Régnié, Brouilly and Côte de Brouilly) can keep a few years. Beaujolais-Villages is a cut above ordinary Beaujolais.

Beaujolais

Vines totally dominate the scene along the northern slopes of the Beaujolais. Of the wine villages, try **Juliénas** with plenty of life and a clutch of restaurants, or **Fleurie** in its open position on the slopes. **Chiroubles** stands in a delightful location too, a theatre of vines above it. The people of Beaujolais have transformed warehouses opposite a railway station into a modern wine museum, Le Hameau du Vin (*open daily 9–6; adm*), at Romanèche-Thorins, an ambitious project presenting winemaking down the ages. There are several films to watch, and the various crafts associated with wine, such as cooperage and glass-making, are also explained before you arrive at the vast tasting and shopping areas. You will find another wine-tasting centre at St-Jean-d'Ardières, **La Maison du Beaujolais** (*open mid-Jan–mid-Dec daily 9am–10pm; adm*), which caters to the masses rushing along the motorway and N6, but also serves as a helpful introduction to the region or as a place to stock up on wines.

Head up the steep slopes from Fleurie, Chiroubles or Villié-Morgon to reach **La Terrasse**, the best-known viewing point in the Beaujolais; on clear days you can see as far as the Jura mountains. From the viewing table you can make out traces of the important Gallo-Roman road from Lyon to Autun that passed this way.

The long main street of the village of **Beaujeu** is crammed along a narrow valley bottom, the steep slopes above reserved for vineyards. An excellent new museum, **Les Sources du Beaujolais** (*open May–Sept daily 10–7; rest of period Mar–Dec daily exc Tues 10–12 and 2–6; adm*), tells the history of Beaujeu and the Beaujolais using modern techniques. Apparently the area has the very tall Claude Brosse to thank for the early marketing success of Beaujolais wine. He took a cart load to Versailles in the 1680s where – being the height of an average man when kneeling – he was purportedly noticed by the king, who asked him what had brought him to the court. A tasting ensued and the trend was set for Beaujolais in the highest circles. You are led around by guides, and at the end treated to a wine tasting.

The **Musée Marius Audin** (*same ticket*) is a more traditional local history museum on the same square. The outstanding stone sculptures were rescued from Beaujeu's old château and church. You are reminded here that Beaujeu hospital was the first in France to initiate charitable wine auctions to raise funds, before the more famous ones at Beaune got underway.

South from Beaujeu the look of the villages changes with a shift from granite to ochre and golden sandstone, although the wine goes somewhat downhill. **Vaux-en-Beaujolais** has a special place in many a Frenchman's heart as the inspiration for Gabriel Chevallier's *Clochemerle*, a classic which in mock-pompous manner pokes fun at French village life. The apartment blocks of Beaujolais' modern capital, Villefranche-sur-Saône, don't appear that welcoming down in the valley; instead, follow the beautiful country roads south via the villages of **Cogny**, **Jarnioux** and **Ville-sur-Jarnioux**, whose houses are built in the most wonderful rich ochre stone. Here in the Pays des Pierres Dorées a decidedly Italianate feel pervades the air. **Theizé** boasts lovely homes, and a whole 17th-century ochre castle, the **Château de Rochebonne**

Getting Around

Lyon's airports lie close by.
Romanèche-Thorins and Villefranche-sur-Saône have reasonable railway links with Paris, Dijon and Lyon, although you will have to change at Mâcon coming south. Bourg-en-Bresse railway station is on the Paris-Gare de Lyon–Geneva line (*just 2hrs from Paris*). A line from Lyon to Bourg-en-Bresse serves smaller stops including Villars-les-Dombes and Marlieux-Châtillon. You can also reach Vonnas on the Bourg-en-Bresse–Mâcon line.

Tourist Information

Beaujeu: Square de Grandhan, t/f 04 74 69 22 88.
Villefranche-sur-Saône: 290 Rue de Thizy, t 04 74 68 05 18.
Châtillon/Pays des Pierres Dorées: Place de la Mairie, t 04 78 47 98 15.
Châtillon-sur-Chalaronne: Place du Champ de Foire, t 04 74 55 02 27, f 04 74 55 34 78.
Bourg-en-Bresse: 6 Av Alsace Lorraine, t 04 74 22 49 40, f 04 74 23 06 28.

Where to Stay and Eat

St-Amour-Bellevue
L'Auberge du Paradis, t 03 85 37 10 26, f 03 85 37 47 92. Lots of angels amongst the sweet decorations of this good little restaurant with old wooden tables (*menus 140–160F*). Closed Jan, Mon eve and Tues.

Juliénas ✉ 69840
★★Chez La Rose, t 04 74 04 41 20, f 04 74 04 49 29 (*inexpensive*). Comfortable, appealing hotel with 10 rooms in a lively Beaujolais village. Restaurant (*menus 98–360F*). Closed Tues exc eve in high season, Mon exc bank hols. Hotel closed Mon exc July and Aug.
Coq au Vin, Place du Marché, t 04 74 04 41 98. Reliable restaurant choice (*menus 98–240F*). Closed mid-Dec–mid-Feb, and Wed.

Chénas ✉ 69840
Les Platanes de Chénas, aux Deschamps, D68, t 03 85 36 79 80. A charming place to eat in the shade of plane trees with vineyard views (*menus 115–265F*). Closed Feb, Thurs lunch, Sept–Mar Wed.

Fleurie ✉ 69820
★★★Hôtel des Grands Vins, La Chapelle des Bois, t 04 74 69 81 43, f 04 74 69 86 10 (*moderate*). In the midst of the vines with 20 decent rooms. Closed Dec and Jan.
Le Cep, Place de l'Eglise, t 04 74 04 10 77, f 04 74 04 10 28. One of the best restaurants in the Beaujolais (*menus 135–260F*). Book. Closed mid-Dec–mid-Jan, Feb hols, Sun and Mon.

Chiroubles ✉ 69115
La Terrasse du Beaujolais, t 04 74 69 90 79. A restaurant in a wonderful location above the vineyards with tremendous views.

(*open June–Oct daily exc Tues; adm*) which is slowly being turned into a cultural centre. The further Pierre Dorée villages of **Oignt** and **Châtillon** look particularly dramatic with towers silhouetted on their heights.

The Bresse

Bresse is synonymous with its AOC blue-legged white-robed *poulets*, reckoned to be the finest chickens in the country. Start exploring at the **Ecomusée de la Bresse Bourguignonne** in the **Château de Pierre-de-Bresse** (*open daily 2–6; adm*). This stupendous moated castle provides the first and the largest surprise in the rather low-key watery flatlands east of the Saône. The castle was built for the Thyard family in the late 17th century. The classically French design, each corner marked by a tower topped by a dome and elegant lantern, is pleasing, as is the pale brick used along the

Beaujeu ✉ 69430
**Anne de Beaujeu, 28 Rue de la République, t 04 74 04 87 58, f 04 74 69 22 13 (*inexpensive*). Classic provincial rooms and dining room (*menus 115–282F*). Closed Sun eve and Mon.

Vaux-en-Beaujolais ✉ 69460
**Auberge de Clochemerle, Rue Gabriel Chevallier, t 04 74 03 20 16, f 04 74 03 28 48 (*inexpensive*). An old stone house in this village of popular literary renown, with a lovely terrace and restaurant (*menus 98–330F*). Closed Tues eve and Wed.

Bagnols-en-Beaujolais ✉ 69620
****Château de Bagnols, t 04 74 71 40 00, f 04 74 71 40 49 (*luxury*). Medieval French castle among the vineyards. This is a stunning place with dreamy rooms, splendid fireplaces and frescoes. Restaurant (*menus 300–510F*). Closed Jan–Mar.

Tarare ✉ 69170
Jean Brouilly, 3 ter Rue de Paris, t 04 74 63 24 56, f 04 74 05 05 48. A very fine restaurant which is a reason in itself for heading across the southwestern corner of Beaujolais to the N7 towards Roanne (*menus 160–380F*). Closed Aug, Feb hols, Sun for lunch, and Mon.

Vonnas ✉ 01540
****Georges Blanc, t 04 74 50 90 90, f 04 74 50 08 80 (*luxury–expensive*). Blanc's brilliance has made this little family inn famous across France. The cuisine is as near to perfection as you're ever likely to taste (*menus 490–900F*). Book in advance. Closed 15 Sept–15 June Wed lunch; 15 June–15 Sept Tues lunch; Mon exc bank hols. The rooms are extremely plush, all with Jacuzzis. Closed Jan. Most of the village now revolves around Blanc's restaurants, hotel and boutique.
L'Ancienne Auberge, t 04 74 50 90 50. At this Georges Blanc inn, the family has recreated a 1900 feel and offers excellent traditional cuisine at much more reasonable prices (*menus 98–240F*). Closed Jan.

Mionnay ✉ 01390
****Alain Chapel, t 04 78 91 82 02, f 04 78 91 82 37 (*expensive*). Named after one of the great late French postwar chefs, and still going strong as one of southern France's best restaurants (*menus 595–800F*), and a luxury hotel with a well-tended garden.

Pérouges ✉ 01800
***Ostellerie du Vieux Pérouges, Place des Tilleuls, t 04 74 61 00 88, f 04 74 34 77 90 (*moderate*). A splendid timberframe and pebbled building on the central square, its outer gallery roofed by corn cobs following Bressan tradition. A beautiful hotel serving fine regional cuisine (*menus 200–500F*).
Chardon, t 04 74 61 12 44. Reasonably priced *chambre d'hôte* in one of the characterful old houses in the village centre.

three wings. One of these is given over to an Ecomusée on the area, presenting its environment, its history, its traditions, its economy.

Louhans has an arcaded main street, a historic hospital which has preserved its old pharmacy, and the church of St-Pierre with its colourful patterned-tile roof. The town goes wild on chicken market days. As you travel around the region, look out for the distinctive old Bressan farmhouses, a mix of timberframe and brick, with broken roofs topped by Saracen chimneys and with large cages to keep corn for feeding the precious chickens.

Below the A40 east of Mâcon you come to the Dombes, another flat land, this one dotted with lakes. Distractions are few beyond the Georges Blanc restaurant at Vonnas (*see* above) and **Châtillon-sur-Chalaronne**, where timberframe houses cluster round the Flemish-looking church and covered market. Ask at the tourist office to see the old pharmacy, or *apothicairerie*, with its old ceramic jars and a Resurrection retable of 1527. A short walk up the hill stand the remnants of the castle, put to good effect on Friday and Saturday nights from early June to late July, when they become the setting for a big outdoor historical drama.

The centre of **Bourg-en-Bresse**, former capital of the whole Bresse, has a few historic streets and a church containing carved choir stalls depicting elegant saints, comical jesters and fighting dogs and dragons. The triple-cloistered **abbey of Brou** (*open April–Sept daily 9–12.30 and 2–6.30; rest of year daily 9–12 and 2–5; adm*), one mile outside the centre, is even better. Under its multicoloured roof, the **church** (1513–32) is a tour de force of Flamboyant Gothic by Loys Van Boghem, an architect from Flanders. Unusual patterns of tracery decorate the main façade. The abbey's founder, Marguerite of Austria, is depicted with her husband Philibert de Savoie, on the tympanum. Inside, the carved rood screen hints of the splendours to come in the choir end. The stalls have an almost neurotic intensity, those on the south side depicting Old Testament stories, those on the north side New Testament ones.

Few more elaborate and dignified lordly tombs have survived in France than those of Marguerite of Austria and Philibert de Savoie. The couple are each represented twice in idealized form, above in finery, below in their death shrouds. On the sole of Marguerite of Austria's foot you can make out the representation of a wound which became infected, leading to her death in 1530. The couple are depicted again in the splendid stained glass, inspired by Albrecht Dürer, and also, in less idealized fashion, in portraits in the **fine arts museum** spread out around the cloisters and in the former monastic cells. Several late-Gothic paintings stand out, and some fine Ancien Régime portraits, while regular exhibitions feature contemporary art.

Hilltop **Pérouges** stands at what must once have seemed a safe distance above the Ain river northeast of Lyon, close to where it joins the Rhône. Nowadays industrial sprawl spreads this far along the valley, but within its ramparts it remains remarkably well preserved. Weaving and wine-making were once the source of its wealth; now it's tourism. The houses are made of the same stones as the cobbled streets; many date from the 15th century, although a few timberframe structures go back even further. The delightful central square, **Place de la Halle**, has a magnificent lime tree of liberty from 1792. Take refuge from the craft shops in the **Musée du Vieux Pérouges** (*open Easter–end Oct; adm*) which fits together pieces of local history; from the top of its tower there are views over Pérouges and the hills around.

The early 17th century **Château de Fléchères** (*should be open at least 12 July–Sept daily 10–12 and 2–6; check on t 04 74 67 86 59; adm*), just north of Fareins by the Saône, is currently undergoing restoration by the dynamic Marc Simonet-Lenglart, who acquired it in 1998. In removing some of the old plasterwork and panelling, whole expanses of the original schemes have been uncovered: Pietro Ricci of Lucca, a pupil of Guido Reni, spent the year of 1632 at Fléchères decorating the interiors. Murals have been discovered everywhere, including depictions of a fantasy hunt that appear at first glance almost like wallpaper. The finest cycle restored so far displays the labours of Hercules, full of power and movement.

The Rhône Valley and the Auvergne

18

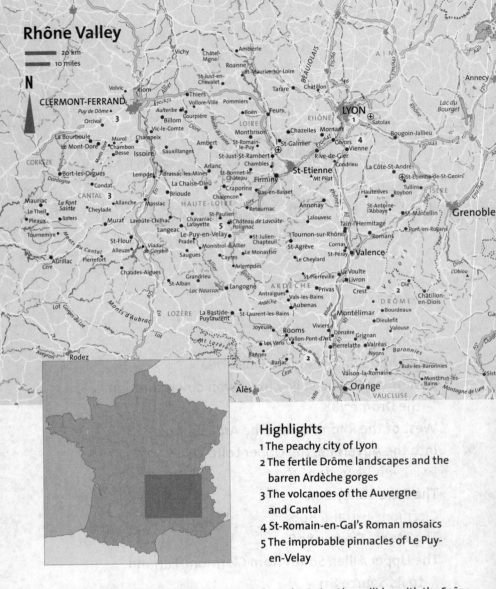

Rhône Valley

20 km
10 miles

N

CLERMONT-FERRAND

LYON

St-Etienne

Grenoble

Valence

Orange

Alès

Highlights

1 The peachy city of Lyon
2 The fertile Drôme landscapes and the barren Ardèche gorges
3 The volcanoes of the Auvergne and Cantal
4 St-Romain-en-Gal's Roman mosaics
5 The improbable pinnacles of Le Puy-en-Velay

At Lyon, the Rhône speeding westwards from the Swiss Alps collides with the Saône heading down from the Vosges, diverting the Rhône dramatically south. This chapter covers the stretch of river between Lyon and Provence. Today, the valley's concentration of industry makes most people pass through quickly. But get off the exasperating main routes and you will be surprised. The first major attraction is Lyon, France's second city (Marseille would quibble; they're about the same size) and a delight to be savoured. The Rhône Valley was one of the great trade routes of antiquity, and the main highway into the interior of Gaul in Roman times; finds are still being unearthed, most notably at Vienne with its superb mosaics.

Food and Drink

Peaches, nectarines, cherries, apricots and a host of other fruit and vegetables grow in profusion along parts of the Rhône Valley and in the Drôme.

Lyon is renowned for the quality of its hearty cooking. Sausages or salami-like *saucissons* remain perennial favourites, along with pigs' trotters, pigs' brawn and tripe. A slice of truffle may be added here and there to impart a subtle flavour to more sophisticated meat dishes. In the southern Drôme, the cuisine becomes distinctly Provençal. Nyons is reputed to grow the best olives in France and to produce the best olive oil, each granted their own *appellations d'origine contrôlée*. The main crop of the rugged Ardèche is chestnuts.

On the upper plateaux of the Auvergne, agriculture becomes somewhat easier. Le Puy-en-Velay has an international reputation for fine green lentils and is also known for herbal teas, notably *verveine* (verbenum). Bottled water is another hugely successful export, Volvic the best known. The slopes of the extinct volcanoes present much more of a challenge for farmers, but in summer cattle graze the high pastures. Five of the region's cheeses have been awarded *appellation d'origine contrôlée* (AOC) status. Look out for traditional makers of St-Nectaire and Cantal. Fourme d'Ambert is the best-known blue cheese, and cone-shaped Gaberon is flavoured with generous amounts of garlic. Salers is an exclusive cow's cheese.

Chestnut purée is used to create many delicious desserts, and fruit tarts and flans are popular. In season try to sample the region's delicious fresh fruits.

In Lyon, the joke goes that three rivers flow through the city – not just the Saône and the Rhône, but also the Beaujolais (just to the north, *see* **Burgundy**); for more on Rhône Valley wines, *see* below.

The fertile Drôme, east of the Rhône below Lyon, boasts some strikingly beautiful countryside. Opposite rises the much poorer and tortured terrain of the Ardèche, a major tourist destination for villages such as Voguë, Rochecolombe, Balazuc, and Labeaume, and for its dramatic gorges and rivers perfect for canoeing. In the 1990s, a group of potholers discovered the exceptional prehistoric cave paintings in what is now known as the Grotte Chauvet. You can't visit the real paintings, but you can see them on film at Vallon-Pont-d'Arc, a place famed up until now for its spectacular natural arch spanning the river.

The green and wildly dramatic extinct volcanoes of the Auvergne provide a dreamy, otherworldly setting surprisingly little known to the outside world. To the east you can explore the upper valley of the Loire, with the historic pilgrimage city of Le Puy-en-Velay. Clermont-Ferrand, the capital of the Auvergne, has the volcanic craters of the Monts Dômes range lined up behind it, where the top of the Puy-de-Dôme offers one of the grandest views in France. Just south of Clermont, dramatic Gergovie is where Vercingétorix and the Gauls had their one great victory against Caesar. Old-fashioned, slightly jaded spa towns are a speciality of the whole Auvergne region.

The distinctive architecture of the Auvergne reflects its extraordinary geology. The builders put the deep grey, even at times black, rocks to use in their constructions. Two unforgettable examples are the soaring coal-black cathedral of Clermont-

Getting There

By plane: Lyon-Satolas and Clermont-Ferrand have good international links. Ryan Air, t 0870 156 9569, has cheap flights to St-Etienne from the UK, and Buzz, t 0870 240 7070, has cheap flights to Lyon from London-Stansted. Valence and Aurillac also have small airports.

By rail: Lyon has excellent rail connections across France and Western Europe, and three main railway stations: Lyon-Satolas, for the airport; Lyon-Part-Dieu, for the TGV; and Lyon-Perrache for the tourist centre. Paris-Gare de Lyon is just 2 hours away. London-Waterloo via Lille is a mere 5 hours away. Continuing down the Rhône Valley, the main TGV stop is Valence. Trains from Lyon also serve the Auvergne. For SNCF rail information, t 08 36 35 35 35.

By road: The busy A7 leads straight down the Rhône Valley to Provence. The much calmer and very beautiful A75 cuts down through the centre of the Auvergne via Clermont-Ferrand. Lyon and Clermont-Ferrand are linked together via St-Etienne by the A47 and A72.

Ferrand and the patterned cathedral of Le Puy-en-Velay with its stairway halfway to heaven. The inventiveness of the Romanesque builders of the region is a delight. The towns and villages around the Cantal have a surprisingly northerly feel: St-Flour or Salers might almost be in Scotland.

Lyon

Picture a crate of ripening peaches, with all its variety of tinges, and you'll have a notion of Lyon's colours. Although most people think of Lyon as the great city of the Rhône, the Saône plays the starring role for visitors. Traditionally, the Saône has been portrayed as the feminine, graceful half of Lyon's partnership, the Rhône as the masculine, labouring one. The two unite south of the historic parts of town, at the end of the long central peninsula, the Presqu'île.

History

A Celtic settlement at the confluence of the Saône and the Rhône existed long before the Romans created Lugdunum in 43 BC, dedicated to Lug, the Celtic divinity who watched over the rising of the sun. Lugdunum rapidly grew into a thriving city on the main river route between southern and northern Europe. The future emperor Claudius, who organized the conquest of England, was born in Lyon. A famous bronze tablet discovered in the city in the 16th century recorded a speech made by Claudius in 48 AD, reassuring the Gaulish tribes that their leaders would be given more access to the Roman political system. The big merchants of Lyon thrived, while the island of Canabae, now part of the Presqu'île, filled with warehouses.

With international trade came foreign religions, including Christianity. Following a popular uprising in 177 many Christian leaders were brutally martyred. Septimus Severus, who served as governor of Lyon from 187 to 188 and would go on to become emperor, also had thousands of Christians massacred. Despite these setbacks, Lyon had one of the first monasteries in France, the monastery of Ile Barbe; by the 12th century it controlled some 40 priories and 100 churches and chapels in France. One Lyonnais merchant, Pierre Waldo or Valdès, caused a stir in the late 12th century with his reforming Waldensian or Vaudois movement; though condemned as heretical in

1185, Waldensian communities survived in the southeast until François I had them massacred in the 16th century.

The archbishops of Lyon held secular power in early medieval times, but from the 13th century the merchants managed to acquire more control for themselves. Near the start of the 14th century, Lyon became a part of the French kingdom, and was granted a municipal charter; a dozen elected councillors from the merchant class were to oversee the running of the city. In the 15th century the city attracted bankers from around Europe. The Medicis were among the Florentine wheeler-dealers to switch their regional centre from Geneva to Lyon, and the skills of silk production were also imported from Italy; silk-weaving would long be a major industry.

By the 16th century Lyon was one of the largest and richest cities in France. Mansions went up in Vieux Lyon, and printing took off spectacularly. Among the books published were the tales of Gargantua and Pantagruel by Rabelais. In the 18th century Bourgelat founded the first veterinary college in Europe. Jouffroy d'Abbans made the first successful experiment with steam navigation in 1783. The following year Joseph Montgolfier and Pilâtre de Rozier took to the air in a hot-air balloon. Lyon's conservative leaders didn't care for the Revolution, and the Parisian National Assembly so detested Lyon that it declared: 'The name Lyon shall be eradicated from all maps of the cities of the Republic.' In 1793 Lyon was besieged by Revolu-tionary troops, and the city was temporarily renamed Ville Affranchie, 'Freed Town'.

Trade took off again with renewed vigour after the Revolution, especially after a local man, Joseph Jacquard, invented his punch-card loom at the start of the 19th century. The Croix-Rousse district became the heart of the silk industry. But the new machines didn't improve the lot of the silk weavers, who rose up unsuccessfully on several occasions. Mechanization and a collapse in trade left many workers in dire straits by the end of the 19th century.

At the start of the 19th century one local weaver, Laurent Mourguet, enjoyed considerable success with his puppet show starring Guignol and other traditional Lyonnais caricatures. And 19th-century Lyon produced that great scientist Ampère, while the Lumière brothers invented the Cinématographe here.

In the Second World War Lyon became one of the major centres for the French Resistance, its key figure, Jean Moulin, eventually falling into the hands of the notorious Gestapo chief, Klaus Barbie, who managed to escape to Bolivia at the end of the war. As a major industrial centre, Lyon inevitably suffered from bombing, but since the war its industries and the business centre of La Part-Dieu have boomed. Now they stand a mere two hours away from Paris by TGV. Klaus Barbie was finally tried in the city in 1987 and condemned to life imprisonment.

The Fourvière Hillside and Gallo-Roman Lyon

The pure white sparkling castle of a church, **Notre-Dame de Fourvière**, is visible on its hillside from many points in Lyon. Head there for a great view down on to the city and to get your bearings. Take the *funiculaire* or cablecar from beside the cathedral to avoid the climb via the steep public gardens. The massive 19th-century basilica was built to the design of the architect Pierre Bossan following the Franco-Prussian War,

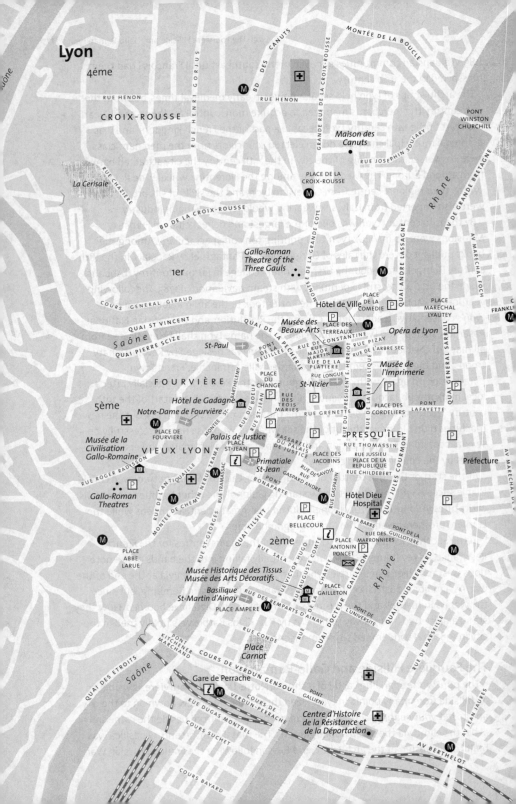

Getting Around

By plane: Air France, **t** 0845 0845 111, *www.airfrance.co.uk*, flies direct to Lyon from London-Heathrow (*Mon–Sat 3 flights daily, Sun 2 flights*) and New York (*once daily*).

Low-cost airline, Buzz, **t** 0870 240 7070, has daily flights to Lyon from London-Stansted.

Lyon-Satolas, or Lyon-St-Exupéry, airport, **t** 04 72 22 72 21, lies some 25km east of the city centre. Buses, **t** 04 72 68 72 17, leave every half-hour or so during the day (*c. 50mins to the centre*). Some planes fly into Lyon-Bron.

By train: Lyon has very good rail connections. By TGV Paris-Gare de Lyon is just 2 hours away, and London-Waterloo (via Lille) is just 5 hours away. For the city centre get off at Lyon-Part-Dieu or Lyon-Perrache.

Lyon has a métro system with four lines. They may be useful to get to the northern and eastern quarters.

By bus: city bus information, **t** 04 72 61 72 61.

By taxi: **t** 04 72 78 77 49; **t** 04 78 52 21 27; **t** 04 78 28 23 23; **t** 04 72 10 15 15; **t** 04 78 26 81 81; **t** 04 72 10 86 86; **t** 04 78 28 13 14.

Tourist Information

Lyon: Place Bellecour, 69002, **t** 04 72 77 69 69, **f** 04 78 42 04 32.

Shopping

There are a number of antique shops on Rue Auguste-Comte; or try the following:

Marché de l'Artisanat. Items by local craftsmen and artists: jewellery, pottery, etc. *Open Sun 7–1*.

Cité des Antiquaires, 117 Bd de Stalingrad. The third largest antiques market in Europe. *Open Thurs, Sat and Sun 9.30–12.30 and 2.30–7; closed Sun in summer*.

Outdoor book market, Quai de la Pêcherie. *Open Sat and Sun 10–6*.

Activities

Navig'Inter's Lyon Croisières, **t** 04 78 42 96 81, **f** 04 78 42 11 09. *Bateaux-mouches* leave from Quai Claude Bernard (between Pont Galliéni and Pont de l'Université). They were invented in Lyon: La Mouche was a naval area on the east bank of the Rhône where the first of these tourist boats were built in the 19th century. The idea was transferred to Paris for one of the Universal Exhibitions.

Where to Stay

Note that the *arrondissement* numbers are given in the addresses.

Lyon ✉ 69000

Luxury

★★★★**La Villa Florentine**, 25–27 Montée St-Barthélémy, 5e, **t** 04 72 56 56 56, **f** 04 78 40 90 56, *florentine@relaischateaux.fr*. In a fantastic location, high on the slope of the Fourvière hill, a former convent converted into a magnificent luxury hotel with its mix of Renaissance and contemporary Italian style. The beautiful terraces have the best views imaginable over the city. The restaurant, Les Terrasses de Lyon, is a splendid place for dinner (*menus 170–400F*).

★★★★**La Tour Rose**, 22 Rue du Boeuf, 5e, **t** 04 78 37 25 90, **f** 04 78 42 26 02. Down in the very heart of Renaissance Lyon below Fourvière, this hotel is set around courtyards with colourful stairtowers. Lyon silks have been used in the sumptuous interior decoration. The restaurant, also known as La Tour de Rose, is excellent (*menus 295–595F*). *Restaurant closed Sun*.

Expensive

★★★★**Royal**, 20 Place Bellecour, 2e, **t** 04 78 37 57 31, **f** 04 78 37 01 36. The most luxurious option in the heart of the Presqu'île.

A handful of really good three-stars stand in elegant buildings in the area of delightful squares and shopping streets in the midst of the Presqu'île.

★★★**Carlton**, 4 Rue Jussieu, Place de la République, 2e, **t** 04 78 42 56 51, **f** 04 78 38 10 71. With its glamorous dome, stands out in the Presqu'île's shopping district.

★★★**Globe et Cécil**, 21 Rue Gasparin, 2e, **t** 04 78 42 58 95, **f** 04 72 41 99 06. Another address with style, all rooms with individual touches.

***Hôtel des Beaux-Arts, 73 Rue du Président E. Herriot, 2e, t 04 78 38 09 50, f 04 78 42 19 19. Behind the very elegant façade, the rooms are more standardized.

Moderate
***Hôtel des Artistes, 8 Rue Gaspard André, 2e, t 04 78 42 04 88, f 04 78 42 93 76. Simply done charm, again right in the centre of the peninsula.

Inexpensive
**Du Théâtre, 10 Rue de Savoie, 2e, t 04 78 42 33 32, f 04 72 40 00 61. Really good value for money for this show of a hotel in the centre of town, some of the rooms with nice views.
**L'Elysée, 92 Rue du Président E Herriot, 2e, t 04 78 42 03 15, f 04 78 37 76 49. Appealing two-star in a traditional building.

Cheap
*d'Ainay, 14 Rue des Remparts d'Ainay, 2e, t 04 78 42 43 42, f 04 72 77 51 90. Excellent location for a cheap one-star. Go for the rooms giving on to Place d'Ampère.

Eating Out

Léon de Lyon, 1 Rue Pléney, 1er, t 04 72 10 11 12, f 04 72 10 11 13. Superb traditional Lyonnais cuisine (*menus 290–750F*). *Closed Sun, Mon and 30 July–21 Aug.*
Pierre Orsi, 3 Place Kléber, 6e, t 04 78 89 57 68, f 04 72 44 93 34. Another classic luxury Lyon restaurant, this one east of the Rhône, just south of the Parc de la Tête d'Or (*menus 240–600F*). *Closed Sun exc hols.*
La Tassée, 20 Rue de la Charité, 2e, t 04 72 77 79 00, f 04 72 40 05 91. A big lively *bouchon* on two levels, but rather classy by *bouchon* standards, especially the upper level with its wall paintings of Beaujolais scenes (*menus 135–280F*). *Closed Sun.*
Le Vivarais, 1 Place Gailleton, 2e, t 04 78 37 85 15, f 04 78 37 59 49. Lots of good Lyonnais pork specialities (*menus 115–180F*). *Closed Sun, 23 July–20 Aug and Christmas.*
De Fourvière, 9 Place de Fourvière, 5e, t 04 78 25 21 15, f 04 72 57 90 12. Traditional Lyonnais cuisine, and great views down on to the roofs of Lyon (*menus 70–180F*).

Les Muses de l'Opéra, 7th Floor of the Opera House, 1 Place de la Comédie, 1er, t 04 72 00 45 58, f 04 78 29 34 01. Extraordinary rooftop location to enjoy fine cuisine (*menus up to 169F*). *Closed Sun.*
Chabert et Fils, 11 Rue des Marronniers, 2e, t 04 78 37 01 94, f 04 78 37 79 18. A picturesque and reliably good *bouchon* (*menus 99–159F*).
Brasserie Georges, 30 Cours de Verdun-Perrache, 2e, t 04 72 56 54 54, f 04 78 42 51 65. Not a *bouchon*, but an enormous and lively Lyonnais culinary institution with outrageous interiors (*menus 98–153F*).
Chez Hugon, 12 Rue Pizay, 1er, t 04 78 28 10 94. A very typical moderately priced *bouchon* (*menus 110–145F*). Book. *Closed Sat, Sun and Aug.*
Café des Fédérations, 10 Rue du Major Martin, 1er, t 04 78 28 26 00, f 04 72 07 74 52. Another recommended *bouchon* (*menus up to 148F*). Book. *Closed Sat, Sun and Aug.*
Les Lyonnais, 1 Rue Tramassac, 5e, t 04 78 37 64 82, f 04 72 41 09 41. A really friendly address down in Vieux Lyon smothered with photos (*menus 58–105F*). *Closed Sun eves, Mon and 20 July–18 Aug.*

Entertainment and Nightlife

Lyon has two miain theatres:
Croix-Rousse Theatre, Place Joannès Ambre, t 04 72 07 49 49, and
Young Years Theatre, 23 Rue de Bourgogne, t 04 72 53 15 15, f 04 72 53 15 19.
Célestins Theatre, 4 Rue Charles Dullin, t 04 72 77 40 00, f 04 72 77 40 06. One of the only theatres in France which can boast two centuries of continuous dramatic activity. New works performed throughout the year.
Institut Lumière, 25 Rue du Premier Film, t 04 78 78 18 95. It was in Lyon in 1895 that the Lumière brothers invented the process of cinematography. The Institut promotes their work and film culture as a whole. Countless exhibitions and screenings. *Open daily 2–6; closed Mons and public hols; adm.* There are usually films shown in their original language at CNP Terreaux, Ambiance, Opéra or Le Cinéma.

Orientation

Of Lyon's four main tourist districts, the oldest, **Fourvière hill** high up west above the Saône, is where you'll find the main Gallo-Roman remains and museum, a massive basilica and copy of the top of the Eiffel Tower. The so-called **Vieux Lyon** down at the bottom of this hill has the medieval cathedral and the UNESCO-listed World Heritage Site of the city's Renaissance quarter. The **Presqu'île**, the peninsula sandwiched between the Saône and the Rhône, has most of Lyon's best museums, several interesting churches, many characterful squares, and the most chic shopping streets. But it also has its grittier quarter to the north, **Croix-Rousse**, the silkweavers' or *canuts'* district. The stars of the newer quarter east of the Rhône are of course the Lumière brothers who made the first film of all time there and gave the world cinema. Other significant stops on the east bank of the Rhône include the museum on the Resistance and the modern art museum, the latter in the spacious Tête d'Or park. Take a trip on a Lyon *bateau-mouche*, and try the *bouchons*, the traditional workers' restaurants which serve solid, traditional Lyonnais food.

in thanks for sparing the city any damage. The exterior is blindingly bright but surprisingly sober, although the ornate west front hints at the extravaganza that awaits inside. The interior, built on huge Hispano-Moorish-looking arches, feels almost Oriental. Mosaics cover the floor and the walls, and much of the decorative scheme is devoted to the life of the Virgin. Ornate stone-carving runs riot. The large crypt is really a second church on the same scale and in the same style. The Musée de l'Oeuvre, a museum of religious articles, has recently been swishly modernized.

The basilica occupies the site where the Gallo-Roman forum of Lugdunum stood until the 9th century. On the hillside you can still admire the remnants of two Gallo-Roman theatres (*open 9–nightfall; adm*) built side by side in a spectacular site. Take care not to trip over the big rough paving blocks of the Gallo-Roman paths. The main theatre was built under Augustus, but was doubled in size under Hadrian, when it would have been capable of seating some 10,000. The smaller theatre, or odeon, was once roofed. You can also learn about Lugdunum at the **Musée de la Civilisation Gallo-Romaine** (*open Wed–Sun daily 9.30–12 and 2–6; adm*), which covers earlier periods of civilization in the Rhône-Alpes region as well, although most of the artefacts explain how Lyon grew so rapidly into such a major Roman political and religious centre. Models recreate some of the grand buildings of the Gallo-Roman town, and there are some splendid mosaics on display.

Vieux Lyon, or Medieval and Renaissance Lyon

At the foot of the Fourvière slope, squeezed in between the Saône and the hillside, lie the cramped, lively streets of Vieux Lyon. The most venerable building in this quarter is the the **Primatiale St-Jean**, the cathedral, mostly built between 1175 and 1275. Marked by two square towers at either end, the cathedral turns its muscular rounded back on the Saône, while its ornate west façade overlooks lovely Place St-Jean. Inside, the tall Gothic nave is soberly grand. By far the most swanky side chapel was decorated for Charles de Bourbon, long-serving archbishop of Lyon in the 15th century, with elaborate vaulting and hanging bosses. In the squat Romanesque apse and in the transepts you can admire 13th-century stained-glass windows, the little religious scenes set against intense deep-blue backgrounds. In the lefthand transept stands a remarkable 14th-century astrological clock, and the separate treasury conceals other marvels. The clatter of the looms of Lyon's early weavers rang out in the St-Georges quarter just south of the cathedral in the mid-16th century.

The powdery-coloured façades of the mansions built for wealthy residents in the 16th century line up along the tight streets north of the cathedral, an area which has been designated a World Heritage Site by UNESCO and extends for around a kilometre along the Saône. Although it is known generally as the Renaissance quarter, a good number of its great houses display late-Gothic features, and in all several hundred late-Gothic and Renaissance mansions have been renovated. This was the quarter where the trade corporations and the bankers were based. Its main artery, the **Rue St-Jean**, heads north from the cathedral, lined with fast-food restaurants and souvenir shops, passing by the imposing Palais de Justice, and then on via sweet little squares. Wander down Rue des Trois Maries and Rue du Boeuf parallel to the Rue St-Jean. No.16 Rue du Boeuf conceals the most famous of all Vieux Lyon's towers, the arch-windowed Tour Rose. One particular feature of the area is the secretive and often dingy covered alleys known as *traboules* (a contraction of the Latin *trans ambulare*, to walk through) which lead from one block of houses to the next. They are often sealed at either end by doorways, but thanks to an agreement between the proprietors and the city, visitors can ring on clearly marked numbers to pass through.

The **Hôtel de Gadagne**, set in a rambling town house on Rue du Boeuf, is the largest Renaissance pile in Vieux Lyon, and now contains two museums: the **Musée Historique de Lyon** (*open daily exc Tues 10.45–6, Fri until 8.30; adm*), which houses some fabulous Romanesque fragments from the former abbey on the Ile Barbe, and the **Musée International de la Marionnette** (*open same hours*). After the Revolution, a silkweaver-cum-entertainer of Lyon, Laurent Mourguet, created the puppets Guignol, Madelon and Gnafron, popular caricatural Lyonnais figures who are now known across France. Wide-eyed Guignol in his tight black headcap is full of silly banter, but also pokes fun at the authorities. His good wife Madelon puts up with him, but grumbles and argues a lot. His great friend Gnafron is a Beaujolais drunkard. The museum contains many different versions of these and other puppets from around the world.

Place du Change, nearby, was where the currency changers set up shop during the Lyon fairs, and where the first exchange in France was built at the start of the 16th century, and redesigned by Soufflot of Paris Panthéon notoriety in the middle of the 18th century. He made the place look like an elegant little theatre. Above the Place du Change, the Romanesque-to-Gothic **church of St-Paul**, one of the oldest Christian buildings in Lyon, now looks a bit sorry for itself; the northern end of Vieux Lyon is still a bit tatty.

The Presqu'île de Lyon

The Presqu'île is Lyon's glamorous peninsula between the Saône and the Rhône. At its north end, on the opposite bank of the Saône from St-Paul, the concave Baroque façade of the church of St-Vincent stands out on Quai de la Pêcherie. The many-fountained **Place des Terreaux** just east of here could be considered the hub of central Lyon, a lively meeting place with café terraces spilling out on to it.

The long, subdued classical façade of the **Musée des Beaux-Arts** (*open daily exc Mon, Tues and public hols 10.30–6; adm*) was originally designed as the sober front for a Benedictine convent, the abbey of Our Ladies of St Peter's, also known as the Palais St-Pierre. After the Revolution it became Lyon's fine arts museum, and it was wholly refurbished in the 1990s. The first floor has a whole wing devoted to antiquities, another to medieval art and *objets d'art* generally, and a third to the Renaissance. Most of the painting, from the late 15th to the 20th century, is on the second floor. One of the masterpieces of the museum, Perugino's *Ascension*, is in the vast entrance hall, a calm, uplifting, colourful work donated by Pius VII in 1816. The monumental Egyptian temple doors from Mehamoud, and the Kore (a representation of a young girl) from the Acropolis of Athens are the highlights of the ancient collections. Vast allegorical dreamscapes typical of Pierre Puvis de Chavannes, a 19th-century native of Lyon, decorate the staircase leading to the second floor, where famous names from the different schools of European painting are represented: Veronese, Tintoretto and Bassano; El Greco and Zurbaràn; Cranach the Elder, Gérard David, Rembrandt and Rubens; Simon Vouet, Philippe de Champaigne, Boucher and Desportes; Delacroix, Géricault, Daumier, Corot and Courbet, Degas and Gauguin. The former abbey church has been turned into a vast sculpture room for works of the 19th and 20th centuries.

The massive town hall overlooks another side of the Place des Terreaux, its façade elaborately redrawn by Jules Hardouin-Mansart and Robert de Cotte after a fire in 1674. Telamones frame the equestrian statue of Henri IV, while grizzly lions rest their paws on globes over the first-floor windows. Behind the town hall rises the brazen **opera house**, its lower parts in classical style recently topped by a modern green barrel vault with glass sides, designed by Jean Nouvel. Major shopping arteries head south from Place des Terreaux, where you will also find the ornate **church of St-Nizier**, with its Gothic forms and its gargoyles scrubbed clean.

Nearby, the **Musée de l'Imprimerie** (*open Wed–Sun 2–6; adm*) on Rue de la Poulaillerie is a highly regarded print museum in a lovely Renaissance mansion with a courtyard. In the first half of the 17th century it was the town hall, until the decision was taken to build the grander one on Place des Terreaux. A plaque shows a male and a female pouring water from an urn, symbols of Lyon's two rivers. The museum contains a rare Gutenberg Bible (*c.* 1454), fine prints from the 15th to the 19th centuries and Doré's famous 19th-century illustrations for Rabelais' *Gargantua*.

Place Bellecour, generally regarded as the centrepiece of the Presqu'île, comes as a bit of a disappointment after the rather glamorous smaller shopping squares to the north, and the town authorities don't seem to know quite what to do with its vast emptiness. The still more sterile **Place Antonin Poncet** adjoining Place Bellecour leads to the Rhône, where the massive dome and façade of the **Hôtel-Dieu** make a grand impression. This hospital was long recognized as one of the leading medical centres in Europe. Rabelais practised here back in the 16th century. The architecture is showy Ancien Régime, designed by Soufflot and his team, and you can visit some of the grandiose interiors as well as the **Musée des Hospices Civils de Lyon** (*open Mon–Fri 1.30–5.30; adm*) which contains fine decorative features and sculptures by Coysevox and Coustou, among others.

South from Place Bellecour, some very chic shopping streets lead to two of Lyon's most famous museums, along Rue de la Charité. You'll get a good feeling for grand 18th-century interiors wandering round the sumptuous **Musée des Arts Décoratifs** (*open daily exc Mon and public hols 10–12 and 2–5.30; combined ticket available with Musée Historique des Tissus; adm; entrance is free to both on Wed*), devoted to Ancien Régime furnishings, and housed in a huge town house thought to have been designed by Soufflot. The **Musée Historique des Tissus** (*open daily exc Mon and public hols 10–5.30; adm; pick up a taped commentary for 10F at the entrance*), in the 18th-century Hôtel de Villeroy, pays homage to textile-making from ancient times to the present day. Much attention is devoted to Lyon's great silk-weaving tradition, but the early sections contain fabulous collections from around the world, and the Middle East in particular. European pieces include Lazarus' shroud from around the year 1000, executed in Hispano-Moorish style with a menagerie of animals and cavaliers on it. The golden age of silk weaving in Lyon was the 18th century, when no one could match the skill of Philippe de Lasalle: his cameo textile portraits look like paintings.

Place Ampère a bit further south pays its respects to André Marie Ampère, born in Lyon in 1775, whose name was given to the basic unit of electric current, the amp. To the west, the heavily restored Romanesque **Basilique St-Martin d'Ainay** formed part of a highly influential Benedictine abbey, and still retains some engrossing Romanesque decoration, including grotesques and animals, and a few capitals carved with Old Testament scenes.

The Northern and Eastern Quarters

On the the hill of **La Croix Rousse**, a short, steep walk north from Place des Terreaux, past the sadly neglected Gallo-Roman theatre of the Three Gauls, is the old silk-weavers' quarter. The weavers settled here after the Revolution, moving from the St-Georges area by the cathedral. The red cross after which the district was named has long disappeared, as have most of the silk-weavers, but some vestiges of old monasteries remain, such as the Chartreux garden which has great views on to the Saône and Fourvière hill. Despite some grand bourgeois 19th-century houses, this area is distinctly working class. **Place de la Croix-Rousse** is its hub. Head north up Grande Rue de la Croix-Rousse (*not* the Boulevard of the same name) and turn right into Rue d'Ivry to visit the **Maison des Canuts** (*open daily exc Sun 8.30–12 and 2–6.30; adm*) where you can see demonstrations of silk-weaving, watch a video on silk-making and admire displays of fine silks. In the mid-19th century a staggering 30,000 master weavers worked in this district. Now there are just 12. You can still buy pieces of fine Lyon silk from the Coopérative des Canuts on the other side of the road.

It's a steep, awkward climb down from the Croix-Rousse district to the Rhône. On the opposite bank, across Pont Winston Churchill, lies the large, flat and restful **Tête d'Or park**, home to the new Interpol headquarters, built in 1989, and to the **Musée d'Art Contemporain**, which hosts temporary exhibitions. You can go boating on the lake and wander through the botanical gardens. The park is named after a story which claimed that a golden head of Christ was buried here. South of it, wide grids of boulevards stretch out from the Rhône.

South again, in the 7th *arrondissement*, the chilling **Centre d'Histoire de la Résistance et de la Déportation** (*open Wed–Sun 9–5.30; adm*) is just a short walk east of the Pont Gallieni on Avenue Berthelot, where the Gestapo had its headquarters during the Second World War. Now you can learn here how Lyon became one of the most vital centres of the Resistance in France, where Jean Moulin – perhaps the greatest of all the French Resistance organizers – did so much to bring together the strands of active protest. The importance of clandestine printing is also emphasized, along with the traumatic issue of collaboration. Lyon saw a massive rounding-up of Jews in August 1942, under the Vichy government, and from November 1942 until liberation the city was at the mercy of the notorious Gestapo chief Klaus Barbie.

You can discover how cinema came to life at the **Institut Lumière** (*open Tues–Sun 2–6; t 04 78 78 18 95, f 04 78 01 36 62; adm*), on Rue du Premier Film, on the corner of the Place Ambroisie Courtois (métro station Monplaisir Lumière), quite far east of the Pont de la Guillotière. In a very grand house, it is part museum, part cinema centre: screening films, inviting speakers and encouraging film studies. You can watch many of the first short films ever made. The first film of all time, shot by Louis Lumière, shows workers emerging from the Lumière factories in Lyon.

Straight Down the Rhône Valley

Dusty old Vienne and neighbouring St-Romain-en-Gal, on the opposite side of the Rhône, harbour one of the most brilliant and unsung Gallo-Roman legacies in France. Below them, the thin strips and patches of northern Rhône Valley vines produce some of southern France's greatest wines. The vineyards mainly rise up the steep slopes of the west bank of the river between Vienne and Valence. This bank, with its cliffs and crumbling hilltop castles, is the more attractive side of the river, although the whole valley is blighted in parts by heavy industry. This section sticks to places within sight of the Rhône river, as far as Montélimar of sticky nougat fame on the Drôme side of the river and Viviers, an almost forgotten little city with a gem of a cathedral, on the Ardèche side. The gorgeous valleys, hills and mountains of the Drôme and Ardèche away from the Rhône are covered in separate sections (*see* pp.788–93 and 794–7).

Vienne and St-Romain-en-Gal

Tatty old **Vienne** was a noble town in Gallo-Roman and early Christian times, built on the site of the main settlement of the Celtic Allobroges tribe. It apparently enjoyed a period of immense trading prosperity from the 1st century AD to the 3rd, as did St-Romain-en-Gal just across the river.

A good way to appreciate Vienne's location is to climb to the 19th-century neo-Gothic **church of Pipet**, from whose terrace there is an excellent view of the Rhône river. The **Roman theatre** (*open April–Aug daily 9.30–1 and 2–6; Sept–Oct daily exc Mon 9.30–1 and 2–6; rest of year Tues–Sat 9.30–12.30 and 2–5, Sun 1.30–5.30; adm*) was fitted snugly into the Pipet hillside. With almost 50 tiers of seats, it was on an impressive scale, one of the largest theatres built in Gaul. A few marble slabs in the stalls show how sumptuous the decorative finish must have been in its heyday. It now hosts the Vienne summer jazz festival and other special events. Some remnants from the theatre and other wonderful classical fragments have been moved to the battered church of St Peter, turned into a **Musée Lapidaire** (*open April–Oct daily exc Mon 9.30–1 and 2–6; rest of year Tues–Sat 9.30–12.30 and 2–7, Sun 2–6; adm*).

In Vienne's centre, the colonnaded Gallo-Roman **Temple of Augustus and Livia** looks slightly battered, many of its channelled columns chipped and shoddy, others restored. The rear apparently dates back as far as the 1st century BC, but most of the temple was rebuilt to honour the Emperor Augustus and his wife. A statue of the emperor would originally have been kept inside.

Vienne was an important Christian centre for many centuries, as its medieval churches attest. The former **cathedral of St-Maurice** somewhat resembles Lyon's cathedral from the front. The three Gothic portals contain some delightful decoration, including lovely musical angels. The scenes in the central doorway illustrate events in Christ's life prefigured in the Old Testament. Inside, Gothic bays were added on to the earlier Romanesque ones down the nave. Some amusing Romanesque carved decoration has survived. Leave by the north door to admire the wonderful stone-carving there.

The **Musée des Beaux-Arts et d'Archéologie** (*open same times as the Musée Lapidaire; adm*) is rather old-fashioned and unappealing. As elsewhere in Vienne, however, there are amazing finds to be made if you are prepared to look beyond the unattractive environment. The more modern **Musée de la Draperie** (*open April–Sept daily 2.30–6.30; open*), in the south of the town, keeps alive the tradition of textile-making, an important local industry which came to an end in the 1980s. Also in this part of town, one last Gallo-Roman remain is worth going out of your way to see: the monument known as the **Aiguille** was said for some time to be the tomb of Pontius Pilate, who – according to legend – was banished to Vienne. In fact the curious arch with its four sides topped by a pyramid probably dates from the 4th century and formed the centrepiece of a Roman circus.

Looking across the river to **St-Romain-en-Gal**, you can see the modern **Musée et Sites Archéologiques de St-Romain-en-Gal-Vienne** (*open daily exc Mon 9.30–6.30; audioguide available in English; adm*) which presents the fabulous Gallo-Roman finds discovered there. St-Romain-en-Gal developed into a quarter for wealthy merchants, with fine villas and large warehouses. It is known that marble, ceramics, oil, fish paste, and even exotica such as dates and figs were imported to the area.

Over 250 mosaic floors have been uncovered in St-Romain-en-Gal and Vienne, making this one of the most prolific areas for such art in the Roman world. Some tell stories from Greek mythology, while others feature decorative geometrical motifs. Some are highly coloured, others black and white. The mosaic of the ocean gods, discovered in 1967, has become the symbol of the museum. There are also some outstanding Gallo-Roman mural paintings, models of Vienne and St-Romain-en-Gal in ancient times, and all the other archaeological finds typically associated with Roman towns – amphorae, statues of gods, tools, and so on – creating an evocative picture of Gallo-Roman life in France. Outside, you can wander around three hectares

Getting Around

Valence is the best railway station along this stretch of the Rhône as the TGV from Paris-Gare de Lyon stops here (*c. 2hrs 30mins*). Smaller stations on the line from Lyon down this part of the valley include Vienne, Tain-l'Hermitage and Montélimar.

From Lyon-Satolas airport you can get a bus to Vienne, Chanas and Valence, with a handful of connections on weekdays.

Tourist Information

Vienne: Cours Brillier, t 04 74 85 12 62, f 04 74 31 75 98.
Condrieu: Place du Séquoia, t 04 74 56 62 83, f 04 74 56 62 83.
Tournon-sur-Rhône: Hôtel de la Tourette, t 04 75 08 10 23, f 04 75 08 41 28.
Valence: Parvis de la Gare, t 04 75 44 90 40, f 04 75 44 90 41.
Montélimar: Allées Provençales, t 04 75 01 00 20, f 04 75 52 33 69.

Where to Stay and Eat

Vienne ✉ 38200

****La Pyramide**, 14 Bd Fernand Point, t 04 74 53 01 96, f 04 74 85 69 73 (*expensive*). Modern Provençal chic in the rooms, but known above all as a temple of *haute cuisine* – the street is even named after the legendary chef who made its name (*menus 470–690F*). Closed Feb; restaurant also closed Tues and Wed.
***Hôtel de la Poste**, 47 Cours Romestang, t 04 74 85 02 04, f 04 74 85 16 17 (*inexpensive*). A reasonable option in the centre.

Estrablin ✉ 38780

***La Gabetière**, 8km east of Vienne off the D502, t 04 74 58 01 31, f 04 74 58 08 98 (*moderate*). A delightful, good-value manor house dating back to the 16th century.

Ampuis ✉ 69420

Le Côte Rôtie, Place de l'Eglise, t 04 74 56 12 05, f 04 74 56 00 20. This restaurant immediately draws attention to itself with its blue front. Inside, it turns out to be a splendid place to try local wines and cuisine (*menus 198–350F*). Closed Mon eves, Tues and Aug.

Chonas-l'Amballan ✉ 38121

****Domaine de Clairefontaine**, t 04 74 58 81 52, f 04 74 58 80 93 (*inexpensive*). Set back in its own garden in a village on the eastern bank of the Rhône, with old-fashioned character and a reputed restaurant (*menus 180–450F*). Closed Sun eves, Tues lunch and Mon.

Condrieu ✉ 69420

*****Hôstellerie Beau-Rivage**, 2 Rue du Beau-Rivage, t 04 74 56 82 82, f 04 74 59 59 36 (*expensive*). A luxury hotel right by the Rhône. Not at all bad value for its location and comfort, although the architecture's a bit of a mixed bag (*menus 310–620F*).

Tournon-sur-Rhône ✉ 07300

Le Chaudron, 7 Rue St-Antoine, t 04 75 08 17 90. A restaurant on a pedestrian street, reputed for its excellent wine list and copious Ardèche-style puddings (*menus 125–170F*). Closed Thurs eves, Sun and 1–15 Aug.

Tain-l'Hermitage ✉ 26600

Rive Gauche, 17 Rue Joseph Péala, t 04 75 07 05 90. An exciting modern restaurant in a modern building by the footbridge across the Rhône (*menus 170–295F*). Closed 1–23 Oct, 22–29 Jan, Sun eves and Mon.

Soyons ✉ 07130

****Domaine de la Musardière and ***La Châtaigneraie**, t 04 75 60 83 55, f 04 75 60 85 21 (*expensive*). Two very good sister establishments side by side just off the N86. The Musardière has a restaurant (*menus 150–350F*).

Baix ✉ 07210

****La Cardinale et sa Résidence**, Quai du Rhône, t 04 75 85 80 40, f 04 75 85 82 07 (*luxury–expensive*). Very smart hotel and restaurant, partly set in a 17th-century house with a wonderful view of the Rhône (*menus 195–450F*). Some of the rooms are in a modern building a few kilometres away. Closed 25 Oct–10 Mar, restaurant also closed Mon and Tues lunch Sept–Oct and Mar–April.

of excavations of the former Gallo-Roman site, where you can make out the lines of Gallo-Roman walls, and see the odd reconstituted colonnaded villa courtyard with small pools, as well as the traces of a crowded market square with stalls.

The Northern Rhône Valley Wine Route from Vienne to Valence

A string of fine little wine-making *appellations* line the west bank between Vienne and Valence. The steepness of the vineyards indicates that tending the vines is quite a feat, but it is worth the effort: the plants lap up the sunshine and are well drained. Their superlative grapes make some of the most exclusive wines in southern France.

Towards the southern end of the St-Joseph wine-producing area, the château at **Tournon-sur-Rhône** stands on solid rock surveying the river at its feet, towers marking the line of its former ramparts. The château has been gradually restored in recent years. Part of it has been turned into law courts, part into a museum. The highlight of the tour is the triptych in the castle's Chapelle St-Vincent, dating from 1555. Christ's Ascension in a ball of flaming light could scarcely be more dramatic. Down in the town, venture into the darkness of the big plain Gothic **church of St-Julien** and feel about for the light switch that will enable you to see the very tender and touching murals in one side chapel, depicting events in Christ's life. You can take a steam train ride up from Tournon into the rugged hills of the Ardèche around Lamastre.

Northern Rhône Valley Wines

The syrah grape makes the powerful, heady red wines, the viognier, marsanne and roussanne varieties the liquorous whites. North to south, you pass through the west-bank vineyards of Côte Rôtie, Condrieu (and tiny Château-Grillet), St-Joseph, Cornas and St-Péray. Hermitage and Crozes-Hermitage spread around the vine-covered hill of Tain-l'Hermitage on the east bank. The wines of the *appellations* of Côte Rôtie, Condrieu and Hermitage are so exclusive that you may not even find it easy to buy them via a *négociant* or wine merchant. The largest *appellation*, St-Joseph, is easier to get your hands on.

The plots producing Côte Rôtie cling precariously to the slopes just southwest of Vienne, between St-Cyr-sur-Rhône and Tupin-et-Semons. At Ampuis, the Guigal family is one of the most famous names in wine-making, but their wines are difficult to get hold of: you are most likely to find them in the local restaurants. Adjoining Côte Rôtie, **Condrieu** is a still more minuscule *appellation*, covering just 70 hectares, but ranking for many wine connoisseurs among the very greatest white wines in the world. The 700 or so hectares of vines allowed to produce *appellation* St-Joseph wines are scattered along some 60 kilometres of the west bank of the Rhône from below Condrieu to the area opposite Valence. The slopes have long produced highly respected wines: the reds have all sorts of flavours of red fruits, but are reckoned to become more 'gamey' with age; the whites have a sweet, strong bouquet and a rounded taste.

M. Chapoutier, 18 Av du Docteur Paul Durand, in Tain, **t** 04 75 08 28 65, **f** 04 75 08 81 70. Sells a good range of wines. *Open every day.*

Below Tournon, follow the Route Panoramique into the hills and you will get a spectacular view in all directions from the heights of **St-Romain-de-Lerps** west of Châteaubourg. **Cornas** back by the river produces more splendid meaty red wines. Its white sibling, **St-Péray**, centred round the sweet little town of the same name, comes sparkling as well as still. The spectacular bone-white ruins of the medieval **castle of Crussol** sit like a huge battered snail's shell on the steep hillside above the town, surveying from on high the wide plain and rolling hills heading east from the Rhône to the barrier of the Vercors mountains. The castle, started in the 12th century, has been in ruins since the 17th. Climb the polished rock paths up to the top of the ruins and you are rewarded with views over Valence and the Rhône valley north and south.

The valley town of **Valence**, built on a series of low terraces above the east bank of the Rhône, perhaps looks more beautiful from up among Crussol's ruins than from down below, but it does have some pleasant pedestrian old streets in its historic heart. One or two ornate façades stand out, notably the sensational Maison des Têtes, but the town's churches are a disappointment, and its museum slightly drab. Valence seems to be proud of the fact that Napoleon stayed here and enjoyed picking the local cherries when undergoing his army training.

On the east side of the river, **Montélimar** means nougat to most. The almonds essential to its making were first imported to the area in the 16th century, and shops selling it have sprung up along the main roads around the town. The old centre, a gently pretty place, has seen its fortunes restored recently. Façades have been repainted in powdery colours, and one of the brightest buildings has been converted into a curious museum dedicated to miniature works of art. Head out of the old centre by the one remaining old gate, the Porte St-Martin, and take the steep path up to the rather severe feudal remains of the **Château des Adhémars** at the very top of the town. This powerful family went on to become lords of the rather more splendid Château de Grignan to the east (*see* p.792). There's a small museum within the walls.

A surprisingly magnificent medieval cathedral crowns the hill of **Viviers**, an episcopal town from the late Roman Empire. From the outside the Gothic choir looks suspiciously like it might be wearing a tiara of stone. Most of the cathedral was rebuilt in the 18th century, but the Romanesque entrance has survived. The interior is staggering, vast and aisleless. A series of extremely rich tapestries showing scenes of Jesus' life adorns the choir.

East of the Rhône Valley from Lyon down through the Drôme

East of the Rhône Valley the hilly landscape is beautiful and unspoilt, rolling down from the Chartreuse and Vercors ranges (*see* pp.856–7) and from the smaller but still spectacular Diois and Baronnies hills. The Isère and Drôme, two major tributaries of the Rhône, weave their way from east to west through wide fruit-growing valleys to join their master. Nature is the main tourist sight in these parts, but there are some small and sometimes eccentric places to entertain you along the way.

Into the Northern Drôme

Music-lovers might care to make a pilgrimage east from Vienne to the pleasant valley-side town of **La Côte-St-André**, set above the amazingly flat Plaine de Bièvre with its seemingly unbroken patchwork of fields. Here the composer's comfortable 18th-century home on the main street has been turned into the **Musée Hector Berlioz** (*open daily exc Tues 9–12 and 3–6; adm*). The museum isn't a cheerful place: a mould of his funerary mask greets you in the entrance hall, while busts of the moody Hector brood over most of the rooms, with their family portraits, the odd frayed family possession and their rare precious letter penned by the genius. The greatest attraction is probably the wide variety of Berlioz recordings on sale in the shop.

The religious centre of **St-Antoine-l'Abbaye**, not far southeast of Hauterives, contains relics of St Anthony, a popular medieval saint who founded the first Christian monastery. In the 11th century the relics were put in the hands of Benedictine monks; a church and a hospital were founded, and in the 13th century the brotherhood became the Order of Hospitallers of St Anthony, or the Antonins. With their headquarters at St-Antoine-l'Abbaye, they went on to found hospices across Europe. Work began on a great Gothic church here in the 13th century, but it would not be completed until the 15th. This was the most successful period in the abbey's history; from the 16th century it went into decline.

A large portion of the complex of buildings has survived, however, and is slowly being restored. Three grand rusticated 17th-century classical arches mark the abbey entrance, topped by roofs with Burgundian-style coloured tiles. The somewhat battered west front of the massive abbey church has kept some of its grandeur, including a 15th-century central portal. Greater riches lie within: remnants of 15th- and 16th-century wall paintings have been preserved in several side chapels. In the choir, a tapestry cycle of finest Aubusson work depicts scenes in the

A Palace of Pebbles

The valleys in the northern half of the Drôme *département* yield large rounded glacial pebbles which are put to good effect in the characteristic squat square farmhouses, often laid out in pleasing herringbone patterns. They are also employed in one of the strangest works of naive architecture in France, the **Palais Idéal du Facteur Cheval**, in the back garden of a quiet Drômois village house at Hauterives (*open 15 April–15 Sept daily 9–7; Feb–14 April and 16 Sept–16 Nov daily 9.30–5.30; Dec–Jan daily 10–4.30; adm*). The local postman, Ferdinand Cheval, fell in love, almost literally, with the stones of the area and for 34 years, beginning in 1879, he used them to build grottoes and cascades. His architectural dreams became increasingly ambitious; after the grottoes came a tomb for the family, in Egypto-Christian style, followed by a Hindu temple guarded by giants. Bizarre creatures and twisted vegetation in stone and cement pop out all over the complex; models of great buildings from around the world have been stuck on here and there. Cheval's folly has become one of the big attractions of the region – and there is even a *son-et-lumière* show during the tourist season.

Getting Around

Romans-sur-Isère and St-Marcellin have railway stations on the line from Valence to Grenoble. Crest and Die are on the line from Valence to Gap and Briançon.

Tourist Information

La Côte-St-André: Place Berlioz, t 04 74 20 61 43, f 04 74 20 29 81.
Hauterives: Place de la Galaure, t 04 75 68 86 82, f 04 75 68 92 96.
St-Marcellin: 2 Av du Collège, t 04 76 38 53 85, f 04 76 38 17 32.
Crest: Place du Dr Maurice Rozier, t 04 75 25 11 38, f 04 75 76 79 65.
Die: Place St-Pierre, t 04 75 22 03 03, f 04 75 22 40 46.
Dieulefit: 1 Place de l'Eglise, t 04 75 46 42 49, f 04 75 46 36 48.
Buis-les-Baronnies: 2 Place du Quinconce, t 04 75 28 04 59, f 04 75 28 13 63.

Where to Stay and Eat

St-Antoine-l'Abbaye ✉ 38160
Auberge de l'Abbaye, Mail de l'Abbaye, t 04 76 36 42 83. In an old building facing the abbey, this restaurant serves excellently executed food at reasonable prices (*menus 120–320F*). *Closed Jan, and Tues Feb–Mar and Oct–Dec.*

Hauterives ✉ 26390
**Le Relais, t 04 75 68 81 12, f 04 75 68 92 42 (*inexpensive–cheap*). A comfortable place

with 17 rooms and a restaurant serving traditional meals (*menus 85–160F*). *Closed 15 Jan–end Feb, Sun eves, restaurant also closed Mon.*
Les Baumes de Tersanne, t/f 04 75 68 90 56 (*inexpensive*). Comfortable B&B rooms in a typical pebble house 3.5km from Hauterives.

Grignan ✉ 26230
****Manoir La Roseraie, Route de Valréas, t 04 75 46 58 15, f 04 75 46 91 55 (*expensive*). Exclusive, luxurious walled property on an estate just on the outskirts of the village. Facilities include a swimming pool, tennis courts and a good restaurant (*menus 195–255F*). *Closed Mon out of season.*
***Le Clair de la Plume, Place du Mail, t 04 75 91 81 30, f 04 75 91 81 31 (*expensive*). A romantic hotel in the village, with rose walls, light blue shutters and rooms overlooking a delightful garden where teas are served in good weather – this is also a splendid *salon de thé*. *Closed Feb.*
Le Poème, Montée du Tricot, t 04 75 91 10 90. Intimate address serving delicious dishes such as the *brandade de morue* with summer truffles (*menus 95–125F*).

Dieulefit ✉ 26220
L'Auberge des Brises, Route de Nyons, t 04 75 46 41 49. Eat stylish country cooking under shady lime trees 1.5km outside town towards Nyons. *Closed Tues, Wed Sept–June.*

Le Poët-Laval ✉ 26160
***Les Hospitaliers, t 04 75 46 22 32, f 04 75 46 49 99 (*moderate*). A wonderful little hotel

life of Joseph. The **Musée de St-Antoine-l'Abbaye** (*open July–Aug daily 11–12.30 and 1.30–6; rest of year daily exc Tues 2–6; adm*) houses a permanent collection on the Antonins and presents a changing programme of temporary art exhibitions.

Cheese enthusiasts might press on to **St-Marcellin**, where there is a museum devoted to the excellent Fromage St-Marcellin. Meandering along the delightful country lanes through the pastures north of town (for example the D71 to Roybon) you will see the big white cattle that produce the St-Marcellin milk grazing by solid farms with wide-brimmed roofs – designed to cope with wintry conditions.

The other side of the Isère river, **Pont-en-Royans** is a busy gateway into the dramatic gorges of the Vercors range (*see p.857*).

occupying a splendid site overlooking the valley towards Dieulefit. The restaurant may have a very limited menu, but the cook concentrates on fine fresh food (*menus 160–340F*). The pool is superbly located. *Closed 16 Nov–14 Mar, plus restaurant closed Mon and Tues except July–Aug.*

Vinsobres
Le Bistrot, t 04 75 27 61 90. Village restaurant spreading out appealingly round a simple fountain and down the pavement.

Nyons ✉ 26110
Le Colombet, Place de la Libération, **t 04 75 26 03 66, **f** 04 75 26 42 37 (*moderate*). With its characterful long façade, a pleasant traditional French provincial hotel-cum-restaurant at the heart of the action (*menus 95–210F*). *Closed 20 Nov–12 Jan.*
Le Petit Caveau, 9 Rue Victor Hugo, **t** 04 75 26 20 21. Restaurant set in the vaulted room of one of Nyons' old houses. The very chatty waitress doubles as a wine expert and is married to the chef, whose cuisine is full of Provençal herbs (*menus 170–250F*). *Closed Sun eves and Mon exc hols, and Christmas.*

Aubres ✉ 26110
***Auberge du Vieux Village, Route de Gap, **t** 04 75 26 12 89, **f** 04 75 26 38 10 (*moderate*). Perched up high in an old village in the hills just east of Nyons, some of the rooms in this hotel built out of the castle ruins have their own terraces as well as fantastic views. The restaurant has a terrace where you'll feel on top of the world (*menus 80–178F*). *Closed*

Jan, plus restaurant closed Wed and Thurs eves out of season.

Les Pilles/Condorcet ✉ 26110
La Charrette Bleue, Route de Gap, **t** 04 75 27 72 33. Cheerful roadside restaurant serving reliably excellent Provençal cuisine (*menus 98–182F*). *Closed Wed, Sun eves Nov–Mar, Tues eves Sept–June, and Jan.*

Valouse ✉ 26110
***Le Hameau de Valouse, **t** 04 75 27 72 05, **f** 04 75 27 75 61 (*moderate*). A gorgeous restored huddle of old houses turned into a delightful hotel in a beautiful location close to the Défilé de Trente Pas, just off the amazing mountainous eastern route between Dieulefit and Nyons.

Mérindol-les-Oliviers ✉ 26170
Auberge de la Gloriette, **t/f** 04 75 28 71 08. South of Nyons, in a village well off the road to Vaison-la-Romaine, a dream of a Provençal cliché, an inn where pottery cats stretch out in the splendid shade of big trees by a splashing fountain. The pies, pizzas and tarts cooked in the wood-burning oven are superlative, as are the melting views. The place has a few quite pleasant modern B&B rooms at the back.

Buis-les-Baronnies ✉ 26170
Sous l'Olivier, Quartier du Menon, **t 04 75 28 01 04, **f** 04 75 28 16 49 (*inexpensive*). Pleasant rooms, plus a pool, tennis court and sauna. There's also an inexpensive restaurant (*menus 100–150F*). *Closed Nov–mid-Mar.*

The Drôme River Valley and the Southern Drôme

Occasionally, adventurous types are allowed to abseil down the side of the 170ft of sheer masonry of **Crest**'s keep. From its towering height there are splendid views east to the Vercors. The keep, dating from the 12th century, is said to be the tallest surviving medieval *donjon* in France. It long served as a prison. East of Crest, patches of Clairette de Die vineyards begin to appear. Pliny the Elder is said to have had a penchant for these wines back in Roman times. Today Clairette de Die is a perfumed sparkling apéritif wine made from the sweetly scented muscatel grape, with some clairette grapes combined.

Colourful **Die**, dwarfed by the massive yellow limestone curtain of the Montagne de Glandasse (nearly 5,000ft), was once a cathedral city. It's hard to believe such a tiny town boasted its own bishop for so long. You can still find traces of Gallo-Roman Die (full title Dea Augusta Vocontiorum) on a wander around town, such as the Porte St-Marcel, a Roman triumphal arch. Gallo-Roman vestiges are displayed in the little town museum, which also covers prehistory in the area and the painful period of religious division and intolerance in the Ancien Régime, when Die suffered as a small Protestant centre. The curious mosaic of which the town is most proud, known as the 'mosaic of the bishop's palace', provides a glimpse into Christian fantasies about the cosmos in the 12th century. The former cathedral is partly built in blindingly white stone, but its interior is filled with a Romanesque darkness.

Half-restored villages, sometimes with the battered ruins of a medieval castle perched above them, hide out in the hill roads leading south from the Drôme river valley. In the valleys, fields of lavender presage the nearness of Provence. The D538 via Saou and Bourdeaux offers a peaceful picture of perfect countryside, the Trois Becs soaring above. Climb the D156 road round their eastern side and fabulous views open out eastwards to the highest peaks of the Alps.

East of Montélimar and Donzère you'll discover something of a pre-Provençal paradise, where elegant mountains slope down to olive groves and cherry and apricot orchards, while lower fields are carpeted with vines and lavender. Between Montélimar and Dieulefit seek out the old hilltop villages of **La Bégude-de-Mazenc** and **Le Poët-Laval**.

Dieulefit ('God made it') has made it rich through modelling clay of its own. The outskirts and the two main streets are filled with potters. The traditional style is of simple glazes in blue, green, yellow or caramel – typically Provençal – but a clutch of more experimental potters have also opened up shop here. The Maison de la Terre holds pottery exhibitions. Take time to explore the little maze of cobbled pedestrian old streets hidden above the high street. The outskirts of Dieulefit are the rather curious location for a Club Med holiday village, which draws a surprisingly glamorous crowd.

The D538 is an irresistible route south to the aristocratic French Renaissance **Château de Grignan** (*open April–Oct daily 9.30–11.30 and 2–5.30; rest of year daily exc Tues, same times; adm*), standing aloof on its rock above the village houses which run around its feet. But it did lose its head at the Revolution, the turrets and tiled roofs decapitated in that period.

Mme de Sévigné, the great court socialite and correspondent of Louis XIV's day, spent three long periods here. Her daughter, Françoise-Marguerite, was also quite a character, and a fine catch, regarded as one of the brightest beauties of the time. La Fontaine dedicated one of his fables to her, the Lion in Love. In 1669 she married François Comte de Grignan who spent most of his time at court, or at Grignan, forking out vast amounts on lavish entertainment. Their daughter, Pauline, would be forced to sell the family castle in 1732 to pay off his terrible debts.

Behind the Renaissance gateway and facade, guides take you on a tour of some 20 rooms, telling stories of the castle's most significant owners and guests. At the end of the tour you'll meet the howling gargoyles of the Adhémar gallery, built in the late-

Gothic period, and go on to what is surely the most decadent and glorious terrace in southern France, placed on the flat roof of the substantial church below. In season beautiful old roses perfume the village streets, where a number of houses have been converted into tourist shops and restaurants. The sweet little **Atelier Musée Livre et Typographie** celebrates the art of book-making, and the works of famous correspondents, including the Marquise de Sévigné, who is buried in the vast Gothic cave of a church pressed against the hillside.

The land between Grignan and Nyons is the most prolific truffle-producing territory in France, with truffle oaks sometimes planted in neat rows to encourage the crop. The village of **Richerenche**, near Valréas, has grown rich on the most important truffle fair in France, held in mid-winter. Olives are the main crop associated with **Nyons**, although cherry and apricot orchards also abound. The experts say that the finest olives in France come from around here – recently granted the rare distinction of their own *appellation d'origine contrôlée*. The friendly little town hosts an international institute of the olive and contains an olive museum. Beyond the stunning single arch of Nyons's medieval bridge, which spans the turquoise waters of the Eygues, the old town is a secretive place beyond the single street of Provençal stores and the old arcaded square. Steep little alleys lead to the Tour Randonne, a crenellated defensive tower which pokes its head out above the rest of the town.

From the Tour Randonne, the town of Nyons seems to have been wedged like a stopper in the entrance to the gorgeous **Baronnies** mountains to the east. Bald-topped Mont Ventoux and Montagne de Lure, guardians of northwestern Provence, loom over the range. The Baronnies mark the historic boundary between the Dauphiné region to the north and that of Provence to the south. Cherry and apricot orchards proliferate, grapes produce Coteaux des Baronnies wine, and lavender finds space to grow. Crumbling, semi-abandoned villages cling to the hillsides. Many are well tucked away in nooks and crannies up the Baronnies slopes. In summer you may encounter a lone goatherd guarding his or her flock. The area produces excellent goat's cheese, *picodons*.

The largest of the many picturesque mountains to climb in the Baronnies is the Mont Angèle, from which you get marvellous views east all the way to the distant peaks of the Alps. Laid-back **Buis-les-Baronnies** attracts a fair crowd of hippies young and old, and there's plenty of plane-tree shade for all to lounge under. It is said that Hannibal passed through here, and that his elephants drank at the fountain. The local speciality comes from the pretty linden or lime trees which line the roads: their young leaves and flowers are gathered and dried to make *tilleul* infusion. Two routes lead east from Buis to that dramatic gateway to Provence, Sisteron. The more northerly route takes you via the **Ouvèze valley** and the **Méouges gorges**. Follow the twisting detour up the **Col de Perty**, if you have time, to enjoy the finest views in the area. The more southerly route through the **Derbous and Jabron** valleys passes along delectable roads lying in the shadow of the brooding masses of the Mont Ventoux and Montagne de Lure. The villages of **Brantes** and **Montbrun-les-Bains** lie in exceptionally dramatic sites.

West of the Rhône Valley: the Ardèche

Heading southwest from Lyon, first come the orchard-covered Monts du Lyonnais and the hidden surprise of a little natural park, the Mont Pilat. The northern half of the *département* of the Ardèche then offers splendid peaceful countryside, but the southern half is more touristy. Even so, the gorges and villages along the Ardèche river valley are simply fabulous. This region was previously known as the Vivarais.

Into the Northern Ardèche

Sandwiched between the industrial Rhône valley below Lyon and the industrial Gier valley leading to St-Etienne, the pine-crested **Mont Pilat** is a beautiful, bucolic surprise, a glorious little haven which has been turned into a small regional nature park. Climb up to the Pilat via the steep roads from Givors, St-Romain-en-Gal or Condrieu, until you come to the D19, which runs along a fertile plateau on the eastern side of the Pilat tops. **Pélussin** hosts the **Maison du Parc**, a centre offering information on the Pilat, its environment and traditions.

North of Pélussin via winding roads, **Ste-Croix-en-Jarez** is the most intriguing destination in the Mont Pilat area, a 13th-century defensive monastery which has been turned into a village since the Revolution. Although some important elements, such as the cloisters, have disappeared, there is still a strong sense of the architectural order of the monastery-turned-village, centred around two large courtyards. It is worth going on the guided tour of this unusual place. To the south, follow the route into the quiet pine forests of the highest peaks of the Pilat, one reaching over 4,000ft. A dramatic road winds northwards down to the village of **Rochetaillée**, with its ruined château set on a precipitous thin crest, ravines either side. From here you can plunge down into industrial **St-Etienne**, not an obvious tourist destination, although a substantial mining museum run by former mine-workers recalls what was until recently the main industry of these parts. If you follow the ring road round the eastern side of town you'll spot the town's **modern art museum**. The tubular-industrial works of Léger stand out, most apt in this context, but there are also provocative works by other major 20th-century figures such as Picasso, Dubuffet and Warhol.

Moving down into the northern Ardèche, the splendid valleys with their semi-abandoned terraces and semi-moribund villages far eclipse the dull towns. **Annonay** is really only worth a stop if you want to pay homage to the Montgolfier brothers, the hot-air balloon pioneers who hailed from here.

The rivers that start on the eastern slopes of Mont Mézenc and Mont Gerbier de Jonc (*see* p.803) rush down to the Mediterranean, hurtling through chicanes of gorges at breakneck speed. Driving along these routes is exhilarating and exhausting. Head down the **Eyrieux valley** from Le Cheylard to Privas, which has a nice little heart made up of small sloping squares. South of Le Cheylard, the route along the **valleys of the Dorne and the Volane** leads to Aubenas, near where the small hilltop village of **Antraigues** is surrounded by towering rocky slopes covered in green lichen. This isolated place became an important centre for the Ardèche Resistance movement in the Second World War. South of here, the busy spa town of **Vals-les-Bains** produces a

Getting Around

The Ardèche has a few tourist trains, but for public transport you really have to rely on the rare bus. To reach the touristy southern Ardèche, it's best to go from Montélimar. One bus line from Montélimar serves Vogüé, Ruoms and Vallon-Pont-d'Arc, another Aubenas, Vals-les-Bains, Joyeuse and Les Vans. There's also a good bus line from Valence via Privas, Aubenas and Vals-les-Bains to Lalevade d'Ardèche.

Tourist Information

Pélussin: Maison du Parc du Mont Pilat, t 04 74 87 52 01, f 04 74 87 52 02.
Privas: Place Charles de Gaulle, t 04 75 64 33 35, f 04 75 64 73 95.
Vals-les-Bains: t 04 75 37 49 27, f 04 75 94 67 00.
Aubenas: t 04 75 35 24 87, f 04 75 89 02 04.
Ruoms: t 04 75 93 91 90, f 04 75 39 78 91.
St-Martin-d'Ardèche: t/f 04 75 98 70 91.

Where to Stay and Eat

Ste-Croix-en-Jarez ✉
Le Prieuré, t 04 77 20 20 09, f 04 77 20 20 80 (*inexpensive*). Four simple, atmospheric rooms set in the gateway into the abbey-village, with a big restaurant below (*menus 60–230F*). Closed Mon, Sun eves out of season, Jan and first half Feb.
Auberge de Vernolon, t 04 77 51 56 58 (*inexpensive*). Basic but good-value B&B rooms, with fine views, plus a spacious barn hung with striking modern art where rustic country cooking is served. Book in advance. *Restaurant closed Mon–Fri exc July and Aug.*

St-Agrève ✉ 07320
**Domaine de Rilhac, t 04 75 30 20 20, f 04 75 30 20 00 (*moderate–inexpensive*). An old stone farm converted into the most charming small hotel in the area. Excellent restaurant (*menus 135–430F*). Hotel closed Jan, and Wed exc summer; restaurant closed Jan and Feb, Tues eves and Wed eves.

Lamastre ✉ 07270
***Château d'Urbilhac, t 04 75 06 42 11, f 04 75 06 52 75 (*expensive*). Very comfortable 19th-century château in mock-16th-century style. Spacious rooms and an extensive terrace for outside dining (*menu 250F*). Some grand views around. *Closed Oct–April; restaurant also closed Mon–Fri lunch.*

Antraigues-sur-Volane ✉ 07530
**Auberge La Castagno, Pont de l'Huile, t 04 75 88 25 01 (*inexpensive*). A pleasant, comfortable hotel with 10 rooms.
Remise, Pont de l'Huile, t 04 75 38 70 74. Serves carefully prepared, good food at very reasonable prices (*menus up to 200F*). Closed Sun eves and Fri exc July-Aug.

St-Julien-du-Serre ✉ 07200
B&B Mas de Bourlenc, t/f 04 75 37 69 95 (*inexpensive*). Lost in the hills a few kilometres above Aubenas, with splendid views. Run by a charming young couple.

La Garde-Guérin ✉ 48800
**La Régordane, t 04 66 46 82 88, f 04 66 46 90 29 (*inexpensive*). A cosy, small hotel in this huddled village. Fare to give you strength for local walks (*menus 100–190F*). Closed Oct–mid-April.

Les Vans ✉ 07140
**Le Carmel, t 04 75 94 99 60, f 04 75 94 34 29 (*inexpensive*). A delightful rambling converted convent above the centre, run with real passion by the owners. No restaurant.
Le Grangousier, Rue Courte, t 04 75 94 90 86. An historic house packed with atmosphere opposite the church. A great place to try regional specialities (*menus 105–260F*). Closed Sun eves and Wed exc July–Aug, and mid-Nov–Feb.

Barjac ✉ 30430
***Le Mas du Terme, Route de Bagnols-sur-Cèze, t 04 66 24 56 31, f 04 66 24 58 54 (*moderate*). An 18th-century silk farm tastefully converted into a relaxing country hotel 3km outside the village. Good cuisine (*menus 170–215F*). Closed Dec–Feb.

sparkling water which was a great commercial success across France long before some of its young upstart – and now more successful – rivals.

Close to the Volane valley, the Bourges river rushes down through another picturesque valley, the highlight of which is the **waterfall of Le Ray-Pic**. There are plenty of gorgeous roads between the Volane and Eyrieux valleys. Arguably the finest takes you through the Glueyre valley with its terraces planted with chestnut trees, in particular between Marcols-les-Eaux and **St-Pierreville**. In a tremendous location surrounded by mountains, St-Pierreville has a pair of small museums – the **Maison de la Châtaigne** fills you in on the importance of the Ardèche chestnuts, which in the past were eaten by families and farm animals alike. They were smoked to be kept in winter, or turned into chestnut flour. Their numbers have dwindled considerably in the 20th century, but here and across the Ardèche you can buy delicious chestnut products, including splendid chestnut jam and luxury *marrons glacés*.

The Ardèche River: through the Central and Southern Ardèche

At **Aubenas** we reach the Ardèche river itself. The town stands far above it, running along a dramatic high crest with views over both the northern and the southern Vivarais. The town's melodramatic silhouette is dominated by a Gothic castle covered with turrets and colourful tiles in the Burgundian fashion, and by a church with a wide cupola. Although the castle dates in part back to the 12th century, the interiors reflect 18th-century good living.

West of Aubenas, a wonderful route leads down the **Chassezac valley** from the northeastern corner of the Cévennes mountains. The plateau village of **La Garde-Guérin** has been beautifully restored, but nothing, not even its tough granite walls, can protect it from the biting winds that cross the high plain. Further down the valley, the charming town of **Les Vans** is set in a fertile bowl of agricultural land. Several picturesque villages lie in the hills around Les Vans, **Chambonas** to the north and **Naves** to the west each with a castle and Romanesque church, and **Bannes** to the south with the ruins of another medieval castle. The well-named **Joyeuse**, with its mountainous surroundings and unspoilt historic centre, has several traditional craft shops along its cobbled streets as well as another museum celebrating the chestnut.

The central and southern Ardèche river valley attracts large numbers because of its splendid riverside villages and dramatic river gorges. **Vogüé**'s square castle, still owned by an aristocratic family, stamps its personality on its delightful old village. Canoeists proliferate here as soon as the season commences. **Balazuc**'s maze of narrow lanes climb steeply up from the river. A couple of craft shops are tucked away in odd corners. The main street in the old grid-planned, fortified town of **Ruoms** is a tourist trap, but the rest of the old town has been spared. **Labeaume**, a short way west, is the most dramatic of the villages in the area, set on one bank of the Beaume river. A small restored castle perches on an unlikely natural spindle of rock above the village houses. Towering, thick plane trees form a vast canopy of shade down beside the river for the hotter half of the year. On the other bank, a row of elephant-man rocks add a surreal touch.

Vallon-Pont-d'Arc is the place to start a trip down the breathtaking **Gorges de l'Ardèche**. Hundreds of thousands do the trip by canoe, although the road that follows the gorges, high in the scrubland on the northern side, offers vertiginous glimpses down the vertical slashes of apricot and grey rock to the river, hundreds of feet below. Vallon itself is pretty, but it's almost always packed out with tourist crowds. Sensational prehistoric cave paintings were found near the town in the mid-1990s – arguably the finest cave paintings ever found, with a greater diversity of animals even than at Lascaux. At Vallon-Pont-d'Arc they've learnt from the mistakes made at Lascaux (*see* p.475), and the Grotte Chauvet won't be opened to the public. However, you can see an excellent half-hour film which shows the cave paintings in all their beauty. As well as the depictions of deer, horses and mammoths that you might expect, there are prides of prehistoric lions, gatherings of prehistoric bears and an unforgettable array of prehistoric rhinos.

Hundreds of grottoes and *avens* (potholes) have been discovered in the limestone of the Gorges. The **Aven d'Orgnac**, the most celebrated one, lies a short way south of Vallon-Pont-d'Arc, lost among scrub and poor vinelands. The extraordinary stalagmites of the vast cavern have been given nicknames which reflect their eccentric forms. Alongside the Aven, there is a substantial museum of prehistory. If you visit just one grotto along the Ardèche valley itself, make it the **Grotte de la Madeleine** as it has the added bonus of a sensational view down to the river. The caverns inside are spectacular, and refreshingly cool in summer.

Into the Auvergne: The Upper Loire Valley

The highlight on the journey along the upper Loire valley to its source is without a doubt the magical pilgrimage city of Le Puy-en-Velay. Some of its most famous monuments stick out above the town on surprising columns of rock. These volcanic chimneys are just one of the many remnants of the explosive activity that makes the landscapes of the Auvergne so distinct from anywhere else in France.

The Upper Loire Valley from Roanne to Le Puy-en-Velay

The upper Loire valley becomes more and more rustic as you head south from industrial Roanne. The east bank road hugs the river, passing the spectacular 13th-century **Château de la Roche** (*open Aug daily 10.30–12 and 2–7; rest of year 2–6; adm*) which stands in the midst of the water, joined to the bank by a low walkway. The recently restored interiors include exhibitions on Loire river trading and the Villerest dam. On the opposite bank, seek out quiet **St-Maurice-sur-Loire** which, along with a 12th-century round keep, has a charming church with cartoonish 13th-century wall paintings. The figure of St Nicholas by the altar recalls that he was patron saint of the Loire mariners in the days when the river was still a major transport route. In the partly walled old village of **Pommiers**, south of the river, a Romanesque church sits proudly above the vegetable plots. The dark interior conceals some surprisingly delicate Gothic wall paintings of New Testament scenes.

To the east of Pommiers, the Loire valley opens out. In the dense area of lakes between Feurs and Montbrison, the **Château de la Bastie-d'Urfé** (*open July–Aug daily 10–12 and 1–6; April–June and Sept daily 10–12 and 2.30–5.30; rest of year daily exc Tues 2–5; adm*) was a medieval manor transformed into an early French Renaissance château; it contains some delightful features, such as the grotto and the chapel, with its ornate gilded ceiling. The pleasant market town of **Montbrison** to the south is tucked into the Vizery valley below the **Monts du Forez** which separate the upper Loire valley from the Dore valley. The highest summit of this little-known range reaches a creditable 5,278 feet above Montbrison.

In the wide Loire valley below Montbrison, worn-down old volcano tops stick out like islands. **St-Romain-le-Puy**'s amazing priory church (*open April–Oct daily 2.30–6.30; adm*) stands on one of these isolated hilltops, like a Mont-St-Michel of the plains. Dating mainly from the late 10th and early 11th centuries, its body has undergone a fair deal of surgery since. The outside of the choir end has a frieze of crudely carved animals and patterns. The interior is utterly startling, with a chaos of floor levels, fragments of medieval wall paintings and bizarre carvings.

The village of **St-Bonnet-le-Château**, above the Loire, is home to the **Musée International Pétanque et Boule** (*open April–Oct weekdays 2.30–5.30, weekends 3–6; adm*), where you can glean all sorts of information on the sport, from its roots in antiquity to the vital difference between *boules* and *pétanque* – basically *pétanque* is more restful as the thrower doesn't move his feet and the game is only played on a short course (so the elderly gentlemen of the south can enjoy the game longer).

The Loire passes through another set of gorges below St-Just-St-Rambert and just west of St-Etienne. On the west bank, you can get commanding views from the superbly sited but ruined **Château d'Essalois**. Down below on the lake, the vestiges of the medieval **Château de Grangent** make an enchanting picture. **Chambles**, the village south of Essalois, has stunning views down on the Loire gorge to compete with its neighbour's. High above Bas-en-Basset, you can only reach the aloof **Château de Rochebaron** by a long, steep hillside walk. Enthusiasts have been cleaning up this isolated medieval fort in recent years. **Retournac** back down by the Loire has recently revived its lace-making traditions, with a museum on the subject. A detour west from Retournac takes you past the sweet village of St-André-de-Chalencon to the hamlet of **Chalencon** in its enchanting wooded valley, with an adorable chequered church.

Not far up river, the darkly picturesque **Château de Lavoûte-Polignac** (*open July–Sept daily 10–12.30 and 2–6.30; June daily 2–5; May weekends and hols 2–5; Easter hols daily 2.30–5; adm*) stands guard over a meander in the Loire. This castle was mostly restored in the late 19th century by members of the Polignac family after it had been abandoned at the Revolution. It still looks very sorry for itself inside, but the guided tour offers an absorbing insight into one of the most hated aristocratic families in France at the Revolution. Although in an even more ruined state, the same family's medieval **Château de Polignac** (*open June–Sept daily 10–7; Easter–May and Oct pm only; adm*) still commands respect on top of its volcanic platform. This tremendous stage-set of a location was the family base until they moved to Lavoûte in the mid-18th century. Its solid towering keep is only 15th century, but some of the substantial

Getting Around

Trains on the Lyon–Clermont-Ferrand line via St-Etienne will take you to St-Romain-le-Puy and Montbrison; you may have to change at St-Etienne.

Tourist Information

Montbrison: Galerie du Cloître des Cordeliers, t 04 77 96 08 69.
Bas-en-Basset: 25 Bd de la Sablière, t/f 04 71 66 95 44.
Chamalières-sur-Loire: Place de la Fontaine, t 04 71 03 44 67.
Le Monastier-sur-Gazeille: 30 Rue St-Pierre, t 04 71 08 37 76.

Where to Stay and Eat

St-Maurice-sur-Loire ✉ 42155
L'Echauguette, Rue Guy de la Mure, t 04 77 63 15 89 (*inexpensive*). B&B rooms in gorgeous village, with views on to the gorges.

St-André-de-Chalencon ✉ 43130
Relais des Seigneurs, Place de l'Eglise, t 04 71 58 41 41, f 04 71 58 41 44 (*inexpensive*).

Caringly renovated little hotel by the church. Special evenings in the restaurant arranged around regional themes at which tourists can meet the locals. A real find.

Polignac ✉ 43000
L'Auberge du Donjon, t 04 71 09 53 63. Simple inn at the foot of the great castle ruins. The **Restaurant de la Tour**, t 04 71 09 68 30, below has panoramic views.

Espaly St-Marcel ✉ 43000
L'Ermitage, 73 Av de l'Ermitage, t 04 71 02 16 29, f 04 71 09 16 59 (*inexpensive*). Tremendous views on to Le Puy-en-Velay from the hillside west out of town. Nicely renovated big rooms and a restaurant (*menus 98–200F*). *Closed Jan and Feb; restaurant also closed Mon.*

Chaspinhac ✉ 43700
La Paravent, t 04 71 03 54 75 (*inexpensive*). Pleasant old B&B, just outside Chaspinhac, with spacious, simple rooms. Run by a woman who's passionate about the area.

Arlempdes ✉ 43490
*Hôtel du Manoir, t 04 71 57 17 14 (*inexpensive*). A large old stone block of a hotel below the castle in this picturesque village.

walls date back to early Romanesque times. From the atmospheric ruins you can look down on the cathedral city of Le Puy-en-Velay, set in the Velay basin surrounded by conical mountains. Before heading into town, make a short detour west to the remains of another impressive castle, the **Château de St-Vidal** (*open July–Aug daily 2–6.30; adm*), which looks a bit like a children's picture-book image of a medieval fort with its square shape and round corner towers, built of the local black volcanic rock.

Le Puy-en-Velay

An enormous pink Virgin stands on top of a finger of volcanic rock in the centre of town, making the skyline of Le-Puy-en-Velay unforgettable. Balanced upon another finger is the chapel of St-Michel d'Aiguilhe, one of the most atmospheric churches in France. The extraordinary cathedral, reached by a daunting stairway, is central Le Puy's other dramatic place of worship, while in the neighbouring community of Espaly, another curious volcanic pinnacle has been topped by a massive statue, this time of Joseph. Lace is a speciality of long standing here, but the town museum offers further attractions for tourists.

Getting Around

Le Puy-en-Velay has a small airport at Loudes, t 04 71 08 62 28, 10mins from the centre, with daily weekday flights to and from Paris-Orly Sud (*exc Aug*).

There's a train from Lyon to Dunières via Le Puy; you might have to change at St-Etienne.

Tourist Information

Pl du Breuil, t 04 71 09 38 41, f 04 71 05 22 62.

Where to Stay

Le Puy-en-Velay ✉ 43000

***Régina, 34 Bd Maréchal Fayolle, t 04 71 09 14 71, f 04 71 09 18 57 (*inexpensive*). On one of the busy boulevards encircling the old city, but quite stylish, completely modernized and very good value. That goes for the cuisine too (*menus 145–240F*). *Restaurant closed Sun eves and Mon Nov–Mar.*

**Le Bristol, 7 Av Maréchal Foch, t 04 71 09 13 38, f 04 71 09 51 70 (*inexpensive*). Quite smart and good value with a friendly boss and a restaurant (*menu 100F*).

Eating Out

Eric et Marc Tournayre, 12 Rue Chênebouterie, t 04 71 09 58 94. Swish restaurant in historic house with vaulted dining room for Auvergnat specialities (*menus 115–350F*). *Closed Sun eves, Mon and Jan.*

L'Olympe, 8 Rue du Collège, t 04 71 05 90 59. Stylish little restaurant in a quiet historic street. Auvergne specialities (*menus 100–310F*). *Closed Sun eves, and Mon exc Aug.*

Le Bateau Ivre, 5 Rue Portail d'Avignon, t 04 71 09 67 20. Cosy restaurant devoted to Auvergne traditions (*menus 110–185F*). *Closed Sun and Mon.*

History

In Gallo-Roman times it seems that a pagan temple existed on at least one of Le Puy-en-Velay's pinnacles of rock. A slab known as the Pierre Fiévreuse, the 'feverish stone', became venerated in the city – it may originally have formed part of a Neolithic dolmen. At the end of the 4th century, as Christianity spread across the Velay, it was said that miracles happened here thanks to the Virgin, and the first church dedicated to her is thought to have gone up in the late 5th century.

Tradition claims that Bishop Gothescalk set out in 950 on the first major pilgrimage from Le Puy-en-Velay to Santiago de Compostela in Spain, and through the Middle Ages, Le Puy became one of the four most important gathering points in France for this journey. Parts of Le Puy's unique Romanesque cathedral had already been built in the mid-10th century. The curious Black Virgin in the cathedral is traditionally said to have been brought here from the Orient by a French king of the early Middle Ages, who was perhaps given her as a gift by a Middle Eastern ruler, but the evidence is unclear. It's now thought that she may in fact be a representation of the Egyptian goddess Isis. Le Puy, along with Chartres, was certainly one of the places where the cult of the Virgin first flourished in France. In the Middle Ages a whole administrative city was built to deal with pilgrims.

The great tradition of lace-making was probably established in the area around the 15th century. Though the trade was largely mechanized in the 19th century, up until the First World War large numbers of women in Le Puy and the surrounding area were employed producing hand-made *dentelles*. Other specialities of the Le Puy area include its excellent green lentils, the first vegetables in France to be granted their own *appellation d'origine contrôlée*, and its verbena teas and liqueurs.

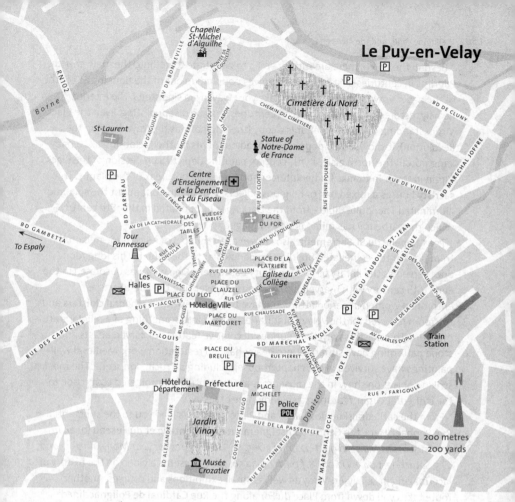

Touring Le Puy-en-Velay

The enormous sickly-pink 19th-century statue of **Notre-Dame de France** (*open May–Sept daily 9–7; rest of year daily 10–5 at least; adm*) on the Rocher Corneille is a typical 19th-century Catholic monstrosity. The Virgin, designed by Jean-Marie Bonnassieux, measures 52 feet in height and weighs in at over one hundred tonnes. Once you've made it up to the statue you can climb inside, although her insides have for a long time been covered head to toe in graffiti.

Steep **Rue des Tables** leads up Mont Anis to the cathedral from Place des Tables. It's one of the most memorable streets in France, and from it the black entrance to the **cathedral** looks like the monstrous mouth of a leviathan. The late 12th-century façade, a sheer wall of masonry, is embellished with patterns of alternating coloured stones and blind columns, a virtuoso display of Romanesque decoration. The massive porch, in itself the size of a decent church, was a clever piece of architecture added on to allow the cathedral to be extended out from the hillside. Rising to the left of the cathedral are the Hôtel-Dieu and the machicolated building behind which hides the cathedral cloister. The whole complex looks like a well-defended holy citadel.

Beyond the porch, there are further steps to negotiate to get into the main church. Pilgrims in centuries past found themselves popping up out of the floor in the centre of the nave. Nowadays you have to make your way in via side stairs. The interior, heavily restored in the 19th and 20th centuries, may be disappointing. Even the Black Virgin standing on the high altar is a copy (the original was destroyed during the Revolution); it shows Jesus popping his head out of his mother's clothing like a baby kangaroo. In the north aisle, a 17th-century painting depicts a procession of the Black Virgin in town, in thanks for her intercession during an outbreak of the plague. The **sacristy** houses a mixed bag of religious objects. You can find out about the splendid illuminated Théodulfe Bible – from the Dark Ages but donated in the 18th century – which the cathedral has miraculously managed to keep.

The **Chapelle du St-Sacrement**, also known as the chapel of relics, is located on the third floor of the crenellated building perpendicular to the church. This long room once served as the library of the university based here. One wall was decorated in the early 16th century with marvellous paintings representing the liberal arts as enthroned women in period attire. You have to pay to visit the **cathedral cloisters** and the room reserved for the Velay's dignitaries, turned into something of a religious art museum. The cloisters with their curious decorative features of carved beasts and stone patterning have suffered from heavy-handed restoration work. Medieval wall paintings have survived in the chapterhouse, including a Crucifixion scene. The most striking object on show in the museum is a 16th-century embroidered coat made for the cathedral Virgin, featuring a splendid Tree of Jesse.

From the cathedral, Rue des Tables and Place des Tables lead you to the substantial **Rue Raphaël**. Here, the **Centre d'Enseignement de la Dentelle et du Fuseau** (*open in tourist seasons Mon–Fri 9.30–12 and 1.30–5.30, Sat 10–5; rest of year Mon–Fri 10–12 and 2–5, Sat 10–12; t 04 71 02 01 68, f 04 71 02 92 56; adm*) presents a video on the history of lace-making in Le Puy-en-Velay as well as small exhibitions and courses. Another route takes you down from Place du For along the **Rue Cardinal de Polignac**, lined with some fine town houses, including that occupied by the mighty Polignac clan from the 17th century to the Revolution. Little **Rue Rochetaillade** boasts some of the oldest houses in Le Puy along its short length. Down below Place de la Platrière, the former Jesuit **Eglise du Collège** adds a twist of Baroque to Le Puy's central slopes.

Adjoining **Place du Clauzel** and **Place du Martouret** constitute the heart of town below the cathedral quarter. The neoclassical Hôtel de Ville was completed in 1766, in time to witness the guillotining of over 40 people, including 18 priests, and the burning in 1794 of the original Black Virgin. An antiques market takes place on Place du Clauzel on Saturday mornings. On the other side of the town hall, **Rue Pannessac**, lined with some splendid old merchants' houses, curves away from Place du Plot. At the end stands the stocky medieval gateway of the **Tour Pannessac**.

Most of the defensive walls surrounding Le Puy came down a long time ago, replaced by boulevards. Just outside these, beyond the town hall, a grand 19th-century civic area was laid out, stretching from the **Place du Breuil** through the shaded **Jardin Vinay**, to the **Musée Crozatier** (*open May–Sept daily exc Tues 10–12 and 2–6; rest of year daily exc Tues and Sun am 10–12 and 2–4; adm*), generously paid for by the sculptor Charles Crozatier. This grand 19th-century museum is crammed with a confusion of artefacts from down the ages. Local traditional arts and crafts take up a large number of the cluttered rooms, with a good display of *dentelles*.

The **Chapelle St-Michel d'Aiguilhe** is isolated in a separate part of town. There are 260 steps up to the chapel, and it's a pretty sheer climb, but it's worth the effort. The story goes that Bishop Gothescalk had the chapel built on his return from his pilgrimage to Santiago de Compostela, and the architecture certainly seems to contain some Spanish-Moorish touches, although it was added to in the 11th century. The curious shape of the church has inevitably been dictated by the very narrow peak on which it stands. Partly held up on comical little columns with wonderful carved capitals, the interior looks a bit cobbled together, but the darkly lit spaces speak of the sacred. The elegant belltower which rises from the chapel appears to have served as a model for that on the cathedral. At the foot of the Rocher de l'Aiguilhe is the rather basic 14th-century **Oratoire St-Grégoire**, and the **Espace St-Michel**, which explains how the Le Puy basin was formed as well as describing the cult of St Michael.

On the boulevards west of the centre, close to the Borne river, the recently restored **church of St-Laurent** – which formed part of a Dominican monastery – is one of the few Gothic edifices in the city. St Dominic came to Le Puy the last year of his life, in 1221. The entrails of the fearsome Hundred Years' War warrior Bertrand du Guesclin ended up here after he died besieging Chateauneuf-de-Randon in 1380, and you can see a tomb effigy of the man in armour.

The Last Leg of the Loire: from Le Puy-en-Velay to its Source

Follow the **D37** out of Le Puy's eastern suburb of Brives-Charensac for a spectacular route along the Loire valley to its source. Along the way you'll be treated to a string of ruined medieval forts. **Arlempdes** has a wonderfully dramatic location, the few remnants of its fort clinging to the back of a monster of a rock which has what looks like the skin of a great wrinkled elephant. The village with its old gateway and its old cross by the church has cobbled charm. At Arlempdes the Loire makes an important turn. To make for the river's source, go east. The first waters of the Loire dribble down the sides of the great pyramid top of **Mont Gerbier de Jonc**. This mountain looks almost man-made in form, seemingly built up of a great mound of boulders, snow-covered or stained with green lichens. Still more impressive than Mont Gerbier is its larger brother, **Mont Mézenc**, to the north.

Directly between Le Puy and Mont Mézenc, the dark purples, blacks and oranges of **Le Monastier-sur-Gazeille**'s former abbey church are the main attraction of this hill-side village east of Chadron. Calmin, a 7th-century count of Auvergne, founded the first monastery and became a saint. Saracens apparently brought down the monastery, but in the early Middle Ages the place came back to life, and the abbey grew into the most influential one in the Velay. Stand at the foot of the flight of steps leading up to the **church** to appreciate the detail of the colourful geometrical patterns of the 11th-century façade, and the animal and human figures set out along the gables, the humans hiding their genitalia with their knees. The stocky **castle** may be less colourful than the church, but with its black volcanic sides and its crinkled red-tiled roofs, it makes quite a pretty picture set in the centre of the village. The insubstantial local history museum occupies the lower floors of the castle. One section inside is devoted to Robert Louis Stevenson, who stayed for a month here in 1878 before heading off on his travels with a donkey.

The Dore Valley

The secretive, steep-sided Dore valley is sandwiched between the upper Loire and the upper Allier, hidden from view by the heights of the Monts du Forez and the Livradois. Although relatively little known, many summits in these ranges reach well over 3,000ft. Thiers, rather precariously situated on a very steep, high slope, is known for knife-making. South of here the stops are quiet and peaceful, the valley remarkably unspoilt by any signs of modernity. At the southern end, La Chaise-Dieu's abbey is now the setting for a highly reputed concert season.

Balanced on something of a knife-edge of a slope, with its knife shops, knife museum and knife house – where you can watch a knife-maker at work – **Thiers'** speciality is pretty obvious: this is the largest cutlery-producing centre in France, dating back to the 14th century. The town rises sharply above the Durolle river, whose waters the locals long used to power the grinding wheels for their knife-making. The **Maison des Couteliers and Musée de la Coutellerie** are both along Rue de la Coutellerie. The other striking speciality of the historic hillside town is the houses with crossed timberframe façades. The heavily restored Romanesque church of St-Genès reveals that Thiers had a life before its knife-making days.

The **Château de Vollore**, south of Thiers, benefits from magnificent views from its delectable terrace. A few remnants still stand of the medieval castle, though in the 19th century a new château arose in different style thanks to the Dumas family. One of the Dumas family members married a descendant of Lafayette, so it is memories of the great general which get the most attention on the short tour.

On the opposite side of the Dore valley, and cut off from any views of the outside world, the **Château d'Aulteribe** is hidden by a curtain of woods. This late-Gothic edifice was long the property of the Lafayette family, but it was transformed into a luxurious dwelling in the 19th century for the Onslow de Pierres. An Onslow family portrait shows the future composer Georges as a boy in his mother's arms. His father, Edward Onslow, was a British diplomat who in 1781 travelled to Clermont-Ferrand, where he met his wife-to-be. The last marquis died without heir, leaving the castle to the state in the 1950s. Highlights of the rich art collections are many accomplished portraits, including Henri IV by Pourbus, Richelieu by Philippe de Champaigne, and an oval painting of Marie-Antoinette and her son by the female artist Vigée Le Brun. Buy a CD of Georges Onslow's works on the way out to discover some of his music, of a rather exquisite Romanticism.

Continuing south along the Dore valley, perhaps the best way to appreciate its quiet beauty is to climb to the barren tops of the Monts du Forez, heading along the maze of country roads below Vollore-Montagne. From the **Col du Béal** you are rewarded with fantastic views in all directions.

Getting Around

Thiers is on the train line between Lyon and Clermont-Ferrand. Otherwise you really need a car to explore this region.

Tourist Information

Thiers: Château du Pirou, t 04 73 80 10 74.
La Chaise-Dieu: Place de la Mairie, t 04 71 00 01 16, f 04 71 00 03 45.

Where to Stay and Eat

Vollore
Château de Vollore, t 04 73 53 71 06, f 04 73 53 72 44 (*expensive*). Excellent B&B.

La Chaise-Dieu ✉ 43160
**Hôtel de l'Echo et de l'Abbaye, Place de l'Echo, t 04 71 00 00 45, f 04 71 00 00 22 (*inexpensive*). A delightfully run small hotel and restaurant right in the abbey complex (*menus 110–380F*). *Closed 13 Nov–3 April.*

Back down in the valley, the small town of **Ambert** is now most closely associated with a blue cheese, Fourme d'Ambert, the Auvergne's pale version of Roquefort. A cheese museum stands in the centre of town, along with attractive timber frame houses with distinctive crossed beams and a late-Gothic church crawling with gargoyles. However, for centuries Ambert was best known for producing paper for the Lyon printing business, and a museum on the subject has been set up in an old paper mill at Moulin Richard-de-Bas, east of town.

An abbey was first founded at **La Chaise-Dieu** in the middle of the 11th century by a canon from Brioude (*see* pp.811-12), Robert de Turlande, who set up a monastic institution following the Benedictine rule on what is still today a remote high plateau – the town stands at an altitude of more than 3,000ft. Robert obtained papal protection for the abbey, and a century after its foundation, the abbey of La Chaise-Dieu ruled over one of the most powerful monastic orders in France. After a crisis in the early 14th century , however, it had to be rescued by a former monk promoted to high places, the Avignon pope Clement VI. He ordered the rebuilding of the church, designed by Hugues Morel, in 1343, just after he'd been elected to the papacy, and his nephew and successor, Gregory XI, saw to its completion after Clement VI had been buried in La Chaise-Dieu's abbey. The abbey managed to keep its head up until the 16th century, when it was decorated, but it became the target of the Huguenots and was then milked for its wealth by various major political figures, including Richelieu and Mazarin. The monks left at the Revolution, and the place was pretty well abandoned through the 19th century. It was slowly restored through the 20th century, and in the 1960s the leading pianist Georges Cziffra founded a music festival here. Since then the Festival de Musique Française has developed into one of the major serious musical events in France.

The **abbey church**, named St Robert after its founder, is a stocky defensive Gothic construction with square towers on the west front. The interior, sober and low, has some exceptional decorations and a fine wood-carved Baroque organ with atlantes and putti. The short nave ends with a rood screen added in the 15th century, topped by a statue of Christ. Beyond the screen, a remarkable tapestry cycle runs round the chancel. The works, made in Arras and Brussels in the early 16th century, depict biblical stories, but the protagonists are dressed in the most exquisite late-Gothic attire. There are wonderful 15th-century carved stalls below the tapestries. In the middle of the chancel lies the tomb of Clement VI, portrayed as a white, frog-eyed figure, with tiny tame lions lying at his feet.

Other parts of the abbey have survived, including remnants of the cloister, while the monks' library now houses the abbey's treasury. In the adjoining square known as the Place de l'Echo, you can not only try out the echoing corners of one chamber, but also visit a waxworks museum with tableaux from La Chaise-Dieu's history. The extraordinary Italianate Tour Clémentine, rising at a strange angle from the end of the choir, now houses the sacristy. In the pleasant streets of the little town, the Musée du Bois celebrates the old traditions of woodwork in these parts. Glass engravers and painters also exhibit their works in nearby shops.

Clermont-Ferrand

Black is the colour of Clermont-Ferrand's lovely heart, and of its cathedral, dwarfed by the black silhouettes of the spectacular Monts Dômes. And it is also the colour of the Michelin tyres which have been linked with the city's industrial growth in the last two centuries. Back in the 17th century, the mathematical genius and philosopher Blaise Pascal proved the weight of air in these parts, and, way back in ancient times, the great Gaulish leader Vercingétorix had a famous victory here. Nowadays Clermont-Ferrand is an attractive town, with its splendid churches and streets, and a fine new art museum.

History

Nemessos, the pre-Roman Celtic settlement, stood high up above Clermont, on the Plateau de Gergovie south of the city. It was the centre of the mighty Arveni tribe. When Vercingétorix managed to unite the Gauls against Caesar's invasion in 52 BC, the Roman leader met with a rare defeat at Gergovie when he tried to besiege the town. Unfortunately, after his victory Vercingétorix pursued Caesar and his men north only to be defeated on another dramatic hilltop, Alésia in Burgundy (*see* pp.744–5). The Gallo-Roman city developed lower down the slopes of the Monts Dômes, where Clermont-Ferrand stands today.

The name Clermont appears on records for the first time in the 8th century, and by the 11th century it was a vibrant city, run by its powerful bishops. At the Council of Clermont in 1095, the city received over 300 European bishops and abbots – it was here that Pope Urban II proclaimed the First Crusade. A large number of knights present at the Council responded with wild enthusiasm, fixing red crosses on their clothes as a symbol of their Christian mission. While the bishops held sway in Clermont, they often came up against the power of the counts of Auvergne, who had a fortress built on a neighbouring slope. Montferrand, as it was known, expanded into a separate *bastide* town in the 13th century. The merchants of both towns started to assert their independence, and they gained still more when the 16th-century French queen Catherine de' Medici took power away from the Clermont bishopric.

Clermont and Montferrand would only officially be merged in the 18th century. In the 17th century, the city saw the birth of a French genius, the scientist and philosopher Blaise Pascal, who conducted some of his experiments on the top of the Puy de Dôme. But the name most associated with Clermont-Ferrand these days is Michelin, whose tyre factories came to dominate the local economy in the 20th century. The company profited enormously from the growth of the car industry, and from one of the most famous corporate logos in the world, Bibendum, the chubby Michelin man with his cheerful rolls of tyre fat. The past few decades have seen a dramatic reduction in tyre production in Clermont-Ferrand, but the creation of an enormous university has somewhat compensated for the industrial decline.

Touring Clermont and Montferrand

The huge, black **cathedral** marks the old city with its looming presence. The twin spires on the front, although built in Gothic style, were in fact only added on in the 19th century, to plans by Viollet-le-Duc. The rest of the structure is original Gothic, built in the second half of the 13th century and the 14th century. Inside, stained-glass windows set within decorative squares illuminate the transepts and choir. The chapels radiating out from the choir ambulatory contain decorative riches, the most famous of which is the gilded statue of the Virgin and child in the lady chapel. The crypt actually dates from an earlier Romanesque church. The Bayette tower leads to the richly endowed cathedral treasury and, if you climb all of its steps, to a panoramic view over the orange-red rooftops.

Major squares surround the cathedral, giving you space to stand back and admire, and giving the cafés the room to spread out away from the building's shadow. A statue of Urban II on Place de la Victoire recalls the First Crusade. The Maison du Tourisme houses the tourist office and the new **Espace Art Roman** (*open June–Sept daily 8.30–7, exc Sun 9–12 and 2–6; rest of year Mon–Fri 8.45–6.30, Sat 9–12 and 2–6, Sun 9–1; adm*), a modern presentation of the colourful Romanesque art which flowered so finely in the Auvergne, including a rousing high-tech spectacle.

Rue des Gras, a magnificent street lined with old mansions turned into shops, slopes down from the cathedral entrance. Along the way, a Chinese face above a doorway signals the entrance to the old-fashioned **Musée Ranguet**, which presents local traditions and crafts, with a section devoted to Pascal and his inventions. The modern covered market lies nearby, a childlike piece of architecture made up of colourful building blocks. Just north of the cathedral, the **Hôtel de Ville** makes its own dramatic statement with its enormous black columns. Beyond it, seek out the black-and-white façade of the sunken **church of Notre-Dame-de-Bon-Port**, tucked away in an old quarter of town. This mosaic of a building dates back to the Romanesque period, although the towers are stylish 19th-century recreations of those destroyed at the Revolution.

Some way south of the cathedral, above the pretty public garden, the **Jardin Lecoq**, lie the twin museums of the **Musée Bargoin** and **Musée du Tapis d'Art** (*open daily exc Mon 10–6; adm*) in purpose-built buildings from the end of the 19th century and the early 20th. These contain some fascinating displays, including ancient Celtic finds and vestiges of the Gallo-Roman city, with statuettes, fragments of mosaics, funeral stelae, sarcophagi, and even a preserved Gallo-Roman tunic. One extraordinary collection consists of ex-votos which were rediscovered in 1968 at the Roches spring at Chamalières up in the western part of the modern town. The splendid 80 or so carpets of the Musée du Tapis d'Art come from the Orient and the Far East. They are works of the highest quality and artistry, beautifully presented in darkened spaces.

The finest museum in Clermont-Ferrand lies out in **Montferrand**, which doesn't have the immediate appeal or cohesive character of historic Clermont, but the grid of old streets close to the **Musée des Beaux-Arts** (*open daily exc Mon 10–6; adm*) has been restored recently, with some very fine old houses bearing carvings on their façades. The museum has taken over a former Ursuline convent which once served as a barracks – but within, the spaces have been superbly adapted to hold the biggest collection of fine arts in the Auvergne. The medieval collection includes some delightful rare objects, including an olifant from the cathedral, a kind of trumpet carved with delicate Romanesque carvings. Two portraits stand out in the Renaissance section, a Clouet woman wearing a huge period ruff and big earrings, and a Bronzino portrait of a rather effeminate young man who might have been envious of such attire. In the 17th-century collection, Philippe de Champaigne is represented by a beautiful angel of the Annunciation, and a masterly portrait of Vincent Voiture.

The Monts Dômes

The crater tops of the Monts Dômes, like so many eggs which have had their tops chopped off by a godly family's breakfast spoons, stand in an extraordinary line above Clermont-Ferrand. The Puy-de-Dôme is the high spot, reaching 4,800ft. Whichever direction you head in from Clermont-Ferrand, you will come upon historic towns, churches and châteaux. Riom to the north was something of a rival as capital of the Auvergne in centuries past. Hillside Volvic is best known for its mineral water but also has a typically delightful church. The Plateau de Gergovie to the south was the one place in Gaul where Caesar really met his match.

Sober as a judge, the darkly historic town of **Riom** has been the centre of the law courts of the Auvergne for centuries. Thanks to the wealth of the lawyers and administrators based here, it's packed with grand mansions, and in the Middle Ages it was at times a rival capital to Clermont. Its roots go back to the 5th century at least, when its first priest, Amable, made his mark, but it seems its name derives from the Latin Ricomagum, indicating it was the site of a Gallo-Roman settlement. Amable was apparently efficacious in putting out fires and frightening snakes, and was declared a saint after his death; pilgrims came to pay their respects. The plan of the fortified town was laid out in the 13th century. In the 14th century the Duc de Berry (given the Auvergne as an apanage) ordered the building of a sumptuous palace for himself on the eastern side of town, virtually all of which has vanished apart from the **Sainte-Chapelle** (*open July–Aug Mon–Fri 10–12 and 2.30–5.30; June and Sept Wed–Fri 3–5; May*

Getting Around

Air France, t 0845 0845 111, has direct flights between Clermont-Ferrand and London-City Airport (*Mon–Fri two flights a day, Sat and Sun one a day*). Clermont-Ferrand's airport, at Aulnat, t 04 73 62 71 00, is 7km east of the city, with limited bus services into the centre.

By train, Clermont-Ferrand can take just 3hrs 30mins from Paris; the fastest direct trains from Lyon-Perrache take 2hrs 30mins.

For local train information, t 04 73 93 54 74.

Tourist Information

Clermont-Ferrand: Place de la Victoire, t 04 73 98 65 00, f 04 73 90 04 11.
Riom: 16 Rue du Commerce, t 04 73 38 59 45, f 04 73 38 25 15.
Volvic: 23 Place de l'Eglise, t 04 73 33 58 73.

Where to Stay and Eat

Clermont-Ferrand ✉ **63000**
★★★**Hôtel de Lyon**, 16 Place de Jaude, t 04 73 93 32 55, f 04 73 93 54 33 (*inexpensive*). Modern standardized rooms in an old building.
★★**Bordeaux**, 39 Av Franklin Roosevelt, t 04 73 37 32 32, f 04 73 31 40 56 (*inexpensive*). Quite appealing rooms, west of Place de Jaude.
Le Bougnat, 29 Rue des Chaussetiers, t 04 73 36 36 98. An atmospheric Auvergnat

address, on a popular street for restaurants, serving hearty, good-value regional fare.
Restaurant Riquier, 11 Rue de l'Etoile, t 04 73 36 67 25. Delightful terrace, stylish interior and good-value regional dishes.

Chamalières ✉ **63400**
★★★**Hôtel Radio**, 43 Av Pierre Curie, t 04 73 30 87 83, f 04 76 36 42 44 (*moderate*). Eccentric hotel perched up high, with great views down on Clermont. Originally a radio station, built in the 1930s. Delightful rooms and ambitious cuisine (*menus 160–330F*).

Pérignat-lès-Sarliève ✉ **63170**
★★★**Hostellerie St-Martin**, t 04 73 79 81 00, f 04 73 79 81 01 (*expensive–moderate*). A lovely country retreat some 6km southeast of Clermont, with its own restaurant (*menus 110–265F*).

Royat ✉ **63130**
Le Paradis, t 04 73 35 85 46, f 04 73 35 64 41. A real eagle's eerie of a restaurant above Royat in a roughly redone block of a medieval castle, with fantastic views.

St-Saturnin ✉ **63450**
B&B Château de St-Saturnin, Place de l'Ormeau, t 04 73 39 39 64, f 04 73 39 09 73 (*expensive*). A spectacular historic castle in which to stay as a B&B guest. Extremely comfortable rooms.

Wed 3–5; *adm*). This lofty aisleless Gothic chapel, with its large expanses of windows, was incorporated into the law courts, built around a grand courtyard in the 19th century. The title Sainte-Chapelle was reserved for religious buildings made to hold a relic directly associated with Christ; this one displayed a piece of the cross. Much restored in the 19th century, the main interest of the Ste-Chapelle now is its stained glass. Five windows have survived from the mid-15th century.

The tightly packed centre of Riom features two museums. The **Musée Francisque Mandet** (*open June–Sept daily exc Tues 10–12 and 2.30–6; rest of year daily exc Tues 10–12 and 2–5.30; adm*), the fine arts museum, has spread out across two substantial granite town mansions set around courtyards. Paintings feature in the first building, including a few hilarious Dutch scenes. Local painters are well represented, notably Alphonse Cornet of Riom, for example with his portrait of Francisque Mandet with Le Puy as the backdrop. A surprise section presents beautiful modern designer objects. The second building takes you back to antiquity with the Richard bequest, left to the town in 1979 by a lawyer from Riom who amassed a fabulous collection of art from ancient cultures. The **Musée Régional d'Auvergne** (*open same times; adm*) close by contains an extensive collection of more prosaic objects associated with traditional life and traditional crafts in the Auvergne. It is worth wandering around the streets of Riom to appreciate the wealth of the individual mansions built in the Ancien Régime. Some have ornate façades with carved stone features or faces. One, above a modern-day optician's shop, displays medallions of topless ladies. Fountains embellish many a corner. The elaborate belfry contains a permanent exhibition on the history of Riom, while the town hall boasts a couple of statues by Rodin and a copy of a letter signed by Joan of Arc, asking the good citizens of Riom to help fund her campaigning. Apparently they were slow to respond.

In neighbouring **Mozac**, the curious black-freckled church conceals amazing treasures, notably some of the most exquisite capitals in southern France. They date from the Romanesque period, when most of the church was built, although it's been much altered since. One of the capitals shows the Marys and Salome visiting Christ's empty tomb, while the guards are superbly rendered as knights asleep in their chainmail. The church also guards a staggering Limoges 12th-century reliquary chest, made for the bones of St Calmin; semi-precious stones decorate the collars and books of the apostles represented on it.

Much better known than its neighbours because of its widely exported spring water, the small hillside town of **Volvic** in fact doesn't have quite the same architectural appeal. Its Romanesque church has been heavily restored, although a few bold carved capitals remain inside. You can tour the town's little art museum, and even tour the Volvic water-bottling plant, but the best place to visit is the **Maison de la Pierre**, for a mostly underground tour through caverns where lava stone was extracted from the Volvic hillside; quarrying apparently began here in the middle of the 13th century to provide the stone for the cathedral of Clermont. The **Château de Tournoël**, a shell of a medieval castle, stands in a dramatic position with plunging views across the whole of the Limagne, the picturesque Allier plains east of Clermont-Ferrand.

Just south of Volvic and west of Clermont-Ferrand rise the **Monts Dômes**. Unfortunately the spectacular **Puy de Dôme**, the crowning volcano of the range, has suffered some indignities. The military have planted a dirty great syringe of a mast on the very pinnacle, and a few tacky tourist attractions have been set up near its foot. You have to pay a toll to take the road up to the summit, and at busy times you'll be forced to park at the bottom and take a shuttle bus to and from the peak. But the view, a panorama of extinct volcanic craters, will blow you away. The summit was a sacred site to the Celts, who had a shrine to Lug here, and in Gallo-Roman times a temple to Mercury was built. There are still a few vestiges of it on the top; the size of the blocks suggests it must have been an impressive structure, perhaps one of the largest temples in Gaul. Some historians wonder whether a monumental statue of Mercury, made by the Greek sculptor Zenodore and described by Pliny, might have been raised on the summit. The temple was destroyed in the Dark Ages, replaced by a

Christian chapel which survived until the 18th century. But what matters up here now are the views – some of the greatest in France.

Just south of Clermont-Ferrand, the **plateau of Gergovie** is where the Gauls under Vercingétorix famously stood up to Caesar's army, as readers of the Astérix books are so frequently reminded. This is another sensational viewing platform. While locals come up here to fly their kites, you can admire an eagle's eye view over the fertile Allier plain to the east, orange-roofed villages dotted around on the tops and slopes of extinct, eroded volcanoes. A little cultural centre, the **Maison de Gergovie**, deals with the geology – going back to a volcanic eruption around 17 million years ago – as well as the Gaulish story.

The Upper Allier:
South from Clermont-Ferrand to its Source

The views are thrilling along the first part of the Allier south of Clermont-Ferrand, the Monts Dômes and Monts Dore standing out to the west, the less well-known but beautiful Monts du Livradois forming the backdrop to the east. Down on the flat by the river, the appealing towns of Issoire and Brioude each possess a magnificent example of Auvergne Romanesque church architecture. Issoire has opened a centre on Romanesque art, while Brioude fêtes its lace-making and salmon-catching traditions. Further south, the village of Lavaudieu celebrates the art of stained-glass-making, while Chavaniac has added the name of its heroic son, Lafayette, to its title to attract tourists to its fine castle. At the start of the Allier's course, the young river passes through narrow gorges which you can follow until you come to the hillside towns of Pradelles and Langogne, the large lake of Naussac below them.

The lively heart of **Issoire**, now encircled by busy boulevards, boasts the splendid, ornate Romanesque church of St Austremoine, built in the 12th century to serve a Benedictine monastery. On the outside, the exuberant east end is decorated with chequered patterns and medallions apparently depicting signs of the zodiac. Much of the colour inside was added in a 19th-century neo-Romanesque redecorating campaign. Some of the original medieval capitals survive, including the Last Supper scene, the table cloth going round the column like a frilly addition. In the narthex a splendid Last Judgement fresco from the 15th century portrays Christ sitting on a rainbow above a cloud of saintly men and women, while the dead are brought back to life to face judgement. In the tall crypt you can admire a reliquary chest made in Limoges in the 13th century, bought by an abbot here to hold relics of the mysterious St Austremoine. The **Centre d'Art Roman** by the church puts on fascinating exhibitions on Romanesque art and architecture. Much of the rest of historic Issoire was destroyed in bitter feuding between Catholics and Protestants in the 16th century.

Usson stands high up on the other bank of the Allier, southeast of Issoire, perched on a hill of basalt columns that look like dark organ pipes. The town's castle was demolished by Richelieu, but there remains a late-medieval church (rarely open) with some fine furnishings. In the atmospheric town of **Brioude**, the walls of the **Basilique**

St-Julien are built out of the local sandstone, with its deep red and ochre tinges, an appropriately bloody colour as this is where the martyr St Julian, the patron saint of the Auvergne, was killed and buried around the start of the 4th century. His tomb quickly became an important place of pilgrimage and great powers were ascribed to his relics. Not only was it said that he could heal the sick, but also that he could control the weather and take revenge on robbers.

The Romanesque to Gothic basilica is one of the most fascinating buildings from these periods in southern France. Although the towers were redone in the 19th century, the narthex and west bays of the nave were built between the end of the 11th and 12th centuries. The elaborate east end, with its large ambulatory and handful of radiating chapels, dates from the early 13th century. There are plenty of curiosities inside – a frighteningly emaciated figure of Christ looking like an Auvergnat peasant, a black Virgin in the ambulatory, even the cobblestone floor, with its petal patterns, added in the 16th century. You have to strain your neck to see the alarmingly carved capitals: winged monsters, animals making music, knights jousting, and an extraordinary number of naked figures. Go on the guided tour to appreciate the paintings of Christ, a host of angels and other scenes perched up high in the narthex; most of the paintings are from the 12th–14th centuries.

Brioude has other attractions. The **Hôtel de la Dentelle** (*open April–Oct Mon–Fri 9–12 and 2–6, or 7 in July and Aug, Sat and public hols 3–6; adm*) presents the traditions of lace-making in the region, emphasizing contemporary creativity. The **Maison du Saumon et de la Rivière** (*open May–Sept; t 04 71 74 91 43 for times; adm*) celebrates the salmon that migrate up and down the Allier, as well as thirty or so other fish that thrive in its waters. The presentation is based around a series of aquariums simulating the river bottom.

With its rustic wooden balconies and porches, its old houses in orange and red-tinged stone and its delightful little river running past the village vegetable gardens, **Lavaudieu** would be charming even without the remnants of its abbey, its arts and crafts museum and its centre on stained glass. The abbey was founded as a Benedictine establishment for women by Robert, the man who created La Chaise-Dieu (*see* above, p.805). The curiously truncated octagonal steeple of the Romanesque **abbey church** lost its top at the Revolution, to be replaced by the strange umbrella of a structure it wears today. Inside, unusually colourful medieval frescoes stand out, painted high up above the arches. One rare scene is supposed to be an allegory of the Black Death which struck in the middle of the 14th century. Look out too for the violent depiction of the martyrdom of St Ursula and her companion virgins. There is only a copy of the Christ of Lavaudieu, a famous medieval sculpture of an oriental-looking Jesus whose head has ended up in the Louvre and whose body has made it to the Metropolitan Museum in New York.

Take the guided tour of the **abbey cloister and refectory** (*open mid-June–mid-Sept 10–12 and 2–6.30; Easter–mid-June and mid-Sept–Oct daily exc Tues 10–12 and 2–5; adm; ticket also valid for the little museum of local arts, crafts and traditions opposite the church*). Single and twin coiled and crinkled columns hold up the arcades. In the

Getting Around

The Clermont-Ferrand–Nîmes line passes via Issoire, Brioude and through the Allier gorges to Langogne and beyond.

Tourist Information

Issoire: Place du Général de Gaulle, t 04 73 89 15 90, f 04 73 89 96 13.
Brioude: Place Lafayette, t 04 71 74 97 49, f 04 71 74 97 87.
Lavoûte-Chilhac: Place du Monument, t 04 71 77 46 57, f 04 71 77 40 11.
Pradelles: Place du Foirail, t 04 71 00 82 65, f 04 71 00 84 21.

Where to Stay and Eat

Varennes-sur-Usson
Chez Mme Verdrier, Les Baudarts, t/f 04 73 89 05 51 (*inexpensive*). Stylish village house, beautifully done up as a B&B.

Sarpoil ✉ 63490
La Bergerie de Sarpoil, t 04 73 71 02 54. The young chef here has built up his success on experimental cuisine often using the finest local ingredients (*menus 120–330F*). Book. *Closed Sun eves and Mon exc July–Aug.*

Lavaudieu ✉ 43100
B&B La Maison d'à Côté, t 04 71 76 45 04, f 04 71 50 24 85 (*inexpensive*). A lovely typical stone house with beautiful terraces by the old bridge in this delightful village.
Auberge de l'Abbaye, t 04 71 76 44 44. Quaint village restaurant serving traditional fare (*menus 100–180F*). *Closed Mon eves, Mon lunch exc 15 July–Aug, Sun eves Sept–15 July.*
Court La Vigne, t 04 71 76 45 79. Good-value, traditional food (*menus 77–150F*). Book. *Closed Tues eves, Wed and Jan.*

St-Haon ✉ 43340
★★Auberge de la Vallée, t 04 71 08 20 73, f 04 71 08 29 21 (*inexpensive–cheap*). Simple and fun on the church square, with comfortable rooms and a restaurant (*menus 80–200F*). *Closed Jan–15 Mar, and Mon Oct–April.*

Langogne ✉ 48300
★★★Domaine de Barres, t 04 66 69 71 00, f 04 66 69 71 29 (*moderate*). A very elegant 18th-century manor by the lake of Naussac, surrounded by a golf course. The interior has been transformed in contemporary style. Excellent value for such comfort, including a covered pool. Gastronomic cuisine too (*menus 98–260F*).

refectory, a very large Christ in Majesty was painted above the Virgin flanked by angels and saints.

A handful of craftspeople work year round in Lavaudieu creating and restoring stained glass. You can see how they work by following the short but fascinating guided tour at the **Carrefour du Vitrail** (*open May–Oct daily 9.30–12 and 2–6.30; adm*) which explains how the lead and glass are prepared and put together, as well as outlining the history of stained-glass making in France. Someone has calculated that France can lay claim to some 65 per cent of the historic stained glass in the world. Apparently fragments have been found dating back to the 8th century, but the craft only really took off from the end of the 12th century. Its most glorious period was through the Gothic period, in particular in the 13th and 14th centuries, and by the 16th century the craft waned in popularity, only to experience a revival in the 19th century.

The US and French flags fly over the **Château de Chavaniac-Lafayette** (*open July–Aug daily 9–6; Mar–June and Sept–mid-Nov daily exc Tues 10–12 and 2–6; adm*) which, like the village, has changed its name in honour of the revolutionary general born here in 1757. In 1916 it was bought by the La Fayette Memorial Inc. Since then it has been well cared for and well furnished, and contains Lafayette memorabilia. The passionate young Lafayette went to America to aid the colonists in 1777, and found himself commanding the troops that trapped the British army at Yorktown, thus ending the war. Back in France, he was an early leader of the Revolution, and wrote a first draft of the Declaration of the Rights of Man – though when the radical Jacobins took power he had to flee to avoid the guillotine. When you've finished the tour you can relax in the beautiful landscaped gardens.

Dramatic twisting roads take you down the **gorges of the Allier** from Brioude to the large artificial lake of Naussac. **Lavoûte-Chilhac**'s wonderful curve of houses follows a meander in the river; its big Gothic church is reached via a concave crescent of buildings, part of a former Benedictine abbey. The wide, aisleless church contains some amusing carved stone figures, some a bit cheeky, like the monkey scratching its private parts. The **Maison des Oiseaux** is dedicated to the bird life of the gorges.

Surrounded by wrinkly rocks, and very popular with canoeists, **Pradelles** is one of the liveliest villages in the Allier gorges, with a lovely chapel with very faded frescoes inside. Amusing rock formations will entertain you on the way south past **Monistrol-d'Allier** and **St-Didier-d'Allier**, both in superb locations.

A detour west takes you to the pleasantly sleepy town of **Saugues** which has a troubled past, as some of its monuments recall. The medieval keep known as the **Tour des Anglais** recalls the English mercenaries who ruled the area by terror after the Hundred Years' War. It now serves as an artists' exhibition space. The new **Musée Fantastique de la Bête du Gévaudan** recounts the mystery of the 'Beast of the Gévaudan', who roamed around the surrounding area in the 1760s, devouring 99 victims, mostly women and children.

Into the Monts Dore

The tallest summit of the Monts Dore, the Puy de Sancy (almost 6,200ft), dominates the countryside for vast distances around its sharp triangular top. The Monts Dore, like the Monts Dômes, form part of the Parc Régional des Volcans d'Auvergne, but their explosive past is nowhere near as obvious – they look more like conventional mountains. The volcanoes in these parts were most active around 2 million to 3.5 million years ago, although the youngest, ones such as Montchal and Montcineyre are only around 6,000 years old. Steep, claustrophobic valleys run below the Monts Dore range, that of the Chambon to the east – with the historic villages of St-Nectaire and Murol – that of the young Dordogne to the west, with the shabbily charming 19th-century spa towns of Le Mont-Dore and La Bourboule. Between them Murat-le-Quaire is making a good effort to make sure local traditions and farming aren't entirely lost, while not far to the north, Orcival conceals one of the Auvergne's most famed Romanesque churches.

The village of **St-Nectaire** is squeezed into the Chambon valley and dominated by its well-known Romanesque church. Dedicated to a companion of St Austremoine, it was built for a Benedictine priory attached to the abbey of La Chaise-Dieu (*see* p.805).

Getting Around

Not much by way of public transport in this mountainous region.

Tourist Information

Le Mont-Dore: Av Libération, t 04 73 65 20 21, f 04 73 65 05 71.
La Bourboule: Place de la République, t 04 73 65 57 71, f 04 73 65 50 21.

Where to Stay and Eat

Le Mont-Dore ✉ 63240
Le Bougnat, 23 Av Georges Clemenceau, t 04 73 65 28 19. A young team not from the region but cooking up tasty local dishes in a lovely stable-turned-restaurant.
B&B Closerie de Manon, t 04 73 65 26 81, f 04 73 81 11 72 (*inexpensive*). A charming place to stay in a typical house between Le Mont-Dore and La Bourboule.

La Barboule ✉ 63150
★★Les Fleurs, Av Gueneau de Mussy, t 04 73 81 09 44, f 04 73 65 52 03 (*inexpensive–cheap*). Chalet of a hotel. Many rooms have balconies and views.
★★Aviation Hotel, Rue de Metz, t 04 73 65 50 50, f 04 73 81 02 85 (*inexpensive–cheap*). Good choice of rooms and facilities.

Inside, the scenes from the Bible carved on the entertaining capitals share the style of those at Issoire – the figures are simple but full of life. The treasury preserves an unusual medieval reliquary arm, said to contain relics of St Nectaire. Below the church, the dark village has a few thermal spa establishments, but St-Nectaire is better known for its cheese.

To escape from the Chambon valley, climb north to **Les Arnats** for sensational views of the Monts Dore, and, closer by, of the **Château de Murol**, an impressively sinister-looking ruin of a castle high above the valley. Constructed as a round within a round, much of it dates from the 15th century, but the great outer wall only went up a century later, under the d'Estaing family. Thanks to the power this family acquired at court, the château was one of the few to be spared from destruction by Richelieu. Its downfall came in the 19th century, when it was abandoned and local people took stones for their own dwellings.

The D5 continues to **Besse-en-Chandesse**, on the southern side of the Monts Dore range, a grey fortified village which sits in a landscape of stark volcanoes and pastures. It's a popular tourist stop, with hotels and boutiques. The Romanesque church turns Gothic at the choir, but before that you can appreciate the decorative scenes on the nave's capitals. The modern ski resort of **Super-Besse** is a bit higher up to the west, set under volcanic peaks, with wide south-facing slopes in a splendid location. From here you can take a chair lift up to the **Puy Ferrand** (nearly 6,000ft), just below the Puy de Sancy, which affords fabulous views. South of Besse, walkers can appreciate a string of curious high lakes set in volcanic craters. The best-known and easiest to reach is the circular **Lac Pavin**, surrounded by woods. In the wide pastures around here the grazing cows produce the milk for St-Nectaire cheese.

The Dordogne valley starts on the north side of the Monts Dore, on the **Puy de Sancy**. A steep, dramatic road takes you from the spa town of **Le Mont-Dore** up close to the peak, with a cablecar operating for the final section of the way. The spa town of Le Mont-Dore far down below has a summer season for rheumatics, asthmatics and ramblers going from May to October. The Celts apparently enjoyed the thermal waters here even before the Romans built substantial baths, vestiges of which survive in the outrageous pastiche 19th-century **Etablissement Thermal**. Forgotten by the outside world for centuries, the waters were rediscovered in the time of Louis XIV; emerging from the lava at between 38°C and 44°C, they are said to be particularly helpful for respiratory problems.

The road north from Le Mont-Dore takes you to **Orcival**, a little village often over-whelmed by tourists. The **Basilique Notre-Dame**, with its octagonal tower and the tiers of its choir end, is the dominating presence, built in the 12th century as a dependency of the abbey of La Chaise-Dieu. One of the finest works of the Auvergnat Romanesque, it is somewhat less lavishly decorated than some others. The one truly remarkable art work inside is an icon-like, silver-coated statue of the Virgin and Child in the severe Auvergne style.

La Bourboule, back down along the Dordogne valley, is Le Mont-Dore's rival – a faded 19th-century spa with several grandiose buildings including its baths, the Grands Thermes, and its casino. Hillside **Murat-le-Quaire**, further up the slopes, is a typical agricultural village that has suffered terribly from changes in agriculture since the war; only two working farms are left in the parish. The **Musée de Toinette**, which is split between two sites, pays its respects to rural life and traditions. The most popular walk from here takes you to the curiously flat-topped old volcano of **La Banne d'Oranche**, another of the many wonderful viewing points over the volcanic land-scapes. The Dordogne river carves its way tortuously west through the steep and wooded **Gorges d'Avèze** to enter the Limousin (*see* **The Southwest**).

Cantal

Below the Monts Dore, the Cantal is basically one huge extinct volcano, apparently the largest one in Europe, with sweet valley roads spilling down its sides like rivulets of sauce trickling down a vast pudding. The top has worn down to reveal a cluster of plugs, notably the Puy Mary, the Puy Griou and the Plomb du Cantal. You can still get a good sense of the shape of the vast volcano from its sloping sides or *planèzes*. Even in the height of summer the high pastures are lush and green, with the handlebar-horned Salers cows adding their ruddy character to the landscapes.

Central and Eastern Cantal

One of the most delightful routes up into the centre of the Cantal volcano and to the Puy Mary is the route winding its way up the Cheylade valley from **Riom-ès-Montagne**, a sweet village best known for producing gentian bitters and for its local cheese. Its medieval church sports a couple of naughty capitals at the entrance to the choir: one appears to depict a religious figure cutting off a lustful man's member.

The lush pastures and open horizons up the Cheylade valley are only interrupted by the odd worn-down volcano plug here and there. Make a special detour to the pilgrimage stop of **La Font-Sainte**, lost in an Irish-looking landscape, the sound of

Getting Around

Aurillac, capital of Cantal, has a little airport with flights to and from Paris: Aurillac-Tronquières, t 04 71 63 56 98; Air Liberté, t 08 03 00 10 00.

Aurillac station, t 04 71 45 61 00, is on the line from Paris-Gare de Lyon. St-Flour station, t 04 71 60 03 37, in eastern Cantal is on the train line from Clermont-Ferrand. A local rail line runs across the Cantal from Brioude on the Upper Allier to Aurillac.

Tourist Information

Riom-ès-Montagnes: Place Charles de Gaulle, t 04 71 78 07 37, f 04 71 78 16 87.
Murat: 2 Rue Faubourg Notre-Dame, t 04 71 20 09 47, f 04 71 20 21 94.
Mauriac: 1 Rue Chappe d'Auteroche, t 04 71 67 30 26, f 04 71 68 25 08.
Salers: Place Tyssandier d'Escous, t 04 71 40 70 68.
Aurillac: Place du Square, t 04 71 48 46 58, f 04 71 48 99 39.

Where to Stay and Eat

St-Flour ✉ 15100
★★Hôtel des Roches, Place d'Armes, t 04 71 60 09 70, f 04 71 60 45 21 (*inexpensive*). The spacious rooms overlooking the cathedral make up for the dull modern decoration.

Lanau ✉ 15260
★★Auberge du Pont de Lanau, t 04 71 23 57 76, f 04 71 23 53 84 (*inexpensive*). By the main road south from St-Flour to Chaudes-Aigues, but a charming stop which has kept some of the character of a 19th-century inn, including the large fireplace dominating the dining room where you can try innovative regional cuisine (*menus 80–280F*). Closed Jan–Feb; restaurant also closed Tues eves and Wed exc July–Aug.

Salers ✉ 15140
★★Hôtel des Remparts, Esplanade de Barrouze, t 04 71 40 70 33, f 04 71 40 75 32 (*inexpensive*). An appealing place to stay with typical architecture, a terrace with a view and a restaurant (*menus 70–165F*). Closed 15 Oct–20 Dec.

Le Theil ✉ 15140
★★★Hostellerie de la Maronne, t 04 71 69 20 33, f 04 71 69 28 22 (*expensive–moderate*). A caringly converted little 19th-century manor in a beautiful valley. A special place to stay with excellent cuisine, but the restaurant is only open in the evenings (*menus 150–280F*). Closed Nov–Mar.

Tournemire ✉ 15310
★★Auberge de Tournemire, t 04 71 47 61 28 (*cheap*). Delightful location looking down on the valley. Simple cheap rooms and hearty cooking (*menus 88–158F*).

jangling cow bells in the air. The church in the delightful village of **Cheylade** itself has possibly the most flower-covered ceiling in France: its three barrel vaults are also covered with angels and naive animals, decorations from the 17th century. A fair walk will take you up to the top of the **Puy Mary**, from where you get a magical view of the whole Cantal volcanic structure and far beyond.

It's a long way round by road from the Puy Mary to the Plomb du Cantal, the highest peak in the Auvergne (just over 6,000ft). The route round to the east takes you via **Dienne**, whose Romanesque church stands aloofly on its terrace outside the village. **Murat** slopes prettily down the Alagnon valley, with irregular old slates on the roofs of its old houses. Pine forests surround the lower resort of **Le Lioran**, but it's from the ski resort of **Super-Lioran** that you can take the cablecar to the top of the **Plomb de Cantal** for fantastic views across the whole of the Cantal and much, much further.

St-Flour, a severe little city, perches way up on a large almond-shaped rock overlooking the Ander and Lescure valleys. The Gothic **cathedral** with its twin towers,

completed at the end of the 15th century, dominates the town. The former **bishops'
palace** next door has been converted into the town hall and museum with interesting religious displays, including a number of wood-carved saints and the treasures
of the cathedral. Other sections are devoted to regional folklore and traditions. The
grandest old mansion in town, the grey Renaissance Maison Consulaire, now contains
the **Musée Douët**, diverse collections of decorative arts brought together by an
enthusiast at the start of the 20th century.

Close to St-Flour, the massive pink-painted metal arch of the **Viaduc de Garabit** is so
bold it comes as no surprise to discover it was built by Gustave Eiffel, in the early
1880s. **Chaudes-Aigues**, an unexpectedly lively little spa town a bit further south,
pulls in the crowds in summer. It claims to have the hottest spa waters in Europe,
coming out of the rock at over 26°C/80°F.

The Western Cantal

More picturesque valleys slide down the western side of the Cantal volcano from
the Puy Mary. The **Vallée du Falgoux** takes you northwest to **Mauriac**, a cheerful-
looking Auvergnat town facing the sunny west. Both its **Basilique Notre-Dame-
des-Miracles** and the **Hôtel d'Orcet** have remarkable Romanesque carved doorways,
and the basilica a colourful carved font. The **Maronne valley** leads you to **Salers**,
a very dour, grey fortified hilltop village surrounded by low walls and suspiciously
surveying the wide vistas around. A splendid array of corner towers and stair towers
compete for your attention on the central square, and you can visit the interiors of
several of the finest old houses. The **Maison des Templiers** typifies the late-Gothic
mansions with which Salers is crammed. As well as showing traditional Auvergnat
interiors, it presents local cheese-making, which is covered more fully at **Les Burons
de Salers**.

The **Doire valley**, harder to reach from the Puy Mary, leads you to the impressive hillside village of Tournemire and the adjoining **Château d'Anjony**, built in the 15th
century for Louis II d'Anjony, a companion in arms to Joan of Arc. One tower contains a
chapel with wall paintings depicting the life of Christ, but still better frescoes are
devoted to chivalric scenes and 16th-century Michel d'Anjony and his wife.
Tournemire and its castle benefit from similar views on to the verdant valley, with
cows and horses grazing on its slopes and speckled-stone villages lying far below.

The **Mandailles valley** takes you directly southwest to **Aurillac**, the quiet, attractive
capital of the Cantal *département*. It lays claim to being the home town of France's
first-ever pope, Sylvester II, who made his meteoric rise from shepherd to pontiff at
the end of the 10th century. His statue stands in a prominent position on Place
Gerbert by the river Jordanne and the old town centre; behind him stretches a pretty
row of riverside houses. The small centre has many fine façades, and a waxworks
museum featuring Sylvestre among other historic figures. On Place St-Géraud, the
Château St-Etienne houses the Musée des Volcans, and in a separate part of town the
Musée d'Art et d'Archéologie presents local archaeological finds, paintings of various
European schools and an array of traditional Cantal interiors.

The Alps and the Jura

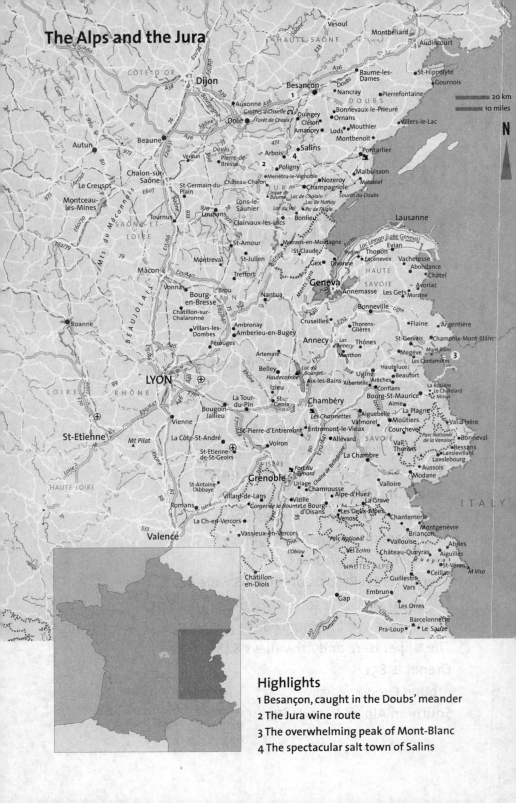

Food and Wine

Most people think of devouring a rich cheese fondue after a long day's skiing when they think of this region: two of the best local cheeses are Comté, made in the Franche-Comté, and Beaufort, made in Savoy. St-Marcellin, a runny mixture of goats' and cows' cheeses, is another excellent regional speciality. Tomme is a general name for cheese in Savoy, and the products sold as Tomme de Savoie are often bland. The Franche-Comté's softer Morbier cheese tries to give itself character by adding a line of ash running through the middle of it, and Bleu de Gex is probably the best blue cheese of these regions. The Reblochon from the Aravis range in Savoy is especially good in a *tartiflette* – served with layers of potatoes, garlic and herbs. But the best way of serving potatoes bears the name of one of the old regions – *Gratin Dauphinois*, slices of potatoes baked with eggs and milk.

Meats are often served in stews, or with rich, mushroom sauces. Game such as venison, wild boar, hare and woodcock is still hunted in these wooded mountainous regions and chefs will often seek out wild *champignons*, particularly morels, chanterelles or ceps, or wild herbs and berries with which to flavour their dishes. Pork *saucissons* and smoked hams traditionally lasted well through the long mountain winters and the pork charcuteries from Morteau in the Franche-Comté are well regarded. River and lake fish often appear on the menus, as do *écrevisses*, the much-prized crayfish plucked from the local streams. With the finest fish dishes in the Jura, a dash of the distinctive local Vin Jaune may impart its character to the sauce.

Some distinctly surprising wines and some positively dangerous liqueurs are produced in the Jura and the Alps. Along the gorgeous Jura wine route, the *vignerons* produce some rather weird wines with funny names (*see* p.830). Vinegrowers in the Bugey close to the Rhône in southern Jura also make a little wine, as do some on the other side of the great river, in the Bauges. The latter, counting among the Vins de Savoie, go into flavouring fondues. Absinthe, made from wormwood macerated in brandy, was long banned for its mind-rotting effects, but has been making a come-back recently. Chartreuse, a dangerous green liqueur made to a secret recipe of the Carthusian monks, is made in the Chartreuse mountain range near Grenoble. Kirsch, made from valley cherries, is a rather friendlier liqueur. Mountain berries taste delicious in tarts from the local pâtisseries, while walnuts put in an appearance in quite a number of traditional desserts. Gâteau de Savoie is a traditional sponge cake.

When Hannibal led his elephants on history's most dramatic expedition through the Alps in 218 BC, the mountains were regarded as a dangerous obstacle. And so they have remained, although the Romantics fell in love with their terrifying beauty, seeing the enormous peaks and troughs as a reflection of life itself, with its exhilarating heights and abysmal depths. Today the French Alps have undergone another metamorphosis, as one of Europe's favourite playgrounds. This chapter starts with the quieter Jura mountains of the Franche-Comté, the 'Free County', where Besançon and other elegant Comtois towns still seem to thrive on their own semi-independence. After the Jura come the French Alpine regions of Savoy and the

Getting There

By plane: The main international airports serving the Alps and the Jura are Lyon and Geneva. There are smaller regional airports at Chambéry/Aix-les-Bains, Annecy and Grenoble. As well as contacting Air France and British Airways about flights to these parts, it's useful to know that Buzz, **t** 0870 240 7070 in Britain, offer low-cost flights to Chambéry. Dole has a regional airport.

By train: Good train services link the French Alps and Paris. There's also a line beloved by keen skiers from Britain taking them to Bourg-St-Maurice via Lille avoiding Paris. For the Franche-Comté, there are reasonable lines to Besançon and Pontarlier in the Jura via Dijon and Dole.

By road: From Paris, branch off the A6 motorway from Paris to Provence to reach the Franche-Comté, Savoy, or the Dauphiné. From the Channel ports, go via Reims, Troyes and Dijon and then branch off the A6.

Dauphiné, stretching from Lake Geneva to Provence. In their eastern portions you'll find the most famous ski resorts and many of the highest places in Europe, including Mont Blanc, rising like an otherworldly meringue high above the other peaks on the Italian frontier. The sheer and weird limestone tops of the Préalpes, a formidable jagged wall when approached from the Rhône Valley, loom above the most interesting towns and the most romantic lakes in the entire Alpine region: Annecy and the Lac d'Annecy, the Lac du Bourget, and Grenoble. East of Grenoble are the major resorts of the Southern French Alps, on the edges of the serrated Ecrins national park. In neighbouring Queyras regional park, the lofty old villages and towns all wear sundials as testimonials to the inordinate amount of sunshine they receive.

The Old Capitals of the Franche-Comté: Dole and Besançon

Dole and Pesmes

Attractive **Dole** on the Doubs river is the main western outpost of the Franche-Comté. The capital of the region in the Middle Ages, it later bagged the Parlement and university. But the French bashed it repeatedly: Louis XI's troops in 1479, then Louis XIV's assaults which brought down the fortifications. Dole's enormous Gothic centrepiece, the **Collégiale Notre-Dame**, survived. There's not much to see inside, except for a fine collection of stone Apostles around the choir. The streets heading off from the Collégiale have tempting shops occupying some of the best houses, some of which sport elegant protruding stair towers. A short walk down towards the Doubs, in the former tanners' quarter, you'll find the **Maison Natale de Pasteur et Musée Pasteur** (*open July–Aug daily exc Sun am 10–6; rest of period April–Oct daily exc Sun am 10–12 and 2–6; adm*), where Louis Pasteur was born in 1822. As well as learning about his family life, you can discover the importance to modern medicine of his work on bacteria and vaccination. The **Musée des Beaux-Arts** (*open July–Aug daily exc Mon and Tues 10–12 and 2–6; rest of year daily exc Mon 10–12 and 2–6; adm*), reached via Rue de Besançon and Rue des Arènes, features local archaeology, paintings by local maestro Courbet as well as experimental landscapes by Auguste Pointelin.

Getting There and Around

By rail, Dole is on the main line from Paris-Gare de Lyon to Bern and Zurich in Switzerland. There are more regular stops on the Paris-Gare de Lyon to Besançon service. Trains from Paris to Dole take around 2hrs; add around another 30mins to reach Besançon. Dole has a small regional airport.

Tourist Information

Dole: 6 Place Jules Grévy, t 03 84 72 11 22, f 03 84 82 49 27.

Pesmes: Grande Rue, t 03 84 31 22 27, f 03 84 31 20 54.

Besançon: Parc Micaud, t 03 81 80 92 55, f 03 81 80 58 30.

Sports and Activities

Besançon: take a **boat trip** along the Doubs from the Pont de la République, with Vedettes Bisontines, t 03 81 68 13 25, f 03 81 68 09 85.

Where to Stay and Eat

Dole ✉ 39100

★★La Cloche, 2 Place Grevy, t 03 84 82 06 06, f 03 84 72 73 82 (*inexpensive*). Central and pretty comfortable.

★★La Romanée, 13 Rue des Vieilles Boucheries, t 03 84 79 19 05, f 03 84 79 26 97 (*inexpensive*). Near the cathedral, serving good Jura cooking in stone-vaulted rooms. *Restaurant closed Wed exc July and Aug.*

Besançon ✉ 25000

★★★Castan, 6 Square Castan, t 03 81 65 02 00, f 03 81 83 01 02 (*moderate*). Wonderfully set in Ancien Régime buildings by the cathedral.

★★Granvelle, 13 Rue du Général Lecourbe, t 03 81 81 33 92, f 03 81 81 31 77 (*inexpensive*). Set back in its own courtyard near the cathedral.

★★Régina, 91 Grande-Rue, t 03 81 81 50 22, f 03 81 81 60 20 (*inexpensive*). Pleasant; set in the central shopping street. *Closed 24 Dec–3 Jan.*

★★★Du Nord, 8 Rue Moncey, t 03 81 81 34 56, f 03 81 81 85 96 (*inexpensive*). Central and appealing.

Mungo-Park, 11 Rue Jean Petit, t 03 81 81 28 01, f 03 81 83 36 97. Inventive and tasty regional cuisine (*menus 195–490F*). *Closed 1–15 Aug.*

La Tour de la Pelote, 41 Quai de Strasbourg, t 03 81 82 14 58, f 03 81 82 37 82. A well-known rendezvous in a 16th-century riverside tower. Good-value menus.

Le Chaland, Promenade Micaud, near Pont Bregille, t 03 81 80 61 61, f 03 81 88 67 42. On a barge on the Doubs. *Closed Sat lunch.*

★★★Le Vauban, Citadelle, t 03 81 83 02 77, f 03 81 83 17 25. Decent restaurant, in vaulted chambers, with a terrace enjoying a great view. *Restaurant closed Sun, Mon eves.*

Due north of Dole, the fortified old village of **Pesmes** stands prettily above the Ognon river. The wide main street leads down to the surviving main gateway and a treasure trove of a **Gothic church** signalled by a typical Comtois tower. The retable in the choir features scenes from Christ's life between red marble columns. Here the pale Virgin swoons; the statue of the Virgin and Child in the exquisite lords' chapel is more forceful, keeping company with a vile relief of the head of Medusa; there's also an amusing kind of peep hole to the main altar.

Besançon

Under the Holy Roman Empire, the Franche-Comté was something of an independent state, and Besançon, in its horseshoe loop in the Doubs, a city state within it. With Hugues de Salins, archbishop in the 1030s, Besançon became a 'free and imperial city' and in 1290 it became a *commune* with far-reaching powers. But when the late medieval Burgundian dukes imposed their authority on the region, Besançon's

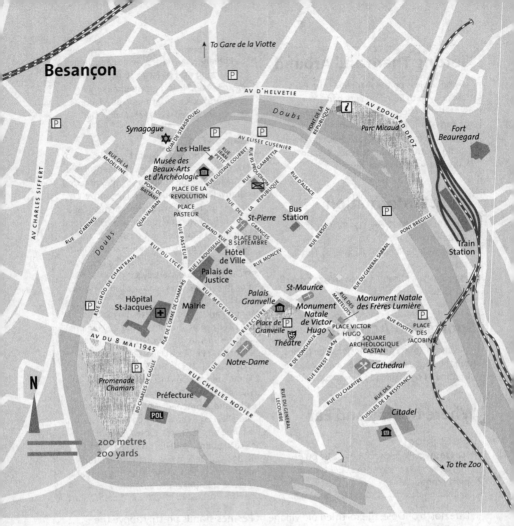

Besançon

To Gare de la Viotte

AV D'HELVETIE

Doubs

PONT DE LA RÉPUBLIQUE

AV EDOUARD DROZ

Parc Micaud

Fort Beauregard

i

Synagogue

QUAI DE STRASBOURG

Les Halles

AV ELISÉE CUSENIER

RUE DE LA MADELEINE

Musée des Beaux-Arts et d'Archéologie

RUE JEAN PETIT

RUE GUSTAVE COURBET

RUE DU GAMBETTA

RUE PROUDHON

RUE D'ALSACE

PONT DE BATTANT

PLACE DE LA RÉVOLUTION

QUAI VAUBAN

PLACE PASTEUR

RUE DES

RUE DE LA RÉPUBLIQUE

St-Pierre

Bus Station

AV CHARLES SIFFERT

RUE D'ARÈNES

Doubs

GRANDE RUE

RUE PASTEUR

RUE DU LYCÉE

RUE J.J. ROUSSEAU

GRANGES

PLACE DU 8 SEPTEMBRE

Hôtel de Ville

RUE BERSOT

PONT BRÉGILLE

Train Station

RUE GIROD DE CHANTRANS

Palais de Justice

RUE MONCEY

RUE DU GÉNÉRAL SARRAIL

Palais Granvelle

St-Maurice

Monument Natale des Frères Lumière

Hôpital St-Jacques

RUE DE L'ORME DE CHAMARS

Mairie

RUE MÉGEVAND

RUE DES MARTELOTS

PLACE DES JACOBINS

Monument Natale de Victor Hugo

PLACE VICTOR HUGO

RUE RIVOTTE

AV DU 8 MAI 1945

RUE DE LA PRÉFECTURE

Place de Granvelle

SQUARE ARCHÉOLOGIQUE CASTAN

Théâtre

R DE RONCHAUX

Notre-Dame

N

Promenade Chamars

BD CHARLES DE GAULLE

RUE CHARLES NODIER

RUE ERNEST RENAN

Cathedral

RUE DU GÉNÉRAL LECOURBE

RUE DU CHAPITRE

RUE DES FUSILLÉS DE LA RÉSISTANCE

Préfecture

POL

Citadel

200 metres
200 yards

To the Zoo

rival, Dole, gained in importance. Between the 1470s and the 1670s the Franche-Comté came under Habsburg control, and Besançon once more became one of the mightiest cities in the Empire. But throughout the 17th century the French coveted it until Louis XIV took the Franche-Comté in lieu of the dowry he had been promised at his marriage to Maria-Teresa of Spain. Imperial forces briefly won back Besançon, but in 1678 Franche-Comté was officially made a part of France through the Peace of Nimègue, and Besançon became undisputed capital of the region: the Parlement and university were moved here from Dole. Famous sons include Victor Hugo, Pierre-Joseph Proudhon and the Lumière brothers; here too the Comte de Chardonnet revolutionized the clothes industry, with the invention of artificial silk, or rayon.

A Tour of Besançon

The **Grande-Rue**, lined with mansions, cuts through the heart of Besançon, extending from the Doubs, past the town hall and the Palais Granvelle, to the cathedral at the foot of the citadel. From the quays on the opposite bank you get some sense of its grandeur. The **Musée des Beaux-Arts et d'Archéologie** (*Place de la Révolution; open daily exc Tues 9.30–12 and 2–6; adm; free on Sun*) occupies the 19th-century corn market. The extensive painting sections include the likes of Titian, Bronzino and Bellini, Cranach and Zurbarán. Courbet contributes a brooding self-portrait and a huge snowy deer hunt showing the bright Jura of mid-winter. The early-20th century canvases include a Renoir and a Matisse. Back on the Grande-Rue, behind the colourful 16th-century town hall, the **Palais de Justice**, by the Dijon architect Hugues Sambin, was where the Franche-Comté Parlement used to meet. Take a short detour along Rue de l'Orme de Chamars to the **Hôpital St-Jacques**, whose chapel, **Notre-Dame-du-Refuge**, is full of flirtatious Baroque playfulness.

The substantial Renaissance façade of the **Palais Granvelle** stretches down one side of the Grande-Rue. The courtyard with its basket-handle arcades has recently been polished up, and an immaculate new **Musée du Temps clock museum** installed inside. Behind the Palais Granvelle, in Rue Megevand, cast an eye over the bold **theatre**, designed by Ledoux (*see p.828*), and the partly Romanesque church of **Notre-Dame**.

The birthplaces of Victor Hugo and the Lumière boys look out on to little **Place Victor Hugo**, in a pretty corner of town. In the shaded **Square Archéologique Castan** you can make out the remnants of a Roman pool in the darkness. Head through a fine remnant of Besançon's Gallo-Roman predecessor Vesontio – a blackened coffered gate, known as the **Porte Noire** – to reach the **cathedral**, whose colourful dome rises above the quarter. Its decoration is sumptuous: a splendidly romantic St John features in the Baroque swirl over the entrance, and the gilded rays, capitals and frames of the Choeur du St-Suaire make an outrageous Baroque show around paintings by the likes of Van Loo, Natoire, de Troy and Sebastian del Piombo. The chapels contain an accomplished Gallo-Roman carving called the Rose de St-Jean and the Virgin and Saints by Fra Bartolomeo, the cathedral's best painting.

To reach the citadel (*open July–Aug daily 9–7; Easter–June and Sept–Oct daily 9–6; rest of year daily exc Tues 10–5; adm*) take the free bus in summer, or the tourist train if you're daunted by the steep climb. It has four museums: the **Espace Vauban**, which concentrates on the history of the citadel and its architect, Vauban; the **Musée Comtois**, which covers the traditions and folklore of the Franche-Comté; the **Musée de la Résistance et de la Déportation**, which deals with the War; and the **Musée d'Histoire Naturelle**. The **zoo** includes an Insectarium, a Noctarium, and the Aquarium Georges Besse. Best of all is the view.

Along the Jura Wine and Salt Routes to Lons-le-Saulnier

The beautiful Jura wine route extends south from Salins-les-Bains, passing gorgeous villages, notably Beaume-les-Messieurs and Château-Chalon. The two salt-producing centres of Arc-et-Senans and Salins-les-Bains are amazing, while Ornans is the birthplace of Gustave Courbet.

Getting Around

The tourist sites lie just off the N83 road. For public transport, there's a bus service between Dole and Lons-le-Saunier (t 03 81 46 40 44, f 03 81 46 65 46 for details). Mouchard north of Arbois and west of Salins-les-Bains has a railway station.

Tourist Information

Ornans: 7 Rue Pierre Vernier, t/f 03 81 62 21 50.
Salins-les-Bains: Place des Salines, t 03 84 73 01 34, f 03 84 37 92 85.
Arc-et-Senans: t 03 81 57 43 21, f 03 81 57 43 51.
Arbois: 10 Rue de l'Hôtel de Ville, t 03 84 66 55 50, f 03 84 66 25 50.
Poligny: Cour des Ursulines, t 03 84 37 24 21, f 03 84 37 22 37.
Château-Chalon: Mairie, Rue St-Jean, t 03 84 44 65 44.
Baume-les-Messieurs: Mairie, t 03 84 44 61 41.
Lons-le-Saunier: Place du 11 Novembre, t 03 84 24 65 01, f 03 84 43 22 59.

Where to Stay and Eat

Ornans ✉ 25290
***Hôtel de France**, 51 Rue Pierre Vernier, t 03 81 62 24 44, f 03 81 62 21 50 (*moderate*). Agreeable if old-styled hotel-cum-restaurant close to the river in the heart of town.

Bonnevaux-le-Prieuré ✉ 25620
***Moulin du Prieuré**, t 03 81 59 21 47, f 03 81 59 28 79 (*moderate*). Restful small country hotel near Ornans in a converted mill, with well-equipped little modern chalets in the grounds. *Closed 10 Jan–10 Feb.*

Lods ✉ 25930
**La Truite d'Or, Rue du Moulin Neuf, t 03 81 60 95 48, f 03 81 60 95 73 (*inexpensive*). A nice, good-value place. *Closed 15 Dec–25 Jan; restaurant closed Oct–April Sun eve and Mon.*

Amondans ✉ 25330
Restaurant du Château d'Amondans, 9 Rue Louise Pommery, t 03 81 86 53 14, f 03 81 86 53 76. A manor-château restored to hold the reputed Institut de Gastronomie Française. Take a cookery course run by a leading French chef, or have a meal (*menus 195–400F*). Reservation obligatory. *Restaurant closed Feb; 13–23 Aug; Sun eve, Tues and Weds.*

Germigney ✉ 39600
****Château de Germigney, t 03 84 73 85 85, f 03 84 73 88 88. A gorgeously converted 18th-century manor along the Loue valley; the best hotel in the Franche-Comté. Rooms decorated with great attention to detail, lovely dining rooms, and a splendid terrace for summer dining (*menus 180–450F*).

From Besançon to Ornans and the Loue

A short way southeast of Besançon is the irresistible riverside town of **Ornans**, with its curving roofs and ramshackle terraces. It provided the inspiration for one of the most provocative painters of the 19th century, Gustave Courbet (1819–77), whose home has been turned into the **Musée Courbet** (*open July–Aug daily 10–6; rest of year daily 10–12 and 2–6; Nov–Mar closed Tues; adm*). Founder of the so-called Realist school, Courbet was a vociferous critic of the art establishment and its obsessions with the Beautiful and the Ideal. His unflinching depictions of modest people in mundane settings (many on display here) were just as controversial in his day; critics compared his fleshy naked women to cart horses.

East of Ornans along the Loue valley, the river gushes through lovely Lods, where the local museum recalls the valley's wine-making traditions – which were wiped out by the phylloxera epidemic of the late 19th century. **Mouthier-Haute-Pierre**, set in a curve in the river, proclaims itself capital of kirsch, the cherry liqueur still made in these parts. The walk to the **Source de la Loue** takes you to one of Courbet's favourite spots.

Salins-les-Bains ✉ 39110
*Des Deux Forts, Place du Vigneron, t 03 84 37 90 50 (*cheap*). A basic, old-fashioned Logis de France in a characterful old house.

Arbois ✉ 39600
****Jean-Paul Jeunet, 9 Rue de l'Hôtel de Ville, t 03 84 66 05 67, f 03 84 66 24 20 (*moderate*). A very smart address in the centre, but the restaurant is the main attraction (*menus 380–550F*). *Closed Dec and Jan; restaurant closed Oct–June Wed lunch, Tues.*

Les Planches-près-Arbois ✉ 39600
***Le Moulin de la Mère Michelle, t 03 84 66 08 17, f 03 84 37 49 69 (*moderate*). A throughly enchanting converted mill near limestone cliffs and a waterfall.

Poligny ✉ 39800
***Domaine de la Vallée Heureuse, Route de Genève, t 03 84 37 12 13, t 03 84 37 08 75 (*moderate*). A converted 18th-century mill, with small, cosy rooms.
**Hôtel de Paris, 7 Rue Travot, t 03 84 37 13 87, f 03 84 37 23 39 (*inexpensive*). Reasonable, central and old-fashioned. No restaurant. *Closed 2 Nov–2 Feb.*

Monts de Vaux ✉ 39800
***Hostellerie des Monts de Vaux, t 03 84 37 12 50, f 03 84 37 09 07. Small exclusive luxury hotel, in a converted stage-coach inn.

Restaurant closed Nov and Dec; July–Aug Tues lunch; Sept–June Wed lunch.

Passenans ✉ 39230
**Domaine de Revermont, t 03 84 44 61 02, t 03 84 44 64 83 (*inexpensive*). Well-located large modern hotel by the vineyards, with pleasant rooms *Restaurant closed Jan and Feb; Oct–Mar closed Sun eve and Mon.*
Auberge de Rostaing, t 03 84 85 23 70, f 03 84 44 66 87. Old house in the vines, with basic yet charming rooms.

Baume-les-Messieurs ✉ 39210
Des Grottes, t 03 84 44 61 59. Delightful restaurant by a waterfall, with simple menus.

Chille ✉ 39570
**Parenthèse et Thélème, t 03 84 47 55 44, f 03 84 24 92 13, just 3km northeast of Lons-le-Saunier (*inexpensive*). A very attractive and inviting large house and garden. *Restaurant closed Sun eve and Mon lunch.*

Courlans ✉ 39570
****Auberge de Chavannes, t 03 84 47 05 52, f 03 84 43 26 53. Reputed and refined little restaurant, 6km west of Lons-le-Saunier (*menus 320–410F*). *Restaurant closed 27 Jun–5 Jul; Jan; Sun eve, Tues lunch and Mon.*

West of Ornans, the village and château of **Cléron** are particularly picturesque. Tucked into the bank of the Doubs west of Quingey, the **Grottes d'Osselle** (*open June–Aug daily 9–7; April–May daily 9–12 and 2–6; Sept daily 9–12 and 2–5; Oct Mon–Fri 2.30–5, Sun 9–12 and 2–5; adm*) is one of the largest series of caves in France, full of colourful columns and pools. Discovered as far back as the 13th century, this was possibly the first cave system to be explored in France.

Salins-les-Bains and the Saline Royale at Arc-et-Senans
Dramatically guarded by a fort perched either side of the steep valley of the Furieuse river, **Salins-les-Bains**, the second town in the Franche-Comté in the 17th century, looks a bit frayed at the edges now. You can still visit the **Salines** (*open July–Aug 10–12 and 2–6; March–June and Sept–Oct daily exc Tues 10–12 and 2–6; adm*), exploited since Gallo-Roman times. Most of the buildings were demolished when the works closed in 1962, but the guided tour will take you into the medieval caverns to

Salt

Salt was precious right up to the time of the Revolution: it was a vital ingredient in preserving food, and – as a commodity which every household needed – it was heavily, often ruthlessly taxed. The *gabelle* (the salt tax) was imposed from the 14th century, and those who produced salt and levied the *gabelle* could make vast fortunes. This corner of the Franche-Comté is located on sedimentary seams rich in salt left over from the geological Secondary Era, when the region was under the sea. The extraction of the salt was a lucrative, but painstaking business. The sedimentary deposits had to be drawn up from far beneath the ground, and then the brine had to be evaporated to produce usable salt. The salt-producing centre was moved from Salins-les-Bains to Arc-et-Senans just before the Revolution as the woods around Salins had been heavily depleted. Arc-et-Senans lies just west of the Forêt de Chaux, which provided the wood needed to heat the brine to evaporate the salt.

see the centuries-old pump which brings up the salt waters from some 780ft below ground. You're invited to a *dégustation*, but you won't want much: it's ten times saltier than ordinary sea water – saltier even than the Dead Sea.

Walk along the main street, lined with fine mansions, as far as the elegant arcaded 18th-century town hall. Behind rises the fat dome of the slightly earlier **chapel of Notre-Dame de la Libératrice**, with its cage of ribs holding up the ceiling. A small **thermal establishment** (*open daily 3.30–6.30; adm*) still operates in the centre. A beautiful route east up into the hills takes you to the **Source du Lison**, springing fully formed from below dramatic walls of rock. There are picturesque walks to the Grotte Sarrazine and Creux Billard.

The bold buildings of the **Saline Royale** (*open July–Aug daily 9–7; April–June and Sept–Oct daily 9–12 and 2–6; rest of year daily 9–12 and 2–5; adm*), stand to one side of quiet unassuming **Arc-et-Senans** on the north bank of the Loue. Planned by the visionary but practical architect Claude-Nicolas Ledoux, and built between 1775 and 1779, they form a grand architectural set piece, classified a World Heritage Site by UNESCO. The salt works at Arc-et-Senans weren't owned by the crown, but had been granted the exclusive royal privilege to exploit the local seams. Ledoux was commissioned to construct a magnificent new salt-producing centre, along with a new town for the workers. This ideal city, Chaux, was never completed, but the hemicycle of buildings that did go up is one of the great expressions of neo-classicism in Ancien Régime France, with imposing Italianate columns and bold decorative details; a recurring theme is of water pouring from pots, symbolizing the blessed brine. The magnificent **Maison du Directeur**, the stocky building which acts as the focal point, boasts the most amazing columns of all, built up from chunky square and rounded blocks. This now houses the **Lieu du Sel**, a permanent exhibition on the salt industry in France down the ages. You can also visit the two long **Bâtiments des Sels**, where the salt was extracted from the brine, one now given over to temporary exhibitions.

Ledoux was one of the most fascinating architects of the 18th century and worked for the likes of Madame du Barry, Louis XV's powerful mistress. Models of his other projects are superbly displayed in the Tonnellerie, the former barrel-makers' building, now converted into the **Musée Ledoux**. At the Revolution, when the *gabelle* was abolished and salt suddenly became cheap, Ledoux found himself in a dangerously ambiguous position as a friend of the Ancien Régime. While in prison he set about writing a book which he hoped would justify his work for posterity. Only one volume of the planned five was published before his death in 1806. His Saline Royale continued to operate through the 19th century, but the depletion of its spring and new means of salt production meant that the works fell into decline.

Along the Jura Wine Route

Set among the vineyards are the brown roofs and yellow and grey stones of the attractive **Arbois**, the capital of Jura wines. The restored remnants of the **Château Pécaud** have been converted into the **Musée des Vins de Franche-Comté** (*open July–Aug 10–12 and 2–6; April–June and Sept–Oct 9–12 and 2–6; rest of year daily exc Tues 2–6*), where you can learn about local wine history, wine traditions and wine making, while neatly kept vines outside illustrate the care of the vineyards. The major monument in Arbois, an orange-tinged bell tower, was tacked on to the Romanesque Gothic St-Just in the 16th century. The wonky nave contains ornate wood carving, including an elaborate organ and pulpit. The town's central **Place de la Liberté** is lined with beautiful 18th-century buildings. Head up Rue Jean Jaurès to the **Musée Sarret-de-Grozon** (*contact tourist office for opening times*) which displays typical bourgeois interiors of the period. Louis Pasteur spent his childhood in Arbois, and he kept his father's home here as a holiday retreat, complete with a laboratory. The **Maison Pasteur** (*contact tourist office for opening times*) has been lovingly restored in the last few years. The guides will tell you about how close he was to his sisters, and how he developed into one of the most important scientists in history, still finding time to work with the local vine-growing community.

South of Arbois a pretty country road leads to **Les Planches-près-Arbois**, a delightful village at the foot of a typical *reculée*, a bite in the Jura plateau, with walls of limestone rising above the village. Another enchanting road takes you along the vine slopes via **Pupillin**, which has a well-regarded wine cooperative, to **Buvilly**.

The small town of **Poligny** was once an important religious centre, but now its institutions have found other uses – for wine, theatre, and so on. Big Gothic St-Hippolyte still serves as a church, and the **Maison du Comté** (*for hours, call t 03 84 37 23 51; adm*) is devoted to another local deity, Comté cheese. South of Poligny, take the route along the vine slopes via a string of adorable villages: **Plasne**, **Passenans**, **Frontenay** and **Menétru-le-Vignoble**, with the hilltop village of **Château-Chalon** as the crowning glory. Only fragments of its medieval abbey remain today, along with the stocky church of St-Pierre with its thick stone ribbing, its baptistry behind bars, curious paintings and a well-displayed treasury. Wander out to the belvedere, for wonderful views along the vine slopes. Vin jaune originated in this area.

A short way south, utterly picturesque **Baume-les-Messieurs** is guarded by a dramatic array of limestone outcrops that frame the famous **abbey**, said to have been planted by the Irish saint Columban. It was developed in the 9th century by abbot Bernon, who went on to found Cluny. From the 16th century, the monks were

Jura Wines

Jura wines are a real peculiarity. Some have odd names like *vin jaune* (yellow wine) and *vin de paille* (straw wine); some are made from odd grape varieties; and the amounts produced are quite small. To cap it all, Jura wines are an acquired taste, and it's difficult to buy the better ones because they're so exclusive. Nutty vin jaune, the region's most famous white wine, comes from savagnin grapes grown around Arbois and Château-Chalon. Vin de paille is a sweet white wine made by drying the grapes on straw before they're pressed, causing the sugar level to be very high. Both can be kept for years, and are generallyexpensive. Many of the ordinary whites come from chardonnay grapes; try the lightly sparkling Chardonnay Crémants de Jura. If you want to play it safe among the reds, look for Pinot Noir; more unusual reds worth trying come from the local poulsard and trousseau grapes .

aristocrats, hence the village's posh suffix. You can wander the abbey's cobbled squares by yourself, or take a guided tour. Although the abbey church is topped by an unfortunate spire in clashing materials, the interior retains all its medieval dignity. Above the nave arches, simple faces are carved in the *culs-de-lampe*. The splendid altarpiece is shielded by the high wrought-iron gates of the choir; you'll need to take the tour to see the fine detail of the central carved scenes and the side panels.

The arcades of Rue du Commerce impart a sense of style to the heart of **Lons-le-Saunier**, another salty spa town known as far back as Gallo-Roman times. Its **Musée des Beaux-Arts** (*open Mon–Fri 10–12 and 2–6, Sat and Sun 2–5; closed Tues; adm*) is a likable small museum, housing two engrossing Breughel the Youngers, one showing Herod's massacre of the innocents set in the snowy Flemish north. But the main emphasis is on pure white statues, mostly by the Jura sculptor Jean-Joseph Perraud. The relatively undistinguished life of Rouget de Lisle, composer of the French national anthem, is celebrated in the little **Musée Rouget de Lisle** in his birthplace on Rue du Commerce. The clock tower in Place de la Liberté plays the *Marseillaise* every hour.

The Big Loop in the Doubs: into Eastern Franche-Comté

The Doubs creates an enormous loop from Besançon back to its source on the picturesque border with Switzerland, where chalets are set below wooded ridges. Here the high spots include the Saut du Doubs waterfall, the Château de Joux in a dramatic pass, and the Mont d'Or, close to the source of the Doubs, which has spectacular views down to the Alps.

At its most northerly points, the Doubs draws two big snail's horns on the map. One horn gets caught around the Germanic industrial town of Montbéliard (*see p.722*), while the other heads around Ste-Ursanne in Switzerland. Ignoring its little detour into Switzerland, you can rediscover the Doubs at pretty **Goumois**, which has a bridge spanning France and Switzerland. South of here the river forms a dramatic border

Getting Around

Pontarlier has a useful train station on the line to Neuchâtel and Bern in Switzerland if you're relying on public transport. A separate train line leads from Besançon to Morteau and Villers-le-Lac.

Tourist Information

Villers-le-Lac: Rue Berçot, t 03 81 68 00 98, f 03 81 68 09 63.

Montbenoît: Route de Pontarlier, t 03 81 38 10 32, f 03 81 38 12 97.

Pontarlier: 14 bis Rue de la Gare, t 03 81 46 48 33, f 03 81 46 83 32.

Malbuisson: t 03 81 69 31 21, f 03 81 69 71 94.

Sports and Activities

Boat trips to the **Saut du Doubs** (the best way to see the cascade from close quarters) leave from Villers-le-Lac. Contact the Saut du Doubs Bateaux Mouches, t 03 81 68 13 25; or CNFS Vedettes Panoramiques, t 03 81 68 05 34.

Where to Stay and Eat

St-Hippolyte ✉ 25190
★★★**Hôtel Bellevue**, Route Maîche, t 03 81 96 51 53, f 03 81 96 52 40 (*inexpensive*). A reliably

good option, with a restaurant, in a popular spot (*menus 130–380F*). *Restaurant closed 21–27 August; Sun eve and Mon exc July and Aug.*

Goumois ✉ 25470
★★★**Taillard**, t 03 81 44 20 75, f 03 81 44 26 15 (*moderate*). A very well-run white chalet on the wooded slopes of this lovely spot along the Doubs valley. Some delightful rooms with balconies. Good cooking too. *Open 6 Mar–Nov. Restaurant closed Wed lunch exc July and Aug; Mar, Oct and Nov Wed eve.*
★★**Le Moulin de Plain**, t 03 81 44 41 99, f 03 81 44 45 70 (*inexpensive*). At the bottom of the valley, another comfortable hotel with restaurant. *Closed 1 Nov–1 Mar.*

Malbuisson ✉ 25160
★★★**Hôtel du Lac**, Grande Rue, t 03 81 69 34 80, f 03 81 69 35 44 (*moderate*). Many rooms with views on to the lake of St-Point in this colourful, well-respected family-run hotel. Excellent dinners (*menus 105–255F*). *Restaurant closed 15 Nov–17 Dec Mon–Fri.*
★★★**Le Bon Accueil**, 10 Grande Rue, t 03 81 69 30 58, f 03 81 69 37 60 (*moderate*). Another good address, with fine regional cuisine from chef Marc Faivre (*menus 165–280F*). *Restaurant closed 3–11 April; 18 Dec–18 Jan; Oct–April Sun eve; Tues lunch and Mon.*

between the two countries. The **Saut du Doubs** is the most famous waterfall in the Franche-Comté, and the best way of reaching it is by boat from scruffy **Villers-le-Lac** (*see* box above). Otherwise, winding routes take you close to the gorges above Villers, but you'll need to leave your car to find the best plunging views. So close to the Swiss border, it's no surprise that this is clock-making territory. At Villers-le-Lac, the **Musée de la Montre** (*open June–Sept daily 10–12 and 3–6; rest of year daily 2–6; closed Jan and Tues; adm*) goes back to the 16th-century origins of the craft. **Montbenoît**, sitting beside rocky cliffs above the Doubs, boasts a famous abbey, of which significant portions survive from the 12th century. The late-Gothic cloisters and choir end of the abbey church are very attractive, but the decorative highlights were added in the 16th century by abbot Ferry Carondelet, a lover of the arts who was influenced by his trips to Italy. The extraordinary carved stalls show lively scenes of women dominating men.

Pontarlier, once known for its absinthe, lies at the meeting point of several valleys, its strategic location underlined by the daunting **Château de Joux** (*open July–Aug daily 9–6; Feb school hols–June and Sept daily 10–11.30 and 2–4.30; Oct–Feb school hols* *daily 10–11.15 and 2–3.30; adm*), a little way south, a formidable fort built on a jagged ridge. Five layers of ramparts encircle the remnants of medieval fortifications, going back to the 11th century. One courtyard is the setting for theatrical performances on summer evenings. On the guided tour you're taken to a **Musée d'Armes Anciennes**, and rooms and cells connected with three remarkable prisoners: Berthe the chatelaine, who, being informed that her husband was killed in the Crusades, took a friend as a lover, only to have her husband return alive and well; the young troublemaking Mirabeau, imprisoned here by his own father until he charmed a local married woman into taking all her husband's money and eloping (they were caught); and most famous of all, Toussaint Louverture, a black officer fired by the French Revolution, who pressed for the independence of Haiti but was captured by order of Napoleon, and brought to Joux to end his days in misery, although Haiti did become the first independent black state in the modern world in 1804. Be warned that the visit involves a lot of climbing, especially down an amazing stairwell of over 200 steps. At the bottom, an enormous well disappears into the bowels of the earth. It was part of the extensive additions made to the fort in the 17th century, after Louis XIV's army had taken the Franche-Comté. The plans were drawn up by Vauban, and a dozen men died in the digging of the well alone.

After the Château de Joux, the long, thin **Lac de St-Point** looks very restful, its gentle slopes dotted with chalet resorts slipping down to small lake ports. The river valley remains open as far as the **Source du Doubs**, in fact just a clear pool of water. For real drama climb to the top of the **Mont d'Or**, which has the best views in the Franche-Comté. To the south rise the distant white tops of the Alps, while the Jura heights cut down to the Swiss plains. The Jura's lake district lies to the west (*see* below).

Central and Southern Franche-Comté; plus the Gex and the Bugey

Many of the most picturesque lakes of the central Jura lake district lie close to the Hérisson (Hedgehog) river, which cascades down into the Ain river. The Col de la Faucille takes you up and over into the Gex, a curious pocket of France staring indiscreetly down on Geneva. Squeezed between the Ain and the Rhône valleys, the Bugey is the little-known southern end of the Jura range. Secretive river gorges are its speciality, with surprising patches of vineyards.

Nozeroy, a Burgundian hilltop village that got away, lies in beautiful agricultural country between Lons-le-Saunier and Pontarlier. It was a stronghold of the Chalons, a great salt-exploiting family in medieval times, and it was the mighty Jean l'Antique de Chalon who had the first castle built here in the 13th century, commanding a major salt route. The medieval village was built on a grid plan, and two major gateways still stand, the Porte Nods and the Porte de l'Horloge. Behind a neoclassical façade, the Gothic church has intriguing paintings celebrating the lives of St Augustine, the hermit St Anthony with his pig, and St François de Sales. The past wealth of the Chalons is evident: works of Flemish art stand out, as does gilded embroidery.

Getting Around

Geneva international airport lies very close to this area, while a railway line from Geneva crosses through the Bugey and heads up through the central Franche-Comté, with stations at St-Claude, Morez, Morbier, St-Laurent-de-Grandvaux and Champagnole.

Tourist Information

Clairvaux-les-Lacs/Pays des Lacs: 36 Grande Rue, t 03 84 25 27 47, f 03 84 25 23 00.
Moirans-en-Montagne: 2 Place Robert Monnier, t/f 03 84 42 31 57.
St-Claude: 19 Rue du Marché, B.P.94, t 03 84 45 34 24, f 03 84 41 02 72.
Ferney-Voltaire: t 04 50 28 09 16, f 04 50 40 78 99.
Nantua: Place de la Déportation, t 04 74 75 00 05.
Seyssel: Maison de Pays, t 04 50 59 26 56.
Belley: 34 Grande Rue, t 04 79 81 29 06.

Activities

If you take your cheese seriously, visit a *fruitière*, the regional name for a cheese-making holding. The **Fruitière 1900 at Thoiria** (*open July–Aug; demonstration at 9am – small fee*) still makes Comté the old-fashioned way.

Where to Stay and Eat

Bonlieu ✉ 39130
**Auberge de la Poutre, t 03 84 25 57 77, f 03 84 25 51 61 (*inexpensive*). The rooms are a right old confusion of tastes and colours, but the chef is a great ambassador of Jura food and wine, and in season goes out picking his own wild berries (*menus 120–320F*). Hotel

closed 11 Nov–11 Feb. Restaurant closed Sun eve, Wed eve and Mon.

Les Rousses ✉ 39220
***Hôtel de France, t 03 84 60 01 45, f 03 84 60 04 63 (*moderate*). A warm and welcoming big family-run chalet in the middle of this pleasant little mountain resort, rooms looking on to the woods. *Closed 24 April–12 May and 20 Nov–15 Dec.*

Col de la Faucille ✉ 01170
***La Mainaz, t 04 50 41 31 10, f 04 50 41 31 77. Well-located hotel high up off the roadside east of the pass, with wonderful views down on Lake Geneva and the Alps, and nicely furnished rooms. You can also enjoy the vistas from the large dining room. *Closed 28 Oct–8 Dec; Sun eve and Mon exc school hols.*

Divonne-les-Bains ✉ 01220
****Château de Divonne, 115 Rue des Bains, t 04 50 20 00 32, f 04 50 20 03 73 (*expensive*). The most luxurious hotel in this casino spa town, actually a 19th-century manor with amazing views across Lake Geneva to the Alps and a golf course close to its spacious grounds. (*Restaurant menus 295–600F*). *Closed Jan.*

Ferney-Voltaire ✉ 01210
**Hôtel de France, 1 Rue de Genève, t 04 50 40 63 87, f 04 50 40 47 27 (*moderate*). The attractive front hides nicely decorated, clean rooms and a rustic restaurant with a terrace where you'll be served refined food (*menus 129–255F*). *Closed 25 Dec–15 Jan.*

Artemare
**Hôtel Michallet, Rue de la Poste, t 04 79 87 39 33, f 04 79 87 39 20. Pleasant, traditional country town hotel with restaurant (*menus 75–270F*). *Closed 17 Dec–9 Jan; Sun eve, Mon.*

Head south via the town of Champagnole and you come to the main lake area of the Jura. From the heights of the **Belvédère des Quatre Lacs** you can look down on the waters of Maclu and Petit Maclu, Ilay and Narlay; for even more spectacular views, climb the frittered grey limestone layers to the nearby rocky promontory of the **Pic de l'Aigle**. The road east from here leads up into the high Jura past Morbier, Morez and Les Rousses; the main road then leads south along the Swiss border to the Col de la Faucille and the Gex (*see* below).

Back close to the Pic de l'Aigle, a footpath of slippery polished stones leads along the beech-shaded **Cascades du Hérisson**, the big steps the river takes down from the Jura plateau. Enjoy a dramatic view down on to **Lac de Chalain** from the belvedere on its eastern side. This is the most touristy lake in the area, a beautiful site surrounded by campers in summer, with a busy, narrow strip of beach and turquoise waters full of *pédalos*. In the early 1900s a drought revealed the vestiges of a Neolithic settlement and you can now see copies of a couple of Neolithic houses on stilts.

Wood-working has long been a speciality here, and pretty **Moirans-en-Montagne** is devoted to the craft of the *tourneurs* who specialize in toys. In the bright blue **Musée du Jouet** (*open July–Aug daily 10–6.30; Feb–June Mon–Fri 10–12 and 2–6, Sat and Sun 2–6; adm*), children can play games, or watch a puppet show in the Ciné-Théâtre.

Wooded valley roads lead to **St-Claude**, with a large white cathedral, half-church, half-château. The cathedral displays a sober grandeur, although the few large putti seem to have freshly coiffed bouffant hair. It pays particular homage to St Claude, a lordly 7th-century archbishop of Besançon who gave up the grand life to became an abbot here. The most famous pilgrim to the tomb of St Claude was Anne de Bretagne, who was married to two French kings. She had had problems conceiving, but after her visit she gave birth to a daughter – named Claude – who went on to marry François I. By the cathedral the old-fashioned **Musée du Diamant et de la Pipe** (*open July–Aug daily 9.30–6.30; May–June and Sept daily 9.30–12 and 2–6.30; Oct and Christmas–April daily 2–6; closed Sun and hols; adm*) dwells on the town's two major industries. Ask at the tourist office about visiting a pipe-maker or diamond-cutter.

The Gex

Beyond St-Claude the roads east head out of the Franche-Comté towards the Gex and the highest ridge of the Jura range, on the Swiss border. From the **Col de la Faucille** you can embark on the GR9, a splendid path with unforgettable views of the Alps. Or you can plunge down by road towards Geneva into the slice of land on the northern side of Lake Geneva which France seems to have poached from Switzerland.

The **Château de Ferney** (*contact t 04 50 28 09 16 for times of visits*) was once home to Voltaire, who spent much of his life on the frontier, ready to slip into exile should he antagonize the royal authorities too much. The castle was rebuilt in classical style for him, and from 1760 became his favourite residence. On the intelligent tour you're given a picture of Voltaire's life here with his niece-cum-lover. He entertained lavishly, but also provided for the local community and encouraged local enterprise. Today the château tries to emulate Voltaire by running a vibrant cultural programme.

The Bugey

The Bugey stretches from Nantua and Bellegarde-sur-Valserine to the triangular tip caused by a dramatic meander in the Rhône below Belley. It long lay under the rule of the dukes of Savoy, but was ceded to Henri IV at the beginning of the 17th century. On the edge of a glacial lake, overseen by limestone cliffs, **Nantua** is a good advert for the Bugey's semi-forgotten towns. The settlement grew up around an 8th-century abbey and the church of St Michael, with its hammered Romanesque doorway and disconcertingly curving pillars. The nave slopes up towards an elegant Gothic choir, where there is a striking St Sebastian by Delacroix (1836).

The gorges of the Ain west of Nantua end at **Ambronay**, with its abbey church founded in the 800s. The restored lintel over the main entrance shows an engrossing Resurrection scene and a pretty Virgin. The cool Gothic interior contains old stained glass, soberly carved wooden stalls and a remarkable stone Crucifixion. A door leads into the beautiful Gothic cloister.

East of the Ain below Nantua you come to the crests of the Bugey range. The pretty road below follows the Rhône valley, with vineyards and typical wine villages, such as **Seyssel**. Precipitous roads climb up to the **Grand Colombier**, where the views are amazing. Close by, you can look down on the Lac du Bourget, but the star of the show is Mont Blanc. On your way to Belley don't miss the picturesque wine village of **Vongnes**, whose reds not only employ gamay and pinot noir, but also the rarer manicle and mondeuse. It also has a little wine museum (*open daily 9–12 and 2–7*). Gorgeous country roads lead down to **Belley**, surrounded by dull industrial buildings. Along the curving main street stands the house of Brillat-Savarin, the town's most famous son, whose work *La Physiologie du Goût* (1826) is a peculiarly French concoction, a meditation on the art of good living and cuisine.

The idyllic village of **Izieu**, at the very bottom of the Bugey, was the setting for an horrific event, recalled in the harrowing **Musée Mémorial** (*open July–Aug daily 10–6.30; rest of year Mon–Fri 9–5, Sat and Sun 10–6; closed Wed; adm*), in a farm above the village. During the war this farm became a secret refuge for Jewish children. But on 6 April 1944 the Gestapo came and took away 44 children and their teachers. Of those arrested, 47 would die in Auschwitz; three others would be shot in Estonia; and just one survived. The barn has been converted into a museum that confronts the ghosts of France's anti-semitism. In all, some 76,000 French Jews, around one quarter of the total living in the country in 1939, were deported under the Vichy regime. The majority ended up in Auschwitz. The museum also explores the notion of crimes against humanity, with a programme of temporary exhibitions.

Into Savoy: Chambéry, Aix-les-Bains, the Lacs du Bourget and Annecy

South of Lake Geneva and east of the Rhône rise the mountains of Savoy, the greatest heights in Europe. The town of Chambéry in the west of Savoy long served as capital of the region, and Savoy only officially became a part of France in 1860. Nowadays the region is divided between two *départements*, Savoie to the south and Haute Savoie to the north.

Chambéry

Delightful Chambéry first acquired some political importance during the 13th century, and was the capital of Savoy until the shift to Turin in the 16th century. A line of counts by the name of Amédée saw to the considerable development of Chambéry

Getting Around

You can fly direct to Chambéry/Aix-les-Bains from London-Stansted with Buzz, t 0870 240 7070 in Britain. Chambéry, Aix-les-Bains and Annecy are all well served by regular trains from Paris-Gare de Lyon. It takes just under 3hrs to reach Chambéry, 3hrs 40mins to get to Annecy.

Tourist Information

Chambéry: 24 Bd de la Colonne, t 04 79 33 42 47, f 04 79 85 71 39.
Aix-les-Bains: Rue Jean Monard, B.P.132, t 04 79 35 15 35/05 92, f 04 79 88 88 01.
Talloires: Rue André Theuriet, t 04 50 60 70 64, f 04 50 60 76 59.
Annecy: 1 Rue Jean Jaurès, Centre Bonlieu, t 04 50 45 00 33, f 04 50 51 87 20.

Sports and Activities

Boat trips on Lac d'Annecy are available from **Croisières du Lac d'Annecy**, t 04 50 51 08 40. Boat or *pédalo* hire, and water-skiing are available from the **Groupement des Loueurs de Bateaux de Haute-Savoie** (Easter–All Saints', t 04 50 52 63 61).

For trips on Lac du Bourget, contact the **Bateaux du Lac du Bourget et du Haut-Rhône**, t 04 79 88 92 09.

Several other companies offer flights from Annecy airport, a magical if *expensive* way of touring the Savoy lakes and Alps: **Avia'Styl**, t 04 72 77 09 90; **Héli-Alpes**, t 04 50 27 35 45, f 04 50 27 31 24; and **Hélijet**, t 04 79 55 69 73, f 04 79 09 77 50.

Where to Stay and Eat

Chambéry ✉ 73000
★★★★**Château de Candie**, Rue du Bois de Candie, t 04 79 96 63 00, f 04 79 96 63 10 (*expensive*). Beautifully furnished converted fortress above town. The modern dining room has trompe-l'œil decorations matched by refined cuisine (*menus 310–410F; closed Sun eve*).

★★★**Les Princes**, 4 Rue de Boigne, t 04 79 33 45 36, f 04 79 70 31 47 (*moderate*). A reliable central option, for comfortable rooms and good classic French cuisine.
★★**Arcantis City-Hôtel**, 9 Rue Denfert-Rochereau, t 04 79 85 76 79, f 04 79 85 86 11 (*inexpensive*). Central hotel with modern interiors in an Ancien Régime house. No restaurant.
Hôtel des Voyageurs, 3 Rue Doppet, t 04 79 33 57 00. Very simple, central, and quite fun.

Les Charmettes ✉ 73000
★★**Aux Pervenches**, t 04 79 33 34 26, f 04 79 60 02 52 (*inexpensive*). A justly popular rural retreat, just southeast of Chambéry, with a good restaurant (*menus 95–195F*).

Challes-les-Eaux ✉ 73190
★★★**Hostellerie des Comtes de Challes**, 247 Montée du Château, t 04 79 72 86 71, f 04 79 72 83 83 (*moderate*). A fortified manor dating back in part to the 12th century, standing above a small spa town 6km southeast of Chambéry with fine views.

Le Bourget-du-Lac ✉ 73370
★★★★**L'Orée du Lac**, La Croix Verte, t 04 79 25 24 19, f 04 79 25 08 51 (*expensive*). Charming manor at the south end of the lake, with comfortable rooms and watersports.

Aix-les-Bains ✉ 73100
★★★**Astoria**, 7 Place des Thermes, t 04 79 35 12 28, f 04 79 35 11 05 (*moderate*). Right in the heart of town, with a great Belle Epoque feel as you walk into its grand reception area. The rooms are quite stylish. *Closed Dec.*
★★★**Le Manoir**, 37 Rue Georges 1er, t 04 79 61 44 00, f 04 79 35 67 67 (*moderate*).Close to the centre of town and the Thermes Nationaux, but calm and surrounded by greenery.
★★**Davat**, 21 Chemin des Bateliers, Le Grand Port, t 04 79 63 40 40, f 04 79 54 35 68 (*inexpensive*). Pleasant traditional hotel by the lake. Meals served in the garden on warm days. *Closed Jan and Feb; Sun eve and Mon.*
★★**Au Petit Vatel**, 11 Rue du Temple, t 04 79 35 04 80, f 04 79 34 01 51 (*inexpensive*). With old-style charm and simple rooms, right by

the Anglican church where Queen Victoria went when she was in town.

Talloires ✉ 74290

★★★★**Auberge du Père Bise, t** 04 50 60 72 01, **f** 04 50 60 73 05, *bise@relaischateaux.fr* (*luxury*). One of the most exceptional hotels in southeastern France, a rival to the Auberge de l'Eridan (*see* below). The sumptuous rooms look out on to lake and mountains. You're unlikely to see lake fish more beautifully dressed up than in the first-rate restaurant (*menus 350–820F*). Private lake-side beach. *Closed 6 Nov–10 Feb. Restaurant closed Wed lunch; Oct and Feb–April Tues.*

★★★★**Les Prés du Lac, t** 04 50 60 76 11, **f** 04 50 60 73 42, *les.pres.du.lac@wanadoo.fr* (*expensive*). Very comfortable rooms scattered throughout the garden which slopes gently down to the lake. Private beach. No restaurant. *Closed 16 Oct–31 Mar.*

★★★**L'Abbaye,** Chemin des Moines, **t** 04 50 60 77 33, **f** 04 50 60 78 81 (*expensive*). An old Benedictine abbey with a piano bar, a solarium, and a private landing stage. The rooms are set around a graceful 17th-century cloister, some adorned with beautiful 18th-century tapestries. *Closed Dec and Jan. Restaurant closed Sun eve and Nov–Mar Mon.*

★★★**Le Cottage Fernand Bise, t** 04 50 60 71 10, **f** 04 50 60 77 51, *cottagebise@wanadoo.fr* (*expensive*). Another classy hotel, but slightly better value. A big chalet set in a garden filled with flowers in season (*menus 175–280F*). *Closed 4 Oct–14 April.*

★★★**Villa des Fleurs,** Route du Port, **t** 04 50 60 71 14, **f** 04 50 60 74 06 (*moderate*). Only 100m from the water, a more secretive little chalet hotel with cute rooms and serving good lake fish. *Closed 12 Nov–16 Dec; 22 Jan–4 Feb; Sun eve and Mon.*

Veyrier-du-Lac ✉ 74290

★★★★**Auberge de l'Eridan – Marc Veyrat,** 13 Vieille Route des Pensières, **f** 04 50 60 24 00, **t** 04 50 60 23 63, *veyrat@relaischateaux.fr* (*luxury*). A fabulous lake-side hotel-cum-restaurant, one of the greatest in France, and one of the most *expensive*. The rooms could scarcely be more luxurious – with

sunny balconies, and double Jacuzzis in some of the bathrooms. Marc Veyrat is one of the best chefs in the country and he knows it, but he still goes foraging in the Alps for authentic ingredients to inspire his imaginative cuisine (*menus 695–995F*). *Closed 16 Nov–9 April. Restaurant closed Tues lunch, Wed lunch and Mon.*

Annecy ✉ 74000

★★★★**L'Imperial Palace,** 32 Av d'Albigny, **t** 04 50 09 30 00, **f** 04 50 09 33 33 (*expensive*). An impressive old-style luxury hotel on the outside, with intriguing modern furnishings within. Very well-located and comfortable.

★★★**Les Trésoms,** 3 Bd de la Corniche, **t** 04 50 51 43 84, **f** 04 50 45 56 49, *tresoms@cybercable.tm.fr* (*moderate*). Charming big house south of the historic centre; many rooms with views of the waters. Panoramic restaurant.

★★**Marquisats,** 6 Chemin de Colmyr, **t** 04 50 51 52 34, **f** 04 50 51 89 42 (*moderate*). Compact, stylish hotel south of the centre. Many rooms have lake views.

★★**Palais de l'Isle,** 13 Rue Perrière, **t** 04 50 45 86 87, **f** 04 50 51 87 15 (*inexpensive*). Best located two-star, in the heart of the old town, one side looking over to the main canal.

★★**Hôtel du Nord,** 24 Rue Sommeiller, **t** 04 50 45 08 78, **f** 04 50 51 22 04 (*inexpensive*). A good central option not far from the railway station.

Le Belvédère, 7 Chemin du Belvédère, **t** 04 50 45 04 90, **f** 04 50 45 67 25. Up on the heights south of the old town, a reputable restaurant with high standards and a splendid view. *Closed 15 Jan–15 Mar; Sun eve and Mon.*

Le Petit Zinc, 11 Rue du Pont Morens, **t** 04 50 51 12 93. Warm, welcoming little restaurant in the heart of old Annecy serving copious Savoie dishes.

Avernoz ✉ 74570

★★**Auberge Camelia, t** 04 50 22 44 24, **f** 04 50 22 43 25, *info@hotelcamelia.com*. Run by a very friendly British couple who have fallen in love with the region and will do their best to ensure that you do too, this simple, village hotel is a real find: comfortable, warm and good value.

from the 14th century. Most famously, in 1453 they came by a shroud said to have been Christ's that drew large numbers of pilgrims until it was moved to Turin in 1578, when François I's troops briefly took Chambéry. The French would be a constant menace, and, in fact, during the Revolution, Chambéry was made capital of the large *département* of Mont-Blanc. But after Napoleon's defeat, the Savoyards regained control until the region voted to join France in 1860.

The core of Chambéry is compact, surrounded by boulevards; one, **Boulevard de la Colonne**, features an absurd but much loved elephant memorial from the 1830s, dedicated to the flamboyant Benoît de Boigne, who funded city improvements with a fortune made in India. The **Musée Savoisien** (*open daily 10–12 and 2–6; closed Tues and public hols; adm*), in a former Franciscan monastery adjoining the cathedral, has displays going back to prehistoric pieces found by Lac du Bourget, such as a beautiful bronze bracelet, Gallo-Roman finds, fragments of a cartoonish 13th-century mural showing an attack on a castle, and ducal coins. The sober late-Gothic Franciscan church turned **cathedral** has a surprising Flamboyant doorway. Neo-Gothic trompe-l'œil scenes embellish the interior, along with some older fragments of wall paintings; the treasury includes a beautiful early-medieval ivory diptych.

From the 19th-century theatre in **Boulevard du Théâtre**, follow the noble curve of **Rue Croix d'Or**, lined with the colourful façades of some of the richest houses in the city. At the end of the street **Place St-Léger** steals the show, with its vibrant façades, fountains and pink cobble stones. Explore the maze of alleyways that lead off the square; you may stumble across some trompe l'œil decoration, a local speciality.

Follow pretty **Rue Basse du Château** to the Gothic castle of the dukes of Savoy, which was restored in the 18th century. The heavily renovated **Sainte Chapelle** is where the Turin shroud was held. Its fine 16th-century stained glass has been preserved; the outrageous 19th-century trompe-l'œil ceiling is by Vicario, the same who decorated the cathedral interior.

The **Musée des Beaux-Arts** (*open daily 10–12 and 2–6; closed Tues and public hols; adm*) is near the tourist office, opposite the law courts. Its Italian collections are particularly rich, a strong reminder of Savoy's connections across the Alps. Gothic highlights include an enchanting retable of St Christopher carrying Jesus by Bartolo di Fredi, and a stunning profile portrait of a young man, attributed to Paolo Uccello. Titian and Giordano also feature, as well as some notable Flemish names and a few well-known French artists, such as de La Tour.

Just a couple of miles south of Chambéry, the **Maison des Charmettes** (*open daily 10–12 and 2–6; Oct–Mar 10–12 and 2–4.30; closed Tues and public hols; adm*) is dedicated to Rousseau and Madame de Warens. Jean-Jacques Rousseau had run away from an unhappy situation in Geneva at the age of 16 and was taken into the bosom of Madame de Warens, an immensely influential figure in his life and his first lover. They lived in Chambéry from 1731 until 1736, Rousseau teaching music to the bourgeoisie, then moved to Les Charmettes, where he developed his *magasin d'idées* through his voracious studies. Charming **Lac d'Aiguebelette** just west of Chambéry is more peaceful than its cousins, and motor boats aren't allowed on it, making it a popular place to swim and sail in summer.

Lac du Bourget

The largest natural lake in France, **Lac du Bourget** is a long expanse of water left over from the last ice age, framed to the southwest by the striking silhouette of the Dent du Chat. The hot sulphorous waters of its main resort, **Aix-les-Bains**, were celebrated by the Celtic Allobroges and it boasted splendid baths in Gallo-Roman times. In the early 1600s Henri IV enjoyed cavorting here and in the 18th century new spa buildings were built, and provision was made for the poor as well as the aristocracy. Napoleon's family took the waters, but the best-remembered French visitor was the sickly young Romantic poet Lamartine, who came in October 1816 and met Julie Charles, a young married woman suffering from tuberculosis, with whom he fell madly in love. They promised to meet up the following season, but Julie was too ill and died before the end of 1817, and the forlorn Lamartine immortalized her in his poetry, notably 'Le Lac', under the name of Elvire. Another famous visitor to Aix-les-Bains on several occasions from 1885 used the subtle pseudonym of Countess of Balmoral. She was none other than Queen Victoria, and a whole English colony followed in her wake. At the end of the century extravagant, Belle Epoque villas were built on the slopes above the town.

Central Aix-les-Bains is something of an architectural jumble now, but it retains a certain style and flair, and that curious spa mixture of sickness and jollity. Outside the Thermes Nationaux stand the remnants of two **Gallo-Roman monuments**, the Arch of Campanus and the Temple of Diana. On the guided tour of the town you're taken through the rather grim **Thermes Nationaux**, which specialize in treatments for rheumatism, to peer at the dark **remnants of the Gallo-Roman baths** beneath. The swanky modern **Thermes Chevalley** have just opened above the old thermal centre, catering in part for those in search of luxury treatments.

Try to have look inside the **Grand Casino** (not to be confused with the Nouveau Casino) not far from the Hôtel de Ville. Some of the original mosaics and stained glass are still in place in this outrageous extravaganza, which was the first place in France to witness Wagner's *Tristan and Isolde*, in 1897. The **Musée Faure** (*open 6 Jan–19 Dec daily 10–12 and 1.30–6; closed Tues and public hols; adm*) contains Impressionist works and sculptures by the likes of Rodin. At the lake-shore you'll find a freshwater aquarium, a beach, and boats for cruising the water. Or take the steep road from Aix up **Mont Revard** (4,920ft), where the plateau offers spectacular views down on the lake and across to Mont Blanc. This plateau is excellent for cross-country skiing, with over 150km of pistes. The **Abbaye de Hautecombe** (*donation; open daily 10–11.30 and 2–5; closed Tues)*, on an east-shore promontory, is accessible by boat from Aix-les-Bains, or by car via the superb lakeside drive. A Cistercian foundation of 1135, two of its abbots became popes in the 13th century, Celestine IV – for just 17 days – and Nicholas III. In the 14th century, a chapel was constructed to house the tombs of the counts and dukes of Savoy. Over 40 members of the family were buried here up until the start of the 16th century when the abbey fell into decline; however, Charles-Félix of the house of Savoy had them sumptuously restored in neo-Gothic style, while a religious community was reinstalled. You can visit some of the extravagant neo-Gothic parts, The last king of Italy, Umberto II of the house of Savoy, was buried here in 1983.

Lac d'Annecy

Lac d'Annecy is one of the most beautiful lakes in Europe. Arrive by the dramatic ridge of the **Montagne de Semnoz** on the western side, or via the **Col de la Forclaz,** the still more perilous route on the eastern side. The highest mountain reflected in its waters, snow-capped **La Tournette**, reaches a heady 7,711ft. On the east shore of the lake, **Talloires** is an extremely chic resort with a swanky port and fabulous array of waterside hotels and restaurants. The **Roc de Chère** promontory north of Talloires is so rich in flora it's been turned into a nature reserve; just beyond it, delightful **Menthon-St-Bernard** is overseen by the many-towered **Château de Menthon** (*open July–Aug daily 12–6; May–June and Sept Thurs, weekends and public hols 2–6; adm*), which claims to have been the birthplace of St Bernard at the end of the 10th century. He did a great deal to encourage piety in the western Alps and cared for mountain travellers, most famously by setting up monasteries at the Petit Bernard and Grand Bernard passes, where the big dogs named after him are trained to help in Alpine rescues.

The historic heart of **Annecy** is as close as any place in France comes to the sheer watery romanticism of Venice. The streets around the town's canals are captivating, with the odd grandiose church façade in white stone rising above the houses. It was purchased in 1401 by Amédée VIII, and from the mid-15th to the mid-17th centuries Annecy was reserved for various junior members of the house of Savoy.

With the Reformation, Annecy suddenly acquired greater importance. Geneva had become the stronghold of Calvinism, and the city's monastic communities were expelled. Many moved to Annecy, which became the seat of a new bishopric for Geneva. One bishop was François de Sales (1567–1622), who devoted his life to gentle but persuasive preaching, advocating a virtuous Catholic life; his *Introduction à la Vie Dévote* became a bestseller across Europe in his lifetime. In 1610 he established the charitable Order of the Visitation with Jeanne de Chantal (grandmother of Mme de Sévigné). François de Sales was buried in Annecy, canonized in 1665, and proclaimed patron saint of writers and journalists in 1923.

The best place to start a tour of Annecy is at the **Pont sur le Thiou,** just in from the lake on the canalized Thiou river. This has the most famous view of Annecy, taking in the **Palais de l'Isle** (*open June–Sept daily 10–6; rest of year daily exc Tues 10–12 and 2–6; adm*), a wonderful boat of a building moored in the river, dating back to the 12th century. Variously a residence, prison, mint, and law courts, it is now the **Musée de l'Histoire d'Annecy**. Nearby, wander along the Quai de l'Ile and Quai de l'Evêché.

The canals make a near-island out of the religious heart of Annecy. By the Pont sur le Thiou, the unmissable scrolled 17th-century front of the **church of St-François de Sales** was the chapel of the first monastery of the Order of the Visitation, where both François de Sales and Jeanne de Chantal were buried. During the Revolution the church was badly damaged and the two saints' tombs demolished. The interior looks sadly grey, the decoration tacky. A short way north, the Dominican Gothic barn of **St-Maurice** is the oldest church in Annecy, but only dating from 1422. Look out for the creepy funeral picture for Philibert de Monthouz and the splendid *Depostion* by Pourbus the Elder. Beyond the choir end of St-Maurice, the stocky town hall is backed by the shady Jardins de l'Europe leading down to the lake.

Head in the other direction down Rue Grenette and Rue Jean-Jacques Rousseau and you come to the **cathedral of St-Pierre**, with a striking Gothic–Renaissance façade. Built for the Franciscans in 1535, it was converted to the bishops' seat with the move from Geneva. In the choir you can make out dramatic chiaroscuro paintings, one showing the liberation of St Peter by Mazzola, another Christ's deposition, attributed to Caravaggio. The **bishops' palace** now houses a major school of music and the Académie Florimontane, a high-minded literary institution co-founded by François de Sales to promote goodness and beauty in art. A slightly leaning Romanesque-style bell tower belongs to the fourth church in the area, **Notre-Dame-de-Liesse**, which was rebuilt after the Revolution and given a classical front topped by a gilded statue of the Virgin and Child. In the Middle Ages, its miracles attracted crowds of pilgrims every seven years. Along arcaded Rue du Pâquier, the **Hôtel de Sales** was built for the de Sales family, and embellished with figures representing the seasons.

South of the Thiou, wonderful arcaded **Rue Ste-Claire** curving around the base of the castle rock was the main thoroughfare of medieval Annecy. The **Porte Ste-Claire**, tightly hemmed in by houses, guarded the way into Annecy from Aix-les-Bains and Chambéry. The **Château d'Annecy** (*open June–Sept daily 10–6; rest of year daily exc Tues 10–12 and 2–6; adm*) lies a short walk up, but a world away from the tourist hordes below. The enormous 13th-century Tour de la Reine forms the oldest part of a massive ensemble from different periods. The 14th–15th-century Gothic Logis Vieux and the 16th-century Renaissance Logis Nemours contain a **regional museum** filled with religious statues and chocolate-box views of Annecy. Many of the rooms are impressive, notably the kitchen with its double fireplace and the guards' room. The **Observatoire Régional des Lacs Alpins** is set apart in the 15th-century Logis Perrière closing off one end of the huge courtyard. It explains the formation of the region's lakes, their fauna and ecology. Up above the castle, the showy white **church of the Visitation** (consecrated in 1949) now holds relics of François de Sales and Jeanne de Chantal, and forms part of the monastery of La Visitation, headquarters of the order.

Not far from Annecy, you can visit the medieval **Château de Montrottier** (*open June–15 Sept daily 9.30–11.30 and 2–5.30; rest of period 15 Mar–15 Oct same times but closed Tues; adm*). The views are especially grand from the top of the round 15th-century keep that rises out of the castle courtyard. Lower down you're shown around the collections of Léon Marès, who bequeathed all to the Académie Florimontane. Among the jaded displays of weapons, tapestries, and Napoleonic objects, the finest works are the Vischers' Renaissance-style bronzes of the Battle of the Centaurs, commissioned by the Fuggers of Augsburg and rejected because they featured too many buttocks. Nearby, the path along the edge of the narrow and precipitous **Gorges du Fier** is best avoided by those who suffer from vertigo.

East of Lac d'Annecy, the **Aravis chain**, rising to around 8,200ft, forms a massive north-south barrier before the Mont Blanc range. Take the picturesque high road via Dingy, Nâves-Parmelan, Villaz and Aviernoz to the **Château de Thorens** (*open July–Aug daily 10–12 and 2–6; May–June and Sept weekends and public hols 2–6; adm*), with its lovely restored towers covered with earth-coloured tiles. The castle was owned by François de Sales the Elder, who had a good eye for art, and acquired beautiful pieces, including a series of early 16th-century Antwerp tapestries. A couple of rooms are devoted to the de Sales' distant descendant, Count Cavour, the headstrong Italian politician who negotiated the ceding of Savoy in 1860 to France in exchange for military help to expel the Austrian army from northern Italy.

From the Château de Thorens a road leads up to the high **plateau of Glières** where a large monument inaugurated in 1973 pays homage to the improbably successful actions of a band of around 500 *maquisards* during the winter of 1944. Vichy made some vain attempts to root them out; over 100 of the *maquisards* were killed, but many more Germans fell, and the tenacity of the Glières Resistance fighters acted both as a spur and a symbol for others. The high meadows of the Glières plateau now provide opportunities for summer walking to the sound of cow bells.

The French Side of Lake Geneva and the Ski Resorts of Haute-Savoie

Lake Geneva

Lake Geneva, or Lac Léman as the French know it, is a little inland sea, where sailing boats tack up and down the great crescent of water. Once past Geneva, most of the south side of the lake is French, strung with beautiful resorts. The best way to get there is the spectacular road over **Mont Salève** which stretches down to Annecy. The views from up top are splendid: the giant fountain in the lake at Geneva is generally visible, and so too are the tallest Alps. On the French side, the little village resorts tip right over into tweedom. **Nernier** occupies a particularly lovely promontory, while **Yvoire** is just too cute, with its old stone houses smothered in flowers in summer. Tourists swarm here in high season to potter around the bazaar. The lakeside is dominated by a castle, its garden now the **Jardin des Cinq Sens** (*open mid-May–mid-Sept daily 10–7; mid-April–mid-May daily 11–6; mid-Sept–mid-Oct daily 1–5; adm*). **Excenevex**, the village just south of Yvoire, boasts the largest, nicest beach on the French side, as well as some of its very poshest villas.

More substantial **Thonon-les-Bains**, once capital of the local Chablais area and much favoured by the lords of Savoy, has a good beach, a sizeable port for boats and yachts and a few old fishermen's cottages. The historic quarter, aloof on its promontory, is connected to the lake by a small cablecar. Here regional culture is celebrated in the **Musée du Chablais** (*contact tourist office for details*). A short way into town lie the interconnecting churches of **St-François de Sales and St-Hippolyte**. The latter is the older, where François de Sales preached to the recalcitrant people of Thonon and won them over. Thonon's lively shopping streets lie nearby.

Surrounded by vineyards east of town, the picturesque **Château de Ripaille** (*contact tourist office for details*) was a hunting lodge of the counts of Savoy. Amédée VIII enlarged it, and retired here with six like-minded gentlemen to devote himself, up to a point, to the holy life, drawing the line at the table; hence the expression '*faire*

Getting Around

Geneva airport is of course very close by. You can reach Thonon and Evian easily by train from Geneva, or from Annecy, Aix-les-Bains or Chambéry to Bourg-St-Maurice. Another train line passing via Chambéry serves the Arc valley, with stops at St-Jean-de-Maurienne and St-Michel-Valloire among others.

Tourist Information

Yvoire: Place de la Mairie, t 04 50 72 80 21, f 04 50 72 84 21.

Thonon-les-Bains: t 04 50 71 55 55, f 04 50 26 68 33.

Evian-les-Bains: t 04 50 75 04 26, f 04 50 75 61 08.

Abondance: t 04 50 73 02 90, f 04 50 73 04 76.

Morzine: t 04 50 74 72 72, f 04 50 79 03 48.

Avoriaz: t 04 50 74 02 11, f 04 50 74 24 29.

Samoëns: t 04 50 34 40 28, f 04 50 34 95 82.

Where to Stay and Eat

Yvoire ✉ **74140**

★★★**Hôtel du Port**, t 04 50 72 80 17, f 04 50 72 90 71 (*moderate*). Irresistible, flower-covered house in stone, by the port and the castle.

Just four rooms, and a restaurant (*menus 170–255F*). *Closed Oct–April, and Wed.*

★★**Le Vieux Logis**, t 04 50 72 80 24, f 04 50 72 90 76 (*moderate*). Ivy-clad hotel up in the village, on the edge of the tourist bazaar. *Closed 1 Dec–14 Mar. Restaurant closed Sun eve and Mon exc July–Aug.*

★★★**Le Pré de la Cure**, t 04 50 72 83 58, f 04 50 72 91 15 (*moderate*). Just outside the main gateway, in an admirable location and with more space. *Closed 16 Nov–2 Mar. Restaurant closed Mar, Oct and Nov, and Wed.*

★★**Les Flots Bleus**, t 04 50 72 80 08, f 04 50 72 84 28 (*inexpensive*). The Hôtel du Port's neighbour and rival, a splendid alternative on the quay, with a few more rooms. *Closed Oct–April.*

Sciez-sur-Léman ✉ **74140**

★★★★**Hôtellerie Château de Coudrée**, t 04 50 72 62 33, f 04 50 72 57 28, coudrée@ relaischateaux.fr (*expensive*). The 12th-century keep of this wonderful lake-side hotel is encased within the wings of the castle. Classic cuisine. *Closed Nov and 24 Jan–3 Mar. Restaurant closed Thurs midday and Weds exc June–Sept.*

Evian-les-Bains ✉ **74500**

★★★★★**Royal** (*expensive*). Outrageous luxury available in this palace, with some

ripaille' for enjoying a hearty banquet. From the early 17th century to the Revolution Carthusian monks settled here. On the tour you're shown their kitchens and wine press. But the bulk of the castle's interiors were redecorated in the 19th and 20th centuries in mock Gothic style with an Art Nouveau twist.

Evian's mineral water was discovered in 1789, beginning its career as a fashionable spa resort. The marina has its share of glamorous boats, and the promenade parterres down by the waterside are immaculately manicured. The rest of the town is a bit of a jumble. The old thermal baths have a somewhat jaded air, while the casino, on the other side, mocks the shape of a Greek-cross church. Up on the main pedestrian street, parallel to the lake, the **Art Nouveau Evian building** cuts a dash. On the street above you can top up on free Evian water at one of the public fountains. •

The Northern Ski Resorts of Haute-Savoie

The pretty roads south from Lake Geneva lead up to the first resorts of the French Alps. The **Dranse d'Abondance valley** takes you up via the little town of Abondance to

spectacular Art Nouveau wall paintings. Highly reputed health and beauty institute, several posh restaurants, beautiful golf course, heliport, and chamber music festival directed by Rostropovich. *Closed 3 Dec–2 Feb.*

****La Verniaz et ses Chalets**, Av d'Abondance, Neuvecelle-Eglise, **t** 04 50 75 04 90, **f** 04 50 70 78 92, *verniaz@relais-chateaux.fr* (*expensive*). Great big luxurious purpose-built rooms spread out in chalets in the well-tended gardens in this plush property above Evian. The restaurant with garden offers very good lake fish. *Closed mid-Feb–mid-Nov. Restaurant closed Tues exc Jul–Aug.*

****Les Prés Fleuris sur Evian**, Route de Thollon, D24, **t** 04 50 75 29 14, **f** 04 50 74 68 75, *presfleuris@relaischateaux.fr*. Another property well located above the lake, this one with many of its rooms enjoying gorgeous views over the waters. The style is of a traditional-style chalet. Refined restaurant. *Closed Oct–May.*

***L'Ermitage**, **t** 04 50 26 85 00, **f** 04 50 75 61 00 (*expensive*). Enormous luxurious early 20th-century hotel close to the Royal, with a luxurious restaurant (*menus 170F–340F*). *Closed 12 Nov–beginning Feb.*

Continental, 65 Rue Nationale, **t** 04 50 75 37 54, **f** 04 50 75 31 11 (*inexpensive*). Central, charming and affordable. No restaurant.

Le Chablais, Rue du Chablais, Publier, c. 4km west of Evian, **t** 04 50 75 28 06, **f** 04 50 74 67 32 (*inexpensive*). Lake view at a reasonable price. Clean rooms, decent meals.

Thollon-les-Memises ✉ 74500

Bon Séjour, **t** 04 50 70 92 65, **f** 04 50 70 95 72 (*inexpensive*). Sweet old-styled family hotel a bit above lake-side village of Meillerie.

Morzine ✉ 74110

***La Bergerie**, Rue du Téléphérique, **t** 04 50 79 13 69, **f** 04 50 75 95 71, *hotelbergerie@portesdusoleil.com* (*moderate*). A very jolly, colourful chalet. No restaurant. *Closed mid-Sep–20 Dec and 15 April–end Jun.*

Samoëns ✉ 74340

Le Moulin du Bathieu, **t** 04 50 34 48 07, **f** 04 50 34 43 25 (*inexpensive*). Picturesque chalet up among sloping meadows, with wonderful views and the merry sound of running water nearby. (From the valley follow signs for Samoëns 1600.)

Les Sept Monts, **t** 04 50 34 40 58, **f** 04 50 34 13 89 (*inexpensive*). A bright and appealing modern chalet down in the centre of Samoëns.

the well-located resort of Châtel by the Swiss border. The pride of Abondance is the vestiges of its Augustinian **abbey**, one of the most important in the Alps in medieval times. Some of its cloisters have been preserved, covered with striking 15th-century frescoes. The treasury museum contains an amusing clutter of religious objects and paintings. **Châtel's** south-facing chalets receive the sun late into the afternoon.

Follow the **Dranse de Morzine valley** south from Thonon-les-Bains to reach the resorts of **Les Gets**, Morzine and Avoriaz. Chic boutiques line the main street of **Morzine**, but somehow the centre lacks character despite the church with its spiked onion dome. In summer, the slopes around Morzine attract mountain bikers. **Avoriaz** is just about the most dramatic of all the modern French Alpine resorts. It stands at the heart of the Portes du Soleil skiing area, which is lively all year round, making the narrow hairpin bends down to the emerald green **Lac de Montriond** all the more dangerous, as they're often crawling with cars.

The wide, fertile **Giffre valley** to the south, peppered with fruit trees and waterfalls, has a scattering of delightful old hamlets, all of which are outdone by Samoëns, reached most dramatically from Morzine via the lofty **Col de Joux**. **Samoëns**, overlooked by the pyramidal tops of the Tuet and Criou, is an old Alpine village which has sprawled out from its centre in a friendly, higgledy-piggledy manner. Beyond the covered market lies the church with a square tower, its door guarded by two Chinese-looking lions at the base of columns, a Lombard conceit common in the old churches here. To one side of the church rises the delightful **Alpine garden** created by a local girl made good who co-founded the Samaritaine department store in Paris. At the **Cirque du Fer à Cheval**, a score of waterfalls drop from great heights.

Mont Blanc and Chamonix

And so to Europe's greatest summit, Mont Blanc, whose 15,767ft peak can surprise you from 100km away and more, suddenly looming in the distance. From up close it makes a truly overwhelming sight. To get there, join the Arve valley from Geneva to Chamonix, or take the prettier (but slower) approach via Mégève, easily reached from Annecy or Albertville.

Getting Around

The Tramway du Mont Blanc, from St-Gervais or from Le Fayet, t 04 50 47 51 83, t 04 50 78 32 75, goes up to 7780ft, at the foot of the Bionnassay glacier.

Tourist Information

Mégève: B.P.24, t 04 50 21 27 28, t 04 50 93 03 09.
Combloux: B.P.38, t 04 50 58 60 49, t 04 50 93 33 55.
St-Gervais: t 04 50 47 76 08, t 04 50 47 75 69.
Chamonix Mont Blanc: B.P.25, t 04 50 53 00 24, t 04 50 53 58 90.

Where to Stay and Eat

La Clusaz ✉ 74220
★★★**Carlina**, t 04 50 02 43 48, t 04 50 02 63 02, carlina@cyberaccess.fr (moderate). Many-gabled modern chalet-style building overlooking the pleasing resort, with lovely south-facing balconies in light wood.

Mégève ✉ 74120
★★★★**Hôtel du Mont Blanc**, Place de l'Eglise, t 04 50 21 20 02, t 04 50 21 45 28 (expensive). Right in the heart of the action, with lovely balconies and luxurious rooms. No restaurant. Closed 1 May–10 Jun.

★★★★**Chalet St-Georges**, 159 Rue Monseigneur Conseil, t 04 50 93 07 15, t 04 50 21 51 18 (expensive). Right by the cablecar in the centre of Mégève, a very bright, light-wood chalet with excellent rooms. Closed end Sept–14 Dec and 24 April–24 Jun.
★★**Chalet des Ours**, 39 Chemin des Roseaux, t 04 50 21 57 40, t 04 50 93 05 73 (inexpensive). A really delightful good-value option in the centre of this pricey resort.
★★**Gai Soleil**, 343 Rue du Crêt du Midi, t 04 50 21 00 70, f 04 50 58 74 50 (inexpensive). Another comfortable option, with more space and some nice balconies in a large chalet to the side of the resort. Closed 16 April–14 Jun and 16 Sep–14 Dec.

Combloux ✉ 74920
★★★**Idéal-Mont-Blanc**, 419 Route du Feug, t 04 50 58 60 54, f 04 50 58 64 50, ideal-mont-blanc@aol.com (moderate). A chalet with splendid views of the Mont Blanc range, including from the covered heated pool and the restaurant. Closed Easter–10 Jun and 21 Sep–19 Dec.

Servoz ✉ 74320
Gîte de l'Alpe, t 04 50 47 22 66. One of a handful of good-value, old-fashioned chalets with simple accommodation in this sprawling village. So close to Mont Blanc, Servoz has wonderful views, but hasn't been as marred by tourism.

The resort of **La Clusaz** in the **Aravis mountain chain**, is modern, but extremely picturesque, its chalets climbing up out of a steep valley bowl. South of La Clusaz, the road via the **Col des Aravis** with its view of Mont Blanc and cutesy chapel takes you to Flumet and **Mégève**. One of the oldest Alpine resorts, it caters to the chic and the flush. Although Mont Blanc lies tantalizingly close, you can only see it if you take a cablecar, or (serious mountain climbers only) make it to the top of Mont Joly. The views of Mont Blanc from **Cordon** and **Combloux** are unimpeded and almost unbelievable, totally filling the end of the Arve valley.

Popular **St-Gervais-les-Bains** is the tradtional base for the ascent of Mont Blanc, although you can't actually see the big mountain from here. Join the mountaineers on the highest train journey in France, the wonderful **Tramway du Mont Blanc** (*see* p.845) up to the Nid d'Aigle (7,78oft) at the foot of the Bionnassay glacier below the peak of Mont Blanc, where you can go walking. For a more peaceful drive through the Arve valley, with better views of Mont Blanc, take the high road via Passy, Plateau d'Assy and Servoz on the north side of the river.

Chamonix-Mont Blanc ✉ 74400

****Auberge du Bois Prin**, 69 Chemin de l'Hermine, Les Moussoux, t 04 50 53 33 51, f 04 50 53 48 75, *boisprin@relaischateaux.fr* (*expensive*). In a way, the most exclusive address in Chamonix, actually on the slopes west above town, facing Mont Blanc, close to the ski slopes and the Téléphérique du Brévent – a lovely little family chalet run to the highest standards, with just 11 rooms. *Closed 25 April–11 May, Nov, and Weds midday.*

*****Le Hameau Albert 1er**, 119 Impasse Montenvers, B.P.55, t 04 50 53 05 09, f 04 50 55 95 48 (*expensive*). The most established luxury hotel in the resort, with a splendid restaurant, but the location isn't that brilliant. *Closed 8–18 May and 5 Nov–5 Dec.*

****Le Mont Blanc**, 62 Allée du Majestic, B.P.135, t 04 50 53 05 64, f 04 50 55 89 44 (*expensive*). Glamorous suites, and some slightly cheaper options. *Closed 20 Oct–15 Dec.*

***Hermitage-Paccard**, Rte des Cristalliers, t 04 50 53 13 87, f 04 50 55 98 14 (*moderate*). Back above town, a comfortable option opposite the Mer de Glace glacier. *Closed 25 Sep–17 Dec and 25 April–16 Jun. Restaurant closed midday in winter exc weekends.*

La Croix Blanche, 87 Rue Vallot, t 04 50 53 00 11, f 04 50 53 48 83 (*moderate*). Nice, and very central. *Closed 3 May–30 Jun.*

***Le Faucigny**, 118 Place de l'Eglise, t/f 04 50 53 01 17 (*inexpensive*). Central and with some mountain views.

***Richemond**, B.P.68, t 04 50 53 08 85, f 04 50 55 91 69 (*inexpensive*). Reasonable, if a tad old-fashioned.

*Le Louvre**, Impasse Androsace, t 04 50 53 00 51, f 04 50 53 70 39 (*cheap*). Centrally located simple hotel; some of the central balconies have fantastic views.

***Eden**, 35 Route des Goudenays, Chamonix-Praz, t 04 50 53 18 43, f 04 50 53 51 50 (*inexpensive*). A stylish option. *Closed 1–15 Jun; Nov; Mon evenings and Thurs out of season.*

***Les Rhododendrons**, Chamonix-Praz (north of the centre) t 04 50 53 06 93, f 04 50 53 55 76 (*inexpensive*). Pleasant big black chalet-style hotel by the roadside.

Le Lavancher ✉ 74400

****Hôtel du Jeu de Paume**, 705 Route du Chapeau, t 04 50 54 03 76, f 04 50 54 10 75 (*expensive*). Lots of balconies make the most of the tremendous views from this chalet on the slopes above the road linking Chamonix with Argentière. *Closed 5 Sep–5 Dec and 5 May–5 Jul.*

***Beausoleil**, t 04 50 54 00 78, f 04 50 54 17 34 (*inexpensive*). Sweet Alpine rooms in a pleasant family-run hotel. *Closed 20 Sep–20 Dec.*

Climbing Mont Blanc

Given the millions of visitors who come here every year, accidents are still relatively rare, but if you want to climb Mont Blanc you must be accompanied by a professional guide or organize your expedition with the authorities. Contact the experts in the Compagnie des Guides, t 04 50 53 00 88. A tour of Mont Blanc by helicopter is a more expensive option. For mere mortals, there are several exhilarating cablecar and train trips up the slopes around Chamonix. None are cheap, but a view of Mont Blanc close up is an unforgettable experience. However, the weather here is often unpredictable, so consider staying a few days for a better chance of seeing the spectacular summit.

The Aiguille du Midi (reserve tickets in advance, t 04 50 53 40 00) is the closest most visitors come to the top of Mont Blanc. If you only have time to take one trip in these mountains, this is the one to choose. The cablecar and lift take you up in three stages. The first viewing platform isn't of much interest, but the second is stupendous, and the third even better. Here you find yourself perched on a platform at roughly 12,000ft. You can see ant-sized climbers, and below the Aiguille du Midi you might make out their tiny camps in the snow. From level two there's the possibility of another exhilarating cablecar ride, which whisks you away across sparkling white glaciers to the Hellbronner peak on the Italian border.

The journey by little red mountain train to the Mer de Glace glacier (from Montenvers station just behind Chamonix's main railway station) is less spectacular and less frightening, taking you up to a mere 6,275ft. In summer the Mer de Glace can look decidedly grubby, with stone débris covering the surface. Its main attraction is an ice grotto, carved afresh each year. The outsized rooms, furnished with ice furniture, wax models, and a couple of live St Bernards, may seem a bit naff, but it is amazing to stare into the transparent top layers of the glacier. Further up, there are displays on crystals and fauna, and a café from which you can watch parties walking on the glacier. Contact the tourist office well in advance if you want to join them.

Many locals will tell you, however, that the finest views of Mont Blanc are to be had from points above the western side of town. Either take the cablecar up to Le Brévent (book in advance, t 04 50 53 13 18) at just over 8,200ft, or go to Les Praz, just north of Chamonix, to take the cablecar for La Flégère. This side of the Arve is for skiers. In 1924 Chamonix hosted the Winter Olympics, and the winter sports facilities have kept up with the times. In summer there are innumerable walking possibilities, especially to the lakes high up west of the Arve. Just don't expect to be alone.

Chamonix is a mountain Mecca, a resort of high drama, dreams and tragedy. Some say that a group of Englishmen put Chamonix on the map in the 1740s. Mountaineering fever gripped the village from 1760, when one Monsieur de Saussure offered a reward to the first person to get to the top of Mont Blanc, otherwise known as the Montagne Maudite (the Cursed Mountain). Messrs Paccard and Balmat were apparently the first to climb Mont Blanc in 1786. De Saussure followed the next year, as did Colonel Beaufoy, the first Englishman. There's some dispute over the first woman to climb Mont Blanc. Marie Paradis reached the top in 1809, but was carried a good deal of the way by friends, so the honour goes to Henriette d'Angerville. Many died trying, and often their frozen bodies were only discovered decades later. Chamonix is still associated with danger. In 1999 heavy snows led to more avalanches than usual, and many more deaths. A fire in the Tunnel du Mont-Blanc the same year killed over 40 people, instigating an array of new safety features.

Argentière, close to the source of the Arve, has slopes for experienced skiers and glaciers, visible in summer by taking the cablecar up to the **Aiguille des Grands Montets** (*reserve tickets in advance,* **t** *04 50 54 00 71*), but you'll need serious mountaineering equipment. The view up the white valley is magical, ending with Mont Dolent whose summit marks the point where France, Switzerland and Italy meet.

The Upper Isère and Arc Valleys

The second great French Alpine range is the Massif de la Vanoise, its centre now a national park. Its highest peaks reach well over 11,000ft. The upper Isère river carves a sensational, jagged path from its source above the Val d'Isère to Albertville, passing roads to Méribel, Courchevel and Tignes – some of the most reputed ski resorts in the world, although most are just architectural messes. Smaller, prettier places include La Rosière or Champagny-en-Vanoise, and down in the valley, Moûtiers or Aime. The less well known but spectacular Arc valley circles the south side of the Vanoise range.

Albertville and the Beaufortain

Set on a big elbow in the Isère, industrial **Albertville's** claim to fame is having hosted the Winter Olympics in 1992. Mainly a modern creation, it was named after its founder in 1836, Charles-Albert of Savoy. It has recently acquired several funky modern buildings, while the central Place de l'Europe is an outrageous apricoty-pink creation in Italian fascist style. On the nearby hillside, the overprettified village of **Conflans** now uses its 14th-century buildings to house craft shops and restaurants. From the esplanade there are wide views of the Isère valley and on to the slope-side 16th-century castle of Manuel de Locatel, now a cultural centre.

East of Albertville, the beautiful cheese-making area around **Beaufort** produces delicious big round *fromages* with concave sides, which you can taste at the cooperative. North of Beaufort, **Hauteluce**, high above the Dorinet river, is one of the prettiest places in Savoy, 'sitting under the gaze of Mont Blanc'. The remnants of a medieval castle lie below the village, and in the centre, the onion steeple of the church stands out. The Baroque interior has a major retable and Crucifixion figures in gilded robes.

Up by the high pass of the Col des Saisies, the well-planned modern resort of **Les Saisies** was built for cross-country skiing. The terrain here proved a good dropping point for munitions for the Resistance in the Second World War. Due south of Beaufort, an idyllic road leads to the villages of Arèches and Boudin. In summer, you can take an austere, almost treeless route east from the nearby **Col de Méraillet**, with its superlative views of Mont Blanc, to Bourg-St-Maurice. There are very few habitations on this high road, and absolutely no ski resorts.

Tourist Information

Albertville: t 04 79 32 04 22, f 04 79 32 87 09.
Beaufort: t 04 79 38 1 3, f 04 79 38 16 70.
Moûtiers: t 04 79 24 04 23, f 04 79 24 56 05.
Val-Thorens: t 04 79 00 08 08, f 04 79 00 00 04.
Méribel: t 04 79 08 60 01, f 04 79 00 59 61.
Courchevel: t 04 79 08 41 60.
Pralognan-la-Vanoise: t 04 79 08 79 08, t 04 79 08 76 74.
La Plagne: t 04 79 09 79 79, t 04 79 09 70 10.
La Rosière: t 04 79 06 80 51, t 04 79 06 83 20.
Val d'Isère: t 04 79 06 06 60, t 04 79 06 04 56.
Bessans: t 04 79 05 96 52, t 04 79 05 83 11.
Aussois: t 04 79 20 30 80, t 04 79 20 37 00.

Where to Stay and Eat

Méribel-les-Allues ✉ 73550
★★★Le Yéti, t 04 79 00 51 15, t 04 79 00 51 73, yeleti@lapaste.fr (*expensive*). This chalet has it all – proximity to the ski lifts, superb views and lovely rooms. *Closed 28 Aug–15 Dec and 26 April–1 July.*
★★Adray-Télébar, t 04 79 08 60 26, t 04 79 08 53 85 (*expensive*). Very popular chalet with a much-loved terrace and simple, though pricey, rooms. *Closed 20 April–20 Dec.*

La Rosière ✉ 73700
★★Plein Soleil, t 04 79 06 80 43, t 04 79 06 83 65 (*inexpensive*). Fabulous views from this cheerful little hotel on the side of the resort.

★★Le Relais du Petit St-Bernard, t 04 79 06 80 48, t 04 79 06 83 40 (*inexpensive*). Great views too beyond the wide parking lot.

Val d'Isère ✉ 73150
★★★★★Christiana t 04 79 06 08 25, t 04 79 41 11 10, christiana-valdisere@laposte.fr (*expensive*). Pine paradise, but you have to pay for the privilege. *Closed 1 May–1 Dec.*
★★★★Le Blizzard, t 04 79 06 02 07, t 04 79 06 04 94 (*expensive*). Loads of balconies and decorative touches give a personal feel. *Closed 8 May–5 Jul and 30 Aug–3 Dec.*
★★★La Savoyarde, B.P.53, t 04 79 06 01 55, t 04 79 41 11 29, moris@infonie.fr (*moderate*). A more traditional-looking large chalet with good amenities (*menu 88F*). *Closed May-Dec.*

Aussois ✉ 73500
★★★Du Soleil, 15 Rue de l'Eglise, t 04 79 20 32 42, t 04 79 20 37 78 (*moderate*). Some warm, cosy rooms in the centre of the village, with an amusing games and relaxation terrace. *Hotel closed 15 April–15 Jun and 1 Oct–17 Dec.*
★★Les Mottets, 6 Rue des Mottets, t 04 79 20 30 86, t 04 79 20 34 22 (*inexpensive*). Plain, central hotel with some very merry Alpine painting inside and good family cooking. *Closed 1 Nov–15 Dec.*

Valloire ✉ 73450
★★Christiania, t 04 79 59 00 57, t 04 79 59 00 06 (*inexpensive*). Cheerful to brash, a popular stopping point in this lively resort. *Closed 20 April–15 Jun and 15 Sep–1 Dec.*

From Moûtiers to Val d'Isère

The Isère valley's steep sides are so densely wooded between Albertville and Moûtiers that there's little to distract you along the way. **Moûtiers**, caught by another elbow turn of the Isère, is an historical town with an Italianate heart. The bishops' palace is now a museum of Baroque art and local traditions.

Val-Thorens lies far down its own separate Alpine valley, an exceptional number of ski lifts strung out along its length, linking it with other valleys. Joined to its more famous neighbours Méribel and Courchevel to the east, this area – **Les Trois Vallées** – boasts the largest interconnecting network of ski runs in the world. Exclusive **Méribel** with its heliport is also tucked away down its own private wooded valley. This is the Isère valley resort with the most style. The high road connecting Méribel and Courchevel passes through that rarity in these parts, a genuine old settlement,

Méribel-Village. The messy resort of **Courchevel** has centres on three levels. The lowest, Courchevel 1550, is much the nicest, with a reputation for glamour in winter.

More delightful little resorts lie east of Courchevel, on the edge of the Vanoise national park. **Champagny-en-Vanoise** is made up entirely of chalets, with an orangey church crowning the hillock in front of it. Inside, the Baroque retable, the silliest in Savoy, looks like it's been attacked by a swarm of pink putti. A precipitous road leads to **Champagny-d'en-Haut** and a delightful flat valley, with a few old hamlets strung along the roadside. Walking paths head into the Vanoise national park. More paths start at **Pralognan-La-Vanoise**, further into the park. The resort is known for cross-country skiing in winter and for walking and climbing in summer.

The valley town of **Aime** has a severe 11th-century Romanesque church, unusual for the region. In the cubic forms of the main church a few fragments of frescoes remain in place, including one of the Creation and another of the Massacre of the Innocents. Head down into the dark depths of the double crypt below. Several clearly inscribed stones recall that a Gallo-Roman settlement grew up here.

Further up, **La Plagne**, a major ski resort, consists of several centres in different styles. At La Roche, you can't miss the huge worm of a bobsleigh track used for the Olympics. Above them, La Plagne 1800 has some stylish architecture, while La Plagne-Aime has monster step-balconied buildings. The beautiful slopes above old Bourg-St-Maurice have been colonized by the three massive new resorts of **Les Arcs**. Its Kilomètre Lancé is legendary among skiers for recording-breaking speeds. Les Arcs 1600 is the oldest of the three, with a pleasant if artificial village atmosphere. Les Arcs 1800 is popular with families both in summer and in winter, offering all manner of activities. Les Arcs 2000 is more remote.

La Rosière, high above Séez, has the most spectacular location of all the Isère valley resorts, overlooking a sharp turn in the river's course. To the west, ridge upon ridge of mountains melt into the distance. To the south, you look down the tight upper Isère valley to Tignes and Val d'Isère. At the nearby **Col du Petit St-Bernard**, a once-important route into Italy, the rather grim-looking remnants of St Bernard's medieval Hospice du Petit-St-Bernard are being restored.

In summer, you might take the vertiginous routes higher up the valley, past perched villages. From La Rosière, the whitewashed church of **Le Châtelard** stands out like a beacon on the slopes. Past the picturesque hamlet of **Le Moulin**, you come to the dark, stepped chalets of **Le Miroir**. By the big, artificial Lac de Chervil, its dam covered by a vast painting, a road leads up to the resort of **Tignes**, where the skiing makes up for the architectural eyesores. **Val d'Isère**, the final, exclusive resort at the end of the valley, has more style, and a glamorous reputation. The Route des Grandes Alpes, linking Lake Geneva with the Mediterranean, takes you south of Val d'Isère by the **Col de l'Iseran**, Europe's highest road pass at more than 9,000ft.

The Arc Valley

Separated by the enormous bulk of the Vanoise range, the rivers Isère and Arc meet a short way south of Albertville. The Arc river starts on the southern side of the Col d'Iseran by the Italian frontier. Its valley is more industrial than the Isère, but the old villages near its source have preserved some delightful churches. **Bonneval-sur-Arc** is very, very pretty, its houses covered with slabs tinged orange with lichen in summer, although many of them have been turned into tourist shops. **Le Villaron**, an irresistible old Alpine hamlet just before Bessans, is only accessible by foot. Over the Arc, the **Avérole valley** offers a calm retreat, covered in a profusion of flowers in summer. Although destroyed in large part in the war, **Bessans** has a church and chapel that mercifully survived on a hillock above town. Start by visiting the **Chapelle St-Antoine** (*small fee*). One outer side is decorated with worn frescoes on which a few noble figures stand out, but not as clearly as two extraordinary beasts, one a bit like a cheetah. Inside, the paintings represent more conventional episodes in Christ's life. The church contains a colourful array of statues of saints, although the main woodworking tradition in the village is of carving devils.

At **Lanslevillard**, try to get into the **Chapelle St-Sébastien** for the charming naive frescoes of the lives of Christ and Sebastian. Lanslevillard's larger twin, **Lanslebourg**, has less charm, but its **Espace Baroque Maurienne** in a former church gives a good introduction to the local Baroque. West of Lanslebourg, the valley becomes industrial, avoidable if you climb to Aussois. This slopes here bristle with **forts**, a few of which you can visit. They were built to defend Savoy from France, but one, Fort St-Gobain close to Avrieux, formed part of the 1930s French Maginot line. **Aussois** is a sunny village resort, facing the summits of the Italian frontier. In the old village, the church has a Baroque interior; after a restrained Annunciation at the entrance and hell-fire Last Judgement in the porch, it's all floating putti within. In summer, Aussois serves as the southern gateway to the hiking tracks through the Vanoise national park, here dominated by the dramatic **Dent Parrachée**. A few kilometres east of Aussois in the woods stands a towering monolith that looks like a giant menhir; other natural menhirs pop their heads out of the surrounding pines. The village of **Avrieux** boasts one of the most extravagant Baroque churches in the valley.

A loop of roads from industrial St-Jean-de-Maurienne leads up to the eastern side of the Belledonne range via the D926 and back down via the D927, offering superb views of Mont Blanc in the distance. Some way north, the Arc finally joins the Isère.

Grenoble

With valleys leading off towards Savoy and Switzerland to the north, Provence and Italy to the south, and the Rhône Valley to the west, Grenoble was an obvious location for the commercial, cultural and intellectual capital of the Dauphiné region. Tarnished with a reputation for being uncompromisingly modern and industrial, it turns out to be a cosmopolitan place, with wonderful squares, and as many museums as there are months of the year, and a fine history.

History

In the Middle Ages, the counts of Albon took over a vast swathe of land stretching from the Rhône to Savoy. One, Guigues IV, was given the name Dauphin, which was

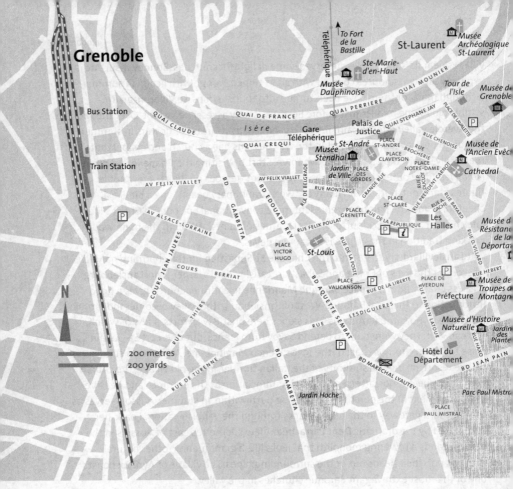

Grenoble

Bus Station

Train Station

Télésphérique

To Fort de la Bastille

St-Laurent

Musée Archéologique St-Laurent

Ste-Marie-d'en-Haut

Musée Dauphinoise

Tour de l'Isle

Musée de Grenoble

QUAI CLAUDE

QUAI DE FRANCE

Isère

QUAI PERRIERE

QUAI MOUNIER

QUAI CREQUI

Gare Téléphérique

Palais de Justice

QUAI STEPHANE JAY

PLACE DE LAVALETTE

Musée Stendhal

St-André

PLACE ST-ANDRE

RUE CHENOISE

Musée de l'Ancien Evêch

AV FELIX VIALLET

AV FELIX VIALLET

RUE DE BELGRADE

Jardin de Ville

RUE MONTORGE

PLACE DES GORDES

RUE BROCHERIE

PLACE CLAVEYSON

PLACE NOTRE-DAME

Cathedral

BD GAMBETTA

BD EDOUARD REY

GRANDE RUE

PLACE ST-CLARE

RUE PRESIDENT CARNOT

RUE A. GACHE

RUE BAYARD

AV ALSACE-LORRAINE

PLACE GRENETTE

RUE DE LA REPUBLIQUE

Les Halles

Musée d Résistano de la Déporta

COURS JEAN JAURES

PLACE VICTOR HUGO

St-Louis

RUE FELIX POULAT

RUE DE LA POSTE

RUE DE LA LIBERTE

PLACE DE VERDUN

RUE HEBERT

Musée de Troupes d Montagn

COURS BERRIAT

BD AQUETTE SEMBAT

PLACE VAUCANSON

LESDIGUIERES

RUE FANTIN LATOUR

Préfecture

RUE THIERS

RUE

Musée d'Histoire Naturelle

Jardin des Plante

200 metres

200 yards

RUE DE TURENNE

BD MARECHAL LYAUTEY

Hôtel du Département

BD JEAN PAIN

N

BD GAMBETTA

Jardin Hoche

PLACE PAUL MISTRAL

Parc Paul Mistra

then adopted by the counts who followed him; by the late 13th century, the whole region was known as the Dauphiné. Philippe VI bought the Dauphiné in 1349, and gave it to his eldest son, and from this time on the eldest sons of the ruling kings of France were known as *dauphins*. In the Wars of Religion, the Protestant leader Lesdiguières secured Grenoble on behalf of Henri IV in 1590. While the Catholic Church hit back in the 17th century by building religious communities around town, this period proved relatively prosperous for the city. Despite an image of aristocratic elegance, Grenoble became a hot bed of sedition as the Ancien Régime tottered. The famed Journée des Tuiles, 7 June 1788, was a riot brought about by the monarchy's attempt to close the regional Parlement. When royalist troops attempted to quell the unrest, many Grenoblois threw tiles from the roofs, an action often portrayed as a precursor of Bastille Day. Henri Beyle, better known by his pseudonym Stendhal, recorded his impressions of the Revolution as a boy in Grenoble.

Industrialization and working class struggles came relatively early to Grenoble. And so did skiing. The first attempts at introducing the sport into France took place at Chamrousse in 1889. A major armaments centre during the First World War, Grenoble

Getting Around

Grenoble is just under 3hrs from Paris-Gare de Lyon. Ordinary trains between Grenoble and Lyon take around 2hrs. The regional airport of Grenoble-St-Geoirs is around 40km northwest of the city but it is handy for the Alpine resorts.

Tourist Information

Grenoble: 14 Rue de la République, t 04 76 42 41 41, f 04 76 00 18 98.

Where to Stay and Eat

Grenoble ✉ 38000

****Park Hôtel, 10 Place Paul Mistral, t 04 76 85 81 23, f 04 76 46 49 88 (*expensive*). Looking out on to the picturesque Paul Mistral park, the luxury option in central Grenoble. *Closed 29 Jul–20 Aug and 23 Dec–2 Jan. Restaurant closed Sun midday and hols.*
***Hôtel d'Angleterre, 5 Place Victor Hugo, t 04 76 87 37 21, f 04 76 50 94 10 (*moderate*). Pleasant and central. No restaurant.

**L'Europe, 22 Place Grenette, t/f 04 76 46 16 94 (*inexpensive*). Central hotel in a Hausmannian-style block with wrought-iron decoration, and modern rooms.
**L'Escalier, 6 Place Lavalette, t 04 76 54 66 16, f 04 76 63 01 58. Excellent restaurant close to the fine arts museum, serving classic French cuisine . *Closed Sat midday and Sun.*
Le Mal Assis, 9 Rue Bayard, t 04 76 54 75 93. A small restaurant in the cathedral quarter, with plenty of atmosphere.
Some of the best options are outside town:

Eybens ✉ 38320

***Château de la Commanderie, 17 Av d'Echirolles, t 04 76 25 34 58, f 04 76 24 07 31 (*moderate*). An historic house set in pleasant grounds just south of Grenoble. Stylish rooms and a terrace for summer (*menus 169–310F*). *Restaurant closed 23 Dec–6 Jan; Sat midday, Sun evenings and Mon.*

Bresson ✉ 38320

****Chavant, t 04 76 25 25 38, t 04 76 62 06 55 (*expensive*). A reputed family hotel and restaurant in this pretty village a short way south of Grenoble (*menus 290–410F*). *Closed 25–31 Dec. Restaurant closed Sat lunch, Mon.*

was then left with a legacy of metal and chemical plants. During the Second World War, Grenoble, as with much of the French Alps, was occupied by the Italians. Although Pétain and other Vichy notables were warmly greeted when they came to the city, Grenoble became the main centre of Resistance in the Alps and was awarded the Croix de la Libération. A large university town, Grenoble is now renowned for its European research facilites. The chemical industry has also developed along its valleys. But pleasure is never far away: the city hosted the Winter Olympics in 1968 and it is the major gateway to the Alpine resorts in the Parc National des Ecrins.

Touring Grenoble

From the heart of town, bubble cars will take you up high over the metallic grey-green waters of the Isère to the **Fort de la Bastille**, which guards the city from the north. From here you'll see how Grenoble sprawls in its flat valley, surrounded by high drama. On clear days you can see Mont Blanc; nearer giants include Taillefer (9,371ft), and Obiou (9,151ft). On the slopes below the fort, Grenoble's oldest church is now the **Musée Archéologique St-Laurent** (*open daily exc Tues 9–12 and 2–6; adm*). From the 4th century a Christian necropolis was established here, just outside the city and protected from the floods of the Isère. At the end of the 5th century a rectangular chapel went up. A rare little funerary church in the shape of a cross, with trefoil ends to each arm, was built on the site in the 6th century. This was transformed in the 8th and 9th centuries, each arm converted into a crypt, with a new church built on top. Then in the 11th and 12th centuries the church was transformed as part of a Benedictine priory. Through its now floorless nave, amid a jumble of gaping tombs, you can make out the rounded ends of the Merovingian church. Alarming swastikas feature on the ceiling; when they were painted in 1910 they were solar symbols. The crypt of St-Oyand, named after a monk from the Jura, has beautiful Carolingian decoration. Wolfish monsters and birds feature among the foliage of the carved capitals.

Outside, the narrow **St-Laurent quarter**, with its massive 14th-century gateway, its 19th-century fortified terraces and ethnic restaurants, is more laid-back than central Grenoble on the other bank. A steep walk up the hill takes you to the **Musée Dauphinois** (*open 2 May–Oct daily exc Tues 10–7; rest of year daily exc Tues 10–6; adm*), which occupies a former convent, Ste-Marie-d'en-Haut, built during the Counter-Reformation by François de Sales' and Jeanne de Chantal's Order of the Visitation (*see* Annecy). Its nuns came from wealthy families, and the architecture has a spacious air, although the interiors are much transformed, having served from the Revolution as prison, school, barracks and housing centre for immigrants. However, the Baroque chapel has survived intact, covered head to toe with paintings depicting the life of François de Sales. The outrageous gilded retable with twisted columns is topped by a figure of God looking like a wild-eyed preacher. The museum has two permanent collections, one on Alpine village life, the other devoted to the history of skiing, while temporary exhibitions on aspects of the Dauphiné are put on in the other spaces.

The main historic centre lies on the other bank. Head first for the grand **Place Notre-Dame**, in the quarter where the bishops of Grenoble held sway in medieval times. The **cathedral** itself looks like it's had to jostle to stay on the square, town houses shouldering in on its sides. The stocky front is topped by a mighty, square brick bell tower which went up in the early 13th century. From inside the cathedral you can visit the adjoining church of **St-Hugues**, a grim and messy early-Gothic building.

While a new tramway was being built here in the 1980s, vestiges were unearthed of earlier episcopal buildings (including a rare 5th-century baptistry) and Gallo-Roman walls, now well housed in the **Musée de l'Ancien Evêché** (*open daily exc Tues 10–7, Wed till 10pm; adm*). The different eras in the Dauphiné's civilizations are covered, starting with prehistoric hunter-gatherers. The section on the Dark Ages boasts the famous Vézeronce helmet, also known as Clodomir's helmet, after a Frankish prince who was killed at the Battle of Vézeronce near the Rhône in 524. With its superb frieze decorated with tiny grapes and birds, it may have been made in Byzantium, and was probably purely ceremonial. The history of the medeival lords of the Dauphiné is covered, and the foundation of three religious orders in the 11th century – the Antonine, the Chalais, absorbed by the Cistercians, and the Chartreuse or Carthusian, founded by St Bruno in the Chartreuse range just north of Grenoble.

The swish modern **Musée de Grenoble** (*open daily exc Tues 11–7, Wed till 10pm; adm*), built in the 1990s, stands on the eastern edge of the historic centre, near the river.

The city's connection with Champollion, who was educated here and went on to decipher hieroglyphics, explains the Egyptian works here. Paintings, however, form the bulk of the collection: among the highlights are Perugino's St Sebastian, Giuseppe Cesari's portrait of an architect. Rubens' Pope Gregory surrounded by saints, and works by Philippe de Champaigne, Vouet and Claude Lorrain (a typically enchanting Italian landscape) and an extraordinary series of New Testament scenes by Zurbarán. David's 1780 *Tête de Femme* looks like a precursor of Lucien Freud. Henri Fanti-Latour, of Grenoble, gets his own space. Grenoble boasts one of the finest modern art collections in France outside Paris. There are good Fauvist and Cubist pieces, a few wonderful Matisses, and canvases by the likes of Léger and Modigliani. The 14th-century Tour de l'Isle, built as the seat of the consuls of Grenoble, has been converted to display drawings, while major sculptors feature outside in the sculpture park.

West of the Musée de Grenoble lie the liveliest, most atmospheric streets of Grenoble. Sumptuous residences built for members of the Parlement stand along Rue Chenoise and Rue Brocherie, which lead to the city's prettiest square, **Place St-André**, overseen by the former **Parlement du Dauphiné**, and by the church of **St-André**. Watch the world go by from the terrace of the Café de la Table Ronde, the second oldest café in France. The adjoining **Place des Gordes** leads to the **Jardin de Ville** created for Lesdiguières. The **Musée Stendhal** (*open daily exc Mon 2–6; adm*) occupies part of Lesdiguières' townhouse; the **Maison Stendhal** (*open daily exc Mon 9–12; adm*), in a house once owned by the writer's grandfather, lies off the Grande Rue. Both museums prove disappointingly dreary for such a passionate Romantic.

Around Grenoble

Surrounded by weird and wonderful limestone summits, Grenoble has one of the most spectacular natural settings of any French town. To the north rises the Massif de la Chartreuse – where the Carthusian monastic order was born and Chartreuse liqueur was invented. East of Grenoble rises the almost impenetrable Chaîne de Belledonne. To the south, between the Isère and Drac valleys, the sheer walls of the Vercors range were important hide-outs of the Resistance.

Chamrousse was one of the earliest ski resorts in France, posted at the south end of the Belledonne chain. Although not well-known these days, it hosted Winter Olympic downhill competitions in 1968, when the legendary skier, Jean-Claude Killy, won three gold medals. Set in splendid grounds, the **Château de Vizille** (*open June–Aug daily exc Tues 9am–10pm; April–May and Sept–Oct daily exc Tues 9–7; rest of year daily exc Tues 10–5; grounds free; adm for château*) was built from 1600 to 1619 for Lesdiguières, and houses an engrossing **Museum of the French Revolution** (*open April–Oct daily exc Tues 10–6; rest of year exc public hols and Tues 10–5; adm*). On 21 July 1788 it hosted the celebrated meeting of the representatives of the three estates of the Dauphiné in a ground-breaking act of independent cooperation between the nobles, the Church and the bourgeoisie. The entrance hall contains a useful timechart, while throughout paintings and models are fused with text to illustrate the stages of the Revolution.

Getting Around

This area isn't easy to explore without your own transport. Ask about bus services.

Tourist Information

Vizille: Place du Château, t 04 76 68 15 16.
Chamrousse: t 04 76 89 92 65.
St-Pierre-de-Chartreuse: t 04 76 88 62 08.
Villard-de-Lans: Place Mure Ravaud, t 04 76 95 50 10.
Correncon-en-Vercors: Place du Village, t 04 76 95 81 75.

Where to Stay and Eat

Uriage ✉ 38410
★★★★**Grand Hôtel**, t 04 76 89 10 80, f 04 76 89 04 62 (*moderate*). A grand Second Empire establishment with a modern hydrotherapy centre, and a fabulous restaurant (*menus 185–360F*). *Closed Jan. Restaurant closed Jan; 27 Aug–9 Sep; Sun and Mon exc July–Aug.*

St-Pierre-de-Chartreuse ✉ 38380
★★★**Beau Site**, t 04 76 88 61 34 (*moderate*). One of a number of pretty, good-value hotels in this village in its bowl surrounded by little mountains. *Closed 17 April–2 May and 15 Oct–23 Dec. Restaurant closed Sun evenings and Mon out of season.*
★**Le Beauregard**, t 04 76 88 60 12, f 04 76 88 65 16 (*cheap*). Above the village, with some of the best views of the limestone tops from the balconies beneath its Victorian eaves.

Villard-de-Lans ✉ 38250
★★★**Le Christiania**, t 04 76 95 12 51, f 04 76 95 00 75. (*moderate*). A big modern chalet with all sorts of family touches within and a son who produces gastronomic cuisine (*menus 139–190F*). *Closed 17 Sep–20 Dec and 20 April–20 May.*
★★★**Le Dauphin**, 220 Av du Général de Gaulle, t 04 76 95 95 25, f 04 76 95 56 33 (*inexpensive*). Cheaper, but still lovingly run.
★★**Villa Primerose**, 147 Av des Bains, t 04 76 95 13 17 (*inexpensive*). A very pretty bargain. No restaurant. *Closed 1 Oct–20 Dec.*

The Belledonne and Chartreuse Ranges

These two dramatic ranges run north from Grenoble on opposite sides of the Isère. The **Belledonne mountains**, geologists say, count among the oldest rocks in France, perhaps dating back 700 million years. Follow the D280 from Uriage up to Allevard, the road known as the **Route des Balcons**, passing orchards and vines below, and sharp snowy peaks above. Branch off for Prapoutel and Pipay, two out of the three little resorts making up the Belledonne skiing terrain of **Les Sept-Laux**. From **Allevard**, a 19th-century spa resort, you can head into the heart of the range along the picturesque road up the **Bréda valley**, past pleasant Alpine villages to the ski resort of **Le Pleyney**, the third of Les Sept-Laux's trio.

'Chartreuse' might conjure up a potent green or yellow liqueur, which is indeed made in these parts. Its recipe, combining dozens of Alpine herbs, is the secret of the Carthusians, founded in 1084 by Bruno, whose headquarters, the Couvent de la Grande Chartreuse, still exist. The monks live cut off from the world, leading an ascetic life, adhering to vows of silence and solitude. From Grenoble, reach the Chartreuse mountains by taking the road via Corenc to the **Fort du St-Eynard**. The precipitous view from here down on to Grenoble induces vertigo, but you can see why the French wanted to fortify it after the disasters of the Franco-Prussian War of 1870 had revealed just how badly prepared many French cities were for foreign invasions.

Charming **St-Pierre-de-Chartreuse** consists of a rash of hamlets, including a little ski resort. The village of **St-Hugues-de-Chartreuse**, a short way south, lies contentedly in a more open valley. The church, converted into a **Musée Départemental d'Art Sacré Contemporain**, contains an intriguing cycle of paintings and decorations, the work of one artist, Arcabas, who came here on three separate occasions, in 1952, 1973 and 1985. The display ends in the apse with the superb drama of the Last Supper, the shadowy figures behind the chequered tablecloth imparting a feeling of brotherhood and of plotting. You can't visit the Couvent de la Grande Chartreuse, but you can get an excellent picture of its history and its monastic life at the **Musée de la Grande Chartreuse** at La Correrie just west of St-Pierre-de-Chartreuse. A beautiful mountain road leads north from St-Pierre-de Chartreuse via the Col du Cucheron, St-Pierre d'Entremont, Entremont-le-Vieux and the Col du Granier to Chambéry (*see* pp.837–8).

To the Vercors

With its ragged-edged peaks, its terrible memories of the Second World War and its spectacularly difficult roads, the Vercors, southwest of Grenoble, has a slightly disturbing air. Bound by the Isère, Drac and Drôme rivers and sheer walls of rock, the upper plateaux, valleys and villages long remained cut off from the outside world. Below the long Montagne de Lans heading down from Grenoble are a string of family ski resorts. Cute **Villard-de-Lans**, surrounded by meadows, is as busy in summer as in winter. The highest line of Vercors mountains reach over 6,560ft. The only way to get close to them is by taking the GR91 from the mountain resort of **Corrençon-en-Vercors** down to Châtillon-en-Diois, by the Drôme valley. From Villard-de-Lans, the road west plunges through the **Gorges de la Bourne**. At the **Grottes de Choranche**, two underground streams converge; the main wonder are the *fistuleuses*, which resemble spaghetti glued to the ceiling. Terrifying roads lead south from the Bourne valley up to the Vercors plateaux. The most notorious takes you along the side of the Vernaison gulley via the **Petits and Grands Goulets**, headspinning distances above and below. Its rival is the route via the **Combe Laval**, with tremendous canyon views.

La Chapelle-en-Vercors was one of the villages martyred by the Nazis in 1944 as they tried to wipe out the Resistance groups hiding on the high plateaux. The wide valley around **Vassieux-en-Vercors**, further south, is overseen by the **Grand Veymont**, the highest peak in the Vercors (7,678ft). Some 600 resistance fighters, along with around 200 villagers, were assassinated by SS soldiers who flew in silently in gliders. Some tensions exist between the old-fashioned **Musée de la Résistance** in the reconstructed village, passionately run by a surviving *maquisard*, and the new-fangled **Mémorial de la Résistance**, snaking down the ridge. Both contain harrowing material.

Southern Alpine Resorts

The highest peaks of the Ecrins, the third major range of the French Alps, reach over 13,000ft. This is an exceptionally sunny part of France – Briançon boasts 300 sunny days a year and has a passion for sundials to prove it. The delightful Italianate towns have impressive fortifications, a legacy of invasion and conflict. The fort at Château-Queyras guards the way up into the higher reaches of the Queyras nature park.

Getting Around

This part of the Alps is quite difficult to get to by public transport, but there is a train line from Livron in the Rhône Valley (a short way south of the TGV station of Valence) which serves Briançon. Trains are infrequent.

Tourist Information

La Grave/La Meije: t 04 76 79 90 05, **f** 04 76 79 91 65.

Serre-Chevalier/La Salle-les-Alpes: t 04 92 24 98 98, **f** 04 92 24 98 84.

Briançon: Maison des Templiers, 1 Place du Temple, **t** 04 92 21 08 50, **f** 04 92 20 56 45.

Névache: t 04 92 21 38 19, **f** 04 92 20 51 72.

Guillestre: Place Joseph Salva, **t** 04 92 45 04 37, **f** 04 92 45 19 09.

St-Véran: t 04 92 45 82 21, **f** 04 92 45 84 52.

Barcelonette: Place Sept Portes, **t** 04 92 81 04 71, **f** 04 92 81 22 67.

Embrun: Place Général Dosse, **t** 04 92 43 72 72, **f** 04 92 43 54 06.

Where to Stay and Eat

La Grave ✉ 053200

★★★La Meijette (*inexpensive*). Most appealing of the collection of hotels here, with wooden balconies. *Closed 20 Sep–20 Feb and 1 May–1 Jun; Thurs exc July–Aug.*

★★Le Castillan, t 04 76 79 90 04, **t** 04 76 79 93 10. Plain but comfortable and with the attraction of a pool tucked into one side. There's a restaurant too (*menus 85–170F*).

Le Monêtier-les-Bains ✉ 05220

★★ Alliey, t 04 92 24 40 02, **t** 04 92 24 40 60 (*inexpensive*). Family-run hotel with cosy rooms, some set around a little garden courtyard, some a little close to the road. *Closed 1 Sept–16 Dec and 21 April–24 Jun.*

★★★Auberge du Choucas, 17 Rue de la Fruitière, **t** 04 92 24 42 73, **t** 04 92 24 51 60. An 18th-century village farm converted into a relaxing inn. The rooms are comfortable, the cuisine inventive. *Closed 3–20 May and 3 Nov–10 Dec. Restaurant closed middays Mon–Thurs in April and June.*

Europe et des Bains, 1 Rue St-Eldrade, **t** 04 92 24 40 03, **f** 04 92 24 52 17. A splashing fountain, attractive terrace, and rustic rooms. *Closed Sept–Dec and April–June.*

Briançon ✉ 05100

★★Edelweiss, 32 Av de la République, **t** 04 92 21 02 94, **f** 04 92 21 22 55 (*inexpensive*). Not far from the Haute Ville, a family hotel with a little garden. Some rooms have views.

★★Auberge Le Mont Prorel, 5 Av René Froger, **t** 04 92 20 22 88, **f** 04 92 21 27 76 (*inexpensive*). Pleasant chalet hotel with a little garden.

Le François Ier, 8 Place du Général Eberlé, **t** 04 92 21 09 18. A beautiful terrace for summer dining, by the ramparts of the Ville Haute.

La Caponnière, 12 Rue Commandant Carlhan, **t** 04 92 20 36 77. Warm surroundings, quite refined cuisine, and a little terrace.

Le Valentin, 6 Rue Mercerie (Petite Gargouille), **t** 04 92 21 37 72. A darkly atmospheric vaulted dining room and local specialities.

Névache ✉ 05100

Auberge Chez Guillaume (*cheap*). A cheap rustic option in an old sun-dialled village.

Embrun ✉ 05200

★★Hôtel de la Mairie, Place Berthelon, **t** 04 92 43 20 65, **t** 04 92 43 47 02 (*inexpensive*). On a beautiful square in the old town. The brasserie serves tasty Provençal-style food. *Closed 8–22 May; Oct and Nov. Restaurant closed Sun evenings and Mon in winter*

St-André-d'Embrun ✉ 05200

Le Nid, Hameau de Siguret, **t** 04 92 43 49 94. A restored old B&B farm north of Embrun where you'll be very well looked after, especially if you try the delicious *table d'hôte*.

The Romanche or Oisans Resorts from Grenoble to Les Ecrins

A winding road leads up from the Romanche valley to **L'Alpe d'Huez** northeast of lively **Le Bourg d'Oisans**. The architectural chaos of the resort has a bit more style than **Les Deux Alpes** opposite. Both resorts have open and high skiing slopes, and the views from L'Alpe d'Huez across to the Massif des Ecrins are hard to match. A sensational road east from L'Alpe d'Huez leads via a 'Route Pastorale' and the Col de Sarenne down to Lac du Chambon along the Romanche valley road.

There are other atmospheric routes in the Oisans which avoid the two major resorts. Follow the road up the **Vénéon valley**, alongside a turquoise stream, deep into the Ecrins range. At picturesque **Venosc**, connected by cablecar to Les Deux-Alpes, you can buy good woodwork and pottery. Beyond St-Christophe-en-Oisans at **Les Etages** you're rewarded with fantastic views of the highest peaks of the Ecrins. Head south from Le Bourg d'Oisans via the D526 and take one of the dead-end roads up either the Valsenestre or Bonne valleys. Continuing east along the Romanche valley, **La Grave** faces the highest peak of the Ecrins, the monumental **La Meije** (just over 13,000ft). There is a fabulous cablecar ride up towards it. The **Col du Lautaret** is the major pass through the northern Dauphiné, allowing you to head over from the Romanche valley to the Guisane valley in the eastern Ecrins. The **Jardin Alpin** grows plants from around the globe. The **Col du Galibier**, just north of the Col du Lautaret, is an amazing link between the northern and southern French Alps. The pass (8,676ft) is often closed, but on a good day it offers one of the finest views in the Alps.

From Serre-Chevalier and Briançon to the Lac de Serre-Ponçon

The ski resorts of **Serre-Chevalier** are strung along the Guisane valley from **Le Monêtier-les-Bains** to Briançon. The slopes cater for all levels of skiers, snowboarding and surfing. **Le Monêtier-les-Bains** (alias Serre-Chevalier 1500), is a resort, a spa and an old monastic centre; a church here holds the **Musée d'Art Sacré**, with statues and finery from some 30 churches in the region. **Villeneuve** (Serre-Chevalier 1400) looks a bit brutal, built below the pretty village of Le Bez, but it has the most facilities of the Serre-Chevalier resorts, including the longest chairlift in the world. From **Chantemerle**, another modern resort adjoining Villeneuve, you can take cablecars up to the 8,100ft peak of Serre-Chevalier itself.

Briançon

The resort on the west side of Briançon is known as **Serre-Chevalier 1200**, but it's eclipsed by historic **Briançon Ville Haute**, supposedly Europe's highest town at some 4,330ft. A settlement has existed up here since early medieval times, but the junction of five valleys down below also made lower Briançon a strategic site in Ligurian and Roman times. Although the king's military engineer Vauban is associated with Briançon, when he arrived here in 1692 the defences around the Ville Haute were already under way. Vauban modified the plans and saw to the construction of new barracks. However, the **Fort du Château**, on the rock above the Ville Haute, was only converted from a tired medieval structure after 1830. You can climb up its various levels to look down on to the rooftops of the Ville Haute. Higher forts, the middle **Fort Dauphin** and the top **Fort des Têtes** (parts open for visits) were added in the 1720s and 1730s and linked to the Ville Haute by the dramatic single-arch **Pont d'Asfeld**, spanning a precipitous gorge above the newborn Durance river. Other little forts are scattered around the town, some added as part of the Maginot Line in the 1930s.

The beautiful Ville Haute was divided into quarters known as Escartons in the 14th century. You have to penetrate several layers of fortifications to arrive at the top of **Grand'Rue**, also known as the **Grande Gargouille** – referring to the water streaming down its central channel. Lined with fine Italian style houses, it leads to the colourful main square, the Place d'Armes. The **Petite Gargouille**, likewise provided with a channel running along its length, runs parallel to the Grande Gargouille. Dominating **Place du Temple** off the Petite Gargouille rise the twin towers of the **Collégiale Notre-Dame**, with an attractive orange and stone façade. But even this church, its backside sticking indecorously out over the ramparts, has a military air, the tops of its towers resembling helmets. It was planned at the end of the 17th century at the same time as the fortifications. A sundial was painted on each tower, with trompe-l'œil atlantes holding them up. Of the previous Romanesque church, only the two pink marble lions were saved, worn-looking creatures either side of the doorway. Inside, elaborate paintings adorn the choir, as do gilded busts and statues above its stalls.

The Place d'Armes features two attractive sundials, although their Latin inscriptions carry the usual sting: one translates roughly as 'Life slips by like a shadow'. From the open terrace high above the Ville Haute's rocky perch, you can look down on the messy modern town. On one side of the terrace rises the former governors' palace, on the other the **Maison du Parc** (*open July–Aug daily 10–7; rest of year daily exc Sun and Mon 10–12 and 2–7; closed late Sept–late Oct; recorded commentary in English*), which presents the Ecrins national park, its wildlife and traditional communities. The disused Franciscan church of **Les Cordeliers** was only handed over to the town by the military in 1980. The original friary went up in the late 14th century, planted in the middle of town to help combat heresy in the valleys around. It was taken over by the army at the Revolution and destroyed, apart from the church which was turned into a military hospital. The town has slowly been converting it into a cultural centre (due to be completed in 2003). In the meantime you should be able to see the two comical curly-haired Lombard lions at the base of the columns and the superbly frescoed chapel from the 1460s. The artist, known as the Master of Briançon, may well have been an Italian, but one who travelled widely. On the ceiling, figures represent the evangelists; St John particularly magnificent, with a ribbon of text flowing out from his desk like a mad computer print-out. The lion of St Mark holds another scroll in his paw. The frizzy sun in the centre represents the light of Christ. The wall frescoes have been more damaged. On the south side are scenes of Adam and Eve. The north wall frescoes are harder to decipher. The top scene is thought to be dedicated to the Virgin, showing her coronation, while the lower scene may show her assumption. Inevitably there's a sundial painted on the outside of the church, added in 1795; the bizarre date given – 5795 – indicates that it was ordered by a masonic lodge which began its calendar with the destruction of King Solomon's temple in 4000 BC.

Around Briançon

The busy road east out of Briançon takes you into Italy via **Montgenèvre**, its main street lined with restaurants and tourist boutiques. But a nicer excursion from Briançon takes in the unkempt villages and picturesque hamlets strung along the road up the Vallée de la Clarée, running parallel to the Italian border. Charmingly scruffy **Névache**, with its sundials, is the centre for information. Surrounded by a walled cemetery, the church has an Annunciation painted over one doorway with a real peasant of a Virgin Mary. The carved wooden doors below feature a Resurrection and Last Judgement, Christ comically seated on his rainbow. In the quirky Gothic interior, the eye is drawn to the gilded Baroque retable in the choir. A charming wooden gallery runs round the other end of the church. North of Névache, the road up the valley is lined by a profusion of wild roses. The landscape becomes increasingly boulder-strewn as you reach the chalets of **Laval**, an excellent place for walks.

An alternative detour west into the Ecrins takes you via the lively village of **Vallouise** to the **Pré de Madame Carle** in the shadow of formidable **Mont Pelvoux**, the second highest peak of the Ecrins range (just over 13,000ft). This is an excellent place for spotting chamois and marmots. The walks up to the **Glacier Blanc** and **Glacier Noir** are very popular. Spectacularly overlooked from afar, Guillestre and Mont-Dauphin stand at the wide junction of the Durance and Guil valleys. At **Guillestre** you can still make out the 14th-century walls, and old gateways lead into the dense network of streets. The porch of Notre-Dame-d'Aquilon is held up by two adorable Romanesque lions, and a chapel contains paintings and gilded statues. The tower has a sundial, but a prettier one decorates one of the houses on the square. The star-shaped fortifications of **Mont-Dauphin**, aloof on its platform of rock west of Guillestre, went up from 1692. A fort was planned to house a garrison and a civilian population to cater for it, and named Mont Dauphin in honour of the heir to the French throne. It is a fascinating place, particularly if you go on one of the lively guided tours. Most of the fort has survived, but some parts, such as the church, were never completed, and others suffered from bombing in 1940. The French army only left in 1980. Since then, a thriving crafts community has established itself. The guides point out the thermal spring and petrifying fountain down in the valley bottom, close to the confluence of the Durance and the Guil.

South of Guillestre you come to the ski resorts of **Vars**: Ste-Catherine, Ste-Marie and Les Claux. Here professionals frequent the most famous record-breaking piste in France, where speeds of over 125 miles (200km) an hour have been achieved.

The Queyras

Tucked into a corner east of Guillestre, **Queyras regional nature park** extends east into Italy. Much appreciated for its beautiful walks, it features a splendid array of Alpine and even Mediterranean flowers in season. Head up the **Guil valley** from Guillestre, or for a choice of beautiful walks in a less crowded area, branch off for the colourful village of **Ceillac**. The narrow, daunting gorges of the Guil, known as the **Combe du Queyras**, focus your attention on the road as you head further into the Queyras. The road is so awkward that coaches frequently get stuck. In summer you can also reach the isolated corner beyond the Guil gorges via the dramatic **Col d'Izoard**, and the startling glacial hill of **Château-Queyras**, topped by a picture-book fort. Parts of the medieval castle have surived, including a keep. Won by the Protestants in 1587, a century later Vauban added impressive new layers of defences.

With its old wooden chalets sporting long balconies for drying crops, its many wood-working shops and its wooden fountains, **St-Véran** is as one of the prettiest traditional villages in the French Alps. It also claims to be the highest village in Europe inhabited year round (at about 6,560ft). At the **Musée Soum**, in a house built in 1641, you can learn something of the harsh pre-war living conditions in the neat little rooms, their different functions explained. Another house, inhabited by two old twins until 1976, has been lovingly preserved by their family as the **Musée de l'Habitat Ancien**. The dark interiors are full of roughly labelled clutter, including such delights as marmot grease, used as a fuel for light, for curing rheumatic pain, and for polishing shoes. In winter the family would sleep in the same room as the horses and pigs, whose heat and manure were much appreciated. Many other houses have been turned into souvenir shops. The extraordinary church, rebuilt at the end of the 17th century, retains its Romanesque lions and a few old capitals carved with primitive little figures. Continuing along the Guil valley, you pass through **Aiguilles**, with its old stone houses and the headquarters of the Queyras nature park, and **Abriès**, with a delightful church containing Baroque retables and choir ribs covered with plaster garlands of grapes. Beyond Abriès, a well-known walk takes you through enchanting Alpine meadows to belvederes over the huge coal-like faces and triangular peak of the Monte Viso just across the Italian frontier.

The Ubaye Valley

South of Guillestre, beyond the Col de Vars, the Ubaye valley offers relatively unspoilt Alpine countryside. **Barcelonette** is the main attraction. The name dates from 1231 when it was founded by the count of Provence and Barcelona. Its narrow old streets are chic and lively, the houses cheerful in fruity tones. A surprising trading link was established between Barcelonette merchants and Central America in the 19th century. Many succeeded and built themselves fancy villas on the outskirts and extravagant tombs in the cemetery. The **Musée de la Vallée**, in a merchant's villa, covers the town's history.

Down in the Ubaye valley west of Barcelonette, the sprightly river is busy with white-water rafters in summer. Two ski resorts lie just south of town. You can easily make out **Pra-Loup**, high on a wooded ridge. While best known for its snow fields in winter, in summer it stays alive with paragliding and other activities. **Le Sauze** and **Super-Sauze** are modest ski resorts, Le Sauze with an older pedigree and more charm. In summer you can walk to the bare mountain tops of Chapeau de Gendarme (Policeman's Hat) and Pain de Sucre (Sugarloaf).

Southwest from Guillestre, **Embrun**, built high over the Durance, now lies at the northeast end of the artificial lake of Serre-Ponçon. The views around Embrun are sensational, but best of all seen from the top of the medieval **Tour Brune** (*adm*) by the cathedral. The delectable cathedral lies just down from the tower. The use of coloured stone shows the Lombard influence, as does the porch, its columns held up by lions. Inside, your eyes will immediately be drawn to the great zebra pelt of a ceiling.

Provence and the Côte d'Azur

20

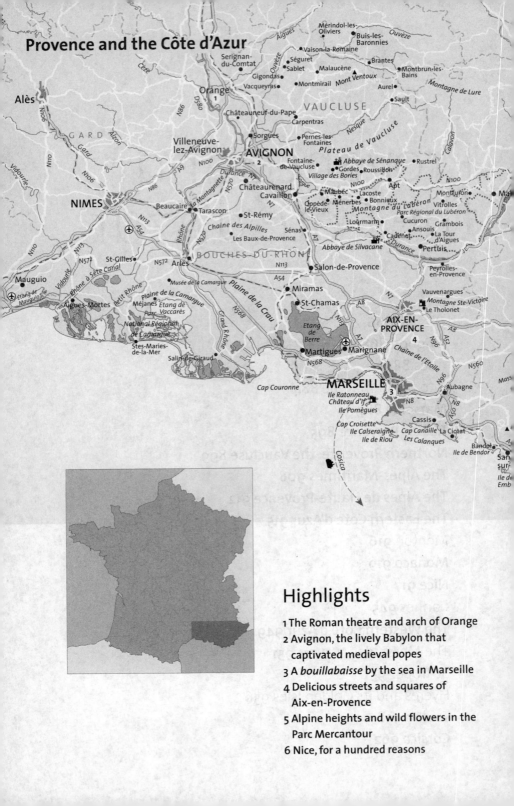

Provence and the Côte d'Azur

Highlights

1 The Roman theatre and arch of Orange
2 Avignon, the lively Babylon that captivated medieval popes
3 A *bouillabaisse* by the sea in Marseille
4 Delicious streets and squares of Aix-en-Provence
5 Alpine heights and wild flowers in the Parc Mercantour
6 Nice, for a hundred reasons

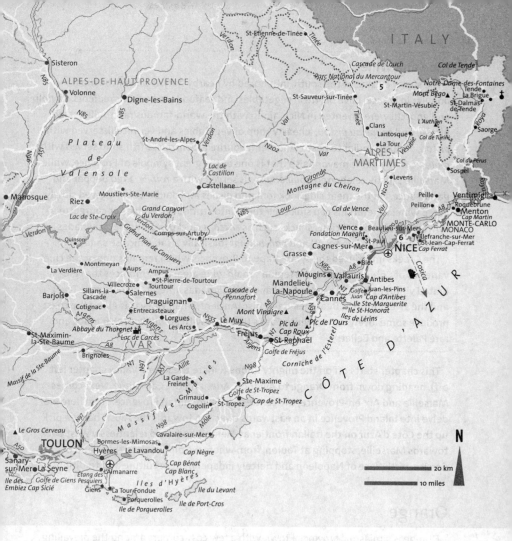

First settled by the ancient Greeks, Provence was the beloved Provincia of the Romans. Even the medieval popes and cardinals in Avignon fell prey to its sensuous *dolce vita*; the voluptuous Mediterranean light inspired Van Gogh, Cézanne, Renoir, Matisse, and the Fauves. After a century of hosting the consumptive and the wealthy in the winter, the Roaring 20s introduced a new fad for turning brown by the sea. The French invented paid summer holidays for everyone in 1936, and the rest is history.

Today, after Paris, Provence and the Côte d'Azur – the French Riviera – are the most visited regions in France. Endowed with a sunny climate, naturally air-conditioned by the mistral wind, replete with dramatic scenery and beaches, fascinating Roman and medieval remains, top-notch art museums, fantastic restaurants and hotels, this 'California of Europe' has its down sides as well: too many holiday villas, too many people, high prices, and too many shop selling lavender soap or *santons*, the omnipresent Provençal crèche figurines. Pick and choose here, and come on the cusp of the season, and you'll better understand what started all the fuss in the first place.

Food and Wine

The sunny cuisine of the south, influenced by nearby Italy, is one of the most popular in France: olive oil, fresh vegetables and seafood are basic ingredients. Ravioli and gnocchi were invented in Nice, along with the world-famous ratatouille, salad niçoise and *soupe au pistou*, a hearty soup of vegetables and vermicelli, served with *pistou*, a sauce similar to pesto. Another favourite is *bourride*, a fish soup served with *aïoli*, a creamy garlic mayonnaise that is one of the great symbols of Provence, while Marseille's justly celebrated *bouillabaisse* is served with a *rouille*, a red pepper and garlic sauce. On the meat side, look for lamb dishes and daubes, beef stewed slowly in red wine; vegetarians can sink their teeth into stuffed vegetables or courgette flowers (*farcies*) or delicious snacks such as *socca*, a chickpea-flour pie, tapenades (olive paste, served on toast) and *pan-bagnat* (basically a salad niçoise sandwich).

The Greeks introduced the syrah grape to Provence, which remains one of the chief varieties of Côtes du Rhône, the region's main wine area; this embraces the celebrated vintages of Châteauneuf de Pape and Gigondas among the reds, rosé Tavel, and the sweet muscat Beaumes-de-Venise. Ancient, small vineyards along the coast produce some lovely wines: white Cassis (the best with *bouillabaisse*), Bandol, and rare Palette and Bellet.

This chapter starts off on the mighty Rhône (where the Rhône Valley chapter left off), heading down from Orange to Avignon, Arles and the Camargue. Next comes Marseille and Aix-en-Provence, the centres of Metropolitan Provence. From here we delve into inland Provence in an eastwards direction towards the Alps. Then we pick up the Côte d'Azur on the Italian frontier at Menton and head relentlessly west back towards Marseille, stopping at Toulon, from where we dip south to the island of Corsica, birthplace of Napoleon and fiercely independent in culture and tradition.

Orange

Orange is a miasmic provincial town with a few cosy corners among the prevailing drabness. Fate, or the lack of a bypass road, has made its streets a kind of Le Mans for heavy lorries. Electing a National Front mayor hasn't helped it either. Nevertheless the prosperous Roman colony that was Orange left it two ancient monuments unmatched in France.

The most unusual page of the city's history, however, was an odd chance that would let Orange lend its colour to the Dutch, the Northern Irish, the Orange Free State and Orange, New Jersey. In 1530, the city became the property of the German House of Nassau, just in time for the Reformation. The Nassaus declared for Protestantism, and Orange rapidly became the dissenters' chief stronghold in Provence. Soon after, William of Nassau – William of Orange – became the first *stadhouder* of the United Provinces and led the fight for Dutch independence. French rule, won by Louis XIV, was a disaster, particularly after the Revocation of the Edict of Nantes, and the city has never really recovered.

The architects of the **Théâtre Antique** (*open summer daily 9–6.30; winter 9–12 and 1.30–5; adm; ticket also valid for Musée Municipal*) might be distressed to hear it, but these days the most impressive part of this huge structure is its back wall. If the old prints in the municipal museum are accurate, this rugged, elegant sandstone cliff facing Place des Frères-Mounet was originally adorned with low, temple-like façades. In its present state, it resembles a typical Florentine Renaissance palace, without the windows. Unlike Greek theatres, which always opened to a grand view behind the stage, those of the Romans featured large stage buildings, serious architectural compositions of columns, arches and sculptured friezes. This is what the great exterior wall is supporting; Orange's stage building (115ft high) is one of two complete specimens that remain to us (the other is at Aspendos in Turkey). Of the decoration, a statue of Augustus remains in the centre.

Other fragments, including an exceptional frieze of satyrs and Amazons, are stowed opposite the theatre in the **Musée Municipal**, one of the most fascinating town

Getting There and Around

The **train** station on Av Frédéric Mistral has direct connections to Paris, Avignon, Arles, Marseille, Nice and Cannes. **Buses** depart from Cours Portoules, t 04 90 34 15 59, for Carpentras, Vaison-la-Romaine and Avignon, and three times daily for Séguret.

Where to Stay and Eat

Orange ⊠ 84100
Arène, Place de Langes, t 04 90 11 40 40, f 04 90 11 40 45 (*moderate*). Pleasant and central with a good restaurant, on a quiet square where you can't hear the lorries.
★★St-Florent, 4 Rue du Mazeau, t 04 90 34 18 53, f 04 90 51 17 25 (*inexpensive*). A decent budget choice.
Le Pigraillet, t 04 90 34 44 25, on Colline St-Eutrope, a wooded park overlooking the Rhône. An unforgettable place to spend a warm summer's night: clients may use the pool before eating, for a fee. *Closed Sun eve and Mon.*

Sérignan-du-Comtat ⊠ 84830
★★★Hostellerie Le Vieux Château, Route de Ste-Cécile, t 04 90 70 05 58, f 04 90 70 05 62 (*moderate*). A grand old place, and all you could ask for in the way of comfort and quiet; there's a pool and restaurant (*110F lunch menu, 160F dinner*).

Vieille Auberge La Vénus, t 04 90 70 08 48. Here 100F will get you a plate of salmon ravioli and duck marinated in Gigondas. *Closed Sat lunch and Sun eve.*

Châteauneuf-du-Pape ⊠ 84230
La Mère Germaine, Place de la Fontaine, t 04 90 83 54 37, f 04 90 83 50 27 (*inexpensive*). It's hard to imagine how such a sweet old place could survive in a tourist trap like Châteauneuf-du-Pape. Fine rooms decorated with antiques, and a restaurant serving tantalizing *millefeuille de morue fraîche* and the succulent *galet de Châteauneuf-du-Pape* (*menus 155F, 195F and 380F*). *Closed Tues eve and Wed.*
★★★★Château des Fines Roches, 2km south on the D17, t 04 90 83 70 23, f 04 90 83 78 42 (*expensive*). For a more luxurious stay, there's this imposing but entirely fake crenellated castle with gardens, set among the vineyards. It's elegant and the kitchen shines in seafood and elaborate desserts (*menus 200 and 290F*). *Closed mid-Dec–Feb.*
★★★La Sommellerie, D17 towards Roquemaure, t 04 90 83 50 00, f 04 90 83 51 85 (*moderate*). In a restored 18th-century sheepfold, with rooms overlooking the pool or vines; the restaurant, presided over by Pierre Paumel, serves delicately perfumed dishes and fish trucked up daily from the coast. Don't miss his reproductions of Van Gogh's paintings – in spun sugar (*menus 170–420F*). *Closed Sun eve, Mon and Nov–Mar.*

museums in Provence (*open summer daily 9.30–7; winter daily 9–12 and 1.30–5.30; adm; ticket also valid for the Roman theatre*). Besides Roman art, it has rooms of Dutch portraits, relics of Nassau rule, and works by the Welsh impressionist Frank Brangwyn (who was in fact born in Bruges).

Rue Victor-Hugo follows the route of the ancient Roman *cardo major* to Orange's other Roman attraction. The **Triumphal Arch**, built around AD 20, celebrates the conquests of the Second Gallic Legion with outlandish, almost abstract scenes of battling Romans and Celts. This is the epitome of the Provençal-Roman style: excellent, careful reliefs, especially in the upper frieze, portraying a naval battle, with a touch of Celto-Ligurian strangeness.

Around Orange: Sérignan-du-Comtat and the 'Virgil of Insects'

Eight kilometres northeast of Orange on the D976 you can pay your respects to the great and delightful entomologist, botanist, scientist, and poet Jean-Henri Fabre (1823–1915). Although born into poverty, Fabre made enough money from writing popular science books to buy an abandoned property in 1879 in Sérignan that he called **L'Harmas**, the 'fallow land' (**t** *04 90 70 00 44; generally open Mon and Wed–Sat 9–11.30 and 2–6; winter 2–5; but ring ahead to make sure; adm*), where he could observe insects. Over the years he wrote ten volumes of *Souvenirs entomologiques*, and was twice nominated for the Nobel Prize for literature. You can see his curious apparatus for observing insects, his collections of fossils, shells, rocks, insects, plants, eggs and coins, and his letters from Darwin.

South of Orange: Châteauneuf-du-Pape

You'll begin to understand why Châteauneuf's wines are so expensive when you pass through the vineyards between Orange and Avignon. Blink and you'll miss them. Every available square inch is covered with vineyards of a rare beauty, so immaculately precise and luxuriant they resemble bonsai trees. The very attractive village that gives the wine its name has not resisted the temptation to become the Midi's foremost oenological tourist trap; along the main street there are few grocers or boutiques, but plenty of wine shops. Brave the hordes and visit the 14th-century **castle**, which the Avignon popes used as a summer residence, to see the huge plain below you, and the Rhône muscling away to the west on its way south to Avignon, or wait till dusk if you can, for a magnificent sunset.

Avignon

Avignon has known more passions and art and power than any town in Provence, a mixture of excitement whipped to a frenzy by the mistral. But even the master of winds has never caused as much trouble as the 14th-century papal court, a vortex of mischief that ruled Avignon for centuries, trailing violence, corruption and debauchery in its wake. 'In Paris one quarrels, in Avignon one kills,' as Hugo put it. Not anymore; Avignon is alive, ebullient and fun.

Getting Around

Avignon's **airport** is at Caumont, t 04 90 81 51 15.

The **train** station is outside the Porte de la République. Avignon is on the Paris–Marseille TGV line, and has frequent links to Arles, Montpellier, Nîmes, Orange, Toulon and Carcassonne.

The **bus** station is next door (Bd St Roch, t 04 90 82 07 35). There are plenty of buses to Carpentras, Cavaillon, St-Rémy and Orange, Arles, Nîmes, one early morning run to Nice, Aix and Cannes, along with six others to Aix and Fontaine-de-Vaucluse, three for Marseille, and some services to the Pont du Gard, Uzès and Châteauneuf-du-Pape. For Villeneuve lez Avignon, take city bus no.11 from in front of the post office.

Travellers of yore always approached Avignon by boat, a thrill still possible on the **tourist excursion boat** *Le Cygne* from Beaucaire, t 04 66 59 35 62, or with a **lunch or dinner cruise** on *Le Miréio*, based at Allées de l'Oulle, t 04 90 85 62 25, f 04 90 85 61 14. In July and August, the **Bateau-Bus** makes regular trips between Avignon and Villeneuve, starting from the Allées de l'Oulle.

Inexpensive **car hire** firms are VEO, 51 Av Pierre Sémard, t 04 90 87 53 43, and Eurorent, 3 Av Saint Ruf, t 04 90 86 06 61.

Tourist Information

Avignon: 41 Cours Jean Jaurès, t 04 32 74 32 74, f 04 90 82 95 03.

Villeneuve-lez-Avignon: Place Charles-David, t 04 90 25 61 33, f 04 90 25 91 55.

Where to Stay

Avignon ✉ 84000

Avignon gets full to the brim in July and August: it's imperative to book ahead, and many places raise their rates. Note that there are also a huge number of chain hotels around the suburbs and major road entrances.

Expensive

★★★★**Hôtel d'Europe**, 12 Place Crillon, t 04 90 14 76 76, f 04 90 14 76 71. Oldest, and still classically formal with its Louis XV furnishings, converted to an inn in the late 1700s. Napoleon stayed here, as did the eloping Browning and Barrett.

★★★★**Cloître St-Louis**, 20 Rue du Portail Boquier, t 04 90 27 55 55, f 04 90 82 24 01, near the station. Built in 1589 as part of the Jesuit school of theology, the beautiful cloister is an island of tranquillity. Rooms are austerely modern; meals are served under the portico or by the rooftop pool.

History

Philip the Fair of France, having just bribed the conclave to elect a Frenchman, Clement V, as pope, also suggested that he flee the anarchy of 14th-century Rome for the safer havens of the Comtat Venaissin, a piece of papal turf picked up after the Albigensian Crusade. Clement V always intended to return to Rome, but when he died the French cardinals elected a former archbishop of Avignon, John XXII (1316–34), who moved the Curia into his old episcopal palace. Although he enlarged the palace with the proceeds, it still wasn't roomy enough for his successor, Benedict XII (1334–42), who replaced it with another palace, or for Clement VI (1342–52), who added another. Meanwhile all the profits that the 14th-century papal machine generated went to Avignon instead of Rome, and overcrowding, debauchery, dirt, luxury, plague, blackmail and crime came with the deal. In 1377 St Catherine of Siena convinced the seventh Avignon pope, Gregory XI, to return to Rome. The pope came, he saw, he sickened, but before he could pack his bags to return to Avignon, he died. The Roman mob seized their chance, and physically forced the cardinals to elect an Italian pope who

****La Ferme Jamet**, Chemin de Rhodes (off Pont Daladier), t 04 90 86 88 35, f 04 90 86 17 72. A 16th-century farmhouse on the Ile de la Barthelasse; rooms range from traditional Provençal to a Gypsy caravan, around a tennis court and a pool.

Inexpensive
****Hôtel du Palais des Papes**, 1 Rue Gérard Philippe, t 04 90 82 47 31, f 04 90 27 91 17. Best views of the Palace, modern sound-proofed rooms and air conditioning.
****St-Roch**, 9 Rue Mérindol, t 04 90 16 50 00, f 04 90 82 78 30. Quiet with a delightful garden just outside the walls of Porte St-Roch.

Cheap
***Mignon**, 12 Rue Joseph Vernet, t 04 90 82 17 30, f 04 90 85 78 46. Bright and charming with small but modernized rooms.
***Splendid**, 17 Rue A. Perdiguier, off Rue de la République, t 04 90 86 14 46, f 04 90 85 38 55. Not too splendid, but cheap.

Eating Out

Expensive–Moderate
Hiély-Lucullus, 5 Rue de la République, t 04 90 86 17 07. Avignon's gourmet bastion for the past 60 years. The kitchen never disappoints

with its *tourte of quail* and foie gras, a legendary *cassoulet de moules aux épinards* and, for dessert, *meringue glacée au chocolat ou café*, accompanied by carafes of Châteauneuf-du-Pape or Tavel (*menus 120–220F and up*). Closed Tues, and Wed lunch.

Moderate
La Fourchette, 17 Rue Racine, t 04 90 85 20 93. Its sister restaurant serves as good for less (*menus from 100F*); a choice of 12 desserts and wine by the carafe. *Closed Sat lunch and Sun.*
Le Bain Marie, 5 Rue Pétramale, t 04 90 85 21 37. Popular and serves traditional French fare (*menus 140F and 165F*).
Le Petit Bedon, 70 Rue Joseph Vernet, t 04 90 82 33 98. Quickly becoming an Avignon institution for well-prepared dishes seldom found elsewhere, like *lotte au Gigondas*, angler-fish cooked in wine (*lunch menu 120F, dinner 180F*).
Woolloomoolloo, 16 bis Rue des Teinturiers, t 04 90 85 28 44. Go global with a feast of 'world cuisine' and live music (*100F and up; cheaper lunch menus*).
Terre de Saveur, Rue St-Michel, t 04 90 86 68 72. For lunch, pop into this vegetarian-orientated place which serves up omelettes and pasta dishes, many recipes using wild mushrooms.

would re-establish the papacy in Rome. When the French cardinals escaped the Romans' clutches, they sparked off the Great Schism by electing a French anti-pope, Clement VII, and went back to Avignon. Finally, the Church decided on one pope, and the Comtat Venaissin was eventually incorporated into France during the Revolution in a blood rite of atrocities. But even as part of France, Avignon has maintained its lively international character. In 1946, actor Jean Vilar founded the Avignon Festival, the liveliest and most popular event on the entire Provençal calendar.

The Famous Half-Bridge
From the Rhône, Avignon is a brave two-tiered sight: in front rise the sheer cliffs of the **Rocher des Doms**, inhabited since Neolithic times, and behind it the sheer man-made cliffs of the Palais des Papes. The ensemble includes the **walls** that the popes wrapped around Avignon: bijou, toothsome garden walls ever since Viollet-le-Duc re-crenellated them in 1860. From the walls, four arches of a bridge leapfrog into the Rhône, sidle up to a waterbound two-storey Romanesque chapel and then stop abruptly mid-river. This is the famous **Pont St-Bénézet**, or simply the Pont d'Avignon,

Around Avignon

★★★**Hostellerie L'Hermitage-Meissonnier**, 30 Av de Verdun, 4km west of Avignon at Les Angles, t 04 90 25 41 68, f 04 90 25 11 68 (*moderate*). Sixteen luxurious rooms and a glorious restaurant specializing in Provençal cuisine of the highest order – even the tomatoes taste better here, especially if you eat out in L'Hermitage's lovely garden (*bargain 100F menu, and others up to 450F*). *Closed Sun eve and Mon; July and Aug Mon lunch only.*

★★★★**Le Jardin des Frênes**, 645 Av les Vertes-Rives, Montfavet, 5 km east (follow the Avenue d'Avignon), t 04 90 31 17 93 (*expensive*). A Relais et Châteaux place, set around a beautiful garden and pool; the rooms are furnished with antiques. Half-board is mandatory in season, but the food is as marvellous as the setting (*lunch menus 205F*).

Villeneuve lez Avignon ✉ 30400

★★★★**Le Prieuré**, Place du Chapître, t 04 90 15 90 15, f 04 90 25 18 20 (*expensive*). Sleep in a 14th-century *livrée*, where the rooms are furnished with antiques, or in the comfortable annexe by the pool; garden, tennis, and a restaurant that does delightful things with seafood and truffles (*lunch menus 200F*). *Closed Nov–Mar.*

★★★★**La Magnaneraie**, 37 Rue Camp-de-Bataille, t 04 90 25 11 11, f 04 90 25 46 37 (*expensive*). Old-fashioned rooms in a former silkworm nursery, or in a modern annexe; with a pool, gardens, and Le Prieuré's rival for the best restaurant in town (*menus 170F and up; menu gastronomique 260F*).

★★**L'Atelier**, 5 Rue de la Foire, t 04 90 25 01 84, f 04 90 25 80 06 (*inexpensive*). A less expensive bit of history in a charming 16th-century building with a walled garden.

★★**Les Cèdres**, 39 Bd Pasteur, t 04 90 25 43 92, f 04 90 25 14 66 (*inexpensive*). A 17th-century house, with a pool and a bungalow annexe. *Closed Nov–Mar.*

Les Jardins de la Livrée, 4 bis Rue Camp de Bataille, t 04 90 26 05 05, f 04 90 25 37 78 (*inexpensive*). Charming bed and breakfast with a walled garden and pool. The restaurant is good too; try the cannelloni stuffed with salmon (*menus 120–150F*).

Aubertin, Place Meissonnier, t 04 90 25 94 84. Intimate place to savour red mullet tartines, with *pistou* and fried aubergines. Book. *Closed Sun, and Mon lunch.*

La Maison, 1 Rue Montée du Fort St-André, t 04 90 25 20 81. An old favourite, with a traditional menu (*menu 120F*). *Closed Wed, Sat lunch and Tues eve.*

begun in 1185 (*open April–Sept daily 9–6.30; Mar and Oct daily 9–5.45; adm*). Originally 22 arches and half a mile long, the bridge enriched Avignon with its tolls, but in 1660 the Avignonnais got tired of the constant repairs it demanded and abandoned it to the monsters of the Rhône. And did they ever 'danse, tout en rond' on their bridge, as in the nursery song? No, the historians say, although they may well have danced under it on the mid-river **Ile de la Barthelasse**, formerly a hunting reserve.

The Palais des Papes

Open April–Oct daily 9–7; Sept till 8; Nov–Mar daily 9.30–5.45; till 9pm during Festival; adm. Optional audio guide in English.

After crossing the **Cour d'Honneur**, the great courtyard dividing Benedict XII's stern Cistercian Palais Vieux (1334–42) and Clement VI's flamboyant Palais Neuf (1342–52), the tour begins in the **Jesus Hall**, decorated with monograms of Christ and now containing a hoard of maps and curios. The most valuable loot would be stored behind walls 10ft thick in the windowless bowels of the **Angels' Tower**.

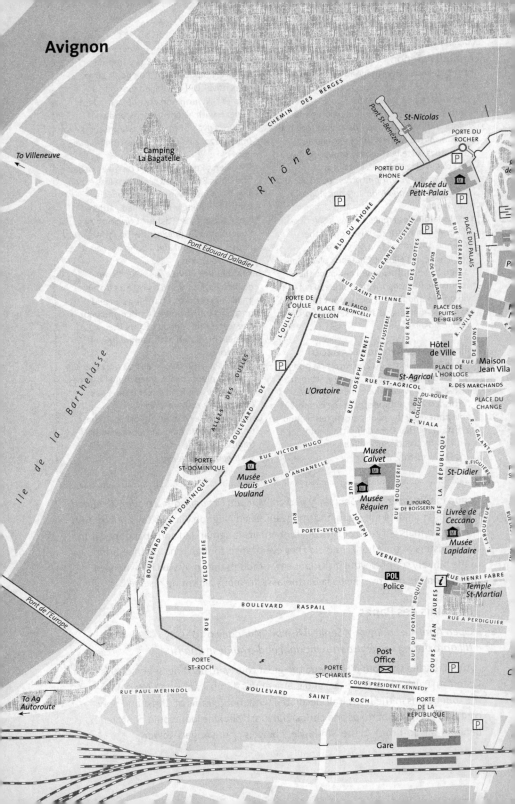

Club Nautique

200 metres
200 yards

N

BOULEVARD DE LA LIGNE

Rocher
des Doms

PORTE DE LA
LIGNE

BOULEVARD DU QUAI SAINT LAZARE

To Carpentras
(A7)

PORTE
ST-JOSEPH

PLACE
ST-JOSEPH

RUE ST-JOSEPH

RUE DES TROIS COLOMBES

R. STE-
ESCALIER ANNE R. BERTRAND

Notre-Dame
des Doms

Palais des Papes

BANASTERIE

RUE SAINTE CATHERINE

RUE DES INFIRMIERES

Cloître

Eglise des
Carmes

RUE CARRETERIE

RUE CARRETERIE

RUE LUCHET

PORTE
ST-LAZARE

RUE ST-BERNARD

Hôtel des
Monnaies

R. ARME DE PONTMARTIN

RUE DE LA CROIX

R. SALUCES

RUE CAMPANE

PLACE DES CARMES

R. ORIFLAMME

R. PORTAIL MATHERON

To
Cimetière
St-Véran

R. PEYROLLERIE

St-Pierre

RUE LOUIS PASTEUR

PLACE
L. PASTEUR

RUE GUILLAUME

RUE NOTRE-DAME DES 7 DOULEURS

on
Vilar

RUE CARNOT

PLACE
CARNOT

Synagogue

RUE DU VIEUX SEXTIER

RUE DES FOURBISSEURS

RUE

R. COLLEGE DE LA CROIX

PLACE
PIE

PLACE
PIGNOTTE

RUE PAUL SAIN

RUE TRIAL

RUE PUY

RUE BUFFON

LIMBERT

PLACE
ST-DIDIER

Les
Halles

La Visitation

R. DU FOUR DE LA TERRE

RUE

BONNETERIE

R. BOURGNEUF

RUE THIERS

PORTE
THIERS

BOULEVARD

RUE DU ROI RENE

RUE SAINT GUILLAUME

RUE PETRAMALE

RUE CHRISTOPHE

RUE SEVERINE

RUE DES 3 FAUCONS

LICES

Chapelle des
Pénitents Gris

RUE DES

RUE BON MARTINET

RUE DES TEINTURIERS

RUE PUY

PLACE DES
CORPS
SAINTS

RUE BARACANE

RUE DE L'AIGARDEN DU PORTAIL MAGNANEN

PORTE
LIMBERT

AVE PIERRE SEMARD

Clôitre
des
Célestins

RUE ST-MICHEL

RUE DU RAMPART ST MICHEL

RUE SAINT MICHEL

PORTE
ST-MICHEL

BOULEVARD SAINT MICHEL

Gare
Routière P

To Airport, Marseille
& Nice (A7)

Next is the **Consistory**, where the cardinals met and received ambassadors; its lavish frescoes and ceiling burned in 1413, and it now displays 19th-century portraits of Avignon's popes and Simone Martini's fresco of the *Virgin of Humility*. In the **Chapelle St-Jean**, dedicated to both Johns, the Baptist and the Evangelist, Matteo Giovannetti of Viterbo, a trecento charmer who left the bulk of his work in Avignon, did the frescoes for Clement VI: saints floating overhead in starry blue landscapes (recall that at the time ultramarine blue paint was even more expensive than gold). The tour continues to the first floor and the huge banqueting hall, or **Grand Tinel**, hung with 18th-century Gobelin tapestries. The adjacent **Upper Kitchen** was large enough to produce Clement VI's coronation feast, in which 3,000 guests consumed 1,023 sheep, 118 cattle, 101 calves, 914 kids, 60 pigs, 10,471 hens, 1,446 geese and 300 pike, topped off by 46,856 cheeses and 50,000 tarts. Off the Grand Tinel, more delightful frescoes by Matteo Giovannetti decorate the **Chapelle St-Martial**.

The tour continues to the pope's **Antechamber**, where he would hold private audiences, and then on to the **Pope's Bedroom**, covered with murals of spiralling foliage, birds and birdcages. It leads directly into the New Palace and the most delightful room in the entire palace, the **Chambre du Cerf**, Clement VI's study. In 1343 he had Matteo Giovannetti (probably) lead a group of French painters in depicting outdoor scenes of hunting, fishing, and peach-picking. The arrows direct you next to the **Sacristy**, crowded with statues of kings, queens and bishops escaped from Gargantua's chessboard, followed by Clement VI's **Great Chapel**, longer even than the Grand Tinel and just as empty. A grand stair leads down to the flamboyant **Great Audience Hall**, where a band of Matteo Giovannetti's Prophets remain intact.

Around the Palace: Notre-Dame-des-Doms

To the left of the palace is Avignon's cathedral, **Notre-Dame-des-Doms**, built in 1150, its landmark square bell tower ridiculously dwarfed by a gilt statue of the Virgin added in 1859, in an attempt to make the church stand out next to the papal pile. The interior has been fuzzily Baroqued, but it's worth focusing on the good bits: the dome at the crossing, with an octagonal drum pierced with light, the masterpiece of this typically Provençal conceit; the 11th- or 12th-century marble bishop's chair in the choir; and in a chapel next to the sacristy, now the **Trésor** (*adm*), the flamboyant *Tomb of John XXII* (d. 1334) by English sculptor Hugh Wilfred. Next to the cathedral, ramps lead up to the oasis of the **Rocher des Doms**, once a *citadela* and now a garden enjoying panoramic views of the Rhône and Mont Ventoux.

Musée du Petit Palais

At the end of Place des Papes, the Petit Palais once housed the cardinal legate and now holds Avignon's medieval art (*open daily 9.30–1 and 2–5.30; closed Tues; June–Sept daily 10–1 and 2–6; adm*). There are fascinating fragments of the 35ft, 8-storey **Tomb of Cardinal Jean de Lagrange** (1389), from Avignon's church of St-Martial, and six rooms glowing with the golden 14th- and early 15th-century Italian Madonnas. Sienese artists (especially Simone Martini and Taddeo di Bartolo), with their more elegant, stylized line and richer colours, were favoured by the popes and strongly influential in the International Gothic style forged at the papal court (room 8). The museum's best-known work, Botticelli's *Virgin and Child*, is a tender, lyrical painting of his youth. Rooms 17–19 are devoted to works by French artists in Avignon, who after 1440 formed one of the most important schools of French Renaissance art; it concentrates on strong, simple images, as in the altarpiece *Virgin and Child between Two Saints* (1450), by the school's greatest master, Enguerrand Quarton.

Place de l'Horloge and Quartier des Fusteries

Just below the Place du Palais, an antique carousel spins gaily in the lively centre of old Avignon: **Place de l'Horloge**, site of the old Roman forum. The windows on the east side of the square are filled with trompe-l'œil paintings of historic personages, who all are linked in some way to the city. Behind the Hôtel de Ville lies the **Quartier des Fusteries**, named for the wood merchants and carpenters who had their work-shops here in the Middle Ages, but were replaced in the 18th century with *hôtels particuliers*. From the Quartier des Fusteries, the steep picturesque lanes of the **Quartier de la Balance** wind back up to the Place du Palais. Off Place de l'Horloge, Rue St-Agricol is named after the Gothic church of **St-Agricol** (1326); its treasure is the *Doni Retable*, a rare Provençal work from the Renaissance.

Museums: Vouland, Calvet, Requien, Lapidaire and Angladon-Dubrujeaud

At the end of Rue St-Agricol curves Rue Joseph Vernet, lined with 18th-century *hôtels particuliers*, antique shops, pricey restaurants and cafés. The kind of overly ornate, spindly furniture, porcelains and knick-knacks that originally filled these mansions is on display nearby in Rue Victor Hugo's **Musée Louis Vouland** (*open May–Oct daily 10–12 and 2–6, otherwise 2–6; closed Sun and Mon; adm*). At 65 Rue Joseph Vernet, a fancy *hôtel particulier* houses the **Musée Calvet** (*open 10–1 and 2–6; closed Tues; adm*), which offers something for every taste: 6,000 pieces of wrought iron, Greek sculp-ture, 18th-century seascapes by Avignon native Joseph Vernet, mummies, tapestries, prehistoric statue-steles, dizzy kitsch paintings of nude men, and an excellent collec-tion of 19th- and 20th-century paintings by Corot, Guigou, Soutine, Daumier, Dufy, Morisot, Utrillo, Seurat, Toulouse-Lautrec, Vlaminck and Rouault.

Adjacent to the Calvet museum, the **Museum Requien** is Avignon's fuddy-duddy natural history collection (*open Tues–Sat 9–12 and 2–6*), where a 81lb beaver found in the Sorgue steals the show. At 27 Rue de la République, in the chilly 17th-century Jesuit chapel, are the sculptures of the **Musée Lapidaire** (*open daily exc Tues 10–1 and 2–6; adm*). It's worth popping in for the 2nd-century BC (or Merovingian) man-eating *Tarasque de Noves*, each hand gripping the head of a Gaul, while an arm dangles from its greedy jaws; or for its statues of Gallic warriors, looking much nattier in their mail than Asterix. There is good Renaissance sculpture as well, but the best is in the nearby church of **St-Didier** (1359), just to the north in Place St-Didier: Francesco Laurana's polychrome reredos of Christ bearing the Cross, called Notre-Dame du Spasme for the spasm of pain on Mary's face.

Nearby, at 5 Rue Laboureur, the treasures of a serious art collector named Jean Angladon-Dubrujeaud have been opened as Avignon's newest museum, the **Fondation Angladon-Dubrujeaud** (*open Dec–Mar Wed–Sun 1–6; April–Nov Tues–Sun 1–6; adm*), with a fine assortment of modern painting never before seen: works by Modigliani, Picasso, Manet, Degas and Cézanne, as well as the only Van Gogh on display in Provence, called *Les Wagons de chemin de fer*. The **Musée du Mont de Piété**, 6 Rue Saluces (*open Mon–Fri 8.30–12 and 1.30–5.30*), the oldest pawnbroker's in France, now houses not only the town archives, but the *conditions des soies*, or silk conditioning equipment, once the wealth of Avignon.

The Eastern Quarters

Rue des Teinturiers, the most picturesque street in Avignon, was named after the dyers and textile-makers who powered their machines on water-wheels in the Sorgue, two of which survive. Petrarch's Laura, who lived in the area, was buried in the Franciscan church here, although only the Gothic bell tower survived the Revolution. Rue des Teinturiers turns into Rue Bonneterie on its way to Avignon's shopping district. Just beyond Place Carnot, **St-Pierre**'s flamboyant façade boasts a set of beautifully carved walnut doors (1551). From Place St-Pierre, Rue Carnot continues to the charming Place des Carmes, dominated by the 14th-century **Eglise des Carmes**, Avignon's biggest church, with a pretty cloister.

Villeneuve lez Avignon

The 10th-century abbey of St-André above Villeneuve lez Avignon was one of the mightiest monasteries in the south of France, and in 1226, when Louis VIII besieged pro-Albigensian Avignon, the abbot offered the king co-sovereignty of the abbey in exchange for royal privileges. But Villeneuve was soon invaded in another way, by cardinals wishing to retreat across the Rhône from the wanton, squalid Avignon of the popes. Though a dormitory suburb these days, Villeneuve still maintains a separate peace, with well-fed cats snoozing in the sun.

In 1307, when Philip the Fair ratified the deal that made Villeneuve royal property, he ordered that a citadel should be built on the approach to Pont St-Bénézet and named after guess who – the **Tour Philippe-le-Bel** (*open Oct–Mar daily 10–12 and 2–5.30; April–Sept daily 10–12.30 and 3–7; closed Mon out of season, and Feb*). From here, Montée de la Tour leads up to the 14th-century **Collégiale Notre-Dame**, now Villeneuve's parish church. The church's most famous work, a beaming, swivel-hipped, polychrome ivory statue of the Virgin carved in Paris out of an elephant's tusk c. 1320, has been removed to safer quarters in the nearby **Musée Pierre-de-Luxembourg** (*same hours as Tour Philippe-le-Bel; adm*). The museum's other prize is the masterpiece of the Avignon school: Enguerrand Quarton's 1454 *Couronnement de la Vierge*, one of the greatest works of 15th-century French painting, commissioned for the Charterhouse (*see below*). Unusually, it portrays God the Father and God the Son as twins, clothed in sumptuous crimson and gold, like the Virgin herself.

In Rue de la République rises what was the largest and wealthiest charterhouse in France, the **Chartreuse du Val-de-Bénédiction** (*open April–Sept daily 9–6.30; Oct–Mar daily 9.30–5.30; adm*). In 1792, the Revolution forced the monks out, and the Charterhouse was sold in 17 lots. Now re-purchased and beautifully restored, it hosts seminars, exhibitions and performances, especially during the Avignon festival. Still, the sensation that lingers in the Charterhouse is one of vast silences and austerity, the hallmark of an order where conversation was limited (originally) to one hour a week. Explanations (in English) offer an in-depth view of Carthusian life. In the Tinel's chapel are 14th-century frescoes by Matteo Giovannetti and his school. The star attraction is **Innocent VI's tomb**, with an alabaster effigy under a Gothic baldachin.

St-Rémy-de-Provence

Enclosed by a garland of boulevards lined with plane trees, St-Rémy's tranquil charms have attracted its share of the famous. Nostradamus was born here, Gertrude Stein spent years here, Princess Caroline drops in for visits (St-Rémy used to belong to the family), and Vincent Van Gogh spent his tragic last year in St-Rémy's asylum.

Nowadays St-Rémy is home to a good many artists, and there are always exhibitions going on. The newest attraction is the bizarre-looking organ in the church of **St-Martin** on Bd Marceau, built only in 1983 and said to be one of the finest in the world. Older attractions are two fine Renaissance palaces, both around Place Flavier. The Hôtel Mistral de Mondragon (1550) contains the **Musée des Alpilles** (local folk life

Getting Around

Although there are no trains, St-Rémy has a decent coach service. All leave from Place de la République, across from the church: at least one a day to Arles, Tarascon, Cavaillon and Aix; more frequently to Avignon. You can easily walk to Les Antiques and Glanum, but buses from St-Rémy to Les Baux are rare and inconvenient. The latter is better connected to Arles, with four or five buses a day.

Tourist Information

St-Rémy: Place Jean-Jaurès, t 04 90 92 05 22, f 04 90 92 38 52.

Where to Stay and Eat

St-Rémy ⊠ 13210
****Le Vallon de Valrugues, Chemin de Canto Cigalo, t 04 90 92 04 40, f 04 90 92 44 01

(*expensive*). On the outskirts. Lovely Provençal-style rooms, pool, sauna, Jacuzzi, and delicious meals, including lots of seafood and truffles in season (*menus from 190F*).
****Château des Alpilles, D31, t 04 90 92 03 33, f 04 90 92 45 17 (*expensive*). Outside the busy one-way rush of traffic round the centre, yet just a few steps out of town, in a park, with a tennis court and pool. It's all mirrors, period furniture and creature comforts; the restaurant caters for hotel guests only.
***Castelet des Alpilles, 6 Place Mireille, t 04 90 92 07 21, f 04 90 92 52 03 (*moderate*). An old country mansion, with pretty rooms and a lovely terrace under a century-old cedar. *Closed Nov–Easter.*
**Villa Glanum, 46 Av Van Gogh, t 04 90 92 03 59, f 04 90 92 00 08 (*inexpensive*). Near the ruins, family-run and has some surprising amenities for its price: a pool and garden. *Closed Nov–Feb.*

and arts) with a special section on Nostradamus (*open daily 10–12 and 2–5; closed 2001*); the Hôtel de Sade has a small but interesting **Musée Archéologique** (*guided tours in French every hour, open daily 10–12 and 2–5; July and Aug till 7; adm; combined ticket with Glanum and Musée des Alpilles available*). St-Rémy is the medieval successor to the abandoned Roman town of Glanum; finds on display here include architectural fragments, statues and reliefs of deities from Hermes to the Phrygian god Attis, and Roman glass and jewellery. The Grimaldi representative in St-Rémy lived in the beautiful 18th-century Hôtel Estrine, in Rue Estrine, now the **Centre Vincent Van Gogh** (*open Tues–Sun 10.30–12.30 and 2.30–6.30; closed Jan–Mar; adm*), where you'll find a permanent exhibit of photos and documents plus a film on Van Gogh's life.

Les Antiques, and Van Gogh's Asylum

Just a 15-minute walk from the centre of St-Rémy, south on the D5, stand two remarkable Roman relics. Originally they decorated the end of the Roman road from Arles to Glanum, the ruins of which lie just across the D5. The **Triumphal Arch** was probably built in the reign of Augustus; its elegant form and marble columns show the Greek sensibility of the artists, far different from the strange Celtic-influenced arches of Orange and Carpentras. Next to it, the so-called **Mausoleum** was really a memorial to Caesar and Augustus, erected by their descendants in the early 1st century AD. There is nothing else quite like this anywhere; the excellent reliefs on the base show mythological scenes including a battle with Amazons, a battle of Greeks and Trojans and a boar hunt.

✶✶Le Cheval Blanc, 6 Av Fauconnet, t 04 90 92 09 28, f 04 90 92 69 05 (*inexpensive*). The centre is noisy, but if you want to look out on to the square as you wake, stay here; the owners are cheerful, and it has a garage.

La Maison Jaune, 15 Rue Carnot, t 04 90 92 56 14. With panoramic terrace; plump for the 255F menu of Provençal specialities (*lunch menu 120F, others 175F and 295F*). Closed Sun eve and Mon, Jan and Feb.

L'Assiette de Marie, 1 Rue Jaume Roux, t 04 90 92 32 14. Vegetarians (and others) will find joy among the bric-a-brac here; try the home-made pasta. Good wine list (*menu 189F*). Closed Tues in winter.

Le Bistrot des Alpilles, 15 Bd Mirabeau, t 04 90 92 09 17. A cheaper place where you'll get generous fresh pasta, great desserts and a pleasant terrace. Closed Sun.

Les Baux ✉ 13520

✶✶✶✶L'Oustau de Baumanière, Route d'Arles, t 04 90 54 33 07, f 04 90 54 40 46

(*expensive*). In magical surroundings in the Val d'Enfer, a restored farmhouse with all the amenities, and a two-Michelin-star restaurant and a spectacular terrace view. There are sumptuous desserts and a formidable wine list (over 100,000 bottles) of Provençal treasures. A memorable splurge, if you can bear the disdainful hauteur (*menus 490F and 750F, but you're just as well off choosing à la carte*). Closed Jan and Feb.

✶✶✶✶Cabro d'Or, D27, t 04 90 54 33 21, f 04 90 54 45 98 (*expensive*). Charming place that offers similar facilities for kinder prices, as well as a chef trained with Ducasse and Robouchon (*menus from 250F*). Closed Mon and Tues lunch.

✶✶✶Mas d'Aigret, below Les Baux (east on the D27), t 04 90 54 20 00, f 04 90 54 44 00 (*moderate*). Some rooms have great views, others open on to the gardens; the *chambres troglodytes* are actually hewn from the rock face. There is a pool, too.

Just across the road from Les Antiques, a shady path leads to the **monastery of St-Paul-de-Mausole** (*open April–Oct Tues–Sun 9.15–6.15; Nov–Mar Tues–Fri 11–5; adm*), in a beautiful setting with gardens all around. Founded in the 900s, the monastery buildings were later purchased for use as a private hospital. This is the place Vincent Van Gogh chose as a refuge from the troubles of life in the outside world, in May 1890, not long after he chopped off his ear. He spent a year here, the most intense and original period of his career, painting as if possessed – 150 canvases and over 100 drawings, including many of his most famous works, such as the *Nuit étoilée* ('Starry Night') and *Les Blés Jaunes* ('Cornfield and Cypress Trees'). The blueish mountains in the background of this work and many others are the Alpilles.

Glanum

Glanum began as a Celtic settlement before the Romans under Marius snatched it around 100 BC. More than anywhere else in France, this is the place to feel really at home in the Roman world. But you'll have to work for it; only the foundations remain, and recreating Glanum will require a bit of imagination (see the museum in the Hôtel de Sade first). From the entrance, to the left are the **Maison des Antes** and the **Maison d'Atys**, two wealthy homes built around peristyle courtyards. The latter had apparently been transformed into a sanctuary of Cybele and Attis; this cult was one of the most popular of the mystery religions imported from the east in imperial times. Across the street are remains of a fountain and the **thermae** (baths), with mosaics, a *palestra* (exercise yard) and a pool. Next door is a building with an exedra that was probably a temple. In this part of the street the **sewers** have been uncovered. The **forum** wasn't very impressive, by Roman standards, and it is hard to make anything out today from the confusion of buildings from various ages that have been excavated. Beyond it, to the right, are foundations of temples; to the left are bases of another fountain and a monument. The street closes at a **gate** from Hellenistic times; the **nymphaeum** is beyond it, to the left.

The Chaîne des Alpilles and Les Baux-de-Provence

In a matter of minutes the five twisting kilometres from St-Rémy to the heart of the Alpilles take you to another world. This world, incredibly, is at most 16km across, and a stone's throw from the swamps of the Camargue and the sea. It is made of thin, cool breezes and brilliant light; its colours are white and deep green – almost exclusively – in an astringent landscape of limestone crags and patches of scrubby maquis.

In the Middle Ages, Les Baux, a steep barren plateau in the centre of the Alpilles, made the perfect setting for the most feared and celebrated of Provence's clans, Seigneurs des Baux, great patrons of the troubadours. By waging incessant warfare on all comers, and occasionally on each other, they gradually became a real power in the region until their castle was demolished by Richelieu in 1632. The village below the castle has been rebuilt in the worst way, and whatever spark of glamour survives here, you will have to run the gauntlet of shops peddling trinkets to reach it.

Up the Rue de la Calade you will come to the Place de l'Eglise, where the 16th-century Hôtel des Porcelet has now become the **Musée Yves Brayer** (*open daily 10–12.30 and 2–5.30; closed Tues; closed Jan–mid-Feb; adm*). Brayer (1907–90), a respected figurative painter, left his major works here, pictures of Spain and Italy as well as Provence; you can get a preview of his work in the 17th-century **Chapelle des Pénitents Blancs** opposite (*same hours*). Also in the village are the **Hôtel Jean de Brion** and the **Hôtel de Manville**, on the Grand-rue. The first houses the **Fondation Louis Jou** (*visit by appointment only, t 04 90 54 34 17; adm*), containing Jou's engravings, as well as ones by Dürer, Rembrandt and Goya. The second is the Hôtel de Ville. The **Citadel** (*open daily 9–7.30, till 9 in summer, till 5 in winter; adm*) has a new museum to keep the tramping tourists from the thing itself: the **Musée d'Histoire des Baux**, with illustrations, archaeological finds and models.

Further up, the ambience changes abruptly – a rocky chaos surrealistically decorated with fragments of once-imposing buildings. The path leads through this 'Ville Morte' to the tip of the plateau, where there is a grand view over the Alpilles. Turning back, the path climbs up to the château itself, with bits of towers and walls everywhere, including the apse of a Gothic chapel cut out of the rock, and the long eastern wall that survived Richelieu's explosives, dotted with finely carved windows. The only intact part is the **donjon**, a rather treacherous climb to the top for a bird's-eye view over the site. Three kilometres further on, the **Val d'Enfer**, the wildest corner of the Alpilles, is a weird landscape of eroded limestone, caves and quarries. The quarries host one of Les Baux's big attractions: the **Cathédrale des Images** (*open daily 10–7; adm*), a slick show where thirty projectors bounce giant pictures over the walls; the theme of the show changes annually.

Arles

Henry James wrote, 'As a city Arles quite misses its effect in every way: and if it is a charming place, as I think it is, I can hardly tell the reason why.' Modern Arles, sitting amidst its ruins, is still somehow charming, in spite of a general scruffiness that seems more intentional than natural. For all the tourists it gets, no town could seem less touristy.

In 49 BC, the local Ligurians, tired of getting raw deals from the Greeks in Marseille, readily gave Caesar the boats he needed to punish and conquer Marseille for siding with Pompey. In return Arles was rewarded the spoils and, most important of all, got all the business that had previously gone through Marseille. The colony became known far and wide for its powerful maritime corporations. At the crossroads of Rome's trading route between Italy and Spain and the Rhône, Arles grew rapidly, each century adding more splendid monuments – a theatre, temples, a circus, an amphitheatre, at least two triumphal arches and a basilica. On the whole, the Dark Ages were not so dark in Arles; from 879 to 1036 it served as the capital of Provence-Burgundy (the so-called 'Kingdom of Arles'), a vast territory that stretched all the way to Lorraine. Most importantly, Arles was a centre of power for Christianity and one of

Getting There and Around

Arles' **train** station is on the northern edge of town, on Av Paulin Talabot. Arles has frequent connections to Paris, Marseille, Montpellier, Nîmes, Aix-en-Provence, and Perpignan; also frequent trains to Avignon and a less frequent service to Orange.

The **bus** station is just across the street, t 04 90 49 38 01. There are about five daily buses to Stes-Maries-de-la-Mer in the Camargue, seven to Salon, Aix and Marseille, five to Avignon, six to Nîmes and two to St-Gilles; in July and August, there are services to Aigues-Mortes. For a **taxi** day or night, call t 04 90 96 90 03.

Tourist Information

Arles: Esplanade Charles de Gaulle, t 04 90 18 41 20, f 04 90 18 41 29, *www.arles.org*, and in the train station, t 04 90 49 36 90. If you intend to see more than two of Arles' monuments and museums, stop here to purchase the 60F global ticket to save money (or you can also pick one up at any of the museums). The tourist office also sells tickets for the two-hour Van Gogh tours of sites associated with the artist (departing every Tues and Fri at 5pm, July–Sept, in French only).

Where to Stay

Arles ✉ 13200

Expensive

****Jules César, Bd des Lices, t 04 90 93 43 20, f 04 90 93 33 47. The luxurious grand-daddy of hotels in Arles occupies a former Dominican monastery with a Caesar-ish temple porch tacked on. The rooms are vast, air-conditioned and furnished with Provençal pieces; the pool is heated and the gardens beautiful. *Closed Nov–23 Dec.*

****Nord Pinus, Place du Forum, t 04 90 93 44 44, f 04 90 93 34 00. With columns from a Roman temple embedded in its façade, the favourite of Stendhal, Mérimée and Henry James now draws top matadors; the premises are full of heavy dark furniture, bull-fighting posters, trophies, and the mounted heads of famous bulls.

---

the bases of the counts of Provence. Arles' cathedral of St-Trophime became the most important church in Provence. After a busy career in the 11th and 12th centuries as a Crusader port and pilgrimage destination, the city's special history ended in 1239 when Raymond Bérenger, count of Provence, evicted Arles' imperial viceroy. As the city declined even the sea abandoned it, leaving the former port stranded between marshes and the rocky plain of the Crau.

The Arles of Van Gogh

When Vincent Van Gogh arrived in Arles in 1888 he found a shabby, ugly town. But he decided to stay, and painted the shabby Arles around him: the Café de nuit with its hallucinogenic lightbulb, La Maison jaune and Le Pont de Langlois (part of a ghastly irrigation project) with colours so intense in their chromatic contrasts they seem to come from somewhere over the rainbow. Van Gogh's dream was to found an art colony at Arles, and he begged his overbearing friend Gauguin to join him, but when Gauguin finally arrived in October he found little to like there. The tension between the two men reached such a pitch in December that the overwrought Van Gogh confronted Gauguin in the street with a razor. Gauguin stared him down and Van Gogh, despising himself, went back to his room and cut off his own ear. Arles breathed a sigh of relief when Van Gogh committed himself to the local hospital, and then to the hospital in St-Rémy. Van Gogh's output in Arles was prodigious (from February 1888 to May 1889 he painted 300 canvases) but not a single one remains in the city today.

★★★**D'Arlatan, 26 Rue du Sauvage, t** 04 90 93
56 66, **f** 04 90 49 68 45. Near the lively Place
du Forum, the 12th–18th-century home of
the Comtes d'Arlatan has been converted
into a magnificent hotel. If you're alone and
can do without a TV and your own bathroom, ask for room 38, located in a converted
chapel. *Closed Jan.*

Moderate
★★**St-Trophime**, 16 Rue de la Calade, **t** 04 90 96
88 38, **f** 04 90 96 92 19. In an old house with
a central court. *Closed mid-Nov–mid-Dec,
and Jan.*
★★**Calendal**, 22 Place Pomme, **t** 04 90 96 11 89,
f 04 90 96 05 84. Rooms overlook a garden
with palm trees.
★★**Hôtel du Musée**, 11 Rue du Grand-Prieuré,
t 04 90 93 88 88, **f** 04 90 49 98 15. A 17th-
century residence opposite the Musée
Réattu. Quiet, subtly chic, and above all
friendly. *Closed Jan–mid-Feb.*

Inexpensive
★★**Gauguin**, 5 Place Voltaire, **t** 04 90 96 14 35.
Just south of Place Lamartine, with simple

but tidy rooms, some with balconies.
Closed Nov.
★**Terminus et Van Gogh**, 5 Place Lamartine ,
t/f 04 90 96 12 32. A bright and very
welcoming place.
★**France**, 3 Place Lamartine, **t** 04 90 96 01 24.
Next door, also good and also slightly
less expensive.

Eating Out

Lou Marquès, in Jules César. Arles' elegant
citadel of traditional *haute cuisine*, featuring
dishes such as *croustillant de St-Pierre* and
carré d'agneau with artichokes, and an excellent wine cellar (*menus 195–380F*).
Le Jardin de Manon, 14 Av des Alyscamps,
t 04 90 93 38 68. *Cuisine provençale* on a
pretty terrace out back (*85F lunch menu,
others 98F, 150F and 200F*).
Vitamine, 16 Rue du Docteur Fanton, **t** 04 90
93 77 36. For a light lunch in the centre, with
50 different salads for under 70F. *Closed Sun,
exc July.*

The Arènes and Théâtre Antique

As enormous as it is, the Roman arena, **Les Arènes** (*open April–mid-June daily
9–12.30 and 2–7; mid-June–end Sept daily 9–7; rest of year daylight hours; closed 12–2*),
10ft wider than its rival at Nîmes, originally stood another arcade higher, and was clad
in marble. An enormous awning operated by sailors protected the audience from the
sun and rain. From the Middle Ages on it sheltered a poor, crime-ridden neighbourhood with two churches and 200 houses, built from stones prised off the amphitheatre's third storey. These were cleared away in 1825, leaving the amphitheatre free
for bullfights, and able to pack in 12,000 spectators. But a different fate was in store
for the **Théâtre Antique** (*same hours as Arènes*), just south of the Arènes: in the 5th
century, in a fury usually reserved for pagan temples, Christian fanatics pulled it apart
stone by stone. A shame, because the fragments of fine sculpture they left in the
rubble suggest that the theatre, once capable of seating 12,000, was much more
lavish than the one in Orange. South of the theatre runs the **Boulevard des Lices** ('of
the lists'), the favourite promenade of the Arlésiens since the 17th century.

Place de la République: St-Trophime and the Crypto-portiques

From Boulevard des Lices, Rue Jean Jaurès (the Roman *cardo*) leads to the harmonious **Place de la République**, an attractive square on the Roman model. Overlooking
it is the Romanesque **cathedral of St-Trophime**. The original church was built in the

5th century, and the great **Portal** was added in the 12th century. Its reliefs describe the Last Judgement; on the left side, St Michael weighs each soul, separating the good from evil – the fortunate are delivered into the bosoms of Abraham, Isaac and Jacob, while the damned, naked and bound like a chain gang, are led off to hell: as in all great Romanesque art, the figures on this portal seem to dance to an inner, cosmic rhythm. After the sumptuous portal, the spartan nudity of the long, narrow nave is as striking as its unusual height. Aubusson tapestries from the 17th century hang across the top. Around the corner in Rue du Cloître is the entrance to St-Trophime's **cloister** (*same hours as the Arènes*). No other cloister in Provence is as richly and harmoniously sculpted as this, carved in the 12th and 14th centuries by the masters of St-Gilles.

Sharing Place de la République with St-Trophime is Arles' palatial **Hôtel de Ville**, built in 1675 after plans by Hardouin-Mansart. Just around the corner on Rue Balze is the cryptoporticus of the forum, the **Crypto-portiques** (*same hours as Arènes; adm*). With the ramparts, this cryptoporticus was the first large construction of the Roman colony. Forming three sides of a rectangle measuring 289 by 192ft, these subterreanean barrel-vaulted double galleries of the 1st century BC were built as foundations for the monumental Forum above.

The Muséon Arlaten, Réattu Museum and Musée de l'Arles Antique

The indefatigable Frédéric Mistral – poet, founder of the Félibrige literary school (the aim of which was to 'safeguard indefinitely for Provence its language, its colour, its easy liberty, its national honour, and its fine level of intelligence, for such as it is, we like Provence'), and the first (and only) writer in a minority language to win the Nobel Prize for literature – began his collection of ethnographic items from Provence in 1896. In 1904 he set up the **Muséon Arlaten** (*29 Rue de la République; open daily 9.30–12.30 and 2–5; June–Aug daily 9.30–1 and 2–6.30; Oct–June closed Mon; adm*). Mistral's aim was to record the details of everyday life in Provence for future generations. The evolution of the traditional Arlésienne costume was one of his obsessions. Most memorable and strange are the life-size dioramas: a Christmas dinner at a *mas*, with a table groaning with wax food, a reed-thatched *cabane des gardians*, and a visit to a new mother and her infant. A **statue of Mistral**, looking uncommonly like Buffalo Bill, stands on Place du Forum.

After the Revolution an academic painter named Jacques Réattu purchased the Priory of the Knights of Malta, and his daughter made it into the **Musée Réattu**, Rue du Grand Prieuré (*same hours as Arènes; adm*). Besides Reattu's own contributions, there are works by Théodore Rousseau and followers of Lorrain and Salvator Rosa. In 1972, the museum was jolted awake with a donation of 57 drawings from Picasso, in gratitude for the many bullfights he enjoyed in Arles. Nearly all date from January 1971 and constitute a running dialogue the artist held with himself on some of his favourite subjects – harlequins, men, women, the artist and his model. Other Picassos in the museum include a beautiful portrait of his mother Maria from the 1920s, donated by his widow Jacqueline, and a sculpture of a woman with a violin.

Arles' newest museum, the **Musée de l'Arles Antique** (*open Mar–Oct daily 9–7; Nov–Feb daily 10–5; adm*), at Presqu'île du Cirque Romain, Avenue de la 1ère D.F.L., is situated in an eerie wasteland slightly out of town (follow the Boulevard des Lices to its western end, and pass under the motorway) and contains the collected contents of several of Arles' old museums. Brilliant architectural models bring the Roman city back to life. Here you'll see how the Roman sailors wired up the sailcloth awning to shade the amphitheatre, how the city centre – the Forum and temples – looked to the man in the street, and much more. Amongst the other exhibits are the pagan statues and sarcophagi of the former Musée d'Art Païen; nearly everything here was made in the Arles region. Also in the museum are the contents of the former Musée d'Art Chrétien, with the best collection of 4th-century Christian sarcophagi anywhere.

The Alyscamps

Because of the legend of St Trophime, who was said to be a disciple of St Paul himself, the Alyscamps (*follow Rue E. Fassin from the Boulevard des Lices, eastwards; a 10min walk from the centre; same hours as the Arènes; adm*) was one of the most prestigious necropolises of the Middle Ages. Burial here was so desirable that bodies sealed in barrels with their burial fee attached were floated down the Rhône. At its greatest extent the necropolis stretched for 2.5km and contained 19 chapels and several thousand tombs, many of them packed five bodies deep. Now, only one romantic, melancholy lane lined with empty, mostly plain sarcophagi remains. Of the 19 chapels, all that's left is a 15th-century chapel that now serves as the ticket booth, along with recently restored Romanesque **St-Honorat** at the far end.

Into the Camargue

To its handful of inhabitants, the Camargue was the *isclo*, the 'island' between the two branches of the Rhône. The river's course has taken many different forms over the millennia, and the present one, with its two arms, has created a vast marshland – France's salt cellar, a treasure-house of water-fowl and the home of some of its most exotic scenery. The Grand and Petit Rhônes build separate deltas, leaving the space in between a soupy battleground where land and sea slowly struggle for mastery.

From the 1600s, cowboys (*gardians*) have created large ranches to exploit the two totem animals of the Camargue: the native black longhorn cattle that thrive on salt grass, and have always been the preferred stock for Provençal bullfights; and the beautiful white horse, believed to have been introduced by the Arabs in the Dark Ages. A true cowboy culture grew up, a romantic image dear to the Provençaux. The government made a Regional Park of the area in 1970 and there are still a few score *gardians* today, keeping up the old traditions.The Regional Park's **Musée de la Camargue** (*open Oct–Mar daily exc Tues 10.15–4.45; April–June and Sept daily 9.15–5.45; July and Aug daily 9.15–6.45; adm*) occupies what not long ago was a working cattle and sheep ranch, 9km southwest of Arles on the D570. The buildings are well restored and documented, giving a feeling of what life was like a century ago. Outside, there are marked nature trails leading deep into the surrounding swampy plain.

For all of us lazy motor tourists, the way to see the best of the Camargue is to take

Getting Around

By train and bus: The only public transport to the centre of the Camargue begins at the bus station in Arles: one or two buses a day each to Stes-Maries-de-la-Mer and Salin-de-Giraud. There are also one or two SNCF trains to St-Gilles from Arles. St-Gilles has regular bus connections to Nîmes (five a day), and a few to Arles.

There are at least two buses daily from Arles to Les Stes-Maries-de-la-Mer (55mins, t 04 90 96 36 25). In July and Aug there are direct services from Stes-Maries to Aigues-Mortes and Montpellier (t 04 67 92 01 43) and others to St-Gilles and Nîmes (t 04 66 29 52 00).

On foot, horseback and by bike and jeep: The Camargue is really quite small – it's never more than 40km from Arles to the coast. It is perfect country for cycling, and there are a few places in Stes-Maries-de-la-Mer to rent some wheels; try Le Vélociste, Place des Remparts, t 04 90 97 83 26 (*open Sept–June*). Horses are even more popular; there are many places to hire one, including, at l'Etang de l'Estagel, L'Etrier, t 04 66 01 36 76. Camargue Safaris in Stes-Maries is one of many firms offering jeep tours of the Camargue, t 04 90 97 86 93. Destination Camargue, t 04 90 96 94 44, organizes day and half-day trips by jeep.

By boat: Blue-Line, t 04 66 87 22 66, and other firms in St-Gilles rent boats fit for a few days' trip through the Petite Camargue. At Stes-Maries and St-Gilles there are excursion boats that make short cruises around the Camargue. From Stes-Maries, the paddle steamer *Tiki III*, t 04 90 97 81 68, offers an hour-long cruise on the Petit Rhône (end Mar–Sept).

Where to Stay and Eat

Les Stes-Maries-de-la-Mer ✉ 13460

★★★**Mas du Clarousset**, 7km north on D85A, the Route de Cacharel, t 04 90 97 81 66, f 04 90 97 88 59 (*moderate*). Little and pink and offers fresh and simple décor. Each room has a private terrace, and there are extras – horses to ride, a pool, jeep excursions and gypsy music evenings in the excellent restaurants (*menus from 250F*).

★★★**Le Pont des Bannes**, 3km north on the D570, t 04 90 97 81 09, f 04 90 97 89 28

the D37, a left turn 4km south of the museum. After another 4km, a side road leads to the **Domaine de Méjanes**, with horse riding and canoes; on summer weekends the gardians put on shows of cowboy know-how, and occasionally bullfights. Further on, the D37 skirts the edges of the **Etang de Vaccarès**, the biggest of the lagoons and centre of the Camargue wildlife preserve. In some places you can see flocks of flamingos year-round. The scenery changes abruptly at **Salin-de-Giraud**, a 19th-century industrial village devoted to the largest saltworks in Europe: a staggering 110 square kilometre network of pans, annually producing 800,000 tonnes of salt. There's a nature centre on the D36, **La Palissade** (*open daily 9–5*), with white horses, bulls, an aquarium, walks etc., and information on the flamingo-filled Etang de Grande-Palun.

Les Stes-Maries-de-la-Mer

Set among the low sand-dunes, lively Stes-Maries-de-la-Mer has an open-armed approach to visitors that long predates any interest in the Camargue, for this is one of Provence's holiest places. The pious story behind it all was promoted to the hilt by the medieval Church: after Christ was crucified, his Jewish detractors took a boat without sails or oars and loaded it with three Marys – Mary Salome (mother of the apostles James and John), Mary Jacobe, the Virgin's sister, Mary Magdalene, Martha and her

(*moderate*). You can sleep comfortably in a *cabane de gardian* with a pool, garden and stables for the total Camargue experience. Similar facilities may be had at the annexe, ★★★**Le Mas Sainte-Hélène**, Chemin Bas-des-Launes, **t** 04 90 97 83 29, **f** 04 90 97 89 28 (*moderate*), spread out along an islet in the Etang des Launes, where you can get eye to eye with the pink flamingos on its water-side terraces.

★**Le Delta**, Place Mireille, **t** 04 90 97 81 12, **f** 04 90 97 72 85 (*cheap*). Good value for the price, and central.

Le Brûleur de Loups, Av Gilbert-Leroy, **t** 04 90 97 83 31. With a terrace overlooking the beach and more delights from the sea, like a seafood mix in white Châteauneuf-du-Pape (*menus from 185F, cheaper for lunch*). *Closed mid-Nov–Mar.*

Hostellerie du Pont de Gau, 4 km north on the Route d'Arles, **t** 04 90 97 81 53. Jolly Provençal décor and a delicious *pot-au-feu de la mer* (*menus from 110F*). *Closed Jan–mid-Feb.*

Le Mangio Fango, Route d'Arles, **t** 04 90 97 80 56. Get a table on their skeeter-free patio for excellent Camargue bull stew (*menus 150F and 195F*).

Aigues-Mortes ✉ 30220

★★★**St-Louis**, 10 Rue de l'Amiral Courbet, just off Place St-Louis, **t** 04 66 53 69 61, **f** 04 66 53 75 92. Gracious and welcoming in a beautifully furnished 18th-century building. Its popular restaurant, L'Archère, is the best in town for steaks and seafood and homemade desserts (*lunch menu 85F, others up to 200F*). *Closed Jan–15 Mar.*

Les Arcades, 6 Bd Gambetta, **t** 04 66 53 81 13, **f** 04 66 53 75 46. Nine attractive *chambres d'hôte*, all with TV, and a good inexpensive restaurant: *viande de taureau* and other local favourites (*menus 130–250F*).

La Camargue, 19 Rue République, **t** 04 66 53 86 88. The Gypsy Kings got their start here, but even in their absence this is the liveliest place in town, with flamenco guitars strumming in the background; seafood and grilled meat (*menus 100–160F*).

Maguelone, 38 Rue République, **t** 04 66 53 74 60. Nearby, bright and blue, with a menu (*145F*) based on local ingredients: *matelote d'anguilles, bourride de lotte* and a *St-Marcel au chocolat croustillant aux coings*. *Closed two weeks Jan.*

resurrected brother Lazarus, St Maximin and St Sidonius. As this so-called Boat of Bethany drifted offshore, Sarah, the black Egyptian servant of Mary Salome and Mary Jacobe, wept so grievously that Mary Salome tossed her cloak on the water, so that Sarah was able to walk across on it and join them. The boat took them to the Camargue, to this spot where the elderly Mary Salome, Mary Jacobe and Sarah built an oratory, while their younger companions went to spread the Gospel. In 1448, during the reign of Good King René, the supposed relics of the two Marys were discovered, greatly boosting the local pilgrim trade. Today Stes-Maries-de-la-Mer is best known for the pilgrimage of Mary Jacobe on 24 and 25 May. This attracts gypsies from all over the world, who have canonized her servant Sarah as their patron saint.

Built in 1130, the **church** at Stes-Maries is the most impressive fortified church in Provence: a crenellated ship with loopholes for windows in a small pond of white villas with orange roofs. Inside are wells that supplied the church-fortress in times of siege; pilgrims still bottle the water to ensure their protection by St Sarah. The capitals supporting the blind arches of the raised choir are finely sculpted in the style of St-Trophime. Under the choir is the **crypt**, where the relics and statue of St Sarah in her seven robes are kept, except on 24 May when the gypsies gather to take her to the sea. From April to mid-November, you can take a stroll below the **bell tower**, with views stretching across the Camargue (*open daily 10–12.30 and 2–6*). This roof walk circles the lavish **upper chapel** (usually closed), dedicated to St Michael, where the coffer holding the relics of the Marys is kept.

To the south in Rue Victor-Hugo the Musée Baroncelli is devoted to zoology, archaeology and folklore. It is named after the Camargue's secular saint, the Félibre Marquis Folco de Baroncelli-Javon (1869–1943), who abandoned all at the age 21 to live the life of a *gardian*. Baroncelli spent the next 60 years herding bulls, writing poetry, and doing all he could to maintain the Camargue and its customs intact.

St-Gilles-du-Gard

West of Arles, the N572 takes you through the drier parts of the Camargue. After crossing the Rhône (you're now in the **Petite Camargue**), it approaches **St-Gilles**, originally a port and the only town for miles in any direction. The cradle of the powerful counts of Toulouse, it had a pilgrimage chapel holding the relics of an 8th-century Greek hermit who lived on doe's milk. Beginning in 1116, this was rebuilt as an **abbey** in one of the most ambitious projects in medieval Provence. During the Wars of Religion the Protestants thought it would look better as a fortress. Rebuilt on a smaller scale in 1650, it suffered further indignities (the loss of many of the figures' faces in the Revolution was nothing short of tragic) but the **façade** remains, miraculously, one of the great ensembles of medieval sculpture, the masterpiece of the 12th-century school of Provence. The other great sight is the Vis, '**the screw**', de St-Gilles, a spiral stair of *c*. 1142 that once led to a bell tower, a tremendous *tour de force* of stones cut so precisely as to form a self-supporting spiral vault.

Aigues-Mortes

In 1241, the Camargue was the only bit of Mediterranean coast held by France. To solidify this precarious strip, Louis IX (St Louis) began construction of a new port. In 1248, the port was complete enough to hold the 1,500 ships that carried Louis and his knights to the Holy Land, on the Seventh Crusade. His successor, Philip III, finished Aigues-Mortes and built its great **walls**, over a mile in length. Aigues-Mortes means 'dead waters', and it proved to be a prophetic name. The sea deserted Aigues and, despite efforts to keep the harbour dredged, the port went into decline after 1350. Attempts to revive it in the 1830s failed, ensuring Aigues' demise, but allowing the works of Louis and Philip to survive undisturbed. Forgotten and nearly empty a century ago, Aigues now makes its living from tourists, and from salt; half of France's supply is collected here, at the enormous **Salins-du-Midi** pans south of town in the Petite Camargue (**t** *04 66 53 85 20; organized visits July and Aug*).

Marseille

Founded by Greek colonists in 600 BC, Massalia (Marseille) boomed from the start. Conquered by Caesar for siding with Pompey, Marseille nearly went out of business.

Getting There

By plane: Marseille's airport is to the west at Marignane; call t 04 42 14 14 14 for flight information. A bus every 20mins (t 04 91 50 59 34) links the airport with the train station, Gare St-Charles, taking 25mins.

By train: There are connections to nearly every town in the south from the main station, Gare St-Charles, and the TGV will get you to Paris in 4hrs 40mins.

By metro and bus: Marseille runs an efficient bus network and two metro lines. Pick up the useful *plan du réseau* at the tourist office or at the RTM (Réseau de Transport Marseillais) information desk by the Bourse, 6–8 Rue des Fabres, t 04 91 91 92 10. Tickets are 9F, valid for an hour, and transferable between the bus and metro. At night a number of buses (Fluobus) run from the Canebière across town.

The coach station, t 04 91 08 16 40, is behind the train station at 3 Place Victor Hugo, with connections to Aix, Cassis, Nice, Arles, Avignon, Toulon and Cannes.

RTM's guided tour bus, the Histobus, leaves from the Vieux Port at 2pm, Sun in winter, daily in summer.

By taxi: Taxi drivers in Marseille tend to be maniacs. If you need one, call t 04 91 02 20 20, and make sure the meter is switched on at the start of your journey.

Car hire: Some car hire firms are in the Gare St-Charles, including Avis, t 04 91 08 41 80. Others include Hertz, 16 Bd Charles Nédelec (1er), t 04 91 14 04 24, and Thrifty, Place Marseillaises, t 04 91 95 00 00.

Tourist Information

Marseille: 4 La Canebière, by the Vieux Port, t 04 91 13 89 00, f 04 91 13 89 20.

Shopping

Rue St-Ferréol and Rue Paradis are the main shopping streets. Marseille holds a remarkable market of clay Christmas crib figures, the Foire aux Santons (end Nov–Jan); at other times, you can find *santons* at **Marcel Carbonel**, 47 Rue Neuve Ste-Catherine, 7e, near St-Victor.

For the best in Provençal food and wine, try **Georges Bataille**, 18 Rue Fontange, t 04 91 47 06 23.

Where to Stay

Marseille ✉ 13000

Marseille's top-notch hotels are the bastion of expense-account businessmen and women, while its downmarket numbers attract working girls of a different kind.

However, in the 11th century, when the Crusaders showed up looking for transport to the Holy Land, Marseille grew fat on the proceeds. It was Europe's greatest port in the 18th century, when its workers did their share in upholding the Revolution: as 500 volunteers set off in July 1792, someone suggested singing the new battle song of the Army of the Rhine. By the time they reached Paris, the 'song of the Marseillais' was perfected and became the hit tune of the Revolution, and subsequently the most rousing and bloodcurdling of national anthems.

Today amid Provence's carefully nurtured image of lavender fields, rosé wine and *pétanque*, Marseille is the great anomaly, the second city of France and the world's eighth largest port. Like New York, it has been the gateway to a new world for hundreds of thousands of new arrivals – especially Corsicans, Armenians, Jews, Greeks, Turks, Italians, Spaniards and Algerians. Many immigrants have gone no further, creating in Marseille perhaps the most varied mix of cultures and religions in Europe. On the down side, Marseille suffers from disproportionately high unemployment and the National Front has generally picked up about a third of the vote here. On the up side, the city is undergoing a vast renovation programme of 3,000 historic

Expensive

****Le Petit Nice Passédat**, off Corniche Kennedy, at Anse de Maldormé, 7e, t 04 91 59 25 92, f 04 91 59 28 08, Marseille's most refined, exclusive hotel, the Relais et Châteaux former villa overlooking the Anse de Maldormé, with a fine restaurant, Le Passédat (*see* below).

Moderate

*****New Hôtel Bompard**, 2 Rue des Flots Bleus, 7e, t 04 91 52 10 93, f 04 91 31 02 14 (bus 61 from ⓦ Joliette or St-Victor). Modern and quiet, set in its own peaceful grounds, with rooms overlooking a garden; the bungalows have their own kitchenette.

*****Mercure Vieux Port**, 4 Rue Beauvau, 1er, t 04 91 54 91 00, f 04 91 54 15 76, overlooking the Vieux Port. Where Chopin and George Sand canoodled – wood-panelled and comfortable with air-conditioned, sound-proofed rooms (but no restaurant).

Inexpensive

****Le Corbusier**, 280 Bd Michelet, 8e, t 04 91 16 78 00, f 04 91 16 78 28. Incorporated into the Unité d'Habitation, this hotel restaurant is a special treat for students of architecture. Book to get one of its 22 rooms.

****Péron**, 119 Corniche Kennedy, 7e, t 04 91 31 01 41, f 04 91 59 42 01, near the Plage des Catalans. An unusual cast-iron façade and good rooms.

****Le Richelieu**, 52 Corniche Kennedy, 7e, t 04 91 31 01 92, f 04 91 59 38 09. The best rooms are nos.28, 29 and 30.

****Moderne**, 30 Rue Breteuil, 6e, t 04 91 53 29 93. Near the Prefecture, with nice rooms with showers and TV.

****Azur**, 24 Cours Roosevelt, 1er, t 04 91 42 74 38, f 04 91 47 27 91. Some frills, such as colour TV and garden views (ⓦ Réformés).

Cheap

***Montgrand**, 50 Rue Montgrand, 6e (off Rue Paradis, behind the Opéra), t 04 91 00 35 20, f 04 91 33 75 89. Good budget choice in a very safe part of town.

***Little Palace**, 39 Bd d'Athènes, 1er, t 04 91 90 12 93, f 04 91 90 72 03. The most benign choice near the Gare St-Charles, at the foot of the grand stair

Eating Out

The Marseillais claim an ancient Greek – even divine – origin for their ballyhooed *bouillabaisse*: Aphrodite invented it to beguile her husband Hephaestos to sleep so that she could dally with her lover Ares – seafood and saffron being a legendary soporific. Good chefs prepare it just as seriously, and display

buildings, and has a new sparkle, as if suddenly awakening to the great potential of its sunny location, its diversity and great reserve of character.

The Vieux Port

Marseille's Vieux Port is now a huge pleasure port with over 10,000 berths; its cafés have fine views of the sunset, though in the morning the action and smells centre around the Quai des Belges and its boatside **fish market**. From the Quai des Belges *vedettes* sail to the Château d'If and Frioul islands (*see* p.895), past the two bristling fortresses that still defend the harbour: to the north **St-Jean**, built in the 12th century by the Knights of St John, and to the south **St-Nicolas**, built by Louis XIV to keep a close eye on Marseille rather than the sea.

A bronze marker in the Quai des Belges pinpoints the spot where the Greeks first set foot in Gaul. And yet Marseille concealed its age until this century, when excavations for the glitzy shopping mall, the Centre Bourse, revealed the eastern ramparts and gate of Massalia, dating back to the 3rd century BC, now enclosed in the Jardin des Vestiges. On the ground floor of the Centre Bourse, the **Musée d'Histoire de**

their *Charte de la Bouillabaisse* guaranteeing that their formula more or less subscribes to tradition: a saffron- and garlic-flavoured soup cooked on a low boil (hence its name), based on *rascasse* (scorpion fish, the ugliest fish in the Med, and always cooked with its leering head attached), which lives under the cliffs and has a bland taste that enhances the flavour of the other fish, especially *fielas* (conger eel), *grondin* (gurnard) and *St-Pierre* (John Dory). When served, the fish is traditionally cut up before you and presented on a side dish of *aïoli* or *rouille*, a paste of Spanish peppers.

Luxury

Le Petit Nice Passédat (*see* above). A haughty gourmet citadel offering ravishing food in its exotic garden (*weekday lunch menu 350F; otherwise menus 800F plus*).

Michel-Brasserie des Catalans, 6 Rue des Catalans, 7e, t 04 91 52 30 63. The best and certainly swankiest *bouillabaisse* is served here, to politicians and showbiz people.

Expensive

Miramar, 12 Quai du Port, 2e, t 04 91 91 10 40. Serves up a reliable, traditional *bouillabaisse* by the Vieux Port; Oscar, next door, does an excellent *bouillabaisse*, too. *Closed Sun, Mon lunch and Aug.*

Chez Fonfon, on the little fishing port at Vallon des Auffes, t 04 91 52 14 38. Overlooking the Château d'If and Frioul islands, you can feast on a renowned *bouillabaisse* from a charter member, which prides itself on the freshness of its fish. *Closed Sun, Mon lunch and Jan.*

L'Epuisette, next door to Chez Fonfon, t 04 91 52 17 82. A Marseille institution for its seafood – try the *filet de roche poêlé aux aubergines confites à l'huile d'olive* (*menus from 195F*). *Closed Sat, Sun eve, Mon lunch.*

Les Mets de Provence Chez Maurice Brun, second floor, 18 Quai de Rive Neuve, 7e, t 04 91 33 35 38. 50-year-old restaurant with an overwhelming four-course lunch menu (*220F*) that starts with eight different hors-d'œuvres and includes a *pichet* of Coteaux d'Aix. *Closed Sun and Mon lunch.*

Moderate

Les Arcenaulx, Cours d'Estienne d'Orves 25, t 04 91 59 80 30. A new favourite in the old arsenal, serving fresh market fare (*menus from 155F*). *Closed Sun.*

L'Atelier, 18 Place aux Huiles, 1er, t 04 91 33 55 00. Dessert mavens flock here, where meals are light to leave room for the exquisite grand finales (*lunch 90F for a plat du jour and dessert, dinner around 160F*). *Closed Sat eve and Sun.*

Marseille (*open Mon–Sat 12–7; adm*) displays models, everyday items from ancient times, mosaics and a 3rd-century BC wreck of a Roman ship, discovered in 1974. Elaborate antique models of later ships that sailed into the Vieux Port and items related to Marseille's trading history are the main focus of the **Musée de la Marine**, in the nearby Bourse, the palatial 19th-century exchange (*open Tues–Sun 10–6; adm*).

Le Panier

The quarter rising up behind the north end of the Vieux Port is known rather oddly as the Panier or 'Basket' after a popular 17th-century cabaret, although its irregular weave of winding narrow streets and stairs dates from the ancient Greeks. During the war this warren of secret ways absorbed hundreds of Jews and other refugees from the Nazis hoping to escape to America. In January 1943, Hitler cottoned on and, in collusion with the French police and local property speculators, ordered the dynamiting of the lower Panier.

Two buildings were protected from the dynamite: the 17th-century **Hôtel de Ville** on the quay, and behind it, in Rue de la Prison, the **Maison Diamantée**, Marseille's 16th-

La Gentiane, 9 Rue des Trois Rois, 6e, t 04 91 42 88 80. One of the city's best vegetarian choices. *Closed Sun and Mon.*

Cheap

Le Marseillois, Quai de Port, a sailing boat moored stern-on, t 04 91 90 72 52. Plenty of atmosphere (*menus 65F and 85F*).

Au Feu de Bois, 10 Rue d'Aubagne, 1er, t 04 91 54 33 96, ⓜ Noailles. Makes some of the tastiest pies in a city that takes pizza seriously. *Closed Sun.*

Le Roi du Couscous, 63 Rue de la République, t 04 91 91 45 46. The best couscous in town. *Closed Mon.*

La Grotte, Calanque de Callelongue, t 04 91 73 17 79. Popular for pizza by the sea.

Entertainment and Nightlife

Marseille has lively after-dark pockets, especially around Place Thiers, Cours Estienne d'Orves and Cours Julien. In the last decade, most of the cultural excitement in Marseille has been generated in its theatres – it has more seats per capita than Paris.

Théâtre National de la Criée, 32 Quai de Rive Neuve, 7e, t 04 91 54 70 54. Performances directed by Marcel Maréchal to wide critical acclaim since 1981.

Théâtre les Bernadines, 17 Bd Garibaldi, 1er, t 04 91 24 30 40. Experimental dance and theatre.

Théâtre du Merlan, Av Raimu, 14e, t 04 91 11 19 30. There's more of the same at Marseille's second national theatre.

Opéra Municipal, Place Reyer, 1er, t 04 91 55 14 99. Italian opera and occasional ballets from the **Ballet National de Marseille** (Roland Petit), 20 Bd Gabès, 8e, t 04 91 32 72 72, f 04 91 71 51 12.

Nightlife in Marseille is concentrated in several distinct zones. Place Jean-Jaurès/Cours Julien and around is the trendiest place.

Espace Julien, 39 Cours Julien, 6e, t 04 91 24 34 10. Jazz, rock and reggae, and a café with live music many nights of the week.

Chocolat Théâtre, 59 Cours Julien, 6e, t 04 91 42 19 29 (*190–230F*). More music, along with chocolates, pastries and *plats du jour*. *Closed Sun.*

Maison Hantée, 10 Rue Vian, off Rue des Trois Mages, t 04 91 92 09 40. The temple of rock.

Le Trolleybus, 24 Quai de Rive Neuve, t 04 91 54 30 45. A great place for a drink or a dance.

Bars and Latin clubs have also sprouted up along the seafront at the Plage de Borély, 8e.

Café de la Plage, 148 Av Pierre-Mendès-France, t 04 91 71 21 76. Trendy café, one of a number of new places at Escale Borély.

century Mannerist masterpiece, named after the pyramidical points of its façade. It holds the **Musée du Vieux Marseille** (*under restoration until 2001; meanwhile guided visits available Wed 3–5.30, Sat 11–2.30*), a delightful attic where the city stashes its odds and ends – Provençal furniture; an extraordinary relief diorama made in 1850 by an iron merchant, depicting the uprising of 1848; 18th-century Neapolitan Christmas crib figures and *santons* made in Marseille; playing and tarot cards, long an important local industry; and poignant photos of the Panier before it was blown to smithereens. The dynamite that blew up the lower Panier was responsible for revealing the contents of the **Musée des Docks Romains**, 2 Place Vivaux (*open winter Tues–Sun 10–5; summer Tues–Sun 11–6; adm*), built over a stretch of the vast 1st-century AD Roman quay. Exhibits describe seafaring in the ancient Mediterranean.

The Panier retains its original crusty character atop the well-worn steps of **Montée des Accoules** and around **Place de Lenche**, once the market or *agora* of the Greeks. Signs point the way through the maze to the top of Rue du Petit-Puits and the elegant **Vieille-Charité**, designed by Pierre Puget, a student of Bernini and court architect to Louis XIV – and a native of the Panier. Built by the city fathers between 1671

Marseille

(map labels)

Cathédrale de la Major
Vieille-Charité
RUE DE L'ÉVÊCHÉ
RUE DES
RUE DE LA RÉPUBLIQUE
BD F. MOISSON
JULES GUESDE
Porte d'Aix
to Coach Station and Gare St-Charles
Ancienne-Major
PLACE DE LA MAJOR
RUE DE TRIGANCE
RUE DES PHOCÉENS
COLBERT
QUAI DE LA TOURETTE
AV. VAUDOYER
RUE DU PETIT PUITS
R. DU PANIER
Le Panier
PLACE SADI CARNOT
RUE D'AIX
ESPLANADE DE LA TOURETTE
MONTÉE DES ACCOULES
Hôpital de l'Hôtel Dieu
RUE MÉRY
Post Office
PLACE L'HÔTEL DES POSTES
PLACE DE LENCHE
RUE CAISSERIE
RUE BONNETERIE
RUE GRAND'
FORT ST-JEAN
R. HENRI TASSO
AV. SAINTE
JEAN
PLACE VIVAUX
PLACE JULES VERNE
Musée César
RUE DE LA RÉPUBLIQUE
Jardins des Vestiges
Centre Bourse
Musée d'Histoire de Marseille
RUE ST-LAURENT
Musée des Docks Romains
RUE DE LA PRISON
Hôtel de Ville
RUE LOGE
Château du Pharo
QUAI DU PORT
Musée de la Marine
COURS BELSUNCE
Parc du Pharo
Q. DES BELGES
VIEUX PORT-HÔTEL DE VILLE
R. DES FABRES
to Palais Longchamp
FORT ST-NICOLAS
Vieux Port
PL. DU GEN. DE GAULLE
Musée de la Mode
Théâtre National de la Criée
QUAI DE RIVE NEUVE
PLACE AUX HUILES
PLACE THIARS
RUE BEAUVAU
RUE NEUVE STE-CATHERINE
RUE ROBERT
R. FORT NOTRE DAME
R. DE LA PAIX
ST
R. FORTIA
SAENS
PLACE REYER
RUE SAINT-FERRÉOL
RUE DE L'ABBAYE
St-Victor
RUE SAINTE
D'ESTIENNE D'ORVES
Opéra
R. LULLI
RUE PARADIS
RUE VENTURE
AV DE LA CORSE
BOULEVARD DE LA CORDERIE
RUE BRETEUIL
RUE GRIGNAN
Musée Cantini
RUE MONTGRAND
RUE DE ROME
COURS PIERRE PUGET
PLACE FÉLIX BERET
BD NOTRE DAME
RUE ANDRÉ AUNE
ESTRANGIN-PRÉFECTURE
Préfecture
500 metres
500 yards
RUE E DELANGLADE
to Notre-Dame de la Garde
RUE SYLVABELLE

---

and 1745 to take in homeless migrants from the countryside, this is one of the world's most palatial workhouses: three storeys of arcaded ambulatories in pale pink stone, overlooking a court with a sumptuous elliptical chapel crowned by an oval dome. It has now been restored as a cultural centre. The Charité's middle gallery houses the excellent **Musée d'Archéologie Méditerranéenne** (*open winter Tues–Sun 10–5; summer Tues–Sun 11–6; adm*), featuring a remarkable collection of Egyptian art (second in France, after the Louvre) and beautiful works from ancient Cyprus, Susa, Mesopotamia, Greece and pre-Roman and Roman Italy. The Charité also houses the **Musée d'Arts Africains, Océaniens et Amérindiens** (*open winter Tues–Sun 10–5; summer Tues–Sun 11–6; adm*), with a fascinating collection of ritual artefacts.

South of the Vieux Port: Quai de Rive Neuve and St-Victor

At 19 Rue Grignan, a *hôtel particulier* houses the modern art collection of the **Musée Cantini** (*open winter Tues–Sun 10–5; summer Tues–Sun 11–6; adm*). Permanent displays include Paul Signac's shimmering *Port de Marseille*, and the first Cubist views of L'Estaque that Dufy painted with Braque in 1908; most of the Cantini's post-1960 works have been moved into the new Musée d'Art Contemporain (*see* below).

On **Quai de Rive Neuve** you'll find ship chandlers' shops, restaurants, and the national theatre, **La Criée**, installed in a former fish auction house. Further along the *quai*, steps lead up to battlemented walls and towers good enough for a Hollywood castle, defending one of the oldest Christian shrines in Provence, the **Abbaye St-Victor**. St-Victor was founded in AD 416 by St Jean Cassien, formerly an anchorite in the Egyptian Thebeaid. A popular account has it that Victor was a Roman legionary who converted to Christianity, and slew at least one sea serpent (see the relief over the door) before being ground to a pulp between a pair of millstones. Cassien excavated the first chapels into the flank of an ancient stone quarry near a Hellenistic necropolis, which he expanded for Christian use. In the 11th century, when the monks of St-Victor adopted the Rule of St Benedict, they added the church on top, turning the old chapels into a labyrinthine **crypt** (*open daily 8–7.15; adm*), with ceilings ranging from 6 to 60ft high. Some of the beautifully sculpted sarcophagi date from the 3rd century AD and were found to contain seven or eight dead monks crowded like sardines, proof of the popularity of an abbey that founded 300 monastic houses in Provence and indeed Sardinia.

Below St-Victor is Louis XIV's **Fort St-Nicolas**, and beyond that, the **Château du Pharo** (bus no.83 from the Vieux Port), built by Napoleon III. The prize 360° view is from Marseille's watchtower hill – an isolated limestone outcrop towering 531ft above the city, crowned by **Notre-Dame de la Garde** (bus no.60, from Place aux Huiles on Quai de Rive Neuve), a neo-Byzantine/Romanesque pile with an unfortunate resemblance to a locomotive crowned in turn by France's largest golden mega-Madonna, 33ft high.

La Canebière

They used to make rope here, and the hemp they used has given its name to Marseille's most famous boulevard. This was the high street of French *dolce far niente*, which could swagger and boast that 'the Champs-Elysées is the Canebière of Paris'. In its day La Canebière sported grand cafés, fancy shops and hotels where travellers of yore had their first thrills before sailing off to exotic lands, but these days La Canebière has suffered the same fate as the Champs-Elysées: banks, airline offices and heavy traffic, plus kebab and pizza stands, but minus the Champs-Elysées' recent improvements and tree plantings.

Palais Longchamp and Environs

In 1834 Marseille suffered a drought so severe that it dug a canal to bring in water from the Durance. This 80km feat of aquatic engineering ends with a heroic splash at the **Palais Longchamp**, a delightfully overblown nymphaeum and cascade, populated with stone felines, bulls and a buxom allegory of the Durance, all slated for restoration in the near future (Ⓜ Longchamp-Cinq-Avenues; bus no.80 from La Canebière). Behind the palace stretch the prettiest public gardens in Marseille; in the right wing of the palace itself, some of the same creatures are embalmed in the **Musée** d'**Histoire Naturelle**, sharing space with their fossilized ancestors (*open winter Tues–Sun 10–5; summer Tues–Sun 11–6; adm*).

The left wing of the Palais Longchamp houses the **Musée des Beaux Arts** (*open winter Tues–Sun 10–5; summer Tues–Sun 11–6; adm*). Local talent is represented by Baroque sculptor, architect and painter Pierre Puget (1671–1745); Françoise Duparc, a follower of Chardin (1726–76), who worked most of her life in England; and the satirist Honoré Daumier (1808–97), who went to prison for his biting caricatures of Louis Philippe's toadies. Here, too, is Van Gogh's roving, bohemian precursor, Adolphe Monticelli (1824–86), who sold his paint-encrusted canvases of fragmented colour for a day's food and drink in the cafés along the Canebière. Also of note are paintings by Provençal pre-Impressionists, especially 18th-century scenes of Marseille's port by Joseph Vernet and sun-drenched landscapes by Paul Guigou.

Heading South: Le Corbusier

To pay your respects to Modular Man, take bus no.21 from the Bourse down dreary Bd Michelet to the Corbusier stop. In 1945, at the height of Marseille's housing crisis, the French government commissioned Le Corbusier to build an experimental **Unité d'Habitation**, derived from his 1935 theory of 'La Cité Radieuse'. Le Corbusier thought the solution to urban *anomie* and transport and housing problems was to put living-space, schools, shops and recreational facilities all under one roof, balanced on concrete *pilotis*, or stilts. Le Corbusier, who guessed the future starring role of cars, intended that the ground level should be for parking.

For a city like Marseille, where people enjoy getting out and about at ground level, the building was a ghastly aberration. But architects were entranced; for the next 30 years thousands of buildings in every city in the world went up on *pilotis*. The Unité's genuinely good points, unfortunately, had few imitators – each of its 337 flats is built on two levels and designed for maximum privacy, each with fine views over the mountains or sea. Of the original extras, only the school, the top-floor gym, and the communal hotel for residents' guests (*see* 'Where to Stay') have survived.

Marseille's Corniche and Parc Borély

From the Vieux Port, you can catch bus no.83, and pass the Parc du Pharo to **Corniche Kennedy**, a dramatic road overlooking a dramatic coast – now improved with artificial beaches, bars, restaurants, villas and nightclubs. Amazingly, until the road was built in the 1850s, the first cove, the picture-postcard **Anse des Catalans**, was so isolated that the Catalan fisherfolk who lived there could hardly speak French. This now has the most popular (and the only real) sandy beach. From the bus stop Vallon des Auffes you can walk down to the fishing village of **Anse des Auffes** ('of the rope-makers'), isolated from the corniche until after the Second World War and still deter-minedly intact. As soon as the corniche was built, the wealthy families of Marseille planted grand villas along it. The corniche then descends to the artificial **Plages Gaston Deferre**, where a copy of Michelangelo's *David* holds court at the corner of Av du Prado. Beyond him opens the cool green expanse of **Parc Borély**, with a botanical garden, duck ponds and the **Château Borély**, an 18th-century palace built according to the strictest classical proportions for a wealthy merchant. Behind it, Av de Hambourg leads into Ste-Anne, another former village, where César's Giant Thumb emerges at the Av d'Haïfa, signalling the vast new **Musée d'Art Contemporain** at No.69 (*open winter Tues–Sun 10–5; summer Tues–Sun 11–6; adm*), with a large collection of post-war art (New Realists, Arte Povera, 'individual mythologies' and more).

The *Calanques* and Grotte Cosquer

To continue along the coast from Parc Borély, you'll need to change to bus no.19, which passes by another beach and the **Musée de la Faïence**, 157 Av de Montredon (*t 04 91 72 43 47; open winter Tues–Sun 10–5; summer Tues–Sun 11–6; adm*), with an exceptional collection of faïence from Neolithic times to the present, concentrating on the famous ware made in Marseille and Moustiers from the 17th century on. More *calanques* follow until the road gives out and the GR98 coastal path to Cassis begins. In 1991, the beautiful jagged **Calanque de Sormiou** made national headlines when local diver Henri Cosquer discovered a subterranean cave above sea level, covered with paintings of running bison, horses, deer and the ancestors of the modern penguin. The **Grotte Cosquer** (named in honour of its discoverer) is now recognized by prehistorians as a contemporary of Lascaux (c. 27,000 BC). To protect the art, the cave has been walled up, but reproductions are on display at the Exposition Grotte Henri Cosquer.

The Château d'If and Frioul Islands

If in French means yew, a tree associated with death, and an appropriately sinister name for this gloomy precursor of Alcatraz built in 1524 (*open daily 9.30–6.30 exc in rough seas; boats, t 04 91 55 50 09, from the Quai des Belges; departures summer hourly 9–6; winter 9, 10.30, 12, 2, 3.30 and 5*). Even when Alexandre Dumas was still alive, people wanted to see the cell of the Count of Monte-Cristo, and a cell, complete with escape hole, was obligingly made to show to visitors. Real-life inmates included a Monsieur de Niozelles, condemned to six years in solitary confinement for not taking his hat off in front of Louis XIV; and, after the revocation of the Edict of Nantes, thousands of Protestants. The other two islands in the Archipel du Frioul are **Pomègues** and **Ratonneau**, now used for a summer festival.

Aix-en-Provence

Elegant and honey-hued, the old capital of Provence is splashed by a score of fountains, a charming reminder that its very name comes from its waters, *Aquae Sextiae*. If tumultuous Marseille is in many ways the great anti-Paris, Aix-en-Provence is the stalwart anti-Marseille – bourgeois, cultured, aristocratic, urbane, slow-paced, convivial, and famous for its university.

Aix was chosen as the capital of Provence by the counts of Provence in the early 13th century. In 1409 Louis II d'Anjou endowed the university; and in the 1450s Aix was the setting for the refined court of Good King René, fondly remembered, not for the way

Getting Around

The **train** station is on Rue G. Desplaces, at the end of Av Victor-Hugo; there are hourly connections to Marseille, and others less often to Toulon. The hectic coach station is in Rue Lapierre, **t** 04 42 91 26 80, with **buses** every 20–30mins to Marseille and direct to the airport, and others to Avignon, Cannes, Nice, Arles and more. For a **taxi**, **t** 04 42 27 71 11; or at night call **t** 04 42 26 29 30. **Bike hire** is available at Cycles Naddéo, Av de Lattre-de-Tassigny, **t** 04 42 21 06 93, and Cycles Zammit, 27 Rue Miguet, **t** 04 42 23 19 53. Parking isn't easy: try the **car parks** in Place des Cardeurs, Place Carnot, or by the bus station (behind the casino).

Tourist Information

Aix-en-Provence: Place du Gén. de Gaulle, **t** 04 42 16 11 61, **f** 04 42 16 11 62.

Shopping

The traditional souvenirs of Aix are its almond and glazed melon confits, *calissons*, which have been made here since 1473; buy them at **Béchard**, 12 Cours Mirabeau, **t** 04 42 26 06 78; or **Confiserie Brémond**, 16 Rue d'Italie, **t** 04 42 27 36 25. **Terre du Soleil**, 6 Rue Aude, **t** 04 42 93 04 54, has local, world-renowned pottery. The better grocers sell the prize-winning *huile d'olive du pays d'Aix*.

Where to Stay

Aix-en-Provence ✉ **13100**

If you come in the summer during the festivals, you can't book early enough; Aix's less pricey hotels fill up especially fast.

Expensive

★★★★**Le Pigonnet**, 5 Av du Pigonnet, on the outskirts, **t** 04 42 59 02 90, **f** 04 42 59 47 77. For luxury, a romantic old *bastide* with rose arbours, pool, lovely rooms furnished with antiques, an excellent restaurant and views out over the Aix countryside.

★★★★**Villa Gallici**, Av de la Violette, **t** 04 42 23 29 23, **f** 04 42 96 30 45. A member of the Relais et Châteaux group, with all the warm atmosphere of an old Provençal *bastide*, with charming rooms, garden, parking and pool.

★★★**Des Augustins**, 3 Rue de la Masse, just off Cours Mirabeau, **t** 04 42 27 28 59, **f** 04 42 26 74 87. A conversion from a 12th-century convent, with soundproofed rooms.

Moderate

★★★**Grand Hôtel Nègre-Coste**, 33 Cours Mirabeau, **t** 04 42 27 74 22, **f** 04 42 26 80 93. Renovated, in an elegant 18th-century mansion, that still hoists guests in its original elevator. No restaurant.

★★★**Mercure Paul Cézanne**, 40 Av Victor Hugo (two blocks from the train station), **t** 04 42 26 34 73, **f** 04 42 27 20 95. Exceptional little hotel, furnished with antiques and serving delicious breakfasts.

★★★**Le Manoir**, 8 Rue d'Entrecasteaux, **t** 04 42 26 27 20, **f** 04 42 27 17 97. Built around a 14th-century cloister.

Inexpensive

★★**Artea**, 4 Bd de la République, near the bus station, **t** 04 42 27 36 00, **f** 04 42 27 28 76. The home of composer Darius Milhaud (who grew up in Aix) is now a comfortable hotel; arrive after 8pm and get a discount.

★★**Le Prieuré Route des Alpes**, 2km from the centre, **t** 04 42 21 05 23, **f** 04 42 21 60 56. In a charming 17th-century priory overlooking a garden designed by Le Nôtre.

he squeezed every possible sou from his subjects, but for the artists he patronized, such as Francesco Laurana, Nicolas Froment and the Maître de l'Annonciation d'Aix, and the popular festivities he founded, especially the masquerades of the Fête-Dieu. When René died in 1486, France absorbed his realm but maintained Aix's status as the capital of Provence, seat of the unpopular king-appointed Parlement. In 1789, the tumultuous Count Mirabeau became a popular hero in Aix when he eloquently

France, 63 Rue Espariat, **t 04 42 27 90 15, **f** 04 42 26 11 47. Cheap and old-fashioned.

Cheap

*Paul, 10 Av Pasteur, near the cathedral, **t** 04 42 23 23 89, **f** 04 42 63 17 80. Good budget choice.

Near Aix

La Petite Auberge du Tholonet, south of the centre on D64E, **t** 04 42 66 84 24. Family-run inn with views over Ste-Victoire, and local produce, good country fare including some vegetarian dishes (*menus 85–250F*). *Closed Sun eve and Mon.*

***Relais Ste-Victoire, 10km from Aix, off the N7 in Beaurecueil, **t** 04 42 66 94 98, **f** 04 42 66 85 96 (*moderate*). Ravishing place to stay or eat, complete with pool, gourmet restaurant with a lovely veranda and, above all, tranquillity. Air-conditioned rooms with terraces. Book early.

Eating Out

Clos de la Violette, 10 Av de la Violette (just north of the cathedral), **t** 04 42 23 30 71. Under the masterful touch of Jean-Marc Banzo, a lovely place that has long been considered the best in Aix, and does wonderful things with seafood and Provençal herbs (*lunch menu 230F, dinner from 300F*). *Closed Sun and Mon lunch.*

Le Bistro Latin, 18 Rue de la Couronne (just north of Place du Général de Gaulle), **t** 04 42 38 22 88. Imaginative variations on local themes such as leg of lamb with herbs (*menus from 87F*). *Closed Sun and Mon lunch.*

Chez Maxime, 12 Place Ramus, **t** 04 42 26 28 51. Dine on a shady terrace or by a cosy fireside on delicious meat or fish dishes, accompanied by a list of 500 wines (*lunch menus*

from 95F, dinner from 130F). *Closed Sun and Mon lunch.*

Trattoria Chez Antoine, 3 Rue Clemenceau (just off Cours Mirabeau), **t** 04 42 38 27 10. Intimate, laid-back, and good for fresh pasta and other Italian and Provençal dishes (*around 130F*).

La Vieille Auberge, 63 Rue Espariat, **t** 04 42 27 17 41. Cosy and popular and serves tasty Provençal dishes at tasty prices (*menus from 84F*).

L'Hacienda, 7 Rue Mérindol (near Place des Cardeurs), **t** 04 42 27 00 35. Eternally popular, offering the best deal in town (*65F menu including wine*).

Le Petit Verdot, 7 Rue d'Entrecasteaux, **t** 04 42 27 30 12. Authentic bistro where red wines by the glass are accompanied by ancient jazz records and simple dishes or charcuterie (*lunch 80F*). *Closed Sun.*

L'Arbre à Pain, 12 Rue Constantin, **t** 04 42 96 99 95. Reasonable vegetarian fare (*lunch from 78F*). *Closed Sun and Mon.*

Entertainment and Nightlife

Outside the festival season, the large student population keeps a number of jazz clubs in business.

Hot Brass, Chemin de la Plaine-des-Verguetiers, west of the centre, **t** 04 42 21 05 57. Jazz club.

L'IPN, 23 Cours Sextius (downstairs). For a good stomp and a beery crowd.

Le Richèlm, 24 Rue Verrerie, **t** 04 42 23 49 29. Similar to the above.

Club 88, at La Petite Calade north on the RN7, **t** 04 42 23 26 88. Club outside town.

Le Mazarin, 6 Rue Laroque, **t** 04 42 26 99 85. Films in their original language.

championed the people and condemned Provence's Parlement as unrepresentative; in 1800, Provence's government was unceremoniously packed off to Marseille.

Cours Mirabeau and Musée Granet

Canopied by its soaring plane trees, decked with fountains and flanked by cafés, banks, pâtisseries, and *hôtels particuliers* of the 17th and 18th centuries, **Cours**

Mirabeau is the centre stage for Aixois society. Laid out in 1649, it begins in Place du Général de Gaulle; at the far end is the **Fontaine du Roi René**, with a statue of the good monarch holding up a bunch of the muscat grapes he introduced to Provence.

South of Cours Mirabeau, the **Musée Granet** (*13 Rue Cardinale; open daily 10–12 and 2–6; closed Tues; adm*) houses Aix's art and antiquities. Downstairs are eerie relics of the Celto-Ligurian decapitation cult from the *oppidum* of Entremont, 3km north of Aix. Holding court upstairs is *Jupiter and Thetis* (1811), arguably Ingres' most objectionable canvas. There are 17th-century portraits of Aixois nobility, made fluffy and likeable by Largillière and Rigaud; Dutch and Flemish masters (Teniers, Brit, Neefs, Robert Campin, Rubens); and the Italians (Alvise Vivarini, Previtali, Guercino, Preti, the mysterious Maître de l'Annonciation d'Aix). But what of Cézanne, who took his first drawing-classes in this very building? For years he was represented by three measly watercolours, until 1984 when the French government deposited eight small canvases here that touch on the major themes of his work.

Vieil Aix

North of Cours Mirabeau, the narrow lanes and squares of Vieil Aix concentrate some of Provence's finest architecture and shopping, especially off the elegant cobbled and fountained Place d'Albertas. In the adjacent Place des Prêcheurs stands the church of **Ste-Marie-Madeleine**, which has a pleasant Second Empire façade and paintings by Rubens and Van Loo, although the show-stopper is the central panel of the *Triptych of the Annunciation*, a luminous esoteric work of 1445, attributed to Barthélémy d'Eyck. Aix's flower market lends an intoxicating perfume to Place de la Mairie, a lovely square framed by the stately, perfectly proportioned **Hôtel de Ville** (1671) and the flamboyant **Tour de l'Horloge** (1510), with clocks telling the phase of the moon and wooden statues that change with the season.

From here, Rue Gaston de Saporta leads to the **Musée du Vieil Aix** at No.17 (*open winter Tues–Sun 10–12 and 2–5; summer Tues–Sun 10–12 and 2.30–6; adm*). It stores some quaint paintings on velvet, a bevy of *santons* in a 'talking Christmas Crib' and 19th-century marionettes.

Cathédrale St-Sauveur and the Tapestry Museum

Rue Gaston de Saporta continues north to Place de l'Université, once part of the forum of Roman Aix, and the **Cathédrale St-Sauveur**, a dignified patchwork of periods and styles. The interior has naves for every taste: from right to left, Romanesque, Gothic and Baroque. The cathedral's most famous treasure, Nicolas Froment's *Triptyque du Buisson Ardent* (1476), is under restoration and can only be viewed between 3 and 4pm on Tuesdays. On the lateral panels are portraits of a well-fed King René, who commissioned the work, and his second wife, while the central scene depicts the vision of a monk of St-Victor of Marseille, who saw the Virgin and Child appear amidst the miraculous burning bush vouchsafed to Moses.

At the back of the cathedral, the 17th–18th-century residence of Aix's archbishops, **L'Archevêché**, is the setting for the festival's operas. It also houses the **Musée des Tapisseries** (*open daily 10–11.45 and 2–5.45; closed Tues; adm*), containing three sets of lighthearted Beauvais tapestries, which were hidden under the roof during the Revolution until the 1840s.

Around Aix: Cézanne and the Montagne Ste-Victoire

Paul Cézanne spent an idyllic childhood roaming Aix's countryside with his best friend, Emile Zola, and as an adult painted those same landscapes in a way landscapes had never been painted before. The **Atelier Cézanne**, 9 Av Paul Cézanne (*open winter Tues–Sun 10–12 and 2–5; summer Tues–Sun 10–12 and 2.30–6; adm*), the studio he built in 1897, has been rather grudgingly maintained as it was when the master died in 1906, with a few drawings, unfinished canvases, his smock, palette, pipe and some of the bottles and skulls used in his still-lifes.

The rolling countryside around Aix is the quintessence of Provence for those who love Cézanne: the ochre soil, the dusty green cypresses, the simple geometry of the old bastides and villages and the pyramidal prow of the blueish limestone **Montagne Ste-Victoire**. This is encircled by the striking 60km **Route Cézanne** (D17), beginning along the south flank in the wooded park and Italianate château of **Le Tholonet** (3km from Aix; take the bus from La Rotonde). Here Cézanne often painted the view towards the mountain, which haunts at least 60 of his canvases. The ascent of the Montagne Ste-Victoire takes about two hours (bring sturdy shoes, a hat and water) and there's a 17th-century stone refuge with water and a fireplace if you want to spend a night. Crowning the precipitous west face, the 55ft **Croix de Provence** (which Cézanne never painted) has been here, in one form or another, since the 1500s. Northerly approaches to the summit of Ste-Victoire begin at Les Cabassols or **Vauvenargues**. The 14th-century Château de Vauvenargues was purchased by Picasso, and he is buried here.

Northern Provence: the Vaucluse

Some of the Midi's most civilized countryside and loveliest villages are in the Vaucluse. These have not passed without notice, of course, and the region is now what the Côte d'Azur was forty years ago: the in-place for both the French and foreigners to find a bit of sun-splashed holiday paradise. Vaucluse's two cities, Orange and Avignon, will be found on pp.866–76. The remainder divides neatly into two areas: the mountainous Luberon, a *pays* of especially pretty villages; and Provence's definitive northern wall, including the dramatic Mont Ventoux and the Dentelles de Montmirail, along with the Roman city of Vaison.

The Luberon

As is the case with many a fair maiden, the Luberon's charms are proving to be her undoing. This is Peter Mayle country, the stage set for his surprise bestseller *A Year in Provence*. The trickle of outsiders who began settling here in the 1950s, permanently or in holiday homes, has now become a flood; if you insist on coming in August, make

Getting Around

Public transport is woefully inconvenient in the Luberon; it's possible to get around the villages, but just barely.

Apt is on an SNCF branch line, with a few trains daily to Cavaillon and Avignon. Buses from Apt leave from the Place de la Bouquerie by the river; there are one or two daily to Roussillon, Avignon and Aix, stopping at Bonnieux and Lourmarin; also one to Digne.

Cavaillon is on the main Avignon–Marseille rail line, and there are also buses to Carpentras (several daily), to Apt and Avignon, and very occasionally to Bonnieux and other western Luberon villages.

Where to Stay and Eat

La Tour d'Aigues ✉ 84240

**Les Fenouillets, just outside the village on the D956, t 04 90 07 48 22, f 04 90 07 34 26 (*inexpensive*). Rooms are simple, but there's a pool nearby, and an inexpensive restaurant with outdoor tables, a good bet for lunch.

Lourmarin ✉ 84160

Lourmarin has some of the best restaurants in the Luberon.

****Le Moulin de Lourmarin, Rue du Temple, t 04 90 68 06 69, f 04 90 68 31 76 (*expensive*). A one-time olive mill with views over the château and nearby hills, now Provençal meets Art Nouveau in its tasteful decoration, and the restaurant serves attractive and delicious Provençal dishes. Book early.

***Hôtel de Guilles, t 04 90 68 30 55, f 04 90 68 37 41 (*moderate*). Just east of the village a similar, immaculately restored farmhouse, beautifully decorated, with lots of antiques and all the amenities: tennis court, pool and gardens.

Le Paradou, Route d'Apt, t 04 90 68 04 05, f 04 90 08 54 94 (inexpensive). In a dreamy setting north of Lourmarin on the D943, at the entrance to the Combe de Lourmarin.

La Villa St-Louis, 35 Rue Henri de Savournin, t 04 90 68 39 18, f 04 90 68 10 07 (*moderate–inexpensive*). A charming *chambres d'hôte* in a 19th-century house run by the warm and affable Mme Lassallette.

La Fenière, Rue du Grand Pré, t 04 90 68 11 79. Expert, innovative cooking with old Provençal favourites: batter-fried courgette flowers and a hearty *daube* (*menus 200–550F*). *Closed Sun eve and Mon, and Tues lunch*.

Le Bistrot, Av Raoul Dautry, t 04 90 68 29 74. A choice of Provençal or Lyonnais cuisine (*menus 88F and 120F*). *Closed Thurs and last two weeks in Aug*.

La Récréation, 15 Rue Philippe de Girand, t 04 90 68 23 73. Fresh Provençal fare and good lamb dishes with garlic on the terrace (*menus 100–135F*). *Closed Wed*.

Cadenet ✉ 84160

**Mas du Colombier, Route de Pertuis, t 04 90 68 29 00, f 04 90 68 36 77 (*inexpensive*). Newish, pleasant place with a pool, in the middle of an old vineyard. *Closed Jan and Feb*.

Stefáni, 35 Av Gambetta, t 04 90 68 07 14. Delicious simple fish and meat dishes are served on the panoramic terrace (*menus from 98F*). *Closed Wed*.

Apt and Around ✉ 84400

***Auberge du Luberon, 17 Quai Léon Sagy, t 04 90 74 12 50, f 04 90 04 79 49 (*moderate*). Rooms and a good resturant on the river; the speciality is rabbit with figs, and other dishes with confit d'Apt (*menus 155–420F*).

**Le Palais in Rue Dr Albert Gros, t 04 90 04 89 32 (*inexpensive*). Includes a pizzeria with other dishes apart from pizza, particularly a good ratatouille (*89F lunch menu*). *Closed Oct–Mar*.

**Relais de Roquefure, on the N100, 4km west, t 04 90 04 88 88, f 04 90 74 14 86 (*inexpensive*). An old stone-built inn with a pool and an inexpensive restaurant. *Closed Jan–mid-Feb*.

Bernard Mathys, 5km northwest in Gargasa, t 04 90 04 84 64. A lovely restaurant in an 18th-century house for a delightful meal with all the trimmings; the vegetables are especially ravishing (*menus 160F, 250F and 350F and 450F*). *Closed Tues and Wed, mid-Jan–mid-Feb*.

Auberge du Presbytère, Place de la Fontaine in Saignon, t 04 90 74 11 50, f 04 90 04 68 51 (*inexpensive*). Two 10th- and 11th-century buildings with a magnificent view over the Luberon, charming rooms and a fine intimate restaurant (*160F menu*); remember to book. *Closed Dec–Jan.*

Roussillon ✉ 84220

★★★**Mas de Garrigon**, t 04 90 05 63 22, f 04 90 05 70 01 (*expensive*). One of the few real luxury places in Roussillon, a well-restored farmhouse with all the amenities, lovely rooms and a gourmet restaurant; but both, unfortunately, are woefully overpriced (*menus 150–380F*). *Restaurant closed Dec.*

★★**Des Ocres**, Route de Gordes, t 04 90 05 60 50, f 04 90 05 79 74 (*inexpensive*). Pleasant and much cheaper, with convenient parking. *Closed mid-Dec–end Jan.*

Le Val des Fées, Rue R. Casteau. t 04 90 05 64 99. For a simple meal, with lovely views over the ochre from its terrace (*menus 120–255F*).

Bonnieux ✉ 84480

★★★**Hostellerie du Prieuré**, t 04 90 75 80 78, f 04 90 75 96 00 (*moderate*). Lovely old hotel in a 17th-century priory in the village centre; the rooms have a view and there's a garden. *Closed Nov–Mar.*

★**Hotel Le César**, on Place de la Liberté, t 04 90 75 96 35 (*cheap*). Inexpensive.

Le Pistou, next door, t 04 90 75 88 01. Local produce on an imaginative menu (*100–200F*).

Le Fournil, on lovely Place Carnot, t 04 90 75 83 62. A dining room excavated in the cliff and light fresh fare (*menus 90–160F*). *Closed Mon and Jan.*

Ménerbes ✉ 84560

★★★**Le Roy Soleil**, Le Fort, along the Route des Beaumettes, t 04 90 72 25 61, f 04 90 72 36 55 (*moderate*). In a 17th-century building in an olive grove overlooking Ménerbes, with a pool and tennis and excellent restaurant. *Closed mid-Oct to mid-Mar.*

Oppède-le-Vieux ✉ 84580

★★**Le Mas des Capelans**, on the N100, t 04 90 76 99 04, f 04 90 76 90 29 (*inexpensive*).

Once a stable, now a pleasant country hotel, with a pool, terrace and playground. Closed mid-Nov–mid-Feb.

L'Oppidum, Place de la Croix, t 04 90 76 84 15. Beneath ruined medieval walls, dine on good-value local produce alongside local works of art (*dinner only, table d'hôte 130F inc wine*).

Gordes ✉ 84220

Gordes is big business; several fancy villa-hotels have sprung up on the outskirts, but the whole scene is over the top, and a bit exploitative of the credulous, who want it and deserve it. The tourist office has a list of the many *chambres d'hôtes* in the area.

★★**Auberge de Carcarille**, southwest of town on the D2, t 04 90 72 02 63, f 04 90 72 05 74 (*inexpensive*). An honest establishment outside the village, a carefully restored *mas* with pretty rooms, some with balconies, and a reasonable restaurant specializing in fish and game (*menus 98F, 150F and 220F*).

Restaurant Tante Yvonne, Place du Château, t 04 90 72 02 54. A solid choice for lunch, with a few unusual specialities (*menus 135–190F*). *Closed Sun eve and Wed.*

Fontaine-de-Vaucluse ✉ 84800

In spite of its touristic vocation, Fontaine-de-Vaucluse is a pleasant place for staying or eating.

★**Hostellerie Le Château**, t 04 90 20 31 54, f 04 90 20 28 02 (*cheap*). In Fontaine's old *mairie*, with a terrace overlooking the Sorgue (behind glass, so you won't get splashed by the water-wheel). Excellent cooking includes delicate sautéed frogs' legs and *rouget à la tapenade* (*menus 119–180F*). Five rooms.

★★**Le Parc**, near the river and centre at Les Bourgades, t 04 90 20 31 57, f 04 90 20 27 03 (*inexpensive*). Simple but pretty hotel wrapped in roses; its restaurant serves some of the best Italian food in Provence (*99–160F*). *Closed Nov–mid-Feb.*

Philip, Chemin de la Fontaine, t 04 90 20 31 81. Mostly trout and other fish (*menus 105F and 155F*), with an outside terrace by the river. *Closed Nov–Easter.*

sure you have your hotel reservations months in advance. In danger of being destroyed by a rash of outsiders and unplanned holiday villas, the Parc Régional du Luberon was founded in 1977, a cooperative arrangement between the towns and villages that covers most of the territory between Manosque and Cavaillon. Park information is available from the **Maison du Parc du Luberon**, 1 Place Jean Jaurès in Apt, with exhibits, slide shows and a gift shop; **t** 04 90 04 42 00, **f** 04 90 04 81 15.

The southern end of the Park, the Pays d'Aigues, is the sleepier corner of the Luberon, a rolling stretch of good farmland sheltered by the Grand Luberon mountain to the north. Of the smaller villages, a few stand out: **Grambois** to the northeast is a neatly rounded hilltop hamlet, a Saracen stronghold in the 8th–10th century and later one of the twelve citadels of Provence. **Ansouis**, north of Pertuis on the D56, is a *village perché* built around the sumptuously furnished Château de Sabran (*open daily 2.30–6; Oct–Easter closed Tues; adm*). For an airier, more pleasant castle without the bric-à-brac, there's **La Tour d'Aigues**, an elegant if roofless Renaissance shell just to the east. Heading west, and still on the south flank of Montagne du Luberon, **Cucuron** was used as the set for *Le Hussard sur le toit* (*The Horseman on the Roof*), the film adaptation of a novel by Jean Giono. Further west, into the heart of the Luberon, **Lourmarin** was the last home of Albert Camus, and he is buried in the cemetery. This is an unusual village, densely packed almost to the point of claustrophobia; many of its houses have tiny courtyards facing the street – too cute for its own good, as few villages even in the Luberon are so beset by tourists.

South of the Durance and 7km from Cadenet is the **Abbaye de Silvacane** (*open April–Sept daily 9–7; Oct–Mar daily exc Tues 10–1 and 2–5; adm*). A Benedictine community had already been established here when the Cistercians arrived in 1147, and made the land flourish until bad frosts in the 1300s killed all the olives and vines, starting Silvacane on its decline. The church is austere and uncompromising; even the apse is a plain rectangle. The cloister now contains a herb garden, around a lovely broken fountain. Note the capitals on the arcades, carved, oddly, with maple leaves.

The narrow roads south of the N100 in the northern Luberon are some of the most beautiful in the region, passing through **Vitrolles** or through **Montfuron**, with its lofty ruined castle, on their way to the Pays d'Aigues. The summit of the Grand Luberon, the **Mourre Nègre**, has views that take in all of the Vaucluse and beyond. **Saignon**, 5km southeast of Apt, is a beautiful *village perché* between two crags, boasting a well-preserved 12th-century church of Ste-Marie.

Apt

The capital of the Luberon (pop. 15,000 and growing) also claims to be the 'World Capital of Candied Fruits'. Everyone comes here for the huge Saturday market, but no one has ever admitted to liking the place. Apt has a good, well-laid-out **Museé d'Histoire et d'Archéologie**, 27 Rue de l'Amphithéâtre (*open June–Sept daily exc Tues and Sun 10–12 and 2–5; Oct–May Mon, Wed, Thurs and Fri 2–5, Sat 10–12 and 2–5; adm*), with archaeological finds going back to the Palaeolithic period, recent Roman and medieval finds from the town centre and a display of Apt's once-flourishing craft of faïence, which had its heyday in the 18th century.

Red Villages North of Apt

Rustrel, northeast of Apt on the D22, was an ochre-quarrying town until 1890. The huge ruddy mess they left is called the **Colorado**; there are marked routes around it for tourists. **Roussillon**, to the southwest, occupies a spectacular hill-top site, and so it should, for centuries of mining have removed nearly everything for miles around. The Association Terre d'Ochres, an organization that wants to get the ochre business going again, has an information centre in the village, and can direct you on a walk through the old quarries.

West of Apt, and south of the N100, is a string of truly beautiful villages that have become the high-rent district of the Luberon, one of the poshest rural areas in France. Don't come here looking for that little place in the country to fix up; it's all been done, as long as 40 years ago, first by the Parisians and then by a wave of outsiders, including many Americans. Biggest and busiest of the villages, **Bonnieux** is also one of the loveliest, a belvedere overlooking all the Petit Luberon. **Lacoste**, west of Bonnieux on the D109, is a trendy *village perché*. Overlooking the village is a gloomy ruined castle, once home of no less a personage than the Marquis de Sade (d. 1814). Continuing along the D109, you come to **Ménerbes**, honey-coloured, artsy and cuter than cute (with an attitude to match). As the former home of Peter Mayle – he's escaped to California – it attracts a constant stream of fans of *A Year in Provence*. From here the D188 continues through grand scenery almost to the top of the Petit Luberon, and **Oppède-le-Vieux**, with its even gloomier ruined castle. To the west, **Maubec** with its Baroque church may be the Luberon village of your dreams.

On the Plateau de Vaucluse

The Plateau de Vaucluse is the high ground that runs between the Luberon and Mont Ventoux to the north. The striking *village perché* of **Gordes** used to make its living from olives. Today, Gordes has found something easier and more profitable: art tourism, with exhibits and concerts in the summer. Gordes was a fierce Resistance stronghold in the war and suffered for it, with wholesale massacres of citizens and the destruction of much of the village. All the damage the Nazis did has been repaired; the village centre, all steep, cobbled streets and arches, is extremely attractive. The château (*open 10–12 and 2–6; adm*) has a superb Renaissance fireplace, the second largest in France, and a hodgepodge of art. The **Village des Bories** just south of Gordes, off the D2 (*open daily 9–sunset; adm*) has a collection of *bories*, or dry-stone huts, restored as a rural museum. Although they resemble Neolithic works, none of the bories you see today is older than the 1600s.

The **Abbaye de Sénanque**, the loveliest of Provence's Cistercian Three Sisters, lies 4km north of Gordes on the D177, built in the warm golden stone of the Vaucluse and

Getting Around

Carpentras is the node for what little there is of **coach** transport in the northern Vaucluse, with good connections to Avignon and Orange, one to Marseille; also one or two a day to Vaison-la-Romaine, Beaumes-de-Venise and Gigondas. There are also several daily SNCF **trains** to Orange and Avignon.

Where to Stay and Eat

Carpentras ✉ 84200

Le Fiacre, 153 Rue Vigne, **t 04 90 63 03 15, **f** 04 90 60 49 73 (*inexpensive*). For something cosy in the centre, an elegant old hotel in an 18th-century building.

*Hôtel du Théâtre, 7 Av Albin Durand, **t** 04 90 63 02 90 (*cheap*). The budget choice; the friendly proprietor may try to corner you into a game of chess.

Le Vert Galant on Rue des Clapiès, **t** 04 90 67 15 50. For original cooking (*150–270F for strictly fresh seafood*). *Closed Sat lunch, Sun, and 2 weeks in Nov.*

Le Marijo, 73 Rue Raspail, **t** 04 90 60 42 65. For less than a 100F note, you won't do better than this popular and friendly place serving traditional Provençal food, or at least a well-cooked trout (*menus 98–150F*). *Closed Sun.*

Malaucène ✉ 84340

Hostellerie La Chevalerie, Rue des Remparts, **t 04 90 65 11 19, **f** 04 90 12 69 22 (*moderate*). Peaceful, and the most comfortable rooms in town; the restaurant has a charming terrace (*menus 90–220F*). *Closed Wed and first week July.*

L'Origan, Cours Isnards, **t 04 90 65 27 08, **f** 04 90 65 12 92 (*inexpensive*). Clean, central, and shipshape; the restaurant offers some hearty cooking – dishes such as guinea-fowl with *morilles* (*menus 85F, 110F and 125F*). *Closed Nov–Mar.*

Le Venaissin, opposite, **t 04 90 65 20 31, **f** 04 90 65 18 03 (*inexpensive*). Similar.

La Maison in Hameau de Piolon, outside Beaumont-du-Ventoux, **t** 04 90 65 15 50. The best cooking in the area, with only one menu (*140F*), though it has a wide selection of dishes, many with a touch of the southwest; try the *pintadeau en croûte*. *Closed Mon lunch, Tues lunch, Wed lunch, and Oct–Easter.*

Around Mont Ventoux: Sault and Aurel ✉ 84390

***Hostellerie du Val de Sault, Ancien Chemin d'Aurel, Sault, **t** 04 90 64 01 41, **f** 04 90 64 12 74 (*moderate*). Handsome new hotel 2,493ft up, facing Mont Ventoux, with only 11 rooms and five suites surrounded by trees and gardens, and equipped with a pool, gym, *salle de pétanque* and good restaurant. *Closed mid-Nov–Mar.*

*Relais du Mont Ventoux, in Aurel, **t** 04 90 64 00 62 (*cheap*). Plain but comfortable rooms and a restaurant with no surprises (*90F menu*). *Closed mid-Nov–mid-Mar.*

---

set among lavender fields and oak groves. The **church** (*open summer daily 10–12 and 2–6; winter daily 2–5; adm*), begun about 1160, shows the same early Cistercian seriousness as Silvacane, and has been changed little over the centuries; even the original altar is present. Most of the monastic buildings have also survived, including a lovely **cloister**, the *chauffoir*, the only heated room, where the monks transcribed books, and a refectory.

The little Vaucluse river called the Sorgue makes its daylight debut at **Fontaine-de-Vaucluse**. In the spring, and occasionally in winter, it pours out at a rate of as much as 200 cubic metres per second. The Fontaine is exquisite, but the 540 or so residents of the town of Fontaine-de-Vaucluse have not been able to keep it from becoming one of Provence's more garish tourist traps. To reach it, from the car park next to the church you walk a noisy 2km gauntlet of *frites* stands to a museum of *santons*.

Chalet-Reynard, on Ventoux, at the corner of the D164 and D974, t 04 90 61 84 55. The only restaurant for miles, a cosy, wood-lined bar where the local lumberjacks tuck into boar and a *pichet de rouge* at lunchtime (*menus from 98F*). *Closed Tues.*

Beaumes-de-Venise/Vacqueyras ✉ 84190

Auberge St-Roch, Av Jules Ferry, in Beaumes, t 04 90 65 08 21. Modest restaurant serving seafood and local dishes. *Closed Dec.*

Mme Bérnard's B&B in the village centre, t 04 90 62 93 98 (*inexpensive*). With lace curtains and balconies.

*Hôtel Restaurant des Dentelles, Vacqueyras, t 04 90 65 86 21, f 04 90 65 89 89 (*inexpensive*). Two-star comfort; so-so restaurant.

**Le Pradet, Route de Vaison, t 04 90 65 81 00, f 04 90 65 80 27 (*inexpensive*). A quiet new complex on the edge of the Vacqueyras.

***Hôtel Montmirail, once part of the spa, t 04 90 65 84 01, f 04 90 65 81 50 (*moderate–inexpensive*). Pool, garden, and restaurant.

Gigondas ✉ 84190

**Les Florets, Route des Dentelles, t 04 90 65 85 01, f 04 90 65 83 80 (*moderate*). In the middle of a Gigondas vineyard, simple rustic rooms and peace and quiet.

L'Oustelet in Place du Portail, t 04 90 65 85 30. In a neoclassical building, serving good beef in wine (*menus 100–140F*). *Closed Sun and Mon.*

Le Mas de Bouvau, Route de Cairanne, just west of Gigondas in Violès, t 04 90 70 94 08, f 04 90 70 95 99. Charming family-run hotel-cum-restaurant in the vines, serving specialities from southeast France: duck *confit*, *magret*, foie gras, pigeon and rabbit (*menus 150–280F*). *Closed Sun eve and Mon.*

La Farigoule, Le Plan de Dieu, Violès, t 04 90 70 91 78. Pleasant B&B in an old farmhouse; they also rent bikes. *Closed Nov–Mar.*

Séguret ✉ 84110

***Domaine de Cabasse, t 04 90 46 91 12, f 04 90 46 94 01 (*moderate*). Part of a Côtes-du-Rhône estate on the D23 towards Sablet; a few comfortable rooms with terraces, a pool, and an excellent restaurant that has truffles in season and other extravagant dishes year-round (*menus 100–170F*). *Closed Jan, Feb and Mar.*

***La Table du Comtat, in the village, t 04 90 46 91 49, f 04 90 46 94 27. Well known for refined dishes such as *julienne de truffe en coque d'œuf* (*menus 170–460F*). *Closed Oct–June Tues evening and Wed.*

Le Mesclun, also in the village, t 04 90 46 93 43. For simpler fare, and an *à la carte* selection of local delights (*menus around 150F*). *Closed Mon.*

Incredibly, many of the attractions are worthwhile. Norbert Castaret's **Musée de Spéléologie (Le Monde Souterrain)** is a 'subterranean world' museum of underground rarities and informational exhibits overseen by France's best-known cave explorer (*open daily 10–12 and 2–6; closed Tues and Christmas–Feb; adm*).

Most surprising of all, in a sharp modern building, is the **Musée d'Histoire 1939–1945** (*open daily 10–12 and 2–6; closed Tues and Oct–Feb; adm*), a government-sponsored institution that recaptures the wartime years vividly with two floors of explanatory displays, newsreels and magazines, weapons and other relics. As at Gordes, Resistance life around Fontaine-de-Vaucluse was no joke. On the way out, peek in at the **Musée Pétrarque** (*open daily 10–12 and 2–6; closed Tues and Oct–Feb; adm*), a subdued look at the life and times of the poet during his stay in the town in the early 1300s.

Carpentras

Perhaps because of its long period under papal rule and its own bishops, Carpentras has character and a subtle but distinct sense of place. It's a lively town, especially when the gorgeous produce of the Comtat Venaissin, 'The Garden of France', rolls in for the Friday market.

Undoubtedly the **Cathédrale St-Siffrein** (*open daily 9–6; closed Sun pm*) is one of the most absurd cathedrals in Christendom. So many architects, in so many periods, and no one has ever been able to get it finished and get it right. Begun in the 1400s, remodellings and restorations proceeded in fits and starts until 1902. Some of the original intentions can be seen in the fine Flamboyant Gothic portal on the southern side, called the **Porte Juive** because Jewish converts were taken through it, in suitably humiliating ceremonies, to be baptized. Just above the centre of the arch is Carpentras' famous curio, the small sculpted *Boule aux Rats* – a globe covered with rats – probably a joke on an old fanciful etymology of the town's name: *carpet ras*, or 'the rat nibbles'. The 28ft Roman **Triumphal Arch**, tucked in a corner between the Cathedral and the Palais de Justice (1640), was built about the same time as that of Orange, in the early 1st century AD. Anyone who hasn't yet seen Orange's would hardly guess this one was Roman at all. Of all the ancient Provençal monuments, this shows the bizarre Celtic quality of Gallo-Roman art at its most stylized extreme, with its reliefs of enchained captives and trophies.

Behind the cathedral and palace, two streets north up Rue Barret, is the broad Place de l'Hôtel de Ville, marking the site of Carpentras' Jewish Ghetto. Before the Revolution, over 2,000 Jews were forced to live here in unspeakable conditions, walled in and obliged to pay a fee any time they wanted to leave. All that remains of the old ghetto is the **Synagogue** at the end of the square. Built in 1741, it has a glorious decorated interior in the best 18th-century secular taste (*open Mon–Thurs 10–12 and 3–5, Fri 10–12 and 3–4*).

Mont Ventoux

Wind-swept **Mont Ventoux**, a bald, massive humpbacked massif over 20km across, is the northern boundary stone of Provence. The base for visiting the mountain is **Malaucène**, a friendly village on the road from Carpentras to Vaison. Further up the mountain, the almost permanent winds make themselves known and vegetation becomes more scarce (despite big reforestation programmes in this century). The D974's big day comes almost every summer, when the Tour de France puffs over it, probably the most tortuous part of the race; it was here that the English World Champion Tommy Simpson collapsed and died in 1967. The top of Ventoux (6,201ft) is a gravelly wasteland, embellished with communications towers and a meteorological observatory. Coming down the eastern side of the mountain takes you into one of the least-visited backwaters of Provence, a land of shepherds, boar and *cèpes*.

Les Dentelles de Montmirail

Montmirail's 'lace' is a small crown of dolomitic limestone mountains, opposite Mont Ventoux on the other side of Malaucène. This is superb walking country, and superb wine country. The D90 takes you into the Côtes-du-Rhône region, beginning with **Beaumes-de-Venise**, the metropolis of the Dentelles. There's a ruined castle to explore, and a small archaeological museum. **Vacqueyras** is a dusty little crossroads devoted entirely to wine. A few kilometres north, **Gigondas**, like so many wine villages in the south, is much smaller than its fame: sweet and small, overlooking the immaculate vineyards, full of shops to *déguster* the eponymous red nectar. **Sablet**, north of Gigondas, is another pretty, hard-working wine village packed on a hill, with old covered lanes to explore. Most of the passing tourists home in on **Séguret**, built on a terrace over the vine-striped Ouvèze plain where it bears the burden of being 'One of the Most Beautiful Villages in France' with a fair amount of grace.

Vaison-la-Romaine

Vaison, in all its 2,400 years, has never been able to make up its mind which side of the River Ouvèze it wanted to be on. Locals have always been wary of the river's mighty potential for destruction, and the town's peregrinations from bank to bank have left behind a host of monuments, including extensive Roman ruins. Such circumspection was proved justified in 1992 when, on the night of 22 September, the Ouvèze burst its banks and swept away houses, caravans, bridges and roads, drowning 30 people in one of the worst French floods this century.

Vaison began on the heights south of the Ouvèze as a Celtic *oppidum*. In the late 2nd century BC, the Romans took control, and moved the town down the hill, where it

Tourist Information

Vaison-la-Romaine: Place du Chanoine Sautel, t 04 90 36 02 11, f 04 90 28 76 04,

Where to Stay and Eat

Vaison-la-Romaine ⊠ 84110

**Hôtel Les Auric, west of Vaison on the D977, t 04 90 36 03 15 (*inexpensive*). Modernized old farmhouse with a pool. *Closed mid-Nov–April.*

***Le Beffroi, Rue de l'Evêché, up in the Haute-Ville, t 04 90 36 04 71, f 04 90 36 24 78 (*expensive–moderate*). Picturesque 16th-century house, furnished to match. A bargain for its quality. *Closed Feb and Mar.*

**Le Burrhus, 1 Place Montfort, t 04 90 36 00 11, f 04 90 36 39 05 (*inexpensive*).

Comfortable rooms with an Art Deco touch, and a shady terrace to relax on. *Closed mid-Nov–mid-Dec.*

Le Brin d'Olivier, 4 Rue du Ventoux, t 04 90 28 74 79. Vaison was something of a gastronomic desert until 1995, when young Olivia and Didier Rogne opened this intimate, romantic restaurant with an inner courtyard, the ideal place to feast on Olivia's fresh, imaginative Provençal cuisine, where fresh herbs hold pride of place (*lunch menu 80F, others 140–200F*). *Closed Wed and Sat lunch, and Christmas.*

La Fête en Provence, Place du Vieux Marché in the Haute-Ville, t 04 90 36 36 43. Serves its own *foie gras de canard*, followed by a *magret* of lamb with olives (*menus 95–240F*). *Closed mid-Nov–mid-April, and Wed.*

prospered spectacularly for the next five centuries. In perhaps the 700s, the counts of Toulouse acquired the site of the old *oppidum* and built a castle on it. Most people abandoned the Roman town for the safety of the heights, the beginnings of what is now the Haute-Ville. In the 1900s, on the move once more, the Vaisonnais were abandoning the Haute-Ville for the river bank.

Between 1907 and 1955 a local abbot uncovered almost 11 hectares of **Roman Vaison's foundations** (*open Nov–Feb daily 10–12 and 2–4.30; closed Tues; Mar–May and Oct daily 10–12 and 2–6; June–Sept daily 9.30–12.30 and 2–7; Site Puymin open July and Aug daily 9.30–7; same adm for both, also includes cathedral cloister*). There are two separate areas, the **Quartier de la Villasse** and the **Site Puymin**. The Villasse is the smaller of the two areas; from the entrance, a Roman street takes you past the city's **baths** (the best parts are still hidden under Vaison's post office) and the **Maison au Buste d'Argent**, a truly posh villa with two *atria* and some mosaic floors. It has its own baths, as does the adjacent **Maison au Dauphin**; beyond this is a short stretch of a **colonnaded street**. The Puymin quarter has more of the same: another villa, the **Maison des Messii**, is near the entrance. Beyond that, however, is an *insula*, or block of flats for the common folk, as well as a large, partially excavated quadrangle called the **Portique de Pompée**, an enclosed public garden with statuary that was probably attached to a temple. On the opposite side of the *insula* is a largely ruined *nymphaeum*. From here you can walk uphill to the **theatre**, restored and used for summer concerts, and the **museum**, with the best of the finds from the excavations.

The fascinating **Cathedral of Notre-Dame-de-Nazareth**, west of the ruins on Av Jules Ferry, was begun in the 6th century. Its **apse** is the oldest part; the rest of the structure dates from a rebuilding that began in the 1100s. Among its many mysteries is a rectangular **maze**, near the top of the façade, and a triangular figure that may be a mystic representation of the sun. The nave is Romanesque at its best, the arcaded apse is magnificent, and in the **cloister**, grinning over the ticket-booth, is Vaison's most famous citizen – Old Nick himself, whose presence here is as enigmatic as is the medieval Latin inscription along the southern cornice.

The **Haute-Ville** – the medieval town – is a splendid sight atop its cliff, a honey-coloured skyline of stone houses under the castle of the counts of Toulouse. Almost abandoned at the turn of the century, it is becoming quite chic now, with restorations everywhere. You reach it by crossing the Ouvèze on a **Roman bridge**, still in good nick after 18 centuries of service (although it had to be repaired after the last floods).

The Alpes-Maritimes

These are real Alps – arrogant crystalline giants, which make their contempt felt as we crawl through the valleys beneath. The best parts have been set aside as the **Parc National du Mercantour**. Established only in 1979, the Parc consists of a central 'protected zone', a narrow strip of the most inaccessible areas, including the Vallée des Merveilles with its prehistoric rock carvings, and a much larger 'peripheral zone' that includes all the villages from Sospel to St-Etienne-de-Tinée and beyond. The most spectacular alpine fauna, and the sort you're most likely to see, are the birds of

Getting Around

In all the hinterlands of Provence, this is the region most difficult to navigate by **car**, and the most convenient for public transport.

One of the best ways to see the Vallée de la Roya is from that alpine rarity – a **train**. The railway line from Nice that runs to Cuneo in Italy offers spectacular scenery and serves all of the local villages: L'Escarène, Sospel, Breil, St-Dalmas and Tende (five each, daily).

Sospel also has four daily **buses** (no.910) to and from Menton, which take 20 minutes. There is a range of buses from Sospel into the smaller valleys (**t** 04 93 04 01 24).

There are no trains in either the Vésubie or the Tinée valleys, and the coach service is sketchy.

St-Martin-Vésubie can be reached by coach from the bus station in Nice (Cars TRAM, **t** 04 93 89 47 14); buses for St-Sauveur and St-Etienne in the Tinée also leave from here.

Roads in this area are difficult, and service stations few.

Where to Stay and Eat

Sospel ✉ 06380

★★Des Etrangers, 7 Av de Verdun, **t** 04 93 04 00 09, **f** 04 93 04 12 31 (*inexpensive*). Only marginally the most expensive of Sospel's hotels, and has a pool. *Closed Dec–Feb.*

★★L'Auberge Provençale, Route de Menton, a mile from the centre, **t** 04 93 04 00 31 (*inexpensive*). Also has a terrace with a magnificent view over Sospel.

Domaine du Paraïs, off the D2566 towards Moulinet at La Vasta (you need a car), **t** 04 93 04 15 78 (*inexpensive*). A villa taken over by officers during the war, which has now been proudly restored as a *chambre d'hôte* by its owners. Book ahead.

L'Escargot d'Or, 3 Rue de Verdon, **t** 04 93 04 00 43. The best place to eat in Sospel, specializing in meat fondues (*menus 68–159F*). Ring to reserve, and to check they're open out of season – they'll close if they anticipate a quiet night.

Saorge ✉ 06540

Le Bellevue, **t** 04 93 04 51 37 (*inexpensive*). The only hotel here.

Lou Pountin, Rue Revelli, **t** 04 93 04 54 90. Excellent pizzas (*menu 75F*). *Closed Wed.*

prey: golden eagles, falcons and vultures. A recent addition, reintroduced from the Balkans after becoming extinct here, is the lammergeyer. On the ground, there's the ubiquitous stoat or ermine, the bulkier marmot, and plenty of boars, foxes, mouflons (wild mountain sheep), chamois and *bouquetins* (ibex). Half the flowers of the whole of France are represented here. The symbol of the park is the spiky *saxifrage multiflora*, one of 25 species found nowhere but here. Edelweiss exists in the park, but is as elusive as anywhere else.

The Vallée de la Roya

Along the road from Nice, **Sospel** greets you with rusty cannons and machine guns, pointing out over the road from Fort St-Roch (*open July and Aug Tues–Sun 2–6; April, May, Sept and Oct weekends only*). The fortress, almost entirely underground, shows only a few blockhouses, in a sort of military Art Deco; it dates from a 1930s counterpart of the Maginot Line. In the last war the town suffered considerable damage, now entirely, and lovingly, restored, including Sospel's landmark, the Pont Vieux, the base of which dates back to the 10th century. The tiny tower in the middle of the bridge was the toll on the salt road; in the Middle Ages, salt from the flats of Toulon and

La Brigue ✉ 06430

★★Le Mirval, Rue St-Vincent Ferrier, **t** 04 93 04 63 71, **f** 04 93 04 79 81 (*inexpensive*). The best choice here; some rooms have views, and the management can arrange a trip (expensive) into the Vallée des Merveilles. *Closed Nov–Mar.*

Levens ✉ 06450

La Vigneraie, t 04 93 79 70 46, **f** 04 93 79 84 35 (*cheap; full board inexpensive*). Friendly auberge on the Nice road below the village. Comfortable rooms, and it would be madness not to take full board at a hostelry that locals travel miles to visit just for Sunday lunch. Lunch alone is possible, if you're not staying (an incredible 120–150F for five courses; book early) – but you'll wish you had a room to sleep in afterwards. *Closed mid-Oct–Jan.*

Lantosque ✉ 06450

★★★Hostellerie de l'Ancienne Gendarmerie, **t** 04 93 03 00 65, **f** 04 93 03 06 31 (*moderate*). On the way up to the Parc Mercantour, the gracious 'former police station' occupies a pretty hillside site, with garden-side rooms and a pool. The restaurant specializes in sea fish and *escargots* (*menus 170F and 300F*). *Closed Oct–Mar.*

St-Martin-Vésubie ✉ 06450

★★La Bonne Auberge, Place Félix Faure, **t** 04 93 03 20 49, **f** 04 93 03 20 69 (*inexpensive*). A welcoming and pretty place with nice rooms and a cosy cellar restaurant with a boar's head over the chimneypiece – grilled chops, *escargots*, *civet de lapin* and profiteroles (*menus 98F and 140F*). *Closed mid-Nov–Jan.*

★Des Alpes, across the square, **t** 04 93 03 21 06 (*cheap*). If the *auberge* is full, settle here. *Closed Jan.*

La Treille, Rue Dr Cagnol, **t** 04 93 03 30 85. Step out for some of the best pizza this side of the border – baked in a proper pizza oven ; also pasta and more ambitious dishes (*90–150F; winter weekends only*).

La Trappa, Place du Marché, **t** 04 93 03 21 50. Mountain fare and heady house wine (*menus 95F and 115F*). *Closed Sun eve and Mon out of season.*

Le Cavalet, outside St-Martin in Le Boréon, **t** 04 93 03 21 46, **f** 04 93 03 34 34. Simple abode in a dreamy lakeside setting, at the forest edge. Half-board compulsory, but the restaurant is excellent (*menus 89–139F*). *Closed Nov.*

Hyères was taken by boat to Nice, and from there by convoys of mules to Piedmont and Lombardy. Make sure you take a wander around the winding streets of the old town, and arcaded Place St-Nicolas with a 15th-century fountain, on the other side of the bridge.

If you travel north beyond Saorge on the N204, there's no way out unless you retrace your steps or continue through the tunnel to Cuneo, Italy. The mountains close in immediately, with the **Gorges de Bergue et de Paganin**; these end at the village of **St-Dalmas-de-Tende**, the gateway to the **Vallée des Merveilles**. From about 1800 BC, the Ligurian natives of these mountains began scratching pictures and symbols on the rocks. They kept at it for the next 800 years, until over 100,000 inscriptions decorated the valley: human figures, religious symbols (plenty of bulls, horns and serpents), weapons and tools. Most defy any conclusive interpretation – circles, spirals and ladders or chequerboard patterns of the kind found all over the Mediterranean. Why they were made is an open question; one very appealing hypothesis is that this valley, beneath Mont Bégo, was a holy place and a pilgrimage site, and that the carvings can be taken as *ex votos* made by the pilgrims. As the prime attraction of the Parc Mercantour, the valley gets its share of visitors these days. Besides the carvings, the landscape itself is worth the hike, including a score of mountain lakes, mostly above the tree line, all in the shadow of the rugged, uncanny **Mont Bégo**, highest of the peaks around the Roya.

Tende, a dour slate-roofed *bourg*, is the only town in the Upper Roya. No longer a dead end since the road tunnel through to Italy was built, it has become a busy place by local standards. On Av du 16 Septembre 1847, the Musée des Merveilles (*open May–mid-Oct daily 10.30–6.30, also Sat till 8pm; mid-Oct–April daily 10.30–5; closed Tues; adm*) has copies and photos of the rock engravings, as well as ethnographic exhibits on prehistoric life up to the 18th century.

East of St-Dalmas-de-Tende, the D143 takes you to **La Brigue**, in a minute region (partly in Italy) that grows apples and pears and raises trout. It has some fine paintings in the late Gothic church of St-Martin: three altarpieces by Ludovico Brea and his followers, along with Italian paintings from the 17th and 18th centuries. Even better are Giovanni Canavesio's wonderful Renaissance frescoes at **Notre-Dame-des-Fontaines**, a rural chapel 4km from La Brigue. Done in the 1490s, these include 26 large scenes of the Passion of Christ in the nave, and on one of the side walls a tremendous *Last Judgement*, a gentle reminder that God wasn't joking. All the tortures of the damned are portrayed in intricate detail, as the devils sweep them into the maw of Hell. Around the choir, on the triumphal arch, he painted scenes from the Life of Mary. The frescoes in the choir itself are by another hand, Giovanni Baleison, done in the 1470s in a more old-fashioned style that still shows the influence of Byzantium.

The Valleys of the Vésubie and the Tinée

The Vésubie flows into the Var near **Levens**, a big walled village high on a small plain with a big church and a scattering of small private art galleries. Beneath it, the main road up the valley, the D2565, follows the scenic **Gorges de la Vésubie**. At the top of the valley, **St-Martin-Vésubie** is the only town for a great distance in any direction, and a base for tackling the upper part of the Mercantour. It's as unaffectedly cute as a town can be; in the delightful and shady town square is an old fountain where the mineral waters of its spa used to flow. The medieval centre is traversed by a lovely street (Rue Dr Cagnoli) with a mountain spring flowing down a narrow channel in the middle, as in a garden of the Alhambra.

There's nothing splashy or spectacular about the Tinée, serenely beautiful even by alpine standards. In the lower part of the valley, the scenery is as much indoors as out; prosperity in the 15th and 16th centuries allowed the villages of the Lower Tinée to decorate their modest churches with fine Renaissance frescoes by artists of the Nice school. You will find examples in the chapels of **La Tour** and **Clans**. Continuing up the valley, the next stop is **St-Sauveur-sur-Tinée**, throbbing metropolis of the valley, with its 496 souls.

The uppermost part of the Tinée, following the D2205, runs through the northern half of the Parc Mercantour. Near the source of the Tinée river is **St-Etienne-de-Tinée**, which has two painted rural chapels.

Getting Around

Buses are so rare they aren't worth the trouble, but it can be fun seeing this region by the scenic, recently modernized narrow-gauge rail-line familiarly called the **Train des Pignes**, from Nice to Digne; it follows the Var, and a few trains stop at villages along the way. This is not the SNCF, but a separate line called Chemin de Fer de Provence (in Digne, call t 04 92 31 01 58, for details).

Where to Stay and Eat

Castellane ✉ 04120

***Nouvel Hôtel du Commerce**, Place de l'Eglise, t 04 92 83 61 00, f 04 92 83 72 82 (*moderate*). Friendly and comfortable. *Closed Nov–April.*

Ma Petite Auberge, 8 Bd de la République, t 04 92 83 62 06, f 04 92 83 68 49 (*inexpensive*). Acceptable for a short stay. *Closed Dec–Mar.*

La Forge, t 04 92 83 62 61, f 04 92 83 65 81 (*inexpensive*). At the foot of the rock next to the church, with a terrace from which to view the village and the walkers going up and down the *roc. Closed mid-Dec–Jan.*

Grand Canyon, 14km east of the village of Aiguines, at the Falaise des Cavaliers, t 04 94 76 91 31, f 04 92 76 92 29 (*inexpensive*). The best views of the Canyon, looking 300m down on to the Verdon from its glassed-in restaurant terrace. *Closed Oct–April.*

Moustiers-Ste-Marie ✉ 04360

****La Bastide de Moustiers**, just outside the village at La Grisolière, t 04 92 70 47 47, f 04 92 70 47 48 (*expensive*). After a day's tramping through the Grand Canyon, you can sleep in comfort and splurge for a memorable dinner at celeb-chef Alain

Ducasse's 17th-century hotel with 12 individually fashioned rooms, Jacuzzi, pool, riding stable, etc. The food is predominantly local, picked from the kitchen garden, and innovative – herb and vegetable tart, spit-roasted baron of lamb followed by cherries baked in batter (*menus from 310F*). *Restaurant closed Jan and Feb.*

Belvédère, t 04 92 74 66 04, f 04 92 74 62 31 (*inexpensive*). Up in the village. *Closed mid-Nov–Jan.*

Les Santons, Place de l'Eglise, t 04 92 74 66 48. Enjoys a gorgeous setting on top of the village overlooking the torrent; the refined Provençal cooking matches the views (*menus 160–300F*). *Closed Mon eve and Dec–Jan; book.*

Quinson ✉ 04500

Relais Notre Dame, in the middle of the Gorges du Verdon at Quinson, t 04 92 74 40 01, f 04 92 74 02 10 (*inexpensive*). A garden and pool, but most importantly a real, warm welcome and very good food. *Closed mid-Dec–mid-Mar.*

Digne ✉ 04000

****Du Grand Paris**, 19 Bd Thiers, t 04 92 31 11 15, f 04 92 32 32 82 (*expensive–moderate*). Distinguished hotel in a restored 17th-century monastery, with an excellent restaurant featuring classic cuisine with truffles. *Closed mid-Dec–mid-Mar.*

Le Provence, 17 Bd Thiers, t 04 92 31 32 19, f 04 92 31 48 39 (*inexpensive*). Central and comfortable, and has a good restaurant.

Petit St-Jean, 14 Cours des Arès, t 04 92 31 30 04, f 04 92 36 05 80 (*cheap*). Looks quaint but the view – if you have one – will be tainted with the whiff of chip oil from the neighbouring restaurant. If you stay here, eat elsewhere.

The Alpes de Haute-Provence

There is something of the Wild West in this *département*, complete with lofty plateaux and canyons, including a Grand one. Provence's wide open spaces are full of lavender fields and fresh air, a place to white-water raft, hang glide, ride, climb or hike.

Castellane, south of Lac du Castillon, is the capital of the Grand Canyon du Verdon, the base for visiting one of the greatest natural wonders in Europe. There is a pretty *mairie* and a church, where the 597ft ascent up the Castellane's landmark square rock begins. Castellane's motto 'Napoleon stopped here. Why don't you?' comes from its spot on the Route Napoléon, the road taken by the emperor on his sneak return from the island of Elba.

The most surprising thing about the **Grand Canyon du Verdon** is that it was not 'discovered' until 1905. The name 'Grand Canyon' was a modern idea; when the French became aware of its existence, comparisons with that grand-daddy of all canyons in Arizona were inevitable. It does put on a grand show: sheer limestone cliffs, snaking back and forth to follow the meandering course of the Verdon; in many places there are vast panoramas down the length of it. There are roads along both sides, though not for the entire distance. Most of the best views are from the **Corniche Sublime** (D71) on the south side; if you want to explore the bottom, ask about trails and the best approaches (it's a long trek) at the tourist office in Castellane.

Directly west of the Canyon, a less spectacular section of the Verdon has been dammed up, forming the enormous **Lac de Ste-Croix**; there is another dam further downstream, and the next 40km of the river valley are under water too: the **Gorges du Verdon**, in parts as good as the Canyon, but sacrificed forever to the beaverish Paris planners.

The **Plateau de Valensole**, north of the Verdon and the Lac de Ste-Croix, is a hot, dry plain of olive and almond trees, and one of the big lavender-growing areas of Provence – come in July to see it in full bloom. **Riez**, in the middle, is an old centre for lavender distilling, now adapted to tourism. Ruined medieval houses have been restored, and artists and potters have moved in, and it can be a good place to dawdle in. At the west edge of town are four standing columns of a Roman Temple of Apollo, and a 6th-century Baptistry that is one of the few surviving monuments in France from the Merovingian era.

To the east, some 15km on the D952, **Moustiers-Ste-Marie** gets all the attention, spectacularly hanging on the west cliffs of the Grand Canyon du Verdon. Another popular base for visiting the Canyon, Moustiers was Provence's main centre for painted ceramics; the blue and yellow faïences were often works of art in their own right. Today potters, some talented and some pretty awful, clutter the village streets, capitalizing on the perfect clay of the region (and on the tourists).

Another of Moustiers' distinctions is the **Cadeno de Moustié**, a 783ft chain suspended between the tops of two peaks overlooking the village. A knight of the local Blacas family, while a prisoner of the Saracens during the Crusades, made a vow to put it up if he ever saw home again; the star in the middle comes from his coat of arms.

Digne means 'worthy'. The capital of the Alpes de Haute-Provence *département*, and the only city in a long stretch of mountains between Orange and Turin, it has one thriving boulevard of cafés and touristic knick-knackery mixed with smart shoe-shops, posh chocolates and bookshops. Out of town is something entirely unexpected: the **Fondation Alexandra David-Neel** (*27 Av du Maréchal Juin; guided tours with her former secretary; July–Sept daily at 10.30, 2, 3.30 and 5; otherwise at 10.30, 2 and 4*), the former home of a truly remarkable Frenchwoman who settled here in her

'Himalayas in miniature' after a lifetime exploring in Tibet. There are exhibits of Tibetan art and culture, photographs and Tibetan crafts on sale; the Dalai Lama has come twice to visit.

At **St Benoit**, the Geology Centre (*open April–Oct daily 9–12 and 2–5.30, Fri till 4.30; Nov–Mar closed Sat and Sun*) houses the largest geology collection in Europe, including an impressive wall of ammonites.

Villages of the Central Var

West of the military town of Draguignan are some of Provence's loveliest and most typical landscapes. Though this area gets its share of summer folk, it isn't as chic or colonized as the Luberon. **Lorgues** is the first village, with a complete ensemble of 18th-century municipal decorations: a fountain, the dignified church of St-Martin, and the inevitable avenue of plane trees, one of the longest and fairest in Provence.

Where to Stay and Eat

Lorgues ✉ 83510
Hôtel du Parc, 25 Bd Clemenceau, t 04 94 73 70 01, f 04 94 67 68 46 (*inexpensive*). A venerable, classy hotel in the centre, a bit down on its luck but still comfortable with a restaurant (*menus 250F*). *Closed Nov.*
Chez Bruno, Campagne Mariette, t 04 94 85 93 93, f 04 94 85 93 99. For something special, book a table at this old *mas*, where the chef does wonderful things with truffles (*menu 300F*). *Closed Sun eve and Mon.* There are also three luxurious rooms and one suite, at prices that extend into the ozone layer (*450F–1,250F*).

Tourtour ✉ 83690
★★★★Bastide de Tourtour, Montée St Denis, t 04 98 10 54 20, f 04 94 70 54 90 (*expensive*). Modern Relais et Châteaux complex with pool, tennis and all the amenities, including a highly reputed restaurant with a blend of Provençal cooking and classic French (*menus lunch 160F, dinner 230–360F*).
★★★Le Mas des Collines, Route de Villecroze, t 04 94 70 59 30, f 04 94 70 57 62 (*expensive; half-board*). Charming and more affordable little hotel, offering tranquillity, air-conditioned rooms and a pretty pool overlooking the valley below Tourtour.
★Les Chênes Verts, 2km on the Route de Villecroze, t 04 94 70 55 06, f 04 94 70 59 35.

Three pricey rooms, but the food is the magnet, featuring lobster, seafood, truffles and game, prepared to classical perfection. *Closed Tues, Wed and June.*
★★★Auberge St-Pierre, 3km east at St-Pierre-de-Tourtour, t 04 94 70 57 17, f 04 94 70 58 04 (*moderate*). An up-to-date working farm built around a hotel; exceptional rooms in an 18th-century house and a fine restaurant, with authentic Provençal food – largely the farm's own produce (*menus 160F and 215F*). Also a pool, gym, tennis, archery and fishing. Beware of the hostess when she is tired. *Closed mid-Oct–Mar.*

Salernes ✉ 83690
★Allègre, 20 Rue Rousseau, t 04 94 70 60 30, f 04 94 70 78 38 (*cheap*). An old establishment, with a bit of faded grandeur and some of its 1920s décor. *Closed Dec–Mar.*
La Fontaine, Place du 8 Mai 1945, t 04 94 70 64 51. For a simple *magret* or stewed rabbit; outside tables too (*menus 98–160F*). *Closed Sun eve, Mon, and Jan.*
Restaurant des Pins, on the D32 in Sillans, ✉ 83690, t 04 94 04 63 26, f 04 94 04 72 71. Very popular restaurant in an old stone house, serving grilled meats with shrimps for openers (*menus 85–210F*). Also a few rooms (*inexpensive*), but book early for summer. *Closed mid-Jan–Feb.*

Further north, there are a number of pretty villages around the valley of the Nartuby: **Ampus**, **Tourtour**, over-restored but up on a height with views down to the sea, and **Villecroze**, with its vaulted lanes, built up against a tufa cliff.

Aups was a Ligurian settlement, and a Roman town. It has a reputation for being different; a monument in the town square records Aups' finest hour, when the citizens put up a doomed republican resistance to Louis Napoleon's coup of 1851. Like the other villages, it has not completely escaped Riviera modernism. The Musée Simon Ségal (*open mid-June–mid-Sept daily 10–12 and 4–7; adm*), founded by the eponymous Russian artist, has his and other 20th-century works. **Salernes**, south of Aups, has been known for over 200 years for its small, hexagonal terracotta floor-tiles called *tomettes* that are as much a trademark of Provence as lavender. Further west, **Sillans** has lately been calling itself Sillans-la-Cascade, to draw attention to the 118ft waterfall just south of the village (it dries up in summer).

South of Salernes, **Entrecasteaux** is dominated by a 17th-century castle, completely restored in the 1970s by a Scotsman named McGarvie-Munn. Further south, the artificial **Lac de Carcès** has been a favourite with fishermen since the dam was built in the 1930s. To the east are the biggest bauxite mines in France, which are playing hell with one of the most impressive medieval abbeys in Provence. This is the **Abbaye du Thoronet** (*open April–Sept Mon–Sat 9–7, Sun 2–7; Oct–Mar Mon–Sat 10–1 and 2–5, Sun 10–12 and 2–5; adm*), the first Cistercian foundation in Provence; the present buildings were begun about 1160. The mines themselves (nearby, but screened by trees) have caused some subsidence, and cracks are opening in the walls. Nevertheless, this purest and plainest of the Cistercian 'Three Sisters' of Provence (with Silvacane and Sénanque) is worth a detour. It displays sophisticated Romanesque architecture stripped to its bare essentials, with no worldly splendour to distract a monkish mind, only grace of form and proportion. Behind the blank façade is a marvellously elegant interior; note the slight point of the arches, a hint of the dawning Gothic. The **cloister** with its heavy arcades is equally good, enclosing a delightful stone fountain-house.

Its inhabitants might be unaware of it, but **Cotignac** is the cutest of the cute, a Provençal village where everything is just right. There are no sights, but one looming peculiarity: the tufa cliffs that hang dramatically over it. In former times these were hollowed out for wine cellars, stables or even habitations; today there are trails up to them for anyone who wants to explore. Westwards on the D13/D560, **Barjols** has little cuteness but much more character. This metropolis of 2,000 souls owes its existence to leather tanning, an important industry here for the last 300 years. It retains an urban and somewhat sombre air: elegant rectangular squares of the 18th century, and moss-covered fountains and *lavoirs* similar to the ones in Aix. At the tourist office you can get a '*circuit des fontaines*' to guide you round all 42 of them.

The Eastern Côte d'Azur

Just west of Italy begins that 20km swathe of Mediterranean hyperbole that represents the favourite mental image of the French Riviera. Although first tamed by

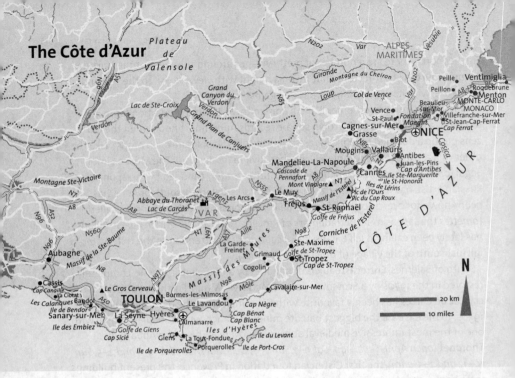

the Romans, this tasty morsel of the Côte d'Azur long remained a world apart, ruled until the mid-19th century by the Grimaldis of Monaco, when bad feelings over Napoleon brought the first English and Russians, with their titles and weak lungs, to winter here. They built hotels, villas and casinos in the fulsome rococo spa style of the period, and to this day the spirit lingers. The scenery is breathtaking, one mighty mountain after another plummeting drunkenly into the sea, traced by hairpinning corniche roads on ledges over vertiginous drops. Where the shores of the eastern Riviera tend to be all shingle, the beaches of the western Côte d'Azur are mostly soft sand. The crowds, cars, art, yachts, boutiques and prices are less intense as well, with the outrageous exception of St-Tropez, the pretty playground of the jet set.

Menton

The Côte d'Azur starts on the Italian frontier, where a wall of mountains blocks out the cold so that lemons can blossom all year. Menton declared its independence from the Grimaldis in 1848 and became part of France in 1860. Soon after, the town attracted a community of 5,000 Brits, led by Queen Victoria herself in 1883. Despite a poor beach and an elderly population, Menton is magnificently situated, sprinkled with some of the coast's finest gardens, and has a healthy attitude to relaxation compared to the hard-edged glamour-pusses to the west.

Getting Around

The *Métrazur* **trains** between St-Raphaël and Ventimiglia, and all others running between Nice and Italy, stop in Menton (Menton-Centre). There's also a stop – Menton-Garavan – behind the port. **Buses** depart from the bus station on the Esplanade du Careï every 15mins to Nice, by way of Roquebrune-Cap-Martin and Monte-Carlo. There's a **taxi** rank outside the Menton-Centre station, or call **t** 04 92 10 47 00.

Tourist Information

Menton: Palais de l'Europe, 8 Av Boyer, **t** 04 92 41 76 50, **f** 04 92 41 76 78. Also at the coach station, Esplanade du Careï, **t** 04 93 28 43 27.

Where to Stay

Menton ✉ 06500

Luxury–Expensive

★★★★Hôtel des Ambassadeurs, 3 Rue Partouneaux, **t** 04 93 28 75 75, **f** 04 93 35 62 32. The last *grande dame* of Menton, gracious, spacious, pink and balconied, and slap bang in the middle of town. There's nearly every luxury you'd expect for the price, but no pool. The restaurant, **La Véranda**, is the best in town.

Expensive

★★★Napoléon, 29 Porte de France, **t** 04 93 35 89 50, **f** 04 93 35 49 22. A delight; the

rooms may be decorated in comfortable dark brown like a favourite great aunt's, but it has a pool, soundproofed, air-conditioned rooms, a private beach, and friendly, obliging staff. *Closed mid-Nov–mid-Dec.*

★★★L'Aiglon, 7 Av de la Madone, **t** 04 93 57 55 55, **f** 04 93 35 92 39. Belle Epoque, stylish and chic, with spindly antiques and high ceilings. By the pool, there is a lovely arbour with wooden beams and rattan blinds. *Closed Nov–mid-Dec.* The restaurant serves traditional regional cuisine in a glassed-in terrace overlooking its pool (*menus 190–300F*).

★★★Royal Westminster, 28 Av Félix-Faure, **t** 04 93 28 69 69, **f** 04 92 10 12 30. Part of a smart hotel group with quiet rooms furnished in cool sea colours, views over the bay, huddles of elderly ladies on the terrace playing poker and scrabble, and a *pétanque* court on the gravel drive.

Cheap

★★Hôtel de Londres, 15 Av Carnot, **t** 04 93 35 74 62, **f** 04 93 41 77 78. Nothing is too much trouble for the cheerful host who will even lend you a cushioned mattress for the stony beach. Rooms are simply but attractively decorated, and some overlook the garden with its little bar and games area. *Closed mid-Oct–mid-Dec.*

Pension Beauregard, 10 Rue Albert Ier, **t** 04 93 28 63 63, **f** 04 93 28 63 79, *beauregard. menton@wanadoo.fr*. A good bargain below the station, a sweet place with a quiet garden. *Closed Nov.*

The Musée Cocteau and Palais Carnolès

Menton is squeezed between the mountains and a pair of shingle-beached bays: the Baie de Garavan, on the Italian side, where villas and gardens overlook the yacht harbour, and the Baie du Soleil which stretches 3km west to Cap Martin. In between these two bays stands a little 17th-century harbour bastion that Jean Cocteau converted into the **Musée Cocteau** (*open daily 10–12 and 2–6; closed Tues; adm*) in the late 1950s, to hold his playful series of *Animaux Fantastiques* and a tapestry of *Judith et Holopherne*, while the happier love affairs of the Mentonnais are portrayed in the *Innamorati* series.

Eating Out

All along Rue St Michel masses of restaurants vie for your attention with tempting displays spilling out into the street that somehow miss the mark.

Moderate

Pierrot-Pierrette, up at Monti, on the Rte de Sospel, t 04 93 35 79 76. Complements the panoramic views with delicious fresh blue trout (*menus 148–195F*). *Closed Mon.*

Darkoum, Rue St Michel 23, t 04 93 35 44 88. Tasty Moroccan dishes. The house speciality is *pastilla*, a fragrant concoction with pigeon and almonds (*menus 90F and 128F*). *Closed Mon in summer.*

La Coquille d'Or, on the corner of Quai Bonaparte, t 04 93 35 80 67. A tourist trap, complete with Gypsy strummers but, surprisingly, also packs in crowds of locals for the *bouillabaisse* (*350F for two*) and paella. *Closed Wed.*

Le Nautic, 27 Quai de Monléon, t 04 93 35 78 74. Bright blue and serves up every possible fish dish, including *bouillabaisse* (*menus from 138F*). *Closed Mon.*

Cheap

Le Merle Blanc, 21 Rue St Michel, t 04 93 35 77 53. Sunny yellow walls, Provençal tablecloths, equally sunny serving staff and serves good value staples like *steak frites* and trout with almonds (*menus from 79F*).

✉ **06190 (Grande Corniche)**

★★★★**Vista Palace**, t 04 92 10 40 00, f 04 93 35 18 94, *vistapalace@webstore.fr* (*luxury*). The ultimate in luxury, hanging on a 1,000ft cliff on the Grande Corniche, with a God's-eye view over Monaco; also a heated pool, squash, gym, and sauna. The hotel's cliff-hanging restaurant, **Le Vistaero**, offers some of the Côte's most talked-about cuisine under the auspices of chef Jean-Pierre Pestre (*menus from 345F*). *Closed Feb.*

★★**Westminster**, 14 Av L.-Laurens, t 04 93 35 00 68, f 04 93 28 88 50, *westminster@ifrance.com* (*moderate*). Down on the poor sinners' level, with a pretty garden terrace near the junction of the lower two Corniches. *Closed Dec–mid-Feb.*

Au Grand Inquisiteur, 18 Rue du Château, Roquebrune, t 04 93 35 05 37. In a former sheepfold cut into the rock, serving well-prepared Provençal dishes like *fleurs de courgette farcies* (*menus from 150F*). *Closed Mon and Tues lunch.*

La Grotte, Place des Deux-Frères, t 04 93 35 00 04. A cheaper troglodyte choice, which also has tables outside at the entrance to the Vieille Ville in Roquebrune, and offers pizzas, pasta and a good value *plat du jour.*

Hôtel des Deux Frères, across the square, t 04 93 28 99 00, f 04 93 28 99 10, *2freres@webstore.fr* (*moderate*). Ethereally light and airy. The rooms are small but white muslin canopies draped over the beds, white-washed walls and endless views make up for the lack of space. Friendly, knowledgeable staff serve excellent regional dishes on the flower-edged terrace. *Restaurant closed Sun eve and Mon.*

This theme of Menton's lovers was first explored by Cocteau in his decorations (1957) for the **Salle des Mariages** (*open Mon–Fri 8.30–12.30 and 1.30–5; adm*), in the Hôtel de Ville in Rue de la République.

At the western end of Menton, the frothy pink and white summer home of the princes of Monaco, the Palais Carnolès (1717), is now an art museum, the **Musée des Beaux-Arts Palais Carnolès**, 3 Av de la Madone (*bus 3; open daily 10–12 and 2–6; closed Tues; adm*). It holds Ludovico Bréa's luminous *Madonna and Child with St Francis*, several oil paintings attributed to Leonardo da Vinci, and all the previous winners from Menton's very own Biennale of painting. Other works were donated by the English landscape and portrait artist Graham Sutherland, who lived part of every year in Menton from 1947 until he died in 1980.

The Vieille Ville, and the Gardens of Garavan

The tall, narrow 17th-century houses of Menton's Vieille Ville are knitted together by anti-earthquake arches that span stepped lanes named after old pirate captains and saints. It's hard to believe that the quiet main street, **Rue Longue** (the Roman Via Julia Augusta), was, until the 19th century, the main route between France and Italy.

From Rue Longue, the shallow stairs of the Rampes St-Michel lead up to the ice-cream-coloured church of **St-Michel** (1675), and the equally charming Baroque **Chapelle des Pénitents Blancs**, headquarters of one of the old Riviera's many religious confraternities. The Montée du Souvenir leads to the top of the Vieille Ville, where the citadel was replaced in the 19th century by the romantic, panoramic **Cimetière du Vieux Château** (*open summer daily 7–8; winter daily 7–6*). From the cemetery, Boulevard de Garavan leads to the **Jardin Exotique Val Rahmeh** (*entrance on the Av St-Jacques; open summer daily 10–12.30 and 3–6; winter daily 10–12.30 and 2–5; adm*), planted with more than 700 tropical and subtropical species from around the world.

The Grande Corniche

Roquebrune-Cap Martin

The medieval village of Roquebrune is all steep, winding, arcaded streets with a fair number of over-restored houses, galleries and ateliers, culminating at the top in the **Château** (*open Oct–Jan daily 10–12.30 and 2–5; Feb–May daily 10–12.30 and 2–6; June–Sept daily 10–12.30 and 2–7; adm*), first erected in the 10th century. The view from the top floor is by far the best of the castle's attractions. Under the castle, Rue du Château, leads to Rue de la Fontaine and Chemin de St. Roch and a remarkable contemporary of the castle: a **1,000-year-old olive tree** with a circumference of 33ft.

In the 1890s a pair of empresses, Eugénie (widow of Napoleon III) and Elisabeth ('Sisi') of Austria, made Roquebrune's peninsula of Cap Martin an aristocratic enclave. Le Corbusier died here in 1965 while swimming off the white rocks beside what is now **Promenade Le Corbusier**. A spectacular path leads from Cap Martin to Monte-Carlo (a four-hour walk).

Monaco

Big-time tax-dodgers agree: it's hard to beat Monaco for comfort and convenience when the time comes to snuggle down with your piggy chips. Rainier III, chairman of the board of Monaco Inc., will probably go down in history as the Principality's greatest benefactor. Through landfill and burrowing he has added a fifth to his realm and on it built more (but certainly not better) than any of his predecessors, creating a Lilliputian Manhattan. Money is the main topic of conversation wherever you go in this security-conscious, sanitized tax haven.

Getting Around

You can **drive** into Monaco along the Corniche Inférieure, or take the **helicopter** from Nice airport if you're in a hurry (7mins, from 402F, Heli Air Monaco, t 92 05 00 50, Monacair t 97 97 39 01). **Buses** leave hourly from Nice Airport (terminal 2; 9am–9pm) or **taxi** (45mins); buses every 15mins between Menton and Nice stop at several points along the Corniche, including right outside the Monte-Carlo casino. The Monaco/Monte-Carlo **train** station is in Av Prince-Pierre, t 93 10 60 15.

Small as it is, Monaco is divided into several towns: Monte-Carlo to the east, Fontvieille by the port, Monaco-Ville on the rock, and La Condamine below, and there's a **public bus** network to save you some legwork. More importantly, free **public lifts and escalators** operate between its tiers of streets.

Tourist Information

Monaco: 2a Bd des Moulins, Monte-Carlo, t 92 16 61 16, f 92 16 60 00, www.monaco-congres.com.
Note: In Monaco, if the telephone number has only 8 digits, you must dial t 00 377 before calling, even from France. If the number has 10 digits, it operates like a French number.

Money: the unit of currency is the French franc; Monégasque coins with Prince Rainier's image are in circulation but are rarely accepted outside the Principality.

Where to Stay

Monaco ✉ 98030, t (00 377–)

Monte-Carlo

★★★★**Hôtel de Paris**, Place du Casino, t 92 16 30 00, f 92 16 38 49, www.montecarloresort.com (luxury; 2,900–3,700F). Opened in 1865 by the SBM for gambling tsars and duchesses, now with direct access to the modern-day Riviera prerequisite, a thalassotherapy centre.

★★★★**Hermitage**, Square Beaumarchais, t 92 16 40 00, f 92 16 38 52 (luxury; 2,700–11,000F). Also owned by the SBM, a beautiful Belle Epoque hotel perched high on its rock, with an Italian loggia and 'Winter Garden' designed by Gustave Eiffel.

★★★**Balmoral** 12 Av de la Costa, t 93 50 62 37, f 93 15 08 69, www.hotel-balmoral.mc (expensive). An old hotel next door, for a third of the price, with a view of the sea.

★★★**Hôtel Alexandra**, 35 Bd Princesse-Charlotte, t 93 50 63 13, f 92 16 06 48 (expensive). More turn-of-the-last-century opulence, gilded and newly refurbished.

History

Lords of Monaco since 1308 and once rulers of a mini-empire including Antibes and Menton, the Grimaldis today own 194 hectares of sea-hugging land. Here Rainier presides as the living representative of the oldest ruling family in Europe, and Europe's last constitutional autocrat.

When the Grimaldis faced bankruptcy in the mid-19th century, Prince Charles III looked for inspiration to the Duke of Baden-Baden, whose casino lured Europe's big-spending aristocrats every summer. Monaco, Charles decided, would be the winter Baden-Baden, and he founded the Société des Bains de Mer (SBM) to operate a casino, with the Principality as the chief shareholder. In 1870 the coffers were so full that Charles abolished direct taxation in Monaco. In another dark, bankrupt period, the 1950s, Rainier III gave his realm a fairy-tale cachet by wedding the American film actress Grace Kelly, bringing in a much-needed injection of socialites and their fat bankrolls. Since then, 'offshore' banking, 'business tourism' and tourism tourism have added to the Principality's riches.

★★★La Maison d'Or, 21 Rue du Portier, t 93 50 66 66, t 93 30 76 00 (*expensive*). Pristine 20th-century copy of a 19th-century villa, with terraces looking out through the yacht masts to the sea.

Monaco-Ville

★★★Abela, 23 Av des Papalins, t 92 05 90 00, f 92 05 91 67 (*expensive*). Modern, air-conditioned, pool, garden, and sea view, a whole floor devoted to non-smokers, and 10 'businesswomen' rooms.

★★★Terminus, 9 Av Prince-Pierre, t 92 05 63 00, f 92 05 20 10 (*expensive*). Another concrete high-rise block, but it has just been refurbished.

★★Le Versailles, 4 Av Prince-Pierre, t 93 50 79 34, f 93 25 53 64 (*moderate*). Near the station, with a reasonable French-Italian restaurant

★★Hôtel De France, 6 Rue de la Turbie, t 93 30 24 64, f 92 16 13 34 (*moderate*). Staid, peachy building in a quiet street full of art galleries.

★★Helvetia, 1 bis Rue Grimaldi, t 93 30 21 71, f 92 16 70 51 (*moderate*). Old-fashioned, over-looking a pedestrianized shopping street lined with orange trees. The least expensive hotel in the principality.

Eating Out

Monaco t (00 377–)

Louis XV, in the Hôtel de Paris, t 92 16 30 01 (*see above*). In Monte-Carlo, those who make it big at the tables, or have simply made it big at life, dine in this incredible golden setting. Edward VII as Prince of Wales, while dining here with his mistress Suzette, was served a crêpe smothered in kirsch, curaçao and maraschino that its 14-year-old maker, Henri Charpentier, accidentally set alight, only to discover that the flambéeing improved it a hundredfold. The Prince himself suggested that they name the new dessert after his companion. Under Alain Ducasse, the youngest chef ever to earn three Michelin stars, the cuisine is once again kingly – made from the finest and freshest ingredients Italy and France can offer, as sumptuous and spectacular as the setting (*menus 840F and 980F, lunch 500F*). *Closed Tues, and Wed lunch.*

Le Vistamar, at the Hermitage (*see above*). Spanking new and offers incredibly fresh fish dishes like the *pescadou à pesca du matin*, which brings the fish from the sea to your plate in under an hour at lunchtime, one of many aromatic creations deftly handled by chef Joël Garrault (*menu 350F*).

Monte-Carlo

Set back in the sculpture-filled gardens of Place du Casino rises the most famous building on the whole Côte d'Azur: the **Casino de Monte-Carlo** (1863) a fascinating piece of Old World kitsch. Anyone over 21 with a passport can visit the *machines à sous* section, with one-armed bandits and other mechanised games. To get past the mastodons at the doorway to the glittering Salon of Europe, you have to fork out 50F; here, American roulette, craps and blackjack tables click and clatter away just as in Las Vegas or Atlantic City. 100F gets you into the *salons privés* (*open from 3pm*) – quieter, more intense – where oily croupiers under gilt, over-the-top rococo ceilings accept limitless bets on roulette and *chemin de fer*.

The casino's bijou opera-theatre, the red and gold **Salle Garnier** (*open only for performances*), was designed by Charles Garnier, inaugurated by Sarah Bernhardt in 1879 and backed by pots of SBM money. SBM's frothy Hôtel de Paris is next door to the casino.

Le St Benoît, 10 ter Av de la Costa (enter the car park and take the lift up), t 93 25 02 34. Superb seafood to go with the views from the terrace, high above the port (*168–235F*). *Closed Mon; July and Aug open Mon eve.*

L'Hirondelle, 2 Av Monte-Carlo, t 92 16 49 30. Gourmets on a diet can take solace here, where lovely fresh and light dishes taste as good as they look, accompanied by swallow-eye views over the sea (*menu 310F*). *Closed eves.*

Loga Café, 25 Bd des Moulins, t 93 30 87 72. Dine sumptuously on Monégasque specialities like *barbagiuan* (a fried cheese and leek-filled pie) or *stocafi* (stockfish stewed with tomatoes, herbs, wine and olives) on the terrace (*menus from 220F*).

Le Texan, 4 Rue Suffren Reymond, t 93 30 34 54, just up from the port. Vivacious, rowdy, Tex-Mex atmosphere. The place to rub shoulders with Crown Prince Albert and Boris Becker over a pizza (*80–200F; cheap beer and Happy Hour*).

Entertainment and Nightlife

Nightlife in Monaco is a glitzy, bejewelled fashion parade. January is the opera, theatre and ballet season. Call t 92 16 22 99 for information.

Monte-Carlo Sporting Club, Av Princesse-Grace. Summer discotheque, Las Vegas-style floor shows, dancing, restaurants and casino.

SBM/Loews Monte-Carlo, 12 Av des Spélugues. Similar offerings.

American Bar at the Hôtel de Paris. Similar offerings.

Jimmy'z, 26 Av Princesse-Grace, t 92 16 22 77. Monte-Carlo's number one, fantastical dance club where entrance is free but the drinks require a small bank loan.

Le Stars N' Bars, 6 Quai Antoine 1er, t 97 97 95 95. Young people from all along the coast drive to this sports bar and club. Open from 10pm.

Flashman's, 7 Av Princesse-Alice, t 93 30 09 03. Beer-drinking in a Brit-run imitation pub. Open till the wee hours.

Ship and Castle, 42 Quai des Sanbarbani, t 92 05 76 72. Pub which also serves food. Open into the early hours.

Cinéma d'été, 26 Av Princesse-Grace, t 93 25 86 80. Open-air cinema which shows a different film in its original language every evening. Open June–Sept 9.30.

La Condamine and Fontvieille

You can see the Prince's very own **Collection de Voitures Anciennes** (*open daily 10–6; adm*); or the **Musée Naval** (*open daily 10–6; adm*). More unusual are the prickly contents of another garden near the Moyenne Corniche, the **Jardin Exotique** (*bus 2; open mid-May–mid-Sept daily 9–7; winter daily 9–6 or nightfall; adm*), with 6,000 succulents planted in the rockface. The same ticket admits you to the adjacent **Grottes de l'Observatoire**, one of the few places in Provence inhabited in the Palaeolithic era.

Up on the Rock: Monaco-Ville

Monaco-Ville, as scrubbed and cute as any town in Legoland, offers the **Historial des Princes de Monaco**, 27 Rue Basse (*open Oct–Jan daily 10–4; Feb–Sept daily 9.30–6; adm*), with waxworks running the gamut from Francesco the Spiteful, founder of the Grimaldi clan, to Caroline and Stéphanie; and the Multi-vision **Monte-Carlo Story**, on Rue Emile-de-Loth (*showings winter 11, 2, 3, 4, 5, summer 11, 1, 2, 3, 4, 5, 6; adm*). Monaco's most compelling attraction is nearby: the **Musée Océanographique de Monaco** in Av St-Martin (*open Oct–Mar daily 10–6; April–Sept daily 9–7; adm*), founded in 1910 by

Prince Albert Ier, who sank all of his casino profits into a passion for deep-sea exploration. To house the treasures he accumulated in his 24 voyages, he built this
museum in a cliff, filling it with instruments, shells, whale skeletons, and on the
ground floor a fascinating aquarium where 90 tanks hold some of the most surreal
fish ever netted from the briny deep.

Monaco to Nice: Grande and Moyenne Corniches

From Monaco, the D53 ascends to the Grande Corniche, a road the Romans called
Via Julia Augusta. The views are precipitous, and you can escape the crowds by
venturing even further inland to Peille and Peillon, two of the most beautiful villages
on the Côte.

La Turbie and its Trophy

The old Via Julia Augusta (Rue Comte-de-Cessole) passes through town on its way
to the **Trophy of the Alps**. This monument, built by the Romans to commemorate
their victory over the Ligurians, originally stood 147ft high, supporting a series of Doric
columns interspersed with statues of eminent generals, the whole surmounted by a
colossal 20ft statue of Augustus flanked by two captives. The still formidable pile of
rubble that remained in the 1930s – after it had been vandalized, ransacked for
building materials and blown up over the centuries – was resurrected to 114ft.

Getting Around

There are three **buses** daily from Nice
(bus station) to La Turbie that continue
up to Peille, but never on Sundays; and
six a day from Monaco. Buses leave less
regularly from Nice to Peillon. Both Peillon
and Peille have train stations, but they lie
several steep kilometres below their
respective villages.

Métrazur **trains** stop at Eze's coastal outpost; a minibus (*navette*) will shuttle you up
to the village.

Bus no.114 from Nice towards Paille stops at
Eze-Grande Corniche twice daily.

There are several buses from Nice (no.112) for
Eze-Village.

All the frequent buses on the Nice–Menton
line stop at Eze-Bord-de-Mer; *navettes* leave
regularly from the Basse Corniche for Eze-
Village and Eze-Grande Corniche.

Where to Stay and Eat

Eze-Grande Corniche ✉ 06360

★★★★**Les Terrasses d'Eze**, Rte de la Turbie, t 04
92 41 55 55, f 04 92 41 55 10, *info@terrasses-
eze.com* (*expensive; half board*). Huge (81
rooms) and '*ultra-moderne*', complete with
sauna and gym. The rooms are not quite big
enough for the price, but the restaurant
offers the best views of the coast to go with
its rich Mediterranean cuisine.

★★**L'Hermitage**, 2km from the village at Col
d'Eze on the Grande Corniche, t 04 93 41
00 68, f 04 93 41 24 05 (*inexpensive*).
Priceless views and traditional décor; an old-
fashioned welcome and monstrous portions
of startlingly good Provençal food (*menus
from 95F*). *Hotel closed 15 Oct–1 Jan; restaurant closed till 15 Feb.*

Eze-Moyenne Corniche

★★★★**Château Eza**, Rue de la Pise, t 04 93 41
12 24, f 04 93 41 16 64 (*luxury; 2,000–
4,000F*). A former prince's residence, actually

Peillon and Peille

The two villages are tiny and lovely; balanced atop adjacent hilltops, both require a wearying climb to reach. **Peillon** is a bit posher, complete with a foyer – a cobbled square with a pretty fountain at the village entrance. Inside are peaceful medieval stairs and arches and a theatrically restored Baroque parish church. But Peillon's big attraction is right at the entrance: the **Chapelle des Pénitents Blancs** (*ring the tourist office to arrange a visit, groups only*) adorned with a slightly faded cycle of Renaissance frescoes on the *Passion of Christ* by Giovanni Canavesio (*c.* 1485).

You can walk to **Peille**, following the Roman road for two hours. More isolated, Peille has more character, and its very own dialect, called Pelhasc. There's an ensemble of medieval streets like Peillon's and a church begun in the 12th century, with an interesting medieval portrait of Peille and its now ruined castle on the wall.

The Moyenne Corniche: Eze

Between Monaco and Nice, the main reason for taking the middle road has long been the extraordinary village of Eze, the most perched, perhaps, of any *village perché* in France, squeezed on to a cone of a hill 430m over the sea. The tight little maze of stairs and alleys was built to confuse attackers, the better to ambush them or spill boiling oil on their heads. The **Jardin Exotique** (*open July and Aug 9–nightfall; adm*), is a spiky paradise created by municipal initiative in 1949. Eze's other non-commercial attraction, the cream and yellow **Chapelle des Pénitents Blancs**, built in 1766, has

a collection of medieval houses linked together to form an eagle's nest, all sharing an extraordinary, perched terrace, with aromatic Niçois and other Provençal specialities to match (*dinner menus from 390F*). *Closed Nov–Mar*.

****La Chèvre d'Or**, Rue du Barri, t 04 92 10 66 66, f 04 93 41 06 72 (*luxury; 1,600–4,200F*). In a medieval castle rebuilt in the 1920s, a romantic Relais et Châteaux with a small park rippling down the mountain-side, a pool, and more ravishing views; chef Jean-Marc Delacourt creates refined, light versions of the French classics, accompanied by one of the Riviera's best wine cellars (*menus lunch from 420F, dinner 680F*). Book well in advance. *Closed mid-Nov–Feb*.

****Le Golf**, Place de la Colette, t 04 93 41 18 50, f 04 93 41 29 93 (*inexpensive*). A more modest choice.

****Auberge des Deux Corniches**, t 04 93 41 19 54, f 04 92 10 86 26 (*inexpensive*). *Closed Nov–Jan*.

Le Troubadour, 4 Rue du Brec, t 04 93 41 19 03. Turbot or *filet de bœuf aux cèpes* go down

nicely, and the price is nice too (*lunch menu 125F, others 175–250F*). *Closed Sun, Mon lunchtime*.

Mas Provençal, just outside the tangle of medieval streets, t 04 93 41 19 53. Completely covered in flowers and ivy, and ensconced in the 19th century; sink into plush red velvet chairs (with antimacassars) and dine on milk-fed pig roasted on a spit, or *risotto aux cèpes* (*menus from 340F*), before ordering the carriage home.

Eze-Bord-de-Mer

****Le Cap Estel**, t 04 92 10 86 26, f 04 93 01 55 20, *www.webstore.fr/capestil* (*luxury; half-board*). Set in a 4-acre park, the luxurious sparkling white Riviera dream built for a Russian princess, has two heated pools and a flight of movie star steps down to the manicured gardens. *Closed Oct–Mar*.

****Eric Rivot**, t 04 93 01 51 46, f 04 93 01 58 40 (*inexpensive*). Family-run with well-priced rooms and gourmet dining (*menus from 140F*).

gathered an eccentric collection of scraps; an old ship's model is suspended from the ceiling, and a disembodied arm brandishes a 13th-century Catalan crucifix. Here too is a 14th-century *Madone des Forêts*, where baby Jesus holds a pine cone. A scenic path to Eze-Bord-de-Mer is called the **Sentier Frédéric-Nietzsche** after the philosopher who walked up it. (It starts at the entrance to the old villlage, down a narrow, almost hidden, path on the left, which also leads to a small observation spot.)

The Corniche Inférieure

To the west of Eze-Bord-de-Mer another wooded promontory, Cap Ferrat, is today's most fashionable address on the Côte d'Azur, crowned by the fascinating Villa

Getting Around

The most amusing way to visit is by way of the Côte d'Azur's equivalent of Hollywood's 'See the Homes of the Stars' bus tours: a 'little train' starts on the quay at Villefranche and chugs around the promontory with a guide calling out, in French and abominable English, the names of the famous who live(d) in the villas.

Tourist Information

Beaulieu: Place Clemenceau, t 04 93 01 02 21, f 04 93 01 44 04.
St-Jean-Cap-Ferrat: 59 Av Denis Semaria, t 04 93 76 08 90, f 04 93 76 16 67.
Villefranche-sur-Mer: Jardins F-Binon, t 04 93 01 73 68, f 04 93 76 63 65.

Where to Stay and Eat

Beaulieu-sur-Mer ⊠ 06310
****La Réserve, 5 Bd Général-Leclerc, t 04 93 01 00 01, f 04 93 01 28 99, *reservebeaulieu@ relaischateaux.fr* (*luxury; 2,950–4,150F*). In the 1870s, when James Gordon Bennett, owner of the New York Herald and the man who sent Stanley to find Livingstone, was booted out of New York society for his scandalous behaviour, he came to the Riviera and ran the Paris edition of his paper from here. One of the most exclusive hotels on the Riviera, it offers guests grand sea views, a beach and marina, heated pool and more delights, including an elegant neo-

Renaissance restaurant (*menus 300–850F*). *Closed Nov–Feb but open for Christmas and New Year.*
***Artemis, 3 Bd Maréchal-Joffre, t 04 93 01 12 15, f 04 93 01 27 46 (*moderate*). Near the station, a modern hotel with rooms with balconies and access to a pool at the back.
**Le Havre Bleu, 29 Bd Maréchal-Joffre, t 04 93 01 01 40, f 04 93 01 29 92 (*inexpensive*). An attractive hotel with pleasant rooms, many with terraces.
*Riviera, 6 Rue Paul-Doumer, t 04 93 01 04 92, f 04 93 01 19 31 (*cheap*). With pretty wrought-iron balconies just up from the Basse Corniche.
Le Catalan, Bd Maréchal-Leclerc, t 04 93 01 02 78. Wood-fired pizzas and delicious pasta (*à la carte*). *Closed Sun, and Mon lunch.*
La Casa, 4 Av Fernand Dunan, t 04 93 76 48 00. Dance the night away with the ageing but still game local retirees; head for the Casino piano-bar and restaurant, with a Cuban orchestra, tapas, Havana cocktails and enormous sizzling barbecues.

St-Jean-Cap-Ferrat ⊠ 06230
****La Voile d'Or, t 04 93 01 13 13, f 04 93 76 11 17, *reservation@lavoiledor.fr* (*luxury; 3,500F*). A charming, voluptuous Italian villa, overlooking the pleasure port. Once owned by film director Michael Powell, who inherited it from his father (and sold it because no one ever paid their bar bills), the Voile d'Or is an ideal first or second honeymoon hotel, with a laid-back atmosphere, a garden hanging over the port, a heated pool, and rooms with every luxury a hotel could need.

Ephrussi de Rothschild and its gardens. To the east, the peninsula and steep mountain backdrop keep Beaulieu so sheltered that it shares with Menton the distinction of being the hottest town in France, while to the west the Corniche skirts the top of the fine old village of Villefranche-sur-Mer.

Beaulieu

'*O qual bel luogo!*' exclaimed Napoleon in his Corsican mother tongue, and the bland name stuck to this lush banana-growing town overlooking the Baie des Fourmis, 'the Bay of Ants', which is so called for the black boulders in the sea. Beaulieu admits to a mere four days of frost a year. The highlight is the **Villa Kerylos** (*open*

Its equally exceptional restaurant is favoured by the tanned and languid yachting set (*menus 280–400F*).

★★★★Grand Hôtel du Cap Ferrat, 71 Bd Général de Gaulle, **t** 04 93 76 50 50, **f** 04 93 76 50 76 (*luxury*). The already luxurious Belle Epoque rooms have been restored in a more airy Riviera style, all set in acres of gardens, lawns, and palms. A funicular lowers guests down to an Olympic-size seawater pool just over the Mediterranean. Its restaurant **Le Cap**, **t** 04 93 76 50 50, on a palatial terrace shaded by parasol pines, serves delicious meals decidedly unhealthy for your wallet (*menus from 430F*).

★★★★Royal Riviera, 3 Av Jean Monnet, **t** 04 93 76 31 00, **f** 04 93 01 23 07 (*luxury*). Sumptuous pale pink Belle Epoque villa set in elegantly landscaped gardens, with the usual Riviera paraphernalia: a sandy beach, watersports, an airy, terraced restaurant serving French and Provençal classics; and a helipad to park the runaround.

★★★Brise-Marine, Av Jean-Mermoz, **t** 04 93 76 04 36, **f** 04 93 76 11 49 (*expensive*). More down-to-earth, with a garden, and large rooms, half with sea views.

★★Clair Logis, 12 Av Centrale, **t** 04 93 76 04 57, **f** 04 93 76 11 85 (*moderate*). Near the centre of the Cap, wonderful, and very reasonable, welcoming villa set back in a lush enclosed garden (*no restaurant*).

★La Bastide, 3 Av Albert 1er, **t** 04 93 76 06 78, **f** 04 93 76 19 10 (*inexpensive*). Not luxurious, but it has a good restaurant (*58–170F*).

Le Provençal, Place Clemenceau, **t** 04 93 76 03 97, **f** 04 93 76 05 39. For a frisson of south coast *hauteur* with your cuisine, go to where you can try delicacies like *fouillis d'asperges aux langoustines au jus de café* (*menus 250–260F*).

Skipper, Port de Plaisance, **t** 04 93 76 01 00. Best for fish (*menus 98–159F*).

Villefranche-sur-Mer ✉ 06230

★★★Welcome, Quai Amiral-Courbet, **t** 04 93 76 27 62, **f** 04 93 76 27 66, *welcome@riviera.fr* (*expensive*). Legendary, although its wild days are over. The newly refurbished rooms are air-conditioned; those on the 5th floor are ravishing. *Closed Nov–Dec; half-board in season.*

★★Provençal, 4 Av du Maréchal-Joffre, **t** 04 93 76 53 53, **f** 04 93 76 53 54 (*moderate*). Unpretentious, family-run. *Closed Dec.*

Le Carpaccio, Plage des Marinières, **t** 04 93 01 72 97. Long a favourite of the Rolls-Royce crowd from Monaco, yet it remains affordable for a night-time splurge or a pizza (*300F à la carte for fish or crustaceans*).

L'Echalotte, 7 Rue de l'Eglise, **t** 04 93 01 71 11. Pretty place with a minuscule terrace and excellent, rich and Provençal food – from sizzling roast suckling pig with figs, to a *noisette de lotte rôtie au thym* (*menus 135–195F*).

Michel's, Place Amélie Pollonnais, **t** 04 93 76 73 24. Has a startling (they are very proud of it) frieze depicting Villefranche, with a lovely terrace looking out over the bay and very friendly staff. Light, local specialities; the melt-in-the-mouth house pâté and the red pepper and aubergine terrine are especially good (*à la carte only*). *Closed Tues.*

July–Aug daily 10.30–7; mid-Feb–mid-Nov daily 10.30–6; mid-Dec–mid-Feb Mon–Fri 2–6, Sat and Sun 10.30–6; closed mid-Nov–mid-Dec; adm; bus stop Hôtel Métropole then a 5min walk), a striking reproduction of a wealthy 5th-century BC Athenian's abode, furnishings and garden, built in 1908 by archaeologist Théodore Reinach, who spared no expense to help his genuine antiquities feel at home. And here this ultimate philhellene lived like an Athenian himself, holding symposia, exercising and bathing with his male buddies, and keeping the womenfolk well out of the way.

St-Jean-Cap-Ferrat

Another retro-repro fantasy, the **Villa Ephrussi de Rothschild** (*a 10min walk from the Corniche Inférieure, or catch the St-Jean bus which passes its entrance; open Nov–Jan daily 2–6; Feb–June and Sept–Oct daily 10–6, July and Aug daily 10–7; adm exp)*, tops the narrow isthmus of bucolic Cap Ferrat. The flamboyant Béatrice de Rothschild was a compulsive art collector and lover of the 18th century, and, after marrying the banker Baron Ephrussi, had this Italianate villa specially built to house her treasures – Renaissance furniture, Florentine bridal chests, paintings by Boucher, rare Chinese screens and furniture, Flemish and Beauvais tapestries, Sèvres and Meissen porcelain, and Louis-Quinze and Louis-Seize furniture. To create the equally eclectic gardens, the isthmus was given a crew cut, and terraced into different levels, all linked together by little pathways and stone steps.

Villefranche-sur-Mer

In the 14th century, the deep, wooded bay between Cap Ferrat and Nice was a duty-free port, hence Villefranche's name. Tall, brightly coloured, piled-up houses line the narrow lanes and stairs; the fine shingle and sand beach with a shallow slope and calm bay is ideal for children. Villefranche's fishermen once stored their nets in the portside Romanesque **Chapelle St-Pierre**, Quai Courbet (*open winter daily 9.30–12 and 2–5; summer daily 10–12 and 4–8.30; closed Mon; adm)*, and in 1957, after a protracted battle with the municipal authorities, Jean Cocteau won permission to restore and renovate it. He frescoed it in 'ghosts of colours' with scenes from the Life of St Peter, plus images of the fish-eyed fishergirls of Villefranche, the Gypsies at Stes-Maries-de-la-Mer, and angels from Cocteau's private heaven.

Nice

The capital of the *département* of Alpes-Maritimes and France's fifth largest town (pop. 400,000), Nice is the Hexagon's most visited city after Paris. Agreeably named and superbly set on nothing less than the Bay of Angels, Nice has a gleam and sparkle in its eye like no other city in France: only a sourpuss could resist its lively old town squeezed between promontory and sea, its markets blazing with colour, the glittering tiled domes and creamy *pâtisserie* 19th-century hotels and villas, the immaculate, exotic gardens, and the famous voluptuous curve of the beach and the palm-lined Promenade des Anglais.

History

Greeks from Marseille founded a commercial colony near the seaside *oppidum* that they named Nikaïa after an obscure military victory. Beset by Ligurian pirates, the Nikaïans asked the Romans for aid. The Romans duly came, and stayed, but preferred to live near the hilltop at Cemenelum (modern Cimiez) close to the Via Julia Augusta. In 1338 Nice allied herself with Savoy, who became firm allies with the English, and by 1755 the first trickle of milords began to discover the sunny charms of a Riviera winter and build the first villas. In 1860, Italy, in exchange for Napoleon III's aid against Austria, ceded Nice and Savoy to France.

In recent years, Nice was the personal fiefdom of the right-wing Médecin family. Jean Médecin reigned from 1928 until 1965, and was succeeded by his flamboyant son Jacques, the man who twinned Nice with Cape Town when apartheid was still on the books. Jacques Médecin had an edifice complex nearly the size of Mitterrand's in Paris. In 1990 the slow, grinding wheels of French justice began to catch up with Médecin, when it was discovered, among other things, that money for the Nice Opera was being diverted into the mayor's bank account. He fled to Uruguay but was extradited to France in 1995 and died in 1998.

Vieux Nice

A dangerous slum in the 1970s, Nice's Vieille Ville, a piquant quarter east of Place Masséna, is busy becoming the trendiest part of the city; the population, once poor and ethnically mixed, is now more than half French and upwardly mobile. Old here means Genoese seaside Baroque – tall, steep *palazzi*, many with opulent 17th- and 18th-century portals and windows.

At its eastern end, the Vieille Ville is closed by **Colline du Château**, the ancient acropolis of Nikaïa and site of the 10th- to 12th-century town and the cathedral of Ste-Marie. You can walk up the steps to the Château, take a mini-train (35F) from the Promenade des Anglais which tours around the Vieille Ville on the way, or pay a few sous to take the lift at the east end of the Quai des Etats-Unis near **Tour Bellanda**. If you descend by way the Montée Eberlé and Rue Catherine-Ségurane, you'll end up in the wide, yellow, arcaded, 18th-century **Place Garibaldi**, named for Nice's most famous native son, who was born here when it was still called Nizza and who had a fit and a half when Napoleon III wheedled it off Italy.

South of Place Garibaldi off Rue Neuve is the old parish church, **St-Martin-St-Augustin**, where a monk named Martin Luther said a Mass during his momentous pilgrimage to Rome in 1514. The dim interior was Baroqued in the 17th century; its treasures include a fine *Pietà* (*c.* 1500) attributed to Ludovico Bréa, and a tatty photocopy of Garibaldi's baptismal certificate. The **Palais Lascaris** at 15 Rue Droite (*open daily 10–12 and 2–6; closed Mon, hols and mid-Nov–mid-Dec*) is a grand 1648 mansion. The ground floor contains a reconstructed pharmacy of 1738; a fantastically opulent

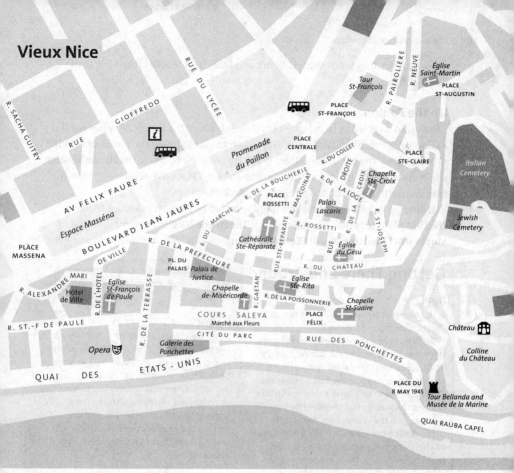

staircase leads up to the *étage nobile*, saturated with elaborate Genoese *quadratura* (architectural trompe-l'œil) frescoes, Flemish tapestries, ornate woodwork, and a 1578 Italian precursor of the pianoforte.

Take Rue Rossetti west to the cafés of pretty Place Rossetti, dominated by Nice's 17th-century **Cathédrale Ste-Réparate**, designed by Jean-André Guibert and crowned with a joyful dome and lantern of glazed tiles in emerald bands.

Cours Saleya and Around the Port

Cours Saleya is an elongated little gem of urban planning, where bars and restaurants line up along the famous outdoor market and the **Chapelle de la Miséricorde**, designed in 1740 by Bernardo Vittone, a disciple of Turin's extraordinary Baroque architects Guarino Guarini and Juvarra, with a superb interior (ask at the tourist office about your chances of getting in).

Overlooking the port is the **Musée de Terra Amata**, 25 Bd Carnot (*buses 32 and 1 from central Nice; open daily 10–12 and 2–6; closed Mon and hols*), which incorporates a cave holding one of the world's oldest 'households', a pebble-walled wind-shelter built by elephant-hunters 400 millennia ago which was discovered in

1966. A fascinating set of models, bones and tools helps evoke life in Nice at the dawn of time.

Up the Paillon

In the old days Nice's laundresses plied their trade in the torrential waters of the Paillon, until the often dangerous river began to vanish under the pavements in the 1830s. Nearest the sea, Jardin Albert Ier is the site of the open-air **Théâtre de Verdure**, while upstream, as it were, vast terracotta-coloured **Place Masséna** is generously endowed with flower-beds and wisteria-shaded benches.

Further up loom a pair of dreadnoughts erected by ex-mayor Jacques Médecin. The first of these is the 282-million-franc **Théâtre de Nice** and the marble-coated **Musée d'Art Moderne et d'Art Contemporain** (*open daily 10–6; closed Tues and hols;*

Getting There and Around

By Plane

The Aéroport Nice-Côte d'Azur is served by flights from around the world.

Buses run every 12 mins between the airport (terminal 2) and Nice coach station, t 04 93 21 30 83, while bus 23 provides links with the train station every 30mins, t 04 93 56 35 40. The bus ticket to town will also give you a free onwards connection on another city bus.

After 10pm the yellow airport bus will detour to the train station if you ask the driver, or else stops in Place Masséna where the night buses depart. There are also several buses daily from the airport to Menton, Monaco, Cannes, Antibes, Grasse, St-Tropez, St-Raphaël and Marseille.

By Train

Nice's train station is in Av Thiers, not far from the centre of town, and has handy left-luggage lockers. Besides *Métrazur* trains between Ventimiglia and St-Raphaël, Nice has frequent connections to Marseille and is on the TGV route to Paris (7hrs).

The Gare du Sud, 4 bis Rue Alfred-Binet, t 04 97 03 80 80, is served by the little *Train des Pignes*, with excursions to Provençal towns high up the Var valley.

By Coach

The coach station is on the Promenade du Paillon, on the edge of Vieux Nice, t 04 93 85 61 81. There are frequent buses to Grasse, Vence, Cannes, Marseille, Aix-en-Provence, St-Raphaël, Cagnes, Antibes, Menton and Monte-Carlo. Bus 17 links the coach and train stations.

By Bus

Pick up a free *Guide Horaire du Réseau Bus* at the tourist office or from SUNBUS's information centre, 10 Av Félix-Faure, t 04 93 16 52 10. Several tourist tickets, called 'Nice by Bus', are available, offering limitless rides for one, five or seven days, including a trip to the airport. Buses stop early, around 9pm, and are replaced by four 'Noctambus' services, all leaving from Place Masséna, which stop at about 1am.

Car Hire

Among the cheapest car hire places is **Rent-a-Car**, opposite the station on Av Thiers, t 04 93 88 69 69, or in the centre of town, t 04 93 37 42 22, or just by the airport at 61 Route de Grenoble, t 04 93 18 82 22.

Avis is at the train station, t 04 93 87 90 11, or at the airport, t 04 93 21 36 33, and **Hertz** is at the airport, t 04 93 21 36 72, and 12 Av de Suède, t 04 93 87 11 87.

Taxis

Call t 04 93 13 78 78.

Tourist Information

Nice: Av Thiers, next to the train station, t 04 93 87 07 07/ 04 93 83 32 64, f 04 93 16 85 16. Also Terminal 1 at the airport, t 04 93 21 44 11, and at 5 Promenade des Anglais,

adm). The building – four concrete towers, linked by glass walkways that seem to smile and frown and afford pleasant views over the city – is an admirable setting for the works of Christo, Niki de Saint-Phalle, Warhol, Dine, Oldenburg, Rauschenberg, Ben and other influential and irreverent figures of the 1960s and '70s.

The view up the Paillon is blocked by Médecin's 1985 congress and art centre and *cinémathèque* called **Acropolis**, 1 Esplanade Kennedy, a gruesome megalithic bunker of concrete slabs and smoked glass. No design could be more diametrically opposed (stylistically and philosophically) to the acropolis in Athens.

West of Place Masséna and the Promenade des Anglais

Important streets fan out from Place Masséna and the adjacent Jardin Albert Iᵉʳ. Nice's main shopping street, **Av Jean-Médecin**, leads up to the train station;

t 04 92 14 48 00. A 3- or 7-day Carte Musées Côte d'Azur can be obtained for 70F/140F from any museum ticket desk or the tourist office, or FNAC bookshop. On the first Sunday of every month, all museums in Nice are free – so everyone goes.

Shopping

The pedestrian zone around Place Masséna has scores of designer clothes shops (mainly on Av Félix-Faure) and cheap boutiques (mainly on Rue Masséna), plus the wonderful **Pâtisserie Vogade** right on the square. In Av Jean-Médecin you'll find Nice's biggest **department store**, Galeries Lafayette, and the Nice Etoile shopping centre.

Provençal fabrics can be found at Ste-Réparate Provence, 1 Rue Ste-Réparate, and Les Olivades, 7 Rue de la Boucherie, and perfume oils for 15F a phial at La Maison de la Lavande, Rue St-Gaétan. Not far away is a landmark, the fabulously rococo premises of **Auer**, 7 Rue St-François-de-Paule, which has been making the region's most celebrated confectionery, jams and fruits confits for almost two centuries.

Where to Stay

Nice ✉ 06000

Nice is packed with hotels of all categories, and in the summer most are just as tightly packed inside. If you arrive without a reservation, the tourist office next to the station will

book rooms for 10F. Get there by 10am in the summer, or risk joining the nightly slumber parties on the beach or in front of the station, where you'll encounter giant cockroaches from hell.

Come instead in the off season, when many of the best hotels offer the kind of rates the French would call *très intéressant*.

Luxury
****Négresco, 37 Promenade des Anglais, t 04 93 16 64 00, f 04 93 88 35 68, *reservations@hotel-negresco.com* (1,750–4,450F). For panache none can top this fabulous green-domed national historic monument, the one hotel in Nice where a Grand Duke would still feel at home, and the last independent luxury hotel on the coast. Its 150 chambers and apartments have all been redecorated with Edwardian furnishings and paintings by the likes of Picasso and Léger. Don't miss the salon royal, lit by a Baccarat chandelier made for the Tsar, and recently topped off with a contemporary sculpture by Niki de Saint Phalle, *Nana Jaune* (*Yellow Girl*).

****Beau Rivage, 24 Rue St-François-de-Paule, t 04 92 47 82 82, f 04 92 47 82 83, *nice beaurivage@new-hotel.com* (*from 1,000F*). If hobnobbing with the rich and famous in the Négresco is out, there's this elegant Art Deco hotel on a pedestrian street in Vieux Nice overlooking Beau Rivage beach; Matisse spent two years here and Chekhov, during his stay, wrote *The Seagull*. The rooms are as luminous and beautiful as a Matisse and there's direct access to the private beach.

Rue Masséna is the centre of a lively pedestrian-only restaurant and shopping zone; and the fabled, palm-lined sweep of the **Promenade des Anglais** around the Baie des Anges is still aglitter through the fumes of the traffic, which is usually as strangled as poor Isadora Duncan was when, after she had bidden her friends farewell with the words '*Adieu, mes amis, je vais à la gloire!*', her scarf caught in the wheel of her Bugatti here in 1927. The long pebble beach is crowded day and night in the summer.

Visitors from the top end of the economic spectrum check into the fabled Belle Epoque **Hôtel Négresco** (No.37), vintage 1906. Next to it is the garden of the **Palais Masséna** (*closed for restoration, expected to reopen mid-2000*), now a *musée d'art et d'histoire*. The ground-floor salons, heavy and pompous, are excruciatingly co-ordinated from ceiling stucco to chair leg. The top floor displays statues of the Ten Incarnations of Vishnu, Spanish earrings, views of Nice, and rooms dedicated to

Expensive

★★★★**Elysée Palace**, 59 Promenade des Anglais, t 04 93 86 06 06, f 04 93 44 50 40, *reservation@elysee-palace.com*. Artsy, stylish hotel with a façade dominated by an enormous bronze Vénus, by Sosno, a 26-metre, 10-ton giantess. Modern comforts, roof-top pool, sauna, and many other amenities.

★★★★**Palais Maeterlinck**, 30 Bd Maeterlink, t 04 92 00 72 00, f 04 92 04 18 10. On the way to Villefranche, a fastidiously refurbished pink and white palace set in beautiful gardens, with a highly acclaimed restaurant, **Le Mélisande**, which serves wonderfully creative dishes on a precipitous terrace (*menus from 300F*).

★★★★**Château des Ollières**, t 04 92 15 77 99, f 04 92 15 77 98, *chateaudesollieres@chateaudesollieres.com*. Flamboyant pink, orange and yellow crenellated folly which once belonged to a Russian prince. Eight heavenly rooms, with antique furnishings, eccentric stained glass and four-poster beds.

★★★**Windsor**, 11 Rue Dalpozzo (behind the Négresco), t 04 93 88 59 35, f 04 93 88 94 57, *windsor@webstore.fr*. Best among the tri-star choices, an idiosyncratic hotel in the midst of a tropical garden, with a pool, an English-style pub, a Turkish hammam, a Thai sitting room and odd frescoes in the rooms.

Moderate

★★★**Vendôme**, 26 Rue Pastorelli, t 04 93 62 00 77, f 04 93 13 40 78, *contact@vendome-hotel-nice.com*. Prettily renovated, air-conditioned rooms, a superb stairway, and a garden.

★★★**La Pérouse**, 11 Quai Rauba-Capeu, t 04 93 62 34 63, f 04 93 62 59 41, *lp@hroy.com*. Halfway up the Colline du Château, a lovely hotel with a pool and good restaurant high above the hubbub (*menus 90–150F*).

★★**Le Petit Palais**, 10 Av Emile-Biekert, in Cimiez, t 04 93 62 19 11, f 04 93 62 53 60. A handsome white Belle Epoque mansion. Rooms vary in size, but the best (at the back) look out over the rooftops of the old town to the sea.

Inexpensive

★★**Hôtel Trianon**, 15 Av Auber, t 04 93 88 30 69, f 04 93 88 11 35. A white grand piano serves as a reception desk, and the sweeping white staircase and little lift with an wrought-iron grille give it a comfortably old-fashioned feel.

Porte Bonheur, 146 Av St-Lambert, t 04 93 84 66 10. Perhaps the best of the cheaper choices; 11-room hotel with a little garden. Apartments (minimum one-week stay) are 165F plus; book well in advance.

★**La Belle Meunière**, 21 Av Durante, t 04 93 88 66 15, f 04 93 82 51 76. Friendly hotel, a stone's throw from the station, and a long-time favourite of budget travellers – it even has parking and a little garden for breakfast.

Eating Out

Expensive

Chantecler, 37 Promenade des Anglais, t 04 93 16 64 00, f 04 93 88 35 68 (*lunch menus 300–620F incl wine*). Gastronomic Nice is

hometown boys Garibaldi and Napoleon's cruel Marshal Masséna. There's the obligatory Napoleana, including Josephine's bed, with a big 'N' on the coverlet.

Fine Arts, and a Russian Cathedral

From the Masséna museum, a brisk 10-minute walk or bus 22 leads to the handsome 1876 villa that is home to the **Musée des Beaux Arts**, 33 Av des Baumettes
(*open daily 10–12 and 2–6; closed Mon; adm*). With the Matisses and Chagalls in
Nice's other museums, the Musée des Beaux Arts is left with the 'old masters of the
19th century'. A room dedicated to Kees Van Dongen includes his entertaining 1927
Tango of the Archangel, which perhaps more than any painting evokes the
Roaring Twenties on the Riviera. Picasso also gets a look-in in this room with a
small collection of the ceramic pieces he created while at Vallauris (*see* p.943),

dominated by the Belle Epoque magnificence of this restaurant snuggling into the
opulent arms of the Négresco. Here, chef
Alain Llorca has succeeded in seducing the
Niçois with his own fabulous versions of
Chantecler favourites like sea bass served
with tomatoes and pesto, roast pigeon with
foie gras ravioli and desserts like the exotic
liquorice-flavoured meringue with raspberry
sorbet. *Closed mid-Nov–mid-Dec.*

Don Camillo, 5 Rue des Ponchettes, t 04 93 85
67 95, f 04 93 13 97 43. Run by a former pupil
of Maximin and Paul Ducasse, already celebrated for its home-made ravioli filled with
Swiss chard *en daube*, and fabulous desserts.
Closed Sun and Mon lunch.

Expensive–Moderate

Auberge de Théo, 52 Av Cap de Croix, t 04 93 81
26 19. One of the best is up in Cimiez, where
you'll find genuine Italian pizzas, salads with
mesclun (Nice's special mixed salad), and
Venetian *tiramisù* for dessert. (*120–300F*).
Closed Mon.

Moderate

La Mérenda, 4 Rue de la Terrasse, no tel, near
the Opera House and the Cours Saleya. Join
the glitterati enjoying Dominique le Stanc's
idiosyncratic Niçois cuisine (*menus
150–180F*). *Closed weekends and school hols.*
No credit cards.

Barale, 39 Rue de Beaumont, t 04 93 89 17 94.
A local institution for dishes full of Provençal
flavour, piled up with a cheerful hotchpotch
of copper pans, old gramophones, vintage
cars and a mechanical piano.

Villa d'Este, 6 Rue Masséna, t 04 93 82 47 77.
The best Italian restaurant in Nice, over
three floors with trompe l'œil Italianate
décor in pretty pastel colours, attentive
service and top-notch pasta. Try the plate
of *antipasti* for a gastronomic feast.

Chez Simon, above Nice in St Antoine de
Ginestière, t 04 93 86 51 62. Serving up local
specialities – *beignets* stuffed with fresh
sardines or courgettes, a melting fricassée of
wild *cèpe* mushrooms in parsley – for four
generations. Rustic wood carvings, and a
lovely terrace in summer. *Closed Mon out
of season.*

Moderate–Cheap

Au Pizzaïolo, 4 bis Rue du Pont Vieux, t 04 93
92 24 79. Specialities include beef *carpaccio*,
farcis niçois and local seafood. The surroundings may be humble, but the food ain't bad
and the staff are very good-natured (*menus
78–140F*). *Closed Tues.*

Cheap

La Fanny, 2 Rue Rossetti, t 04 93 80 70 63, in
Vieux Nice. A new venture by two genuinely
charming local boys. The lamb melts in the
mouth, and the seafood is wonderfully
fresh, but best of all is the virulent green
eau-de-vie made from basil which is offered
at the end (*menus from 68F*). *Closed Mon
and Tues lunch.*

Voyageur Nissart, 19 Rue Alsace-Lorraine,
between the station and Av Jean-Médecin,
t 04 93 82 19 60. Two wide-ranging menus
(*67–109F*). *Closed Mon.*

while the cheerful Raoul Dufy's early Fauve works are his finest, especially the 1908 *Bateaux à l'Estaque*. One room is devoted to Nice's own fluffy Belle Epoque lithographist, Jules Chéret.

In 1865, the young Tsarevich Nicholas was brought to Nice, and, like so many consumptives who arrived in search of health, he quickly declined. The luxurious villa where he died was demolished to construct the **Cathédrale Orthodoxe Russe St-Nicolas**, located a few blocks from the west of the train station at 17 Bd du Tzarévitch, just off Bd Gambetta (*bus 7 and 15; open daily exc Sun am and services 9–12 and 2.30–5; no shorts or sleeveless shirts; adm*). Paid for by Tsar Nicolas II and completed just before the Bolshevik Revolution, its onion domes glow with colourful glazed Niçois tiles; inside are frescoes, woodwork and icons.

Denis le Niçois 'La Véritable Socca', 4 Rue St-François, **t** 04 93 13 98 23, has entertaining service and cheap *beignets*; opposite is a Brazilian and Tunisian restaurant with huge beef steaks if you need something more substantial.

La Taverne de l'Opéra, 10 Rue St-François-de-Paule, **t** 04 93 85 72 68. Excellent socca and other delights, plus jazz on summer Fri nights. *Closed Jan.*

Pasta Basta, Rue de la Préfecture, **t** 04 93 80 03 57. Looks ordinary but offers *bruschetta*, salads and salmon *agnolotti* with rich tomato sauce cheaper than anywhere in trendy Cours Saleya.

Fenocchio, Place Rossetti. 99 varieties of ice cream. Lavender cream, jasmine sorbet and the bitterest chocolate imaginable make a heavenly combination.

Entertainment and Nightlife

You can find out what's happening in Nice in the daily *Nice-Matin*. Other sources covering the entire Côte are *7 jours/7 nuits*, distributed free in the tourist offices, the *Semaine des Spectacles* (Wed), or Radio Riviera, the coast's English-language station broadcast out of Monaco at 106.3 and 106.5.

Rialto, 4 Rue de Rivoli, one block from the Négresco, **t** 04 93 88 08 41. For films in their original language.

Nouveau Mercury, 16 Place Garibaldi, **t** 08 36 68 81 06. For films in their original language.

Cinémathèque de Nice, 3 Esplanade Kennedy, **t** 04 92 04 06 66. For films in their original language.

Opéra de Nice, 4–6 Rue St-François-de-Paule, **t** 04 93 13 98 53. Operas, concerts and recitals at various locations including the Acropolis; the Théâtre de Nice (Esplanade des Victoires); and the Théâtre de Verdure.

Théâtre de Verdure, Jardin Albert 1er. From April onwards rock, jazz, and other concerts take place in this outdoor theatre.

Nice's nightlife is divided between expensive clubs and bland piano bars, and the livelier bars and clubs of Vieux Nice, which come and go like ships in the night.

Chez Wayne, 15 Rue de la Préfecture. Noisiest of the jumping ex-pat joints, a British-owned pub and restaurant with live music every night (*open 10am–midnight, reservations obligatory at weekends*).

De Klomp, 6 Rue Mascoïnat, near Place Rossetti. Funky Dutch hangout with live jazz and a hedonistic atmosphere (not for teetotallers or anti-smokers).

Hole in the Wall, 3 Rue de l'Abbaye. Small hole serving large beers, big fresh burgers, and live music on an unfeasibly small stage.

Jonathan's beer cellar, 1 Rue de la Loge, in the north of Vieux Nice. Food, candles and the 1970s-inspired 'live' music hosted by Jonathan himself.

Cimiez: Chagall, Matisse and Roman Ruins

On the low hills west of the Paillon, where wealthy Romans lived the good life in Cemenelum, modern Niçois do the same in Cimiez, a luxurious 19th-century suburb dotted with the grand hotels, now genteel apartment buildings. Bus 15 from the Gare SNCF will take you to the main attractions, beginning with the **Musée National Message Biblique Marc Chagall** on Av du Docteur Ménard (*open Oct–June daily 10–5; July–Sept daily 10–6; closed Tues; adm*), built to house Chagall's cycle of 17 paintings based on stories from the Old Testament. The paintings are divided into three sections: *Genesis*, *Exodus* and the *Songs of Solomon*; they have been hung, as Chagall requested, chromatically rather than chronologically and are paired to complement each others' rich glowing emeralds, cobalts and magentas. They leap with Chagall's idiosyncratic symbolism – tumbling flowers, fish, angels and rabbits. Best of all, in an adjacent, octagonal gallery is the rapturous red, red, red series of the *Song of Songs*.

Henri Matisse died in Cimiez in 1954 and left the city his works, displayed in the **Musée Matisse**, set in the olive-studded Parc des Arènes (*take bus 15, 17, 20 or 22 from the Promenade des Anglais or Av Jean-Médecin; open April–Sept daily 10–6; Oct–Mar daily 10–5; closed Tues and some hols; adm*). Matisse's last work, the gargantuan paper cut-out *Flowers and Fruit*, 1952–3, dominates one whole side of the entrance hall. The main collection begins with some of his early bronze sculptures. There is also a lyrical series of back studies (*Dos*), an obsession to which he returned again and again throughout his career. Even in these early works, colours sing out, especially in the sultry *Odalisque du Coffret Rouge* (*Odalisque with a Red Box*, 1926); others include the soft, dreamy *Figure Endormie* (*Sleeping Figure*), and the famous *Nature Morte aux Grenades* (*Still Life with Pomegranates*, 1947).

Adjacent to the Matisse Museum is the new **Musée Archéologique** (*open April–Sept daily 10–12 and 2–6; Oct–Mar daily 10–1 and 2–5; closed Mon and some hols; adm*), entered through the excavations of Roman Cemenelum. These include the baths, a marble swimming pool, and the amphitheatre, with seating for 4,000 (small for a population of 20,000, but perhaps the Romans here were too couth for gladiators). The museum houses vases, coins, statues, jewels, and models of what Cimiez looked like 2,000 years ago.

From here, walk back past the Matisse museum and across the Jardin Public to the **Musée Franciscain, Eglise et Monastère de Cimiez** (*open daily 8.30–12.30 and 2.30–6.30; closed Sun*). The Franciscans have been here since the 1500s; their church was heavily restored in 1850, although it still has two beautiful altarpieces by Ludovico Bréa: the *Vierge de Piété* and a *Crucifixion*.

Cagnes

The bloated amoeba of Cagnes is divided into three cells – overbuilt Cros-de-Cagnes by the sea with a Hippodrome; Cagnes-sur-Mer, further up, site of Renoir's house, the happiest of all artists' shrines in the south; and medieval Haut-de-Cagnes on the hill, notorious in the 17th and 18th centuries for its indecorous pastimes and the brilliant

Getting Around

There are **train** stations in both Cagnes-sur-Mer and Cros-de-Cagnes and a continuous service of minibuses from Cagnes-sur-Mer station up the steep hill to Haut-de-Cagnes. **Buses** from Nice to Vence stop in Cagnes-sur-Mer.

Tourist Information

Cagnes-sur-Mer: 6 Bd Maréchal-Juin, t 04 93 20 61 64, f 04 93 20 52 63.

Where to Stay and Eat

Haut-de-Cagnes ✉ 06800

★★★**Le Cagnard**, Rue Pontis-Long, t 04 93 20 73 21, f 04 93 22 06 39, *www.le-cagnard.com*

(*luxury; 950–2,600F*). Sumptuous comforts discreetly arranged to fit in with the 14th-century architecture. Nearly every room has a private terrace, but the largest and most magical belongs to the Michelin-starred restaurant (*menus from 300F*), which also has a coffered Renaissance-style ceiling that opens up in summer. Among the delicacies served up beneath it are pigeon stuffed with morels and foie gras and crispy red mullet with garlic and rosemary. *Restaurant closed Nov–mid-Dec.*

Les Peintres, 71 Montée de la Bourgade, t 04 93 20 83 08. The walls are covered with paintings and the tables with warm home-made bread and Provençal dishes (*menus 148 and 188F*). *Closed mid-Nov–mid-Dec, and Mon in winter.*

parties held in its castle before the Revolution, beginning a long tradition of artsy decadence on the Mediterranean.

Cagnes-sur-Mer: Musée Renoir

There is only one thing to do in sprawling Cagnes-sur-Mer: from central Place Général-de-Gaulle follow Av Auguste-Renoir up to Chemin des Colettes, to **Le Domaine des Colettes** (*open daily 10–12 and 2–5; May–Sept daily 10–12 and 2–6; closed Tues; adm*), where Renoir spent the last 12 years of his life. Stricken with rheumatoid arthritis, Renoir followed his doctor's advice to move to warmer climes,where he produced paintings even more sensuous and voluptuous than before; there's no contrast more poignant than that of the colour-saturated *Les Grandes Baigneuses* (in the Philadelphia Museum of Art) and the photograph in the museum of the painter's hands, so bent and crippled that they're painful even to look at. It was also in Cagnes that Renoir first experimented with sculpture, by proxy, dictating detailed instructions to a young sculptor. In 1989, the museum's collection of portraits of Renoir by his friends was supplemented with 10 canvases the master himself painted in Cagnes.

Haut-de-Cagnes

Spared the worst of the tourist shops, intricate, medieval Haut-de-Cagnes has become instead the fiefdom of contemporary artists, thanks to the UNESCO-sponsored Festival International de la Peinture. The crenellated **Château-Musée Grimaldi** (*open winter daily 10–12 and 2–5; summer daily 10–12 and 2–6; closed Tues and Nov; adm*) was built by the first Rainier Grimaldi in the 1300s. This contains a **Musée de l'Olivier**, and the **Donation Suzy Solidor** – 40 paintings donated by the Paris cabaret star, all of herself and each by a different artist – Van Dongen, Dufy,

Kisling, Friesz, Cocteau, and so on. On the next floor, the **Musée d'Art Moderne Méditerranéen** is dedicated to a rotating collection of works by painters who have worked along the coast.

St-Paul-de-Vence and Vence

Inland from Cagnes are two towns as bound up with contemporary art as any in the whole of France. St-Paul-de-Vence is the home of the wonderful Fondation Maeght, while Vence has a unique chapel painted by Matisse.

St-Paul-de-Vence and the Fondation Maeght

Formerly a '*ville fortifiée*' that still preserves a watchtower dating from the 12th century and ramparts built by François 1, St-Paul-de-Vence is now clogged with visitors and artsy trinket shops. In the square is the restaurant **La Colombe d'Or**, whose first owner fell in love with modern art and for 40 years accepted paintings in exchange for meals from the impoverished artists who flocked here after the First World War – including Picasso, Derain, Matisse, Braque, Vlaminck, Léger, Dufy, and Bonnard. By the time he died he had accumulated one of France's top private collections but strictly for viewing by those who can at least afford a meal.

Getting There

There are frequent buses from Cagnes-sur-Mer to La Colle-sur-Loup, St-Paul-de-Vence and Vence, and connections almost hourly from Nice. For bus times, call SAP, **t** 04 93 58 37 60.

Tourist Information

St-Paul-de-Vence: 2 Rue Grande, **t** 04 93 32 86 95, **f** 04 93 32 60 27.
Vence: Place du Grand Jardin, **t** 04 93 58 06 38, **f** 04 93 58 91 81.

Where to Stay and Eat

St-Paul-de-Vence ✉ 06570
To stay in St-Paul-de-Vence, have buckets of money and book months in advance in the summer.
***La Colombe d'Or**, Place des Ormeaux, **t** 04 93 32 80 02, **f** 04 93 32 77 78 (*luxury*). Book early to sleep here among the 20th-century art. With earthy stone, low tiled roofs, and rustic shutters; the rooms are full of character, the pool heated, the stone-arcaded terrace lovely. The restaurant (*à la carte only,*

around 400F), serves groaning platters of hors-d'œuvres and grilled meats. *Closed Nov–Dec.*
****Le St Paul**, 86 Rue Grande, **t** 04 93 32 65 25, **f** 04 93 32 52 94, *stpaul@relaischateaux.fr* (*luxury; 900–3,500F*). In the centre, in a 16th-century building: the interior designers let their hair down to create unusual but delightful juxtapositions of medieval, surreal, Egyptian and Art Deco elements. Its equally attractive restaurant is in an ancient vault (*lunch menus 320–580F*). *Closed Tues, and Wed lunch.*
***La Grande Bastide**, 1350 Route de la Colle, **t** 04 93 32 50 30, **f** 04 93 32 50 59, *stpaullgb@lemail.fr* (*expensive*). Just outside the village, a stylishly renovated 16th-century manor with a pool and sun terrace, and welcoming *patronne*. *Closed Nov–April.*
***Le Hameau**, 528 Rte de La Colle, **t** 04 93 32 80 24, **f** 04 93 32 55 75 (*expensive*). Lovely, with wide views over the orange groves from its low-beamed rooms decked out in cheery Provençal fabrics, and a small pool.
Café de la Place, **t** 04 93 32 80 19. With its own *boules* court, large covered terrace and grand Parisian-style mirrored interior. A good lunch or coffee stop.

Set back in the woods up on Route Passe-Prest, the **Fondation Maeght** (*open July–Sept daily 10–7; Oct–June daily 10–12.30 and 2.30–6; adm*) is the best reason of all for visiting St-Paul. Its fairy godparents, Aimé and Marguerite Maeght, art dealers and friends of Matisse and Bonnard, wanted to create an ideal environment for contemporary art, and they hired Catalan architect José-Luis Sert to design the perfect white luminous setting. The permanent collection, which includes around 6,000 pieces by nearly every major artist of the past century, is removed during the Foundation's frequent exhibitions and retrospectives. But you'll always be able to see the works that were incorporated into the walls and gardens: Chagall's first mosaic, *Les Amoureux*, sparkling on an exterior wall, and Miró's dreamy *Labyrinth* of winding garden paths lined with delightful sculptures. Braque's blue-mosaiced fountain basin, *Les Poissons*, and Calder's *Humptulips* were also created specifically for the Foundation. The works in the sculpture garden at the entrance to the Foundation rotate, but usually among them are Miró's great *Monument*, an airy *Stabile* by Calder, Jean Arp's *Large Seed*, and a wet and wobbling tubular steel fountain by Pol Bury. On the other side of the museum, opposite the entrance hall, is Giacometti's sculpture courtyard. The Foundation also has a cinema and a studio for making films, art workshops, and one of the world's most extensive art libraries.

Le Ste Claire, Espace Ste-Claire, t 04 93 32 02 02. Sturdy Provençal décor to match its cuisine, which is well-priced (*50–150F*) and served up on a panoramic terrace.

Vence ✉ 06140

****Château St-Martin**, 3km from Vence on Rte de Coursegoules, t 04 93 58 02 02, f 04 93 24 08 91, *st-martin@webstore.fr* (*luxury; 3–4,000F*). A set of villa-*bastides* built around a ruined Templar fortress. The 12-hectare park has facilities for riding, fishing, tennis and a heart-shaped pool installed at the request of Harry Truman. The restaurant is equally august, with prices to match (*lunch menu 400F*). *Closed Nov–Jan.*

****Relais Cantemerle**, 258 Chemin Cantemerle, t 04 93 58 08 18, f 04 93 58 32 89, *info@relais-cantemerle.com* (*expensive*). Decorated with Art Deco bits from the gutted Palais de la Méditerranée in Nice and set in its piney garden, with terraces and a pool. The Cantemerle's restaurant serves some of the finest food in Vence – *St-Pierre à la fondue de poivrons et tomates* (*menu 220F*). *Closed Oct–Mar.*

***La Roseraie**, 14 Av H.-Giraud, t 04 93 58 02 20, f 04 93 58 99 31 (*expensive– moderate*). In a garden of magnolias and cedars, with an enormous home-made breakfast, by an impeccable pool. Antiques, Salernes tiles a-plenty, and lovely ironwork, but beware the two topmost rooms, which are noisy and cramped.

****Le Mas de Vence**, 539 Av Emile Hughes, t 04 93 58 06 16 (*moderate*). Be treated like one of the family; there is a decent pool and the restaurant is one of the best places to try real Niçois ravioli (*menu 160F*).

***Closerie des Genêts**, 4 Impasse Marcellin-Maurel, t 04 93 58 33 25, f 04 93 58 97 01 (*inexpensive*). Hidden in the centre of Vence, charming yet unpretentious, with quiet rooms and a shady garden where you can bring your own picnic.

Les Templiers, 39 Av Joffre, t 04 93 58 06 05. Traditional lamb, foie gras and fish; Provençal surroundings and warm service (*menus 205–320F*). *Closed Mon.*

Le Vieux Couvent, 37 Rue Alphonse Toreille, t 04 93 58 78 58. Hearty helpings of locally produced, well-prepared regional dishes (*menus from 260F*). *Closed Wed.*

Le Pêcheur du Soleil, on Place Godeau (behind the church), t 04 93 58 32 56. Fine, as long as you won't be dazzled by the choice of 500 different pizza toppings.

Vence and Matisse's Chapelle du Rosaire

Vence lies 3km from St-Paul and 10km from the coast, sufficiently far to seem more like a town in Provence than a Riviera fleshpot. The Vieille Ville has kept most of its medieval integrity, partly because the citizens were granted permission to build their homes against the ramparts in the 15th century. Enter the walls by way of the west gate, the fortified Porte du Peyra, now yet another art gallery, the **Château de Villeneuve–Fondation Emile Hughes** (*open July–Sept daily exc Mon 9.30–12.30 and 1.30–6.30; Oct–June daily exc Mon 10–12.30 and 2–6; adm*) which displays a comprehensive collection covering the artist's fluttering career. Just inside the walls, the **Place du Peyra** was the Roman forum, and is still the site of the daily market.

Roman tombstones are incorporated in the walls of the **Ancienne Cathédrale**, a rococo church full of little treasures, the best of which are the stalls with lace-fine carvings satirizing Renaissance customs and mores, sculpted by Jacques Bellot in the 1450s.

Matisse arrived in Vence in 1941 to escape the bombing along the coast, and fell seriously ill. The 'White' Dominican sisters nursed him back to health, and as a gift he built and decorated the simple **Chapelle du Rosaire** for them (*open Tues and Thurs 10–11.30 and 2–5.30, school hols also Mon, Wed and Sat 2–5.30; adm*). Matisse worked on the project well into his 80s, from 1946 to 1951, using long bamboo poles to hold his brushes when he was forced to keep to his bed, designing every aspect of the chapel, down to the priest's robes. He considered the result his masterpiece, an expression of the 'nearly religious feeling I have for life'. Probably the most extraordinary thing about these decorations by the most sensual of Fauves is their lack of colour, except in the geometrically patterned stained glass windows that occupy three walls and which give the interior an uncanny, kaleidoscopic glow. The other walls are of white faïence, on which Matisse drew sweeping black line drawings of *St Dominic holding a Bible*, the *Virgin and Child*, the *Crucifixion* and the *Fourteen Stations of the Cross*.

Back towards the Coast: Biot, Antibes, Juan-les-Pins and Vallauris

Biot, now known for its Légers, was synonymous with pots since Roman times, while Antibes started out as the Greek trading colony of Antipolis, 'the city opposite' Nice. But these days it's also the antithesis of the Nice of retired folks: Antibes belongs to the young, who scoot and skate to *lycée*, and the aspiring young who frequent the mega-white boats that measure over a hundred yards long. On the other side of luxurious Cap d'Antibes are the sandy beaches of Juan-les-Pins, where you can swing all night, especially to the tunes of the Riviera's top jazz festival. Inland is Vallauris, another ceramics village, this one synonymous with Picasso.

Getting There

Biot's train station is at La Brague, a steep 5km walk up to the village, although buses approximately every hour from Antibes stop at the station en route to Biot.

Antibes' train station is at Place P. Semard, about a 10-minute walk from the centre. The station in Juan-les-Pins is centrally located on the Av de l'Esterel.

There are frequent *Métrazur* and TGV trains from both stations to Nice and Cannes. Buses from Antibes (t 04 93 34 37 60) for Cannes, Nice, Nice airport, Cagnes-sur-Mer, and Juan-les-Pins depart from Place de Gaulle; others leave from Rue de la République.

Tourist Information

Antibes: 11 Place de Gaulle, t 04 92 90 53 00, f 04 92 90 53 01.
Juan-les-Pins: 51 Bd Guillaumont, t 04 92 90 53 05, f 04 92 90 53 01.
Vallauris: Square du 8 Mai 1945, t 04 93 63 82 58, f 04 93 63 13 66.

Where to Stay and Eat

Biot ☑ 06410
**Auberge du Jarrier, Passage de la Bourgade, t 04 93 65 11 68. For a special feast, reserve a table at least a week in advance. In an old jar-works, with a magical terrace and a superb four-course seasonal menu that puts the Côte's *haute cuisine* budget-busters to shame (*menus 180–380F*). *Closed Tues, Wed and Thurs lunch.*

*Arcades, 16 Place des Arcades, t 04 93 65 01 04, f 04 93 65 01 05 (*moderate*). A delightful old hotel in a 15th-century building, furnished with antiques. The popular artsy restaurant below does a genuine *soupe au pistou* and other Provençal favourites (*menus from 170F*). *Closed Sun eve, Mon.*

3615 Code Café, 44 bis Impasse St-Sébastien, t 04 93 65 61 61. A large sunny garden, with a 55F *plat du jour* for a quick lunch. *Closed Mon lunch and Tues lunch.*

Antibes ☑ 06600
****Hôtel du Cap Eden Roc, Bd Kennedy, Cap d'Antibes, t 04 93 61 39 01, f 04 93 67 76 04, www.edenroc-hotel.fr (*luxury; 2,500–6,500F*). Still very much there, brilliantly white and set in an idyllic park overlooking the dreamy Iles de Lérins. No hotel on the Riviera has hosted more celebrities, film stars or pluto-crats; you could easily drop 1,000F at the exalted restaurant, the **Pavillon Eden Roc**. *Closed mid-Oct–April.*

****Imperial Garoupe, 770 Chemin de la Garoupe, t 04 92 93 31 61, f 04 92 93 31 62,

Biot

Set in a couple of miles from the sea, Biot (rhymes with yacht) is a handsome village endowed with first-rate clay – in Roman times it specialized in large wine and oil jars. In 1955, Fernand Léger purchased some land here in order to construct a sculpture garden of monumental ceramics, then died 15 days later. In 1960 his widow used the land to build the superb **Musée National Fernand Léger** (*open Oct–May 10–12.30 and 2–5.30; June–Sept 10–12.30 and 2–6; closed Tues; adm*), hard to mistake behind its giant ceramic-mosaic designed for the Olympic stadium of Hannover. Inside are the 348 paintings, tapestries, mosaics and ceramics that trace Léger's career from his first flirtations with Cubism back in 1909 – although even back then Léger was nicknamed the 'tubist' for his preference for fat noodly forms. After being gassed in the First World War, he recovered to flirt with the Purist movement founded by his buddies Le Corbusier and Amédée Ozenfant, a reaction to the 'decorative' tendencies of Cubism. Purism was to be the cool, dispassionate art of the machine age, emotionally limited to a 'mathematical lyricism', and Léger's scenes of soldiers and machines fitted the bill. After teaching at Yale during the Second World War, he returned to

www.imperial-garoupe.com (luxury; 2,700–5,000F). Not quite in the same class but a sumptuous peachy villa with impeccable rooms and opulent marble bathrooms set in tranquil gardens above the sea and a private beach. Breakfast is served at your private terrace, or overlooking the pool. There is a restaurant (menus from 280F).

★★★La Gardiole, 74 Chemin de La Garoupe, t 04 93 61 35 03, f 04 93 67 61 87 (expensive). In Cap d'Antibes, with large, luminous rooms set in a pine wood and a magnificent wisteria over the terrace. Rooms vary greatly in price. Closed Nov–Feb.

★★★Mas Djoliba, 29 Av de Provence, t 04 93 34 02 48, f 04 93 34 05 81, info@hotel-pcastel-djoliba.com (moderate). A serendipitous mas in a small park with a heated pool. Closed Nov–Jan (May–Sept half-board compulsory).

★L'Auberge Provençale, 61 Place Nationale, t 04 93 34 13 24, f 04 93 34 89 88 (inexpensive). Cosy house under the plane trees, with Provençal furniture, canopied beds, and rattan-shaded tables. There are only 7 rooms, so reserve far in advance.

★Le Nouvel Hôtel, 1 Av du 24-Août, t 04 93 34 44 07, f 04 93 34 44 08 (inexpensive). Near the bus station, 20 soundproofed rooms which fill up rapidly in summer.

De Bacon, Bd de Bacon, Cap d'Antibes ,t 04 93 61 50 02. As stylish and elegant as its perfectly prepared seafood and bouilla-baisse, at classy prices (menus from 280F). Closed Mon and Tues lunch and Nov–Jan.

La Bonne Auberge, on the N7 near La Brague, t 04 93 33 36 65. Renowned Chef Jo Rostang's son Philippe has inherited the kitchen, and has already made a name for his salade de homard aux ravioles de romans and millefeuille bonne auberge (lunch menu 220F). Reserve long in advance. Closed Mon and mid-Nov–mid-Dec.

Les Vieux Murs, Promenade Amiral-de-Grasse, t 04 93 34 06 73. Near the Picasso museum, cool and spacious, with wooden décor, and serves traditional food made modern – try the pissaladière and the crème brûlée à la lavande (menu 220F).

Le Sucrier, 6 Rue des Bains, t 04 93 34 85 40. The chef is proud to be the great-great-nephew of Guy de Maupassant and spirits up traditional French classics with an exotic twist in a cavernous stone setting (menus from 125F). Astonishingly for this part of the world there is even a vegetarian menu. Closed Tues in winter.

Chez Olive, 2 Bd Maréchal-Leclerc, t 04 93 34 42 32. Good Provençal favourites and a truly succulent fresh ravioli (menus 86–164F). Closed Mon out of season.

L'Oursin, 16 Rue de la République, t 04 93 34 13 46 (menus begin at 105F). Famous for fresh fish, and does particularly fine things with shellfish. Closed Sun eve.

France with a keen interest in creating art for the working classes, using his trademark style of brightly coloured geometric forms to depict workers, factories, and their pastimes.

The presence of the museum has boosted the local ceramic and glass industry; across from the museum at **La Verrerie de Biot**, you can watch workers make glass suffused with tiny bubbles (verre à bulles). More ceramics and glass can be seen in the charming **Musée d'Histoire et de Céramique Biotoises** in the walled town (open Wed–Sun, 10–6; adm). Guarded by 16th-century gates, Biot itself has retained much of its character, especially around central Place des Arcades, albeit crammed with art and pottery galleries.

Antibes and the Musée Picasso

Inlanders regard Antibes with jaundiced eyes: instead of 'go to hell' they say 'Vai-t'en-à-n-Antibo!' Yet Antibes still retains an authentic vivacity all its own, drawing in crowds of bright young things who disdain the hollower charms of Juan-les-Pins. A relic of Antibes' earlier incarnation as France's bulwark against Savoyard Nice are its

Juan-les-Pins ✉ 06160

****Juana, in a lovely garden on Av Georges Gallice La Pinède, **t** 04 93 61 08 70, **f** 04 93 61 76 60, *www.hotel-juana.com* (*luxury; 2,000F*). A grand survivor from the 1920s: a beautiful Art Deco hotel, a private beach and heated pool.

****Belles Rives, Av Baudouin, **t** 04 93 61 02 79, **f** 04 93 67 43 51, *belles.rives@atsat.com* (*luxury; 1,750–3,200F*). De luxe rooms, vintage 1930, facing the sea. There's a private beach and jetty, and a good restaurant (*menus start at 390F and rise steeply*), with a fine view over the gulf, or you can eat on the beach.

***Des Mimosas, in Rue Pauline, 500m from the sea, **t** 04 93 61 04 16, **f** 04 92 93 06 46 (*moderate*). The rooms have balconies overlooking the pool and garden.

***Welcome, 7 Av Docteur Hochet, **t** 04 93 61 26 12, **t** 04 93 61 38 04, *contact@hotelwelcome.net* (*moderate*). Lives up to its name and has sunny terraces and a garden.

La Terrasse, **t** 04 93 61 20 37 (*lunch menus 290–590F, or à la carte; gourmet evening menu 690F*). The resort's top restaurant, a luxurious place that boasts delicate dishes imbued with all the freshness and colour of Provence, and excellent wines to match from the region's best vineyards. *Closed Mon and Thurs lunchtime, and Wed.*

Le Bijou, directly on the sea on Bd du Littoral, **t** 04 93 61 39 07. An excellent array of sea and land dishes fill the menu; during the Cannes festival it's a good place to find the stars tucking into a *bouillabaisse* (*380F for one, 300F each for two*).

Le Capitole, 26 Av Amiral-Courbet, **t** 04 93 61 22 44 (*menus at 105F*). A charming welcome and generous seafood menus. *Closed Tues lunch in summer, and Nov.*

Eden Beach, Av E. Baudoin, **t** 04 92 93 71 71. Excellent 100F lunch menu, which includes coffee and wine. Seaside terrace and in the evenings, *thés dansant*.

Entertainment and Nightlife

In Antibes, the famous **La Siesta**, on the road to Nice, **t** 04 93 33 31 31, operates as a beach concession by day and at night turns into an over-the-top nightclub and casino where thousands of people flock every summer evening to seven dance-floors, fountains, and fiery torches.

The whole of Juan swings during the jazz festival. In Juan '*ça bouge*,' the young say; they move it at **Whisky à Gogo**, La Pinède, **t** 04 93 61 26 40; older shakers and movers bop at **Le Village**, 1 Bd de la Pinède, **t** 04 92 93 90 00.

sea-walls, especially the massive 16th-century **Fort Carré**. The handsome 17th- and 18th-century houses of Vieil Antibes look over their neighbours' shoulders towards the sea, obscuring it from **Cours Masséna**, the main street of Greek Antipolis, which holds a morning market.

The best sea views are monopolized by the **Château Grimaldi** – a seaside castle built by the same family who ran most of this coast at one time or another, including Antibes from 1385 to 1608. For six months in 1946, the owner, Romuald Dor, let Picasso use the second floor as a studio. Picasso, glad to have space to work in, quickly filled it up in a few months, only later discovering to his annoyance that all along Dor had intended to make his efforts into the **Musée Picasso** (*open summer 10–6 and Fridays 10–10; winter 10–12 and 2–6; closed Mon and hols; adm*). Because of the post-war lack of canvases and oil paint, Picasso used mostly fibro-cement and boat paint. You can't help but feel that he was exuberantly happy, inspired by the end of the war, his love of the time, Françoise Gillot, and the mythological roots of the Mediterranean, expressed in *La Joie de vivre*, *Ulysse et ses sirènes* and 220 other works.

Cap d'Antibes

Further south along the peninsula (follow the scenic coastal D2559) the delightful, free, sandy (and therefore packed) beach of **La Salis** marks the beginning of Cap d'Antibes, scented with roses, jasmine and the smell of money. The **Plateau de la Garoupe** is the highest point of the headland, with the ancient seamen's **Chapelle de la Garoupe**. Further west, a 12th-century tower holds the **Musée Naval et Napoléonien**, Av Kennedy (*open 9.30–12 and 2.15–6, closed Sat afternoons, Sun and Oct*), with ships' models and items relating to Napoleon's connections with Antibes. The cape is practically synonymous with the **Grand Hôtel du Cap**, built in 1870, where the Murphys and F. Scott and Zelda Fitzgerald frolicked in the Roaring 20s, and played a major role in the creation of the Riviera's summer season.

Juan-les-Pins and Vallauris

Created in the 1920s as a French-style Miami Beach, Juan-les-Pins flourished when it suddenly become desirable to bake brown on the beach. By 1930 it was the most popular and scandal-ridden resort on the Riviera, where women first dared to bathe in skirtless suits. The presence of Edith Piaf and Sidney Bechet boosted its popularity in the 1950s; all the young came here from Antibes and further. It's still going strong, not a beauty but a brash and sassy tart of a resort, with nightclubs, strings of minuscule private beaches, and a magnificent jazz festival in the last two weeks of July.

Two kilometres inland from Golfe-Juan, **Vallauris**, like Biot, was famous for its pottery, but in this case useful household wares. Because of competition with aluminium, the industry was on its last legs in 1946 when Picasso rented a small villa in town and met Georges and Suzanne Ramié, owners of the Poterie Madoura. Playing with the clay in their shop, Picasso discovered a new passion, and spent the next few years working with the medium. He gave the Ramiés the exclusive right to sell copies of his ceramics, and you can still buy them at **Madoura**, just off Rue du 19 Mars 1962. Thanks to Picasso, 200 potters now work in Vallauris, some talented, others trying. In 1951, the village asked Picasso if he would decorate a deconsecrated chapel next to the castle. The result is the famous plywood paintings of *La Guerre et la Paix*, now known as the **Musée National Picasso**, Place de la Libération (*open Oct–May 10–12 and 2–6; June–Sept 10–6.30; closed Tues and hols; adm*).

Grasse

Grasse's most important industry throughout the Middle Ages was tanning imported sheep-skins and buffalo-hides, using aromatic herbs that grew nearby. From this, the Grassois moved on to making fine perfumed gloves at the request of Catherine de' Medici. When gloves fell out of fashion after the Revolution they became simply *parfumeurs*. Today, this picturesque but unglamorous hilltown, with approximately 30 *parfumeries*, leads the world in perfume-making.

Getting There

There are no trains, but there are frequent buses from Cannes and Nice to Grasse. The bus station (t 04 93 36 37 37) is on the north side of town, at the Parking Notre-Dame-des-Fleurs. Leave your car here: Grasse's steep streets are narrow for motorists.

Tourist Information

Grasse: Palais des Congrès, t 04 93 36 66 66, f 04 93 36 86 36.
Mougins: 15, Av Mallet, t 04 93 75 87 67, f 04 92 92 04 03.

Where to Stay and Eat

Grasse ✉ 06130

★★★**Best Western Hôtel des Parfums**, Bd Eugène-Charabot, t 04 92 42 35 35, f 04 93 36 35 48, *www.hoteldesparfums.com* (*expensive*). Pretty views, a pool, sauna and Jacuzzi. It offers a 1½hr 'Introduction to Perfume' that takes you into the secret heart of the smell biz, lending you a 'nose' to help create your own perfume.

★★**Hôtel du Patti**, in the medieval centre on Place du Patti, t 04 93 36 01 00, f 04 93 36 40 (*moderate*). Very comfortable rooms, all with air-conditioning and TV.

Bastide Saint Antoine, 48 Rue Henri-Dunant, t 04 93 70 94 94. For a sumptuous Tuscan feast in glorious al fresco surroundings (*menus 250, 550, 700F*).

Les Arcades, Place aux Aires, t 04 93 36 00 95. For a reasonably priced lunch underneath the arches (*menus 90–145F*), with Provençal dishes and fishes.

★★★**Auberge du Colombier**, 15km east at Roquefort-les-Pins, t 04 92 60 33 00, f 04 93 77 07 03 (*expensive*). A delightful white *mas* with cheerfully decorated rooms, expansive gardens with a pool, and an extraordinary restaurant – try the ravioli stuffed with wild mushrooms and scattered with roasted hazelnuts (*menus 150–195F*).

Mougins ✉ 06250

★★★★**Le Moulin de Mougins**, Notre-Dame-de-Vie, t 04 93 75 78 24, f 04 93 90 18 55,

www.moulin-mougins.com (*luxury–expensive*). In 1969 chef Roger Vergé bought a 16th-century olive mill near Notre-Dame-de-Vie and made it into the internationally famous luxury restaurant, which also has three rooms and two apartments overlooking the sculpture gardens and wisteria-covered terraces. Of late, France's gourmet bibles have been sniffing that the mild-mannered celebrity chef, author of *The Cuisine of the Sun* (1979), has lost a bit of his touch – and little faults seem big when you shell out 1,000F for a meal. But it's still a once-in-a-lifetime experience for most, in the most enchanting setting on the Côte. *Closed mid-Dec–mid-Jan.*

L'Amandier, Place du Com.-Lamy, t 04 93 90 00 91, If you can't get a table at Le Moulin, Vergé has a simpler restaurant, located up a winding staircase in a 14th-century olive-oil mill above his shop. The ivy-covered terrace is utterly romantic, and menus start at 155F. In the shop, **Les Boutiques du Moulin**, you can stock up on a selection of the master's sauces and compotes. For those that still haven't had enough Vergé, he has also opened a cookery school above L'Amandier; t 04 93 75 35 70 for details.

★★★★**Les Muscadins**, 18 Bd Courteline, t 04 92 28 28 28, f 04 92 92 88 23, *muscadins@alcyonis.fr* (*luxury–expensive*). Individually decorated sumptuous bedrooms of charm and character. The nouvelle cuisine and chocolate desserts are excellent (*menus 185F and 250F*). *Closed Nov–mid-Dec.*

Brasserie de la Méditerranée, Place de la Mairie, t 04 93 90 03 47. Grilled *gambas* with ginger and other seafood delights accompanied by heavenly home-made bread (*lunch menus 138–227F, evening menus 172–227F*).

Bistrot de Mougins, t 04 93 75 78 34. For traditional dishes like roast quail, beef stew and aubergine caviar, in a vaulted, wooden-beamed dining room (*menus 175–248F*). Don't miss the fig tart. *Closed Wed and Sat lunch.*

Le Rendez-vous de Mougins, Place du Village, t 04 93 75 87 47. Long a local favourite, with aromatic dishes like beef with wild mushroom sauce and sea bass with truffles (*lunch menus from 98F, evening menus 138–238F*).

The arcaded **Place aux Aires** near the top of the town in the Vieille Ville is the main meeting point for all and holds a morning food and flower market. From here Rue des Moulinets and Rue Mougins-Roquefort lead to the Romanesque **Cathédrale Notre-Dame-du-Puy**. The art is to the right: the *Crown of Thorns* and *Crucifixion* painted by Rubens at the age of 24, before he hit the big time; a rare religious subject by Fragonard, the *Washing of the Feet*; and, most sincere of all, a reredos by Ludovico Bréa. The Cannes road leads into Grasse's promenade, Place du Cours, with pretty views over the countryside. Just north of the Cours, at 2 Rue Jean Ossola, the **Musée d'Art et d'Histoire de Provence** (*same hours as Villa Fragonard*) exhibits Gallo-Roman funerary objects, *santons* and furniture in all the Louis styles and an exceptional collection of faïence from Moustiers and Apt. At 8 Cours Honoré-Cresp, the **Musée International de la Parfumerie** (*same hours as Villa Fragonard*) displays lots of precious little bottles from Roman times to the present.

It's hard to miss the *parfumeries* in Grasse. The alchemical processes of extracting essences from freshly cut mimosa, jasmine, roses, bitter orange etc. are explained – you learn that it takes 900,000 rosebuds to make a kilo of rose essence. Tours in English are offered by **Parfumerie Fragonard** at the 18th-century converted tannery at 20 Bd Fragonard, **t** 04 93 36 44 65, and at the spanking new factory at **Les 4 Chemins**, on the Route de Cannes.

Mougins

Cooking, that most ephemeral of arts, is the main reason most people make a pilgrimage to Mougins, a luxurious, fastidiously flawless village of *résidences secondaires*, with more gastronomy per square inch than any place in France, thanks to the magnetic presence of Roger Vergé (*see* box to left).

Cannes

The English and Russians started arriving in Cannes in the mid-19th century. By the 1920s the byword was: 'Menton's dowdy. Monte's brass. Nice is rowdy. Cannes is class!' Less enthusiastic commentators mentioned the dust, the bad roads, the uncontrolled building, and turds bobbing in the sea. If nothing else, the French Riviera proper ends with a bang at Cannes.

Besides ogling the shops, the shoppers and their dogs there isn't much to see in Cannes. Characterless luxury apartment buildings and boutiques have replaced the gaudy Belle Epoque confections along the fabled promenade **La Croisette**. The shore-line is divided into 32 sections (you can get a map), as memorably named as 'Waikiki', 'Le Zénith' and 'Long Beach' (which is all of several metres long). One rare public beach is in front of the fan-shaped **Palais des Festivals**. The **Vieux Port**, with its bobbing fishing-boats and plush, luxury craft, is on the other side of the Palais des Festivals. Cannes' cramped old quarter, **Le Suquet**, rises up on the other side of the port, where the usual renovation and displacement of the not-so-rich is just beginning. At the city's highest point, the monks of St-Honorat built a square watchtower, the Tour du

Birth of a Festival

In 1939 a film festival at Cannes was established to rival Mussolini's new Venice film festival. Cannes' historians cite 1954 as the year when everything coalesced, when the essential ingredients of sex and scandal were added to the glamour of film: the décolletage of newcomer Sophia Loren made a big impression, grabbing attention and headlines away from Gina Lollobrigida. Another well-endowed starlet (English this time) named Simone Silva went on to the Iles de Lérins for a photo session with Robert Mitchum and removed her brassiere. Two hours later she was told to leave Cannes and a few years later, no longer able to find work because of her precocious gesture, she committed suicide. Cannes should have made her an honorary citizen. Two years later, the new sensation was Brigitte Bardot, who coyly spun her skirts around to reveal her dainty *petites culottes*. Nowadays would-be starlets strip down completely and bump and grind on the Croisette hoping to attract attention. Although the big American studios have traditionally shunned the festival, the importance of the international entertainment market has brought a growing stream over from Hollywood. But the wheeling and dealing that goes on has not diminished expectations of fun and wild times.

Mont Chevalier, in 1088; their priory is now the **Musée de la Castre** (*open 10–12 and 2–6; 3–7 July–Sept ; 2–5 Oct–Mar; closed Tues and Jan; adm*), with an archaeological and ethnographic collection, containing everything from Etruscan vases to pre-Columbian art and a 40-armed Buddha. A good way to get Cannes into proportion is to see it by night. Climb up through Le Suquet to **La Tour**, and join the lovers to look beyond the white boats and lights.

The Iles de Lérins: St-Honorat and Ste-Marguerite

When Babylon begins to pall, you can take refuge on a delightful pair of green, wooded, traffic-free islets just off the coast. (Take water and a picnic, for there is only a smattering of expensive little shops and cafés on Ste Marguerite and just one restaurant on St-Honorat.) They are named after two saints who founded religious houses on them: **St Honorat** landed on the islet that bears his name in 375. The island became a beacon of light and learning in the Dark Ages, producing 20 saints among its alumni, including Patrick. The 29 monks who live there now cultivate part of the island, producing a delicious golden liqueur called Lérina.

Larger **Ile Ste-Marguerite** has nicer beaches, especially on the south end of Chemin de la Chasse. On the north end stands the gloomy **Fort Royal** (*open Oct–Mar 10.30–12.15 and 2.15–4.30, April–Sept 10.30–12.15 and 2.15–5.30,closed Tues and hols; adm*), with a little aquarium and a **Musée de la Mer** which displays finds from submarine archaeological digs. The fort, built by Richelieu, served mainly as a prison, especially for the mysterious Man in the Iron Mask. Speculation about the man's identity continues: was he Louis XIV's twin, as Voltaire suggested, or, according to a recent theory, the gossiping son-in-law of the doctor who performed the autopsy on Louis XIII and discovered that the king was impotent?

Getting There

By plane: The frequent Métrazur between St-Raphaël and Menton, and every other train whipping along the coast, calls into the station at Rue Jean-Jaurès.

By bus: There is a multiplicity of private bus companies, all arriving and departing from different places; though there is one central number: t 04 93 45 20 08.

By boat: Every hour in the summer, the glass-bottomed boat, *Nautilus*, at Jetée Albert-Edouard, departs for tours of the port; tickets 70F, call t 04 93 39 11 82.

Boat trips out to the Iles de Lérins, t 04 93 39 11 82, depart from the Gare Maritime, Allées de la Liberté, approximately every hour, and much less frequently between October and June. The general tour is a whirlwind trip; you're best off going to one island at a time.

Tourist Information

Cannes: Palais des Festivals, 1 La Croisette, t 04 93 39 01 01, f 04 93 99 84 23; another office is in the Gare SNCF, t 04 93 99 19 77.

Where to Stay

Cannes ✉ 06400

Although there are sizeable discounts if you come in the off-season, you can't book too early for the film festival or for July and August. Cannes' two tourist offices offer a free reservation service, but they won't be much help at that time of year.

Luxury

★★★★Carlton, 58 La Croisette, t 04 93 06 40 06, f 04 93 06 40 25, www.interconti.com (2,225–4,090F). A Riviera landmark, with its two black cupolas, said to be shaped like the breasts of the *grande horizontale* Belle Otero, the Andalusian flamenco dancer and courtesan of kings. Renovated by its new Japanese owners, the 7th floor has a pool, casino and beauty centre, and more.

★★★★Majestic, 14 La Croisette, t 04 92 98 77 00, f 04 93 38 97 90, www.lucienbarriere.com (2,270–4,200F). The movie stars' favourite

with its classic French décor, heated pool, private beach, etc.

★★★★Martinez, 73 La Croisette, t 04 92 98 73 00, f 04 93 39 67 82, martinez@concorde-hotels.com. This has kept its Roaring 20s character, but now has all imaginable modern comforts, including tennis courts, a heated pool and, from the 7th floor, grand views over the city (*rooms 2,000–3,000F; discounts for stays over five days*).

Expensive

★★★Bleu Rivage, 61 La Croisette, t 04 93 94 24 25, f 04 93 43 74 92, info@cannes-hotels.com. A renovated older hotel amidst the big daddies on the beach, where rooms overlook the sea or the garden at the back.

★★★Molière, 5–7 Rue Molière, t 04 93 38 16 16, f 04 93 68 29 57. Sitting in the midst of a garden, with bright rooms and terraces. *Closed mid-Nov–mid-Dec.*

★★★ Hôtel Vendôme, 37 Bd d'Alsace, t 04 93 38 34 33, f 04 97 06 66 80, hotel.vendome@wanadoo.fr. This ice-cream-pink 19th-century villa has recently been attractively renovated and sits in a private garden in the heart of the town.

Moderate–Inexpensive

If you aren't in Cannes on an MGM expense account, there are other alternatives.

★★Sélect, 16 Rue Hélène-Vagliano, t 04 93 99 51 00, f 04 92 98 03 12. A quiet, modern choice with air-conditioned rooms, all with bath.

Le Chanteclair, 12 Rue Forville, t/f 04 93 39 68 88. Good doubles with showers. *Closed Nov.*

Youth hostel, 35 Av de Vallauris, t/f 04 93 99 26 79. To the west, in Cannes la Bocca. *Closed Christmas and New Year.*

Eating Out

Luxury–Expensive

La Palme d'Or, Martinez hotel (*see* above), t 04 92 98 74 14. The Alsatian chef, Christian Willer, prepares dishes including *salade de pigeonneau* or a succulent *agneau de Sisteron persillé* (*menus 390, 450 and 750F*), served in a fabulous Art Deco dining room.

Closed mid-Nov–Dec, and Mon–Tues; open daily during Festival.

La Belle Otero, on the 7th floor of the Carlton (*see above*), t 04 92 99 51 10. The seventh heaven of gastronomy; if *loup de Méditerranée en croustillant de parmesan poêlée de légumes niçois* doesn't make your mouth water, then be guided by numbers – it shares two Michelin stars with the Palme d'Or (*lunch 290F, eves 410 and 620F*). *Closed Sun, Mon, and Tues lunch time out of season.*

La Villa des Lys, Hôtel Majestic (*see above*), t 04 92 98 77 00. Chef Bruno Oger creates inspired variations on French classics impeccably served on the palatial terrace (*menus 280–780F*). *July and Aug eves only.*

Moderate–Cheap

Lou Souléou, 16 Bd Jean-Hibert, t 04 93 39 85 55. For affordable seafood and fine views of its original habitat; try *bouillabaisse* and a pretty good *aïoli* (*menu 145F*). *Closed Mon and Wed lunch times in season.*

Le Coin de Clyve, 23 Bd Alexandre III, t 04 93 43 06 34. A homely, welcoming little place off the beaten track, with delicious *jambon persillé en gelée* and a splendid apple and almond tart (*lunch menu from 75F, evening menus from 100F*). *Closed Wed out of season.*

L'Envol, at the Hôtel Crystal, 13–15 Rond Point Duboys d'Angers, t 04 93 39 45 45. A wide-ranging menu with an Italian accent which includes truffled eggs, *Estouffade provençale* with fresh tagliatelle. The great views from the 6th floor make up for the slightly old-fashioned décor (*menus 78–150F*).

Au Bec Fin, 12 Rue du 24-Août, t 04 93 38 35 86. Good food and plenty of it near the station (*menus 69–125F*). *Closed Sun.*

Hôtel Brasserie du Marché, 10 Rue Monseigneur-Jeancard, Cannes le Bocca, t 04 93 48 13 00. Retains the ambience of the old village and has tasty daily specials like lamb with wild mushrooms and *cuisses de grenouilles* (*62–80F*).

Grand Boulevard, 25 Bd Carnot, t 04 93 39 16 06. This is connected to a butcher's, so it comes as no surprise to find meaty specialities like *boudin* with apple (*plat du jour 55F*).

La Pizza, 3 Quai St-Pierre, t 04 93 39 22 56. Fine pizzas *saltimbocca à la Romana*, a very passable *tarte aux pommes* and a congenial

atmosphere (*lunch 62–115F*). *Open until 2–3am in the summer.*

Le Grand Café, Rue Félix-Faure, t 04 93 99 93 10. With a promenade view for people-watching, and grilled sardines and huge margaritas served by an assortment of chatty young waiters.

Entertainment and Nightlife

Film

For stars on celluloid, sometimes in their original language:

Les Arcades, 77 Rue Félix-Faure, t 04 93 39 00 98.

Olympia, 16 Rue Pompe, t 08 36 68 00 29.

Star, 98 Rue d'Antibes, t 04 93 68 18 08.

Casino

The casinos draw in some of the highest rollers on the Riviera, although the adjoining casino discos are fairly staid:

Casino Croisette, Palais des Festivals, t 04 92 98 78 00.

Casino Club, Carlton Hotel, t 04 92 99 51 00.

Bars and Clubs

To get into the most fashionable clubs (those with no signs on the door), you need to look like you've just stepped off a 100ft yacht to get past the sour-faced bouncers.

Jimmy's, at the Casino in the Palais des Festivals, t 04 92 98 78 00, after 11pm t 04 93 99 78 79. A glitzy showcase billing itself '*La discothèque des stars*'; it's certainly for those with stars in their eyes – gamblers, their ladies and mainstream music (*11pm–dawn*).

La Chunga, 72 La Croisette, t 04 93 94 11 29. There's usually live music to go with the food (*meals about 300F*). *8.30pm–dawn.*

Le Whisky à Gogo, 115 Av de Lérins, t 04 93 43 20 63. A well-heeled crowd.

Brooms Bar, Hôtel Gray d'Albion. With a piano bar. It also has a disco on Sunday night – **Jane's Club**, t 04 92 99 79 59.

Zanzi-Bar, 85 Rue Félix-Faure, t 04 93 39 30 75. A gay bar of long standing (*6pm–6am*).

Disco 7, 7 Rue Rougière, t 04 93 39 10 36. Dancing and a transvestite show (*90F cover charge*). *11.30pm–6am.*

The Western Côte d'Azur

Between the mountainous porphyry-red Esterel and the Massif des Maures are St-Raphaël and Fréjus: St-Raphaël has more beaches, holiday flats and yachts; its venerable neighbour Fréjus (Forum Julii) is a market town and naval port, founded by Julius Caesar to rival Marseille.

St-Raphaël

St-Raphaël's once glittering turn-of-the-century follies and medieval centre were bombed to smithereens in the war, all except the Victorian-Byzantine church of **Notre-Dame de Lépante** in Bd Felix-Martin, and the **Eglise des Templiers** or St-Pierre (1150), with its Templar watchtower, in Rue des Templiers. This is the third church to occupy the site, re-using the same old Roman stones. If the church is closed, pick up the key at the adjacent **Musée Archéologique** (*open April–Sept daily 9–7; Oct–Mar Tues–Sun 9–12 and 2–5*). This holds finds from a Roman shipwreck full of building materials (not a sunken city as everyone thought), brought up by Jacques Cousteau. There is also a reconstruction of a Roman galley, and a room devoted to the strange menhirs and dolmens of the eastern Var region. This is much the prettiest part of town, with a little maze of streets hemmed in by peeling houses.

Fréjus: the Roman Town

Founded in 49 BC, Forum Julii was the first Roman town of Gaul, but not the most successful; the site was malarial and hard to defend, and eventually the river Argens silted up, creating the vast sandy beach of Fréjus-Plage but leaving the Roman harbour, once famous for its size, high and dry a mile from the sea. The fragments of Forum Julii are a long hike across the modern town. Best preserved is the ungainly, greenish **Amphithéâtre Romain**, Rue Henri-Vadon (*open winter Mon–Sat 10–12 and 1.30–5.30; summer Mon–Sat 10–1 and 2.30–6.30; adm*), flat on its back like a beached whale with the rib arches of its vomitoria exposed to the sky. Arches from a 40km **aqueduct** still leapfrog by the road to Cannes; north, on Av du Théâtre Romain, the vaults of the **Théâtre Romain** (*same hours as amphitheatre; adm, free Sun*) survived, although the seating had to be replaced.

When the Saracens had left and the coast was clear in the 12th century, the Fréjussiens rebuilt their **Cathédral St-Léonce** in Place Formigé, and in the 16th century gave it a superb pair of Renaissance doors carved with sacred scenes, a violent Saracen massacre, and portraits of aristocratic ladies and gents. The cathedral was the centre of a mini **cité épiscopale** incorporating a defence tower, a chapterhouse and a bishop's palace (*guided tours April–Sept 9–7, other times 9–12 and 2–5; closed Mon; adm*), all built with the warm red stone of the Esterel. The tour includes the **baptistry**, the one bit of Fréjus the Saracens missed: late 4th century, octagonal and defined by eight black granite columns with white capitals lifted from the Roman forum. Fairest of all is the 12th-century **cloister**, with slim marble columns and a 14th-century ceiling, coffered into 1,200 little vignettes. Upstairs, the **Archaeology Museum**

Getting Around

St-Raphaël is the terminus of the *Métrazur* trains that run along the coast to Menton. Other trains between Nice and Marseille call at both St-Raphaël and Fréjus stations, making it easy to hop between the two; St-Raphaël also has direct connections to Aix, Avignon, Nîmes, Montpellier and Carcassonne, and TGVs from Paris. Both towns have **buses** for Nice airport and Marseille (bus station, t 04 91 50 57 68) and for St-Tropez and Toulon (SODE-TRAV, t 04 94 95 24 82). Les Bateaux de St-Raphaël, t 04 94 95 17 46, **sail** regularly to St-Tropez and Port Grimaud, and make day excursions to the Iles de Lérins and Ile de Port Cros (summer only), as well as jaunts around the Golfe de Fréjus and its *calanques* (creeks); reserve ahead in July and Aug.

Tourist Information

St-Raphaël: Rue Waldeck Rousseau, t 04 94 19 52 52, f 04 94 83 85 40.
Fréjus: 325 Rue Jean-Jaurès, t 04 94 51 83 83, f 04 94 51 00 26.

Where to Stay and Eat

St-Raphaël ✉ **83700**

*****Golf de Valescure**, Av des Golfs, t 04 94 52 85 00, f 04 94 82 41 88, *info@golf-hotel-provence.com* (*expensive*). In the same family for five generations, with tennis and a pool when you're not on the links; golf packages are available.

*****San Pedro**, Av du Colonel Brooke, t 04 94 19 90 20, f 04 94 19 90 21, *www.hotel-sanpedro*

.com (*expensive*). Very reasonable option in the old artists' quarter.

****Les Pyramides**, 77 Av P. Doumer, t 04 98 11 10 10, f 04 98 11 10 20 (*inexpensive*).Budget choice with a little garden. *Closed Dec–Feb.*

L'Arbousier, 6 Av de Valescure, t 04 94 95 25 00 (*menus 145–320F*). The most genial place to eat, combines charm and excellent, aromatic gourmet food for half the price you'd pay elsewhere. *Closed Sun eve, Mon eve and Wed.*

Pastorel, 54 Rue de la Liberté, t 04 94 95 02 36. In the same family since 1922, with a pleasant no-nonsense proprietress and an attractive garden terrace. Friday special 160F *aïoli* menu (*other menus 170 and 210F*). *Closed Sun eve and Mon.*

Fréjus ✉ **83600**

*****Aréna**, 139 Rue du Gal. de Gaulle, t 04 94 17 09 40, f 04 94 52 01 52, *info@arena-hotel* .com (*expensive*). Colourful, air-conditioned rooms, a pool, and good food in old Fréjus. *Closed Nov.*

***Le Bellevue**, by the cathedral in Place Paul-Vernet, t 04 94 17 27 05, f 04 94 51 20 41 (*inexpensive*). The best of the cheapies, and quiet.

Le Mérou Ardent,157 Bd de la Libération, is t 04 94 17 30 58. Overlooking the beach and boats, dine on monkfish with prawns and spices, and a heart-warming *fondant au chocolat* (*menus 89–139F*). *Closed Mon lunch and Thurs lunch in season.*

Le Resto Cave, Place des Tambourinaires, t 04 94 17 21 22. A wine-cellar/restaurant hybrid: there are hearty portions of classic dishes like *navarin d'agneau aux haricots*, and a heavenly *millefeuille* (*menus from 55F for plat du jour with wine and coffee*).

(*open summer 10–1 and 2.30–6.30; winter 10–12 and 1.30–5.30; closed Tues and Sun; adm*) has a collection of finds from Forum Julii, among them a perfectly preserved mosaic, a fine head of Jupiter, and a copy of the superb two-faced bust of Hermes discovered in 1970.

Just off the N7, in the Tour de la Mare district of Fréjus, is **Notre-Dame de Jérusalem** (*open Nov–Mar Mon–Fri 2.30–6.30, Sat 10–1 and 2.30–6.30; April–Oct Mon–Fri 1.30–5.30, Sat 9.30–12.30 and 1.30–5.30; adm*), an octagonal chapel designed by Jean Cocteau in the 1960s. He died before its completion; his partner, artist Edouard Dermit, finally painted the chapel himself from Cocteau's plans. Inside is an anarchic flurry of colour and form; limbs radiate from the glass window in the dome (symbolising the Resurrection of the Dead) and colours bounce off the walls from the brilliant stained glass windows.

The Massif des Maures

Between Fréjus and Hyères, the coast bulges out and up to form the steep hills and arcadian natural amphitheatres of the Massif des Maures. For centuries its chestnut and cork trees were the main source of income, while the coast was defended by the bravos of St-Tropez.

Ste-Maxime and Port Grimaud

In the seaside conurbation spread between Fréjus and St-Tropez, the only place that may tempt a detour is **Ste-Maxime**, a modern resort town with a shady, older nucleus by the port and a beach of golden sand facing St-Tropez. It willingly takes the overflow of fashionable and bankable holidaymakers from the latter, linked by frequent boats; St-Tropez may not look far away but it's two hours' traffic jam in high season. Ten kilometres north towards Le Muy on the D25, the remarkable **Musée du Phonographe et de la Musique Mécanique** in the wooded Parc de St-Donat (*open Easter–Sept 10–12 and 3–6; closed Mon and Tues; adm*) has exhibits that include one of Edison's original phonographs of 1878, an accordion-like 'Melophone' of 1780, and an audio-visual 'Pathégraphe' to teach foreign languages, built in 1913.

From Ste-Maxime, the road passes through **Port Grimaud**, a pleasure port designed in 1968 by Alsatian entrepreneur François Spoerry, inspired by the lagoon complexes around St Petersburg, Florida, where home-owners, like Venetians, can park their boats by the front door. The traditionally styled, colourful houses are a preview of the real McCoys in St-Tropez.

St-Tropez

It made the headlines in France when St-Tropez's mayor forced the discos to close at 2am and declared the beaches off limits to dogs, inciting the fury of 'Most Famous Resident' Brigitte Bardot, that crusading Joan of Arc of animal rights who married a National Front politician and in a recent autobiography referred to her son as a 'tumour'. But then again BB has always been a bit ahead of the rest of us, ever since she came down here to star in Roger Vadim's *Et Dieu créa la femme* in 1956 and incidentally made this lovely fishing village into the national showcase of free-spirited fun, sun and sex. The French fondly call this St-Trop' – pronouncing the 'p', not as if it's St-Too Much, though in the summer it really is. At other times of the year it's easier to understand what started all the commotion in the first place.

Pre-BB, St-Tropez was discovered by painters in the early 1900s. Writers, most famously Colette, joined the artists' 'Montparnasse on the Mediterranean' in the 1920s. The third wave of even more conspicuous invaders, Parisian existentialists and

Getting Around

SODETRAV **buses (t** 04 94 97 88 51) link St Tropez to St-Raphaël, Grimaud, Cogolin and Hyères and to the nearest TGV stop at Les Arcs. There's also a regular bus from Toulon. You may be better off catching a **boat** to St-Tropez from St-Raphaël (**t** 04 94 95 17 46), or Ste-Maxime (MMG, **t** 04 94 96 51 00).

The ghastly traffic makes **bike and moped hire** an attractive alternative (M.A.S, 5 Rue Quaranta, near St-Tropez's Pl Carnot, **t** 04 94 97 00 60).

Other villages in the Massif des Maures are much harder to reach by public transport: two buses a day go from Le Lavandou to La Garde-Freinet, and there's but one linking La Garde-Freinet and Grimaud to Toulon.

Tourist Information

St-Tropez: La Maison du Tourisme du Golfe de St-Tropez/Pays des Maures, **t** 04 94 55 22 00, **f** 04 94 55 22 01, at the N98/D559 junction just before the traffic gridlock, and at Quai Jean-Jaurès, **t** 04 94 97 45 21, **f** 04 94 97 82 66.

Shopping

Although many boutiques are now owned by chains, a few exclusive shops remain: **Gas**, Place Sibilli, specializing in coral and turquoise jewellery; **Rondini**, 16 Rue G. Clemenceau, for the famous *sandales tropéziennes*, invented in 1927; **Sugar**, Rue Victor-Laugier, for cotton tops and shorts, and **Galeries Tropéziennes** for fabrics, espadrilles, and everything else. For de luxe chocs, try **La Pause Douceur**, 11 Rue Allard; for Provençal specialities, there is **Autour des Oliviers**, Place de l'Ormeau.

Where to Stay and Eat

Ste-Maxime ✉ 83120

****La Belle Aurore. 4 Bd Jean-Moulin, **t** 04 94 96 02 45, **f** 04 94 96 63 87, *www. belleaurore.com* (*luxury*). For all the usual comforts, including parking, pool, private beach and a fine gastronomic restaurant (*menus 210–450F*). *Closed Oct–Mar*.

***Parc Hotel Jas Neuf, t 04 94 96 51 88, **f** 04 94 49 09 71. A comfortable huddle of Provençal style buildings around a swimming pool (*expensive*).

Le Revest, 48 Av Jean-Jaurès, **t 04 94 96 19 60, **f** 04 94 96 32 19 (*moderate*). Central, with a pool. *Closed Nov–Easter*.

***Domaine du Calidianus, Bd Jean Moulin, **t** 04 94 96 23 21, **f** 04 94 49 12 10 (*expensive*). Glam and newly refurbished. *Closed Jan and Feb*.

***Mas des Brugassières, Pont-de-la-Tour, **t** 04 94 55 50 55, **f** 04 94 54 50 51 (*expensive*). Delightful farmhouse which doesn't require a king's ransom but makes you feel like royalty anyway. Some rooms open on to the gardens and pool. *Closed mid-Oct–Mar*.

St-Tropez ✉ 83990

If you haven't already booked a hotel long ago, forget about arriving in St-Tropez on the off-chance between June and September. There are acres of campsites in the area, although in the summer they are about as relaxing as refugee camps. As for prices,

glitterati came in the 1950s, when Françoise '*Bonjour Tristesse*' Sagan and Bardot made St-Trop the pinnacle of chic. Joan Collins, George Michael and Elton John have houses here.

If everything about St-Tropez fills you with dismay, let the **Musée de l'Annonciade** (*open Oct–May 10–12 and 2–6, June–Sept 10–12 and 3–7, closed Tues, holidays and Nov; adm*) be your reason to visit. It concentrates on works by painters in Paul Signac's St-Tropez circle, post-Impressionists and Fauves – colour-saturated paintings that take on a life of their own with Vlaminck (*Le Pont de Chatou*) and Derain (*Westminster Palace* and *Waterloo Bridge*), along with works by Braque, Matisse, Vuillard, Bonnard,

expect them to be about 20 per cent higher per category than anywhere else on the coast. And if you come in the off season, beware that most hotels close in the winter.

****Byblos, Av Paul Signac, **t** 04 94 56 68 00, **f** 04 94 56 68 01, *st-tropez@byblos.com* (*luxury; 2,700–3,950F*). If money's no object, there's the Byblos, built by a Lebanese millionaire, designed like a *village perché*, with rambling corridors, patios, and opulent rooms. In the middle there's a magnificent pool, and the nightclub is one of most desirable to be seen in. *Closed mid-Oct–Easter.*

****Résidence La Pinède Plage de la Bouillabaisse, **t** 04 94 55 91 00, **f** 04 94 97 73 64, *www.relaischateaux.fr/pinede* (*luxury; 3,135–8,690F*). The *luxe, charme et volupté* of the Relais et Châteaux has given it the current fashion edge; gourmet restaurant (*menu 490F*). *Closed Nov–Mar.*

****Bastide de St-Tropez, Rte des Carles, **t** 04 94 55 82 55, **f** 04 94 97 21 71, *www.bastide-saint-tropez.com* (*luxury; 2,200–4,350F*). Similarly swish, but perched on a hill, with an even better, Michelin-starred restaurant, **L'Olivier** in a garden of oleander, figs, palms, eucalyptus and parasol pines. The food is flamboyant, generous and exceptionally delicious; *morue demi-sel en ratatouille minute* or *carré d'agneau au riz parfumé et sa brochette d'abats* (*menus 310–450F*).

****Les Yacas, 1 Bd d'Aumale, **t** 04 94 55 81 00, *www.hotel-les-yacas.fr* (*luxury; 1,500–2,700F*). Once home to Colette and before her to Paul Signac. A rambling but very very chic fusion of three small cottages; most of the rooms look inwards to a courtyard bursting with flowers. The staff are so discreet they are virtually invisible. The restaurant has menus at 350F. *Closed mid-Oct–Easter.*

****La Ponche, 3 Rue des Remparts, **t** 04 94 97 02 53, **f** 04 94 97 78 61, *hotel@laponche.com* (*luxury*). Picasso's old watering hole, located in a group of old fishermen's cottages – a charming, romantic nook to entice your special darling. *Closed Nov–Mar.*

***Le Sube Continental, **t** 04 94 97 30 04, **f** 04 94 54 89 08 (*expensive*). Sleep in the port overlooking the yachts at the oldest hotel in town and an historic monument to boot. *Closed Jan.*

***Lou Troupelen, Chemin des Vendanges, **t** 04 94 97 44 88, **f** 04 94 97 41 76, *troupelen@aol.com* (*moderate*). Quiet rooms in an old farmhouse. *Closed mid-Oct–Easter.*

Les Lauriers, in the centre at Rue du Temple, **t 04 94 97 04 88, **f** 04 94 97 21 87 (*moderate*). Modern rooms in a garden. *Closed mid-Oct–mid-Mar.*

Les Chimères, Port du Pilon, **t** 04 94 97 02 90, **f** 04 94 97 63 57 (*inexpensive*). At the entrance of town, no star but it does have a restaurant. Ask for a room on the garden.

Leï Mouscardins, 1 Rue Portalet, **t** 04 94 97 29 00. For atmosphere and creative food, book a table overlooking the harbour. Laurent Tarridec's remarkable cuisine may be one of the high points of your holiday (*menus 365F*). *Closed lunch July and Aug.*

Chez Maggi, **t** 04 94 97 16 12. Busy, fashionable, gay bar/restaurant, serves up good and inexpensive Franco-Italian cuisine, like delicious *petits farcis provençaux*, to a youthful clientèle in a small room adjoining the raucous bar area (*menu from 130F*).

Van Dongen and Dufy. Just outside the museum, the port is edged with the colourful pastel houses that inspired the Fauves. The view is especially good from the Môle Jean Réveille, the narrow pier that encloses the yacht-filled port. Seek out **Place de l'Ormeau**, **Rue de la Ponche** and **Place aux Herbes**, poetic corners of old St-Tropez that have refused to shift into top gear. The rambling little **Quartier de la Ponche**, with several coolly chic restaurants and bars, folds itself around the shore and the tower of the now defunct Château de Suffren. The narrow Rue de la Ponche leads out to a point surmounted by the Old Tower, with a little beach which is very nice for a quick dip. Another essential ingredient of St-Tropez is the charming Place Carnot, better

La Voile Rouge, on Plage de Ramatuelle, t 04 94 79 84 34 (*à la carte from 270F*). The current fashionable favourite beach restaurant.

Ramatuelle ✉ 83350

****Château de la Messardière**, Rte de Tahiti, t 04 94 56 76 00, f 04 94 56 76 01, *hotel@messardiere.com* (*luxury; 2,200–3,500F*). For self-indulgence, you can't beat this late 19th-century folly; ultra comfortable, with a superb panoramic restaurant and exquisite, exotic dishes you'll find nowhere else (*menus 360–520F*). *Closed Oct–Feb.*

***La Figuière**, Rte de Tahiti, t 04 94 97 18 21, f 04 94 97 68 48 (*expensive*). Relaxing old farmhouse in a vineyard, tennis, and a pool. *Closed Oct–Easter.*

***Hostellerie Le Baou**, Rue Gustave-Etienne, t 04 94 79 20 48, f 04 94 79 28 36, *hostellerie.lebaou@wanadoo.fr* (*luxury–expensive*). The views are enchanting among the vineyard terraces; also a heated pool and restaurant serving sunny Provençal treats like *dos de loup au caviar d'aubergine* (*menus 190–360F*). *Closed Nov–Mar.*

Grimaud ✉ 83310

***Hostellerie du Coteau Fleuri**, Place des Pénitents, t 04 94 43 20 17, f 04 94 43 33 42, *coteaufleuri@wanadoo.fr* (*moderate*). A comfortable stone inn, hidden by flowers and ivy, with grand views over the vineyards and the Maures; its restaurant serves reliably good Provençal dishes – *filet de rouget au pistou*, and *carré d'agneau* (*menus 195–300F*). *Closed mid-Nov–mid-Dec. Restaurant closed Tues.*

Le Verger, Rte de la Collobrières, t 04 94 43 25 93, f 04 94 43 33 92 (*expensive*). Old low Provençal building lost in the countryside. French windows lead out into the gardens, and dinner by the pool (*menus 150–250F*). *Closed Nov–Feb.*

***La Boulangerie**, Rte de Collobrières, t 04 94 43 23 16, f 04 94 43 38 27 (*moderate*). Great views and silence, plus a pool, tennis and a video library. *Closed Oct–Easter.*

Les Santons, Rte Nationale, t 04 94 43 21 02. In dining rooms full of *santons*, indulge in a gourmet spread of lobster salad, seafood, or thyme-scented *selle d'agneau* (*menus from 215F*). *Closed Tues, Wed and Thurs lunch in season, and Jan–mid-Mar.*

Café de France, Place Neuve, t 04 94 43 20 05. Pennywise, the best bet for food in an old stone house with a summer terrace and an average 129F menu.

Entertainment and Nightlife

The bars in Place des Lices provide an entertaining sideshow, especially the resolutely old-fashioned **Café des Arts**, t 04 94 97 02 25, with its zinc bar and crowd of St-Germain-des-Prés habitués (*closes after the Nioulargue*).

By the port, **Sénéquier**, t 04 94 97 08 98, is a St-Trop institution. Younger bars include **La Bodega de Papagayo**, on Quai d'Epi, t 04 94 97 76 70.

Dancing and much besides goes on until dawn at St-Trop's clubs. Try the **VIP Room** by the new port, t 04 94 97 14 70, or **Les Caves du Roy** at Hôtel Le Byblos, t 04 94 97 16 02.

---

known by its old name of **Place des Lices**, an archetypal slice of Provence with its plane trees, Tuesday and Saturday market, cafés and eternal games of *pétanque*.

Although the **beaches** begin even before you enter St-Tropez, those famous sandy strands where girls first dared to bathe topless (circumventing local indecency laws by placing Coke bottle tops over their nipples) skirt the outer rim of the peninsula. In the summer minibuses link them with Place Carnot, a good idea as beach parking is as expensive as the beaches themselves. **Plage des Graniers** is within easy walking distance of town, but it's the most crowded. A path from here skirts Cap de St-Tropez and, in 12km, passes **Plage des Salins** (4km direct from St-Tropez), the gay beach

Neptune, and ends up at the notoriously decadent **Plage de Tahiti**, the movie stars' favourite. Tahiti occupies the north end of the 5km **Plage de Pampelonne**, lined with cafés, restaurants, and luxury concessions where any swimming costume at all is optional. On the other side of Cap Camarat, Plage de l'Escalet is hard to reach, but much less crowded and free (take the narrow road down from the D93); from L'Escalet you can pick up the coastal path and walk in an hour and a half to the best and most tranquil beach of all, Plage de la Briande.

Into the Massif des Maures

Beckoning just a short drive from the coastal pandemonium are the quiet chestnut woodlands of the Massif des Maures, or at least what's left of them after a quarter of the forest burned in 1990; note that some of the roads that penetrate the mountain may be closed in dry summers.

Perhaps by now you've noticed signs advertising pipes from **Cogolin**; they've been making them for over two centuries (visits at Courrieu Pipes, 58 Av G.-Clemenceau, *open Mon–Fri 9–12 and 2–5, Sat 9–12 and 2–6*). Other crafts particular to Cogolin are hand-knotted wool rugs, top-quality reeds for saxophones, and furniture. Unlike Cogolin, nearby **Grimaud** is all aesthetics and boutiques. A former Saracen and Templar stronghold, it can hold its own among the most perfect *villages perchés* on the coast, crowned by the ruined castle of the Grimaldis, after whom the village is named. From the Romanesque church of St-Michel, Rue des Templiers, lined with arcades of 1555, passes the House of the Templars, one of their few surviving structures in Provence.

When Charles Martel defeated the Moorish invaders at Poitiers in 732 and pushed them back to Spain, a few managed to give the Franks the slip and escape into Provence. Their strongholds, or *fraxinets*, gave their name to **La Garde-Freinet**, a large village full of medieval charm and British expats. A path, past chestnuts said to be 1,000 years old, ascends to the site of a Saracen fortress (the standing walls are from the 15th century). Six kilometres off the D14 from Grimaud stands the moody, ruined **Chartreuse de la Verne** (*open 11–6, 11–5 in winter, closed Tues and religious feast days and Jan; adm*), founded in 1170 in one of the most romantically desolate corners of France – a vast and impressive Carthusian complex. The air is sweet in the biggest settlement of the western Maures, **Collobrières**, an attractive old village full of quirky fountains and scented with chestnuts being ground into paste and purée or undergoing their apotheosis into delectable *marrons glacés*.

The Corniche des Maures: Cavalaire, Bormes-les-Mimosas and Le Lavandou

The bay on the underside of the St-Tropez peninsula, with its clear coves and large beaches of silken sand, has been given lock, stock and barrel to the property promoters. The longest beach, however, at **Cavalaire-sur-Mer**, remains more popular with families than movie stars. Near by, the **Domaine du Rayol**, Av des Belges (*open Feb–June and Sept–mid-Nov daily 9.30–12.30 and 2.30–6.30; mid-Nov–Jan by appointment; July, Aug Tues–Sun 9.30–12.30 and 4.30–8; adm*) is well worth a stop for its

Mediterranean gardens. Persevering west past Cap Nègre and the exclusive villages of Pramousquier and Cavalière you find the big boys on the Corniche-des-Maures, the fishing port and resort of **Le Lavandou** and **Bormes-les-Mimosas**, a cute hyper-restored medieval enclave that added the mimosas to tart up its name in 1968. Le Lavandou, where Bertolt Brecht and Kurt Weill wrote *The Threepenny Opera* in 1928, is a good place in which to empty your wallet on seafood, watersports, boutiques and nightclubs. There are twelve beaches here, and a '*petit train*' trundles between them.

Hyères and its Golden Isles

Hyères claims to be the original resort of the Côte d'Azur, with a pedigree that goes back to Charles IX and Catherine de' Medici, who wintered here in 1564. In the early 19th century, people like Empress Josephine, Pauline Borghese, Victor Hugo, Tolstoy and Robert Louis Stevenson built villas here, before it faded genteelly from fashion in the 1880s. For despite its mild climate and lush gardens, Hyères was, unforgivably, three miles from the seaside.

Hyères and the Giens Peninsula

There isn't much to do in Hyères but take a brief wander into the **Vieille Ville**, beyond Place Massillon. Here stands the Tour des Templiers, a remnant from a Templar's lodge, and on top of a monumental stair, the church of St-Paul (1599) with

Getting There and Around

By plane: Hyères-Toulon Airport is served mainly by Air France from Paris.

By train: Hyères is a dead end, linked to Toulon but nowhere else; the station is 1.5km south of town, but there are frequent buses into the town centre.

By bus: Buses can be tricky. Telephone first. SODETRAV, 47 Av Alphonse Denis, **t** 04 94 12 55 12, serves destinations west to Toulon and east to Le Lavandou. City buses (from the bus station in the town centre) link Hyères to Hyères-Plage and the Giens peninsula.

By boat: Boats for all three of Hyères' islands depart at least twice a day, year-round, from Port d'Hyères (**t** 04 94 12 54 40) and Le Lavandou (**t** 04 94 71 01 02), with additional sailings in the summer. There are more frequent connections from La Tour-Fondue, at the tip of the Giens peninsula, to Porquerolles (**t** 04 94 58 21 81), and in summer boats also sail from Toulon to Porquerolles. Be warned that inter-island connections are rare.

Tourist Information

Hyères: Rotonde Jean-Salusse, Av de Belgique, **t** 04 94 01 84 50, **f** 04 94 01 84 51.

Where to Stay and Eat

Hyères Town ✉ 83400

***Les Pins d'Argent**, Bd de la Marine, **t** 04 94 57 63 60, **f** 04 94 38 33 65, *pins.dargent@wanadoo.fr* (*moderate*). Near the sea, surrounded by trees, with a pool and warm welcome, and delicious food at fair prices (*menus 110–190F*). Hotel closed Oct–Mar; restaurant closed Sun eve and Mon out of season.

Les Orangers, 64 Av Iles d'Or, **t** 04 94 00 55 11, **f** 04 94 35 25 90, *www.var-provence.com*, *orangers@var-provence.com* (*inexpensive*). A sturdy Provençal-style building houses one of the prettiest and most comfortable hotels in town.

*La Reine Jane**, by the sea at Ayguade, **t** 04 94 66 32 64, **f** 04 94 66 34 66 (*inexpensive*).

400 ex votos dating back to the 1600s and a set of *santos* too large to move. The Renaissance house next to St-Paul doubles as a city gate, through which you can walk up to Parc St-Bernard. At the upper part of the park, the **Villa de Noailles** was designed as a *château cubiste* for art patron Vicomte Charles de Noailles. Austere cement on the outside, furnished with pieces commissioned from Eileen Gray and designers from the Bauhaus, this vast villa was a busy hive of creativity between the wars. The Noailles' garden has been recently linked to that of Edith Wharton, author of *The Age of Innocence*, who lived on the same slope in a former convent of Ste-Claire, spread over 28 terraces (*open daily 8–7; free*). Further up the hill are the hollow walls and towers of the **Vieux Château** with an overview of Hyères' peninsula. Originally the island of Giens, it has been anchored to the continent by two sand-bars whose arms embrace a salt marsh. Although the link is dodgy – Giens became an island again in the storms of 1811 – it hasn't stopped people from building villas and hotels. The barren west arm, dotted by shimmering white piles of salt, is traversed by the narrow *route du sel* beginning at Plage de l'Almanarre. The salt road ends in little Giens, under a ruined castle.

The Iles d'Hyères

Hyères' three islands are voluptuous little greenhouses that have seen more than their share of trouble. In the Middle Ages they belonged to St-Honorat by Cannes, and attracted pirates like moths to a flame; in 1160, after the Saracens carried off the entire population, the monks gave up and just let the pirates have the islands. In the

---

Good rooms and food at bargain prices (*lunch 200F*). *Closed Jan.*

Le Bistrot de Marius, 1 Place Masillon, t 04 94 35 88 38. Tiny establishment with big plates of Provençal fare and a jolly host (*menus 92–195F*). *Closed Tues.*

Jardin de Bacchus, 32 Av Gambetta, t 04 94 65 77 63. For gourmet dining, on rich, flavour-some Provençal dishes (*menus 151–300F*) in quietly elegant surroundings. *Closed Sun eve and Mon.*

Ile de Porquerolles ✉ 83400

There are seven hotels, all priced above the odds and all booked months in advance.

****Mas du Langoustier, t 04 94 58 30 09, f 04 94 58 36 02, *langoustier@compuserve.com* (*luxury; half-board*). A romantic old inn between the woods and long sandy beach, with lovely rooms and a superb restaurant, serving Porquerolles' famous rosé (*menus from 330F*). *Closed mid-Oct–April.*

**Auberge Les Glycines, Place d'Armes, t 04 94 58 30 36, f 04 94 58 35 22 (*expensive; half-*

board). Small and charming, with rooms decorated in Provençal fabrics set around a tranquil courtyard.

**Relais de la Poste, Place d'Armes, t 04 98 04 62 62, f 04 94 58 33 57, *www.relais-de-la-poste.com* (*moderate*). The island's first hotel: Provençal-style rooms with loggias and a simple crêperie. *Closed Oct–Mar.*

Il Pescatore, t 04 94 58 30 61. For all things fish: not just the predictable *bouillabaisse* but carpaccio and sashimi. Eat on the restful terrace overlooking the boats bobbing in the port (*menus 85–120F*). *Closed Nov–Feb.*

Port-Cros ✉ 83400

***Le Manoir, t 04 94 05 90 52, f 04 94 05 90 89 (*luxury; half-board*). The only choice on paradise: pricey, tranquil and casual, an 18th-century mansion set among the eucalyptus groves, which also has an outdoor pool and a fine little restaurant (*menus from 265F*). Book months in advance. *Closed Nov–Mar.*

late 19th century, they were used to quarantine veterans of the colonial wars and as Dickensian orphanages. In 1892 the navy bought Le Levant and blew it to pieces as a firing range. In the 1890s fires burned most of the forests on Porquerolles and Port-Cros. Fortunately, the French government has since moved decisively to protect the islands; strict laws protect them from the risks of fire and developers.

Largest of the islands, **Porquerolles** stretches 7km by 3km and has the largest permanent population, which in the summer explodes to 10,000. Its main village, also called Porquerolles, was founded in 1820 as a retirement village for Napoleon's finest soldiers and invalids. It still has a colonial air, especially around the central pine-planted Place d'Armes, the address of most of Porquerolles' restaurants, hotels and bicycle hire shops. Although the cliffs to the south are steep and dangerous, there are gentle beaches on either side of the village, especially the white **Plage Notre-Dame** to the east and **Plage d'Argent** to the west.

Although barely measuring a square mile, **Port-Cros** is the most mountainous of the islands, and since 1963 it has been a national park, preserving not only its forests of pines and ilexes, but nearly a hundred species of birds; brochures will help you identify them as you walk along the mandatory trails. The surrounding waters, rich in fish and plant life, are also part of the park ; even divers have an underwater 'trail' to follow. The French navy still hogs almost all the flowering **Ile du Levant**, the third island, and uses it to test aircraft engines and rockets. The island's remaining quarter is occupied by Héliopolis, France's first nudist colony (1931).

Toulon

Thanks to an abundance of murex shells, Toulon was a centre for dyeing cloth from Phoenician times, until Louis XIV changed the town forever by making it the chief port of France's Mediterranean fleet. As such it has had more than its share of history. In 1793, when Toulon's royalists had confided the city to the English and their allies, they were driven out by a ragamuffin Revolutionary army led by a young Napoleon Bonaparte, beginning his meteoric career. In 1942, Vichy Admiral Laborde scuttled the entire Mediterranean fleet rather than let it fall into the hands of the Germans. In August 1944, after flattening the old port with aerial bombing raids, the Allies landed and the French army recaptured Toulon. Over the last few years the shipyards in La Seyne have closed down, putting thousands out of work, while the ugly forces of reaction elected France's first National Front deputy, followed by the election of a National Front mayor whose xenophobic, anti-cultural antics have been a national affront.

From the train station, Avenue Vauban continues down to the large bleak square of Place d'Armes, decorated with ordnance from the adjacent arsenal, one of the biggest single employers in southeast France with some 10,000 workers. Alongside the arsenal in Place Monsenergue, the **Musée de la Marine** (*open April–Oct daily 10–6.30; Nov–Mar 10–12 and 2–6, closed Tues; adm*) displays models of the ships that it once made. Baroque sculptor Puget started out in Toulon carving figureheads for the ships,

Getting Around

By plane: Toulon's airport, with flights to Paris, Corsica, and Brittany is out near Hyères (for information, t 04 94 00 83 83).

By train: The train station is on the north side of Toulon in Place Albert 1er, with four daily TGVs to Nice and Marseille, four also direct to Paris (just over 5hrs), and frequent links along the coast and to Hyères.

By bus: For St-Tropez and the coast between Hyères and St-Raphaël, catch a SODETRAV bus in the bus station (next to the train station), t 04 94 18 93 40. Littoral buses (from Av Vauban, south from the station), t 04 94 74 01 35, will take you to Bandol.

By boat: Companies on Quai Cronstadt offer boat tours of Toulon's anchorages and the surrounding coasts and islands: Trans-med 2000, t 04 94 92 96 82 (daily commentated tours to the Ile de Porquerolles); Bateliers de la Rade, t 04 94 46 24 65 (year-round tours of the anchorages and summer crossings to all three Iles d'Hyères).

Tourist Information

Place Raimu, t 04 94 18 53 00, f 04 94 18 53 09.

Where to Stay

Toulon ✉ 83000

***La Corniche, 17 Littoral F.-Mistral, at Mourillon, t 04 94 41 35 12, f 04 94 41 24 58 (*moderate*). The most elegant place to sleep and eat in Toulon, a cleverly designed modern Provençal hotel, air conditioned and near the beach. The restaurant, **Le Bistrot**, is built around the massive trunks of three maritime pines, serves refined seafood and dishes such as *selle d'agneau en rognonnade* (*menus 156–240F*).

**Le Grand Hôtel du Dauphiné, 10 Rue Berthelot, t 04 94 92 20 28, f 04 94 62 16 69, *dauphine83@hotmail.com* (*inexpensive*). In the pedestrian zone, not far from the opera, a comfortable friendly older hotel, air conditioned, with guarded parking.

*Le Jaurès, 11 Rue Jean-Jaurès, t 04 94 92 83 04, f 04 94 62 16 74 (*cheap*). Nearby, friendly and the top bargain choice; the rooms, a tad gloomy, all have baths.

La Résidence de Cap Brune, Chemin de l'Aviateur Gayraud, off Corniche Gén. de Gaulle, t 04 94 41 29 46 (*moderate*). A magical old white villa, set on a cliff beyond the beaches of Mourillon, a world away from the urban hubbub of Toulon; it has a small pool and a steep path down to the shore. *No restaurant. Closed Nov–Mar.*

Eating Out

Le Lingousto, Rte de Pierrefeu, t 04 94 28 69 10. Very popular place outside town in an old *bastide*, where the freshest of fresh local ingredients are transformed into imaginative works of art (*menus 250–400F*). *Closed Sun eve and Mon, and Jan–Feb.*

Le Lido, Av Frédéric Mistral, t 04 94 03 38 18. Nice, nautical décor, and a window on to the kitchen where you can watch your fresh fish being prepared in a variety of ways (*menus 140 and 190F*). *Closed Sun eve and Mon in winter.*

La Frégate, 237 Av de la République, t 04 94 92 97 60. *Moules* and good home-made *frites* for a thrifty 45F. Pizzas come at about the same price, and, if not exactly glamorous, it's one of the few places in Toulon where you can eat late. *Closed Sun.*

La Chamade, 25 Rue Denfert-Rochereau, t 04 94 92 28 58. Serious fixed three-course menu prepared by chef Francis Bonneau. *Closed first three weeks in August.*

and the museum has works by his followers, while Puget's chisel left the two Atlantes (1657) on Quai Cronstadt, Force and Fatigue. Off the Quai, Rue d'Alger, now a popular evening promenade, used to be the most notorious street in Toulon's Vieille Ville, or 'Le petit Chicago', the pungent pocket of the pre-war town. Some of the narrow streets around 'the gut', as it's known, are still unsavoury after dark, even as the shifty bars and shabby flats give way to fashionable cafés and boutiques.

Toulon looks better from a distance. Bus 40 will take you to Bd Amiral-Vence in Super-Toulon, site of the terminus of the little blue **funicular** that runs (*daily 9–5.30, later in summer, closed winter 12–2*) to the top of 535m **Mont Faron**. Buses 3 and 13 from in front of the station or Av Général-Leclerc go to the Plage du Mourillon, Toulon's largest beach and site of the city's oldest fort, Louis XII's Grosse Tour.

West of Toulon: Bandol, La Ciotat and Cassis

Sheltered from the ravages of the mistral, **Bandol** is a typical, pretty Côte d'Azur town. But Bandol has something most of the Riviera hotspots lack – its own excellent wine and a little island, **Ile de Bendor**. A barren 6-hectare rock when Paul Ricard bought it with his pastis fortune in 1950, it is now a little adult playground. There's a diving and windsurfing school, a nautical club that organizes yacht races, an art school and gallery, a business centre, hotels, and the **Exposition Universelle des Vins et Spiritueux** (*open Easter–Sept 10–12 and 2–6, closed Wed; adm free*), with displays of 8,000 bottles and glasses from around the world. Apart from wine, Bandol offers its visitors pink flamingos, toucans, cockatoos, and Vietnamese pigs in a lovely exotic garden of tropical flora at the **Jardin Exotique et Zoo de Sanary-Bandol**, 3km east (*open winter daily 8–12 and 2–6, closed Sun am; summer daily 8–12 and 2–7; adm*).

La Ciotat has given the world two momentous pastimes. First, motion pictures, pioneered here in 1895, when Auguste and Louis Lumière filmed a train pulling into La Ciotat station (*L'Entrée d'un train en gare de La Ciotat*), a clip that made history's first film spectators jump out of their seats; the Eden Théâtre where it was shown, on 28 December 1895, is the oldest surviving cinema. And second, *pétanque*, that most Provençal of sports, which came into being here in 1907 when one old-timer's legs became paralysed and he could no longer take the regulation steps before a throw. Most visitors to La Ciotat keep to the beaches and pleasure port around La Ciotat-Plage, but it's the Vieux Port that affords the best loafing. Take bus no.3 to the cliff-top Parc du Mugel. Avenue de Figuerolles continues from here to the red pudding-stone walls and pebble beach of the Calanque de Figuerolles.

The old coral-fishing village of **Cassis**, with its fish-hook port, white cliffs, beaches and quaint houses spilling down steep alleyways, was a natural favourite of the Fauve painters. In the summer so many tourists descend on the now chic little port that it's often elbow room only here and on the pebbly **Plage de Bestouan**. The sheer limestone cliffs that stand between Cassis and Marseille are pierced by startling tongues of lapis lazuli – mini-fjords known as *calanques*, or creeks. The nearest *calanque*, **Port-Miou**, is accessible by car or foot (a 30min walk): here the hard, white stone was cut for the Suez Canal. Another mile's hike will take you to **Port-Pin**, with a pretty beach, and another hour to **En-Vau**, the most beautiful of them all (you can also reach En-Vau with less toil from a car park on the Col de la Gardiole). Take a picnic and plenty of water. Note, however, that after being ravaged by forest fires in 1990 the paths to the *calanques* are strictly off limits from the beginning of July to the second Saturday in September, when the only way to visit is by motor boat from Cassis port.

Getting Around

Bandol is on the Toulon–Marseille TGV. SODETRAV buses, t 04 94 18 93 40, run from Toulon to St-Tropez and St-Raphaël, and Littorals Cars, t 04 94 74 01 35, leave Toulon from Rue Vauban for Bandol. La Ciotat is a main stop for trains between Marseille and Toulon; regular buses cover the 3km from the station to the Vieux Port. Cassis' train station is just as far from the centre but has less frequent services; if you're coming from Marseille, take one of the frequent coaches instead.

Where to Stay and Eat

Bandol ✉ 83150

★★★**Master Ker Mocotte**, 103 Rue Raimu, t 04 94 29 46 53, f 04 94 32 53 54 (*expensive; half-board*). Delightful villa that once belonged to the Toulon-born Raimu – the best actor in the world, according to Orson Welles. It has a seaside garden, private beach and pool, and offers facilities for water sports. The restaurant offers a summer grill in gardens above the Mediterranean (*menus from 220F*). *Open all year*. Its cheaper annexe, the villa ★★**Coin d'Azur**, looks directly over the beach.

★★**Bel Ombre**, Rue de la Fontaine, t 04 94 29 40 90, f 04 94 25 01 11. Hidden down a residential street and friendly (*moderate; half-board*). *Closed mid-Oct–Mar.*

L'Auberge du Port, 9 Allée J.-Moulin, t 04 94 29 42 63. Bandol's gourmet rendezvous, specializing in seafood. Go the whole hog on a 260F *menu dégustation* (*other menus from 128F*).

Le Jerôme, t 04 94 32 55 85. Seafront restaurant and pizzeria serving huge portions at attractive price. The Provençal salad has a selection of delicious olive tapenades and a sumptuous aubergine caviare, topped with crusty toasted bread (*menu 90F*).

Ile de Bendor ✉ 83150

★★★**Delos**, t 04 94 29 11 60, f 04 94 32 41 44, *www.hoteldelos.fr* (*expensive*). Ricard's, with big, comfortable rooms decorated in extravagant bad taste – but the views of the sea

below and the many watersports make up for it. *Closed Jan–Feb.*

Hôtel Soukana, t 04 94 25 06 06, f 04 94 25 04 89 (*expensive*). Lots of activities and an occasionally raucous but cheerful clientèle. *Closed Nov–April.*

La Ciotat ✉ 13600

★★★**Miramar**, 3 Bd Beaurivage, t 04 42 83 09 54, f 04 42 83 33 79 (*moderate*). Classy, updated old hotel by the beach; half-board mandatory in the summer, but its restaurant, **L'Orchidée**, t 04 42 83 09 54, is the best in town (*menus from 125F*).

République Indépendante de Figuerolles, a *chambres d'hôte* (*inexpensive*) on the beach at the Calanque de Figuerolles, t 04 42 08 41 71, f 04 42 71 93 39. The good restaurant becomes Russian in Nov–May (*a great 120F menu*).

Cassis ✉ 13260

★★★★**Les Roches Blanches**, Av des Calanques, t 04 42 01 09 30, f 04 42 01 94 23 (*expensive*). Most spectacular, on the promontory overlooking the bay. Rooms are a tad small, but very comfortable; there's a private beach; half-board is mandatory in season.

★★★**Les Jardins de Cassis**, Rue Favier, t 04 42 01 84 85, f 04 42 01 32 38 (*moderate*). Set amid lemon groves and bougainvillaea, a lovely oasis, with a pool. *Closed Nov–Mar.*

★★**Grand Jardin**, 2 Rue Pierre Eydin, t 04 42 01 70 10, f 04 42 01 33 75 (*inexpensive*). More reasonable, but book months in advance.

La Fontasse, Col de la Gardiole, t 04 42 01 02 72. West of Cassis, in a magnificent setting over the *calanques*, France's most remote youth hostel is a dusty drive an hour's walk from town or a bus ride (bus stop Les Calanques on the Marseille–Cassis road). Beds, lights and cold water are the only creature comforts (*50F a head, bring your own food*).

Chez César, 21 Quai des Baux, t 04 42 01 75 47. On the waterfront with reasonably priced food served in Marcel Pagnol décor. *Closed Mon eve, Tues, Jan.*

Nino, 1 Quai Barthélemy, t 04 42 01 74 32. Tasty fish soup and grilled prawns on a summery seaside terrace (*menus from 150F*). *Closed Sun eve, Mon.*

Corsica

During the long centuries that Paris spent 'perfecting' France's borders, it received a special offer from Genoa on an uppity piece of property outside the confines of the mystic Hexagon. The Corsicans, for their part, argued that Genoa had no right to sell what was no longer hers, because under Pascal Paoli they had declared themselves an independent republic. But the year was 1769, long before republics commanded much respect. The French defeated the politically precocious but defiant islanders and married Corsica to the mainland. A couple of months later, Mme Bonaparte gave birth to a bouncing baby boy named Napoleon – but then again, the island was always famous for its vendettas.

'I would recognize my island with my eyes closed, by nothing more than the smell of the maquis carried on waves,' Napoleon once remarked. For the most part, however, he turned his back on Corsica. Neglect, in fact, would characterize French policy until the 1980s, when Corsican separatist pressure (and violence) and a measure of

Getting There and Around

There is a wide variety of slow and fast ferries to Corsica's ports, but don't think you can just pop down on the spur of the moment in the summer, when cars especially have to be booked months in advance. Lines are Corsica Ferries (from Nice, t 04 92 00 43 76), and SNCM (from Nice, Toulon or Marseille), t 08 36 67 95 00. Flights to Bastia, Ajaccio and Calvi depart from Nice, Marseille and Paris Orly.

A *micheline* train links Calvi, Bastia, Ajaccio and Corte, but faster coaches provide most of the somewhat infrequent public transport on the island.

In summer, the mountains offer some of the most spectacular walking in France, especially along the legendary GR20 trail.

Tourist Information

Bastia ✉ 20200: Place St-Nicolas, t 04 95 31 81 34, f 04 95 55 96 00.
Calvi ✉ 20260: Port de plaisance, t 04 95 65 16 67.
Ajaccio ✉ 20000: Rue du Roi-Jérôme, t 04 95 51 53 03, f 04 95 51 53 01.
Porto-Vecchio ✉ 20137: Rue du Député de Rocca Serra, t 04 95 70 09 58.

Where to Stay and Eat

Bastia ✉ 20200
La Citadelle, 6 Rue du Dragon, t 04 95 31 44 70. Near the top of Bastia and serving some of the best innovative and classic French dishes in Corsica in a vaulted old olive mill (*menu 180F, à la carte 250F*). *Closed Sun and Mon lunch.*

Erbalunga ✉ 20222
***Castel' Brando, t 04 95 30 10 30, f 04 95 33 98 18 (*moderate*). One of the nicest places to stay near Bastia is this 19th-century villa built by a Corsican who made good in Santo Domingo. The garden has a pool and old palm trees; rooms have many of their original furnishings and air conditioning. *Open Apr–mid-Oct; pricey in high season.*

Calvi ✉ 20260
****La Villa, Chemin de Notre Dame de la Serra, t 04 95 65 10 10, f 04 95 65 10 50 (*expensive*). A member of the Relais et Châteaux, in a hilltop garden; luminous and elegant rooms in an updated version of a Roman villa, with lovely views over the bay. Two pools, tennis, fitness centre, hammam and sailing on the beach a kilometre away; the hotel organizes four-wheel-drive excursions into the Balange. It has a good restaurant, too.

common sense brought about change. Nowadays, not only has Corsica been granted an array of privileges, but the government has even put a modest degree of autonomy in the pipeline, igniting the dreaded explosion of me-tooism from independent-minded Bretons, Basques, Catalans and overseas territories. Whether or not autonomy can also put an end to the feuding on Corsica remains to be seen, as some nationalist groups have developed links to organized crime.

This tug of war takes place in a setting that the word 'romantic' was invented for. Corsica is the fourth largest island in the Mediterranean, with the second highest mountains (after Etna in Sicily). A natural park encompasses a third of its deeply forested slopes, while the shore melts into sandy beaches or dive bombs to the sea in sheer cliffs. A central mountain chain, capped by 8,810ft Monte Cinto, divides Corsica into two: the north and east is *Diqua dei monti* ('this side of the mountains', now the *département* of Haute-Corse, or 2B); the south and west is *Dila dei monti* ('beyond the mountains', now the *département* of Corse du Sud, or 2A). The more fertile *Diqua dei monti* is historically the *Terra di commune*, a land of independent-

**Les Arbousiers, Rte de Pietramaggiore, t 04 95 65 04 47, f 04 95 65 26 14 (*inexpensive*). A simple but pleasant beach hotel, 5 minutes' walk from the sea.

Corte ✉ 20250

La Restonica, t 04 95 46 09 58, f 04 95 61 15 79 (*moderate*). Very comfortable rooms by the river, all with TV; it also has a pool and a delightful restaurant, serving omelettes with *bruccio* (Corsican cheese) and fresh mint, and other delights in a magical setting. Half-board (*425F*) is mandatory in season. *Closed Sun eve, Mon lunch and Nov–Mar.*

U Museu, Rampe Ribanelle, t 04 95 61 08 36. Wonderful Corsican restaurant where each hearty dish is packed full of the island's flavours in every dish from soup to trout to boar *daube* with myrtle, served with a fine house wine (*menus from 89F*).

Ajaccio ✉ 20000

***Fesch, 7 Rue Cardinal Fesch, t 04 95 51 62 62, f 04 95 21 83 36 (*moderate*). Traditional old hotel in the centre, recently refurbished; all rooms air conditioned and with TVs.

***Du Golfe, 5 Bd Roi-Jérôme, t 04 95 21 47 64, f 04 95 21 71 05 (*moderate*). Modern, on the port, a short walk from the ferries and buses; soundproofed, air-conditioned rooms.

Da Mamma, Passage Guinghetta, t 04 95 21 39 44. Off Cours Napoléon and the best

option in town for authentic Corsican cuisine (*menus from 65F*).

Porto-Vecchio ✉ 20137

***Belvedere, Rte de Palombaggia, t 04 95 70 54 13, f 04 95 70 42 63 (*moderate*). Just what a seaside hotel should be, on the beach among the parasol pines, with 16 air-conditioned rooms and a lovely and excellent restaurant terrace with fossils embedded in the walls and dishes such as *aubergines confites* with *bruccio* (*menus 300–450F*).

A Cantina di l'Orriu, Cours Napoléon, t 04 95 72 14 25. A chaming wine bar serving at least 12 Corsican wines by the glass, with plates of local charcuteries, cheese or toasts topped with dried mullet roe, *boutargue*.

Bonifacio ✉ 20169

***La Caravelle, 37 Quai Comparetti, t 04 95 73 00 03, f 04 95 73 00 41 (*moderate*). Occupies a handsome 19th-century house overlooking the marina. The restaurant, in a 13th-century chapel, has a terrace under the palms and specializes in seafood prepared with a masterly touch (*menus from 120F*). *Closed mid-Oct–Mar.*

U Castille, up in the Haute Ville on Rue Simon Varsi, t 04 95 73 04 99. There's no view, so the cooking has to be good, served by the aimiable Marcel in traditional old stone dining room. Delicious *soupe de poisson* on the 120F menu. *Closed Sun.*

minded peasantry whose frequent rebellions had a strong flavour of natural, unideo-
logical socialism. *Dila dei monti*, the wild land of maquis, was the *Terra dei signori*, the
battleground of feudal barons – sometimes patriots but more often petty gangsters
on the make – warring against the Pisans, Genoese and French, but most of all
against each other.

Corsica annually receives six tourists for each of its 250,000 inhabitants, yet
remains remarkably unspoilt, thanks in part to the separatist penchant for blowing
up holiday homes. Like many islands, it is a miniature continent, with its own traditions, language (close to medieval Tuscan), music, cuisine and granite architecture. It
is a highly distinctive place, and intends to remain so; if all the trappings of globalization and homogenized corporate culture get you down, come here. Only avoid July
and especially August, when it's packed to the gills.

Bastia and Diqua dei Monti

Bastia, the bustling main port of the north, was founded by the Genoese and looks
it, with tall narrow houses and Baroque churches crowded over the old port; like
Genoa itself it was heavily bombed in 1944 by the Americans, this time by mistake, a
few days after Corsica became the first part of France to be liberated. Besides general
atmosphere, the main things to soak up in town are the historical and geological
collections in the newly remodelled **Musée d'Ethnographie Corse** (*open 9–12 and 2–6,
June 9–6.30, July and Aug 9–8; adm*) in the 15th-century Palais des Gouverneurs.
Bastia is also the gateway to Cap Corse, the narrow, steeply mountainous peninsula
that seems to point so accusingly northwards to France. Its villages have always lived
from the sea, and now from vineyards; much of the west coast plunges dramatically
into the sea. **Erbalunga**, **Maciaggio** and **Centuri-Port** are among the few seaside
hamlets along the Cap equipped to take more than a handful of visitors.

Just south and west of Bastia, the agricultural region of the **Nebbio** is rich in Pisan
Romanesque churches, the architectural jewels of Corsica: the best is San Michele
(1280), 1km from the village of **Murato**. Below the Nebbio, framed in a beautiful gulf,
the chic resort and marina of **St-Florent** has another excellent Pisan church to go with
its pretty beaches. The **Désert des Agriates**, just to the west, is an uninhabitable bulge
of rock, light and maquis, although at the west end of it, above the port resort of **l'Ile
Rousse**, you'll find the **Balagne**, known as the 'garden of Corsica', at least when there
were enough men to cultivate its wheat fields and olive groves. Closing off the northeast corner of the island is the striking sun-bleached citadel of **Calvi**, with an almost
feasible claim to being the birthplace of Christopher Columbus; a long sandy beach
below has made the town a big holiday favourite.

Where the Balagne ends, the northern border of the **Parc Naturel Régional** begins,
encompassing the spectacular coastline of the **Scandola Nature Reserve**, accessible
only by boat from Calvi or **Porto**. Porto, set amid a fantastic tumble of red rocks, makes
a fine base for visiting some of Corsica's renowned beauty spots. Just south, one of
the most extraordinary roads in Europe weaves through the fantastical pinnacles and

cliffs of the **Calanche** to **Piana** (in July and August, it becomes one of Europe's worst traffic jams), while inland you can explore the magnificent **Gorges de Spelunca** and the **Forêt d'Aitone**, where 500-year-old Laricio pines, once prized by the Genoese for masts, tickle the sky. Further up the road into the interior is the austere, fire-scarred mountain enclosure of the **Niolo**, where only goat herds can make a living; the Niolo's main village, **Calaccuia**, hosts the most traditional of Corsican festivals in early September, complete with singing and archaic poetry competitions.

In the centre, surrounded by magnificent mountain gorges, atmospheric grey granite **Corte** was chosen by patriot Pascal Paoli in the 18th century to be the capital of Corsica's short-lived republican government and (now revived) university. The new **Museu di a Corsica** (*open summer daily 10–8, mid-Sept–Mar Wed–Sat 10–6; adm*), at the top of the town, has excellent changing exhibitions on all aspects of the island, as well as an important ethnographic collection. A narrow road from Corte penetrates the magnificent **Gorges de la Restonica**, which rise towards glacial lakes and the island's second peak, **Monte Rotondo**.

Between Corte and the east coast are the picturesque mountain villages of the **Castagniccia**, where the Genoese established a thriving chestnut tree economy; once an island staple, the chestnuts are now used for sweets, fattening wild pigs and brewing a tasty chestnut beer called Pietra. After the mountains, the citrus and vine-covered **Eastern Plain** south of the Castagniccia is rather dull, but here you'll find **Aléria**, founded by the Greeks in 564 BC, who nicknamed the island Kallisté, 'the most beautiful'. Later the island's Roman capital, the ruined city can be visited, but best of all is the nearby **Musée Jérôme Carcopino** (*open daily 8–12 and 2–5, to 7pm in summer*), filled with a prize collection of Greek vases found on the site.

Ajaccio and Dila dei Monti

Sunny **Ajaccio**, Corsica's little Paris, gave the world Napoleon Bonaparte, and has laid low ever since. The locals tend to view their ambitious famous son as a sell-out to the French, but he's what the punters come to see, so Ajaccio obliges with a plethora of embarassing statues, the shrine-like **Salon Napoléonien** in the Hôtel de Ville, and his birthplace, the **Maison Bonaparte** (stripped of most of its original furnishings). Best of all is the **Musée Fesch** (*closed Mon Oct–Mar*), housing the art collection accumulated by Cardinal Fesch, Madame Bonaparte's half-brother, who picked up plenty of masterpieces 'liberated' by his nephew's Grand Armée, including a Botticelli, a Veronese and a Titian. Sandy coves line the road from Ajaccio to the pretty **Iles Sanguinaires**; bigger beaches rim the gulf around **Porticcio**.

Corsica's most intriguing prehistoric site, **Filitosa** (*open Easter–Oct daily 9–7; adm*), is well signposted off the main N196 from Ajaccio to Propriano. Of all the Neolithic peoples in the Mediterranean, the Corsicans sculpted the most naturalistic human features on their statue-menhirs. But who do they represent? According to archaeologist Roger Grosjean, they are portraits of Corsica's Bronze Age invaders, the Torréens, who arrived c. 1700 BC. The Torréens later used these supposed portraits of themselves to build the walls of their citadel. The whole is shrouded in mystery, emphasized by the faces staring out of the night of time.

Nearby **Propriano** is a brash overbuilt resort by Corsican standards. In contrast, just south, the stalwart granite town of **Sartène** was labelled by Prosper Mérimée as 'the most Corsican of Corsican towns', where barons feuded and vendettas consumed the passions of generations; more benignly, it is now a key place in the revival of the island's ancient choral music, or polyphonies, sung by the Scola di cantu di Sarté, under Ghjuvan-Paulu Poletti. The Sartène region is also rich in Neolithic and Torréen sites, which you can learn about in the town's **Musée de la Préhistoire Corse** (*closed Sun; also Sat from Oct to May*). The most important of these is the 1500 BC Torréen site of **Pianu di Levie**, inland from Sartène (*t 04 95 78 48 21 for opening hours*). The spectacular mountain scenery in these parts culminates in the famous granite needles and wind-tormented pines of the **Col de Bavella**, along the D268.

On Corsica's southeast coast the big noise is **Porto-Vecchio**, a handsome medieval walled citadel town that over the past two decades has spread to become the most flagrant holiday target on the island, especially popular with Italians (Corsica, after all, is only 70km from Livorno, compared to 300km from Marseille); the gorgeous beaches to the south are only a short drive away. The south tip of Corsica – an hour's ferry ride from Sardinia – is guarded by **Bonifacio**, one of the most remarkable towns in France, where lofty medieval houses balance precariously on a narrow ridge over a fjord of white cliffs and sea caves, which you can visit by boat.

Languedoc-Roussillon

21

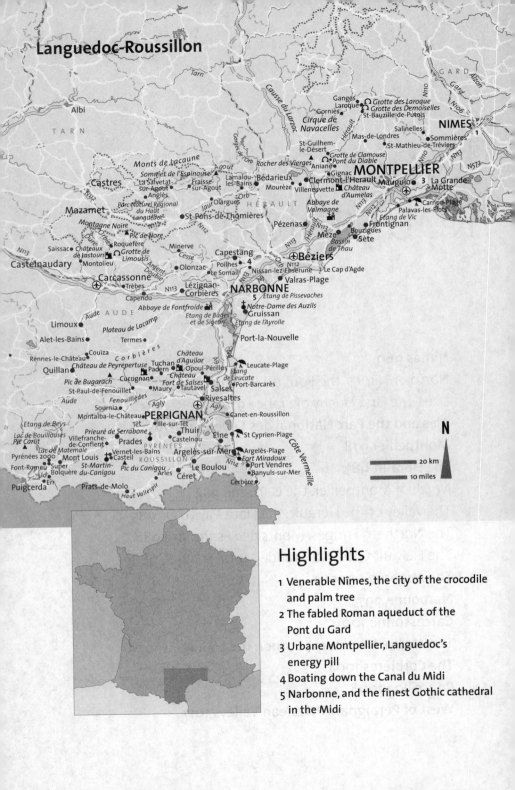

Languedoc-Roussillon

Highlights

1 Venerable Nîmes, the city of the crocodile and palm tree
2 The fabled Roman aqueduct of the Pont du Gard
3 Urbane Montpellier, Languedoc's energy pill
4 Boating down the Canal du Midi
5 Narbonne, and the finest Gothic cathedral in the Midi

N

20 km
10 miles

Food and Wine

Castelnaudary's beans, combined with pork, sausage and *confits*, go into *cassoulet*, the totem dish of Languedoc; in second place comes *brandade de morue*, a salt cod purée with garlic. In the old days that was about it in France's 'culinary desert'. Now arty influences from Provence and Catalan *nouvelle cuisine*, the rage in Barcelona, have met and collided in Languedoc, and you'll find no end of Mediterranean surprises. The biggest revolution of all has been in the wines: a fresh emphasis in quality rather than quantity has made the region one of the rising stars on the French wine charts: Corbières and Minervois are the two biggest regions, but don't neglect smaller regions like Fougères and La Clape, or Banyuls, France's answer to port.

Languedoc-Roussillon is France's 'other' Mediterranean province, with rugged sun-baked scenery, long sandy beaches, and more vineyards producing more tons of wine than any other region in France. It flourished under the Romans – *see* Nîmes, below, and the Pont du Gard, p.974 – and under the counts of Toulouse, until the 13th-century Albigensian Crusaders destroyed its civilization (the name Languedoc comes from its language, Occitan, where *oc* meant yes). When the region began to revive in the 16th century, it embraced Protestantism. The subsequent Wars of Religion and Revocation of the Edict of Nantes were tremendous setbacks; in the 19th century phylloxera destroyed the wine industry and brought economic ruin.

In 1959, Leo Larguier of the Académie Goncourt wrote of Languedoc, 'Talent has never flowered again, and the genius is forever dead.' His obituary now seems premature: the dawn of the 21st century finds Montpellier one of the most dynamic and progressive cities in France, with Nîmes nipping at its heels. The handsome cities of Narbonne, Béziers and Perpignan have rubbed the sleep from their eyes. As Provence begins to seem all full up (and expensive), Languedoc-Roussillon is gaining a reputation as the great alternative; come here to discover the lazy charms of the Canal du Midi; the art towns of Collioure, Céret, Uzès, and Pézenas; the impossible Cathar castles of the Corbières; the National Park of the Cévennes; Carcassonne, Canigou, mysterious Rennes-le-Château, and Castelnaudary's ultimate mess of beans.

Nîmes

Geography dealt Nîmes a pair of trump cards: first, a mighty spring, and second, a position on the road from Italy to Spain. The Romans paved it and called it the Via Domitia, and turned Celtic Nîmes into their Colonia Nemausensis. Augustus endowed Nîmes with the Maison Carrée, a sanctuary, an aqueduct (the Pont du Gard) to augment the water supply, and its walls.

Nîmes, like much of Languedoc, got into trouble with the Church in the early 13th century by taking up the Cathar heresy, although at the approach of the terrible Simon de Montfort the city surrendered without a fight. Catholicism never went down well in Nîmes, and when the Protestant alternative presented itself in the 16th century,

Nîmes

RUE STEPH. MALLERME

Tour Magne

Mt Cavalier

Nymphée

Temple de Diane

Jardin de la Fontaine

RUE MENARD

RUE DE LA LAMPEZE

RUE DE LA TOUR MAGNE

ROUGET DE L'ISLE

RUE PASTEUR

PONT DE VIERNE

QUAI DE LA FONTAINE

DE LA PLACE A. BRIAND

QUAI

RUE GRETRY

RUE DES CHASSAINTES

RUE DE LA LAMPEZE

RUE BADUEL

RUE DU FORT

Castellum

RUE DE LA BAUME

CLERISEAU

PLACE DE LA REVOLUTION

Carré d'Art

St Paul

SQUARE ANTONIN

RUE DUGNON COUVENT

R. DU MURIER D'ESPAGNE

RUE LITTRE

PLACE D'ASSAS

BD A. DAUDET

RUE AUGUSTE

Maison Carrée

PLACE DE LA MAISON CARREE

Théâtre

PLACE DE L'HORLOGE

RUE DE LA MADELEINE

RUE GENERAL PERRIER

Post Office ✉

BOULEVARD GAMBETTA

PLACE ST CHARLES

R. DU CHATEAU FADAISE

RUE STANISLAS CLEMENT

RUE EMILE JAMAIS

RUE DELON SOUBEYRAN

RUE BECDELIEVRE

RUE DU MAIL

RUE EMILE ZOLA

RUE LA PLACETTE

RUE BIGOT

RUE ST MATHIEU

RUE PORTE DE FRANCE

RUE L'HOTEL DIEU

RUE DAGOBERT

BD VICTOR HUGO

RUE DE L'ETOILE

RUE DE L'ASPIC

PLACE AUX HERBES

Les Halles

PLACE BELE CROIX

RUE NATIONALE

Notre-Dame-et-St-Castor

R. LACROIX

Musée du Vieux Nîmes

RUE DU CHAPITRE

RUE DOREE

Hôtel de Ville

RUE DES GREFFES

PLACE DE LA SALAMANDRE

PLACE DU MARCHE

PLACE DES ARENES

Palais de Justice

Les Arènes

BD DES ARENES

PLACE DES ARENES

RUE A. DUCROS

RUE REBOUT

PLACE DU CHATEAU

Porte d'Auguste 🏛

PLACE D'AUGUSTE

RUE CURATERIE

GRAND RUE

R. POISE

St-Ignace

RUE AMIRAL

Musée Archéologique 🏛

Ste-Perpétue

BD DE LA LIBERATION

ESPL. CH. DE GAULLE

BD DE PRAGUE

Synagogue ✡

RUE CARNOT

AVENUE PRADIER

RUE ROUSSY

BD ET SAINTENAC

St-Baudile

RUE VINCENT FAITA

RUE DE BEAUCAIRE

RUE SEGUIER

RUE NOTRE-DAME

RUE FENELON

AVENUE FEUCHERES

P

P

Chapelle

Post Office ✉

BD DE BRUXELLES

POL Police

Gare

AVENUE FEUCHERES

RUE JEANNE D'ARC

RUE MARC

RUE BRICONNET

BD DE BRUXELLES

BOULEVARD TALABOT

AVENUE JEAN JAURES

AVENUE GEORGES POMPIDOU

R. FRANÇOIS IER

RUE ERNEST RENAN

RUE DU CIRQUE ROMAIN

PLACE SEVERINE

RUE HENRI ESPERANDIEU

AVENUE JEAN JAURES

RUE DHUODA

RUE HENRI IV

RUE GENERAC

PLACE MONTCALM

St François-de-Salles

RUE DE JAQUEDUC

RUE CHARLES MARTEL

RUE DE LA REPUBLIQUE

RUE ST REMY

RUE HENRI IV

RUE SAINT

RUE BOURDALOUE

RUE DE LA CITE FOULC

Musée des Beaux-Arts 🏛

RUE BOSSUET

RUE DE ST GILLES

LE PLANAS

CHARLEMAGNE

RUE

RUE ANDRE SIMON

BOULEVARD SERGENT TRIAIRE

RUE PIERRE GAMEL

RUE DE PLANAS

RUE

FELICITE

Gare Routière

RUE DE MARRONNIERS

SAINTE

RUE DU DR CALMETTE

RUE DE LA TOUR DE LEVEQUE

N

300 metres
300 yards

To Aquatropique ↙

To Airport ↓

To L'Orangerie & Arles ↘

Getting Around

By air: Air France has 3 to 4 flights a day from Paris-Orly to Nîmes-Garons airport, t 04 66 70 49 49. Ryanair flies from London-Stansted to Nîmes once a day, t 04 66 70 49 51. Shuttle buses run 8km from between the airport and Nîmes (Palais de Justice).

By train: Nîmes' station, at the south end of Av Feuchères, has direct trains to Carcassonne, Montpellier, Arles, Orange and Marseille; and TGVs to Paris and Lille.

By bus: destinations include the Pont du Gard, Uzès, St-Gilles, Aigues-Mortes, Le Grau du Roi, La Grande Motte, Avignon, and Montpellier.

Tourist Information

Nîmes: 6 Rue Auguste, t 04 66 58 38 00, f 04 66 21 81 04, www.ot-nimes.fr. Also in the train station, with a hotel booking service, t 04 66 84 18 13.

Where to Stay

Nîmes ☒ 30000

★★★★**Impérator Concorde**, Quai de la Fontaine, t 04 66 21 90 30, f 04 66 67 70 25 (*expensive*). An old dowager with a recent facelift; a lovely garden, TVs, air-conditioning, and Nîmes' top restaurant, **L'Enclos de la Fontain** where the chef cooks up classics and imaginative dishes like veal with fresh fig *beignets* (*menus 155 (lunch only)–360F*).

★★★**New Hotel La Baume**, 21 Rue Nationale, t 04 66 76 28 42, f 04 66 76 28 45. Stylish modern rooms (*moderate*) in a 17th-century mansion with a garden terrace and restaurant (*menus 90 and 110F*).

★★★**L'Hacienda**, Chemin du Mas de Brignon, Marguerittes (☒ 30320), 8km northeast on N86, t 04 66 75 02 25, f 04 66 75 45 58 (*moderate*). A large farmhouse in the *garrigue*, converted into a hotel with an equally spacious swimming pool, terraces, and an excellent restaurant (*menus 195 and 265F, dinner only*).

★★**Le Lisita**, 2 Bd des Arènes, t 04 66 67 29 15, f 04 66 67 25 32 (*inexpensive*). Next to the amphitheatre, the *toreros'* favourite is owned by an enthusiastic bullfighting fan, who has given his rooms Spanish and rustic Languedocien furnishings.

★★**Royal**, 3 Bd Alphonse-Daudet (just off Place d'Assas), t 04 66 67 28 36, f 04 66 58 28 28 (*inexpensive*). A delightful Art Deco hotel with artistic rooms and a palm-fronded lobby; reserve early in the summer.

three-quarters of the population switched. After nearly being ruined by the Revocation of the Edict of Nantes by Louis XIV, Nîmes went back to its second concern after religion: textiles. Its heavy-duty blue *serge de Nîmes* was reduced to the more familiar 'denim' in 1695, in London – where many of the Protestants went in exile – and it was exported widely. Some of it found its way to California, where in 1848 a certain Levi Strauss discovered it to be perfect for outfitting goldrushers.

Built of stone the colour of old piano keys, Nîmes disputes with Arles the title of the 'Rome of France'. With its new Carré d'Art designed by Sir Norman Foster, the city also vies for avant-garde cultural supremacy in this corner of France with Montpellier. But what really makes the juices flow in Nîmes is not modern architecture, but bulls. Nîmes is passionate about its *ferias*, featuring top matadors from France, Spain and Portugal.

Les Arènes and the Maison Carrée

Twentieth in size, but the best-preserved of the 70 surviving amphitheatres of the Roman world, the **arena** at Nîmes (late 1st century AD) is just a bit smaller than its twin at Arles (*open 9–6.30; winter 9–12 and 2–5; Oct–April free guided tours; closed*

★★Plaza, 10 Rue Roussy (off Bd Amiral Courbet), t 04 66 76 16 20, f 04 66 67 65 99 (*inexpensive*). Old house, now an air-conditioned hotel with retro furnishings.

★★L'Amphithéatre, 4 Rue des Arenes, t 04 66 67 28 51, f 04 66 67 07 79 (*inexpensive*). Sweetly restored 18th-century building, with antiques and big bathrooms.

Auberge de Jeunesse, Chemin de la Cigale, t 04 66 23 25 04, f 04 66 23 84 27. On a hill 2km from the centre (bus no.2 from the station or no.8 from town; bus stop: Stade Villeverte).

Eating Out

Magister, 5 Rue Nationale, t 04 66 76 11 00. A smart restaurant (the *brandade* and stuffed pigeon are recommended), and a good local wine list (*menus 185–280F*).

Jardin d'Hadrien, 11 Rue Enclos Rey, t 04 6 6 21 86 65. A current favourite, with its beamed dining room and veranda; try the cod simply cooked with olive oil or courgette flowers stuffed with *brandade* (*menus 95–150F*).

Aux Plaisirs des Halles, 4 Rue Littré, t 04 66 36 01 02. Cosy little bistro near the market for *aïoli* with vegetables or *brandade* with truffles and black olives (*menus: lunch 88–190F, dinner 140–250F*).

Nicolas, Rue Poise, just off Bd Amiral Courbet, t 04 66 67 50 47. One of the more affordable fine restaurants in town, and always busy (*menus 70–142F*).

La Belle Respire, 12 Rue de l'Etoile, t 04 66 21 27 21. Fine cooking in the unusual decor of Nîmes' former bordello, in the historic centre (*menus 69–128F*).

Au Flan Coco, 31 Rue du Mûrier d'Espagne, t 04 66 21 84 81. Delightful and tiny, run by two *traiteurs* alongside their shop; the food comes fresh from the market and is whipped up before your eyes (*menu 94F*). *Closed eves, except Sat, and mid-Aug.*

Entertainment and Nightlife

Tickets and reservations for events at Les Arènes are available from the Bureau de Location des Arènes, Rue Alexandre Ducros, t 04 66 67 28 02. In town the hottest spots are **Café Napoléon** and **Café de Petite Bourse**, both on Boulevard Victor Hugo.

La Movida, on La Placette, t 04 66 67 80 90.For music, cafe-theatre and tireless animation with a flamenco flair. *Closed Sun and three weeks in Aug.*

public hols and days of concerts; adm). Like the Maison Carrée, it escaped being cannibalized for its stone by being put to constant use – as a castle for the Visigoths and the knightly militia of the Frankish viscounts, then after union with France, as a slum, housing some 2,000 people.

When new, the arena could accommodate 24,000 people, who could reach or leave their seats in only a few minutes thanks to an ingenious system of five concentric galleries and 126 stairways. Near the top are holes pierced in the stone for the supports of the awning that sheltered the spectators from sun and rain – an idea revived in 1988, but with a mobile plexiglass and aluminium roof that allows it to host events year round. The event that has packed the crowds in since 1853 is the *corrida*, a sport always close to the hearts of the Nîmois.

To the north stands Nîmes' ragamuffin **Cathédrale Notre-Dame-et-St-Castor**, which was consecrated in 1096 but flattened by rampaging Huguenots in 1597 and 1622, who spared only the campanile to use as a watchtower. Across the façade runs a vigorous frieze of Old Testament scenes. There's another good Romanesque frieze nearby, in Place aux Herbes, this time adorning a rare, well-preserved 12th-century house (**Maison Romane**).

Then there's the best-preserved Roman temple anywhere, the graceful little 1st-century BC **Maison Carrée** just off the Via Domitia (*open summer 9–6.30; winter 9–12.30 and 2–6*). Built by the great General Agrippa, who also built the Pantheon in Rome, the temple was dedicated to the imperial cult of Augustus' grandsons, Caius and Lucius. Known as 'Carrée' or square, because of its right angles and 'long' square shape (85 by 50ft), its *cella* (cult sanctuary) and the Corinthian columns of the porch are perfectly intact. Nîmes always found it useful for something, most notably as the meeting hall of the Consuls and least notably as a stable. It now houses a small museum which includes a 1st-century painting of *personnages grotesques* discovered in 1992 when Carré d'Art was built.

The Maison Carrée is overlooked by Sir Norman Foster's **Carré d'Art** (*open 10–6, closed Mon, adm; the museum also offers free guided tours Mon–Fri at 4.30, weekends and holidays 3 and 4.30*). Inaugurated in May 1993, this palace of glass and steel houses a modern art museum, audiovisual centre and extensive library. The ancient columns of the Maison Carrée are reflected in Sir Norman's own slender columns of steel; the walls and even the stairways are of glass to let light stream through the building. Inside, the **Musée d'Art Contemporain** on the first floor contains post-1960 works.

Jardin de la Fontaine and the Tour Magne

A short stroll to the west down Quai de la Fontaine is the great spring that origi-nates in the karst caverns of the *garrigue* to gush out at the foot of Mont Cavalier. It was domesticated in the 18th century as the lovely **Jardin de la Fontaine**, a kind of neo-Roman nymphaeum; of the many Roman sanctuaries here only the ruins of a temple of Diana survive. Paths wind up Mont Cavalier to the oldest Roman monu-ment in Gaul, the octagonal 106ft **Tour Magne** (*open summer 9–7, winter 9–5; adm*). No record of its origin has survived: it may have been a trophy dedicated to the opening of the Via Domitia, or a signal tower, or simply the mightiest of the 30 towers in the city wall, originally standing some 150ft high.

Museum-crawling

Two museums share the former Jesuit college at 13 bis Blvd Amiral Courbet: the **Musée Archéologique**, with a striking Celtic lintel found at Nages, with a frieze of galloping horses and human heads, and the old-fashioned **Musée d'Histoire Naturelle et de Préhistoire**, home to a collection of two-headed lambs and so on, and those mysterious menhirs-with-personality, the statue-steles (*both open 10–6, closed Mon; joint adm*). For the **Musée de Vieux Nîmes**, with an exceptional collection of 19th-century textiles and 500 print designs from Nîmes' wool and silk industries, follow Grand' Rue behind the museums, north to Rue Lacroix (*open 10–6, closed Mon; adm*). The **Musée des Beaux-Arts** is in Rue Cité-Foulc (*open 10–6, closed Mon; adm*). The ground floor is dedicated to an enormous Roman mosaic, while upstairs is a worthy provincial array of Venetian, Dutch and French paintings.

North of Nîmes: the Pont du Gard

By 19 BC, the spring of Nemausus could no longer slake Nîmes' thirst and a search was on for a new source. The Romans were obsessed with the quality of their water, and when they found a crystal-clear spring called the Eure near Uzès, the fact that it was 50km away hardly mattered to antiquity's star engineers. The resulting aqueduct, built under Augustus' son-in-law Agrippa, was like a giant needle hemming the landscape, piercing tunnels through hills and looping its arches over the open spaces of the *garrigues*, all measured precisely to allow a slope of .07 centimetres per metre.

No matter how many photos you've seen before, the Pont du Gard's three tiers of arches of golden stone without mortar makes a brave and lovely sight; since the 1920s the natural setting and river have been maintained as intact as possible. What the photos never show are the two million people who come to pay it homage every year, and you may well find it more evocative if you arrive very early in the morning or about an hour before sunset. As you walk over it, note how it's slightly curved (the better to stand up to floods) and how the Roman engineers left cavities and protruding stones to support future scaffolding. In the 18th century, the bottom tier was expanded to take a road, now fortunately limited to pedestrians, due to the damaging vibrations caused by cars.

Uzès, the First Duchy of France

Few towns of 8,000 souls have so bold a skyline of towers, or so little truck with the modern industrial world. Uzès seems to have been vacuum-packed when its wealthy Protestant merchants of cloth and silk stockings packed their bags and left at the Revocation of the Edict of Nantes. 'O little town of Uzès', wrote André Gide (whose father was a Uzètien) 'Were you in Umbria, the Parisians would flock to visit you!' Now they do, more or less. Houses tumbling into ruin have been repaired, creating the perfect stage for films like *Cyrano de Bergerac*.

Uzès' café life engulfs most available space around Place Albert I, just under the **Duché**, residence of the first dukes of France who picked up the title when the Duc de Montmorency lost his title and head in 1632 (*daily guided tours July–mid-Sept 10– 1 and 2–7, mid-Sept–June 10–1 and 2–6; adm exp*). The rectangular donjon called the **Tour Bermonde** was built over a Roman tower in the 10th or 11th century. The Renaissance façade in the central courtyard was built in 1550 and bears the dukes' motto: *Ferro non auro* ('iron, not gold' – i.e. they were warriors, not financiers).

Uzès is a lot smaller than it seems, and a short wander will soon bring you to the delightfully irregular, arcaded **Place aux Herbes**, for centuries the centre of public life. Set apart from the rest of the old town on a terrace, the **Ancien Palais Episcopal** (1671) was the seat of the powerful bishops of Uzès (64 bishops reigned here between the 5th century and the Revolution). A restoration attempt in the 1970s caused the interior to cave in, although the right wing is in good enough nick to hold the eclectic collections of the **Musée Municipal** (*open 3–6, closed Mon and Jan*) with its fossils,

Getting Around

Uzès is linked by frequent buses to Nîmes, Bagnols-sur-Cèze, Avignon, Alès and the Pont du Gard, t 04 66 22 00 58, or STD Gard, t 04 66 29 27 29.

STDG (t 04 66 29 27 29) coaches from Nîmes, Uzès, and Avignon pass within a kilometre of the Pont du Gard 8 or 9 times a day. Canoe and kayak hire is available upstream at Collias: contact Kayak Vert, t 04 66 22 80 76.

Tourist Information

Uzès: Chapelle des Capucins, Place Albert 1er, t 04 66 22 68 88, f 04 66 2 2 95 19.
Remoulins: 30210 Rue du Moulin d'Aure, t 04 66 37 22 34, f 04 66 37 22 01.

Where to Stay and Eat

Uzès ✉ 30700

***D'Entraigues, 8 Rue de la Calade, t 04 66 22 32 68, f 04 66 22 57 01 (*moderate*). A fine old hotel fit for a duke in a 15th-century building, with a pool suspended over the dining room and air conditioning; try to get a room near the top.

**Le Saint Genies, Route de St-Ambroix, t 04 66 22 29 99, f 04 66 03 14 89 (*inexpensive*). An oasis of tranquillity half a mile from the centre, with a charming pool and three-star rooms. *Closed Jan–mid-Feb.*

**La Taverne, 7 Rue Sigalon (just off Place Albert I), t 04 66 22 13 10, f 04 66 22 45 90 (*inexpensive*). Renovated rooms in the centre

of town, and the chance to dine at the restaurant, on a pretty garden terrace (*four good courses for 105F*).

Les Jardins de Castille, Place de l'Eveché, t 04 66 22 32 68. An elegant hotel-restaurant, with a classy 168F lunch menu – avocado salad with turkey gizzard *confits* (better than they sound) and roast guinea hen on a bed of braised cabbage.

Coté Jardin, Place Dampmartin, t 04 66 22 47 08. Menu changes daily; in the evening there's pizza, too (*menus 75–130F*). *Closed Sun and Mon out of season.*

Around Uzès ✉ 30700

***Marie d'Agoult, 4km west at Arpaillargues et Aureillac, t 04 66 22 14 48, f 04 66 22 56 10 (*moderate*). Marie d'Agoult was Liszt's muse and a frequent guest at this 18th-century château. Antique beds, pool, tennis courts, and the garden restaurant serves a fine 145F menu and, for a bit more, dishes with truffles. *Closed Nov–Mar.*

L'Auberge de St-Maximin, St-Maximin, 6km south of Uzès, t 04 66 22 26 41. Some of the best food in the area is served on this garden terrace, where they do wonderful things with asparagus and other local products (*menus 150–250F*). *Closed Mon and Tues except evenings in summer, and Nov–Mar.*

Jean and Diane Donnet's bed and breakfast, La Capelle-Masmolène, t 04 66 37 11 33, f 04 66 37 15 21. Owned by a hot-air balloon pilot, this comes complete with a pool. Also contact Jean Donnet about flights over Uzès in his *montgolfière*.

ceramics, paintings, and memorabilia of the Gide family. Behind stretches the pleasant **Promenade des Marroniers**, while adjacent is the **Cathédrale St-Théodorit**, built in 1663. The quaint neo-Romanesque façade was tacked on in 1875, with the idea of making a better partner to the stunning 12th-century **Tour Fenestrelle** spared by the Protestants only because they found it useful as a watchtower. Unique in France, the 137ft tower is encircled by six storeys of double-lit windows, inspired by the Romanesque campaniles of Ravenna and Lombardy. The cathedral's interior was severely damaged during the Revolution, when it was converted into a Temple of Reason, leaving only the peculiar upper gallery with its wrought-iron railing and the cathedral's pride and joy: a splendid **organ** of 1670, the only one in France to have retained its original painted shutters.

Bagnols-sur-Cèze

North of Uzès, Bagnols-sur-Cèze is the traditional gateway to Languedoc, and although it's not much in itself, its **Musée de Peinture Albert André** (*open 10–12 and 2–6, summer 3–7; closed Tues, Feb and hols; adm*) was nothing less than the first provincial museum of contemporary art in France, thanks to André, a friend of Renoir's. In 1924, however, it all burned down during a firemen's ball. It was a blessing in disguise: André sent an SOS out to the French art world, and was able to cover his walls with works by Bonnard, Marquet, Matisse, Picacco, Renoir, Signac, and Gauguin.

Alès and the Parc National des Cévennes

The big town of the northern Gard, **Alès**, was known as the Ville Noire or 'Black Town' for its coal mines and industry; events here inspired Zola's *Germinal*. Since 1980, however, this little piece of Lorraine in the south has pretty much closed shop; for a

The Camisards

Louis XIV may have been the Sun King, but nearly everything he did eclipsed the rest of France. One of his greatest blunders was the Revocation of the Edict of Nantes in 1685, undoing all the good work of his grandfather Henri IV, who declared for religious tolerance. As absolutist Louis saw it, French power depended on the country's universal Catholicism. As all the Protestants who could left for exile in Germany, England and Holland, greatly benefiting those countries, many parts of France, including Languedoc, faced bankruptcy. Those who remained in France faced severe repression. The shepherds of the Cévennes were fervent Huguenots who had nowhere else to go, were persecuted, and at the end of the 17th century, were swept by a religious revival that brought forth prophets, declaring that the dark days would soon come to an end. To speed up the process, they revolted in 1702, determined to destroy their Catholic oppressors. Known as the Camisards for the white shirts (*camisas*) they wore to identify themselves while fighting at night, they were led by a baker's apprentice, Jean Cavalier, a brilliant guerilla leader, ambushing the king's armies and defeating his finest regiments, hiding out in the mountains that they knew so well, and enjoying the support of the local population. Louis responded with a policy of extermination, destroying hundreds of villages and killing all their inhabitants. Cavalier's loss of his arsenal forced him to ask for a truce in 1704, but as the king still refused to let the Protestants worship in peace, his followers deserted him and he was forced to flee (he went on to become a brigadier general in the British Army). Without him, the revolt wound down, although resistance continued right up to the Edict of Tolerance in 1787.

The best places to learn about the Protestant resistance is the Musée du Désert at the Mas Soubeyran, 11km from St-Jean-de-Gard (*open Mar–Nov daily 9.30–12 and 2.30–6, July and Aug without break*). Desert was the biblical name the Protestants gave the Cévennes as the wilderness of their exile, and the museum poignantly brings the hard cruel years to life.

vivid lesson in industrial archaeology, you can take a tour of the galleries of an abandoned mine at the **Mine Témoin**, just outside town at Rochebelle (*open Apr–Nov 9–12.30 and 2–5.30; June–Aug 9.30–7; arrive at least 90 minutes before the closing time; adm*). Today Alès would prefer to be known as the southern gateway to the Cévennes, the wild and mostly mountainous country of upper Languedoc. It prospered in past centuries, when the Crusaders brought back the secret of silk; mulberry trees were planted everywhere, and the industry reached its peak in the 19th century, then dwindled with the invention of synthetics. The last mill closed in 1965. A wholesale rural exodus has left it one of the most unspoiled areas of France, and in 1970 the **Parc National des Cévennes** was created to protect its rich range of flora and fauna, both in an inaccessible core area, but also in a wide peripheral area that encompasses much of the northern Gard and southern Lozère, including the Gorges du Tarn (*see* p.535). One fun way to explore it is to follow the tracks of Robert Louis Stevenson, who was fascinated with the Camisards, and spent 12 days walking along a trail now named after him, with a donkey named Modestine: the origin of his *Travels with a Donkey in the Cévennes* (1879); contact the park office in Florac for details of local donkey stables and maps.

Sommières

Between Nîmes and Montpellier, hidden under the cliffs of the river Vidourle, Sommières only suffers moderately from the usual plagues besetting picturesque southern villages: the Parisians, the English, the trinket shops – it even has to do without a famous writer, since longtime resident Lawrence Durrell died in 1990. Its streets and squares are well worn and well lived in, with faded shop signs, flowers under every window and huge plane trees.

Before Sommières, there was Sommières' **bridge**, built by Tiberius between AD 19 and 31. Oddly, almost half of the bridge is now hidden inside the town; medieval Sommières expanded into the dry parts of the river-bed, and eventually an embankment was built. **The Tour de l'Horloge**, the entrance to the town, was built over the bridge's fifth arch in 1659. The other arches of the bridge lie under Rue Marx Dormoy, the street leading from the bridge to **Place des Docteurs Dax**, a lovely 12th-century market square that everyone in Sommières still calls by its old name, the **Marché-Bas**. The houses are all built on stone arcades: in the old days, the square would be

Tourist Information

Sommières: Rue Général-Bruyère, t 04 66 80 99 30, f 04 66 80 06 95.

Where to Stay and Eat

Sommières ✉ 30250

Hôtel d'Orange, Chemin du Château Fort, t 04 66 77 79 94, f 04 66 80 44 87 (*moderate*). A 17th-century building, lovingly converted into a guesthouse, with a pool and garage, but only six rooms, so book; ask to see the *baume*, or cave.

***Auberge du Pont Romain, 2 Av E. Jamais, t 04 66 80 00 58, f 04 66 80 31 52 (*inexpensive*). Lovely, spacious rooms in a 19th-century herbal distillery close to the river, with a pool, and a gourmet restaurant serving the house foie gras and other delights on a peaceful garden terrace (*menus 125–250F*). *Closed mid-Jan–mid-Mar*.

L'Olivette, 11 Rue Abbe Fabre, t 04 66 80 97 71. A local favourite, serving regional cuisine with an orignal twist, such as duck with balsamic vinegar and *oeufs en meurette langeudocienne* (eggs cooked in red wine; *menus 75–185F*).

Manoir du Cazalet, Route de Junas, t 04 66 80 87 60, f 04 66 80 87 65. In a 16th-century *mas*, a good classic restaurant (*menus from 125F; the 395F menu offers a six-course feast, each course with its own wine*).

L'Evasion, 6 Rue Paulin Capmal, t 04 66 77 74 64. At lunchtime, watch the life of the Marché Bas pass by from an outdoor table; the menu is none too complicated: medallion of veal, frog legs and pizza (*46–98F*). *Closed Sun eve and lunch*.

underwater every spring, forcing the market up two streets to the **Marché-Haut** (now Place Jaurès). The web of lanes radiating from these squares have their share of handsome 17th-century *hôtels particuliers*.

Montpellier

Montpellier's reputation as a centre of medicine began in the 13th century with the formation of a *Universitas Medicorum*, and later a *studium* of law. In 1349 the Catalan Kings of Majorca sold Montpellier to France for 120,000 golden écus. A period of relative peace and prosperity followed until the 1560s, when the university academics and tradesmen embraced the Reformation. For the next 70 years much of what Montpellier had achieved was wiped out. In 1622 Louis XIII came in person to besiege the city and reassert royal authority.

Putting its merchant republic days behind it, Montpellier settled down to the life of a university town and regional capital of a wine region. The Revolution passed without kicking up much dust; a far bigger crisis for Montpellier occurred in the 1890s, when phylloxera knocked out the vineyards. Until 1977 and the election of the irrepressible Socialist Mayor Georges Frêche (now in his fifth term), Montpellier was a pleasant, sleepy university backwater of fawn-coloured stone. With his Paris-sized projects, notably the monumental new quarter called Antigone, Frêche has made Montpellier a European model for innovative and effective city government. Now trumpeted as the 'Capital of Southern Europe' and 'the Rome of Tomorrow', this is one live-wire of a city, progressive, fun and friendly.

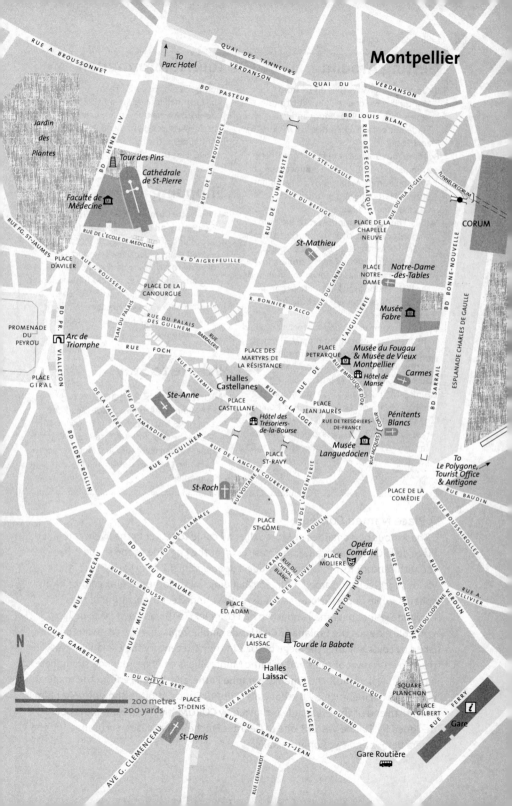

Getting Around

By air: British Airways flies direct from Montpellier to London daily. Air Littoral serves Nice, Lyon, Strasbourg and Bordeaux, or take Air France to Paris, t 04 67 20 85 00.

By train: You can race here from Paris in 4hrs 40mins on the TGV, or catch direct trains to Avignon, Nîmes, Marseille, Nice, Perpignan, Béziers, Narbonne, Agde, Lunel, Sète, Carcassonne and Toulouse.

By bus: The coach station, next to the train station, t 04 67 92 01 43, has buses to Nîmes, La Grande Motte, Béziers, Aigues-Mortes, etc.; every 20mins bus no.17 trundles down to the sea at Palavas. In town, you may find the little Petibus vans useful to get around the pedestrian zones of the Ecusson and Antigone.

By tram: In summer 2000 Montpellier opened the first stage of its tram project. The first line crosses the city centre from southwest to northeast. Information from TAM, t 04 67 22 87 87, or the tourist office.

Car hire: The big firms are at the airport, or try Avis at 900 Av Prés-d'Arènes, t 04 67 92 51 92, or Hertz France, 18 Rue Jules-Ferry, t 04 67 58 65 18. For a less expensive used car try A.D.A., 58 bis Av Clemenceau, t 04 67 58 34 35.

Tourist Information

Montpellier: Allée du Tourisme, Le Triangle, just off the Place de la Comédie, t 04 67 60 60 60, *www.herault-en-languedoc.com*. Also in the station, t 04 67 22 08 80, and at Antigone, at the motorway exit, t 04 67 22 06 16, f 04 67 22 38 10.

Shopping

Caves Notre Dame, 1348 Av de la Mer, t 04 67 64 48 00, is an excellent source for local wines and offers tastings; others, along with a good range of local food products from olive oil to caviar, are sold at the Maison Regionale des Vins et des Produits du Terroir, 34 Rue Saint-Guilhem, t 04 67 60 40 41. For English books and videos, there's Steve Davis' Bookshop, 4 Rue de l'Université, t 04 67 66 09 08.

Where to Stay

Montpellier ⊠ 30400

★★★★Alliance Métropole, 2 Rue Clos-René, t 04 67 58 11 22, f 04 67 92 13 02 (*expensive*). Top of the line: antique-furnished, with a quiet garden courtyard and air conditioning, between the train station and Place de la Comédie.

A Place Named Comédie

The various personalities of Montpellier all come together in the lively, café-lined **Place de la Comédie**, locally known as *l'Œuf*, or the Egg, due to the shape it had in the 18th century. Its ornaments include a *doppelgänger* of the Paris Opera, and various 19th-century larded bourgeois buildings with domes reminiscent of bathyspheres, while opposite looms a modern glass-and-steel semi-ziggurat, the **Polygone**, a shopping mall and town hall complex. To the north of Place de la Comédie extends the **Esplanade Charles de Gaulle**, replacing the city walls demolished by Louis XIII after the siege of 1622. In the 18th century the Esplanade was planted with rows of trees and became Montpellier's chief promenade; along here is a rare survival of 1908, the **Cinématographe Pathé**, a little palace from the magical early days of cinema (now the Rabelais Cultural Centre; it often shows foreign films). The north end of the Esplanade is flanked by **CORUM**, 'the House of Innovation' designed by Claude Vasconi, one of Georges Frêche's showcases, encompassing the Opéra Berlioz and two congress halls.

***Demeure des Brousses**, Rte des Vauguières, 4km east on the D24 towards the Château de la Mogère, t 04 67 65 77 66, f 04 67 22 22 17 (*moderate*). If you have a car, the most charming place to stay is this 18th-century ivy-covered *mas*, surrounded by a vast park. It has an excellent restaurant to boot (*menus 145–280F*).

***La Maison Blanche**, 1796 Av de la Pompignane (off the route to Carnon), t 04 99 58 20 70, f 04 67 79 53 39. Another gem requiring your own transport: 38 rooms in a big, balconied house that escaped from the French quarter of New Orleans, surrounded by a 5-hectare park. The restaurant has a menu for 150F.

Parc, 8 Rue Achille Bège, t 04 67 41 16 49, f 04 67 54 10 05 (*inexpensive*). An 18th-century *hôtel particulier*, fitted out with air conditioning, TVs, etc.

Palais, 3 Rue du Palais, t 04 67 60 47 38, f 04 67 60 40 23 (*inexpensive*). A recently restored building, with a charming breakfast room.

Nice, 14 Rue Boussairolles, t 04 67 58 42 54 (*inexpensive*). Very pretty and flowery, on a dull street near the station.

*Les Arceaux**, 35 Bd Arceaux, t 04 67 92 03 03, f 04 67 92 05 09 (*cheap*). Clean and comfortable, with a small garden.

*Les Fauvettes**, 8 Rue Bonnard, t 04 67 63 17 60, f 04 67 63 09 09 (*cheap*). Good value for money near the Jardin des Plantes, with

quiet rooms overlooking interior courtyards. *Closed 20 Dec–3 Jan and 20 July–10 Aug.*

*Etuves**, 25 Rue des Etuves, t 04 67 60 78 19 (*cheap*). Cheap and comfortable.

Eating Out

Le Jardin de Sens, 11 Av St-Lazare (off the N113 towards Nîmes; bus no.4), t 04 99 58 38 38. One of the best restaurants in Languedoc, run by twins Jacques and Laurent Pourcel. Try the squid stuffed with ratatouille and crayfish tails, *bourride* and traditional *oreillette* pastries (*menus: lunch 290F, evening 495–715F*).

Le Chandelier, 3 Rue Leenhardt (off Rue du Grand St Jean), t 04 67 15 34 38. Another culinary temple (complete with columns), featuring well-polished versions of the classic French repertoire (*menus: lunch 155F, evening 220 and 400F*).

Le Petit Jardin, 20 Rue J Rousseau, t 04 67 60 78 78, f 04 67 66 16 79. In the centre, where you can dine in a delightful large shady garden with a view of the cathedral. Good local fish, salads, pasta (*menus 120–170F*).

L'Olivier, 12 Rue Aristide Olivier, t 04 67 92 86 28. A popular restaurant bang on the new tramway; Art Deco style, smooth service, classic cuisine and the best local wine, of course (*menus 185–200F*).

Antigone

East of Place de la Comédie lies another Frêche initiative: **Antigone**, a mostly moderate-income quarter with housing for 10,000 people, and shops and restaurants, all designed by trendy Barcelona architect Ricardo Bofill in 1979 and spread along a huge formal axis down to the river Lez. Bofill understood just what a Rome of Tomorrow needs: Mannerist neo-Roman arches, cornices, pilasters, and columns as big as California redwoods. On a bad day, Antigone looks like the surreal background to a De Chirico painting; on a good day, it seems like a delightful place to live, especially for kids, who can play football in the monumental Place du Millennium and still hear their parents call them in for lunch.

Musée Fabre

On Boulevard Sarrail, between the Cinématographe and CORUM, the Musée Fabre (*open 9–5.30, until 5 Sat and Sun, closed Mon; adm*) was long the main reason for visiting Montpellier, with one of the most important collections of art in provincial

Lively Rue des Ecoles Laïques and Place de la Chapelle Neuve make up Montpellier's Latin Quarter, where the colours, smells and live music from the Turkish, Greek, Spanish and Tunisian restaurants collide in gleeful discord.

Le Vieil Ecu, 1 Place de la Chapelle Neuve, t 04 67 66 39 44, f 04 67 72 71 01. Good food, served in the old chapel (*menus: lunch 70F, evening 110 and 135F*).

Les Puits Ste-Anne, 9 Rue de l'Amandier, t 04 67 60 82 77. A vast choice for its 56F menu, or you can splurge and get an extra course for 90F, with wine.

Tripti-Kulai, 20 Rue Jacques Cœur. A vegetarian restaurant and tea room that offers some exotic dishes: a good spot for an *inexpensive* light lunch.

Pizzeria du Palais, 22 Rue du Palais des Guilhem, t 04 67 60 67 97. Italian-run, with a wide choice of pizzas and other dishes, and always crowded (*about 70F*).

Entertainment and Nightlife

To find out what's going on, get a copy of the city weekly *La Gazette*; or visit FNAC, in the Polygone, which has tickets for most events. During the year, there are performances at the CORUM, t 04 67 61 66 16, home of L'Orchestre Philharmonique de Montpellier and Montpellier Danse, and the old Opéra Comédie, t 04 67 60 19 99, still puts on opera and theatrical performances.

In a city where a quarter of the population are students, nightlife is never going to be dull. One of the most lively clubs in Montpellier is Mimi la Sardine, out of the centre at 131 Avenue de Toulouse, t 04 67 99 67 77, offering music and dancing, pool and games. Otherwise head for the life-size red Cadillac implanted in the wall at Le Rockstore down from Place de la Comédie on Rue de Verdun, t 04 67 58 70 10. Most dance-nights there is free entry and drinks are inexpensive. On weekends and often weekdays there's live jazz, blues or world music at **Le Cargo**, 5 Rue du Grand St Jean, t 04 67 92 56 05; **Sax'Aphone**, 24 Rue Ernest-Michel, t 04 67 58 80 90; **l'Antrouille**, 12 Rue Anatole-France, t 04 67 58 75 28; **Le Fil**, 16 Rue du Pila St-Gély, t 04 67 66 20 67; **Cotton Pub**, 9 Place Laissac, t 04 67 92 21 60.

The latest thing in Montpellier are 'philosophy cafés', where certain nights are appointed for discussions from anything from astrology to theology. Try the following and check the local press or *La Gazette* for details: **Brasserie Le Dome**, 2 Av Clemenceauy, t 04 67 92 66 70; **Le Jam**, 100 Rue F. de Lesseps, t 04 67 02 75 52; **Café des Arts**; **Brasserie du Corum**, t 04 67 61 67 61.

France. The museum has six levels, with floors devoted to 17th-century painting, ceramics and painters from Montpellier. The superb collection on **Floor 5** was donated by the museum's great benefactor, Alfred Bruyas (1821–77). Born into a Montpellier banking family, Bruyas resolved the frustration of not being able to paint himself by befriending many of the artists of his day and asking them to paint him – there are 24 portraits of the red-bearded patron in this museum alone, lined up one after another, including examples by Delacroix and Alexandre Cabanel of Montpellier (1823–89). Four are by Gustave Courbet (1819–77), who became Bruyas' friend, and whose works are the highlight of the museum.

Into the Ecusson

There is nothing as compelling as the Musée Fabre in Montpellier's historic centre, the Ecusson; much was lost in the Wars of Religion, and even the many 17th- and 18th-century *hôtels particuliers*, as stuccoed and ornate as many of them are inside, show mostly blank walls to the street. But few cities in the south of France manage to be as pleasant and lively. The entire Ecusson is a pedestrian zone, and it's a delightful place for walking. One of the major crossroads of the Ecusson is Place Notre-Dame, under the cool gaze of the neoclassical **Notre-Dames-des-Tables** (1748). At the Hotel de Varennes in Place Pétrarque there's a pair of small museums devoted to the good old days. The **Musée du Fougau** ('the Foyer', *open Wed and Thurs 3–6*) preserves the arts and traditions of old Montpellier. The **Musée de Vieux Montpellier** (*open Tues–Sat 9.30–12 and 1.30–5; adm*) exhibits portraits of notables, and plans and views of the city from the 1500s on. At 7 Rue Jacques Cœur is the **Musée Languedocien** (*open daily exc Sun 2–5, July and Aug 3–6; guided tours on request; adm*), with Greek vases and pre-historic finds from the Hérault; an excellent collection of Romanesque sculpture; three 12th-century Islamic funeral steles, and a major collection of 16th- to 18th-century faïence made in Montpellier to round things off.

Western Quarters: the Promenade du Peyrou

Since the late 17th century the lofty west edge of Montpellier has been devoted to tons of mouldy fol-de-rol glorifying Louis XIV, beginning with an **Arc de Triomphe** (his triumphs include digging a canal, wrestling the English lion to the ground and conquering heresy with the bigoted Revocation of the Edict of Nantes). Beyond stretches the **Promenade du Peyrou**, a nice park spoiled by an equestrian statue of his megalomaniac majesty as big as the Trojan Horse. At the edge of the promontory stands the far more elegant **Château d'Eau**, a neoclassical temple designed to disguise the reservoir of the **Aqueduc St-Clément** (1771).

The waters feed the unicorn fountain in the nearby **Place de la Canourgue**, a charming 17th-century square. It looks down on the medieval monastery college of St-Benoît, built by papal architects from Avignon, used since 1795 as the **Faculté de Médecine**, housing an enormous medical library, and the **Musée Atger** (*open Mon, Wed and Fri 1.30–5.45, closed Aug; adm*), with a hoard of drawings mostly by the likes of Rigaud, Fragonard and Mignard but also by Flemish, Dutch, German and Italian schools of the 15th–18th centuries. Adjacent, the former monastic chapel has been Montpellier's **Cathédrale de St-Pierre** ever since the see was transferred here in 1563, although its status didn't spare it the usual depredations in the Wars of Religon and the Revolution. The cathedral's greatest distinction is its unusual porch, supported by two conical turrets. Beyond lies the lovely **Jardin des Plantes** (*open 10–7 in summer; 10–5 the rest of the year; closed Mon*), the oldest botanical garden in France, founded by a decree of Henri IV in 1593. It has several magnificent 400-year-old trees, exotic succulents, plants from the *garrigues*, and an *orangerie* .

The Hérault

For devotees of rural France, this seemingly innocuous area may be the ultimate find. Just enough tourists come for there to be plenty of country inns and *fermes-auberges*, though in most villages foreigners are still a novelty. The food is good; and there's enough wine to make anyone happy; the Hérault is the most prolific wine-producing region in France. It can be a perfect alternative to overcrowded and overpraised Provence: just as beautiful, more real and relaxed, full of things to see – and considerably less expensive.

North of Montpellier: the Garrigue

On a map, you'll notice lots of blank space in this region, a *pays* without a name. It is a geographer's textbook example of *garrigue*, a dry limestone plateau with sparse vegetation, where even sheep only just get by. The few villages seem huddled, closed into themselves.

From Montpellier, the best approach to the *garrigue* is by way of the D17 to St Mathieu-de-Tréviers, where you can pick up the D1/D122 west, a scenic high road that passes below **Pic St-Loup**, a lone, striking 2,110ft exclamation point. The D122 passes through the typical *garrigue* village of **Le Mas de Londres** before arriving at **St-Martin-de-Londres** (25km direct on the D986 from Montpellier). St-Martin is a surprise package. Passing the tiny, densely built village on the road, you would never guess it conceals one of the most exquisite medieval squares anywhere, picturesquely asymmetrical and surrounded by houses that have not changed for centuries. The ensemble has a **church** to match, an architecturally sophisticated 11th-century building with a rare elliptical cupola. South of St-Martin, in a military zone just off the D32, a 5,000-year-old settlement was discovered at **Cambous** in 1967 (*t 04 67 86 34 37 (Société des Monuments Historiques) for further info; open weekends only Sept–Jun 2–6 pm, July–Sept open daily 2–7pm except Mon and Thurs*). With considerable intelligence and dedication, the archaeologists have made the site into a veritable recreation of Neolithic life.

From St-Martin, the main D986 leads northwards towards the Cévennes. From the village of St-Bauzille-de-Putois there is a steep side road to the **Grotte des Demoiselles** (*open daily summer 9–12 and 2–6.30, July and Aug 9–7; winter 9.30–12 and 2–5; adm*) with one of France's most spectacular displays of pipe-organ stalactites and stalagmites, in the staggeringly enormous 'Cathedral of the Abysses'. Visits are by subterranean funicular.

Ganges is the only real town around, and quite a pleasant one. In the 18th century, it was France's capital of silk stockings. Like most of the Cévennes, Ganges was and remains a mostly Protestant area; the old part of town is crisscrossed by *chemins de traverse*, labyrinthine passes laid out to confuse Catholic troops, and it has an imposing, peculiar seven-sided Protestant 'temple', built in 1850. Just south, the village of **Laroque** is prettily set on the river and offers another stalactite cave to visit, the **Grotte de Laroque** (*open daily Easter–1 Nov 10–6; July–Aug 10–7*). Follow the D25 west of town to the end, and you come to the famous **Cirque de Navacelles**. A cirque looks like a deep lunar crater, though it is in fact a loop dug deep into the limestone of the *garrigue* by the meandering river Vis long ago. There are many in the *causses* and *garrigues* of the Midi, and this is the most striking, with steep, barren walls and a rocky 'island' in the centre.

Tourist Information

Ganges: Plan de l'Ormeau, t 04 67 73 00 56, f 04 67 73 63 24.

Where to Stay and Eat

St-Martin-de-Londres ✉ 34380
Les Muscardins, 19 Route des Cévennes, t 04 67 55 75 90. For years gourmets from Montpellier have driven up especially to feast at Les Muscardins, which offers fancy terrines and pâté, game, formidable desserts and a selection of the best regional wines on a choice of four menus (*170–390F*). *Closed Mon, Tues lunch and Feb.*

La Pastourelle, 350 Chemin de la Prairie, t 04 67 55 72 78. Serves delicious dishes based on local cèpes, lamb, and seafood (*menus: lunch 110F, evening 170 and 280F*). *Closed Tues eve and Wed.*

★★Hostellerie le Vieux Chêne, Causse de la Selle, west of Frouzet, t 04 67 73 11 00, f 04 67 73 10 54 (*inexpensive*). This has three luxurious rooms and a good restaurant serving French classics on a pretty terrace (*110F*). *Closed mid-Nov–Feb.*

Auberge de Saugras, Argelliers, south of St-Martin-de-Londres, t 04 67 55 08 71, f 04 67 55 04 65 (*cheap*). A stone *mas* with several rooms and gourmet menus from 99 to 420F. You'll need to book ahead and ask for directions!

La Ferme des Moreaux, t 04 67 73 12 11. For something extra special, attend a supper concert on the unique patios of 'Chapelle Musicale'. Madame Moreaux prepares a tasty meal based on medieval recipes and seasonal ingredients (*menus: lunch 135F,*

evening 195F) while guests are regaled with everything from Gregorian chant to jazz with an electronic touch; dress up, bring a sweater, don't smoke and be quiet (*June–Oct, nightly at 9pm, reservations mandatory; no children*).

Ganges ✉ 34190
★★Hôtel de la Poste, 8 Plan de l'Ormeau, t 04 67 73 85 88, f 04 67 73 83 79 (*inexpensive*). Prettily restored by its friendly new owners, Marie and Jean-Yves, who are mines of information about the area. *Closed Jan.*

Joselyn Mélodie, Place Fabre d'Olivet, t 04 67 73 66 02. A more intimate place in the old town, named after its two charming owners, who will fill you with good French cooking for less than 100F. *Closed Wed.*

Chez Maurice, Pont d'Hérault, 11km north of Ganges, t 04 67 82 40 02. The best *cuisine terroir* around (*good value menus for 128–280F*). Book.

Le Parc aux Cedres, Laroques, south of Ganges, t 04 67 73 82 63, f 04 67 73 69 85 (*inexpensive*). With a garden and pool, and menus for 80–175F.

Gorniès ✉ 34190
★★★★Château de Madières, 7km west of Gorniès, t 04 6773 84 03, f 04 67 73 55 71 (*expensive*). Combine the austerity of the *garrigue* with style and creature comforts in a 14th-century fort; a park, pool, fitness centre, and beautiful vaulted dining room (*menus 195 and 295F*) are some of the amenities. *Closed Nov–Mar.*

La Baume Auriol, St-Maurice-de-Navacelles, t 04 67 44 62 67. Good, reasonably priced food to go with a matchless view over the cirque (*menus 95–175F*).

The Valley of the Hérault: the Haut Pays d'Oc

The Hérault slices dramatically through the *garrigue*, and the atmosphere is clear, luminous, otherwordly: the perfect landscape for saints and pilgrims, and wine.

St-Guilhem-le-Désert

'Desert', in French or English, originally meant *deserted*, and this is still as lonely a region as it was when the hermit St Guilhem came here, in the reign of Charlemagne. The little village northwest of Montpellier is stretched on the edge of a ravine and has changed little since medieval times. The abbey **church** (*open Mon–Sat 8–12 and 2–5.30, to 6.30 in summer; Sun 11–4, closed for Mass*) is a remarkably grand and lovely specimen of Lombard architecture. The interior, lofty and dark, has lost almost all of its decoration. Some fragments of frescoes survive in the side chapels, and niches in the pillars around the choir once held the relics of St-Guilhem and a bit of the True Cross, a gift from Charlemagne. The cloister is ruined, and most of its capitals have ended up at the Cloisters Museum in New York.

The steep **Gorges de l'Hérault** extend on both sides of the village, and can be followed on the D4. With all this eroded limestone about, you would expect caves, and there are several. The most impressive, 3km south, is the **Grotte de Clamouse** (*open July and Aug 10–6; otherwise to 5pm; guided tour; adm*), one of the big tourist attractions of the Hérault, with its lovely aragonite crystals. Some 500 yards to the south, don't miss the massive stone bridge of 1030, the **Pont du Diable**.

Aniane and Gignac

Everyone who studies medieval history has trouble untangling the two Benedictine Benedicts. The first, Benedict of Norcia, founded the order. In the time of Charlemagne, Benedict of **Aniane**, St Guilhem's mentor, reformed it, forcing the poor Benedictines back to the original precepts of obedience, hard work and no fooling around. The **abbey** he built in his home town was thoroughly wrecked by the Protestants and rebuilt in the 17th century. The church, **St-Sauveur**, was rebuilt under Louis XIV, and in drab little Aniane it comes as quite a shock, with its glorious Baroque façade framed in big volutes, one of the best in the south. The interior is typically divided into two parts: one for the monks and one for the villagers.

South of Aniane on the D32, the bustling market town of **Gignac** enjoyed a period of prosperity in the 17th and 18th centuries; its best-known monument is outside town, over the Hérault: the **Pont de Gignac**. This bridge, begun in 1776, is every inch a product of the Age of Enlightenment, strong and functional architecture without a trace of Bourbon curlicues.

Southeast of Gignac, off the main N109, the **Château d'Aumelas** occupies a romantically isolated hilltop. This castle, built sometime before 1036 by the Lords of Montpellier, is on a dirt track and difficult to reach, but it's a wonderful place to explore; parts of the noble residence, chapels and other buildings are still substantially intact. South of the château on a rocky track, is a beautiful and austere Romanesque church, **St-Martin-de-Cardonnet**, set amidst the ruins of the monastery that once surrounded it. To the west, on the D139, the circular fortified village of **Le Pouget** is just north of the colossal **Dolmen Gallardet**.

Clermont-l'Hérault

Clermont is a peacefully bovine and prosperous town, living off the wine and table grapes of this more fertile part of the Hérault valley. Its medieval centre, on a hill top, is large and well preserved, including a tall and graceful Gothic church, **St-Paul**, begun in 1276. The 10th–11th-century **castle** around which the town grew up is also in pretty good nick.

Tourist Information

St-Guilhem-le-Désert: Rue de la Font du Portal, t/f 04 67 57 44 33.

Gignac: Pl Général Claparède, t 04 67 57 58 83, f 04 67 57 67 95.

Clermont-l'Hérault: 9 Rue Doyen R-Gosse, t 04 67 96 23 86, f 04 67 96 98 58.

Lodève: 7 Pl de la République, t 04 67 88 86 44, f 04 67 44 07 56.

Where to Stay and Eat

St-Guilhem-le-Désert ✉ 34150

**Hostellerie St-Benoit, Aniane, t 04 67 57 71 63, f 04 67 57 47 10 (*inexpensive*). A comfortable motel with a pool and a good restaurant specializing in trout and crayfish (*menus 115–185F*). *Closed Jan–Feb.*

Auberge sur le Chemin, 38 Rue Fond de Portal, t 04 67 57 75 05. A medieval inn serving tasty regional treats (*menus 72–110F*), but only in season.

Gignac ✉34150

Ferme-Auberge Le Pélican, Domaine du Pélican, t 04 67 57 68 92 (*inexpensive*). Rooms, but also a wonderful 115F menu – guinea-hen stuffed with olives, duck in honey vinegar, home-made desserts and their own wines; booking essential. *Open every eve in July–Aug; otherwise Sat eve and Sun lunch only.*

**Capion, Bd de l'Esplanade, t 04 67 57 50 83, f 04 67 57 50 60. Run by the same family for almost a century, this popular hotel-restaurant with an outdoor terrace eschews simple local cooking in favour of complex seafood fantasies like *salmon à trois façons* (*menus 190–300F*). *Closed Sun eve and Mon out of season. Rooms 250–300F.*

Liaisons Gourmandes, 3 Bd de l'Esplanade, t 04 67 57 50 83, f 04 67 57 50 60. Well worth a visit for its inventive regional cooking: for example, chicken with truffles and marinaded sardines (*menus 98–260F*).

Clermont-l'Hérault ✉ 34800

**Sarac, Rte de Nebian, t 04 67 96 06 81, f 04 67 88 07 30 (*inexpensive*). A pleasant Logis de France with views over the vineyards. *Open Mar–mid-Nov.*

L'Arlequin, Place St-Paul, in the medieval centre, t 04 67 96 37 47. The best of the restaurants, serving smoked trout, *confits* and good Faugères wine in a refined candle-lit room (a good bargain, too, with 78–128F menus). *Closed Mon.*

**La Source, Place Louis XIV, Villeneuvette, 4km southwest, t 04 67 96 05 07 f 04 67 96 90 09 (*inexpensive*). A refreshing stopover: a charming rural retreat with a pool and tennis with an impressive restaurant, specializing in salmon and truffles (*menus 100–199F*). *Closed mid-Nov–mid-Dec and 5 Jan–5 Mar.*

Ferme-Auberge de la Vallée du Salagou, towards Salascon on the D8, t 04 67 88 13 39 (*inexpensive*). A comfortable bed and breakfast with lovely views; the restaurant serves a filling 90F menu, with grilled lamb or steaks and wine from Octon.

**Les Hauts de Mourèze, 8km from Clermont, t 04 67 96 04 84, f 04 67 96 25 85 (*inexpensive*). Overlooking the cirque, with beautiful views. *Closed Dec–Feb.*

To the south lie weirdly eroded rock formations in the **Cirque de Mourèze**, a long, stretched-out cirque with the dusty village of Mourèze and its ruined castle at the centre. Between the cirque and Clermont lies **Villeneuvette**, founded only in 1670 and a manufacturing centre for *londrins*, printed linen cloth. Though the works are now closed (since 1954), Villeneuvette is still the very picture of an old French paternalistic company town. The factories remain, behind the gate with the big inscription *Honneur au Travail*.

North of Clermont, the N9 heads into the *causses* of deepest France, passing **Lodève**, a comfortable, somewhat isolated town wedged between two rivers. Like Clermont-l'Hérault, Lodève has an impressive Gothic church with a lofty tower as its chief monument; **St-Fulcran**, begun in 1280, and turned into a fortress during the Hundred Years' War. Lodève's textile-manufacturing past is recalled in a local workshop of the famous Parisian tapestry factory, the **Atelier National de Tissage de Tapis de Lodève**, (*ring ahead to visit; t 04 67 96 40 40; open Tues, Wed, Thurs 2–5*). Lodève was a Roman town, and its **Musée Fleury**, in Rue de la République (*open 10–12 and 2–6, closed Mon*), has finds from that age.

The Northern Fringes: Monts de l'Espinouse

The natural beauty of the Espinouse – rough canyons, trout streams and chestnut groves – never did it much good; even forty years ago, this was a poor area, losing its population. The creation of the Parc Régional du Haut Languedoc in the 1960s has made all the difference; *tourisme vert*, as the French call it – hiking, canoeing or just relaxing – increases every year.

The only big road in this region, the D908, runs west from Clermont-l'Hérault across the base of the mountains. The first town is **Bédarieux**, a humble enough market town. **Lamalou-les-Bains**, 10km further west, has been a thermal spa since the 1600s and made it big when the railroad arrived in 1868. The prosperity of the next three decades – dukes and counts, famous actresses, even a sultan of Morocco checked in for the cure – brought Belle Epoque hotels and villas, cafés, a casino and a theatre. Either town is a good base for exploring the eastern half of the Espinouse: the **Gorges d'Heric**, a hiker's paradise, and the **Gorges de l'Orb**.

The loveliest village of the Espinouse, **Olargues**, has two medieval monuments, a striking 11th-century bell tower on a hill and a humpbacked bridge. Next, **St-Pons-de-Thomières** is the little capital of the Espinouse, surrounded by forests. Its landmarks are a **cathedral**, with a Romanesque portal and a tremendous 18th-century organ, and its **Musée Municipal de Préhistoire Régionale** (*open daily 10–12 and 2.30–5.30; adm*). Never suspecting they were in a future Regional Park, Neolithic people made St-Pons and the Espinouse one of their favourite haunts in France. St-Pons is also the perfect base for visiting the **Parc Naturel du Haut Languedoc**, spread over a wide area of the Espinouse, on the borders of the Hérault, Tarn and Aveyron, where there is a wide choice of hiking trails in the mountains. North from St-Pons, the valley of the Agout spreads across the heart of the park; the roads that follow it, the D14 and D53, make a delightful tour, through beautiful villages like **La Salvetat-sur-Agout** and **Fraisse-sur-Agout**, which has a curious statue-menhir in situ, carved with a serpent and egg. The D53 continues towards the 3,651 ft summit of the Espinouse.

The Hérault Coast: La Grande Motte to Agde

West of the Camargue, the lagoons continue for another 80km, dotting the coast like beads on a string. Unlike the Camargue, almost all of this coast is easily accessible by car; there are beaches and resorts in abundance, and attractions like salty Sète, medieval Maguelone and Agde.

Getting Around

Except along the coast, public transport is rudimentary; the coastal SNCF line runs from Montpellier through Frontignan, Sète, Agde and Béziers on its way to Narbonne and Perpignan, with as many as 22 trains a day. The only train service in the interior is from Béziers northwest to the Espinouse, taking a roundabout route through Bédarieux, Lamalou-les-Bains, Olargues and St-Pons on its way to Castres in the Tarn.

St-Pons is also connected by bus to Béziers, via St-Chinian. Coach lines from the bus station in Montpellier have regular services to Gignac, Clermont-l'Hérault and Lodève; there are additional buses to some tourist attractions (like St-Guilhem-le-Désert) in the summer (t 04 67 06 03 67).

Tourist Information

Lamalou-les-Bains: 2 Ave Dr. Ménard, t 04 67 95 70 91, f 04 67 95 64 52.
Olargues: Place de la Gare, t 04 67 97 71 26, f 04 67 97 78 93.
St-Pons-de-Thomières: Place du Foirail, t 04 67 97 06 65. Maison du Parc Régional du Haut Languedoc, 13 Rue du Cloître, t 04 67 97 38 22.

Where to Stay and Eat

Lamalou-les-Bains ✉ 34240
***Belleville, 1 Av Charnot, t 04 67 95 57 00, f 04 67 95 64 18 (*inexpensive*). Excellent value

for relative luxury: some bathrooms come with Jacuzzi.
**De la Paix, 18 Av Daudet, t 04 67 95 63 11, f 04 67 95 67 78 (*inexpensive*). This 100-year-old hotel has been prettily renovated; it serves old French favourites in the restaurant (*menus 85–245F*), and offers wine tastings in the summer.

Olargues ✉ 34390
***Domaine de Rieumégé, 3km out on the St-Pons road, t 04 67 97 73 99, f 04 67 97 78 52 (*moderate*). An enchanting place to stay: a 17th-century building set in a 20-acre estate, with a pool and tennis. If you don't stay, at least eat in the superb restaurant : seafood, *boeuf en croûte* and a big wine list (*menus: lunch 98F, evening 135F*).

St-Pons-de-Thomières ✉ 34220
**Le Somail, 2 Av de Castres, t 04 67 97 00 12. A simple place in town.
La Route du Sel, 15 Grand' Rue, t 04 67 97 05 14. A little restaurant, specializing in original, well-prepared dishes such as foie gras gilded with jerusalem artichokes (*topinambours*) (*menus from 95F*). *Closed Sun eve, Mon, and Sat lunch out of season.*
Les Bergeries de Ponderach, 1 km outside St-Pons towards Narbonne, t 04 67 97 02 57, f 04 67 97 29 75 (*moderate*). A haven of peace in the hills, with a rustic restaurant (*menus 98–230F*), rooms with terraces and country views, summer concerts and even an art gallery.

Built in 1963, **La Grande Motte** looks like no other resort in the world – its hotels and apartments rising in colourful triangles and roller-coaster curves – but it is a great success as a resort, offering countless sports facilities and a casino. For you fogies, a more old-fashioned beach holiday can be spent at **Carnon-Plage** or **Palavas-les-Flots**, 15km down the dune-lined coast. Built around a narrow canal full of boats, Palavas is an endearingly humble resort with some 8km of good beaches.

Maguelone, 4km from Palavas, became a papal holding in the 12th century, valued for its salt pans. Though almost no trace of the town remains today, the impressive **Cathedral St-Pierre** was saved from ruin and restored in the 1870s (*open daily, 9–7*). Built, and built well, by Lombard masons in the 1170s, it is an austere building;

Tourist Information

La Grande Motte: Place de la Mairie, t 04 67 29 03 37, f 04 67 29 03 45.

Palavas-les-Flots: Blvd Joffre, t 04 67 07 73 34, f 04 67 07 73 58.

Sète: 60 Grand Rue Mario Roustan, t 04 67 74 71 71, f 04 67 46 17 54.

Agde: Place Molière, t 04 67 94 29 68, f 04 67 94 03 50.

Cap d'Agde: 11 Impasse du Hourier, t 04 67 01 04 04, f 04 67 26 22 99.

Where to Stay and Eat

La Grande Motte ✉ 34280

★★★Grand M'Hotel, Quartier Point Zero, t 04 67 29 13 13, f 04 67 29 14 74 (*expensive*). The fanciest hotel, right on the front, with a thalassotherapy centre and balconied rooms with good sea views.

★★★Mercure, Rue du Port, t 04 67 56 90 81, f 04 67 56 92 29 (*expensive–moderate*). A splashy address on the Big Lump, looming over the marina; rather charmless, but a chance to meet that segment of the fast crowd who avoid the Riviera, and it does have a nice terrace fish restaurant (*menus 120–160F*).

Alexandre, Esplanade de la Capitainerie, t 04 67 56 63 63. A splurge for refined regional specialities in an especially elegant setting

(*menus from 200F*). Closed Sun eve and all Mon.

La Cuisine du Marché, 89 Rue Casino, t 04 67 29 90 11. Good fresh fish served in classic style (*menus 139–199F*). Small, so you'll need to book.

Palavas-les-Flots ✉ 34250

★★Mas de Couran, Route de Fréjorgues, Lattes ✉ 34970, t 04 67 65 57 57, f 04 67 65 37 56 (*moderate*). It's worth coming inland to Lattes for this special place, set in a beautiful park, with swimming-pool and restaurant (*menus 110–240F*).

La Passerelle, Quai Paul-Cunq, t 04 67 68 55 80. This couldn't be simpler, its menu limited to piles of fresh inexpensive shellfish. *Open May–Sept.*

L'Escale, 5 Bd Sarrail, on the seafront, t 04 67 68 24 17. Here you can have *sèche à la rouille* for starters, or a mixed shellfish extrava-ganza, *panaché de coquillages*—the bill can go up to 300F before you recover your reason (*menus 160–380F*).

Sète ✉ 34200

★★★Grand Hôtel, 17 Quai Lattre de Tassigny, t 04 67 74 71 77, f 04 67 74 29 27 (*moderate*). Right on Sète's 'Grand Canal', it almost deserves its name, with plenty of the orig-inal decor from the 1920s. If you can't swing

the bell tower offers views down the coast. Inside are fragments of the bishops' tombs and inscriptions.

Sète

Gritty, salty, workaday Sète is an attractive town, laced with canals, and livelier and more colourful than any place on the coast, save only Marseille. France's biggest Mediterranean fishing port, it also claims the Bassin de Thau, one of the largest lagoons along the Mediterranean, with salt-pans here, and now huge oyster and mussel farms. Businesslike freighters from Sète carry French sunflower and rape-seed oil to every corner of the globe.

The bustling centre of Sète is its 'Grand Canal', the **Canal de Sète**, lined with quays where the ambience ranges from boat-yards and ship chandlers to banks and boutiques. At the southern end of the canal, the **Vieux Port** handles most of the fishing fleet, as well as offering tourist fishing boats and excursions around the Thau lagoon. From the Vieux Port it's a bit of a climb up to the **Cimetière Marin**, where the Sètois poet Paul Valéry was buried in 1945. The adjacent **Musée Paul Valéry** (*open daily*

the Danieli in Venice, this will do fine. The hotel's **Rotonde** restaurant (t 04 67 74 86 14) is refined and serves rewarding menus at 115 and 235F.

★★L'Orque Bleue, 10 Quai Aspirant-Herber, t 04 67 74 72 13, f 04 67 74 72 13 (*moderate*). Anyone who grew up in the '70s will feel at home here.

★★Les Abysses, 47 Grand' Rue Mario Roustan, t 04 67 74 37 73, f 04 67 74 24 82 (*inexpensive*). Small and central.

La Palangrotte, Rampe Paul Valéry, t 04 67 74 80 35. Quality seafood on the lower end of the Canal de Sète (*menus 150–300F*): grilled fish, and several styles of fish stew, including *bourride sètoise. Closed Sun eve and Mon, except in July and Aug.*

Le Chalut, 38 Quai Gérard Durand, t 04 67 74 81 52. The seafood, including many *sètois* specialities, is as tasty as the décor (*menus from 130F*). *Closed Wed, and Jan.*

Terrasses du Lido, Rond-Point de Europe, along the Corniche road, t 04 67 51 39 60. A pretty Provençal-style villa serving authentic Sètoise dishes from *bourride* to *bouillabaisse* (*menus 150–320F*).

Bouzigues ✉ 34140

Côte Bleue, Av Louis-Tudesq, t 04 67 78 30 87. A large family restaurant overlooking the Bassin de Thau which is the best place to sample a vast variety of shellfish, mussels, langoustines and the local Bouzigues oysters (*menus 98–250F*).

Agde ✉ 34300

★★La Galiote, 5 Place Jean Jaurès, t 04 67 94 45 58, f 04 67 94 41 33 (*inexpensive*). Some rooms in this old bishop's palace overlook the river; there's a bar full of English beer, and an excellent restaurant (*menus 88–248F*): seafood or roast lamb with thyme, and alcoholic ices between courses.

★★Le Donjon, Place Jean Jaurès, t 04 67 94 12 32, f 04 67 94 34 54 (*inexpensive*). The second choice in town, with old-fashioned, comfortable rooms.

★★★La Tamarissière, 21 Quai Théophile-Cornu (D32E), t 04 67 94 20 87, f 04 67 21 38 40 (*expensive*). A real charmer amid century-old parasol pines and roses 4km down the Hérault, with quiet, stylish, well-equipped rooms, a pool, and the best restaurant in the area: fresh, colourful dishes such as saint-pierre baked with stuffed baby courgettes and saffron (*menus 175–390F*).

Cap d'Agde ✉ 34300

Le Brasero, Port Richelieu, t 04 67 26 26 75. With a vine-covered terrace, classic French food including lots of fish of course, and regional wines (*menus 80–270F*).

exc Tues, 10–12 and 2–6; adm) contains exhibits on the poet, and on the history of Sète. Sète's other contribution to French culture, modern troubadour Georges Brassens (died 1981), is buried in the **Cimetière de Py**, under the Pierres Blanches, overlooking the Etang de Thau; the nearby **Espace Georges Brassens**, 67 Blvd Camille-Blanc (*open 10–12 and 2–6, to 7pm July and Aug, closed Mon Oct–May; adm*), has photos and exhibits relating to his life.

Abbaye de Valmagne

Valmagne (*8km north of Mèze on the D161; guided tours; in summer open daily exc Tues, 3–6, the rest of the year Sun and holidays only, 2.30–6*) is not your typical Cistercian church. St Bernard would have frowned on architectural vanities like the porch, the bell towers and the sculpted decoration. Its size is astonishing: a 370ft nave, and great pointed arches almost as high as Narbonne cathedral's. Most of the work is 14th-century, in a straightforward but sophisticated late Gothic. The relatively few monks who lived here would hardly have needed such a church; here too, architectural vanity seems to have overcome Cistercian austerity.

Agde, the 'Black Pearl of Languedoc'

If Sète is a brash young upstart, Agde, a lovely grey town, built almost entirely of volcanic basalt from nearby Mont St-Loup, has been watching the river Hérault flow down to the sea for some 2,500 years. Founded by Greeks from Phocis, in medieval times it was an important port, despite occasional visits by Arab sea-raiders. The stern basalt **Cathédrale St-Etienne** was begun about 1150. Its fortress-like appearance is no accident; Agde's battling bishops used it as their citadel. From the quay along the Hérault, Rue Chassefière leads into the *bourg*, or medieval addition to the city. On Rue de la Fraternité, the **Musée Agathois** (*open daily exc Tues 10–12 and 2–7; adm*), is the best of the south's town museums, encapsulating nearly everything about Agde's history and traditions in a few well-arranged rooms.

Cap d'Agde, 4km away, is the biggest beach playground in all Languedoc. The original 1960s plan even accommodated the *naturistes*; the camp called **Héliopolis** on the northern edge of town has become the biggest nudist colony in Europe. One surprising attraction is a fine, small archaeological collection at the **Musée de l'Ephèbe** (*open daily exc Tues and Sun am out of season 9–12 and 2–6.30; adm*), the star of which is the *Ephèbe d'Agde*, a Hellenistic bronze of a boy, discovered in 1964.

Pézenas

If Carcassonne is Languedoc's medieval movie-set, Pézenas has often been used for costume dramas set in the time of Richelieu or Louis XIV. Few cities have a better ensemble of buildings from what the French (rather over-enthusiastically) used to call the 'Golden Age'.

Roman *Piscenae* was known for wool, the best in Gaul. In the 1200s, it became a possession of the French crown. Later, the troubles of Béziers and Narbonne in the Albigensian Crusade and the Hundred Years' War would prove lucky for Pézenas and the town replaced Narbonne as seat of the Estates-General of Languedoc after 1456. The royal governors of the region followed, bringing in their wake a whole wave of wealthy nobles, clerics and jurists, who rebuilt Pézenas in their own image, with new churches, convents, government buildings and scores of refined *hôtels particuliers*. For the next two centuries they remained, until it all came to an end with the Revolution.

The tourist information office offers a brochure with a detailed walking tour of the town and its 70-odd listed historical buildings. From the Renaissance through to the 1700s, Pézenas really did develop and maintain a distinctive architectural manner; this can best be seen in the *hôtels particuliers*, with their lovely arcaded courtyards and external staircases. Molière spent some seasons in Pézenas in the 1650s, when his troupe was employed by the governor, the Prince de Conti. On Rue Alliès, the **Musée de Vuillod-St-Germain** contains memorabilia of the playwright and his time here, along with collections of tapestries, faïence and paintings (*open 10–12 and 3–7, closed Sun am and Mon out of season; adm*).

Getting Around

Béziers is on the main coastal rail line, and it's easy to get to Narbonne, Sète and Montpellier. The other line from the city heads north for Castres, passing through Bédarieux and St-Pons. The bus station has regular connections to Pézenas (and to everywhere the trains go), and less regular ones to villages of the eastern Hérault.

Tourist Information

Béziers: Palais des Congrès, 29 Ave Saint-Saëns, t 04 67 76 47 00, f 04 67 76 50 80.
Pézenas: Place Gambetta, t 04 67 98 35 45, t 04 67 98 36 40, f 04 67 98 96 80.

Where to Stay and Eat

Béziers ✉ 34500
***Imperator, 28 Allées Paul Riquet, t 04 67 49 02 25, f 04 67 28 92 30 (inexpensive). This has the best location in town and there's a garage, too.
**Champ de Mars, 17 Rue Metz, t 04 67 28 35 53, f 04 67 28 61 42 (inexpensive). A good value place, nice and central but on a quiet street, with recently renovated rooms.
**Paul Riquet, 46 Allées Paul Riquet, t 04 67 76 44 37, f 04 67 49 00 37 (cheap). Small, pleasant and considerably cheaper.
Le Jardin, 37 Av Jean Moulin, near Place 14 Juillet, t 04 67 36 41 31. The finest ingredients go into the wide-awake cuisine (menus 100–310F). Closed Sun eve and Wed.
Le Framboisier, 12 Rue Boieldieu, off Bd Paul Riquet, t 04 67 49 90 00. Local gourmets head here for delicacies like fricassee of asparagus and eggs with truffles or rouget with black olive tapenade (menus 170–380F).
Le Bistrot des Halles, Place de la Madeleine, t 04 67 28 30 46. Has 88 and 137F menus often including smoked salmon, and home-made desserts. Closed Sun and Mon.
Brasserie Le Mondial, 2 Rue Solférino, t 04 67 28 22 15. Packed most evenings, not so much for its food but its concerts, usually Wed–Sat nights. Closed Sun.

Pézenas ✉ 34120
**Genieys, 9 Av Aristide Briand, t 04 67 98 13 99, f 04 67 98 04 80 (inexpensive). Outside the historic centre, but the only good hotel in town; demi-pension obligatory in July and Aug.
***Hostellerie de St-Alban, 31 Rte d'Agde, Nézignan l'Evêque, just south of Pézenas, t 04 67 98 11 38, f 04 67 98 91 63 (moderate). A quiet 19th-century villa in the vines, with a pool, tennis and restaurant (menus 145–300F).
Côté Sud, Place 14 Juillet, t 04 67 09 41 74. For a shellfish feast this place comes up with the goods (lunch 45F, other menus 70 and 99F).
Le Pre Saint-Jean, 18 Av du Maréchal-Leclerc, t 04 67 98 15 31. Has a pretty terrace and serves classics like stuffed squid and carré d'agneau en croute (menus 90–190F).
Maison Alary, Rue St-Jean 9. Pézenas' spool-shaped petits pâtés take French visitors by surprise ('what is this, half-sweet and half-mutton?'): the recipe was introduced in 1770 by the Indian chef of Lord Clive, Governor of India, who spent a holiday in Pézenas. They still make them here; eat them warm.

Béziers

This city's history is succinct: a rude interruption and a second chance. In 1209, at the beginning of the Albigensian Crusade, a large number of Cathars took refuge in the city and were besieged. The troops stormed the city, and found that the entire population had taken refuge in the churches. The Crusaders' ayatollah, the Abbot of Cîteaux, had ordered the massacre of the Cathars. Asked how to distinguish them from the Catholics, he replied, 'Kill them all, God will know his own.' From all accounts, that is exactly what happened; in his report to Rome, the papal legate bragged that some 20,000 people were put to death. Not surprisingly, Béziers languished for centuries. The second chance came in the 1660s, with the building of the Canal du Midi. A new Béziers has grown up since, a busy port and industrial town of 90,000.

Life in Béziers centres along the the **Allées Paul Riquet**, a promenade of plane trees named after the city's great benefactor, the builder of the Canal du Midi. Besides a statue of Riquet, there is a handsome 19th-century theatre, and a monument to Resistance hero Jean Moulin (another Bitérois) at the top of the romantic **Plateau des Poètes**. From the other end of the Allées Paul Riquet, any of the streets to the west will take you up to the medieval centre.

Someone must have been left in Béziers after 1209, for the city spent the next two centuries working on its grandiose **cathedral**, replacing the original that was wrecked in the sack. Its grim, fortress-like exterior seems a foreign presence, the citadel of an occupying force. Behind the cathedral, the **Musée Fabregat** in Place de la Révolution, houses Béziers' fine arts museum, founded in 1859 (*open Tues–Sat 9–12 and 2–6, Sun 2–6; adm*), with something for every taste. Many of the fine modern works (de Chirico, Soutine, Friesz) were purchased by Jean Moulin; the great Resistance leader posed as a designer and art dealer under the name of Romanin. Just north, the **Musée Fayet**, in a delightful 17th-century *hôtel particulier* at 9 Rue du Capus (*open Tues–Fri 9–12 and 2–6; same adm*), contains several rooms of 18th- and 19th-century paintings and decorative arts. On a belvedere on the south side of Béziers is the **Musée du Biterrois** (or de St-Jacques) (*open daily summer 10–7, winter 9–12 and 2–6, closed Mon; adm*). The museum divides its space between regional archaeological finds, medieval capitals and other bits, ethnography (especially wine-making), science and ceramics.

The Canal du Midi

The best thing to do in Béziers is go west for one of Languedoc's best-kept secrets. This canal, one of very few in the south, remains serene and relatively unburdened by tourism, and is planted its entire length with parallel rows of great plane trees. Paul Riquet's canal is also an early monument of economic planning, from the days of Louis XIV's great minister Colbert, when everything in France was being reformed and modernized. Riquet was a local baron and the state's Tax Farmer (*fermier-général*) for Languedoc. He conceived the idea for the 235km canal that would link the Mediterranean to the Atlantic by way of the Garonne and sold it to Colbert, then saw through its construction with remarkable single-mindedness, inventing ingenious tricks to get the canal over the highest stretches, paying a third of the expenses himself, and even sacrificing his daughters' dowries to the cause. From 1666, as many as 12,000 men worked on the project, which required over 100 locks. It was completed 39 years later; Riquet died bankrupt a few months before the opening.

Oppidum d'Ensérune

Seven km southwest of Béziers on the N9 Narbonne Road is one of the most important pre-Roman towns of southern Gaul (*open April–Oct 9–12 and 2–6, July and Aug*

Getting Around

Forget about buses and trains; you'll need a car to get around here, or better a mountain bike (VTT in French); the shady tow paths are lovely for cycling. Best of all, hire a small boat (ask at any of the villages). The canal is open for navigation March–Nov.

Tourist Information

Nissan-lez-Ensérune. t 04 67 37 14 12, f 04 67 37 63 00.

Where to Stay and Eat

Poilhes ✉ 34310

La Tour Sarrasine, Bd du Canal, t 04 67 93 41 31. Imaginative *haute cuisine*: pigeon stuffed with foie gras, steaks in a sauce of wine and marrow and the like make a memorable dinner (*menus at 130–235F*). *Closed Sun eve out of season, and Mon.*

Nissan-lez-Ensérune and Around ✉ 34440

★★Résidence, 35 Av de la Cave, t 04 67 37 00 63, f 04 67 37 68 63 (*inexpensive*). Antiquated charm, with a more modern annexe.

★★Via Domitia, Colombiers, t 04 67 35 62 63, f 04 67 35 62 00 (*inexpensive*). Offers creature comforts, with TVs and air conditioning.

Homps and Le Somail ✉ 11120

Les Tonnaliers, by the port in Homps, t 04 68 91 14 04. The terrace is a favourite stop for lunch or dinner; try the marinated salmon (*menus 80–185F*).

Auberge de l'Arbousier, 50 Av de Carcassonne, Le Somail, t 04 68 91 11 24, f 04 68 91 12 61 (*inexpensive*). A charming hotel-restaurant in an old *mas* on the banks of the Canal du Midi; the kitchen specializes in cooking with local Minervois wine, as well as serving it (*menus 85–210F*).

Bed and breakfast, Le Somail, t 04 68 46 16 02 (*inexpensive*). In a charming 17th-century house. *Open April–Oct.*

Trèbes ✉ 11800

Château de Floure, 1 Allée Gaston Bonheur, t 04 68 79 11 29, f 04 68 79 04 61 (*expensive*). Just east of Trèbes, this ivy-covered chateau was originally a Romanesque abbey; it has an elegant French garden, a pool, tennis, comfortable rooms and a good restaurant (*menus 230–280F*). *Closed Nov–1 April.*

9.30–7, otherwise 10–12 and 2–4; guided tours; adm). Initially settled in the 6th century BC, the Oppidum d'Ensérune began as a fortified trading village under Greek influence. It revived again under Roman rule but was largely abandoned by the 1st century AD. Not much remains of the town: the foundations of the wall, cisterns and so on, but the excellent **museum** in the centre of the excavations has a collection of ceramics, including some fine Greek and Etruscan works. Just outside the town, where an ancient column with an unusual, trapezoidal capital has been re-erected, you can take in one of the oddest panoramas in France, a gigantic surveyor's pie. This was the **Etang de Montady**, a circular swamp reclaimed in the 13th century, when the new fields were divided by drainage ditches radiating from the centre.

The Minervois

This is a *pays* with plenty of character, though not many people. With typical French irony, the Minervois suffered grievously from poverty and rural depopulation throughout the 20th century – then, just when everyone was gone, vintners improved the quality of their Minervois wines. They have become increasingly popular across France, and the region's prosperity has returned. The country is ragged and wild, with outcrops of eroded limestone, and there is a sense of strange isolation.

West of Béziers, the narrow D10 will take you up into the heights of the Minervois, to **Minerve**, a town as old as any in Languedoc. The Celts and the Romans built the town, and in the Middle Ages it was a feudal stronghold with a Cathar slant. Minerve accepted refugees from the sack of Béziers in 1209; Simon de Montfort followed them, and took the town after a siege, followed by the usual butchery and burning of 140 Cathars at the stake. All that is left of the château is a slender, octagonal tower; the Minervois call it the '*candela*'. There are narrow medieval alleys, gates and cisterns, and a simple 12th-century church with a white marble altar from 456, said to be the oldest in Europe. The real attractions are in the country. A short walk from town, there are **'natural bridges'** – really more like tunnels, eroded through the limestone by streams. To the west extends the narrow, blushing pink **Canyon de la Cesse**.

The **seven-sided church of Rieux-Minervois**, one of the most uncanny medieval monuments in France, is in the village of Rieux. The seven-pointed star is the recurring mystic symbol of the Midi. Just what it means has never been adequately explained; neither has anyone ventured an explanation for the presence in this unremarkable Minervois village of what may be the only seven-sided church anywhere. Dedicated to the Virgin, the church was built sometime in the late 12th century. The ambition of the builders of this church, and their resources, are seen in the sculptural detail inside, entrusted to the Master of Cabestany. Building in heptagons certainly must have tried the patience and mathematical know-how of a 12th-century mason; we can admire their careful work, especially the seven-sided belfry, directly over the altar, and the tricky toroid vaulting that connects the heptagon with the 14-sided exterior wall.

The Montagne Noire

Even wilder than the Minervois, if not as unusual, the bleak, brooding Black Mountain is a 30km-wide stretch of peaks, taller than their neighbours and difficult to access until modern times. All the routes into it follow narrow parallel valleys leading up from the river Aude. The **valley of the Orbiel** (D101) is the most populous of the region, and perhaps the most beautiful. It also contains the region's landmark, the **Châteaux de Lastours** (*open daily Oct 10–5, April, May, June, Sept 10–6, July and Aug 9–8, Feb, Mar, Nov, Dec, weekends only 10–5; adm*) – not one, but four castles, in various states of picturesque ruin, all on the same hilltop to defend the Montagne Noire's mineral richness. The Lords of Cabardès, the bosses before the arrival of de Montfort in 1211, built the castles of Cabaret and Quertinheux; the two between, Surdespine and Tour Régine, were added by the French kings after Montfort.

To the east of Lastours is a remarkable cave, the **Grotte de Limousis**, with unique formations of gleaming white aragonite crystals (*open daily Mar–June and Sept 10–12 and 2–5.30; July and Aug 10–6; adm*). Further up the valley are two of the most beautiful and unspoiled villages of the region: **Roquefère** and **Mas-Cabardès**. Mas-Cabardès has some half-timbered houses and a 16th-century church with a rugged belfry. In the village centre, note the carefully carved stone **cross**, typical of Montagne Noire villages.

Tourist Information

Minerve: t 04 68 91 81 43.
Rieux-Minervois: Place de l'Eglise, t 04 68 78 13 98, f 04 68 78 32 32.

Where to Stay and Eat

Minerve and Olonzac ✉ 34210
***Relais Chantovent**, 17 Grande Rue, t 04 68 91 14 18, f 04 68 91 81 88 (*inexpensive*). The only hotel in Minerve, with just 7 rooms; also a fine restaurant with a terrace overlooking the gorges, serving truffles, *cèpes*, and some seafood (*menus 100–225F*). *Closed mid-Nov–mid-Mar, Sun and Mon out of season.*
Auberge de St-Martin, south of Minerve in Beaufort, t 04 68 91 16 18. A sweet old *mas* with a shady terrace, offering wood-fire grilled meat and fish (*menus 120–150F*).

Rieux-Minervois ✉ 11160
****Logis de Merinville**, Av Georges Clemenceau, t 04 68 78 12 49 (*inexpensive*). An atmospheric 19th-century stone inn in the village centre, with lovely rooms, 1930s furniture and a good restaurant (*menus 69–180F*). *Closed Tues eve, Wed and Jan.*
*****Château de Violet**, Route de Pepieux, outside Peyriac-Minervois, t 04 68 78 10 42, f 04 68 78 30 01 (*expensive–moderate*). The Minervois' luxury resort: a restored farmhouse, elegant and sumptuously furnished, with pool and gardens. A bit expensive for its rating, it also has a restaurant with 100–250F menus.
****Hôtel d'Alibert**, Place de la Mairie, Caunes-Minervois, t 04 68 78 00 54 (*inexpensive*). A sweet little place to stay or eat, with good regional food in the restaurant (*menu 120F*). *Closed Dec–Feb.*

In the valley furthest west, that of the Vernassonne, **Saissac** is another lovely village, built over a ravine and surrounded by forests. Saissac too has its romantically ruined, overgrown fortress, and a 10ft **menhir**, just to the north off the D4. To the south, **Montolieu**, balanced over the gorges of the the Alzeau and Dure, has become a centre of the local bookmaking trade: in the centre, the **Montolieu, Village du Livre** (*open 10–12 and 2–6; adm*), traces the history of bookbinding and printing.

Narbonne

The Roman colony of *Colonia Narbo Martius*, a good site for a trading port along the recently built Via Domitia, was founded in 118 BC. It rapidly became the most important city of southern Gaul, renowned for its beauty and wealth. In the 12th century, Narbonne entered its second golden age, which lasted until the 14th century when wars, plagues and the harbour silting up led to its ruin. By the end of the century, the city had shrunk to a mere market town. Now Languedoc's capital, Narbonne has a local economy largely fuelled on plonk – the bountiful vineyards of the Corbières and other nearby regions – and the city is also finding a new vocation as an industrial centre. With its impressive medieval monuments, boulevards and lively streets, it is quite a happy and contented place – one of the Midi's most agreeable urban destinations – with an excellent museum, and the best cathedral in the south.

The City Centre

Follow Rue Jean Jaurès from near the train and bus stations and you'll be following the **Canal de la Robine** into the centre of the city, lined with a delightful park called the

Getting Around

Narbonne is on the main Bordeaux–Toulouse–Nice rail route across the Midi; there are frequent connections (about 12 a day) to Perpignan, Toulouse, and Béziers and the other coastal cities to the east. The bus station offers coach services that largely duplicate the trains; there will also be a bus or two a day to Gruissan and Leucate.

Tourist Information

Narbonne: Place Roger-Salengro, t 04 68 65 15 60, f 04 68 65 59 12.

Where to Stay

Narbonne ✉ 11100

★★★**La Dorade**, 44 Rue Jean Jaurès, t 04 68 32 65 95, f 04 68 65 81 62 (*inexpensive*). But for the lack of parking and a bit of street noise, this would be perfect. Narbonne's old 'Grand Hôtel', with marble telamones holding up the balcony, is still well kept, centrally located overlooking the canal, and a bargain.

★★★**Languedoc**, 22 Bd Gambetta, t 04 68 65 14 74, f 04 68 65 81 48 (*inexpensive*). Another gracious old establishment, a bit fancier and more expensive, this is now part of the Mapotel chain. It has a restaurant (*menus 125 and 360F*).

★★★**La Residence**, 6 Rue du 1er Mai, t 04 68 32 19 41, f 04 68 65 51 82 (*inexpensive*). An old

hôtel particulier, with calm, well-equipped rooms and a garage.

★★**Will's Hôtel**, 23 Av Pierre Semard, t 04 68 90 44 50 (*inexpensive*). It's not run by a Will, and the present owners can't imagine who Will might have been, but it is still a comfortable and extremely friendly place.

★★**Hôtel du Lion d'Or**, Av Pierre Semard, t 04 68 32 06 92, f 04 68 65 51 13 (*inexpensive*). A small, family-run hotel with a good line in wine-tastings.

★**De la Gare**, 7 Av Pierre Semard, t 04 68 32 10 54 (*cheap*). Very nice for its price.

Eating Out

L'Eglefin, 22 Rue de l'Ancienne Porte de Béziers. East of the centre, near a delightful park called the Place Thérèse et Léon Blum, this restaurant specializes in seafood, as its name implies – an *eglefin* is a haddock, and he appears on the menu cooked in cider, along with grilled *loup* and other delights (*60, 100 and 120F menus*).

La Baie d'Along, Place Bistan, in old Narbonne, t 04 68 65 58 83. For Chinese-Vietnamese cooking, very correct and tasty too, this is the best in town; there's a 98F menu, though you may want to splurge for the elaborate starters.

Table St Crescent, Rte de Perpignan, t 04 68 41 37 37. One of Narbonne's top restaurants is outside town at the Palais du Vin, with a vine-covered terrace specialising of course in the best regional wines and dishes (*menus 100–258F*).

Jardin Entre Deux Villes. Narbonne's centre is the busy **Place de l'Hôtel de Ville**. Facing the square, the twin façades of the **Palais des Archevêques** were blessed with a romantic Gothic restoration by the master himself, Viollet-le-Duc, in the 1840s. The passage between the two buildings (the Palais Neuf on the left, and the Palais Vieux on the right) leads to a small courtyard, and the entrances to Narbonne's two excellent museums, the **Musée d'Art et d'Histoire** and the **Musée Archéologique** (*both open daily 10–12 and 2–5; April–Sept, 9.30–12.15 and 2–6*). The Musée d'Art et d'Histoire's **Grande Galerie** contains some of the best paintings in the museum: an intense *St Jerome* by Salvator Rosa, a Canaletto and, among many Dutch and Flemish pictures, a *Wedding Dance* by Pieter Breughel the Younger. In the **Salle des Faïences** 18th-century painted ceramics come mostly from well-known French centres like Moustiers and Varange, but also from Marseille and Montpellier. It is only luck that made Nîmes the 'French Rome', while only one of Narbonne's monuments has survived. There is, however, no shortage of remaining bits and pieces, and the best of them have been assembled in the Musée Archéologique: reliefs from three triumphal arches and the gates of its walls, milestones from the Via Domitia, funeral monuments, and a model of a Roman house.

Narbonne's one Roman monument is a warehouse or **Horreum**, on Rue Rouget de Lisle (*open 9–12.15 and 2–6, closed Mon Oct–mid-May; adm*). Typical of the state-run warehouses of any Roman city, this is the only complete one anywhere. Just a small part has been excavated, a maze of tiny chambers; the original structure was over 500ft long.

Cathédrale St-Just

This can be entered through the fine 14th-century **Cloister**, a Gothic quadrangle with leering gargoyles. A better way, though, is to circumnavigate the huge bulk of the cathedral and palace complex towards the west front, and the **Cour St-Eutrope**, a spacious square that occupies the unfinished two-thirds of the cathedral itself.

This is the third church to occupy the site and was begun in 1272, at the height of the city's fortunes. To extend the new cathedral to its planned length, it would have been necessary to rebuild a section of the city wall, but a lawsuit between the city and the church brought construction to a halt. Just the same, this one-third of a cathedral is by any measure the finest on the Mediterranean, the only one comparable to the magnificent Gothic structures of the Ile-de-France. The short nave, in fact, heightens the exuberant verticality of the 131ft apse and choir, exceeded in height only by those of Amiens and Beauvais. Throughout, the structural lines are accented with ribbing or with protruding stone courses, as if the builders wanted to leave a gentle reminder of the technical skill that made such a building possible.

Inside, the best features are in the ambulatory and its chapels. Near the altar, facing the chapels, are two remarkable archepiscopal tombs. The **Tomb of Cardinal Briçonnet** (1514) has a mix of Renaissance refinement and ghoulish, grinning skeletons, typical of that age. The other, the **Tomb of Cardinal Pierre de Jugie**, is an exquisite Gothic work of 1376. The ambulatory chapels are illuminated by lovely 14th-century glass; the central **Chapelle de la Vierge**, has something really special, unique polychrome reliefs of the late 1300s. Ruined and covered in a Baroque remodelling of 1732, these were rediscovered in the last century, and are currently being restored. In the **Cathedral Treasury** (*open daily May–Sept Mon–Sat 10–5, Sun and out of season by appointment only, t 04 68 33 70 18; adm*) are medieval reliquaries, a 10th-century carved ivory plaque, and two 16th-century Flemish tapestries.

The Bourg

This is Narbonne's medieval extension across the river (now across the canal). Behind the city's popular covered **market**, the deconsecrated 13th-century church of Notre-Dame-de-Lamourguier now houses the **Musée Lapidaire**, a large collection of architectural fragments from ancient Narbonne, displayed at random (*open July and Aug 9.30–12.15 and 2–6; adm*). The **Basilique St-Paul-Serge** was first built in the

5th century and dedicated to the first bishop of Narbonne. The present building was begun in 1229, an imposing monument that was one of the first in the south to adopt the new Gothic architecture.

Narbonne's Coast

The coastal road, more or less following the path of the Roman Via Domitia, cannot follow this complicated shoreline; some detours on the backroads will be necessary to see it. Beyond **Narbonne-Plage**, a bright, modern, characterless resort, the landscape rises into the **Montagne de la Clape**, once an island and still a world in itself. Parts are lush and pine-clad, others rugged and desolate. Near the top, the chapel of **Notre-Dame-des-Auzils** has a fascinating collection of sailors' ex votos – ship models, paintings and the like, many over a century old (*get the key from the tourist office at Gruissan*). Most of those sailors came from **Gruissan**, south of La Clape. One of Narbonne's ports in the Middle Ages, Gruissan today is surrounded by lagoons and salt-pans; the charming village is set in concentric rings around a ruined 13th-century castle, built to defend the approaches to Narbonne. Gruissan's other landmark is the Plage des Pilotis, where beach cottages hang in the air. The sea regularly covers the sand here, and over a century ago people began building their houses on stilts.

Abbaye de Fontfroide

Down the D613 southwest of Narbonne, a marked side road leads to the **Abbaye de Fontfroide** (*open for guided tours only July and Aug 9.30–6, every half-hour except*

Tourist Information

Gruissan: 1 Blvd Pech-Maynaud, t 04 68 49 03 25, f 04 68 49 33 12.
Sigean: Place de la Libération, t 04 68 48 14 81.

Where to Stay and Eat

Narbonne-Plage ✉ 11100
★★Hôtel de la Clape, Rue des Flots Bleus, t 04 68 49 80 15, f 04 68 75 05 05 (*inexpensive*). Hardly upmarket, but a wonderful address from which to write home.
★★Les Trois Caravelles, Av Front de Mer, t 04 68 49 13 87, f 04 68 49 85 22 (*inexpensive*). Slightly better. *Closed Oct–Easter.*
Domaine d'Hospitalet, Route de Narbonne Plage, t 04 68 45 34 47, f 04 68 45 23 49 (*expensive–moderate*). A wine domaine on the Clape Massif, this incorporates an *auberge* with pretty rooms, a restaurant (*menus 135–180F*), and caves and wine tastings.

Gruissan ✉ 11430
L'Estagnol, t 04 68 49 01 26. A popular converted fishermen's cottage at the entrance to the village, it offers sumptuous sea-food and fish menus for 130–170F.
★★Hôtel Corail, Quai Ponant in Gruissan Port, t 04 68 49 04 43, f 04 68 49 62 89 (*inexpensive*). Has a fine restaurant specializing in *bouillabaisse* (*several menus from 92F*). *Closed Nov through Jan.*

Abbaye de Fontfroide
David Moreno, t 04 68 01 86 00. Abbaye de Fontfroide has also become a gastronomic halt, with chef David Moreno installed in his eponymous restaurant and serving such *nouveau* delights as pig's trotter and oyster croquettes (*menus 198–380F*). *Open eves only.* For lunch you might try the tuna steak-frites at the bistro version of David Moreno, **Les Cuisiniers Vignerons**, in an old abbey *bergerie* (*menus 84–148F*).

1pm; April–July and Sept–Oct 10–12 and 2–5, every 45 minutes; Nov–Mar 10–12 and 2–4, every hour; adm). Fontfroide was founded in 1145, and until its suppression in 1791, it was one of the richest and most influential of all Cistercian houses in the south. The best part of the tour is Fontfroide's lovely 13th-century **cloister**, with its broad arches inset with smaller ones. The 12th-century **church** impresses with its proportions and Romanesque austerity. Fascinating abstract collages of old stained-glass fragments can be seen in the **dormitory**, brought here from northern French churches wrecked during the First World War.

Carcassonne

After running north down from the Pyrenees, the river Aude makes a sharp right turn for the sea, thus conveniently providing not only an easy natural route into the mountains, but also one across the 'French isthmus', between the Mediterranean and the Atlantic. The river's angle, one of the crossroads of France since prehistoric times, is an obvious site for a fortress; there seems to have been one nearby since the 8th century BC. From 1084 to 1209 Carcassonne enjoyed a glorious period of wealth and culture under the Trencavels, a family who were also viscounts of Béziers and Nîmes, and very sympathetic to the Cathars. Under them the cathedral and the Château Comtal were begun. Simon de Montfort, realizing the importance of the town, made it one of his first stops in the Crusade of 1209. The last viscount Trencavel was captured and probably poisoned by Montfort, who declared himself viscount and used Carcassonne as his base of operations until his death in 1218. When France gobbled up the province of Roussillon in 1659, this mighty bastion no longer had any military purpose, and it was allowed to fall into disrepair. Today's Carcassonne has a split personality: up on its hill, the pink towers of the lovingly restored *cité* glitter like a dream. No longer impregnable, its 750 inhabitants are invaded by over 200,000 visitors each year, while down below, the workaday Ville Basse gets on with the job.

The Walls of the Cité

Most visitors come in through the back door, by the car parks and the bus stop, at the **Porte Narbonnaise**. Between the two walls of the *cité*, you can circumnavigate Carcassonne through the open space called **les Lices**, the 'lists', where knights rained, and where tournaments were held. The **outer wall** is the work of Louis IX; note how it is completely open on the inside, so that attackers who stormed it would have no protection from the defenders on the **inner wall** – parts date back to the Romans.

To the right of the Porte Narbonnaise, the first large tower is the mighty **Tour du Trésau**. Beyond it, the northern side of the inner wall is almost completely Roman, with the characteristic rounded bastions used all over the Empire. The walls to the left of the Porte Narbonnaise were almost completely rebuilt under Philip III, a long stretch of impressive bastions culminating in the great **Tour St-Nazaire**. Atop both the inner and outer walls, almost everything you see today – the crenellations, wooden

Getting Around

There are **trains** to Toulouse and Narbonne (11 a day), and from there to all the coastal cities; also a few trains down the Aude valley to Limoux and Quillan. Several **buses** a day go to Narbonne and Castelnaudary, three to Toulouse, and a rare few to outlying towns like Limoux. Some buses to villages in the Montagne Noire and Minervois leave from the Café Bristol in front of the rail station. To get up to the *cité*, take the no.4 city bus (every 30 minutes) from the rail station or from Place Gambetta.

Tourist Information

The main office is at 15 Bd Camille Pelletan, opposite Place Gambetta, in the centre of the Ville Basse; **t** 04 68 10 24 30, **f** 04 68 10 24 38, *www.tourisme.fr/carcassonne/*. In the *cité* (*summer only*), by the Porte Narbonnaise, **t** 04 68 10 24 35, **f** 04 68 10 24 37.

Where to Stay

Carcassonne ✉ 11000

Stay in the *cité* if you can, but it's not cheap.

★★★★De la Cité, Place St-Nazaire, **t** 04 68 71 98 71, **f** 04 68 71 50 15 (*luxury*). In a pretty garden under the walls, this hotel occupies the former episcopal palace, restored in 1909, with marble baths, a pool and a restaurant (*menus 80–160F*).

★★★Du Donjon, Rue du Comte Roger, **t** 04 68 71 08 80, **f** 04 68 25 06 60 (*moderate*). In another charming old mansion of the *cité*, with a small garden and a fine restaurant where even the humble *cassoulet* reaches new heights (*menus 89–130F*).

★★Hôtel du Pont Vieux, 32 Rue Trivalle, **t** 04 68 25 24 99, **f** 04 68 47 62 71 (*inexpensive*). One of the closest hotels to the *cité*, and one of the best. No restaurant.

Auberge de Jeunesse, Rue Vicomte-Trencavel, **t** 04 68 25 23 16, **f** 04 68 71 14 84. In the centre; fax or write to reserve in summer. *Closed mid-Jan–mid-Feb.*

All of the rest are down in the Ville Basse, near the train station or Bd Jean Jaurès.

★★★Trois Couronnes, 2 Rue des Trois Couronnes, **t** 04 68 25 36 10, **f** 04 68 25 92 92 (*moderate*). A modern hotel by the river in the lower town, which makes up for its unprepossessing appearance with a stupendous view of La Cité, and a very good restaurant (*menus 125–160F*).

galleries (*hourds*) and pointed turrets that make up Carcassonne's memorable skyline – is the work of Viollet-le-Duc. As in all his other works, the pioneer of architectural restoration has been faulted for not adhering literally to original appearances. This is true, especially concerning the pointed turrets and northern slate roofs, but Viollet-le-Duc worked in a time before anyone could have imagined our own rigorous, antiseptic approach to recreating the old. His romantic, 19th-century appreciation of the Middle Ages made possible a restoration that was not only essentially correct, but creative and beautiful.

The defences are strongest on the western side because here, the *cité's* three lines of defence – the outer and inner walls and the citadel, the **Château Comtal** – are closely compressed. Probably the site of the Roman governors' palace, it was rebuilt by the Trencavels for their own palace, and expanded by King Louis IX (*open Nov–Mar 9.30am–5pm; Apr, May and Oct 9.30am–6pm; Jun–Sept 9.30am–7.30pm; adm*). You have a choice of **guided tours** of the walls and towers (*40 or 90 minutes, usually on the hour, schedule posted at the entrance*) which begin with a room-sized model and continue, in fascinating, excruciating detail, through an advanced course in medieval military architecture. Louis' builders laid many traps for invaders – for example the

★Astoria, 18 Rue Tourtel, t 04 68 25 31 38, f 04 68 71 34 14 (*cheap*). A friendly, family-run place, with a comfy *decor à l'anglaise*.

★★★★Domaine d'Auriac, Rte St-Hilaire, south of town, t 04 68 25 72 22, f 04 68 47 35 54 (*expensive*). A Relais et Châteaux hotel in a stately, ivy-covered 18th-century mansion set in a large, immaculately kept park. There's a pool, tennis, and even a golf course close by. Also an elegant and highly-rated restaurant, featuring some seafood but mostly traditional dishes of the Aude, such as pigeon with truffles (*dinner 250–400F*). *Hotel closed Sun and Mon Oct–May; restaurant closed mid-Nov–Feb.*

★★★Auberge du Château de Cavanac, Cavanac, 4km south on the Rte St-Hilaire, t 04 68 79 61 04, f 04 68 79 79 67 (*moderate*). A big farmhouse in a garden, with an excellent restaurant serving a unique five-course 198F menu with wine and all the works, starting with a kir and a choice of foie gras, smoked salmon or lobster. *Closed mid-Jan–mid-Feb; restaurant only open eves, closed Sun, closed Mon out of season.*

Eating Out

Jardins de la Tour, 11 Rue Porte d'Aude, t 04 68 25 71 24. A pretty, idiosyncratic restaurant with garden dining and authentic regional dishes and fish (*menus 80–100F*). Book.

Le Pont-Levis, t 04 68 25 55 23. Has a terrace near Porte Narbonnaise and specializes in langoustines in various guises (*135–280F menu*). *Closed Sun eve and Mon.*

Dame Carcas, 3 Place du Château, t 04 68 71 23 23. Delicious wood-fired food (*menus 85 and 145F, dinner only*). *Closed mid-Jan–mid-Feb, and Mon.*

Le Languedoc, 32 Allée Iéna, t 04 68 25 22 17. A popular restaurant with a patio, famed for its *cassoulet* with *confit de canard* and foie gras salad (*menus 135–250F*).

L'Oeil, 32 Rue de Lorraine, t 04 68 25 64 81. In the Ville Basse, feast on smoked duck *magret* and southwest fare (*menus 85–120F*). *Closed Sat lunch, Sun, and Aug.*

Escalier, 23 Bd Omer Sarraut, t 04 68 25 65 66. Something of an institution in Carcassonne, where Tex Mex, pizza and moussaka collide (*menus 100 and 120F*).

Terminus, 2 Av Maréchal Joffre, t 04 68 20 93 33, f 04 68 72 53 09 (*inexpensive*). For a touch of class at economy prices, used as a set in a number of French films; this is an inexpensive restaurant close to the railway station (*menus 60F and à la carte*).

stairways where each riser is a different height. Your ticket also includes the **Musée Lapidaire**, which fills much of the palace. Old prints and paintings give an idea of the half-ruined state of the *cité* before Viollet-le-Duc went to work on it, with houses half-filling les Lices and windmills along the walls.

Erected in 1096, the cité's **Basilique St-Nazaire** took shape as an austere, typically southern Romanesque cathedral. The French conquerors had more ambitious plans, and in 1270 rebuilt the transepts and choir in glorious, perpendicular Gothic. The windows illuminate the interior (*open summer 9–12 and 2–7, July–Aug 9–7; winter 9.30–12 and 2–5.30*) with beautiful 16th- and 17th-century stained glass. In the right aisle, you can pay your respects to the devil himself, at the **Tomb of Simon de Montfort**, marked by a plaque.

The Aude's Northwest Corner: the Lauragais

West of Carcassonne and the Montagne Noire lies a region called the Lauragais, a mostly flat expanse of serious farming of the humbler sort: beans, barley and pigs.

Windmills are a chief landmark, as is the shady blue and nearly straight ribbon of the Canal du Midi en route to Toulouse. Rugby makes the juices flow in these parts, but in the old days it was Catharism.

Castelnaudary, Famous for Beans

French cookery books claim that a *cassoulet* requires four things: 'white beans from Lavelanet, cooked in the pure water of Castelnaudary, in a casserole made of clay from the Issel, over a fire of furze from the Black Mountain'. Back in the 1570s, Castelnaudary's *cassoulet* was prescribed to Queen Margot as a cure for sterility, unfortunately without success. Today, housewives are torn between making their own, which takes hours, or succumbing to the allure of the canned version. With *cassoulet*, the charms of Castelnaudary are nearly exhausted. There is the 14th-century church of **St-Michel**, with a steeple that dominates the city; also the **Moulin de Cugarel**, a restored 17th-century windmill, one of over 30 that once spun in the vicinity (*open summer 10–12 and 3–7*), and the port of the Canal du Midi.

The Corbières

Thanks to wine, the Corbières has finally found its vocation. This scrubby, mountainous area has been the odd region out since ancient times. As a refuge for disaffected Gauls, it was a headache to the Romans. In the Middle Ages, sitting astride the boundaries of France and Aragon, it was a permanent zone of combat. Local *seigneurs* littered the landscape with castles in incredible, impregnable mountain-top sites. Some of these became the last redoubts of the persecuted Cathars; nearly all of them are ruined today. For anyone with clear lungs and a little spirit, exploring them will be a challenge and a delight.

Castles, Gorges and the Fenouillèdes

The humble D611 and D14 were the medieval main routes through the Corbières, connecting with the passes over the Pyrenees to Spain, and castles occur with the frequency of petrol stations on a motorway. **Tuchan**, a typically stark and dusty Corbières village, has no fewer than three ruined castles; the best of them, the **Château d'Aguilar**, saw plenty of action: Simon de Montfort stormed it in 1210, but the French had to take it again from rebellious barons 30 years later; over the next 200 years the Spaniards regularly knocked at the gate.

West of Tuchan the landscapes become higher and wilder. **Padern** has another castle, ruined despite rebuilding work in the 18th century; so does **Cucugnan**, a colourful little village. Both these towns offer scenic detours – from Padern, north through the **Gorges du Torgan**, and from Cucugnan, south through the spectacular **Grau de Maury**, the Corbières' back door. Cucugnan's landmark is obvious from a distance, the picture-postcard **Château de Quéribus** (*open daily 10–6, July and Aug till 8pm, in Feb, Mar, Nov, and Dec weekends only 10–5, closed Jan; adm*), balancing nonchalantly on a slender peak, a half-mile in the air. The best-maintained of the Corbières castles, Quéribus was the last redoubt of the Cathars after Montségur (*see* p. 618); a small band of bitter-enders held out for months here in 1255.

Castles atop mountains will be nothing new by now, but nowhere else, perhaps, is there a bigger castle atop a taller, steeper mountain than the **Château de Peyrepertuse** (*open April–Sept 10–7, July and Aug 9–8; adm; at other times, free – there's no gate*). From Cucugnan, it is an unforgettable sight, a white, limestone cliff rising vertically in the clouds, crowned by a stretch of walls and towers over 777ft long. Close up, from the bottom of the cliff, you can't see it at all. Begun in the 10th century, Peyrepertuse was expanded by St Louis in the 1240s. As important to the defence of France's new southern border as Carcassonne, Peyrepertuse was intended as an unconquerable base; attacking the place would be madness; no one ever tried. The vertiginous road to the castle starts from Duilhac; from the car park it's an exhausting 20-minute struggle up to the walls. The entrance leads into the **Château Vieux**, the original castle, rebuilt by St Louis. Nearly everything is in ruins; the keep is still in good shape, and a large cistern and the ruined chapel can be seen directly behind it. The **Château St-Georges**, with another keep and chapel, is on top.

There are no easy roads in any other direction from Peyrepertuse, but if you're heading west, rejoin the main route by way of the D7 and the white cliffs of the **Gorges de Galamus**, the most impressive natural wonder of the Corbières, a deep gorge with wonderful stone pools for swimming and canyoning.

Descending from Opoul to the southwest, the D9 passes through some romantically empty scenery towards **Tautavel**, a pretty village under a rocky escarpment. Human bones have been found around here from as far back as 450–680,000 BC, making 'Tautavel Man' a contender for the honour of First European. Palaeolithic bones have become a cottage industry – over 430,000 have been found, especially in a cave called the **Caune de l'Arago** (*north of the village, open June–Aug for guided tours*) – the best being displayed in the village's archaeological museum, **Musée de la Prehistoire** (*open April–June 10–7, July and Aug 9–9, Sept 10–6, Jan–Mar and Oct–Dec 10–12.30 and 2–6*).

The Agly valley and the mountains around it make up the **Fenouillèdes**. Though equally mountainous, its scenery makes a remarkable contrast to the dry and windswept Corbières. Here, limestone gives way to granite, and much of it is covered by ancient virgin forest.

The Valley of the Upper Aude, and Rennes-le-Château

Near the castle of Puilaurens, the D117 joins the course of the Aude, passing northwards through a spectacular canyon, the **Défilé de Pierre-Lys**. The *pays* that begins here is called the **Razès**, a sparse, scrubby, somewhat haunted region, the back door to the Corbières. **Quillan**, the first town after the Pierre-Lys canyon, makes its living from manufacturing shoes; it has an odd, perfectly square castle from the 1280s, and does its bit to cash in on the Cathars with models of the castles and exhibits at the **Espace Cathare,** by the tourist office in Place de la Gare (*open daily 10–12 and 2–6; adm*).

Whatever is haunting the Razès, it resides in **Rennes-le-Château,** a woebegone mountain-top village above Couiza. The fun began in the 1890s, when the young parish priest, Berenger Saunière, began spending huge sums of money on himself

Getting Around

SNCF rail-lines make a neat square around the Corbières, but none of them ventures inside the region. The only useful one is from Carcassonne, stopping at Limoux, Alet-les-Bains, Couiza, Quillan and St-Paul-de-Fenouillet on its way to Perpignan. Don't count on buses either. There are some services from Perpignan's bus station up the Agly valley to Maury, St-Paul and Quillan, and one a day through the heart of the Fenouillèdes to Sournia.

Tourist Information

Lézignan-Corbières: Cours de la République, t 04 68 27 05 42.
St-Paul-de-Fenouillet: t 04 68 59 07 57.
Quillan: Place de la Gare, t 04 68 20 07 78, f 04 68 20 04 91.

Where to Stay and Eat

For tourism, the Corbières is virgin territory; accommodation is fairly scarce.

Lézignan-Corbières ✉ 11200
★★Le Tassigny, Place de Tassigny, t 04 68 27 11 51, f 04 68 27 67 31 (*inexpensive*). Has a restaurant, Le Tournados (*menus 75–140F*). *Closed Mon and Sun eve.*
Le Patio, Bd Général Sarrail, on the outskirts, t 04 68 27 42 23. Best for seafood (*menus 75–185F*). *Closed Sun eve and Mon out of season.*
Stromboli, 43 Cours Lapeyrouse, t 04 68 27 00 81. A popular pizzeria.

Maury ✉ 66460
L'Auberge du Grand Rocher, Rue Eloi Tresserres, Caramany, t 04 68 84 51 58. This simply furnished restaurant in a pretty hill town is

well worth the 20min drive from Maury; the terrace has lovely views over the valley. The husband-and-wife team prepare perfectly cooked local specialities at moderate prices: *confit de canard* with potatoes roasted in duck fat (the best in the region), or roast lamb with thyme. Leave room for *crème catalan* and a glass of Banyuls (*menus 80–165F*). Always call ahead.
★★Hôtel des Graves, 9 Bd Jean-Jaurès, Estagel near Tautavel on the D117, t 04 68 29 00 84, f 04 68 29 47 04 (*inexpensive*). If you're passing by you can eat and/or sleep well and economically at this hotel owned by the local wine barons; Catalan specialities served with wine from you know where (*menus 79–139F*).

Cucugnan ✉ 11350
★★Auberge du Vigneron, 1 Rue Achille-Mir, t 04 68 45 03 00, f 04 68 45 03 08 (*inexpensive*). Cosy rooms and a restaurant in a former wine cellar serving simple but fragrant dishes (*menus from 100F*). *Closed Mon, Sun eve in the off season.*

St-Paul-de-Fenouillet ✉ 66220
★★Le Chatelet, Rte de Caudies, t 04 68 59 01 20, f 04 68 59 01 29 (*inexpensive*). A Logis de France hotel, with a pool and restaurant (*menus 80–180F*).
★Relais des Corbières, 10 Av Jean Moulin, t 04 68 59 23 89 (*inexpensive*). Smaller, central and also Logis de France.

Tautavel ✉ 66720
Le Petit Gris, Route d'Estagel, t 04 68 29 42 42. Popular family restaurant, especially for Sunday lunch, so you'll need to book. There are great views of the plain from big windows, and they serve grilled dishes including an excellent Catalan *cargolade* of snails, pork, lamb and sausages cooked on your own grill (*menus 70–170F*).

and on embellishing his church. The story, and the speculation, hasn't stopped unfolding since. Rennes-le-Château's one permanent business is an occult bookshop, where you can pick up a copy of the 1970s bestseller *Holy Blood, Holy Grail* that attracted international attention to Rennes, describing Jesus' problematical but well-publicized European tour after a faked crucifixion. It has been a recurring theme in French and English legend from the beginning ('And did those feet in ancient time,' etc.). Here, the idea is that Jesus came to Gaul with his wife Mary Magdalene; both may have been buried in Rennes, and their descendants were the lazy 'do-nothing' Merovingian kings of France, deposed in the 8th century by a shady deal between the popes and Carolingians. Supposedly, the blood line has survived to this day.

Did Saunière discover proof of Jesus' tomb and make his fortune by blackmailing the Vatican? Or did he find the Holy Grail, or the treasure of the Visigoths, the Merovingians, or the Templars? The most fashionable theory these days leans towards the fabulous treasure of the Jews, stolen from Jerusalem by Titus in AD 10, and pillaged in turn by the Visigoths, before ending up in safekeeping in the impregnable fortress at Rennes. Saunière used his money to pave the road up to Rennes and redo the **church** dedicated (naturally) to Mary Magdalene, with unorthodox imagery, beginning with a statue of Asmodeus, the gaurdian of King Solomon's treasure (*open 10.45–6.45*). An adjacent **museum** (*open 10–6 in summer;, 10–5 in winter; adm*) relates some of this to the Cathars, who had a mysterious treasure of their own that they slipped out of Montségur and hid in parts unknown before the bitter end.

Into the Limousin

Before its right turn at Carcassonne, the Aude traverses a lovely, modest stretch of open rolling country, the Limousin. Most of the roads here are still graced with their long arcades of plane trees – there isn't enough traffic yet to threaten them.

On the Aude, **Alet-les-Bains** is one of the most beautiful and best-preserved medieval villages of Languedoc. A small spa since Roman times, Alet owes its prominence to the popes, who made it a bishopric in 1318. Its two jewels are the 14th-century church of **St-André** with frescoes and a fine west portal, and the nearby impressive Benedictine **abbey**, founded in the 9th century and wrecked in the Wars of Religion. Even before you notice the vineyards, the civilized landscapes suggest wine. **Limoux**, the capital, is an attractive town, with a medieval bridge across the Aude, the

Pont Neuf; this meets the apse and steeple of **St-Martin**, a good piece of Gothic, if anachronistic – though the church was begun in the 1300s, most of the work is from three centuries later. The centre is the arcaded **Place de la République**.

To the east of Limoux, a pretty side road (the D104) takes you to **St-Hilaire d'Aude** (*open July–Sept for guided tours,* **t** *04 68 69 41 15*), an abbey founded in the 8th century; its Benedictine monks invented the bubbly Blanquette de Limoux. A graceful, double-columned Gothic cloister survives, along with the Romanesque abbey church, containing the white marble sarcophagus of St Sernin (d. 250), the patron of Toulouse, sculpted by the Master of Cabestany – one of his masterpieces. South of St-Hilaire, the monastery of **St-Polycarpe** is just as old, though not as well preserved.

Roussillon

Heading for the southernmost angle of the French Hexagon, you'll begin to notice a certain non-Gallic whimsy in the names of the towns. The further south you go in Roussillon the stranger they become: Llivia, Llous and Llupia, Eus and Oms, Molitg, Politg and Py. Streets signs appear in two languages, and on your restaurant table impossibly sweet wines will appear. You are among the Catalans, in the corner of Catalunya that, for military considerations in the 17th century, was destined to become part of France. Perpignan is the capital, and around it stretches the broad Roussillon plain, Collioure and the delectable Côte Vermeille, and spectacular valleys that climb up into the Pyrenees.

The Roussillon Coast and the Côte Vermeille

A geographical oddity, the northern Roussillon coastline is nearly perfectly straight, and runs due north–south for 40km, from Port-Barcarès to Argelès. It isn't the most compelling landscape, but it is almost solid beach, and has been greatly developed since the 1940s. After Argelès, the shoreline, now called the Côte Vermeille, changes dramatically, climbing into the Pyrenees. The red clay soil of the ubiquitous olive groves lends the area a vermilion tint, and there is a remarkable mix of light and air. Henri Matisse spent one summer here, at Collioure, and the result was a milestone in the artistic revolution called Fauvism.

The Roussillon Coast

New government-planned resorts at Leucate-Plage and Port-Leucate initiate the least attractive stretch of Languedoc's coast, continuing for 8km down to **Port-Barcarès**. Inland behind the Etang de Salses appears the last, lowest, and least spectacular of this region's many castles – but the **Forteresse de Salses** was the most important of them all (*guided tours on the hour daily except Tues, open July and Aug 9.30–7, June and Sept 9.30–6.30, April, May and Oct 9.30–12.30 and 2–6, winter 10–12 and 2–5; adm*). Built in 1497 by Ferdinand the Catholic, first king of united Spain,

Getting Around

The coastal railway from Narbonne to Spain passes through Leucate, Salses and Rivesaltes, dipping inland for Perpignan before returning to the coast; there are frequent services to Elne, and then Collioure and Cerbère.

There are buses from the station in Perpignan to resorts where the train doesn't go, such as Canet and Port-Barcarès, as well as frequent services to the Côte Vermeille. In the summer a Bus Inter-Plages stops at all ten resorts, from Barcarès and Cerbère.

Tourist Information

Salses: Place de la Répubique, t 04 68 38 66 13, f 04 68 39 60 83.
St-Cyprien: Quai Arthur Rimbaud, t 04 68 21 01 33, f 04 68 21 98 33.
Elne: 2 Rue Docteur-Bolte, t 04 68 22 05 07, f 04 68 37 95 05.
Collioure: Place du 18 Juin, t 04 68 82 15 47, f 04 68 82 46 29.
Port-Vendres: Quai Forgas, t 04 68 82 07 54, f 04 68 82 53 48.
Banyuls-sur-Mer: Ave de la République, t 04 68 88 31 58, f 04 68 88 36 84.

Where to Stay and Eat

St-Cyprien ✉ 66750

★★★**Mas d'Huston**, t 04 68 37 63 63 f 04 68 37 64 64 (*expensive; 535–770F*). Adjacent to the golf course; also with a pool and tennis, and two excellent restaurants: **Le Mas** (*menus 185–270F*) and **Les Parasols** (*menus 160–270F*).

★★★**L'Almadin**, Bd de l'Almadin, t 04 68 21 01 02, f 04 68 21 06 28 (*expensive*). Air-conditioned rooms, tennis, pool, all on its own little island. The restaurant is considered one of the best on the coast, with stylish treatment of Catalan dishes, such as *carré d'agneau* with garlic *jus*, and shrimps *escalivada* marinaded in olive oil (*menus 210–395F*). *Restaurant closed Mon and Tues Oct–mid-April.*

Elne ✉ 66201

★★**Le Weekend**, 29 Av Paul Roig, t 04 68 22 06 68, f 04 68 22 17 16 (*inexpensive*). A delightful place with only eight rooms and a garden terrace far from the crowds; good home cooking, too (*menus 93 and 130F*). *Closed Nov–mid-Feb.*

Argelès-sur-Mer ✉ 66700

Auberge de Roua, Chemin du Roua, t 04 68 95 85 85, f 04 68 95 83 50 (*moderate*). A little Catalan *auberge* with a terrace. The cooking adds a twist to Mediterranean classics; try

Salses was the last word in castles. It was meant to guard Perpignan and the coast but did not have a chance to do so until 1639. The Spaniards, caught by surprise, had only a small garrison at Salses; nevertheless, it required 18,000 Frenchmen and a month's siege to take it. The same year, a Spanish army spent 3 months regaining it.

Back on the coast, **Canet-en-Roussillon** is the favourite resort of the Perpignanais. After taking a beating in the last war, it has been rebuilt without much distinction. South, past a long stretch of wild beach, you'll find **St-Cyprien-Plage**, which looks just like Canet, only more so. South again, **Argelès-Plage** makes some claim as the European Capital of Camping with 84 sites and a capacity for 100,000 happy campers. Between these last two resorts, set a little way inland atop a steep hill, the citadel of **Elne** has guarded the Roussillon plain for at least 2,700 years. Through the Middle Ages, and until the 1500s, Elne remained the most important city in Roussillon and seat of the archbishops. Its **cathedral**, a fortified church begun in 1069 with a wonderful stage presence, has a crenellated roof-line and stout, arcaded tower. The **cloister**

monkfish with orange and almonds (*menus 165–280F*).

Collioure ✉ 66190

★★★Casa Païral Impasse des Palmiers, t 04 68 82 05 81, **f** 04 68 82 52 10 (*expensive–moderate*). For an agreeable stay in the centre; a dignified, Mansard-roofed palace a few streets from the shore. There is a wide choice of rooms, from the simple to the luxurious; also a pool and enclosed garden. *Closed Nov–April.*

★★★La Frégate, Av Camille Pelletan, **t** 04 68 82 06 05, **f** 04 68 82 55 00 (*inexpensive*). This pink and jolly place is on the busiest corner of Collioure, but has been soundproofed and air-conditioned; it has a good restaurant, decorated with *azulejos* (*mostly seafood; menus from 100–190F*).

★★Les Templiers, Quai de l'Amiranté, **t** 04 68 98 31 10, **f** 04 68 98 01 24 (*inexpensive*). Picasso, Matisse, Dufy and Dalí all stayed here, and owner Réné Pous was friend to them all. Each room has its own charm; reservations are imperative. The bar is a friendly local hang-out, festooned with paintings, and the restaurant is excellent, with a terrace and imaginative dishes like cod with aioli and pine nuts (*menu 120F*).

Boramar, 19 Rue Jean-Bart, on the Plage du Faubourg, **t** 04 68 82 07 06 (*inexpensive*). A simple budget choice overlooking the busiest beach. *Closed Nov–Mar.*

Ermitage Notre-Dame-de-Consolation, above Collioure on the D86, **t** 04 68 82 17 66 (*inexpensive*). A pleasant B&B.

Neptune, Rte Prt Vendres, **t** 04 68 82 02 27. One of the best restaurants in town, with wonderful canopied sea views and the full *nouvelle* Catalan cuisine on the order of lobster ravioli with cardamon vinaigrette. Ravishing desserts include poached figs and rosemary sorbet (*menus 185–330F*).

La Marinade, Place 18 Juin, **t** 04 68 82 09 76. Delectable seafood from simple *sardines en papillote* to an elaborate Catalan *bouillabaisse* (*menus from 78 to 156F*).

Banyuls-sur-Mer ✉ 66650

★★Les Elmes, Plages des Elmes, **t** 04 68 88 03 12, **f** 04 68 88 53 03 (*moderate–inexpensive*). Pleasant seaside rooms and an excellent restaurant serving Catalan dishes (*menus 90–175F*); half-board is excellent value.

★★La Pergola, 5 Av Fontaulé, by the port, **t** 04 68 88 02 10, **f** 04 68 88 55 45 (*inexpensive*). Immaculate rooms and good fish (*menus 80–200F*).

★La Plage, on the beach strip, **t** 04 68 88 34 90. Serves satisfying seafood; set menus at 130F include *sole meunière*, grilled salmon or *parillade*, a Catalan mixed grill.

Chez Rosa, Rue St-Pierre, **t** 04 68 88 31 89. A lace-curtained neighbourhood favourite for lunch; tasty roast pork, couscous, chicken, and mushrooms (*85F menu*).

(*open daily except during services April–May 9.30–6, June–Sept 9.30–7, Oct–Mar 9.30–12 and 2–5; adm*), is perhaps the best in the Midi, and also the best-preserved. Capitals and pillars are decorated with imaginative, exquisitely carved arabesques and floral patterns. The sides were completed in different periods, in 50-year intervals.

The Côte Vermeille: Collioure and Beyond

It's hard to believe, looking at the map, but in the Middle Ages the village of **Collioure** was the port for Perpignan; with no good harbours on the dismal and (then) unhealthy coast to the north, Perpignan's fabrics and other goods had to come to the Pyrenees to go to sea. In the 14th century Collioure was one of the biggest trading centres of Aragon, but nearly the whole town was demolished by the French after they took possession in 1659. In 1905 it was discovered by Matisse and Derain. Many other artists followed, including Picasso, but these two were the most inspired by the place. The village has created the *Chemin du fauvisme*, placing copies of their works on the spots where the two set up their easels. In a peaceful villa on the south edge of town over a lovely terraced olive grove, the **Musée d'Art Moderne** (*open daily June–Sept, closed Tues Oct–May; adm*), has works by lesser-known artists in the style of the Fauves, as well as an intriguing collection of Moorish ceramics.

Collioure is a thoroughly Catalan town, and the red and yellow striped Catalan flag waves proudly over the **Château Royal**, dominating the harbour (*open daily 10–6 in summer, 9–5 in winter; adm*). First built by the Templars in the 13th century, it was expanded by various Aragonese kings. The outer fortifications, low walls and broad banks of earth, were state-of-the-art in 1669. From the castle, cross the small stream called the Douy (usually dry and used as a car park) into the Mouré, the old quarter that is now the centre of Collioure. There is an amiable shorefront, with a small beach from which a few anchovy fishermen still ply their trade. At the far end you'll see Collioure's landmark, painted by Matisse and others: the church of **Notre-Dame-des-Anges**, built in the 1680s to replace the church destroyed by the French. The best thing about the church is that you can hear the waves of the sea from inside, a profound *basso continuo* that makes the celebration of Mass here a unique experience. The next best are the five retables (1699–1720) by Joseph Sunyer and others. The second of Collioure's beaches lies right behind the church; it connects the town with a former islet, the **Ilot St-Vincent**, crowned with a tiny medieval chapel. High above, you'll see **Fort Miradoux**, the Spanish King Philip II's addition.

Port-Vendres is a real port, modern-style, with none of the charm of Collioure; its main business is anchovy fishing. **Banyuls-sur-Mer** (Banyuls de la Marenda in Catalan) is the next town along the picturesque coastal N114, a sleepy resort with a beach and mini-golf right at the centre. The heart of the Banyuls wine region, it is also the home of the **Fondation Arago**, an oceanographic laboratory affiliated to the University of Paris. Their excellent Aquarium of Mediterranean species was built in 1883 (*open daily 9–12 and 2–6.30, till 10 in July and Aug; adm*). As for art, Banyuls has a good 11th-century Romanesque church, **La Rectorie**, on Ave du Puig-del-Mas and takes credit for Aristide Maillol, perhaps the best-known French sculptor of the 19th century after Rodin, born here in 1861. His tomb, documents tracing his life, and a few copies of works are in his old farm house, La Métairie, now the **Musée Aristide Maillol**, 4km up the Col de Banyuls road (*open 9–12, 2–5, closed Tues and hols; adm*).

If you don't care to go to Spain, there's an extremely scenic route through the mountains back to Collioure, along the steep and narrow D86. Several abandoned fortresses come into view. The **Tour Madeloc** is the highlight, a signal tower, part of a communications network that kept the medieval Kings of Aragon in close contact with their borders.

Perpignan

PERPIGNAN DEAD CITY is the slogan the local anarchists write on the walls, and if that's slightly premature, you can't help wondering about a town named after a reactionary murderer, one that has let its most beautiful Gothic monument become a

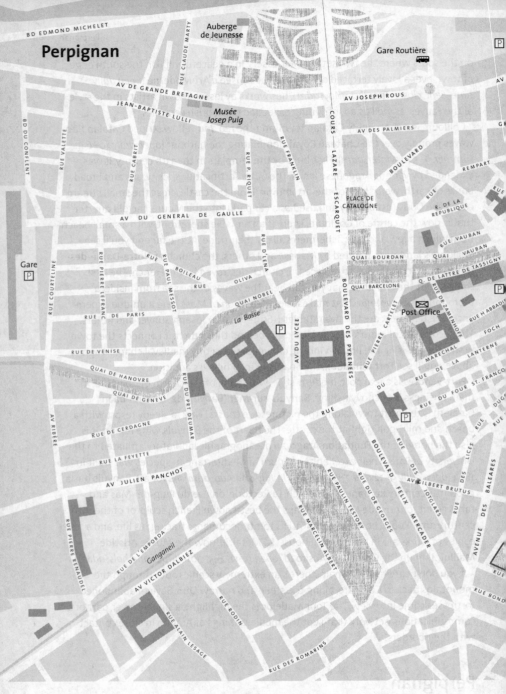

Perpignan

hamburger franchise, and which highlights its tourist brochure with a photo of its trucking terminal. Perpignan is named after Perperna, a lieutenant in the Roman army who murdered his boss, the great 1st-century BC populist general, Quintus Sertorius. The city enjoyed its most brilliant period in the 13th century when Jaime I,

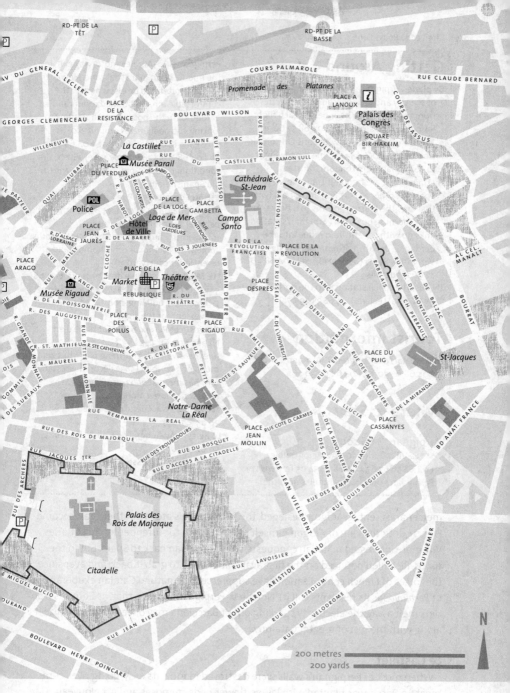

king of Aragon and conqueror of Majorca, created the Kingdom of Majorca and
County of Roussillon for his younger son Jaime II. This little kingdom was absorbed by
the Catalan kings of Aragon in the 14th century, but continued to prosper until 1463,
when Louis XI's army came to claim Perpignan and Roussillon as payment for

Getting Around

By plane: Perpignan's airport is 7km northwest of the city and linked by aerobus *navettes* from the station an hour before each flight (info from the airport on t 04 68 52 60 70). There are connections with Paris Orly on Air Liberté and AOM. Ryanair has a daily flight to Perpignan from London-Stansted.

By train: There are frequent trains down to the Spanish border at Port Bou and a new TGV that cuts the journey to Paris to 6 hours. An early morning bus from Perpignan's station links up with *Le Petit Train Jaune* into the Cerdagne, departing from Villefranche-Vernet-les-Bains (*see* p.1018); call t 04 68 96 22 96 for details.

By bus: The coach station is to the north, on Av Général Leclerc, t 04 68 35 29 02.

Tourist Information

In the Palais des Congrès, Pl. Armand-Lanoux, t 04 68 66 30 30, f 04 68 66 30 26.

Where to Stay

Perpignan ✉ 66000

****La Villa Duflot**, 109 Av Victor Dalbiez, t 04 68 56 67 67, f 04 68 56 54 05 (*expensive*). Perpignan's only luxury hotel is near the Perpignan-Sud–Argelès motorway exit, in the middle of an industrial zone. However, you can pretend to be elsewhere in the comfortable air-conditioned rooms and garden, or in the popular restaurant overlooking the pool (*meals around 250F*).

***Le Park**, 18 Bd Jean-Bourrat, t 04 68 35 14 14, f 04 68 35 48 18 (*inexpensive*). Plush, air-conditioned, sound-proofed rooms with an old Spanish flair.

***Hôtel de la Loge**, 1 Rue Fabrique d'en Nabot, t 04 68 34 41 02, f 04 68 34 25 13 (*inexpensive*). Nicest in the centre, in a 16th-century building, this has pretty rooms, some with TV and air conditioning, and a lovely inner courtyard.

Le Maillol, 14 Impasse des Cardeurs, t 04 68 51 10 20, f 04 68 51 20 29 (*inexpensive*). In a 17th-century building: not too noisy, and convenient for the sights.

La Poste et Perdix, 6 Rue Fabrique d'en Nabot, t 04 68 34 42 53, f 04 68 34 58 20 (*inexpensive*). This charming place has kept much of its original 1832 décor; the restaurant has menus for 62–110F. *Closed Feb; restaurant closed Mon.*

Le Helder, Av Général de Gaulle, t 04 68 34 38 05 (*cheap*).

*Le Berry**, 6 Av Général de Gaulle, t 04 68 34 59 02 (*cheap*).

Auberge de la Jeunesse, Av de Grande-Bretagne, t 04 68 34 63 32 (*cheap*). A small

mercenaries sent to Aragon. Besieged, the Perpignanais ate rats rather than become French, until the king of Aragon himself ordered them to surrender. In 1493 Charles VIII, more interested in Italian conquests, gave Perpignan back to Spain. But in the 1640s, Richelieu pounced on the first available chance to grab it back, and ever since the forces of French centralization have suppressed the natural Catalan exuberance of *Perpinyà* (as its residents call it). Not a few Perpignanais hope that, as Europe's frontiers melt away, the electricity sparking out of Barcelona may once again galvanize it along with the rest of greater Catalunya.

Le Castillet

When most of Perpignan's walls were destroyed in 1904, its easy-going river-cum-moat, La Basse, was planted with lawns, flower-beds, mimosas and Art Nouveau cafés. Only the fat brick towers and crenellated gate of **Le Castillet** were left upright; built in 1368 by Aragon to keep out the French, it became a prison once the French got in. Le Castillet now houses a cosy museum of Catalan art and traditions, the **Musée**

youth hostel; bed and breakfast 70F (book in summer). *Closed 20 Dec–20 Jan.*

Eating Out

Le Chapon Fin, Park Hôtel (*see above*). Perpignan's finest restaurant, as well as one of the prettiest with its Catalan ceramics. But it's the *tartare de saumon* and ravioli stuffed with scallops that keep its folks coming back for more, even all the way from Spain (*menus 130–300F*). *Closed Sun.*

Les Trois Soeurs, 2 Rue Fontfroide, t 04 68 51 22 33. By the cathedral, a fashionable restaurant with fancy Catalan cooking: monkfish with *mousserons* (wild mushrooms), sea bass with sesame seeds, lamb with honey, and spiced pears (*menus 80–150F*).

Côte Theatre, 7 Rue Theatre, t 04 68 34 60 00. Elegantly converted restaurant in the old town, celebrated for its refined treatment of regional food, especially fish; the squid and artichoke salad is sensational (*menus 148–340F*).

Brasserie l'Arago, Place Arago, t 04 68 51 81 96. Packed day and night; good food and pizza – not always a strong point with the Catalans (*menus from 80F*).

Casa Sansa, 3 Rue Fabriques Couvertes, near Le Castillet, t 04 68 34 21 84. Lively, with excellent food from Catalan *escargots* to rabbit with *aïoli*, and more than its share of Catalan flair: occasional live music and wine tasting in a 14th-century cellar (*around 150F, lunch 49F, book Fri and Sat nights*). *Closed Sun and Mon lunch.*

Les Expéditeurs, 19 Av Général Leclerc, t 04 68 35 15 80. The classic 65F lunch with wine; hearty Catalan cooking and a tasty paella on Wed.

Entertainment and Nightlife

On evenings from June to September in Place de la Castellet, the Perpignanais come to dance *sardanas*, the national Catalan dance.

Nightlife is mostly concentrated on students, but try the following:

Le Goya bar, Rue Talrich, t 04 68 51 80 84. Heavy metal every Friday and Saturday night till 2am.

L'Estaminet, 10 Rue Grande-la-Monnaie, t 04 68 34 91 50, is a popular student bar with exhibitions of painting and photography, and poetry evenings.

Le Zinc, 8 Rue Grand-des-Fabriques, t 04 68 35 08 80, offers jazz and cocktails.

Check the listings at the **Cinema Castillet**, 1 Bd Wilson, t 04 68 51 25 47, or drive out to Mas Sabole, 11km south, for first-run films at **Le Drive-In-Ciné**, an American-style drive-in cinema (first show at 9.45pm).

Pairal (*open daily exc Tues 9–6, summer 9.30–7; adm*), with items ranging from casts of Pau (Pablo) Casals' hands to a kitchen from a Catalan *mas*. Place du Verdun, by Le Castillet, is one of Perpignan's liveliest squares, while, just outside the gate, the **Promenade des Platanes** is lined with magnificent plane trees.

Loge de Mer to the Musée Rigaud

In Place de la Loge stands Perpignan's most beautiful building, the Gothic **Loge de Mer**, or Llotja, built in 1397 by the king of Aragon. This proud and noble building of ochre stone, with its Venetian arches and loggia and ship-shaped weathercock, fell on hard times. But Perpignan takes good care of its monuments – the city rented it to a fast-food chain.

The neighbouring 13th-century **Hôtel de Ville** has been spared the Llotja's humiliation, probably because it still serves its original purpose. To the right, the **Palais de la Députation Provinciale** (1447) is a masterpiece of Catalan Renaissance, formerly the seat of Roussillon's parliament and now housing dismal municipal offices. South of the Députation, in Rue de l'Ange the **Musée Rigaud** is named after Perpignan native Hyacinthe Rigaud (1659–1743), portrait painter to Louis XIV (*open daily exc Tues 12–7; adm*). Hyacinthe, master of raising the mediocre and unworthy to virtuoso heights of rosy-cheeked, debonair charm and sophistication, is well represented, as are works by Picasso, Dufy, Maillol and Miró.

Cathédrale de St-Jean, the Dévôt Christ and the Quartier St-Jacques

Just east of Place de la Loge unfolds Place de Gambetta, site of Perpignan's pebble-and-brick **cathedral**, topped by a lacy 19th-century wrought-iron campanile. Begun in 1324 but not ready for use until 1509, the interior is a success because the builders stuck to the design provided in the 1400s by Guillem Sagrera, architect of the great cathedral of Palma de Majorca. Typical of Catalan Gothic, it has a single nave, 157ft long, striking for its spacious width rather than its soaring height. The chapels, wedged between the huge piers, hold some unique treasures, the oldest of which is a marble **baptismal font** (first chapel on the left). The cathedral is proudest of its exquisite retables: on the high altar, the marble *Retable de St-Jean*, carved in a late Renaissance style in 1621 by Claude Perret; at the end of the left crossing, the *Retable des Stes Eulalie et Julie* (1670s); in the apsidal chapels, the painted wood *Retable de St-Pierre* (mid-1500s), and to the right, the lovely, luminous *Notre-Dame de la Mangrana* (1500). A door in the right aisle leads out to a 16th-century chapel constructed especially to house the extraordinary **Dévôt Christ**. Carved in the Cologne region in 1307, this wasted Christ, whose contorted bones, sinews and torn flesh are carved with a rare anatomical realism, is stretched to the limits of agony on the Cross, almost too painful to behold.

The piquant neighbourhood south of the cathedral was once the Jewish quarter of Perpignan. After the Jews were exiled, the quarter was renamed St-Jacques, and inhabited by working men's families and Gypsies, and most recently by Algerians. The 12th–14th-century church of **St-Jacques** is opulent and rich inside: there's a 'Cross of Insults', a statue of St James in Compostela pilgrimage gear (1450) and more fine retables.

The Palace of the Kings of Majorca

Enclosed in a vast extent of walls, later enlarged by Vauban, Louis XIV's military genius, the **Palais des Rois de Majorque** (*entrance in Rue des Archers; open daily May–Sept 10–6, winter 9–5; adm*) is the oldest royal palace in France, begun in the 1270s by Jaime the Conqueror and occupied by his son Jaime II after 1283. Yet for all its grandeur, only three kings of Majorca were to reign here before Roussillon, Montpellier, the Cerdagne and the Balearic islands were reabsorbed by Aragon in 1349. The scale of magnificence that they intended to become accustomed to survives, including a mastodonic but elegant Romanesque-Gothic courtyard, but not much else. The palace is now a favourite venue for events.

West of Perpignan: Pyrenean Valleys

There are two major valleys: the **Conflent** (the valley of the river Têt) and the **Vallespir** (of the river Tech), sloping in parallel lines toward the Spanish border. Don't think that this butt end of the Pyrenees consists of foothills; in between the valleys stands snow-capped **Canigou**, not the highest (a mere 9,134ft) but certainly one of the most imposing peaks of the chain.

The Conflent (Têt Valley)

The narrow D48 wiggling west of **Castelnou**, a perfectly preserved medieval village, is unabashedly beautiful. At **Ille-sur-Têt**, an attractive old village at the gateway to the mountains, art from the 11th to 19th centuries from Roussillon's churches has been assembled in a 16th-century hospital, the **Centre d'Art Sacré** (*open daily mid-June–Sept 10–12 and 2–7, otherwise 10–12 and 3–6, closed Tues, and Sat and Sun morning*). The D2 northwest of Ille to Montalba-le-Château takes you very quickly to some surprising scenery: orange eroded 'fairy chimneys' called the **Orgues**, with a forgotten ruin of a 12th-century tower on top.

Seeing the finest medieval sculpture in Roussillon at the **Prieuré de Serrabonne** requires dedication: the most direct route requires 13km of hairpin turns, starting from the D618 at Bouleternère, just west of Ille, and ending in a remote spot on a mountain called Roque Rouge. The solemn, spare shape and dark schist of Serrabonne's church (*open daily 10–6; adm*) are not promising, making the surprise inside that much the greater. The best efforts of the 12th-century Catalan sculptors were concentrated in the single gallery of the cloister and especially in the **tribune**, in rosy marble from Canigou. Perfectly preserved in its isolated setting, this includes a fantastical bestiary, centaurs, a grimacing St Michael, and reliefs of the four Evangelists.

Prades, a typical stolid Catalan town, is known for its music festival (late July–early August) founded in 1951 by Pau Casals. A few kilometres up through orchards is **St Michel-de-Cuxa**, one of the most important monasteries of medieval Catalunya (*open 9.30–11.50 and 2–6, to 5pm in winter, closed Sun am; adm*). Even in its reduced, semi-ruined state, the scale is impressive; this was one of the great monastic centres from which medieval Europe was planned and built. St Michel is occupied by a small community of Benedictine monks from Montserrat, the centre of Catalan spiritualism and nationalism. The Romanesque architecture is Catalan as well, especially in the more-than-semicircular 'Visigothic' arches in the nave. Other notable features include the massive but elegant bell tower, and an unusual circular crypt, built in the 11th century. The crypt is covered by toroid barrel-vaulting, with a mushroom-like central column almost unique in medieval architecture. In the cloister, you can see galleries and capitals with monsters from the medieval bestiary; the rest are in New York.

Canigou, with its distinctive Phrygian cap of snow, is the 'fortunate mountain' of the Catalans, and if you feel its famous magnetism working on you, don't resist the call. You can make two thirds of the climb – 7,053ft – by car, on a forest road that begins at the east end of Prades. This leaves you at the **Chalet-Hôtel des Cortalets** refuge (*open May–Sept; call t 04 68 96 36 19 to book a bed; 80F a night, meals 90F*). From here it's a

Getting Around

The coach and train service is good, but it won't help you see rural monuments like St-Michel or Serrabonne. From the bus station in Perpignan there are 10 or 12 buses a day to Prades and Villefranche-de-Conflent; a few continue on to Font-Romeu and Latour-de-Carol. At Villefranche you can pick up *Le Petit Train Jaune*, a scenic narrow-gauge train that runs twice a day into the Cerdagne, practically unchanged since 1910. For the Vallespir, there are frequent daily buses to Arles-sur-Tech and Amélie-les-Bains-Palada, with a few pressing on further up the valley to Prats-de-Mollo.

Tourist Information

Prades: 4 Rue Victor Hugo, t 04 68 05 41 02, f 04 68 05 21 79.
Vernet-les-Bains: 6 Pl de la Mairie, t 04 68 05 55 35, f 04 68 05 60 33.
Villefranche-de-Conflent: 38 Rue St-Jacques, t 04 68 92 22 96, f 04 68 96 23 93.
Font-Romeu: 33 Av E.-Brousse, t 04 68 30 68 30, f 04 68 30 29 70.
Céret: Av Clemenceau, t 04 68 87 00 53, f 04 68 87 00 56.

Arles-sur-Tech: Rue Barjau, t 04 68 39 11 99, f 04 68 39 11 99.

Where to Stay and Eat

Prades ✉ 66500

Les Glycines, 12 Rue Gén. De Gaulle, t 04 68 96 51 65, f 04 68 96 45 57 (*inexpensive*). Tucked in a quiet courtyard, with comfortable rooms and a decent restaurant (*menus 70 and 120F*). *Closed Sat lunch, Sun except July and Aug.*
★**Hostalrich,** 156 Rue Général De Gaulle, t 04 68 96 05 38 (*cheap*). A big neon sign makes it easy to find, and all rooms have TV and shower; some have balconies.
Jardin de L'Aymeric, 3 Av du General de Gaulle, t 04 68 96 53 38. The best bet for stylish regional cooking and an excess of neon (*menus 98–170F*).
L'Hostal de Nogarols, Chemin Nogarols, on the way to St-Michel-de-Cuxa, t 04 68 96 24 57. A good stop before music concerts, serving excellent wood-fired pizzas, as well as Catalan classics like *petit gris* snails and rabbit (*menus 105–190F*).

fairly easy three- to four-hour walk to the summit, requiring only a decent pair of walking shoes and windbreaker. There's a second, hair-raising forest road up to the refuge from the D27, practical only in a four-wheel drive. The Prades tourist office has a list of tour operators with jeeps.

Vernet-les-Bains, a bustling modern spa, has most of the accommodation in the area, and hot sulphuric waters that are good for your rheumatism and respiratory problems. From nearby Casteil, Canigou's second medieval monument, **St-Martin-du-Canigou,** is a taxing though lovely 40-minute walk up (*open daily in summer, closed Tues in winter, tours at 10, 11.45 (12 on Sun), 2, 3, 4 and 5 in summer, 10, 11.45, 2.30, 3.30 and 4.30 in winter; adm*). An innovatiave architect named Sclua designed this monastery complex in the early 11th century, making it a rustic acropolis, as a series of courtyards and terraces, spectacularly sited with views around Canigou and the surrounding peaks. The church, with its immense, fortress-like bell tower, has two levels, an upper church dedicated to St Martin and a lower crypt for a certain obscure subterranean Virgin Mary: *Notre-Dame-sous-Terre*. Some good white marble capitals can be seen in the cloister, and medieval tombs survive in the upper church.

Villefranche-de-Conflent, the most logical place from which to defend the Têt valley, has had a castle at least since 1092. In the 17th century it took its present form, as a

Vernet-les-Bains ✉ 66820

***Le Mas Fleuri**, 25 Bd Clemenceau (the road up to St Martin), t 04 68 05 51 94, f 04 68 05 50 77 (*moderate*). At the top of the list, this century-old hotel is set in a pretty park, with a pool; rooms are air conditioned. *Closed mid-Oct–mid-May.*

***Comte Guilifred**, t 04 68 05 51 37, f 04 68 05 64 11 (*inexpensive*). This modern place is the training ground for the local hotel school; ask for a room in the back overlooking the garden. The restaurant has menus for 88 and 165F.

****Princess**, Rue Lavandières, t 04 68 05 56 22, f 04 68 05 62 45 (*inexpensive*). A pleasant Logis de France (*menus 85 and 170F*). *Closed Dec –mid-Mar.*

Villefranche-de-Conflent ✉ 66500

****Auberge du Cèdre**, Domaine Ste-Eulalie, outside the walls, t 04 68 96 05 05 (*inexpensive*). Nine comfortable rooms, an adequate restaurant (*menus from 75F*) and two fat, friendly ginger cats in the garden. *Open all year.*

Auberge St-Paul, Place de l'Eglise, t 04 68 96 30 95. The chef at this lovely restaurant fetches from Canigou the basic ingredients for *filet mignon de sanglier* (boar) and beef with morels (*menus 140–500F*). *Closed Mon; Mon and Tues in winter.*

Au Grill, 81 Rue St-Jean, t 04 68 96 17 65. Solid traditional cuisine (*plat du jour 50F, menus 95 and 130F*). *Closed Tues and Wed eve.*

Mont-Louis ✉ 66210

****Le Clos Cerdan**, t 04 68 04 23 29, f 04 68 04 23 79 (*inexpensive*). Get a room with a view at this grey stone hotel on a cliff overlooking the valley; modern but comfortable. The restaurant has menus for 79–150F. *Closed Nov.*

Lou Roubaillou, Rue des Ecoles-Laïques, t 04 68 04 23 26, f 04 68 04 14 09 (*cheap*). By the ramparts, family-run and serving delicious food specializing in mushrooms in various guises (*menus 125–195F*). *Closed May, Nov and Dec.*

Font-Romeu ✉ 66120

****Clair Soleil**, Rte Odeillo, t 04 68 30 13 65, f 04 68 30 08 27 (*inexpensive*). With a view, a swimming pool and a restaurant (*menus 100 and 195F*).

model Baroque fortress-town, rebuilt by Vauban. You can tour his **ramparts** with their walkway built through the wall (*daily June–Sept 10–7; April, May and Oct 10–12 and 2–6; Nov–Dec 2–7; Feb–Mar 2–5; closed Jan; adm*) and if you have sufficient puff and military curiosity, climb up the remarkable 1,000 subterranean rock-hewn steps to **Fort Liberia** (*open daily 9–8; 10–6 in winter; adm*), another Vauban opus. A survivor from the pre-Vauban Villefranche, the church of **St-Jacques** is a fine 12th-century building with capitals from the workshop of St-Michel-de-Cuxa; inside there's another retable by Sunyer.

The Cerdagne

The lofty plateau of the Cerdagne (*Cerdanya* in Catalan) was an isolated and effectively independent county in the Middle Ages, split between Spain and France in the 1659 Treaty of the Pyrenees. The building of the Little Yellow Train, in 1911, brought French Cerdagne into the modern world, and skiing has made it rather opulent today.

After Villefranche, the main N116 climbs dramatically into the mountains. Climb, climb, climb and at last you'll reach the gateway to the Cerdagne, **Mont-Louis**, another work of Vauban's and the highest fortress in France (5,250ft), named after Louis XIV. The army still resides here, though only to look after a pioneer **solar furnace** (*open 10–12.30 and 2–6; adm*), built in 1953. To the north, D118 carries you to the isolated plateau and hiker's wonderland of the **Capcir**. The best parts lie to the west, on the slopes of the **Pic Carlit**; there you will find the sources of both the Têt and the Aude (above the D60, in the Forêt de Barrès).

The western road (D618) will take you through more pine forests to **Font-Romeu**, one of the biggest ski resorts in France with its satellites, Super-Bolquère and Pyrénées 2000. It has the World's Largest **Solar Furnace**, 'stronger than 10,000 suns!', the successor to the one in Mont-Louis. With its curved mirror, covering an entire side of the nine-storey laboratory building, it reflects the Pyrenees beautifully while helping scientists work out all sorts of high-temperature puzzles (*open daily 10–6 in summer; 10–12.30 and 2–6 in winter; adm*). South of Font-Romeu, along the N116, road signs startle with town names like Llo and Err; linguists say they're evidence that the Basques lived here in remote times. You can visit the **Musée de Cerdagne** (*open summer daily 10–1 and 3–7; winter 10–12 and 2–6, closed Tues*) in a 17th-century farm, dedicated to the pre-ski trades of the plateau – shepherding and farming.

The Vallespir

The valley of the Tech, the southernmost valley of Roussillon, winds a lonesome trail around the southern slopes of Canigou. Known for its mineral waters since Roman times, it now lives by tourism, with some francs on the side from cherries and cork oak. The D115 streaks up the valley from Le Boulou to the cherry orchards surrounding **Céret**, a laid-back town under enormous plane trees, with perfect little squares (especially the **Plaça dels Nou Raigs**), medieval gates, a big Baroque church, a war memorial by Maillol, and an elegant 14th-century **bridge** over the Tech. Visit Céret before visiting the **Musée d'Art Moderne**, 8 Blvd du Maréchal Joffre (*open 10–6, closed Tues Oct–April; adm*), and you'll be surprised at how many scenes you'll recognize. Céret found its artistic destiny at the start of the 20th century, thanks to Picasso, Braque, Gris, Manolo, Matisse, Soutine, Kisling, Masson, Tzara, Lhote, Marquet and others who spent time here up until 1940, and whose works now fill the rooms.

Sulphurous waters, good for your rheumatism, have been the fortune of **Amélie-les-Bains** since ancient times; a Roman swimming-pool with a vaulted roof has been uncovered, and the spa, rising on either side of the river Tech, still does a grandstand business. Just west, **Arles-sur-Tech**, the ancient capital of the Vallespir, is a curious old village built on a narrow maze of lanes. Its 11th-century church of Ste-Marie was originally the centre of a monastery; its Dark Age anonymous saint – an empty 4th-century sarcophagus dripping holy water known as Sainte-Tombe – was once a major pilgrimage attraction and is outside the front door.

Some towns just ask for it. As if having a name like **Prats-de-Mollo** weren't enough, this tiny spa advertises itself as the 'European Capital of Urinary Infections'. Prats-de-Mollo's other claim to fame is a European record for rainfall, 33 inches in 16 hours on 15 October 1940.

Language

Everywhere else in France the same level of politeness is expected: use *monsieur, madame* or *mademoiselle* when speaking to everyone (and never *garçon* in restaurants!), from your first *bonjour* to your last *au revoir*.

General

hello *bonjour*
good evening *bonsoir*
good night *bonne nuit*
goodbye *au revoir*
please *s'il vous plaît*
thank you (very much) *merci (beaucoup)*
yes *oui*
no *non*
good *bon (bonne)*
bad *mauvais*
excuse me *pardon, excusez-moi*

Can you help me? *Pourriez-vous m'aider?*
My name is... *Je m'appelle...*
What is your name? *Comment t'appelles-tu?* (informal), *Comment vous appelez-vous?* (formal)
How are you? *Comment allez-vous?*
Fine *Ça va bien*
I don't understand *Je ne comprend pas*
I don't know *Je ne sais pas*
Speak more slowly *Pourriez-vous parler plus lentement?*
How do you say ... in French? *Comment dit-on ... en français?*
Help! *Au secours!*

Where is (the railway station)? *Où se trouve (la gare)?*
Is it far? *C'est loin?*
left *à gauche*
right *à droite*
straight on *tout droit*

entrance *l'entrée*
exit *la sortie*
open *ouvert*
closed *fermé*
WC *les toilettes*
men *hommes*
ladies *dames* or *femmes*

doctor *le médecin*
hospital *un hôpital*
emergency room *la salle des urgences*
police station *le commissariat de police*
tourist information office *l'office de tourisme*

How much is it? *C'est combien?*
Do you have...? *Est-ce que vous avez...?*
It's too expensive *C'est trop cher*
bank *une banque*
money *l'argent*
change *la monnaie*
traveller's cheque *un chèque de voyage*
post office *la poste*
stamp *un timbre*
postcard *une carte postale*
public phone *une cabine téléphonique*
shop *un magasin*
central food market *les halles*
tobacconist *un tabac*
pharmacy *la pharmacie*
aspirin *l'aspirine*
condoms *les préservatifs*
insect repellent *l'anti-insecte*
sun cream *la crème solaire*
tampons *les tampons hygiéniques*

Transport

airport *l'aéroport*
aeroplane *l'avion*
go on foot *aller à pied*
bicycle *la bicyclette/le vélo*
mountain bike *vélo tout terrain, VTT*
bus *l'autobus*

bus stop *l'arrêt d'autobus*
coach station *la gare routière*
railway station *la gare*
train *le train*
platform *le quai*
date-stamp machine *le composteur*
timetable *l'horaire*
left-luggage locker *la consigne automatique*
car *la voiture*
taxi *le taxi*
subway *le métro*
ticket office *le guichet*
ticket *le billet*
single to... *un aller* (or *aller simple*) *pour...*
return to... *un aller et retour pour...*
What time does the ... leave?
  A quelle heure part...?
delayed *en retard*
on time *à l'heure*

Accommodation

single room *une chambre pour une*
  personne
twin room *une chambre à deux lits*
double room *une chambre pour deux*
  personnes
bed *un lit*
blanket *une couverture*
cot (child's bed) *lit d'enfant*
pillow *un oreiller*
soap *du savon*
towel *une serviette*
booking *une réservation*
I would like to book a room *Je voudrais*
  réserver une chambre

Months

January *janvier*
February *février*
March *mars*
April *avril*
May *mai*
June *juin*
July *juillet*
August *août*
September *septembre*
October *octobre*
November *novembre*
December *décembre*

Days

Monday *lundi*
Tuesday *mardi*
Wednesday *mercredi*
Thursday *jeudi*
Friday *vendredi*
Saturday *samedi*
Sunday *dimanche*

Time

What time is it? *Quelle heure est-il?*
month *un mois*
week *une semaine*
day *un jour/une journée*
morning *le matin*
afternoon *l'après-midi*
evening *le soir*
night *la nuit*
today *aujourd'hui*
yesterday *hier*
tomorrow *demain*
day before yesterday *avant-hier*
day after tomorrow *après-demain*

Numbers

one *un*
two *deux*
three *trois*
four *quatre*
five *cinq*
six *six*
seven *sept*
eight *huit*
nine *neuf*
ten *dix*
eleven *onze*
twelve *douze*
thirteen *treize*
fourteen *quatorze*
fifteen *quinze*
sixteen *seize*
seventeen *dix-sept*
eighteen *dix-huit*
nineteen *dix-neuf*
twenty *vingt*
twenty-one *vingt et un*
twenty-two *vingt-deux*
thirty *trente*

forty *quarante*
fifty *cinquante*
sixty *soixante*
seventy *soixante-dix*
seventy-one *soixante-onze*
eighty *quatre-vingts*
eighty-one *quatre-vingt-un*
ninety *quatre-vingt-dix*
hundred *cent*
two hundred *deux cents*
thousand *mille*

Deciphering French Menus

Many of the restaurants in this book don't translate their menus, so we've included the decoder below; try the sections on regional specialities in the regional chapters if an item isn't listed below.

Hors-d'œuvre et Soupes (Starters and Soups)

amuse-gueule appetizers
assiette assortie plate of mixed cold *hors d'œuvre*
bisque shellfish soup
bouchées mini *vol-au-vents*
bouillabaisse famous fish soup of Marseille
bouillon broth
charcuterie mixed cold meats, salami, ham, etc.
consommé clear soup
coulis thick sieved sauce
crudités raw vegetable platter
potage thick vegetable soup
tourrain garlic and bread soup
velouté thick smooth soup, often fish or chicken
vol-au-vent puff-pastry case with savoury filling

Poissons et Coquillages (Crustacés) (Fish and Shellfish)

aiglefin little haddock
alose shad
anchois anchovies

anguille eel
bar sea bass
barbue brill
baudroie anglerfish
belons flat oysters
bigorneau winkle
blanchailles whitebait
brème bream
brochet pike
bulot whelk
cabillaud cod
calmar squid
carrelet plaice
colin hake
congre conger eel
coques cockles
coquillages shellfish
coquilles St-Jacques scallops
crabe crab
crevettes grises shrimp
crevettes roses prawns
cuisses de grenouilles frogs' legs
darne slice or steak of fish
daurade sea bream
ecrevisse freshwater crayfish
eperlan smelt
escabèche fish fried, marinated and served cold
escargots snails
espadon swordfish
esturgeon sturgeon
flétan halibut
friture deep-fried fish
fruits de mer seafood
gambas giant prawns
gigot de mer a large fish cooked whole
grondin red gurnard
hareng herring
homard Atlantic (Norway) lobster
huîtres oysters
lamproie lamprey
langouste spiny Mediterranean lobster
langoustines Norway lobster (often called Dublin Bay prawns or scampi)
limande lemon sole
lotte monkfish
loup (de mer) sea bass
louvine sea bass (in aquitaine)
maquereau mackerel
merlan whiting
morue salt cod
moules mussels
oursin sea urchin
pagel sea bream

palourdes clams
petit gris little grey snail
poulpe octopus
praires small clams
raie skate
rascasse scorpion fish
rouget red mullet
saumon salmon
St-Pierre John Dory
sole (meunière) sole (with butter, lemon and
    parsley)
stockfisch stockfish (wind-dried cod)
telline tiny clam
thon tuna
truite trout
truite saumonée salmon trout

Viandes et Volailles (Meat and Poultry)

agneau (de pré-salé) lamb (grazed in fields by
    the sea)
ailerons chicken wings
aloyau sirloin
andouillette chitterling (tripe) sausage
autruche ostrich
biftek beefsteak
blanc breast or white meat
blanquette stew of white meat
bœuf beef
boudin blanc sausage of white meat
boudin noir black pudding
brochette meat (or fish) on a skewer
caille quail
canard, caneton duck, duckling
carré the best end of a cutlet or chop
cassoulet haricot bean stew with sausage,
    duck, goose, etc.
cervelle brains
chair flesh, meat
chapon capon
châteaubriand porterhouse steak
cheval horsemeat
chevreau kid
chorizo spicy Spanish sausage
civet meat (usually game) stew, in wine and
    blood sauce
cœur heart
confit meat cooked and preserved in its
    own fat
côte, côtelette chop, cutlet
cou d'oie farci goose neck stuffed with pork,
    foie gras and truffles

crépinette small sausage
cuisse thigh or leg
dinde, dindon turkey
entrecôte ribsteak
epaule shoulder
estouffade a meat stew marinated, fried
    and then braised
faisan pheasant
faux-filet sirloin
foie liver
frais de veau veal testicles
fricadelle meatball
gésier gizzard
gibier game
gigot leg of lamb
graisse or gras fat
grillade grilled meat, often a mixed grill
grive thrush
jambon ham
jarret knuckle
langue tongue
lapereau young rabbit
lapin rabbit
lard (lardons) bacon (diced bacon)
lièvre hare
maigret (or magret) (de canard) breast
    (of duck)
manchons duck or goose wings
marcassin young wild boar
merguez spicy red sausage
moelle bone marrow
mouton mutton
museau muzzle
navarin lamb stew with root vegetables
noix de veau (agneau) topside of veal (lamb)
oie goose
os bone
perdreau (or perdrix) partridge
petit salé salt pork
pieds trotters
pintade guinea fowl
plat-de-côtes short ribs or rib chops
porc pork
pot au feu meat and vegetables cooked in
    stock
poulet chicken
poussin baby chicken
quenelle poached dumplings made of fish,
    fowl or meat
queue de bœuf oxtail
ris (de veau) sweetbreads (veal)
rognons kidneys
rosbif roast beef
rôti roast

sanglier wild boar
saucisses sausages
saucisson dry sausage, like salami
selle (d'agneau) saddle (of lamb)
steak tartare raw minced beef, often topped
   with a raw egg yolk
suprême de volaille fillet of chicken breast
   and wing
taureau bull's meat
tête (de veau) head (calf's). fatty and usually
   served with a mustardy vinaigrette
tortue turtle
tournedos thick round slices of beef fillet
travers de porc spare ribs
tripes tripe
veau veal
venaison venison

Légumes, Herbes, etc.
(Vegetables, herbs, etc.)

ail garlic
aïoli garlic mayonnaise
algue seaweed
aneth dill
anis anis
artichaut artichoke
asperges asparagus
aubergine aubergine (eggplant)
avocat avocado
basilic basil
betterave beetroot
blette Swiss chard
bouquet garni mixed herbs in a little bag
cannelle cinnamon
céleri (-rave) celery (celeriac)
cèpes ceps, wild boletus mushrooms
champignons mushrooms
chanterelles wild yellow mushrooms
chicorée curly endive
chou cabbage
chou-fleur cauliflower
choucroute sauerkraut
choux de bruxelles Brussels sprouts
ciboulette chives
citrouille pumpkin
clou de girofle clove
cœur de palmier heart of palm
concombre cucumber
cornichons gherkins
courgettes courgettes (zucchini)
cresson watercress
echalote shallot

endive chicory (endive)
epinards spinach
estragon tarragon
fenouil fennel
fèves broad (fava) beans
flageolets white beans
fleurs de courgette courgette blossoms
frites chips (French fries)
genièvre juniper
gingembre ginger
haricots (rouges, blancs) beans (kidney, white)
haricot verts green (French) beans
jardinière with diced garden vegetables
laitue lettuce
laurier bay leaf
lentilles lentils
maïs (épis de) sweetcorn (on the cob)
marjolaine marjoram
menthe mint
mesclun salad of various leaves
morilles morel mushrooms
moutarde mustard
navet turnip
oignons onions
oseille sorrel
panais parsnip
persil parsley
petits pois peas
piment pimento
pissenlits dandelion greens
poireaux leeks
pois chiches chickpeas
pois mange-tout sugar peas or mangetout
poivron sweet pepper (capsicum)
pomme de terre potato
potiron pumpkin
primeurs young vegetables
radis radishes
raifort horseradish
riz rice
romarin rosemary
roquette rocket
safran saffron
salade verte green salad
salsifis salsify
sarriette savory
sarrasin buckwheat
sauge sage
seigle rye
serpolet wild thyme
thym thyme
truffes truffles

Fruits et Noix (Fruit and Nuts)

abricot apricot
amandes almonds
ananas pineapple
banane banana
bigarreau black cherries
brugnon nectarine
cacahouètes peanuts
cassis blackcurrant
cerise cherry
citron lemon
citron vert lime
coco (noix de) coconut
coing quince
dattes dates
figues (de Barbarie) figs (prickly pear)
fraises (des bois) strawberries (wild)
framboises raspberries
fruit de la passion passion fruit
grenade pomegranate
groseilles redcurrants
lavande lavender
mandarine tangerine
mangue mango
marrons chestnuts
mirabelles mirabelle plums
mûre (sauvage) mulberry, blackberry
myrtilles bilberries
noisette hazelnut
noix walnuts
noix de cajou cashews
pamplemousse grapefruit
pastèque watermelon
pêche (blanche) peach (white)
pignons pinenuts
pistache pistachio
poire pear
pomme Apple
prune plum
pruneau prune
raisins (secs) grapes (raisins)
reine-claude greengage plums

Desserts

Bavarois mousse or custard in a mould
biscuit biscuit, cracker, cake
bombe ice-cream dessert in a round mould
bonbons sweets, candy
brioche light sweet yeast bread

charlotte sponge fingers and custard cream dessert
chausson turnover
clafoutis batter fruit cake
compote stewed fruit
corbeille de fruits basket of fruit
coulis thick fruit sauce
coupe ice cream: a scoop or in cup
crème anglaise egg custard
crème caramel vanilla custard with caramel sauce
crème Chantilly sweet whipped cream
crème fraîche slightly sour cream
crème pâtissière thick pastry cream filling made with eggs
gâteau cake
gaufre waffle
génoise rich sponge cake
glace ice cream
macarons macaroons
madeleine small sponge cake
miel honey
mignardise same as *petits fours*
mousse 'foam': frothy dessert
œufs à la neige floating island/meringue on a bed of custard
pain d'épice gingerbread
parfait frozen mousse
petits fours sweetmeats; tiny cakes and pastries
profiteroles choux pastry balls, often filled with chocolate or ice cream
sablé shortbread
savarin a filled cake, shaped like a ring
tarte, tartelette tart, little tart
tarte tropézienne sponge cake filled with custard and topped with nuts
truffes chocolate truffles
yaourt yoghurt

Fromage (Cheese)

brebis (fromage de) sheep's cheese
cabécou sharp local goat's cheese
chèvre goat's cheese
doux mild
fromage (plateau de) cheese (board)
fromage blanc yoghurty cream cheese
fromage frais a bit like sour cream
fromage sec general name for solid cheeses
fort strong

Cooking Terms and Sauces

à point medium steak
bien cuit well-done steak
bleu very rare steak

aigre-doux sweet and sour
aiguillette thin slice
à l'anglaise boiled
à la bordelaise cooked in wine and diced
  vegetables (usually)
à la châtelaine with chestnut purée and
  artichoke hearts
à la diable in spicy mustard sauce
à la grecque cooked in olive oil and lemon
à la jardinière with garden vegetables
à la périgourdine in a truffle and foie gras
  sauce
à la provençale cooked with tomatoes, garlic
  and olive oil
allumettes strips of puff pastry
au feu de bois cooked over a wood fire
au four baked
auvergnat with sausage, bacon and cabbage
barquette pastry boat
beignets fritters
béarnaise sauce of egg yolks, shallots and
  white wine
bordelaise red wine, bone marrow and
  shallot sauce
broche roasted on a spit
chasseur mushrooms and shallots in white
  wine
chaud hot
cru raw
cuit cooked
diable spicy mustard or green pepper sauce
emincé thinly sliced
en croûte cooked in a pastry crust
en papillote baked in buttered paper
epices spices
farci stuffed
feuilleté flaky pastry
flambé set aflame with alcohol
forestière with bacon and mushrooms
fourré stuffed
frais, fraîche fresh
frappé with crushed ice
frit fried
froid cold
fumé smoked
galantine cooked food served in cold jelly
galette flaky pastry case or pancake
garni with vegetables

(au) gratin topped with browned cheese and
  breadcrumbs
grillé grilled
haché minced
hollandaise a sauce of egg yolks, butter
  and vinegar
marmite casserole
médaillon round piece
mijoté simmered
mornay cheese sauce
pané breaded
pâte pastry, pasta
pâte brisée shortcrust pastry
pâte à chou choux pastry
pâte feuilletée flaky or puff pastry
paupiette rolled and filled thin slices of fish
  or meat
parmentier with potatoes
pavé slab
piquant spicy hot
poché poached
pommes allumettes thin chips (fries)
raclette melted cheese with potatoes, onions
  and pickles
sanglant rare steak
salé salted, spicy
sucré sweet
timbale pie cooked in a dome-shaped
  mould
tranche slice
vapeur steamed
véronique green grapes, wine and cream
  sauce
vinaigrette oil and vinegar dressing

Miscellaneous

addition bill (check)
baguette long loaf of bread
beurre butter
carte non-set menu
confiture jam
couteau knife
crème cream
cuillère spoon
formule à 80F 80F set menu
fourchette fork
fromage cheese
huile (d'olive) oil (olive)
lait milk
menu set menu
nouilles noodles
pain bread

œufs eggs
poivre pepper
sel salt
service compris/non compris service included/not included
sucre sugar
vinaigre vinegar

Snacks

chips crisps
crêpe thin pancake
croque-madame toasted ham and cheese sandwich with fried egg
croque-monsieur toasted ham and cheese sandwich
croustade small savoury pastry
frites chips (French fries)
gaufre waffle
jambon ham
pissaladière a kind of pizza with onions, anchovies, etc.
sandwich canapé open sandwich

Boissons (Drinks)

bière (pression) beer (draught)
bouteille (demi) bottle (half)
brut very dry
chocolat chaud hot chocolate
café coffee

café au lait white coffee
café express espresso coffee
café filtre filter coffee
café turc Turkish coffee
demi a third of a litre
doux sweet (wine)
eau (minérale, plate ou gazeuse) water (mineral, still or sparkling)
eau-de-vie brandy
eau potable drinking water
gazeuse sparkling
glaçons ice cubes
infusion (or tisane) (verveine, tilleul, menthe) herbal tea, (usually either verbena, lime flower or mint)
jus juice
lait milk
menthe à l'eau peppermint cordial
moelleux semi-dry
mousseux sparkling (wine)
pastis anis liqueur
pichet pitcher
citron pressé/orange pressée fresh lemon/orange juice
pression draught
ratafia home-made liqueur made by steeping fruit or green walnuts in alcohol or wine
sec dry
sirop d'orange/de citron orange/lemon squash
thé tea
verre glass
vin blanc/rosé/rouge white/rosé/red wine

Glossary

abbaye: abbey

abside: apse

arc-boutant: flying-buttress

ardoise: slate

arrondissement: city district

auberge: inn

autel: altar

bas-côté: aisle (which can also be a *collatéral*)

basse-cour: (for château) outer courtyard; (for farm) farmyard

bastide: a new town founded in the Middle Ages; usually rectangular, with a grid of streets and an arcaded central square; sometimes circular in plan

beffroi: tower with a town's bell

bergère: wing chair (more frequently means shepherdess, though)

bien national: property of the state

boiserie(s) (en plis de serviette): (linenfold) wood panelling

cachot: prison cell; dungeon

canonnière: loophole for gun

castelnau: a village, often planned, that grew up around a seigneur's castle (often the parish church will be on the edge of a castelnau instead of at its centre)

castrum: a rectangular Roman army camp, which often grew into a permanent settlement (like Bordeaux and many others)

chaire: pulpit

châtelain(e): lord of a château (lady of a château)

chemin: path

chemin de ronde: parapet walk, wall walk, rampart walk

choeur: choir (architecturally speaking)

cintre: arch (also coat-hanger)

clef (or clé) de voûte: keystone or boss (architecturally speaking)

clocher-mur: the west front of a church that rises high above the roofline for its entire width to make a bell tower; a common feature in medieval architecture in many parts of southwest France

col: pass

colimaçon (escalier en): spiral (staircase)

collégiale: collegiate church

colombage: half-timbering (not to be confused with colombier)

colombier: dovecot (not to be confused with colombage)

(les) combles: attic, loft, garret; roof timbers

commanderie: local headquarters of a knightly order (like the Templars or Knights Hospitallers), usually to look after the order's lands and properties in an area

commune: in the Middle Ages, the government of a free town or city; today, the smallest unit of local government, encompassing a town or village

(les) communs: outbuildings

corps de logis: main building

côte: coast; on wine labels *côte, coteaux* and *costières* mean 'hills' or 'slopes'

cour: court; courtyard (a *cour d'honneur* is the principal courtyard of a château)

cours: wide main street, like an elongated main square

couvent: convent or monastery

croquant: peasant guerilla in the anti-French revolts of the 17th and 18th centuries

cul-de-lampe: sculpted pendant at the bottom of a rib or vault

domestique: as an adjective, domestic, but just as commonly used as a noun meaning servant

donjon: castle keep

douves (sèches): (dry) moat

ecluse: canal lock

enceinte: defensive enclosure (also means pregnant)

enfeu: niche in a church's exterior or interior wall for a tomb

enfilade: series of linked rooms

estampe: engraving (*sur bois* = woodcut)

fabrique: folly (more commonly manufacture or factory)

fenêtre à meneaux: mullioned window

fossé: ditch

fraise: strawberry, but also ruff

fusain: charcoal

géminé: twin

gentilhommière: a small country château, especially popular in Périgord in the 18th century

gisant: a sculpted prone effigy on a tomb

gîte: shelter

gîte d'étape: basic shelter for walkers

Grande Randonnée (GR): long distance hiking path

grange: farm

herse: portcullis; (in agriculture) harrow

historié: historiated (decorated with flowers or figures or animals, often telling a story in pictures)

hôtel: originally the town residence of the nobility; by the 18th century became more generally used for any large, private residence; also a hotel

investir: to invest, but also to besiege

lavoir: communal fountain, usually covered, for the washing of clothes

lucarne: dormer, attic or gable window

mairie: town hall

la maison: ordinary word for a house, but also a euphemism for a château, which it would be too vulgar to refer to directly

maquis: Mediterranean scrub; also used as a term for the French Resistance during the Second World War

mascaron: an ornamental mask, usually one carved on the keystone of an arch

mécène: patron

modillon: a stone projecting from the cornice of a church, carved with a face or animal figure

ogive: diagonal rib (in architectural vaulting); an *arc en ogive* is a lancet arch; an *ogive nucléaire* is a modern instrument of the Apocalypse, a nuclear warhead

parlement: a regional law court before the Revolution, with members appointed by the king; by the late Ancien Régime *parlements* exercised a great deal of influence over political affairs

particule (nom à): name with a handle (i.e. nobleman's name indicated by a 'de' or 'du' in front of the surname)

pech: hill

pignon: gable (*avoir pignon sur rue* = to be prosperous, or to have a shop in a prime position)

pleurant: weeper, mourner

pont-levis: drawbridge

porte cochère: carriage entrance

poudre de succession: 'powder of inheritance' (euphemism for poison)

poutre: beam

presqu'île: peninsula

primitif: early master (in painting)

puy: high point (also *pujol*)

retable: a carved or painted altarpiece, often consisting of a number of scenes or sculptural ensembles

rez-de-chausée (rc): ground floor (US first floor)

rinceau(x): ornamental foliage, foliated scroll

romain: Roman (note difference from *roman* in French; a *roman*, as a noun, is a novel)

sablière: beam, stringer

sens de la visite: generally not sense of the visit, but direction to follow on the visit

sens interdit: no entry

sens unique: one way

tomber en quenouille: to pass into the female line or fall to the distaff

tourelle: turret

transi: in a tomb, a relief of the decomposing cadaver

travée: bay (in church architecture); span (of bridge)

trumeau: the column between twin doors of a church portal, often carved with reliefs

tympanum: semicircular panel over a church door; often the occasion for the most ambitious ensembles of medieval sculpture

verdure: tapestry representing trees or foliage as the main motif (more commonly means greenery or salad vegetables)

vieille ville: historic, old quarter of town

village perché: hilltop village

visite libre: unaccompanied visit, not free visit (which would be *visite gratuite*)

vitrail (plural: vitraux): stained glass window(s)

voûte: vault or arch (*en anse de panier*: basket-handle arch; *d'arête*: groined vault; *en berceau*: barrel vault; *en éventail*: fan vault; *d'ogives*: ribbed vault; *en plein cintre*: semicircular arch)

Chronology

BC

c. 1,000,000: Arrival of first people in France
35,000–9,000: Palaeolithic cave painting
c. 4500: Beginnings of Neolithic civilization
c. 1000: Beginnings of Celtic migration
c. 600: Marseille founded as a Greek colony
121: Roman conquest of Provence
58: Julius Caesar begins the conquest of Gaul

AD

260–76: Incursions of Alemanni and Franks
c. 397: Death of St Martin of Tours
406: Germanic tribes breach the Rhine
c. 450: Celtic refugees from Britain begin to
  settle in Brittany
455: Visigothic kingdom established in
  Aquitaine, Franks occupy much of northern
  Gaul, Burgundians the Rhône Valley
475: Formal end of the Western Roman Empire
      Clovis (482–511) Merovingian
      Frank rules most of Gaul
511: Division of Frankish kingdom between
  Clovis' four sons
578: Gascons (Basques) begin to settle what
  is now Gascony
687: Pepin of Herstal reunites the three
  Merovingian kingdoms
732: Charles Martel stops the Arab invasion
  at the Battle of Poitiers
      Pepin the Short (751–68)
754–6: Frankish invasions of Italy in support
  of the Pope
      Charles I (Charlemagne, 768–814)
800: Charlemagne crowned Emperor in Rome
      Louis I (the Pious, 814–40)
843: Treaty of Verdun, division of the
  Carolingian Empire into three parts
845: First Viking raid on Paris
      Charles II (the Bald, 843–77)
885: Count Eudes repels Vikings from Paris
      Eudes (888–98)
896: Vikings begin to settle in Normandy
911: Duchy of Normandy created under
  Norman Duke Rollo

Hugues Capet (987–96)
1066: Duke William of Normandy
  conquers England
1095: First Crusade proclaimed at Clermont
1115: Foundation of the first Cistercian abbey at
  Clairvaux, by St Bernard
      Louis VII (1137–80)
1140: St-Denis begun, first Gothic church
1142: Death of Peter Abelard
1152: Louis divorces Eleanor of Aquitaine, who
  in turn marries Henry II of England
      Philippe II Auguste (1180–1223)
1190: Building of the original Louvre
1204–8: Philippe Auguste wrests control
  of Normandy, Anjou and the Touraine
  from the English
1209: Albigensian Crusade begins
1214: French victory at the Battle of Bouvines
1218: Death of Simon de Montfort at the Siege
  of Toulouse
      Louis VIII (1223–6)
      Louis IX (St Louis, 1226–70)
1249: Louis's crusade to Egypt results in his
  capture in battle
      Philippe IV (the Fair, 1285–1314)
1302: First meeting of the Estates-General
1305: Papacy moves to Avignon
      Louis X (1314–16)
      Philippe V (1316–22)
      Charles IV (the Fair, 1322–28)
      Philippe VI (1328–50)
1328: Edward III of England proclaims himself
  King of France; Hundred Years' War begins
1346: Battle of Crécy
1347–9: The Black Plague
      Jean II (the Good, 1350–64)
1358: Revolt of Etienne Marcel
      Charles V (1364–80)
      Charles VI (1380–1422)
1392: Beginnings of the factional strife of
  Armagnacs and Bourguignons
1420: English occupy Paris
      Charles VII (1422–61)

1438: Pragmatic Sanction places the French Church under royal control
1453: English chased out of France

Louis XI (1461–83)

1482: Burgundy becomes part of France

Charles VIII (1483–98)

1494: First invasion of Italy

Louis XII (1498–1515)

François I (1515–47)

1515–47: Wars in Italy
1525: François I captured in battle by imperial forces at Pavia

Henri II (1547–59)

1559: Treaty of Cateau-Cambrésis; end of French designs in Italy

François II (1559–60)

Charles IX (1560–74)

1562: Beginning of the Wars of Religion
1572: St Bartholomew's Day massacre of Protestants

Henri III (1574–89)

1589: Assassinations of the Duc de Guise and the King

Henri IV (1589–1610)

1594: Henri IV converts to Catholicism, enters Paris
1598: Edict of Nantes proclaimed; end of religious wars

Louis XIII (1610–43)

1610–24: Regency of Marie de' Medici
1624: Cardinal Richelieu becomes minister
1627–8: Siege of Huguenot La Rochelle

Louis XIV (1643–1715)

1643: Cardinal Mazarin becomes minister
1659: Treaty of the Pyrenees with Spain; France gains Roussillon
1682: King abandons Paris for newly built Palace of Versailles
1685: Revocation of the Edict of Nantes
1701–19: War of the Spanish Succession

Louis XV (1715–74)

1715–23: Regency of Philippe d'Orléans
1720: Bursting of John Law's 'Mississippi Bubble'
1756–63: Seven Years' War; France loses most of its American possessions to Britain

Louis XVI (1774–92)

1789: Beginning of Revolution; convocation of the Estates-General, storming of the Bastille
1791: Old provinces abolished; France divided into *départements*
1792: First Republic proclaimed

1793: The Terror; execution of Louis XVI
1795–9: Rule of the Directoire
1799: 'Coup de Brumaire'; Napoleon seizes power

Napoleon I (Emperor, 1804–15)

1814: Allies enter Paris; Napoleon sent to Elba

Louis XVIII (1814–24)

1815: The Hundred Days; Battle of Waterloo

Charles X (1824–30)

1830: Revolt of the 'Trois Glorieuses' overthrows Charles X

Louis-Philippe (1830–48)

1848: 'Revolution of contempt'; Second Republic formed
1851: Coup of Louis-Napoleon

Napoleon III (Emperor, 1852–70)

1870: Franco-Prussian War; disaster at Sedan, siege of Paris
1871: Paris Commune; Third Republic proclaimed at Versailles
1889: Paris Exposition, opening of Eiffel Tower
1894: 'Dreyfus Affair' begins
1914–18: First World War; France loses 10 per cent of its population
1919: Treaty of Versailles
1920: Newly elected President Paul Deschanel goes mad, falls off a train in the middle of the night and wanders through France in his pyjamas
1927: Construction starts on the Maginot Line
1934: Stavisky scandals: demonstrations and riots
1936: Election of Popular Front government
1940: Defeat by the Nazis; 'French State' government set up at Vichy in the unoccupied zone under Marshal Pétain
1943: Germans occupy all of France
1944: Normandy landings
1946: Fourth Republic; De Gaulle in power 1946–8
1954: Defeat in Vietnam at Dienbienphu
1958: Return of De Gaulle to power
1962: Retreat from Algeria, followed by the migration of a million *pied noirs* into France
1968: Students' revolt; De Gaulle resigns the following year
1968: Opening of space port at Kourou, French Guiana
1981: Election of first Socialist President, François Mitterrand
1995: Jacques Chirac elected president
1996: Death of François Mitterrand

Further Reading

Ardagh, John, *France Today* (Penguin, 1987). One in Penguin's informative paperback series on contemporary Europe.

Bonner, Anthony, *Songs of the Troubadours* (Allen & Unwin, 1973). Introduction to the troubadours, with some verse translations.

Briggs, Robin, *Early Modern France: 1560–1715* (OPUS). A readable, very reliable study of the period in this much recommended series.

Brown, Frederick, *Zola*. Stunningly intelligent and beautifully written study of Zola's life and his period. Gripping from start to finish.

Buisseret, D.J., *Henry IV*. Such an appealing figure with his sensual passions as well as his will to unite the country, Henry IV is well served by this introduction.

Caesar, Julius, *The Conquest of Gaul* (Penguin Classics). Cool and sharp account of his victories over the Celtic tribes of France.

Cézanne, Paul, *Letters* (London, 1941).

Cobb, Richard, *The French and their Revolution*. By a serious historian who delves into the darkest reaches (for example morgue records) to reveal fascinating insights into the lower strata of French society.

Cook, Theodore A., *Old Provence* (London, 1905). A classic traveller's account of the region, out of print and hard to find.

Cronin, Vincent, *Louis XIV*. A still highly readable and useful biography, despite its age.

Cronin, Vincent, *Napoleon*. Classic on the megalomaniac.

Daudet, Alphonse, *Letters from my Windmill* (Penguin, 1982). Bittersweet 19th-century tales of Midi nostalgia by Van Gogh's favourite novelist.

Dumas, Alexandre, *The Count of Monte Cristo*. A romantic fantastical tale of revenge.

Durrell, Lawrence, *The Avignon Quintet* (Faber). Lush wartime sagas in Avignon and around.

Ferguson, Niall, *The Pity of War*. Provocative recent study of the First War World by this ambitious young historian, arguing that Britain should never have involved its army.

Fitzgerald, F. Scott, *Tender is the Night*. 1920s Riviera decadence based on personal research.

Fortescue, Winifred, *Perfume from Provence* (1935). Poor, intolerable Lady Fortescue's misadventures with the garlicky peasants.

Giono, Jean, *To the Slaughterhouse, Two Riders of the Storm* (Peter Owen, 1988). Giono is a major 20th-century novelist of Provence, whose deep pessimism contrasts with the sunnier views of his contemporary Pagnol.

Gramont, Sanche de, *The French: Portrait of a People* (Putnam, New York, 1969). One of the funnier attempts at the favourite French pastime: national self-analysis.

Greene, Graham, *J'Accuse: The Dark Side of Nice* (Bodley Head, 1982). Mafia connections and graft in the government of discredited mayor Jacques Médecin.

Gregory of Tours, *The History of the Franks* (Penguin Classics). Rip-roaring totally unreliable romp through the violent centuries by this 6th-century bishop of Tours. A great read.

Hibbert, Christopher, *The French Revolution*. Successful popular history, not as up-to-date or flamboyant as Schama, but shorter.

Howard, Michael, *The Franco-Prussian War* (Routledge). First-rate explanation of this most important but overlooked conflict between Prussia (later Germany) and France, by the doyen of military historians.

Hugo, Victor, *Les Misérables*. Injustice among the galley-slaves and basis for the musical.

Keegan, John, *The First World War*, and *The Second World War* (both Hutchinson). A solid introduction to the subject. Unusually, at the end of the First World War tome Keegan puts up an unfashionable defence of the war generals, but this bizarre argument is totally undermined by all the evidence he produces in the rest of the work.

Knecht, R.J., *The Rise and Fall of Renaissance France*. A serious study of this century of excess: the first part focuses on François I, France's answer to Henry VIII, at the start of the century; the second part delves into the later turmoil of the Wars of Religion.

Knecht, R.J., *Catherine de' Medici.* This recent work gives an intelligent picture of this complex woman so villified as wickedest of queen mums by popular memory.

Ladurie, Emmanuel Leroy, *Love, Death and Money in the Pays d'Oc* (Scolar, 1982).

de Larrabeiti, Michael, *The Provençal Tales* (Pavilion, 1988). Troubadours' tales told by shepherds around the camp fire.

Lugand, Jacques, Robert St-Jean and Jean Nougaret, *Languedoc Roman* (Zodiaque, 1975). The best of Languedoc's Romanesque architecture, with plans, lots of photos and an English translation.

McDonald, Lynn. Any of her titles. Pioneering approach to the Great War, concentrating on the real life of the soldiers and the tragedy of their lives by unearthing the treasure trove of diaries, letters and records they had left, rather than coldly analysing the generals' strategies.

Mayle, Peter, *A Year in Provence* and *Toujours Provence* (Sinclair Stevenson/Pan, 1989 and 1991). The entertaining bestsellers on ex-pat life in the Luberon.

Mistral, Frédéric, *Miréio* and *Poème de la Rhône.* Poems by the Nobel prize-winning Félibre, available in French or Provençal.

Mitford, Nancy, *The Sun King.* The other classic on Louis XIV still going strong as a good read. Also wrote on the Marquise de Pompadour, Louis XV's mistress.

More, Carey and Julian, *A Taste of Provence* (Pavilion, 1987). Father and daughter team up to evoke the countryside and gastronomy of Provence in words and photographs.

Morris, Edwin T., *Fragrance: The Story of Perfume from Cleopatra to Chanel* (Charles Scribner & Sons, 1984).

Pagnol, Marcel, *Jean de Florette and Manon of the Springs, The Days were too Short* (Picador, 1960). Autobiography by Provence's most beloved writer.

Petrarch, Francesco, *Songs and Sonnets from Laura's Lifetime* (Anvil Press, 1985).

Pope Hennessy, James, *Aspects of Provence* (Penguin, 1952). A fussy but lyrical view of the region in the '40s and '50s.

Schama, Simon, *Citizens.* Splendidly readable account of the French Revolution and its causes, studied via major personalities.

Madame de Sévigné, *Selected Letters* (Penguin Classics). Charming courtier from the age of Louis XIV giving her views on pressing subjects from hot chocolate to politics.

Seward, Desmond, *The Hundred Years War* (Constable and Company). In fact any history book by Seward can be recommended.

Smollett, Tobias, *Travels through France and Italy* (London, 1776). The irrepressible, grouchy Tobias 'Smellfungus' makes modern travel writing look like advertising copy.

Süskind, Patrick, *Perfume* (Penguin, 1989). Thrilling and fragrant murder in the 18th-century perfume industry in Grasse.

Tapié, V.-L., *France in the Age of Louis XIII and Richelieu.* Really good study of the period, giving a flavour of all the court intrigue as well as sound historical judgement.

Tuchman, Barbara, *A Distant Mirror* (Papermac). Thoroughly researched, huge gripping novel based around the life of one of the lords of Coucy-le-Château in Picardy, giving a minutely detailed picture of his age, as indicated in the subtitle, *The Calamitous Fourteenth Century.*

Van Gogh, Vincent, *Collected Letters of Vincent Van Gogh* (New York, 1978).

Vergé, Roger, *Cuisine of the Sun* (London, 1979). The owner of the Moulin de Mougins tells some of his secrets of Provençal cooking.

Warner, Marina, *Joan of Arc: The Image of Female Heroism* (Vintage). Fascinating, meticulous study to try and sort out the true story of Joan of Arc's life and of the multitude of myths to which she gave rise.

Weber, Eugene, *Paris 1900.* Delightful evocation of Belle Epoque life before the First World War, across a wide social spectrum.

Weir, Alison, *Eleanor of Aquitaine* (Pimlico). Hugely popular recent history on 12th-century Eleanor and the Plantagenets.

Whitfield, Sarah, *Fauvism* (Thames and Hudson, 1991). A good introduction to the movement that changed art history.

Wylie, L., *Village in the Vaucluse* (Harvard University Press, 1971). A very readable sociologist's classic based on Roussillon.

Zeldin, Theodore, *France 1845–1945* (Oxford University Press, 1980). Five well-written volumes on all aspects of the period.

Index

Page references to maps are in *italics*.

Acknowledgements

Philippe Barbour

I would like to dedicate this book to all my French family, who have made France such a very happy place for me.

My first enormous thank you goes to all the press officers of the French *départements* and to all the guides at the countless sites who helped me with such bounding enthusiasm in the preparation of this book. Thank you also to Eurotunnel and to Hoverspeed for helping in the research with a free Channel crossing each.

I'd like to say a very special thank you to my friends who came out to see me: John Lotherington for his inspiration and support and for sharing the most amazing moonrise; Claire Lofting for fine conversation over *tilleul tisane* under starlit skies; Aruna Vasudevan for putting up with mounds of post and sleepless nights; Kate Berney and David Steward for coming out of their way from Arabia; Karin Galil for stopping by on her way round the world. I'd also like to thank the members of my family who've looked after me so wonderfully at various stages in the journey, especially Ninan, Tata Dine and Tonton René, and Yann and Catherine and their children; and *un grand merci* to Mme Aubert for always being so kind and thoughtful. As ever, the biggest thanks of all goes to my parents for providing me with love, encouragement and support, and with one of the most beautiful offices in the world, in their adoptive Drôme.

I would like to thank Cadogan for giving me the opportunity to do this wonderful cultural Tour de France, and to thank Catherine Charles, my editor, for her cheerfulness, which I greatly appreciated during the enormous task of completing the writing.

Dana Facaros and Michael Pauls

We acknowledge, most truly, Our Editor Kitty,
Who toils in the mournful plains of White City.
Under dreadful conditions she despatched her brief,
And now she'll have Christmas, and timely relief.

Cadogan Guides

The publishers would like to thank Robert Gallagher for his expertise in the First World War and northern France, Nick Rider and Edward Clarke for their valuable contributions, Judith Wardman, Lorna Horsfield and everyone at Map Creation for all their hard work on this guide; and a special thank you to the whole editorial and design teams at Cadogan for mucking in and making it happen.

Also Available from Cadogan Guides...

Country Guides

Amazon
Antarctica
Central Asia
China: The Silk Routes
Germany: Bavaria
Greece: The Peloponnese
Holland
Holland: Amsterdam & the Randstad
India
India: South India
Ireland
Ireland: Southwest Ireland
Ireland: Northern Ireland
Japan
Morocco
Portugal
Portugal: The Algarve
Scotland
Scotland: Highlands and Islands
South Africa, Swaziland and Lesotho
Tunisia
Turkey
Yucatán and Southern Mexico
Zimbabwe, Botswana and Namibia

The France Series

France
France: Dordogne & the Lot
France: Gascony & the Pyrenees
France: Brittany
France: The Loire
France: The South of France
France: Provence
France: Corsica
France: Côte d'Azur
Short Breaks in Northern France

The Italy Series

Italy
Italy: The Bay of Naples and Southern Italy
Italy: Bologna and Emilia Romagna
Italy: Italian Riviera
Italy: Lombardy and the Italian Lakes
Italy: Rome and the Heart of Italy
Italy: Tuscany, Umbria and the Marches
Italy: Tuscany
Italy: Umbria
Italy: Northeast Italy

The Spain Series

Spain
Spain: Andalucía
Spain: Northern Spain
Spain: Bilbao and the Basque Lands

Island Guides

Caribbean and Bahamas
Corfu & the Ionian Islands
Crete
Greek Islands
Greek Islands By Air
Jamaica & the Caymans
Madeira & Porto Santo
Malta
Mykonos, Santorini & the Cyclades
Rhodes & the Dodecanese
Sardinia
Sicily

City Guides

Amsterdam
Barcelona
Brussels, Bruges, Ghent & Antwerp
Bruges
Edinburgh
Egypt: Three Cities – Cairo, Luxor, Aswan
Florence, Siena, Pisa & Lucca
Italy: Three Cities – Rome, Florence, Venice
Japan: Three Cities – Tokyo, Kyoto and
     Ancient Nara
Morocco: Three Cities – Marrakesh, Fez, Rabat
Spain: Three Cities – Granada, Seville, Cordoba
Spain: Three Cities – Madrid, Barcelona, Seville
London
London–Amsterdam
London–Edinburgh
London–Paris
London–Brussels
Madrid
Manhattan
Paris
Prague-Budapest
Rome
St Petersburg
Venice

Cadogan Guides are available from good bookshops, or via **Grantham Book Services**, Isaac Newton Way, Alma Park Industrial Estate, Grantham NG31 9SD, t (01476) 541 080, f (01476) 541 061; and **The Globe Pequot Press**, 246 Goose Lane, PO Box 480, Guilford, Connecticut 06437–0480, t (800) 458 4500/f (203) 458 4500, t (203) 458 4603.

France
touring atlas

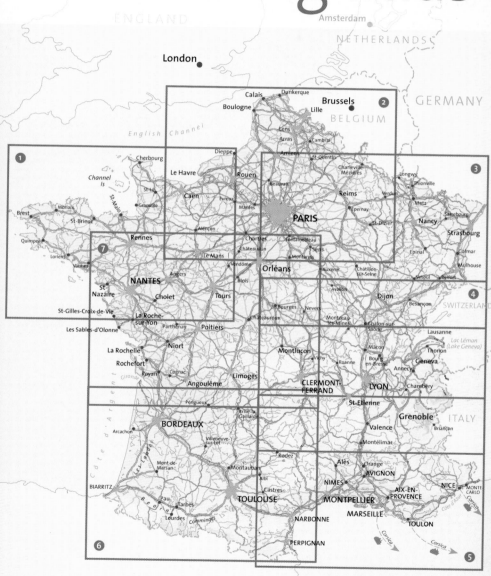

20 km
10 miles

N

BELGIUM

Tourcoing
Roubaix
Armentières
Lille
Bethune
Carvin
Hénin-
Beaumont
St-Amand-
les-Eaux
ame-
ette Aubigny
Lens
Vimy
Douai
Denain
Valenciennes
NORD
Arras
Bavay
Maubeuge
Hautmont
Le Quesnoy
Cambrai
Caudry
Le Cateau
Ors
Avesnes
Givet
Bapaume
Albert
Peronne
Le Catelet
Bony
Bohain-en-V
Haybes
Fumay
Revin
Monthermé
St-Michel
Rocroi
St-Quentin
Guise
Guise
Vervins
Charleville-
Mézières
Sedan
Roye
Crécy
Poix-Terron
Mouzon
Avioth
Montdidier
Noyon
Chauny
Laon
Sissonne
ARDENNES
Montmédy
elay-
gny
AISNE
Coucy-le-
Château
Filain
Craonne
Vendresse
Rethel
Stenay
Compiègne
Blérancourt
Vouziers
Buzancy
Forêt de
Compiègne
Pierrefonds
Soissons
Aisne
Montfaucon
d'Argonne
Etain
Crépy-en-
Valois
Villers-
Cotterêts
La Ferté-Milon
Reims
Marfaux
Pourcy
Verzenay
Verzy
Verdun
enlis
Nanteuil
Ermenonville
Hautvillers
Ay
Marne
Ste-
Menehould
Fresnes-
en-W
MEUSE
Château-
Thierry
Epernay
Châlons-en-
Champagne
St-Mihiel
Meaux
La Ferté-s/s-
Jouarre
Vertus
MARNE
Revigny
Bar-le-Duc
3
Disneyland
Paris
Coulommiers
Mondemont-
Montgivroux
Fère-
Champenoise
Commercy
NS
Sézanne
Vitry-le-
François
St-Dizier
Melun
SEINE-ET-
MARNE
Provins
Romilly
Lac de Der
Chantecoq
Wassy
Joinville
Grand
Forêt de
Fontainebleau
Aube
Lac du
Temple
Brienne-
le-Château
Cirey-sur-
Blaise
Vignory
Nemours
Troyes
AUBE
Lac
d'Orient
Colombey-les-
Deux-Églises
Andelot
Sens
Bar-sur-Aube
Clairvaux
HAUTE-MARNE
Chaumont
Villeneuve-sur-
Yonne
Chaource
Bar-sur-Seine
Essoyes
Arc-en-
Barrois
Montargis
Courtenay
Joigny
Flogny
Les Riceys

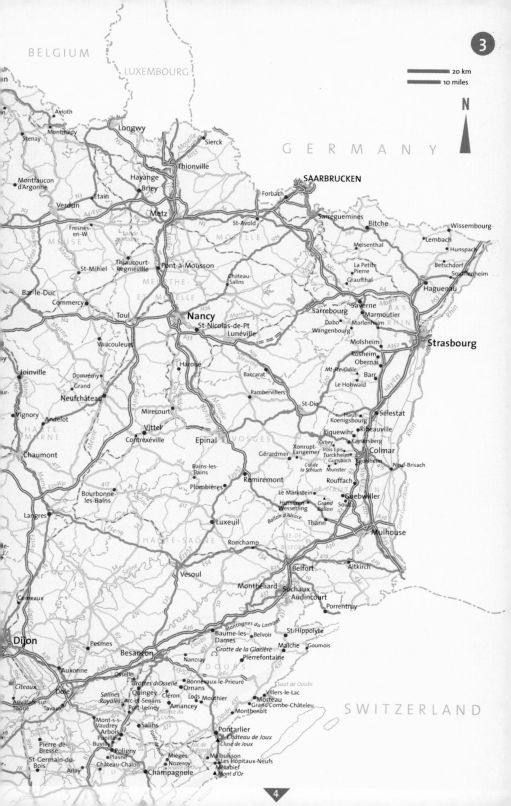

20 km
10 miles

N

BELGIUM

LUXEMBOURG

GERMANY

Avioth
Stenay
Montmédy
Longwy
Sierck
Thionville
Montfaucon
d'Argonne
Hayange
Briey
SAARBRUCKEN
Etain
N3
Forbach
Verdun
A4/E50
Metz
Fresnes-
en-W
St-Avold
Sarreguemines
Bitche
Wissembourg
MOSELLE
N3
Meisenthal
Lembach
Hunspach
MEUSE
Thiaucourt-
Regniéville
Pont-à-Mousson
La Petite
Pierre
Betschdorf
Soufflenheim
St-Mihiel
Château-
Salins
Graufthal
Haguenau
Bar-le-Duc
Commercy
MEURTHE-
ET-MOSELLE
Toul
N74
Nancy
Sarrebourg
Saverne
Marmoutier
Dabo
Marlenheim
RHIN
Vaucouleurs
St-Nicolas-de-Pt
Lunéville
Wangenbourg
Molsheim
A352
Strasbourg
A33
Harouë
Rosheim
Obernai
Joinville
Domrémy
Grand
Baccarat
Mt-ste-Odile
Barr
Le Hohwald
Neufchâteau
Rambervillers
Vignory
Andelot
Mirecourt
St-Dié
HAUTE-
MARNE
Vittel
Contrexéville
Epinal
VOSGES
Haut-
Koenigsbourg
Sélestat
Chaumont
Gérardmer
Xonrupt-
Langemer
Riquewihr
Ribeauvillé
Orbey
Trois Epis
Turckheim
Kaysersberg
Colmar
Col de
la Schluch
Gunsbach
Munster
Eguisheim
Neuf-Brisach
Bains-les-
Bains
Plombières
Remiremont
Rouffach
Bourbonne-
les-Bains
HAUT-RHIN
Le Markstein
Guebwiller
Langres
Husseren-
Wesserling
Grand
Ballon
Soultz
Luxeuil
Ballon d'Alsace
Thann
Mulhouse
HAUTE-SAÔNE
Ronchamp
TERRE-DE-
BELFORT
A36
Vesoul
Belfort
Altkirch
Montbéliard
Sochaux
Audincourt
Gemeaux
Porrentruy
Dijon
Pesmes
Montagnes du Lomont
St-Hippolyte
Baume-les-
Dames
Belvoir
Besançon
Nancray
Grotte de la Glacière
Maîche
Goumois
Pierrefontaine
Auxonne
Osselle
DOUBS
Citeaux
Grottes d'Osselle
Bonnevaux-le-Prieuré
Saut de Doubs
Dole
Quingey
Ornans
Lods Mouthier
Villers-le-Lac
Auvillars-sur-
Saône
Salines
Royales
Arc-et-Senans
Cléron
Amancey
Morteau
Grand'Combe-Châteleu
Tavaux
Port-Lesney
source du
Lison
Montbenoît
SWITZERLAND
Mont-s-s-
Vaudrey
Salins
Arbois
Pontarlier
Pupillin
Buvilly
Château de Joux
Pierre-de-
Bresse
Poligny
Mièges
Nozeroy
Malbuisson
Les Hôpitaux-Neufs
St-Germain-du-
Bois
Château-Chalon
Plasne
source de l'Ain
Métabief
Arlay
Champagnole
Mont d'Or

Montbéliard
Sochaux
Audincourt
Porrentruy
Gemeaux

Montagnes du Lomont
Baume-les-Dames · Belvoir · St-Hippolyte
Pesmes · Nancray · Grotte de la Glacière · Maîche · Goumois
Besançon · Pierrefontaine

DOUBS

20 km
10 miles
N

Auxonne · Osselle
Citeaux · Grottes d'Osselle · Bonnevaux-le-Prieuré · Villers-le-Lac
Dole · Forêt de Chaux · Quingey · Clerons · Ornans · Mouthier · Morteau
Auvillars-sur-Saône · Salines Royales · Arc-et-Senans · Amondans · Lods · Grand'Combe-Châteleu
Tavaux · Germigney · Amancey · Montbenoit
Mont-s-s Vaudrey · Port-Lesney · Source du Lison
Pierre-de-Bresse · Arbois · Salins · Pontarlier
St-Germain-du-Bois · Buvilly · Pupillin · Château de Joux
Passenans · Poligny · Cluse de Joux
L'Étoile · Plasne · Château-Chalon · Mièges · Nozeroy · Malbuisson · Les Hôpitaux-Neufs · Métabief
Courlans · Cirque de Baume · Champagnole · Mont d'Or
Lons-le-Saunier · Cascades du Hérisson · Chaux-Neuve
Louhans · Clairvaux-les-Lacs · Thoiria · Bonlieu · Pic de l'Aigle · Source du Doubs

SWITZERLAND

Montpont · St-Trivier-de-Courtes · Col de la Savine · Morbier · Morez
Lausanne
St-Amour · Morans-en-Montagne · Parc Nat Reg
St-Julien · Lac de Vouglans
Lac Léman (Lake Geneva)
Montreval · Treffort · St-Claude · Col de la Faucille · Evian · Meillerie · St-Gingolph
du Haut Jura · Gex · Excenevex · Thonon · Vacheresse
Bourg-en-Bresse · Oyonnax · Nernier · Sciez · Abondance · Châtel
Ferney-Voltaire · La Dranse d'Abondance
Nantua · St-Julien-en-G · Geneva · Annemasse · Avoriaz · Morzine · Les Gets
Bellegarde-s-V · Collonges
HAUTE SAVOIE
Pont-d'Ain · Plateau de Retord · Cruseilles · Bonneville · Cluses · Samoëns · Cirque du Fer à Cheval
Ambronay · Seyssel · Thorens-Glières · Villaz · Col de la Colombière · Flaine · Cascade de Rouget · Argentière
Ambérieu-en-Bugey · Lochieu · Le Grand-Bornand · Servoz · Le Lavancher · Aiguille des Grands Montets
Pérouges · Artemare · Grand Colombier · Annecy · Nâves-Parmelan · Les Praz-de-Chamonix
Rumilly · Thônes · Combloux · Chamonix-Mont-Blanc
Belley · Sévrier · Menthon · Aiguille du Midi · Le Nid d'Aigle
Hautecombe · St-Jorioz · La Tournette · Megève · Mont Blanc
Satolas · Izieu · Lac du Bourget · Col de la Forclaz · Flumet · Les Saisies · Les Contamines
Aix-les-Bains · Albertville · Ugine · Hauteluce · Beaufort
Bougoin-Jallieu · Le Bourget · Le Châtelard · Aréches · Roignais · Cormet de Roselend · Col du Petit St-Bernard
St-Genix · Mt Revard · Conflans · Bourg-St-Maurice · Col du Frêne · Aime · Les Arcs · Le Miroir
La Tour-du-Pin · Chambéry · Challes · Landry · La Plagne · Mt Pourri
Le Pont-de-Beauvoisin · Les Charmettes · Aiguebelle · Valmorel · Moûtiers · Tignes · Val d'Isère
La Côte-St-André · St-Pierre-d'Entremont · Col du Granier · Col de la Madeleine · Pralognan-la-Vanoise · Grande Casse · Col de l'Iseran
Voiron · Entremont-le-Vieux · Allevard · Méribel · Parc National de la Vanoise · Bonneval
St-Étienne-de-St-Geoirs · Col du Cucheron · Val Thorens · Dent Parrachée · Bessans
Roybon · Fort du St-Eynard · La Chambre · Lanslebourg · Aussois · Col du Mt Cenis
St-Antoine-l'Abbaye · Grenoble · Zybens · Col du Glandon · Col de la Crox de Fer · Modane
St-Marcellin · Pont-en-Royans · Uriage · Chamrousse · Valloire
Parc · Vizille · **ITALY**
Combe Laval · Gorges de la Bourne · Le Bourg-d'Oisans · Alpe-d'Huez · La Grave · Col du Galibier · Névache · Plampinet
Grands Goulets · La Ch-en-Vercors · St-Christophe-en-Oisans · Les Deux-Alpes · Col du Lautaret · Le Monetier · La Salle · Col de Montgenèvre
Col de la Bâtille · Vassieux-en-Vercors · Venosc · Les Écrins · Chantemerle · Serre Chevalier · Montgenèvre
Vercors · Le Grand Veymont · Corps · Mt Pelvoux · Briançon
Col de Roussel · L'Obiou · Parc National des Écrins · Vallouise · Col d'Izoard · Aiguilles · Parc Nat Reg Queyras · Château-Queyras
Die · Vieux Chaillol · du Queyras
Saillans · Col de Menée · Col de Grimone · Mont-Dauphin · M Viso
DRÔME · Châtillon-en-Diois · Col de la Croix Haute · Col du Festre · Risoul · Goillestre · Vars
Bourdeaux · Col Bayard · St-André-d'Embrun · Ceillac · Les Vaux
HAUTES-ALPES · Embrun · St-Sauveur · Col de Vars
Dieulefit · Gap · Les Orres
Valouse · Barrage de Serre-Ponçon
Condorcet · Ubaye · Barcelonnette
Pra-Loup · Le Sauze

La Côte-St-André
Voiron
St-Laurent-du-P.
Allevard
Méribel
Pralognan-la-Vanoise
Parc National de la Vanoise
Bonneval
St-Etienne-de-St-Geoirs
St-Pierre-de-Chartreuse
Val-Thorens
Dent Parrachée
Bessans
Tullins
Le Pleyney
La Chambre
Lanslebourg
Col du Mt Cenis
Roybon
Pipay
Col du Glandon
Aussois
Avrieux
St-Antoine-l'Abbaye
Prapoutel
Col de la Crox de Fer
Modane
Fort du St-Eynard
Grenoble
Eybens
Valloire
St-Marcellin
Uriage
Chamrousse
Pont-en-Royans
Villard-de-Lans
Vizille
Alpe-d'Huez
Col du Galibier
Gorges de la Bourne
Le Bourg-d'Oisans
La Grave
Combe Laval
National
Les Deux-Alpes
Nevache
Plampinet
Grands Goulets
La Chien-Vercors
Venosc
La Meije
Le Monetier
Col de Montgenèvre
St-Christophe-en-Oisans
La Salle
Montgenèvre
Vassieux-en-Vercors
du
Les Chantemerle
Col de a Bataille
Vercors
Massif des Ecrins
Ecrins
Serre
Briançon
Col de Rousset
Mt Pelvoux
Chevalier
Corps
Parc National des Ecrins
Vallouise
Col d'Izoard
Parc Nat Reg
Abriès
L'Obiou
Aiguilles
ITALY
Château-Queyras
lle
Col de Menée
Vieux Chaillol
du Queyras
St-Véran
Saillans
Col de Grimone
Mont Dauphin
Ceillac
M Viso
Châtillon-en-Diois
HAUTES-ALPES
Guillestre
Drôme
Col de la Croix Haute
Col du Festre
Risoul
Vars
DRÔME
Col Bayard
St-André-d'Embrun
Les Claux
Saou
Bourdeaux
Embrun
St-Sauveur
Col de Vars
Gap
Les Orres
Dieulefit
Col de Cabre
St-Sauveur
Barrage de
Serre-Ponçon
Valouse
Condorcet
Barcelonnette
Aubres
Les Pilles
Pra-Loup
Le Sauze-
Super-Sauze
Nyons
Baronnies
Le Chapeau de Gendarme
Mérindol-les-Oliviers
Buis-les-
St-Etienne-de-Tinée
Vaison-la-Romaine
Baronnies
Brantes
Malaucène
Montbrun-les-Bains
Sisteron
Parc National du Mercantour
Col de Tende
Montmirail
Aurel
ALPES-DE-HAUT-PROVENCE
St-Sauveur-sur-Tinée
Mont Bégo
Tende
Notre-Dame-des-Fontaines
VAUCLUSE
Sault
Montagne de Lure
St-Martin-Vésubie
St-Dalmas-de-Tende
Carpentras
Volonne
Digne-les-Bains
Clans
L'Authion
Saorge
Pernes-les-Fontaines
Plateau de Vaucluse
St-André-les-Alpes
MARITIMES
Lantosque
La Tour
Col de Turini
Col du Pérus
Abbaye de Sénanque
Roussillon
Rustrel
Plateau
Levens
Sospel
Village des Bories
Maubec
Lacoste
Apt
de
Peille
Ménerbes
Bonnieux
Montfuron
Valensole
Castellane
Montagne du Cheiron
Peillon
Menton
Senas
Cucuron
Grambois
Manosque
Riez
Moustiers-Ste-Marie
Col de Vence
Vence
Ventimiglia
Cadenet
Ansouis
La Tour d'Aigues
Lac de Ste-Croix
MONTE-CARLO
Abbaye de Silvacane
Pertuis
Quinson
Grand Plan de Canjuers
Comps-sur-Artuby
Cagnes-sur-Mer
Grasse
MONACO
St-Jean-Cap-Ferrat
Salon-de-Provence
Montmeyan
La Verdière
Aups
Ampus
Mandelieu
Mougins
NICE
Cap Ferrat
St-Chamas
Peyrolles-en-Provence
Villecroze
Tourtou
Draguignan
La-Napoule
Antibes
Vauvenargues
Barjols
Salernes
Mont Vinaigre
Cannes
Juan-les-Pins
AIX-EN-PROVENCE
Le Tholonet
St-Maximin-la-Ste-Baume
Cotignac
Entrecasteaux
Le Muy
Pic de l'Ours
Cap d'Antibes
Etang de Berre
Abbaye du Thoronet
Torgues
Les Arcs
Pic du Cap Roux
Fréjus
St-Raphaël
COTE D'AZUR
Marignane
Brignoles
La Garde-Freinet
Ste-Maxime
MARSEILLE
Aubagne
Grimaud
Cap de St-Tropez
Ile Pomègues
Massif de la Ste-Baume
Cogolin
St-Tropez
Cap Croisette
Cassis
Le Gros Cerveau
Cavalaire-sur-Mer
Cap Canaille
La Ciotat
Le Lavandou
Cap Nègre
Les Calanques
Bandol
TOULON
Hyères
Sanary-sur-Mer
La Seyne
L'Almanarre
Cap Bénat
Cap Blanc
Ile des Embiez
Cap Sicié
Giens
La Tour-Fondue
Ile du Levant
Porquerolles
Ile de Port-Cros
Corsica
Ile de Porquerolles

20 km
10 miles
N

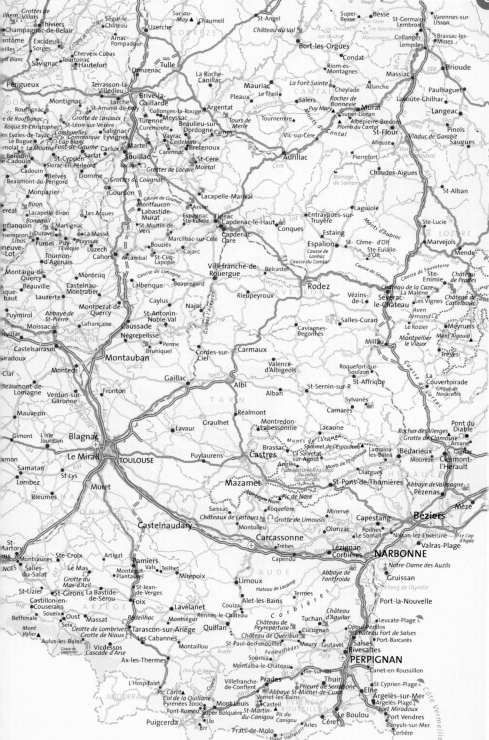